PAINTING IN QUEBEC
1820-1850

PAINTING IN QUEBEC
1820-1850

New Views, New Perspectives

Under the direction of

Mario Béland
Curator of Early Quebec Art

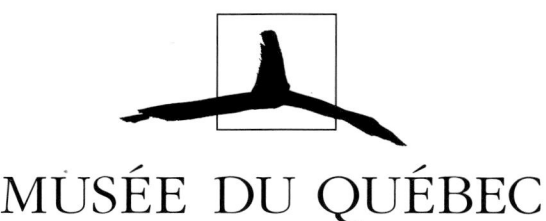

MUSÉE DU QUÉBEC

This publication was produced for the exhibition entitled
Painting in Québec, 1820-1850. New Views, New Perspectives
presented at the Musée du Québec from October 16, 1991 to January 5, 1992.
The exhibition and the catalogue accompanying
it were prepared by a scientific team
led by Mario Béland, Curator of Early Quebec Art,
and made up of Paul Bourassa, Laurier Lacroix, John R. Porter and Didier Prioul.
The exhibition catalogue was produced by the
Communications Department, Musée du Québec.

Publishing: Pierre Murgia, Musée du Québec
Translations: Cabinet de Traduction Dialangue
Graphic design: Guimar
Layout: Couthuran
Production: Louis Gauvin, Musée du Québec
Word-processing: Denise Agaliotis, Musée du Québec
Electronic editing: Nancy Trépanier, Musée du Québec
Photo engraving: Point de trame
Printing: Interglobe

The *Painting in Quebec, 1820-1850* exhibition
benefited from the generous support of the American Express Foundation,
the Department of Communications (Canada)
under the Museum Support Program,
as well as of the Amis du Musée du Québec.

A special financial contribution from Communications Canada
has greatly helped us in fulfilling our publication objectives,
making this project available to all English-speaking Canadians.

Work reproduced on the book jacket:
John Richard Coke Smyth, *View of Québec* (see cat. 216)

The exhibition is being presented at the following locations:

Musée du Québec, Quebec City, October 16, 1991 - January 5, 1992
National Gallery of Canada, Ottawa: January 31 - March 29, 1992
Vancouver Art Gallery: April 29 - June 23, 1992
Art Gallery of Nova Scotia, Halifax: August 1 - September 27, 1992
Montreal Museum of Fine Arts: October 29, 1992 - January 3, 1993

ISBN 2-551-12970-2
Legal deposit, 4th quarter 1992
Bibliothèque nationale du Québec
National Library of Canada

FOREWORD

It is with great anticipation and pride that the Musée du Québec presents the catalogue and the exhibition Painting in Quebec, 1820-1850. New Views, New Perspectives. *This project is a major event in the year marking the reopening of the expanded Musée du Québec. A team of specialists has worked on this exhibition for several years. It was led by Mr. Mario Béland, Curator of Early Quebec Art, and was composed of Mr. Paul Bourassa, Assistant to the Curator of Early Quebec Art, of Mr. Laurier Lacroix, professor at the Université du Québec à Montréal, Mr. John R. Porter, professor at the Université Laval, and guest Chief Curator at the Montreal Museum of Fine Arts, and of Mr. Didier Prioul, Curator at the Montreal Museum of Fine Arts.*

The exhibition and its accompanying publication are significant in terms of the breadth of research conducted, and in terms of their relationship to the main and foremost mandate of the Musée du Québec. Indeed, an essential aspect of our aim to conserve and promote the art of Quebec from all periods, is hereby beautifully fulfilled. This exhibition is, beyond doubt, the largest and most ambitious project of early Canadian Art to have been realized in many years. Furthermore, it is one of the major historical, scientific and museological event to have been produced by our institution.

More than forty private collectors and public institutions have generously supported our project by lending important works of art for the duration of the exhibition in Quebec and on tour, in Canada. Amongst them, may we thank the National Archives of Canada, the National Gallery of Canada, the Royal Ontario Museum, the Musée du Séminaire de Québec, the McCord Museum of Canadian History, the Musée du Château Ramezay, and the Montreal Museum of Fine Arts, as major lenders. Our sincere thanks also go to many other museums, to several parishes, and to all the private collectors who have supported us.

Following its Quebec City showing, the exhibition will be presented in four Canadian venues, with the financial support of the Museum Assistance Program, Communications Canada, and the participation of the American Express Foundation. We wish to sincerely thank our colleagues, directors of Canadian museums for their enthusiasm and dedication in presenting the exhibition to their visitors, throughout 1992: Mrs. Shirley Thomson, from the National Gallery of Canada, in Ottawa, Mr. Willard Holmes, from the Vancouver Art Gallery, Mr. Bernard Riordon, from the Art Gallery of Nova Scotia, in Halifax and Mr. Pierre Théberge, from the Montreal Museum of Fine Arts.

I also hereby wish to thank Les Amis du Musée du Québec, for their unfailing support, and all those who directly and indirectly have made this exhibition and this publication a success. Special thanks must be addressed to Mr. Mario Béland and to his collaborators. Their work has born fruits of great quality, in the name of history, culture and society at large.

Andrée Laliberté-Bourque
General Director

MEMBERS OF THE SCIENTIFIC COMMITTEE

MARIO BÉLAND

Mario Béland, who has been the Curator of Early Quebec Art at the Musée du Québec since 1985, holds a Ph.D. in history from Université Laval. After having collaborated in 1984, as assistant to the guest curator, of *Le Grand Héritage* exhibition, organized for the visit of Pope Jean-Paul II to Québec, he prepared in 1986 the *Louis Jobin, Master Sculptor* exhibition and wrote the accompanying catalogue, for which he obtained an honorable mention from the Société des musées québécois. The author of the works *Marius Barbeau et l'art au Québec* (1985) and *Le Musée du Québec: les expositions des origines à 1990* (1991), he has also published numerous articles in various specialized magazines.

PAUL BOURASSA

Initially trained in the science field, Paul Bourassa obtained a master's degree in art history from Université du Québec à Montréal in 1986. He is currently preparing Ph.D. at Université Laval. He participated in the conception of an exhibition on painter Louis Dulongpré and in the preparation of the accompanying catalogue, presented at the McCord Museum of Canadian History in 1988. Having worked as Docent at Université du Québec à Montréal, he has held the position of Assistant to the Curator for Early Quebec Art at the Musée du Québec since May 1989.

LAURIER LACROIX

Laurier Lacroix is a professor of art history and museology at Université du Québec à Montréal. He is very much interested in the questions of drawing, landscapes, collections and public art as applied to Québec and Canadian art of the 19th and 20th centuries. Occasionally, he delves into contemporary art. His numerous writings have been published in the *Journal of Canadian Art History, Continuité, Vie des Arts* and *Musées*. He has pursuing exhibitions on François Baillairgé, Suzor-Côté and Irene F. Whittome, to name but a few. He is pursuing research on the Montreal artists of the "Montée Saint-Michel" and is currently working on an exhibition devoted to Ozias Leduc to be presented at the Montreal Museum of Fine Arts in 1994.

JOHN R. PORTER

A full professor at Université Laval and guest chief curator at the Montreal Museum of Fine Arts, John R. Porter holds a Ph.D. from Université de Montréal. In his 20-year career, he has made a name for himself through the diversity of his works, the scope of his achievements and the quality of the art historians he has trained. His summaries, monographs, catalogues, articles, research projects, seminars and conferences in Canada and abroad have done much to contribute to the advancement of knowledge and the influence of art in Québec.

DIDIER PRIOUL

Didier Prioul did his art history studies at Université Laval. As part of his doctorate thesis on the landscapes of Joseph Légaré, he focussed his research on the ties between European art and painting in Québec. His interests have dealt, in particular, with the "copy" phenomenon, to which he devoted an exhibition in 1990 at the Musée du Séminaire de Québec. Since 1986, he has oriented his work towards British landscape artists active in Québec during the 18th and 19th centuries. In this volume readers will find an initial summary of this research. Having been a teaching assistant at Université Laval, he became the Curator of the Musée du Séminaire de Québec, a position that he held from 1988 to 1991. There he developed research on the history of the collections. Since September 1991 he has been the Curator of European Art (1300-1800) at the Montreal Museum of Fine Arts.

AUTHORS

MEMBERS OF THE SCIENTIFIC COMMITTEE

Mario Béland (M.B.)
Curator of Early Quebec Art, Musée du Québec, Quebec City

Introduction: *New Views, New Perspectives*; notices: 6-7, 8-9, 14-16, 18-19, 38-41, 53, 105-108, 109-110, 112-113, 126, 128, 131, 132, 134-135, 136, 149, 178, 186, 190, 203, 205, 207, 211, 221, 248, 259, 267.

Paul Bourassa (P.B.)
Assistant to the Curator of Early Quebec Art,
Musée du Québec, Quebec City

Essay: *A Look at Likeness: Portraiture in Lower Canada*; notices: 12, 17, 22-24, 25, 26, 27, 88-89, 90, 116, 117 (collaboration of), 129, 152, 175, 177, 180 (collaboration of), 183, 185, 191-192, 197-198, 206, 208, 218, 219, 242, 245, 253, 256-257 (collaboration of), 260-261.

Laurier Lacroix (L.L.)
Professor, Université du Québec à Montréal

Essay: *Yesterday's Standard, Today's Fragment: Element of Esthetics in Quebec, 1820-1850*; notices: 1-2, 3-4, 5, 36, 115, 118, 119, 120-121, 122, 130, 147, 148, 151, 153-154, 155-156, 173, 181, 193, 200, 201-202, 204, 217, 227, 228, 229, 231, 237, 250, 251, 255, 258, 264-265 (collaboration of).

John R. Porter (J.R.P.)
Full Professor, Université Laval, and Guest Chief Curator,
Montreal Museum of Fine Arts

Essay: *The Market for Paintings: Basic Needs Versus Artistic Taste*; notices: 87, 125, 133, 137, 138, 158, 160, 166, 168, 169 (collaboration of), 176, 182, 184, 187-188, 189, 196, 220, 239, 240, 247, 266.

Didier Prioul (D.P.)
Curator of European Art (1300-1800),
Montreal Museum of Fine Arts

Essay: *British Landscape Artists in Quebec: From Documentary Views to a Poetic Vision*; notices: 20-21, 28-29, 32, 33, 34, 42, 43, 44-45, 51, 54-58, 59, 60, 61-62, 63-64, 67, 68-71, 72-75, 76, 77-78, 79-81, 82, 83, 84-86, 91-92, 93-95, 96-99, 103-104, 111, 141-142, 143-145, 146, 157, 159, 161, 162, 163-164, 165, 167, 169 (collaboration of), 170, 171-172, 174, 179, 209-210, 212-213, 214-215, 216, 225, 226 (collaboration of), 230, 233-235, 236, 238, 241, 252, 256-257 (collaboration of).

OTHER COLLABORATORS

Mary Allodi (M.A.)
Curator, Canadian Art, Royal Ontario Museum, Toronto

Notices: 13, 35, 47-50, 150, 246.

Victoria Baker (V.B.)
Assistant Curator of Canadian Art
National Gallery of Canada, Ottawa

Notices: 222-223, 224.

Denis Castonguay (D.C.)
Research Assistant, Musée du Québec, Quebec City

All the artist's biographies except the ones of the J. Hankes and T.P. Jones; notice: 30-31.

Joanne Chagnon (J.C.)
Art Historian

Notices: 52, 117 (collaboration of), 180 (collaboration of), 226 (collaboration of), 232, 249, 254, 262-263.

Lydia Foy (L.F.)
Documentary art and photography division,
National Archives of Canada, Ottawa

Biographies of J. Hankes and T.P. Jones; notices: 37, 139-140, 243 and 244.

Gilbert Gignac (G.G.)
Documentary art and photography division,
National Archives of Canada, Ottawa

Notice: 114.

Yves Lacasse (Y.L.)
Curator of Canadian Art (painting and sculpture before 1960),
Montreal Museum of Fine Arts

Notices: 123-124, 194, 195, 199.

Eva Major-Marothy (E.M.M.)
Documentary art and photography division,
National Archives of Canada, Ottawa

Notice: 46.

Denis Martin (D.M.)
Curator of Prints and Drawings,
Musée du Québec, Quebec City

Notices: 10-11, 65-66, 100-102, 127.

Stanley G. Triggs (S.G.T.)
Curator of Photography, Notman photographic archives,
McCord Museum of Canadian History, Montreal

Notice: 264-265 (collaboration of).

LENDING INSTITUTIONS

Archevêché de Québec
Archives nationales du Québec, Quebec City
Art Gallery of Hamilton
Art Gallery of Ontario, Toronto
Basilique Notre-Dame de Montréal
Bishop's University, Lennoxville
City of Quebec
Congrégation de Notre-Dame, Musée de la Maison Saint-Gabriel, Montreal
Corporation professionnelle des Médecins du Québec, Montreal
Dr Guy Marcoux, Beauport
Institut Canadien de Québec
McCord Museum of Canadian History, Montreal
McGill University, Montreal
Metropolitan Toronto Reference Library
Montreal Museum of Fine Arts
Musée d'art de Joliette
Musée du Château Ramezay, Montreal
Musée de l'Hôpital général de Québec
Musée des Augustines de l'Hôtel-Dieu de Québec
Musée des Soeurs grises de Montréal
Musée des Ursulines de Québec
Musée du Saguenay-Lac-Saint-Jean, Chicoutimi
Musée du Séminaire de Québec
Musée Pierre-Boucher, Séminaire de Trois-Rivières
National Archives of Canada, Canada
National Gallery of Canada, Ottawa
Power Corporation of Canada/Power Corporation du Canada, Montreal
Royal Ontario Museum, Toronto
Séminaire de Nicolet
Société des établissements de plein air du Québec (Manoir Montmorency), Quebec City
Vancouver Art Gallery
and various Private Collections

ACKNOWLEDGMENTS

We wish like to express our gratitude to all those who assisted us in preparing this exhibition and the accompanying catalogue. Our thanks first go to the management of the Musée du Québec which always gave its full support to this project, in particular to Andrée Laliberté-Bourque, Director, Gaétan Chouinard, Assistant to the Director, and Michel V. Cheff, Chief Curator.

The cooperation of our colleagues of the Musée du Québec was remarkable. We thank the following members of the Curatorial Department: Denis Castonguay whose devotion warrants special mention, Denis Martin, Louise Allard and Louise Dubois of the curatorial section; Lise Nadeau, Suzanne Breen, Catherine Perron, Suzette Brousseau, Nathalie Thibault, Claude Bilodeau, Patrick Altman, Jean-Guy-Kérouac and Daniel Mercier; of the Registrar's section; Pierre Bouvier, Denis Allison and Danielle Lessard of the exhibition design sector; and Suzanne Michaud and Nathalie Maynard for their first-rate secretarial work. Of the Education and Cultural Events Department: André Marchand, Lucille Fréchet, Marie-France Tremblay, Mireille Galipeau, Michel Nadeau and Jean-Pierre Labiau. Of the Commmunications Department: Lise Boyer and Joanne Trudel of the information and public relations sector, Pierre Murgia, Louis Gauvin, Nancy Trépanier and Myriam Young of the publishing sector.

For the restoration of works of art and frames, we were able to count on the services of Claude Belleau and Achille Murphy of the Musée du Québec, Anita Henry, Jim Bourdeau and Michel Pelletier, as well as of Michel Cauchon, Roger Roche, Joan Rathbone-Roche, Suzanne Holm and Marthe Olivier, of the Centre de conservation du Québec. We also wish to express our gratitude to Renée Gagnon-Guimond, Jacques Blanchet and Hélène Basque of the Amis du Musée du Québec for their continuous support.

Throughout the various conception, research and production stages associated with this exhibition, we were able to count on the support and expertise of several colleagues from various museums and of members of lending institutions.

In Chicoutimi, Renée Wells and Guy Coutu of the Musée du Saguenay-Lac-Saint-Jean. In Halifax, Bernard Riordon and Susan Foshay of the Art Gallery of Nova Scotia. In Hamilton, Robert F. Swain, Ross Fox and Agnes Richard of the Art Gallery of Hamilton. In Joliette, Michel Perron and Michel Huard of the Musée d'art de Joliette. In Lennoxville, Dr Hugh Scott and Monique Nadeau-Saumier of Bishop's University. In Montreal, Dr Augustin Roy and Dr Jacques Brière of the Corporation des Médecins du Québec; Pierre Théberge, Yves Lacasse and Louise d'Argencourt of the Montreal Museum of Fine Arts; Pierre Brouillard, Monique Laliberté and André Délisle of the Musée du Château Ramezay; Luke Rombout, France Gascon, Conrad Graham, Moira McCaffrey, Pamela Miller, Stanley G. Triggs and Nicole Vallières of the McCord Museum of Canadian History; Paul Desmarais, Serge Joyal, Serge Pizem of Power Corporation of Canada; Bruce Whiteman and Norma Morgan of McGill University. In Nicolet, Marie Pelletier of the archives du Séminaire de Nicolet. In Ottawa, Lilly Koltun, Jim Burant, Gilbert Gignac, Lydia Foy, Eva Major-Marothy, Patricia Kennedy, Elizabeth Krug, Brian Carey, Eldon Frost, Sylvie Gervais and Anne Goddard of the National Archives of Canada; Shirley L. Thomson, Charles C. Hill, Victoria Baker, Rosemarie Tovell, René Villeneuve, Pierre B. Landry, Michael Pantazzi and Katherine Laing of the National Gallery of Canada. In Quebec City, Yvan Dussault, Monique Laurent, Jacques Morin, Claude Boudreau and Céline Villeneuve of the Archives nationales du Québec; Jean Payeur of the Institut canadien; André Juneau, Joanne Chagnon, Sonia Mimeault, Pauline Grégoire and Gaétan Gagné of the Musée du Séminaire de Québec; Michel Noël de Tilly and Réjean Laberge (Manoir Montmorency) of the Société des établissements de plein air du Québec; Mayor Jean-Paul L'Allier, Michel Choquette, Jacques Genest and Michelle Allard of the City of Québec. In Toronto, John Crosthwait of the Metropolitan Toronto Reference Library; William Withrow, Glenn Lowry, Dennis Reid and Christine Boyanovski of the Art Gallery of Ontario; Mary Allodi and Donald B. Webster of the Royal Ontario Museum. In Trois-Rivières, Françoise Chainé of the Musée Pierre-Boucher du Séminaire de Trois-Rivières. In Vancouver, Willard Holmes and Ian Thom of the Vancouver Art Gallery.

Our thanks also go to several members of the religious communities and the clergy who agreed to lend their works, as well as to the private citizens who, for the most part, wished to remain anonymous. In Beauport, Dr Guy Marcoux, in Montreal, Sister Thérèse Cloutier of the Congrégation de Notre-Dame au musée de la Maison Saint-Gabriel; Monsignor Fernand Lecavalier of the Parish of Notre-Dame; Sisters Jeannette Gagnon, Réjeanne Grandmaison and Gaétane Chevrier of Les Soeurs grises. In Quebec City, His Eminence Cardinal Louis-Albert Vachon, Monsignor Maurice Couture and Father Armand Gagné of the Archdiocese; Sisters Rita Caron and Corinne Cloutier of the monastère des Augustines de l'Hôpital général; Sisters Claire Gagnon and Alvine Bouillé of the monastère des Augustines de l'Hôtel-Dieu; Sister Gabrielle Dagnault of the monastère des Ursulines.

Other persons provided us with a great deal of assistance in a number of ways and we thank them. In Calgary, Patricia Ainslie and Chris Jackson of the Glenbow Museum. In Detroit, Nancy R. Shaw of the Detroit Institute of Arts. In Fredericton, Ian Lumsden and Tom Smart of the Beaverbrook Art Gallery. In Lille (France), Arnauld Brejon de Lavergnée, Paul Rouzé and Dr Marcel Héraud. In London, Karen Taylor of Sotheby's. In Montréal, Michel Doyon, Denise Roy; Daniel Olivier of the Bibliothèque municipale de Montréal, salle Gagnon; Father Claude Turmel of the Diocese of Montreal; Édith Morin of the Jardin botanique de Montréal; Sister Thérèse Payer of the monastère des religieuses de Saint-Joseph. In Nicolet, Marthe Taillon. In Ottawa and in Quebec City, René Chartrand and Yvan Fortier of the Canadian Parks Service; in Ottawa, Émile Mongrain of Communications Canada. In Quebec City, Lynda Robitaille, Andréanne Bolduc, Daniel Drouin, Madeleine Godin, Micheline Huard, Ginette Laroche-Joly, Claudine Villeneuve, Marianna O'Gallagher; of the Musée de la Civilisation, for the loan of ethnological objects during the presentation of the exhibition in Quebec City, Richard Dubé, Thérèse Latour, Lydia Imreh, Marie-Paule Robitaille and Guy Toupin; and finally, Guy-André Roy, of ministère des Affaires culturelles, whose dedication warrants special mention.

Mario Béland
Curator of Early Quebec Art
Paul Bourassa
Assistant to the Curator of Early Quebec Art
and the members of the scientific committee

TABLE OF CONTENTS

NOTICE
TO THE READERS

This publication is composed of two parts. The first one includes four essays on the fondamental questions raised by painting of the period from 1790 to 1860; the second, a catalogue of the exhibited works, is divided into three parts, respectively entitled Emergence, devoted to the 1790-1820 period; Affirmation, to the 1820-1850 period, and Perspectives, to the 1850-1860 period. For each of these periods, the artists are presented in alphabetical order and their works in chronological order.

Due to the constraints related to the conservation of works on paper, the latter are not presented at each venue. Abbreviations under the reproductions indicate those museums where the works are presented. All the titles of the exhibited works have been standardized and translated into English. The dimensions are given in centimetres and, as is customary, the height precedes the width. The spelling of the inscriptions and the quotes has, insofar as possible, been respected without further indication, The translated passages are clearly identified by a "Translation" note.

The bibliographical references of the catalogue are given in abbreviated form: in the case of books and articles, the name of the author is given first, followed by the year of publication and the page; in the case of exhibitions, we first mention the city in which the exhibition was presented, then the year and the number of the work in the catalogue. Readers will find full references in the general bibliography and the list of exhibitions appearing at the end of this work. However, this bibliography includes only the printed sources and directly related to the works of the catalogue. The other references are given in their entirety in the notes.

ABBREVIATIONS

alb.	album
b.	back
d	denier (pence)
f.	front
i.	initialed
l.c.	lower centre
l.l.	lower left
l.r.	lower right
£	pound, Quebec currency
n.d.	not dated
s	shillings
s.	signed
s.d.	signed and dated
u.c.	upper centre
u.l.	upper left
u.r.	upper right

AGNS	Art Gallery of Nova Scotia, Halifax
AGO	Art Gallery of Ontario, Toronto
AMHDQ	Archives du monastère de l'Hôtel-Dieu de Québec
AMMCH	Archives of the McCord Museum of Canadian History, Montreal
AMUQ	Archives du monastère des Ursulines de Québec
ANQM	Archives nationales du Québec, Montreal
ANQQ	Archives nationales du Québec, Quebec City
ANQTR	Archives nationales du Québec, Trois-Rivières
ASGM	Archives des Soeurs grises de Montréal
ASQ	Archives du Séminaire de Québec
DCB	Dictionary of Canadian Biography
HDQ	Hôtel-Dieu de Québec
HGQ	Hôpital général de Québec
MAJ	Musée d'art de Joliette
MCR	Musée du Château Ramezay, Montreal
MMCH	McCord Museum of Canadian History, Montreal
MMFA	Montreal Museum of Fine Arts
MSQ	Musée du Séminaire de Québec
MQ	Musée du Québec, Quebec City
NAC	National Archives of Canada, Ottawa
NGC	National Gallery of Canada, Ottawa
PC	Private collection
RACAR	Revue d'art canadien / Canadian Art Review
ROM	Royal Ontario Museum, Toronto
VAG	Vancouver Art Gallery

INTRODUCTION

NEW VIEWS, NEW PERSPECTIVES

LANS FOR AN EXHIBITION on the art of painting in Quebec (1820 to 1850) began taking shape in fall 1986. After organizing a retrospective on Louis Jobin, master sculptor of the late 19th century, I turned to a completely different discipline and period: painting in the first half of the 1800s. Since recent studies had targeted the most prominent Quebec painters of this time, I chose to delve deeper into an area which had been largely ignored by the experts and was little known to the public, namely, the work of foreign professional artists who settled in Quebec between 1790 and 1860. However, early on in project planning, I was faced with two major problems in defining the body of work to be exhibited. First, we needed to define the concept of "foreign" painter; and then establish the connection between foreign painters and Quebec artists. It is difficult to compare the work of artists such as Louis Dulongpré, James Duncan, William Berczy and Cornelius Krieghoff, who settled in Canada to pursue their career, to that of travelling artists such as John James, James Bowman and Samuel Palmer, whose stay here was only cursory. Another challenge was to address the new, complex relationships which developed between these foreign painters and local artists. After much thought, in January 1987, the idea that the exhibition be an overview of pictorial production in Quebec between 1790 and 1860 by both foreign and Quebec artists seemed natural. During the period in question, painting in Lower Canada experienced such an unprecedented boom that some art historians qualify it as "the Golden Age of painting in Quebec."

Since the 1960s, with the publication of *La peinture traditionnelle au Canada français* (1960) by Gérard Morisset and *Painting in Canada: A History* (1967) by John Russell Harper, no serious overview had targeted this prominent period. In the opinion of Morisset and Harper, this era marked a renewal in Quebec art as well as the birth (1790-1820) and coming of age (1820-1860) of a characteristically Canadian painting tradition. Generally considered pioneers in their field, the two art historians are credited with unveiling many previously unknown works and artists, often based on first-hand information. Although their studies are still considered compulsory reference works, they nonetheless contain documentary flaws and interpretational errors and, more importantly, espouse a now-outdated perception—based precisely on the idea of a "Golden Age"—of the period 1790-1860. In addition to underestimating the importance of religious painting, Morisset and Harper divided up schools of art, groups of artists, the genres they worked in, and the media used. For example, they dealt with local and foreign artists separately from British soldiers, amateur watercolourists, miniaturists and silhouettists; landscapes and genre scenes were treated as distinct from portraits, and so forth.

In the early 1970s, the study of Quebec's early art history reached a turning point and was no longer the exclusive realm of a few isolated researchers like Morisset and Harper. Interest in early Quebec art flourished under favourable conditions characterized by a collective awakening to Quebec's heritage, resulting from the prevailing nationalist social and political context, by new professional practices in art museums, and by specialized university courses and programs. The collective efforts of museum curators and university professors revitalized this field and generated numerous studies focusing on 19th-century Quebec painting. The 1970s and 1980s saw more inventories of art collections, catalogues, monographs and artists' biographies -particularly with the publication of the *Dictionary of Canadian Biography*—briefs, theses and background articles on art schools or artists' groups, in-depth studies of the production of a given artist, of a given medium, theme, or even region, scientific articles on a specific work, issue or phenomenon, and so on. In this respect, the *Journal of Canadian Art*, first published in 1974, was instrumental in disseminating new-found knowledge. And, in this context, it was important that such a large-scale project as *Painting in Quebec, 1820-1850* be undertaken by a team of experts rather than by one person alone.

The Scientific Committee

In winter 1987, after project submission and approval, a scientific committee, originally composed of John R. Porter, full professor at Université Laval in Quebec City and, since summer 1990, guest head curator at the Montreal Museum of Fine Arts, Laurier Lacroix, professor at Université du Québec à Montréal, and myself, was set up. We three had worked on *Le Grand Héritage*, a major exhibition of religious art organized by the Musée du Québec in 1984 on the occasion of Pope John Paul II's visit to Quebec. John R. Porter and Laurier Lacroix need no further introduction—both are well-known throughout Canada for their scholarship and publications in the field of Quebec art in general, and of early Quebec art in particular. In 1981, John R. Porter defended a doctoral thesis on Quebec painter and collector Joseph Légaré, a prominent figure from the first half of the 19th century; Laurier Lacroix is preparing to submit his on the "Tableaux Desjardins" (Desjardins collection), which had a major influence on the history paintings of this period. In fall 1987, our team welcomed the addition of Didier Prioul, then curator at the Musée du Séminaire de Québec and, since summer 1991, curator at the Montreal Museum of Fine Arts. In recent years, Didier Prioul has been furthering his study of British military artists in Canada, primarily in the form of a doctoral thesis entitled *Joseph Légaré, paysagiste*, to be submitted in the near future.

During phase one of the project—seeking out and making a preliminary selection of works—Lynda Robitaille, assistant curator from August 1987 to September 1988, helped with research and was responsible for the exhibition titles (artists, works, collections). During phases two and three—research, final selection, loan requests and photography of the selected works—Paul Bourassa joined the scientific committee as a curatorial assistant and member in May 1989. His many tasks were often tedious and demanding: drafting information cards, compiling an extensive bibliography and list of exhibitions, creating a file for each work and supervising the borrowing and photographing of the pieces. He also drew our attention to a number of significant discoveries—a previously unshown work, the attribution of a work to a given artist, the identification of a piece. Finally, Denis Castonguay joined the team in August 1990 as researcher and assistant for certain scientific and technical aspects, concentrating, in particular, on drafting most of the artists' biographies.

The existence of a scientific committee and the combined efforts of Messrs. Porter, Lacroix, Prioul, Bourassa and myself enabled us to turn our respective interests and knowledge in various fields to good account. This teamwork also made for more dynamic discussion on decisions regarding every project phase, be it research, the preliminary selection of the works to be showcased, or the final version of the catalogue and actual exhibition. Our many exchanges and discussions during the twenty-five or so meetings held over the past four and a half years were frank and at times heated, but always very productive and imbued with team spirit and humour.

The first three committee meetings, held in spring 1987, enabled us to establish a general concept, determine the periods and territory to be covered, define the approaches and levels of interpretation required - based on the artists, works and milieux -, identify the phenomena or factors specific to the era and, finally, draw up a preliminary list of themes, sub-themes, and landmark works or "musts".

Geographical Context and Chronology

We chose to focus on works produced in Lower Canada between 1820 and 1850. However, we also felt that an introduction and conclusion, covering the periods 1790-1820 and 1850-1860 respectively, were necessary to illustrate the era's characteristics. We thus divided our analysis into three different periods (each characterized by specific changes) covering a total of 70 years, although some trends may have begun prior to 1820 and others may have continued after 1850. These dates and boundaries are not meant to be restrictive—they are not hard-and-fast divisions in time and space. They should be considered geographical and temporal indicators marking events and movements specific to a given location at a given time. The reader should not be surprised to find that this catalogue includes works that were either produced abroad by or for Quebeckers or produced during the 1850s but considered within the decades 1820-1850, since they are merely a continuation of certain practices characteristic of this period.

The introduction is generally devoted to 1790-1820, a period which marked the emergence of painting in Lower Canada. The 1790s witnessed the return of François Baillairgé and François Beaucourt, the first Canadian artists to study in France under British rule, and the arrival of two talented foreign painters, Frenchman Louis Dulongpré and German William Berczy. Furthermore, during their stay, a group of landscape artists who worked in watercolour—British-born James Peachey, Thomas Davies and George Heriot—introduced the tradition of English-style landscape portrayals to Lower Canada and ensured their popularity. And finally, there was the influence of the periodic presence of English and American portrait painters such as Gerrit Schipper, Eliab Metcalf and John James, who travelled about doing miniatures, silhouettes and pastels.

The main body of the work covers the decades from 1820 to 1850, a period during which painting came into its own, blossomed, and eventually enjoyed a high point. In 1817 and 1820, Abbé Philippe-Jean-Louis Desjardins rescued some 180 canvases—mostly religious portrayals—from the ravages of the French Revolution, and sent them to Canada. The arrival of these works, mainly of the French school, not only stimulated and encouraged a new generation of local artists, but also considerably transformed the art market and pictorial practices. Quebec painters such as Jean-Baptiste Roy-Audy, Joseph Légaré, Antoine Plamondon and Théophile Hamel began their career and reached artistic maturity during these thirty years. Furthermore, several painters from various countries came to Lower Canada to practice their trade. Some, such as Irish-born James Duncan and Dutchman Cornelius Krieghoff, were well known; others, such as Robert Clow Todd, Samuel Palmer, James Bowman, Henry D. Thielcke and William F. Wilson, were less so. Some of these professional artists, like miniaturists Anson Dickinson and Gerome Fassio, travelled from town to town, offering their services as portrait painters.

The marked presence of British troops contributed to the production of watercolour landscapes, first during the 1820s by Charles R. Forrest, John E. Woolford and John C. Young, military men who were among Lord Dalhousie's contemporaries—the dominant figure in this initial group of artists definitely being James Pattison Cockburn. Then the Rebellion of 1837-1838 resulted in the arrival of a number of British soldiers in the colony, some of whom were landscape painters known as the "Group of 1838," which included Philip J. Bainbrigge, Henry W. Barnard, William R. Herries and, of course, Lord Durham's drawing master, John R. Coke Smyth. Various wives of soldiers or civil servants—Elizabeth F. Hale, Katherine J. Ellice, Millicent M. Chaplin and Elizabeth F. Durnford among them—took up painting for pleasure, and became the first women artists in Quebec's history. The works of amateurs, such as Jean-Joseph Girouard,

R.-S.-M. Bouchette and William S. Sewell, also bear witness to the artistic vitality of this period.

The decade 1850-1860, which is dealt with in the conclusion, was a transitional phase, marked by significant change, if not major upheaval. Several renowned Quebec artists were already deceased or died during this period (Louis Dulongpré, Jean-Baptiste Roy-Audy and Joseph Légaré), or were retired (Antoine Plamondon). Théophile Hamel and Cornelius Krieghoff settled in Quebec City and began a brilliant new phase in their career, while Napoléon Bourassa, upon his return from Europe, began his own career in Montreal and introduced a new esthetic trend and different practices to the art world. Another generation of European landscape artists, Otto R. Jacobi among them, settled in Montreal, ushering in a new era in Quebec painting. During this time, Antoine-Sébastien Falardeau was being recognized in Italy for his talents as a copyist. However, the landmark event was without question the development and popularity of photography, signalled by the opening of the Notman studios in Montreal and the Livernois studio in Quebec City. This phenomenon brought about drastic changes, and even a fragmentation in the field of visual arts and, consequently, pictorial production.

Over the 70 years in question, artists both renowned and unknown, in general very versatile, created works of particular interest on a wide variety of themes, using different procedures, styles and subjects: portraits, religious paintings, landscapes, genre scenes, still lifes, history paintings, altar ornaments, coats of arms, panoramas, miniatures, silhouettes, etc. This diversified body of work, which comprises watercolours, drawings and oils, bears witness to our redefinition and new perspective of the period 1790-1860 in general and the decades 1820-1850 in particular.

Choosing a Title

The works produced between 1790 and 1860 illustrate a series of specific phenomena and factors that we first lumped together under the theme and temporary title *Passages* which, although appropriate, has been overworked, especially recently. Like *Passages*, the title *New Views, New Perspectives* calls to mind the presence of numerous foreign artists (British, French, Italian, American) in Lower Canada; the exchanges between these artists and their local counterparts; the travels of various Quebec artists (François Baillairgé, François Beaucourt, Antoine Plamondon, Théophile Hamel, etc.) in Europe and the United States; their travels throughout Lower Canada; the dissemination (imports, exports and collections) of works from various sources, and finally the diversification of production on all levels. These artistic trends shed light on the historical context of the era as a whole: the socioeconomic and religious situation, the cultural context, the training and status of the artists and their work, the bourgeoisie and the art of portrait painting, religious painting and the clergy, the group of British landscape artists and their perceptions of the country, the world of reproductions, esthetic trends, and stylistic influences.

This new perspective also allow us to situate the creation of these works and their use within a given context. Rather than focusing on an artificial sphere based on the image of a "Golden Age," which relegates secondary figures and utilitarian works to the fringes while glorifying renowned artists and so-called "noble" subjects, we chose a more dynamic approach to the painting of this era in order to illustrate its entirety and universality, focusing on its strong points, popular manifestations, impact and developments. Little-known amateur artists rub elbows with big names, and "pot-boilers" are displayed beside major genre paintings and works considered masterpieces. More than mere illustrations documenting the Quebec of 1790-1860, these works have proven to be veritable beacons guiding us through the cultural and artistic universe of this era. Reflecting a society in full development, whose pluralist, fragmented ideology is manifested in a quest for identity, a desire to preserve the past, and curiosity and openness on the world, our project, in keeping with the concerns of contemporary Quebec society, targets this same openness, especially through the integration of a number of foreign artists and comparison with works from other countries.

Avenues of Research

During phase one of the project, which was devoted to seeking out possible works for the exhibition, we drew on a number of holdings, including the Inventaire des oeuvres d'art de Gérard Morisset, housed in the Musée du Québec's documentation centre, collection inventories drawn up by the Ministère des Affaires culturelles (in Quebec City and Montreal), a body of work excerpted from old newspapers, and an iconographic directory of art works produced under the supervision of John R. Porter. We also relied heavily on the computerized inventory of the Canadian Heritage Information Network. While gathering data, we compiled an extensive bibliography on painting during the period under study, based on general and specialized works. These various research tools enabled us to draw up exhaustive lists of collections and artists, and use these lists to establish files on the works. During phase two, we systematically sorted through public and private collections and examined works in detail, with the assistance of a number of curators, archivists and collection administrators, whose knowledge and advice were invaluable. I would like to acknowledge the exceptional contribution of Jim Burant and Gilbert Gignac of the National Archives of Canada (Ottawa), Rosemarie Tovell of the National Gallery of Canada (Ottawa), Mary Allodi of the Royal Ontario Museum (Toronto), Yves Lacasse of the Montreal Museum of Fine Arts, Conrad Graham of the McCord Museum (Montreal), Didier Prioul of the Musée du Séminaire de Québec, and Denis Martin of the Musée du Québec. Finally, I would like to thank Guy-André Roy of the Ministère des Affaires culturelles in Quebec City for helping us with certain collections from parish churches and religious communities.

This research into various holdings and collections enabled us to create an impressive visual bank of several thousands of works. From the outset, we purposely excluded engravings, since they belong to an entirely different sphere and, moreover, have recently been studied in depth by Mary Allodi. Our selection of works from the visual bank occurred in stages, focusing first on phenomena, issues, and themes specific to the era, and then on artists and collections. This method ensured a more well-balanced choice and greater representativeness of painters, subjects, media and periods.

Obstacles and Constraints

At this critical point in the project, we ran into major problems and constraints regarding works' availability and condition. We had to consider the duration of the loans, since the exhibition runs almost fifteen months: inaugurated at the Musée du Québec in October 1991, it will travel across Canada throughout 1992, thanks to a generous grant from Communications Canada. The tireless efforts of Michel V. Cheff, chief curator at the Musée du Québec, will allow the exhibition to be shown in four other major Canadian art institutions: the National Gallery of Canada (Ottawa), the Vancouver Art Gallery, the Art Gallery of Nova Scotia (Halifax), and the Montreal Museum of Fine Arts. The latter replaced, on short notice, the Art Gallery of Ontario (Toronto), which will be unable to host the exhibition due to major expansion work. The exhibition's lengthy circulation forced us to consider various alternatives for the selection of works on paper which have low light tolerance—generally a maximum of six months over a period of five years. Consequently, rather than replacing the originals with facsimiles or designing overly elaborate display cases, we planned a second selection of works for the latter half of the tour. After being exhibited in Quebec City and Ottawa (four months), all the works on paper will be replaced with equivalents by the same artist for the exhibitions in Vancouver, Halifax and Montreal (six months). Needless to say, this option makes the selection, borrowing, crating and transportation of the works more complicated, but it has the advantage of offering the cities on the second half of the tour a selection of new works, representing one third of the entire exhibition. As a result, the exhibition as presented in Montreal will be quite different from the one shown in Quebec City. The exhibition catalogue includes 267 works, of which the Quebec City public will see 207.

In addition to this constraint inherent to works on paper, we had to work around exhibitions being presented at the same time as ours, among them the retrospective of William Berczy mounted by the National Gallery of Canada, and the exhibitions organized as part of Montreal's 350th anniversary celebrations. This explains the under-representation in our exhibition of works by Berczy—despite an important discovery made recently (Cat. 18 and 19)—and of landscapes and views of Montreal. Finally, given the exhibition's planned itinerary, we had to consider the condition of the works, both those belonging to public institutions, such as the Musée du Québec, and those housed in parish churches and religious communities. This explains the absence of some artists, such as James Bowman, and of major works such as Jacques Viger's album, (at the Montreal municipal library) and Théophile Hamel's *Abbé Patrick McMahon* (Musée du Québec, Fig. 137A)—which deserves in-depth study in itself—and especially the under-representation of a significant component of the art history of this period: large-format religious painting. Our efforts in this area were largely in vain, both in tracing works suitable for exhibition and in finding sponsors

or other solutions for the restoration of a number of works in various Quebec parishes. The problem lay not in any unwillingness on the part of the parish churches and religious communities, but rather in a lack of sufficient funds, since restoration is extremely costly. If steps are not taken soon to conserve large-format religious paintings, this entire facet of our artistic heritage will be doomed, if not to disappearance, then at least to deterioration beyond repair. Thanks to the generous financial support of the Amis du Musée du Québec, whose remarkable commitment to art conservation merits the highest of praise, we were able to restore some fifteen major works in our collection (Cat. 53, 115, 116, 122, 134, 135, 153, 159, 168, 177, 193, 200, 201, 221, and 253)—some of which had never before been shown publicly—as well as J.-B. Roy-Audy's work entitled *The Baptism of Christ* (Cat. 203), owned by the Saint-Joseph de Deschambault parish and stored at the Musée du Québec. Finally, a number of important or previously unseen works housed in other public institutions (e.g. Cornelius Krieghoff's *Merrymaking*, which belongs to the Beaverbrook Art Gallery, and Henry Daniel Thielcke's *Elizabeth Durnford*, owned by the National Archives of Canada) could not be loaned, either because they were too fragile or because they had been reserved for other exhibitions. We would like to point out, however, that the absence of these works is offset by illustrations in the essays of the first part of the exhibition catalogue and by comparisons made in the catalogue entries.

A Representative Body of Work

Despite such difficulties, we still managed to collect an imposing body of work marked by diversity and quality, and generally quite representative of painting in Quebec between 1790 and 1860. The exhibition assembles, for the first time, over 200 well-known or previously unshown works—paintings, drawings, watercolours, miniatures, albums, and photographs—attributed to 70 artists and loaned by some 40 individuals and institutions. Naturally, the Musée du Québec's rich collection is well represented, with close to 70 works. However, we would also like to emphasize the invaluable contribution of several public institutions, which agreed to loan a number of major works from their collections for an extended period of time. Among these institutions are the National Archives of Canada (which loaned 39 works), the Royal Ontario Museum (34), the National Gallery of Canada (27), the Musée du Séminaire de Québec (23), the McCord Museum (11), the Château Ramezay Museum (9), and the Montreal Museum of Fine Arts (8), as well as other museums and galleries, religious communities, parish churches and private collectors.

Major names from the artistic community of this period have been highlighted: Théophile Hamel (25 works), Antoine Plamondon (23), Joseph Légaré (15), François Baillairgé and James Pattison Cockburn (11), James Duncan and Cornelius Krieghoff (10), Louis Dulongpré, Robert Clow Todd and Gerome Fassio (6), and finally François Beaucourt, Philip J. Bainbrigge and John R. Coke Smyth (5).

Several works acquired or discovered recently are also being exhibited or reproduced for the first time. The most important of these are Samuel Palmer's portraits of *Alfred*

Hawkins and *James Turnbull Senior* (Cat. 175 and Fig. 175B), William Berczy's *Pierre-Amable de Bonne* and his wife (Cat. 18 and 19), Théophile Hamel's *Narcisse-Fortunat Belleau, Abbé Joseph-David Déziel* (Cat. 137 and Fig. 137B), and *Portrait of a Young Indian Girl* (Cat. 131), Cornelius Krieghoff's *Doctor Daniel Arnoldi* (Cat. 149), François Beaucourt's *Mrs. Daniel Sutherland* (Cat. 13), Antoine Plamondon's *The Despair of Cain* (Cat. 182) and *The Little Gardeners* (Cat. 267), Ignace Plamondon's *The Bagpiper* (Cat. 200), Robert Clow Todd's altar ornament (Cat. 226), John Richard Coke Smyth's views of Quebec City (Cat. 216) along with those of William F. Wilson (Cat. 231), the interior scenes of the Ursuline chapel (Cat. 214 and 215), and various landscapes by British soldiers, such as the panorama of Quebec City (Cat. 241)— until recently, these detached sheets were thought to be four separate works!

A number of new attributions have also been made; for example, the famous view of Montreal, formerly attributed to Duncan (Cat. 238), and several miniatures and silhouettes (Metcalf, Fassio, Berczy and Peale). New identifications have been proposed—for Hamel's portraits of *Alphonse Colas* and *Jean-Mathieu Nisen* (Cat. 120 and 121), for instance—and changes have been suggested to several dates, especially for the landscapes done by British soldiers. We had to exclude several well-known works, such as the *Self-Portrait*, presumedly by Francis Matte, at the Detroit Institute of Arts, whose identification has proven unfounded, as well as the portrait of *Mère Marguerite d'Youville* belonging to the Musée du Québec which, despite the signature, turned out to be not a work by Beaucourt painted in 1792, but a copy probably done by Plamondon as late as 1873 (Cat. 12)! In short, this exhibition, which includes both well-known and unknown works shown together for the first time as part of a major overview and not confined to the traditional categories of landscapes, portraits, and religious painting, bears eloquent witness to the diversity and quality of pictorial production between 1790 and 1860, while offering an original and unprecedented interpretation of this era's art production as a whole.

A Monumental Publication

In addition to this introduction, the exhibition catalogue includes four essays on fundamental issues related to painting in 1790-1860, short biographies of the artists, and in-depth catalogue entries for each work selected. The essays were authored by members of the scientific committee: John R. Porter on the painting market, Paul Bourassa on portraits, Didier Prioul on British landscape artists, and Laurier Lacroix on esthetics. Although Denis Castonguay penned the biographies, and the scientific committee the catalogue entries, we called on the following outside collaborators to help with some of the texts: Mary Allodi of the Royal Ontario Museum, Victoria Baker of the National Gallery of Canada, Joanne Chagnon, formerly of the Musée du Séminaire de Québec, Yves Lacasse of the Montreal Museum of Fine Arts, Denis Martin of the Musée du Québec, Lydia Foy, Gilbert Gignac and Eva Major-Marothy, all three of the National Archives of Canada, and Stanley G. Triggs of the McCord Museum. Like the exhibition, the catalogue is the result of a collective effort by members of the scientific committee and outside researchers.

In keeping with the exhibition, this expansive catalogue, with its 600-or-so pages and 500 illustrations, will, we hope, become not only the most important synthesis ever published on painting between 1790 and 1860, but also a reference work on Quebec art in the 19th century. More than just an overview or summary of what is known at present, it updates the research conducted over the past twenty years and provides a new interpretation, a redefinition, and a new perspective on painting in the period under study. The work as a whole, with its in-depth essays and well-documented entries, sheds new light on the context, career and production of the artists featured. New perspectives, original interpretations, recent discoveries, and comparisons which take into account the works' history and iconography as well as the artists' style will contribute greatly to advancing and renewing knowledge, while proposing new areas for study. Thanks to the most recent developments in research, analysis and contemporary issues, the works in question, analyzed in the context of their production, take on new meaning— especially through the many comparisons with American and European painting—and should prove a veritable revelation for the public as a whole and specialists in particular. Quebec art's openness to outside influences becomes evident, above all, through methodical, in-depth study. The result of ongoing, exacting efforts, this exhibition on painting in Quebec and the accompanying catalogue should be important landmarks in the dissemination of knowledge on Quebec's artistic heritage. It is within this perspective that my colleagues and myself toiled long and hard and gave the best of ourselves.

Mario Béland
Coordinator, Scientific Committee

ESSAYS

THE MARKET FOR PAINTINGS:
BASIC NEEDS VERSUS ARTISTIC TASTE

by John R. Porter

"Painting is such a great gift—when in its highest form, it is such a wonderful endowment for a society in which a liking for this divine art reigns, that anyone who loves his country and fellow countrymen must commend a project likely to produce these desirable effects, and do everything in his power to ensure its success" [1](*Le Canadien*, 1838). (Translation)

"...painting, one of those fine arts of which so little is known and which is so ill-appreciated in this country where basic needs outweigh all other concerns..." [2] (François-Xavier Garneau, 1855). (Translation)

T HE TITLE OF THIS ESSAY, like the two quotations which preface it, reflects the evolution of painting in Quebec between 1820 and 1850—an ongoing process marked by contrast and opposition. Like society, and the cultural milieu in particular, artists, their clients and their works vacillated constantly between the necessity for meeting basic needs and the growing appeal of a certain artistic freedom. This leitmotif necessarily affects our exploratory approach, which is aimed at identifying and understanding a fairly complex area of painting. Given the status of research and the considerable changes to our own perception in recent years, we intend to proceed with caution and reserve in our global overview of the situation. Having finally succeeded in discarding some generalized or ill-founded conceptions, it would be ill-advised to create new ones! Our approach, therefore, is designed to emulate the contrasting and complementary brush strokes of a work in progress rather than the glossy surface and sometimes deceiving shine of the finished work.

Defining the prospects for marketing paintings in Quebec between 1820 and 1850 means examining a period characterized by sweeping changes that cannot be understood without taking a look at the periods immediately preceding and following, that is, the years 1790-1820 and 1850-1860. It also entails exploring a specific social, economic, political and cultural context, as well as a changing geographical arena whose boundaries shifted with the government's relocations and the artists' careers. Naturally, it requires a look at the artists' clients, their means, expectations, needs and tastes. It also involves recognizing the highly variable status of hundreds of painters made unique by their training, versatility or specialization. Finally, it necessitates the study of a wide variety of subjects and a large body of work produced within a competitive context in which cost was often as important a criterion as quality.

A Colonial Context

Between approximately 1790 and 1860, Quebec was known as Lower Canada, a name which persisted despite the official adoption of the term Canada East in 1840. Lower Canada was a colony in every sense of the word, especially with regard to its administrative, commercial, military and cultural structures, and seems to have been underpopulated when compared to its American neighbours to the south: in 1851, there were barely 890 261 inhabitants in all of Quebec, with the largest cities being Montreal (pop. 57 715) and Quebec City (pop. 42 052). In 1825, these same cities numbered 25 976 and 20 386 inhabitants respectively.[3] With the British Conquest of 1759, the colony's population became linguistically mixed, as a constant flow of British immigrants boosted the percentage of English-speaking inhabitants. In 1831, over 44% of the population of Quebec City—the capital—was English-speaking, as was over 51% of that of Montreal.

Under the Constitutional Act passed by England in 1791, the province of Lower Canada was given a parliamentary system of government consisting of a House of Assembly and a Legislative Council, which were responsible for passing laws under the authority of the Governor representing the British Crown. The House of Assembly soon became the site of confrontations between the French-speaking "Canadiens" and the English-speaking members who, although fewer in number, were closely connected to the true wielders of power, the Governor-controlled Legislative Council and Executive Council. In 1837 and 1838, economic problems, tensions between English-speaking merchants and French-speaking professionals, the consequences of immigration and cholera epidemics, as well as the impossibility of effecting a comprehensive reform of government structures, resulted in a major political crisis. After the failure of the rebellions and Lord Durham's report, the imperial government united Upper and Lower Canada (Act of Union passed in 1840 and ratified in 1841), thereby meeting the long-standing expectations of Lower Canada's English minority. In the new United Provinces of Canada, Lower Canada had less representation, proportionally speaking, than Upper Canada. English henceforth became the country's only official language and Assembly members could not control public funds. It was not until 1848 that French once again became one of the two official languages of the House and the principle of responsible government was finally approved. Tensions between the French— and English-speaking populations, however, remained acute:

Ill. 1.
Jarvis F. Hankes,
*George Ramsay,
9th Earl of Dalhousie,*
c. 1828;
black paper cutout,
bronze paint and
grey wash on paper
29.4 × 22.5 cm.
National Archives
of Canada,
Ottawa, (C-95138)

Ill. 2.
James Smillie,
*Ticket or Admission
Card to the Chasseur's
Museum,* c. 1826;
engraving,
15.1 × 11.4 cm.
Archives du
Séminaire de Québec
(polygraphy 8, no. 46)

one year later, discontented English Tories, outraged that Governor Elgin had agreed to approve the Rebellion Losses Bill, under which Lower Canadians received compensation for losses suffered during the rebellions of 1837-1838, set the Parliament Buildings in Montreal afire.

Some of these events had direct repercussions on the location of the colonial government and, by extension, on the social, economic and artistic life of the cities to which the government moved. With the passage of the Act of Union in 1841, Quebec City lost its status as capital city to Kingston in Upper Canada (Ontario) until 1844. Montreal then became the capital until the Parliament Buildings were burned in 1849, at which time the seat of government moved to the cities of Toronto (Upper Canada, 1850-1851, 1855-1859) and Quebec City (Lower Canada, 1851-1855, 1859-1865).

Although Lower Canada was dependent on the British Crown, it was not cut off from the outside world. In fact, during the years under study, the British colony was generally open to many outside influences and, to a certain extent, the arrival of foreigners from Europe or the United States. Also, there was the constant and periodically renewed presence of a British garrison, with its cultivated officers enamoured of art, science, theatre and literature.

Until the early 1840s, Quebec City, the capital, was not only a major administrative, commercial, religious and military centre, it was also an appealing intellectual nucleus, home to a small elite interested in developing the arts and sciences, apart from the fundamental daily concerns of the population. Under the aegis of the Governor, Lord Dalhousie (Ill. 1), the Literary and Historical Society was founded in Quebec City in 1824 and, five years later, was united with its French-language counterpart, the Société pour l'Encouragement des Arts et des Sciences en Canada, created in 1827. These associations helped foster artistic initiative while promoting an interest in the arts. Like many of his successors, Dalhousie proved a great art enthusiast. Many talented watercolourists and landscapists, such as John Elliot Woolford, John Crawford Young and James Pattison Cockburn, became part of his entourage. Dalhousie was also the patron of

the young James Smillie (1807-1885), the first engraver to ply his trade in Quebec City in the 19th century.

Despite his skill, near-monopoly and versatility (his portfolio included both utilitarian works and truly artistic endeavours), Smillie's talents were under-utilized and he lived in constant insecurity,[4] which caused him to leave for New York in 1830, where he was confident that his professional future would be ensured. This is a good indication of the difficulties and limitations of the art market in Quebec City, at least during the 1820s. Although a colonial capital such as Quebec City might have offered relative advantages, it could not rival European or American capitals which enjoyed a well-established artistic tradition, a larger clientele and infrastructures more favourable to the development of the arts. The first museum to open in Quebec City (and, indeed, in Canada), was a museum of natural history, the result of the personal initiative of gilder Pierre Chasseur in 1824 (Ill. 2).[5] In 1829—or a little before—painter Joseph Légaré reached an agreement with the Literary and Historical Society to exhibit his small collection of European canvases temporarily in the Society's ground floor premises in the Union Hotel. Again, this was a private initiative and, despite the efforts of a small group of art devotees, neither Quebec City nor Montreal was to see the establishment of a true art museum during the period under study,[6] likely due to the lack of collectors.

Nor was there an academy or school of fine arts in Quebec City or the rest of Lower Canada. Where local artists were concerned, knowledge was passed down from master to apprentice, based on the old system inherited from the French regime. One did not attain the status of professional artist by means of a specific rule. This situation inspired the following commentary by the editor of Montreal's *Le Populaire*, following a visit to the studio of Thomas Valin, pupil of painter James Bowman:

When we consider all that this country lacks to help and stimulate those who have devoted themselves to science and the arts; when we realize that painters are ignorant of the works of the great

Ill. 3.
William Berczy,
*Saint Michael and
the Dragon*, 1810;
287 × 252.7 cm.
Church of
Saint-Michel
de Vaudreuil.

masters, of the differences between the various schools; that they cannot draw from the round, that they have no accurate information about architecture, perspective and colour ranges; that they have no models from which to study the effects of nature, the reflection of light, the texture of fabrics, we must agree that, to produce even anything passable in Canada, one must have taste, innate talent and an artist's soul.[7] (Translation)

This same article mentioned Valin's hope to "perfect his talents" in Europe the following year and reported on the encouragement he had received to date from clergymen and religious communities, as well as "several Britons."[8] (Translation) It is not surprising that the latter remark refers to the two mainstays of the colonial painting market at that time: copies of religious subjects and portraits of members of the clergy and leading citizens. Evidently, Lower Canadian society was not very stimulating to the artistic imagination. As talented as they may have been, most artists depended on a limited clientele with specific requirements in order to make a living from their art. Most commissions had either a religious or social function. Copies of religious paintings or engravings had to meet the immediate needs of church authorities who were looking to decorate their churches. Although artists such as Légaré and Plamondon produced remarkable landscapes, genre scenes, history paintings and still lifes, their religious works clearly overshadowed their respective achievements. As well, many foreign painters, whose training and experience had not prepared them for this, were required to produce religious works in order to meet their clients' expectations. Although this trend was already evident between 1790 and 1820, with artists such as François Beaucourt and William Berczy (Ill. 3), it became more widespread in later years.

Portraits of clerics, leading citizens, and members of the bourgeoisie and middle class largely dominated the field of secular art. Among those who commissioned portraits were Assembly members, councillors and civil servants, who made up the bulk of artists' clientele. The tangible effects of the capital's periodic relocation beginning in the 1840s must be taken into account when ascertaining the impact of this action

and identifying the boundaries of the colonial market in question. Obviously, the presence of the government and related institutions attracted many individuals while stimulating trade and promoting an active social and cultural life.

In 1836, it was only "at the repeated urging of several of Montreal's leading citizens" (Translation) that Antoine Plamondon agreed to leave Quebec City for the summer to work on new commissions. A few years later, when Parliament moved to Montreal, the city became even more interesting, boasting a number of Anglophone artists belonging to the Montreal Society of Artists.[9] Due to the lack of art enthusiasts in Quebec City, Plamondon indicated his intention to take advantage of the opening of the new session of the House of Assembly in November 1848 by selling the six works by master artists in his collection in Montreal. Two months earlier, Légaré had exhibited several of his own canvases as well as works from his collection in a shop located near that of Joseph Boulanget on Rue Notre-Dame. Painter Théophile Hamel had set up his studio at Boulanget's in November 1847, where he mounted a permanent exhibition of portraits as well as copies of Italian and Flemish works.[10] Added to these indications of the importance of the market catering to Canadian parliamentarians are Hamel's many moves to Kingston and Toronto, Krieghoff's arrival in Quebec City in 1853, and the closing of Légaré's art gallery in 1840 and its reopening in 1852, which coincided with the departure and return of parliamentarians and civil servants to Quebec City.[11] Obviously, the art market was not limited to the parliamentary capital and, given the context just described, it is clear that itinerancy was a requirement for the several hundred Canadian or foreign artists who worked for varying lengths of time in the cities and villages of Lower Canada between 1790 and 1860.

Imports, Art Enthusiasts, Exhibitions and Clients

The microcosmic art world of Lower Canada cannot be fully understood without taking the existence, influence, market and even the competition of European art in the

Ill. 4.
*Catalogue of Oil
Paintings & Books
to be Sold
at the Chambers
of J.C. Reiffenstein,*
Front page of a
special insert in the
Quebec Mercury,
26 August 1823.

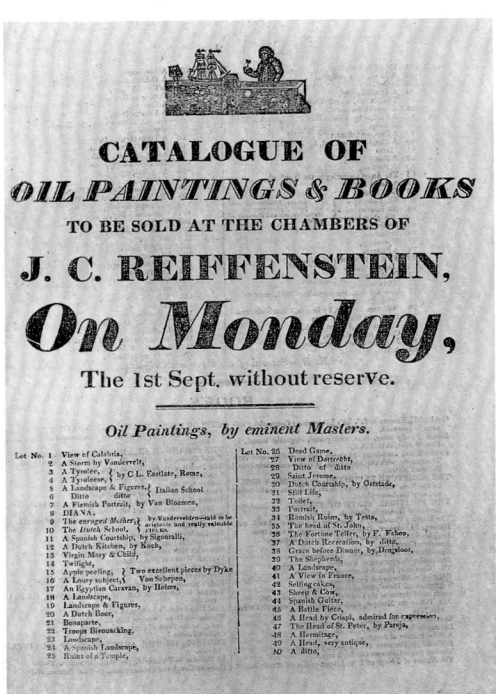

Ill. 5.
*Advertisement for the
Public Opening of
Joseph Légaré's first
Quebec Picture
Gallery,* in 1833,
printed on page 3
of the newspaper
Le Canadien,
22 November 1833.

colony into account. The presence of this art and its dissemination allows us to compare to some extent paintings executed within an atmosphere of artistic freedom for pure enjoyment with those designed to be useful and functional. However, this a minor consideration since, ultimately, it is the eye of the beholder which makes a religious work, for example, appreciated more for its plastic qualities than for its ability to evoke piety or repentance! The fact remains that one is always more inclined to discern artistic taste among lovers of landscapes or still lifes than in someone who merely commissions his own portrait or that of his wife.

Despite the fact that it lacked an art museum housing the works of great European masters, Lower Canada was not totally bereft in this area. Prior to the British Conquest of 1759, it was common practice for parish church authorities, missions and religious communities to have religious canvases and engravings sent from France.[12] These included well-done copies of canvases by the great masters, as well as original works of great value. To these reverently guarded works were added the famous Desjardins collection in 1817 and 1820, a set of 180 canvases which were among those seized by the revolutionary government in Paris and environs between 1793 and 1795. Following his return to France in 1802 after a ten-year exile in Lower Canada, Abbé Philippe-Jean-Louis Desjardins acquired the works in 1803 and shipped them to Quebec City to his brother, Abbé Louis-Joseph Desjardins, for resale. Once unpacked, mounted, restored and exhibited, these works by 17th—and 18th-century French masters found buyers not only in the parishes—sometimes served by French refugee priests (Abbé V.-C. Fournier in Baie-du-Febvre and

Abbé Jean Raimbault in Nicolet) or by Canadian-born priests (Abbé Louis-Marie Cadieux,[13] stationed in Trois-Rivières)—and religious communities—such as the Ursuline nuns of Quebec City, protégées of Abbé L.-J. Desjardins—but also among budding art enthusiasts and collectors such as Joseph Légaré.[14]

It was in this manner that religious communities and parishes such as Notre-Dame de Québec, Notre-Dame-des-Victoires, Saint-Roch de Québec, Saint-Michel de Bellechasse, Verchères and Saint-Denis-sur-Richelieu came to play a role akin to that of museums during the 19th century. The Séminaire de Québec chapel was considered by art enthusiasts and artists alike to be a veritable treasure trove of works by European masters,[15] while in 1876, the church at Oka (the former Sulpician mission of the village of Lac-des-Deux-Montagnes) was still reputed to house paintings that were among the "most beautiful [...] in Canada."[16] (Translation)

While the Desjardins canvases were well-known, they were not the only ones to be imported. Merchants such as Johan Christopher Reiffenstein, Joseph Cary and Giovanni Domenico Balzaretti flooded the colony's market with canvases and engravings to satisfy the expectations of any art enthusiast. By studying excerpts from several newspapers dating from between 1815 and 1855, we were able to estimate the number of paintings and engravings imported from Europe at no less than 442 and 18 536 respectively.[17] Although most of the engravings depicted religious subjects, such was not the case for paintings, since the majority were landscapes, followed by religious canvases, genre scenes, portraits, mythological subjects, battle scenes, and so forth. During a

Ill. 6.
Théophile Hamel,
*Denis-Benjamin
Viger*, c. 1848;
oil on cardboard,
30.5 × 25.3 cm
(irregular
measurements).
Musée du Séminaire
de Québec
(portfolio 159-G,
folio 66).

single auction held in September 1823, Reiffenstein sold no fewer than 118 secular and religious canvases of the Flemish, Dutch and Italian schools (Ill. 4).[18]

Joseph Légaré was among those lovers of European art who did business with Reiffenstein, and the number of works he purchased through the latter is estimated at 38.[19] At the time of his exhibition at the Union Hotel, his collection boasted 70 works. This number had climbed to 97 by the time his first gallery opened (1833-1835), and reached its peak of 162 at the inauguration of his third gallery in 1852.[20] In the absence of a real museum, the establishment of a gallery of European paintings and engravings in Quebec City in 1833 was very well received, both by art devotees and artists who could then directly study the works of the "leading painters of Europe" (Ill. 5). The initiative was hailed by Governor Aylmer, as it was later by Lord Elgin in 1852. At the Literary and Historical Society, art lover and humanist Daniel Wilkie praised Légaré's good taste and generosity, and made an appeal to the art-loving public which, it must be said, was limited. The second art gallery opened by Légaré, with attorney Thomas Amiot in 1838, attracted only a small number (58) of subscribers, both Francophone and Anglophone.[21] Many indications lead us to believe that Légaré connoisseurs and potential buyers of his works were primarily Anglophones.[22]

In 1852, the catalogue of his collection was published in English only and, on September 28, the editor of the *Journal de Québec* noted "the visit of a large number of foreigners" and indicated his regret "to learn that his fellow citizens were generally indifferent." (Translation)

Newspapers of the day lead us to believe that Légaré's many initiatives to develop artistic taste among his fellow countrymen were less than successful. Nonetheless, research conducted to date on the collectors of European art in Lower Canada does not allow us to draw a final conclusion in this regard. We really know very little about the collections of timber merchant Henry Atkinson,[23] the "beautiful oil paintings" of William Gildard,[24] the 70 landscapes, seascapes and still lifes of Judge Jean-Baptiste-Édouard Bacquet[25] (Cat. 156), the "beautiful collection of works" of Seigneur and parliamentarian Denis-Benjamin Viger[26] (Ill. 6), the "small Collection of Oil Paintings, several by Italian Masters" of Montreal merchant Benaiah Gibb[27] or that other unidentified Montreal collector whose collection of 80 works by European masters was put up for auction in April 1847. This is a whole new chapter that warrants further exploration and study, since more knowledge of this aspect would probably shed new light on the evolution of art in Lower Canada.

A number of European-art lovers were also interested in local contemporary works. Around 1833, the well-to-do Henry Atkinson, a man of good taste and patron of the arts, agreed to exchange a work entitled *Baccahanale*, attributed to Caravaggio, in return for works by Légaré, probably the four "Views of Carouge" ("Redcliffe") mentioned in the Spencer Wood auction catalogue of 1851.[29] Other collectors were probably not as openminded about Canadian art, conscious as they were of the difference between it and "great art." Anxious to foster the development of authentic Canadian art, newspaper editors confessed that they were often torn between the lack of respect for European standards and the laudable efforts of talented artists lacking formal training.[30] When Joseph Légaré exhibited some of his works in October 1848, a kindly art enthusiast made the following lucid and revealing comment:

And to those who would criticize the paintings of Mr. Légaré, I say, without embarking on a long debate, that if they expect to witness the birth of a Raphael or a Michelangelo, without forefathers, predecessors, masters and schools, they may have to wait a thousand years...[31] (Translation)

Fifteen years earlier, a reporter from *Le Canadien* thought it a good omen "that drawing is taught in some of our colleges," and wondered "whether, with time, people will refer to the Canadian School, just as they talk today of the French School, the Flemish School, etc."[32] In a letter addressed to Joseph Légaré in 1839 in which he discussed the illustrated album he was to assemble, famous Montreal collector Jacques Viger confided, "I am trying to make it as Canadian as possible, both in the selection of subjects and in the Artists I am employing."[33] Five years later, when notary Archibald Campbell bought Légaré's *The Engagement* and *The Despair of an Indian Woman* (Cat. 167) even before they were completed, he saw his purchase "primarily as a future monument to the first works of the Canadian school."[34] The few informed art enthusiasts in Lower Canada were obviously not interested only in the self-taught Légaré, and their activities took many forms. For example, Antoine Plamondon, trained in Quebec City and Paris, received a commission for an original religious work by patron of the arts Denis-Benjamin Viger, who intended it for his Ile-Bizard tenants; the painting, entitled *Tobie and Raphael*, was composed and sketched in 1847 based on the advice of Abbé Jérôme Demers, a "very exacting" connoisseur who forced the artist to excel. The work subsequently brought a large sum from the client and was very favourably commented upon by the artist's mentor, journalist Joseph-Édouard Cauchon.[35]

The colonial government's vacillation is also highly indicative of the Lower Canadian society's artistic values. An examination of the government's attitude does not consist in assessing the role it apparently refused to play in terms of vocational training, or the fact that it provided a studio for artists such as Plamondon and Thielcke and occasionally loaned its premises for temporary exhibitions (Ill.7).[36] Rather, it involves evaluating its performance in commissioning works of art. It seems that, while clumsily attempting to please everyone, government authorities were also torn between the appeal of foreign works and the necessity of taking local art into account.

In 1844, it was likely painter Antoine Plamondon who protested under the name of Cauchon that the Speaker of the House of Assembly had awarded Andrew Morris, a Montreal artist of Scottish origin, the contract for "two large-format works representing Trade and Agriculture, intended to decorate the Assembly meeting room" (Translation) in the Parliament Buildings in Montreal (see Cat. 173). The author of the *Journal de Québec* article indicated his surprise that a competition was not held, but he did not succeed in convincing the editor of the *Montreal Gazette*. On the contrary, not only did this newspaper maintain its opposition to a competition on the pretext that Canadian artists were incapable of producing preliminary sketches, it even went so far as to recommend that the Legislature import European works to decorate its premises!

Essentially the same arguments were used regarding the commission for portraits of Queen Victoria. After Légaré had tried in vain in 1845 to sell the government his excellent copy of *Queen Victoria* (1839), based on an original by the American Thomas Sully, for the sum of £75, Cornelius Krieghoff had to be content with a mere £40 for a copy (1847) based on George Hayter's work which was graciously offered to Parliament by a private individual. However, in 1848, the Assembly agreed to pay the tidy sum of 400 guineas for an original portrait of the Queen painted by Englishman John Partridge.[38]

The imminent return of Canadian parliamentarians to Quebec City in 1851 was the pretext for the many renovations in the old buildings of the House of Assembly. *The Quebec Mercury* published a long description of this work on August 31 of the following year, which was reprinted in French in the September 9 edition of *Le Journal de Québec*. This text is enlightening in that it summarizes in a few lines the artistic choices made by the government over the years, choices which were somewhat conventional, certainly, but which fluctuated once again between colonial and metropolitan works. In the Lower Chamber, the Speaker's chair was located next to old but valuable[39] portraits of the late King George III and Queen Charlotte, painted by the famous English painter Joshua Reynolds; however, the windows of the galleries were decorated with very recent works, in this case "magnificent transparencies representing the [parliamentary] cities

Ill. 7.
August Köllner,
Parliament House, Quebec, C., 1848;
(?) ink and watercolour on paper.
National Archives of Canada, Ottawa (C-13427).

of Quebec, Montreal, Toronto and Kingston" (Translation), painted by Robert Clow Todd and John Murray of Quebec City. In the Upper Chamber, near the Governor's throne, was a portrait of *George IV* painted in 1829 by Joseph Légaré (Cat. 160)—based on a work by Wheatley, which in turn was inspired by a canvas by Englishman Thomas Lawrence—as well as the *Queen Victoria* copied a few years earlier by Krieghoff. In a reception room were two works by Partridge: the full-length portrait of Queen Victoria—which had been rescued from the flames in Montreal in 1849—and the portrait of a former House Speaker, Sir Allan MacNab. One year later, in 1853, the government commissioned Théophile Hamel to complete a major series of portraits of parliamentarians, with the first set to be of the successive speakers of the legislative assemblies of Upper and Lower Canada, and the second, the speakers of the legislative councils of both provinces.[40]

Group commissions for official portraits were also made by educational institutions, citizens satisfied with the work of their mayor and parishioners acknowledging the zeal of their pastor, with the size of the commission and the finish of the work largely dependent upon the clients' generosity. For the most part, what was important to those commissioning the work was not so much the portrait's pictorial qualities or composition, but rather the pose and the quality of the likeness. The same held true for religious works which parish church authorities commissioned for worship purposes. Not all priests boasted an artistic taste as refined as that of Vincent, Raimbault, Cadieux, Narcisse-Charles Fortier,[41] Desjardins or Demers. In Lower Canada, it is obvious that, to ordinary mortals, copies—even passable ones—of a religious work were worth as much as an original, especially when that original was soiled or considered too expensive.

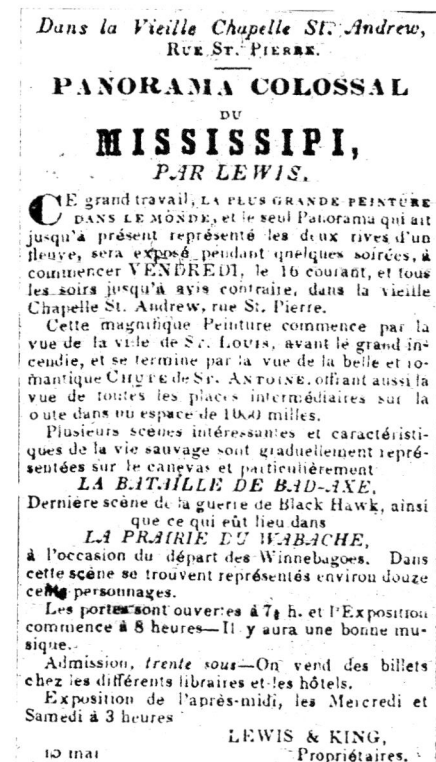

Ill. 8.
*Panorama Colossal du
Mississipi, par Lévis*
Advertisement Printed on
page 2 of the newspaper
La Minerve,
15 May 1851.

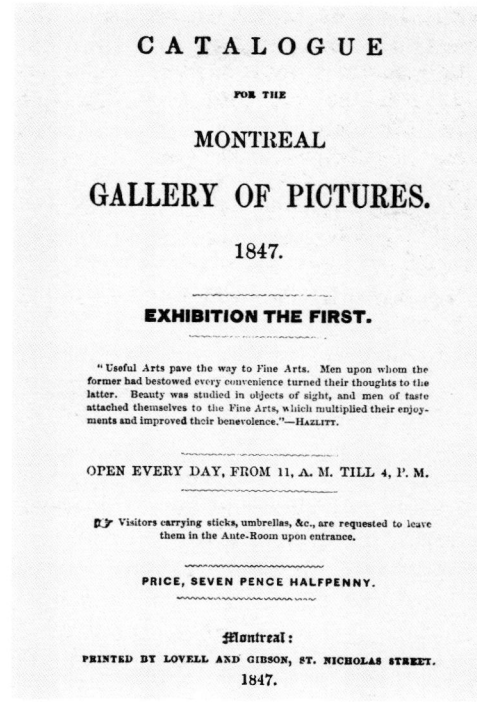

Ill. 9.
*Catalogue for the
Montreal Gallery of
Pictures 1847*,
Title page of an 1847
publication
by Lovell and
Gibson, Montreal.
Copy conserved
at the Agnes
Etherington Art
Centre, Kingston.

This can clearly be seen in the condescending words of Abbé Jérôme Demers in a letter addressed to the priest in Verchères on September 24, 1825:

I have just seen the four works which one of our young Quebec City artists recently completed for you. I hope you are happy with them. These paintings are certainly not the work of a Raphael, Lebrun, Rubens or Van Dyck; and you should not expect that; but as they are, they will please you, and please your former parishioners, and I am convinced that whichever of the "Grand Vicaires" responsible for examining them will be very pleased to allow them to be hung in your church.[42] (Translation)

The burden of necessity, the lack of an art museum and the dearth of artwork in the everyday world were not factors likely to awaken and develop artistic taste in the ordinary citizen. One almost had to be an art expert to be able to distinguish between the essential and the superfluous in the concert of superlatives which almost unfailingly hailed the slightest presentation of works of art. Everything tended to be given equal treatment, from the exhibition of the portrait of a king, bishop, politician or criminal, to the presentation of a panorama or a diorama, not to mention auctions, lotteries, annual meetings of societies of all sorts or agricultural and industrial exhibitions. To find his treasure, an attentive enthusiast had no choice but to make the rounds of hotels, bookstores, the headquarters of various associations, notaries' offices, auction rooms, artists' studios, music halls, private homes, municipal buildings, religious communities, newsrooms, the stock exchange, churches and the House of Assembly, not to mention Légaré's art gallery!

However, the most appreciated exhibitions were certainly panoramas and dioramas, those immense painted canvases—sometimes brought to life by lighting effects—which travelled on the continent from one city to another and were presented in rotundas where illusion reigned. On these very popular premises, stupefied visitors could find themselves in the thick of the battles of Waterloo, Algiers or Trafalgar, visit the cities of London, Dublin or Moscow, attend the feast of Belshazzar, witness the destruction of Babylon or the funeral of Napoleon, view the wonders of the Great Exhibition of 1851 in London at a fraction of the cost, or have a bird's-eye view of the St. Lawrence and the Great Lakes or even the Mississippi River, through the magic of "the largest painting in the world" (Ill. 8). (Translation) Aside from these occasional exciting moments, just what was the attitude of ordinary members of the Canadian bourgeoisie when directly invited to the few true exhibitions of Canadian works of art organized in Quebec City or Montreal, especially during the 1840s? For example, in August 1842, Légaré presented an exhibition and sale over four or five days in the drawing rooms of Madame Saint-Julien on Rue Saint-Gabriel in Montreal. This initiative earned him some favourable comments from Joseph-Guillaume Barthe, editor of *L'Aurore des Canadas*. After criticizing a few canvases, the latter reported "a variety of other works from which people of taste can choose" (Translation) and concluded his remarks by making the following flattering and optimistic appeal:

We therefore hope that the members of Montreal's privileged classes, who have always shown good taste and have always been pleased and proud to sponsor the fine arts, will hasten to welcome, honour and encourage them in a fellow countryman. It is not enough to glorify our men of talent, we must also pay to deserve them.[43] (Translation)

It is not known whether this appeal received much of a response, but it is highly doubtful, given the comments made about the exhibition of 179 works organized five years later by the Montreal Society of Artists (Ill. 9). This group of seven artists associated with Montreal's English-speaking community intended to make its members known, stimulate an interest in the arts in the city and build up a clientele which would enable the artists to make a living from their work.[44] As part of a long critique published in *The Pilot and Journal of Commerce* on January 29, 1847, a physician, who signed H.N., made a rather discouraging diagnosis of the fine arts situation in Montreal, emphasizing the lack of vitality, interest and encouragement, the fact that Canada was well behind the United States, that infrastructures were non-existent, that talented artists wishing to perfect their art in Europe lacked the finances to do so, and that the response to certain type of works was lukewarm whereas, in other countries, they would be very highly thought of.

One year later, some of the comments about a more modest exhibition mounted in the foyer of the former building of the House of Assembly in Quebec City were similar to those about the Montreal exhibition. Organized by Légaré, this exhibition boasted several of his own works as well as some canvases from his European collection; of these works, 31 were to be the subject of a lottery.[45] The newspapers' enthusiastic reception was coupled with an appeal to public pride, as can be seen in the conclusion of this article published in *Le Journal de Québec*:

We hope that Mr. Légaré will succeed in selling all his lottery tickets and that the citizens of Quebec City and other towns and villages will not show themselves as members of a society which owes its origins to the nation of arts "par excellence," but which lets the latter die here through lack of encouragement.[46] (Translation)

As in Montreal, the Quebec City exhibition was not as successful as hoped. A reader of *Le Canadien* indicated he was as impressed by the quality of the exhibition as he was disappointed by the lack of names entered on the list of lottery subscribers. Annoyed, he even reprimanded the government for its unwillingness to establish an art museum that would benefit artists and the public alike:

But why should we be surprised by this indifference when the example is set from so high up? If the government does not protect the arts, there is no point in depending on the support of individuals.[47] (Translation)

In October 1847, journalist Napoléon Aubin made a frankly pessimistic assessment of the market open to Lower Canadian artists:

With the exception of family portraits, painters receive commissions only for the occasional church painting, for which they are still paid only the cost of the canvas, paints and their hours of work as if they were common labourers, their talent, studies, and imagination counting for nothing. [...] Quebec boasts distinguished painters skilled in various art forms; two of them [Antoine Plamondon and Théophile Hamel] travelled to Europe to draw inspiration from the indispensable lessons of the great masters. Upon their return, their fellow citizens could find nothing more beautiful, noble and gracious to offer the artists' skillful brushes, their imaginations freshly stimulated by the brilliant works of ten centuries of genius [...] than their own faces, of which they are asked to produce a more or less faithful and flattering copy. It seems to us that, as well as family subjects, whose attractions we wish neither to deny nor condemn, they could have been commissioned to reproduce some of the magnificent scenes of the Canadian landscape, to interpret a few of the brilliant, touching and

patriotic pages of our heroic history which no painter has yet undertaken. Do we lack the resources or artists with sufficient skills? Not at all. [...]
Why then do we allow talents, of which we should be proud, to remain dormant; why do we leave ourselves open to remarks by all distinguished travellers who visit us to the effect that there are no more Canadians in Canada? Let it be said once again: because those who can set the tone for society are misguided in where they place their pride and their ostentation. [...]
Let us suppose that a traveller, a painting enthusiast, visits the home of one of our leading citizens. He is shown into the drawing room where he finds soft carpets, mahogany furniture, gilded chandeliers, marble fireplaces, thick drapes and, for decoration, a thousand insignificant trinkets showing neither good taste nor talent, and nary a painting in sight. [...] But if he were to find your walls decorated with works painted in Canada, showing a scene representing local customs, a landscape, a historical event; were these paintings to show the slightest bit of originality, they would not fail to be the subject of an interesting conversation and would give the visitor a favourable view of Canadian high society, of the advancement of arts among us, and perhaps he might wish to take home some artistic souvenir from this country.[48] (Translation)

While these comments may seem excessive, they all strike a similar note: in the early 1850s, the market for artists working in Lower Canada was still limited to certain "useful or functional" art forms, despite the initiatives of a few painters and enthusiasts in favour of diversification. It is therefore not surprising that the latter sang an oft-repeated refrain, deploring the indifference and lack of taste among members of the bourgeoisie and the well-heeled, "the number of important obligations [continue to] relegate drawing, music and other decorative arts to the boudoirs of the fair sex."[49]

But, aside from these general observations, what could really be found on the walls of these "parlours" and "drawing rooms"? Although it is difficult to answer such a question with any degree of accuracy, many indications lead us to believe that engravings were considered very important, an aspect of the daily visual universe which we too often neglect or relegate to obscurity.[50] It is important to remember the very large number of English, French or other engravings imported by merchants during the period under study.[51] And there is no doubt that the members of the Lower Canadian bourgeoisie were epicures of the subjects they depicted at affordable prices: religious or historical themes, portraits of famous people, romantic views, genre scenes, sentimental subjects, and so on. Here again the best and the worst can be found, including those "bad lithographs coloured red and blue" deplored in a critique in 1842.[52] Nor must those engravings of Canadian content disseminated both within the colony and among our neighbours to the south or in Europe be forgotten.[53] This limited body of work nevertheless comprises a fairly wide variety of subjects, including landscapes, architectural views, scenes from daily life, a few religious subjects and, of course, political and religious personalities, which were considered fashionable to hang in the home.[54]

The Artist's Changing Profile:
A Reflection of Market Demands

Such was the pictorial landscape in which hundreds of artists evolved for better or for worse between 1820 and 1850. This

Ill. 10.
Louis-Hubert Triaud,
*The Martyrdom of
Saint Andrew*, 1821,
oil on canvas,
approx.
275 × 185 cm.
Church of
Saint-André
de Kamouraska.

Ill. 11.
Louis-Hubert Triaud
(attr. to),
Hector-Simon Huot,
c. 1825;
oil,
29.2 × 22.9 cm.
Unknown location.

rather checkered group included a few prominent figures, whose well-defined profile contrasts sharply with that of obscure artists about whom nothing is known other than their names—their artistic endeavours long since lost in the dark reaches of oblivion.[55] Between these two extremes are painters who have recently been rediscovered through research and to whom it will now be possible to attribute tangible works: in short, a small, complex universe in which individuality quickly overrode general trends. To the diversity of artists' national origins (Canada, England, United States, France, Italy) must be added the disparity in training, the varying degree of specialization or versatility, a geographically fluctuating field of activity, differing lengths of time spent in Lower Canada, a professional status which grew with the number of clients and type of work, etc. Take, for example, the many contrasts between travelling portraitists such as the self-taught Jean-Baptiste Roy-Audy and the brilliant Samuel Palmer, between a versatile artist such as Todd and a haughty Plamondon who refused certain types of work, between an insignificant drawing master such as Victor Ernette and a great portraitist of Théophile Hamel's stripe, between a fine miniaturist such as Gerome Fassio and the versatile explorer named Légaré! This sampling accurately reflects Lower Canada's artistic mosaic, a somewhat fragmented reality which we nevertheless will attempt to study from the perspective of four revealing phenomena: versatility, itinerancy, competition and professional hierarchies.

In the late 18th century, the colony's diverse elementary needs combined with an obvious lack of human resources to fulfill them meant that an artist of François

Baillairgé's mettle was required to work on several fronts without necessarily mastering all the tasks for which he was hired. Although comfortable in the fields of sculpture and architecture, he was hesitant when commissioned to produce religious works or painted portraits. An excellent drawer, he apparently managed to acquit himself well with portraits in pastels and miniatures, but it is highly doubtful that he was as successful when restoring or painting theatre sets.

Many painters practising their craft in Baillairgé's wake between 1820 and 1850, faced with colonial constraints and the specific expectations of certain clients, agreed to expand their field of activity. This forced versatility is reflected somewhat in the body of work of several Canadian or foreign artists, but it is clearly obvious in the work of painters such as Louis-Hubert Triaud, Joseph Légaré and Robert Clow Todd.

Presumed to have arrived in Quebec City in late 1819, Triaud quickly distinguished himself by his adaptability, despite the fact that his previous career in England had been dominated by portraiture.[56] A protégé of Abbé Louis-Joseph Desjardins, he proved to be an excellent restorer of early works, and agreed to execute a large painting for the high altar of the church in Saint-André-de-Kamouraska (Ill. 10), based on a European work hanging in the Notre-Dame church in Quebec City,[57] and to complete a coat-of-arms for the nuns of the Hôtel-Dieu de Québec hospital (Cat. 229), sets for the Théâtre royal de Québec, and a festive painting on satin for the Confrérie des imprimeurs de la ville. As well, he continued to paint portraits, as proved by his painting of attorney Hector-Simon Huot, executed around 1825[58] (Ill. 11).

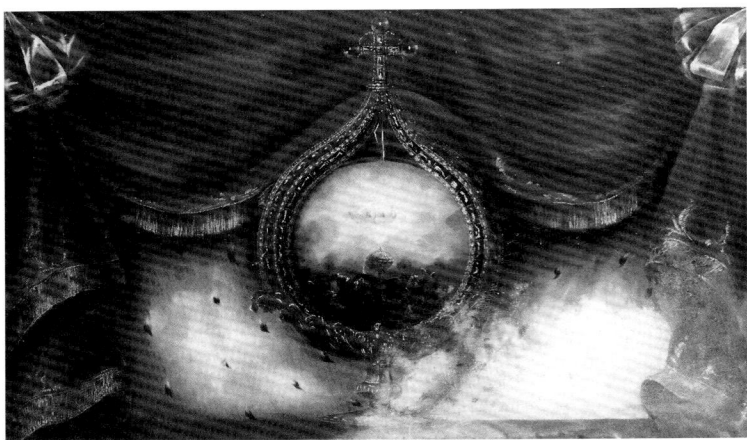

Ill. 12.
Joseph Légaré,
Antependium, 1832;
oil on canvas, 62.5 × 97 cm.
Musée de l'Hôpital général de Québec.

Unlike Triaud, Légaré did not benefit from the advantages of a formal education. After serving as the apprentice of a "painter and varnisher," he took advantage of a favourable economic context to become an artist around 1818. Probably because of his modest, self-taught status, or his versatility acquired during his twofold training, he subsequently made himself available for any task at the slightest request. Coats-of-arms, banners, altar frontals (Ill. 12), restoration work,[59] theatre sets, statue colouring—no task seemed too daunting. What is more, his artistic production as such shows remarkable diversity, comprising numerous copies of religious engravings or paintings, a few portraits, several landscapes, history paintings, genre scenes, still lifes, etc.[60] The many constraints inherent in the artist's composite clientele, sometimes French-Catholic and clerical, sometimes English-Protestant and secular, must be kept in mind when considering this wide variety of works. The obligation to serve and satisfy this essentially conservative clientele, and their very different tastes, needs and interests, often forced Légaré to conceal some of his religious[61] or political beliefs, and appear conformist or moderate in his public behaviour. An opportunist, Joseph Légaré occasionally managed to turn his sociopolitical commitment to advantage in order to land a few attractive contracts. However, certain errors in judgement where market opportunities in the Lower Canadian colonial community were concerned left him with major works on his hands.[62]

The career profile of an artist like Robert Clow Todd bears many similarities to Légaré's.[63] Although most of his clients came from his own social and linguistic community, this English artist managed to make important breakthroughs into a field of activity which was by no means guaranteed from the start. He distinguished himself with a varied body of work which, like that of Légaré, was regularly mentioned in the local press. "Sign painter" and "artist" (Translation), he painted not only coats-of-arms but also portraits, religious subjects—including one of the Holy Family on an *Antepen-*

dium for the Séminaire de Québec (Cat. 226)—patriotic banners, landscapes, portraits of racehorses, emblematic transparencies and genre scenes.[64]

It is quite possible that the versatility of Triaud, Légaré and Todd enabled them to carve out a career in Quebec City without having to wander too far from their home port. Such was not the case, however, for the majority of their colleagues, especially portraitists. Beginning in the 1790s, Lower Canada was visited by dozens upon dozens of miniaturists and silhouettists. Natives of the United States or various European countries, these travelling artists moved from city to city throughout North America. Their sojourns were of varying lengths—from a few days to several months—depending on their reception and the interest manifested in them. It goes without saying that their work is generally as difficult to identify as their route is complex to reconstruct. One has only to think of Gerritt Schipper, for example, whose career took him to Amsterdam, Paris, Charleston, Boston, Salem, Hartford, New York, Quebec City, and so on. It can therefore be seen that the geographic area in which artistic creation—or at least portraits—flourished was not confined to Lower Canada and varied greatly from painter to painter.

The same holds true for those Canadian artists who sought additional training elsewhere. For a self-taught artist such as Roy-Audy, the problem was presented in another way. Unable to compete with his more talented colleagues, he took to the road, avoiding the major centres, confident of finding in their outskirts or in more remote villages members of the bourgeoisie who would like their portrait done, or priests willing to commission works at affordable prices for their church. Moreover, he did not hesitate to travel beyond the colony's borders in his search for a market.[65] Another interesting case is that of James Bowman, who travelled through Europe, the United States and the British North American colonies.[66] Although he worked primarily in the field of portraiture, he attempted, with mixed success, to diversify his body of work, even venturing along the dangerous paths of religious composition. A clever man, he managed to land an attractive contract to complete six paintings intended for the side chapels of the new Notre-Dame church in Montreal in summer 1833. One of them, *Christ Identifying Saint Roch as Protector Saint Against the Plague* (Ill. 13), illustrates his limitations, the importance of the religious painting market and the constant influence of European prototypes, in this case, an engraving based on a work by Peter Paul Rubens.[67]

The arrival of a foreign artist such as Bowman in the colony probably offended Canadian painter Antoine Plamondon, whose tolerance was inversely proportional to his pride and ambition. Annoyed by the successes of the American Bowman on the portrait and religious painting market since 1831, Plamondon finally had the opportunity to get back at him when William Kemble, editor of *The Quebec Mercury*, solicited his opinion on the Quebec City showing of a diorama entitled *La Chapelle des Capucins à Rome* and executed by his competitor.[68] Identifying himself as a "student of the French school," Plamondon hastened to ridicule Bowman's work, calling it "genuine caricature,"[69] which earned him a scathing reply from Kemble, a reply to which the

Ill. 13.
James Bowman,
*Christ Indentifying
Saint Roch as
Protector Saint
Against the Plague*,
oil on canvas,
203 × 185.5 cm.
Notre-Dame Basilica,
Montreal.

artist could not prevent himself from answering with contempt and disdain:

It is very important for the advancement and perfection of the fine arts to point out the failings and qualities of any work shown to the public in order to enlighten and shape public tastes.[70] (Translation)

Aside from his verbal outbursts, Plamondon's attitude is an excellent indicator of the competitive climate which characterized the tiny world of artists in Quebec City during this period. Although Légaré was naturally inclined to maintain cordial relations with his fellow Canadian or foreign artists, Plamondon had a tendency to be on his guard against the encroachments of his colleagues in the field of "history painting," if not in that of teaching drawing and painting. Englishman Henry Daniel Thielcke and Frenchman Victor Ernette each in turn paid the price for a rash venture into the preserve of the irascible Antoine Plamondon.

Thielcke's misfortunes began in 1835 when he attempted to break out of his restrictive English-speaking market by producing a religious work, *The Baptism of Christ*, which he exhibited in his studio—next to Plamondon's—on the premises of the House of Assembly. Vexed by the work's favourable reception on the part of the editors of *Le Canadien* and *The Quebec Mercury*, our artist wrote an open anonymous letter under the pseudonym "Des Amateurs" (Art Lovers), in which he gave a vitriolic analysis of his competitor's composition, cheerfully contrasting its supposed weaknesses to the great qualities of Claude-Guy Hallé's *The Baptism of Christ*, which hung in the outdoor chapel of the Séminaire de Québec.[71] All evidence shows that this controversy imposed a severe constraint on Thielcke's efforts to diversify his market.

Poor Ernette committed the offense of being chosen over his rival as drawing master for novices at the Hôpital général de Québec, in addition to landing a similar job with the Ursuline nuns. Soon after his arrival in Quebec City in 1842, he also suffered from the anonymous wrath of our

"enemy of Charlatanism on behalf of fine arts" (Translation) in *Le Canadien* of March 14. The following excerpt clearly shows the xenophobic tone of the attack:

When a great foreign charlatan finds his way into a country, into a city, especially a city like Quebec, inhabited with honest citizens, to filch the people's money, it is necessary for one of these citizens, if he has any conscience at all, to bring this shameful practice to light.[72] (Translation)

Outraged, Ernette beat a retreat and returned to France a few weeks later.

The mere fact that artists spent part of their time teaching not only emphasizes the lack of a fine arts academy or school in the colony, but also bears witness to their need to seek additional income enabling them to make ends meet. We have lost count of the number of artists—of various origins and backgrounds—who worked as drawing, miniature or painting masters, either in educational institutions or giving private lessons to young ladies and interested gentlemen. Baillairgé, Roy-Audy, Triaud, Martyn, Ignace and Antoine Plamondon, Woodley, Bowman, Fassio, Thielcke, Somerville, Hamel, Todd and many others did not hesitate to add this string to their bow.

Some masters were better known that others. As well, the small artistic community in the colony had an internal hierarchy based on reputation, specialty, training, body of work or clientele, rather than on tradition and regulations as in Europe. Status sometimes varied depending on the fields of art in which the artists were involved and whether basic needs were satisfied. When Plamondon attacked Bowman's diorama in 1833, he went so far as to advertise himself as the spiritual heir of "Phidias, Michelangelo, Raphael, Le Sueur, Poussin, David, Guérin, etc.," thereby relegating his rival to the lower rungs of the profession:

We hope we never have to degrade ourselves to the point of painting theatre sets [...]. Theatre painters are not on the same level as history painters. It is monstrous to draw this comparison.[73] (Translation)

Ill. 14.
Louis Dulongpré,
*Descent from the
Cross,* after
Charles Le Brun,
1804;
oil on canvas,
approx.
305 × 213 cm.
Church of
Sainte-Croix,
Lotbinière.

Ill. 15.
Antoine Plamondon,
*Descent from the
Cross,*
after Pieter Paul
Rubens, 1840;
oil on canvas,
approx.
245 × 142 cm.
Chapel of the
Augustines,
Hôtel-Dieu,
Quebec.

Such a diatribe could only serve to rub artists such as Triaud, Schinotti and Légaré the wrong way.

Joseph Légaré's regular commissions for works of a rather utilitarian nature[74] and his status as a self-taught artist, deprived of the prestige attached to European training, probably constituted a serious handicap despite the artist's versatility. As the editor of *Le Canadien* wrote in 1833:

We have always regretted that this Gentlemen did not have the opportunity to go to Europe to spend some time under the tutelage of some great master and be exposed to magnificent works. The same could be said of some other Canadians who work with mixed success in this field.[75] (Translation)

Although the above sheds some light on the overall situation of artists working in Lower Canada, more details are required. This is why, now that we have placed the painters and their clients within the colonial context, we intend to examine a little more closely the characteristics of and changes in the main facets of the artists' work, beginning with the two dominant genres, religious painting and portraiture.

Religious Painting

"As we have already stated, the Catholicism which reigns in this country provides a constant and ever-growing market for holy paintings; and consequently acts as a spur to genius in this fine art."[76] (Translation)

After the British Conquest of 1759, copying truly began to gain ground in Canada.[77] Under the French regime, it was common to import paintings needed in the colony from France, a practice which naturally did not promote the emergence of local talent. Deprived of its traditional source of supply after the Conquest, the former French colony was then forced to learn to become self-sufficient in the field of pictorial art. By the end of the 18th century, the practice of copying was well established, with artists systematically using models—painted or engraved—conserved from the *Ancien Régime.* Cut off from the major centres of European art and unable to benefit from the resources of an academy, several Quebec artists learned the rudiments of their art by analyzing and copying the only European canvases and engravings at their disposal. Having acquired certain tricks of the trade, they were able to fulfill the community's needs, which continued to grow as new parishes were established.

Given this context, it is not surprising that the arrival of the Desjardins collection in 1817 and 1820 provided new resources and was apparently the event which launched the artistic careers of Légaré and Roy-Audy. Unable to purchase certain original works, several parishes turned to available painters for copies. Between 1820 and 1825, Légaré painted some thirty religious works, especially for the churches of Saint-Roch-des-Aulnaies, Trois-Rivières, Bécancour and Sainte-Foy, as well as for the Hôpital général de Québec chapel. Many of them were based on the works which arrived in 1817 or 1820. Roy-Audy was not far behind, copying Philippe de Champaigne's *The Pentecost* in 1818, *Saint Peter Freed from his Prison* (then attributed to Charles de la Fosse) in 1819, Samuel Massé's *Christ with the Doctors of the Church* in 1821 and Charles Monnet's *Christ on the Cross* in 1825, all part of the Desjardins collection.

Market opportunities for copies of religious works were such that many foreign artists also tried to take advantage of them, but with mixed success. Generally, copyists of religious subjects—or "history painters," to use a common enough term of the time—had to take advantage of established models, either painted or engraved. In such cases, copies had to be very close to the original to be accepted. In 1845, much to his chagrin, Plamondon was reminded of this fact when the Chambly parish church authorities refused his *Saint John the Baptist* because it "in no way resembled the model provided."[78] A few beautiful works by European masters hanging in churches or chapels were especially prized, to such an extent that a whole range of copies by different artists are still in existence.[79] In some cases, Lower Canadian painters had to work from "a wretched engraving."[80] The editor of Montreal's *Le Populaire* admitted to being impressed by the religious works which Thomas Valin was to paint in his studio located on the premises of the Grey Nuns of Montreal in 1837:

All of Mr. Valin's works are based on small, inferior engravings, in which the composition is often truncated, proportions disregarded and drawing careless, but notwithstanding all these obstacles, his works are well executed, his details are accurately reproduced, his contours are soft and gracious, his colours are vibrant without being unrealistic.[81] (Translation)

To better understand the copying process, the prestige of certain models and the role of various participants, we studied the two works of the *Descent from the Cross* commissioned from Louis Dulongpré in 1804 and from Antoine Plamondon in 1840 to decorate the high altar in the Hôtel-Dieu de Québec hospital chapel. These deceptively simple examples illustrate the diversity of the means by which a specific iconography is conveyed as they quickly lead us to other works distributed throughout a pictorial network which is very complex.

The history of our paintings begins with Jacques Dénéchaud, a French physician who arrived in Quebec City in 1752 and worked at the Hôtel-Dieu hospital from 1769 until his death in 1810. His portrait, which was probably the work of fellow Frenchman Louis Dulongpré, is still hanging in the hospital. In 1805, Dénéchaud donated a series of paintings representing the twelve apostles and the evangelists St. Mark and St. Luke to the Hôtel-Dieu nuns. They are probably works by Dulongpré repainted by Triaud in 1830-1831. The configuration of the apostles is directly based on works by Rubens engraved between 1646 and 1650 in the studio of Bolswert and Pieter Clouwet.[82] In 1804, this generous physician gave the Hôtel-Dieu a large *Descent from the Cross* painted by Dulongpré, which is now hanging in the Sainte-Croix church in Lotbinière (Ill. 14). The work is clearly based on a painting that has been hanging since the first half of the 18th century in the Sulpician mission church in the village of Lac-des-Deux-Montagnes (Oka), in this case, an excellent copy painted directly from an original by Charles LeBrun (circa 1680) now housed in the Musée des beaux-arts de Rennes in France.

In 1811, Dulongpré returned to visit the Sulpician mission church to make copies, as indicated in a letter dated August 28 from Abbé Louis-Joseph Desjardins to Sulpician Candide-Michel Le Saulnier.[83] The artist knew Abbé Desjardins well because he had painted his portrait three years earlier. During his visit, he copied another version of the *Descent from the Cross*, this time an excellent copy made from the original by Jean Jouvenet (1708), which is still located in the Saint-Maclou church in Pontoise.[84] Dulongpré painted this work for the parish of Saint-Martin de l'Ile-Jésus.[85] A few years later, between 1836 and 1839, Antoine Plamondon used the same prototype, probably at the suggestion of Sulpician Joseph-Vincent Quiblier, to complete one of the paintings of the Way of the Cross intended for the new Notre-Dame church in Montreal.[86] In the meantime, painter Yves Tessier

also visited the village of Lac-des-Deux-Montagnes to find models for some of the works he was to deliver to the Saint-Marc-sur-Richelieu church in 1824. He copied *The Flagellation of Christ*,[87] as well as *Descent from the Cross*, inspired by LeBrun (Fig. 218A).

Thanks to the kindness of Abbé Jérôme Demers, Plamondon obtained authorization to move his studio in 1838 to the garret of the Hôtel-Dieu de Québec hospital, where he had all the space he needed to execute his 14 large paintings for the Way of the Cross. Once his work was finished, and before moving yet again, our artist complied with Abbé Louis-Joseph Desjardins' invitation, and painted a large *Descent from the Cross* (Ill. 15), which was to replace the canvas completed by Dulongpré in 1804. However, for the composition of this work, he did not work from the prototypes based on the paintings by LeBrun and Jouvenet. Instead, he used an engraving based on the central panel of Rubens' triptych hanging in the Antwerp cathedral (1612)![88] Consciously or unconsciously, Plamondon had returned to the source with the series of apostles inspired by Rubens which Dulongpré had painted 35 years earlier.

Aside from their literal copies of paintings or engravings, painters of religious canvases would sometimes utilize only a part (of varying sizes) of the original work. They also occasionally integrated elements borrowed from various models into a new composition.[89] Aside from the fact that copying was a common, well-established practice, it seems that church authorities were too poor to commission original compositions which, according to our data, would have cost at least twice as much as copies. To use one of Plamondon's expressions, parishes were only able to pay "the cost of a day's work of a labourer"[90] for paintings they commissioned. Echoing Plamondon's complaints, the editor of *L'Aurore des Canadas* in 1843 regretted that "wealthy church authorities allow churches to be stripped, denuded, or decorated with caricatures which only God in all his infinite goodness can endure!"[91]

Over the course of his long career, Plamondon was often spurred on by foreign competition. Since he wanted at all cost to protect his privileged status with church authorities and religious communities, he was occasionally required to re-examine his pictorial compositions with regard to religious works, as can be seen in a long, obviously biased article by Joseph-Édouard Cauchon about a work entitled *Saint Lucie, Praying for Her Mother's Cure on Saint Agatha's Tomb* (Ill. 16). The gift of a rich individual, the canvas in question was intended for the high altar of the Sainte-Luce-de-Rimouski church and still bears the unequivocal inscription (A. Plamondon inventit/1842) which Plamondon used to confirm his creatorship. Cauchon, the artist's mentor and confidante, concluded his partisan commentary published in *Le Journal de Québec* in May 1843 as follows:

This is the first true composition he has had to execute. Many times he has been required to make major changes in some compositions, and he has always been happy with his attempts. Often he has had to compose all the colours, as in the fourteen paintings of the "Way of the Cross" for the huge church in Montreal; and everyone knows how pleasing and surprising were the richness and magic of his brush revealed in each painting in various and always more ravishing forms. However, it can be said that colour and composition are two distinct qualities, and that often a great colourist is a poor composer, and a good composer is sometimes a poor colourist. Mr. Plamondon has just shown his composition to disbelievers today, to those who judge what a man can do by what he usually does, when he has not yet been given the opportunity to display his full talent.[92] (Translation)

Readers would be justified in seeing in this passage an allusion to the conflict which, a few years earlier, had set our artist in opposition to English painter Henry Daniel Thielcke. Be that as it may, four years later Plamondon was to put the final touches to *Tobie and Raphael*, a painting commissioned by Denis-Benjamin Viger and which he executed with great difficulty. This was apparently to be his last original composition.[93] The artist was later to return to his former life as a copyist while attempting, with mixed success, to maintain his share of activities as a "history painter." It was during this time that the Canadian clergy began to show interest in Italian painters and their works. Although they were not well received because of their poor quality, the paintings of the Way of the Cross by Giovanni Salvagni, which arrived in Montreal in 1847—to replace Plamondon's works which the Sulpician Quiblier had to refuse—presaged a long line of paintings which soon changed the face of religious art in the country.[94]

Beginning in the 1850s, the artistic "catch-up" process in Canada stepped up considerably, promoting greater openness on the rest of the world. In Quebec, the Church became steeped in a triumphalist atmosphere. In an attempt to make itself omnipresent, it tried to provide a material equivalent to its growing spiritual and temporal power. Monseigneur Ignace Bourget, the influential, ultramontane bishop of Montreal, showed an overpowering and contagious predilection for European art. Shared by a growing number of clergymen, his specific fondness for Italian art was certainly a measure of his strong attachment to the Holy See.

Ill. 17.
A.-Sébastien Falardeau,
The Triumph of Charity over Christianity,
after Federico Barocci, 1860; oil on oval panel, 37.5 × 37 cm with four miniatures representing *Christ*, after Carlo Maratta (1861), *Beatrice Cenci*, after a painting formerly attributed to Guido Reni (1861), *Music*, after Giovanni Martinelli (1861), and *A Sybill*, after Guido Reni (1861). Musée du Québec, Quebec (34.707).

Impressed by the wall decorations and paintings they could admire in the Old World, certain clerics wished to recreate in Quebec church decorations resembling those in Europe. To this end, they often encouraged Italian, French and German artists to come to Canada, or they systematically imported European works. Overcome by events, painters like Plamondon soundly denounced the blind admiration of certain clients for such works. On September 3, 1861, Plamondon used the recent acquisition by the Sisters of Charity of Quebec City of an impressive canvas, measuring 27 feet high and executed by Parisian painter Alexandre Legrand, to express his resentment, going so far as to say that this *Sacred Heart* lacked inspiration, since "to paint a holy subject well, the painter must be raised a Roman Catholic![95] And in August 1862, he reacted significantly to the recent success enjoyed by his fellow countryman Antoine-Sébastien Falardeau (Ill. 17). Jealous of the reception which several painting enthusiasts gave to this famous copyist during his one-month stay in Canada—the first since his departure for Italy in 1846—he published a scornful critique of Falardeau's works without even deigning to name him.[96]

Given the small number of religious paintings contained in this catalogue, readers will realize that we have, to some extent, overemphasized this side of Lower Canadian artistic work in this essay. This is a conscious and deliberate attempt to counterbalance the under-representation of religious works caused by the poor condition of church paintings and their scarcity within public collections. In its quest for originality, the historiography of Quebec painting between 1790 and 1860 has augmented this distortion, giving unfair priority to the development of portraiture over the history of copying holy subjects.

Portraiture

When reviewing the historiography of painting in Quebec during the first half of the 19th century, especially portraiture, one automatically thinks of Antoine Plamondon. For well over 15 years following his return from Paris in 1830, this confirmed bachelor proved to be a sensitive painter of "family subjects."[97] Parents and their children were obviously not the only ones to knock at his studio door:[98] clergymen, military men and members of the episcopacy could also be found there. His clientele was drawn from various levels of the middle class: politicians, professionals, English and French merchants, etc. All appreciated the close resemblance and classical treatment of the facial features painted by this "student of the French school." Despite many Canadian and foreign competitors, Plamondon was first in his field until Théophile Hamel's return from Europe in 1846. From that time on, Hamel quickly cornered a large share of the market previously taken for granted by his former master. Before Plamondon and Hamel, itinerant artists such as Dulongpré and Roy-Audy had already managed to tap the portrait market by travelling from town to town, visiting priests, seigneurs, landowners, officers and proud members of the bourgeoisie, not to mention those elderly ladies whose coquetry allowed them to forget the ravages of time while they posed.

Before switching to oil portraits, Dulongpré used pastels in the late 18th century, a process offering the twofold advantage of being faster and less costly. At that time, he was seeking clients of more modest means who were looking for a fair likeness. It was therefore logical that in spring 1794 he inform readers of *The Quebec Gazette* that he had "lately arrived from the Colonies, where he has improved in the Art of Drawing under the best Academicians [and] acquaints the Public, That he will Paint in Miniature and in Crayons, Pastels."[99] (Translation) At the time, the United States were expanding rapidly, and the nation's demographic growth soon enabled artists to gain access to a significant proportion of the population which was comfortably well off. Proud of its new status, this social class wanted to call attention to itself, but within its means. This is where pastellists, miniaturists or painters who were less skilled, but capable of producing a close resemblance at affordable prices, came into play. Naturally, this extraordinary development in the portrait market among our neighbours to the south had an impact on the colonies of British North America, facilitating the emergence of several travelling portraitists who, faced with growing competition, did not hesitate to expand their field of activity in the hope of finding new markets.

Similarly, a significant number of European artists decided to leave the old country to try their luck in new pastures, even if it sometimes meant banking on the easy prestige conferred by a list of accomplishments almost too wonderful and too embellished to be true! It would take a clever person to verify the accuracy of the declarations of "Mr. Hervé, of the Cities of London and Edinburgh" when, after arriving in Quebec City in 1817, he claimed that he had completed no fewer than 35 000 portraits in the capital of the British Empire alone. However, the citizens of the Canadian capital were quite free to use his diligent services as their purses would permit. His fees were as follows: miniatures at

Ill. 18.
Gerome Fassio,
*Marie-Angélique
Chaboillez*, c. 1834;
watercolour, gouache
and gum arabic on
ivory, 6.8 × 5.5 cm.
National Gallery
of Canada,
Ottawa (35515).

20 piastres and up, coloured miniatures in profile at 4 piastres and up, silhouettes at 1 écu—or 1 piastre for 4 silhouettes of the same person—and profiles in bronze at 2 piastres and up.[100]

Full faces, profiles or silhouettes, all types of artistic endeavour were represented, with some travelling artists stressing their low prices or the quality of their work, while others emphasized their "style which is superior to most profile drawings" or "their unique, excellent style."[101] But they all had to guarantee the accuracy or fidelity of the "likeness." After all, the main objective was to create "a permanent souvenir of friends and relations."[102] The plastic qualities of such portraits ranged from virtually nil to remarkable, depending on the artist's talents and the client's expectations. A simple comparison of the somewhat plain, if not mechanical, profiles of Metcalf (Cat. 38 to 41) with the refined silhouettes of Hankes (Cat. 139 and 140) and Édouart (Cat. 100 to 102) is sufficiently convincing.

With miniatures, as with all types of portraits, the primary criterion was the quality of the likeness. Evidently, Italian miniaturist Gerome Fassio was one of those who distinguished themselves in this difficult field, combining accuracy of features with a personal style, which could not fail to please his Montreal, Quebec City and Trois-Rivières clients (Ill. 18). A fine conversationalist and talented artist, Fassio patiently added to his store of delicate effigies for some fifteen years before ending his career in Bytown (Ottawa) in 1850. Ten years earlier, an enthusiast hailed his arrival in Montreal in these evocative terms:

Signor Fassio's exquisite brush is certainly among the most marvellous in this field, and all lovers, pretty women and fashionables who let this opportunity slip by will regret it.[103] (Translation)

In 1845, *Le Journal de Québec* continued in the same vein:

The miniature offers indisputable advantages. With a relative or a friend far away, one often feels the need to send him or her a likeness of oneself, or one's husband, wife, child, etc. especially when the price is within reach of everyone.[104] (Translation)

Given this context of quasi-utilitarian art in which clients were most interested in the portrait's likeness, the invention and development of photography by Frenchmen Nicephore Niepce and Jacques Daguerre had a decisive impact. In April 1839, Daguerre's invention was already all the talk in Quebec City. A year and a half later the daguerreotype came to the capital with the arrival of some travelling portraitists from the United States.[105] On October 13, 1842, the daguerreotypist Prosch made a frontal attack on the miniaturists' market, with an advertisement published in *The Quebec Mercury*:

"Miniature Portraits taken by the Daguerreotype process in a few minutes surpassing for correctness of likeness anything that can be done by the art of painter".

A few weeks later, the editor of *Le Canadien* commented on an advertisement by painter Samuel Palmer and emphasized:

Until we find the secret of reproducing natural colours through daguerreotypes, this marvellous instrument will not replace the paintbrush.[106] (Translation)

The miniaturists' market was hardest hit by the arrival and progressive improvement of photographic processes.

In his January 21, 1843 edition, the editor of *Le Journal de Québec*, who had just witnessed a camera in action, confessed his surprise at the "ease with which a likeness, perfect in every way, is transferred to the plate" (Translation) before issuing the following invitation to the public:

Individuals about to depart on a voyage who wish to leave a lasting remembrance of themselves, patients unable to leave their rooms, poor men or frugal lovers who want to send their portraits to their sweethearts who want them [...] close to their hearts [...], all will find this invention invaluable. (Translation)

As anticipated, a craze soon ensued, and an advertisement published by L.M. Cyrus in May 1844 reported "2500 portraits taken in Kingston and Montreal over the last 7 months."[107] (Translation). And Cyrus added:

Considerable improvements have made it possible to offer Quebec City residents portraits far superior to any done to date, since he has managed to reduce the time required to pose to *one second*, in moderate light and in any weather, which enables him to reproduce family groups with children of all ages, leaving expressions sweet, and endowing portraits of ladies especially with a beauty which art can never imitate. (Translation)

Evidently, competition was fierce, to such an extent that the columnist for *Le Journal de Québec* in Montreal ridiculed it in his December 20, 1845 edition:

About a dozen daguerreotypists and other portrait painters came to Montreal this year, and the newspapers are still announcing the arrival of a few more; that's too many, far too many. It seems that these Gentlemen do not want to hold a monopoly. The difficulty today is not having your portrait done, but deciding who should do it since, for a few shillings, you can have one done and redone and, what is more, it will never be unflattering. (Translation)

The situation was such that poor Fassio, who had already cut his prices in half in 1844, had to lower them again in 1847 and 1848 in the vain hope of checking the draining of his market.[108] Yet more proof that photography was gaining ground: on May 23, 1848, Governor Lord Elgin agreed to pose for "daguerreotypist" T.C. Doane of Montreal (Ill. 19) in order to distribute a steel-plate engraving.[109]

Portraitists such as Plamondon and Hamel, however, seemed barely affected by the new competition. As noted by the columnist for *The Morning Chronicle* following a visit to Hamel's studio in 1858:

"Daguerreotypes are pretty memorials to possess of absent friends, neat tokens of affection and regard; but they shrink into comparative insignificance before the noble emanations of the canvas and the brush from the hands of polished Artists".[110]

At the very most, Hamel occasionally employed daguerreotypes to help paint the features of a handful of subjects (Cat. 253), although he usually used a live model in his work.

However, qualities other than mere resemblance in the features painted by Plamondon and Hamel, as well as those by competitors such as Palmer and Valin,[111] came to be viewed with a critical eye. In July 1841, a journalist commenting on the "portraits of the most respectable families" (Translation), which Hamel had just brought back from parishes downriver from Quebec City, took the opportunity to invite studio visitors to appreciate "the artist's use of colour, the position in which he places his subjects, the manner in which he illuminates the subjects' heads to make them stand out from the canvas, how he defines the contours and reproduces the flesh tints."[112] Aside from a certain amount of verbosity, it can be seen that this is a similar approach to the one taken by Plamondon when executing his famous portraits of nuns the following month (Cat. 196).[113] Six years later, a columnist for *Le Journal de Québec* provided an insightful description of this difficult transition from a world where basic needs dominated to one based on more esthetic consid-

Ill. 19.
Thomas Coffin
Doane,
James Bruce,
8ᵗʰ Earl of Elgin,
and 12ᵗʰ Earl
of Kincardine, 1848;
daguerreotype.
National Archives
of Canada,
Ottawa (C-291).

Ill. 20.
Théophile Hamel,
Michel-Eustache-
Gaspard-Alain de
Lotbinière,
after a portrait
attributed to Louis
Dulongpré, 1854;
oil on canvas,
110 × 84.4 cm.
Speaker's Office,
House of Commons,
Ottawa.

erations. Making special mention of the many portraits which Hamel had been called upon to paint since his return from Europe, he wrote:

These portraits all bear a striking resemblance to the originals, although perhaps some are more faithful than others; and, what is more important for an artist or enthusiast, they are generally painted carefully and skillfully.[114] (Translation)

Hamel did not limit himself to family portraits. Familiar with the great names of his time and especially with politicians, he managed to garner a number of prestigious contracts, creating in particular a beautiful series of official full-length portraits in the early 1850s (Cat. 137 and 138). In 1853, he also landed the highly coveted government contract to paint the speakers of the assemblies and councils of the two Canadas. To successfully perform this task, which he was to complete in 1861,[115] he sometimes had to use works by his predecessors as models, as in the case of his *Alain Chartier de Lotbinière* (Ill. 20), copied from a work attributed to Louis Dulongpré and now part of a private collection in Ontario. Others before him had already had the opportunity to copy the likeness of a sovereign or bishop, including Légaré, who painted *George III, George IV* (Cat. 160) and *Victoria*, and the many artists who conveyed the likeness of Monseigneur Plessis[116] (Cat. 181). The many replicas of noteworthy clergymen sometimes by a single artist in keeping with the desires of relatives, friends, parishes or religious communities wanting to augment their portrait gallery should not be forgotten. Examples include the portraits of Monseigneur Lartigue by Valin and those of Monseigneur Pierre-Flavien Turgeon by Plamondon.[117] Finally, in a broader context, we must bear in mind all the engraved portraits of various leading figures in the colony—Plessis, Papineau, Panet, Symes, Girouard, Perrault, McMahon, Chiniquy, Elgin, etc.— by such talented artists as James, Sproule, Tessier, Thielcke, Fassio, Aubin, Plamondon and Hamel, that were sometimes widely disseminated.[118]

Landscapes and Visual Records

Beginning on November 21, 1833, painter Joseph Légaré published in Quebec City's French—and English-language newspapers an advertisement at the end of which he claimed he "will always be ready to execute all orders wich may be given him for Church Paintings, Landscapes, &c., &c."[119] On December 13, the interest he manifested in landscapes was highly commended by an enthusiast in a long article published in *The Quebec Gazette*. The following is an excerpt:

"Of Mr. Légaré himself, professionnally, I deem it quite unnecessary to add aught of enlogizing mention of mine to the established favorable opinion of the public; but I cannot refrain from expressing the satisfaction I have felt, in my different visits of late to his *studio,* to see that, latterly, he has devoted much of his time and art to the charmfull and romantic scenery of his own beautiful forest-land, and he has been exceedingly happy in the delineation. He has emerged from the dusty and prozing society of vigilworn Saints, and other goodly canonized notables, to give his pencil a revel amid the fair and fresh of nature's loveliness; and he is now, as I love to see him, surrounded by heaps of mountains, and sunny vallies, and dear grey hills of his own country. À propos, may I be permitted to mention here, that it has often excited my wonder, that our native painters have not devoted some part of their time and study to the scenery of Canada. —To their shame, be it spoken, they have not; and truly, they have neglected a field from which rich laurels will yet be won. Even in the late instance of Colonel Cockburn's sketches, published in London, and which have met, I am credibly informed, with a most extensive patronage and sale—it proves that such a style and choice of subject would tell to a solid purpose of fame and emolument. But no; old worn copies upon copy of European landscape, or anything else, seems to be preferable to the rich and novel *material* which our own picturesque land affords to the ready pencil; and where does the blame lie?—alas! but in the proper tact of our artists. —At no very distant day some wanderer brush will take up this thing, and ample as deservedly will be the reward. Only think of the heaps upon heaps of subject afforted to the '*true talent*' of the enterprizing and fanciful artist. Our winter views—breaking thro' the ice—Indian camps by night—the mounted Sioux, chief of the Western wilderners, and the bivouac on the prairie—hillock—the chase of the buffalo—the council tent—the savage and his forest wigwam—and a thousand others which I could mention; and why, I ask, are scenes and subjects like these not taken up, and echo answers and repeats 'why are they not'"?[120]

Such admiration was surely due to Reverend Daniel Wilkie, who made similar comments during a speech six days later before members of the Quebec City Literary and Historical Society.[121] The fact that the author was a minister of the Scottish Presbyterian church explains the unique tenor of his remarks regarding the "dusty and prozing society of vigilworn Saints". In his speech, Wilkie referred to the two series of six coloured aquatints—one of Niagara and the other of Quebec City—which Lieutenant-Colonel James Pattison Cockburn published in England. This reference to works by the officer/watercolourist is particularly relevant given that Légaré's interest in landscapes began as a result of his contact with British topographical painters stationed in Quebec City, of which Cockburn was one of the best. He alone left a few hundred watercolours and drawings of views of Quebec City and its environs.[122] It is possible that an exhibition such as the one held at the Quebec City ladies' bazaar in April 1828 stimulated Légaré's interest in landscapes. In fact, this can be seen in the drawings and watercolours by Cockburn and another soldier stationed in Quebec City. The following excerpts from *The Quebec Mercury* and Montreal's *La Minerve* reflect the glowing terms in which this exceptional exhibition was reported:

"There where however some contributions from Gentlemen, particularly a book of Sketches, by an Officer of Rank in the Royal Artillery, who holds a distinguished place amongst Artists in Water Colours, and some very charming detached sketches of scenes in and about Quebec [...] It has often occured to us that Canadian views and subjects, in the hands of the Engraver, would form matter for an entertaining graphick volume that could not fail in becoming popular, and would remunerate those who might undertake it, as it would be purchased, for the reminesences it would call up in those who had visited these Provinces, and if delineated with the strict fidelity, which so eminently marks the works of the Officer whose, contributed, sketches are the object of our present remark, would become a valuable acquisition to the Port-folio of the Amateur or encourager of the Fine Arts. We are sure that if the Officer, referred to, would dedicate his leisuure[*sic*] to such a work he would add greatly to his fame as an Artist [...]".[123]

This wish was fulfilled in 1831 when Cockburn published, through Thomas Cary, a short guide to Quebec City and the surrounding area, illustrated with a few engravings made from his drawings.

The last of Wilkie's wishes expressed in 1833 were to remain unfulfilled for 15 to 20 years, when Cornelius Krieghoff arrived in the colony and became fascinated by the various facets of Amerindian life. As for Légaré, he was almost the only one among his fellow Canadians who continued to develop his pictorial taste for waterfalls, rivers, forests, country houses, urban landscapes and scenes from everyday life or special occasions. Unlike Légaré, his former disciple Plamondon preferred to limit himself mainly to religious paintings and portraits and refused to take up the challenge issued by journalist William Kemble during the artist's altercation with diorama painter James Bowman in 1833. During

Ill. 21.
Joseph Légaré, *Landscape with a Momument to Temperance, Beauport*, 1842, oil on cardboard, 43.1 × 53.5 cm.
Musée du Collège Sainte-Anne-de-la-Pocatière.

the summer, Bowman visited the Lac-des-Deux-Montagnes church to paint the ceremony of "the distribution of presents given by the Pope to the savages of that village."[124] In order to judge the respective merits of the two artists, the editor of *The Quebec Mercury* wanted the proud Antoine to undertake a similar subject:

"we invite him to try his skill in the same style of painting, and propose to him as a subject the interior of the Paroisse of Quebec: it is worth transferring to canvas, and will afford Mr Plamondon the opportunity of shewing his skill and exhibiting, to the untravelled, the glories of a splendid Diorama".[125]

It would be totally inappropriate to speak of a landscape market when referring to the work of military landscape artists and other British watercolourists who stayed in the colony for varying lengths of time, save perhaps in terms of some of their paintings which were disseminated through engravings or lithographs. In short, the world of watercolour landscapes was a parallel universe based on practices entirely different from those of artists the likes of Légaré or Todd. The same can be said for John Elliott Woolford's very specific work for Governor Dalhousie, which was documentary in nature and subject to the specific requirements of a client who wanted to keep a visual record of his colonial sojourn.[126]

Essentially the same desire to obtain pictorial souvenirs seemingly motivated several commissions for landscape artist Légaré. His landscapes were mostly commissioned by British officers posted in Canada, as well as Anglophone enthusiasts and "foreign connoisseurs" visiting Quebec City.[127] In order to procure a picturesque view of their visit to the colony, some preferred to purchase paintings, while others chose a set of oil-on-paper sketches. It was works of this type which were commissioned by Montreal collector Jacques Viger, according to a laboriously worded proposal made to him by Légaré in December 1839:

Right now I have some charming, small Sketches in oil on paper of the right size for your album, since the largest is at most 6 or

Ill 22.
Joseph Légaré, *Caldwell Manor and the Etchemin Mills*, c. 1843;
oil on canvas, 58.4 × 87.6 cm.
Musée du Québec, Quebec (56.04).

Ill. 23.
Cornelius Krieghoff, *The Lumber Trade*, c. 1860; a series
of nine paintings decorating the seat of the Chairman of the House of
Assembly in the Quebec Parliament, destroyed by fire in 1833;
early photograph. Archives du Séminaire de Québec (Ph.87.669).

7 inches by 5 inches. I have already made a similar set for a lady from Liverpool, they are as follows: two views from different points of La Puce Falls, a view of Cape Tourment taken from the La Puce River, a view of the Ste Anne du Mont River Falls, a slip where Vessels were being repaired at Lévis Point, Niagara Falls, St-Féréole Falls, the Montmorency Falls in Winter, a view of Quebec City taken from Lévis Point. The price of these small items is ten shillings Each and would not Cost you much because you do not need to reduce them for your album. I have a larger version (2 feet by 3) of the Montmorency Falls. (Translation)

Légaré had less success with his paintings of tragic events experienced by his fellow citizens: the cholera epidemic of 1832 (Cat. 158), the landslide of 1841 and the fires of 1845 (Cat. 168). Aside from the paintings of the fires, which we know were refused by the municipal corporation of Quebec City,[129] the context in which these works were executed and their ultimate purpose are largely unknown. Such is not the case for "utilitarian" works such as the first seal of Quebec City, *Le Canadien* (Cat. 159), or the banners for the Société Saint-Jean-Baptiste de Québec, all works based heavily on landscape techniques.[130] Similarly, we can now associate the *Landscape with a Monument to Temperance, Beauport* with a ceremony held in that parish in March 1842 to honour Abbé Chiniquy, a temperance advocate (Ill. 21).[131]

No exception to the rule, Légaré's allegorical landscapes were sometimes drawn from motifs borrowed from various sources or plastic influences assimilated with mixed success. His landscapes also include panoramic works such as *Caldwell Manor and the Etchemin Mills*, which seem to reflect a specific facet of colonial society in Lower Canada (Ill. 22). This type of work betrays as much a desire on the part of the client to distinguish himself by his property, as the wish to keep a tangible souvenir of it. Otherwise, why would Henry Atkinson, for example, commission from Légaré four views of his property of "Carouge" ("Redcliffe") and Captain John Walker order from Krieghoff a view of his country

residence near Quebec City (MQ)? And what about the two panoramic views (Cat. 222 and 223) which Allan Gilmour, another timber merchant, commissioned from Robert Clow Todd? Such landscapes display limited artistic freedom, inasmuch as they were executed to testify to the client's success and perpetuate the image of property acquired through perseverance and skill. This is all part of the world of appearances which, among the wealthiest, was not confined to painted physiognomies. In this sense, Gilmour's paintings are portraits of material possessions rather than pure landscapes. The paintings of trotters *Corbeau* (Cat. 224) and *Fraser* (Cat. 152) by Todd and Krieghoff should probably be viewed in the same way. They flaunt property and lifestyle, as much as they commemorate triumphs on racecourses. Good taste, leisure, fortune and the joys of superfluity commingle in these works.

During the 1850s, artists such as Cornelius Krieghoff and James Duncan helped to significantly expand the market for landscapes, after planning to collaborate on a "magnificent panorama of Canada which [would have included] all the most remarkable views along the St. Lawrence and the lakes upriver."[132] (Translation) In 1853, Krieghoff settled in Quebec City, where he enjoyed undeniable success for a dozen years, diligently satisfying the expectations of an Anglophone clientele fond of landscapes as picturesque and varied as our seasons. In the early 1860s, some of his compositions betrayed the influence of photographers such as Samuel McLaughlin, whose series entitled *The Photographic Portfolio: A Monthly View of Canadian Scenes and Scenery* contained views and scenes much appreciated by the public (Cat. 262 and 263). During the same period, Krieghoff obtained a contract to execute a set of vignettes in a large, carved wooden frame to be hung behind the Speaker's chair in the House of Assembly in the new Parliament Buildings.[133] This set of nine paintings was reduced to ashes in 1883, but a recently discovered photograph has made it known to us (Ill. 23). It marvellously illustrates one of the favourite subjects of the

Ill. 24.
Cornelius Krieghoff, *Death of a Moose*, 1859;
oil on canvas, 36 × 53 cm.
Glenbow Museum, Calgary (87.71.1).

Ill. 25.
Cornelius Krieghoff, *Merrymaking*, 1860;
oil on canvas, 88.9 × 121.9 cm.
Beaverbrook Art Gallery, Fredericton.
Beaverbrook Canadian Foundation.

artist and his rich clients: the timber trade.[134] It must be remembered that this activity was of primary importance in the economic life of the colony, creating jobs and generating profits, from felling trees in the forest to their assembly in the Sillery cove, the final step before the timber was shipped across the Atlantic.

Genre Scenes, Fancy Pictures and History Paintings

Soon after his arrival in Lower Canada in 1846, Krieghoff began to take an interest in the Amerindians and their way of life. Subsequently, a growing portion of his work portrayed scenes of canoeing or portaging along the rapids, encampments in the forest, hunting or fishing, not to mention type characters, from the basket seller to the Native guide accompanying Whites in their expeditions into the forest (Ill. 24). Krieghoff was the undisputed master of these subjects, which were midway between landscapes and genre scenes. Martin Somerville certainly attempted them, but with less diversity, consistency and brilliance. Légaré's contribution in this field was basically limited to works of imaginary customs, such as *The Engagement of an Indian Girl* and *The Despair of an Indian Woman* of 1844, "two scenes taken [...] from the life of savages and which depicts both its sweet ease and terrifying energy" (Cat. 167).[135] (Translation)

A native of Northern Europe, Krieghoff proved faithful to his roots in his pronounced taste for genre scenes. He thoroughly explored the various facets, each as colourful as the next, of the theme of "Canadiens," the very people whom the English-speaking inhabitants of the colony familiarly, and somewhat condescendingly, called *habitants*. He painted to his heart's content their would-be shortcomings, the rustic nature of their lifestyle in remote areas, their picturesque faces and clothing, their disregard for the law, and even their drinking binges filled with "joie de vivre" (Ill. 25). This iconography which borders on caricature does not,

however, lack for charm or pictorial qualities, and was considered novel in the Canadian context of the time. It was therefore a delight to the artist's Anglophone friends and clients.

This clientele also proved fond of more conventional "fancy pictures," to the point that Krieghoff did not hesitate to paint copies of popular subjects based on European prints and paintings, and even photographs. He was not the first to tap this lucrative market: he was beaten to it by Antoine Plamondon, whose few "bits of fancy" (Translation)—*Lost in the Wood* in 1836 (Cat. 190), *The Little Savoyards* in 1844 (Cat. 199) and *The Little Gardeners* in 1857 (Cat. 267)—were based on the same anecdotal and sentimental sources. In 1853, the same year in which this artist was to put the finishing touches on *The Pigeon Hunt* (Cat. 266), painter Robert Clow Todd held a lottery to try to liquidate "25 cabinet-size oil paintings" before his departure from Quebec City (Ill. 26). Among these paintings were a large number of copies of genre scenes and other everyday subjects which give us a glimpse into an additional piece of colonial pictorial history. Similarly, the cityscapes, market scenes and views of Montreal life—often in watercolours—left by James Duncan should not be disregarded, inasmuch as they bear witness to changing tastes and sensibilities (Cat. 93 to 95 and 249).

Duncan was also interested in portraits and historical events. Responding to collector/archivist Jacques Viger's invitation, he painted the features of various notables in Canadian history using painted or engraved prototypes recommended to him, and attempted to reconstruct specific events dating back to the period of New France. Some of his fellow painters in Quebec City also worked in this area. Recall, if you will, Théophile Hamel's many copies (beginning in 1847) of the "historical" portrait of Jacques Cartier painted by Frenchman François Riss[136] (Cat. 127); or the so-called likeness of Jesuit and New France historian Pierre-François-Xavier de Charlevoix, which was copied in turn by Légaré,

PAR LOTERIE.

25 Tableaux de Cabinet a l'huile,

CONSISTANT EN :

Prix.		£	s.	D.
1 Jeunes Paysans Espagnols—cadre doré—l'après Murillo.		12	0	0
2 La Médisance—d'après Soleman.		10	0	0
3 Le Trefle, la Rose et le Chardon—cadre doré—C. Baxter.		9	0	0
4 La Chasse au Faucon—cadre doré—d'après Landseer, de l'Acad. Royale.		9	0	0
5 Il fut un grand Chasseur devant le Seigneur—A. Cooper de l'A. R.		7	0	0
6 Retour de la Grève—d'après J. M. Mole.		7	0	0
7 La Famille du Pêcheur Napolitain—d'après Riedel.		7	0	0
8 L'Enfance—cadre doré—d'après sir Thomas Lawrence.		5	0	0
9 Fruits—cadre doré,		5	0	0
10 Vieillard Aveugle—cadre doré,		5	10	0
11 et 12 S ut de Montmorenci, en été et en hiver—cadres dorés,		5	0	0
13 Chien d'arrêt—cadre doré,		4	10	0
14 Cupidon et l'Abeille—cadre doré—Porter,		4	0	0
15 Montmorenci vu de l'Anse des Sauvages, Pointe-Lévi,		3	10	0
16 Noël avec sa Bûche,		3	0	0
17 La Dignité et l'Impudence—Gravure—cadre doré,		3	0	0
18 Branche de Gui de Chêne—cadre,		2	10	0
19 Goëlette Gitana, de l'escadre des yachts royaux,		2	10	0
20 Lac inférieur de Killarney et Château de Ross,		2	0	0
21 Château de Chillon,		2	0	0
22 Asture—d'après les Beautés de Byron—cadre,		1	0	0
23 Un Paysage,		1	0	0
24 Un Paysage,		1	0	0
25 Château de Windsor, vu de la Tamise—cadre,		2	10	0
		£114	0	0

Cent-quatorze Souscripteurs a £1 chacun.

Cette LOTERIE sera tirée à l'HOTEL RUSSELL le MERCREDI 27 avril, à SEPT heures du soir.

Ces tableaux sont exposés au n° 4, rue Sainte-Angèle, où il y a des billets à vendre.

Un Notaire présidera au tirage de la loterie.

R. C. TODD,

N° 4, rue Sainte-Angèle.

Québec, 4 avril 1852.

Ill. 27.
Joseph Légaré, *The Battle of Sainte-Foy*, c. 1854;
oil on canvas, 50 × 74.5 cm.
National Gallery of Canada, Ottawa (18489).

New Views, New Perspectives

"Useful Arts pave the way to Fine Arts. Men upon whom the former has bestowed every convenience turned their thoughts to the latter. Beauty was studied in objects of sight, and men of taste attached themselves to the Fine Arts, which multiplied their enjoyments and improved their benevolence. —Hazlitt." (Introductory quotation in the 1847 catalogue of the Montreal Society of Artists).

In concluding this brief overview, I should stress the fact that many aspects of the development of painting in Quebec between 1790 and 1860 remain to be explored. Much against our will, we have omitted dozens of artists whose specific contribution is still unknown to us as a result of the vagaries of historiography and research. What do we really know about the contribution of women to the art world of this era? We know little about individuals such as Madame Clouet (the only women to subscribe to the Quebec Picture Gallery in 1838[138]), Madame Joseph-Ulric Tessier (whose personal album included works by Légaré and Hamel as well as literary texts by P.-J.-O. Chauveau, F.-X. Garneau and J.-C. Taché[139]), Madame Saint-Julien of Montreal, who opened her drawing room doors to a "brilliant exhibition" of works by Légaré in 1842,[140] and artists such as Miss Deming[141] and Miss Dunkin[142] who, with "a Lady," took part in the exhibition organized by the Montreal Society of Artists in 1847. The same holds true for all those women "artists and enthusiasts" who, like Amélie Panet and the Misses Malone, autographed the page reserved for them by Jacques Viger in his album. Viger's vivid description of the contents of his album in a letter to Joseph Légaré in 1839 alone sheds light on some of the types of painting we have had to overlook in this essay:

Right now, I am making an Album, but in my own way, that is, not as small, light and insignificant as this sort of book usually is; I am trying to make it as Canadian as possible, both in the selection

Plamondon and Hamel.[137] Of all these artists, it was Légaré who went the furthest in the yet untouched field of history painting. Cheerfully plumbing the depths of his collection of paintings and engravings, he created, with mixed success, images of historical events such as *The Martyrdom of Françoise Brunon* circa 1827 (MMFA), *Massacre of Hurons by the Iroquois* circa 1827-1828 (Cat. 157), *The Martyrdom of Fathers Brébeuf and Lalemant* circa 1843 (Cat. 165), and *The Battle of Sainte-Foy* circa 1854 (Ill. 27). Like the canvas entitled *Conference Between Jacques Cartier and the Natives of Stadacona (6 May 1536)* which Samuel C. Hawksett painted in 1859 at the invitation of history buff Georges-Barthélemi Faribault (Cat. 254), Légaré's reconstructions were the forerunners of the historical works which were to become so popular in Quebec during the final decades of the 19th century.

of subjects and in the Artists I am employing. Artists and Enthusiasts, everyone who knows how to draw or paint in Montreal has been included. I already have almost a hundred pieces, of which a large number are certainly worthwhile; but I still do not have anything of Quebec City, that will come. I have everything in this book: flowers, fruit, animals, landscapes, buildings, monuments, medallions, bas-reliefs, portraits, etc. I have happy pictures, sad pictures, sweet pictures, frightening pictures, religious pictures, secular pictures [...] but decency is the main consideration. Finally, I also have engravings, pen-and-ink and pencil drawings, mezzotints, wash drawings, watercolours and gouache—and even découpage. (Translation)

And despite anyone's opinion of such work, there was at the time a "market"—limited certainly—for "vases of flowers, fruit, birds and butterflies" on paper or wood,[145] along with more noble still lifes painted on canvas by Légaré (Cat. 155), Plamondon (Cat. 193), Somerville, Todd, Krieghoff (Cat. 148) and others. This, too, is a part of the history and development of taste.

Apart from these reservations, painting between the years 1820 and 1850 in Quebec, if viewed both as a whole and in its various forms, is not as foreign as one might first think. In fact, it underscores the still-timely dilemma between what is everyday routine and what transcends it, this question of necessity versus the ideal, which tries to surpass it. This endeavour to transcend the various requirements of daily life is omnipresent in the progress and work of the artists, just as it is in the reflections of the few art enthusiasts and critics of the first half of the 19th century. In a context of transition, passage, change, affirmation and opening onto the world, a closer look at this small, teeming world of fine arts in the not-so-distant past can help put us in touch with many of our contemporary sensibilities, provided, of course, that we agree to discover, question and understand them, and allow them to reach us through the boundaries of time, as a journalist of *La Minerve* so touchingly emphasized in 1849:

Are not fine arts called upon to regenerate a country, excite the imagination of its people by one of those powerful disturbances which transform existence? They can awaken in the soul a host of mysterious impressions, evoke innocent emotions, foster in the heart of man a million sympathies: in a word, slipping through all the chinks of his workaday existence, like those lilies of the field which are mixed with its painful harvest.[146] (Translation)

Around 1850, the artistic landscape changed considerably: views changed again, and perspectives broadened. Many indications point to a willingness to break down boundaries and become reunited with our European heritage. Onlookers rejoiced to see numerous artists leaving to study in Europe, just as they deplored Canada's deficiencies in artistic education:

Deprived as we are in this still comparatively new country of special schools where one can train in the study and especially the practice of fine arts, we are forced to recommend a trip and a sojourn in Europe to those whose special abilities, decided vocation and auspicious beginnings promise certain success. To date, those whose taste and inner voice have pushed them from Canada to the capitals of fine arts, Rome and Paris, have brought back what they never found among us, a feeling for true beauty which is acquired only by contemplating works by great masters.[147] (Translation)

Despite past disappointments, the tone tended towards optimism from then on, if the following extract from an article published in *Le Canadien* of April 14, 1852, is any indication.

A decided talent and taste for painting is developing in this country, which is undoubtedly due in part to the works, both copies and originals, of the great masters which decorate some of our churches or are found in private collections, and especially to those which Abbé Desjardins [...] sent to this country following his return to France, and of which a great many can still be found in Joseph Légaré's beautiful, valuable collection. Quebec has already produced a large number of distinguished artists in this genre; it is enough to mention those who are still among us: Joseph Légaré, who did not have the advantage of visiting Europe and owes the rank to which he has risen as an artist to his genius alone; Antoine Plamondon, who studied in Paris under the great names of the French school; Théophile Hamel, who also studied art in Italy and Belgium; and Sébastien Falardeau, who is still in Italy and who [...] was named a member of the Académie de Parme and created a Knight, First Class, of the Order of St. Louis for a work he painted in that city. Another young man from Quebec City, a son of our fellow citizen Mr. Mimee, has been in Rome for a few years, studying painting; and Napoléon Bourassa, a student of Hamel, will be heading there this spring. (Translation)

The works which Falardeau brought back from Italy in 1862 were all the more prized by collectors as they were executed, not based on "wretched engravings" or intermediary works, but directly after the originals of great masters.[148] Copies of works of all types thus became popular once again in the wake of initiatives taken by artists such as Krieghoff who, beginning in 1847, exhibited in Montreal eight copies executed in Paris, at the Musée du Luxembourg and the Louvre.[149] We must also acknowledge the increasingly marked presence of Italian art in the country at this time. Thanks to initiatives taken by Bishop Bourget, the names of artists such as Pietro Gagliardi soon became familiar, while it became fashionable for clergymen and members of the upper classes to call upon the artful devices of an Italian brush to immortalize their faces. The traditional portrait market, already in decline, was then hit even harder by the development of photographic processes, to the point where photographic artists such as Notman in Montreal and Livernois in Quebec City used painters to enhance the artistic worth of their snapshots.

For their part, landscapes gained in popularity and artistic freedom, becoming increasingly appreciated for their intrinsic picturesque qualities. The stimulating proximity of photographers and the arrival of foreign artists such as William Raphael and Otto Jacobi (Cat. 255) changed the way of looking at and understanding them. Considered a marginal art form until the mid-1840s, genre painting benefitted from the work of artists such as Krieghoff, and a growing craze spurred on by engravings from all sources. This area of interest, however, underscored a marked socio-ethnic division between Francophones and Anglophones, since the two groups rarely shared the same perceptions and sensibilities. A similar gap continued to widen among enthusiasts and collectors of European art.[150]

Even before these orientations and trends were manifested or became established, painting in Quebec between 1820 and 1850 had already been marked by an undeniable movement of affirmation, by changes of all sorts and by a growing openness in its outlook. In the 1850s, there is little doubt that the artistic context had changed considerably from the time—not so long before—when François Baillairgé, lacking confidence in his abilities, was left to execute the pressing commissions for religious paintings by himself. In December 1856, encouraged by the progress made and optimistic about the future, the editor of the Montreal newspaper *Le Pays* could finally write:

Now that the axe has pushed the forests back from the edges of our rivers and lakes; now that the way has been cleared for natural population growth and immigration, both by land and by sea—since rich, densely populated cities form many stops along the traveller's route—it is time to hope that the development of artistic taste and needs, created through superfluity, will soon give impetus to the cultural arts.[151] (Translation)

Notes

1. *Le Canadien*, September 5, 1838, p. 2. Excerpt from a commentary published on the occasion of the opening of an art school headed by Henry Daniel Thielcke as part of the new Quebec Picture Gallery owned by painter Joseph Légaré and attorney Thomas Amiot.

2. François-Xavier Garneau quoted in *BELLERIVE 1925*, p. 21.

3. Montreal became more densely populated than Quebec City around 1815.

4. "I struggled along, doing everything and anything", he acknowledged in 1829 (*ALLODI AND TOVELL 1989*, p. 27).

5. The Government agreed to acquire it in 1836, but the collection was destroyed in the fire of the House of Assembly building in 1854.

6. See *PORTER 1977/2*, pp. 75-82.

7. *Le Populaire*, quoted in *Le Canadien*, October 27, 1837, p. 2.

8. The journalist indicated that these clients of "Briton" or British extraction were "practically the only ones who knew how to put a price on the dissemination of arts and science". (Translation) Farther on, he specifically mentioned the name of Stanley Bagg.

9. We are referring to Krieghoff, Somerville, Morris, Sawyer, Duncan, Wilson and Howden (*TRUDEL 1900/2*, pp. 61-87). See Endnote 44.

10. *PORTER 1981*, pp. 231, 233, 234, 243 and 244.

11. *PORTER 1981*, pp. 178, 226 and 350.

12. See *PORTER 1987/1*, pp. 529-539.

13. About the fate of Abbé Cadieux's paintings, see *PORTER 1981*, p. 163.

14. *LACROIX 1989/1*, pp. 43-46.

15. See *Les Mélanges religieux*, July 11, 1848, p. 317.

16. See John R. Porter and Jean Trudel, *Le Calvaire d'Oka* (Ottawa: National Gallery of Canada, 1974), pp. 92-93.

17. These are obviously the lowest figures, since the newspapers did not always specify the quantities involved in the various shipments of works of art. These figures are the results of a compilation by Didier Prioul in April 1979 based on our data.

18. *PORTER 1981*, pp. 47-48.

19. *PORTER 1981*, p. 49.

20. John R. Porter and Didier Prioul, "Beaux-Arts, prestige et politique: la galerie de peintures de Joseph Légaré," *Cap-aux-Diamants*, No. 25 (Spring 1991), pp. 14-16.

21. *PORTER 1981*, pp. 171-172.

22. For example, advertising exclusively in English in May 1838 (The *Quebec Mercury*, May 19, 1838, p. 1). See also *PORTER 1981*, pp. 157-158.

23. *PORTER 1981*, pp. 126-127.

24. *Le Canadien*, March 31, 1852, p. 3. (Translation)

25. *PORTER 1981*, pp. 353, 354 and 419.

26. *Les Mélanges religieux*, November 19, 1847, p. 17. (Translation)

27. *TRUDEL 1990/2*, p. 74.

28. *TRUDEL 1990/2*, pp. 74-75.

29. *PORTER 1981*, pp. 126-127; Renée Gagnon-Guimond, "Henry Atkinson, gentilhomme et baron du bois," *Cap-aux-Diamants*, Vol. IV, No. 3 (Autumn 1988), pp. 19-22. See lots 19 and 20 in the catalogue.

30. A similar attitude was observed among Toronto journalists around 1833. See Angela Carr, "Georges Théodore Berthon (1806-92): portraiture, patronage and criticism in nineteenth century Toronto," *Journal of Canadian Art History*, Vol. XI, No. 1-2 (1989), p. 25.

31. *Le Canadien*, October 13, 1848, p. 2.

32. *Le Canadien*, November 25, 1833, p. 2. (Translation)

33. ASQ, Fonds Verreau, letter from Jacques Viger to Joseph Légaré, November 23, 1839. (Translation)

34. *Le Castor*, April 18, 1844, p. 2 (Translation.

35. *PORTER 1990/1*, pp. 923-924.

36. See the conclusion of an article signed "Polymetis" in the October 13, 1848 edition of *Le Canadien*, as well as *PORTER 1977/1*, pp. 13-24.

37. *PORTER 1977/1*, pp. 19-20.

38. *PORTER 1981*, pp. 449-450; Angela Carr, *loc. cit.*, p. 52 and *HARPER 1979*, p. 23; *The British Colonist*, July 18, 1848, p. 1.

39. They were then appraised at £700 each.

40. The exact number of portraits varies from source to source and author to author. See Raymond Vézina, "Trente-cinq tableaux inédits de Théophile Hamel," *RACAR*, Vol. IX, No. 1-2 (1982), pp. 47-56.

41. Priest at Saint-Michel de Bellechasse and subscriber to Légaré's art gallery in 1838.

42. Bibliothèque nationale du Québec à Montréal, Fonds J.-M. Beauregard, box 6/10 (2), Verchères file, typewritten copy of a letter from Abbé J. Demers to Father Kimbert, September 24, 1825.

43. *L'Aurore des Canadas*, August 20, 1842, p. 2; Porter 1981, pp. 239-240.

44. According to a compilation made by Jean Trudel, 35 of the paintings exhibited had typically Canadian subjects, while an equivalent number were copies. Of the 179 works, only 27 were offered for sale. A total of 17 professional and amateur artists took part in the exhibition. The seven members of the Montreal Society of Artists did not exhibit an equal number of works. Cornelius Krieghoff exhibited the most (48 works), followed by Martin Somerville (21) and Andrew Morris (21), William Sawyer (16), James Duncan (13), William F. Wilson (7) and Robert T. Howden (2). Henry Samuel Davis, honorary Society member, British officer and topographical painter, exhibited 20 works (Trudel 1990/2).

45. See Porter 1981, pp. 231-232. On the eve of his departure from Quebec City for Toronto in 1853, painter R.C. Todd also held a lottery to try to sell "25 oil Cabinet-size paintings" (*Le Canadien*, April 4, 1853, p. 3). (Translation)

46. *Le Journal de Québec*, October 10, 1848, p. 2.

47. *Le Canadien*, October 13, 1848, p. 2.

48. *Le Canadien*, October 15, 1847, p. 2. This commentary on the decor of drawing rooms must be compared with the one found in Montreal's *La Minerve* in 1842: "Look at our drawing rooms. Aside from a few families who, from their travels in Europe, have brought back a few beautiful paintings, a few beautiful sculptures, what do we see? A few bad lithographs coloured red and blue" (reprinted in *Le Canadien* of December 26, 1842, p. 1). (Translation)

49. *Le Canadien*, July 26, 1833, p. 3. (Translation)

50. For example, we can refer to three estate inventories drawn up in 1860 and 1861 of the property of legislative councillor Joseph Dionne of Saint-Pierre-les-Becquets (ANQTR, official records of notary Valère Guillet, January 9, 1860), the last companion of the eccentric Moses Hart (1768-1852) of Trois-Rivières (ANQTR, official records of notary Valère Guillet, January 30, 1861), and the widow of merchant Philéas Méthot of Quebec City (ANQQ, official records of notary Joseph Petitclerc, April 22, 1860). Dionne's inventory mentions, in order, his portrait, the paintings (apparently portraits) of "the Lady of Victory," "My Lord Pépin" and "Monseigneur Cooke" (Translation), a painting of the Assumption, a "picture of St. Joseph" (Translation), three "pictures" representing respectively "Our Lord" (Translation), St. Joseph and Bonaparte, "paintings" (probably engravings, according to estimates) of "the Seigneurial Court," "Queen Victoria," "Pius IX," "Mr. Joliette," "Monseigneur Plessis" and "Monseigneur Panet" (Translation), and finally, various "small pictures". (Translation) The inventory for Mary McCarthy *alias* Brown lists an image of St. Patrick and "a painting of Monseigneur Cooke" (engraving) (Translation), "paintings" of Queen Victoria and Prince Albert, a "Portrait of Pius IX," "six gilded frames, containing various landscapes and subject[s]" (Translation), two large frames representing "Caravans in the desert" (Translation) and the portraits of the late Moses Hart and his mother. The house—and especially the "small drawing room" (Translation)—of the Méthot family contained only engravings representing Queen Victoria, Prince Albert, a view of Washington, card players and "various views" (Translation), not to mention "a set of engravings," "a set of secular & holy engravings," and "a set of various engravings & patterns". (Translation)

51. To the minimum figures quoted earlier can be added the plausible observations of Jean Trudel based on Montreal newspaper excerpts from 1847 (Trudel 1990/2, pp. 72, 73 and 78).

52. See Endnote 48.

53. See Allodi 1980 and Claudine Villeneuve, "Le portrait dans l'estampe diffusée au Bas-Canada entre 1825 et 1850: essai d'analyse stylistique," master's thesis submitted to Université Laval in December 1989.

54. See the comments made in connection with the publication of the engraved portraits of the late Monseigneur Lartigue (*L'Ami du Peuple*, May 30, 1840), Pope Gregory XVI (*Le Canadien*, September 4, 1843, p. 3) and Abbé Chiniquy, temperance advocate (*L'Ami de la religion et de la patrie*, November 8, 1848, p. 766).

55. What do we really know about Alexis-Charles Boucher dit Belleville (1808-1885), that "painter" who apparently painted signs and to whom Émile Falardeau attributed a handful of portraits in a brief exploratory essay published some fifty years ago? See *Artistes & artisans du Canada*, second series, *Boucher* (Montreal: G. Ducharme, 1942), 86 p.

56. The text which follows is largely based on Triaud's biography in Karel 1988, pp. 941-943.

57. Entitled *Christ Attended by Angels*, this work was destroyed in the fire at the Quebec City cathedral in 1922. Around 1820, it also served as the model for a work by Légaré intended for the church in Saint-Roch-des-Aulnaies. See Porter 1978/1, p. 113 (Repr.).

58. This portrait, until recently housed in the Archives de la Province de Québec, cannot be traced. Based on the identification of a Office du film photograph held in the Inventaire des oeuvres d'art, the portrait appears to be signed "L.T." in the lower right-hand corner. Based on this single photograph, it is tempting to compare it with the painting we identified in 1978 as the self-portrait of Joseph Légaré. See Porter 1978/1, pp. 29-30 (Repr.).

59. See Porter 1981, pp. 39, 103, 104 and 132. A statement of account conserved in the Archives du Séminaire de Québec indicates that he restored some 33 works on behalf of collector J.-B.-E. Bacquet in 1837, 1840, 1841, 1842, 1844 and 1852 (non-inventoried document dated May 25, 1855 and brought to our attention by Didier Prioul).

60. See Porter 1978/1, passim.

61. Like L.-J. Papineau, Légaré was anti-clerical and an atheist. See Porter 1981, pp. 210-211.

62. As in the case of his series of works on the Quebec City fires in 1845. See Porter 1981, pp. 246, 273 and 274.

63. It is certain that these two men knew each other, because in 1850, Légaré rented Todd one of his houses on Rue Sainte-Angèle (ANQQ, official records of notary Michel Tessier, February 14, 1850, No. 7003).

64. See Porter 1981, pp. 263-264.

65. Documents show that he stayed in Rochester in 1836. William F. Pect, *The Semi-Centennial History of the City of Rochester* (Syracuse: D. Mason & Co. Publishers, 1884) (see Cat. 208).

66. See Lacasse 1983/2, pp. 74-90.

67. We owe this unpublished information to our colleague Yves Lacasse. The work in question is entitled *Saint Roch Interceding for the Plague Victims*; it dates from 1623-1626 and decorates the altar dedicated to St. Roch in the Saint-Martin d'Alost church in Belgium. It was engraved by Gérard Audran, Cornelis Meyssens and Paulus Pontius. See Hans Vlieghe, *Corpus Rubenianum Ludwig Burchard*, t. VIII, Vol. II (London/New York: Phaidon, 1972), pp. 142-144, No. 140 (Repr.).

68. The work had already been shown in Montreal in March 1833 (Lacasse 1983/2, p. 76).

69. *Le Canadien*, July 24, 1833, p. 2. (Translation)

70. *Le Canadien*, August 7, 1833, p. 1. That same year, he went on to set himself up as a great connoisseur and teach a lesson to editors of Montreal and Quebec City newspapers who had the misfortune of extolling the merits of a set of works by masters of the Italian and Flemish schools (*Le Canadien*, September 27, 1833, p. 2).

71. *Le Canadien*, September 2, 1835, p. 2. In September 1838, Thielcke challenged Plamondon to produce an "Original History Painting, and a Landscape from nature" in order to "leave no doubt as to which [of the] two ranks first" (*Le Canadien*, September 26, 1838, p. 2). (Translation) Plamondon declined the invitation haughtily. See Porter 1984, pp. 17-19.

72. *Le Canadien*, March 14, 1842, p. 2. See also *Le Fantasque*, February 7, 1842, pp. 581-582, and April 7, 1842, p. 4.

73. *Le Canadien*, August 7, 1833, p. 1.

74. See Porter 1981, p. 263. An article published in *Le Canadien* of June 9, 1843 (pp. 2-3) tells us that the completion of the banners of various sections of the Société Saint-Jean-Baptiste de Québec was entrusted to Légaré "after other Canadian painters in this city were offered the opportunity to take their brush to a national work so that the society could not be accused of sponsoring one artist exclusively". (Translation)

75. *Le Canadien*, November 25, 1833, p. 2.

76. *Ibid.*

77. This section is largely based on one of our previous texts on copying, and repeats some of its passages (Porter 1984, pp. 3-4).

78. Lacasse 1983/1, p. 104, See Endnote 184. (Translation)

79. See Porter 1984, pp. 5-10.

80. Porter 1984, pp. 11-15. (Translation)

81. *Le Populaire* of October 23, 1837, reprinted in *Le Canadien*, October 27, 1837, p. 2.

82. Didier Bodard, *Rubens e l'incisione* (Rome: De Luca Editore, 1977), No. 98 and following (Repr.).

83. "I am very pleased about Mr. Dulongpré's undertaking, he has everything to gain by copying your beautiful paintings of the lake" (John R. Porter and Jean Trudel, *op. cit.*, p. 92). (Translation)

84. *Ibid.*, pp. 88, 90 and 91 (Repr.).

85. Completed in 1812, it was rescued from a fire in 1942. Since 1966, it has been conserved, rolled up, at the Musée du Québec. Although there is no photograph of it, its composition is known to us thanks to an excellent description by Gérard Morisset (*Lacasse 1983/1*, pp. 68 and 103, Endnote 162).

86. John R. Porter and Jean Trudel, *op. cit.*, pp. 91-92 (Repr.).

87. *Ibid.*, pp. 84-86 (Repr.).

88. Didier Bodard, *op. cit.*, No. 448 (Repr.).

89. *Porter 1984*, p. 15.

90. *Le Journal de Québec*, August 2, 1862, p. 2. (Translation)

91. *L'Aurore des Canadas*, August 24, 1843, reprinted in *Le Journal de Québec*, September 12, 1843, p. 3. (Translation)

92. *Le Journal de Québec*, May 16, 1843, p. 1.

93. *Porter 1984*, pp. 19 and 21. It is significant that the commissions for *Sainte Lucie* and *Tobie* were given by wealthy individuals. The first work was donated to the Sainte-Luce parish by Madame Luce-Gertrude Drapeau—widow of Thomas Cazeault—, the *seigneuresse* of the area. This only goes to prove the considerable difference in cost between a copy and an original canvas.

94. See *Lacasse 1983/1*, pp. 41-45 (Repr.).

95. *Le Journal de Québec*, September 3, 1861, p. 2. (Translation)

96. *Le Journal de Québec*, August 2, 1862, p. 2; see also *Le Journal de Québec*, July 22, 1862 and *Le Canadien*, August 13, 1862 (p. 2.).

97. The expression is borrowed from Napoléon Aubin (*Le Canadien*, October 15, 1847, p. 2). (Translation)

98. In October 1842, the editor of *L'Encyclopédie canadienne*, Mr. Bibaud, visited the artist's studio and was impressed by the quality of half-length portraits "of an entire Quebec City family, father, mother, son, daughter, etc." (Translation)

99. *The Quebec Gazette*, April 10, 1794.

100. *The Quebec Mercury*, August 26, 1817, p. 266.

101. See *La Minerve*, September 25, 1828, p. 4, and *Le Canadien*, May 10, 1833, p. 2.

102. *Le Canadien*, May 10, 1833, p. 2. (Translation)

103. *L'Aurore des Canadas*, October 6, 1840, p. 2.

104. *Le Journal de Québec*, November 6, 1845, p. 3.

105. *Le Canadien*, October 7, 1840, p. 3.

106. *Le Canadien*, December 9, 1842, p. 3.

107. *Le Canadien*, May 31, 1844, p. 3.

108. See *Karel 1985*.

109. See *The Quebec Mercury*, August 24, 1848, p. 3, and *L'Ami de la religion et de la patrie*, June 11, 1849, p. 3.

110. *The Morning Chronicle*, July 28, 1858.

111. When visiting Valin's studio, the editor of *L'Aurore des Canadas* (December 22, 1842, p. 2) noted the presence of portraits "painted with exquisite taste and polish". (Translation)

112. *Le Canadien*, July 5, 1841, p. 3. (Translation)

113. See *Le Canadien*, August 20, 1841, p. 2, and *Le Fantasque* of August 23, 1841, pp. 436-439.

114. *Le Journal de Québec*, January 16, 1847, p. 2.

115. See *Vézina 1975/2*, pp. 104 and 111.

116. We should also mention the copy which Plamondon made of a portrait of Pope Gregory XVI painted in 1841 by Pietro Gagliardi and housed at that time in the bishop's palace in Montreal. Plamondon's work (1842) today hangs in the bishop's palace in Quebec City.

117. See, respectively, *Le Canadien* of October 27, 1837, p. 2, and *Le Canadien* of June 19, 1835, p. 2.

118. See *Allodi 1980* and C. Villeneuve, *op. cit.*, 1989.

119. *The Quebec Gazette*, November 27, 1833, p. 1 (advertisement reprinted on November 2 and 18); *Le Canadien*, November 22, 1833, p. 3 (advertisement dated November 21 and reprinted 12 times until January 31, 1834); *The Quebec Mercury*, November 21, 1833, p. 1.

120. *The Quebec Gazette*, December 13, 1833, p. 2.

121. *The Quebec Mercury*, December 19, 1833, p. 1.

122. See *Cameron and Trudel 1976*.

123. *The Quebec Mercury*, April 8, 1828, p. 169.

124. See *Lacasse 1983/1*, pp. 77 and 87 (Endnotes 19 and 20).

125. *The Quebec Mercury*, July 27, 1833, p. 3. In the same vein, see Endnote 71 above.

126. See Didier Prioul's essay.

127. See *Porter 1981*, pp. 165, 173-175, 269 and 270.

128. ASQ, Fonds Verreau, letter from Joseph Légaré to Jacques Viger, December 6, 1839 (box 61, No. 4). Among his fellow countrymen, our landscapist seems to have had to content himself with critical success. See *Porter 1981*, p. 269.

129. *Porter 1981*, pp. 246 and 272-274.

130. See *Porter 1978/1* and *Porter 1981*, *passim*.

131. *Porter 1981*, pp. 199, 264 and 265. We are grateful to Denis Castonguay for drawing our attention to the existence of this work.

132. *La Minerve*, July 17, 1851, p. 2 and July 31, 1851, p. 2. See also *Harper 1979*, pp. 57, 58 and 91.

133. See *Harper 1979*, pp. 92, 94 and 184.

134. *Harper 1979*, p. 184, Endnote 32.

135. *Le Castor*, April 18, 1844, p. 2.

136. See *Martin 1988*, pp. 80-81 (Repr.).

137. *Porter 1978/1*, pp. 132-133 (Repr.); *Martin 1988* (pp. 4-5) explains how Jacques Viger appealed to Duncan to execute a watercolour copy for his album.

138. Madame Clouet, née Marie-Joseph Lépine, became a widow in 1836 upon the death of merchant and Assembly member Michel Clouet. She was definitely interested in art and artists. In 1840, she rented a room in a house located at 20 Rue Buade to painter Théophile Hamel who, in May, opened his first studio there. See *Porter 1981*, pp. 172 and 403.

139. *Porter 1981*, pp. 454-456.

140. *Porter 1981*, pp. 239-240.

141. She exhibited seven works, consisting of five miniatures painted on ivory and two chalk drawings. These works included a copy of a painting by Joshua Reynolds ("Shepherd Boy") and one of a Correggio ("Madonna") (*Trudel 1990/2*).

142. She exhibited 4 landscapes: 2 copies based on Joseph Vernet's work, a "View on the Rivière du Loup" and a "View of the Falls of Niagara" (*Trudel 1990/2*).

143. She exhibited a work entitled *Country Girl* painted in watercolours, as well as two "Views in Devonshire" (*Trudel 1990/2*).

144. ASQ, Fonds Verreau, letter from Jacques Viger to Joseph Légaré, November 23, 1839 (box 62, No. 227).

145. An advertisement by French painter Victor Ernette confirms this. *Le Fantasque*, February 7, 1842, pp. 581-582.

146. *La Minerve* quoted in *Le Canadien*, December 26, 1849, p. 1.

147. *Le Canadien*, October 11, 1847, p. 3.

148. In Europe at that time, a quality copy was still considered an important work of art. On the history of the view of copies, see the editorial of No. 21 of *Revue de l'art*, published in 1973 (pp. 5-31). This article is by François Chamoux, Tania Velmans, Louis Grodecki, Marie-Madeleine Gauthier, Antoine Schnapper, Bruno Foucart and André Chastel. Pages 23 to 29 are especially insightful. About the various interpretations which could be made about an original or a copy, see the article in *Le Journal de Québec* (June 7) published on the Quebec Industrial Exhibition of 1853. There are also some interesting comments on the hierarchy of genres and processes, with watercolours being deemed "the dregs of painting"! (Translation)

149. *Trudel 1990/2*, p. 67.

150. It must be remembered that in the 1850s, it was primarily Anglophones who attended Légaré's third art gallery in Quebec City. In the words of collector Edward Taylor Fletcher, who met "most of the Quebec artists and picture fanciers" there, this gallery "was a delightful place of resort" (Archives of the Montreal Museum of Fine Arts, John W.H. Watts Papers, Scrapbook, p. 344).

151. *Le Pays*, quoted in *La Minerve*, December 6, 1856, p. 2.

A LOOK AT LIKENESS:
PORTRAITURE IN LOWER CANADA

by Paul Bourassa

L IKENESS was unquestionably the primary criterion by which 19th-century portraits were judged;[1] the term was used time and again by critics expressing their opinion on the quality of a given work. The notion of likeness or resemblance[2] is the jumping-off point for our study of portraiture and its significance in Quebec society between 1790 and 1860, and more specifically between 1820 and 1850, and this essay will focus on whether likeness should be judged on physical, psychological or ideological grounds. On the one hand, unless there is an existing photo of the subject, physical resemblance is impossible to confirm and, even if it were possible, it would serve little real purpose. On the other hand, physiognomy—the study of a person's character based on outward appearance—seems to be a rather outdated avenue of exploration.[3] Even if a painter could reveal the sitter's personality or temperament by interpreting physical traits based on a codified list of facial expressions,[4] the artist's own character and the viewer's perceptions would introduce distortion on at least two levels. Though certain portraits lend themselves to this type of analysis better than others,[5] such an analysis actually reveals very little, unveiling only a fraction of the sitter's individuality. As for ideological analysis, it can be summed up as follows: "Portraiture expresses not so much ideas as ideals."[6] Indeed, of all the types of paintings defined by their subject matter, the portrait probably best reflects social values and, consequently, most faithfully mirrors the ideology determining their codification or typology.[7] While portraits were obviously a means of expressing the sitter's individuality, the main objective was to identify the person whose portrait was being painted with a specific group or social class by emulating certain models. These models were less a reflection of actual social categories than of a desire on the part of some to achieve the same status as others. Members of the bourgeoisie who wished to consolidate their position in society thus adopted an aristocratic lifestyle and method of representation, while aristocrats, in turn, modelled their image after that of the king or his courtiers.[8] The codification or conventions governing portraiture did not reveal the sitter's individuality or social standing as much as they manifested the ideology underlying his behaviour.

Although the portrait was subject to certain restrictions based on its function, uses, and the client's expectations, its esthetic value is nonetheless significant. Before the artist and the person commissioning his portrait entered into any contract, certain decisions were made. The prospective sitter would first decide, based on financial means and status—

or the one to which he aspired—whom he wished to pose for: a painter, miniaturist, silhouettist or photographer. If he opted for a painting, and chose a particular artist over another, it was likely for very specific reasons. He may have been familiar with the artist's reputation and was flattered to be painted by him, as others in his set had been, or he may have liked the artist's paintings and preferred his style over another's. Both subject and artist benefitted from this arrangement. For the artist, gaining access to a clientele of a higher station than that to which he himself could lay claim raised him to an equivalent status.[9] Of modest origins, he thus became a member of the bourgeoisie, rising to this privileged status through the relationships he was able to establish through his painting.[10]

"Likeness", then, as employed in Quebec portraiture in the first half of the 19th century, will be approached mainly from the perspective of the complex relationship between the portrait's social and esthetic value.

A Bourgeois Lifestyle

The social, economic, political and artistic conditions in Quebec between 1820 and 1850 were particularly favourable for portraitists, this period being characterized by the rise of the bourgeoisie.[11] Facts show that members of this multi-faceted group represented only a very small percentage of the working population,[12] but that they maintained a very high profile in society, becoming involved in every field of activity in order to validate or maintain their status. Their ascent was concrete (the advantages of economic or political power), abstract (the quality of intellectual or spiritual authority) and conspicuous (social behaviour displaying the possession of this "advantage" or "quality"). The portrait came into play in this quest for prominence, being one of a number of means used by members of the bourgeoisie to flaunt their social standing.

The elite in Lower Canada (seigneurial classes, rich business classes, senior civil servants and officers) enjoyed approximately the same privileges,[13] with only slight qualitative and quantitative differences in their economic status.[14] Compared to other groups and previous years, the elite's wealth increased auspiciously during the first half of the 19th century[15] and was most obvious in private life. As evidenced by estate inventories of deceased members of the bourgeoisie, their huge homes—often worth between £500 and £2000—contained many chambers, including a drawing room,

Ill. 28.
Unidentified artist, *Five Gentlemen Drinking Around the Table*, c. 1845;
watercolour over graphite on paper, 12.2 × 20.4 cm fol. 22 of
Lady Belleau's Album. National Archives of Canada, Ottawa (C-23331).

a dining room, an office or study, an average of five bed-rooms and sometimes even a games room. The contents usually included a vast array of luxurious furniture, exceptional lighting, more-than-adequate heating, overflowing wardrobes, well-stocked libraries and enough china to serve a multitude.[16] Luxury items also constituted a portion of this wealth, often accounting for more than 20% of the goods in a bourgeois home, and being worth more than £90 on average.[17] These included some very costly items: jewellery, clocks, watches, carpets, musical instruments (particularly pianos, which were fashionable in these circles), games (such as billiard tables or backgammon boards), silver and, of course, artwork. Many of these goods, especially gold and silver pieces, might have been considered safe, long-term investments, but their real value was as symbols of social success. The bourgeois home was the setting for various social events; it was there that friendships were formed and, more importantly, where one established a network of business contacts. It was not unusual to find portraits of the master and mistress of the house hanging prominently in the drawing room, dining room or study to foster feelings of trust in guests and potential clients (Ill. 28). In 1808, Judge Pierre-Amable De Bonne commissioned portraits from William Berczy (Cat. 18 and 19) to "decorate his parlour".[18] (Translation) While Napoléon Aubin complained, in one article, that the drawing rooms of the country's "upper crust" contained "soft carpets, mahogany furniture, gilded chandeliers, marble fireplaces, thick drapes, and for decoration, a thousand insignificant trinkets showing neither good taste nor talent, and nary a painting in sight" (Translation), this must be seen as the observation of an artistically sensitive soul anxious to see a greater variety of work. Aubin had earlier noted that artists received commissions only for "family subjects, whose attractions we wish neither to deny nor condemn."[19] Portraits, then, along with a few European canvases and numerous prints, were the works favoured by the bourgeoisie of the era. Estate inventories drawn up after the death of wealthy landowners show that they often owned 15 or more "framed prints."[20]

The bourgeoisie was not alone at the top of the social ladder; this rung was shared with the clergy. The very structure and manner in which the Church carried out its activities were reminiscent of society's own hierarchy. The clergy had both its elite and those who worked behind the scenes. The senior members of the clergy, important parish priests and leaders of religious communities held undeniable social sway. Most were from the same class as civil servants, magistrates and important businessmen. Monseigneur Jean-Jacques Lartigue was Louis-Joseph Papineau's cousin, Abbé David-Henri Têtu was the brother of important merchants. In general, priesthood was synonymous with social recognition. Even the simple country priest had a privileged status.

It was these members of the bourgeoisie and clergy who saw the portrait as a means of establishing and consolidating their identity and living on after death. Several options were available, and the client's choice depended on the portrait's purpose.

The Use and Purpose of the Portrait

Portraits produced in Quebec between 1790 and 1860 served every possible purpose and came in every possible form, from the very official full-length portrait to the extremely personal miniature. These uses in turn determined the codes or conventions that were followed to ensure that the portrait fulfilled the desired function. Absolute definition is impossible, however, given that the various categories sometimes overlapped.

The Official Portrait

Several examples of full-length portraits existed in Lower Canada, most of them painted by Théophile Hamel. These portraits were customarily reserved for people in administrative positions and were usually commissioned to commemorate an extraordinary achievement.[21] They were not destined to grace the walls of bourgeois homes, but were intended to be displayed where the subjects carried out their regular duties. The portraits of James Bruce, 8th earl of Elgin and 12th earl of Kincardine (Cat. 138), Narcisse-Fortunat Belleau (Cat. 137), Abbé Patrick McMahon (Fig. 137A) and Abbé Joseph-David Déziel (Fig. 137B) conform to this definition. All followed a standard formula: dignity of bearing; official garments where called for; commemoration of an event either by an inscription or by the presence of a map on partially unrolled parchment; an elaborate setting. This formula is taken directly from royal[22] and aristocratic portraits, some of which—such as the copy of the portrait of King George IV by Joseph Légaré in 1834 (Cat. 160)—were well known in the country. When it came to having their portraits done, members of the bourgeoisie and clergy could receive the same treatment as the governor of the colony or the monarch.

This codification was used for other institutional commissions, but followed different rules. In his portrait, John Bethune (Cat. 245) is wearing his robes as rector of McGill University and shown full-length, seated in a chair. John Samuel McCord is wearing his robes as chancellor of Bishop's University. William Notman took two full-length photographs of him (Fig. 251A) and ultimately favoured a

Ill. 29.
François Baillairgé,
(attr. to)
*Louis Fromenteau de
la Boucherie*, c. 1812;
oil on canvas,
76.9 × 61.5 cm.
Musée du Québec,
Quebec (76.195).

Ill 30.
Théophile Hamel,
*Commodore Richard
Israël Alleyn*, 1846;
oil on canvas,
84.8 × 69 cm.
Montreal Museum
of Fine Arts.
Purchase, Horsley
and Annie Townsend
Bequest (1975.20).

tighter composition for the final work, which was touched up by John A. Fraser (Cat. 251). The same was done for certain portraits of bishops or priests holding administrative positions. Abbé Louis-Jacques Casault, rector of Université Laval, was also portrayed wearing his robes.[23]

The Professional Portrait

The conventions mentioned above applied not only to officially commissioned works or full-length portraits, they were also observed for professional portraits, which feature the subject in his workplace or carrying out his duties. Clothes, books and other accessories had a symbolic value in such paintings. Clergy—bishops in particular—were portrayed wearing their most elaborate vestments (cape, surplice, rochet, stole, cross), symbolizing religious as well as social prestige. Secular figures such as René-Edouard Caron (Fig. 188A), Louis-Joseph Papineau (Cat. 188) and Elzéar Bédard (Cat. 197) wore robes and bands indicating their role in society. This role is further confirmed by the names of philosophers, politicians or jurists appearing prominently on the binding of the books surrounding the subjects. In other paintings, the symbolism is subtler. The portraits of Joseph Papineau (Cat. 90) and Dr. Daniel Arnoldi (Cat. 149) suggest their respective professions of notary and doctor. Archibald Campbell's portrait (Cat. 125) highlights the notary's involvement in shipbuilding, while that of Daniel Wilkie (Cat. 176) discreetly suggests his activities as pastor, teacher and philanthropist. Certain occupations were governed by specific principles. Military portraits, for example, showed the subject in uniform near a battlefield. The portrait of *Melchior-Alphonse d'Irumberry de Salaberry* (Cat. 133) is rather understated in this regard, but for confirmation one need only look at the portrait of Louis Fromenteau, attributed to François Baillairgé (Ill. 29). Navigators and shipbuilders alike could be portrayed spyglass in hand, as were Commodore Richard Israël Alleyn, in an 1846 painting by Hamel (Ill. 30), and James McKenzie, in an 1843 work by Palmer (MQ). Finally, artists often resorted to the use of the written word to highlight a specific event. Jean-Baptiste Roy-Audy referred di-

rectly to the political role played by Louis Bourdages (Cat. 205) in the formulation of the Ninety-Two Resolutions through an inscription on the paper held by the sitter. The same was done in the portrait of Ludger Duvernay (Fig. 205A), who is portrayed holding a copy of a scathing text which he had published in *La Minerve* in 1832. These portraits could be used either for public display or in private homes. Surrounded by an assortment of luxury items, the portraits reflected the self-assurance of the master of the house and convinced visitors of his credibility and social standing.

At first glance, certain pictures seemed to have been destined for a specific room in the house. The study or "office," where business or intellectual pursuits were carried out, was often chosen to display professional portraits; even the term used to designate them ("cabinet-size") is significant. It is possible that the portraits of Alfred Hawkins (Cat. 175) and James Turnbull (Fig. 175B) were originally painted for this purpose. The imagery used points to their philanthropic activities (which were nonetheless not completely devoid of business considerations): Hawkins' publication of a map and Turnbull's art collection and patronage.

The Half-Length or Head-and-Shoulders Portrait

The portrait, though always indicating a certain degree of prestige, could also be somewhat less formal. In such cases, openness, integrity and honesty, as they related to the subject's respectability, became the significant values. The half-length portrait lent itself well to this end. The Renaissance set the standard: a three-quarter view of the subject looking directly at the viewer to establish a "sincere" relationship. Often, the lower part of the arm and hand on the side of the body nearest the viewer were used to close the lower part of the composition.[24] Most portraits of the 1790-1860 period followed this standard; one need simply look at the portrait of James McGill by Louis Dulongpré (Fig. 17A) and that of Amable Dionne by Théophile Hamel (Ill. 31). The portraits painted by Antoine Plamondon between 1830 and 1835 (Cat. 183) also conform to this general rule, establishing the "authority" of the bourgeois gentleman, be he merchant or magistrate. In these, the model adopted a full-frontal pose with the light striking the face, creating strong shadows and sharp contrast to give a more sculpted look. Over the years, this very direct approach gradually gave way to a less austere interpretation. By changing the centering, the artist had greater freedom and could, at the same time establish a certain distance between the subject and viewer. The ease of the pose and the decorative aspect of the painting thus reflected the assurance gained by both the painter and the member of the bourgeoisie portrayed.

The 1842 portrait of François-Xavier Paradis (Ill. 32) shows a well-established member of the bourgeoisie, proud of his success, good taste and manners. Paradis, whose diverse investments in the timber, food, real estate and insurance industries guaranteed him a substantial income, was a typical example of the business class living in the Saint-Roch district of Quebec City. Like any good middle-class gentleman, he was a member of philanthropic organizations, such as the *Société bienveillante de Québec.* At the time of his wife's death in 1846, he possessed a vast fortune, including belongings valued at £503.[25] Plamondon often received the patronage of these members of the middle class, who shared a similar lifestyle and who were often related to one another. In 1841-1842, for example, the artist's studio was visited by Paradis' daughter Caroline (Ill. 34), her husband, Joseph

Ill. 35.
Antoine Plamondon
*Joseph Guillet dit
Tourangeau*, 1842;
89.2 × 74.3 cm.
Musée du Québec,
Quebec (53.77).

Ill. 36.
Antoine Plamondon,
*Mrs. Joseph Guillet
dit Tourangeau,
née Judith Kemner,*
1842;
oil on canvas,
91.5 × 76.5 cm.
Musée du Québec,
Quebec (77.04).

Ill. 37.
Antoine Plamondon,
Soeur Saint-Joseph,
1841;
oil on canvas,
88.9 × 71.1 cm.
Musée de l'Hôpital
général de Québec.

The Family Portrait

In looking once again at the portraits of Louis-Joseph Papineau, Elzéar Bédard and René-Edouard Caron, and those of their wives, certain 19th-century ideas about family roles become evident.[26] Generally speaking, inasmuch as men, in a desire to affirm their self-worth, relied on their occupations, portrayals of women focused on their appearance and maternal aspects.[27] By holding the musical score bearing the name of her young daughter, who is sitting primly at the piano, Madame Papineau's role as educator of her family is stressed (Cat. 187). In sharp contrast, the portrait of Madame Bédard wearing a ball gown and carrying evening gloves highlights her role as a worldly socialite (Cat. 198). Madame Caron and her daughter (Ill. 38), enveloped in yards of fabric, carefully posed and surrounded by tasteful objets d'art, are luxury and grace personified—the privilege of womanhood.[28]

It should be pointed out that motherhood and childhood were new concepts in the society of this era. The impact of Rousseau's notions on family devotion and education were felt here, as well as in Europe.[29] In New France, portraits of children were almost unheard of, and in the rare ones that existed, children were portrayed as miniature adults. As in 15th—and 16th—century Europe, children were not seen as distinct entities but simply as incomplete adults, and childhood was considered an awkward age. This view, due in part to extremely high infant mortality, led to the rejection of anything resembling a child's form and structure.[30] With the importance attached to at-home education in the late 18th century,[31] and the emotional links developed within "the intimate sanctuary" (Translation) of the home, children gained status as individuals, which led to the development of new conventions. The "family" was also venerated by the bourgeoisie, who, since the end of the *Ancien Régime,*[32] had seen it as the basic component of the whole social structure. Plamondon portrayed the serious, studious side of children (*Cyprien Tanguay*, Cat. 184 and *Mrs. Louis-Joseph Papineau, née Julie Bruneau, and Her Daughter Ézilda*, Cat. 187) while

Guillet dit Tourangeau (Ill. 33), his parents, prosperous baker Joseph Guillet dit Tourangeau (Ill. 35) and his wife, née Judith Kemner (Ill. 36), as well as their two daughters, who became nuns, sisters Sainte-Anne (Cat. 196) and Saint-Joseph (Ill. 37). A dozen years later, in 1854, he authored the portraits of two more Tourangeau children, Josephine (MQ), who joined the Ursuline convent that year, and Émilie, Madame François-Narcisse Gingras (MQ). The less formal character of these portraits is evident in the more relaxed pose, the absence of details revealing the subject's occupation, the solid background and the clothing which, while sober, is relatively stylish. In short, the portraits revealed nothing about social or professional standing. These middle-class citizens did not need to show how they had achieved their financial success, but simply that they had succeeded and were guaranteed social prestige as a result. The portraits merely confirmed the fact.

Ill. 38.
Théophile Hamel,
*Mrs. René-Edouard
Caron, née Joséphine
de Blois, and Her
Daughter*, 1846;
oil on canvas,
122.9 × 99.7 cm.
Musée du Québec,
Quebec (47.129).

Ill. 39.
Théophile Hamel,
*Mrs. Charles-Hilaire
Têtu, née Elizabeth
O'Brien, and Her
Son, Eugène*, 1841;
oil on canvas,
115.1 × 97.2 cm.
Montreal Museum
of Fine Arts.
Anonymous gift
(1968.1585).

Ill. 40.
James Bowman, (attr. to) *Celina and Rosalvina Pelletier*, c. 1838; oil on
canvas, 63.5 × 76.2 National Archives of Canada, Ottawa (C-99707).

Ill. 41.
William Berczy,
*The McGillivray
Family*, 1806;
oil on canvas,
120 × 90 cm.
McCord Museum
of Canadian History,
Montreal (M18683).

Hamel depicted a more playful, though still earnest, aspect (Ill. 39). One example that clearly illustrates the new concept of family devotion is the work entitled *Mrs. William Burns Lindsay, née Maria Jones, and Her Son fils John* (Cat. 219) by Henry Daniel Theilcke. This concept's application to portraiture had been developed in England by Joshua Reynolds and Thomas Lawrence.[33] Children were shown at play and portrayed tenderly, as innocents. By expressing profoundly human behaviour through their attitudes, actions and facial expressions, children were the embodiment of the adults they were to become,[34] without the inhibitions—at least in paintings.[35]

The sentiments conjured up in childrens' portraits also correspond to typically bourgeois values. Samuel Palmer, a devotee of the British tradition, depicts these values in his portrait of the Turnbull children (Cat. 177 and Fig. 177A). The presence of a dog in the portrait of the young girls

stresses children's natural affection and their closeness to nature.[36] The portrait of Célina and Rosalvina Pelletier (Ill. 40) used similar conventions: the presence of an animal and an affectionate gesture made by one of the two sisters.[37] The sensitivity expressed by this portrait is accentuated by its warm colours. The two sisters are wearing red gowns and necklaces of red coral, a symbol of protection against childhood illness. Although this era finally heralded the portrayal of children, either alone or with their mothers, the family portrait *per se* was not as common. Exceptions include the famous painting of the Woolsey family (Fig. 18-19A) by William Berczy, which presents a hierarchical image of the family structure using precise geometrical composition. Another example is the original version of the McGillivray family portrait, also done by Berczy (Ill. 41), which illustrates the joys of family life. The painting shows them in a natural setting, in accordance with the ideals espoused by Rousseau.[38]

Ill. 42.
Cornelius Krieghoff, *John Budden*,(?) 1847;
oil on canvas, 58.4 × 73.7 cm. Private collection.

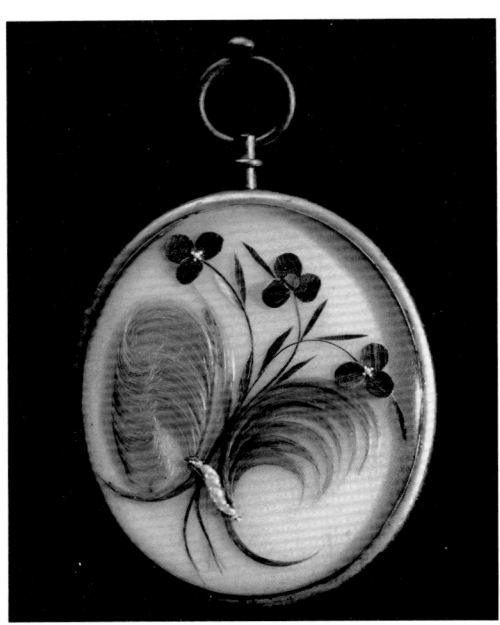

Ill. 43.
Reverse side of a
miniature
by William Berczy,
*Pierre-Amable
De Bonne*, 1808;
hair, hair pigment,
gold thread, pearl
seeds, 6.3 × 5 cm.
Musée du Québec,
Quebec.

The Private Portrait

Portraiture could also be adapted to fulfill more private purposes. As a fixed image used to replace an absent loved one and keep a memory alive, the portrait took on a less formal tone and sometimes carried hidden symbolism. The romantic style sometimes used for childrens' portraits—a style which expressed the profound love of nature so important to Jean-Jacques Rousseau—was never used extensively in adult portraiture in Quebec. The landscapes surrounding the subjects portrayed were used strictly as backdrops. Portraits of American Indians, whether painted by Légaré, Plamondon or Hamel, followed the same rules when the artist's intention was to portray the individual. The painting of John Budden (Ill. 42), however, is a remarkable exception. Done by his friend, artist Cornelius Krieghoff, Budden's portrait shows man's relationship with his environment as a sign of his morality. The oval shape underscores the intimacy of the scene. Budden is seen in profile, seated on the ground and leaning on one hand, in *contrapposto*, showing more of his back than his face, a pose completely at odds with the conventional poses adopted at the time. Wearing checkered pants, studded shoes and spats, the gentleman hunter has laid down his top hat, rifle and game bag—which form an evocative still life—and has paused with his dog in the middle of the pathway. In the half-light passing through the leaves above, Budden can, to quote Rousseau, "drink in nature's attractions at his leisure". (Translation) Here, hunting is not killing, but rather, a diversion for a genteel member of the bourgeoisie whose sensitivity blossoms when confronted with his natural surroundings, causing him to become lost in noble "fantasies." In terms of ideas and inspiration, a relationship exists between Krieghoff's portrait of John Budden and that of Sir Brooke Boothby, painted by Joseph Wright of Derby in 1781, in which Rousseau's ideology is even more clearly illustrated.[39] While exceptional in the Quebec of the era, this example

shows that there was an interest in this type of portraiture, in which nature was perceived as an object of esthetic emotion, expressing harmony between man and his universe.

However, the private portrait differs from works shown publicly or displayed in the homes of the upper classes mainly in its small size. Whether on canvas, wood, paper or ivory, the image is frank and unaffected. The portrait of Georges-Barthélemi Faribault (Cat. 237) demonstrates these qualities. His relaxed pose, with his arm thrown over the back of the chair, suggests a certain insouciance. By definition, the miniature is an intimate form. Its evolution, however, reflects the esthetic changes that took place in England and bestowed upon the miniature a different role. The dimensions and delicate, subtle colours of the miniature depicting *Basilique-Benjamin Trottier Desrivières Beaubien* (Cat. 46), by James Peale, is typical of late 18th-century productions. First designed as jewellery, the miniature was set in a medallion or locket which could be kept in a gentleman's waistcoat pocket or worn around a lady's neck (see *Mrs. Ignace Trottier dit Desrivières, née Marguerite Mailhot*, Cat. 14). The miniature's symbolic use, as a token of affection, was often reinforced by adding a lock of hair or the initials of the person portrayed to the back of the medallion. The lock of hair could be braided (sometimes with those of the person receiving the locket) or arranged to form a fan or floral motif by adding dyes, gold threads and seed pearls.[40] Judge Pierre-Amable de Bonne, for example, gave William Berczy "a lovely locket," in which to paint his likeness (Ill. 43).[41]

In early 19th-century England, under the influence of artists such as Andrew Robertson (1777-1845), the technique used to paint miniatures on ivory was changing. With its new format (larger and often rectangular), increased use of gum arabic, and use of glazes over richer, more intense colours, the miniature more closely resembled the oil painting—the actual objective. The miniature thus became an exhibition piece,[42] as exemplified by the works of American Anson

Ill. 44.
Gerome Fassio,
Portrait of a Woman,
c. 1845;
watercolour on paper,
13.4 × 10.6 cm.
National Gallery
of Canada,
Ottawa (18181).

Ill. 45.
Jarvis F. Hankes and
Emmanuel Reynolds,
Thomas Porteous,
c. 1828;
black paper cutout,
bronze detail and
grey wash on paper,
25.3 × 20.5 cm.
National Archives
of Canada,
Ottawa (C-104257).

Dickinson (Cat. 88 and 89) and was also displayed differently, often in wooden or black papier maché frames topped by a ring so that it could be hung on the wall. The works of Gerome Fassio were generally displayed in this manner (Cat. 107 to 110). Some miniatures were kept in Moroccan leather boxes with hinged lids and latches. The earliest miniatures in this new style were small and oval, lending themselves to the same uses as the medallion (Cat. 52). However, the rectangular format, which could be displayed on a table, gained in popularity, particularly with the arrival of the daguerreotype (Cat. 105 and 106). Subject portrayal also changed. The figures depicted by Fassio in the 1840s were more or less "posed," as if seeking to lend themselves a certain bearing, and the artist followed the usual conventions of the painted portrait (Ill. 44). These changes illustrate the capriciousness of this fragile art form, which was affected by the sudden changes occurring in portraiture during the same period. Originally an intimate object, the miniature sought to more closely copy the painted portrait, and then had to compete with the cheaper likeness produced by the daguerreotype.

The Silhouette

The silhouette is a rather special type of portrait. While resemblance and immediate recognition were the ultimate criteria for perfection in portraiture, these "shades," as they were sometimes called, gave the model a fleeting, otherworldly appearance. Three phenomena gave rise to the silhouette: physiognomy, mechanical procedures and the lure of novelty. Throughout history, the profile was often used in portraiture because it clearly showed the most significant physical characteristics of the face: the forehead, nose, mouth and chin. It was also used by artists in ancient Greece, medal makers and early Renaissance painters. The silhouette was originally a diversion for amateurs, as shown in the portraits of the Hale family (Cat. 243 and 244). Very early on, though,

the postulations of physiognomists made it a pseudo-scientific discipline which allowed characterization through examination of facial features.[43] Goethe, who collaborated with Johann Kaspar Lavater on his works in physiognomy, said of the silhouette that it was the "emptiest yet most faithful image of a man possible". (Translation) However, it was the invention of devices allowing the outline of the face to be quickly traced and then reduced that led to the immense popularity of this type of portrait. The silhouette's popularity rapidly spread throughout Lower Canada because it was decorative, amusing and relatively cheap, and because anything new was avidly sought during that era. However, silhouettes were done mainly by itinerant artists, most of them European or American. American Eliab Metcalf (Cat. 38 to 41) was one of those who introduced the use of a "patent physionotrace," as mentioned in his advertisements, while Augustin Édouart (Cat. 100 to 102) and Jarvis Hankes (Cat. 139 and 140) were among those noted for their rapidity and dexterity in cutting out silhouettes using nothing more than "a pair of ordinary scissors", as their advertisements claimed. While they produced the customary profiles, these two artists were best-known for their full-length silhouettes. In certain cases, Hankes and his associate, Emmanuel Reynolds, highlighted the silhouettes with gold or bronze detailing (Ill. 45) and affixed them to paper which had been gray-washed to give the impression of a background (Ill. 1).

A Question of Cost or Taste?

It is difficult to determine whether each type of portraiture corresponded to a specific clientele, or what led a person to pose for Jean-Baptiste Roy-Audy rather than for Antoine Plamondon. What is certain is that the artist's accessibility played a key role. Artists who travelled to towns and villages had a different clientele than those who settled in the capital. When Louis Dulongpré painted his many pastels of the lower middle class in the Richelieu region, he probably went door-to-door to offer his services. This is what Louis-Joseph-Amédée Papineau may have been referring to when he wrote, "here in Canada, a venerable gentleman by the name of Du Longpré, who came with Lafayette to fight for the Independence of the Republic, calls upon various families and, in exchange for their hospitality, produces likenesses of the most important members of the family, usually the elders".[44] (Translation) Did Jean-Baptiste Roy-Audy do this as well? It seems likely, given that the portraits to his credit include both country folk and city dwellers. William Berczy, Antoine Plamondon and Théophile Hamel, once well-established, worked strictly in larger communities, seeking out wealthy members of the bourgeoisie who moved in political circles.

The cost of a portrait in the early 19th century differed considerably depending on the technique used. Cost was also based on the artist's reputation and the clients sought. In 1818, Louis Dulongpré charged £6, 5s [$25][45] for a half-length portrait of Judge Thomas McCord.[46] He charged approximately the same price (£7, 10s [$30] each) for four versions of a portrait of Joseph Papineau (Cat. 90) in 1825.[47] Ten years earlier, when William Berczy produced his portraits of Judge Pierre-Amable De Bonne (Cat. 18 and 19), he had mentioned that "according to the price I set for my work, a half-length portrait costs 12 guineas for labour," in other words, £14 [$56].[48] According to information drawn from the accounts of Théophile Hamel, the artist probably charged from $50 to $200 for a similar portrait during the 1850s. Napoléon Bourassa, however, reprimanded him saying, "I will not forgive you if you continue to repeat the same types of portraits requested by your clients, averaging two hours per session and 50 piastres for labour."[49] However, these prices could vary depending on the importance of the commission. When Hamel obtained a government contract in 1853, he was guaranteed £100 [$400] per canvas.[50] The fees charged for oil portraits were similar to those charged for the most expensive furniture and jewels in a bourgeois home of the era. These portraits, then, were the purview of society's most affluent members.

Miniatures on ivory were also relatively expensive and reserved for the very wealthy. The high cost was associated mainly with the basic material but the technique used and time involved also had some bearing. Berczy's miniatures—worth £8 [$32] each—were as costly as half-length oil portraits.[51] Anson Dickinson seems to have charged $25 for his works from the beginning of his career on.[52] When another American, William Dunlap, visited Canada in 1820, he charged $30 for his miniatures and between $25 and $120 for his oil portraits, depending on the format.[53] Gerritt Schipper offered a wide variety of portraits, ranging from "Miniature painted on ivory... price 20 dollars," to "Couloured crayon" for 6 dollars, to "Watercolours, suitable for lockets, breast pins, &c." for 3 dollars, to drawings in "Black crayons" for 1 dollar.[54]

These small watercolours and pencil and pastel drawings on paper made the portrait accessible to a greater public. It became even more so with the advent of the silhouette in the 1820s, and especially with the arrival of the daguerreotype in the 1840s. Prices were based on the rapidity of the execution and the existence of mechanical devices to make the work easier. Eliab Metcalf, who used the physiognotrace and could cut out silhouettes in less than a minute, charged "thirty sous [$.50] for two likenesses."[55] A certain W.H. Morgan advertised "PROFILES Cut, 2 for One Shillings [.20$]",[56] while American Thomas Charles Bell (active between 1811 and 1831) offered "Miniature Coloured 7s 6d [1.50$] to 10s [2$]" and "Black Profiles, in relief—3s [.60$]".[57] As for Jarvis Hankes, the admission fee for his "Papyrotomia or Gallery of Paper Cuttings," was 2s 6d [$.50] for adults and half price for children, and included for each visitor "a portrait—an amazing likeness cut in only seconds, without the aid of a machine."[58] For full-length silhouettes, Hankes charged between three and five dollars, depending on whether or not they were highlighted with bronze detailing (See Cat. 138 and 139). In the United States, Augustin Édouart charged 5 shillings [$1] for a full-length silhouette (3 shillings [$.60] for a duplicate) and 1 shilling [$.20] for a head-and-shoulders.[59]

The daguerreotype burst onto the scene in Quebec in 1840. On June 21, 1841, *Le Fantasque* announced that an "artist, newly arrived from France, would, beginning Monday, make portraits using a Daguerreotype […]. Each portrait would cost 4 piastres".[60] (Translation) Cost became an incentive, and almost a threat, in certain ads:

What a deal!!

At the urging of many of his close friends, Mr. M. Desnoyers has decided to reduce his prices for DAGUERREOTYPE portraits to half of what they were in Montreal. The prices will be:

Regular size, 7s6 [$1.50] to 10s [$2.00].

Large size, 10s [$2.00] to 12s6 [$2.50].

By reducing his prices so drastically, he hopes to gain public support and encourage his fellow countrymen to have their portraits done. If, after an ample trial period (say, one month), Mr. Desnoyers does not receive the encouragement due his efforts, he will be forced to return to his regular prices.

Since price is no longer a consideration, it is to be hoped that people will allow themselves to be guided by their taste for art.[61] (Translation)

In 1845, a columnist made the following observation:

The difficulty today is not having your portrait done, but deciding who should do it since, for a few shillings, you can have one done and redone and, what is more, it will never be unflattering.[62] (Translation)

Even with greater accessibility and democratization, those who had portraits done cannot be divided into set categories. Important dignitaries like Lord Elgin agreed to pose for Théophile Hamel as readily as for photographer T.C. Doane (Ill. 19). Lord Dalhousie was attracted by the prodigious Master Hankes and commissioned five silhouettes (Ill. 1 and Cat. 139). Louis-Joseph Papineau was immortalized on canvas by renowned artists such as Hamel, Plamondon (Cat. 188) and Bourassa (Cat. 248), as well as by the camera of William Notman and many others. Members of the seigneurial class like Louis-Ignace-Michel-Antoine d'Irumberry de Salaberry had silhouettes done by Metcalf and his ilk (Cat. 39) and their features captured on ivory by people such as Dickinson (see Cat. 89).

Ill. 46.
Antoine Plamondon,
Portrait of a Lady,
1834;
oil on canvas,
75.5 × 65 cm.
National Gallery
of Canada,
Ottawa (30239).

Ill. 47.
Jean-Baptiste
Roy-Audy,
*Mrs. Alexis
Désaulniers,
née Julie Bélair*,
c. 1830;
oil on canvas,
66.3 × 56.5 cm.
Musée du Québec,
Quebec (81.271)

Personal taste also determined the choice of artist or of a particular type of portrait. Esthetic considerations, as well as financial ones, explain why two ladies of similar standing would choose to have their portraits done by different artists, say Plamondon (Ill. 46) versus Roy-Audy (Ill. 47). Seen through the eyes of viewers of that era—uninitiated to the figurations and images with which we are constantly in contact—the precision of a canvas done by Roy-Audy is mesmerizing. One journalist remarked to his readers that "the finish on his portraits is extremely meticulous, and the fabric is lovely."[63] The specific qualities of these portraits, obtained through simplified forms and painstaking attention to finish, can be attributed both to the preferences of those who commissioned the work, and to the artist's technical inadequacies. How else can we explain the proliferation of this type of portrait, both here and in the United States, when the finest artists were using a more academic style? Changes in demographic patterns and greater access to a certain socioeconomic status resulted in a broader market, paving the way for the portrait to solidly establish the new bourgeoisie's social identity. In the United States, William Matthew Prior (1806-1873) offered his clients two possibilities: a two-dimensional portrait in a "primitive" style or, for a higher price, a version which met the academic standards of perspective and relief.[64]

By choosing Plamondon, people identified themselves with the "intellectual" art of the capitals of the world, sacrificing "meticulous finish" for technical brilliance. At the dawn of the 1840s, Plamondon and his exegetes had developed a new esthetic discourse on the portrait. While still present, the criterion of resemblance in the appreciation a work became of secondary importance.[65] The value of *mimesis* or illusion was now determined by strictly artistic qualities: light, colour, brush stroke, etc. On August 20, 1841, three famous portraits of nuns by Plamondon (Cat. 196 and Ill. 37) drew raves from a "Friend of the Arts" (Translation) in the newspaper *Le Canadien.* On the topic of light, the author—undoubtedly Joseph-Édouard Cauchon, then editor of the *Canadien*—wrote:

In a constant effort to produce relief, which is so evident in nature, he never lights his portraits from the front, which is utterly ridiculous, but always from a two-thirds or three-quarters position [...]. Were he to light his portraits from the front, contours and illusions would disappear, and the viewer would see nothing but paint. However, in his paintings, light and shadow form a beautiful contrast and, as in nature, it is impossible to tell the two apart because the artist has pored over the contours, and because from one extreme to the other, the colour changes are imperceptibly subtle. (Translation)

A reply in *Le Fantasque* signed, ironically, "Friend of the Artists,"[66] sparked an esthetic debate:

This depends a great deal on people's tastes—some do not wish to be portrayed weighed down by unnatural-looking shadows—and on the painter's talent, which is all the greater if he can produce illusion and relief without recourse to unnatural lighting, which should be reserved for historical paintings rather than portraits. If Quebec art enthusiasts are to be believed, the great master, Van Dyck, is little more than a ludicrous simpleton for having chosen not to follow Mr. Plamondon's style, and for having dared, on the contrary, to light a great number of his paintings from the front. If he had lit them from behind, he would have been lauded by our FRIEND OF THE ARTS. [...] I saw, at the studio of Mr. Th. Hamel, portraits which resembled their subjects, showed perfect relief and natural colour, and yet which were illuminated from the front [...] and they were at least as pleasing to the eye and heart as portraits which seem to have been painted in crypts by the light of funeral torches. (Translation)

The criticism goes on to deal with the rendering of the fabric and the poses, transcending laconic comments or elements unrelated to the work. Another passage in the article supporting Plamondon stresses how the quality of his execution can be seen not only when looking at the portrait as a whole, but also when examining its parts:

Now that you have seen all the portraits, look at them more closely, see how painstakingly every detail is rendered, look and see if you can find the brush strokes. Try as you might, you will not be able to, and this is another secret of skilled artists, who manage to conceal the paint before your very eyes, so that all you see is nature […]. Move closer and see how the artist has captured the eye's dampness, the tear that has just left the tear duct, the crystalline quality of the transparent cornea. Without these details, the painter has achieved nothing because he has not succeeded in breathing life into his painting, he has produced nothing but the dead orb of a statue. (Translation)

According to these critics, painting's power of illusion is reflected even in the tactile quality of the objects portrayed. When he visited Plamondon's studio in 1842, a journalist for *L'Encyclopédie canadienne* noticed a series of portraits, probably those of the Tourangeau family (Ill. 33 to 36):

Among the half-length portraits, I noted, in particular, those of an entire Quebec family, father, mother, son, daughter, etc. I stepped away, I drew a step nearer, it was not only the people themselves I imagined there before me, but the actual fabrics, the fine draperies, velvet, silk, batiste, lace, ribbon, jewellery, etc. Again, it is not merely from a distance that you see and believe yourself capable of touching these things, but from close up, from a hair's breadth away. (Translation)

These new esthetic criteria, probably formulated by Plamondon himself, dictated the conduct and tastes of art enthusiasts based on an analytical process. Paintings were henceforth judged on their power of illusion and on the artist's technical skill, showcased by the work. Debates on the esthetic qualities of the portrait aimed to develop the tastes of potential clients. Certain preferred the Plamondon "school", others favoured the Hamel "school", and still others preferred the realism of Roy-Audy.

Thus, the portrait was subject to different imperatives which governed formulation, codes, uses, cost and esthetics. To delve more deeply into these phenomena would require a study which does more than merely scratch the surface. It would require a treatise placing them in a more global, detailed context. There are many avenues of portraiture still to explore, but this short analysis unveils certain aspects of the Lower Canadian bourgeoisie, and the factors and ideals which dictated the dissemination of their image. This image is neither the grotesque, overblown mask of a society, nor its death mask, a sort of fossil from the past, but rather, in the words of Baudelaire, "a dramatized biography" (Translation) of its actors. The lights have dimmed, the play is over; now it is time to apply its message to our own day and age.

Notes

1. Many avenues in the field of portraiture remain open to investigation. Few studies, either European or Canadian, have actually focused on this art form, except for the background work by Pierre and Galienne Francastel, *Le portrait, 50 siècles d'humanisme* (Paris: Gallimard, 1959). Quebec possesses only a few texts by Gérard Morisset, the work by Laurier Lacroix on religious portraiture in LE GRAND HÉRITAGE 1984 (pp. 109-112) and Éric Nicolaï's master's thesis on children's portraits (see NICOLAÏ 1990).

2. The *Webster's Ninth New Collegiate Dictionary* defines resemblance as "the quality or state of resembling; esp.: correspondence in appearance or superficial qualities." For more on resemblance, see E.H. Gombrich, *L'art et l'illusion. Psychologie de la représentation picturale* (Paris: Gallimard, 1971), first section: *Les limites de la ressemblance*, pp. 57-123. This topic as it related to *Self-Portrait in the Studio* by Théophile Hamel, was examined in BOURASSA 1989-1990, p. 46. Resemblance obviously refers back to the notion of *mimesis* and to the concept of imitating nature. Perfect resemblance was attained when an illusion of the reality imitated was achieved. Not only did the viewer recognize the person depicted, but he saw the subject "come to life" on the canvas.

3. Physiognomy made its appearance in the 13th century with the Aristotelian treatise *Physiognomonica*. Johann Kaspar Lavater (1741-1801) studied the topic, devoting his *Essays on Physiognomy*, which appeared in 1789, to it. Basing his essay on humanist ideals, Lavater reconciled scientific data with a philosophy influenced by mysticism. He compiled a veritable inventory of characteristics based on the human profile. This type of study was very much in vogue in 14th-century Europe and was responsible for the huge popularity of the silhouette (see below). The related science of phrenology, a study of the human character based on the shape of the skull, is also a result of this interest.

4. The study of expressions and a knowledge of anatomy as a basis for human representation were particularly favoured by academicians. The drawings of heads illustrating different expressions developed by Charles Le Brun in the 17th century and their codification to express emotions (*La méthode pour apprendre à dessiner les passions*), based on a Cartesian system (*Traité des Passions*), were used by academies until the 19th century. *Principles of Beauty Relative to the Human Head* (1778) by Alexander Cozens, also deals with this, as do similar works in which physical traits are codified according to a scale of characteristics, which are based on moral values. See Kim Sloan, *Alexander and John Robert Cozens. The Poetry of Landscape* (New Haven and London: Yale University Press, 1986), pages 63-68.

5. For example, when they are based on convincing testimony to the subject's personality (*James Sinclair*, Cat. 26) or if the person is known by, or more importantly is a close friend of, the artist (*Louis-Joseph Papineau*, Cat. 248).

6. Desmond Shawe-Taylor, *The Georgians. Eighteenth-Century Portraiture & Society* (London: Barrie & Jenkins, 1990), p. 31.

7. Roland Recht and Marie-Jeanne Geyer, *A qui ressemblons-nous? Le portrait dans les musées de Strasbourg* (Cat.) (Strasbourg: Éditions Les Musées de la ville de Strasbourg, 1988), pp. 9 and 11. The authors say of the portrait that "of all types of illustrations, it is the one most influenced by outside factors and thus, the one that most immediately confronts the viewer with ideology as a means of representation." (Translation)

8. *Ibid.*, p. 11. The following passage helps clarify our premise. In discussing the origin of codification in portraiture, the authors provide a definition which, although generalized, explains the repeated use of the same principles by painters who may not even have realized their scope and significance: "The origin can be traced back to the point of greatest power; the king and the royal portrait provided the absolute model. It was the privileged relationship between the prince and the artist, who was naturally chosen from among the best of that century, that gave rise to these codes. The aristocrat then seized on them, with the result that the aristocratic portrait could neither vary from this model, nor neglect the encoded rules that it establishes. When the bourgeoisie began to have their portraits done, the aristocratic portrait was taken as a model. What changed were not the codes, even if, occasionally, they were reduced or simplified, but rather the painters […]. In no other type of art was the client's wealth so ostentatiously displayed." (Translation)

Hermann Broch, in a conference on *Kitsch* ("Quelques remarques à propos de l'art tape-à-l'oeil"), defined the ideological position of the bourgeoisie, which explained its behaviour toward the aristocracy, as follows: "The bourgeoisie entered the 19th century as the ruling class on its way up. In accordance with this role, they were required, on the one hand, to carry on the traditions of the aristocracy, which was on its way out and, on the other hand, to consolidate their formerly revolutionary position." (Translation) The author reveals the aristocracy's esthetic tradition and its impulsive and dissolute behaviour, which contrasts sharply with middle class ethics and asceticism (Counter-Reformation and French Revolution). The bourgeoisie, in a way, sublimated their impulsiveness through romantic idealism, kitsch being the degenerative result of this. See Hermann Broch, *Création littéraire et connaissance* (Paris: Gallimard, 1966), pp. 311-325.

9. In Europe, painting was raised to the status of a liberal art, thus elevating the artist's standing, at the same time that the individual portrait was developed in the 14th century. A somewhat similar phenomenon occurred in Quebec in the first half of the 19th century.

10. Hamel, Plamondon and Roy-Audy all came from families of tradesmen or farmers. As with the bourgeoisie of the era, their social status was based on the network of influential people they reached through the practice of their art and through other means of advancement (societies and associations, military ranks, marriage). However, social mobility was not a concept relevant to the Quebec of the era (especially as concerns Montreal); instead, we should refer to a radical transformation in the social relationships characteristic of a pre-industrial society. See Robert Sweeny, "Un passé en mutations: bilan et perspectives pour une histoire socio-économique de Montréal au XIXᵉ siècle" in *Montréal au XIXᵉ siècle. Des gens, des idées, des arts, une ville*, proceedings from a symposium organized by the Montreal Historical Society (fall 1988) (Ottawa: Leméac, 1990), pages 25-26.

11. It might be wise to specify how this word should be interpreted. There are three possibilities, corresponding to three levels of meaning: a historical meaning, as defined by the people of the era; a historiographic one, as set out in historical writings; and a technical one, as used regularly by historians (see Michel Peronnet, "Bourgeois et bourgeoisie d'après les textes contemporains" in *Bourgeoisies de province et révolution*, Actes du colloque de Vizille [1984], Presses universitaires de Grenoble, 1987), pp. 13-26. Literally, "bourgeois" (noun) should be defined as a city dweller who has a certain amount of wealth ("bourgeoisie" referring to the group as a whole) and "bourgeois" (adjective) as the quality of such an individual. The industrial revolution and Marxist theory conferred on the bourgeoisie the tools of production. In a 19th-century, Lower Canadian context, it would perhaps be more correct to speak of a mainly urban "social group" made up of individuals whose economic activities (trade, industry, finance, services) brought them wealth and influence in political, military, and even religious circles. Their social, cultural and family practices gave the group a sense of values and identity. However, this definition assumes a certain homogeneity within a clearly identifiable group, which was far from the case in the bi-cultural, heterogenous and diverse colony that was post-Conquest Quebec. Strictly speaking, there was no united "bourgeoisie" in Lower Canada. On the contrary, events characterizing the period from 1790 to 1860 can be explained in part by the differences between the various groups of bourgeois in a constantly changing society.

The concept of bourgeois as defined here can also refer more generally to "leading citizen" or "leading citizenry," but the historical, historiographic and even technical ramifications of this popular nomenclature are poorly defined. Do they refer to influential people, wealthy landowners or people with strong personalities? (for more on the ambiguity of the term, see Pamela M. Pilbeam, *The Middle Classes in Europe, 1789-1914. France, Germany, Italy and Russia* (London: Macmillan, 1990), pp. 10-11. In France, this group of leading citizens (leading citizens is distinguished from leaders of society) can be defined as having legal status and a political role. The psychological and social characteristics of this group are informative in terms of the behaviour and ideologies of the upper classes in general: despite certain social antagonisms (conservatism vs. liberalism), all were defined by their influence in society. This influence was linked to their wealth and especially to their displays of it, which were not only tangible (real estate), but also artificial and ostentatious (see André-Jean Tudesq, *Les Grands Notables en France 1840-1849. Étude historique d'une psychologie sociale* (Paris: Presses universitaires de France, 1964), Vol. I, pp. 13-14 and 475; Vol. II, p. 1239. In Quebec, the term "leading citizen" classified seigneurs, nobles and priests in the same group as businessmen, magistrates, lawyers, doctors or notaries, traditionally recognized as bourgeois (see *COURVILLE 1990*, pp. 134-138 and Jean-Claude Robert, "Les nota-

bles de Montréal au XIXᵉ siècle," *Histoire sociale*, Vol. VIII, No. 15, May 1975, pp. 54-76). In this sense, the term is more historically accurate. Despite its intrinsic ambiguity, and its current pejorative connotation, we have kept the term "bourgeois," but expanded its meaning. Technically, "bourgeois" seems more likely to convey the ideology of the members of this group, who often had widely dissimilar interests but who were characterized by their status and behaviour.

12. The 1825 Montreal census showed 8656 people, or 38.4% of the population, had an "occupation." Of these, more than 40% were day labourers or domestics. The rest were mainly small merchants, shopkeepers or tradesmen. The most lucrative jobs (overseas trading, transportation and industry) accounted for only a small percentage of the total. The city had only 173 professionals (lawyer, notary, doctor, clerk, apothecary, dentist, surveyor), that is, barely 2% of the labour force (0.5% of the total population). Quebec City's make-up was slightly different given the number of positions in the public service, but professionals, though increasingly numerous, still accounted for only 2% of the working population throughout the first half of the 19th century. This period also saw the phenomenal expansion of the village as a geographical and social entity of the Quebec countryside. From 1815 to 1851, the number of communities rose from 30 to 300. It was within these semi-urban centres that the leading citizens or "countrified" bourgeoisie wielded their influence. Here again, the numbers representing this upper crust of society remained the same. There were an average of two leading citizens per village in 1831 and less than four in 1851. This corresponds to about 7% of the working population of the village. However, this percentage falls to less than 1% if farmers in the outlying regions, who constituted 60% of the rural population, are included. See Jean-Paul Bernard, Paul-André Linteau and Jean-Claude Robert, "La structure professionnelle de Montréal en 1825," *Revue d'histoire de l'Amérique française*, Vol. XXX, No. 3 (December 1976), pp. 383-415; *COURVILLE 1990*, pp. 121-148; Fernand Ouellet, *Le Bas Canada 1791-1840* (Ottawa: Éditions de l'Université d'Ottawa, 1980), pp. 286-287.

13. Jean-Pierre Wallot and Gilles Paquet identify "seven groups which seem to constitute the structural groups of Lower Canadian society at the turn of the 19th century." (Translation) These were: 1. the bureaucratic and military aristocracy (senior civil servants and officers); 2. the seigneurial classes; 3. the rich business classes; 4. the upper middle and middle classes; 5. the urban working classes; 6. the rural working classes; 7. the clergy. See Gilles Paquet and Jean-Pierre Wallot, "Groupes sociaux et pouvoir: le cas canadien au tournant du XIXᵉ siècle," *Revue d'histoire de l'Amérique française*, Vol. XXVI, No. 4 (March 1974), pp. 509-564. We want to avoid referring to an upper middle, middle and lower middle class, since this presupposes a prior categorization of the iconographical representations of members of these groups. In fact, the distinctions between these groups are not necessarily based on typological differences. Rather, it was economic means which determined access to one type of portraiture rather than another.

14. George Bervin, "Environnement matériel et activités économiques des conseillers exécutifs et législatifs à Québec, 1810-1830," *Bulletin d'histoire de la culture matérielle*, No. 17 (1983), pp. 45-62; Gilles Paquet and Jean-Pierre Wallot, "Structures sociales et niveaux de richesse dans les campagnes du Québec: 1792-1812," *Ibid.*, pp. 25-44.

15. To provide a basis for comparison, a survey of occupations shows that members of the upper class usually possessed an average of over £450 worth of possessions, small merchants, about £75 and farmers, £48. George Bervin, "Espace physique et culture matérielle du marchand-négociant à Québec au début du XIXᵉ siècle (1820-1830)," *Bulletin d'histoire de la culture matérielle*, No. 14 (spring 1982), p. 16.

16. *Ibid.*, pp. 5-16.

17. George Bervin shows, in the 11 examples chosen from among the legislative and executive counsellors, that the value of luxury items varied from £17 for John Young (whose household items were worth more than £233) to £277 for Judge Pierre-Amable De Bonne (whose items were valued at more than £991). George Bervin, "Environnement matériel...," *loc. cit.*, p.47.

18. Archives de l'Université de Montréal, Collection Baby, Papiers Berczy, U/1473, letter from William Berczy senior to his wife, Quebec, September 21, 1808 (published in "William von Moll Berczy," *Rapport de l'archiviste de la Province de Québec pour 1940-1941*, (Quebec: Rédempti Paradis, 1941), p. 49). According to the list of Judge De Bonne's possessions drawn up after his death at the request of Charles-Michel de Salaberry, (Cat. 89) as attorney for Marie-Anne Hervieux, wife of Jean-Baptiste

Melchior Hertel de Rouville and of Jean-Baptiste Hervieux, her brother—"the only heirs presumptive" (Translation) of this judge, who was known for his libertine behaviour—the notary found "in the parlour [...] portraits of Mr. Debonne, Mrs. Debonne, and Mrs. Debonne's mother [which] were left to said widow Debonne" (Translation) and which were not appraised. In addition, "a painting of High Constable de LesDiguères and a portrait of Mr. Debonne's mother were left to the abovementioned Charles Michel De Salaberry Ecuyer for his constituents, without being appraised." (Translation) This explains why the portrait of *François de Bonne, duc de Lesdiguères, Connétable de France* painted by François Baillairgé in 1799 passed from the De Bonne family to the Salaberry family, where it remained until it was acquired by the Château Ramezay in 1940. In addition to the paintings, the room contained 12 chairs, two small sofas, a stool, a stove, a pedestal table, six pairs of curtains, four large mirrors, two games tables, "eight small, gilt-edged tables," (Translation) an "old, common pianoforte," (Translation) a "guitar and case" (Translation) and an organ appraised at £30. This shows the refinement of the main parlour of the château de la Canardière. ANQQ, Notarial records of Joseph B. Planté, No. 7108, October 8, 9, 10, 11, 12, 14, 15, 16 and 17, 1816, "Succession de feu l'honorable Pierre-Amable Debonne."

19. *Le Canadien*, October 13, 1848, p. 2. (Translation)

20. Thus, when rich merchant-trader, military officer and legislative councillor William Burns (circa 1755-1829) died, his parlour contained "a portrait of the late Honourable William Burns, in a gilt frame," (unappraised), as well as "a print (*Nelson's Victory at Cape St. Vincent*) with a gilt frame, appraised at one pound, ten shillings" (Translation) and "four engravings (naval battles) with gilt frames appraised at fifteen shillings each." (Translation) In the dining room, the notary found "eight large prints with gilt frames appraised at one pound each" (Translation) and "nine small, framed engravings worth five shillings each." (Translation) There were also "two engravings of scenes from Quebec, appraised at five shillings for the two" (Translation) in a chest in one of the bedrooms. ANQQ, Notarial records of Errol Boyd Lindsay, No. 1158, September 30, 1829, "Inventaire de la propriété et des effets appartenant à la succession de feu l'Honorable William Burns."

21. The *Portrait of Young Man of the Taché Family*, though not a life-size portrait (Cat. 128), is a notable exception to this rule and should be classified as an informal portrait, which will be discussed later.

22. For example, the portrait of Louis XVI engraved by Charles-Clément Balvay after Callet (see Claudette Hould, *Images of the French Revolution* Cat., (Quebec: Musée du Québec and Les Publications du Québec, 1989), p. 114, Repr.) or the one of Napoléon I, engraved by A. Boucher Desnoyers after François Gérard (See Sara Stevenson, *A Face for any Occasion. Some Aspects of Portrait Engraving*, Cat. (Glasgow: Scottish National Portrait Gallery, 1976), p. 52, Repr.).

23. *VÉZINA 1975/1*, p. 99 (Repr.).

24. Roland Recht and Marie-Jeanne Geyer, *op. cit.*, p. 142.

25. Jean-Pierre Hardy, "Niveaux de richesse et intérieurs domestique dans le quartier Saint-Roch à Québec," *Bulletin d'histoire de la culture matérielle*, No. 17 (1983), pp. 72-73.

26. The excellent analysis of the symbolism contained in the portrait of the Papineau couple found in the entry written by John R. Porter (see Cat. 187 and 188) will not be repeated here.

27. An exception to this was the portraits of the Cyrice Têtu couple (Cat. 134 and 135), in which the father is shown in the company of his daughter. The roles, nonetheless, seem well defined. The solicitous father allows his daughter to play with his watch, a sign of his wealth and social success (the gold pocket watch and chain was the most costly piece of jewellery at the time, often appraised at more than £5 in estate inventories), while the affectionate mother ensures her son's education by guiding his hand over a passage in a book.

28. Could the sculpture under glass shown in the painting symbolize the handing down of feminine cultural values in the family? The three caryatids could perhaps be the three Graces, representing the qualities which enrich a man's life. They are holding a basket filled with fruit which may symbolize youth, since it is often present in children's portraits, particularly those by Hamel (see the portrait of *Flore and Olympe Chauveau*, Cat. 136).

29. Rousseau's theory of education extolled the virtues of learning in a family context over an education based on social behaviour or manners, a system promoted by Erasmus in the 16th century. Rousseau's plea in favour of natural, moral education was published in *Emilius*, in which he

held that only in intimate surroundings could children develop "sensitivity and learn moral behaviour. A new form of child-rearing and education must be implemented within the family. Rousseau suggests that children learn best within natural and private relationships—with blood kin—and that these will result in the fullest possible expression of the child's nature and personality." (Translation) See "Les usages de la civilité," by Jacques Revel in *Histoire de la vie privée. De la Renaissance aux Lumières*, Book III, under the direction of Philippe Ariès (Paris: Éditions du Seuil, 1986), p. 207.

30. According to Montaigne, children possessed "neither spirituality, nor a recognizable physical form" (Translation) (*Essais*, II, p. 8, quoted by Roland Recht and Marie-Jeanne Geyer, *op. cit.*, p. 223). They were therefore perceived as part of a single social entity and never as individuals, merely ensuring the continuation of the family. As the concept of individual awareness developed, new emotions arose with regard to children, who became the perpetuation of the individual. This marked the passage from the extended family to the nuclear family. See "L'individualisation de l'enfant" by Jacques Gélis in *Histoire de la vie privée...*, *op. cit.*, pp. 311-328.

31. See "Les refuges de l'intimité" by Orest Ranum in *Ibid.*, pp. 211-265 and Philippe Ariès, *L'enfant et la vie familiale sous l'Ancien Régime* (Paris: Édition du Seuil, 1973), p. 267, which shows that "the evolution of family sentiment parallels the evolution of private life." (Translation)

32. Roland Recht and Marie-Jeanne Geyer, *op. cit.*, p. 224.

33. Desmond Shawe-Taylor, *op. cit.*, pp. 183-201.

34. *Ibid.*, pp. 203-221.

35. A good example of these inhibitions was provided by William McGillivray who, in 1820, requested that American painter William Dunlap repaint part of a portrait showing him in the company of his wife and son. The canvas was painted around 1806 by William Berczy (MMCH). The original image, revealed by X-rays, shows McGillivray presenting a basket of fruit to his wife in an affectionate gesture. In the scene repainted by Dunlap, he is holding a gun and is presenting his wife with proof of his hunting prowess; the symbolic meaning of the work is thus changed. See *DEROME, BOURASSA ET CHAGNON 1988*, pp. 12, 14 and 15 (Repr.).

36. In England, the dog was often closely associated with portraits of women, and sometimes of men, to stress the same qualities. See Desmond Shawe-Taylor, *op. cit.*, pp. 69-71 and 137-138.

37. The treatment of the fabric, the contouring of the face and, in particular, the gracious smiles of the subjects lead us to attribute this work to James Bowman—after comparing it with the painting of young *Cyprien Tanguay* (Fig. 184B) and *Mère Saint-Henry McLaughlin* (See *LACASSE 1983/2*, p. 86, repr.)—rather than to Théophile Hamel, who was given credit until recently. In fact, other portraits of the Pelletier family, until now attributed to Hamel or Plamondon, should be reviewed in light of this new information. The portraits of *Mrs. Pierre Pelletier, née Élizabeth Moreau* (MMFA) and *Marie-Louise-Émilie Pelletier* (PC), in our opinion, bear a closer resemblance to the works of Bowman than to those of Plamondon.

38. English painters, specifically Thomas Gainsborough, popularized this type of portrait, in which worldly men adopted casual poses in idyllic landscapes or strolled across their estates with their wives. In the painting of the McGillivray family, the presence of the dogs demonstrates the couple's fidelity, while the top hat on the ground reinforces the precedence of intimacy over social graces, as Mr. McGillivray's original gesture also suggested (See note 35).

39. See Desmond Shawe-Taylor, *op. cit.*, pp. 76-80; Frederick Cummings, "Boothby, Rousseau and the Romantic Malady," *Burlington Magazine*, Vol. CX, No. 789 (1968), pp. 659-666. The portrait by Wright of Derby is considered a prototype for the portrait in which the subject is portrayed in a casual, intimate and natural manner in an outdoor environment suggesting fantasy, relaxation and individualism, as well as a physical and spiritual oneness with nature. The same qualities are evident in the portrait of Goethe by Johann Heinrich Wilhelm Tischbein. See Rudolf M. Bisanz, "Goethe and Tischbein in Italy: An Epigonic Painting Reconstructed," *Gazette des beaux-arts*, Vol. CXIII, No. 1441 (February, 1989), pp. 105-114.

40. See the examples reproduced in Dale T. Johnson, *American Portrait Miniatures in the Manney Collection* (New York: The Metropolitan Museum of Art, 1990), p. 31. The intimate purpose of the miniature is also reinforced by the European tradition whereby lovers exchanged miniatures of one of their eyes (full-size). There are no examples of this type in Canada or the United States. However, an example of a modified version

exists in *Beauty Revealed* by American artist Sarah Godridge (1788-1853). This self-portrait, showing only the miniaturist's breasts, was a present for her "friend," Senator Daniel Webster. See *ibid.*, pp. 126-127, No. 89, Plate 19.

41. Archives de l'Université de Montréal, Collection Baby, Papiers Berczy, U/1470, letter from William Berczy senior to his wife, Quebec, September 3, 1808 (published in "William von Moll Berczy," *op. cit.*, p. 45).

42. Dale T. Johnson, *op. cit.*, pp. 22-23.

43. See Note 3. In his American advertisements, Augustin Édouart used the following argument to promote the advantages of his freehand method, since his "Likeness are produced by the Scissors alone, and are preferable to any taken by Machines, inasmuch as by the above method the expression of the Passions, and peculiarities of Character, are brought into action, in a style wich has not hitherto been attempted by any other Artist". Andrew Oliver, *Auguste Édouart's Silhouettes of Eminent Americans, 1839-1844* (Charlottesville: University Press of Virginia/National Portrait Gallery, 1977), p. xv.

44. For a complete transcript of this document, see *Derome, Bourassa et Chagnon 1988*, p. 91.

45. One pound, in the provincial currency, was equivalent to 20 shillings worth 12 pence each. This was the equivalent of 24 old francs (20 sous/franc). In 1805, the British pound sterling was worth 1/9 more than the provincial pound. In addition, £1, 3s, 4p was the equivalent of one English guinea (the guinea being worth 1/6 more) and 5 shillings equalled a dollar (or 4 dollars for £1). Source: *The Quebec Almanac and British American Royal Kalendar, For the Year, 1805* (Quebec, J. Neilson, 1805, pp. 119-120). For example, in Montreal in the 1830s, a piece of land with a house and outbuildings was worth about £200. Rent for a single-storey wooden house in Montreal's suburbs was between £10 and £20 a year, while a three-storey stone house was rented for £80 to £150. Though the value of money fluctuated, and variations in the cost of living are not considered, a dollar value for all monetary amounts mentioned is included in parentheses to facilitate comparison.

46. AMMC, "Reçu de Louis Dulongpré à Thomas McCord," May 2, 1818 (see *Derome, Bourassa et Chagnon 1988*, p. 19).

47. ANC, MG 24, B2, Vol. XXXIX, File 1, "Reçu de Louis Dulongpré à Louis-Joseph Papineau," June 24, 1825.

48. Archives de l'Université de Montréal, Collection Baby, Papiers Berczy, U/1473, letter from William Berczy senior to his wife, Quebec, September 21, 1808 (Published in "William Moll von Berczy," *op. cit.*, p. 49).

49. Letter from Napoléon Bourassa to Théophile Hamel, December 1852, quoted in *Vézina 1975/1*, p. 61.

50. Antoine Plamondon—once again—protested the commission, "The government just gave three thousand louis to a portrait painter for thirty portraits!! Thirty portraits!... Yes, one hundred louis per portrait." (Translation) (*Le Courrier du Canada*, March 21, 1860). On April 15, 1856, Hamel wrote, "I flatter myself that the sum of £100 will not be considered excessive, as the price of each portrait", given that he is "entitled to receive as a proper remuneration for my service, and the disbursements necessary to be made in my journies to different places, namely to Montreal, Cobourg, Toronto, Hamilton & New York". In November, he did indeed receive payment for 14 portraits of the speakers of the Legislative Assembly, at £100 each (ANC, RG 14, C5, Vol. XII, "Legislative Assembly, Vouchers").

51. On August 31, 1808, Berczy announced, "I have raised the price for all my work and will charge 6 guineas for all half-length portraits executed in oils or in any other manner." (Translation) For all the portraits commissioned by Judge De Bonne, the artist calculated his revenue at 39 guineas (see Note 48). This means 24 guineas for the half-length portraits and, if we assume he charged 3 guineas for the retouches, that leaves 12 guineas for the miniatures, or £8 each. In his letter of August 31, Berczy points out that market conditions played some role in the prices he set for his paintings since, in Quebec, he received "two louis more than in Montreal." (Translation) Archives de l'Université de Montréal, Collection Baby, Papiers Berczy, letter from William Berczy senior to his wife, Quebec, August 31, 1808 (quoted in *Trudel 1976*, p. 18).

52. *Dearborn 1983*, p. 4.

53. *Rosenfeld 1981*, pp. 111-121.

54. *The Montreal Gazette*, October 31, 1808, p. 4.

55. *La Gazette de Montréal*, October 10, 1808, p. 4. Metcalf also declared in his advertisement that his "profile likenesses [are] on fine vellum, and [he] decorates them in the most tasteful and fashionable manner. [...] They can be painted or gold-enamelled most elegantly." (Translation) The

price is exactly the same as that requested by one B. Lyon, who ran a similar advertisement in the same newspaper on August 28, 1809. As for Joseph Morand, a former apprentice of Louis Dulongpré (in the ad, his name was spelled "Moran"), he requested the same amount for two silhouettes in an advertisement which appeared on December 5, 1808, again in *La Gazette de Montréal*.

56. *The Quebec Mercury*, October 13, 1820, p. 6.

57. *The Quebec Mercury*, September 14, 1819, p. 295.

58. *La Gazette de Québec*, March 27, 1827. (Translation)

59. Andrew Oliver, *op. cit.*, p. xv. The artist reduced his price to 3s 6d for full-length silhouettes of children under eight and to 2s 6d for doubles.

60. *Le Fantasque*, June 21, 1841, p. 340. (Translation)

61. *L'Avenir*, October 14, 1848.

62. *Le Journal de Québec*, December 20, 1845, p. 3.

63. *La Minerve*, November 22, 1830.

64. John and Catherine Ebert, *American Folk Painters* (New York: Charles Scriber's Sons, 1975), pp. 14 and 76-82.

65. This may have been a reaction to the competition offered by the daguerreotype. A journalist for the newspaper *Le Fantasque* informed his readers on June 21, 1841, that using this process, "one can obtain a portrait on silver, under glass, more delicate than anything the lightest engraving could have produced until now," but that this "exact image [...] could perhaps be criticized only for being too faithful." (Translation)

66. The author seems to leap to the defence of the young painter Théophile Hamel, who had just left his mentor and who seemed to be targeted by certain remarks made by Plamondon's supporter. Hamel is the object of the remark made by "Friend of the Artists," who speaks of "a young artist who combines real talent, which has already been recognized, with modesty, a quality he could teach someone in exchange for lessons already given him." (Translation) See *Le Fantasque*, August 23, 1841, pp. 437-439.

BRITISH LANDSCAPE ARTISTS IN QUEBEC: FROM DOCUMENTARY VIEWS TO A POETIC VISION

by Didier Prioul

"My natural inclination led me to landscapes [...] I determined to draw after nature. But I soon found, that this great and sublime master does not explain himself clearly but to those who have learnt to comprehend him. My precision in following him every where led me astray". Salomon Gessner, *A Letter to M. Füslin on Landscape Painting*[1].

T HE BRITISH LANDSCAPE ARTISTS who spent time in Quebec from the late 18th to mid-19th centuries have often been classified, for the sake of convenience, under the general qualifier "topographical artists". If we take this term in a narrow sense, such as the one given by Henry Ogden, it would fit many drawings produced in Quebec: "topographical landscape, as distinguished from ideal, is the representation of actual scenery and of specific places—usually named. The artist intends the spectator to recognize the place he depicts".[2] It is not at all difficult to apply this definition to James Peachey's *A View of the City of Montreal* (Cat. 43): from the high vantage point atop Mount Royal, Peachey portrays the city in all its detail—a military artist taking an inventory of the British Crown's new possessions. His superiors have demanded that he show acute observation and absolute truth in his rendering of the subject matter.[3] The principles of geometric composition are strictly applied so as to produce an image that respects set standards, independent of the artist's personal vision.

Site Description

Drawing for military purposes was based on strict, ongoing training handed down by generations of teachers who honed their skills based on the first principles of topography developed a century earlier. In discussing topography and the military artists in an attempt to understand how the latter perceived a new country reference must be made to Wenceslaus Hollar (1607-1677). Hollar was one of the first artists to introduce this art form to Great Britain, largely in the form of engravings, which provided other artists with examples that could be copied,[4] hence the unwavering composition of works such as *Tangier From the South-West* (Ill. 48). As "King's scenographer" or "designer of Prospects", Hollar accompanied an expedition to Tangier in 1669 to take a topographic survey of this new British possession (1662). He set an example to be followed by all military topographical artists by judiciously integrating elements serving a strictly military purpose

(location of roads, strategic position of city, ramparts) into a composition in which the landscape plays a unifying role.

James Peachey's *A View of the Quebec Citadel* (Cat. 42) should be seen in the same light. He, too, portrayed the contours of the land in order to emphasize Quebec City's topography. The figures and secondary elements serve as a counterpoint to the artist's primary objectives; Wenceslaus Hollar used them in a similar fashion to highlight a hillock or reinforce a diagonal. "Embellishing" the topography in this way made the final composition much less dry. Conversely, in the work of Sempronius Stretton (Cat. 51), we find the raw version of topographical observation: graphite lines or pen and ink are used to outline the design with the obvious aim of giving it a cold finish.

Peachey faithfully applied the teachings of the previous century. Other artists, such as George Heriot, allowed themselves more freedom in depicting their subjects, while showing they understood the principles. The watercolour *Montreal, Quebec Gate* (Ill. 49) is another work that demonstrates an exact topographical interpretation. The fortifications, through which the Quebec Gate opens on the left, encloses and protects Montreal. The foreground is uncluttered, except for a few figures which serve as a link between the two horizontal strips defining the composition. This very codified type of representation became highly conventional around 1793, the same year Heriot surveyed the site.[5] The principal subject is given full force in the middle ground, laid out as it is based on a series of parallel planes, which fade as the viewer's eye draws closer to the city. The background is composed of two lateral vistas used to show that this specific site is merely part of a larger environment. Heriot probably studied at the Woolwich Military Academy and we can safely assume that this is where he learned the rules of composition for works of this type. But he is also an excellent example of how difficult it is to classify artists. One has only to look at his *Ferry on the Jacques Cartier River* (Cat. 34) to see that he does not observe the same rules as in *Montreal, Quebec Gate* and yet, we still have before us a well-identified site, named by the artist on the back of the drawing, in keeping with the definition by Henry Ogden given above.

Portraying Nature: from Reality to Resemblance

In his letter discussing landscape art addressed to Johann Casper Fuseli, from which we have quoted below, Salomon Gessner (1730-1788) did not have topographical artists in

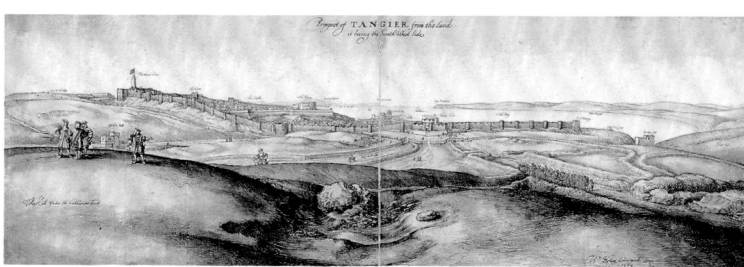

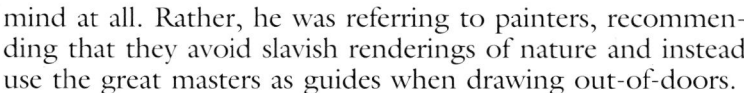

Ill. 48.
Wenceslaus Hollar, *Tangier From the South-West*, 1669;
pen and ink, grey wash and watercolour on paper,
British Museum, London (240886).

Ill. 49.
George Heriot, *Montreal, Quebec Gate*, c. 1793;
watercolour over graphite on paper, 23.9 × 36.5 cm.
National Gallery of Canada, Ottawa (16676).

mind at all. Rather, he was referring to painters, recommending that they avoid slavish renderings of nature and instead use the great masters as guides when drawing out-of-doors.

"[…] Like the bee I search'd honey from many flowers. I consulted, I imitated […] But the two Poussins, and Claud Lorrain, at last possessed me entirely. It was in their works I found dignity and truth united".[6]

Immediately upon seeing *View of Quebec* (Cat. 29) by George Bulteel Fisher, one can guess that Gessner's advice was being followed by a military topographical artist. The reference to Claude Lorrain (1600-1682) is woven into the very fabric of the landscape. Quebec City is surrounded by greenery and relegated to the middle ground. The grandeur of the landscape gives it full authority, while the figures—hunters in search of game—could easily replace the nymphs and shepherds in classic 17th-century landscape paintings. Considering the prints published by Fisher in London (Cat. 28 and 29), in which all the sites are scrupulously accompanied by a description, it must be conceded that his work resembles that of topographical artists. The explanation is simple: the term "topography" does not refer to a strict category. Eighteenth century Britain witnessed the emergence of various trends that blurred the line between ideal landscapes, in which the imagination prevailed, and topographic landscapes, which were limited to copying reality.

At the forefront of these trends was a vision of nature based on a classical education, nurtured by the Italian landscape painters of the 17th century. The terms of landscape painting established by Claude Lorrain, Gaspard Dughet, Nicolas Poussin and Salvator Rosa (1615-1673) during the 17th century had become the inevitable references used to render a natural landscape which had never yet been portrayed. Peter Bicknell summed up this new approach perfectly in a telling image:

"The work of the topographers was almost universally picturesque, in the sense that in recording nature they converted it into compositions of ideal landscape; in fact they "cooked" nature in the man-

ner of Claude, Salvator and Poussin, with occasionally a leaven of Zuccarelli or Vernet".[7]

William Gilpin (1724-1804) was one of those admirers of Claude Lorrain who took the approach to near-theorization. In his *Three Essays: on Picturesque Beauty, on Picturesque Travel; and on Sketching Landscape*, published in London in 1792, he included two illustrations of the same landscape, one based on the principles of beauty (Ill. 50) and the other on the qualities of the picturesque (Ill. 51). In the first illustration, uniformity rules the artist's portrayal of nature, thus preserving the site's natural characteristics. The overall image is unbroken and the curved lines drawing the viewer off into the distance lend a sense of harmony to the picture. The picturesque landscape, on the other hand, is just the opposite: the broken lines are the result of a constant concern for highlighting the irregularity and roughness of the textures. The foreground is broken up by a road along which two figures are walking, and the eye is unable to move steadily toward the background without being intercepted by either the valley in the middle ground or by the strong contrast in light. The words of William Gilpin and, in a broader sense, the notion of picturesque, were to have considerable impact. The discovery of aquatint around 1768-1769 and its quick rise in popularity in England resulted in a wide dissemination of drawings.[9] While this technique made it possible to obtain subtle hues, ranging from deep blacks and browns to light greys and blackish-browns, its greatest advantage was to enable artists to retain the pictorial quality of drawings when reproducing them in engravings. As a result, aquatint was the favoured form of illustration for travel accounts, and publishers sought out artists or art enthusiasts that could keep them supplied with suitable models.

In this context, we must mention the significant role played by engravers in the reproduction and dissemination of the topographic landscape artists' images. We have intentionally chosen to illustrate this role with an Italian view to emphasize how these images were manipulated. In the spring of 1816, 1817 and 1818, James Pattison Cockburn travelled

Ill. 50.
William Gilpin, *Non-picturesque Mountain Landscape*, 1792; aquatint on paper, 21.5 × 14 cm, Illustrating *Three Essays: on Picturesque Beauty, on Picturesque Travel; and on Sketching Landscape*. Yale Center for British Art, New Haven. Paul Mellon Collection (ND1340/65).

Ill. 51.
William Gilpin, *Picturesque Mountain Landscape*, 1792; aquatint on paper, 21,5 × 14 cm, Illustrating *Three Essays: on Picturesque Beauty, on Picturesque Travel; and on Sketching Landscape*. Yale Center for British Art, New Haven. Paul Mellon Collection (ND1340/65).

Ill. 52.
James Pattison Cockburn, *L'Isola dei Pescatori, Lake Maggiore*, 1816-1818; brown ink and brown wash on paper, 13.3 × 30.8 cm. Castle Museum, Norwich (17.L1976.19).

Ill. 53.
James Duffield Harding, after J.P. Cockburn, *L'Isola dei Pescatori, Lake Maggiore*, 1821; aquatint on paper, plate XLVIII of *Views to Illustrate the Road of the Simplon* (1822). University of New Orleans, Earl K. Long Library, New Orleans.

to Italy to produce a series of drawings of Pompeii to be included in a major publication.[10] While travelling south, Cockburn sketched *L'Isola Dei Pescatori, Lake Maggiore* (Ill. 52) in brown ink and then, in 1821, asked James Duffield Harding (1797-1863) to reproduce it in a lithograph (Ill. 53).[11] The British engraver was a master lithographer, breathing poetry into Cockburn's somewhat unpolished rendering. He first outlined the main subject and added a foreground to the original work. Then, while respecting the basic architectural lines of the houses on fishermen's island and the silhouette of the mountains, he softened the sharpness of the original drawing by shrouding the mountains in a veil of mist. This decorative tendency and gradual leaning towards poetic renderings is common in Quebec art, its purpose being to depict faraway lands in a flattering light for the enjoyment of those who have never seen them. It is for this reason that Fisher depicted Quebec City in terms of a classical landscape. The works of Charles Ramus Forrest and many of the

watercolours of James Pattison Cockburn should also be considered in a similar light.

Training Landscape Artists

At this point, we will take a look at the basic training given at the military academy, since this is where the majority of landscape artists visiting Lower Canada learned the rudiments of their art. At Woolwich (Ill. 54), it was the second master who taught drawing, both for figure drawing "from Drawings by the Master" and for the theory of perspective and its initial application. The first master taught drawing from nature:

"Putting Perspective in Practice by copying from Drawings, which qualifies them from Drawing from nature; teaches them the effect of Light and Shade; and makes them acquainted also with Aerial Perspective. Then to proceed to take views about Woolwich and other places; which teaches them at the same time to break ground, and forms the eye to the knowledge of it".[12]

Ill. 54.
R. Havell, after J.P. Cockburn, *View of the Royal Military Academy, Woolwich*, aquatint colored by hand on paper, 29 × 48 cm. National Army Museum, London (7504-83).

Ill. 55.
R. Pollard and J.C. Stadler, *The Siege of Copenhagen*, (plate V), 1807; aquatint colored by hand on paper, 34.5 × 49.5 cm. National Army Museum, London (7102-33-124).

Ill. 56.
Paul Sandby, *View of the Town through the Gateway, from the Castle Hill*, c. 1770; watercolour over graphite, pen and black ink on paper, 31.7 × 46.7 cm. The Royal Library, Windsor. Reproduced with special permission of Her Majesty, Queen Elizabeth II (14546).

This type of training found its practical application in British military campaigns, as seen in the series of five aquatints illustrating the siege of Copenhagen in 1807 (Ill. 55), after drawings by Cockburn. The panoramic landscape is laid out based on his on-site observations and the composition enhanced through the addition of specific locations: the city and castle were certainly taken from two separate drawings. The overall harmony dominating the works of Duncan, for example, (Cat. 91 to 99) is totally foreign to an approach of this kind. Rather, the term "paysage cartographié", or "mapped landscape images",[13] appears more accurate, since the sole purpose is to render the site visible to the viewer. This vision and portrayal of a new country, midway between cartography and topography, finds its justification in the concise statement of the inspector general of the Marlow Military College:

"Everything which is put down in writing of necessity takes on some colour from the opinion of the writer. A sketch map allows of no opinion".[14]

Cadets were not judged according to the same criteria as those applied to artists, since their objectives were different. Instead, they were expected to master the science of drawing for purposes of description—land surveys, identification of communication routes or fortification proposals—as was the case with Philip John Bainbrigge. In fact, the Woolwich Military Academy clearly established what was expected of cadets in terms of skill:

"As Drawing is an accomplishment which depends in a great measure upon genius, it is not to be expected that every Gentleman Cadet should become an expert draftsman; and as their knowledge of the French language must be considerably affected by their previous education, it is not to be supposed that they can all be proficients alike in this branch of the studies".[15]

Indeed, learning French made contact with 19th-century Quebec easier, as witnessed by personal diaries such as that of Butler.

However, the quality of the training also depended on the abilities of the teacher. The military authorities were apparently aware of this fact since, in 1768, they appointed Paul Sandby (1731-1809) to replace Gamaliel Massiot.[16] Sandby was a highly renowned artist when he took over the drawing course at Woolwich. In keeping with the academic tradition, he taught from his own works, which he had his students copy. His *View of the Town through the Gateway, from the Castle Hill* (Ill. 56), which dates to Sandby's early teaching years at Woolwich, corresponds fairly closely to the models given to the students. The principal components of the drawing are lightly sketched in lead pencil. Pen and ink are then used to outline, and light shades of watercolour set off the drawing. The composition is built around a central vanishing point, with figures added to give life to the architectural structures. This process provided the less-skilled students with a composition grid that could easily be applied to any new site, while the more talented students put this basic knowledge to work to produce masterpieces. But this is a generalization: it must not be assumed that the accomplishments of a lifetime depend solely on what is learned in one's youth.

1820-1830
Lord Dalhousie and his Circle of Artists

We are accustomed to studying British landscape artists as an isolated group, candidly executing drawings in a new country. The numerous connections that formed over the course of meetings and during garrison life are often forgotten. Charles Ramus Forrest's stay in Exeter (Cat. 171) is a prime example of how one artist can be influenced by another's work, such as that of Francis Towne (1739/1740-1816). The same holds true for James Pattison Cockburn during his six years at the Norfolk garrison. A member of the Norwich school of landscape artists,[17] like his teacher John Thirtle (1777-1839) and John Sell Cotman (1782-1842), Cockburn developed a more flexible approach to nature drawing, one which displayed new poetic overtones and was imbued with greater sensitivity. This new artistic approach had a significant impact on the landscapes Cockburn created in Quebec; for example, his watercolours like *Devil's Tower Norwich* (Ill. 57) should serve as a basis for comparison to *Quebec Viewed from the Round Tower on the Saint Charles River Above Dorchester Bridge* (Cat. 79). Other factors of development, such as instruction books for amateurs, dissemination through engravings of basic models that offered new perspectives on nature drawing, and a growing number of exhibitions in which watercolours were showcased in their own right, also explain the medley of visions evident even in apparently simple works, such as those of John Crawford Young or William Herries.

It is not surprising, then, to see circles of artists forming in Quebec during this period, one of which is the first network created around Lord Dalhousie, who arrived in Quebec City in 1819.[18] Two of Dalhousie's followers were John Elliott Woolford (Cat. 233 to 235) and Charles Ramus Forrest (Cat. 111), first aide-de-camp to the governor. As illustrator for Lord Dalhousie, Woolford accompanied him on his inspection tours. Woolford and Forrest probably first exchanged drawings in late summer 1821. They were not, however, slavish copies. Forrest employed the uncommon blue wash technique,[19] which leads us to believe that he sought not so much to reproduce a given site, but rather to understand the composition of natural surroundings which were totally foreign to him. He then used this codification for his large-scale landscapes in watercolour. Following the departure of Forrest in 1823, John Crawford Young became Lord Dalhousie's new aide-de-camp. Woolford, who settled in Novia Scotia, virtually broke ties with Quebec City. However, a new string of connections developed between Young and Cockburn. The former's album contains a number of landscapes that bear an amazing similarity to those of Cockburn, particularly in the way he frames the central scene with tall trees on either side.

The leading figure in this initial circle of artists remains James Pattison Cockburn. His past accomplishments, age and experience easily won him the respect of his colleagues, as evidenced by a quote from a letter Lady Aylmer wrote to her nieces in England in 1831:

Ill. 57.
James Pattison Cockburn, *Devil's Tower Norwich*, c. 1809-1814; watercolour on paper, 21.6 × 16.5 cm.
Castle Museum, Norwich (72.235.951).

"he [Cockburn] has travell'd much in all the Countries we have seen, and in many where we have not been, he has an immense and most Valuable collection of his own drawings in every part of the world he has travell'd over and some color'd from Nature".[20]

Cockburn also drew from nature with second lieutenant Thomas George Marlay (1809-1837), who arrived in Quebec in April 1829. Relations between the two military men probably lasted the two years Marlay was in Quebec City (April 1829 to June 1831). Their works bear numerous similarities. Marlay sketched and engraved the frontispiece for the brochure Cockburn published in 1831, *Quebec and Its Environs; Being a Picturesque Guide to the Stranger*.[21]

The many connections between the artists are, no doubt, due to the political and economic situation in Lower Canada during this period. The instability resulting from the War of 1812 gave way to true economic prosperity, particularly in Quebec City. Leisure time became more common, enabling the soldiers stationed at the garrison to travel more outside the city. More and more individuals were drawn by the idea of visiting the countryside, even if just for the simple pleasure of enjoying some picturesque landscape. People became so familiar with the area that it led to comparisons with some of the most famous sites in history:

"From the top of the signal house, the splendid panorama of the city and country needs no remark—it is unrivalled; indeed the boasted bay of Naples will no gain much in comparison".[22]

James Pattison Cockburn, who spent several summers in Naples, was speaking from experience. In keeping with the idea of becoming familiar with a new country, is this quote from Frederic Tolfrey, hunting enthusiast:

"A little beyond the village of Old Lorette, on the high road to Jacques Cartier—wich is in fact the *grande route* to Montreal—woodcocks will we found in plenty, especially in a little covert to the left between the village itself and the Curé's habitation.

Ill. 58.
James Pattison Cockburn, *Falls of the Saint Anne River*, 1827;
sepia over graphite on paper, 34.8 × 52.7 cm.
Musée du Québec, Quebec (69.74).

Ill. 59.
James Hope-Wallace, *Falls of the Saint Anne River*, 1839;
watercolour over faint graphite lines on paper, 22.9 × 33.2 cm.
Royal Ontario Museum, Toronto (951.45.50).

I once took up my quarters in this little hamlet for a week or two beneath the comfortable roof of the wheelwright and waggon-builder of the place, who wisely added to his exchequer by letting a wing of his snug cottage to those who felt disposed to inhale a little pure air during the summer and autumnal months. In a mossy bog in front, as well as the rear of the building on both sides the high road, the snipes are, or rather were, in great abundance, I say *were*, for the march of improvement may have enlightened the minds of the landholders; and the quagmire of 1817 may now be as dry as the Macadamized thoroughfare of Regent Street in the dog-days".[23]

Tolfrey visited Lower Canada in 1816 and 1817. The above lines were written twenty-eight years later, in 1845. In the meantime, a completely new generation of watercolourists drastically changed past ways of thinking.

Two Visions of the Same Falls: Poetic and Sublime

What is commonly called true-to-life nature often depends on the sensibility of the artist putting this theory into practice. If we compare *Falls of the Saint Anne River* by James Pattison Cockburn (Ill. 58) with similar works by James Hope-Wallace (Ill. 59, Cat. 145, Fig. 145A and 145B), we can see that both artists use the same diagonal composition. In his sepia wash drawing dated August 1827, Cockburn reproduces the various levels of the falls on the Sainte-Anne river. He purposely depicts the various levels of rock and their stair formation, which offer a resting place for his diminutive figures. His vision, characterized by a concern for detail, is also reflected in his portrayal of the vegetation, where the conventional depiction of crossed trees "idealizes" the "wilderness" aspect of nature. Similarly, the lightly applied washes help avoid abrupt passages from one point to the next, and their beautiful luminosity softens the geometric lines. James Hope-Wallace, on the other hand, uses contrasting shades of watercolour: his opaque washes create masses that confront each in clashing bright hues. His more impressionist style shuns the meticulous, dry technique of the topographical artist. Dense and impenetrable, the woods are closed to visitors. The rocks are disproportionate, as if the result of a sudden upthrust. The artist has chosen to illustrate only a part of the landscape, neglecting detail in favour of a sublime landscape which sends a shiver down the viewer's spine.

Both the sublime and poetic visions of landscape painting took root in a new awareness of nature and an entirely revamped approach to watercolour. The tinted drawing, that is, the use of pen and ink to draw pictures before adding watercolour, can be traced back to the works of Paul Sandby and continued in those of James Peachey (Cat. 42 to 45), George Heriot (Cat. 32 to 35) and James Pattison Cockburn (Cat. 72 to 82). This technique corresponds to nature as seen from the outside like a static model, part of a fixed universal order. In this respect, the works reflect an idealized vision of nature, in accordance with the standards of the period, set by Claude Lorrain, Salvator Rosa and Peter Paul Rubens (1577-1640). The turn of the century saw the development of a totally different concept of nature. Influenced by the development of new sciences such as geology (Cat. 170) and meteorology (Cat. 171 and 172), viewers were faced with a world in perpetual motion. This acceptance of continual change replaced the previous notion of universal order. Landscape artists gave it expression through a more dynamic watercolour technique, which gave rise to greater spontaneity in artistic expression. The white of the drawing paper was used to depict space; scraping and rubbing techniques were used to heighten the ephemeral effects of light; colour was henceforth applied in multiple layers, with the addition of gouache or gum arabic for more subtle effects. The British landscape artists arriving in Quebec in the mid-1830s were to view nature in a much different light than their predecessors.

Ill 60.
John Richard Coke Smyth, *Saint Joseph, Pointe Lévis*, 1838;
graphite and watercolour on paper, 16,7 × 26 cm.
Royal Ontario Museum, Toronto (950.114.12).

Ill. 61.
Henry William Barnard, *Village of Pointe Lévis*, 1838;
sepia over graphite on paper, 27.3 × 34.3 cm.
National Archives of Canada, Ottawa (C-11923).

1836-1842: Creating a New Image

The Troubles of 1837-1838 brought a new generation of British watercolourists to Quebec. The arrival of British troops and the recall of companies stationed outside Quebec (Cat. 141 and 142) breathed new life into landscape art. Known as the "Group of 1838",[24] these artists established highly complex relations amongst themselves, which we are only just beginning to understand.

John Richard Coke Smyth was at the forefront of the newcomers. Hired by Lord Durham, Coke Smyth came to Quebec in 1838 as drawing master to the governor's family. Despite the sarcastic remark recorded in Katherine Jane Ellice's diary in April 1838 while the ship bound for Quebec was being boarded in Portsmouth, "*Mr. Smythe*, drawing *Master or Artist*",[25] it was indeed as an artist that Coke Smyth made his mark in Quebec. But it was especially his portfolio of lithographs (Cat. 212 and 213) that influenced other artists more than any direct contacts Coke Smyth might have established during his short stay.[26]

It is through Henry William Barnard that several watercolourists working during this period met. Coke Smyth appears to have shared certain affinities with Barnard, as seen in the two drawings of Pointe Lévis (Ill. 60 and 61), which were done from nature at the same time. Coke Smyth has chosen a vantage point slightly outside the village, from behind a hill crowned with a tree that serves as a foil. The composition is bold and plays on the crossing of the two diagonals: the one formed by the tree is set off by the road leading to the village. Barnard draws from the same spot, but his composition is not nearly as skillful. His subject is drawn using a series of parallel lines, slightly on the diagonal, with the entire left side of the page remaining empty. The tree is

merely one element among others in Barnard's composition, which is less forcefully structured than that of Coke Smyth. His architectural lines are clumsy, showing that the artist has far from mastered perspective. Barnard does make an attempt, however, to imitate Coke Smyth's nervous pencil strokes. In a sense, such a comparison shows the similarities and differences between the work of a talented amateur and that of a professional artist. In May 1841, Henry William Barnard returned to Quebec, where he established ties with artists such as James Hope-Wallace that he may not have met the first time round. Together, they went on a fishing trip on the Jacques-Cartier river, from July 7 to 23, 1841, during which they did a number of drawings. At the time, the style of the two artists was so similar (Ill. 62 and 63) that it was difficult to determine the degree of mutual influence. Although Hope-Wallace's work is more vibrant, both artists have a subtle, easy manner of grasping the essence of a landscape.

Perhaps it was Hope-Wallace who introduced Barnard to Millicent Mary Chaplin. The album compiled by Chaplin (Cat. 68 to 71) carries an important message, telling of the complex relations that marked the presence of the watercolourists in Quebec City between 1839 and 1842. Perhaps it is a testament to the meetings of a circle of amateur artists, in the manner of The Sketching Society in England.[27] An illustration such as *Wolfe and Montclam Monument*, copied by George St. Vincent Whitmore (Fig. 54-58B) and Millicent Mary Chaplin (Fig. 54-58C) after a work by Philip John Bainbrigge (Fig. 54-58A), certainly leads us to think so. However, all known drawings copied repeatedly during this period would have to be inventoried, and attributions and dates of execution carefully checked, before any conclusion can be reached. Nothing proves, for example, that Bainbrigge did not give his drawings to Whitmore, as well as to Chaplin.

Ill. 62.
James Hope-Wallace, *Bridge over the Jacques Cartier River*, 1841;
watercolour over graphite on paper, 22.8 × 33 cm.
Royal Ontario Museum, Toronto (951.45.52).

Ill 63.
Henry William Barnard, *Bridge on the Jacques Cartier River*, 1841;
watercolour over graphite on paper, 24.1 × 34 cm.
Royal Ontario Museum, Toronto (949.41.40).

Ill. 64.
Charles Wright, *Looking towards Quebec from the Saint Louis Road*, 1837;
watercolour over graphite, on paper, 22.8 × 30.1 cm.
Royal Ontario Museum, Toronto (951.67.4).

Ill. 65.
Millicent Mary Chaplin, *View outside St. Louis Gate, Quebec*, 1840;
watercolour over graphite, on paper, 20.3 × 30 cm.
National Archives of Canada, Ottawa (C-862).

And the same could be said for *Looking towards Quebec from the Saint Louis Road* (Ill. 64) by Charles Wright (1793-1866), which is dated 1837 but was copied by Chaplin in 1840 (Ill. 65). To complicate our example, Wright left Quebec in July 1838.[28] However, his daughter Fanny Amelia (1814-1891) had just married Henry Woolsey Bayfield (1795-1885), a land surveyor and, like his wife, an amateur artist. It is perhaps through them that Wright's *Looking towards Quebec from the Saint Louis Road* came into the hands of Millicent Mary Chaplin.

There is so much overlapping here that we feel it is too early to draw any conclusions. Several pieces are still missing from the puzzle; for instance, the collection of Archibald Acheson (1776-1849), second count of Gosford and governor of Lower Canada from 1835 to 1838, still

needs to be studied. We are only beginning to be able to guess at the size of this collection, thanks to works that are turning up at auctions.[29] The works appearing in this collection, by watercolourists such as Philip John Bainbrigge, Charles Wright and George St. Vincent Whitmore, many of whom were soldiers stationed in Quebec during Acheson's term as governor, also appear in Chaplin's album. However, by going into further detail, we may risk reducing this carefully woven fabric of relationships to a jumble of ill-assorted influences.

Years of Change

Henry William Barnard, James Hope-Wallace, Philip John Bainbrigge and Millicent Mary Chaplin all left Quebec in fall

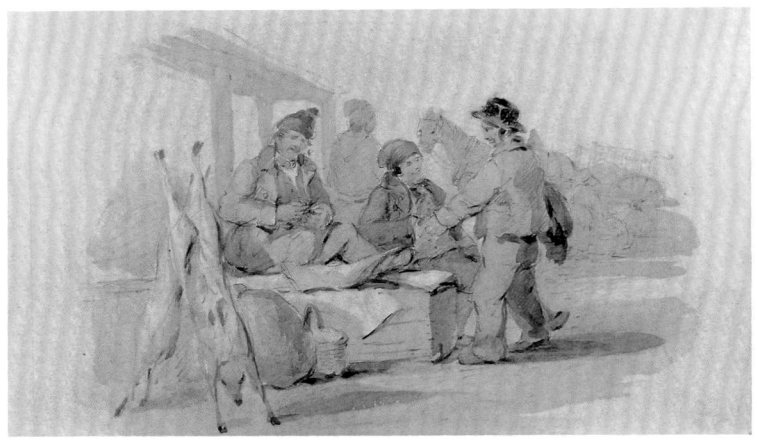

Ill. 66.
James Duncan, *Frozen Sheep at Montreal Market*, c. 1840-1845;
watercolour over graphite on paper, 23.3 × 33.5 cm.
Royal Ontario Museum, Toronto (951.158.6).

Ill 67.
Amelia Frederica Dyneley, *Market Scene, Montreal*, 1850;
watercolour and graphite on paper, 17.8 × 25.8 cm.
National Archives of Canada, Ottawa (C-040275).

1842. Some were promoted to administrative positions in the military. James Pattison Cockburn, for example, was appointed director of the Royal Arsenal of Woolwich's Royal Laboratory in 1838, and Philip John Bainbrigge taught fortifications at the same institution beginning in 1854. Others carried on in active service, sometimes perishing in battle—William Robert Herries was killed at the battle of Moodkee (India) in 1845 at the tender age of twenty-seven; sometimes succumbing to cholera—William Henry Barnard died during the siege of Delhi in 1857. For James Hope-Wallace, on the other hand, military life was only a digression from which he returned to civilian life to start a family.

The mid-1840s, marked a break in the presence of watercolourists in Quebec. The network of relations crumbled following the return of some to Great Britain and the posting of others elsewhere. This change was to affect, and even herald the end of, the heyday of landscape painting in Quebec. Regardless of the quality of the works, it is figures like George Seton (Cat. 209 and 210) who carried an understanding of nature similar to that of the early topographical artists into the late 19th century. Henry James Warre employed the same watercolour technique as the one we already know from the works of James Hope-Wallace. In fact, Warre is a prime example of the changes that occurred around 1845. Until this time, it was entirely possible to study the development of watercolour landscapes solely in the Quebec context, thanks to the presence of numerous artists and their production of major works. The marked interest in Western Canada was to drastically modify the geographical context of artistic production. In a sense, Henry James Warre laid the basis for

this new vision, which was characterized by a growing curiosity about unexplored territory. We have chosen to use his sketchbook on moose hunting (Cat. 230), dated 1842, to illustrate a given period in his production. The border disputes with the United States in 1845-1846 took Warre westward, to the Rockies and the state of Oregon, producing new drawings at every stop along the way. But it was the introduction of photography in the late 1850s that finally brought about real changes in artists' visions and perspectives.[30]

Although much in Quebec's art history during the period 1840-1850 remains a mystery, further major discoveries in the area of watercolour seem unlikely.[31] Connections between artists hold more potential; for instance, take Amelia Frederica Dyneley (1830-post-1860), who copied one of James Duncan's *Frozen Sheep at Montreal Market* (Ill. 66 and 67).[32] This example shows that we still have much to learn about the milieu in which Duncan worked. It is too early yet to compile a complete and final overview of the British landscape artists working in Quebec; we have instead chosen to illustrate, through a body of carefully chosen works, as many of the gradual changes that occurred as possible, changes that, when taken together, allow us to broaden our traditional views. If some of the major names one expected to find are missing—William Henry Bartlett, for example—it is because our focus is elsewhere. Bartlett is known above all for his engravings; his place amongst watercolourists is merely a result of circumstance and classification. And if new names appear—i.e. William Edmond Logan—it is precisely in order to create new openings in an approach that to date has perhaps been excessively compartmentalized.

Notes

1. Quoted from Luke Herman, *British Landscape Painting of the 18th Century* (London: Faber & Faber, 1973), p. 84. The original text was published in German in 1770. Two translations were published in Great Britain: London (1776) and Edinburgh (1798). Johann Casper Fuseli was the father of painter Henry Fuseli (1741-1825).

2. Henry V. Seton Ogden and Margaret S. Ogden, *English Taste in Landscape in the Seventeenth Century* (Ann Arbor: University of Michigan Press, 1955), p. 57.

3. It should be noted right away that, as mentioned later on, the various categories are not totally restrictive. Thomas Davies shows greater freedom in his landscapes than in his military works.

4. For further reading on Wenceslaus Hollar, see Katherine S. van Eerde, *Wenceslaus Hollar. Delineator of His Time* (Charlottesville: University Press of Virginia, 1970).

5. The same compositional layout can be seen in Wenceslaus Hollar's *Wurzbourg View*, engraved in 1636 (*Ibid*, p. 10, Fig. xx, repr.).

6. Quoted from Luke Hermann, *op. cit.*, p. 84. The two Poussins mentioned by Salomon Gessner refer to Nicolas Poussin (1594-1665) and Gaspard Dughet (1615-1675).

7. Peter Bicknell, *Beauty, Horror and Immensity. Picturesque Landscape in Britain, 1750-1850* (cat.), (Cambridge: Fitzwilliam Museum, 1981), p. XII.

8. *Three Essays: on Picturesque Beauty, on Picturesque Travel; and on Sketching Landscape* was published in 1792. For more on William Gilpin, see Carl Paul Barbier, *William Gilpin. His Drawings, Teaching, and Theory of the Picturesque* (Oxford: Clarendon Press, 1963). See also Malcolm Andrews, *The Search for the Picturesque. Landscape Aesthetics and Tourism in Britain, 1760-1800* (Stanford: Stanford University Press, 1989) for an application of this notion to travel accounts.

9. Aquatint was probably invented by Jean-Baptiste Le Prince (Marianne Roland Michel, *Le dessin français au XVIIIᵉ siècle* [Paris: Office du Livre/Éditions Vilo, 1987], p. 168). However, Paul Sandby was so quick to use the technique to reproduce his drawings in engravings that he was credited with its invention.

10. *Delineations of the celebrated City of Pompeii; consisting of Forty Picturesque Views, on a large scale, from accurate Drawings made in the Year 1817. By Major Cockburn, of the Royal Artillery.* For more on the context in which this publication was produced and the difficulties related to its production, see Cecilia Powell, *Turner in the South. Rome, Naples, Florence* (New Haven and London: The Paul Mellon Centre for Studies in British Art, 1987), p. 81.

11. *Views to Illustrate the Route of the Simplon. Drawn from Nature by Major Cockburn and on Stone by J. Harding* (London: Rodwell and Martin, 1822). This collection of fifty plates is among the first of Harding's lithographies. Harding did not make his first trip to Italy until 1824 (Martin Hardie, *Water-colour Painting in Britain. The Victorian Period* [London: B.T. Bastsford Ltd., 1979], pp. 24-27).

12. H.D. Buchanan-Dunlop, Ed., *Records of the Royal Military Academy 1741-1892* (Woolrich: F.J. Cattermole, 1892), p. 33.

13. The term comes from Svetlana Alpers: "They were founded significantly by artists who were on the road looking, artists who were not staying at home listening to travellers' accounts [...] These works are descriptions, but not in the rhetorical sense, for description in these cases is not a rhetorical but a graphic thing. It is description, not narration." (*The Art of Describing. Dutch Art in the Seventeenth Century*, Chicago: The University of Chicago Press, 1983 p. 147).

14. Michael Clarke, *The Tempting Prospect. A Social History of English Watercolours* (London: British Museum Publications Limited, 1981), p. 96.

15. Buchanan-Dunlop, *op. cit.*, p. 45.

16. For a brief description of the role of drawing teachers in a military academy, see Martin Hardie, *op. cit.*, pp. 216-217. Massiot taught from 1744-1768 (F.G. Guggisberg, *"The Shop". The Story of the Royal Military Academy*, [London: Cassell and Company, 1900], p. 263).

17. *PRIOUL 1988*, p. 209. Andrew W. Moore's *The Norwich School of Artists*, Norfolk Museums Service, 1985, is the most complete overview on the subject. A number of Cockburn's drawings resemble those of his teacher so closely that they were mistakenly exhibited under Thirtle's name. See Marjorie Allthorpe-Guyton, *John Thirtle 1777-1839. Drawings in Norwich Castle Museum* (Cat.), Norfolk Museum Services, 1977, No. 120, Repr. Pl. 56.

18. *ALLODI AND TOVELL 1989*, pp. 5-8.

19. The combination of blue wash and India ink was employed by a number of topographical artists, such as Edward Dayes (1763-1804) (Martin Hardie, *Water-colour Painting in Britain. The Eighteenth Century* [London: B.T. Batsford Ltd., 1975], pp. 180-181).

20. An excerpt from Lady Aylmer's diary, *Recollections of Canada*, appeared in the *Rapport de l'archiviste de la province de Québec pour 1934-1935* (Quebec: Rédempti Paradis, 1935), p. 283.

21. A facsimile appears in the exhibition catalogue published by Michael Bell and Martha E. Cooke in Kingston in 1978, pp. 17-32. Thomas George Marlay appears in a watercolour painted by Cockburn to commemorate a fishing trip on lake Saint-Charles (*CAMERON AND TRUDEL 1976*, p. 154, No. 141, Repr.).

22. James P. Cockburn, *Quebec and Its Environs; Being a Picturesque Guide to the Stranger* (quoted from *BELL AND COOKE 1978*, p. 19). The vantage point referred to by Cockburn corresponds to the drawing by Sempronius Stretton (Cat. 51A).

23. Frederic Tolfrey, *The Sportsman in Canada* (London: T.C. Newby, 1845, Vol. II), pp. 53-54.

24. One of the first people to identify these artists was Mary Allodi (1974). Also see the excellent overview by Jim Burant, "The Military Artist and the Documentary Art Record", *Archivaria*, No. 26 (Summer 1988), pp. 33-51.

25. Patricia Godsell, Ed., *The Diary of Jane Ellice* (Oberon Press, 1975), p. 18.

26. We are referring specifically to Cornelius Krieghoff (*HARPER 1979*, pp. 46-47).

27. Jean Hamilton, *The Sketching Society, 1799-1851* (Cat.), (London: Victoria and Albert Museum, 1971). See also Martin Hardie, *op. cit.*, 1979, pp. 12 and 57.

28. *COOKE 1983*, p. 8.

29. *Topographical Paintings, Watercolours and Drawings*, Sotheby's auction sale, London, November 4, 1987, lots 41 to 54. See also *Un moment dans l'histoire*, 1991, p. 95 (entry by Lydia Foy) and *MARTIN AND GRANDBOIS 1991*, p. 64.

30. On the topic of artists and Western Canada with respect to watercolour/photographic production, see the extremely well-documented exhibition catalogue entitled With Lens and Brush. Images of the Western Canadian Landscape 1845-1890. (Calgary: Glenbow Museum, 1989).

31. We are, of course, not including here the very real changes that came about later on with Henry Sandham, Charles Jones Way or Aaron Allan Edson.

32. *COOKE 1983*, pp. 70-79.

YESTERDAY'S STANDARD, TODAY'S FRAGMENT: ELEMENT OF ESTHETICS IN QUEBEC, 1820-1850

by Laurier Lacroix

This text is dedicated to the memory of the wives of the British landscape painters, travelling artists and importers of art in Lower Canada.

"And to those who would criticize the paintings of Mr. Légaré, I say [...] that if they expect to witness the birth of a Raphael or a Michelangelo among us, without forefathers, predecessors, masters or schools, they may have to wait a thousand years; for if a man is to grow strong, he must be well-fed and nurtured as a child; and if our neighbours the Yankees had not encouraged their first artists and bought their mediocre canvases, they would not have a Powell or a Brown today"[1] (Polymetis, *Le Canadien*, October 13, 1848, p. 2). (Translation)

B ROACHING THE QUESTION OF ESTHETICS[2] means attempting to understand the visual contemplation[3] of beauty, to penetrate an internal experience which manifests itself through attitudes, reactions, and comments, but first and foremost through expression. For beauty in art is defined above all by the artist. It is the artist who draws on his or her personal experience to make a proposal or formulate a project for later evaluation. Esthetics are thus based on a given work and on the conditions of its production, but also on its reception, and the public's ability to accept, appreciate and understand it.[4] Seeking a more in-depth definition of esthetics implies establishing criteria so that judgment can operate and determine the beauty of a work.

Understanding the vision of the artist, art lovers and viewers of a given work requires not only the work itself, but also verbal or written testimony reflecting the sensory, emotional and intellectual message it conveys. Defining an esthetics based solely on a body of work results in a knowledge of the creators' quest and production. Being able to draw on information recorded by individuals from various periods provides answers that are essential to defining an esthetics.

Analyzing esthetics from this perspective (what choice do we have?) means situating it in our own context, in the Kantian tradition of esthetics, with the priority going to the viewer.[5] It must be remembered, however, that the object of our study is pre-Kantian. The Lower Canadian public was not familiar with these theories; it believed that art was subject to invariable standards and that beauty could be defined in absolute terms and pre-established doctrines which set forth its precepts for all eternity. In order to appreciate the works, some knowledge of art is essential to defining the tastes of the Lower Canadian public. This knowledge is based on principles which link esthetics to morals, associating beauty with good. The purpose of art was to elevate people above the human condition; it had to obey certain rules and conventions governing the genre, structure and organization of the works; and to imitate specific models. In order to exist as a quality, beauty had to observe certain formulas which determined its composition. These beliefs were not exclusive to Lower Canada; rather, they were the result of the academic tradition which had developed in 16th-century Italy[6] and which was codified at France's Académie des beaux-arts in the 17th century, before spreading throughout the Western Hemisphere.

This does not mean that the Canadian public was unable to experience the esthetic process as described by Kant—in fact, many records suggest the contrary—but it does appear that the quest for pleasure was secondary to the type of work which could inspire such an experience. Not just any painting could conjure up an esthetic emotion. Only after the criteria governing a work of art had been understood and mastered could art lovers permit themselves to appreciate it.

An attitude such as this, which reflects insecurity or a lack of experience with esthetic objects, speaks volumes about a specific artistic education and a lack of familiarity with art. The definition of a painting differed both in meaning and scope for the English and French of Lower Canada. For the Catholics, the rules governing history painting, made up almost exclusively of religious canvases, were considered to be at the top of the artistic hierarchy: the relation between subject and form in religious art made the latter the ideal genre.[7] Other genres, especially portraits, were produced, but were perceived as inferior art forms. The English, on the other hand, saw landscapes as the ultimate contemporary art form, having been primed by British theorists and essayists, as well as by a different culture and different religious practices, to be more confident in their own perception, while also basing their appreciation on other principles of art.[8] Their appreciation of religious works of art and their decision to import them was based mainly on the formal, stylistic and historical qualities of the works rather than on their subject. The bases of comparison are therefore different for these two ethnic groups.

Analyzing the esthetics of a historical period with a colonial setting is not easy given that the criteria for appreciating and judging the beauty of art were subjective, and that certain individuals dominated the scene, while others received little exposure.[9] There are a considerable number of sources which help us define these criteria for taste, but they are often contradictory and even incoherent. The predominant trend, easily identifiable, can be too readily explained by Lower Canada's backwardness and dependence on criteria and requirements established elsewhere, thereby preventing us from attempting to describe or analyze local practices. Other manifestations of taste which might help form an overall view often appear marginal, either as a contrast, in the unsaid, in the absence of records or the disappearance of works.

Attempting to define esthetics means imposing uniformity, based on personal opinion and judgment, on a society, on different social groups, and on a historical period which is complex by definition. It implies attributing the experience of a few individuals to a collectivity, in the hope that what the former felt and thought applies to the latter. Uniformity and the chronological organization of heterogeneous and often contradictory events is a necessary part of writing history. It is this miscellany of fragmented, disjointed historical facts which I will try to organize, structure and arrange into some semblance of order.

1820-1850

Any attempt to define the esthetics of the period 1820-1850 presupposes a certain homogeneity within the era and the qualification of various sensibilities—in this case those of nearly two generations—in generic terms: two generations of local artists of French descent and of new Canadian artists who crossed over from Britain. We believe that these thirty years share common characteristics, and we have chosen them as the exhibition focus based on the observation of artistic and pictorial phenomena that are not linked to ideological or social changes, which are often considered to have greater influence on mentalities and attitudes.[10] The exhibition centres around events and activities which affected the pictorial production of the first half of the 19th century, an era which is depicted as being governed by its own specific rules.

The landmark dates of 1820 and 1850, although they happen to refer to specific decades, should not be taken to be restrictive. The studies carried out in preparation for this exhibition highlighted the disparity of artistic practices during this period. Some existed even before 1820, while others continued after 1850. For example, the production of military landscape painters and travelling artists who stayed in Lower Canada only a short time doing mainly silhouettes and miniatures dates to before 1820, while the Nazarene esthetic did not reach its zenith until the 1880s. Similarly, other activities which add to the understanding of this period did not extend over the full thirty years.

The inclusion of an introduction on the years 1790-1820 and a conclusion covering the years 1850-1860 clearly shows that artistic practices did not change solely within the thirty years under study; on the contrary, they began before the period and continued for some time afterward. In other words, any division that is to provide a more complete view of the development of painting in Quebec would be impossible without some discussion of phenomena that cover a longer period and reflect different realities from those occurring from 1820 to 1850.

Ill 68.
A. Borum, after Cornelius Krieghoff, *Place d'Armes, Montreal,* 1848; lithography, published by Th. Krammerer, 34.5 × 48.6 cm. McCord Museum of Canadian History, Montreal (M11910).

The year 1820 heralded the emergence of a new generation of local artists who were fired by the religious canvases sent from France by Abbé Philippe-Jean-Louis Desjardins in 1817 and 1820[11] and who characterized these thirty years with their production of history paintings, portraits and landscapes, the latter becoming the dominant trend in the second half of the century. At the other end, 1850 marked the development of photography,[12] which opened up a whole new field in the visual arts. The popularity of this new medium and the emigration of European artists from countries other than Britain transformed Quebec's artistic tastes. Cornelius Krieghoff's settling in Quebec City (Cat. 151, 152 and 256-259) in 1853, Napoléon Bourassa's return from Europe (Cat. 248) in 1855, and the opening of photographer William Notman's studio (Cat. 251, 264 and 265) in 1856, where several recently emigrated artists worked, were representative of this transformation. Montreal became the new artistic hub of the province, ousting Quebec City. The type of change which occurred will help us characterize the esthetics of the period 1820-1850.

On the formal and symbolic levels, several proposals formulated over these thirty years modified the taste in art and bear witness to the scope of the transformations to which Canadians had to adapt. In architecture, for example, classical and Palladian forms, which were evident in many buildings of neo-classical style (Ill. 68),[13] co-existed with the emergence of the neo-Gothic architectural style, which came to the fore with the construction of Montreal's Notre-Dame church in 1829. Not only did the urban landscape change considerably during this period, which marked the onset of industrialization in Canada, but the Regency and Victorian architectural styles, with their eclectic adaptations, introduced elements borrowed from past styles, especially in private homes.[14]

Among the difficulties and limits we encountered in defining our subject, there were, of course, the sources and documentation,[15] which were referred to earlier. Indeed, whose rendering is to be believed, whose statements lead to a more complete interpretation of the period in question? The art historians of this era, who became more vocal after 1830, appear to have alternated between a celebration of the artists and their works and a denunciation of the pitiful state of public support. Unconditional support,[16] "encouragement," a popular term of the day,[17] and praise stood in opposition to scathing remarks on the indifference and apathy shown toward the arts in Lower Canada and the public's lack of taste.[18] Could a more "objective," more easily understandable reality, somewhere in between adulation and self-punishment, not be defined? What may be perceived as a double message is actually one and the same way of supporting the artists, either by stressing the quality of their work or by deploring the lack of viewers of which they were victims.

Another issue stems from the more specific problem of designating the production of this era as a body of artwork. The paintings which have been conserved from this period can be perceived as works of art from many different viewpoints. The reception given these works through the years shows that their appreciation was influenced by external criteria. Several views and portraits were, until recently, seen as documentary or decorative works; the landscapes done by British soldiers were considered the work of amateurs; portraits produced using mechanical means, often by self-taught or travelling artists, were commissioned mainly to record the model's facial features for posterity; and historical portrayals were often deemed of poor quality by members of the high clergy or by artists. Everything would seem to indicate that the passage of time, the current sensitivity to art, the influence of modern art and the scarcity of early works on the market have made it easier for us to accept the production of this era as works of art. We are especially moved by the direct qualities of these often unpretentious portrayals and the nostalgia they conjure up.

Although the landscapes produced by British soldiers remained unexhibited for over a century, the rising interest in Canadian history during the 1920s and 1930s led to their collection to fill a gap in the country's iconography. Family portraits were also dusted off and added to the collections of history buffs and history museums, before being admitted into art museums. This distinction was made gradually, beginning with portraits of members of the upper classes, painted in a more orthodox manner, and then growing to include the works of unidentified artists and portraits of unknown models. Including works by such diverse artists as Plamondon and Desrochers or Coke Smyth and Henry James Warre in the same museum gallery would have been unthinkable for preceding generations. While for us they may represent the diversity and richness of an era, they also point to significant changes in the ability and methods used to define and judge works of art.

The Ability to Judge a Work of Art

Our reflections on the ephemeral nature of cultural objects led us to wonder about the public for such objects. Two questions immediately arose: who had the ability to define art? and who was likely to benefit from an esthetic experience based on art? In general, it was agreed that everyone had the

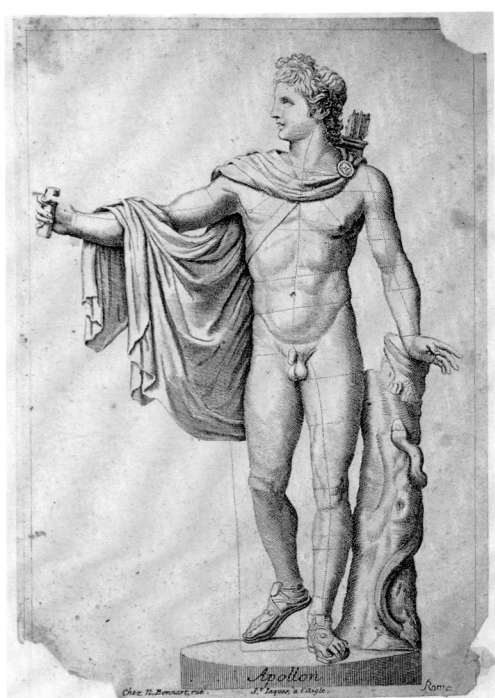

Ill. 69.
Nicolas II Bonnart,
Apollo Belvedere,
engraving.
Archives du
Séminaire de Québec
(P983.100).

ability to benefit from a work of art. Numerous appeals to public opinion indicate that, either through ignorance or simple resignation, the decision on what constituted beauty was left to the public.[20] However, the frequent distinctions made between bad taste and the tastes of the public and connoisseurs indicate that not all works were evaluated according to the same principles. Such was the case for distinctions between beauty as defined by the public, which was expressed in street performances and celebrations displaying artwork of an ephemeral nature,[21] and beauty as defined by other social classes, in whose homes richly coloured canvases and engravings seemed to be representative of bad taste:

Picture these crude engravings, and crudely illuminated to boot, to which gawkers and lovers of bright, tawdry colours flock in droves.[22] (Translation)

The artistic production of this period as a whole bears witness to the coexistence and plurality of tastes. Although it was agreed that everyone had a sense of esthetics, not everyone was able to develop it; this conclusion had also been drawn by Alexander Pope (1688-1744) in his work published in 1711.[23] In his opinion, the educated were better qualified than others to pass judgment.[24] It was up to them to establish the standards of reference for the intentions of God or nature. A limited education in art[25] and a conservative opinion appear to have been the basis for the prevailing tastes in Lower Canada. The portfolio of drawings and engravings by the drawing masters at the Séminaire de Québec (Ill. 69), compiled throughout the 19th century, tells a great deal about the tendency to consistently draw on models from Antiquity and the Classical period for basic references in establishing principles of drawing and composition.[26] Casts of early sculptures were not imported until the late 1850s,[27] but engravings were already being used to convey the principles of Greek and Roman statuary.

Ill. 70.
Edmund Willoughby Sewell, *Quebec City, from the St. Lawrence River,*
oil on canvas, 38.4 × 53.3 cm.
National Archives of Canada, Ottawa (C-11045).

In the absence of a recognized art school, artists were trained under the traditional method of apprenticeship.[28] Artists such as Légaré, Plamondon, Hamel and Bourassa and their followers adopted this method, as did many others. What appeared most important for the development and support of an artistic production, however, was the presence of an informed, knowledgeable public, able to develop its skills or interests and provide a receptive, critical sounding board.[29] The essential role of educating society to recognize the contribution of artists fell to private instruction. A practical knowledge of the rules of drawing was considered the basis of a well-rounded education. The increase in the number of drawing teachers and courses is a good indication of the type of needs to be met: additional income for the artists and precepts for the public. The involvement of teachers was nevertheless somewhat limited, judging from the duration of their teaching contracts and the programs, which were often ill-prepared.[30] We have little information on the students who took these classes, but the innumerable works on paper, especially in albums, shows that many amateurs studied drawing and watercolour, helping to create a context which was more conducive to the appreciation of works of art. Members of the clergy and of the bourgeoisie, who were avid travel, history and literature enthusiasts, made up albums. Collective works, those mixtures of correspondence, poetry and reflections, were decorated with views of well-known sites and monuments, portraits of celebrities and friends, and still lifes. The result of several years' work, they reflected the personality of their owners and authors.[31]

The notion of "art enthusiast" gave way to "amateur artist" during the period 1820-1850.[32] The British soldiers already familiar with the medium of watercolour and the rules of landscape portrayal formed a circle of artists which attracted a number of interested parties. Fascination with nature was manifested through trips and excursions during moments of leisure and favoured the development of drawing and watercolour, which the availability of material[33] and teaching methods[34] facilitated.

Elizabeth Durnford is a typical example of this type of amateur, for whom the practice of an art form was both an essential complement to an active life and a mark of social standing. Her father, military engineer Elias Walker Durnford (1774-1850), lived in Quebec City from 1816 to 1831[35] and oversaw construction of the Citadel. Involved in rebuilding the Porte du Palais, Durnford also supervised the expansion of Fort Lennox and repairs made to the Cathedral of the Holy Trinity. An amateur geologist, his only regret, according to his daughter Mary, was that he was not an accomplished musician like his wife. His responsibilities and rank—he was promoted to lieutenant general—brought him into contact with members of high society, such as Judge Jonathan Sewell (1766-1839). On October 24, 1842, Elizabeth married Sewell's son Edmund Willoughby (1800-1890), an amateur artist (Ill. 70) like his brother William Smith Sewell (Cat. 211). Jonathan Sewell, a fervent art enthusiast, travelled in Europe in 1826 and 1827 with his family. An actor and patron of the theatre, he founded the Théâtre royal in 1832, for which Légaré, Triaud, Schinotti and Woodley created sets. He also played music[36] and painted. A founding member of the Quebec Literary and Historical Society in 1824, he was a friend of Cockburn (Cat. 72 to 82) and Fassio (Cat. 105 to 110), whose company he enjoyed. It is in this family and cultural context that Elizabeth Durnford first began drawing.[37] She may even have accompanied Cockburn on his visits to Montmorency Falls in the winter of 1828-1829.[38]

Henry Daniel Thielcke (Cat. 219 and 220) left us a superb portrait of Elizabeth Durnford Sewell, done in 1843

Ill. 71.
Henry Daniel
Thielcke,
*Elizabeth Durnford
Sewell*, 1843;
oil on panel,
33 × 25.4 cm.
National Archives
of Canada,
Ottawa (C-134491).

(Ill. 71). It shows an elegant young woman holding a handkerchief and sitting in front of a drawing table. She is painting a watercolour, shown by the paintbrushes and water glass which are very much in evidence, and is posed in a classical setting against a summer backdrop dominated by a stormy sky. Instead of a view, her drawing portrays a woman with her skirt blowing in the wind. The neo-classical subject juxtaposed against a vast landscape brings together two traditions which inhabited the imagination of Lower Canadians.

There were other ways of developing one's knowledge and taste and refining one's judgment. The educated public had access to newspapers which reported on artistic happenings in Europe and provided information on the main events taking place in the colony.[39] The lectures organized by social groups or scientists,[40] activities proposed by the artists, who opened their workshops to the public, and the formation of a group of new Canadian artists in the Montreal Society of Artists in 1846[41] are only a few examples of events which helped promote artistic concepts and the work of painters.

History Painting or Adapting the Great Tradition

In an article on good and bad church paintings, Antoine Plamondon, who enjoyed the prestige of having studied abroad, sums up the essential of what he had learned in Paris:

Well-done paintings are the most magnificent, majestic, noble, educational, and edifying of ornaments, those that touch our hearts and, consequently, those which should be favoured above all others. (Translation)

He points out that the main quality of church paintings lies in the drawing, which must satisfy the rules of "proportion of the parts among themselves as compared to the whole, and of the suitability of to the attention and feeling attributed to the model being portrayed." (Translation) He also emphasizes the importance of facial expressions and character, as well as the garments. He concludes:

Here ends my explanation of some of the qualities which make up a good painting, but this is only an overview, for I did not speak of colour schemes, chiaroscuro [...] I did not mention shadow and light [...] nor the effects of air.[42] (Translation)

The artist's message sums up the "objective" concepts formulated during the 17th century and accepted by all persons of culture as the basis of an informed opinion. The fundamental notions of composition, drawing, the expression of emotions, light and colour[43] were part of the everyday vocabulary of educated people. It is highly probable that the debate surrounding these notions, which had occupied Europe's most cultivated minds for two centuries, was largely unknown in Quebec; however, people were definitely familiar with its underlying principles, and some members of the clergy even participated actively in this debate, which was beneficial to the Catholic Church. These principles were dealt with by Monseigneur J.-O. Plessis in his writings about works displayed in churches and the standards they had to meet. The lack of properly trained artists and models to follow handicapped the country, forcing it to accept inferior works of art. The prelate observed:

Little can be expected from a student of Mr. Dul. [Dulongpré?] [...] [The paintings] can be displayed in your church along with the high altar painting. Such works of art are acceptable in a country without artists.[44] (Translation)

A similar remark was made by Abbé Philippe-Jean-Louis Desjardins concerning the effects of the paintings he sent to Quebec City: "However, I am distressed for [François] Baillairgé. These works will be harmful to him, as people will see what real art is".[45] (Translation) Abbé Desjardins seemed to realize that comparison with superior works of art would likely stimulate the public and establish standards of quality which would harm the local art market. The paintings sent by Abbé Desjardins were mostly French and Italian works from the 17th and 18th centuries, which means that they provided a French-influenced view of history and vaunted the merits of this school and of its main source of inspiration: Italian art.

Comparing local art to European works appears to have been essential to the artistic process, both for artists and art enthusiasts. The quality of local production was measured against these works and for this reason, the opinion of European travellers and tourists was highly respected. Their experience with different cultures and their knowledge, which was never questioned, resulted in people quoting their expressions of surprise, and occasionally of longing, to describe the works imported to Lower Canada and also local works, which they sometimes purchased.

Trips to America and Europe by members of the liberal professions, the clergy, and physicians for the purpose of study, business or simple pleasure, were another means of enriching their visual experience and comparing and appreciating the "development of the arts" in Lower Canada.[46] Constant pressure was placed on local artists to complete their training abroad, and those who did so found their return to Canada especially gratifying, since critics never missed an opportunity to mention where they had studied. The fact that Légaré succeeded in developing his talent as an artist in Quebec rather than abroad was often cited as a major achievement.[47] Foreign artists enjoyed particular prestige and generally obtained commissions immediately upon their arrival in Canada.

These examples confirm that a knowledge of esthetics was especially important with regard to history paintings; the influence of the clergy was thus evident in the establishment of artistic standards. We are not sure that the message contained in the following text is representative of the general situation,[48] but it nevertheless clearly illustrates the differences in taste which existed among members of a single community, depending on each individual's training and aspirations. We have quoted it in its entirety to demonstrate the viewpoint of the churchwardens who were opposed to the authority and proposals of Abbé Gatien, priest of the Cap-Santé parish.[49]

Shortly after having completed the painting for the Sainte-Anne chapel [1825], Mr. Plamondon, who knew that Monsieur le Curé did not like the painting displayed above the high altar, (*Holy Family* by Charles Dusaultchoy, 1781-1852), generously made the following offers. He would replace the painting, of which we have already provided an idea in these memoirs,[50] and the merit of which can be judged upon seeing it, with a faithful copy of the magnificent portrayal of the Adoration of the Magi, which is at the chapel of the Séminaire de Québec (by Michel-Honoré Bounieu, 1740-1814),[51] under conditions to be determined, in exchange for the removal of the current painting with oversized figures, three louis to cover the cost of the material required for the new painting, and a guarantee that he would be considered for the production of the other two paintings to be hung in the two chapels, for which, including their frames, he would be paid twenty louis each, the subjects and size of these paintings to be chosen by the priest. Thus, for three louis and the painless sacrifice of the painting above the high altar, a superb copy of one of the most magnificent paintings in all the country could be obtained. A more generous and more advantageous proposal to the parish could not have been made. The priest was certainly thankful, and almost anyone would have accepted such a proposal with haste and gratitude. However, far from doing so, the churchwardens rejected it scornfully and indignantly. Transformed suddenly and as if by enchantment into fervent admirers of their life-size painting, and especially charmed by the brilliance of its colours which they alone could see, and asking with ironic concern if the new painting would be as brilliant and vividly coloured as the old, for these were the only things that seemed to matter to them; in a word, appearing to despair of ever having in the church anything approaching the perfection of their lovely canvas, the churchwardens, rejecting the proposals of Mr. Plamondon, stubbornly refused to give up the masterpiece embellishing their high altar.

This conduct on the part of the churchwardens was the result of the ill will of a few, which had been conveyed to the rest. It was not difficult for the priest, after this stormy meeting during which painting was discussed in such an original manner, to show the churchwardens where they had been led astray, and how they had managed to cover themselves in utter ridicule. They were ashamed of having allowed themselves to be influenced by prejudices foreign to them. (Translation)

The cooperation between Abbé Gatien and Antoine Plamondon was beneficial to the artist. Not only did he render a service to the priest, but he also received an original work[52] and the promise that other works would be commissioned from him. Abbé Gatien denounced the churchwardens' opinion—which was not unanimous, according to him—of a painting whose colour scheme, proportion and size in relation to the architecture were not to their liking. While the churchwardens accepted the painting—or became used to its bright colours, size and disproportionate figures—and wished to keep it, the priest wanted to replace the original with the copy of a painting which had been approved by his superiors and with which he was familiar from his studies at the Séminaire de Québec.

Creating by Copying

During the period 1820-1850, copying was tremendously popular. The copyist's work was held in high esteem and copies were hailed as works of merit, receiving the same recognition as the original if the composition was balanced and if facial expressions and colour harmony met established standards.[53] Since there was only a limited number of original works around, copies were considered acceptable and even recommendable substitutes, given that the models had already passed the test of public recognition. Artists looked for work as copyists as part of their training, of course, but especially because it allowed them to gain commissions more easily. Whether artists produced exact replicas or added their own personal touch (Cat. 153 and 155), copies were a means of measuring their talent against that of a master and even of surpassing themselves.[54] The choice of the work to be copied did not necessarily depend on the reputation of the artist who had painted it, although Raphael was often mentioned. It was more the subject and the accessibility of the work to be copied that influenced the choice of artists and art lovers alike. This attitude changed in the late 1840s, when the public began seeking famous sources and works by well-known artists. The freedom which had previously reigned due to the limited number of imported images and subjects gave way to increased knowledge in the field of art history, and therefore a greater demand for specific artists.

Ill. 72.
Joseph Légaré,
*Saint Philip
Baptizing Queen
Candice's Eunuch*,
1821;
oil on canvas,
290.8 × 171.5 cm.
National Gallery
of Canada,
Ottawa (18615).

Ill. 73.
Antoine Renou,
*The Presentation
of Mary in the
Temple*, 1775;
oil on canvas,
approx.
280 × 150 cm.
Church of
La Présentation,
Quebec.

In this respect, the flattering attributions and misquoted names appearing in the lists of imported works in Quebec guidebooks describing canvases hanging in churches,[55] or in Joseph Légaré's Quebec Picture Gallery,[56] bear witness to the era's tastes or to what stood in their stead. Copies and attributions reflect the era's taste, knowledge, and esthetic appreciation, as do fake paintings, on which Mark Jones wrote:

"The key point about detected fakes is that, [...] they once deceived but deceive no longer. Because they successfully deceived they can tell us more about the perceptions of those who were deceived by them than any number of genuine objects or honest imitations can ever do. [...] These are concrete visual evidence of exactly what scholars and collectors saw in and sought from the past, evidence which until now had remained almost completely unexploited".[57]

We can conclude that a more in-depth study of art in Lower Canada should consider foreign works and public perception of them an essential tool in learning not only about the works imported but also about the taste in art that they reflected.

Religious paintings, whether originals or copies, were chosen to embellish churches on the basis of their imagery. The goal was to constitute a homogeneous whole based not on style but on subject matter.[58] The work's role of promoting piety remained essential. Certain themes from the life of Christ, such as his baptism and crucifixion, and works inspired from the life of the Virgin Mary and Holy Family were especially in demand. Imported engravings and paintings supplied the market with works and artists with models.[59]

Since imports were rather scarce, artists had limited material to work from, depending on the requests of those commissioning their works. As a result, members of the clergy had a limited choice of subjects. However, originality was not a concern, the preference being for tried-and-true formulas and well-known models. For example, although Abbé Philippe Desjardins sent a wide variety of religious paintings, a single one (*The Baptism of Christ* by Hallé) inspired some twenty reproductions. Two other canvases portraying baptismal images, *Saint Philip Baptizing Queen Candice's Eunuch* (Ill. 72) and *The Baptism of Saint Augustin* were copied a number of times. Only four other paintings were copied at least four times.[60] Commissions for a new subject were rare and the competition fierce.[61] For example, Plamondon's hostility toward James Bowman, Victor Ernette and Henry D. Thielcke resurfaced each time he felt that they were about to encroach on a market he considered rightfully his.

Beginning in the French colonial period, church authorities and religious communities purchased works or obtained them through networks of donors. This custom was renewed in the 19th century after having been abandoned for a short time due to the political problems which marked the beginning of the British regime. The arrival in Quebec City between 1817 and 1820 of 180 religious works sent by Abbé Philippe-Jean-Louis Desjardins to Abbé Louis-Joseph Desjardins (Cat. 154 and 202) was the key to this renewal, which was in keeping with the high clergy's wishes.[62]

Importers and merchants were aware of this preference for foreign works and took advantage of any opportunity to import them. In 1820,[63] La Présentation church (near

Ill. 74.
Antoine Renou,
The Annunciation,
c. 1775;
oil on canvas,
approx.
310 × 155 cm.
Church of
La Présentation,
Quebec.

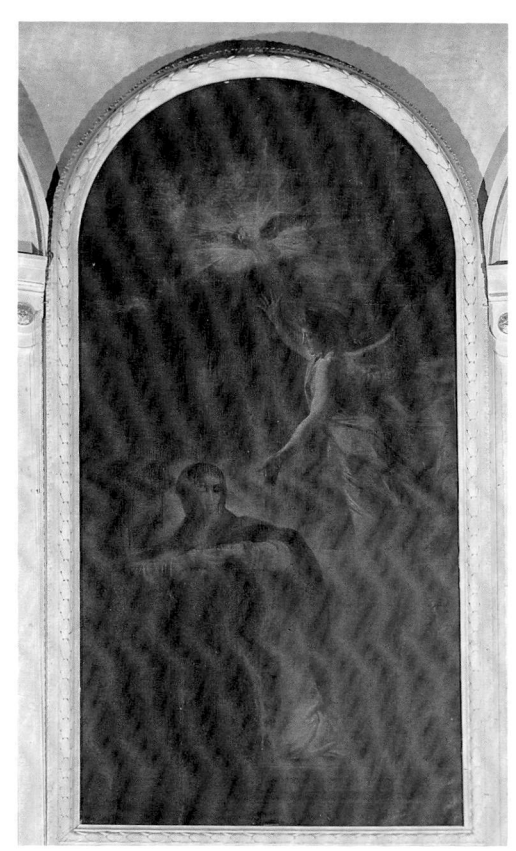

Ill. 75.
Antoine Renou,
*The Assumption
of the Virgin,* 1777;
oil on canvas,
approx.
310 × 155 cm.
Church of
La Présentation,
Quebec.

Saint-Hyacinthe) acquired six paintings imported by Reiffenstein. They were being sold at the Union Hotel, a place often used for auctions. The canvases advertised for public sale in the October 25, 1819 edition of *The Quebec Gazette* did not appear in the edition of the 28th, when the sale was to have taken place. Could they have been withdrawn and purchased directly by the church authorities? The advertisements contain the following descriptions: "of masterly execution," "a beautiful composition that leaves nothing to be desired," "guaranteed original," "A masterful composition with a luminous effect, in which can be seen the talent of Philippe de Champaigne, one of the greatest painters of the Flemish school." Besides being a publicity strategy, these comments reveal a knowledge of the stylistic vocabulary and the notions of the history of painting.

Three of the paintings put up for sale were by Antoine Renou (1731-1806)[64] and formed a series portraying the life of the Virgin Mary. *The Annunciation* and *The Presentation of Mary in the Temple* (1775) were exhibited at the Salon de 1775, whose catalogue indicates that they had been executed for the church in Saint-Germain-en-Laye. *The Assumption of the Virgin*, painted in 1777, probably belonged to the same series (Ill. 73 to 75). These three monumental compositions with simple planes, depicting figures in flowing robes in the foreground, are excellent examples of the neo-classical style. The exhibition of these paintings in Quebec City must surely have brought back memories to François Baillairgé, who was a student at the Academy while Renou was teaching there (Cat. 1 to 4).

Works by other contemporary artists appeared in Quebec at that time. Charles Monnet (1732-1794), Jean-Jacques Lagrenée (1739-1821), Michel-Honoré Bounieu (1740-1814), François Guillaume Ménageot (1744-1816), Laurent Guillot (1756-1806), and Jérôme Preudhomme (popular between 1763 and 1797)[65] were academicians or renowned painters whose work reflected the most recent trends of history painting in France. Besides the three works by Renou, four other canvases were put up for sale, three of which hang in the La Présentation church: *The Last Communion of Saint Claire* by Frère Luc (1614-1685),[66] *Christ on the Cross* by Jean Restout (1692-1768),[67] and *The Presentation of Jesus in the Temple* (artist unknown).

In public sales, little distinction was made between original works from different periods and schools, and copies; the common denominator was the subject portrayed. Quantity appears to have been the main criterion: buyers acquired works with a view to amassing series or collections. Taste was thus reflected by the number, and not the quality, of works. Rarely did church authorities or art enthusiasts exchange or sell works, even after learning more about art, as in the above-mentioned example of the Cap-Santé church. The heterogeneous nature of art collections reveals the limits of public appreciation, which was influenced by a secondary market in a colonial setting. However, the fact that individuals and institutions collected art illustrates the efforts made to give the country a cultural infrastructure largely ignored by the public sector. The addition of locally produced paintings to collections of imported works enabled collectors to showcase Canadian talent while increasing public knowledge about and appreciation of Canadian-born artists.[68] The collections could be seen in public places: churches,[69] conference halls, clubs, hotels, private homes and, thanks to Légaré, in spaces especially provided for this purpose. Major exhibitions bear witness to the results of these unstructured initiatives. Légaré's art gallery—open from 1833 to 1835, from 1838 to 1840, and then from 1852 on—was the predecessor of the museum-like institutions which mushroomed during the 1870s, such as the Pinacothèque of the Séminaire de Québec and the Art Association of Montreal. Similarly, the Montreal Society of Artists' exhibition in 1847 of 177 original works and copies—inspired by Canadian and European subjects—by professional and amateur artists was the precursor of various art associations and annual exhibitions which were to become more numerous in the second half of the century.

The Portrait or
"Recording Living Memories for Posterity"

Before discussing "the other" genre, landscapes, I will briefly touch on the portrait, which was the most popular and most practised art form of the period. For public administrators and senior civil servants, merchants, professionals, and well-heeled citizens, the main link with art was through portraits.[70] The number of artists who offered their services as portrait painters is astonishing. Many of them were travelling artists who offered to reproduce faces or silhouettes—often using the latest mechanical procedures [71]—or painters who have left us a significant body of work and who specialized in portraits, such as Berczy, Dulongpré, Plamondon, and Hamel.

Portraits were perceived as a means of confirming social prestige in the present and ensuring immortality for the future. They were a ritual marking important events, such as marriage or a promotion. Portraits also fulfilled a documentary role for the models and their contemporaries. Artists were skilled at embellishing their models; in 1841, Antoine Plamondon wrote, "Nature is not always what it should be," thereby echoing the ideas of Roger de Piles.[72] Aside from their narcissistic role, portraits provided a more fundamental proof of people's existence, of the "I was," to paraphrase Roland Barthes. The portrait was an object of contemplation for the model and for his or her family, friends and admirers.

The most sought-after quality in portraits was likeness[73] coupled with a certain idealized realism,[74] effects which were achieved more easily with the daguerreotype than with the paintbrush.[75] But painting offered the advantages of colour and a large format, and the main purpose in having one's portrait done was to have the artist bring the model to life on canvas. Viewers wanted to believe that a portrait reflected not only the model's physical characteristics, but also his or her personality. People's expectations of painted portraits are expressed in the theories of Johann Kaspar Lavater (1741-1801), who believed that a person's physical characteristics mirror the personality and that artists were capable of improving upon it or portraying the most flattering aspects, using a direct gaze, the suggestion of a smile or an air of confidence. Neutral backgrounds emphasized the model's facial features, and the portrayal of clothing and accessories was yet another way of confirming the model's good taste and social standing. The familiar objects which were depicted along with the

model added to his or her credibility and social and cultural standing. Jewellery, books or a writing desk were used to convey an idea of the model's possessions, knowledge and activities.

The naivete with which portraitists had their models pose, and with which the models in turn played the game, is disarming. The experience was fascinating for the subject, who appeared to be watching the artist attentively so as to miss nothing. Energy was channelled into this tension between the artist and the model, who gave him or herself up entirely. The artist could not disappoint the model. Public figures gaze to one side or off into the distance, rendering themselves inaccessible to viewers. Female models also seem to have refused this contact with the viewer on occasion, and this reticence gives them a more reserved air and confines them to a private place rife with dreams and melancholy. These portraits conjure up elements other than the quest for resemblance: the links of complicity between the male artist and his model of the "fair sex"[76] (Translation) were often evident to viewers.[77] The portrait thus becomes a means of situating the role of women, not as artists but as participants in the artistic process and the main element in the promotion of art in everyday life.

"No one possessed a keener sense of enjoyment for the beauties of nature".

This observation made by Mary Durnford about her father, military engineer Elias Walker Durnford,[78] could have been made by thousands of her contemporaries. At the turn of the 19th century, human nature, deemed the most faithful reflection of the highest principles of beauty, was obliged to share its supremacy with the landscape. The links which were established between the soul and the landscape led people to consider all of nature as a new model, an idea which was developed in Dutch and Italian painting and echoed in literature by Goethe and Rousseau. It laid the foundations for the romantic movement which was to influence Canada's esthetic vision thanks to the British landscape artists. Witnessing nature in all its glory was unanimously hailed as one of the greatest esthetic experiences, and its portrayal on canvas was governed by set principles and an idealized vision of beauty.[79]

The predominance of this trend influenced recreational activities. Travel guides pointed out the strategic location of Quebec City, the proximity of the rivers and falls in its environs (Ill. 76), the beauty of the St. Lawrence River and of its cliffs, and the unique location of the island of Montreal, which could be observed from Ile Sainte-Hélène and from Mount Royal which overlooked it. Views of nature which lent themselves well to paintings were sought after, and emotions were linked to this outdoor experience.[80] The sites depicted became the trademark images of Canada for nearly half a century.

The statement made by art enthusiast Philippe-Jean-Louis Desjardins upon seeing Montmorency falls typifies the general enthusiasm: "Never has a vision so moved me".[81] (Translation) Although the object of admiration was nature, it was clearly contemplated from a cultural viewpoint based on the principles of beauty arising from art theories.[82] Picturesque nature was confirmed as the greatest source of esthetic

Ill. 76.
Unidentified Artist, *Montmorency Falls,* 1833; graphite, pen and ink
on paper, (drawing made with Claude's Glass), 19.4 × 26.5 cm.
National Archives of Canada, Ottawa (C-89522).

Ill. 77.
Philip John Bainbrigge, *View from my Window,* 1840; graphite and
watercolour on paper, 18.8 × 26.8 cm.
National Archives of Canada, Ottawa (C-011884).

emotion.[83] Nature's imposing dimensions, with its rocks, crevices, trees and water which made a laughing-stock of well-tended French gardens, and its tumult of water crashing to the bottom of the falls which contrasts with the placid pool forming further on, were the object of strong emotions and profound reflections.

Travellers or emigrants—whether British soldiers, civil servants or merchants—were the first to seek out and acknowledge the beauty of Canadian nature and marvel at it,[84] influencing settlers who subsequently became familiar with nature and learned to perceive it as an object of wonder, admiration and learning.[85] The increase in commissions for landscapes from local and foreign artists during the first half of the 19th century bears witness to this art form's popularity.[86] The resulting awareness manifested itself in specific trends among British landscape artists[87] and Canadian and new-Canadian artists. In large-format portraits, it was a common practice to have male models pose against a landscape, thereby associating them with their natural surroundings (Cat. 117, 133, 194). Artists frequently integrated their signature into the forms of a stone or tree trunk, as if identifying themselves with their subject (Cat. 155) and acknowledging landscapes as a major source of inspiration.

The artists of Lower Canada were especially influenced by the topographic artists who plied their trade in the 1830s. The works of Canadian landscape artists resemble those of these topographers in that they are more descriptive, with their anecdotes of Canadian life, more down-to-earth observations (Ill. 77), and more common landscapes, reflecting a fuller integration into society. The accidents and tragedies which occurred in Quebec City (cholera, fire, Cat. 158 and 168, and landslides) and the highly structured landscape of

The Pigeon Hunt (Cat. 266) enshrined as a major art form what had been treated cursorily by Duncan (Cat. 249), or what soon would be by periodical illustrators.

These changes reflect an approach to nature which differs from the one characterizing the works of the topographic artists during the decades 1790-1830. Nature was now less idyllic and more closely resembled everyday life. Although still the scene of breathtaking panoramas and an object of study destined to fill albums or satisfy the demands of tourists, it was also becoming a place where local history was being made and recorded. In this sense, John R. Coke Smyth (Cat. 212 and 213), Joseph Légaré (Cat. 158) and Cornelius Krieghoff (Cat. 258) were merely delving deeper into what Cockburn had already heralded discreetly in his observations of urban life. Krieghoff's popular subjects combined a sharp sense of observation with a sense of humour on the grandiose backdrop of nature painted in autumn or winter colours. His depiction of rural subjects in settings typical of the Canadian topography won him a special place in the history of artistic taste and in Canadian history books. Thus, it took some two centuries for European tradition to perceive and begin to record on canvas the uniqueness of life in Canada: a reality which took shape during the period 1820-1850, and which we are still learning to master.

Conclusion

The quantity of the data gathered and the quality of the works amassed here clearly show that we still have much to learn about the decades 1820-1850. Our discoveries and the relations established between the works on display will no doubt encourage further study of this period in years to come.

While we feel we have shed new light on the subject, it still seems like we have done little more than scratch the surface; several monographs and overviews on specific aspects will be required to round out the information we have offered here. Better tools and methods are needed to fully understand the production context and art market and the connections between the artists themselves, whether they were travellers, emigrants or native-born Canadians. The scientific studies and observations made during restoration work will be indispensable, and more analyses will have to made of works using different approaches if we are to carve out a niche for the fine arts in the history of culture.

In my opinion, contrary to other socioeconomic, sociopolitical or cultural practices, the visual arts of 1820-1850 appear to be the breeding ground for common practices through which the coexisting French and British could communicate. Could this viewpoint be coloured by my perception of the current political climate, which acknowledges differences and yet aspires to greater harmony? It seems to me that the objectives of both producers and consumers coexisted harmoniously within this form of non-verbal communication.

For the English—and French-speaking elite, art, and painting in particular, was a means of expressing and satisfying a need for identity, education and leisure. Painting was intimately linked to the predominant social groups' desire to establish a local culture, identify its components and develop the creative forces within the community. Artists, collectors and art enthusiasts formed various associations so as to better promote their own interests, whether it be the link—fleeting, but oft-repeated—between a portraitist and his model, or the more lasting ties formed by artists and art enthusiasts who sought either to better defend their market or to improve their skills and convey a message through their shared passion.

Through its historical portrayals, portraits and landscapes, painting in Lower Canada provided a meeting ground for two traditions, which was of paramount importance in the structuring and development of art history. Painting was seen and appreciated by each of the ethnic groups as a means of moulding the colony to fit its own image: a double image, combining British allegiance and a need for a national identity. History painting, which enjoyed renewed popularity beginning in 1820, conferred a unique status on Francophones living in American territory. The presence of masterpieces from past centuries and the inspiration they provided gave artists and art patrons a sense of confidence, while art enthusiasts were able to appreciate the plastic qualities of these works.

For the British, landscapes served as propaganda while slaking their thirst for discovery. This art form bears witness to England's authority and the control she exercised over nations, territories and knowledge. Learning to paint the local landscape was for Francophones a means of cultural integration which was subsequently denied them. But that is another story, and one which should not affect our perception of the stimulating interaction that characterized this "Golden Age" of painting in Quebec.

Notes

1. We can only marvel at Polymetis' erudition in his choice of comparisons. Is it sarcasm or lucidity? The analogy between human and artistic development was often used by critics and essayists up until the 20th century. But is the author going too far in comparing Légaré's works to the first "mediocre canvases" produced in the United States? His choice of artists requires an explanation, given that they are little known today. Mather Brown (1761-1831) worked mainly in England, and his contemporaries by the name of Powell are little known today; I doubt that he is referring to William Henry Powell (1823-1879), since there is nothing noteworthy about the artist's production as a history painter.

2. The use of the term "esthetics" raises certain problems, given its etymology, history, and meaning (Francis Sparshott, *The Theory of the Arts* [Princeton: Princeton University Press, 1982]). The purpose of using this concept is not to cultivate a paradox, but rather to identify what can be retained as fundamental in the artistic experience of the public during the period under study.

3. The selection and juxtaposition of a number of works in an exhibition and a catalogue will provide material on which to base the notion of esthetics during the period 1820-1850. The interpretations offered in light of recent research are mainly factual, historic, formal and, occasionally, ideological. They do not take into account current concerns, which focus on the relationship between the historian and his or her subject, a relationship marked by the sex, ethnic community and social class to which the historian belongs. For the preparation of this catalogue, the members of the scientific committee—all men—made up a homogeneous group as concerns education and methodology. This exhibition has been developed in a context where history is being rewritten. It is now possible, for example, for nationalist* Quebec historians to study the contribution of artists from non-francophone ethnic communities and integrate it into Quebec's history.

4. Although I do not agree entirely with the structure of P.A. Michelis's esthetic judgment nor its foundations, I must admit that it clarifies my remark: "As concerns esthetic judgment, I must first distinguish between the artist's esthetic judgment at the time of creation and the judgment of the same artist after the work has been completed.

The artist's esthetic judgment once a work has been completed is not the same as during the actual creation process; rather, it resembles more that of an informed viewer. Once the work has been completed, the artist simply looks at the result and judges the beauty of it, whereas during the creation process the artist strives to make it beautiful, struggling with the material, the medium and the composition at the same time. During the first phase, the artist judges the esthetics with a specific goal in mind, while in the second phase he judges the esthetics of the result achieved, within itself, independently of any goal. In the first phase, the artist's judgment helps the imagined beauty to manifest itself; in the second phase, it acknowledges the manifested beauty" ("Le jugement esthétique" (1958), *Études d'esthétique* [Paris: Éditions Klincksieck, 1967], p. 47). (Translation)

5. In "Critique of Aesthetic Judgement", taken from his *Critique of Judgement*, Kant observes: "The judgment of taste is therefore not a cognitive judgment; consequently, it is not logical but rather aesthetic, that is, the principle determining it is purely subjective. Portrayals and even feelings can always be considered in relation to objects (and it is this relation which constitutes the real element of an empirical portrayal); but in this case it is no longer a question of their relation to feelings of pleasure or pain, which says nothing about the object and everything about the state of the subject affected by the portrayal" (Paris: Éditions Hatier, 1983, p. 56). (Translation)

6. Robert Klein, "*Giudizio* et *Gusto* dans la théorie de l'art au Cinquecento" (1961), *La forme et l'intelligible* (Paris: Gallimard, 1970), pp. 341-352.

7. Joseph Légaré attempted to secularize history painting, mainly with his canvases painted during the 1840s depicting tragic episodes in the history of Quebec City (Cat. 158 and 169), and with allegorical portrayals (Cat. 161). Like his American and European contemporaries, he used landscapes and recent events to portray modern history.

8. Iain Pears, *The Discovery of Painting: The Growth of Interest in the Arts in England, 1680-1768* (New Haven: Yale University Press, 1988), pp. 27-50.

9. For example, Antoine Plamondon was omnipresent. The anonymity of the majority of newspaper articles, an important documentary source,

makes it all the more difficult to determine the roles of the various key players and witnesses of the period.

10. In political history, the rebellions of 1837-1838 and the Union of the Canadas in 1840 influenced the first half of the 19th century, before the signing of the British North America Act of 1867. In economic history, 1850 heralded the impact of industrialization, which transformed the economic base. In addition, the Catholic Church's rise to power, which began in 1840, had a lasting impact on the French Canadian mentality.

11. These artists were Jean-Baptiste Roy-Audy, Joseph Légaré, his apprentice Antoine Plamondon, and Ignace Plamondon. The work of artists Yves Tessier, Thomas Valin, Francis Matte, Ursuline Nuns Mother Saint-François de Borgia, Mother Sainte-Cécile, and new Canadians Louis-Hubert Triaud and James Bowman was influenced by the market created by the Desjardin works.

12. The August 14, 1845 edition of *La Minerve* published an article on Vital Desrochers and advertised his work, which indicates some of the major changes that occurred over this thirty-year period in art. Vital Desrochers offered his services to "take your portrait, either in painting or using the Daguerreotype process." He is described as a portrait painter and student of Plamondon, but also as having studied in New York with photographers Plumb and Ferry. The painter was thus familiar with the technique of photography. The major American cities were considered the equivalent of European cities for both training and production. See Louise Désy on the popularity of the photographic medium, *L'histoire de la photographie au Québec à travers les périodiques: 1839-c.1880*, master's thesis submitted to the Université du Québec à Montréal, 1984, 342 pp.

13. The *Précis d'architecture* by Abbé Jérôme Demers, written in 1828, bears witness to this Canadian theorist's debt to the French classical treatises, especially Blondel's *Cours d'architecture*. See Marc Grignon, "Le précis d'architecture de Jérôme Demers. Une théorie déchirée," *Journal of Canadian Art History*, Vol. XI, nos. 1-2 (1988), pp. 1-20. See also four Parks Canada (Ottawa) publications in the collection "Canadian Historic Sites: Occasional Papers in Archaeology and History": Mathilde Brosseau, *Gothic Revival in Canadian Architecture* (1980); Leslie Maitland, *L'architecture néo-classique au Canada* (1984); Nathalie Clerk, *Le style palladien dans l'architecture au Canada* (1984); and Janet Wright, *L'architecture pittoresque au Canada* (1984).

14. Examples appear in Christina Cameron and Monique Trépanier, *Vieux Québec: son architecture intérieure* (bilingual edition) (Ottawa: National Museum of Man, 1986) (Collection "Mercure", No. 40). The works produced in Quebec during the period in question reflect a number of pictorial trends. Classical art, naturalism, romanticism, and the troubador and Nazarene styles marked genre scenes, history paintings and landscapes.

15. Unlike the United States, we do not have a historical compilation like William Dunlap's *History of the Rise and Progress of the Arts of Design in the United States*, which was published in New York in 1834. Based on the model established by Vasari, Dunlap presents the development of the arts in the young republic through a series of biographies.

16. "Canada is so poor in the area of fine arts that it is a veritable feat to see some of her sons devote themselves to an unappreciated, miserable career in this field. Our remarks apply more specifically to the wretched position of the artist struggling against poverty in a thankless career. However, it gives us great pleasure when we are able to call public attention to the works of our artists" (*Le Journal de Québec*, February 20, 1845, p. 2). (Translation)

17. *PORTER 1977/1.*

18. Several comments on this topic deserve mention, such as the following: "On a visit to the workshop of Mr. Plamondon, one of our fine Canadian artists, a few days ago, we were greatly dismayed to see several canvases of merit produced by his talented hand and which we have noticed, it is true, with renewed pleasure for the last ten or twelve years, but which should long ago have found a place in the drawing room of some of our citizens who, through their fortune and position, are responsible for setting an example for all of society. With the exception of family portraits, painters receive commissions only for the occasional church painting, for which they are still paid only the cost of the canvas, paints and their hours of work as if they were common labourers, their talent, studies and imagination counting for nothing. [...] we cannot help but note, however, that people lack far less in taste than they do in money. Considerable sums are spent on superfluous masses of gilt which convey no message to the mind and which will give our descendants a dismal idea of our evolution in the field of fine arts, while other masterly paintings, produced here, enjoy a

considerable following, speak both to the eye and to the heart, mirror the lofty precepts of religion by powerfully perpetuating the events which established them [...] A boor made wealthy by the hazards of fortune can commission the richest, most colourful objects from his cabinet maker; but it is up to sensitive, educated citizens of good standing to suggest well-chosen subjects to artists for their paintings" (*Le Canadien*, October 15, 1847, p. 2). (Translation)

19. Portraits were found in the homes of the descendants of the models or in institutions, where they played a decorative or symbolic role attached to the building's history. The Antiquarian and Numismatic Society of Montreal, founded in 1862, collected portraits in hopes of establishing a history museum. The Archives nationales du Québec acquired their first portraits in 1934 with a view to documenting history, and the Montreal Museum of Fine Arts did not begin collecting them until after 1950.

20. For example, the November 27, 1839 edition (p. 2) of *Le Canadien* invited the public to see Plamondon's stations of the cross, destined to "embellish the most beautiful building in all of British North America," Notre-Dame church in Montreal. "The fourteen paintings were to be of equal dimensions on all sides, which meant that the artist had the same amount of space for each of the different subjects portrayed. A great deal of skill and prowess was required to overcome this difficulty, and we feel that he has acquitted himself marvellously. Having neither the time, space nor knowledge necessary to examine the topic in detail, we leave this task to the public". (Translation)

21. Using an article from *La Gazette de Québec*, the November 28, 1821 edition (p. 359) of *Le Canadien* describes the following event: "Last Wednesday evening the entire city was lit up in honour of the Coronation. The entire Upper and Lower Town, the St-Roch, St-Jean and St-Louis districts, and even part of Pointe-Lévis were illuminated. The Château, the courthouse, the Jesuit dormitories, the Palais épiscopal, the seminary and public buildings contributed to the general splendour. A number of private homes sported beautiful transparencies, most of them depicting a crown, G.R. IV, God Save The King, or Vive le Roi. The building occupied by the military offices on Rue St-Louis particularly stood out because of a transparency of this type, and the home of the chief justice, on the same street, was notable for its group of Chinese lanterns portraying a crown and the letters G.R.

At 8 o'clock, which was the time fixed for the lights to go on, there was a display of fireworks at the square across from the Château which lasted approximately an hour, and attracted an immense number of spectators. *The flares were magnificent.* The Tuesday night frost had dried off the roads, which were bustling with residents of the town and the districts *enjoying the newness and beauty of the display* which, all things considered, *surpassed anything of its kind ever seen before in this city.* However, many people, and especially the ladies, were considerably disturbed by the gunshots, flares and firecrackers, nuisances prohibited by police legislation, which was never so poorly observed as on this occasion" (Translation) (The underlines are our own). See also endnote 24.

22. This comment was made by the Montreal correspondent for the *Journal de Québec* in the June 22, 1847 edition (p. 2), concerning the portrait of Queen Victoria, "manufactured by an English painter" and which was displayed in the reading room of the Legislative Council. Abbé Gatien - whose text will be quoted further on - associated his churchwardens' lack of taste with the bright colours of the painting hanging over the high altar in the Cap-Santé church.

23. His *Essay on Criticism* (1711) was often referred to.

24. This ability to pass judgment was also attributed to artists. "Chemical dioramas (presented by Robert Winter). We have not said one hundredth of what could have been said about these exhibitions, for fear of degenerating into exaggeration and "puff". They must be seen to be believed. People who came all the way from isolated rural communities, influenced by what they had heard from their friends, assured us that never had the cost of travel been so worthwhile. We believe that most Quebec City residents have visited and revisited these exhibitions, and we have yet to encounter a single person who did not say that it was the most beautiful display they had ever seen. The finest artists, such as Légaré and Plamondon, in other words, those most apt to judge, speak of it with great enthusiasm" (*Le Canadien*, October 6, 1845, p. 2). (Translation)

25. "In which school, and under which master, did he study drawing? Where did he learn osteology and myology? Who showed him linear perspective? He has learned nothing of all this. And despite this he wants to

criticize paintings! What presumption! What stupidity!" Antoine Plamondon (*Le Canadien*, August 7, 1833, p. 1) (Translation), in response to an article in *The Quebec Mercury* on the James Bowman's diorama of the *The Interior of the Capuchins Chapel at Rome* exhibited in Quebec City.

26. Marie-Dominic Labelle, "Au-delà du langage des mots. L'enseignement du dessin au Séminaire," *Cap-aux-Diamants*, Vol. IV, No. 1 (Spring 1988), pp. 29-32.

27. In 1882, the Art Association of Montreal received from the Institut canadien five sculpture casts, namely, the *Apollo Belvedere*, the *Laocoon*, the *Venus of Milo*, *Diana* (high relief), and a chandelier. The annual report of the Art Association (pp. 6 and 7) states that they were "originally sent out to their Society from Paris by Prince Napoleon as a gift, and for the encouragement of the fine Arts in Canada. [...] The first three of these important reproductions are examples of the highest Art the world has known, and are especially valuable as casts, taken at the instance of the French Government, from the original marbles".

28. "When one considers all that is lacking in this country to assist and stimulate those who devote themselves to the arts and sciences; when one realizes that our painters have no knowledge of the works of the great masters and the differences between the great schools; that they cannot draw from the round, that they have no exact notions of architecture, perspective, or colour distribution; and that they cannot have models pose for them to study the effects of nature, the reflections of light, or the texture of materials, one must agree that, to produce something even passable in Canada, one must have good taste, skill, and soul" ("Atelier de M. Valin", *Le Canadien*, October 27, 1837, p. 2, taken from *Populaire*). (Translation)

29. "Here are some of the immediate or future advantages we can enjoy first from the establishment of this (drawing) class, and then from the establishment of a school of fine arts. For a number of young people who have a taste for drawing, this will be an opportunity to spend a few hours during our long winter nights enjoying an exercise which is pleasant when one is interested in it and which will prove useful later on, even if only to judge a work of art based on some knowledge. We are often called to judge a painting or statue, and from time to time even have the opportunity to acquire an object of this type; it is therefore a good idea to be informed when doing so. Otherwise, we risk exposing ourselves to ridicule, like those who mistake Chapelain for Racine. I know some fine people here who took the trouble to send for a few paintings, which they call *their collection*! They would be astonished and even insulted if they were told that they have nothing but a pile of *crusts* with a *collection of gilt wood*. Painting is perhaps the thing which has fooled the most good people, even those who are educated and intelligent" (Napoléon Bourassa, quoted in the article "École des Beaux-Arts—Lecture de M. Bourassa à l'École Normale Jacques-Cartier," *Journal de l'Instruction publique*, Vol. V, No. 12, December 1861, p. 208). (Translation)

30. Among the drawing masters inventoried between 1820 and 1850 are (in alphabetical order): William Andrews, 1823, Quebec City; Mrs. Andrews, 1830, Quebec City; James Bowman, 1833, Quebec City; George R. Brown, 1831, 1840, Quebec City; C.G. Crehen, 1847, Montreal; Vital Desrochers, 1836, Montreal; James Duncan, 1845, Montreal; Adolphe Ernette, 1842-1844, Quebec City, Montreal; Gerome Fassio, 1835-1836, 1842, 1844, 1848; Mrs. Fitzgerald, 1831, Quebec City, Montreal; Louis Gegorgewskoi, 1834, Montreal; J.G. Kendirk, 1827, Montreal; Cornelius Krieghoff, 1847-1850, Montreal; John Martyn, 1847, Quebec City; J. Moron, 1831, Quebec City; M. Pierce, 1835, Montreal; Antoine Plamondon, 1833, Collège de Sainte-Anne-de-la-Pocatière, 1833-1835, 1841-1851, Séminaire de Québec; Ignace Plamondon, 1833, Collège de Chambly; Jean-Baptiste Roy-Audy, 1820, Quebec City; F.A. Schmeltz, Quebec City, 1841; Martin Somerville, 1847-1850, Montreal; Henry D. Thielcke, 1838, Quebec City; Robert C. Todd, 1842-1843, Quebec City; Louis-Hubert Triaud, 19820-1821, Quebec City; Wilson, 1829, Quebec City; Woodley, 1830-1831, Quebec City. Unless otherwise noted, these were all private classes. The January 4, 1820 edition of *The Quebec Mercury* (p. 3), provides us with an example of how these classes were advertised. Jean-Baptiste Roy-Audy and Louis-Hubert Triaud offered their services as instructors in "the art of drawing and painting in all its aspects using the method followed in the French and English academies". (Translation)

31. This is how Father Charles-François Painchaud (1782-1838) imagined an encounter with Chateaubriand in Niagara, "the material proof of which he had included in his album, beautiful in both shape and substance and the most precious ornament of his drawing-room, which had other

lovely decorations such as family portraits and various works of art which reflected the diversity and refinement of his tastes" (J.G. Barthe, *Souvenirs d'un demi-siècle ou Mémoires pour servir à l'histoire contemporaine* [Montreal: J. Chapleau & Fils, 1885], pp. 99-100). (Translation) The most famous album of all is undoubtedly that of Jacques Viger, housed in the Montreal Municipal Library and described as follows: "A distinguished patron of the arts and letters, Jacques Viger paid them ingenious homage in a magnificent ALBUM, each page of which is illustrated with a souvenir, landscape or character renowned in the country. May he long continue this gallery of famous Canadians, which begins with our earliest days and hopefully will never end" (*Le Canadien*, December 18, 1848, p. 2, taken from *L'Avenir*). (Translation) See Huguette Pierrard-Boivin, *L'Album Jacques Viger*, master's thesis submitted to the Université du Québec à Montréal, 1991.

32. See the chapter by Michael Clarke devoted to this subject in *The Tempting Prospect. A Social History of English Watercolours* (London: British Museum Publications Ltd., 1981), pp. 103-122.

33. *LEVENSON 1983*.

34. A number of methods, developed both in the academies and by artists such as Gilpin and Ackerman, are mentioned in advertisements for drawing classes.

35. André Charbonneau, DBC, Vol. VII (1988), pp. 287-289. Mary Durnford ed., *Family Recollections of Lieut. General Elias Walker Durnford, a colonel commandant of the Corps of Royal Engineers*, Montreal, John Lovell, 1863. The copy at the Montreal Municipal Library is decorated with a lithographed portrait of E.W. Durnford done by David Weil, after a pencil drawing by Elizabeth Durnford Sewell. The same drawing is reproduced in a photography by Ellisson. Another photograph by Ellisson reproduces the portrait of Elias Durnford, "reduced by his granddaughter Elizabeth Sewell."

36. A violinist, he conducted an orchestra at the request of Prince Edward Augustus. See the entry by F. Murray Greenwood and James H. Lambert, DCB, Vol. VII (1988), pp. 847-858.

37. Still according to Mary Durnford, we know that the older brothers, who spoke several languages, saw to their sisters' education. The oldest, Lieutenant Elias Durnford, was "travelling through Italy and France, and in the course of his journey frequently employing his pencil in sketching" (p. 162).

38. Her album contained drawings by Cockburn and was up for sale at Sotheby and Co. (Canada) Ltd., on June 13 and 14, 1972 (lot 81). Mary Durnford (1863) wrote: "In March of this year, 1828, the cone, formed every winter at the foot of the falls of the river Montmorency, rose to the height of 120 feet, or forty in excess of its usual accumulation; and an accomplished amateur artist, colonel Cockburn, of the artillery, then commanding that corps in Canada, was never weary in studying it from different aspects". A coloured aquatint by Cockburn entitled *View of the Cone of Montmorency as it appeared in 1829* was published in London by Ackerman in 1833. See *CAMERON AND TRUDEL 1976*, p. 163 (Repr.).

39. Newspapers often reprinted articles published in British and French dailies. For example, in its page 2 column entitled "Fine Arts", the February 24, 1818 edition of *The Quebec Mercury* published a summary of a lesson on colour given by Benjamin West of the Royal Academy. "Mr. West then reminded the students of the great advantages they possessed in the Elgin marbles and the Cartoons of Raphael; and after advising them to attend to the cultivation of their minds as much as to the attainment of facility in manual execution, concluded his lecture by expressing his intention of publishing, at some future period, a more full and minute explanation of the principles he had slightly indicated". The article stressed the importance of studying the works of the masters, an invitation often repeated (*Le Canadien*, October 11, 1847, p. 3) to artists who were encouraged to study in Europe.

40. On December 18, 1833, Daniel Wilkie (Cat. 176) gave a lecture on the progress of arts and literature, during which he referred to the work of Plamondon and Légaré (*The Quebec Mercury*, December 19, 1833, p. 1). The Société de discussion was set up in Quebec City in 1843. Plamondon, who participated, gave a two-part lecture in January and February 1845 entitled "Origine de la peinture" (*Le Journal de Québec*, January 7, 1845, p. 2, and February 6, 1845, p. 2).

41. *TRUDEL 1990/2*.

42. *Le Journal de Québec*, February 23, 1850. p. 2. In the September 2, 1835 edition of *Le Canadien*, "Des Amateurs" (could this have been a pseudonym used by Antoine Plamondon?) wrote in reply to an article published in the August 29 edition of *The Quebec Mercury* concerning Thielcke's *Baptism of Christ*. The attack launched against a foreign artist

who dared penetrate the field of religious painting was coupled with a reminder of the academic rules governing correct composition. "Farewell, esteemed editor of *The Mercury*, farewell in this province to correct composition, accuracy in drawing, to nobility and truth in facial expressions, to grace, to good taste in garments, and to the beauty and variety of colour schemes, if you continue to praise canvases which have none of these qualities and which are worth nothing. Beware, Mr. Editor, of giving foreign artists the impression that Canadians are lacking in taste and too ignorant to be able to distinguish between good and bad works or art, especially where the difference is so pronounced". (Translation)

43. This is how the text *Sentiments des plus habiles peintres sur la pratique de la peinture et sculpture mis en table de préceptes* (Paris, 1680) codified the components of a work of art. See Moshe Barasch, *Theories of Art from Plato to Winckelmann* (New York: New York University Press, 1985), pp. 338 and following.

44. Archives of the Archevêché de Québec, Registre des lettres, Vol. IX, p. 61. Letter from Monseigneur J.-O. Plessis to Joseph-Norbert Provencher, November 11, 1816.

45. ASQ, *Polygraphie 18*, No. 35. Letter from Abbé Philippe-Jean-Louis Desjardins to Abbé Antoine-Bernardin Robert, Paris, May 8 and June 25, 1803.

46. During his trip to Europe in 1819-1820, Monseigneur Plessis spent a great deal of time visiting monuments. In Paris, he visited a painter and a sculptor whose names are unknown (H. Têtu, Ed., *Journal d'un voyage fait dans les années 1819-1820 en Europe par Monseigneur Joseph-Octave Plessis*, 3 vol., Quebec City: Pruneau et Kirouac, 1903). Also, the remarks made in retrospect by François-Xavier Garneau concerning his stay in Paris in August 1831 reflects the critical spirit he developed as a result: "After having gone through the (Mazarine) library with a fine-tooth comb, I visited a faithful follower of Charles X and the Restoration, Paulin Guérin, one of France's most eminent artists, under whom our excellent Antoine Plamondon studied. He gave me a warm reception, showed me his workshop which contained many fine canvases, and spoke to me of his former student with interest. However, M. Guérin's education made M. Plamondon too good a painter for Canada, because he has been forced to abandon his easel for farming. A perfectionist, he gave his works a polish that went unappreciated and which took too much time for the prices offered him. Commercialism is too ingrained in America for the fine arts to flourish there. Simple sketches are hailed as masterpieces; people need only know how to promote them. Canada has had no experience with painters trained under French masters. We do not know if Mr. Hamel, who replaced Mr. Plamondon in Quebec City and who studied in Rome, will be more fortunate" (Translation) (François-Xavier Garneau, *Voyage en Angleterre et en France dans les années 1831, 1832 et 1833*, Paul Wyczynski Ed. [Ottawa: Éditions de l'Université d'Ottawa, 1968], p. 206). This text first appeared as articles in 1854 and 1855 and was published in 1855.

47. "It is unfortunate that this gentleman [Légaré] never had the opportunity to spend some time in Europe studying with the great masters and models. The same goes for a number of other Canadians who are working in this area with limited success" (*Le Canadien*, November 25, 1833, p. 2). (Translation)

48. The bishops' insistence on approving the paintings to be hung in churches indicates that they did not trust members of the clergy to make an informed decision, and churchwardens were hardly fit to advise them, if the example given below is any indication. Good taste was often associated with plastic qualities that made them seem more like virtues. Modesty and decency thus governed the censoring of figures, which were hidden under shades of modesty (Cat. 201).

49. Félix H. Gatien, *Mémoires Historiques sur la Paroisse et Fabrique de Cap Santé depuis son Établissement jusqu'en 1831*, a manuscript housed in the Fabrique de Cap-Santé archives, 337 p., pp. 181-185. The document was published in 1899 by Abbé David Gosselin and republished in 1955 by Abbé J.-Albert Fortier. The excerpt quoted was reprinted in *MORISSET 1980*, pp. 206-208.

50. "This painting, which is unfinished and which was sent from France merely as a protective covering for other works of arts, was sold to them for 25 louis. Fortunately, the churchwardens knew nothing of painting, otherwise they would be sorely to blame for such an acquisition" (Félix H. Gatien, *op. cit.*, p. 144). (Translation)

51. Plamondon wrote an enthusiastic description of this work in a letter to the editor published in the February 23, 1850 edition of *Le Journal de*

Québec. The canvas was destroyed in the fire of the seminary chapel in 1888.

52. It appears that artists used this method to exchange originals for copies. The example was set by public figures such as Abbé Louis-Joseph Desjardins, who took advantage of the poor condition of the works and the lack of knowledge of church authorities to make this type of bargain. Légaré acquired a number of canvases for his collection this way (*PORTER 1978/1*, pp. 25-26), and three paintings were "sacrificed" to Roy-Audy by the Saint-Antoine de Longueuil church after he copied them in 1822 (*CAUCHON 1971*, p. 74).

53. "This painting of Christ (*Christ on the Cross* after Van Dyck, Notre-Dame de Québec), we repeat fondly, is a magnificent work, which fools even the most skilled eye; for copies of this calibre often fetch the price of the original works" (Edmond de Fenouillet, "Beaux-Arts. Deux tableaux de la cathédrale et du Séminaire de Québec," *Journal de l'Instruction publique*, Vol. I, No. 2, February 1857, p. 37). (Translation)

54. With respect to Plamondon's copy of the composition after Mignard entitled *Saint Charles Borromeo Giving the Communion to the Plague Victims of Milan* (Fig. 87B) for the church in Joliette (l'Industrie), *Le Journal de Québec* of October 15, 1846 (p. 2) remarked: "The composition is by Mignard; but the colour scheme is that of Mr. Plamondon, whose talents are well known in this respect [...] The artist copied a miserable engraving and consequently had to add everything himself, from the expression to the colour scheme". (Translation)

55. For example, in *BOURNE 1829*, the following little-known—and incorrectly spelled—names appear: Fleuret, Chatis, Hutin, Panocel d'Avignes, Bourieu, Vigneau, Restaut, Menageat.

56. Attributions to François Chauveau, Lanfranco, Poussin, Hubert Robert, Lebrun, Agostino Carraci, Poelenburg, etc., appear in Joseph Légaré's *CATALOGUE 1852*.

57. Mark Jones, *The Burlington Magazine*, June 1989, p. 424.

58. During the second half of the 19th century, artists from Germany and Italy allowed clergy to commission decorative ensembles which were homogeneous both with regard to style and imagery.

59. The art market and collections had been flourishing in England since the early 1790s. Importing works was looked on highly, as pointed out by British art merchant William Buchanan: "The late Mr. President [Benjamin] West used to remark, that next to the merit of having painted a picture which should do honour to the art, and become an ornament to the state, wherein it was produced, was the credit of having brought from foreign countries works of the great masters. The importation of such works tends to enrich the nation which receives them, it holds out a bright example for imitation, and rouses and calls into action the native talents of those who feel the sacred flame of emulation". (*Memoirs of Painting with a chronological history of the importation of Pictures by the Great Masters since the French Revolution* [London: Ackerman, 1824], Vol. I, p. 9). On imports to Quebec, an unpublished study by Didier Prioul, *Les importations de gravures et de peintures dans la première moitié du XIXe siècle—1816-1855* (1979, 151 p.) retraces the number and type of works imported based on advertisements for public sales.

60. They were *Saint Francis of Paola Raising his Sister's Child from the Dead* by Simon Vouet, *The Virgin and Child-Jesus Appearing to Saint Anthony of Padoua and to Saint Francis of Assisi* by Daniel Hallé (Saint-Henri de Lévis), *Christ on the Cross* by Charles Monnet, and *The Vision of Saint Jérome* by Pierre Dulin (MSQ).

61. "Mr. Duvernay—I saw in your newspaper an advertisement dated May 1, 1830, concerning a painting of the Adoration of the Magi in Bethlehem, which is said to have "sparked praise from connoisseurs in the United States, and which due to exceptional circumstances is being let go for a quarter of its actual value as estimated in Baltimore or Philadelphia." I invite those who took the time to examine this painting in detail during its exhibition at the parish church of this city to go to Mr. Tessier's workshop opposite St-Jacques church, where they will see a work of the same composition, copied in this country, from the very same original as the painting in question. It is true that it did not come from the United States, that it was not painted by an "artist of distinction," that it did not spark "the praise of connoisseurs" abroad. However, art lovers will be able to judge the difference for themselves" (*La Minerve*, August 9, 1830, p. 2). (Translation)

62. These works were to have been imported as early as 1803. However, the quest for a safe, economical means of transporting the works, the

continental blockade, and the imprisonment of Abbé Philippe-Jean-Louis Desjardins postponed the first shipment.

63. Archives de la Fabrique de La Présentation, *Livres de comptes 1807-1874*, for 1820: "six large canvases approved in writing by Monseigneur de Telmesse". (Translation)

64. A student of Vien and Pierre, Renou was received into the Academy in 1766. Appointed assistant secretary in 1776 and academician in 1781, he became, for a short period in 1790, secretary for life. He painted three canvases for the Petit Trianon in 1773, and participated in the decoration of the Fontainebleau chapel in 1775.

65. Charles Monnet painted *Christ on the Cross*, which was destroyed in the Séminaire de Québec chapel fire in 1888, but which was known through copies done by Roy-Audy (1823, Musée du Québec; 1825, Boucherville) and Plamondon (1830, Saint-Roch de Québec; 1851, Saint-Michel de Sillery); Jean-Jacques Lagrenée painted *The Burying of Christ* (1770) and *The Incredulity of Saint Thomas* (1770), Musée du Québec (both from Baie-du-Febvre), and *Christ and the Samaritan* (1770), destroyed in the Séminaire de Québec chapel fire of 1888; Michel-H. Bounieu produced *The Adoration of The Shepherds*, also destroyed in the Séminaire de Québec chapel fire; François Guillaume Ménageot painted *The Virgin Placing Saint Theresa Under the Protection of Saint Joseph* (1787), convent of the Augustines at the Hôtel-Dieu hospital in Quebec City; Laurent Guillot painted *The Hermits of the Thébaïde*, Séminaire de Québec; and Preudhomme authored *An Anachorite Imploring for a Penitent the Admission in a Monastery* (1786) and *The Bishop Nonnus Receiving the Penitent Pélagie* (1787), Convent of the Ursulines de Québec.

66. This painting, attributed at the time of the sale to Philippe de Champaigne, is actually a major work by Frère Luc. Unfortunately, it has now deteriorated considerably.

67. Two other versions of Restout's painting exist in France (at the Hospice de Vernon and the Notre-Dame church in Vitry-le-François). The composition was probably exhibited at the Salon de 1737. See Pierre Rosenberg, Antoine Schnapper, *Jean Restout (1692-1768)* (Rouen: Musée des beaux-arts de Rouen, 1970), pp. 188, 209, No. 12 and 13 (Repr.).

68. The September 12, 1844 edition of *Le Castor* published the following article, signed "Canadien", concerning the painting commissioned from Morris by the Legislative Assembly: "We are not aware of the situation in Montreal, but in Quebec City we have art collections which would be the envy of any European artist; we also have Canadian-born and other artists whose work has been admired and sought after by European art enthusiasts: we leave it to them to judge this evaluation of this country's taste in fine arts". (Translation)

69. "A remarkable taste for painting has developed in Quebec City. This same city has also produced a number of Canadian-born artists whose works are much admired, not only by their compatriots, but also by art enthusiasts from other countries. We could mention the names of Légaré, Plamondon, Hamel and others, who are living proof that Canadians are exceptionally gifted in the areas of the arts and science, and in painting in particular. What probably contributed largely to the development of a taste for painting in Quebec City is the fact that the city possesses collections of works, exhibited for all to see in the churches, of a quality rarely seen elsewhere in America" ("Beaux-Arts," *L'Aurore des Canadas*, December 1, 1846, p. 2, excerpted from *Le Canadien*). (Translation)

70. "Quebec boasts talented painters skilled in various art forms; two of them travelled to Europe to draw inspiration from the indispensable instruction of the great masters. Upon their return, their fellow citizens could find nothing more beautiful, more noble, more gracious to offer these artists' skilful brushes, their imagination freshly engraved with the brilliant work of ten centuries of genius... than their own faces, of which they are asked to produce a more or less faithful and flattering replica" (*Le Canadien*, October 15, 1847, p. 2). (Translation)

71. The decades preceding the invention of photography saw the development of a number of procedures used to copy facial features, which facilitated the execution of the portrait and lowered prices, as seen in this advertisement which appeared on page 2 of the May 10, 1833 edition of *Le Canadien*: "Miniatures and profiles painted. In the apartments above the shop owned by Mrs. Fergus, Preserves Maker, at the corner of Rue Saint-Jean and Rue Saint-Stanislas, through a branch of the establishment now located in Montreal. Likenesses in profile taken on a machine using set principles, and finished in their own excellent style, for one écu. Portraits of all types copied and renewed, frames at low prices. The artists will be here this week and next week only, so do not pass up this opportunity

to obtain a lasting souvenir of friends and relatives... Children half price". (Translation)

72. See endnote 75. Roger de Piles, *Cours de Peinture par principes* (1708) (Paris: Gallimard, 1989), pp. 131 and following.

73. For those who questioned the resemblance of the copy of the portrait of *Grégoire XVI* after Pietro Gagliardi done by Plamondon in 1842, the October 7, 1843 edition (p. 2) of *Le Journal de Québec* gleefully published a letter written on August 26 and sent from Rome by Théophile Hamel, in which he clears up any doubts: "Mr. Hamel, who has seen His Holiness in person, states that the portrait done by Mr. Plamondon is an exact likeness; a categorical response for those who asserted the contrary". (Translation) On the topic of resemblance, see Philippe Dubois, "De la vérisimilitude à l'index," *L'Acte photographique* (Brussels: Éditions Labor, 1983), pp. 17-53, and Sarah Kofman, "La ressemblance des portraits: l'imitation selon Diderot," *La mélancolie de l'art* (Paris: Galilée, 1985), pp. 35-70. An adapted version of this publication appeared in *L'imitation, aliénation ou source de liberté?* (Paris: La Documentation Française, 1985), pp. 215-230 (Coll. "Rencontres de l'École du Louvre").

74. The following remark was made concerning the portraits of the nuns at the Hôpital général: "Do not think, however, that the beautiful effects of painting are easily achieved, and that all the artist has to do is to mechanically reproduce what he sees before him; you would be wrong, for nature is not always what it should be. Some of its shapes are more beautiful than others, some of its arrangements are, if you will permit the expression, more natural, true and beautiful, at least as compared to models or garments, and there are often elements of beauty in nature which the unskilled painter is incapable of reproducing, because he does not possess the secret of his art, in other words, because he has no feeling for nature. For nature is the book of all great artists; they pore over it and study it in depth, thereby uncovering its wealth of treasures, while mediocre painters merely scratch the surface, deforming and changing beyond recognition anything of beauty they may find. Artists follow the same process as men of letters; before dealing with a subject, they study it, ponder over it, examining all that is intrinsic to it as well as anything lacking. This lack is what they try and compensate for, and through their efforts they often achieve magnificent results [...] see how lovingly the artist portrayed his subject, look and see if you can find the brush strokes. Try as you might, you will not be able to, and this is another secret of skilled artists, who manage to conceal the paint before your very eyes, so that all you see is nature; [...] As for Mr. Plamondon's palette, which is the greatest of his talents, it is unequalled even on the other side of the ocean. These remarks are not ours alone, but are echoed by many foreign art connoisseurs and persons of taste" ("Un ami de la peinture," *Le Canadien*, August 20, 1841, p. 2). (Translation) A reply to this article from "un ami des peintres" appeared in the August 23, 1841 edition of *Le Fantasque*, pp. 437-439, stating that the author of the article in *Le Canadien* was "a friend of the painter," since it was obvious that it had been written under the supervision of Plamondon.

75. See note 12.

76. As used by *Le Canadien*, July 26, 1833, p. 2.

77. "Mr. Plamondon should congratulate himself on being able to count a number of lovely ladies among his visitors and, moreover, on having enchanted them with his artwork; this is the most conclusive proof of its perfection, given the refined taste and perception of the elite of humanity. We must record here the words spoken by a fair damsel in the enthusiasm of the moment. "I would be extremely happy," she told us, "to be painted by such a brush!" We are sure that Mr. Plamondon would be no less happy, for he would convey to the canvas a revelation of true beauty by depicting such a model; [...] We have also learned that many distinguished families had planned to avail themselves of the services of Mr. Plamondon, anxious as they were to have an expert Canadian hand record their living memory for posterity" (*L'Aurore des Canadas*, December 24, 1842, p. 2). (Translation)

78. Mary Durnford, *op. cit.*, p. 83.

79. On this topic, see two background works: Christopher Hussey, *The Picturesque Studies in a Point of View* (London: Frank Cass and Company Limited (1927), 1983), and Samuel H. Monk, *The Sublime* (Ann Arbor: The University of Michigan Press (1935), 1960); see also the introduction and anthology of texts compiled by Marie-Madeleine Martinet in *Art et Nature en Grande-Bretagne au XVIIIe siècle. De l'harmonie classique au pittoresque du premier romantisme* (Paris: Aubier-Montaigne, 1980).

80. Proof of James Pattison Cockburn's knowledge of and love for the Quebec City region was the guide he published in 1831, entitled *Quebec and*

Its Environs; Being a Picturesque Guide to the Stranger, illustrated with 7 engravings (BELL AND COOKE 1978). See also Nicolas Grimaldi, "L'esthétique de la belle nature. Problèmes d'une esthétique du paysage," *Mort du Paysage? Philosophie et esthétique du paysage*, directed by François Dagognet (Seyssel: Éditions du Champ Vallon, 1983), pp. 113-131.

81. In a letter to de Varicourt, Quebec City, May 6, 1793, reprinted in "Quelques prêtres français en exil au Canada," *Rapport de l'archiviste de la province de Québec*, Tome XLIV, (Quebec City, 1966), pp. 147-149.

82. The famous *Discourses* by Reynolds published as of 1778 provided a contemporary basis for this viewpoint. See Robert R. Wark ed., *Sir Joshua Reynolds Discourses on Art London* (New Haven: Yale University Press, 1975).

83. In 1882, James MacPherson LeMoine published *Picturesque Quebec* (Montreal: Dawson Brothers). In Chapter One, LeMoine compiled an anthology of descriptions of Quebec City and its surroundings, one of which was written by author Susanna Moodie (1803-1885) after a trip she made on September 22, 1832: "Never shall I forget that short voyage from Grosse Isle to Quebec. What wonderful combinations of beauty and grandeur and power, at every winding of that noble river!

Every perception of my mind became absorbed into the one sense of seeing, when, upon rounding Point Levis, we cast anchor before Quebec. What a scene! Can the world produce another? Edinburgh had been the *beau idéal* to me of all that was beautiful in nature—a vision of the Northern Highlands had haunted my dreams across the Atlantic; but all these past recollections faded before the present of Quebec. Nature has ransacked all our grandest elements to form this astonishing panorama There, frowns the cloud-capped mountain and below, the cataract foams and thunders; woods and rock and river combine to lend their air in making the picture perfect, and worthy of its Divine originator. The precipitous bank upon which the city lies piled, reflected in the still, deep waters at its base, greatly enhances the romantic beauty of the situation. The mellow and serene glow of the autumn day harmonized so perfectly with the solemn grandeur of the scene around me, and sank so silently and deeply into my soul, that my spirit fell prostrate before it, and I melted involuntarily into tears".

84. Thomas Davies, in the watercolour depicting the Chaudiere Falls (1787, NGC), portrays an artist sketching the landscape. In *Death of a Moose* (1859, Ill. 24), Cornelius Krieghoff is depicted carrying a portfolio and accompanying his fellow hunters.

85. "I cannot refrain from expressing the satisfaction I have felt, in my different visits of late to his studio, to see that, latterly, he has devoted much of his time and art to the charmful and romantic scenery of his own beautiful forest-land, and he has been exceedingly happy in the delineation. He has emerged from the dusty and prozing society of vigilworn Saints, and other goodly canonized notables, to give his pencil a revel amid the fair and fresh of nature's loveliness; and he is now, as I love to see him, surrounded by heaps of mountains, and sunny valleys, and dear grey hills of his own country. A propos, may I be permitted to mention here, that it has often excited my wonder, that our native painters have not devoted some part of their time and study to the scenery of Canada" ("An Amateur," *La Gazette de Québec*, December 13, 1833, p. 2).

86. "Poetry and painting, two art forms of inspiration and genius, also began to spread their wings and develop their forces [...]. Fondness for the latter has transformed unskilled brushes into fertile palettes from which lovely landscapes spring, glorifying new canvases from year to year and proving, contrary to Raynal's belief, that we are sensitive to the beauty of nature" ("Observations sur le changement qui s'est opéré dans le caractère et les habitudes des Canadiens depuis qu'ils ont passé sous la domination britannique," *Le Journal de Québec*, May 25, 1844, pp. 1-2). (Translation)

87. See the essay by Didier Prioul, pp. 50-59.

CATALOGUE

TITLES OF WORKS

The figures refers to catalogue numbers

François Beaucourt
Mrs. Daniel Sutherland, née Margaret Robertson (cat. 13)

George Bulteel Fisher
View of Quebec (cat. 29)

George Heriot
View of Quebec (cat. 35)

Thomas Davies
A View of Château-Richer, Cape Torment, and Lower End of the Isle of Orleans near Quebec (cat. 20)

Charles Ramus Forrest
Falls of the Saint Anne River (cat. 111)

Théophile Hamel, after Pieter Paul Rubens
Education of the Virgin (cat. 124)

Joseph Légaré, after Matthias Stomer
The Vision of Saint Roch (cat. 153)

Antoine Plamondon
Mrs. Louis-Joseph Papineau, née Julie Bruneau, and Her Daughter Ézilda (cat. 187)

Antoine Plamondon
Mrs. Thomas B. Wragg, née Mary Ann Wilkins (cat. 191)

William Robert Herries
The 43rd Regiment on March from New Brunswick to Canada Accross the Madawaska Portage (cat. 141)

Henry William Barnard
Landing Place at Sorel (cat. 59)

Joseph Légaré
Josephte Ourné (cat. 166)

Antoine Plamondon
Zacharie Vincent (cat. 194)

Théophile Hamel
Portrait of a Young North American Indian Girl (cat. 131)

Henry Daniel Thielcke
Presentation of a Newly Elected Chief of the Huron Tribal Council of Lorette (cat. 220)

Joseph Légaré
Quebec Viewed from Pointe Lévis (cat. 162)

Robert Clow Todd
**The Timber and Shipbuilding Yards of Allan Gilmour and Company at Wolfe's Cove, Quebec,
Viewed from the West** (cat. 222)

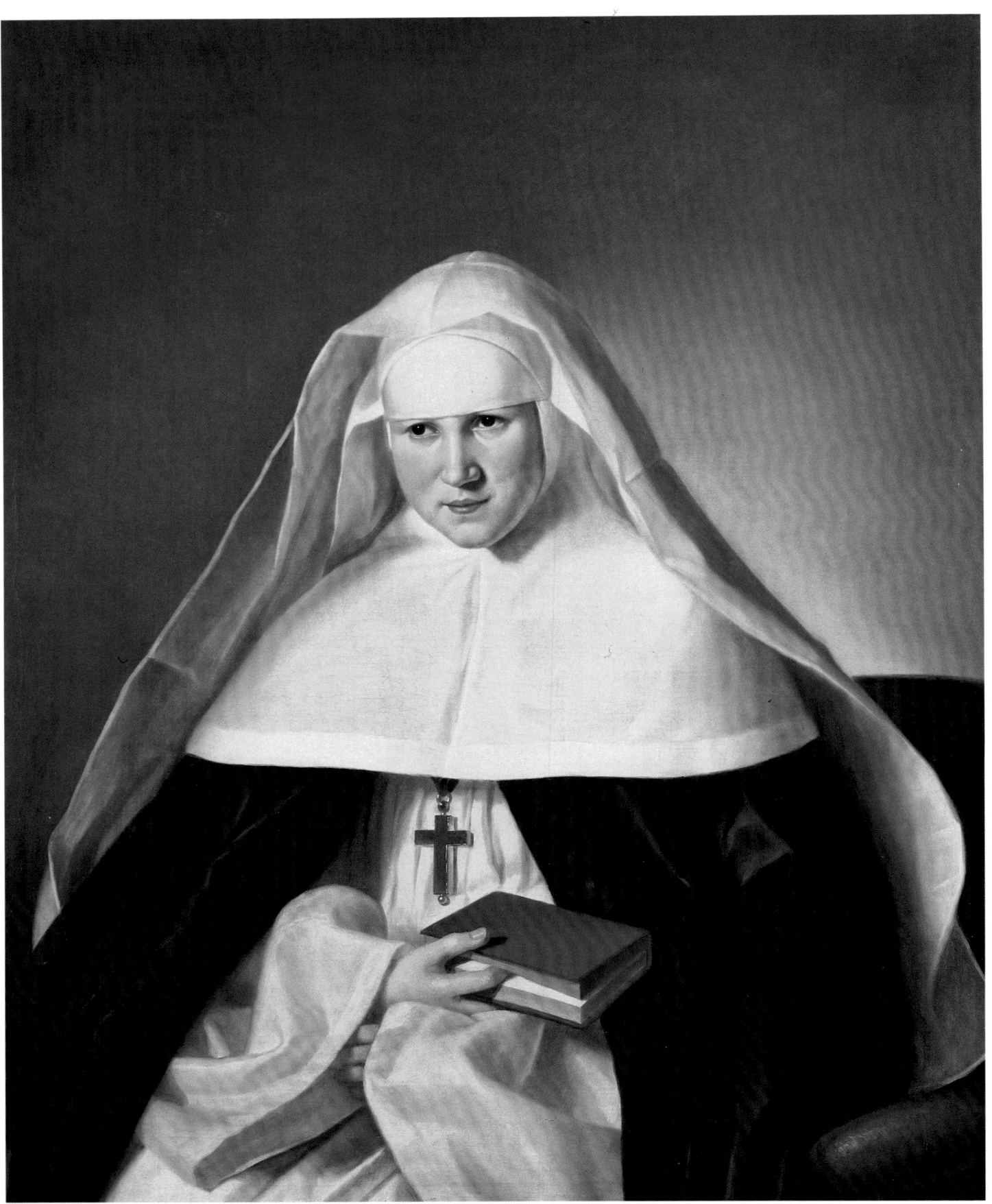

Antoine Plamondon
Sœur Sainte-Anne (cat. 196)

Théophile Hamel
Self-Portrait a Landscape (cat. 117)

James Pattison Cockburn
Quebec Seen From the West Bank on the Saint Charles River (cat. 81)

Joseph Légaré
Country House of Philippe Panet on the Little Saint Charles River (cat. 163)

Antoine Plamondon
Lost in the Wood (cat. 190)

Cornelius Krieghoff
"Fraser", With Mr. Miller Up (cat. 152)

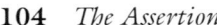

Jean-Baptiste Roy-Audy
Monseigneur Rémi Gaulin (cat. 208)

Gerome Fassio
(?) Mrs. Pierre-Antoine Doucet,
née Delphine Bruneau (cat. 108)

Gerome Fassio
Joseph Rouleau (cat. 110)

John Richard Coke Smyth
The Pulpit of the Church of the Ursuline Convent, Quebec (cat. 214)

James Hope-Wallace
Camping Near Quebec (cat. 146)

Théophile Hamel
James Bruce, 8th Earl of Elgin and 12th Earl of Kincardine (cat. 138)

Théophile Hamel
***Mrs. Cyrice Têtu, née Caroline Dionne,
and Her Son Amable*** (cat. 134)

Théophile Hamel
Cyrice Têtu and His Daughter Caroline (cat. 135)

Antoine Plamondon, after Edward Magnus
The Little Gardeners (cat. 267)

Napoléon Bourassa
Louis-Joseph Papineau (cat. 248)

James Duncan
The Gavazzi Riot (cat. 249)

THE EMERGENCE
1790-1820

FRANÇOIS BAILLAIRGÉ was born in Quebec City on January 21, 1759 and was introduced to art while apprenticed to his father, Jean Baillairgé (1726-1805), a sculptor and carpenter. François apparently studied sculpture under Antoine Jacson and drawing under a certain Nicol, a Swiss engineer and his father's journeyman. In July 1778, at age 19, Baillairgé left for France, where he stayed until August 1781. He received his academic training at the Académie royale de peinture et de sculpture and in the studios of such artists as sculptor Jean-Baptiste Stouf (1742-1826) and painter Simon Julien (1735-1800).

A diary kept by Baillairgé from 1784 to 1800 has made it possible to trace part of the artist's career and output. He produced at least 30 religious paintings around the turn of the century. In one of his first works, *Saint Peter and Saint Paul* (1785), the artist presented a personal composition. On September 20, 1785, the *Quebec Gazette* quoted Baillairgé as follows: "Being deprived in this country of the lessons needed to guide me in this art, I hope that the criticism and advice of experts will lead me to the perfection to which I aspire." (*Translation*) The series of eight canvases he painted for the church of Sainte-Famille on île d'Orléans between 1802 and 1805 was certainly the largest commission he received from a parish church. According to his diary, François Baillairgé did portraits in paint, pastel and miniature. He also painted theatre sets, did some restoration work and taught drawing. Jean-Joseph Girouard and Joseph Bouchette were among his students.

Baillairgé was more successful as a sculptor than as a painter. Among other works, we owe him the interior decoration of the churches of Islet (1782-1787), Notre-Dame de Québec (1787-1793), Baie-Saint-Paul, and Saint-Joachim (ca. 1816-1826). His father assisted him for the first two churches, while his son took over for the last two. He began carving the altarpiece in the church of Baie-Saint-Paul in 1818. As demonstrated by the plaster vault of Notre-Dame de Québec, Baillairgé instilled a sense of harmony into his architectural works and even made a number of formal or technical innovations.

François Baillairgé was an active man who took an interest in music, science and history. A friend of Father Jérôme Demers, he was also in fairly close contact with other artists such as Louis Dulongpré and William Berczy as well as with goldsmiths François Ranvoyzé (1739-1819) and Laurent Amiot (1764-1839). Baillairgé died in Quebec City on September 15, 1830.

FRANÇOIS
BAILLAIRGÉ
1759-1830

Main sources

KAREL, NOPPEN AND THIBAULT 1975; KAREL, NOPPEN AND PARADIS 1981; FRANÇOIS BAILLAIRGÉ 1985.

VAG, AGNS, MMFA

1.
Apollo Belvedere, c. 1778-1781
Red chalk and graphite on paper, 60.9 × 45.9 cm

Provenance
Mrs. Marie-Ange D. Lamy, Trois-Rivières; acquired by the National Gallery of Canada, Ottawa, 1976.

Exhibition
Montreal 1985, No. 21r.

Bibliography
FRANÇOIS BAILLAIRGÉ 1985, pp. 25, 34 and 35 (Repr.); *HILL AND LANDRY 1988,* p. 31 (Repr.).

Collection
National Gallery of Canada, Ottawa (18704)

F RANÇOIS BAILLAIRGÉ was already familiar with the rudiments of sculpture when he arrived in Paris in September 1778. In going to France he hoped to obtain more systematic instruction from masters, using recognized models. Baillairgé studied several subjects at the same time: drawing and its corollaries anatomy and perspective, as well as sculpture and painting.

The two drawings shown here attest to the similarity between the teaching methods of the Académie royale de peinture et de sculpture, where Baillairgé en-

roled in 1779, and of the private studio of his sculpture teacher, Jean-Baptiste Stouf. Drawing from sculpture was an essential part of the artist's training: immobile forms allowed him to practice rendering volumes on paper. By studying the techniques of other artists, whose works were presented as models, Baillairgé learned about different ways of treating the human body. Owing to the choice and repetition of subjects, a particular tradition was established and maintained.

The *Apollo Belvedere* is so named on account of its location in the Belvedere court of the Vatican, where it was placed by Jules II in 1511, shortly after its discovery. This 2nd century Roman sculpture was probably based on a Greek original from the 4th century BC. Restoration work replaced its missing left forearm and right hand. It was this version of the statue that was known until the 20th century.[1] François I commissioned a copy of the work in 1540 for Fontainebleau. The Académie royale de peinture et de sculpture had a copy that provided the inspiration for a number of exercises.[2] The fact that the sculpture was a Roman copy in no way diminished its popularity, as shown by the many engravings and reproductions of the statue in different materials. The sculpture was considered a masterpiece from antiquity and it was appropriate that it depict the sun god in idealized forms.

Baillairgé sketched the sculpture from an angle that captured its dynamic nature: the leg movement, turned head, and position of the hand, which has just released an arrow, breathe life into the drawing. The apprentice sculptor's attention was drawn to elements with the most relief: the tree trunk, drapery and hair. On the other hand, the figure's smooth muscles have been rendered with almost no volume. The unbroken, uniform line around the figure hardens the contours and contrasts with the drapery's more supple texture. The parallel lines shading the background are designed to achieve an equilibrium between the various forms and stabilize the model in the upper middle part of the composition. By omitting the genital organs covered by the customary fig leaf, the figure has been emasculated. Combining superfluousness with inutility, this part of the drawing seems to have been prudishly altered.

Students prepared to draw live models by exploring sculpture's rich vocabulary. Their academic training was designed to teach them to render the wide range of nonverbal signals expressed by the human body and, in particular, to portray the character as it is revealed by facial expressions. It is not surprising, therefore,

MQ, NGC

Fig. 2A.
Jean-Baptiste Stouf,
L'Affliction, 1814;
marble.
Musée d'Orsay, Paris
(RF1695).

2.
Bust of a Young Girl in Three-Quarters View, c. 1778-1781

After Jean-Baptiste Stouf
Red chalk and traces of graphite on paper, 46 × 31.4 cm (irregular dimensions)

Provenance
Descendants of the artist; Charles Baillairgé, Quebec City; Louis de Gonzague Baillairgé, Quebec City; Mrs. Victor Baillairgé, Trois-Rivières; acquired by the Musée du Québec, Quebec City, 1975.
Exhibitions
Quebec City 1975, No. 7; Montreal 1985, No. 29r.
Bibliography
KAREL, NOPPEN AND THIBAULT 1975, p. 16, No. 7 (Repr.); *Au fil des événements,* March 14, 1975 (Repr.); PARADIS 1979, p. 492 (Repr.); FRANÇOIS BAILLAIRGÉ 1985, pp. 28 and 41, No. 29r (Repr.); BÉLAND AND BOURASSA 1990, pp. 5, 8 and 18 (Repr.).
Collection
Musée du Québec, Quebec City (75.253)

that Baillairgé drew this ***Bust of A Young Girl in Three-Quarters View*** after a work by Jean-Baptiste Stouf. The arm, which is cut off below the shoulder, indicates that the source work was a sculpture. Stouf ex-

hibited *Jeune Fille affligée* at the Salon of 1785 (No. 244).[3] Although this sculpture has not been located, its title corresponds to the subject of Baillairgé's drawing. The dramatic facial expression, tear on the cheek, tormented eyes, partly open mouth, dishevelled hair, and raised shoulder convey the young girl's despair. Using softer lines, parallel strokes and crosshatching in combination with stumping, Baillairgé has rendered the model with great sensitivity.

These drawings reveal that Baillairgé's training exposed him not only to classical subjects but also to contemporary sculpture. Moreover, based on the drawings he brought back with him from Paris, he seems to have studied the sculptors of the French school in depth: Pierre Puget (1620-1694), Antoine Coysevox (1640-1721), Edme Bouchardon (1698-1762) and Jean-Antoine Houdon (1741-1828).[4]

L.L.

Notes
1. Francis Haskell and Nicholas Penny, *Taste and the Antique* (New Haven: Yale University Press, 1981), pp. 148-151.
2. KAREL 1974, pp. 165 and 523, Fig. 14. Baillairgé also drew from the sculpture *Capitoline Antinoüs;* see catalogue entries 22 and 23 by Jean-Pierre Duchesne in FRANÇOIS BAILLAIRGÉ 1985, pp. 36-37.
3. As shown by several other sculptures presented at the various Salons, Stouf drew inspiration from this theme. In 1785 he exhibited *Jeune Fille affligée* (No. 244), whose date of production is closest to the time of Baillairgé's stay in Paris. *Jeune Fille pleurant* was presented in 1789 (No. 254) and the marble *La Tristesse* in 1791 (No. 452). *L'Affliction,* exhibited at the 1814 Salon (No. 1141), is currently in the Musée d'Orsay collection (Fig. 2A). An analysis of this marble reveals that Stouf's model resembled the sculpture drawn by Baillairgé around 1780. Perhaps Stouf always depicted the same subject, merely varying it somewhat each time. For example, although the young girl portrayed in *L'Affliction* is wearing a veil, she has the same facial expression as the figure in Baillairgé's drawing. See catalogue entries 29 and 30 by Anne Page in FRANÇOIS BAILLAIRGÉ 1985, pp. 41 and 42.
4. These drawings can be associated with the following works: *Perseus Rescuing Andromeda* (1684, Louvre) by Pierre Puget; *Fame* (1700-1702) by Coysevox; certain parts of *Fountain of the Seasons* (1739-1745), a fountain on Rue de Grenelle in Paris, by Bourchardon; and *L'Écorché* (1767) and *Henri IV trampling on the Hydra of Anarchy* (1780) by Houdon. Another sculpture by Stouf, representing a deer (1778), is also known from a drawing by Baillairgé. See the catalogue entries on these works in FRANÇOIS BAILLAIRGÉ 1985.

MQ, NGC

3.
Academic Study of a Seated Man Depicted in Three-Quarter View from the Back with Head Bent Forward, c. 1778-1781

Red chalk and traces of graphite on paper, 53.7 × 38.6 cm (irregular dimensions)

Provenance
Descendants of the artist; Charles Baillairgé, Quebec City; Louis de Gonzague Baillairgé, Quebec City; Mrs. Victor Baillairgé, Trois-Rivières; acquired by the Musée du Québec, Quebec City, 1975.

Exhibitions
Quebec City 1975, No. 13; Montreal 1985, No. 33.

Bibliography
KAREL, NOPPEN AND THIBAULT 1975, p. 18, No. 13 (Repr.); *FRANÇOIS BAILLAIRGÉ 1985*, pp. 29 and 43-44, No. 33 (Repr.); *BÉLAND AND BOURASSA 1990*, p. 4 (Repr.).

Collection
Musée du Québec, Quebec City (75.238)

ACCORDING TO THE METHODS followed by the academy, students were taught to draw from live models only in the last stages of their drawing course. Prior to this, they drew from two-dimensional models (prints and drawings) and then from sculpture (Cat. 1 and 2) to assimilate basic techniques and the formal vocabulary of classical poses and models. For both historical and moral reasons, the male model was the preferred subject of study. Drawing from live models and applying the canon of masculine proportions were essential to training artists during the Renaissance. The Royal Academy, which had the right to use nude models, made this practice a distinctive part of its instruction. Metonymy came into play and the term *académie*, or nude, came to be associated with the institution or place where this type of drawing was practised.[1] Prior to the Revolution, the refusal to use female models was based not only on tradition but also on the fear that a woman's presence could lead to debauchery.

The main role of the teacher in charge of drawing classes was to assign a pose to the model. The repertoire of forms offered to students varied not only with the teacher's interests and preferences,[2] but also with the position of the artist in relation to the model. The two drawings shown here, which along with five other nudes were in the portfolio that François Baillairgé brought back after studying in Paris, raise several questions about his training and level of instruction. It is very possible that they were done in a studio, probably that of his private sculpture teacher Jean-Baptiste Stouf, rather than in the school of the academy. The proximity of the model and the angle from which it was drawn indicate that the artist was on approximately the same level as the subject: slightly lower in the case of **Academic Study of a Seated Man** and slightly higher in that of **Academic Study of a Man Lying on the Right Side.** It would have been impossible for Baillairgé to occupy such a position in relation to the model in the drawing classes of the academy, where places were assigned on the basis of certain privileges and the quality of a student's work, judged regularly through competitions.[3]

The composition of **Academic Study of a Seated Man** is quite unusual. The angle of the artist in relation to the model is not very advantageous and has complicated the task of articulating the various parts of the body, which are viewed asymmetrically. The movement from the shoulders to the left thigh is unified even though the muscles have been timidly rendered. The artist has had problems,

4.   VAG, AGNS, MMFA

Academic Study of a Man Lying on the Right Side with Left Arm Stretched Out, c. 1778-1781

Red chalk and traces of graphite highlighted with white chalk on paper, 44.8 × 58.6 cm (irregular dimensions)

Provenance
Descendants of the artist; Charles Baillairgé, Quebec City; Louis de Gonzague Baillairgé, Quebec City; Mrs. Victor Baillairgé, Trois-Rivières; acquired by the Musée du Québec, Quebec City, 1975.

Exhibitions
Quebec City 1975, No. 14; Montreal 1985, No. 37.

Bibliography
KAREL, NOPPEN AND THIBAULT 1975, p. 18, No. 14 (Repr.); DE ROUSSAN 1982, p. 30 (Repr.); *FRANÇOIS BAILLAIRGÉ 1985*, pp. 30 and 45-46, No. 37 (Repr.).

Collection
Musée du Québec, Quebec City (75.239)

The pose of the figure in *Academic Study of a Man Lying on the Right Side* is also complicated. Certain weaknesses can be detected in the way the body has been twisted to face the floor and in the position of the legs lying on their side. Since the head is partially hidden by the figure's right arm, the artist did not have to draw the entire face. Once again, Baillairgé has had problems with the composition. In addition, owing to lack of space, he has only sketched the hands and feet. The artist has paid considerable attention to lighting, accentuating areas of light and dark. Relatively dense parallel lines have been used to suggest the underlying bone and muscle. The outline is sensitive, varying in strength and thickness. The pose is reminiscent of *The Death of Abel* (Fig. 4A), a marble exhibited by Jean-Baptiste Stouf at the Salon of 1785 (No. 243) and presented to the academy as a diploma piece. It is not known whether Baillairgé did this drawing from a live model or from a drawing by his teacher.

When Baillairgé returned to Quebec City in late summer 1781, after studying and working in Paris for over three years, he in turn began to teach drawing. There is no proof, however, that these drawings were used as models by his students, except for the traces of wear attesting to considerable handling. Perhaps they were used to show the extent of his skills to more advanced students, since Baillairgé certainly did not use live models in his classes.

L.L.

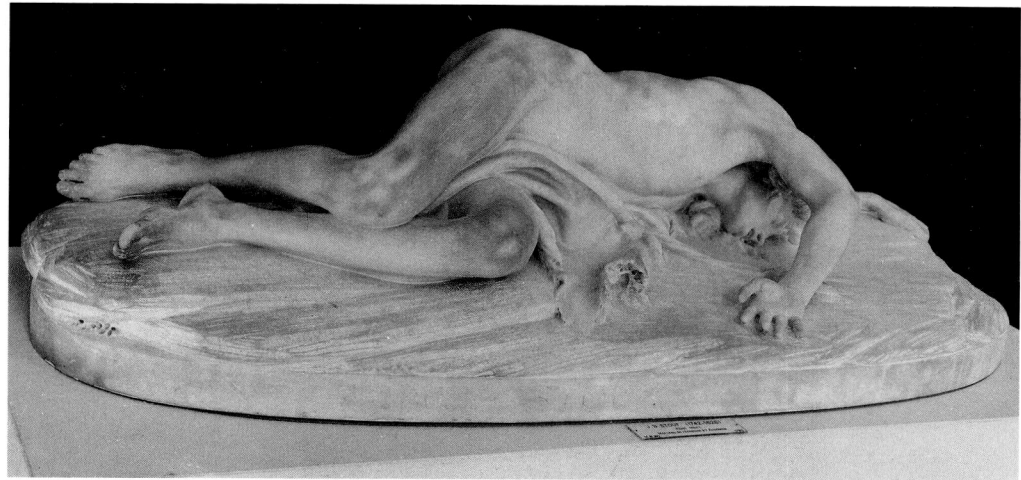

Fig. 4A.
Jean-Baptiste Stouf,
The Death of Abel, 1785;
marble.
Musée d'Orsay, Paris (MN 80).

Notes

1. See Henry James Rubin, *Eighteenth Century French Life Drawing* (Princeton: Princeton University Press, 1974). Members of the academy were allowed to have models pose in their studio for themselves or their students. This practice spread in the 18th century.

2. This is discussed in Chapter 15 of Karel's thesis (KAREL 1974).

3. The four instances where we know the standing Baillairgé achieved in the competition deciding students' place in the classroom indicate that his work was increasingly appreciated as his skills improved: 51st out of 112 in February 1779, 40th out of 112 in September 1779, 36th out of 102 in April 1780, and 28th out of 101 in October 1780. Archives de l'École nationale supérieure des beaux-arts, Paris, Jugement des places.

however, integrating the other parts of the body. The seated figure, with its head bent forward, fills the entire work, thereby emphasizing the gigantic proportions of the model. The distorted long legs and huge torso give an almost unreal appearance to this human figure surmounted by a tuft of hair, while the bench, half of which is missing, makes the work look even more unusual. Finally, the lifeless drapery and overly heavy outline give a static appearance to the model, whose volumes have been evoked by a network of parallel lines and stumping.

MQ, MMFA

5.
View of Paris from François Baillairgé's Room, 1780
Charcoal and graphite on paper, 41 × 24.3 cm

Inscriptions
(l.c., in ink) *fr. Baillairgé a Dessiné cette vue
Perspective en la Ville de Paris en 1780, d'une/des
fenêtres qu'il occupoit en l'aille lateralle a gauche
de la cour de la Maison de M*/Hardelle maître
menuisier; le Coté marque A, est une des fenêtres
de la chambre-/qu'il a occupé ensuitte jusqu'a son
depart pour Quebec, par l'Angleterre en 1781.;* (c.l.,
in ink) *A.*

Watermark
[?] *TINDE*/[?].

Provenance
Descendants of the artist; Charles Baillairgé,
Quebec City; Louis de Gonzague Baillairgé,
Quebec City; Mrs. Victor Baillairgé, Trois-Rivières;
acquired by the Musée du Québec, Quebec City,
1975.

Exhibitions
Quebec City 1975, No. 20; Montreal 1985,
No. 40; Quebec City 1991, No. 1.

Bibliography
KAREL, NOPPEN AND THIBAULT 1975, p. 20, No. 20
(Repr.); *FRANÇOIS BAILLAIRGÉ 1985,* pp. 31 and 47-
48, No. 40 (Repr.); *PORTER AND BÉLISLE 1986,*
p. 167 (Repr.); *MARTIN AND GRANDBOIS 1991,*
pp. 41-43, No. 1 (entry by Denis Martin) (Repr.);
NADEAU 1991, p. 58 (Repr.).

Collection
Musée du Québec, Quebec City (75.237)

I N THIS DRAWING, François Baillairgé attempted to put into practice the principles of perspective learned at the Académie royale de peinture et de sculpture in Paris. By choosing a subject as familiar as the view from his window, he worked on a motif that he could study at leisure while producing a tangible souvenir of his stay in Paris.

In the autobiographical notes he wrote in 1801, Baillairgé gave the following description of his studies abroad:

Left Quebec City on July 26, 1778 when nearly twenty with Serot de Rondeau & his wife, Thérèse Dubeau & Cousin Parant & went to France, where studied drawing, Painting and Sculpture, arrived in Paris on September 19, 1778, at Mr. [in margin: (illegible) Stouf][1] Hout's & the Académie Royalle, taking lessons at the same time, during the last three months of my stay in Paris, with Mr. Julien[2] history painter, worked under Mr. Ruis, another painter, & studied with [word crossed out] the Mr. Julien mentioned above Messrs. Maugendry and a Hunchback were also, etc. took two Anatomy Courses with Mr. Sue[3] and his Son, a Course in Perspective with the Master in Ordinary of the Academy,[4] as a protégé of Mr. Lagrenée the Younger,[5] Painter and Teacher at the Académie Royalle de Peinture & Sculpture; left Paris on the eighth of March seventeen hundred and eighty-one arriving in London on the fourteenth; left London on the sixth of April; arrived in Quebec City on the twenty-fourth of August the same year, after 109 days at sea & in various ports, an absence of three years and twenty-six days from Quebec

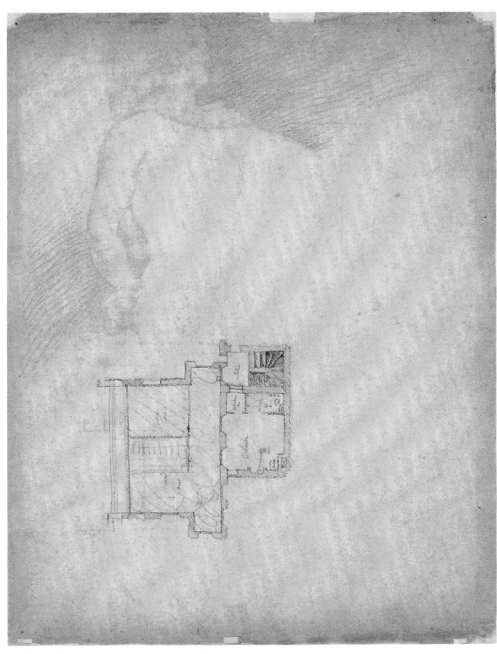

Fig. 5A.
François Baillairgé,
Sketch of François Baillairgé's Room, 1778-1781;
black ink, graphite and red chalk on paper,
60.9 × 45.9 cm.
National Gallery of Canada, Ottawa (18704
back).

City, a stay of two years, five months and seventeen days in Paris, and a stay of twenty-three days in London.[6] (*Translation*)

According to David Karel, "when François studied [perspective] with him [Leclerc], the class used to walk with the master to sites within a short distance of the academy to study perspective motifs."[7] (*Translation*) Baillairgé integrated the principles he had learned into this "Perspective view," (*Translation*) as it is identified in the drawing caption. He pursued his interest in architecture in this work. However, owing mainly to the awkward combination of different vantage points, space has not been treated in a coherent manner. Although he has clearly rendered the general organization of the different buildings, using oblique lines and tones merging into one another, the elements in the lower part of the drawing have not been well integrated into the composition. The effect of depth that Baillairgé wanted to achieve is counteracted by the cobblestones drawn without any perspective and the foreshortening of the planks and boards set out to dry in the carpenter's yard.

This drawing was done from Baillairgé's second apartment on Rue de Sèvres in Paris, where the artist lived with master carpenter Antoine-Louis Hardelle. He had shared the first apartment with master mason Brely.[8] The studio of his sculpture teacher, Jean-Baptiste Stouf, was also on

this street, near the Séminaire des Missions étrangères, where Baillairgé's mentor, Father de Villars, lived.[9] Baillairgé pursued his daily activities within a narrowly defined area, only venturing outside its limits to attend the academy school at the Louvre on the right bank of the Seine. By living with other master craftsmen in the field of construction, Baillairgé remained in a familiar milieu that may have reminded him of his home environment.

A floor plan of the room in which Baillairgé lived appears on the back of the *Apollo Belvedere* drawing (Fig. 5A). It depicts a modest dwelling on the second floor overlooking the courtyard and consisting of a room with two windows separated from the landing by an antechamber. The main room, which was equipped with a stove, opened onto an alcove that was scarcely larger than the bed it contained. The caption indicates that Baillairgé later moved into a room at the back of the house looking out onto the main courtyard.

The artist does not seem to have done this type of drawing when he returned to Quebec City. Although soldiers and amateur artists produced numerous views of the city from streets or windows, Baillairgé did not leave any urban scenes or cityscapes.

L.L.

Notes

1. Jean-Baptiste Stouf (1742-1826), see Cat. 2.

2. Simon Julien (1735-1800) was certified by the academy in 1783.

3. Jean Süe Senior, surgeon and teacher. See Jean Locquin, *La peinture d'histoire en France de 1747 à 1785 (...)* (Paris: Henri Laurens, éditeur, 1912). Rptd. (Paris: Arthena 1978).

4. Leclerc (?-1785).

5. Jean-Jacques Lagrenée (1739-1821). Three works by this artist arrived in Quebec City in 1817 with the first shipment of paintings from Abbé Desjardin's collection. Dating from 1770, they had been executed for the abbey of Montmartre. *The Burying of Christ* and *The Incredulity of Saint Thomas* are in the Musée du Québec collection (provenance: Baie-du-Fèvre); *The Christ and the Samaritain* was destroyed when the chapel in the Séminaire de Québec burned down on January 1, 1888.

6. Handwritten text on a sheet of paper glued to the inside front cover of the Baillairgé family album (MQ). This text originally appeared on the cover of an account book belonging to François Baillairgé.

7. *KAREL, NOPPEN AND THIBAULT 1975*, p. 55. Three preliminary perspective studies of staircases in the Tuileries Gardens bear witness to these teaching practices (MQ). See also *NOPPEN AND GRIGNON 1983*, pp. 64-65 (Repr.).

8. See catalogue entries 21 and 40 by Monique Nadeau-Saumier in *FRANÇOIS BAILLAIRGÉ 1985*, pp. 34-35 and 47-48.

9. In 1780, Baillairgé had the opportunity to assist Stouf in carving sculptures for the Missions étrangères church.

Inscription
(s.d., c.l., pen and black ink) *François Baillairgé/ Invenit & Delinxit/1793.*

Watermark
*J*WHATMAN.

Provenance
Descendants of the artist; Charles Baillairgé, Quebec City; Louis de Gonzague Baillairgé, Quebec City; Mrs. Victor Baillairgé, Trois-Rivières; acquired by the Musée du Québec, Quebec City, 1975.

Exhibition
Quebec City 1975, No. 22.

Bibliography
ANQQ, *Journal de François Baillairgé, 1784-1800,* Fol. 137, 140, 141, 142, 144 and 145 (December 28, 1792, January 10, March 23, April 10, April 19, May 11, May 13, May 15, October 3, October 5, November 4 and November 6, 1793); ANQQ, Fonds Girouard, manuscript of J. J. Girouard, "Famille Baillairgé", 1853, Fol. 10; KAREL, NOPPEN AND THIBAULT 1975, pp. 21, 22 and 25-26, No. 22 (Repr.); DE ROUSSAN 1975, p. 22 (Repr.); PARADIS 1979, pp 428-432, 438-443 (Repr.); BÉLISLE 1982, pp. 5-7 (Repr.); BÉLISLE 1984, pp. 36-37 (Repr.); PORTER AND BÉLISLE 1986, pp. 224, 264, 305-308, 311, 318 and 454-455 (Repr.); DEROME, BOURASSA AND CHAGNON 1988, p. 65; BÉLAND AND BOURASSA 1990, pp. 8 and 22 (Repr.).

Collection
Musée du Québec, Quebec City (75.255)

MQ, NGC

6.
Figure-Head Design for the Ship "Royal Edward" (Starboard Side), 1793
Ink, watercolour and traces of graphite on paper,
39.5 × 53 cm (irregular dimensions)

F RANÇOIS BAILLAIRGÉ was very active in the field of naval sculpture and monopolized this new market during the late 18th century. According to his diary, he worked for the major ship-builders in Quebec City. Through government contracts signed with John Craigie (1757-1813), private secretary to the Lieutenant-Governor and commissioner-general of the British army in Canada, Baillairgé decorated some 20 ships, including six provincial navy vessels.

The artist was awarded a number of commissions,[1] including three important figureheads, when Prince Edward Augustus (1767-1820), future Duke of Kent and Strathearn and father of Queen Victoria, stayed in Quebec City. Edward lived on Rue Saint-Louis, not far from Baillairgé's studio. The Prince had frequent contacts with the artist and seems to have taken a keen interest in his work. In 1792-1793 and 1800, Baillairgé carved three effigies of the Prince, all of which were to be used as figureheads. His diary describes all the stages involved in preparing the statues, from the moment they were commissioned to the time of their delivery.[2]

In late 1792, or more precisely on December 28, Baillairgé received a commission from the colonial government to decorate the King's ship the *Royal Edward*. This 18-cannon schooner was under construction in Saint-Jean-sur-Richelieu, the site of a major shipyard since the American War of Independence. The Prince was to be the main subject of the vessel's ornamentation. Captain Fisher, a royal engineer, provided the sculptor with detailed "drawings and measurements" for the project.

On January 10, 1793, the artist prepared a preliminary clay model of the sculpture "representing Prince Edward with the two provinces of Upper and Lower Canada and their attributes." (*Translation*) As Baillairgé noted on March 23 and April 10, he submitted a first and then a second drawing based on this rough model to John Craigie:

[March 23] delivered the drawing of figures Mr. Cragy requested for the bow of a vessel in Fort Saint jean, for which I claimed the Sum of forty Current Halifax louis d'or: These figures will Represent Prince Edward standing on the bow with the two provinces of Upper and Lower Canada kneeling beside him in the friezes, the rest of which will be filled with trophies.
Wednesday, [April] 10 [...] I did a Second drawing for the Royal Edward which I also submitted to Mr. Cragy who then gave both drawings to the Engineer Capt fisher who approved them except for the trophies he wants Replaced today they were presented to His Royal Highness who also approved them along with the engineer's suggestions, they were immediately given back to me by Mr. Cragy and the engineer who had presented them and they ordered me to make a Model.[3] (*Translation*)

These two drawings correspond to the watercolours in the Musée du Québec collection and come from Baillairgé's portfolio. As mentioned above, they had been returned to the artist after having been approved except for a few minor details.

The preparatory drawings show both sides of the bow of the ship. They are full-length portraits of Edward Augustus in a military uniform with a fur hat and a red cutaway coat with gold epaulettes. This was the uniform of the colonel of the regiment that had accompanied the Prince from Gibraltar to Quebec City, namely the 7th infantry regiment known

MQ, NGC

7.

Figure-Head Design for the Ship "Royal Edward" (Port Side), 1793

Ink, watercolour and traces of graphite on paper,
38.7 × 51.3 cm (irregular dimensions)

Inscriptions
(s.d., c.r., pen and black ink) *françois Baillairgé Invenit, &/Delinxit. 1793 Quebec.;* (b.) sketch of a face.

Provenance
Descendants of the artist; Charles Baillairgé, Quebec City; Louis de Gonzague Baillairgé, Quebec City; Mrs. Victor Baillairgé, Trois-Rivières; acquired by the Musée du Québec, Quebec City, 1975.

Exhibition
Quebec City 1975, No. 23.

Bibliography
ANQQ, *Journal de François Baillairgé, 1784-1800,* Fol. 137, 140, 141, 142, 144 and 145 (December 28, 1792, January 10, March 23, April 10, April 19, May 11, May 13, May 15, October 3, October 5, November 4 and November 6, 1793); ANQQ, Fonds Girouard, manuscript of J. J. Girouard, "Famille Baillairgé", 1853, Fol. 10; KAREL, NOPPEN AND THIBAULT 1975, pp. 25-26, No. 23 (Repr.); PARADIS 1979, pp 428-432, 438-443 (Repr.); BÉLISLE 1982, pp. 5-7 (Repr.); RICHARDSON AND AL. 1984, p. 131 (Repr.); BÉLISLE 1984, pp. 35 and 36-37 (Repr.); PORTER AND BÉLISLE 1986, pp. 224, 264, 305-308, 311, 318 and 454-455 (Repr.); HARE, LAFRANCE AND RUDDEL 1987, p. 141 (Repr.); DEROME, BOURASSA AND CHAGNON 1988, p. 65; BÉLAND AND BOURASSA 1990, p. 22.

Collection
Musée du Québec, Quebec City (75.256)

as the "Royal Rifles." Standing with his right foot on the scroll at the tip of the bow, the military officer is about to unsheathe his sword with his right hand. This full-length portrait of the Prince was probably executed after an engraving or a drawing.

The Duke of Kent is accompanied by two kneeling female figures looking up at him from the trail boards between the cheeks. These allegorical figures represent Upper Canada, on the starboard side, and Lower Canada, on the port side. These two provinces had just been created by the Constitutional Act, sanctioned on June 10, 1791 and brought into force on December 26. The reverential, and even submissive, attitude of the two provinces toward the British Crown is evoked by the position of the two figures, which are less upright than the Prince located at the tip of the triangle formed by the bow. Upper Canada is personified by an Amerindian with long braided hair, wearing a traditional dress, moccasins and a bracelet. Lower Canada is symbolized by a barefooted woman in a pale blue dress modelled on the robes of classical antiquity and

possibly intended to evoke France. Wearing crowns of leaves and small fruit, the two allegorical figures are followed by a beaver, the newly adopted symbol of Canada, and by many trophies of war: a red flag and a cannon on a four-wheeled carriage on the starboard side, and a white flag, drum, cymbals, horn, sword and musket on the port side.

Jean Bélisle advanced the following interpretation of Baillairgé's design. First published in the magazine *Neptunia* (1984), it was later included in a study he prepared with John R. Porter, *La sculpture ancienne au Québec* (1986):

The relative complexity of the ornamentation between the cheeks reflects the designers' desire to deliver a message based on the prevailing political context [...] the Constitutional Act passed in London divided the old British colony into two separate provinces: Lower Canada, with a predominantly Francophone population, and Upper Canada, which was mainly English-speaking. The Act of 1791 also created the first elected House of Assembly.

To fully understand the iconography of the *Royal Edward,* it should also be mentioned that the densely populated United States had won their independence in 1783 and elected their

first president in 1789. In this context, the presence of a member of the British royal family in Quebec City in 1791 was tangible evidence of England's interest in its North American colony. Very popular with Francophones, Prince Edward was perceived as the living symbol of the union of Canada's two linguistic communities. Portrayed by Baillairgé in the process of unsheathing his sword, the Crown's representative appears to be the defender of the colony's two provinces. Since the *Royal Edward* was to navigate Lake Champlain near the American border, we are justified in thinking that the symbolic message conveyed by the bow of the ship was addressed not only to Canadians but also to the citizens of the United States. While reflecting the indestructible union of Upper and Lower Canada, Baillairgé's design was probably also intended to make it clear that London had no intention of tolerating any attempt by the Americans to expand their territory northward. (*Translation*)

Baillairgé's two drawings attest to his remarkable ability to render three-dimensional, decorative designs on paper. They make it possible to visualize the structure of the vessel's bow and the volume of the statues and other carved ornaments. The watercolours offer a foretaste of the rich polychromy, highlighted with gold, that was to cover the sculpture as a whole. The drawings bear the stamp of an artist trained according to academic methods where the study of anatomy and perspective and, above all, drawing formed the very basis of painting and sculpture.

M.B.

Notes

1. For further reading on Prince Edward, see W. S. MacNutt, DCB, Vol. V (1983), pp. 325-326. As revealed by his diary, Baillairgé benefited greatly as a painter and sculptor from Edward Augustus' stay in Quebec City. On November 11, 1791, he received a commission "from Mr. Arner Captain Talbot's chief steward for a transparency of a crown and Prince Edward's monogram with "Vivat!" underneath to be illuminated on the 2nd of this month." (*Translation*) The following January 17, shortly after having noted in his diary that the Act creating the provinces of Upper and Lower Canada had come into effect, Baillairgé gave a detailed description of a special commission related to the constitutional event, consisting of four transparent allegorical paintings commissioned for the Château Saint-Louis by a certain Langlois, chef of General Clarke. The theme of these works was intended to mark the coming into force of the new constitution and to pay tribute to the Governor-General and the Prince. From May 1792 to February 1794, the artist received a number of payments for various purchases and work related to the decoration and finishing of vehicles belonging to His Royal Highness, in particular, two carioles (April 24), two cabriolets (May 3 and 7), one phaeton (May 25) and various other carriages including one by the name of "Guigne" (July 2, August 9 and February 17).

2. In addition to this project, the sculptor was also commissioned in 1792 to decorate the *Prince Edward*, a merchant vessel built in Saint-Roch by John Black. This large contract included the carving of a figurehead of the Duke of Kent, holding a sword; two trophies on the ship's bow; two quarter galleries or badges; and two catheads. Between January 7 and September 11, 18 diary mentions reported on various stages of the work. May 8, Baillairgé mentioned the execution of a "drawing." On February 3, 1800, John Craigie asked Baillairgé to do sketches for a statue of His Royal Highness in armour, accompanied by Glory. Five days later, the sculptor began carving this new figurehead after a drawing approved by His Excellency Peter Hunter (1746-1805), commanding officer of the armed forces of Upper and Lower Canada and lieutenant-governor of Upper Canada.

3. On April 19, Baillairgé purchased two pounds of yellow wax and made a final wooden and wax model of the friezes and the group of figures. He finished the model on May 11. Two days later, Craigie authorized him to select the pieces of wood needed to sculpt the figures from the King's woodyard. The same day the sculptor paid to have the pieces sawn and delivered to his studio. He paid a certain Cocherie and his son on May 15 for rough-hewing a statue of the Prince (2 days) and again on June 22 for giving the preliminary shape to another figure and some drums (2 days). On August 6, he bought two packets of gold sheets for gilding the main figure. Less than two months later, on October 3, Baillairgé wrote in his diary that, after having worked for 105 days, supplied gold, wax, wood, oil, colour and varnish, paid his assistants' salaries, and covered the cost of transporting the wood, he had finished carving, painting and gilding the group of figures. The artist immediately informed Craigie that the work was complete and ready to be delivered to the shipyards. On November 2, the sculptures were packed in four crates and, four days later, shipped to Saint-Jean on Lake Champlain. See the complete transcript of Baillairgé's diary entries on the *Royal Edward* in KAREL, NOPPEN AND THIBAULT 1975, pp. 25-26 and in PORTER AND BÉLISLE 1986, pp. 454-455. Notary Jean-Joseph Girouard, a nephew of the artist, mentioned this figurehead in a handwritten text: "I remember having seen, as a child, the statue of Prince Edward with two Glories at his feet for the bow of a ship, and I believe that the wax model is still in the possession of his son." (*Translation*)

VAG, AGNS, MMFA

8.
Figure-Head Design for the "Earl of Moira", 1803
Grey wash, ink and graphite on paper, 25.8 × 40.3 cm

Inscriptions
(u.r, in pen and brown ink) *No. 1/This is a Sketch of a Figure by Mᴱ.Baillarge/that may be placed on the vessel following the/dimensions as given by Capᵗ Steel –;* (u.r.,in graphite) *89a;* (l.c., in pen and black ink) scale in feet (from 0 to 10) and inches (0, 3, 6, 9, 12); (b.,r., in pen and brown ink) *In Mr. Craigue's 24ᵗ Oct 1803 –;* (b.,u.c., in graphite) *90.*

Provenance
Transferred from the Manuscript Division to the Picture Division; Public Archives of Canada, Ottawa, 1982.

Exhibitions
Quebec City 1975 No. 24; Saint-Lambert 1982.

Bibliography
NAC, Manuscript Division, RG 8, series C, "British Military and Naval Records", Vol. DCCXXVI, pp. 87-88, letter from John Craigie to James Green, October 24, 1803; *KAREL, NOPPEN AND THIBAULT 1975*, p. 26, No. 24 (Repr.); *BÉLISLE 1982*, p. 7; *BÉLISLE 1984*, pp. 32 and 38-40 (Repr.); *PORTER AND BÉLISLE 1986*, pp. 225-226 and 307-308 (Repr.).

Collection
National Archives of Canada, Ottawa (1983-10-4 back)

Fig. 8A. François Baillairgé,
Study for the Figure-Head Design for the "Earl of Moira", 1803
(reverse side of *Design No. 1,* right half of the sheet); sepia wash on paper, 25.8 × 40.3 cm. National Archives of Canada, Ottawa (C-15228).

AS DEMONSTRATED by John R. Porter and Jean Bélisle in *La sculpture ancienne au Québec* (1986), the preparatory work involved in sculpting a figurehead was essential and fairly complex. As in the case of the *Royal Edward* figurehead (Cat. 6 and 7), this stage could involve making watercolour drawings, rough clay models, and wooden and wax maquettes. The drawings submitted for approval were sometimes subject to fairly major changes that could modify the original design. Figureheads for government-built military vessels were usually based on iconographic models that were as strict as they were limiting; the sculptor merely executed the design prescribed by the client. Although the iconography of the *Earl of Moira* figurehead was much simpler than that of the *Royal Edward,* it nonetheless reveals the importance of how the subject was represented. Baillairgé even

submitted two different proposals for the design of this figurehead, which he drew in 1803.

On December 31, 1802, the ship-builder Alex Munn submitted the plans for a vessel to Commissioner-General John Craigie who in turn presented them to a certain Captain Steel. The 90-ton military vessel was to be built in Kingston, located at the eastern end of Lake Ontario and, like Saint-Jean-sur-Richelieu, the site of a major shipyard. Over eight months later, on September 9, 1803, Steel gave Baillairgé a naive sketch showing the general appearance of the ship's bow as well as the size and colour of the various ornaments. In October, Baillairgé did a life study showing the general outlines of the model (Fig. 8A). He then did a wash drawing on the back of the same sheet of paper, showing a preliminary proposal in which the figure was located at the bow of the

ship. A comparison of the two drawings reveals that the artist made the figure lean much further forward in the wash drawing than in the original sketch. In addition, the figure followed the curved line of the stem, and thereby adopted the general shape of the cutwater. The sculpture was so well integrated that it seemed to be part of the ship's structure, to the detriment of the subject portrayed. This probably explains why Captain Robe gave Baillairgé another preliminary sketch of both the starboard and port sides which straightened the figure out slightly and thereby made it stand out from the bow (Fig. 8B). Based on this drawing, the sculptor submitted a final proposal in the form of a watercolour, which seems to have been approved despite the fact that it involved minor changes to the ship's construction. Compared with the figure in Robe's drawing, the one proposed by Baillairgé still leans further forward so

Fig. 8B. Captain William Robe,
Figure-Head Design for the "Earl of Moira"
(port-side), 1803;
ink and watercolour on paper.
National Archives of Canada, Ottawa
(C-15229).

as to retain the general movement of the personage portrayed.

In a letter accompanying the three drawings, dated October 24, 1803 and addressed to Major James Green (1751-1835), military secretary to Lord Dorchester, John Craigie described the various stages in designing the figurehead and explained the reasons for the changes made in the three consecutive proposals:

I had the honour to write to you on the 6th and 17th instant. I have now to acknowledge the receipt of your letters of the 19th 22nd 26th 28th 29th and 30th ult

In compliance with the Generals desire signified in your letter of the 26th ult° I have endeavoured to obtain information in respect to a suitable figure Head for the Earl of Moira and have now the honour to inclose three Sketches which I request you will lay before the General The First n 1 is a sketch by Mr Baillairgé sculptor here to be placed so as to answer the dimensions given by Capt Steel. It being however thought that a Figure so placed would not in execution be found correct and suitable to the position a General Officer ought to have Capt Robe undertook to give the out-

lines of a Figure to be differently placed and in our idea more consistent with propriety this is N° 2 and from this outline Mr Baillairgé has proposed a Plan N° 3, that may be executed conformable to the rules of sculpture, but if this is adopted an alteration will be necessary in the *cutwater* which is described in the Plan, and may be made, it is judged, without injury to the appearance of the vessel.

I have no doubt from past experience that Mr Baillairgé will be able with Capt Robe's assistance to execute such a figure as may be satisfactory to the General—The Price would be from Twenty five to Thirty Guineas. I would be necessary Mr Baillairgé should receive his order early in January to be able to compleat the figure so as to be sent here on the first opening of the communication—perhaps by having them sooner, it might be sent up on the winter roads. I shall endeavour in the meantime to procure a likeness of the Earl of Moira—

N.B. If the Plans are to be worked upon they must be sent back.

Plan No. 3 therefore marked the beginning of the work and served as a guide for the sculptor. The actual carving

of the figure was done in January 1804 so that it could be transported easily to Kingston by the winter road. The sculpture was probably mounted on the ship shortly before the vessel was launched the following spring.

As shown by Craigie's letter, the figurehead, which was the most elaborate of the ship's sculpted ornaments, occupied a prominent position below the bowsprit, where the main structural lines of the vessel converged. The silhouette and inclined position of the figure had to be well integrated with the structure of the ship while breathing life into the personage portrayed. Above all, the sculpture of the *Earl of Moira* was intended to show the subject off to advantage by providing a faithful portrait of the Earl rather than merely adding another decorative element to the ship. First Marquess of Hastings and second Earl of Moira, the Irishman Francis Rawdon (1754-1826) took part in almost all the battles of the American War of Independence. After returning to England,

9.
Figure-Head Design for the "Earl of Moira", 1803
Watercolour, pen and black ink with traces of graphite on paper, 26 × 40.2 cm

he sat in the Irish House of Commons and was promoted to various ranks in the army, including that of general in 1803, the year the figurehead was carved.[1]

In the sketch submitted to Baillairgé by Captain Steel, the Earl of Moira brandished a sword in his right hand while holding a document in the other, probably in support of a treaty or cause. The rolled parchment evokes one of the famous speeches delivered by the Earl in the House of Lords in London. A half-length portrait of a figure blowing a horn or a trumpet at his feet probably represents Glory and highlights Rawdon's military exploits. Various other motifs, in particular two flags, a small cannon and a horn of plenty, symbolize the benefits derived from the actions of this soldier and politician. In his first proposal, Baillairgé eliminated the Glory and the various ornaments in the trail boards. In addition, with regard to the main figure, he did away with the general's hat, placed his left hand on the handle of the sword resting in its sheath, and gave prominence to the document in his right hand. To gain his client's approval for the final proposal, Baillairgé made some minor changes: he portrayed the officer wearing a cocked hat with a feather and moved the sword and left hand further back, placing the hand on the figure's hip. The artist added a special touch to the final proposal by setting the figurehead against a mountainous landscape in the background.

M.B.

Note

1. Leslie Stephen and Sidney Lee, eds., "Hastings, Francis Rawdon," *Dictionary of National Biography 9* (London: Oxford University Press, 1917), p. 117.

Inscriptions
(u.r., in pen and brown ink) *No. 3./This is a figure proposed by Mr Baillargé on the outlines proposed by/cap^n Robe's sketch –;* (u.r., in graphite) *89;* (l.c., in pen and brown ink) scale in feet (from 0 to 9) and in inches (0, 3, 6, 9, 12); (b.,r., vertically, in pen and brown ink) *In Mr Craigue's 24' Oct 1803.*

Provenance
Transferred from the Manuscript Division to the Picture Division; Public Archives of Canada, Ottawa, 1982.

Exhibitions
Quebec City 1975, No. 25; Saint-Lambert 1982.

Bibliography
NAC, Manuscript Division, RG 8, series C, "British Military and Naval Records", Vol. DCCXXVI, pp. 87-88, letter from John Craigie to James Green, October 24,1803; KAREL, NOPPEN AND THIBAULT 1975, p. 26, No. 25 (Repr.); BÉLISLE 1982, p. 7; BÉLISLE 1984, pp. 38-40 (Repr.); PORTER AND BÉLISLE 1986, pp. 225-226, 307-308 and 386, No. 18 (Repr.).

Collection
National Archives of Canada, Ottawa (1983-10-3)

10.
The Resurrection, c. 1804
After Antoine Coypel
Ink and watercolour on paper, 31.8 × 26 cm (irregular dimensions)

Inscriptions
(f., in ink on the four sides) figures from 1 to 14 and 1 to 17 for the scale; (b.,l.,vertically, in pen and black ink) *J'ai exécuté Ce Tableau pour le Cœur de l'église de la paroisse de la Sᵉ. Famille en l'isle d'orléans, en Septembre/et Octobre 1804, L'aurore a été fait de laque et de blanc rompue de Jone, et au dessus, j'ai ajouté du bleu et dimin [...]/laque; puis de jone, et augmenté de blanc. La gloire de blanc, de jone, et de vermillon, puis diminuée de rouge, se terminant avec un peu de bl [...]/un gris sanguin, retouché ca et la de jonatre. Les bordures des nuées de blanc et de jone seulement, puis avec un peu de bleu et l [...]/et ainsi continuant a les ombrer et ajoutant du jone et du rouge plus brun, et les terminant de roux gris bleuatre ou jonatre c. les bor [...]/extérieurs ou inf [t?]érieurs. Ce qui a produit des nuances très douces et très légèrres.*

Provenance
Descendants of the artist; Charles Baillairgé, Quebec City; Louis de Gonzague Baillairgé, Quebec City; Noémie Baillairgé, Quebec City; acquired by the Musée de la Province de Québec, Quebec City, 1959.

Exhibition
Quebec City 1975, No. 31.

Bibliography
MORISSET 1960/1, p. 60; KAREL, NOPPEN AND THIBAULT 1975, p. 29, No. 31 (Repr.); HARPER 1966, p. 64 (Repr.); *Nos racines,* No. 45 (1979), p. 888 (Repr.); PARADIS 1979, pp 299-300 (Repr.); KAREL, NOPPEN AND PARADIS 1987, p. 28; BÉLAND AND BOURASSA 1990, pp. 6, 8 and 28 (Repr.).

Collection
Musée du Québec, Quebec City (59.77)

A CCORDING TO THE diary kept by Baillairgé from 1784 to 1800 and his various extant works, he did many religious paintings for parishes on the outskirts of Quebec City. The Musée du Québec's prints and drawings collection includes three squared-off watercolours from the Baillairgé family album, acquired in 1959, that not only shed light on how the artist worked but also on the tradition of borrowing and copying from which his pictorial practices derived. The three studies shown here are ***The Resurrection,*** done in preparation for a canvas to be hung in the choir of the church of Sainte-Famille on île d'Orléans (Fig. 10A), ***The Guardian Angel,*** and *The Repentance of Saint Peter* (Fig. 10-11A).[1]

Of the three watercolours in the Musée du Québec collection, ***The Resurrection*** is the only work that can be dated precisely, owing to a long inscription on the back of the painting. This watercolour was part of a much larger series of eight works commissioned for the church of Sainte-Famille on île d'Orléans and executed between 1802 and 1805. The series included *The Martyrdom of Sainte Thècle, Christ on the Cross, The Healing of a Crippled by the Apostles Peter and John, Saint Francis Xavier Preaching,*[2] and two other paintings, *The Guardian Angel* and *Saint Anthony,* sold to the parish church of Saint-François in 1807. Baillairgé's annotations on the colours used in ***The Resurrection*** and the numbering of the lines squaring off and providing a scale for the original watercolour make it possible to better appreciate the care with which the artist elaborated this composition, which has been qualified as "ambitious" in comparison with the other religious paintings attributed to him.

The watercolour ***The Resurrection*** is even more revealing, however, with regard to Baillairgé's ability to copy and transform the iconographical models and themes used in engraving. Both this watercolour and his final work are based on

Fig. 10-11A.
François Baillairgé,
The Repentance of Saint Peter, 1800-1805;
ink and watercolour on paper, 35 × 25.4 cm.
Musée du Québec, Quebec City (59.76).

Fig. 10A.
François Baillairgé,
The Resurrection, 1804;
oil on canvas, 235 × 120 cm.
Fabrique de Sainte-Famille de l'île d'Orléans.

Fig. 10B.
Jean Audran after Antoine Coypel,
The Resurrection of Jesus Christ, c. 1702;
engraving with burin, 66 × 37.5 cm (plate).
Cabinet des estampes de la Bibliothèque
nationale, Paris.

The Resurrection painted by Antoine Coypel (1661-1722) in 1702 for the chapel in Meudon castle. Coypel's work was reproduced the same year as an engraving by Jean Audran (1667-1756); however, the composition of this reproduction was reversed in relation to that of the original painting (Fig. 10B).[3] The composition of Audran's engraving must in turn have been reversed when it was copied during the 18th century, since Baillairgé's watercolour is presented the same way round as the work by Coypel. In Baillairgé's work, however, some of the elements from the engraving have been rearranged and certain details left unfinished. The Roman soldier protecting himself with his shield is no longer in the foreground but behind the entangled figures of the other guardians of the tomb. His left leg is superimposed on that of the figure in the centre of the composition and on the robe of the angel lifting the slab of stone. The round shield is now under the arm of the soldier lying on the ground while his helmet is superimposed on that of the soldier who has fallen down in the left side of the wa-

tercolour and who, in the engraving, rests his head and arm on the chest of his comrade-in-arms. Obviously, Baillairgé wanted to group the various elements in Coypel's original work and Audran's engraving closer together. However, the vigorous composition and openness of Coypel's *The Resurrection* are not reflected very well in the watercolour by the Quebec artist. By lowering the angel in the centre of the composition, Baillairgé diminished the effect of depth created by the wings emerging from the stone slab covering the tomb and by the oblique lines of the angel's body. Certain details in the engraving, such as the figures of Mary and Martha in the background and the shrub clinging to the walls of the tomb, have only been roughly sketched in the watercolour and were completely eliminated in the painting for the church of Sainte-Famille.[4] It is also interesting to note that, in June 1814, the Bishop of Quebec, Monseigneur Joseph-Octave Plessis, ordered that Baillairgé's *Resurrection* and *Christ on the Cross,* located on either side of the high altar in the church of Sainte-Famille, "be removed or covered

immediately with Curtains."[5] (*Translation*) The Bishop no doubt considered it indecent that the artist had represented Christ shielded only by a cloud, particularly in *The Resurrection.* The loincloth hiding the Saviour's nude body seems, moreover, to have been added later, perhaps by Thomas Baillairgé who offered to touch up the "condemned" paintings for the priest of Sainte-Famille free of charge.

Almost invariably, Baillairgé copied or borrowed elements from other works in painting the thirty or so religious compositions attributed to him. His models included famous works of such painters as Domenichino, Rubens, Annibale Carracci,[7] and of engravers like Claude Mellan, as well as certain paintings he may have seen in the religious communities and churches of Quebec City. ***The Guardian Angel,*** in particular, reveals the impact of these various influences on Baillairgé's work. This squared-off sketch was probably done in around 1800-1805 in preparation for another painting for the church of Sainte-Famille on île d'Orléans. It is known that the Sainte-Famille parish church sold two

VAG, AGNS, MMFA

11.
The Guardian Angel, c. 1800-1805
Ink, watercolour and traces of graphite on paper,
29.2 × 25.2 cm (irregular dimensions)

Inscriptions
(f., in ink on the four sides) figures from 1 to 10 and 1 to 11 for the scale; (b., in graphite) sketched version of the child.

Provenance
Descendants of the artist; Charles Baillairgé, Quebec City; Louis de Gonzague Baillairgé, Quebec City; Noémie Baillairgé, Quebec City; acquired by the Musée de la Province de Québec, Quebec City, 1959.

Exhibition
Quebec City 1975, No. 32.

Bibliography
KAREL, NOPPEN AND THIBAULT 1975, pp. 22 and 29, No. 32 (Repr.); *Perspectives,* March 22, 1975, p. 24 (Repr.); MORRIS 1980, p. 2 (Repr.); *Nos racines,* No. 114 (1982), p. 2273 (Repr.); DE ROUSSAN 1982, p. 10 (Repr.); KAREL, NOPPEN AND PARADIS 1987, p. 29; MARTIN 1990, pp. 267-268 (Repr.); BÉLAND AND BOURASSA 1990, p. 28.

Collection
Musée du Québec, Quebec City (59.78)

of Baillairgé's paintings to the parish of Saint-François in 1807, one representing a *Saint Anthony* and the other, a *Guardian Angel*. The watercolour in the Musée du Québec may well have been a preparatory study for the guardian angel painting. This canvas, which has since disappeared, is the only work that Baillairgé painted on this theme, at least according to the documents consulted. The painting still existed in 1814, since it was expressly mentioned in an order issued that year by Monseigneur Signay, calling attention to the "indecency" of the work:

Since the portal statues are unbecoming owing to their State of damage and decay, we recommend that they be repainted. We make the same recommendation with regard to the painting above the Altar of the Blessed Virgin and to that of the guardian Angel, whose portrayal by the artist is indecent.[8] (*Translation*)

It appears, therefore, that François Baillairgé's *Guardian Angel* offended the sensibilities of the Bishop, who judged the work was as sternly as Monseigneur Plessis had *The Resurrection*.

The sources from which Baillairgé borrowed elements for his watercolour *The Guardian Angel* reveal that he adhered to a firmly established iconographical tradition. He was obviously familiar with the painting *The Guardian Angel* (Fig. 11A) in the convent of the Hôtel-Dieu de Québec and drew inspiration from it. This work, which has long been attributed to the painter Michel Dessaillant, was proba-

bly painted in France by an unknown artist at the end of the 17th century and provides an excellent example of the relationship between painting and engraving.[9]

Certain details of François Baillairgé's *Guardian Angel,* whose composition is reversed in relation to that of the painting in the Hôtel-Dieu, suggest that the artist integrated elements from the late 17th-century work: the position of the angel, standing with his legs slightly apart, the design of one of his wings, the general treatment of the clothing, the drapery movement, and even the trees in the background. Baillairgé may also have borrowed the shape of the long cape hanging from the angel's shoulders from an engraving published by Jean Mariette (1660-1742) in Paris after a painting by Carlo Maratta (1625-1713) (Fig. 11B). However, the artist borrowed most of the elements in his watercolour from another work, namely an engraving produced by Jean Couvay (1622-ca. 1675-1680) around 1650-1660 (Fig. 11C) after a painting by Charles Le Brun, *The Guardian Angel Leading a*

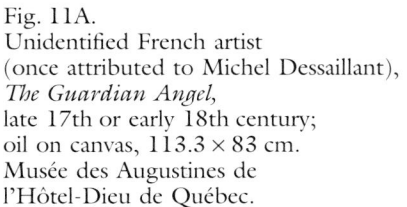

Fig. 11A.
Unidentified French artist
(once attributed to Michel Dessaillant),
The Guardian Angel,
late 17th or early 18th century;
oil on canvas, 113.3 × 83 cm.
Musée des Augustines de
l'Hôtel-Dieu de Québec.

Fig. 11B.
Jean Mariette, publisher, after Carlo Maratta,
The Guardian Angel, c. 1690-1700;
engraving with burin, 26 × 19.2 cm (plate).
Archives du monastère des Augustines de
l'Hôtel-Dieu de Québec.

Fig. 11C.
Jean Couvay,
*The Guardian Angel Leading a
Child by the Hand,* c. 1650-1660;
engraving with burin.
Cabinet des estampes de la
Bibliothèque nationale, Paris.

Child by the Hand, executed for the chapel in the Collège des Grassins in Paris.[10] Baillairgé literally borrowed the personage of young Tobie and the face of the archangel Raphael from this engraving. He also depicted the angel wearing the same type of sandals. However, he reversed the position of his figures' hands in relation to those in the work by Charles Le Brun, on which Couvay's engraving was based. Moreover, he used either the painting in the Hôtel-Dieu or another engraving combining the elements in the works already presented as possible sources to interpret the shape and direction of the angel's wings, his clothing, now covering his chest, and the landscape features in the foreground and background.

    The original iconographic model for all these representations of the guardian angel is still unknown; however, it is plausible that it dates from the second half of the 17th century when devotion to this protective figure grew to a considerable extent. In the artistic world of the 17th and 18th centuries, it is not surprising that

a particular work served as the source of a series of other works or, as in the case of François Baillairgé's **Guardian Angel,** as the final repository of elements borrowed or copied from various works. By using models already in existence for over a century in his watercolours **The Resurrection** and **The Guardian Angel,** Baillairgé, whose academic training was based on copying famous works, adhered to an artistic tradition that was firmly established in Europe, and even in Canada, during the French regime.

D.M.

Notes

1. Originally given an approximate date, the watercolour *The Repentance of Saint Peter* was eventually associated with a painting done by Baillairgé for the church of Saint-Pierre de Montmagny. This hypothesis was presented in the catalogue LE MUSÉE DU QUÉBEC 1983 p. 239, No. 291. The date then assigned to the watercolour was based on excerpts from the artist's

diary, where he stated that he had been commissioned to do a painting of Saint Peter for the high altar of the church of Saint-Pierre de Montmagny. Although he did the painting between 1796 and 1798, he obviously used a different model from that for the watercolour in the Musée du Québec (see Gaétan Chouinard, *Les églises de Saint-Pierre de la Rivière-du-sud* (Quebec City: Ministère des Affaires culturelles, 1978), p. 19, Repr.). Baillairgé may have drawn several preparatory studies before painting the *Repentance of Saint Peter* for Montmagny; however, the way in which the artist squared off the watercolour seems to indicate that he used it to prepare another work, perhaps the eighth picture in the series he painted for the church of Sainte-Famille on île d'Orléans between 1802 and 1805. It should also be mentioned that the Soeurs du Bon-Pasteur de Québec owned a certain number of drawings that had served as studies for religious paintings. In a letter addressed to Supérieure générale, Soeur Saint-Vincent-de-Paul, on September 6, 1884, Louis de Gonzague Baillairgé wrote: "Please accept these few sketches, drawings and plans by Canadian artists François and Thomas Baillairgé for your painting department. These coloured sketches were done 3/4 of a century ago, not surprising that the "[?] colour" has faded completely with time and that the red (vermilion) is still intact thus spoiling the drawings today nearly 70 to 80 years later. These pictures were done in different parishes in and around Quebec City, Montreal and 3 Rivières and give some idea of what painting was like at the time. I would be pleased if these works could be of any use to your skilled artists." (*Translation*) Unfortunately, all these drawings were destroyed when the building housing the painting studio burned down in 1927 (document and information given to Mario Béland by Soeur Yvette Labrecque, s.c.i.m., archivist at the Maison généralice des Soeurs du Bon-Pasteur).

2. See Guy-André Roy and Andrée Ruel, *Le Patrimoine religieux de l'île d'Orléans* (Quebec City: Ministère des Affaires culturelles, 1982), pp. 85-87, Nos. 69-72 (Repr.).

3. See Nicole Garnier, *Antoine Coypel (1661-1722)* (Paris: Arthena, 1989), p. 145, No. 82 (Jean Audran's engraving is reproduced in this work: Fig. 163). For further reading on this engraving, see also Roger-Armand Weigert, *Inventaire du fonds français. Graveurs du XVIIe siècle* (Paris: Bibliothèque nationale, 1938), Vol. I, p.161, No. 43, and Daniel Wildenstein, "L'oeuvre gravé des Coypel-II," *Gazette des beaux-arts,* Vol. LXIV (September 1964), p. 145, No. 24 (Repr.).

4. Antoine Plamondon also used Coypel's *The Resurrection*, or one of its engraved versions, as a model. One of Plamondon's first versions of the *The Resurrection*, dated 1859, is located in the church of Saint-Jean-Chrysostome; contrary to the composition of the two works by François Baillairgé, that of Plamondon's work corresponds exactly to Coypel's composition. A second, undated *Resurrection* (oil on canvas, 145.5 × 97 cm; L-88-003-P), is also in the collection of the Musée d'art de Joliette.

5. Archives de la Fabrique de Sainte-Famille de l'île d'Orléans, *Livres et comptes (1767-1870),* June 18, 1814. This information on the "condemnation" of Baillairgé's *Resurrection* and the "indecency" of the painting *The Guardian Angel* (see above) was kindly provided by Mr. Guy-André Roy.

6. Archives de la Fabrique de Sainte-Famille de l'île d'Orléans, untitled collection of documents (the first document is entitled *Extrait des registres des conseil supérieur*). These documents include *Le Retable* signed around 1820 by Abbé Joseph Gagnon, who wrote the following: "Remember that young Baillairgé offered […] to touch up, free of charge, the paintings condemned by the Bishop, since they had been done by his father." (*Translation*)

7. Archives de la Fabrique de Saint-François de l'île d'Orléans, *Livre de comptes pour l'église de St-François-de-Sales commencé en l'année 1789,* p. 142.

8. On September 9, 1798, Baillairgé entered the following statement in his diary: "Last Saturday, received a print under glass from Sieur Plésis, parish Priest of quebec city; based on a painting by Anibal caracche representing the Blessed Virgin with the body of christ lying on her knee, Accompanied by three other women. to make a large Copy in oil for the notre dâme de pitié Chapel in the parish Church of quebec; for the sum of three hundred francs" (*Translation*) (ANQQ, *Journal de François Baillairgé, 1784-1800,* Fol. 176).

9. An engraving of a guardian angel, published by Jean Mariette after a painting by Carlo Maratta, has already been identified as one of the models that Baillairgé used for this work. This engraving, now in the Musée des Augustines de l'Hôtel-Dieu de Québec hospital, bears certain similarities to the painting. However, the latter's composition as a whole and, in particular, the position and gestures of the angel are too different from those of the engraving to be associated with this work alone. Another source seems more likely, namely an engraving by René Lochon, dated 1672, that appears on the title page of *Chroniques de l'Ordre des Ursulines,* published by Jean Henault in Paris in 1673 and kept at the Archives du monastère des Ursulines de Québec. Since the composition of Lochon's engraving is reversed in relation to that of the painting, it was probably based on the work used as a model for the anonymous painting in the Hôtel-Dieu de Québec hospital. For further reading on the history of this work, see MARTIN 1990, Vol. 1, pp. 265-268.

10. For further reading on this engraving by Jean Couvay and on the painting by Le Brun, see Daniel Wildenstein, "Les oeuvres de Charles Le Brun d'après les gravures de son temps," *Gazette des beaux-arts,* Vol. LXVI (July-August 1965), p. 4. Fig. 13 (Repr.), and Roger-Armand Weigert, *Inventaire du fonds français. Gravures du XVIIᵉ siècle* (Paris: Bibliothèque nationale, 1954), Vol. III, p. 207, No. 43.

F̲RANÇOIS M̲ALEPART DE B̲EAUCOURT was born in La Prairie, Quebec on February 25, 1740. He probably started painting under the tutelage of his father, Paul Malepart de Grand Maison, *dit* Beaucourt (1700-1756), a soldier and himself a painter. In 1773, Beaucourt married Benoîte Camagne, daughter of decorative painter Joseph-Gaëtan Camagne, in Bordeaux. There, he painted some stage sets for the Bordeaux theatre as well as a number of religious works.

After a failed attempt to enter the *Académie de Peinture, Sculpture et Architecture Civile et Navale de Bordeaux* in 1775, Beaucourt was finally accepted into the academy in 1784. Over the next eight years, he apparently visited various cities in Europe before returning to the United States, where he spent the winter of 1792 in Philadelphia. A series of advertisements published in the *Montreal Gazette* beginning June 7, 1792 announced his return to Canada. In them, he described himself as a "Canadian Painter, Member of the *Académie de Peinture, Sculpture and Architecture de Bordeaux,* which is affiliated with the Paris academy," stating that he did oil paintings, history paintings and landscapes; that he was starting to paint stage sets, and was particularly interested in geometric and aerial landscapes, having met with considerable encouragement in several cities in Europe including Paris, St. Petersburg, Nantes, and Bordeaux, where he made a living from such genres; that he was skilled at decorating homes in the most elegant, most fashionable and richest manner, respecting the architecture and bas relief or the most sensible taste; and that he would accept pupils in any form of painting they wished.

While in and around Montreal, Beaucourt painted portraits as well as a number of religious works, of which only a few examples remain; among them, parts of *Marie, Secours des chrétiens* (1793), painted for the church of Saint-Martin, Ile Jésus, and the four canvases from the church of Sainte-Anne-de-Varennes representing the Doctors of the Church. All of Beaucourt's Canadian works date from the last two years of the artist's life. He died in Montreal on June 24, 1794.

FRANÇOIS BEAUCOURT
1740-1794

Main sources
M̲AJOR-F̲RÉGEAU *1979;* M̲AJOR-F̲RÉGEAU *1980.*

12.
Mère Marguerite-Thérèse Lemoine-Despins, 1792
Oil on canvas, 75.7 × 60.2 cm

Inscription
(s.d., l.r.) *F∴ Beaucourt∴ pinxit/A Montreal∴ 1792∴*.

Bibliography
ASGM, G5/11C44, *Mémoires particuliers (Ancien journal)*, No. 1 (1688-1857), 4ᵉ cahier, "Tableaux", p. 296; *Notes biographiques sur nos Sœurs décédées de 1741 à 1848*, "Sœur Marie-Louise Lepellé-Mézière", pp. 33-35; ANNUAIRE *1880*, p. 41; MORISSET *1941/1*, p. 58; MORISSET *1941/3*, p. 897; MORISSET *1950/1*, pp. 26 and 50 (Repr.); MORISSET *1956/1*, p. 23; MORISSET *1960/ 1*, p. 46; MORISSET *1965*, p. 198; TRUDEL, JUNEAU AND MASSEY *1967*, p. 14; HARPER *1970*, p. 21; MAJOR-FRÉGEAU *1979*, pp. 38, 43, 65-66, 76 and 141 (Repr.); MAJOR-FRÉGEAU *1980*, p. 549.

Collection
Musée des Sœurs grises de Montréal (73-A-007)

O N JUNE 6, 1792, following the death of Reverend Mother Thérèse Lemoine-Despins (1722-1792), the Sisters of Charity of the Montreal General Hospital (today the Grey Nuns of Montreal) commissioned François Beaucourt to paint her portrait. Mother Despins was the second superior of her religious community. Beaucourt was probably asked to paint the portrait of *Mère Marguerite d'Youville* (Fig. 12A)[1] at the same time. According to *Mémoires particuliers*, written between 1840-1860, Sister Louise Lepellé-Mézière commissioned the portraits of D'Youville and Despins, as well as that of Father Claude Poncin.[2]

This portrait of Reverend Mother Despins falls within the tradition of post-mortem portraits. A number of portraits dating from the period of early Quebec art were painted posthumously, including those of Catherine de Saint-Augustin, attributed to Father Hugues Pommier (1668); Marie de l'Incarnation, also attributed to Father Pommier (1672); Marguerite Bourgeois, by Pierre Le Ber (1700); Louise Soumande de Saint-Augustin, by Michel Dessaillant (1708); and Marguerite d'Youville, by Philippe Liébert (1771),[3] to name but a few. At the time, it was not uncommon to see devout Catholics refuse to have their portrait painted so as not to succumb to the sin of vanity, but rather to obey the religious principles of abnegation and renunciation.[4] While some artists truly portrayed their subjects as deceased, others brought them back to life, as it were, by portraying them in a traditional pose worthy of their rank.

This was the position adopted by François Beaucourt in his portrait of Mother Despins, shown seated at a table, facing a crucifix, her hands folded over an open book, the background partially hidden behind a drape. At the same time, the portrait betrays the subject's passing: the hard facial features have a ghostly air about them and the hands a cadaverous stiffness. The clothing is less austere, however. The material is vibrant and the lighting on the sleeve suggests volume and movement.

In this particular portrait, death is not expressed solely through the subject herself: various symbols are used to recall her passing or death itself. The crucifix, placed on a diagonal opposite the cross worn by Mother Despins, associates the nun with prayer and a life of submission and contemplation. The skull at the base of the crucifix is a reminder of triumph over death.[5] This image finds its iconographic equivalent in the reliquary or pro-

Fig. 12A.
François Beaucourt,
Mère Marguerite d'Youville, 1792;
oil on canvas, 75.5 × 59.5 cm.
Musée des Sœurs grises de Montréal
(73-A-025).

fessional cross worn by the subject, who is thereby united with Christ in a perfect imitation of his life and virtues. Throughout her life, Mother Despins lived according to the precepts of the Holy Scriptures. While the open book lying on the table could be reminiscent of her devotion, more probably it symbolizes her obedience to the rules set by her predecessor, Mother d'Youville, for the religious community. Mother d'Youville was portrayed by François Beaucourt holding a quill, her hand resting on a similar book. Together, these elements impart a deathly quality on the portrait of Mother Despins, but they also make her a model of religious perfection.

P.B.

Notes

1. There are two existing versions of this oil portrait, painted 50 years after the death of Marguerite d'Youville (née Marie-Marguerite Dufrost de la Jemmerais, 1701-1771) after a watercolour by Philippe Liébert: the one owned by the Grey Nuns of Montreal and the one owned by the Musée du Québec. Although both works have traditionally been attributed to Beaucourt, there are significant differences between the two, both in the treatment of the subject matter and the colour scheme. Given the obvious similarities between the portrait owned by the Grey Nuns and the portrait of Mother Despins, the former could be considered authentic.

An inscription hidden under thick layers of paint (retouching), which recent restoration was unable to eliminate, can be made out at the bottom of the painting. The Musée du Québec portrait, however, although signed "F. Beaucourt pinxit./ A Montréal. 1792", has a greater affinity with portraits from the late 19th century. It is actually a copy most likely executed by Antoine Plamondon around 1873. In June of that same year, "the 6th, Monsieur De Boucherville, who had borrowed the portrait of Mother d'Youville, returned it along with another painted canvas of S. Jean l'Evangéliste, which she [sic] had donated to the community." (*Translation*) The treatment of the subject matter in this painting, signed by Plamondon and dated 1871, resembles that of the Musée du Québec's Mother d'Youville: the preference for warm colours such as red, and the broad brushstrokes used in certain parts are common to both works. According to Gérard Morisset, the portrait of Mother d'Youville was acquired "from the De Boucherville family, who were related to the Dufrosts de la Jemmerais" in 1956. It is possible that someone from the Boucher family, perhaps Georges de Boucherville (1814-1894), asked Plamondon to produce a copy of the painting by Beaucourt and that the artist, as much out of respect for the original work as out of a sense of unconscious imitation, included the signature, which was still visible at the time. See, among other works, *MAJOR-FRÉGEAU 1979*, pp. 65, 74 and 95 (Repr.), and *LE GRAND HÉRITAGE 1984*, p. 116, No. 93 (entry by François-Marc Gagnon). See also the Archives des Soeurs grises de Montréal, Correspondance générale, G5/ 11C21A, document 578, circular from Soeur Stubenger to the nuns in Saint-Boniface, June 15, 1873, and the Archives du Musée du Québec, Préarchivage, Box 141, letter from Gérard Morisset to M.H. Drikwater, July 17, 1964.

2. These memoirs fill several notebooks, with no special order, and contain memories, document transcriptions, customs, etc. dealing with the order's history. They were written by Sister Mc-Mullen, née Élizabeth Forbes (1806-1875), Sister Olier, née Louise Pope (1816-1893) and Sister Sainte-Croix, née Pommainville (1811-1847). The nuns' attribution of the works to François Beaucourt probably came from reading the records of accounts and, more specifically, from an oral tradition that still exists within the community.

3. See, respectively, *MARTIN 1988*, pp. 37-40; *MARTIN 1988*, pp. 41-46; *LE GRAND HÉRITAGE 1984*, p. 117; *Ibid.*, p. 114; *L'Église de Montréal, 1836-1986: aperçus d'hier et d'aujourd'hui* (Montréal: Éditions Fides, 1986) p. 244c.

4. *LE GRAND HÉRITAGE 1984*, pp. 109-112 (entry by Laurier Lacroix).

5. In Christian iconography, a skull at the base of the crucifix may have several meanings. Apart from the fact that Golgotha symbolizes death, it also recalls the Biblical words: "the earth shook, and the rocks were split; the tombs also were opened". Furthermore, legend has it that Adam was buried at Golgotha. His skull thus makes it possible to link the first man to Jesus, this new Adam, uniting the concepts of original sin to that of redemption. See Louis Réau, *Iconographie de l'art chrétien, tome second, Iconographie de la Bible*, Tome II, *Nouveau Testament* (Paris: Presses Universitaires de France, pp. 488-489).

13. (See colour reproduction, p. 81)
Mrs. Daniel Sutherland, née Margaret Robertson, 1792
Oil on canvas, 81.8 × 61.4 cm

Inscription
(s.d., c.r.) *F.: Beaucourt:. pinxit/A Montreal:. 1792.*

Provenance
Descendants of the Sutherland, Hallowell and Wood families; private collection; gift to the Royal Ontario Museum, Toronto, 1988.

Bibliography
ROYAL ONTARIO MUSEUM 1988, p. 10; *ALLODI 1990*, pp. 5-6 (Repr.).

Collection
Royal Ontario Museum, Toronto. Gift of the Jeanne T. Costello and William White foundation (988.96.1)

F RANÇOIS BEAUCOURT's portraits are especially enchanting because of their naive and decorative qualities, and the straightforward statement he makes about his subjects. The portrait of Margaret Sutherland reveals a prosperous and cultivated woman. She was the daughter of Marie-Louise Réaume and Colonel Daniel Robertson of Montreal. In 1781 she married Daniel Sutherland (1756?-1832), a wealthy Montreal merchant. She is depicted in a formalized oval setting—a technique often used by Beaucourt—, dressed in her best muslins and ribbons, and wearing a ring, a wedding band and a pearl necklace. The artist has shown her in a moment of arrested action, pausing in her letter writing to glance somewhat beguilingly at the viewer. Beaucourt's sitters are commonly depicted surrounded by re-vealing attributes from their daily lives: playing cards for men, tea services for women (Cat. 14, 15 and 16), books and crucifixes for members of religious orders (Cat. 12) and for Margaret Sutherland, a quill pen and ormolu-mounted malachite writing set.

Beaucourt was known as a decorative painter for the theatre and private homes; although these works have not survived, and thus cannot be used for illustration, his talent in this area is evident in his portraits. Elements of costume are rendered in enthusiastic detail, including lace borders, embroidered vests, watchfobs and chatelaines, jewelry and ribbons. This decorative tendency is carried through to the face, which is disarmingly made-up, showing a very pale complexion with red lips and cheeks and long dark eyelashes. The large almond-shaped eyes, and the hands carefully finished in brushpoint outline, are found in other Beaucourt portraits. The colour is restrained and theatrically effective: the subject holds the spotlight, dressed in white and pink; the background details are rendered in subdued olive green, with some browns and yellows, while the upholstered chairback is a deep blue-green. X-ray examination shows that some adjustment was made to the costume, eliminating a ruffled over-sleeve; and that the face was first painted without its alluring makeup.

M.A.

14.
**Eustache-Ignace Trottier
dit Desrivières,** 1793
Oil on canvas mounted on fibreboard,
79.5 × 63.8 cm

15.
**Mrs. Eustache-Ignace Trottier
dit Desrivières, née Marguerite-Alexis
Mailhot,** 1793
Oil on canvas mounted on fibreboard,
79.9 × 64.1 cm

Fig. 15A.
François Beaucourt (attr. to),
Portrait of a Woman, c. 1792-1794;
oil on canvas, 66 × 53.5 cm.
Musée du Québec, Quebec City (83.09).

Inscription
(s.d., l.l.) *F.. Beaucourt pinxit/A Montreal 179* [2
or 3].
Provenance
Mrs. Jean-Paul Fortin, Quebec City; acquired by
the Musée de la Province de Québec, Quebec
City, 1956.
Exhibitions
Bordeaux 1962, No. 1; Ottawa 1965, No. 16;
Vancouver 1966, No. 16; Toronto 1966; Quebec
City 1967, No. 4; Sherbrooke 1975, No. 7;
Quebec City 1977, No. 12; Quebec City 1983-
1984, No. 45.
Bibliography
Morisset 1959/1, p. 39; *Morisset 1960/1,* pp. 32g
and 57-58 (Repr.); *Martin-Méry 1962,* pp. iv and
5, No. 1 (Repr.); *Harper and Hubbard 1965,*
p. 39, No. 20; *Shadbolt 1966,* No. 16; *Harper
1966,* pp. 54 and 56-57 (Repr.); *Trudel, Juneau
and Massey 1967,* pp. 14-15, No. 4 (Repr.);
Ostiguy 1970, p. 105; *Lord 1974,* pp. 31-32
(Repr.); *Portraits anciens 1975,* No. 7; *Godsell
1976,* p. 29; *Thibault, Galarneau and Noppen
1977,* p. 25, No. 12 (Repr.); *Robert 1978,* p. 20
(Repr.); *Nos racines,* No. 44 (1979), p. 880b
(Repr.); *Major-Frégeau 1979,* pp. 38, 43, 67-68,
83, 90-91, 139 and 141 (Repr.); *Major-Frégeau
1980,* p. 549; *Le Musée du Québec 1983,* p. 53,
No. 45 (entry by Claude Thibault, Luc Noppen
and Michel Doyon) (Repr.); *Comeau 1983,* p. 27;
*Les Cahiers d'Histoire de la Société d'Histoire de
Beloeil – Mont-Saint-Hilaire,* No. 16 (February
1985), p. 31 (Repr.); *Hill and Landry 1988,*
p. 69; *Derome, Bourassa and Chagnon 1988,*
p. 74; *Béland and Bourassa 1990,* p. 20; *Ruddel
1990,* p. 50; *Nadeau 1991,* p. 15 (Repr.).
Collection
Musée du Québec, Quebec City (56.297)

Inscription
(s.d., l.r.) *F.. Beaucourt.. pinxit/Montreal.. 1793.*
Provenance
Mrs. Jean-Paul Fortin, Quebec City; acquired by
the Musée de la Province de Québec, Quebec
City, 1956.
Exhibitions
Paris 1958; Vancouver 1959, No. 96; Ottawa
1959, No. 1; Toronto 1966; Ottawa 1967/1,
No. 40; Toronto 1971, No. 3; St-John's 1972;
Sherbrooke 1972; Sherbrooke 1975, No. 8;
Quebec City 1977, No. 13; Quebec City 1983-
1984, No. 46.
Bibliography
Ayre 1956, p. 17 (Repr.), attr. to François
Baillairgé; *Morisset 1959/1,* pp. 39, 41 and 44,
No. 96 (Repr.); *Morisset 1959/2,* No. 1 (Repr.);
Morisset 1960/1, pp. 57-58 and 64a (Repr.);
Harper 1962/3, pp. 9; *Harper 1966,* pp. 55 and
56-57 (Repr.); *Harper 1967/1,* pp. 68 and 69
(Repr.); *Hubbard and Ostiguy 1967,* pp. 28 and
33, No. 40 (Repr.); *Collections 1967,* No. 19
(Repr.); *Soucy 1969,* p. 40 (Repr.); *Reid 1973,*
p. 45 (Repr.); *Lord 1974,* pp. 31-32 (Repr.);
Portraits anciens 1975, No. 8 (Repr.); *Godsell
1976,* pp. 28-29 (Repr.); *Thibault, Galarneau
and Noppen 1977,* p. 26, No. 13 (Repr.); *Le
Musée du Québec 1978,* pp. 26-27 (Repr.);
Robert 1978, pp. 20 and 21 (Repr.); *Major-
Frégeau 1979,* pp. 38, 43, 67-68, 78-82, 90, 139,
141 and 143 (Repr.); *Nos racines,* No. 42 (1979),
p. 840b (Repr.); *Lamontagne 1980,* pp. 20 and 21
(Repr.); *Major-Frégeau 1980,* p. 549; *Mellen
1981,* pp. 110-111 (Repr.); *Le Musée du Québec
1983,* pp. 53 and 54, No. 46 (entry by Claude
Thibault, Luc Noppen and Michel Doyon)
(Repr.); *Comeau 1983,* p. 27; *Ruddell 1987,* p. 50
(Repr.); *Hill and Landry 1988,* p. 69; *Derome,*

Bourassa and Chagnon 1988, p. 74; *Lacroix
1989/2,* p. 74 (Repr.); *Béland and Bourassa
1990,* pp. 6, 9 and 20 (Repr.); *Nadeau 1991,* p. 15
(Repr.).
Collection
Musée du Québec, Quebec City (56.298)

16.
*Eustache-Ignace Trottier
dit Desrivières*, 1792
Oil on canvas, 84 × 68 cm

Inscription
(s.d., c.r.) *F.·. Beaucourt.·. pinxit/A. Montreal. 1792.*

Provenance
Descendants of the Trottier Desrivières Beaubien, Bouthillier and Routh families; Herbert T. Schwarz, Bragg Creek (Alb.); acquired by the National Gallery of Canada, Ottawa, 1975.

Bibliography
Galerie nationale 1976, pp. 70, 71 and 98 (Repr.); *Mellen 1981*, p. 111; *Major-Frégeau 1979*, pp. 69 and 84 (Repr.); *Hill and Landry 1988*, p. 69 (Repr.).

Collection
National Gallery of Canada, Ottawa (18251)

W E KNOW LITTLE about the life and career of Eustache-Ignace Trottier (1727-?).[1] Merchant in Montreal then later at the mission in Lac-des-Deux-Montagnes, he traded furs in 1780-1790, particularly in the Abitibi and Témiscamingue lakes region. Stiff competition from British merchants forced Trottier to abandon this activity and concentrate almost exclusively on his retail business at Lac-des-Deux-Montagnes. Married in November 17, 1759, Eustache Trottier and Marguerite Mailhot (1735-ca. 1806) were approximately 65 and 57 respectively when they had their portraits painted by François Beaucourt soon after his return from the United States.

Although the last figure of the date written on the portrait of Eustache Trottier is difficult to read, both portraits are considered to have been painted in 1793. Two other versions of the portrait of Mr. Trottier exist: one is still in a private collection while the other, acquired by the National Gallery of Canada in 1975 and shown here, is signed and dated 1792.[2] The latter portrait unquestionably served as a model for later copies, in all likelihood commissioned from Beaucourt by a close relative or friend of Trottier's. It is also possible that the artist painted additional versions of his portrait of Madame Trottier.

Regardless, the two Musée du Quebec paintings are among the earliest matching portrayals of a husband and wife. The well-dressed couple are depicted enjoying their favourite pastimes in an interior setting, a rare feature in portraits at the turn of the 19th century in Lower Canada. In this respect, they are valuable testaments to bourgeois life at the time.

Both figures, slightly turned toward the imaginary centre of the double composition, are seated at a table, looking at the viewer. Dressed in their finest attire and surrounded by objects attesting to their wealth and social standing, the Trottiers are shown enjoying a special moment of leisure: the husband is playing cards, while his wife is about to serve tea. Both portraits have been painted in shades of pastel, mainly warm green, blue, pink and gold tones.

Eugene Trottier is seated in a red-back chair, hair powdered and dressed in the fashion of the day: a navy-blue velvet redingote with large gold buttons, a white silk shirt embroidered with gold thread, and an intricate lace jabot. Hanging from his belt is a piece of gold jewelry that would appear to be a chatelaine, a watch chain with fobs on it worn by men particularly in the 18th century. In his left hand Trottier is holding five cards, waiting to

play his next trump, having already played his best card: the ace of hearts. On the table, beside his right hand, is a pile of gold louis and coins. The colours used in the Musée du Quebec and the National Gallery of Canada portraits are similar, as is the manner in which the subjects are depicted. Only a few details differ, such as the top of the chairback, the position of the playing cards and coins and the sitter's facial features (eyes, nose, mouth and hairstyle). The features in the National Gallery of Canada portrait are more accentuated and harder, making the subject appear older.

The back of the chair in which Marguerite Mailhot is seated is finely worked. The sitter is wearing a blue dress with a bodice jacket of the same colour with lace around the cuffs. Over her shoulders is a fichu, a light triangular scarf, made of transparent fabric, adorned with fine stitching and edged with lace. On her head, the lady is wearing a dormeuse, a white bonnet with upturned, jagged edges that was commonly worn indoors. Overall, her attire recalls that worn by the elderly woman depicted in a portrait attributed to Beaucourt and acquired by the Musée du Quebec in the early 1980s (Fig. 15A). The miniature set in a medallion tied at her neck with a ribbon could be either one of her sons (Cat. 46) or her husband. Madame Trottier is about to open a small gold jewelry case, a snuffbox or a tin of tea.

Infrared photographs and X rays taken in 1956, followed by somewhat radical "cleaning" in 1958, revealed a curtain hanging diagonally to the subject's right— one of the first times this artificial pictorial device was used in Canada—plus a tea service set on a pedestal table and treated like a true still life. More than likely this is the result of retouching by a "painter-restorer" rather than an afterthought on the part of the original artist. Indeed, along with Beaucourt's plate of tropical fruit in *The Negress* (1786, MMCH), this tea service is one of the artist's most elaborate still lifes. It includes a hot water urn made of silver and enamel—the term samovar would be anacronous—a silver ewer or cream jug, a china cup and saucer, and a silver spoon. The enamel plating on the hot water urn takes on the blue tint of Madame Trottier's dress.

The costumes and household accessories in the portraits of the Trottier couple obviously reflect their respectability and wealth, but they also testify to the artist's skill and mastery in rendering both the variety of textures and fabrics and the quality of the lighting. This is particularly evident in the delicacy of the lace, conveyed through a few nimbly added touches (ja-bot, headdress and fichu), in the rich velvet of Monsieur Trottier's jacket, in the shining reflections on the components of the still life, the coins, the buttons of the frock coat and on the embroidery on Monsieur Trottier's shirt. The long, thin, graceful hands of the sitters are typical of Beaucourt's portraits. These two particular paintings do include a few anatomical errors, however, notably the awkward foreshortening of Madame Trottier's right hand and the strange position of the Monsieur Trottier's eyes.

The Trottiers are a sterling example of the French-Canadian merchant class. It is not surprising that, compared with portraits of prominent citizens, seigneurs or members of the liberal professions, the portrait of this wealthy Montreal merchant gives an entirely different impression. The portrait of Monsieur Trottier is more intimate, more familiar and, consequently, not as solemn or official as that of Judge P.-A. De Bonne, for instance, painted by William Berczy (Cat. 18) some fifteen years later. The seigneur of Beauport is also shown enjoying a moment of leisure; instead of playing cards, though, he is engrossed in the writings of an Enlightenment philosopher. Unlike the two portraits by Beaucourt, which endow the sitters with an entirely human quality, both in their pride and their weakness, the portrait of Judge De Bonne reveals absolutely no sign of character in this highly controversial figure. The artist's sensitivity allows him to paint a psychological profile of his two sitters, both of whom aspire to the life of the French-Canadian aristocracy and nobility: Monsieur Trottier feigns the calm assurance of a merchant who is proud of his success, while his wife displays the courtesy of the perfect hostess as she does the reserve and gentleness of the ideal spouse.

The refined style and careful execution of these two portraits, along with the natural ease of the sitters' pose, reveal something of the influences affecting Beaucourt's work. The first Canadian painter to have developed his technique in Europe, Beaucourt carried on the legacy of a career practised not in the major cities of Europe or in keeping with the major artistic trends, but rather in the provincial cities where he stayed, whether Bordeaux or Philadelphia.

M.B.

Notes

1. See the short biography of his son, Eustache-Ignace, by Raymond Dumais in DCB, Vol. V (1983), pp. 828-829. Although Trottier senior's real name was actually Eustache Trottier Desrivières Beaubien, we have purposely used the name habitually given him in the title of the portrait.
2. See *MAJOR-FRÉGEAU 1979*, p. 68.

WILLIAM BERCZY was born in Wallerstein (Saxony, Germany) in December 1744. Born Johann Albrecht Ulrick Moll, it was not until he was in his mid-thirties, after breaking all ties with his family, that he changed his name.

By age 47, Berczy had already travelled to several European countries. Raised amidst diplomats and aristocrats, he moved to Vienna with his family in 1745 where, in 1762, he registered at the city's academy of fine arts. Four years later, at the age of 21, he returned to Germany to study at the University of Jena. He later travelled back and forth between Germany, Poland and Hungary, settled in Bern from 1779 to 1780 and then in Florence from 1780 to 1784, where he was accepted into the academy of fine arts in 1781. Berczy married Jeanne-Charlotte Allamand on December 1, 1785 near Lausanne. He and his wife then moved to London, where they both showed their works at the Royal Academy of Arts.

In 1791, a group of British speculators hired Berczy to oversee the colonization of a vast territory in western New York state. He gathered together a group of peasants from his homeland and sailed to America with his family in May 1792. In 1794, following some misunderstandings with the representative of the investors group, and given the new interest in developing Upper Canada, Berczy and his colonists left New York and settled in the township of Markham, near York (Toronto). With all the trials plaguing him during these three years, Berczy had little time to paint.

His first stay in Quebec City was in 1798-1799, when he had to plead his case concerning the confiscation of his land by the Executive Council of Upper Canada. During this year, he painted several miniatures. He then returned to London for a final attempt to ply his trade. Somewhere around 1805, he once again joined his wife in Montreal, where she had been living since 1798, and there began the most productive period of his artistic career. From 1798 to 1811, he painted portraits (*James McGill*, Cat. 17) as well as religious canvases, such as *The Archangel Saint Michael* (Vaudreuil) and *The Assumption of the Virgin* (Notre-Dame church in Montreal). Back in Quebec City in 1808-1809, Berczy was barely able to fill his orders, despite assistance from his son, William junior. It was during this time that he painted the portraits of Monsieur and Madame De Bonne (Cat. 18 and 19; Fig. 17C and 17D) and *The Woolsey Family* (Fig. 18-19A). Berczy occasionally gave drawing lessons and did some architectural work, designing the plans for Christ Church, the Anglican cathedral in Montreal, in 1803.

Berczy was as interested in North American politics as he was in the political upheavals taking place throughout Europe. He was sufficiently drawn to literature and the science of topography to produce a few manuscripts, which, unfortunately, he was never able to get published. He moved in the same circles as artists François Baillairgé and Louis Dulongpré, topographical painters George Heriot and Joseph Bouchette, surveyor Jean-Baptiste Duberger and collector Jacques Viger, as well as several other art enthusiasts. William Berczy died on February 5, 1813 in New York City, at the age of 68.

WILLIAM BERCZY
1744-1813

Main sources
Trudel 1976; Staggs 1983; Stock 1983; Lesser 1984; Allodi, Moogk and Stock 1991.

VAG, AGNS, MMFA

17.
James McGill, c. 1805-1811
Watercolour, gum arabic highlighted with
white gouache on ivory, 6.5 × 5.2 cm

Inscription
(b., on the cardboard protecting the back of the
work, in graphite) *Jas McGill/Founder of McGill/
university − died/19^" Dec 1813 −/age 69 −.*

Bibliography
ALLODI, MOOGK AND STOCK 1991, p. 198, No. 68
(Repr.).

Provenance
Descendants of the Trottier Desrivières and
Reynolds families; R. A. Reynolds & Son,
Windsor; George F. Macdonald, Windsor; gift to
the McGill University, Montreal.

Collection
Department of Rare Books and Special
Collections, McGill University, Montreal

JAMES MCGILL (1744-1813) belonged to the influential Scottish community that controlled the commercial fur trade in the late 18th century. In association with Isaac Todd (Fig. 27A), among others, he was a partner in Todd McGill and Company and the North West Company. With the signing of the Treaty of Paris in 1783, and the subsequent ceding of Ohio to the United States, McGill lost the important market centred around the city of Detroit. As a result, he began diversifying his commercial activities, and the timber trade and, more specifically, land speculation became his major sources of income. McGill also played a key role in public affairs, as justice of the peace (1776), major (1787) then colonel (1810) in the first militia battalion of the city of Montreal, member of the House of Assembly (1792, 1796 and 1800), and executive councillor (1796) and interim chairman of the Executive Council (1813). At his death, McGill was one of the wealthiest men of the day. He bequeathed £10 000, along with Burnside, his estate at the foot of Mount Royal, for the creation of a college or university that would bear his name. His donation led to the founding of McGill University, whose charter was obtained in 1821 and which opened its doors to students in 1829.

The known portraits of James McGill show a man who, although experienced in the world of business, remains generous and humble. The work by Louis Dulongpré (Fig. 17A) is somewhat austere. Although the canvas is bare apart from the sitter himself, there is a sense of warmth and ease created through the use of rich colours and a unique facture. This portrait was not only copied—by William Raphael, among others—, it was also reproduced, in 1859, in an engraving by Albert W. Graham, under the direction of James Duncan and at the request of McGill University.[1] It also appears in the portrait of John Bethune (Cat. 245), second principal of McGill University, hanging on the back wall of the room in which Bethune is sitting.

The *James McGill* portrayed in the two known miniatures, i.e. the ones owned by McGill University and the McCord Museum of Canadian History (Fig. 17B),[2] is less formal and more accessible, while remaining dignified with his silk tie and periwig. Because miniatures are for personal use, they do not have to conform to the same conventions as oil portraits, which are for public use. To date, the McGill University miniature has been attributed to John Ramage (circa 1748-1802), an Irish artist who plied his trade in Lower Canada between 1794 and 1802.[3] Although various historical circumstances associate Ramage with the McGill family—he died at the residence of a Desrivières family,

perhaps related to the Montreal merchant—, it is highly unlikely that he is really the artist of these two miniatures. The attribution of the portraits to Ramage dates from 1930 and was based on a comparison between the McCord Museum miniature and works by Ramage housed in the Metropolitan Museum of Art (MMA) in New York. If we compare the McGill miniature to the miniature portrait of Elijah Boardmen (circa 1790) owned by the MMA, the relation is shaky at best.[4] The treatment of the hair, background and, especially, the clothing is totally different from their treatment in the two miniatures of James McGill. The same reservations must be held if the comparison is extended to include other works by Ramage.[5] In fact, William Dunlap, one of Ramage's contemporaries, described the artist's work as follows: "His miniatures were in the line style, as opposed to the dotted." This description reveals a trademark style of the artist that holds no affinities with the miniatures of McGill, i.e. the use of multiple, tiny brushstrokes that let the ivory, translucid in its thinness, shine through.

The artistic techniques and style of the two miniatures of McGill make it possible to link them to those of Judge Pierre-Amable de Bonne (Fig. 17C) and his wife (Fig. 17D), both definitely the work of William Berczy and executed between September and November 1808, at the

Fig. 17A.
Louis Dulongpré,
James McGill, before 1813;
oil on canvas, 83.8 × 67.8 cm.
McCord Museum of Canadian History,
Montreal (M970x.106).

Fig. 17B.
William Berczy,
James McGill, c. 1805-1811;
watercolour, gum arabic highlighted with
gouache on ivory, 6.7 × 5.5 cm.
McCord Museum of Canadian History,
Montreal (M1150).

Fig. 17C.
William Berczy,
Pierre-Amable De Bonne, 1808;
watercolour, gum arabic highlighted with
gouache on ivory, 6.3 × 5 cm.
Musée du Québec, Quebec City (91.103).

Fig. 17D.
William Berczy,
*Mrs. Pierre-Amable De Bonne, née Louise-
Élizabeth Marcoux*, 1808;
watercolour, gum arabic highlighted with
gouache on ivory, 6.5 × 5.2 cm.
Musée du Québec, Quebec City (91.104).

creased use of gum arabic. A few highlights of white gouache emphasize the lighting on lace, puckers in the jabot and jacket buttons. A close examination of the two miniatures of James McGill would seem to show that the McGill University miniature is slightly less refined than the McCord Museum one but that they are, in fact, two versions by the same artist. This makes it further possible to put a date to the McGill portrait: both versions date from Berczy's stay in the Montreal area, between 1805 and 1811, excluding 1808-1809, which the artist spent in Quebec City.

P.B.

Notes

1. See DEROME 1981-1982, p. 45.

2. This version will be shown in the 1991-1992 exhibition *William Berczy,* organized by the National Gallery of Canada.

3. After completing his training as a goldsmith in Dublin, Ramage settled in America around the 1770s. Between 1775 and 1794, while in the United States, he painted numerous oblong miniatures, for which he made the frames himself. Financial difficulties forced him to move to Montreal in July 1794. Although his letters clearly show that he produced various works during his stay in Canada, it is impossible to attribute any to him with any certainty. See Ramage's letters to his wife, Montreal, September 9, 1794 and March 23, 1795, quoted in John Hill Morgan, *A Sketch of The Life of John Ramage Miniature Painter* (New York: The New York Historical Society, 1930) pp. 37 and 39.

4. Robin Bolton-Smith and Dale T. Johnson, "The Miniature in America", *Antiques,* Vol. CXXXVIII, No. 5 (November 1990), p. 1047 (Repr.).

5. See John Hill Morgan, *Op. cit.* and Nos. 305, 928, 1315, 1618, 1626 and 2091 of the *Catalogue of American Portraits in the New York Historical Society* (New Haven: Yale University Press, 1974).

6. In his letters, however, the artist specifies that his son, William Berczy junior, assisted him in his work: "He is intent on doing his best to help me complete my work, especially the miniatures for Monsieur DeBonne where he can do much since he has the original oil portraits as reference" (*Translation*) (Archives de l'Université de Montréal, *Collection Baby,* Papiers Berczy, U/1473, letter from William Berczy senior to his wife, dated September 21, 1808, published in "William von Moll Berczy", *Rapport de l'archiviste de la province de Québec pour 1940-1941,* Quebec, Rédempti Paradis, 1941, p. 50). Nevertheless, the finished portraits reflect mainly the style of William Berczy senior, recalling the technique used in his watercolour portraits. Only the backgrounds differ. In the two versions of the McGill miniature, the brushstrokes are longer and the effects of colour gradation, less refined.

same time as the large oil versions (Cat. 18 and 19).[6] It is also possible to establish similarities between the two miniatures and another work attributed to Berczy, the portrait of Jean-Marie Mondelet (MCR). In all five cases, the flesh tones are rendered using tiny strokes of white, grey and pink. The backgrounds are painted in shades of grey, green and blue that blend with the shadows created by the facial features and clothing folds. The richly coloured fabrics are generally enhanced through an in-

18.
Pierre-Amable De Bonne, 1808
Oil on canvas, 81 × 66 cm

Inscriptions
(on the page of the book) *DE L'ESPRIT DES LOIS/LIV. XII/D;* (on the edge) [?]/D/MONT/T.I

Provenance
Louise-Élizabeth Marcoux, 1816; Abbé André-Amable Marcoux, his nephew, c. 1848; Descendants of the Marcoux family; Dr. Guy Marcoux, Beauport; gift to the Musée du Québec, Quebec City, 1991.

Exhibition
Ottawa 1991-1992, No. 79 (Presented in Quebec City only).

Bibliography
Archives de l'Université de Montréal, Collection Baby, Papiers Berczy, U/1470, U/1473, U/1474 and U/1475, letters from William Berczy senior to his wife; September 3 and 21, November 12 and 23, 1808 (published in "William von Moll Berczy", *Rapport de l'archiviste de la province de Québec pour 1940-1941*, Quebec City, Rédempti Paradis, 1941, pp. 45-65); *BETCHERMAN 1962*, pp. 70-73 and 117; *HARPER 1966*, p. 70; *ALLODI, MOOGK AND STOCK 1991*, pp. 72, 212-214, No. 79 (Repr.).

Collection
Musée du Québec, Quebec City. Gift from Dr. Guy Marcoux, Beauport (91.113).

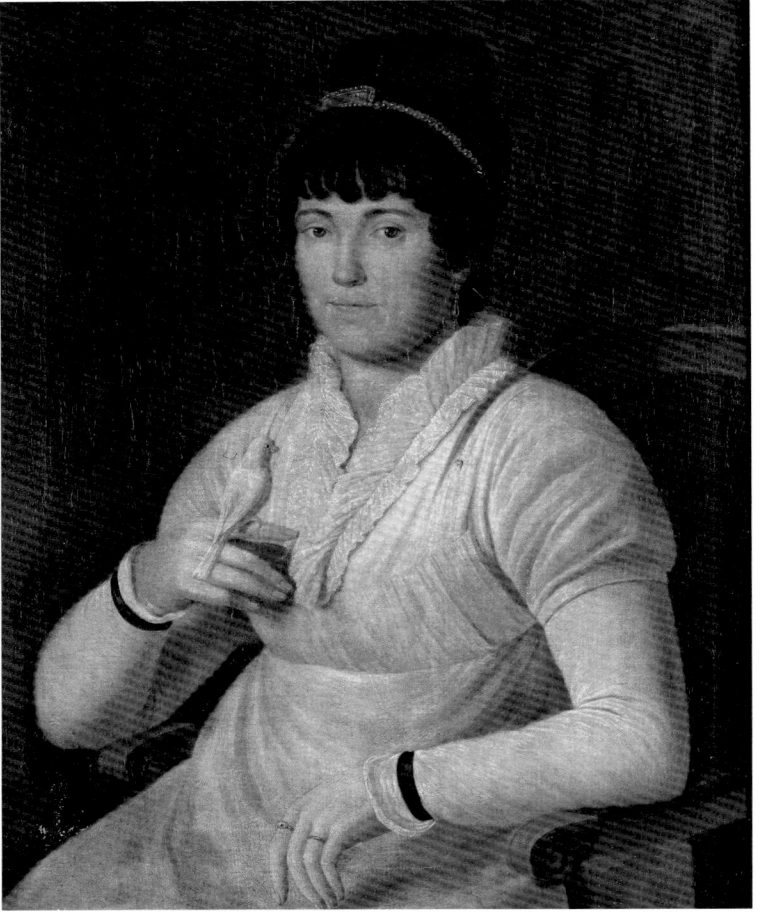

19.
*Mrs. Pierre-Amable De Bonne,
née Louise-Élizabeth Marcoux,* 1808
Oil on canvas, 81 × 65.8 cm

Provenance
Louise-Élizabeth Marcoux, 1816; Abbé André-Amable Marcoux, his nephew, c. 1848; Descendants of the Marcoux family; Dr. Guy Marcoux, Beauport; on deposit at the Musée du Québec, Quebec City, 1991.

Exhibition
Ottawa 1991-1992, No. 80 (Presented in Quebec City only).

Bibliography
Archives de l'Université de Montréal, Collection Baby, Papiers Berczy, U/1470, U/1473, U/1474 and U/1475, letters from William Berczy senior to his wife; September 3 and 21, November 12 and 23, 1808 (published in "William von Moll Berczy", *Rapport de l'archiviste de la province de Québec pour 1940-1941*, Quebec City, Rédempti Paradis, 1941, pp. 45-65); *BETCHERMAN 1962*, pp. 70-73 and 117; *HARPER 1966*, p. 70; *ALLODI, MOOGK AND STOCK 1991*, pp. 72, 212-214, No. 80 (Repr.).

Collection
Musée du Québec, Quebec City. Deposit from Dr. Guy Marcoux, Beauport (DLT-91.203)

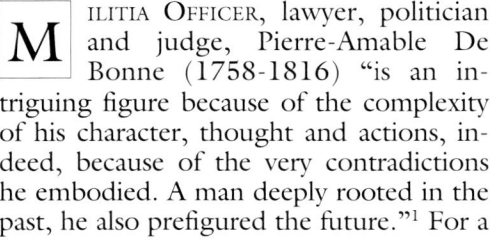ILITIA OFFICER, lawyer, politician and judge, Pierre-Amable De Bonne (1758-1816) "is an intriguing figure because of the complexity of his character, thought and actions, indeed, because of the very contradictions he embodied. A man deeply rooted in the past, he also prefigured the future."[1] For a long time, De Bonne led the life of a libertine, which led to several run-ins with the Catholic clergy. Yet, this "honest man" also kept company with the upper crust and participated in community cultural life. After completing his classical studies, De Bonne studied law and obtained a commission as a lawyer in 1780. The following year he married Louise Chartier de Lotbinière in Vaudreuil; unfortunately, the marriage went downhill rapidly, ending in a spectacular breakup just one year later. He remarried in 1805, this time to Louise-Élizabeth Marcoux, who was only 23. As seigneur of half of Sault-Sainte-Marie since 1781, De Bonne had accumulated

Fig. 18-19A.
William Berczy,
The Woolsey Family,
1808-1809;
oil on canvas,
60.3 × 87 cm.
National Gallery of
Canada, Ottawa.
Gift of Major Edgar
C. Woolsey, 1952
(5875).

increasing amounts of land over the years. In 1794, he purchased the *sub-fief* of Grandpré, on the Route de la Canardière near Quebec City and had a mansion built there the following year. These property transactions, along with his lifestyle, suggest unquestionable financial independence.

The years 1790-1794 proved to be the most prosperous for this member of the liberal professions. Considered to be Lower Canada's first professional "politician", from 1788 on De Bonne continued to add new positions to his resumé: justice of the peace, clerk of the register of landed property, assistant to the French secretary and translator for the governor and Lower Canada Council, judge of the Court of Common Pleas and the Court of King's Bench for the District of Quebec and, finally, executive councillor. He was an elected member of the Assembly from 1792 to 1810 for various townships, including Trois-Rivières and Quebec City, and leader of the governing party in the House of Assembly, that is, the British administrators, merchants, etc. under the helm of Governor James Henry Craig (Cat. 49). He was called a traitor by his fellow Frenchmen and hated by the members of the *Parti canadien*. De Bonne was a founding member of the *Courrier de Quebec*, which denounced, among other things, the party and its mouthpiece, *Le Canadien*. In order to rid themselves of De Bonne, the *Parti canadien* tabled legislation that forbade judges to be members of the House of Assembly. In 1812, after a much-criticized political and legal career, De Bonne resigned and retired to his estate of La Canardière, in Beauport, of which the mansion and gardens were extolled by Joseph Bouchette.[2]

While De Bonne had his roots in the *Ancien regime,* he was no less a man of his time. His voluminous library reveals a man impregnated with the spirit of the Enlightenment: Voltaire and Rousseau alone accounted for over 50 books and he even owned a copy of the *Dictionnaire des beaux-arts.*[3] De Bonne also liked theatre. He was a director of the *Théâtre de société de Montréal,* which during its opening season, in 1789-1790, put on *Le Médecin malgré lui,* despite threats of Church censorship. Painter Louis Dulongpré participated in the theatre's founding as stage manager and by painting three stage sets in the first year.[4] Other than Dulongpré, De Bonne also met François Baillairgé, from whom he commissioned a full-length portrait of François De Bonne, Duke of Lesdiguières (1543-1626) and constable of France, and of whom the justice purported to be a descendent.[5]

It was perhaps through his colleague Pierre-Louis Panet (1761-1812), also a justice of the Court of King's Bench for the District of Montreal and member of the Executive Council, that De Bonne was introduced to William Berczy. At Panet's instigation, the Montreal painter had moved to Quebec City on July 22, 1808, primarily to paint an important group portrait, the John William Woolsey family, with all its eight members (Fig. 18-19A). During this same year, he accepted numerous other commissions: religious canvases for the Ursuline nuns and, particularly, head-and-shoulder and life-size portraits in oil or miniature portraits in watercolour on ivory, such as the one of M.-E.-G.-A. Chartier de Lotbinière, De Bonne's ex-brother-in-law.

The abundance of letters (in French) that Berczy and his wife, Jeanne-Charlotte Allamand, wrote to each other provide many details on the artist's stay in Quebec City and the circumstances sur-

rounding the order for and execution of the portraits of Judge De Bonne and his wife. Berczy was accompanied by his son, William junior, who helped mix colours, clean paintbrushes and, on occasion, work on certain areas of his paintings, particularly by completing the background on his miniatures.

In a letter to his wife dated September 3, 1808, Berczy tells of twice stopping for refreshments at the home of Judge De Bonne—with whom he seems to have already made acquaintance—during a trip to Montmorency Falls. During their meeting, the two men agreed on the terms of the commission:

In a week from today, I have agreed to come and spend a week at the home of Monsieur De Bonne, during which time I shall paint, or at least commence, four life-sized oil portraits of himself and Madame De Bonne; as well as the same in miniature (he already bought a very pretty locket today for one of them). I further promised to retouch and make corrections to the portrait of one of his elderly relatives [the mother of L.-É. Marcoux, *née* Louise Bélanger] which bears enough resemblance but which is very badly painted being the work of Bayargé [sic]. I expect to be well advanced by week's end since our son William has offered to pour his heart and soul into helping me. (*Translation*)

On September 21, the artist wrote another letter, mailed directly from "Monsieur De Bonne's country estate", stating that he had left Quebec City in order to spend a week or so at the home of the seigneur of La Canardière:

I arrived at my present place of residence where I was received with open arms—at least, they were anxious to see me settled in as the owner very much wants to receive the paintings he has commissioned me to do and which he wishes to use to add more decoration to his Parlour.

Early Monday morning, I immediately set to work getting together all that was necessary to begin painting, and by evening I had completed a sketch for Monsieur De Bonne's portrait that bore a very good resemblance; at least, enough to be to the family's liking. The size of the canvas forces me to paint a Half-length portrait including the two hands which makes for more work, but which at the same time adds to my yield since according to the prices set for my work, a Half-length portrait pays 12 guineas such that my stay here will pay me 39 guineas or £45.10, including the portrait of Madame De Bonne's mother, which I retouched. Tuesday I sketched Monsieur De Bonne's entire body and it was so good that from a short distance they thought it was a finished canvas, all the more so since they are unaccustomed to seeing finished paintings that are so effective. As Monsieur De Bonne had to go into town today to the Criminal Court, I sketched his wife in his absence. I was as

Fig. 19A.
William Berczy,
Maria Sutherland Hallowell, c. 1805;
oil on canvas, 79 × 61 cm.
Royal Ontario Museum, Toronto (988.96.2).

successful with her as I was with her husband and they are just as pleased with this piece of work—they are astonished at the rapidity with which I work [...] it took me such a short time that I had a lot of time left. (*Translation*)

Further on in his letter, Berczy talks about his activities, about what time they sit down for meals "à la française", and about the pool games with either William junior or the De Bonnes. He adds that he "has a very good time with the lord of the manor who is very educated and who likes to talk." (*Translation*) Other than that, he continues, "since I do not claim to be his friend, I enjoy his good qualities without concern for whether or not what some say about him is true or false." (*Translation*) On November 12, back in Quebec City, Berczy informed Charlotte that "business [...] is progressing. The three large portraits of Monsieur De Bonne have been varnished and will be framed tomorrow; and I have only half of the miniature of his wife left to do [...]. William will work on the miniatures." (*Translation*) Finally, on November 21, after hearing some ugly gossip regarding the judge's mental health—the judge had been gone for eight weeks—, the artist went to La Canardière to verify the allegations, but moreso, to deliver his portraits:

I had already resolved to go see Monsieur De Bonne as soon as the portraits were completely finished and I had no more than one day's

work left when the day before yesterday I received a very polite note from him saying that as soon as the portraits were ready they were anxious to send someone for them. His note did not appear to be written by someone who was crazy [...]. I answered it immediately assuring him that I would come the next day, hopefully with the two miniatures [...]. Although I was unable to fully complete the miniature of Madame De Bonne, I set out [...] in a carriage with young William and the two miniatures yesterday morning.

I am very pleased to have finished the paintings for Monsieur De Bonne since now I can spend all my time on the family portrait, which I hope to make progress on quickly.

Thus, while carrying out his numerous other activities, Berczy took exactly two months to complete the two oil portraits and copies in miniature. De Bonne received the paintings just a few days prior to his fiftieth birthday on November 25.[6]

As agreed, Pierre-Amable De Bonne and his wife, aged 50 and 25 respectively, were painted in life-sized, half-length (hands showing) portraits. They are shown in a three-quarter profile set against a neutral background, each seated in a classical-style armchair. The chairs are covered in velvet—one pink, the other blue—, the backs finely worked, with scroll-shaped handrests. The couple face each other in near-symmetrical positions.

In a pose somewhat similar to that of Peter Russel in the portrait painted by Berczy in 1803 (PC), De Bonne holds an open book in his right hand, with "*DE L'ESPRIT DES LOIS*" written across the top of one of the pages. More than familiar with the writings of the philosophers and authors of the Age of Enlightenment, the judge owned two different editions of Montesquieu's *De l'Esprit des lois,* one in three volumes, the other in four. This magistrate and political figure thus wished to be seen as an endorser of the liberal ideas of the famous French moralist.

Just like Julie Lemoine in the painting of the Woolsey family, Louise-Élizabeth Marcoux is dressed in the latest Empire style. Her gown is reminiscent of ancient times and she is wearing a tiara in her hair. Her high-waisted, white gown[7] has sleeves fitted below the shoulder, black velvet ribbon around the wrists and a starched collar folded into two rows of pleats. Her hair is arranged in a chignon on top of her head, with ringlets across her forehead. A pearl tiara decorated with a gold bar completes the ensemble. The fashion of wearing a tiara was started by the empress Josephine. Madame De Bonne is also wearing drop earrings and two rings on her left hand: a wedding band on her

ring finger and a ring with a gemstone on her left index finger. The young woman is also holding a pale yellow pet bird, possibly a canary, on her right index finger. In the style of his portrait of Louis Genevay (ca. 1803, MSQ), the drooping, slightly twisted left hand shows that Berczy, while charging extra for painting hands, was not always able to render them correctly. Finally, the subject is portrayed in somewhat similar fashion to *Maria Sutherland Hallowell,* painted by the same artist circa 1805 and recently acquired by the Royal Ontario Museum in Toronto (Fig. 19A).

These two portraits are an exceptional pair in the artistic production of William Berczy. Along with the five other known works, these two paintings are among the rare life-size, oil portraits that have survived. Their recent discovery is of capital importance for the understanding of both Berczy's work and Quebec painting in the early 19th century as a whole.

M.B.

Notes

1. Pierre Tousignant and Jean-Pierre Wallot, DCB, Vol. V (1983), p. 230.
2. In 1849, Judge De Bonne's property was sold in order to build an asylum in Beauport. The judge's former residence appears in a painting hanging in the institution (now the Robert-Giffard hospital).
3. See "La bibliothèque du juge DeBonne", *Le Bulletin des recherches historiques,* Vol. XLII, No. 3 (March 1936), pp. 136-143.
4. DEROME, BOURASSA AND CHAGNON 1988, pp. 82 and 86. In 1811, Dulongpré apparently also made a caricature of De Bonne for printer John Neilson. The judge is shown with a pair of horns growing out of his forehead with the caption "EN VOILÀ ENCORE DE BONNES" (A play on words loosely translated into English as "That's a good one.") (MQ, Centre de documentation, artist's file).
5. Today housed in the Musée du Château Ramezay. See the entry lifted from Baillairgé's *Journal* in KAREL, NOPPEN AND THIBAULT 1975, p. 31 (Repr.).
6. Following Judge De Bonne's death at his residence in 1816, Louise-Élizabeth Marcoux kept the portraits until 1848, the year she tragically committed suicide at the asylum where she was residing. In her will, written before notary Charles-M. DeFoy and dated March 16, 1844 (No. 4425), Louise-É. Marcoux bequeathed her silverware and family paintings to her nephew, André Amable Marcoux, a priest. The family paintings do not appear on the inventory of her estate drawn up the Mr. DeFoy and dated October 17, 1849. Nevertheless, the four works by Berczy were to remain in the possession of the descendents of the family until now.
7. Initially pink the same as in the miniature (Fig. 170), the organic pigments have faded over time.

T HOMAS DAVIES entered the Royal Military Academy at Woolwich (London) on March 1, 1755, during Gamaliel Massiot's term as drawing master. Davies was promoted several times during his long career, rising in rank from sublieutenant (1756) to lieutenant-general (1803). Davies made four trips to North America, probably returning to England between them. During his first posting, from 1757 to 1762, he was promoted from sublieutenant (1757) to assistant captain (1762), and was stationed in Halifax (1757), Louisbourg (1758), Fort Frederick (1758, 1759), Lake Champlain, Montreal (1759, 1760), Lake Ontario, in the state of New York (1761), Lake George, Lake Champlain and again in Montreal (1762).

During his second trip to North America, from 1764 to about 1767, Davies was stationed in the state of New York and in Canada. On his return to England, he was made a captain in 1771 and aide-de-camp to General Sir Jeffrey Amherst in 1772 and 1773. He actually dedicated a series of engravings entitled *Six Views of North American Waterfalls*, published in London in 1768, to the general. He also exhibited his work at the Royal Academy of Arts in 1771. From 1773 to approximately 1779, he was transferred from Halifax (1773, 1774) to Boston (1774-1776), back to Halifax (1776) and, finally, to New York state, while continuing to supply the Royal Academy with his work. Once again back in England, he was appointed aide-de-camp to General Amherst for a second time, from 1778 to 1783, and promoted major (1782) and lieutenant-colonel (1783). He was in Gibraltar in 1783 and 1784 and, on his way back from the West Indies (1786), was posted to Quebec City from 1786 to 1790. As aide-de-camp to Prince William Henry, he participated in a royal visit to Halifax, Quebec City and Montreal. From 1793 to 1796, Davies was colonel (1794) then major-general (1796) at Plymouth. He again showed his work at the Royal Academy in 1793, 1794, 1798, 1799 and 1806. He died in Blackheath, near Woolwich, on March 16, 1812.

THOMAS DAVIES

circa 1737-1812

Main sources
HUBBARD 1972/1; HUBBARD 1972/2; COOKE 1983.

MQ, NGC

20. (See colour reproduction, p. 84)
A View of Château-Richer, Cape Torment,
and Lower End of the Isle of Orleans near Quebec, 1787
Watercolour over traces of graphite on paper, 35.4 × 52.7 cm

Inscriptions
(b.,c., in graphite, in the artist's hand) *A View of Chateau Riché Cape Torment and lower end of the Isle of Orleans near Quebec 1787;* (b.,u.r., in graphite, by another hand) *13.*

Provenance
Collection of the Earl of Derby, Knowsley (Lancashire), England (sold by Christie's, London, October 19, 1953, lot 137); acquired by the Frank T. Sabin Gallery, London, England, 1953; acquired by the National Gallery of Canada, Ottawa, 1954.

Exhibitions
Vancouver 1959, No. 117; Ottawa 1972/1, No. 49.

Bibliography
HIGHLY IMPORTANT 1953, p. 25, No. 137; *FENWICK AND STACEY 1956*, p. 275b (Repr.); *BARBEAU 1957* (Repr.); *MORISSET 1959/1*, p. 55, No. 117 (Repr.); *MORISSET 1960/1*, p. 73; *HARPER 1966*, p. 43; *VAUGEOIS AND LACOURSIÈRE 1970*, p. 243 (Repr.); *HUBBARD 1972/1*, p. 43 (Repr.); *HUBBARD 1972/2*, pp. 37 and 121, No. 49 (Repr.); *MOOGK 1977*, p. xx (Repr.); *SEARS 1978*, p. 106 (Repr.); *COMEAU 1983*, p. 72; *BROWN AND LINTEAU 1988*, pp. 288d and 288e (Repr.); *HILL AND LANDRY 1988*, p. 258 (Repr.).

Collection
National Gallery of Canada, Ottawa (6275)

T HESE two pages originally belonged to an album of over fifty watercolours by Thomas Davies housed in the Earl of Derby's library in Knowsley Park (Lancashire). Sold in London in 1953, the album was bought by Frank T. Sabin, who took it apart to sell the pages individually to various art museums in North America. The National Gallery of Canada purchased some twenty works, leaving strictly American subjects for the Old Print Shop in New York City. The bulk of our knowledge on Davies' Canadian works comes from this body of work.

It is not known how the Earl of Derby came to own this album,[1] nor whether it was put together by Davies himself or by someone else who merely assembled a number of separate works. The sales catalogue is of no help in trying to understand the album's original composition. It is therefore not known whether the watercolours were presented in chronological order according to when they were completed[2] or not. A brief look at its contents, from what we know of it today, leaves many questions unanswered.

First, we wonder whether these works constitute the principle milestones in Davies' artistic career as a whole, perfectly situated in time. Probably not. The album indeed marks the major periods in Davies' military career, from the view of Halifax dated 1757 to the view of Montreal, executed in 1812, but nothing makes it possible to confirm that the date marked on the drawings corresponds to their date of completion. While the question of possible confusion between the date of the studies and the date of the actual composition had already been raised by Robert H. Hubbard,[3] the latter failed to discuss the implications in his monography on the artist. Adding further doubt is the fact that all fifty or so watercolours are on paper of similar format, except for a few rare cases in which the sheets differ by a few centimetres.[4] Rosemarie L. Tovell pointed out one of the fundamental problems involved in conducting research on Davies by noting that the type of paper used in *View of Montreal*, which dates from 1762 according to the signed inscription on the back, did not even exist until 1780.[5] In other words, how are we to understand Davies' work if there are scarcely any solid facts to work from?

With no chronological dates provided, we must rely on the works themselves and what they show. The first point worthy of note is that the recent discovery of a sketchbook,[6] put together primarily during Davies' posting in New York state

MQ, NGC

21.
A View of the River La Puce, near <u>Quebec</u>, North America, 1789
Watercolour over graphite on paper, 34.1 × 51.9 cm

Inscriptions
(b.,c., in graphite, in the artist's hand) *A View on the River La Puce near Quebec North America 1789;* (b.,l.r., in graphite, by another hand) [5 or 3]*9.*

Provenance
Collection of the Earl of Derby, Knowsley (Lancashire), England (sold by Christie's, London, October 19, 1953, lot 137); acquired by the Frank T. Sabin Gallery, London, England, 1953; acquired by the National Gallery of Canada, Ottawa, 1954.

Exhibitions
Mexico City 1960-1961, No. 77; Ottawa 1967/2, No. 174; Ottawa 1972/1, No. 53; Austin 1973, No. 2.

Bibliography
HIGHLY IMPORTANT *1953,* p. 25, No. 137; MORISSET *1960/1,* p. 73; HUBBARD *1960,* p. 48 (Repr.); ARTE CANADIENSE *1960,* No. 77 (Repr.); PALL MALL *1967,* p. 344 (Repr.); STRONG *1967,* p. 242, No. 174 (Repr.); HUBBARD *1972/1,* p. 50 (Repr.); HUBBARD *1972/2,* pp. 37 and 125, No. 53 (Repr.); HUBBARD AND FRYE *1973,* pp. 40 and 41, No. 2; LORD *1974,* pp. 64 and 65 (Repr.); HARPER *1974,* p. 137 (Repr.); GODSELL *1976,* pp. 33 and 35 (Repr.); PAQUET AND WALLOT *1983,* p. 32 (Repr.); HILL AND LANDRY *1988,* p. 258 (Repr.)

Collection
National Gallery of Canada, Ottawa (6282)

between 1776 and 1779, reveals a somewhat different artist: while the faithfulness with which this topographical artist reproduced minute detail is familiar, we discover, in particular, the manner used to render the motif. Compare the sketch for *A View Near Morris House Looking Down Harlem Creek Towards New York* (Fig. 20-21A) with the resultant watercolour (Fig. 20-21B), found in the album acquired by the Earl of Derby. Although Davies added a few fishermen and his customary vegetation to the foreground of the finished watercolour, he recorded the topography of the site exactly as in his sketch. Davies' immediate mental image of the site was conveyed on paper, producing a coherent, definitive, codified composition. After capturing the view instantaneously, Davies enhanced the sketch in the resultant watercolour by deepening the perspective—

a near-general feature of his finished works—and improving the pictorial quality and colour scheme.

Davies' *A View of Château-Richer, Cape Torment, and Lower End of the Isle of Orleans near Quebec* and *A View of the River La Puce, near Quebec, North America,* for which no preliminary sketches exist, should be viewed similarly. The previous theory of watercolours painted from nature no longer holds; these works were actually produced in the studio. They clearly reproduce the vocabulary of drawings from nature, while using a refined technique whereby reality is conveyed much more subtly. The panoramic approach to *A View of Château-Richer* allows Davies to include all the components: from a high vantage point, he takes in the entire landscape from the Beaupré coast to Cap Tourmente. Once the land-

scape has been broken down into successive planes, the artist concentrates on detail: houses, fields, enclosures, rocky foreground, freshly cut stump, etc. Furthermore, the symbolic aspect of this work is important: the judicious positioning of the figures, the animals in the foreground and the huge fir tree all indicate a peaceful, prosperous countryside.

A View of the River La Puce embodies a different approach to nature, in which the topographical artist becomes a landscape artist. Davies has constructed his view of the river based on a large diagonal that cuts through the entire composition, separating the rocky plateau from the wooded background. As of the late 18th century, this type of composition was extremely popular with British artists. The motif of waterfalls framed on either side was developed by Dutch and Flemish

Fig. 20-21A.
Thomas Davies,
A View Near Morris House Looking Down
Harlem Creek Towards New York, c. 1776-1779;
watercolour, black wash, pen and ink,
graphite on paper, 11.4 × 18.6 cm.
National Gallery of Canada, Ottawa (26954).

Fig. 20A.
Gaspard Dughet,
The Cascade, c. 1671-1673;
black chalk hightened with white chalk
on blue-green paper, 22.0 × 35.7 cm.
National Gallery of Canada,
Ottawa (14690).

Fig. 20-21B.
Thomas Davies,
New York, Long Island, etc., 1778;
watercolour on paper, 34.4 × 51.5 cm.
Private collection, New York.

artists in the early 17th century. It was later used in Italy in the occasional drawing by Claude Lorrain (1600-1682) and was painted in an entirely new approach by Gaspard Dughet (1615-1675), particularly in his fresco in the *palazzo Colonna* (Fig. 20A). Davies has therefore chosen to paint the river by way of a composition that is based on the principles of the idealized landscape. In this way, the work becomes familiar to his contemporaries, as the reference to the idealized landscape stimulates the imagination, allowing the viewer to partake in the complex game of associations.

This forces us to rethink the long-held view of Davies as a "primitive" artist, based solely on the linear contour and colour scheme of his works. A close look at the composition of Davies' drawings shows that the naive view of the Canadian landscape has given way to a "skilful topographical view" produced after much reflection.

D.P.

Notes

1. While not one of the largest in England, the Earl of Derby's collection was nevertheless famous in the late 18th century. In 1782, the 12th Earl of Derby purchased the most important painting by Nicolas Poussin in England, *Landscape with the Ashes of Phocion collected by his Widow.*

2. It is possible that Frank T. Sabin made a detailed record of the order in which the watercolours appeared before taking the album apart. However, we do not know if such a record still exists. Furthermore, given the many unanswered questions, we have chosen to retain the dates generally given to the works.

3. *HUBBARD 1972/2,* p. 23.

4. While it would be inappropriate to embark upon a detailed study of Davies here, we feel this would be an important point on which to base any future studies on the artist.

5. *Dessins de maîtres du Musée des beaux-arts du Canada* (Cat.), (Ottawa: National Gallery of Canada, 1988), p. 238. See *HILL AND LANDRY 1988,* p. 257, Inv. 6272 for illustration.

6. Acquired by the National Gallery of Canada in 1981 (26954, p. 17R).

L OUIS DULONGPRÉ was born in Saint-Denis (near Paris) on April 16, 1759. His enlistment in the French army during the American War of Independence brought him to North America. In 1784, two years after hostilities ended, Dulongpré met some Canadian merchants in Albany, New York who urged him to move to Montreal, where he pursued his artistic career. Three years later, on February 5, 1787, Dulongpré wed Marguerite Campeau at Notre-Dame church in Montreal.

Soon after moving to Montreal, Dulongpré became actively involved in the city's cultural life. He gave private music lessons up to 1792 and helped found the *Théâtre de société* in November 1789 by assuming the positions of stage manager and decorator—he painted three different stage sets. In 1791 he advertised "the establishment of a Boarding School for Young Ladies" offering a comprehensive education that included needle-work, music, dance and drawing. Perhaps after acquiring some basic training in painting, Dulongpré returned to the United States in 1793-1794, mainly to Baltimore, Maryland, to perfect his skills.

According to his obituaries, it would seem that Dulongpré was a prolific artist, with three to four thousand portraits (oil and pastel) to his credit. He also did religious paintings, including six large canvases for the Berthierville church in 1797-1798. Spreading his talent far beyond the Montreal area, he painted three series of canvases for the churches in Saint-Jean-Port-Joli, La Pocatière and Rivière-Ouelle between 1796 and 1806. He worked with sculptor Louis Quévillon and, on more than one occasion, met with William Berczy, François Baillairgé and the American painter William Dunlap, who stayed in Montreal in 1820.

A versatile artist, Louis Dulongpré also did gilding and mar-bling. In 1809, he submitted a "general decorating plan for N.-D. church in Montreal." (*Translation*) He opened a factory for making oiled floor-cloths in 1812 and, after joining the militia, was a soldier in the War of 1812. Dulongpré died at the Dessaulles manor house in Saint-Hyacinthe on April 26, 1843.

LOUIS DULONGPRÉ
1759-1843

Main sources
BAZIN 1988; DEROME, BOURASSA AND CHAGNON 1988.

MQ

22.
François Noiseux, 1796
Pastel on paper mounted on canvas,
36.5 × 28.8 cm

Inscription
(written in ink, on a paper that protected the back of the work, cut at the time of restoration and entered in the file) *François Noïseux fils D'étienne Noiseux Et De marie/Jeanne Malet ne à S^{te} foi Proche Quebec le 8 fevrier 1729./Marié a charles Bourg Le 14 janvier1748. Peint Par Mr Louis/Dulongpré. Le 29 juillet 1796-.*

Provenance
Miss Alice Nolin, Montreal, before 1941; Jean Nolin, Westmount, by inheritance; acquired by the Musée du Québec, Quebec City, 1978.

Exhibition
Quebec City 1983-1984, No. 290.

Bibliography
Nos racines, No. 51 (1979), p. 1012; *ACQUISITIONS 1979-1980*, p. 154, No. 39 (Repr.); *LA CHRONIQUE 1979*, p. 30, No. 144 (Repr.); *LE MUSÉE DU QUÉBEC 1983*, pp. (35) and 239, No. 290 (entry by Guy Paradis) (Repr.); *DEROME, BOURASSA AND CHAGNON 1989*, pp. 56, 78 and 86; *MARTIN AND GRANDBOIS 1991*, p. 19.

Collection
Musée du Québec, Quebec City (78.84)

MMFA

23.
Abbé François Cherrier, c. 1795-1798
Pastel on paper mounted on canvas,
39 × 30.8 cm

Inscription
(b., on a mounted paper) *Mon cher...*

Provenance
Maurice Corbeil, Montreal, before 1973; gift to the Montreal Museum of Fine Arts, 1984.

Exhibition
Ottawa 1973/1, No. 8.

Bibliography
ALLAIRE 1905, p. 136 (Repr.); *HUBBARD 1973*, pp. 52 and 53, No. 8 (Repr.).

Collection
Montreal Museum of Fine Arts. Gift from Maurice Corbeil (1984.43)

IN THE SPRING following his return from the United States, Louis Dulongpré placed an advertisement in the April 10, 1794 edition of the *Quebec Gazette* announcing: "[that he has] lately arrived from the Colonies, where he has improved in the Art of Drawing under the best Academicians" and "gives notice that he will paint in Miniature and in Crayons, Pastels." His first known work was a pastel portrait of Marguerite Parent-Leprohon (MCR) dated 1793. A miniature of this portrait is held at the Musée du Québec. Unfortunately, there exists only one example of this type of twofold production and only this particular miniature can be attributed to Dulongpré. It would seem that Dulongpré began his career as an itinerant artist by making pastel por-

traits of the bourgeoisie. Beginning in the 1800s, he gradually dropped this medium in favour of portraits in oil, which won him a new clientele.

Most of his portraits in pastel follow a number of technical and stylistic conventions. Sketched on beige or blue paper and mounted on canvas, probably by the artist himself, the majority are of average size, measuring about 40 × 30 centimetres. Profiles are rare: nearly all his subjects are depicted at a full-face, head-and-shoulders or three-quarter angle. Dulongpré showed a predilection for white, ultramarine, brown ochre, black, vermilion, yellow ochre and green. The artist probably applied layers of pastel—most likely pastel crayons—in small strokes, then softened the tones by smudging, except in a

few places, particularly for lace, where he highlighted textures using strokes of white. Black chalk was sometimes used to accentuate lines and heighten certain areas. The plain backgrounds are often hatched with diagonal strokes, most often in shades of blue and brown ochre.

The works shown here illustrate not only the common features of Dulongpré's portraits, but also their inconsistencies. *François Noiseux*, which dates from 1796 according to an early inscription, is marked by warm colour tones and shows a generally soft, nervous execution, despite a certain stiffness in the facial features and contours. Similar features, such as the angular lines and the application of the pastel, are found in the portrait of *Abbé François Cherrier*. The proposed date of

Fig. 23A.
Louis Dulongpré,
Louis-Joseph Papineau, c. 1796;
pastel on paper, 38.2 × 30.5 cm.
National Archives of Canada,
Ottawa (C-96268).

NGC

24.
Self-Portrait, c. 1805
Pastel on paper, 23.2 × 20.4 cm

Inscriptions
(b.,u.c., on the frame, in ink) *Cd Dulongpré Peint par lui-même, à l'âge de 40* [a word crossed out] *an* [a word above] *ans Compliment à Son amie M*[d]. [a word that is illegible]. *archambault. en succession à sa fille Julie de Martigny S-Hyacinthe Le 1er janvier 1806.;* (b.,c., on the paper that was used to protect the back of the work, saved in the file) *Cd Dulongpré, Peint par lui-même à l'âge de 80 ans/Com*[plime]*nt à son amie M^{de}.. Archambault − en Succe*[ss]*ion/à sa fille Julie de Martigny. S^t.. Hyacinthe − 1er.. janvier 1806.*

Provenance
Gift from the artist to Mrs. Amable Archambault, née Marie-Anne Bourgault, 1806; Mrs. Hugues Lemoine de Martigny, née Julie Archambault, by inheritance; Louis Carrier, Sainte-Anne-de-Bellevue; acquired by the National Gallery of Canada, Ottawa, 1961.

Exhibition
Ottawa 1969-1970, No. 2.

Bibliography
HARPER *1962/3,* p. 414 (Repr.); LA CHRONIQUE *1963,* p. 65; HARPER *1966,* pp. 61 and 62 (Repr.); READY *1969,* No. 2; LORD *1974,* pp. 40-41 (Repr.); AMTMANN *1976,* pp. 288 and 288a (Repr.); HILL AND LANDRY *1988,* p. 285 (Repr.); DEROME, BOURASSA AND CHAGNON *1988,* pp. 5, 9, 49-53, 56, 70 and 86 (Repr.).

Collection
National Gallery of Canada, Ottawa (9673)

execution (circa 1795-1798) concurs with the apparent age of the subject at the time and is in keeping with the stylistic techniques of the day. Father Cherrier (1745-1809) was parish priest in Saint-Denis, on the banks of the Richelieu River, from 1774 until his death. From 1797 on, he was also vicar-general of the parishes south of Montreal. He kept company with the most influential families of the day, including the Vigers and Papineaus. The Montreal Museum of Fine Arts and the National Archives of Canada both hold pastel portraits, attributed to Dulongpré, of the priest's brother, Joseph-Marie Cherrier, two of his sisters, Perrine-Charles Cherrier (MMFA) and Marie-Anne Cherrier (NAC), and Louis Joseph Papineau at age ten, when he was a student at the

Séminaire de Québec (Fig. 23A). The latter work confirms the suggested dating of this series since the age given Papineau in the portrait's inscription would situate its completion around 1796. Dulongpré apparently worked in the Richelieu area often; the region experienced incredible growth after the merchant class set up business there. A dozen portraits of the Cartier family, a prestigious family of local merchants and ancestors of Georges-Étienne Cartier, have survived to this day (MCR, Séminaire de Saint-Hyacinthe and PC). Finally, based on the inscription on the back of the frame, Dulongpré's *Self-Portrait* can be dated circa 1805,[1] which corresponds to the subject's clothing: a jacket whose narrower collar and lapels are decorated with an M-shaped notch, a shirt

with a jabot and starched collar whose ends point up towards the subject's cheeks and around which the artist has gathered a tie that has neither a bow nor a knot. The subtle treatment and rich textures of this work are evident despite its state of advanced deterioration. Because this portrait was not a commission, but rather for personal display, the artist enjoyed more freedom and its execution reveals Dulongpré's potential talent as a pastellist.

P.B.

Note
1. See the discussion of this inscription in DEROME, BOURASSA AND CHAGNON *1988,* p. 52.

25.
Mère Thérèse-Geneviève Coutlée, c. 1800
Oil on canvas, 72.5 × 64.8 cm

Inscription
(b.,l.r.,in ink, before the new backing covered the inscription) *Portrait de Mère T.G. Coutlée/–1791-1821-/par M^r^. Dulomprez- artiste-/au frais de Sr. Mézières.*

Exhibitions
Montreal 1967/1, No. 80; Quebec City 1984-1985, No. 96.

Bibliography
ASGM, G5/11C44, *Mémoires particuliers (Ancien journal),* No. 1 (1688-1857), 4e cahier, "Tableaux", p. 296; *Morisset 1960/1,* p. 69; *Harper 1966,* pp. 59 and 61 (Repr.); *Harper 1967,* pp. 68 and 69 (Repr.); *Carter 1967,* No. 80 (Repr.); *Le Grand Héritage 1984,* pp. 118 and 119, No. 96 (entry by Laurier Lacroix) (Repr.); *Duclos 1987,* p. 185; *Derome, Bourassa and Chagnon 1988,* p. 33; *Simard 1989,* pp. 182 and 183 (Repr.).

Collection
Musée des Sœurs grises de Montréal (73-A-024)

O N June 9, 1792, Mother Marie-Thérèse-Geneviève Coutlée (1742-1821) became the third general superior of the Grey Nuns of Montreal, succeeding Mother Marguerite-Thérèse Lemoine-Despins (Cat. 12), who had died three days earlier. It was under her direction that the Montreal General Hospital created or renovated various workshops for making objects used in religious celebra- tion: embroidery, braiding, liturgical and wax decorations, bookbinding, gilding, etc. In light of the financial hardships faced by the community, Mother Coutlée always helped with various manual duties, there- by remaining ever humble. Perhaps this is why she agreed, unlike her precursors, to have her portrait painted without feeling she was shirking her obligations. Dulong- pré has portrayed her embroidering a ma- niple similar to the one housed in the Grey Nuns museum.[1]

Very few portraits from the period of early Quebec art that broke with recog- nized conventions succeeded in being so personalized. Later in the 19th century, a few painters depicted their subjects sur- rounded by insignias of their profession or, more often, portrayed them in an arti- ficial setting with various attributes indica- tive of their office or intellectual qualities. In this portrait, however, Mother Coutlée is shown with objects that are more than mere symbols; they actually serve a pur- pose. The composition is built around contrasts of stability and dynamism. The static quality of the subject's pyramid- shaped face is offset by the three-dimen- sional effects implied by the diagonal drop of the shoulders and tilt of the head, by the skilful foreshortening of the right hand, and by the movement evoked by the ma- niple. The stark background and sombre clothing contrast with the bright colours used for the flesh tones, cross, thimble and maniple.

Since the community's books make no specific mention of the portrait of Mother Coutlée, it can be assumed that it was paid for by a third party. The inscrip- tion, no longer visible, would have it that Sister Louise Lepellé-Mézières commis- sioned the portrait, as she did those of Mother d'Youville and Mother Despins. While the remaining sources available on the subject make no mention of this issue, they corroborate the attribution to Louis Dulongpré suggested by the same inscrip- tion. A passage in *Mémoires particuliers* (1840-1860), the annals of the communi- ty, reveals that from among the paintings belonging to the nuns, "the one of Mr. Roux [Jean-Henry-Auguste Roux] and that of Mother Coutlée were done by Mr. Du- lonprez-." (*Translation*) These attribu- tions were probably based on an oral tradition still existing within the religious community.[2]

Although Philippe Liébert and François Beaucourt both had close ties with the community founded by Mother d'Youville, it would be difficult to attribute the portrait of Mother Coutlée to either of them. The fluidity and technical skill with which the portrait was executed im- mediately disqualifies Liébert. Various cir- cumstances do suggest Beaucourt could possibly have been the artist. In 1792, Mother Coutlée, then age 50, was ap- pointed Mother Superior of the communi- ty, a perfect occasion to have her portrait painted, in keeping with her two precur- sors. *Mémoires particuliers* also reveals that Beaucourt provided the drawing for an altar facing embroidered by Mother Coutlée. Given that she is depicted em- broidering, the theory that Beaucourt is the artist is appealing. However, compared with Beaucourt's other religious portraits, the colours here are brighter—particularly the flesh tones, in which the red practically lights up the nun's face; the subject mat- ter, richer and livelier, is rendered with short brush strokes; the style is nervous, more compact and less subservient to the drawing; the technique used to make the fingernails shine and highlight the joints is different. All these features show greater affinities with the technique of Dulong- pré. Mother Coutlée's facial features make it impossible to date the portrait with any accuracy. Her jovial expression, plump face and self-confident gesture show her to be no older than sixty, which makes it highly unlikely that the portrait was completed later than 1805. Dulongpré's artistic pro- duction is difficult to date: points of defi- nite comparison are rare and the artist's stylistic inconsistencies cloud the issue.[3] Nevertheless, this portrait stands apart from the pictorial production of the time in its originality and is generally thought to be a major work in Dulongpré's career.

P.B.

Notes
1. *Simard 1989,* p. 183 (Repr.).
2. Unfortunately, the portrait of Father Roux, still held by the Grey Nuns, appears to have been largely repainted, making it difficult to distinguish the artist's technique. However, another portrait of the Sulpician can be found at Maison Saint-Gabriel (Notre-Dame congregation). Dated 1823, it is also attributed to Dulongpré. This portrait conforms with the artist's style, which tends to confirm the accounts of the author of the Grey Nuns' memoirs.
3. *Derome, Bourassa and Chagnon, 1988,* pp. 34 and 56.

26.
James Sinclair, 1808
Oil on canvas, 68 × 55 cm

Inscriptions
(b., on the canvas, four documents attached by James Sinclair) 1° Letter from the Honourable Hector Theophilus Cramahé to James Sinclair, September 15, 1775, in which Sinclair is given the rank of *Quarter Master with the Rank of Lieutenant in the British Militia at Quebec;* 2° Letter from Guy Carleton to James Sinclair, September 15, 1775, in which Sinclair is given the same rank as above; 3° Letter from Lord Dorchester to James Sinclair, May 2, 1787, in which Sinclair is given the same rank as above; 4° Autographic biography, July 2, 1808, beginning with this sentence *On the other Side, is the Portrait of James Sinclair Esqʳ. now in his 76 year of/Age; − done by Louis Dulongpré Esqʳ. − Master Limner in all Canada −.*

Provenance
Private collection, London (sold by Sotheby & Co., London, February 28, 1962, No. 101); acquired by the Royal Ontario Museum, Toronto, 1962.

Exhibitions
Toronto 1978/2; Toronto 1982-1983; Montreal 1988-1989.

Bibliography
CATALOGUE 1962, p. 18, No. 101; *ALLODI 1978,* pp. 20 and 21 (Repr.); *LEVENSON 1983,* p. 35; *DEROME, BOURASSA AND CHAGNON 1988,* pp. 5, 9, 33, 34, 42, 43, 44, 70, 86, 92 and 93.

Collection
Royal Ontario Museum, Toronto (962.260)

THE SUAVE ELEGANCE of this portrait illustrates the degree of accuracy with which Louis Dulongpré was able to paint the psychological profile of his subjects around 1810. The documents attached to the back of the canvas by James Sinclair himself show a proud man who had led a simple life and fulfilled his obligations: his respectable age allows Sinclair to proudly display his achievements. After listing several of his feats of arms, both in Scotland—battle of Culloden, 1746—and in America—siege of Louisbourg, 1758; Battle of the Plains of Abraham, 1759; battle of Sainte-Foy, 1760; blockade of Quebec, 1775-1776—, he ends his autobiography with these words: "I am now in the 76th year of my Age; I do not wish to see any more War by I do sincerely wish and Hope, I will depart this life, when my benevolent Geneator pleases in peace with God and Man." Yet this Scot, born in 1732, was to live another 13 years before dying at the age of 89, in 1821.

Louis Dulongpré's portrait of Sinclair, who lived in Trois-Rivières, displays a nobleness that comes with age, a certain bourgeois *savoir faire* and the outmoded luxury of near-feminine grace. The high, shiny forehead, the decided look, the pursed lips, powdered hair and made-up face, the dignified pose, refined jabot, the rose in the buttonhole and gold-knob cane, in short, the entire personality of James Sinclair is exposed on canvas. The artist has succeeded in organizing these few elements in a work whose warm hues, filtered lighting and full-toned palette add to the near-excessive refinement of the sitter.

The gold-knob cane is reminiscent of the portrait of Dr. Jacques Denéchaud (Fig. 26A), which was once attributed to François Baillargé but is actually the work of Dulongpré. Denéchaud was a major donor to Quebec City's Hôtel-Dieu hospital and commissioned major works from Dulongpré to decorate the chapel.[1] As in the portrait of James Sinclair, Denéchaud's face stands out against a finely shaded background that resembles a cloudy sky. Inherited from the British tradition, this convention was also used by painter Robert Field, who worked in the United States from 1794 to 1808 and in Halifax from 1808 to 1818, notably in his portrait of lieutenant-general George Prevost (MSQ).[2] This compositional device seems to have been used especially in portraits of army officers.[3] It can be found in the works of two American artists who were contemporaries of Dulongpré: Rembrandt Peale

Fig. 26A.
Louis Dulongpré (attr. to),
Doctor Jacques Denéchaud, c. 1805;
oil on canvas, 73.5 × 61 cm.
Musée des Augustines de
l'Hôtel-Dieu de Québec.

(1787-1860) and John Trumbull (1756-1843).[4] Research to date shows that Dulongpré, perhaps trained in this technique during his stay in the United States, was one of the rare artists to have adopted and used it in Lower Canada.

Executed in 1808—according to the documents Sinclair mounted on the back of the canvas—this portrait is considered to have been painted at the height of Dulongpré's artistic career. It was during this period that he mastered the effects of texture, lighting and the psychological analysis and development of his subjects. In this portrait, Dulongpré blends beguiling charm and pictorial realism, without seeking the monumental stature achieved by such artists as Antoine Plamondon in the early 1830s (Cat. 183).

P.B.

Notes
1. See *BOISCLAIR 1977,* pp. 102-103 and 105-109, Nos. 151 and 153-166.
2. *CAUCHON 1971,* p. 126 (Repr.) and Alice Hoskins, *Robert Field* (Halifax: Novia Scotia Art Gallery, 1978), pp. 60-61, No. 29 (Repr.). See also Nos. 6, 39, 40 and 41.
3. See Desmond Shawe-Taylor, *The Georgians. Eighteenth-Century Portraiture & Society* (London: Berrie & Jenkins, 1990), Chap. II.
4. On Trumbull, see Nos. 484 and 2222 and, on Peale, Nos. 80, 466, 1071 and 1589 of the *Catalogue of American Portraits in The New-York Historical Society* (New Haven: Yale University Press, 1974).

27.
Abbé François Boissonnault, 1810
Oil on canvas, 67.3 × 54.5 cm

Inscription
(b.,u.c., on the canvas before the new backing covered the inscription) *SF^r Boissonault p^{tre} curé de S^t. Pierre de Sorel/peint le 23 Janvier 1810 à l'age de 34 ans 23 Jours par m^r L^s Du-/longpré* [Peintre] *Montréal.*

Provenance
Henri Fournier, Saint-Jean-Port-Joli; Louis-Philippe Morneau, Saint-Jean-Port-Joli; acquired by the Musée du Québec, Quebec City, 1968.

Exhibitions
Quebec City 1980/1; Quebec City 1983-1984, No. 52; Montreal 1988-1989.

Bibliography
Nos racines, No. 49 (1979), p. 972 (Repr.); *FAILLANT-DUMAS 1980*, pp. 58-64, 70 and 74 (Repr.); *CHEERS 1980*, p. 13; *AU MUSÉE 1980*; *LEVENSON 1983*, p. 35; *LE MUSÉE DU QUÉBEC 1983*, p. 58, No. 52 (entry by Claude Thibault, Luc Noppen and Michel Doyon) (Repr.); *DEROME, BOURASSA AND CHAGNON 1988*, pp. 5, 9, 30, 31, 33, 34, 36, 70, 76, 77, 86 and 93 (Repr.); *BÉLAND AND BOURASSA 1990*, pp. 6, 8 and 32 (Repr.); *LACROIX 1990*, p. 21; *UN MOMENT 1991*, p. 191.

Collection
Musée du Québec, Quebec City (68.150)

THE PORTRAIT of Father François Boissonnault by Louis Dulongpré can be dated with accuracy thanks to an inscription on the back of the canvas possibly written by the subject himself—it is often through inscriptions of this kind that we are able to identify and date Dulongpré's paintings. Born December 31, 1775, Father Boissonnault had no trouble identifying his age to the day, indicating at the same time the exact date on which Dulongpré, who at the time was plying his trade in Montreal, painted the portrait. Boissonnault was parish priest at Saint-Pierre-de-Sorel and Ile Dupas from 1806 to 1814, then in Saint-Jean-Port-Joli from 1814 to 1843. It was there that he died in 1854, after retiring. His portrait was found in a private home—possibly belonging to a descendent of the family that took him in during the last years of his life—and not in the parish rectory as originally thought.

Although the pose is conventional, it confirms Boissonnault's status. Using his index finger to hold open his breviary, which is decorated with a headband sewn directly to the spine, the sitter, wearing a powdered periwig and silk belt, is taking a momentary break from his reading. Caught in a moment of reflection, he slides one hand into his cassock and pulls out a fine silk tie. These components paint a portrait that is far from the image of the good parish priest; indeed, Father Boissonnault displays the dignity of his rank and the nobility of the educated. He is portrayed more as a member of the elite whose influence extends beyond his own parish and into the religious community as a whole.

To endow the sitter with the presence he warrants, Dulongpré uses a series of technical and stylistic means which tend to be characteristic of his oeuvre. The subject is set against a plain background lit from the left. The artist lends subtlety to his textures using various artistic techniques: the stiff collar and lapel; the delicate tie; the heavy fabric, cinched in with a belt; the rich gilding on the breviary; and the powder shining on the wig and shoulder pad. Similar to the portrait of Mother Coutlée (Cat. 25), the composition is built on contrasts: the very compressed left hand and the foreshortening of the breviary contrast with the broad movement of the right arm.

This portrait is not without certain weaknesses, however. The facial contours and lines have a heaviness about them that contrast with the fine rendition of the portrait of James Sinclair (Cat. 26), dated two years earlier. But the shadowing

Fig. 27A.
Louis Dulongpré,
Isaac Todd, 1800;
oil on canvas, 84.8 × 68.1 cm.
Musée du Québec, Quebec City (56.299).

around the beard and eyebrows was accentuated at an unknown time and these additions were not removed during the restoration carried out in 1980. Much more characteristic, on the other hand, is the difficulty Dulongpré experienced rendering hands: they appear artificially chubby, the anatomy is incorrect, and the wrist joint is not realistic enough. The portraits of Mother Coutlée (Cat. 25), James Sinclair (Cat. 26), Joseph Papineau (Cat. 90), Dr. Jacques Denéchaud (Fig. 26A), Isaac Todd (Fig. 27A) and James McGill (Fig. 17A) show similar difficulty with the hands.

Louis Dulongpré's notion of portraiture definitely remains faithful to the values of the *Ancien regime*, perpetuating certain esthetic canons of pre-revolutionary France. His work nevertheless lacks the mannered charm of François Beaucourt, who was trained under these principles. The works of Dulongpré combine dignity, nobility and gracefulness, while retaining sobriety and realism. The influence of his year of training in Baltimore, in 1793, no doubt contributed to this adherence to established norms that also characterized American portraiture at the time.

P.B.

GEORGE BULTEEL
FISHER
1764-1834

GEORGE BULTEEL FISHER was born in Peterborough, England on March 16, 1764 and grew up in a stimulating family environment, with two brothers, John and Benjamin, who were also watercolourists. John, the eldest child, Bishop of Salisbury and friend of George III, had developed privileged relations with British artists. George chose to serve in the army and began his training in the drawing room of the Tower of London, where James Hunter (well-known between 1777 and 1792), another topographical painter who visited Quebec in 1778-1779, had also studied. Fisher and his brother Benjamin exhibited together at the Royal Academy of Arts in 1780 and again in 1781. George Bulteel Fisher completed his training at the Royal Military Academy at Woolwich. On July 1, 1782, he was appointed sublieutenant of the Royal Artillery and was later promoted to the ranks of captain, then brevet colonel in June 1814 and major-general in May 1825.

After being sent to Gibraltar in 1790, Fisher sailed to Lower Canada in 1791 as part of the staff of Prince Edward Augustus, future Duke of Kent (Cat. 6 and 7). In spring 1792, he travelled to Upper Canada, where he painted several views of Niagara Falls. His work drew the attention of Elizabeth Posthuma Simcoe (1766-1850), wife of the lieutenant-governor of Upper Canada and herself an amateur watercolourist. Fisher left Canada for the West Indies in 1794 before returning to England. He arranged for John William Edy to produce aquatint engravings of his *Six Views of North America...* and also published a larger scale aquatint of a Niagara Falls view. In March 1809, Fisher served in the war fought in Spain, during which time he produced a series of watercolours depicting Spanish landscapes. After returning to Woolwich, he was appointed commanding officer of the garrison on February 10, 1827, a position he held until his death on March 8, 1834.

Main sources
COOKE 1983; COOKE 1987.

View on the St. Ann's or Grand River.

28.
View of the Saint Ann's Falls, 1796
Engraved by John William Edy After George Bulteel Fisher
Aquatint on paper, 49,7 × 67 (plate)

Inscriptions
(l.l., under the image) *G.B. Fisher delin.*; (l.c., under the image) *Pub¹. Feb². 1. 1796. by J.W. Edy, No... 2, Romney Row, S¹. John's, Westminster./VIEW ON THE S¹. ANN'S OR GRAND RIVER.*; (l.l.,under the image) *J.W. Edy Aquatinta.*; (u.r., above the image) *e.*

Provenance
Séminaire de Québec; on deposit at the Société du Musée du Séminaire de Québec, 1983.

Exhibition
Ottawa 1967/2, No. 161 (British Museum version, London).

Bibliography
JEFFERYS 1948, No. 397; *SPENDLOVE 1958*, pp. xviii, 22-24 (Repr.); *LORD 1965*, p. 28; *STRONG 1967*, pp. 231-232, No. 161 (Repr.); *DE VOLPI 1971*, pl. 35; *FINLEY 1983*, pp. 49-50 and 64 (Repr.).

Collection
Musée du Séminaire de Québec (Pf 990.3)

G EORGE BULTEEL FISHER'S stint in Lower Canada arose from his position as a member of Prince Edward Augustus' staff (Cat. 6 and 7) and was very short. He arrived at Quebec in 1791, probably in the spring, and left in 1794 to take part in the capture of Martinique during the war with France. Immediately upon his return to England in 1795, Fisher joined forces with John William Edy (active between 1780 and 1820), a specialist in landscape engravings, to publish a series of aquatints after his drawings from nature done in Quebec. Fisher accompanied each engraving with an inscription describing the exact site and aiding the viewer to interpret the work. His *View of the Saint Ann's Falls,* fourth in the series

of views dedicated to Prince Edward, bore the following description:

The peculiar boldness of the present scene is particularly striking. The river which runs through these wild and rugged banks, takes its rise on the very summits of the mountains, and descends by a multiplicity of cataracts into the river St. Lawrence. Within the distance of one mile may be reckoned six falls; some of them of the height of fifty or sixty feet. The access to this river is extremely difficult, as the banks are every where very steep and rugged, and in some places of a stupendous height. The situation of this river is eighteen miles below Quebec, and at the extremity of the settled country on the north shore of the river St. Lawrence.

This collection of six aquatints holds major significance in the field of North American landscape art. As far as it

MQ, NGC

29. (See colour reproduction, p. 82)
View of Quebec, c. 1795
Watercolour over graphite on paper, 54.8 × 76.6 cm

(See technical data on the next page).

is known, this is the first time Quebec landscapes were reproduced in engravings based on the principles of the Picturesque.

In order to fully understand Fisher's vision of landscape portrayal, notably his emphasis on the "wilderness" aspect of a site, clearly isolated from "civilization", it is necessary to consult the publications which were popular in Great Britain at the time. In 1794, the year before Fisher did his *View of the Saint Ann's Falls,* William Sotheby had published *Tour through Parts of Wales* in London. This guide was illustrated with a series of aquatints by S. Alken after drawings by John "Warwick" Smith (1749-1831).[1] If George Bulteel Fisher had never seen this book, his publisher surely had, since *Melincourt Cascade* (Fig. 28A)

has much in common with *View of the Saint Ann's Falls.* The high horizon, the rock wall and cascading waterfalls in the middle distance, the play on light and shadow, and the strong luminosity emphasizing the sublime atmosphere of the site, where three figures have come in quest of the imposing landscape, are all common to both Edy's and Alken's engravings. Edy's technique of inserting something of the North American landscape into a standard vision of nature that was familiar to his British contemporaries was unprecedented. As Gerald Finley has so well illustrated,[2] these aquatints were to have a profound influence on other artists, particularly George Heriot and his works after 1797.

Fisher's North American views are a perfect example of poetic landscape, whereby a specific site is totally subordinate to an esthetic principle that governs every last detail. His huge *View of Quebec,* held at the National Archives of Canada, is based entirely on such principles. This spectacular watercolour illustrates the artist's desire to create an exceptional work. Quebec City is portrayed in a geometric composition, strictly laid out according to the rules of the classical landscape. The two tall, vertical trees in the foreground frame a succession of horizontal planes parallel to the pictorial plane. Fisher was surely familiar with the works of Claude Lorrain (1600-1682), either directly, or indirectly through Richard Earlom's (1743-1822) recent

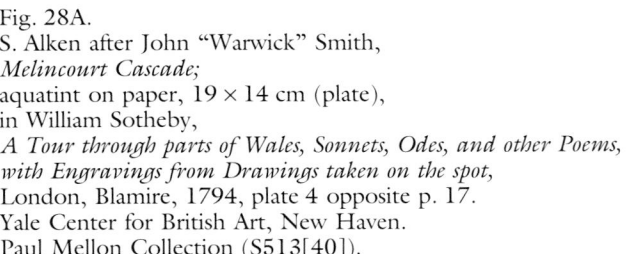

Fig. 28A.
S. Alken after John "Warwick" Smith,
Melincourt Cascade;
aquatint on paper, 19 × 14 cm (plate),
in William Sotheby,
A Tour through parts of Wales, Sonnets, Odes, and other Poems,
with Engravings from Drawings taken on the spot,
London, Blamire, 1794, plate 4 opposite p. 17.
Yale Center for British Art, New Haven.
Paul Mellon Collection (S513[40]).

Fig. 29A.
Richard Earlom after Claude Lorrain,
Landscape with the Metamorphosis of the Apulian Shepherd, 1777;
mezzotint engraving, 20.3 × 26 cm (plate size),
in Claude Lorrain,
Liber Veritatis, Vol. II, Fol. 142.
Yale Center for British Art, New Haven.
Paul Mellon Collection (L200[f.142]).

publication of two thick volumes of two hundred mezzotint engravings after the drawings of *Liber Veritatis*.[3] A comparison of *Landscape with the Metamorphosis of the Apulian Shepherd* (Fig. 29A), from the Duke of Sutherland's collection, and the watercolour by Fisher shows compositional affinities between the two works. ***View of Quebec*** also gives the foreground full importance, making it the principal site of activity, and makes use of the overall luminosity in which the trees contrast with the hazy distance. Fisher probably did this watercolour following his return to England. Judging by its size and the extreme care given the finished product, he must have intended to exhibit it. The artist had already shown his works at the Royal Academy of Arts in 1780 and 1781. The letters exchanged between the artist's nephew, John Fisher, and painter John

Constable (1776-1837) reveal that George Bulteel Fisher often solicited comments on his landscapes.[4]

D.P.

Notes

1. See Peter Bicknell, *Beauty, Horror and Immensity. Picturesque Landscape in Britain, 1750-1850* (Cat.) (Cambridge: Fitzwilliam Museum, 1981), No. 139.

2. *FINLEY 1983*, pp. 49-52.

3. On *Liber Veritatis* and Richard Earlom's engravings, see Michael Kitson, *Claude Lorrain: Liber Veritatis* (London: The Trustees of the British Museum, 1978).

4. For further reading on the relationship between G.B. Fisher and J. Constable, see Martin Hardie, *Water-Colour Painting in Britain* (London: B.T. Batsford Ltd., 1968) [1979]), Vol. III, pp. 264-265.

View of Quebec, c. 1795

Technical data

Inscription
(b.,l.c., in graphite) *View of the City of Quebec by G. B. Fisher/circa 1795.*

Provenance
E. Parsons & Sons, London; acquired by the Public Archives of Canada, Ottawa, 1922.

Bibliography
MORISSET 1960/1, p. 73.

Collection
National Archives of Canada, Ottawa (1989-593-1X)

JEAN-JOSEPH GIROUARD, grandson of Jean Baillairgé, was born in Quebec City on November 13, 1794. Following the death of his father in September 1800, Girouard went to live with his grandfather and, like his father, had the opportunity to be apprentice to the famous Quebec carpenter and sculptor as well as to his uncles, François and Pierre-Florent. Jean Baillairgé died five years later, in 1805. In 1811, Girouard was hired as a clerk in the office of notary Joseph Maillou, completing his training under Pierre-Rémi Gagné immediately after the War of 1812. He settled in the parish of Saint-Benoît (Deux-Montagnes township) after receiving his commission as a notary on June 13, 1816.

Over the years, Girouard took up the cause of the *Patriotes*, striking up friendships with various party members. In 1831, he became a member of the Assembly for the new constituency of Deux-Montagnes and, in 1834, supported the Ninety-Two Resolutions and campaigned for office during that year's "stormy" elections. A questionable decision by the returning officer in Girouard's favour enabled him to return to the House of Assembly until 1837.

During the rebellion of November 1837, Girouard was jailed in the new Montreal prison from December 26, 1837 to July 16, 1838 and again from early November to December 27, 1838. It was during this time that he did the series of portraits of his fellow prisoners, all valuable witnesses to and principal players in the uprisings (Cat. 112 and 113). When the hostilities ended, Girouard, aged forty-four, had lost everything. He went back to his professional career, devoting his final years to building a convent for the education of young girls and care for the elderly in Saint-Benoît. Jean-Joseph Girouard died at Saint-Benoît on November 13, 1855.

JEAN-JOSEPH GIROUARD
1794-1855

Main sources
LAURIN 1973; CHASSÉ 1985.

MQ, NGC

VAG, AGNS, MMFA

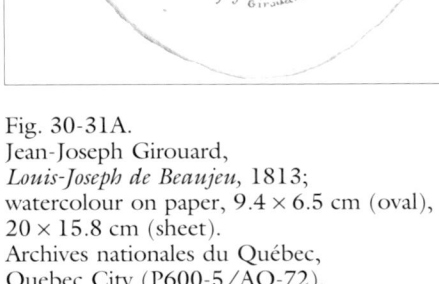

30.
Eustache-Ignace Trottier Desrivières Beaubien, 1813
Watercolour on paper, 9.2 × 6.4 cm (oval);
20 × 15 cm (sheet)

Inscriptions
(l. c., on the mat, in pen and black ink) *Pinx by J. Girouard – 1813;* (b.) *Beaubien.*

Provenance
Pierre-René Boucher de La Bruère; Dr. Pierre-Claude Boucher de La Bruère; the Honourable Pierre Boucher de La Bruère; Alice de La Bruère-Fortier; gift to the Archives de la Province de Québec, Quebec City, 1942.

Exhibitions
Vancouver, 1959, No. 144; (?) Archives de la Province de Québec, Quebec City, 1966.

Bibliography
MORISSET 1959/1, p. 45; *LAURIN 1973*, p. 5.

Collection
Archives nationales du Québec, Quebec City (P600-5/AQ-71)

31.
Pierre-René Boucher de La Bruère, 1813
Watercolour on paper, 9.3 × 6.6 cm (oval);
20 × 15 cm (sheet)

Inscriptions
(l. c., on the mat, in pen and black ink) *Pinx J. Girouard 1813;* (b.) *No.. 76/Pierre Boucher de la Bruère?/Major Pierre René Boucher/de la Bruère.*

Provenance
Dr. Pierre-Claude Boucher de La Bruère; the Honourable Pierre Boucher de La Bruère; Alice de La Bruère-Fortier; gift to the Archives de la Province de Québec, Quebec City, 1942.

Exhibitions
Vancouver, 1959, No. 144; (?) Archives de la Province de Québec, 1966.

Bibliography
MORISSET 1959/1, p. 45; *LAURIN 1973*, p. 5; *CHARTRAND 1986-1987*, p. 38.

Collection
Archives nationales du Québec, Quebec City (P600-5/AQ-73)

Fig. 30-31A.
Jean-Joseph Girouard,
Louis-Joseph de Beaujeu, 1813;
watercolour on paper, 9.4 × 6.5 cm (oval),
20 × 15.8 cm (sheet).
Archives nationales du Québec,
Quebec City (P600-5/AQ-72).

J EAN-JOSEPH GIROUARD's best-known work is a series of silhouette portraits of fellow prisoners jailed during the 1837-1838 uprisings (Cat. 112 and 113), as well as a few pencil and pastel portraits of members of the Baillairgé family. There are at least three existing portraits—all of officers in the War of 1812—dating from his early career as an artist.[1] Girouard himself took part in the conflict: after leaving his position as notarial clerk in Sainte-Geneviève-de-Pierrefonds, he enlisted, initially as a volunteer, in the militia at Lachine. In November 1812, at

the age of eighteen, he joined the Lavaltrie battalion. Girouard painted watercolour portraits of officers ***Pierre-René Boucher de La Bruère*** (1770-1855), ***Eustache-Ignace Trottier Desrivières Beaubien*** (1761-1816) and *Louis-Joseph de Beaujeu*[2] (Fig. 30-31A) probably to occupy his spare time. Boucher de La Bruère held the ranks of captain (May 1812) then major (March 1813); Desrivières Beaubien, son of Eustache Trottier Desrivières and Marguerite Mailhot (Cat. 14, 15 and 16), and brother of Basilique-Benjamin Trottier Desrivières Beaubien (Cat. 46), was promoted from

major to second lieutenant-colonel in September 1813.[3]

All three officers served in the famous Battle of Châteauguay on October 26, 1813, under the command of Lieutenant-Colonel Charles-Michel de Salaberry (Cat. 89). They knew each other since Ignace Desrivières Beaubien was married to Boucher de La Bruère's sister and Beaujeu had previously been captain of the Second Select Embodied Militia battalion alongside Boucher de La Bruère.[4] While posted in Laprairie, Beaujeu would have lunch and tea with Madame de La Bruère, who had accompanied her husband on his mission.[5] The portraits remained in the La Bruère family until their donation. Having distinguished himself in the Battle of Châteauguay, La Bruère left his family two flags given to his battalion by Princess Charlotte, George III's daughter. It is thus possible that the portraits were executed during this Battle, since La Bruère and Beaujeu were majors in the Second Select Embodied Militia battalion, and Desrivières Beaubien was second lieutenant-colonel of the sedentary militia at Verchères.

From age six to ten, Jean-Joseph Girouard lived with his grandfather, Jean Baillairgé, where he learned "the rules of finding cubic content" and, by the same token, the rudiments of drawing. He no doubt continued drawing in the years that followed, probably learning on his own some techniques in the art of miniatures.[6] In some respects, the three portraits in question form a set,[7] not only because they depict three officers who were closely associated, but also because they shed light on Girouard's artistic development in the art of miniature portraiture. They reveal an artist with definite talent, but one who is still trying to understand and exploit the qualities of this technique.

By painting the three officers in their scarlet redingotes with chamois collars and lining, the artist is already showing a concern for originality. Each of the sitters is shown in a different profile: full silhouette for Beaujeu; almost full-face for La Bruère, his right hand inside his jacket; and three-quarter profile for Desrivières

Beaubien. The latter portrait shows the most technique. While the facial features are rendered in detail in all three portraits, those of Desrivières Beaubien are the most luminous. Girouard has used a richer palette to paint the flesh tones, the light, saturated grey of the background creating greater contrast, thereby better setting off the officer's face. In addition, the technique used to render the officers' uniforms and wash the grey background is far more effective in the portrait of Desrivières Beaubien. Although Girouard has attempted to create a certain effect by increasing the number of brushstokes around Beaujeu's face, the result is somewhat dull and makes the profile harder to distinguish. Unlike in the portrait of Beaujeu, Girouard has succeeded in giving more volume to Boucher de La Bruère's coat and has painted the middleground more skilfully.

Girouard seems to have found his greatest inspiration in times of trouble—the War of 1812 and the 1837-1838 uprisings—; in fact, many of the works attributed to the artist are closely tied to these events. Perhaps Girouard felt the need to turn his talents as a drawer to good account by immortalizing the portraits of some of the key players in these events. Even if, as far as we know at least, only four portraits date from this initial period, they nonetheless reveal the artist's skill as a drawer and watercolourist. Girouard remains one of the few French-Canadian artists of his time to have painted portraits in miniature.[8]

D.C.

Notes

1. The literature also makes mention of a fourth miniature painted by Girouard: a portrait of Louis-Édouard Hubert, lieutenant in the Second Select Embodied Militia battalion in the War of 1812. See *Laurin 1973*, p. 5; Marie-Paule R. LaBrèque, DCB, Vol. VII (1988), pp. 421-422; *Catalogue 1887*, p. 19.

2. Made captain in May 1812, De Beaujeu was promoted major in October of the same year. Nicknamed the "knight of Beaujeu", he spent his final days in the army as lieutenant of the Royal Canadian Regiment. He never married.

3. For details on the various military ranks, see L. Homfray Irving, *Officers of the British Forces in Canada during the war 1812-1815*, s.l., Canadian Military Institute, 1908, pp. 122, 189, 195-196.

4. Louis-Édouard Hubert was a lieutenant in the same battalion.

5. Beaujeu even attended the christening of one the couple's children on February 16, 1813, in Laprairie. For more on Boucher de La Bruère, see Montarville Boucher de La Bruère, "Le livre de raison des seigneurs de Montarville", *Cahier des dix*, No. 4 (1939), pp. 243-270.

6. A small portrait of Jean-Joseph Girouard, dated 1814, exists and was previously attributed to François Baillairgé. See *Laurin 1973*, p. 4.

7. In 1959, Gérard Morisset discussed the three portraits as one catalogue number (*Morisset 1959/1*).

8. Girouard lost all his artist's materials used to paint pastels and miniatures when his house burned down during the 1837-1838 uprisings. The inventory of his losses, drawn up in 1846, includes a number of engravings as well as four paintings depicting the Doctors of the Church by François Beaucourt. See Paul-André Linteau, "Documents inédits", *Revue d'histoire de l'Amérique française*, Vol. XXI, No. 3 (December 1967), pp. 478-479).

GEORGE HERIOT

1759-1839

EORGE HERIOT was born in Haddington, Scotland in 1759, and studied at the Royal High School in Edinburgh from 1769 to 1774, possibly learning some drawing and painting there. In 1777, Heriot went to London in the hope of rapidly completing his artistic training, taking with him a letter of introduction addressed to architect Robert Adam (1728-1792). Little is known about this period in Heriot's life; there are no documents clearly explaining why Heriot suddenly left England for the West Indies that same year. On his return to Britain in 1781, he published *A Descriptive Poem Written in the West Indies* in London and then entered the Royal Military Academy at Woolwich. He was appointed to Woolwich's Ordinance Department in 1783 and seven years later, in September 1792, was transferred to Quebec City. He remained with the Department for the duration of his stay in Canada.

On October 18, 1799, Heriot took on a new position, replacing Hugh Finley as deputy postmaster general of British North America, a position he held for nearly seventeen years. Heriot returned to Britain twice; the first time in 1796-1797—in spring 1797, he exhibited three of his works, including two Canadian landscapes, at the Royal Academy of Arts. In 1804, he published the first history of Lower Canada in English. In 1806, he made his second trip back to England and in 1807, published *Travels through the Canadas…*, an account of his numerous travels throughout Upper and Lower Canada illustrated with plates based on his own watercolours.

After several attempts to improve the country's postal service, but also owing to conflicts with both his superior in London and certain members of the colonial administration, Heriot resigned from his position at the post office in January 1816. The following summer he returned to England and spent the many years remaining in his life painting and travelling to various countries in Europe, including France, Austria and Italy. George Heriot died at Chelsea (London) on July 22, 1839.

Main sources
COOKE 1983; FINLEY 1983; FINLEY 1988.

VAG, AGNS, MMFA

32.
West View of Château-Richer, c. 1792

Watercolour over graphite, pen and brown ink on paper.
18th Century mount with black and grey lines on beige wash, 21.4 × 32.3 cm

Inscriptions
(i., l.r.) *GH;* (l.c., on a mount from the 18th century, in pen and black ink, in the artist's hand) *West View of Chateau Riché.*

Provenance
Sold by Maggs Bros., London, 1929, No. 16; William Hugh Coverdale collection, Manoir Richelieu, Tadoussac, before 1940; acquired by the National Gallery of Canada, Ottawa, 1971.

Exhibitions
Montreal 1940, No. 1092; New York 1942, No. 60; Quebec City 1942-1943, No. 141; Kingston 1973, No. 12; Kingston 1978-1979, No. 54.

Bibliography
Maggs Bros., catalogue 514, 1929, No. 16 (Repr.); *CATALOGUE 1940,* p. 8, No. 1092; *CATALOGUE 1942,* p. 19, No. 60; *GODENRATH 1942,* p. 20, No. 141; *REID 1973,* pp. 27 and 28 (Repr.); *SMITH 1973,* No. 12; *HARPER 1977/1,* p. 52 (Repr.); *FINLEY 1978,* p. 40, No. 54; *FINLEY 1983,* pp. 44, 56 and 233, No. 15 (Repr.); *McDOUGALL 1988,* p. 32.

Collection
National Gallery of Canada, Ottawa (16674).

I N HIS MONOGRAPH on George Heriot, published in 1983, Gerald Finley dated this particular watercolour circa 1792, making it one of the artist's first Canadian pieces, since Heriot arrived in Quebec City to work as a clerk in the Ordinance Department only in September 1792. This is a highly plausible date for this watercolour and nothing allows us to continue including it as part of the artist's production of 1805-1806, as the catalogues for the Coverdale collection did for so long.

The actual focus of this composition is the ruins of the convent of the Sisters of Notre-Dame Congregation. Built in the early 1690s on property belonging to the Séminaire de Québec, the convent was destroyed in August 1759 when the Beaupré coast was captured by British troops.[1] In 1777, the population of Château-Richer launched an attempt to reconstruct the building in an effort to reinstate its initial purpose as an educational institution; however, this time the Séminaire de Québec refused to make any financial contribution and the project was abandoned.[2] For years the ruins of the convent, a two-storey stone building, remained standing just below the parish church; Cockburn even painted it around 1830.

There is an obvious simplicity about this work. A series of horizontal planes draw the viewer's attention across a number of focal points as the planes gradually fade off in the distance: peasants and livestock, trees, convent ruins, parish church and the mountains in the background. The drawing is meticulous and the colours reduced to a minimum. The fact that the artist deliberately left areas of the two-tone (blue and beige) drawing paper blank is of essential importance. Only the occasional ochre highlights set off the rocks in the foreground, the roofs of the houses and the cluster of trees on the slope just left of the convent.

Heriot's arrival in Quebec City marked the end of nearly a decade in Woolwich (1783-1792).[3] As suggested by Gerald Finley, this period in Woolwich undoubtedly made it easier for the artist to meet up with Paul Sandby,[4] from whom he learned the principles of the panoramic view, portrayed in a purified spatial structure. However, nothing indicates that Heriot was influenced by Paul Sandby alone, since this particular type of composition was specific to a period in which the works of Paul and his brother, Thomas Sandby, were indistinguishable.[5] Furthermore, there is every indication that his work was influenced by other artists as well: the colour scheme, notably the dominant blues, echoes the work of Edward Dayes (1763-1804)[6] and the ochre highlights are reminiscent of the Italian influence on British watercolourists of the late 18th century, such as John "Warwick" Smith (1749-1831), for example.[7]

Gerald Finley has shown in no uncertain terms Heriot's technique of taking nature's fundamental qualities and portraying them in simple, rational images. This is probably one of the reasons the view of Château-Richer so resembles an English park. The three scrawny trees and the lone ruins sitting atop a hillock have the symbolic strength of a "décor perdu".

D.P.

Notes

1. Noël Baillargeon, *Le Séminaire de Québec de 1685 à 1760* (Quebec City: Les Presses de l'Université Laval, 1977), pp. 234-236.

2. Noël Baillargeon, *Le Séminaire de Québec de 1760 à 1800* (Quebec City: Les Presses de l'Université Laval, 1981), pp. 231-233.

3. While Heriot's presence in Woolwich in 1783 has been confirmed by an archival document (*FINLEY 1983,* p. 209, Note 16), it is highly possible that he had been living there since 1781-1782 as a student at the Royal Military Academy.

4. *FINLEY 1983,* pp. 21-23. The works from this period nevertheless remain the only tangible proof.

5. See A.P. Oppe, *The Drawings of Paul and Thomas Sandby in the collection of His Majesty the King at Windsor Castle.* Oxford and London: The Phaidon Press Ltd., 1947, No. 31 (Paul) and No. 54 (Thomas).

6. M. Hardie, *Water-Colour Painting in Britain* (London: William Clowes and Son, 1975), Vol. I, pp. 179-180.

7. See *SS Giovanni e Paolo, Rome, with S. Stefano Rotondo in the distance,* in Lindsay Stainton, *British Landscape Watercolours, 1600-1860* (London: British Museum Publications Ltd., 1985), No. 52, Pl. 21 (Repr.).

Fig. 33A.
Michael Angelo Rooker,
Buildwas Abbey, Shropshire;
watercolour over graphite on paper,
The Whitworth Art Gallery,
Manchester, England (D.1892.15)

MQ, NGC

33.
Ruins of the Intendant's Palace, 1799
Watercolour, pen and brown ink over graphite on paper laid on strong cardboard,
26.8 × 37.8 cm

Inscription
(b.,c., on a strip of paper cut from the 19th century mount and laid down, in pen and black ink, in the artist's hand) *Ruins of the Intendants Palace./ 1799.*

Provenance
Old Print Shop, New York; acquired by the Royal Ontario Museum, Toronto, 1953.

Exhibitions
Charlottetown 1964, No. 19; (?) Vancouver 1966, No. 25; Ottawa 1967/1, No. 41; Kingston 1978-1979, No. 63.

Bibliography
SPENDLOVE *1958*, pp. xvii and 26a (Repr.); HUBBARD *1959/2*, p. 127 (Repr.); (?) HUBBARD *1963*, p. 50; HARPER *1963*, pp. 22 and 23, No. 19 (Repr.); (?) SHADBOLT *1966*, No. 25; HUBBARD AND OSTIGUY *1967*, pp. 32 and 33, No. 41 (Repr.); (?) REID *1973*, p. 27; ALLODI *1974/1*, Vol. I, No. 821; FINLEY *1978*, p. 42, No. 63; FINLEY *1979*, pp. 16 and 18; FINLEY *1983*, pp. 52, 69 and 238, No. 60 (Repr.); COMEAU *1983*, p. 128.

Collection
Royal Ontario Museum, Toronto (953.132.24)

THE INTENDANT'S PALACE stood on the banks of the Saint-Charles River, in Quebec City's Lower Town. In addition to the palace itself, rebuilt by Chaussegros de Léry in 1726 after being razed by a fire, were a magazine, a building for potash, stables, various sheds and a very large garden. Since it was left untouched by the 1759 bombings, Richard Short was able to leave a record of its size and appearance. Unfortunately, however, the building was destroyed during the Bostonians' siege of Quebec City in 1775-1776. Invested by American troops, the palace became the target of attacks which led to its destruction. The ruins remained standing until 1870.[1]

Ruins of the Intendant's Palace is part of a series of four watercolours done in 1798 and 1799.[2] Of similar treatment, they depict the palace ruins from various angles. In *Ruins of the Intendant's Palace*, the building's facade faces the mouth of the Saint-Charles River: sailing ships can actually be seen through the first-floor window. Based on Chaussegros de Léry's architectural plan, the artist probably recorded the scene from the chapel.[3] The background is sectioned off by the gable, with its bull's-eye window. It is a faithful reproduction of the site and the concern for topographical accuracy is obvious. Compared with *West View of Château-Richer* (Cat. 32), which is essentially the

view of a landscapist who merely inserts architectural structures into the natural setting, *Ruins of the Intendant's Palace* shows more of the topographical artist's painstaking attention to the exact location of buildings.

Unlike Gerald Finley, who considers this watercolour to have been influenced by Thomas Girtin (1775-1802),[4] we feel that the treatment of the motif—e.g. the attention to detail, the meticulous lines and precision of the rockbeds, the entire building bathed in soft light and sunlight, and the pastel colour scheme—has much in common with the depiction of architectural ruins by Edward Dayes (1763-1804) and Michael Angelo Rooker (1746-1801) (Fig. 33A). It is possible that Heriot was in direct contact with the works of these artists during his visits to England or was familiar with them through engravings.

D.P.

Notes
1. For an overview of the architectural history of the intendant's palace, see NOPPEN, PAULETTE AND TREMBLAY *1979*, pp. 290-294.
2. ROM, Nos. 953.132.25, 26 and 27.
3. See NOPPEN, PAULETTE AND TREMBLAY *1979*, p. 108, Pl. 16.
4. FINLEY *1979*, p. 16, Fig. 2, and FINLEY *1983*, p. 52.

VAG, AGNS, MMFA

34.
Ferry on the Jacques Cartier River, 1807
Dark brown wash over graphite on paper, 12.6 × 18.8 cm (irregular dimensions)

Inscription
(b.,u.c., in pen and brown ink, in the artist's hand)
Ferry on the Jacques Quartier/20ᵗʰ September 1807.

Provenance
Old Print Shop, New York; acquired by the Royal
Ontario Museum, Toronto, 1953.

Exhibition
Windsor 1967-1968, No. 17.

Bibliography
ALLODI 1974/1, Vol. I, No. 835; *FINLEY 1983,*
p. 253, No. 156.

Collection
Royal Ontario Museum, Toronto (953.132.7)

A CCORDING TO JOSEPH BOUCHETTE, "the River Jacques Cartier, viewed with a military eye, forms a most powerful natural barrier, and may be termed one of the outworks to the city and environs of Quebec."[1] The site is definitely pristine: the river is hemmed in by virtually inaccessible rocky slopes and the swift current makes crossing a perilous adventure. Heriot has depicted the point where the main road, which runs along the seigneury, joins the Jacques-Cartier River and the ferry crossing, "of about 160 toises broad, where, on account of the violence of the stream, the boats are traversed from side to side by means of hawsers stretched across."[2]

Dated September 20, 1807, this watercolour marks Heriot's return to Lower Canada after spending the winter of 1806-1807 in England and the early summer in Nova Scotia and New Brunswick. When *Ferry on the Jacques Cartier River* was done, Heriot had fully mastered his technique. His watercolours from the very early 1800s had already established the rules for compositions in three parallel plans.[3] In this respect, *Ferry on the Jacques Cartier River* presents nothing new. The highly contrasting foreground draws immediate attention. The buildings, in light washes, occupy the middleground and the eye is drawn to a thin mountainous strip in the central opening. Heriot's visit to the Atlantic provinces in the summer of 1807 allowed him, in particular, to refine his style of expression and gain new confidence in his increased technical skills.[4] *West View of Partridge Island from Parsborough, Bay of Fundy* (Fig. 34A), drawn from nature on June 24, 1807, shows an artist demonstrating a different sensitivity: the unique shapes of the trees disappear in the contrasting play on light, and the light brushstrokes soften the edges of both the foliage and the somewhat abrupt rocky ridge. With just cause, Gerald Finley describes these landscapes as marked with "Virgilian severity and pastoral simplicity."[5]
Reverend William Gilpin's influence on Heriot through his writings has been

Fig. 34A.
George Heriot,
*West View of Partridge Island from Parsborough,
Bay of Fundy,* 1807;
watercolour over graphite on paper,
13.5 × 18.6 cm.
Royal Ontario Museum, Toronto (953.132.19).

well documented. The artist meditated on the principles of the Picturesque espoused by Gilpin's works, either based on descriptions, or by studying the aquatints used to illustrate its application.[6] The overall harmony of the landscape is of utmost importance and is achieved primarily by eliminating any elements likely to stand out: no scrawny trees, spruce or rocks that might destroy the unity. For example, trees are identified primarily with forests; the fact that forests are made up of different species is of little importance. According to Gilpin, representation by analogy is one of the principal characteristics of the Picturesque. Heriot made it one of the distinctive features of his North American landscapes, turning the specific topography of a site into ideal images that rule the vision. This approach owes much to the monochromatic brown washes that play on the colour gradation and impregnate the drawn landscape with a pictorial quality. Heriot's portrayal of nature is therefore in no way servile. It is not a question of copying nature for the sake of copying, but rather of grasping its poetic content. In keeping with the principles of the ideal, the artist forsakes reality for beauty.

D.P.

Notes
1. *BOUCHETTE 1815,* p. 389.
2. *Ibid.,* p. 390.
3. See, in particular, *The Whirlpool, Niagara River,* dated 1801 (ROM, No. 953.132.23).
4. *FINLEY 1983,* pp. 124-125.
5. *FINLEY 1979,* p. 19.
6. On William Gilpin, see Carl Paul Barbier, *William Gilpin. His Drawings, Teaching, and Theory of the Picturesque* (Oxford: Clarendon Press, 1963).

35. (See colour reproduction, p. 83)
View of Quebec, c. 1805
Oil on canvas, 109.2 × 73.7 cm

Provenance
William H. Coverdale, New York; Old Print Shop, New York; Dr. Sigmund Samuel, Toronto; gift to the Royal Ontario Museum, Toronto, 1955.

Exhibitions
Charlottetown 1964, No. 24; Montreal 1967/1, No. 301; Kingston 1978-1979, No. 92; Toronto 1984, No. 169.

Bibliography
HARPER 1964, pp. 25 and 26, No. 24 (Repr.) attr. to Richard G. A. Levinge; HARPER 1966, pp. 48 and 49 (Repr.) attr. to Richard G. A. Levinge; CARTER 1967, No. 301 (Repr.) attr. to Richard G. A. Levinge; CARTER 1967-1968, pp. 14 and 15 (Repr.) attr. to Richard G. A. Levinge; FINLEY 1978, p. 51, No. 92 (Repr.); FINLEY 1983, pp. 43, 54 and 230-231, No. 1 (Repr.); WEBSTER 1984, pp. 37 and 163, No. 169 (Repr.); BROWN AND LINTEAU 1988, p. 288g (Repr.); DE ROUSSAN 1989, p. 11; ALLODI, MOOGK AND STOCK 1991, p. 70 (Repr.).

Collection
Royal Ontario Museum, Toronto (955.227)

D URING THE WINTER MONTHS, the citizens of Quebec City took advantage of the frozen river for sleighing, both for business and for pleasure. This picturesque scene was recorded by many of the British topographical painters, and remains one of the liveliest and most pleasing subjects in early Canadian art. As early as 1781, James Peachey was painting watercolour views of sleighing near Quebec, using the ice cone at Montmorency Falls as a background. As early as 1781, James Peachey was painting watercolour views of sleighing, using the ice cone at Montmorency Falls as a background.[1] Sleigh scenes with city backdrops became popular subjects for military topographers such as James Pattison Cockburn in the 1820s, and 1830s. Professional artists were painting the theme in oil by the 1840s (See Cat. 231 by William F. Wilson; and Cat. 93 by James Duncan, c. 1850).

In this painting, perhaps the earliest oil painting of winter sleighing at Quebec City, the artist has included elegant pleasure sleighs, a childrens' dog-drawn sled, and in the distance a couple of sledges of the type used for the transport of goods; one of these is drawn by an ox. A panoramic view of Quebec City occupies the background, and depicts the walled town as it was during the first decade of the 19th century; the buildings shown are carefully described, and correspond to the buildings in the Duberger scale-model of the city which was constructed between 1806 and 1808.[2] On the shore at the right can be seen the ruins of the old Intendant's Palace; the skyline is dominated by the spires of Notre-Dame de Quebec church on the left, and the Anglican cathedral on the right.

The painting was formerly said to be by Sir Richard Georges Augustus Levinge and dated 1838. The attribution was most probably based on the fact that Levinge, who painted Canadian views in watercolour, published a lithograph showing the meeting of a sleigh club at Saint John, N.B. in 1838. A study of the information contained in the painting reveals a much earlier date for both architecture and costume. The Intendant's Palace, although a ruined shell, is shown in the Duberger model to have further deteriorated by 1808. Thirty years later, it was in a much more tumble-down state.[3]

George Heriot is best known as a painter in watercolour, a medium in which he excelled. This view of Quebec is the only known oil painting of a Canadian subject by Heriot.[4] However, he was experimenting with oil paints while in Canada; in 1810, he told a friend that he was finishing an oil of "a naked Venus and two Cupids," with which he was quite pleased.[5] The oil view of Quebec relates in subject matter to watercolours painted by Heriot in 1798-1799. A 1798 watercolour depicts a similar theme of sleighing on

the ice against a Quebec City background. In 1798 and 1799, Heriot painted close-up watercolour studies of the ruins of the Intendant's Palace (Cat. 33). The little dog in the left foreground is repeated in a watercolour of circa 1799. And the ox pulling a load of wood was the subject of a watercolour dated circa 1799.[6] Stylistically, the oil painting corresponds to Heriot's topographical watercolour compositions: the scene is divided into tonal planes which become lighter towards the horizon, to indicate distance; and a silhouetted diagonal *coulisse* in the foreground leads the eye into the composition.

M.A.

Notes

1. James Peachey, *A Winter View of the Falls of Montmorency, from the Road on the Ice fronting it, taken 12th April 1781* was engraved in etching with aquatint by J. Wells, and published in London in 1785 (NAC C-13696 ROM 950.68.2).

2. This large model, scale 24 feet to the inch, (Collection Canadian War Museum, Ottawa; on exhibition at Artillery Park National Historic Site, Quebec) was constructed by Lieutenant Jean-Baptiste Duberger (1767-1821) under the supervision of Captain John By (1781-1836). In a letter of 1810, By stated that the model was "closed" in the year 1808, that is, it did not show constructions built after that date. (War Office, WO55, Series 859.) See also Bernard Pothier: *The Quebec Model.* National Museum of Man Mercury series, Canadian War Museum #9, Ottawa 1978.

3. This discrepancy was first noticed by John Bland, professor of architecture, McGill University, in 1969. And the costume of the couple in the elegant central sleigh indicates a fashion dating somewhere between 1803 and 1817, rather than 1838. The composition corresponds to the work of George Heriot, who was active in Canada from 1791 until 1816.

4. Two oil paintings of Scottish views are known. See *FINLEY 1983*, p. 231, Nos. 2-3.

5. New Brunswick Museum, Winslow Papers, Vol. X, Fol. 2, Georges Heriot, Quebec, to Judge Edward Winslow, Kingsclear, N.B., July 25, 1810.

6. *FINLEY 1983*, p. 62 (Repr.); *FINLEY 1983*, p. 110 (Rep.); *FINLEY 1983*, p. 112 (Repr.)

JOHN JAMES

active between 1811 and 1845

ITTLE IS REALLY KNOWN about American portraitist John James' artistic career in the United States. Only William Dunlap mentions that a certain James from New York City apparently painted until after 1800 and plied his trade in Quebec City. James did, in fact, move to the Old Capital in 1815, where he published the following advertisement in the September 7 edition of the *Quebec Gazette:* "A recent arrival to the city is in need of a *Room in which to paint portraits.* If you are able to help, please leave a message with this Office to the attention of J.J. Quebec City, August 30, 1815." (*Translation*) James also had a foothold in the art market: in the November 27, 1817 edition of the same newspaper, he put up for sale "Four beautiful paintings, two from the Italian School, one from the French School and one from the Flemish School, all selected by one of London's Men of good taste as samples for this Country." (*Translation*).

James received at least two prestigious commissions. Sometime around 1824, the residents of Quebec City's Saint-Roch parish ordered a large portrait of their former priest and benefactor, Monseigneur Joseph-Octave Plessis, which they presented to the latter on January 24, 1825 to mark the 24th anniversary of his consecration (MQ). Earlier that same year, James had painted the portrait of Joseph Signay, then priest at Notre-Dame church in Quebec City. A few years later, the population of Quebec City encouraged him to paint the portrait of another illustrious Canadian, Louis-Joseph Papineau, Speaker of the Assembly. It was then suggested that the portrait be reproduced in an engraving. The painting was not completed until 1832, as James was soliciting the support of new subscribers to engrave the work. Apart from these few dates, James' artistic production remains a mystery.

Main source
HARPER *1970.*

Fig. 36A.
John James (attr. to),
Samuel Neilson Junior, 1816;
oil on a panel, 18 × 12.7 cm.
Royal Ontario Museum,
Toronto (983.234.1).

36.

Joseph-Martin Chinic, 1815
Oil on panel 19.5 × 14.3 cm

Inscriptions
(b.,u.c., on the panel, in ink) *Jos Martin/Chinic Jnr à l'age de vingt/deux ans & sept mois/Quebec 1er novembre/1815/Jos M Chinic Jr;* (below, in another hand) *Dcédé à Champlain/le 24 Mai 1828.*

Provenance
Descendants of the Chinic family; Eugène Chinic, Quebec City; Jean Palardy, Montreal; acquired by the Musée de la Province de Québec, Quebec City, 1956.

Bibliography
MORISSET 1960/1, p. 138; *COMEAU 1983,* p. 137.

Collection
Musée du Québec, Quebec City (56.384)

J OSEPH-MARTIN CHINIC (1793-1828) hailed from a family of mariners, shipowners and merchants:[1] four generations of Chinics were among Quebec City's most noted businessmen. Joseph-Martin was the son of Martin Chinic (1770-1836) and Julienne-Claire Énouille, *dit* Lanois.

Chinic entered business in January 1815 with a future brother-in-law, Alexandre-Augustin Vézina, as a commission merchant and auctioneer, and later with another relative, Joseph Measam.[2] Chinic married Julie Measam in Quebec City on January 8, 1816.

Chinic & Measam auctioneers was located at 9 Rue du Sault-au-Matelot. They imported and sold mainly dry goods: hardware and notions (nails, paint, linseed oil, paper, leather, soap, putty, window-panes, thread, buttons, measuring tapes, etc.) and foodstuffs (tea, tobacco, mustard, lard, etc.).[3] The newspapers show that the competition in Quebec was fierce: they mention numerous other importers and merchants, including Joseph-Martin's father, Martin Chinic.[4]

It was Gérard Morisset who suggested, in 1960, that this portrait could be the work of John James. The thought is appealing, since it would make this the first identified portrait by the artist, who had arrived in Quebec City only two months earlier. The early inscription on the back of the canvas dates the painting November 1, 1815, which concurs with the advertisement published in the *Quebec Gazette* on September 7 indicating that John James was looking to rent a room *in which to paint portraits.*

The application of a thin layer of paint on a panel of untreated wood adds great purity to the work. The layers of oil become thicker, making the brushstrokes more visible, thereby accentuating the highlights of white lighting on the collar, forehead and around the lips. The composition is set slightly off to the right of the canvas, lacking symmetry and creating the impression that the painting was done very quickly. The efficient treatment and masterful technique suggest that the artist was well trained; the format is similar to that of large miniatures or portraits executed for a modest sum.

The portrait of Joseph-Martin Chinic could be compared to another portrait of somewhat similar format, that of Samuel Neilson junior (Fig. 36A), also painted in oil on wood. On the back is the inscription "Quebec 3 August/1816." The two portraits bear a number of common stylistic features: the composition, obviously, but also the very apparent physical presence of the sitters. The artist seems to have had the same difficulty rendering the ears, which appear disproportionate and poorly attached to the head. Based on these characteristics, James could also be thought to have painted the portrait of Joseph Légaré,[5] for which a plausible date would be about 1818.

L.L.

Notes
1. David Roberts, "Martin Chenneque", DCB, Vol. VI (1987), pp. 134-135; "Martin Chinic", DCB, Vol. VII (1988), pp. 176-177; Huguette Filteau and Jean Hamelin, "Guillaume-Eugène Chinic", DCB, Vol. XI (1982), pp. 189-191.

2. David Roberts, *Loc. cit.,* p. 176.

3. See, for example, the detailed advertisement published in *Le Canadien* over the course of an entire month, starting October 9, 1822.

4. Among the other busiest importers between 1815 and 1828 were Joseph Cary, Jean-Baptiste Martinucio, Wurtele & Fraser, Balzaretti, and Reiffenstein & Phillips.

5. Reproduced as *Self-portrait* in *PORTER 1978/1,* p. 29, No. 7.

T.P. JONES

active c. 1808

JONES WORKED as a silhouettist around 1808 in Schenectady, New York, and the surrounding area. His method consisted in tracing the sitter's silhouette with a pantograph and then cutting it out. Sometimes, he would use ink to highlight certain details such as costume and hair. The few pieces of his work that have survived bear the artist's stamp "*T.P. JONES FECIT.*" Another silhouettist, identified as F.P. Jones, worked in New England at the turn of the 19th century and may, in fact, be T.P. Jones. The misunderstanding is thought to have resulted from an improper reading of the artist's stamp, with the T.P. having been mistaken for an F.P.

L.F.

Main sources
CARRICK 1928; BAKER 1947; GROCE AND WALLACE 1957; YOUNG 1968; MCKECHNIE 1978.

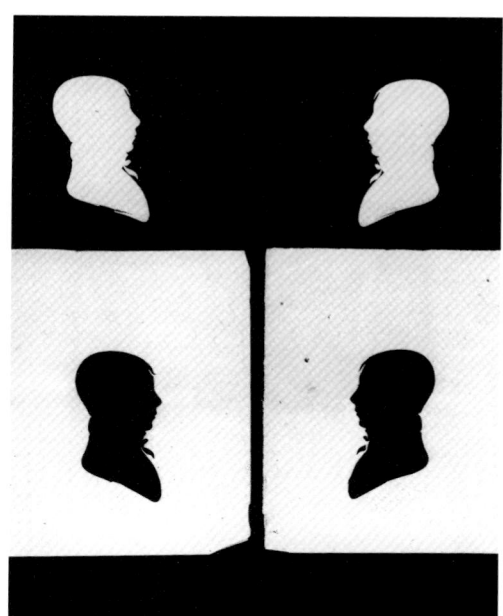

MQ, NGC

37.

Portrait of a Boy of the Claus Family, c. 1810

Paper cutout, 12.5 × 10.1 cm (cutout, left profile); 12.6 × 10.2 cm (cutout, right profile); 5.6 × 3.5 cm (cuttings)

Inscription
(on two cutout sheets, at the bottom of the cut, artist's seal highlighted) *T.P. JONES/FECIT.*

Provenance
Descendants of the Claus family; Mrs. E. Claus, Montclair, New Jersey, United States; acquired by the Federal Archives Bureau, Ottawa, 1919.

Collection
National Archives of Canada, Ottawa. Collection of the Claus family (1990-485-3X to 6X)

T HESE SILHOUETTES, along with several others by T.P. Jones, were discovered among the papers of the Claus family at the National Archives of Canada. The papers contain correspondence and documents pertaining to the activities of Daniel Claus (1727-1787),[1] who was a superintendent of the Indian Department in Canada, and his son William Claus (1765-1826),[2] who also served in the Indian Department and later became a member of the Legislative Council of Upper Canada. The Jones silhouettes are early-18th century and likely depict members of the William Claus family and that of his wife Catherine, the daughter of Jacob Jordan (1741-1796),[3] prosperous businessman and owner of the seigneury of Terrebonne.

There is no evidence to suggest that Jones visited Canada. The only information known is that he worked in Schenectady, New York, around 1808. As it happens, William and Catherine Claus sent two of their sons, William Jr. and Daniel J., to Union College in Schenectady where they also had several relatives among the Willard family.[4] In 1807, William Jr. wrote from Schenectady to his mother in Niagara telling her that a profile of Daniel had been sent to her.[5] It is possible this profile was a silhouette by Jones and possibly the one shown here. Daniel was the youngest of the William Claus children. In 1807, he was 14 years old, since by 1810 he was serving with an army regiment at Trois-Rivières.[6] However, any identification of the sitter must remain tentative, since it is possible that the profiles are those of Willard family members. The only identified silhouette by Jones in the Claus collection is that of Ann Jordin Willard.

Jones cut his silhouettes using a tracing machine or pantograph, which outlined and reduced the sitter's features, leaving a miniature profile outline on a white piece of paper. The profile was then cut out of the paper and removed, leaving the sheet with a hole. The sheet was then backed with black paper or cloth to create a silhouette which could then be framed. The white paper silhouettes were usually discarded or kept as models for making duplicates, but were not displayed. In the case of the present silhouette, we are able to see both the hollow-cuts and the white paper silhouettes. Jones has created two copies of the silhouette, probably by folding the paper in two and cutting two outlines at once. Like many profile cutters, Jones appears to have cut only bust-length portraits, foregoing the challenge of creating full-length silhouettes, such as those of Edouart (Cat. 100 to 102) and Hankes (Cat. 139 and 140). Jones' silhouettes, however, demonstrate a certain competence. The outlined details, such as the boy's knotted necktie and the shock of hair falling over his forehead, as well as a delicately cut eyelash, create a simple and charming profile.

L.F.

Notes
1. Douglas Leighton, DCB, Vol. IV, pp. 154-155.
2. Robert S. Allen, DCB, Vol. VI, pp. 151-153.
3. A.J.H. Richardson, DCB, Vol. IV, pp. 402-403.
4. NAC, Claus family papers, MG19FI, Vol. 16, pp. 59, 65, 155-156, letters from William Claus Jr. to his mother, dated in August and October 1807 at Union College, Schenectady, New York, and Vol. 17, p. 52, letter from Edward C. Willard to his cousin, Daniel J. Claus, dated December 20, 1811 at Albany, New York, in which he mentions their school days together at Union College.
5. NAC, Claus family papers, MG19FI, Vol. 16, p. 65, letter from William Claus Jr. to his mother, dated October 18, 1807 at Union College, Schenectady, New York.
6. NAC, Claus family papers, MG19FI, Vol. 17, part 1, pp. 22-24, letter from Daniel J. Claus to his mother, dated July 21, 1810 at Trois-Rivières.

ELIAB METCALF

1785-1834

ELIAB METCALF was born in Franklin, Massachusetts on February 5, 1785. A specialist in portraiture (miniatures and especially silhouettes), Metcalf was an itinerant artist. He spent 1807 and part of 1808 in Guadeloupe before moving to Montreal in fall 1808. The following spring, he left for Quebec City, where he apparently did not stay for long, since he was living in Halifax in 1810. That same year he went to New York City to perfect his technique under Samuel Lovett Waldo (1783-1861), who trained in London between 1806 and 1808 and was one of the founders of the National Academy of Design. It would seem Metcalf also studied with William Jewett (1795-1873), as well as being Waldo's assistant and later his associate (1820-1854).

While in Quebec City, he advertised his services in the March 16, 1809 edition of the *Quebec Gazette,* stating that he could reproduce profiles of a perfect likeness "in a style of superior elegance" (*Translation*) using a physiognotrace. The ad continues: "He prides himself in the fact that, after long practice and having shown a special interest in this art and having received much encouragement (producing over 5000 portraits in the past six months), he is able to guarantee universal satisfaction." (*Translation*) Although the number of portraits seems somewhat high, it possible due to the rapidity of this simple, inexpensive technique.

After some health problems, Metcalf seemed to have recovered almost fully by the fall of 1817. After 1819, however, his fragile health no doubt led him to travel south, to New Orleans and even the Caribbean. He reportedly returned to New York every year, where he showed his works at the National Academy. Metcalf died in New York City on January 15, 1834.

Main sources
HARPER 1970; FIELDING 1974.

MQ, NGC

38.
Pierre-Ignace Aubert de Gaspé, 1809
Beige paper cutout highlighted with black
ink on black paper, 7.6 × 7.6 cm

Fig. 38A.
Label of Eliab Metcalf on the back of the
portrait of *Pierre-Ignace Aubert de Gaspé.*

Inscriptions
(b., artist's printed label) THE PORTRAIT OF/ [in pen
and black ink, in the artist's hand] *Père*/ [?] *Gaspé*
[written over]/*Père*/ [printed]DRAWN IN ONE MIN
[UTE]/WITH THE/PATENT PHYSIOGNOTR [ACE]/BY/
E. METCALF,/No... 20,/Buade Street,/QUEBEC,/
1809.; (on the same label, to the left, vertically, in
pen and black ink, in another hand) *Father of
author of/"Les Anciens Canadiens".*

Provenance
Honourable Justice Georges Baby; acquired by
the Château Ramezay, Montreal, 1904.

Bibliography
MCR, *Registre des acquisitions 1895-1974,* p. 185,
No. 2520, October 27, 1904; O'LEARY 1907,
p. 50, No. 95; O'LEARY 1917, p. 48, No. 95;
O'LEARY 1920, p. 50, No. 94; O'LEARY 1922,
p. 51, No. 94; O'LEARY 1923, p. 50, No. 94;
O'LEARY 1926, p. 55, No. 94; CATALOGUE 1927/2,
p. 55, No. 94; CATALOGUE 1928, p. 55, No. 94;
CATALOGUE 1931, p. 77, No. 94; CATALOGUE 1936,
p. 79, No. 94; CATALOGUE 1937, p. 76, No. 94;
CATALOGUE 1948, p. 79, No. 94; CATALOGUE 1954,
p. 79, No. 94; CATALOGUE 1956, p. 79, No. 94;
CARRIER 1957, p. 131, No. 1827; CARRIER AND
LEFEBVRE 1962, p. 143, No. 1827; SELECTED
CATALOGUE 1985, p. 66, No. 151 (entry by Roslyn
Rosenfeld).

Collection
Musée du Château Ramezay, Montreal (2520)

N UMEROUS MINIATURISTS and silhouette artists came to Lower Canada
to ply their trade during the
decades 1800 to 1820. A number of
portraitists specializing in silhouettes,
commonly referred to as profiles or
"shadows", have been identified through
advertisements placed in Quebec City and
Montreal newspapers. Unfortunately, the
little that is known about most of these
itinerant artists comes entirely from the
information provided in these ads: the vast

majority of surviving silhouettes are neither
signed, nor dated, with the exception of a
few works that have a label or stamp
identifying the artist on the back of the
picture (Cat. 37, 139 and 140).[1] Such is
the case with the works of American
silhouettist Eliab Metcalf, who made his
career in Lower Canada from 1808 to
1809.

PROFILE PAINTING.—E. Metcalf, Has the honor
respect-fully, to acquaint the Ladies and Gentlemen of the city that he occupies an appart-
ment in the house lately occupied by Joseph
Mathon, where by means of the Patent PHYSI-
OGNOTRACE he will cut or paint the most perfect LIKENESSES in PROFILE and execute them in
a new, and superior style of elegance.

He also takes the liberty to inform the Military
Gentlemen in particular that, he has a new
method of distinguishing the Military dress
which he is confident will meet their approbation. He flatters himself from his long practice
and particular attention to the art, and from
the encouragement he has received (having
taken upwards of 5000 within the last six
months past) that he will be able to give universal satisfaction.

Ladies and Glentlemen are respectfully solicited to call at his room, where specimens may be
seen and where he will attend every day (Sun-
days excepted) (for a few weeks only), from
nine, till three o'clock.

He has, for sale, suitable frames, lockets &c. of
all descriptions.

Metcalf spent the fall of 1808 in
Montreal, where he advertised his services
in the *Montreal Gazette* from September 5
to November 7. At the end of December,
the studio Metcalf had rented was occupied
by a certain Cromwell, profile painter and
former student of Benjamin West. In spring

1809, Metcalf was in Quebec City, where
he placed advertisements describing his
specialty in the local papers. His very first
notice, published in the *Quebec Gazette* on
March 16 and reprinted in French in *Le
Spectateur* on April 4, tells much about
the type of services offered:

In the May 25, 1809 edition of
the *Quebec Gazette,* the profile painter,
whose studio was located at 20 Rue Buade,
stated that he could cut a silhouette "in
just one minute" and notified the population that he would be leaving Quebec City
in a few days time. He apparently stayed
longer than planned, however, since in
mid-June, Metcalf was still placing ads in
the papers, this time accompanying the
French version with a sample female profile and the English version with a male
profile. It was during this three-month
period that he did the portraits of *Pierre-
Ignace Aubert de Gaspé* (1758-1823),
*Ignace-Michel-Louis-Antoine d'Irumberry
de Salaberry* (1752-1828), *Mrs. Ignace-
Michel-Louis Antoine d'Irumberry de
Salaberry, née Françoise-Catherine Hertel de Saint-François,* and *John Neilson*
(1776-1848), his wife and their three
children: *Samuel Neilson* (1800-1837),
Isabel (1800-1873) and Mary.

Father of the well-known author
of *Les Anciens Canadiens* and fifth seigneur of Port-Joly, Pierre-Ignace Aubert
de Gaspé was 51 when he had his portrait
done, and was militia officer and justice of
the peace for the District of Quebec. He
had useful connections in political,
military as well as social circles.[2] Irumberry
de Salaberry, age 57 and seigneur of
Guillaudière, held the same positions as

VAG, AGNS, MMFA

VAG, AGNS, MMFA

39.

Ignace-Michel-Louis-Antoine d'Irumberry de Salaberry, 1809

Black, grey and red ink with traces of scraping out on paper, 9.3 × 6.8 cm

Provenance
Louis Mulligan, Montreal; acquired by the McCord Museum, Montreal, 1972.

Exhibitions
Montreal 1981; Montreal 1987/1.

Bibliography
BRIERLEY 1988, p. 331 (Repr.); *BOURASSA 1990*, p. 84.

Collection
McCord Museum of Canadian History, Montreal (M972.81.21.1)

40.

Mrs. Ignace-Michel-Louis-Antoine d'Irumberry de Salaberry, née Françoise-Catherine Hertel de Saint-François, 1809

Black and grey ink on paper, 9.3 × 6.8 cm

Provenance
Louis Mulligan, Montreal; acquired by the McCord Museum, Montreal, 1972.

Exhibitions
Montreal 1981; Montreal 1987/1.

Bibliography
LESSARD 1987/2, p. 42 (repr. – version in a private collection identified as *Silhouette de femme inconnue*); *BRIERLEY 1988*, p. 331 (Repr.).

Collection
McCord Museum of Canadian History, Montreal (M972.81.21.2)

Aubert de Gaspé as well as being inspector of forests for Lower Canada and member of the Assembly for Huntingdon. A member of the seigneurial gentry, Salaberry was a close friend of Prince Edward Augustus (Cat. 6 and 7) and father of the famous colonel Charles-Michel, who distinguished himself as a hero in the Battle of Châteauguay (Cat. 89).[3] John Neilson (Cat. 53) was a bookseller, printer and publisher, and owner of the *Quebec Gazette*, the daily in which Metcalf advertised his services during his stay in Quebec City. Four years after engaging in politics in 1818, Neilson turned the management of his company over to his eldest son, Samuel.

In 1809, Samuel was nine and attending Daniel Wilkie's Grammar School (Cat. 176), where he got a solid education. He had his portrait painted seven years later, in 1816, probably by the American painter John James (Fig. 36A).[4]

Glued to the back of the circular frame of the silhouette of Aubert de Gaspé, held at the Château Ramezay, is a label with Metcalf's name and temporary address in Quebec City (Fig. 38A). The inscription says that the portrait was drawn in one minute using a physionotrace. Room was left on the label to identify the sitter. The engraved seal apparently came from the printing shop belonging to John Neilson.

The portraits of the five Neilson family members now belong to various public and private collections, including the Royal Ontario Museum (Isabel; Fig. 41A) and the Musée du Québec (Samuel). The remains of the decorative label are still glued to the back of the circular frames of the silhouettes of Isabel and Samuel. The portraits of Irumberry de Salaberry and his wife are set in rectangular frames, probably more recent, and there is no trace of a label.

As indicated in Metcalf's advertisements and on his printed label, all the silhouettes were done using a physionotrace, a mechanical device invented by French

MQ, NGC

41.

Samuel Neilson Junior, 1809

Beige paper cutout highlighted with black ink on black silk, 8.6 × 8.6 cm

Inscription
(b., on the panel protecting the back of the work, in black ink) SAMUEL NEILSON.

Provenance
Descendants of the Neilson family; Gordon Anthony Neilson inheritance; on deposit at the Archives de la province de Québec, 1942; Ian Satow; John L. Russell, Gananoque, Ontario; gift to the Musée du Québec, Quebec City, 1984.

Bibliography
BÉLAND AND BOURASSA 1990, p. 5 (Repr.).

Collection
Musée du Québec, Quebec City (84.45)

Fig. 41A.
Eliab Metcalf,
Isabel Neilson, 1809;
beige paper cutout highlighted
with black ink on black silk, 8.6 × 8.6 cm.
Royal Ontario Museum, Toronto.
Gift from John L. Russell (984.103.1).

scissors: the profiles are painted entirely in black directly onto the support and enhanced with grey and red ink highlights to indicate the coiffure and the shirt and blouse. De Salaberry's jacket collar has been outlined through light scratches in the paper that continue beyond the profile. In the portrait of Aubert de Gaspé, the head and shoulders have been cut out in beige paper and placed on a black paper background, with the details of the jacket collar and jabot drawn in black ink on the blank paper between the two cutouts. The silhouette of Samuel Neilson uses the same technique as the portrait of Aubert de Gaspé except that the beige paper is on black silk rather than on another sheet of paper. In all four cases, the contour of the hair is washed with ink, suggesting a curl for Madame de Salaberry and a pigtail in the style of the *Ancien regime* for her husband. The four silhouettes have been embellished just below the shoulders with a motif of curved lines, a feature that is almost a trademark of Metcalf's.

Metcalf's miniature head-and-shoulder portraits and his simple, hastily cut out black profiles do not have the quality of the full-length silhouettes, depicted in an interior setting or against a landscape, produced by the likes of Hankes or Édouart, or of certain profiles embellished with watercolour, or gold or silver streaks.

M.B.

engraver Gilles-Louis Chrétien (1754-1811) in 1786. Derived from the pantograph, this "machine for making profiles" was the tool most used by North American silhouette artists of the day. Newspaper ads show that it was commonly used by profile painters passing through Lower Canada, notably T.H. Bell, Peter M. Choice, Luke Kent and Joseph Morand. The subject was placed in a dark room, seated on a chair placed in front of a transparent screen lit by a candle. The portraitist would trace the outline of the shadow cast on the screen from behind and then reduce or enlarge it to the desired size on a sheet of paper. The adjust-

able bars of the physionotrace made it possible to trace a perfect outline of the head and shoulders very quickly and then enlarge or reduce it as wished. It also allowed the artist to make several copies: a second version of the portrait of Madame d'Irumberry de Salaberry is held in a private collection.[5] Not only was the technique therefore fast and inexpensive, it also guaranteed a perfect likeness. The artist completed the portrait by working and then highlighting the profile using different chromatic processes, witness these four silhouettes by Metcalf.

The two silhouettes of Irumberry de Salaberry and his wife show no trace of

Notes
1. See the chapter entitled "Portraits pour le grand public," pp. 115-119 in HARPER 1966, as well as ROSENFELD 1981 and Roslyn Rosenfeld, "An index of miniaturists and silhouettists who worked in Montreal", *Journal of Canadian Art History*, Vol. V, No. 2 (1981), pp. 111-121.
2. See Jacques Castonguay, DCB, Vol. VI (1987), pp. 16-17.
3. See Céline Cyr and Michelle Guitard, DCB, Vol. VI (1987), pp. 341-344. Two other miniatures of De Salaberry exist: see Cat. 89 and BOURASSA 1990, p. 84.
4. See Sonia Chassé, Rita Girard-Wallot and Jean-Pierre Wallot, "John Neilson", and Claude Galarneau, "Samuel Neilson", DCB, Vol. VII (1988), pp. 644-650.
5. See LESSARD 1987/2, p. 42 (Repr.).

JAMES PEACHEY

known c. 1773-1797

T HE PRINCIPAL DATES in the artistic career of James Peachey essentially correspond to his period of production in North America, where he stayed during three different intervals. Around 1773, he was employed as a draughtsman under the surveyor general of the Province of Quebec and of the Northern District of North America, Samuel Holland (circa 1728-1801). Peachey returned to England in 1775 to prepare for the publication of their surveys in a book by Holland. Although the project never materialized, the maps did appear in *The Atlantic Neptune,* a book by J.F.W. Des Barres published in 1777. Peachey is thought to have participated in the publication.

Peachey returned to Quebec City a second time in 1780. Records of his travels and their respective dates often come from his artistic works. In 1783, as deputy surveyor under Samuel Holland, he was assigned to survey and plot lands for refugee loyalists and retired army officers. The same year, at Holland's request, Peachey surveyed the north shore of Lake Ontario, likely receiving support from General William Tryon (1729-1788) and the governor-in-chief of Canada, Sir Frederick Haldimand (1718-1791). In 1784, Peachey surveyed the St. Lawrence River (Cat. 44 and 45) and accompanied Haldimand on a trip to England. There, he published a number of his Canadian views in aquatints in 1785-1786. In 1786 and 1787, he exhibited some Canadian subjects at the Royal Academy and illustrated two books, for which he also etched the frontispiece.

Peachey's third stay in North America began in August 1788, after obtaining an ensign's commission in the 1rst battalion of the 60th Foot a year earlier. He had come to join his regiment, which was stationed at Niagara and, in 1790, was transferred to the Montreal area. Peachey continued his work as deputy surveyor under Holland. In October 1793, he was promoted to the rank of lieutenant and transferred to a new regiment in Quebec City, then to Halifax the following year. The date Peachey left Canada is uncertain: it is thought to have been after he was promoted captain in 1795, but it was more likely following his transfer to the 43rd Foot in February 1797. He died in Martinique on November 24, 1797, while on duty with his new regiment.

Main source
COOKE 1983.

A View of the Citadel at Quebec with the Outworks taken from the Heights of Abraham Oct. 29 1784

MQ, NGC

42.
A View of the Quebec Citadel with The Outworks Taken from The Heights of Abraham, 1784
Watercolour, pen and black ink on paper, 36.5 × 56.4 cm

Inscriptions
(s., l.l., in pen and black ink) *James Peachey*; (l.c., on the border, in pen and black ink, in the artist's hand) *A View of the Citadel at Quebec with the Outworks taken from the Heights of Abraham Oct'. 29 1784.*

Provenance
Charles H. Ault, New York; acquired by the Federal Archives Bureau, Ottawa, 1913.

Exhibitions
Quebec City 1918; Ottawa 1972-1975, No. 79.

Bibliography
BELL 1972, No. 79 (Repr.); *THIBAULT, GALARNEAU AND NOPPEN 1977*, p. 108 (Repr.); *NOPPEN, PAULETTE AND TREMBLAY 1979*, p. 255 (Repr.); *CHARBONNEAU, DESLOGES AND LAFRANCE 1982*, p. 64 (Repr.); *HUARD 1986/2*, p. 30 (Repr.).

Collection
National Archives of Canada, Ottawa (1989-217-3X)

T HIS VIEW OF the left slope of the citadel was drawn from the Plains of Abraham. The entire middle-ground is given over to the fortifications, with their blockhouse, redoubts, tenailles and covered roads lined up beginning at Anse-des-Mères bay. The structures mould the topography, forming terrepleins and taluses; and their outline can still be seen today.

Peachey has shown the citadel as it was following its construction between 1779 and 1783[1] by William Twiss, chief engineer for Canada. The year 1775 marked the beginning of the American Revolution and the invasion of Quebec City by American troops. In reaction to the resulting instability and to France's entry into the conflict in 1778, Governor Sir Frederick Haldimand, decided to reinforce Quebec's defence system by building a new citadel. Using the wall already built by French engineer Chaussegros de Léry, Twiss designed a structure that would reinforce the initial fortifications and correct the weaknesses resulting from the fact that they had not been completed. Work

began in October 1779; however, Twiss, like Chaussegros de Léry, never saw his project finished since Great Britain signed a peace treaty in 1783. The Treaty of Versailles officially recognized the United States' independence and greatly reduced British holdings in North America. The new Canada-U.S. border ceded all territory south of the Great Lakes to the United States. With peace came the end of the citadel's reconstruction and William Twiss's return to Great Britain.

Peachey's *A View of the Quebec Citadel With The Outworks Taken from The Heights of Abraham* is characteristic of topographical drawings in the style of Wenceslaus Hollar (1607-1677). The composition is built on three separate planes, enhanced with a play on "coulisses". The technique is obvious: the artist has captured the essence of the site using a minimum of means. The singular use of the pen freely scallops the land, accentuating shadows. Drawing from a distant vantage point, in this case the heights of the Plains of Abraham, is typical of the first British topographical artist, who carried on

the traditions of Hollar and Francis Place (1647-1728) into the 19th century. The focal point of the composition is shown within its immediate natural surroundings by way of a more or less complex series of hills and dales. The viewer can immediately locate the citadel's network of defence strategies: the city and plains on one side and the river on the other.

Peachey liked to enhance his drawings with various elements that serve more than just a decorative purpose. In this work, done a year after the end of conflict with the United States—it is dated October 29, 1784—, Peachey has painted an image of renewed peace, witness the two figures enjoying a moment of relaxation, on the hillock in the foreground, as well as renewed activity on the river and the assurance symbolized by the livestock out to pasture.

D.P.

Note
1. *CHARBONNEAU, DESLOGES AND LAFRANCE 1982*, pp. 62-65 and 160-162.

MQ, NGC

43.
A View of the City of Montreal, Taken from the Top of the Mountain, 1784
Watercolour, pen and black ink over graphite on paper, 17 × 36.9 cm

Inscriptions
(s., l.l.) *J. Peachey;* (l.c., on the border, in pen and black ink, in the artist's hand) *A View of the City of Montreal taken from the Top of the Mountain, the 15th October, 1784.*

Provenance
Henry Stevens & Stiles, London; acquired by the Federal Archives Bureau, Ottawa, 1917.

Exhibitions
Quebec City 1918; Quebec City 1985.

Bibliography
(?) MORISSET 1960/1, p. 73; BELL 1973/1, p. 79 (Repr.)

Collection
National Archives of Canada, Ottawa (1989-218-2X)

A CCORDING TO the date indicated on *A View of the City of Montreal, Taken from the Top of the Mountain,*[1] this work was produced just a few days before *A View of the Quebec Citadel With The Outworks Taken from The Heights of Abraham* (Cat. 42). Peachey's position as deputy surveyor under Samuel Holland had just terminated, on October 10.[2] The artist had most likely been granted a short vacation prior to his imminent departure for England. A year earlier, from May 1783 to April 1784, Peachey had surveyed the land along the north shore of Lake Ontario, beginning at Cataraqui, in order to plot lands for refugee loyalists.[3] Samuel Holland had briefly described the conditions of the survey in a letter to General William Tryon, letting show the extreme fatigue resulting from the exercise.[4]

Peachey's *A View of the City of Montreal* is one of the first depictions of the city from atop Mount Royal. The high vantage point enables the artist to paint a bird's-eye view of Montreal and the outlying areas.

The first terrace, bordering the St. Lawrence River, is one of the earliest inhabited sites in Lower Canada. Delineated by the ramparts, the terrace boasts the city's most important buildings along Rue Notre-Dame, from the citadel on the left to Place d'Armes on the right. The second terrace, more a suggestion than actually apparent in the topography, marks the beginning of the rise towards Mount Royal. In 1784, the city was still separated from the plain by the Saint-Martin river, whose bridge can be seen opposite Place d'Armes. Having become an open sewer, the river was filled in in 1837 to make way for Rue Craig. This watercolour also shows the first signs of Montreal's urban development. The Quebec suburb is developing to the east, in line with the port of the same name. The countryside extending northward along the road perpendicular to the river towards the Saint-Laurent parish is to become the Saint-Laurent suburb. And finally, to the west, the Récollet suburb extends the life inside the monastery walls to the outside world. The plain was populated based on access to the city and the relations between the two areas were very separate.

This work established Peachey as a professional topographical artist well-acquainted with pictorial conventions. Bird's-eye views had long ago made military topography one of the compositional bases for depicting a given site in relation to its natural surroundings. This foundation can then be built upon using a wide range of possible combinations: communication routes, natural vegetation and outcrops, distribution and density of buildings, recognition of nerve centres, etc. Hence not much importance is given to the foreground. Mount Royal's only purpose is to create the idea of a high promontory affording a view overlooking the plain. The anecdotal role Peachey gives the hunters and the emblematic aspect of the tall tree rising above the plain is highly reminiscent of the Flemish tradition introduced by Pieter Bruegel the Elder (circa 1525/1530-1569), developed between 1600 and 1620 and exploited in England by Jean Siberechts (1627-circa 1703).

Another version of this watercolour is housed in a private collection in London. Peachey improved upon his original composition by making the fence lines separating the fields to the left converge toward a single vanishing point. The foreground is also fuller, taking half the composition horizontally.

D.P.

Notes

1. Peachey dates his watercolours according to when the sketch was done, and not to when the work was completed. For the purposes of this entry, dates have been interpreted in the same way.

2. NAC, RG 1 E 15A, Public Accounts: Board of Audit, Vol. 27 (1784), "List of the Gentlemen employed in the Surveying Department of the year 1784".

3. *Ibid.,* Vol. 26 (1784).

4. NAC, MG 11 CO 42 Series Q, Vol. 16, letter from Samuel Holland to General Tryon, August 21, 1784, Folio 230-233.

44.
A View of the Basin of Quebec, with Ile d'Orléans, Pointe Lévis and Falls of Montmorency, 1784

Watercolour, pen and black ink on paper, 10.8 × 37.6 cm

VAG, AGNS, MMFA

45.
A View of Grosse Ile with the Church of Kamouraska, 1784

Watercolour, pen and black ink on paper, 11.2 × 32.6 cm
(enlarged to the right by a 6.4 cm strip of paper)

VAG, AGNS, MMFA

Inscriptions
(s., l.l., in pen and black ink) *J. Peachey;* (l.c., in pen and black and yellow ink, in the artist's hand) *taken from I. Marked in the Plan/A View of the Bason of Quebec, with the Island of Orleans, Point Levi, & Fall of Montmorenci.;* (l.l., in pen and black ink, in the artist's hand) *a. Fall of Montmorenci./ b* corresponding with the letter "a" on the drawing.

Provenance
Henry Stevens & Stiles, London; acquired by the Federal Archives Bureau Ottawa, 1916.

Exhibition
Quebec City 1918.

Collection
National Archives of Canada, Ottawa (1989-218-6X)

Inscriptions
(s., l.l., in pen and black ink) *J. Peachey;* (l.c., in pen and black ink, in the artist's hand) *A View of the Gros Isle, with the church at Kamouraska, Bearing S. distance 1 League/to the Church 2 Leagues. 17ᵗʰ No.vʳ. 1784*

Provenance
Henry Stevens & Stiles, London; acquired by the Federal Archives Bureau Ottawa, 1916.

Exhibition
Quebec City 1918.

Collection
National Archives of Canada, Ottawa (1989-218-13X)

J AMES PEACHEY left Quebec on November 16, 1784, sailing aboard the British ship *Atalanta.*[1] He was accompanying the governor, Sir Frederick Haldimand, on a vacation to London. His departure had been planned for several months, probably on the recommendation of General William Tryon according to a letter to Tryon from Samuel Holland: "he [Peachey] thanks your Excelency for the Present you intended him, thinking himselve highly Honoured, with you[r] approbation, as he is to go to England with the General."[2] During the first two days of the trip, Peachey did a series of ten watercolours detailing the coastline of the St. Lawrence valley, concentrating on a few specific sites in particular: Ile d'Orléans and its immediate surroundings, Cap Tourmente, Ile Madame and Ile aux Rats; Malbaie and Ile aux Coudres; the Kamouraska mountains, Grosse-Ile, the neighbouring islands, and the area around Ile aux Lièvres. All the watercolours are the same format and several have alphabetical references that possibly refer to a map. With the inclusion of a map bearing, ***A View of Grosse Ile with the Church of Kamouraska*** is the only work that today establishes such a direct link. It is for this reason that

this work is being discussed here, even if it has practically faded.

Given that no in-depth research has ever been conducted on this series of watercolours, it would be dangerous to try and reach a hasty conclusion. The coherence of the ten watercolours gives the impression they may be the remains of a more ambitious project, one that probably included a map of the St. Lawrence valley.[3] It is not known whether the drawings were cut off after the map had been drawn or whether the initial project was aborted before the map had been completed. An exhaustive study of the collection of topographical works from the library of George III, acquired in 1828 by the British Library, would provide answers to a number of questions.

These watercolours alone illustrate a specific aspect of the topographer's trade. They provide an example of naval topography as taught by the military academies. The objective is simple: to provide a faithful rendition of the coastline in order to provide reliable navigation aids. The topographical artist translates the intellectual information on maps into visual information. Peachey is a skilful draughtsman: the carefully drawn outlines are traced over in

pen, thereby meeting the requirements of naval topography, i.e. a servile rendering of the site. In addition, he has taken his meticulousness a step further by using washes to highlight an escarpment or to hollow out a rocky crevice. And yet, the three-tone colour scheme (blue, yellow and pink) eliminates any trace of local colour, in keeping with the colour's sole purpose of description. These works are consistent with the illustrations in the *Atlantic Neptune,* a project that spanned the period 1777-1784 under the direction of Joseph Frederick Wallet Des Barres (1722-1824).[4]

D.P.

Notes
1. *Quebec Gazette,* November 18, 1784.
2. NAC, MG 11 CO 42 Series Q, Vol. 16, letter from Samuel Holland to General Tryon, August 21, 1784, Folio 233. Quoted from the transcription of the letter in the artist's file at the NAC.
3. See COOKE 1983, p. 158.
4. *Ibid.* A number of stylistic similarities lead us to believe that Peachey collaborated on the book, either directly or indirectly through his drawings.

JAMES PEALE
1749-1831

BORN IN Chestertown, Maryland, American artist James Peale was the younger brother of painter and engraver Charles Willson Peale (1741-1827). Following in his brother's footsteps, James was initially a cabinetmaker, learning to paint from his sibling in the late 1760s. Charles had studied in Boston under John Singleton Copley (1737-1815), one of the greatest American painters of the time. James Peale's artistic career was interrupted for at least three years, beginning in 1776, when he enlisted in the Maryland Regiment and served under Washington during the American Revolution. Soon after the war ended, Peale wed Mary Claypoole, sister of another painter from Philadelphia, and settled down there to be near his family. At about that time, he apparently went back to his painting, specializing in portraits in miniature. His brother Charles painted James' portrait in 1822, showing him seated at his work table examining one of his own miniatures (*The Lamplight Portrait,* Detroit Institute of Arts). Over the years, Peale added large-format portraits and landscapes to his repertoire, while continuing to paint miniatures. He is one of the artists that introduced the tradition of still lifes to the United States. Although he spent the greater part of his life in Philadelphia, Peale worked in the southern states on occasion. He was also a member of the Maryland Society of Cincinnati.

Around 1818, he gave up painting altogether due to vision problems. His daughters Anna (1791-1878) and Sarah (1800-1885), and son James (1789-1876) carried on the family tradition. The Peale name was widespread throughout American art circles through Charles Willson's offspring, Raphael (1774-1825), Rembrandt (1778-1860) and Rubens (1784-1864), named in honour of the European masters. James Peale died in Philadelphia on May 24, 1831.

Main sources

GROCE AND WALLACE 1957; FIELDING 1974; AMERICAN FOLK PORTRAITS 1981; NYGREN 1986.

MQ, NGC

46.
Basilique-Benjamin Trottier Desrivières Beaubien, 1792
Watercolour on ivory, 5.1 × 4 cm

Inscription
(i.d., l.l.) *IP/1792.*

Provenance
Descendants of the Trottier Desrivières Beaubien, Bouthillier and Routh families; Randolph Routh, Montreal (sold by Pinney's, Montreal, March 22, 1988, No. T139); acquired by the National Archives of Canada, Ottawa, 1988.

Bibliography
ART CANADIEN *1988,* pp. 64 and 65, No. T139 (Repr.); GAUTHIER *1988,* pp. 77 and 79 (Repr.).

Collection
National Archives of Canada, Ottawa
(1988-42-2)

T HE IDENTIFICATION OF Benjamin Beaubien as the subject of this miniature is based on an inventory made by his grandson Charles Frontenac Bouthillier in 1924. The inventory comprises a list of pictures hanging in his residence, the Bleury house, and the first item on it is "a small picture [of] Benjamin Basilic Trottier de Beaubien," which is almost certainly this miniature.[1] Beaubien's only child, Louise, married Louis-Tancred Bouthillier, and their son Charles Frontenac Bouthillier married Emmy Sills, *née* Routh. There being no surviving children from this marriage, the estate was inherited by the Routh family, the maternal side of Emmy Sills (Cat. 16).

Benjamin Beaubien (1776-1834) was the youngest son of Marguerite-Alexis Mailhot (Cat. 15) and Eustache-Ignace Trottier Desrivières Beaubien (Cat. 14 and 16), a merchant in Lac-des-Deux-Montagnes. Prior to embarking on a career in law, he had gone to the United States to complete his education "at one of the best

Universities."[2] (*Translation*) From about 1796 to 1801, he worked as a clerk in the office of Montreal lawyer Louis Charles Foucher to fulfil the educational requirements of this profession, and applied for a commission to practise law in Montreal in September 1801.[3] The granting of the commission was publicly announced in November of the same year.[4] In 1806, he married Geneviève Sabrevois de Bleury.[5] He served as captain of the second militia battalion of the city of Montreal during the War of 1812 and was promoted major in 1814. In 1820, he became major in the first battalion of the city.[6]

Beaubien was a well-respected Montreal lawyer whose strong ideas of democracy had been forged during his studies in the United States. Nevertheless, he did not take an active part in public affairs until the last few years of his life.[7] An eloquent address, delivered in April 1834 at a public assembly in Montreal, reveals his political stance.[8] Sharing the podium with Robert Nelson and C.S.

Cherrier, Beaubien praised the British institutions because they guaranteed the rights of their subjects, proclaimed his support for the Ninety-Two Resolutions and advocated bypassing the governor in order to deliver the grievances of the French-Canadian populace directly to the King.[9] Unfortunately, he died on July 31, 1834, a victim of the cholera epidemic of that summer, just as he might have entered the public forum.[10]

This charming miniature of the young Beaubien is signed I P and dated 1792, both inscriptions positioned by the left shoulder of the sitter. It was painted by the prominent American miniaturist James Peale, the younger brother of Charles Willson Peale. The elder Peale gave up painting miniatures in 1786 in order for James to take over the market, and the latter specialized in this form of portraiture for the rest of his career.[11] Both the substitution of the archaic I for J and the position of the inscriptions are typical of James Peale. Other stylistic devices also confirm Peale as the artist. They include the high placement of the figure in the oval, the wiry, linear treatment of the hair, combining light and dark strands, the use of a pair of dark curved lines to indicate the edge of the eyelid and the crease of the flesh where the eyelid folds into the socket, and finally, the small, tightly pursed lips with upturned corners.[12] The portrait is very similar to other Peale miniatures of young men from the early 1790s, such as *Captain Thomas Yorke Sprogel,* 1791 (R.W. Norton Art Gallery, Shreveport, La.) or *George Richards,* 1792 (American Philosophical Society Library). Unfortunately, unlike his meticulous older brother, James Peale did not keep records of his sitters, so we are unable at this time to determine the exact circumstances of this commission.[13]

Beaubien was only 16 years old when this miniature was painted. If he studied in Philadelphia, where there was a large French community, he could easily have sat for Peale, who lived and worked there. However, Peale did travel in the Eastern States occasionally to fulfil commissions. The exact connection between the artist and sitter remains to be discovered.

Beaubien was not the first French Canadian to be portrayed by a member of the Peale family. In 1776 Charles Willson Peale painted miniatures of four French Canadians who had fought on the side of the English during the American War of Independence and were prisoners of war at the time.[14] Perhaps Beaubien's parents knew of these miniatures, since they moved in the same social circles. Whatever the origin of the commission, Beaubien must have sent the miniature almost immediately to his mother, who is seen proudly wearing it in the portrait François Beaucourt painted of her the following year (Cat. 15). The miniature is a sign of a special affection between the youngest son and Madame Trottier, who was 41 years old at the time of Benjamin's birth.

E.M.M.

Notes

1. "Bleury Pictures in Dining Room," photocopy of a manuscript, NAC, Documentary Art and Photography Division, curatorial files.

2. *La Minerve,* August 4, 1834. p. 2.

3. NAC, RG 4 B8 Vol. 18, p. 6422 microfilm reel H-1415; Letter from Benjamin Beaubien to Robert Shore Milnes, September 21, 1801.

4. *Quebec Gazette,* November 12, 1801. p. 2.

5. Marriage certificate. ANQQ, 206-7/7. Ste-Famille de Boucherville.

6. NAC, MG 30 D1, François Joseph Audet Biographical Notes, Vol. 3, pp. 629-630.

7. *La Minerve,* August 4, 1834.

8. *La Minerve,* April 3, 1834. p. 2.

9. *Ibid.*

10. *La Minerve,* August 4, 1834.

11. Lillian B. Miller (ed.) *The Selected Papers of Charles Willson Peale and his Family* 2 vols. (New Haven & London: Yale University Press, 1983), Vol. I, p. 390 and *The Peale Family: Three Generations of American Artists* (Detroit: Wayne State University Press, 1967), pp. 29-31 and 73-85.

12. Letter to the author from Linda Crocker Simmons, Corcoran Gallery of Art, February 4, 1991.

13. Telephone conversation with Rose Emrich, from the "Peale Papers Project," National Portrait Gallery, Washington, D.C., February 8, 1991.

14. Lillian B. Miller, *op. cit,* Vol. I, pp. 175-176 and N° 138. The four were Joseph-Dominique-Emmanuel Le Moyne de Longueuil, François-Marie Picotté de Belestre, Jean-Baptiste des Bergères de Rigauville and Eustache Gaspard Chartier de Lotbinière. The location of these miniatures is not known at this time.

GERRITT SCHIPPER

1770-1825

BORN IN AMSTERDAM, Schipper apparently studied in Paris around 1790, during the French Revolution. Without knowing who his masters ·were, it is certain that he learned the art of miniatures, silhouettes and pastels in Paris. A specialist in portrait painting, Schipper plied his trade as an itinerant painter from 1790 to 1800. He left Europe for the United States where, beginning in 1802, he visited various cities including Charleston, Boston, Salem and Hartford. In 1808, he went to Lower Canada, where he spent two years, building up an impressive clientele boasting important artists (Cat. 50), businessmen (Cat. 47 and 48) and government figures, including the governor general of the Canadas, Sir James Henry Craig (Cat. 49). Schipper left Lower Canada in late summer 1810, perhaps to supervise the engraving of his portrait of Craig. In an advertisement published on April 26, of the same year, he gives notice that "only the number of engravings that have been ordered will be shipped over to this Province." (*Translation*) In the fall of 1810, Schipper was living in London and it would seem he spent the remainder of his life in England. He died at Camden Town (London) in 1825.

Main sources
GROCE AND WALLACE 1957; HARPER 1970; ALLODI, MOOGK AND STOCK 1991.

NGC

47.
Charles Chaboillez, c. 1808-1810
Pastel on paper, 22.8 × 19.8 cm

Inscriptions
(b., on the panel protecting the back of the work)
unidentified newspaper clippings giving the
obituary notice of Charles Chaboillez and label
relating the history of the work.

Watermark
Crowned coat of arms

Provenance
Descendants of the Chaboillez, Berthelet and
Larocque families; Louis Carrier, Sainte-Anne-de-
Bellevue; acquired by the National Gallery of
Canada, Ottawa, 1962.

Exhibition
Toronto 1968.

Bibliography
ANDRE 1967, pp. 99 and 136f (Repr.); HILL AND
LANDRY 1988, p. 83 (Repr.).

Collection
National Gallery of Canada, Ottawa (9674)

MMFA

48.
Benaiah Gibb Junior, c. 1808-1810
Pastel on paper, 17.5 × 13.4 cm

Provenance
John Gibb-Carsley, Montreal; gift to the McCord
Museum, Montreal, 1983.

Exhibition
Montreal 1987/1

Bibliography
ANDRE 1967, pp. 99 and 136c (Repr.).

Collection
McCord Museum of Canadian History, Montreal
(M983.228.2)

I N THE YEARS immediately preceding
1812, at least forty prominent residents of Montreal and Quebec
City were portrayed in pastel profile: their
portraits are to be found in various public
and private collections. Representative of
this style of portraiture are the following
likenesses: *Sir James Henry Craig* (1748-
1812), Governor-in-Chief of British North
America from 1807 to 1811; *Charles
Chaboillez* (1772-1812), wealthy fur
trader from Montreal; *Behaiah Gibb Jr.*
(1798-1877), who was to inherit his father's merchant-tailoring business; and
Louis Dulongpré, the best known portrait

painter in the province. Although these
pastel profiles have been attributed to various artists (notably William Berczy and
Louis Dulongpré), recent studies[1] show
that they are most probably the work of a
relatively unknown itinerant artist named
Gerrit Schipper.

Schipper, a native of Holland,
studied art in Paris during the French
Revolution, and in 1794 began his travels
as a practising portrait painter.[2] He had
arrived in the United States by 1802, and
visited towns and cities from North Carolina to Massachusetts, painting profile
portraits in pastel. At least fifty of his

American portraits have survived, and are
very similar in style and format to the Canadian profiles. Schipper arrived in
Montreal in the fall of 1808, and advertised his specialty:[3]

NEW METHOD OF PAINTING IN CRAYONS

"G. Schipper, Miniature painter, who lately arrived in this city, has by a new experiment
adopted to take likenesses in Crayons, in a small
size; which he warrants not to fade or change
their colours, so he has prepared the Crayons
himself, avoiding each ingredient, which by
experience will not stand. The price is Six Dollars, (an elegant gold frame with glass, included); and if not approved of, no payment will
be requested."

VAG, AGNS

49.
Sir James Henry Craig, 1811
Aquatint on paper, 29.8 × 23.6 cm (plate).

Inscription
(l.c., under subject) *HIS EXCELLENCY/SIR JAMES HENRY CRAIG,/CAPTAIN-GENERAL, AND GOVERNOR IN CHIEF./in and over the Provinces of Lower Canada, Upper Canada, NovaScotia,/New Brunswick and their Several Dependencies, &c, &c, &c,*

Provenance
Séminaire de Québec; on deposit at the Société du Musée du Séminaire de Québec, 1983.

Bibliography
La Gazette de Québec, April 26, 1810, p. 2, May 31, 1810, p. 3 and July 4, 1811.

Collection
Musée du Séminaire de Québec (Pf 990.4)

Fig. 49A.
Gerritt Schipper,
James Henry Craig, c. 1810;
pastel on paper, 22.7 × 20 cm.
Art Gallery of Ontario, Toronto.
Gift from George E. Kingsford, 1955 (55.19).

He remained in Montreal for at least six months, and probably longer, drawing profiles in pastel. One portrait which varies slightly from his usual format is the profile of **Benaiah Gibb Junior.** It is a half-length composition with the body presented at a three-quarter angle, although the head remains in profile; the boy is seated at a table or ledge, holding a recorder in one hand and a sheet of paper in the other. The musical instrument is carefully drawn, but the hands lack volume and show that Schipper was not accustomed to this departure from his usual bust-in-profile formula. The same awkward rendering of hands can be seen in his portrait of *Bishop Jean-Olivier Briand,* which was copied from an oil painting in Quebec City in 1810 (MSQ).

By April 1810, Schipper was living in Quebec City, where he published a protest against a Montrealer who intended to publish an unauthorized print after a Schipper portrait of Sir James Craig; he declared:

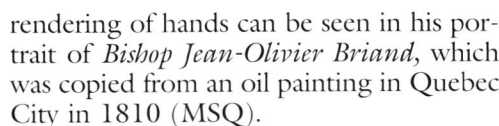

"I believe the likeness above alluded to, to be a Copy of a Copy sold by me, and by no means sufficiently finished to serve as a model for an Engraving (...) As I have the honour to be the painter of the original Portrait, I propose to publish (...) A Likeness of His Excellency Sir James Henry Craig, to be Engraved in Colours by one of the first mezzot into engravers in London, from a Likeness which I painted for that purpose, and which is now in my possession."[4]

Schipper probably sailed for England in August 1810;[5] in December of the same year he was established in Camden Town, London. He must have made immediate arrangements to have the Craig portrait printed and sent to Canada. On July 4, 1811, the *Quebec Gazette* announced the arrival from London of

MQ

50.

Louis Dulongpré, c. 1809
Pastel on paper, 23 × 20 cm

Inscriptions

(u.c., on the panel protecting the back of the work, entered in the file) *Louis Dulongpré-/peintre.;* (l.c., on a label once mounted on the panel protecting the back of the work, removed and entered in the file, in the hand of Abbé Amédée Gosselin) *a vécu au Canada de longues/années, y a fait une mul-/titude de portraits./Né à St Denys, près de Paris, le/16 avril 1754 – Venu en Amérique avec/Rochambeau, fit la guerre de l'indépen-/dance, vint après au Canada, et se/fixa à Montréal.-/Décédé à St. Hyacinthe le 26/avril 1843./A.E.G.*

Provenance

Jacques Viger, Montreal; Damsels Lennox, 1858; acquired by Abbé Hospice-Anthelme Verrault, Quebec City, 1860; bequeathed to the Séminaire de Québec, 1901; on deposit at the Société du Musée du Séminaire de Québec, 1983.

Exhibitions

Montreal 1887, No. 51; Montreal 1892, No. 261; Toronto 1945, No. 40; Albany 1946, No. 12; Quebec City 1952, No. 11; Vancouver 1959, No. 101; Quebec City 1973.

Bibliography

CATALOGUE 1887, p. 11, No. 51; *MACDONALD 1892*, p. 16, No. 261; *LAVAL UNIVERSITY 1905*, p. 33, No. 51; *UNIVERSITÉ LAVAL 1906*, p. 43, No. 30; *UNIVERSITÉ LAVAL 1908*, p. 43, No. 30; *CARTER 1908*, p. 39, No. 239; *UNIVERSITÉ LAVAL 1909*, p. 45, No. 239; *LAVAL UNIVERSITY 1909*, p. 49, No. 239; *BAZIN 1934*; *MORISSET 1935/8*, p. 5 (Repr.); *MORISSET 1936-1937*, Vol. I, pp. 99, 102a and 103-104 (Repr.) and Vol. II, p. 75; *MAHEUX 1939*, p. 879; *MORISSET 1941/1*, p. 85; *HUBBARD 1945*, p. 18, No. 40; *PAINTING IN CANADA 1946*, p. 21, No. 12 (Repr.); *MORISSET 1952*, p. 24, No. 11; *MORISSET 1959/1*, pp. 42 and 55, No. 101 (Repr.); *MORISSET 1960/1*, p. 136; *ANDRE 1967*, pp. 99 and 136d (Repr.); *SOUCY AND THIBAULT 1974*, p. 105; *PARIZEAU 1975*, pp. 31 and 403; *PARIZEAU 1976*, pp. 157 and 159 (Repr.); *RICHARDSON AND AL. 1984*, p. 244 (Repr.); *DEROME, BOURASSA AND CHAGNON 1988*, pp. 51, 52-53 and 78; *LESSARD 1989*, p. 57 (Repr.).

Collection

Musée du Séminaire de Québec (Pf984.25)

"striking LIKENESSES of Sir James Henry Craig, and of Joseph Octave Plessis, printed in colours according to the present stile." The aquatint of Craig is printed in red, blue and yellow\orange, with the addition of hand colouring in some impressions. Although these aquatint prints are not inscribed with the name of the artist, the image of Craig is obviously modelled after the pastel portrait by Schipper (Fig. 49A). (The pastel of Plessis has not been found). It is interesting to see that Schipper chose to publish as a pair the portraits of two powerful adversaries, the Bishop of Quebec and the Governor-in-Chief of the Canadas.

The use of pastel had reached its golden age in 18th-century France (where Schipper studied), and at that time it was often called "crayon painting." Schipper's profiles follow a basic formula: a half-length likeness is sharply defined against a dark background, with a diagonal shaft of light used to provide a contrast with the darker costume. The subject is inscribed in either

an oval or an octagonal format. The portraits are drawn with precision and clarity, in the neoclassical cameo pose favoured in the late 18th century. The face is outlined in black, and may have been drawn with the help of a psysionatrace, and reduced to small size by using a pantograph.

Schipper blends his strokes of pastel, rather than laying them side by side, so that a uniform surface is achieved for the basic colour areas. In some places the colour is applied thickly and burnished or rubbed to a smooth, glossy finish. Over the blended tones, lighter graphic touches are applied to give texture and definition to the hair and costume. The eyes, nose and mouth are accentuated with touches of red-brown. The facial structure is indicated with grey shading. In some areas (such as costume) he moistened the pastel, so that it acquired either an opaque gouache-like consistency, or a more transparent and flowing texture like watercolour.

M.A.

Notes

1. Paper given by M. Allodi at the Royal Ontario Museum Research Colloquium, November 22, 1988. For a resumé of this paper, see National Gallery of Canada exhibition catalogue *Berczy*, Ottawa 1991, Appendix B.

2. See the typescript autobiography by the artist's eldest son Nicholas Shipper (*sic*), "The Life of Nicholas L. Shipper, written by himself, embracing a period of sixteen years, until his arrival in America in the year 1826," Frick Art Reference Library, New York. See also Richard Hyer, "Gerrit Schipper, Miniaturist and Crayon Portraitist" in *New York Genealogical and Biographical Record*, Vol. 83, April 1952, pp. 70-72; and Jeanne Rigerne, "New Light on Gerrit Schipper, the Painter" in *The Clarion* (Museum of American Fold Art: New York), Vol. 13, Ab. I, Winter 1990, pp. 65-70.

3. *Montreal Gazette*, November 28, 1808.

4. *Quebec Gazette*, April 16, 1810.

5. Schipper's last known commission in Quebec City was for pastel copies of portraits of bishops François de Montmorency Laval and Jean-Olivier Briand, for the Seminaire de Quebec. His receipted invoice is dated August 3, 1810. See ASQ file 121, No. 238.

SEMPRONIUS STRETTON

1781-1842

BORN IN 1781, Sempronius Stretton, like several other amateur painters from Britain, came to Canada after enlisting in the British army. Made lieutenant of the 49ᵗʰ Foot in 1801, Stretton arrived in North America in 1803, at the age of 22. He was stationed at York (Toronto) from 1803 to 1805 and then transferred to the Quebec City garrison. He painted views of York and Queenston as well as Quebec City and its environs. His sketchbook also includes some studies of birds (Cat. 51).

Stretton left the country in 1806. His older brother, Severus William Lynam Stretton (1793-1884), also worked in Canada after 1818. Sempronius Stretton continued his military career, particularly distinguishing himself during the war in Spain beginning in 1812, and at Waterloo in 1815. He died at Croydon (London) on February 5, 1842, after being promoted colonel.

Main source
COOKE 1983.

51.
Sketchbook, 1803-1806
20.8 × 16.5 cm

Inscriptions
(on front cover, upper section, in graphite) *Lt. Stretton' Sketch Book No...1./Case VII a;* (c., in graphite) *Canadian Sketches/Executed 1803-1806./By Lieut. (afterwards Colonel)/Sempronius Stretton co.[?] 40th and 64th Regts.*

Provenance
Descendants of the Stretton family; W. de C. Stretton, S. Devon, England; acquired by the Public Archives of Canada, Ottawa, 1930.

Exhibition
Ottawa 1988 (Fol. 36).

Bibliography
COOKE *1983,* p. 193; WILSON *1988,* p. 147.

Collection
National Archives of Canada, Ottawa (1990-336X)

MQ

A. *View of the Signal House on Cape Diamond* (Fol. 22), 1805
Pen and black ink, and gey wash on paper, 13.3 × 20 cm

Inscription
(l.c., in pen and black ink, in the artist's hand on an identical inscription in graphite almost erased) *View of the Signal house on Cape Diamond with the bay of Quebec/the Isle of Orleans, the falls of Montmorency &, from Cape Diamond Quebec July 20. 1805.*

Fig. 51A.
Edward Walsh,
A View of the City of Montreal from the McTavish Monument on the top of the Mountain, 1806;
watercolour over graphite on paper,
35.5 × 52.3 cm.
Royal Ontario Museum, Toronto (952.217).

S EMPRONIUS STRETTON arrived in the Canadas at the beginning of his military career, in 1803, which makes this sketchbook the work of a young amateur, then aged twenty-five. It includes over forty drawings, in ninety-five folios, with topographical surveys, studies of costumes and bird drawings. The sketchbook is divided into two distinct sections. The first includes the main topographical drawings, which are numbered in order from one to seventy-four, but not dated chronologically (Cat. C, D and E). The second section, which totals some twenty folios, is a series of watercolours of birds: the drawings are dated chronologically beginning with the last folio and working towards the centre. These last drawings were done while Stretton was stationed in Québec City, using stuffed birds he had killed on hunting trips during his posting in York from 1803 to 1805. These observations make it difficult to confirm, among other things, the actual dating of the sketchbook, traditionally considered to be from the artist's Quebec period.

Two theories are plausible. First, Stretton could have disregarded the page order of the sketchbook and merely drawn anywhere, leaving a series of blank pages between certain drawings (folios 16 to 19 are blank). Second, he could have gone back and used the sketchbook at a later date to copy drawings from nature done in Quebec. Given the scarcity of data from which to work and the lack of studies on the artist, the years 1805-1806 have been retained for the drawings executed in Quebec, since these dates correspond to the soldier's work during this time.

The artist's approach is candid. Stretton has given us a frank view of the sites he visited (Cat. D); at least, this is the first impression the viewer gets from his sketchbook which, along with the sketchbook of George Heriot, housed in the McCord Museum of Canadian History,[1] is one of the earliest known collections of Quebec views. The strictly topographical surveys are accompanied by descriptions that are almost ethnographic in nature. His costume studies (Cat. E and F), for example, recall the drawings of John Lambert, who visited Quebec City a few months after Stretton's departure. Drawings of specific buildings, such as the ones on Cap Diamant (Cat. A and B), are described in true military fashion, i.e. with more con-

cern for detailing the immediate surroundings than for conveying them in esthetic terms. It would seem from Stretton's sketchbook that the artist showed no interest in the prevailing influences of the day, such as the Picturesque. Consequently, although Stretton was in Quebec City at the same time as Edward Walsh (1756-1832) (Fig. 51A), his drawings show no hint of contact between the two. What is more, the view of Quebec City (Cat. C) recalls the very beginnings of topography, when it shared land surveys and hydrography with the science of cartography.

D.P.

Notes
1. Heriot's sketchbook includes a number of drawings of Quebec dated circa 1810 (M 6357).

NGC

B. *View of the Hanging Magazine and Part of the Old French Work on Cape Diamond* (Fol. 24), 1805

Pen and black ink, and grey wash on paper, 13.4 × 20 cm

Inscription

(on the drawing, in pen and black ink, in the artist's hand on an identical inscription in graphite almost erased) *View of the hanging Magazine & part of the old french works on the/Cape with the river S̄ Laurence below & the opposite shore taken from/the signal house Cape Diamond Quebec July 20. 1805 Looking up the river.*

Bibliography

NOPPEN, PAULETTE AND TREMBLAY *1979*, p. 150 (Repr.); CHARBONNEAU, DESLOGES AND LAFRANCE *1982*, p. 270 (Repr.).

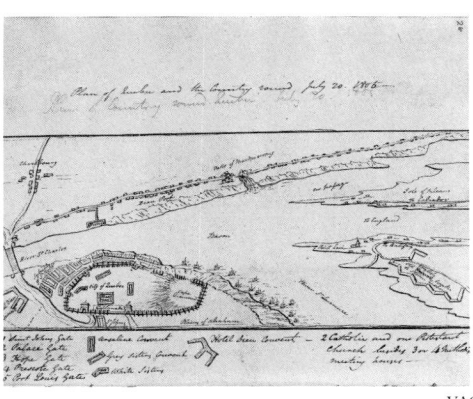

VAG

C. *Plan of Quebec and the Country Around* (Fol. 26), 1805

Pen and black ink on paper, 8.5 × 20 cm

Inscriptions

(above the drawing, in pen and black ink, in the hand of the artist on an inscription) *Plan of Quebec and the Country round July 20. 1805*, *Plan of Country round Quebec, July 20. 1805;* (below the drawing) legend of the plan.

AGNS

D. *Two Shops opposite my Lodgings in Quebec* (Fol. 36), 1806

Pen and black ink, and grey wash on paper, 12.8 × 20 cm

Inscriptions

(below the drawing, in pen and black ink, in the artist's hand) *Two Shops opposite my lodgings in Quebec, a Tanners, & a merchants,/all Canadian Shops are built after this manner /In St John's Street – June 29* [?] *1806;* (in Fol. 37, in pen and black ink, in the artist's hand) *The rooms of the left hand shop are the lodging of L̇. Johnston 49 Reḡ.*

Exhibition
Ottawa 1988.

Bibliography

NOPPEN, PAULETTE et TREMBLAY *1979*, p. 49 (Repr.); WILSON *1988*, pp. 146-147 (Repr.)

MMFA

E. *A Canadian Man and Woman in their Winter Dress* (Fol. 38), 1805

Pen and black ink, watercolour on paper, 20 × 16 cm

Inscription

(u.c., in pen and black ink, in the artist's hand) *A Canadian man and woman in their winter Dress. Quebec/Canada No.ṿ 21. 1805.*

Bibliography

BELL *1973/1*, p. 66 (Repr.); AGENDA D'ART *1982* (Repr.).

MMFA

F. *A Canadian Man and Woman in their Winter Dress, Back View* (Fol. 39), 1805

Pen and black ink, and watercolour on paper, 20 × 16 cm

Inscription

(u.c., in pen and black ink, in the artist's hand) *Back view of the above.*

Bibliography

BELL *1973/1*, p. 66 (Repr.); AGENDA D'ART *1982* (Repr.).

UNATTRIBUTED WORKS

MQ, NGC

52.

Portrait Tought To Be of Thomas Baillairgé, 1816

Watercolour, gum arabic highlighted with gouache on cardboard, 7.5 × 6 cm

Inscription
(b., in ink) *Peint en septembre/1816. par un Français/qui etait venu avec/La belle Abine* [?]-.

Provenance
Doctor Bacon; gift to the Séminaire de Québec, c. 1945; on deposit at the Société du Musée du Séminaire de Québec, 1983.

Exhibitions
Quebec City 1952, No. 31; Vancouver 1959, No. 93; Quebec City 1989-1990.

Bibliography
UNIVERSITÉ LAVAL 1933, No. 615; *MORISSET 1952*, p. 28, No. 31; *MORISSET 1959/1*, pp. 41 and 55, No. 93 (Repr.); *MORISSET 1960/1*, p. 61; *KAREL, NOPPEN AND THIBAULT 1975*, p. 30, No. 33 (Repr.); *O'GALLAGHER 1979*, p. 32b (Repr.); *O'GALLAGHER 1981*, p. 19 (Repr.); *NOPPEN AND GRIGNON 1983*, p. 76 (Repr.); *RICHARDSON AND AL. 1984*, p. 139 (Repr.); *LESSARD 1987/2*, p. 42 (Repr.).

Collection
Musée du Séminaire de Québec (Pf984.13)

T HE LONG-HELD BELIEF that this miniature is a portrait of sculptor and architect Thomas Baillairgé (1791-1859) is based on a single document. At first glance, the undated manuscript seems to be of some significance, since it is signed by the work's benefactor, "L(?)C(?)G Bacon md", who wanted to establish the authenticity of the portrait:

This small portrait, set in a red leather medallion, is the [word missing] of Jean-Thomas Baillairgé, son of François Baillairgé and M. Louise Cureux of St-Germain. He was a lawyer—having never practised.—sculptor, cabinetmaker [...] Jean Thomas B. studied in France with his cousins for several years, some ten or so. [word illegible] In addition to the portrait of J.T.B., the Procureur also received from Dr. Bacon the Chevalier de St.G. medallion belonging to Ls. de G. Baillairgé.[1] (*Translation*)

However, perusal of this document reveals that Dr. Bacon has confused Thomas with his cousin Louis de Gonzague Baillairgé.[2] This imbroglio forced us to try and learn more about Dr. Bacon, but our research was inconclusive. Bacon did, on the other hand, donate other works to the

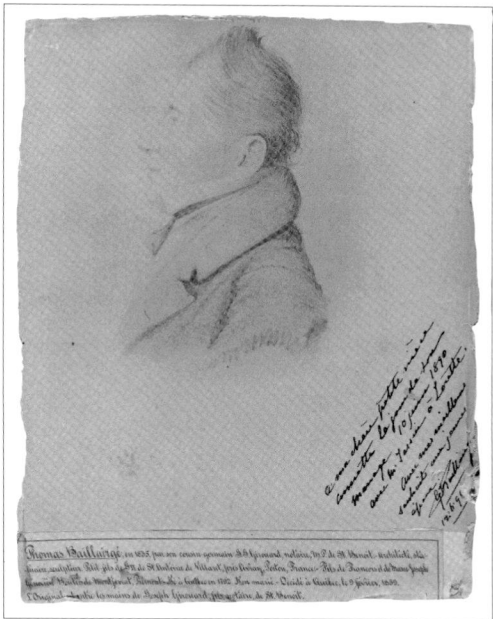

Fig. 52A.
Jean-Joseph Girouard,
Thomas Baillairgé, c. 1837;
old photograph of a portrait in graphite.
Private collection.

Séminaire de Québec that are directly tied to the Baillairgé family, one of which is the *Portrait of Pierre-Florent Baillairgé*[3] by François Baillairgé. This red pencil drawing is easily identified as Pierre-Florent and attributed to François thanks to the sitter's son, Louis de Gonzague, who clearly identified the portrait as that of his father and done by his uncle.[4] This particular work compares easily to other red pencil drawings by Baillairgé. Although they do not share enough affinities to positively identify the sitter in the miniature, the coherence of the works donated by Bacon must be acknowledged.[5] Furthermore, the red pencil drawing was sent to the Séminaire in November 1945,[6] making it possible to assume that the miniature was donated in the same period.

This raises questions as to whether the portrait is indeed of Thomas Baillairgé. The inscription on the back of the miniature leaves no doubt as to the date of execution. Confirmed by the sitter's obvious youth, "*Septembre/1816*" allows for the possibility that it could be Thomas Baillairgé at the age of twenty-five. Compare the figure in this particular portrait to the portrait of the sculptor drawn by Jean-Joseph Girouard (Fig. 52A): one wonders if they are really the same man. Although the contours of the nose, lips and chin are obviously similar, this hastily sketched drawing alone is not enough to establish that the miniature actually depicts Thomas Baillairgé. In short, without enough proof that the figure in this portrait is indeed Thomas Baillairgé, at best, we can only assume that it is.

The miniature was drawn freehand, and not with the use of a physionotrace as originally believed.[7] The inscription "*Peint* [...] *par un Français*" (painted by a Frenchman) on the back of the watercolour provides the only information known about the artist, i.e his nationality. The lack of similarities with other works, the format and the subject matter lead us to believe that it is the legacy of one of the many itinerant miniaturists who visited the colony in the early 19th century.

J.C.

Notes

1. MSQ, file on the portrait.

2. Trying to correct all the errors in this document would be too time-consuming. We would like to mention only that Marie-Louise Cureux of Saint-Germain was the mother of Louis de Gonzague, who was a lawyer: Thomas never exercised this profession, nor did he ever study in France.

3. MSQ (Pf984.20). *See* KAREL, NOPPEN AND THIBAULT 1975, p. 27, No. 26 (Repr.).

4. Signed "*L G B*" in pencil in the lower right-hand corner of the back of the drawing. The authenticity of the signature can be confirmed by comparing it with documents signed by Louis de Gonzague Baillairgé.

5. At the same time as the red pencil drawing, Dr. Bacon donated *Portrait of Louis de Gonzague Baillairgé*, thought to be by Jean-Joseph Girouard. However, research conducted to date does not make it possible to establish the exactitude of the identification and attribution of this pastel portrait (MSQ, Pf984.21).

6. MSQ, document signed by Dr. Bacon, File No. Pf984.20.

7. MORISSET 1960/1, p. 61; LESSARD 1987/2, p. 42.

53.
John Neilson, c. 1820
Oil on canvas, 74 × 58.5 cm

Provenance
Descendants of the Neilson family; Gordon Anthony Neilson inheritance; on deposit at the Archives de la Province de Québec, 1942; Ian Satow; John L. Russell, Gananoque, Ontario; acquired by the Musée du Québec, Quebec City, 1984.

Exhibition
Vancouver 1959, No. 156.

Bibliography
MORISSET 1959/1, p. 46, No. 156; *Nos racines,* No. 71 (1979), p. 1403 (Repr.); *GALARNEAU 1986,* p. 5 (Repr.); *BÉLAND AND BOURASSA 1990,* pp. 6, 8 and 38 (Repr.).

Collection
Musée du Québec, Quebec City. Restored in 1991 with the assistance of the Amis du Musée du Québec (84.30)

J OHN NEILSON (1776-1848) carved out a remarkable career for himself in the early 1800s. Born in Scotland, Neilson came to Quebec City in 1791 to help his brother Samuel run the printery founded by their uncle, William Brown. Following his brother's death in 1796, John took over the business, becoming owner and publisher. Between 1800 and 1820, his company was the largest publishing concern in the province of Quebec. Most of its income came from government and private contracts and from the publication of the *Quebec Gazette,* a bilingual newspaper founded by Neilson's uncle in 1764. Not only did Neilson publish the largest existing weekly, but he also owned the main bookstore. Educated, perfectly bilingual and extremely cultivated, Neilson was active in cultural, educational and agricultural affairs and took an avid interest in colonization.

Neilson was also a brilliant politician. A reformist or moderate liberal, he entered politics in 1818 and became so involved that four years later, in 1822, he was forced to hand over two thirds of his company to his eldest son, Samuel (Cat. 41). Championing the cause of the French Canadians and their institutions, Neilson ran for office as a member of the *Parti canadien* and was elected in the Quebec City riding. He twice travelled to London in an attempt to have the rights of the French Canadians recognized. His first trip was in 1823, when he and Louis-Joseph Papineau (Cat. 188) submitted the petitions from Lower Canada against the proposed union. He went again in 1828, this time with Denis-Benjamin Viger and Augustin Cuvillier, when he was delegated to state the Assembly's grievances against Lord Dalhousie's administration.

In March 1830, Papineau publicly thanked Neilson for all that he had done and less than two years later, his fellow citizens organized a banquet in his honour in Quebec City. He was presented with a commemorative silver urn commissioned from a silversmith in England (MQ). But a deep gulf was already separating Neilson and Papineau, who had become head of a more radical faction. The final break came in 1834, with the adoption of the Ninety-Two Resolutions. Neilson was called a traitor and was defeated in the elections that same year. He nevertheless continued to be an active member of various associations until his death. He left behind a considerable fortune and a reputation as an honest and fair man.[1]

Fig. 53A.
Unidentified artist,
Philémon Wright, 1800-1810;
oil on canvas, 71.0 × 52.1 cm.
National Archives of Canada,
Ottawa (C-11056).

Fig. 53B.
Unidentified artist,
*Judge Joseph-Rémi Vallières
de Saint-Réal*, c. 1830;
oil on canvas, 76.7 × 63.2 cm.
Musée du Québec, Quebec City (34.547).

This extremely sobre portrait of Neilson is free of any pictorial device and shows him in a three-quarter, head and shoulders, close-up profile; he is gazing off to the left, beyond the composition. The halo and the illuminated face define the subject's head against the plain background, whose dark brown tones merge with the deep blacks of the sitter's costume in the lower section of the canvas. This tight, bare, even somewhat austere, composition was designed to set off Neilson's facial expression and the whiteness of his shirt. This same artistic style can be found in the portrait of *Philémon Wright*, painted by an unknown artist circa 1800-1810 (Fig. 53A) and in that of *Judge Joseph-Rémi Vallières de Saint-Réal*, until just recently attributed to painter Théophile Hamel (Fig. 53B).[2] All three portraits were likely painted by the same artist.

The sitter's age (40-45) as well as certain details of his attire—e.g. the ascot folded around his neck and high jacket collar with an M-shaped notch—make it possible to date the portrait circa 1815-1820. Gérard Morisset once attributed this unsigned work to American painter John James, who worked in Quebec City be-

tween 1815 and 1830 and about whose artistic production little is known. Although there were indeed some professional ties between James and the Neilsons, there are no documents certifying that he is in fact the artist. Moreover, the quality of the portrait of Neilson shows that it was done by a much more skilful artist than the only two oil portraits by James known in Quebec, i.e. the one of Monseigneur Plessis (1824), formerly held in the Saint-Roch de Québec rectory (MQ) and the one of Father Joseph Signay (1824), until recently housed in the Notre-Dame de Québec cathedral (MSQ, deposit). The portrait of Neilson could have been done by any one of the many foreign, itinerant artists who plied their trade in Lower Canada around 1820. Indeed, in 1809, Neilson had already had his silhouette, as well as that of his wife and three children, cut by Eliab Metcalf, an American artist working in Quebec at the time (Cat. 41). Since the name of the artist, who was obviously a talented professional probably trained in the English School, is unknown, it is best to leave the portrait anonymous.[3]

M.B.

Notes

1. Sonia Chassé, Rita Girard-Wallot and Jean-Pierre Wallot, DCB, Vol. VII (1988), pp. 644-649.
2. This unsigned, undated canvas cannot be attributed to Théophile Hamel for several reasons. First, Vallières de Saint-Réal (1787-1847) appears no older than 45, which would mean that the portrait was done between 1830 and 1835, at which time Hamel was only an apprentice. Second, the portrait of *Vallières de Saint-Réal* painted by Hamel for the government in 1854 bears an artist's inscription indicating that it is a copy (House of Commons, Ottawa), probably copied from the painting held at the Musée du Québec. Finally, with the exception of the portrait of *Wolfred Nelson* (MMCH), the position of the sitter in this painting is extremely rare for the artist.
3. John Neilson had his portrait painted on two other occasions. The first is a profile possibly corresponding to the miniature exhibited at Château Ramezay in 1887 and 1892, and the second is likely another version of the painting shown here, painted much later, circa 1865, and commissioned from Théophile Hamel by the government for its portrait gallery. For further reading on the profile and miniature, see *Le Bulletin des recherches historiques*, Vol. VIII, No. 8 (August 1902), p. 246; *Cap-aux-Diamants*, Vol. V, No. 3 (Fall 1989); CATALOGUE *1887*, p. 38 (No. 719) and MACDONALD *1892*, p. 29 (No. 423); on the painting by Hamel, see VÉZINA *1975/1*, pp. 111 and 115; VÉZINA *1976/1*, p. 55; 1977, p. 397.

THE AFFIRMATION
1820-1850

PHILIP JOHN
BAINBRIGGE
1817-1881

LDEST SON OF GENERAL Sir Philip Bainbrigge, Philip John was born in Stafforshire, England, on January 16, 1817. Coming from a military family, he studied at the Royal Military Academy in Woolwich (London) from 1830 to 1833. He spent his entire career in the army as part of the Royal Engineers. After leaving Woolwich, Bainbrigge went to work for the topographical services, but as of 1835, he offered to go overseas. Arriving in Canada on June 25, 1836, he aided in suppressing the 1837-1838 insurrections in the Richelieu valley and at Saint-Eustache. Following the hostilities, Bainbrigge travelled to various regions in the provinces to inspect fortifications and other defence systems. His visits included Quebec City, Amherstburg, Chatham (Ontario), and locations along the Rideau Canal and near the Saint John river in New Brunswick.

Bainbrigge remained in Canada until August 1842, when he returned to England to enjoy a prosperous career teaching fortifications and then heading the department at Woolwich. He was promoted colonel in 1861 and then major-general two years later. Bainbrigge died at Blackheath on October 23, 1881.

Main sources
HARPER 1970; COOKE 1983.

MQ, NGC

VAG, AGNS, MMFA

54.
Montmorency and Isle of Orleans
from a Hill Below Point Levi, Quebec, 1836
Watercolour over graphite on paper, 18.7 × 26.7 cm

Inscriptions
(b.,l.c., in graphite, in the artist's hand) *Montmorency & I. of Orleans from a hill below P'. Levi./Sept 8ᵗʰ 1836.;* (below;, in graphite, by another hand) *Montmorenci from the Hills/1836.*

Provenance
E. Parsons & Sons, London; acquired by the Public Archives of Canada, Ottawa, 1921.

Collection
National Archives of Canada, Ottawa (1983-47-116X)

55.
*Crossing Lake Etchemin on Ice,*1836
Watercolour on faint graphite lines with scraping out on paper, 17.5 × 25.2cm

Inscriptions
(b.,c., in pen and black ink) *Crossing Lake Etchemin on the Ice/Dec. 12ᵗʰ. 1836.;* (below, in graphite, in the artist's hand[?]) *Sir Randolph Routh farm;* (b.,l.c., in graphite, by another hand) *Lake Etchemin 1836.*

Provenance
E. Parsons & Sons, London; acquired by the Public Archives of Canada, Ottawa, 1921.

Bibliography
AGENDA D'ART 1982 (Repr.); *COOKE 1983*, p. 12.

Collection
National Archives of Canada, Ottawa (1983-47-123X)

PHILIP JOHN BAINBRIGGE, like James Pattison Cockburn, received his training at the military academy in Woolwich. He entered it at the age of thirteen and graduated with honours. His extraordinary talent marked his entire life, as evidenced by the obituary published in *The Royal Engineers Journal* on January 2, 1882:

At Woolwich Academy, where his career was a most distinguished one, he took sixty places, and obtained his commission as 2nd Lieutenant in the Royal Engineers in 1833.

Unlike the Royal Artillery, which was easier to enter, acceptance into the Royal Engineers was difficult.[1] After completing his basic training, Bainbrigge embarked on what was to be an unswerving career. In 1845, he was hired as fortifications master at Woolwich and then full professor ten years later.

At his own request, he was transferred to Quebec on June 25, 1836, his first posting overseas, at the age of nineteen. This remark is significant since his portrayal of Quebec landscapes was directly linked to his training at Woolwich, i.e, it is doubtful that he had the time to assimilate any artistic style other than that of Thales Fielding (1793-1837), Bainbrigge's drawing master at Woolwich. Fielding taught at the military academy for nearly ten years, beginning in 1828, having just returned from Paris after spending eight years working in the engraving studio of his brother, Newton Fielding (1799-1856).[2] During these critical years, the British landscape tradition was spreading throughout France. Thales Fielding, Richard Parkes Bonington (1802-1828) and Louis Francia (1772-1839) all collaborated on the publications put out by the Paris publishing firm owned by the Osterwald brothers.[3] It was also during this period that Bonington and Eugène Delacroix (1798-1863) worked together and shared a studio.[4] Thales Fielding thus came from a tradition of topographical art that was clearly different from that of Paul Sandby: his more fluid style left greater room for light effects.

Bainbrigge put the instruction received from Fielding at Woolwich into practice in his depiction of Quebec landscapes. He showed little interest in recording life inside city walls, never painting the buildings or neighbourhoods that were important to city life as James Pattison Cockburn did (Cat. 72 to 75). Taking the comparison between these two artists a step further, it could be said that Cockburn is much more analytical. His landscapes are "dissected" into their component parts: trees, rocks and architectural structures stand alone in the final composition. Conversely, Bainbrigge's style is synthetic: he sacrifices detail for the whole.

This is a fundamental characteristic of Bainbrigge's oeuvre, and one that changed little during his six years in Quebec garrisons. There is little difference between his watercolours dating to the fall of 1836, such as *Montmorency and Isle of Orleans From A Hill Below Point Levi, Quebec,* and his landscapes of 1841, such as *Mount Saint-Hilaire,* either in the composition or the handling. Many of his

VAG, AGNS, MMFA

56.

Fort and Church Chambly, 1838

Watercolour over graphite with some traces of scraping out on paper, 15.3 × 22 cm

Inscription
(b.,l.c., in graphite, in the artist's hand) *Fort & church Chambly - 1838.*

Provenance
E. Parsons & Sons, London; acquired by the Public Archives of Canada, Ottawa, 1921.

Exhibition
Ottawa 1972-1975, No. 12.

Bibliography
BELL 1972, No. 12 (Repr.); *AGENDA D'ART 1982* (Repr.); *SENIOR 1985,* p. 76 (Repr.); *COURVILLE 1990,* p. 92 (Repr.).

Collection
National Archives of Canada, Ottawa (1983-47-68X)

MQ, NGC

57.

Saint Paul's Bay, Saint Lawrence, 1841

Watercolour on paper, 13.1 × 17.5 cm

Inscriptions
(b.,c., in graphite, in the artist's hand) *Sky from nature;* (below, in graphite, in the same hand) *S*. *Pauls Bay. S* *Lawrence 1841.*

Provenance
E. Parsons & Sons, London; acquired by the Public Archives of Canada, Ottawa, 1921.

Bibliography
AGENDA D'ART 1982 (Repr.); *COURVILLE 1990,* cover p. (Repr.).

Collection
National Archives of Canada, Ottawa (1983-47-42X)

landscapes are built on three parallel planes, with the first slightly on a diagonal. The pictorial quality is rich and layers of colour washes merely suggest shape rather than define it with exaggerated application. The wayside cross in ***Montmorency and Isle of Orleans From A Hill Below Point Levi, Quebec*** is a good illustration. On the back of the watercolour is a pencil drawing of the same cross. It stands straight on a square base and is decorated in keeping with the strict codification of the symbols of the Passion.[5] Bainbrigge, on the other hand, limits his watercolour to the essential. His wayside cross takes on the role of picturesque motif with a local flavour: leaning strongly to the left, barely in the ground, it frames the composition on the right and draws the eye back to Montmorency Falls, aided by the long shadows of the fenceposts, the figure and the tree. Bainbrigge shows little penchant for bright, contrasting colour tones. The pale ochres of the ground merge with the yellowish-greens of the mountains in the distance. The empty surface of the drawing paper

helps create visual schemes: the white of the peasant bearing an axe echoes the white of the falls. All these features are repeated in ***Mount Saint-Hilaire,*** both with respect to the composition and the colour scheme. Yet, this work was done at the end of Bainbrigge's stay in Quebec, as evidenced by the inclusion of the national and religious monument, which was erected on the mountain in 1841. The temperance cross was blessed by Monseigneur De Forbin-Janson, bishop of Nancy, on October 6, 1841.[6]

Bainbrigge builds his landscapes in segments, and ***Crossing Lake Etchemin on Ice*** is probably the clearest example. The inscription on the back of the watercolour, "*Sir Randolph Routh farm*", reminds the viewer that this is a view of a very specific location. Furthermore, it can be assumed that the drawing was not done while Bainbrigge was out on a casual stroll, but rather that the artist made the trip on purpose, since Sir Randolph Isham Routh (1782-1858) "was in charge of all the financial transactions of the army in the

Canadas and was guardian of a military chest with resources often equalling or surpassing those of Lower Canada's provincial treasury."[7]

Around 1836, Routh moved his large family—four sons and five daughters—onto a farm bordering the Etchemin River, then far from city life. To convey this isolation, Bainbrigge chose to depict the farm as a lone, inhabited oasis surrounded by near-impenetrable nature. In the foreground, the figures bundled up in their winter coats have their backs turned to the viewer. This detail, coupled with the tracks in the snow, forcibly draws the viewer directly into the scene, thereby accentuating the feeling of grandeur. Bainbrigge often used this type of composition to indicate progression towards an ultimate goal, sometimes less successfully than in this particular watercolour.[8] The work is stark and, using a minimum of means, the artist has succeeded in creating a feeling of solitude and cold. Grey wash is used to show thinning of the ice on the frozen lake, while scraping along the riverbanks

VAG, AGNS, MMFA

58.
Mount Saint Hilaire, 1841 or 1842
Watercolour over graphite on paper, 15.7 × 22.4 cm

Inscriptions
(b.,c., in graphite, in the artist's hand[?]) *Belanil Mountaine;* (below, in graphite, by another hand) *Belœuil & S*. *Hilaire.*

Provenance
E. Parsons & Sons, London; acquired by the Public Archives of Canada, Ottawa, 1921.

Collection
National Archives of Canada, Ottawa (1983-47-43X)

Fig. 54-58A.
Philip John Bainbrigge,
Wolfe Monument;
watercolour over graphite on paper, 18.3 × 25.4 cm.
National Archives of Canada, Ottawa (C-11893).

marks an accumulation. The occasional touch of colour—the blue of the mountains and winter coats; yellow of the driver's fur coat and the houses on the hill—serve to enliven an otherwise rather dull composition. The deep blacks used to accentuate the shadows on the seated figures clash with the white of the empty surface in the foreground, which is given limited treatment. This is the work of a careful observer, the same quality found in *Saint Paul's Bay,* in which the artist is concerned less with depicting a given landscape than with conveying an effect through the use of colour. The shapes in the foreground have been painted with a lack of precision only to draw the viewer's eye to the sunlight peeking through the clouds. The light, indicated by the surface left blank, hits the thin line of the horizon, outlining the contours of the church steeple. Thin strokes of blue-grey sweep the sky to define the rays of light.

The basis of all of Bainbrigge's watercolours are a few, simple composition grids. *In Fort and Church, Chambly,* the eye is drawn to the background focusing on an astonishing outline of a ship, which appears as an extension of the long horizontal of the quay. This is the only dramatic effect the artist indulges in as the rest of the composition makes common use of horizontals: the line of the quay is repeated in the alignment of buildings in the far middleground. The strictness of the composition is attenuated by the triangle of highly textured ground in the foreground. Bainbrigge's work shows a constant concern for depicting the principal contours of the landscapes being rendered. Perhaps this is a legacy of his engineering training. Supporting this theory is the fact that he went on numerous tours, inspecting fortifications and surveying the borders between the United States and New Brunswick. His Journal[9] includes a number of specific ex-

amples in which the artist has noted map bearings and made a quick sketch of the landscape on the same page.

A number of Bainbrigge's watercolours were exchanged amongst amateurs, although we have no clear picture of the relationships. An identical copy of *Crossing Lake Etchemin on Ice* was done by captain George St. Vincent Whitmore (1798-1851).[10] Contact between the two men was probably facilitated by the fact that Whitmore had received similar military training at the Woolwich academy. The practice of copying warrants further discussion, and the *Wolfe Monument* will serve to illustrate the process. The original watercolour is by Bainbrigge (Fig. 54-58A). It includes all the characteristics found in his oeuvre as a whole: skilful composition, confident use of washes and frank, long shadows. The copiers attempt to capture the science of his technique and copy it faithfully, with no concern for adjusting

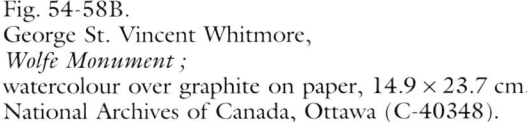

Fig. 54-58B.
George St. Vincent Whitmore,
Wolfe Monument ;
watercolour over graphite on paper, 14.9 × 23.7 cm.
National Archives of Canada, Ottawa (C-40348).

Fig. 54-58C.
Millicent Mary Chaplin,
Wolfe Monument ;
watercolour over graphite on paper, 16.4 × 26.6 cm.
National Archives of Canada, Ottawa (C-839).

perspective to fit the format of the paper they are working on. Thus, Whitmore (Fig. 54-58B) places emphasis on the monument, while shortening the fence to the left. The wider column is also taller and leaves only a thin strip at the top of the page for the sky. A similar situation can be found in the copy by Millicent Mary Chaplin (Fig. 54-58C): to offset the fact that her composition is too small, she is forced to lengthen the fence to the left. The inscription at the bottom of the drawings by Whitmore and Chaplin, "*Here died Wolfe victorious*", indicates that Bainbrigge probably gave his work to the two amateurs to copy together. But why? Perhaps Whitmore and Chaplin were merely looking for models to copy during their spare time to fill their albums. Or perhaps Bainbrigge's style, like that of Hope-Wallace (Cat. 143 to 146) or Henry William Barnard (Cat. 59 to 62), offered something new and was therefore appealing. If so, it should have encouraged watercolourists like Whitmore and Chaplin to try and understand the principles of his technique. If this theory were to prove true, then we would be looking at a veritable circle of watercolourists, however modest their results.

D.P.

Notes

1. In 1833, 19 brevets were awarded by the Royal Artillery, compared with 9 by the Royal Engineers (F.G. Guggisberg, "*The Shop*", The Story of the Royal Military Academy, London, Cassell and Company, 1900, p. 269).

2. Martin Hardie, *Water-Colour Painting in Britain. The Romantic Period* (London: B.T. Batsford Ltd., 1979), pp. 223-224, and Idem, *The Victorian Period*, pp. 36-37.

3. *Louis Francia, 1772-1839* (Cat.) (Calais: Musée des Beaux-Arts (1988-1989), pp. 60 and 136.

4. Marcia Pointon, *Bonington, Francia & Wyld* (London: B.T. Batsford Ltd., 1985), pp. 39-41.

See also Arlette Serullaz and Régis Michel, *L'aquarelle en France au XIXᵉ siècle* (Cat.) (Paris: Musée du Louvre, 1983), No. 43 (Repr.).

5. For an overview of this topic, see the text by John Porter entitled "La croix de chemin" in *Le Grand Heritage 1984*, p. 282. The author also reproduces a watercolour by Bainbrigge depicting a road cross at Lévis.

6. *Allodi 1980*, pp. 150-153.

7. Biographical entry by Elinor Kyte Senior, DCB, Vol. VIII (1985), p. 778.

8. Reference is to *Artillery Returning to Montreal*.

9. NAC, Maps and plans department, "Roads along the Frontiers and in Upper Canada". *Journal* is the generally accepted term for this manuscript.

10. For more on Whitmore, see Eva Major-Marothy, "Captain George St. Vincent Whitmore: A Newly Discovered Military Artist", *Archivaria*, No. 29 (Winter 1989-1990), pp. 168-172, and *Un Moment 1991*, pp. 95-97. The copy of *Crossing Lake Etchemin on Ice* was reproduced in *Cooke 1983*, p. 12, No. 28.

HENRY WILLIAM
BARNARD
1799-1857

ALTHOUGH OF IRISH ANCESTRY, Henry William Barnard was born in Wedbury, England in 1799. His father was an Anglican minister in the county of Buckinghamshire and an amateur artist, while his grandfather had been a bishop of Derry, Ireland. After completing his studies at Westminster College, Henry chose a career in the army. He trained at Ireland's Royal Military College of Sandhurst, where he learned the rudiments of military drawing, including the art of designing fortifications. In 1814, Barnard was promoted ensign in the Grenadier Guards. He later attained the ranks of captain (1822), lieutenant-colonel (1831) and colonel (1846).

Barnard fought in the Napoleonic wars, primarily during the Allies' entry into Paris in late March 1814. He then served in the West Indies. He came to Canada in May 1838, immediately following the 1837-1838 uprisings, as an officer of the 2nd battalion of the Grenadier Guards. During the four years his battalion was stationed in Canada, Barnard spent only a year and a half there, from May 1838 to May 1839 and from May to October 1841. Health problems forced him to return to England from June 1839 to April 1841 and again during the fall of 1841. During his stay in Canada, Barnard sat on the bench of the court martial established at the end of the Rebellions of 1837. Outside of his military activities, Barnard played an active role in Quebec City's social life.

After leaving Canada, Barnard held various positions, both in England and abroad. In the Crimean War, he was appointed head of staff under General Simpson. His final posting, in 1857, was to Bengal, during the Sepoy Mutiny. Prior to this, Barnard had been made Knight Commander of the Order of Bath. He died of cholera during the siege of Delhi in 1857.

Main sources
ALLODI 1974/1; UN MOMENT 1991.

MQ, NGC

59. (See colour reproduction, p. 91)
Landing Place at Sorel, 1838
Watercolour over graphite on paper, 18.5 × 28.5 cm

Inscriptions
(b.,u.l., in pen and black ink, in the artist's hand
[?]) *Landing place at Sorell./Sir J. Colborne's in the
distance;* (below, in graphite) *44.*

Provenance
Walker's Galleries, London; acquired by the Royal
Ontario Museum, Toronto, 1949.

Bibliography
ALLODI 1974/1, Vol. I, No. 94 (Repr.).

Collection
Royal Ontario Museum, Toronto (949.41.6)

T HE VILLAGE OF SOREL is located at the confluence of the Richelieu and St. Lawrence rivers. Under the French regime, Sorel was considered a strategic point and made a part of planned defence systems.[1] With the arrival of British troops and the American War of Independence, efforts were stepped up, notably through the construction of barracks capable of housing a few thousand soldiers.[2] Sorel's geographical location also allowed it to play an active role in the economy, particularly the wheat trade. When Joseph Bouchette published *The British Dominions in North America,* in 1832, Sorel was developing along with other villages (Saint-Hyacinthe, Berthier, L'Assomption), increasing its activities so as to become a nerve centre for the surrounding region.[3]

For the British troops arriving in Quebec during the 1837-1838 uprisings, Sorel signified a stopover point and barrack life. James W. Butler stayed there on January 20, 1838, on his way to Montreal. He recorded a brief topographical survey of the site in his *Journal* (Cat. 67), indicating in particular the fact that the Richelieu River was the site of careening during the winter for steamships travelling between Quebec City and Montreal.[4] It was one of the places for taking ships out of the water for the winter as depicted in ***Landing Place at Sorel.*** The river cannot be seen for the steamship leaning on its starboard side, and the intense activity of the site is skilfully suggested by the horse, the boat and the fresh ruts in the ground. It is perhaps late fall 1838, when everything is being stored for the winter. The annotation apparently written by Barnard himself on the back of his drawing, "*Sir J. Colborne's in the distance*", could well support this theory. The commander of the Canadian troops is possibly depicted as the diminutive figure in red trousers just below the ship's stern.[5] In November 1838, Sir John Colborne led the counter-attack against the *Patriotes* uprisings, which led in particular to the capture of the Beauharnois manor house (Cat. 103 and 104), undoubtedly passing through Sorel.

Barnard has roughly outlined the principal contours of his drawing starting from a central vanishing point—indicated with a pencil star just below the horizon—and drawing toward the foreground of the composition, confirming that the watercolour is actually a study from nature. The imposing wooden building creates a mass on the right, while the long diagonal of the stockade, the horse and the boat prolong the perspective to the left. The figures, placed conspicuously along the vanishing point, indicate the scale of the ship, whose stern alone is visible. The nervous lines show the rapidity with which Barnard sketched the site. The artist has made no attempt to cover up the hastily drawn lines with paint. In fact, he is almost incisive in his use of brown to highlight his pencil lines on the ground and hillside. Barnard uses limited means to conserve the memory of the ***Landing Place at Sorel.*** Pure yellows are used to create highly luminous areas and are covered with a layer of muted sienna to convey patches of shadow. An occasional touch of bright colour—red of clothing and ultramarine of the river—enhance the drawing.

It is possible that Barnard learned to master the art of both drawing and colour during his training at the Sandhurst military academy. However, from what is known about his oeuvre, his teacher, Andrew Wilson (1780-1848), was primarily an artist who reproduced a specific site following the principles of the ideal landscape.[6] In this respect, he has virtually nothing in common with Barnard. The latter likely inherited his artistic style from his father, Reverend William Henry Barnard (1767-1818).[7] An amateur artist, Reverend Barnard took lessons from John Baptist Malchair (1731-1812) at Oxford. Malchair's teaching consisted in providing his students with manual skill that could later be used as an "alphabet" with which to draw from nature.[8] Malchair emphasized understanding the motif through colour tones, avoiding the use of lines to convey contours since "natural objects have, strictly speaking, no outline and may be imitated without the help of lines in painting".[9] His students especially learned to discern a specific motif, such as a window or tree branch, from a spot of colour or a crayon mark on the paper.[10] This was a very unconventional approach for a period which made copying from masters its primary teaching method. Helped by his father's experience, Henry William Barnard must have benefited from such teachings during his youth. It is possible that he remembered the principles for a long time since we can see a hint of them in **Landing Place at Sorel,** primarily in the broad lines that refuse to outline the motif and in the indication of masses using shadow and colour.

D.P.

Notes

1. CHARBONNEAU, DESLOGES AND LAFRANCE 1982, p. 125.

2. CHARBONNEAU, DESLOGES AND LAFRANCE 1982, pp. 382-383. Sorel was renamed William Henry in 1787 in honour of Prince William Henry (the future William IV), who was then on a royal visit to Canada during his term in the navy.

3. COURVILLE 1990, p. 188. A general breakdown of the growth of suburbs shows that the number of houses in Sorel rose from 150 in 1815 to 251 in 1831, and to 534 in 1851. In 1831, it was the largest village in the District of Montreal, followed by La Prairie (214 houses).

4. "Ye steam boats plying between Quebec & Montreal are laid up in ye winter at Sorel in ye Richelieu. There are now seven" (Quoted from the transcription of Butler's diary done by the National Archives of Canada (p. 26). Butler also describes his visit to the inside of the steamship *John Bull* (pp. 26-27).

5. Contrary to what is written in the ROM catalogue on Barnard's watercolours—"near the landing place at Sorel was a lodge serving as residence for the Governor in summer, which may be the indistinct building in this view referred to as 'Sir J. Colborne's'" (ALLODI 1974/1, Vol I, No. 94)—, we do not feel that this inscription corresponds to a building painted by Barnard. Although of modest size, the governor's summer residence had a central square with two side wings that served as kitchen and servants' quarters (see Raymonde Gauthier, *Les manoirs du Québec,* Québec City, Éditeur officiel du Québec/Fides, 1976, pp. 62-63, Repr.).

6. H.L. Mallalieu, *The Dictionary of British Watercolour Artists up to 1920,* The Antique Collector's Club, 1984, Vol. II, p. 548. See also the catalogue entry on James Hope-Wallace (Cat. 43 to 45), Notes 2 and 3.

7. H.L. Mallalieu, *Op. cit.,* Vol. I, p. 24, and Vol. II, p. 304.

8. Martin Hardie, *Water-colour Painting in Britain. The Victorian Period* (London: B.T. Batsford, 1979), Vol. III, pp. 228-234.

9. Quoted from M. Hardie, *Ibid.,* p. 230.

10. Malchair took up teaching again in 1791 with a treatise that was to remain unpublished: *Observations On Landskipp Drawing with many and various Examples Intended for the use of beginners.* In addition to M. Hardie, see Leslie Parris, *Landscape in Britain, c. 1750-1850* (London: The Tate Gallery, 1973), p. 52, No. 88.

E RECTING A MONUMENT in honour of the two generals who lost their lives in the Battle of Abraham was the idea of Lord Dalhousie. At a meeting at the Château Saint-Louis on November 1, 1827, Dalhousie made a brief statement on his intention:

A monument worthy of General Wolfe, and worthy of England, has been placed in Westminster Abbey. My only object is to remove a subject of general regret, that in Quebec, nothing is found to honor the memory of Wolfe, nothing more than if his great achievements had been effected in other countries distant or unknown to us.[1]

In the mind of the governor-in-chief of British North America, then, is it possible that James Wolfe and Louis-Joseph de Montcalm, heros through their death in Quebec City on September 13, 1759, were not united in posterity? John Crawford Young's sketches for the monument were tabled at the meeting of November 1. The design was the outcome of the artist's discussions with Lord Dalhousie during their daily walks in the winter of 1826-1827, when Crawford was the governor's aide-de-camp.[2] Dalhousie's trip to Egypt,[3] coupled with a passion for Egyptian decoration, possibly affected the artist's choice of an obelisk standing on a sarcophagus-shaped base.

The cornerstone was laid on November 15, 1827 during an impressive ceremony. The greystone monument, which is an exact replica of Crawford's drawing, "is thirteen feet from the ground [to the top of the surbase]. On this rests the Sarcophagus, seven feet three inches high. The obelisk measures forty-two feet eight inches, and the apex two feet one inch, making in the whole an altitude of sixty-five feet from the ground."[4] The inauguration took place on September 8, 1828, the day of Dalhousie's departure, when the top stone was placed during an official ceremony. In his diary, Dalhousie confided that "I am vain enough to think it in some respects, a monument to my own name, at the last hour of my Administration of the Government in this Country."[5]

The site chosen to erect the monument was highly symbolic. The enclave was located in the upper section of the governor's gardens, along Rue Carrières and was actually to become one of the oldest public esplanades in the city, providing an unimpeded view over the St. Lawrence River. Standing alone, the monument at once became an automatic reference point for panoramic views of the city. Alfred Hawkins described it as follows:

VAG, AGNS, MMFA

Fig. 60A.
R. Wallis after William Henry Bartlett,
*Wolfe and Montcalm Monument
in Quebec*, 1840;
engraving, 22.8 × 29.2 cm (plate).
National Gallery of Canada, Ottawa (15015).

60.
Wolfe and Montcalm Monument, Quebec, 1838-1839 or 1841
Watercolour over graphite on paper, 18.6 × 25.6 cm

Inscription
(b.,c., in graphite) *Wolfe Monument/Quebec.*
Provenance
Walker's Galleries, London; acquired by the Royal
Ontario Museum, Toronto, 1949.

Bibliography
ALLODI 1974/1, Vol. I, No. 81.
Collection
Royal Ontario Museum, Toronto (949.41.7)

The Monument is a conspicuous object from
the River; but on account of the numerous
spires which rise around it in a distant view, it
is seen to the best advantage from the centre
of the channel between the Lower Town and
Pointe Lévi.[6]

The monument can be perceived
as much more than a mere tourist stop.
The possibilities were endless for watercolourists; for example, they could use it
to pay a posthumous tribute or see it as a
symbol of possession.

For James P. Cockburn, it was essentially just a monument in the city: we
are given an indication of its size by its
immediate setting. The artist has it situated in the middle of the park, half hidden
by the trees, or at the crossroads of two
streets.[7] During his stay in Quebec City in
1838, William Henry Bartlett (1809-1854)
painted the monument, focusing on its
moral values by depicting a soldier explaining the inscription to a young boy
(Fig. 60A). Like James Hope-Wallace
(Cat. 144), Bartlett does not ignore the
monument's commanding position overlooking the river; however, the spirit of his

work differs. Bartlett likes to give his sites
a dramatic overtone to throw the viewer
off with the unexpected association of ideas.
He had assimilated certain teachings of
Joseph Mallord William Turner (1775-
1851), notably the highly contrasting use
of light and dark. He made this one of the
main elements of his artistic vocabulary,
thereby indicating a certain precariousness.
At the other extreme is James Hope-
Wallace, whose monument to Wolfe and
Montcalm stresses permanency. Well anchored to its base, the obelisk shows no
contradictions: no figures fill the space and
the dark shadows cast on the ground only
serve to set off its direct, powerful presence. One might ask where Barnard's watercolour fits in in all this. It must be
acknowledged that it does not have the
strength of James Hope-Wallace's rendition. The composition is similar, with the
monument in the centre and a row of trees
framing the composition on the right, but
no attempt is made to correct the weaknesses of the overall scene. The obelisk,
too big for its narrow base and with little
linking it naturally to the sarcophagus on

which it sits, appears lopsided. The wavy
form of the tree trunks and the condensed
foliage do not provide the viewer with a
powerful image. The composition focuses
on the monument as a meeting place and
shows it in full sunlight, with no attempt
to create an effect. The eye follows the
diagonal alley, which is clearly reinforced
by the umber-coloured ground and grass
border. The lined-up grenadiers, probably
the regimental band, recall the principles
of James P. Cockburn based on a different
esthetic. Thus, *Wolfe and Montcalm
Monument, Québec* is essentially merely a
visual record, one of the basic principles of
topographical views. For this reason, it is
difficult to date it accurately to either of
Barnard's stays in Quebec.

D.P.

Notes
1. Quoted from *HAWKINS 1834*, p. 268.
2. *HAWKINS 1834*, p. 268.
3. See catalogue entry on John Elliott Woolford
(Cat. 233 to 235).
4. *HAWKINS 1834*, pp. 276-277.
5. Quoted from Peter Burroughs, "George Ramsay, 9th Earl of Dalhousie", DCB, Vol. VII
(1988), p. 731. It must be acknowledged, however, that Dalhousie was also a sponsor in this
initiative.
6. *HAWKINS 1834*, p. 276.
7. *CAMERON AND TRUDEL 1976*, pp. 100-102,
Nos. 76-78 (Repr.).

Fig. 61A.
James Duncan,
Notre-Dame Street, Montreal, 1841;
watercolour over graphite on paper,
17.4 × 26.1 cm.
National Gallery of Canada, Ottawa (28067).

MQ, NGC

61.
Notre-Dame Street, Montreal, 1841
Watercolour over graphite with touches of gouache on paper, 20.5 × 30.9 cm

Inscriptions
(b.,u.l., in pen and black ink, in the artist's hand[?]) [?] *Notre Dame -/Montreal*; (b.,l.r., on the mount, i,n graphite) *Notre Dame Street/ Montreal. Canada/1840.*

Provenance
Walker's Galleries, London; acquired by the Royal Ontario Museum, Toronto, 1949.

Bibliography
ALLODI 1974/1, Vol. I, No. 87 (Repr.).

Collection
Royal Ontario Museum, Toronto (949.41.1)

T HE TWO VIEWS ABOVE were executed from a purely topographical perspective. Barnard has chosen a central vantage point for **Notre-Dame Street, Montreal,** drawing from the governor's gardens. The two similar buildings, set slightly back on the north side of the street, are the new prison, with the guards in front, and the courthouse. A little farther on can be seen the spire of the Anglican church and tower of the former Notre-Dame parish church. The Nelson pillar, on the south side of the street, stands next to the governor-in-chief's house, which:

being very old, and an early specimen of the unpolished architecture of the province, it is not much entitled to notice; it is however, kept in good repair, and furnished as an occasional residence of the governor-in-chief, when he visits the upper district.[1]

The west tower of the new Notre-Dame church had just been completed during the summer of 1841 and was to be consecrated on November 4.[2] The spire of the former church of the *Récollets monastery,* attended primarily by the Irish Catholics,[3] can just barely be made out at the very back of the drawing.

Barnard has given us a detailed inventory of the city's busiest street.[4] If he has used the same vantage point as other artists, notably Robert Auchmuty Sproule (1799-1845) circa 1829-1830,[5] it is because it is the only one that allows the artist to get so many buildings into limited space. James Duncan did a watercolour of the same view (Fig. 61A) the same year as Barnard. While Duncan's rendition shows greater skill and includes more figures, a few specific points warrant some discussion. First, it is surprising to see the same three figures appear in the lower right-hand foreground. Second, what is to be made of the group of people turning the corner of Rue du Marché, on the left, with the horse-drawn cart leading the crowd in both cases. And third, both works have a carriole in the middleground guiding the eye in the desired direction. Even if these elements are essentially no more than artificial pictorial devices used by topographical artists to mark a change in planes and progression into the distance, the coincidence is astonishing.

At this point, it is essential to ask whether the watercolour by Barnard is merely a copy of Duncan's version. In our opinion, it is not. Barnard has clearly marked his vanishing point on the horizon with a pencil point and outlined his perspective, proving that the watercolour is actually based on a study from nature. Any doubts are erased by comparing it to *Landing Place at Sorel* (Cat. 59), which Barnard unquestionably drew from nature using the same technique. The ties between Barnard and Duncan, then, are more than just a copyist/model relation. Our opinion is that they drew their views together, each according to his own vision, which resulted in two entirely different compositions.

Essentially a topographical artist, Henry William Barnard has used figures for the sole purpose of marking the focal points of the view as a reminder of the place and the scale of the buildings. Duncan, on the other hand, had been living in Montreal for about ten years and was not looking to create a memento. For him, buildings indeed identify a city, but cannot exist without the many individuals who inhabit them and breathe some life into them. It is also in this respect that one must view the greater proliferation of vegetation in his work; compared with Duncan, Barnard has transformed his trees into glorified feathers.

VAG, AGNS, MMFA

62.
View from the Backyard of the Jesuit Barracks, Quebec, 1841
Watercolour over graphite highlighted with gouache on paper, 24.4 × 36.4 cm

Inscriptions
(b.,u.l., in pen and black ink, in the artist's hand, quoted after *ALLODI 1974/1*, as the mount does not allow a clear reading of the inscription) *View from the back yard of the Jesuit college, Quebec-now used as a Barrack;* (l.r, on the mount, in graphite) *Part of the Jesuit Barracks. Quebec/then occupied by the 2ᵈ Battⁿ Grenads Guard/1838.*

Provenance
Walker's Galleries, London; acquired by the Royal Ontario Museum, Toronto, 1949.

Bibliography
ALLODI 1974/1, Vol. I, No. 67 (Repr.).

Collection
Royal Ontario Museum, Toronto (949.41.34)

The same, marked interest for a strict topographical recording of a site can be found in Barnard's **View From the Backyard of the Jesuit Barracks, Quebec.** The artist is drawing from the barracks' backyard, his back to Rue Sainte-Anne.[6] The entire lower-third of the composition is given over to the bare yard, which was previously the gardens of the Jesuit monastery but is now used for drill exercises:

but these [the gardens], to the great regret of many, have been destroyed since the house, in common with the other property of the order, has reverted to the crown, and now form a place of exercise for the troops: indeed, no one could view without much reluctance the fall of some of the stately and venerable trees, yet untouched by decay, that were the original tenants of the ground at the first foundation of the city".[7]

The buildings form a straight band across the picture, from the barracks on the right, across the roofs of the houses along Rue Saint-Jean and Côte de la Fabrique, to the spire of the Hôtel-Dieu hospital chapel on the left. Again, the artist uses figures only to help define the composition: the tight row of Grenadier Guards is one of the rare diagonals in this work.

Only the datation of these works remains to be determined. Henry William Barnard returned to Quebec in May 1841, after two years' absence. His second stay was short, however, since health problems forced him to return to England in October of the same year.[8] While there is no difficulty establishing that **Notre-Dame Street, Montreal** was done during these few months, given the inclusion of the new tower of Notre-Dame church and the connection with Duncan,[9] it is not so easy to date **View From the Backyard of the Jesuit Barracks, Quebec.** The answer comes partially from the series of copies of Barnard's watercolours done by Millicent Mary Chaplin.[10] All are dated 1841, signifying there were connections between the two artists at this time, and raising questions about the date of 1838 appearing on the mount of Barnard's watercolour. In the context of copying, it is likely the date was added *a posteriori*, when the album was being assembled.[11] If it actually was the date of execution, why would Henry William Barnard have brought works done during his first stay in Canada back with him in May 1841. More simply, it seems justified to advance that he made his most recent drawings available to Chaplin and also had close ties with James Hope-Wallace during the same summer (1841).

D.P.

Notes
1. *BOUCHETTE 1832*, pp. 226-227.
2. *ALLODI 1980*, p. 149.
3. *BOUCHETTE 1832*, p. 227.
4. *BOUCHETTE 1832*, p. 216. See also Jean-Claude Robert, *Montréal 1821-1871. Aspects de l'urbanisation*, doctoral thesis submitted to the École des Hautes Études en Sciences Sociales, Paris, March 1977, p. 369.
5. *ALLODI 1980*, p. 68 (Repr.).
6. For further reading on the relation of this section of the barracks to the rest of the Collège des Jesuits buildings, see *NOPPEN, PAULETTE AND TREMBLAY 1979*, p. 219, Fig. 8 and 9.
7. *BOUCHETTE 1832*, p. 249.
8. This biographical datum was recently established by Eva Major-Marothy in *UN MOMENT 1991*, p. 120, Endnote 2.
9. As well as the copy by M.M. Chaplin in 1841 held at the ROM (*ALLODI 1974/1*, Vol. I, No. 258).
10. M.M. Chaplin's copy of **View From the Backyard of the Jesuit Barracks, Quebec** appears on Folio 22 of her album (NAC, I-27). The other copies based on Barnard's works are No. I-103, I-25 and I-26. Only the *House of Assembly, Quebec (North Front)* (I-23) is dated 1842. However, it is not thought that M.M. Chaplin copied it directly from a work by Barnard. A number of varying details lead us to believe that it was copied from a second work.
11. A second watercolour, *Grenadier Guards at Quebec* (*ALLODI 1974/1*, Vol. I, No. 68, Repr.), also copied by M.M. Chaplin in 1841 (NAC, I-26), bears a similar inscription. The second battalion of the Grenadier Guards was stationed in Lower Canada from 1838 to 1842.

JOSEPH
BOUCHETTE
1774-1841

JOSEPH-FRANCIS
BOUCHETTE
1800-1881

SON OF a navy officer and merchant, Joseph Bouchette was born in Quebec City on May 17, 1774. Here, he struck up ties with a number of British authorities; among them, Guy Carleton, Governor-in-Chief of Canada. In 1788 and 1789, he worked with William Chewett's team of surveyors in the Montreal area. While training at the office of the surveyor general of Quebec, he met James Peachey and attended classes given by François Baillairgé. On March 25, 1791, he became a surveyor but, from 1791 to 1796, chose to work with his father, who at the time was a commander on the Great Lakes. On his return to Montreal and as an officer of the Royal Canadian Volunteer Regiment, he received command of a ship assigned to the St. Lawrence. It was not until 1801 that he returned to work under his uncle by marriage, Samuel Johannes Holland, surveyor general of Lower Canada. Following Holland's death, Robert-Shore-Milnes used his authority and influence to have Bouchette named surveyor general in 1804. In 1814, Bouchette went to London to publish a map and *A Topographical Description of the Province of Lower Canada...* (1815), for which a London association awarded him an honorary medal in 1816.

After returning to North America, Bouchette became a member of various committees, through which he helped found the Literary and Historical Society of Quebec in 1824 and the Society for the Encouragement of Art and Science in Canada three years later. From 1826 to 1829, he collected data for more books, which were published in 1832: *The British Dominions in North America; or a Topographical Description of the Provinces of Lower and Upper Canada* (2 volumes) and *A Topographical Dictionary of the Province of Lower Canada*. After that, he travelled to France and Italy before returning to Canada in 1834. In the fall of 1840, Bouchette retired and settled in Montreal, where he died a year later, on April 8, 1841.

Joseph Bouchette's eldest son, Joseph-Francis, was born in Montreal on July 27, 1800. Much less is known about Joseph-Francis than about his father or his brother, Robert-Shore-Milnes. Qualified a surveyor in 1824, Joseph-Francis became deputy surveyor general of Lower Canada. He also published two technical works: *Table des solutions trigonométriques,* published in the 1820s, and *Tables concernant la longitude de l'Atlantique au Pacifique,* published in Toronto in 1857. During his father's absence from 1829 to 1834, Joseph-Francis replaced him as surveyor general of the province. He took over as head of the survey department after the post of surveyor general was abolished and the related responsibilities turned over to the commissioner of crown lands.

Like his brother, Joseph-Francis Bouchette contributed to the books published by his father in London in 1832, either through survey reports, landscape drawings (Cat. 64) or maps. Bouchette died at Pont-Rouge (Portneuf township) on February 24, 1881 and was buried in Quebec City.

Main sources
HARPER 1970; BOUDREAU AND LÉPINE 1988.

63.
Long's Farm on Lake Témiscouata, c. 1814

Joseph Bouchette
Ink and watercolour on paper laid on cardboard, 21.6 × 36 cm

Inscription
(s., l.r., in pen and black ink, in the artist's hand[?])
Bouchette.

Provenance
David Ross McCord, Montreal; McCord Museum, Montreal, 1929.

Exhibitions
Montreal 1962-1963, No. 83; Ottawa 1967/1, No. 56.

Bibliography
HARPER 1962/1, p. 60, No. 83 (Repr.); HUBBARD AND OSTIGUY 1967, pp. 40 and 41, No. 56 (Repr.); VAUGEOIS AND LACOURSIÈRE 1970, p. 277 (Repr.); ROBERT 1978, p. 23 (Repr.).

Collection
McCord Museum of Canadian History, Montreal (M10493)

THE WATERCOLOURS OF Joseph Bouchette and Joseph-Francis Bouchette, father and son, are visual testaments to their work as surveyors. The numerous maps and books published by Joseph Bouchette greatly contributed to the understanding of Lower Canada's topography. His watercolours are primarily scientific in nature, which is why they are included here, much the same as the works by William Edmond Logan (Cat. 170).

In 1815, Joseph Bouchette published *A topographical description of the province of Lower Canada, with remarks upon Upper Canada, and on the relative connexion of both provinces with the United States of America* in London. The book was illustrated with a number of engravings of Bouchette's drawings from nature, including ***Long's Farm on Lake Temiscouata.***[1] The watercolour provides the reader with a better understanding of what isolated areas looked like:

From the main road of the St. Lawrence, where the portage road branches off, to Long's Farm on the bank of Lake Timiscouata, the distance is thirty-seven miles: the direction of the road is generally to the eastward, but it has numerous turns and windings to avoid ascending several very lofty and rugged hills, or crossing deep swamps; as it is, about twenty-four miles of the distance is over a succession of mountains, many of them rough and very steep. However, none of the formidable impediments exist that were formerly considered so insurmountable; and indeed a little exertion, with an expense not very considerable, would render this road as good and convenient for travelling as can be reasonably expected in a wild and unsettled country.

Lake Témiscouata is located on the former trade route between Lower Canada and New Brunswick and «Long, the proprietor of it [the farm], has a large family: himself and his sons are the ferrymen of the lake, and have always bark canoes ready to take passengers from one side to the other». But the farm is isolated and Joseph Bouchette does not hide this fact from his readers:

In this spot, so far removed from the habitations of man and the pleasures of society, the farm, though but an humble one, becomes an object of considerable interest; it consists only of a cottage, a barn, and two or three small out-houses, surrounded by a few cultivated fields and a garden. In summer time the scenery around it is various, and uncommonly pleasing, but it can hardly compensate for the dreary solitude of winter.

Belonging to the same tradition of topographical artists of the strictest

MQ, NGC

64.
Trading Post on the Rivière-aux-Rats, 1828
Joseph-Francis Bouchette
Ink and watercolour on paper laid on cardboard, 21.2 × 37.3 cm

Inscriptions
(s., l.r., in pen and green ink) *J F Bouchette;* (l.l., in pen and green ink) *Trading Post on the River Aux Rats.*

Provenance
Davies Book Co. Ltd., Montreal; acquired by the Musée de la Province de Québec, Quebec City, 1959.

Bibliography
BÉLAND AND BOURASSA *1990,* pp. 7, 8 and 46 (Repr.); MARTIN AND GRANDBOIS *1991,* p. 53.

Collection
Musée du Québec, Quebec City (59.342)

allegiance as James Peachey (Cat. 42 to 45), Bouchette has produced a faithful record of the site. The sole purpose of his drawing is to show the exact location of the farm in relation to its natural surroundings and anything too characteristic of the landscape is neglected in favour of a more or less arbitrary codification. Bouchette's primary objective is to reproduce a likeness of the location. Claude Boudreau's research[2] on Bouchette's 1831 map of Lower Canada shows how the latter conveyed his observations (hills, rivers, convents, etc.) in iconic and graphic form. On his map, bodies of water are identified according to their size.[3]

The same reasoning could be applied to the watercolour in question, since what he has actually done is merely provided the spatial organization of the components. Thus, the thick forest is suggested by rolling hills of trees, while the far distance is indicated merely by applying a layer of wash over the mountains. Specific details of a pristine nature are lacking, apart from the occasional fir tree on the right, suggesting the proximity of unlogged territory.

Joseph-Francis Bouchette followed in his father's footsteps. His *Trading Post on the Rivière-aux-Rats,* done in 1828 during an expedition along the Saint-Maurice River,[4] differs little from his father's portrayals. However, this watercolour does show a little more flexibility in the treatment and application of colour washes. The trading post was located near the present-day town of La Tuque.

D.P.

Notes
1. Joseph Bouchette had his drawings engraved in London. An aquatint of *View of Long's Farm on Lake Temiscouata at the extremity of the Portage* was reproduced on pages 540-541 of his book. For a description of the shores of Lake Témiscouata and Long's farm, see pp. 537-541.

2. Claude Boudreau, *L'analyse de la carte ancienne, essai méthodologique: la carte du Bas-Canada de 1831 de Joseph Bouchette* (Quebec City: CELAT, December 1986) (Coll. "Rapports et Mémoires de recherche" No. 7).

3. *Ibid.,* p. 102.

4. This series of three watercolours, held at the Musée du Québec, was the subject of a recent study by Denis Martin (see MARTIN AND GRANDBOIS *1991,* pp. 52-53). For this reason, it will not be discussed further in this catalogue.

BORN IN QUEBEC CITY on March 12, 1805, Robert-Shore-Milnes Bouchette was the youngest son of Joseph Bouchette. He was brought up in a privileged family environment: his father was surveyor general of Lower Canada and his godfather none other than Lieutenant-Governor Sir Robert Shore Milnes, his namesake. He studied under Reverend Daniel Wilkie (Cat. 176), then entered the offices of Andrew Stuart to study law. At the age of eighteen and at the request of Lord Dalhousie, he went to New York to produce maps of the Canada-U.S. border.

On his return to Canada, he received a commission as a lawyer in 1826, but soon left to join his father, among other things, to assist in the topographical survey of the Ottawa area. In 1829, he accompanied his father to London to complete the two volumes the latter published in 1832. Once back in Canada, he returned to practising law, but discovered a new passion: politics. He actively espoused the cause of the Patriotes, much to his father's chagrin. He founded the bilingual Quebec City newspaper *Le Libéral/ The Liberal*, in which he published a number of viscous articles. On December 6, 1837, he took up arms to fight in the skirmish at Moore's Corner (Saint-Armand-Station). Jailed in Montreal, he was among the *Patriotes* Lord Durham exiled to the Bermudas in June 1838. Following a stay in Vermont, he returned to the Canadas in 1845. Initially employed as clerk in the office of the attorney general of Canada East in March 1851, he was later appointed commissioner of customs, a position he held until 1875. He also sat on several parliamentary committees, notably the one on the *Exposition universelle de Paris* of 1867, to which he and Joseph-Charles Taché were delegates.

Following the example of some of his ill-fated fellow countrymen who were jailed in the Pied-du-Courant prison as a result of the 1837 uprisings, Bouchette cultivated a taste for drawing and watercolour (Cat. 65 and 66). He had probably learned the rudiments from his father. Some of his works were reproduced in lithographs, such as the sketchbook of views of the Ottawa region (1827) and a view of Quebec City drawn September 29, 1829 and published in his father's book *The British Dominion in North America* (1832). Bouchette died in Quebec City on June 4, 1879. In 1903, his son Errol published his *Mémoires,* which covered the period 1805-1840.

ROBERT-SHORE-MILNES
BOUCHETTE

1805-1879

Main sources
TESSIER 1972; ALLODI 1974/1; ALLODI 1980.

MQ, NGC

65.

Bouchette in prison, 1838

Watercolour and traces of graphite on paper, 13 × 18 cm

Inscriptions
(i., l.r., in brush and black ink) *RSMB*; (l.r., in green ink, by another hand) *Bouchette en prison*; (b., on a gummed paper) *Watercolour Portrait of Robert Shore Milnes Bouchette, Painted by him-self while in Montreal prison 1838 He was the youngest son of Joseph Bouchette, Surveryor-general of Lower Canada. This painting was done for Lady Lafontaine and was part of a collection she had of the prisoners.*

Provenance
William P. Wolfe, Montreal; acquired by the Musée de la Province de Québec, Quebec City, 1959.

Exhibition
Vancouver 1959, No. 106.

Bibliography
Morisset 1959/1, p. 42, No. 106 entitled *Bouchette dans sa cellule de prisonnier politique*; *Nos racines*, No. 67 (1979), p. 1333 (Repr.); Béland and Bourassa 1990, pp. 7, 8, 60 and 62 (Repr.); Martin and Grandbois 1991, pp. 66 and 67 (Repr.); Un Moment 1991, pp. 193 and 194.

Collection
Musée du Québec, Quebec City (59.10)

VAG, AGNS, MMFA

66.

Les Captifs, 1838

Watercolour and traces of graphite on paper, 15.3 × 16.7 cm (irregular dimensions)

Inscriptions
(i., l.r., in graphite) *RSMB.*; (l.c., in graphite) *Les Captifs*; (l.l., in graphite) *15. Fev*r. *1838.*

Provenance
Mrs. Jean-Paul Fortin, Sillery; acquired by the Musée de la Province de Québec, Quebec City, 1956.

Exhibition
Quebec City 1991/1, No. 12.

Bibliography
Nos racines, No. 67 (1979), p. 1333 (Repr.); Béland and Bourassa 1990, p. 62; Martin and Grandbois 1991, pp. 65-67, No. 12 (entry by Denis Martin) (Repr.); Un Moment 1991, pp. 193 and 194; Nadeau 1991, p. 59 (Repr.).

Collection
Musée du Québec, Quebec City (56.302)

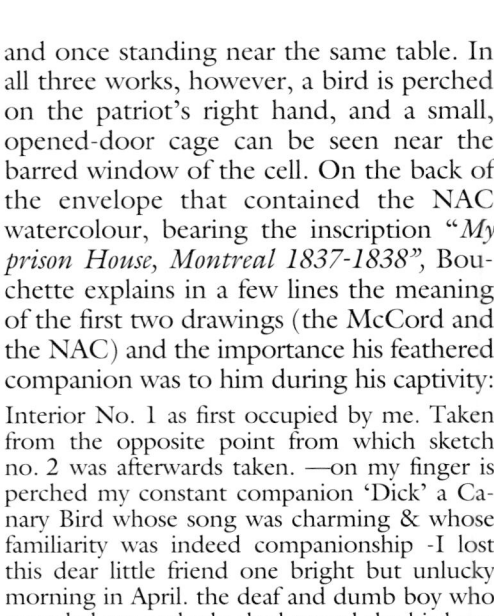

T O OUR KNOWLEDGE, Robert-Shore-Milnes Bouchette produced four drawings depicting himself inside his cell at the so-called Pied-du-Courant prison in Montreal. He had been imprisoned there a few days after being wounded and taken prisoner during a skirmish between the *Patriotes* and the British troops at Saint-Armand-Station near the United States border. The drawings in question were produced between December 1837 and June 1838. The first is a rough sketch belonging to the McCord Museum of Canadian History entitled *The Wounded Captive Knight*.[1] Bouchette is undoubtedly referring here to his own wound as well as to the poem "The Wounded Captive" that he wrote at the Ile aux Noix fort in December 1837 while waiting to be escorted to the Montreal prison, and which

is in some respects a lament to the Freedom lost under "British rule."[2]

In the McCord Museum drawing, Bouchette gives a different view of his cell from the one provided in three small watercolours, one of which is owned by the National Archives of Canada (Fig. 65-66A)[3] and the other two, i.e. *Les Captifs* and *Bouchette in prison,* by the Musée du Québec. The McCord drawing is a very schematic view of the inside of Bouchette's prison cell, drawn from the right corner of the room, and in which the position of the furniture is reversed. The NAC watercolour, dated 1837, and the two Musée du Québec watercolours, dated early 1838, are drawn from the left corner of the cell and show only minor differences with respect to the furniture. Bouchette has twice depicted himself seated at his work table

and once standing near the same table. In all three works, however, a bird is perched on the patriot's right hand, and a small, opened-door cage can be seen near the barred window of the cell. On the back of the envelope that contained the NAC watercolour, bearing the inscription "*My prison House, Montreal 1837-1838*", Bouchette explains in a few lines the meaning of the first two drawings (the McCord and the NAC) and the importance his feathered companion was to him during his captivity:

Interior No. 1 as first occupied by me. Taken from the opposite point from which sketch no. 2 was afterwards taken. —on my finger is perched my constant companion 'Dick' a Canary Bird whose song was charming & whose familiarity was indeed companionship -I lost this dear little friend one bright but unlucky morning in April. the deaf and dumb boy who attended me and who had tamed the bird not

Fig. 65-66A.
Robert-Shore-Milnes Bouchette,
Imprisonment of R.S.M. Bouchette, Montreal, 1837,
or *My prison House, Montreal 1837-1838;*
watercolour on paper, 12 × 15.2 cm.
National Archives of Canada, Ottawa (C-21554).

heading that Dick was at large opened the Window and soon to his great dismay discovered the little captive perched on one of the outside Bars. He drew my attention to the danger. Both he & I tried every device to entice him inwards with our Canadian Canary Xwise flying low in various directions & Dick followed resting Wherever he could on the way & finally disappeared over the —Gaol walls without any possibility of our following him Captives as we were![4]

In these three watercolours, including the one actually entitled ***Les Captifs,*** Robert-Shore-Milnes Bouchette was no doubt looking to symbolize his hope of getting his freedom back, after fighting so bravely for it. This cultivated lawyer had turned his cell into a relatively comfortable office/studio, witness the books, drawing portfolio and guitar depicted in one or other of his drawings. During his few months of captivity, he drew not only his prison cell, but also other sketches and watercolours. As reported in his *Mémoires:*

I decorated my room using my paintbrush, reproducing landscapes from my sketches on the walls. On one side, I painted the Montmorency Falls and on the other, the home of Mr. Atkinson in Cap-Rouge [Cat. 76]. Around the arched window, a vine and honeysuckle are intertwined. The other two walls, as my room was the shape of an irregular pentagon, were taken up with bookshelves and my

small set of pots and pans, dishes, coffee pot, etc., all arranged so as not to disturb the overall harmony. In one corner of the room were my portfolios; in the other, my guitar. The ceiling was obviously painted sky blue.[5] (*Translation*)

In a letter written one month prior to his exile, Bouchette admitted to colonel Dundas that "Drawing was of great resource during my solitude."[6] (*Translation*) From the drawings executed by the artist during his imprisonment, the Musée du Québec holds a watercolour dated January 30, 1838, depicting the gardens of Tivoli in Italy (56.304), and another entitled *The Frightened Horse* (56.303), after an engraving of a work by Carle Vernet.[7] The three watercolours entitled ***Les Captifs, Bouchette in prison*** and *My Prison House…* are, in our opinion, among the most significant work of this ardent patriot.

These works form the basis of a series of drawings and watercolours bearing witness to the rebellions of 1837-1838, which include the pencil portraits of *Patriotes* drawn by Jean-Joseph Girouard (1795-1855), who was in jail at the same time as Bouchette. Girouard even did a beautiful profile of Bouchette (Cat. 112).

D.M.

Notes

1. MMCH, John Samuel McCord Papers, Miscellaneous Books, Box 2, "Cards etc.".

2. *Ibid.* We owe this information to Mary Allodi, of the Royal Ontario Museum.

3. See LORD *1974,* pp. 38-39 (Repr.).

4. NAC, C-21553 (overleaf). In his *Mémoires,* Bouchette wrote about the bird he depicted in his three watercolours: "I was permitted to hire the services of a young deaf lad who was imprisoned for petty theft. This child was very useful to me. He grew attached to me and gave me a canary named Dick. Dick soon became my friend. He perched on my shoulders and shared my meals. Every morning, I awoke to the sound of his song. For four months we were inseparable, but one fine April morning, he flew out the open window, which is now barred, and, despite my calls, he never came back." (*Translation*) (*Mémoires de Robert-S.-M. Bouchette, 1805-1840, recueillis par son fils Errol Bouchette et annotés par A.-D. Decelles,* Montreal, La Cie de publication de La Revue Canadienne, 1903, p.60).

5. *Ibid.,* pp. 59-60. Quoted in part in *Nos racines,* No. 67 (1979), p. 1333.

6. Letter from Bouchette to Colonel Dundas, from prison, Montreal, June 9, 1838, quoted in *Ibid.,* p. 69.

7. The Musée du Québec collection also includes a number of pencil drawings depicting travels, engraved maps and some prints reproduced from works produced by Bouchette prior to his imprisonment and following his return from exile.

JAMES WANDESFORD BUTLER

1815-1863

JAMES WANDESFORD BUTLER's family was of the British nobility. Son of the 19th earl and first marquis of Ormonde, Butler was born in May 1815. With rebellion seething in Upper and Lower Canada, he came to the Canadas in 1837 as a soldier of the 85th regiment stationed in Saint John, New Brunswick. In the winter of 1837-1838, Butler set out with three regular army regiments on a long march from Saint John to Montreal to reinforce the scanty military troops in Lower Canada. The main document left by the artist is without question his diary and sketchbook (Cat. 67), which he worked on during this epic march. He arrived at Quebec City on January 5, 1838. On January 15 he left for Sorel and arrived in Montreal on January 22. With Butler on the march that winter were Sir Richard George Augustus Levinge, member of the 73rd regiment, and William Robert Herries. After returning to England, Butler married Lady Rachel Russel, daughter of the Duke of Bedford, in April 1856. He died on April 13, 1863.

Main source
HARPER 1970.

67.

Journal "March from St. Johns, N.B. to Quebec undertaken in consequence of the disturbances in Canada in the year 1837", 1837-1838

Pen and black ink; graphite and watercolour on paper
9.8 × 16.5 × 1.6 cm

Inscription
(s.d., in pen and black ink on the back of the upper side) *J.W. Butler/1837*.

Provenance
Acquired by the Public Archives of Canada, Ottawa, 1932.

Collection
National Archives of Canada, Ottawa (MG 24, F35).

MQ

A. *Montmorency Falls*
Watercolour on paper

Fig. 67A.
Charles Beauclerk,
*Back view of the Church of St-Eustache and Dispersion of the Insurgents,
14th December 1837*, 1840;
lithograph published by A. Flent,
27.8 × 36.8 cm.
Archives du Séminaire de Québec
(bibliothèque, fonds ancien).

T HE DIARY OF James Wandesford Butler is of great value to our understanding of the arrival of the British troops from New Brunswick in Lower Canada during December 1837. As shown by the events that followed, the defeat of the *Patriotes* at Saint-Eustache on December 14, 1837 (Fig. 67A) and the subsequent suppression by Sir John Colborne's army constituted a turning point in the insurrection. The renewed hostilities in 1838 (Cat. 141 and 142) marked less of a revolutionary awakening than it did the continuation of a shock wave triggered long before.[1]

James Butler left Saint John on December 21, 1837: "Ten sleighs were provided for ye men, 8 on each. One for yᵉ offᵗˢ and baggage & one for blankets &c. My sleigh followed" (p. 1).[2] He recorded the daily events in his diary, systematically jotting down the time and place of departure, their midday stop and the point of arrival, and commenting on the various activities of the day. On day one, for example:

I got on well—but my sleigh went wrong twice—this was remedied and after tickling up the horses who thought 35 miles too long for the first days journey arrived at dusk at Gooldings (p. 1).

Sometimes it was the picturesque landscape that drew his attention: "Ye Town (Gage Town) is on yᵉ right bank on a rise from yᵉ river. Yᵉ hill is crowned by a pretty church and the scene wᵈ have made a capital picture for Vemeulen" (p. 2). The reference to Adam-Frans Van der Meulen (1632-1690) reveals much about Butler's culture and state of mind. Van der Meulen painted *Conquêtes de Louis XIV* and, as a painter, accompanied the French troops to their various battlegrounds, drawing cities and strongholds.[3] The dissemination of his work through engravings helped earn him a name, which is possibly how Butler came into contact with it. It is further possible that engravings based on Van der

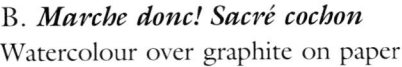

B. *Marche donc! Sacré cochon*
Watercolour over graphite on paper

Fig. 67B.
James W. Butler,
Near Dingee, 1838,
Sepia on paper.
National Archives of Canada,
Ottawa (C-30976).

Meulen's oeuvre were used in teaching topographical painting in British military academies.

Butler's diary therefore tells us of the route taken to Lower Canada. The troops followed along the Saint John River: Woodstock, Aroostook River crossing, Grand Falls, then across the Saint John River to Madawaska. They entered Lower Canada via Lac Témiscouata, down the Saint-François and Du Loup rivers to join up with the St. Lawrence River at Saint-André de Kamouraska (Cat. 141). Unlike Robert Herries and Richard Levinge, who recorded the stages of the march through pictures rather than words (Cat. 141 and 142), Butler did not see fit to illustrate his diary with drawings showing the difficulties encountered during the journey from Saint-John to Montreal. Only a night in Dingee (Fig. 67B) serves as a reminder:

We drove to Dingee's — civil people, not very well put up. Browns the first house being ye best. The next page contains a sketch from near yᵉ house, yᵉ river runs at about a couple of hundred yards from it (p. 6).

The troops were travelling so fast— twelve days in all from Saint John to Saint-André de Kamouraska—that Butler obviously did not have the time to get out his paper and paintbrushes.

Once the troops arrived in Quebec City, however, things changed. The men were able to enjoy a few days off and the

soldier cum tourist seemingly took in the usual sites: monument to Wolfe, tour of the city and Montmorency Falls (Cat. A):

The underneath sketch of the Montmorenci Falls was taken from immediately under the Fall owing to ye spray which fell very thick & froze on me. I cᵈ take but little time about it. The cone had only commenced to form but yᵉ river was quite frozen below and covered with yᵉ spray rose in hillocks of some height down which we coasted. Nothing cᵈ be finer than looking up at yᵉ fall 240 fᵗ immediately above when yᵉ mist suddenly cleared away and left yᵉ tremendous mass of water thundering down with yᵉ sun shining full on it. It was a glorious sight (p. 20).

The interest of Butler's diary lies precisely in descriptions of this type. It is a total break from the usual watercolours— drawings of cities or picturesque landscapes—which are designed to please the eye. Butler's images have a private quality about them and are a direct extension of the artist's personal life. They are not as finely structured as the drawings of Philip John Bainbrigge (Cat. 54 to 58) or Henry William Barnard (Cat. 59 to 62) and, what is more, his diary probably never served the same purpose as the album of Katherine Jane Ellice, who circulated it amongst friends in order to record their impressions (Cat. 103 and 104).

Butler's illustrations, then, were closely tied to daily events. While Butler never gave any explanation for *Marche*

donc! Sacré cochon (Cat. B), the drawing speaks for itself. On the other hand, in the style of an itinerant traveller, Butler depicts his surroundings as seen through his hotel window. One of the two views of the south shore of the St. Lawrence at Montreal (Cat. C and D) was drawn from the Rasco hotel, Rue Saint-Paul. Although Butler got some pleasure out of the place, it was apparently not the ideal spot for relaxation according to Katherine Jane Ellice: "Such a nasty, dirty, pot house looking place. Such a smell of Bad tobacco, & such a large bug on my pillow."[4]

Butler is more philosophical about the matter, however:

I was tired and glad to return to Rasco's wh is not very comfortable with bad attendᶜᶜ. we pay (3 of us) a dollar daily each rations & fuel for our board & private sitting room. We have met with great civility here, many people calling & asking us to parties (p. 28).

Window views are common in British imagery.[5] The examples left by Millicent Mary Chaplin express great feeling (Cat. 69), whereas those of Sempronius Stretton are basically cold, technical surveys (Cat. 51). Butler's works more closely resemble those of Stretton; only the difference in technique allows for a more fluid rendition.

D.P.

VAG, AGNS

C. *Bank of the Saint Lawrence, Opposite Montreal*
Watercolour on paper

Notes

1. Fernand Ouellet, *Histoire économique et sociale du Québec, 1760-1850* (Montreal: Fides, 1971). pp. 427-435.

2. Quoted from the National Archives of Canada's transcription of Butler's diary. For easier reference, we have noted the page number at the end of the quote.

3. Laure C.-Starcky, Paris, *Mobilier national. Dessins de Van der Meulen et de son atelier* (Paris: Éditions de la Réunion des musées nationaux, 1988) (Inventory of French government collections, No. 33).

4. Patricia Godsell, ed., *The Diary of Jane Ellice* (Oberon Press, 1975), p. 50.

5. We cannot go without mentioning the magnificent watercolours by Thomas Jones (1742-1803), drawn from his Neapolitan residence (Lindsay Stainton, "La terra classica": pittori inglesi a Napoli nel Settecento e nell'Ottocento" in *All'ombra del Vesuvio, Napoli nella veduta europea dal Quattrocento all'Ottocento,* Cat. (Naples: Castel Sant'Elmo, 1990), pp. 71, 198-199 and 402).

MMFA

D. *From my Window at Rosco's Hotel, Montreal*
Watercolour on paper

MILLICENT MARY
CHAPLIN

active between 1838 and 1842

Wife of Thomas Chaplin, lieutenant-colonel of the 2nd Foot—the Coldstream Guards—Millicent Mary (born Reeve) accompanied her husband on his posting to Canada in 1838. She produced landscapes depicting the areas of Ottawa, Quebec City and the Maritimes. The fact that she copied works by James Hope-Wallace, Henry William Barnard and Philip John Bainbrigge would seem to show that she knew several watercolourists of the day. Her own watercolours depict the life of *habitants*, local customs and local landscapes.

Main sources
Bell 1972; Allodi 1974/1.

VAG, AGNS, MMFA

68.
Our House No. 13 St. Ursule Street, Quebec,
from July 1838 to September 1842, c. 1842
Watercolour over graphite with traces of scraping out on paper, 29.8 × 37.6 cm

Inscription
(i., l.l., in brush and brown wash) *m.mc.*

Provenance
R. C. Chase, England; acquired by the Public Archives of Canada, Ottawa, 1953.

Bibliography
BARBEAU 1957 (Repr.).

Collection
National Archives of Canada, Ottawa (1956-62-44)

W HEN MARIUS BARBEAU used many of Millicent Mary Chaplin's watercolours to illustrate his 1957 book *I Have Seen Quebec,* he came close to making her a "pioneer" in the history of Quebec landscape art. Actually, these watercolours all came from one album, acquired by the Public Archives of Canada in 1953 and dismantled for exhibition purposes.

The album in question is a particularly complex collection of nearly 130 drawings on 90 folios. While most of them were done by Millicent Mary Chaplin herself, some are the work of other artists active in Quebec City at the same time. The names Sir Henry William Barnard (Cat. 54 to 58) and Philip John Bainbrigge (Cat. 59 to 62) are more than familiar, but there is also a drawing by Charles Philip Wilbraham (active 1828-1840), *View of the Lake Saint Charles,* dated July 13, 1840.[1] The National Archives holds a small album of Wilbraham's drawings which show a great feel for composition, but which are unfortunately too fragile to be exhibited.[2] The other names in the album, such as Miss A. Kirby[3] and Prof. Renwick,[4] are less known. The contribution of numerous artists makes this album all the more interesting. A second *View of the Lake Saint Charles,* this time drawn and signed by Millicent Mary Chaplin, bears the inscription "*color'd by Col. Hope*"[5] on the back, undoubtedly referring to James Hope-Wallace. This holds further significance since it places Chaplin's album at the basis of a string of data that help establish the beginnings of the "Group of 1838", as coined by Mary Allodi in 1974. A few watercolours and repeated copies provide us with the names of the principal watercolourists working in Quebec City during the summer of 1838: Sir Henry William Barnard, Philip John Bainbrigge, James Hope-Wallace. A recent study completed the picture by identifying captain George St. Vincent Whitmore as the man behind some twenty watercolours heretofore recognized by a trademark signature.[6] This provides an idea as to how the members of a small drawing society working in close contact can influence each other.

As mentioned, this album contains over a hundred works, spanning the period spent by the artist in Quebec. There are numerous landscapes, panoramic views drawn from atop the Citadel and Pizeau point and walks leading to nearby falls and Indian campsites. All this is commonplace and nothing sets the album apart if not for the very personal view it presents. The most valuable thing in Millicent Mary Chaplin's album is "the desire to take in" everyday life.

Chaplin arrived in Quebec City in spring 1838. She was accompanying her husband, lieutenant-colonel Thomas Chaplin, officer of the Coldstream Guards, on his recent posting to Lower Canada. The couple rented a house on Rue Sainte-Ursule (Cat. 68 and 211), where they lived until September 1842. The house was built by Richard Goldsworthy circa 1802 and was probably left vacant following his death in 1836.[7] The house has changed little, aside from the large front porch which has since gone. The main, Palladian-style door divides the first floor symmetrically and the roof has a double row of gable windows. The chimneys and gable walls rise above the roofline to form fire walls. The windows overlooking the garden provided Chaplin with an observation site; from her dressing room, she could look out over the Ursuline convent (Cat. 69).[8] The structure of the composition—framed on either side by the vertical steeples of the Anglican cathedral and Presbyterian church—was dictated by

VAG, AGNS, MMFA

69.
View from Mrs. Chaplin Dressing Room Window, 1839
Watercolour over graphite with some traces of scraping out on paper, 22.8 × 38 cm

Inscriptions
(i.d., l.r., in brush and brown wash) *mmc./1839.;*
(b.,l.c., in pen and black ink, in the artist's hand[?])
View from Mrs C-s dressing room Window. Quebec.
Provenance
R. C. Chase, England; acquired by the Public
Archives of Canada, Ottawa, 1953.
Bibliography
BARBEAU *1957* (Repr.).
Collection
National Archives of Canada, Ottawa
(1956-62-47)

the window frame. The Saint-Augustin wing occupies the first plane on the right. The drawing shows the convent with the new floor that was added in 1832, with the kitchen wing of the main building extending into the gardens and ending with the stair tower and its imperial-style roof. The foreground shows the convent property, divided into a yard and space reserved for the gardens. It ends in a high stone wall that isolates the nuns from the outside world, as Joseph Bouchette observed in 1815: "The religieuses live very recluse, and are more rigid in their manner than any other in the province."[9] The roofs of the cityscape make up the first horizon of this window view. The diagonal of the Laurentians, fading from purple above Beaupré to blue at Cap Tourmente, serves both as a final visual barrier and an opening out onto the river. The panorama is superb and shows keen, extremely controlled observation, mixing uniform washes with layered brushstrokes of colour. The trees in the garden combine autumn shades of dark green, oranges and crimson. On the hills along the Beaupré coast, purples and blues melt into browns to create the atmospheric perspective. This watercolour is dated 1839 and marks a stylistic period of Chaplin's that differs from her landscapes, which used broad brushstrokes and were closer to the style of Barnard and Bainbrigge.

The two views of the garden at 13 Rue Sainte-Ursule (Cat. 70 and 71) are unexpected, almost unusual. At first glance, they would appear to be two halves to a pair of pictures that use the same site to illustrate Quebec's extreme seasonal differences. However, a closer look shows a more subtle connection, as evidenced by the reconstructed album as proposed by Deborah McNeill in 1979.[10] To the two views reproduced here must be added a third, depicting the backyard and stables in winter (Fig. 70-71A). Done in December 1838, this is actually the first watercolour of the series. It merely sets forth the basic winter vocabulary: scrawny trees, blocked entranceways, sleigh for collecting snow. Millicent Mary Chaplin went back to this subject on February 17, 1842 to illustrate the previous evening's snowstorm. It was no longer the daily winter activities she wished to depict—however surprising they may be at one's first encounter—but a natural phenomenon. This watercolour records the exaggeration of winter: the snow that has accumulated in just a few hours, blocking every pathway. The affinities between these works would come into play later on when Millicent Mary Chaplin assembled her album. It was probably with this in mind that she drew the view over the garden in summer. Dated August 1842, just a few weeks before Chaplin's return to Europe, this watercolour is the

last in her series of garden views from the window of her home. However, it appears second in the album, immediately following the view of the facade of her home. Anyone perusing the album would thus turn the pages, going from the front of the house (Cat. 68) to the garden in summer (Cat. 70), only to see it buried under the snow during the first winter (Fig. 70-71A) and then the sudden effects of a snowstorm (Cat. 71). With just a few images, Millicent Mary Chaplin depicted the world in which she had lived.

D.P.

Notes
1. NAC (neg.) C-930.
2. NAC, 1984-176.
3. NAC (neg.) C-898, 912 and 913.
4. NAC (neg.) C-916-917.
5. NAC, 1956-62-82.
6. Eva Major-Marothy, "Captain George St. Vincent Whitmore: A Newly Discovered Military Artist", *Archivaria*, No. 29 (Winter 1989-1990), pp. 168-172.
7. Madeleine Gobeil-Trudeau, "Maison Malenfant", *Les CHEMINS DE LA MÉMOIRE 1990*, Vol. I, p. 185.
8. James Pattison Cockburn had depicted somewhat the same point of view twelve years previously, from the gardens of the Ursulines convent.
9. *BOUCHETTE 1815*, p. 445.
10. See NAC file on M.M. Chaplin. It also contains photographs of the watercolours, mounted between the pages of the original album.

MQ, NGC

70.
Stable Yard (13 Sainte-Ursule Street) After Snow Storm,
Night of February 16th 1842, 1842
Watercolour over graphite on paper, 27.9 × 41.8 cm

Inscriptions
(i.d., l.l., in brush and grey wash) *mmc/1842.;*
(b.l,.c., in pen and black ink, in the artist's hand[?])
*Stable Yard after Snow Storm night of Feb*ʳ
*16*ᵗʰ *1842.*

Provenance
R. C. Chase, England; acquired by the Public
Archives of Canada, Ottawa, 1953.

Collection
National Archives of Canada, Ottawa
(1956-62-96)

MQ, NGC

71.
Stable Yard (13 Sainte-Ursule Street), Quebec, 1842
Watercolour over graphite on paper, 28.6 × 37.8 cm

Inscription
(i.d., l.r., in brush and brown wash) *mmc./August 1842.*

Provenance
R. C. Chase, England; acquired by the Public Archives of Canada, Ottawa, 1953.

Collection
National Archives of Canada, Ottawa (1956-62-45)

Fig. 70-71A.
Millicent Mary Chaplin,
Col. C. Stable & Yard, Quebec, Dec. 1838;
watercolour over graphite on paper,
20.4 × 33 cm.
National Archives of Canada, Ottawa (C-892).

JAMES PATTISON
COCKBURN

1779-1847

J AMES PATTISON COCKBURN was born of British parents in New York on March 18, 1779. His father was a member of the Royal Artillery. On March 19, 1793, after Cockburn returned to England, he enrolled as a cadet in the Royal Military Academy of Woolwich; Paul Sandby (1725-1809) was drawing master there at the time. During his military career, Cockburn was promoted to various ranks: captain in June 1806, colonel on January 10, 1837 and major-general on November 9, 1846. His participation in various battles led him to travel quite extensively. He was at the Cape of Good Hope in 1795 and took part in campaigns against Manilla and Copenhagen in 1798. He was in Antwerp in August and September 1807 and again in August 1809. His works were first published in November 1807. They consisted of a series of five coloured aquatints depicting the siege of Copenhagen. Between military campaigns, Cockburn was stationed in various garrisons in England, first Colchester and then, beginning in November 1808, Norwich, in the county of Norfolk, where he came into contact with the Norwich school of landscape artists. In summer 1809, he exhibited some 17 watercolours, painted in the Cape of Good Hope and Bengal, with the Norwich Society of Artists. Cockburn was back in Colchester between 1814 and 1817.

Between 1816 and 1822, Cockburn made several trips to the continent, in particular to Italy and Switzerland, on behalf of English publisher and engraver William Bernard Cooke.

Cockburn's first stay in Canada lasted from November 1822 to June 1823. He returned in August 1826 for six consecutive years as commanding officer of the Royal Artillery in Canada. Most of his Canadian works, sepia drawings and watercolours, date from this period. During visits to Upper and Lower Canada, he painted numerous landscapes. On August 2, 1832, the year before leaving Quebec City, he published *Quebec and Its Environs; Being a Picturesque Guide to the Stranger,* illustrated with seven engravings.

On October 10, 1838, six years after returning to England, Cockburn was appointed director of the Royal Arsenal of Woolwich's Royal Laboratory, a post from which he retired on November 15, 1846. Cockburn died in Woolwich the following spring, on March 18, 1847.

Main sources
CAMERON AND TRUDEL 1976; PRIOUL 1988.

MQ, NGC

72.
Jesuit Barrack and Quebec Market Place, 1829
Watercolour, pen and brown ink over graphite on paper, 33.4 × 47.5 cm

Inscriptions
(b.,l.r., in pen and black ink, in the artist's hand) *Jesuit Barrack and Quebec Market Place/1829. J.C.;* (b.,l.c., on the mount, in pen and brown ink, by another hand) *Jesuit Barracks.;* (b.,l.l., in graphite) *72.*

Provenance
Mrs. Russell Barrington, Kensington England (sold by Sotheby & Co., London, April 27, 1927, No. 118); L. Kashnor, The Museum Book Store, London, 1927 (acquired by Spencer); Ward C. Pitfield, London; acquired by the Royal Ontario Museum, Toronto, 1942.

Bibliography
CATALOGUE 1927/1, No. 118; ALLODI 1974/1, Vol. I, No. 345 (Repr.); CAMERON AND TRUDEL 1976, p. 114, No. 91 (Repr.)

Collection
Royal Ontario Museum, Toronto (942.48.72)

J AMES PATTISON COCKBURN was stationed in Quebec City on two occasions. His first posting was short, from November 1822 to June 1823, and very few works date from this period. His second posting lasted six years, from 1826 to 1832, and during it he conducted what virtually amounted to a systematic survey of the city's streets and buildings. Over 70 of these street scenes are found in the collections of the National Archives of Canada and the Royal Ontario Museum alone. In Cockburn's time, the military presence in Quebec City was strongly reflected in the urban network. Although traditional areas, such as Artillery Park, have retained their original function, others, like

the Jesuits' college, have taken on a new role. When the fortifications were rebuilt between 1820 and 1830, the open space along Rue d'Auteuil became an esplanade for parade drill. As a result, secondary streets were used more frequently, and soldiers and civilians were in constant contact. Cockburn witnessed this phenomenon daily and portrayed it in his watercolours.

From the outset, the artillery barracks (Cat. 73 and 74) were one of Cockburn's favourite subjects. He rendered them in detail from every possible angle: from their entrance gate, inner courtyard, or the surrounding ramparts and gardens. Jesuit ***Barrack and Quebec Market Place***

VAG, AGNS, MMFA

73.
Artillery Barracks, Quebec, 1831
Watercolour and traces of graphite on paper, 14.8 × 23.5 cm

Inscription
(b.,l.r., in ink) *Artillery Barracks Quebec/20" June/ 1831/Last of Marlay.*
Provenance
Séminaire de Québec; on deposit at the Société du Musée du Séminaire de Québec, 1983.
Collection
Musée du Séminaire de Québec (Pf986.60)

MQ, MMFA

74.
Artillery Barracks, Quebec, 1831
Watercolour over graphite on paper, 15.3 × 24 cm

Inscriptions
(b.,l.r., in pen and black ink, in the artist's hand) *John & his son in the/Garden;* (in another hand [?]) *The building on the left is the dauphine Barracks/where the officers of artillery live an slept —/The front is the Com^d. officers' quarters & their/adjutant. The Men's continue further/to the right. The distance is the country thro'/which the St. Charles River flows -;* (below, in the artist's hand) *Artillery Barracs - Quebec./Augt. 1831. J.C.*

Provenance
Acquired by the Royal Ontario Museum, Toronto, before 1960.
Exhibition
Kingston 1978, No. 38.
Bibliography
ALLODI 1974/1, Vol. I, No. 352; CAMERON AND TRUDEL 1976, p. 134, No. 115 (Repr.); BELL AND COOKE 1978, p. 44, No. 38 (Repr.).
Collection
Royal Ontario Museum, Toronto (960x276.18)

is a typical example of the view of a military artist. This watercolour illustrates Notre-Dame market and the old Jesuits' college, converted into a barracks after the Conquest, at the end of Rue Buade. This area, which was also the site of the cathedral, one side wall of which frames the right side of the painting, was one of the most animated parts of the city. For James Pattison Cockburn, the street was a theatre with strict rules. Contrary to the situation described in newspapers of the period, it was hardly the scene of turmoil and excitement. Of course, Cockburn drew several market scenes and religious processions. However, they cannot really be said to reflect a firm interest in local customs. It would be unwise, therefore, to generalize from watercolours such as *Lower Town Church and Market Place, Quebec* which symbolizes, above all, a particular moment in time where an often stereotyped, and even repressed, notion of social life dominates the image.

Cockburn has left us an incomparable visual record of Quebec City in the 1830s. Owing, in particular, to the number of works he produced, architectural historians have often emphasized the pertinence

VAG, AGNS, MMFA

75.
Lower Town Church and Market Place, Quebec, c. 1831
Watercolour over graphite on paper, 15.3 × 23.9 cm

Inscriptions
(c.l., on the first sign) ALIVE CROCODILE/ALLIGATOR.; (c.l, on the second sign) SOLD./T.G; (c.l., on the fourth sign) GARRISON THEATR[E]/LORD [A]ND LADY AYLMER/BOMBASTES FURIO../MILLER... MEN; (b.,l.r., in ink, in the artist's hand) *Lower Town Church & Market Place/Quebec J Cockbu*[rn].

Provenance
Séminaire de Québec; on deposit at the Société du Musée du Séminaire de Québec, 1983.

Exhibitions
Quebec City 1952, No. 15; Vancouver 1959, No. 113; Ottawa 1965, No. 36; Quebec City 1974, No. 104.

Bibliography
MORISSET 1950/4, p. 26 (Repr.); *MORISSET 1951/2*, p. 100 (Repr.); *MORISSET 1952*, p. 25, No. 15; *BARBEAU 1957* (Repr.); *MORISSET 1959/1*, p. 42, No. 113; *MORISSET 1960/1*, p. 48d (Repr.); *MORISSET 1962*, p. 37 (Repr.); *HARPER AND HUBBARD 1965*, pp. [18] and 46, No. 36 (Repr.); *THIBAULT 1974*, p. 30, No. 104; *CAMERON AND TRUDEL 1976*, p. 61, No. 42 (Repr.); *DUVAL 1977*, p. H-6 (Repr.); *TOUPIN 1977*, p. D-19 (Repr.); *NOPPEN, PAULETTE AND TREMBLAY 1979*, p. 177 (Repr.); *TÊTU DE LABSADE 1990*, p. 247 (Repr.).

Collection
Musée du Séminaire de Québec (Pf984.30)

of his work. Moreover, many authors have devoted efforts to identifying the subjects he portrayed,[1] an objective fully justified by the focus of Cockburn's work. In his street scenes, Cockburn may be seen as perpetuating the coloured-drawing tradition. Lines are used to define and separate. Initially drawn in graphite, contours were retraced with pen and brown ink and then covered with colour washes. Such washes embellish the composition, but do not structure its forms. Streets are umber coloured and sidewalks bluish grey. The sole purpose of strong colours, such as crimson for clothing or bricks for the roofs, is to bring out simple geometric forms. Similarly, Cockburn bathes his works in uniform light, almost totally ignoring the shadows cast by the various elements.

Cockburn structures his work and, above all, the image itself. An analysis of the perspective grid of *Jesuit Barrack and Quebec Market Place* reveals a network of orthogonal lines—lines perpendicular to the picture plane—which meet at the vanishing point, located just left of the middle. This grid highlights the *coulisse* of Rue Desjardins, opening onto the marketplace. The illusion of scale created by the differ-

ent sized figures is not maintained for long. While the size of the soldier leaning against the cathedral wall is fairly compatible with that of the other elements in the watercolour, such as the harnessed horse and the couple with their back to the viewer, the same cannot be said of the size of the other figures on Rue Buade. In fact, the artist has juxtaposed two series of orthogonal lines instead of one: the first begins at the cathedral and crosses the covered market, while the other is parallel to the façades on Rue Buade. The figures obey this perspective grid, which is designed to convey a feeling of depth. Unlike Duncan, for example (Cat. 93 to 95), Cockburn rarely uses architecture as a backdrop to scenes from daily life. Rather, it is the focal point of his work.

By depicting its streets one after the other as well as its many squares, Cockburn prepared a faithful record of Quebec City. The dozens of different images he produced could be juxtaposed and combined to form panoramic views. These street scenes might even be equated with insets around a map. Such a comparison will no doubt come as a surprise. However, to support this statement, we should

mention the Dutch tradition of including a descriptive text and a series of small-scale topographic views of main buildings on city maps.[2] James Pattison Cockburn's figures obey the rules of geometry while his colours reflect a symbolic adaptation of reality that sharpens the image in unshadowed light. Consequently, his drawings play a merely descriptive role and are similar to the insets included on maps up to the 19th century.[3]

D.P.

Notes

1. James Pattison Cockburn's interest in illustrating Quebec City has already been established. Christina Cameron and Jean Trudel (1976) and W. Martha E. Cooke (1978) have discussed the main aspects.
2. See, in particular, the views of Amsterdam and Delft reproduced in *Opkomst en bloei van het Noordnederlandse stadsgezicht in de 17de eeuw/ The Dutch Cityscape in the 17th Century and Its Sources* (Cat.) (Amsterdam and Toronto, 1977), pp. 116-117.
3. A map of this type was published on New Orleans and its environs in 1815 (Gloria Gilda Deak, *Picturing America, 1497-1899* (Princeton: Princeton University Press, 1988), No. 292, Repr.).

MQ, NGC

76.
"Cap-Rouge" Cottage Near Quebec, 1831
Watercolour over graphite on paper, 15.4 × 24.2 cm

Inscriptions
(b.,l.r., in graphite, in the artist's hand) *H-Atkinsons - Cape Rouge/24ᵗʰ June - 1831 - J.C.*; (l.r.,on the base, in graphite, in another hand, hidden at the time of mounting) *Rideau Rivier;* (b.,l.r.) *Atkinsons House near Quebec.*

Provenance
Mrs. Russell Barrington, Kensington England (sold by Sotheby & Co., London, April 27, 1927, No. 118); L. Kashnor, The Museum Book Store, London, 1927; Ward C. Pitfield, London; Gift from Leonard Milberg, New York, to the Royal Ontario Museum, Toronto, 1987.

Bibliography
CATALOGUE *1927/1*, No. 118.

Collection
Royal Ontario Museum, Toronto (987.12.1)

THIS WATERCOLOUR appeared recently on the market during the sale of Ward C. Pitfield's collection in Montreal in 1986. Its provenance is the same as that of the watercolour in the Royal Ontario Museum (Cat. 72). In 1927, four albums of around 360 of Cockburn's drawings went on sale in London. The many pictures sold at the time explains the interest his work has long aroused. Purchased by an English merchant, the drawings were offered to the Public Archives of Canada. However, owing to their price and the fact that Ottawa was unable to purchase all the albums, it was agreed that the four portfolios would be divided up and the watercolours sold separately. Arthur G. Doughty, then archivist with the federal government, concluded an agreement with Ward C. Pitfield, a Montreal collector, to share a large number of works between them. The London merchant prepared a list of the watercolours before the albums were divided up. *"Cap-Rouge" Cottage Near Quebec* was found in Volume II of Folio 58.[1]

The principle of grouping works into albums was, of course, not exclusive to Cockburn. Many other artists and collectors stored them in this way. Based on the lists drawn up in 1927, the sole purpose of these albums was to group Canadian scenes together, without classifying them according to location or separating sepia drawings from watercolours. What is important, however, is that these portfolios contained both sketches and finished watercolours (Cat. 72). *"Cap-Rouge" Cottage Near Quebec* belongs to the first category.

The National Archives of Canada holds a series of pencil drawings known as the Cockburn-Wiggin Album.[2] Two of these works, depicting the area around the Henry Atkinson estate on the Cap-Rouge heights, are directly related to the watercolour in the Royal Ontario Museum (Figs. 76A and 76B). These drawings are of sketchbook format and very similar in size. The fact that they bear the same date as the watercolour in Toronto, i.e. June 24, 1831, proves that the three works are re-lated. It should be specified immediately that these drawings do not correspond to rough notes taken in preparation for studio work. Drawn from nature, they are works in their own right; their composition is perfect and colour alone is lacking. They were probably done using a *camera lucida*, which allowed the artist to weed out the unessential elements of a landscape and focus on the main lines of a composition. *"Cap-Rouge" Cottage Near Quebec* is the final version of these works. First, a pencil drawing was done outdoors, as shown by the holes left by the pins stuck in the corners of the paper to attach it to a support while the artist worked.[3] This practice was essential when using a *camera lucida* to prevent the wind from disturbing the artist. Watercolour washes, probably applied later, added the crowning touch to the work, which Cockburn considered the most representative of the series. This is a particularly fine work. The choice of vantage point alone allowed the artist to accurately render the scale of the villa, heralding the description by James

Fig. 76A.
James Pattison Cockburn,
Cap-Rouge, 1831;
graphite on paper, 13 × 23.8 cm, *Wiggin Album.*
National Archives of Canada, Ottawa (C-12661).

Fig. 76B.
James Pattison Cockburn,
Cap-Rouge, 1831;
graphite on paper, 13 × 23.8 cm, *Wiggin Album.*
National Archives of Canada, Ottawa (C-12668).

Macpherson LeMoine in 1865: "a magnificent avenue glides along the high bank under centennial, ever-verdant pines, whose far outspreading branches, under the influence of winds, sigh a plaintive but soothing music."[4] The colour fully expresses the pleasure experienced by the artist: strong greens contrast with one another against a mixed background; darker browns have been used to depict ruts in the road; tree bark is rendered with long, parallel strokes designed to enhance its roughness, while the villa walls, fully exposed to the light, have been painted in chalky tones. The shadows, particulary those in the foreground, were also outlined in graphite beforehand as though the artist were afraid of forgetting their importance.

Henry Atkinson gained recognition in the timber trade in Quebec City, where he purchased wood on behalf of the Royal Navy. He rapidly accumulated an enormous fortune that enabled him to build "Cap-Rouge" around 1820. This L-shaped villa had a large veranda extending toward the river; it also had one of the first hothouses in the city.[5] The villa was surrounded by a garden with flowerbeds and fountains. Paths led to orchards, the forest, a stream, or a pavilion on the cliff overlooking the river. Although Atkinson lived on his estate for only about ten years, his landscaping foreshadowed that of "Spencer Wood" in 1834.[6] He had purchased this property in London during a four-year grand tour of Europe in the early 1830s in search of works of art, "objets d'art" and plants for his collections.

The "Cap-Rouge" villa was rarely illustrated (see Cat. 65 and 66). Prior to the discovery of this watercolour, it was known only through an anonymous engraving from the 1850s.[7] The watercolour also made it possible to identify a drawing by Joseph Légaré on the back of an oil on paper in the Musée du Séminaire de Québec collection.[8]

D.P.

Notes

1. NAC, RG 37, Vol. CCXCVIII, James Pattison Cockburn file.

2. NAC, 1948-77-1 to 43.

3. It should also be mentioned that a pencil sketch of a house with a sign appears on the back of this watercolour. It does not seem to be related, however, to the "Cap-Rouge" villa.

4. James MacPherson LeMoine, *Maple Leaves. Canadian History and Quebec Scenery* (Quebec: Hunter Rose & Co., 1865), 3rd series, p. 98.

5. *GAGNON-PRATTE 1980*, pp. 292-293.

6. *GAGNON-PRATTE 1980*, pp. 208-210. H. Atkinson brought a gardener, Peter Lowe, over from Scotland in 1846 to remodel the grounds of "Spencer Wood" after an English garden.

7. *DE VOLPI 1971*, p. 124 (Repr.).

8. Although not very well executed, this drawing is currently the only known example of Légaré's four views of "Carouge" commissioned perhaps by Atkinson and remaining in his collection until it was put up for auction in 1851. For further reading, see Renée Gagnon-Guimond, "Henry Atkinson, gentilhomme et baron du bois," *Cap-aux-Diamants*, Vol. IV, No. 3 (fall 1988), pp. 21-22.

VAG, AGNS, MMFA

77.

Village of Jeune Lorette, a Huron Settlement Near Quebec c. 1831

Watercolour over graphite highlighted with gum arabic and traces of scraping out on paper laid on strong cardboard, 43.9 × 66.6 cm

Inscription
(b.,l.c., in graphite) *The Village of Lorette near Quebec/a Huron Settlement.*

Provenance
Frank T. Sabin Gallery, London; acquired by the Royal Ontario Museum, Toronto, 1953.

Bibliography
SPENDLOVE *1967*, p. 10 (Repr.); ALLODI *1974/1*, Vol. I, No. 302 (Repr.); CAMERON AND TRUDEL *1976*, p. 153, No. 140 (Repr.).

Collection
Royal Ontario Museum, Toronto (953.131.5)

T HE VARIOUS FALLS on the outskirts of Quebec City soon became a centre of attraction for the British. Montmorency Falls was illustrated from the outset. The city's proximity and the presence of Sir Frederick Haldimand's residence undoubtedly prompted James Peachey to draw Montmorency Falls around 1781-1784.[1] After 1850, which marks the end

of the period covered by this exhibition, the falls were included in Samuel McLaughlin's portfolio of photographs (Cat. 261). It is not without some irony, therefore, that they appear only incidentally in the works presented here.[2] Visitors also flocked to the Chaudière Falls from a very early date; they were just as popular, in fact, as Montmorency Falls. Writings of the period particulary praised their picturesque character and breathtaking view, extolling the enjoyable walks that could be taken nearby. Both these sites were charged with history. Montmorency Falls occupied a prominent place in a series of engravings published in London in 1760. Based on drawings by Hervey Smyth, there were intended to illustrate the sites of the battle of Québec.[3] When George Bulteel Fisher included a panoramic view of the Chaudière Falls in his 1796 portfolio of aquatints, he accompanied it with a quotation recalling Benedict Arnold's march: "It was by the River Chaudière that General Arnold took his route, when he made an attempt on Quebec in the year 1776".[4]

In James P. Cockburn's time, these sites were very accessible and history was merely a fleeting reference to the past. *Village of Jeune Lorette, a Huron Settlement Near Quebec* illustrates this phenomenon well. In *Quebec and Its Environs*, Cockburn takes pleasure in quoting Pierre-François-Xavier de Charlevoix and taking the reader back 100 years to appreciate

the changes the country had undergone. In 1831, the modern traveller reached Lorette in an hour, passing through cultivated fields and inhabited countryside. For Charlevoix, who wrote the following passage in his *Histoire et description générale de la Nouvelle-France* in 1774, the situation was completely different:

We are surrounded with the vastest woods in the world; in all appearance, they are as ancient as the world itself, and were never planted by the hand of man. Nothing can present a nobler or more magnificent prospect to the eyes; the trees hide their tops in the clouds, and the variety of different species of them is so prodigious, that even amongst all those who have most applied themselves to the knowledge of them, there is not, perhaps, one who is not ignorant of at least one half of them.[5]

Such comparisons of 18th- and 19th century Quebec raise another issue altogether. People were gradually becoming aware of the chaotic deforestation of land. The picturesque traveller enjoyed visual contrasts, in particular: cultivated fields surrounded by dense forest and hollow trees beside majestic pines. However, the clearing of land for colonization was sometimes at odds with landscaping. The former, with its ensuing visual chaos, created by partially felled trees and branchless trunks, was contrary to the esthetic principle of skilfully contrasted harmony and often offended British travellers.[6] Reforestation prizes were awarded annually in Great Britain following the increased enclosure of land between 1750 and 1815, which radically changed the English countryside.[7]

The Falls on the Saint-Charles River cannot be disassociated from the neighbouring Huron village indicated in the title. Moreover, the viewpoint chosen by Cockburn shows the village off to advantage: "the best view is from the opposite bank, having the fall in the foreground, with the church and village of the Indians behind it."[8] James Pattison Cockburn has carefully structured the image, dividing it into three separate planes. The overly prominent horizontal in the foreground is offset to an extent by a slight incline; the clump of trees framing the watercolour on the left echoes the vertical lines of the buildings on the right. Cockburn has deliberately emphasized contrasts by drawing the buildings with a ruler and compass and reserving freehand strokes for the trees and the cascading water of the falls, depicted mainly by the white of the drawing paper. Like *Quebec From Below Aubigny Church, Pointe Lévis* (Cat. 82), this watercolour is a studio work. Should it too be

MQ, NGC

78.
The Chaudière Falls, c. 1831
Watercolour over graphite and traces of scraping out on paper, 43 × 66 cm

interpreted as a work prepared for an engraver? Cockburn's original project[9] included a series of 12 engravings, including *The Falls on the Saint-Charles River*. However, when the number of works in the series was reduced by half, Cockburn had to eliminate certain subjects, one of which was probably this view of the Saint-Charles River. Nevertheless, the quality and size of this watercolour suggest that it was intended for the original project.

This might also be the case for **The Chaudière Falls** from the McCord Museum. It has all the characteristics of a work intended for reproduction. The vantage point corresponds to a site mentioned by Joseph Bouchette:

The woods on the banks of the river, notwithstanding its vicinity to the capital, are so impervious as to render it necessary for strangers who visit the falls to provide themselves with a competent guide. Few falls can be compared with this for picturesque beauty. The best view is to the left from a ledge of rocks that project into the basin; from this spot the scene is surprisingly grand. The next point of view is from a parallel ledge behind the former.[10]

This is a splendid work. Cockburn has placed small figures on the edge of the cliff overlooking the water, thereby suggesting the dizziness they must have experienced. The open area in the foreground and the scrubby trees hanging from the cliff are also used to evoke this feeling. Cockburn learned this composition tech-

nique from Joseph Mallord William Turner (1775-1851). At the time of Lord Dalhousie's departure in 1828, Cockburn prepared an album of drawings of various Canadian falls for Lady Dalhousie. The entire foreground of one of these drawings, *The Ice Cone, Montmorency Falls, Quebec,* was borrowed from an engraving by Turner, *Little Devil's Bridge over the Reuss above Altdorf.*[11] It depicts a narrow ravine plunging toward the base of the falls, conveying the same dizzy sensation as **The Chaudière Falls.** This might be interpreted, essentially, as a means of embellishing an overly bare foreground. However, it is tempting to believe that Cockburn's intentions were more far-reaching. Lady Aylmer, who used to admire the Chaudière Falls from the same vantage point, recorded her impressions in a diary: "I prefer some of the Swiss falls, and certainly think Terni finer in many respects, but the tout ensemble of the picture here is very fine."[12] Foreign countries, such as Switzerland or Italy, were often used as a basis of comparison in travellers' journals of the period. Perhaps, Cockburn wanted to evoke, in some of his drawings, elements of certain well-known, much appreciated sites. This practice is entirely in keeping with association theory and takes advantage of the different levels of interpretation offered by topographic views.

D.P.

Provenance
Charles J. Beadon; David Ross McCord, Montreal, 1920; McCord Museum, Montreal.

Exhibition
Montreal 1962-1963, No. 105.

Bibliography
HARPER 1962/1, p. 70, No. 105 (Repr.).

Collection
McCord Museum of Canadian History, Montreal (M371)

Notes

1. GAGNON-PRATTE 1980, pp. 278-279.

2. Montmorency Falls had originally occupied a prominent place in the exhibition and were represented by the magnificent panoramic view by Charles Ramus Forrest, *Quebec City and Montmorency Falls,* from the National Gallery of Canada. However, owing to conservation decisions, this watercolour had to be withdrawn at a later date, once the choice of works was final.

3. DE VOLPI 1971, Pl. 7.

4. DE VOLPI 1971, Pl. 37.

5. James Pattison Cockburn, *Quebec and Its Environs; Being a Picturesque Guide to the Stranger.* Quoted from the facsimile of this guide in BELL AND COOKE, 1978, p. 25.

6. Bruce Robertson presents an overview of this question in *Views and Visions. American Landscape before 1830* (Cat.) (Washington: The Corcoran Gallery of Art, 1986), pp. 204-206.

7. See Ann Bermingham, *Landscape and Ideology. The English Rustic Tradition, 1740-1860* (Berkeley and Los Angeles: University of California Press, 1986).

8. J.P. Cockburn, *op. cit.,* p. 24.

9. See Cat. 82 for details.

10. BOUCHETTE 1832, p. 300.

11. For a reproduction of Cockburn's drawing, see BELL AND COOKE 1978, No. 47. For Turner's engraving, see Gerald Wilkinson, *Turner on Landscape. The Liber Studiorum* (London: Barrie & Jenkins, 1982), p. 60, Pl. 19 (Repr.). The album offered to Lady Dalhousie was put up for sale at Sotheby's in London on May 24, 1965 (lot 67). It is currently part of a private collection. It should also be mentioned that the painting of Niagara Falls on the frontispiece of this album was literally copied by Joseph Légaré (PORTER 1978/1, pp. 53-54, No. 31, Repr.).

12. Quoted from the transcript of Lady Aylmer's diary, *Recollections of Canada,* in the *Rapport de l'archiviste de la Province de Québec pour 1934-1935* (Quebec: Rédempti Paradis, 1935), p. 306.

MQ, NGC

Fig. 79A.
James Smillie after James Pattison Cockburn,
Quebec from the Old Mill, c. 1828-1830;
engraving, 11.4 × 16.2 cm (image).
Musée du Québec, Quebec City (78.386).

79.
Quebec Viewed from the Round Tower on the Saint Charles River, above Dorchester Bridge c. 1828-1830

Sepia, pen and brown ink over graphite on paper, 11.5 × 19.2 cm

Inscription
(b.,c., in pen and brown ink) *Quebec from the Round Tower/on the River S*. *Charles above Dorchester/Bridge - March 1831*.

Provenance
(?) Mrs. Russell Barrington, Kensington England (sold by Sotheby & Co., London, April 27, 1927, No. 118); (?) L. Kashnor, The Museum Book Store, London, 1927; Henry Stevens, Son and Stiles; W. H. Coverdale, Manoir Richelieu, Tadoussac; acquired by the Public Archives of Canada, Ottawa, 1970.

Exhibition
Ottawa 1973-1977, No. 42.

Bibliography
(?) CATALOGUE *1927/1*, No. 118; GODENRATH *1939*, p. 12, No. 1729; BELL *1973/2*, No. 42 (Repr.); BELL AND COOKE *1978*, pp. 45-46; COOKE *1983*, p. 50, No. 110 (Repr.); ALLODI AND TOVELL *1989*, p. 80.

Collection
National Archives of Canada, Ottawa (1970-188-1729)

T HIS VIEW OF QUEBEC CITY, with a circular tower in the foreground, was drawn from the banks of the Saint-Charles River, or more precisely, from Pointe aux Lièvres. This point was located on land purchased in 1667 by Charles Aubert de la Chesnaye who, in the late 17th century, built a residence, secondary buildings and three windmills on his property.[1] Cockburn chose one of these windmills, without its vanes, as the main foreground motif of a series of panoramic views of Saint-Roch suburb and Quebec City. Few topographers took an interest in this subject. A watercolour by Thomas Davies, *A View of Quebec, taken near Beauport Ferry in 1787*,[2] painted from a similar angle, is another work in which the circular tower frames the right-hand side of the composition. In a watercolour dated June 8, 1830, James Pattison Cockburn depicts the abandoned windmill beside a

two-storey house and the bay formed by the river (Fig. 79-81A).

The sepia drawing from the National Archives of Canada (Cat. 79) inaugurates the series. The background is occupied by Quebec City, surrounded by its fortifications. A large building on the beach, in front of the city walls, probably corresponds to a warehouse owned by Matthew Bell, whose commercial activities revolved around the import-export trade.[3] The houses of Saint-Roch parish line the riverbank, bearing witness to the growing number of lots granted outside the ramparts. The presence of timber depots below the tower can be explained by the economic activity associated with John Goudie's shipyard. *Quebec Viewed from the Round Tower on the Saint Charles River Above Dorchester Bridge* exhibits highly controlled use of topography. After tracing the outlines in graphite, Cockburn applied

brown washes of growing intensity as he approached the foreground. He then used a pen to obtain greater definition or to emphasize texture. James Smillie (1807-1885) reproduced these effects in the engraving he produced around 1825-1830 (Fig. 79A). He followed Cockburn's drawing very closely, modifying only minor details, and did not alter the composition or use of light.

In 1832, James Pattison Cockburn reproduced his original idea in a larger watercolour (Cat. 80). He chose especially thick paper that allowed him to fully exploit his washes by mixing and superimposing colours, without being hampered by a weak support. The watercolour rectified the composition of the original drawing by eliminating the gap created by the road on the right. This watercolour illustrates the traditional composition inherited from classical landscape, in which the open area

MQ, NGC

Fig. 79-81A.
James Pattison Cockburn,
*The Saint-Charles River
from Dorchester Bridge,* 1830;
watercolour on paper, 13.3 × 20.9 cm.
Royal Ontario Museum, Toronto (942.48.31).

80.
Quebec Viewed from the Round Tower on the Saint Charles River above Dorchester Bridge, 1832

Watercolour over graphite on paper, 33.7 × 47.4 cm

Inscription
(b.,l.r., in pen and brown ink, in the artist's hand)
Quebec from S. *Charles River/Jas. Cockburn./1832.*

Provenance
(?) Estate of Mrs. Waddel; acquired by the Public Archives of Canada, Ottawa, 1947.

Exhibition
Ottawa 1975-1976, No. 12.

Bibliography
BELL AND COOKE 1975, No. 12 (Repr.); *Le Journal de Québec,* July 3, 1975, p. 9 (Repr.); *Progrès-Dimanche,* July 6, 1975; p. 12-C (Repr.); *Le Nouvelliste,* July 7, 1975, p. 21 (Repr.); *Le Réveil,* July 8, 1975, p. 24 (Repr.); *Quebec Chronicle Telegraph,* July 9, 1975, p. 10 (Repr.); BELL AND COOKE 1978, p. 45; COOKE 1983, p. 50; ALLODI AND TOVELL 1989, p. 80.

Collection
National Archives of Canada, Ottawa (1947-5-1).

in the centre is framed by vertical planes in the foreground. The circular tower now encloses the composition while the *coulisse* of the road in the foreground merely suggests what the preparatory drawing actually depicted. By changing the rafts into large timber floats, Cockburn has intensified riverfront activity. In going from the sepia drawing to the watercolour, he has paid more attention to drawing and technique. The city in the background is shown in great detail and the buildings are more clearly defined. Basically, however, these elements serve as a support for the foreground, which has captured the landscape artist's undivided attention. Cockburn has increased the size of the tower, which is now compressed by the sides of the paper. He has also emphasized its state of decay: the masonry is cracked, some stones are dislodged and the window is wide open. Cockburn has paid special at-

tention to technique and made the drawing more expressive by taking advantage of the rugged shapes. He has used watercolour washes carefully, mixing brick tones and light ochres with greyish greens, the whole highlighted with orange accents. The foliage, which is dominated by browns tinged with olive, has been meticulously constructed with small juxtaposed strokes. The topography is now only one of the many elements in the landscape. In particular, Cockburn has obtained an attractive decorative effect by turning the remains of the windmill into a majestic ruin. He thereby echoes William Gilpin, who recommended that artists use their imagination to reorganize overly natural elements into a more harmonious whole.

At first glance, this large watercolour from the Royal Ontario Museum seems to apply this approach, typical of the picturesque style. However, on closer analysis,

differences can be detected, some of which are significant enough to suggest that another philosophy underlies the work. Contrary to the two previous works, this landscape is not dated. The date traditionally assigned to it—circa 1830—is not very plausible. ***Quebec Seen From the West Bank on the Saint Charles River*** (Cat. 81) obviously concludes the series. Owing to its composition and technique, this watercolour cannot be immediately associated with the landscape paintings of the 1831-1832 period, in particular with the preparatory watercolours for the engravings (Cat. 82). Certain stylistic elements allow it to be dated much later, around the 1840s, when Cockburn was back in England. This statement is confirmed by a large watercolour, of exactly the same dimensions, of Montmorency Falls dated 1843.[4] The artist wrote on the back of the work that it was done expressly for Wm. Beadon

MQ, NGC

81. (See colour reproduction, p. 100)
Quebec Seen from the West Bank on the Saint Charles River, c. 1840
Watercolour over graphite withh some traces of gum arabic on paper, 44.4 × 67 cm

Inscription
(b.,c. in graphite) *View of Quebec with the Timber Depot.*

Provenance
Frank T. Sabin Gallery, London; acquired by the Royal Ontario Museum, Toronto, 1953.

Exhibitions
Ottawa 1967/1, No. 66; Kingston 1978, No. 43.

Bibliography
DUVAL 1954, p. 3 (Repr.) entitled *View of Quebec; SPENDLOVE 1967*, p. 6 (Repr.) entitled *View of Quebec with Timber Depot; HUBBARD AND OSTIGUY 1967*, p. 46, No. 66 entitled *View of Quebec with Timber Depot; HUBBARD AND FRYE 1973*, pp. 9 and 10 (Repr.) entitled *View of Quebec with Timber Depot; ALLODI 1974/1*, Vol. I, No. 299; *BELL AND COOKE 1978*, pp. 45-46, No. 43 (Repr.) entitled *Quebec from the Round Tower on the St. Charles River above Dorchester Bridge; BLANCHET 1987*, p. 12 (Repr.); *ALLODI AND TOVELL 1989*, p. 80

Collection
Royal Ontario Museum, Toronto (953.131.6)

Esqr.[5] Cockburn was therefore not inactive when he returned to England. On the contrary, he obviously reproduced certain works, either as presents or at the request of friends or patrons. We suggest that **Quebec Seen From the West Bank on the Saint Charles River** be considered in this light. Once again, the composition is modified. The narrower central vista between the tower and the trees reduces the city with its bluish architecture to an horizon line. The foreground alone is important. The circular tower in the far right foreground overlooking the river has recovered its full importance and no longer acts as a repoussoir. With its conical roof and straight sides, it proudly announces its position. The decay of the tower has given way to ochred light masking its imperfections. The surrounding vegetation, rendered with a refined range of reddish-browns to olive greens, has enabled Cockburn to hide the bulging masonry at its base. As in the original drawing, the window has recovered its lustre. A crack in the wall beneath the window alone foreshadows its future decay. We are tempted to believe, for a moment, that the seated

figure at the foot of the tower is the proud owner of the structure and that he spends his days here peacefully.

This highly refined landscape is based on traditions largely abandoned by landscape artists of the 1840s. The motif of tall birch trees with broad, powerful trunks extending beyond the edge of the painting is reminiscent of works done by John Robert Cozens (1752-1797) after his stay in Italy between 1776 and 1779.[6] The realism with which Cockburn has painted the cart drawn by a team of differently coloured horses is unusual. Although the names of Thomas Gainsborough (1727-1788) and John Constable (1776-1837) immediately come to mind, it would be unwise to draw too many comparisons. It should be remembered that, in the 19th century, artists in search of *beaux motifs* to incorporate into their works were not at a loss for sources of inspiration. In 1806, William Henry Pyne (1769-1843) published *Microcosm: or, a Picturesque Delineation of the Arts* in London, placing examples of groups of figures, animals and vehicles at the disposal of artists to highlight the picturesque character of their land-

scapes.[7] Like many of his contemporaries, James Pattison Cockburn may have consulted this repertoire to embellish **Quebec Seen From the West Bank on the Saint Charles River.**

D.P.

Notes
1. *HARE, LAFRANCE AND RUDDEL 1987*, p. 73. (use small capitals)
2. *HILL AND LANDRY 1988*, p. 258, No. 6277 (Repr.).
3. Michel Bédard, André Bérubé and Jean Hamelin, "Matthew Bell," DCB, Vol. VII, 1988, pp. 70-75. See also *CAMERON AND TRUDEL 1976*, p. 29, No. 10.
4. *A Morning View of the Falls of Montmorency* (ROM, 959.159.1).
5. William Beadon was James P. Cockburn's son-in-law, having married his daughter Jessie.
6. See, in particular, *View of Windsor from the South West* reproduced by Kim Sloan in *Alexander and John Robert Cozens. The Poetry of Landscape* (New Haven: Yale University Press), 1986, p. 160, Fig. 185.
7. One of the plates from this publication is reproduced in the exhibition catalogue *Beauty, Horror and Immensity. Picturesque Landscape in Britain, 1750-1850* (Cat.) (Cambridge: Fitzwilliam Museum, 1981), No. 169, Pl. 86.

82.
Quebec From Below Aubigny Church, Pointe Lévis, c. 1831
Watercolour over graphite highlighted with gouache and some traces of scraping out on paper laid on strong cardboard, 40.7 × 64.2 cm

Inscription
(b.,c., in graphite) *Quebec from Point Levi./the artiste has introduced his own figure, sketching, into this view.*

Provenance
Frank T. Sabin Gallery, London; acquired by the Royal Ontario Museum, Toronto, 1953.

Exhibitions
(?) New York 1942, No. 79; Vancouver 1966, No. 27; Toronto 1978/1, No. 4.

Bibliography
(?) CATALOGUE *1942*, p. 21, No. 79; SHADBOLT *1966*, No. 27; SPENDLOVE *1967*, p. 9 (Repr.); ALLODI *1974/1*, Vol. I, No. 289 (Repr.) entitled *The Artist Sketching Quebec from Pointe Lévis;* CAMERON AND TRUDEL *1976*, p. 20, No. 1 (Repr.); ADAMSON *1978*, pp. 5 and 19, No. 4.

Collection
Royal Ontario Museum, Toronto (953.131.2)

J AMES PATTISON COCKBURN invariably sought to have his works reproduced as engravings. As early as 1807, he took advantage of his participation in the siege of Copenhagen to publish a series of five coloured aquatints based on drawings from nature. He continued this practice in later years, having not only a military map (1809) but also picturesque views of trips to Italy and Switzerland (1820, 1822 and 1823) made into engravings. He also contributed to William Bernard Cooke's major work on Pompeii (1818/1819 and 1827).[1] It is only natural, therefore, that Cockburn's stay in Canada allowed him to pursue these interests. In writing about the success of the Ladies' Bazaar, which had just opened on April 7, 1828, a columnist for the *Quebec Mercury*, was justified in recommending that the officers present, who were skilful watercolourists, consider the possibility of publishing their work:

There were however some contributions from Gentlemen, particularly a book of Sketches, by an Officer of Rank in the Royal Artillery, who holds a distinguished place amongst Artists in Water Colours, and some very charming detached sketches of scenes in and about Quebec [...] It has often occured to us that Canadian views and subjects, in the hands of the Engraver, would form matter for an entertaining graphick volume that could not fail in becoming popular, and would remunerate those who might undertake it, as it would be purchased, for the reminesences it would call up in those who had visited these Provinces, and if delineated with the strict fidelity, which so eminently marks the works of the Officer whose, contributed, sketches are the object of our present remark, would become a valuable acquisition to the Port-folio of the Amateur or encourager of the Fine Arts. We are sure that if the Officer, referred to, would dedicate his leisure to such a wok he would add greatly to his fame as an Artist.[2]

The enthusiastic response to Georges Bourne's work *Picture of Quebec* in 1829 confirmed the interest aroused in some segments of society for this type of endeavour.

James Pattison Cockburn left Quebec City on August 2, 1832, a year after publishing *Quebec and Its Environs; Being a Picturesque Guide to the Stranger.* This opuscule, which in no way compares with his major European publications of the 1820s, was the outcome of efforts initiated in 1826.[3] He was thus preparing the

Fig. 82A.
James Pattison Cockburn,
Quebec from Aubigny Church, Pointe Lévis;
Sepia on paper of the album *Recollections of Canada,* by Lady Aylmer.
Archives nationales du Québec, Quebec City (P363/AQ-30).

Fig. 82B.
H. Pyall after James Pattison Cockburn,
Quebec from Below Aubigny Church, Point Levi, 1833;
aquatint published by Ackermann & Co., 52 × 72 cm.
Musée du Québec, Quebec City (INC.2).

public to seek out larger samples of his work. In March 1832, Cockburn announced his intention in the newspaper to have two series of 12 engravings published in London: one on Niagara Falls and the other on Quebec City and its environs. A notice in the *Quebec Mercury* on March 19, 1833 informed subscribers that the artist had reached an agreement with Ackermann & Co. However, the original plan to publish 12 views in each series had been reduced to six. It is not known what prompted this decision. Perhaps the project did not arouse as much interest as anticipated or the price asked by the publisher was too high.

Cockburn therefore concluded an agreement with a leading London publisher, who produced high-quality work. For his series on Quebec City, he decided to include mainly panoramic views: Lower Town and the river, the Château gardens, Montmorency Falls in summer and winter, Quebec City viewed from Pointe à Pizeau, and the ice bridge between Quebec City and Lévis with a panoramic view of Quebec.

Quebec From Below Aubigny Church, Pointe Lévis belongs to this series. The site depicted in this work was highly appreciated by artists. We are familiar with several of Cockburn's drawings executed at various points along the road descending toward the river. Lady Aylmer's album contains a sepia drawing (Fig. 82A) which, regardless of whether it is the original study or a later reproduction, already contains all the elements of the finished work. Subsequent modifications affected only minor details: for example, the left side of the composition was closed, river activity intensified and the vegetation refined. The seated figure in the foreground, making sketches of the site, became a veritable artist at work in the final version of the watercolour.

Cockburn prepared the watercolour meticulously, allowing the engraver very little freedom to make changes (Fig. 82B). Nonetheless, the engraver adjusted the perspective to obtain a more coherent interpretation of the two foreground levels, changing, in particular, the size of the figures walking down the path. He also defined the vegetation more clearly, replacing the anarchical profusion of watercolour with the radiant light of a garden. The changes are minor, however, even with regard to the more clearly delineated patterns of light. Certainly, James Pattison Cockburn was anxious for the undertaking to be a success. In accordance with the wish expressed in 1828 by the columnist quoted above, he wanted the aquatint to have the same visual impact as a direct record of the site itself.

D.P.

Notes

1. For further reading, see *PRIOUL 1988,* pp. 210-211.

2. *Quebec Mercury,* April 8, 1828, p. 169.

3. See *ALLODI AND TOVELL 1989,* pp. 8-11, 20, 27, 98-99, 108, Cat. 55, 55a-f, 64, 66.

W. HENRY COTTON

1817-1877

W. HENRY COTTON is thought to have been born in St. Petersburg, the son of William Miles Cotton, an Englishman living in Russia. He was not yet twenty years old when he arrived in Canada; and in 1837, he married Eleanor Ross, daughter of David Ross. Until 1841, Cotton held a position in the Upper Canada civil service. After that, and at the time of the unification of the two provinces, he served the governor general in Quebec City. After Confederation, his duties with the governor general's office took him to Ottawa, where he died in 1877. A number of the views he did of Quebec City were published as lithographs in 1850 by Sarony & Major of New York.

Main sources
HARPER 1970; ALLODI 1974/1.

MQ

83.
Montréal, View from "Temple Grove", after 1843
Watercolour over graphite on paper, 26.7 × 39.4 cm

Provenance
David Ross McCord; McCord Museum, Montreal.
Exhibition
Kingston 1990-1991, No. 7.
Bibliography
FARR 1990, p. 42, No. 7 (Repr.).
Collection
McCord Museum of Canadian History, Montreal (M1859)

W E KNOW VERY LITTLE about Henry Cotton, and the works attributed to him are few.[1] His ties with the McCord family stemmed from his marriage to Eleanor Ross, whose sister, Anne, had wed John Samuel McCord. In 1836, the year before Henry Cotton married, John Samuel McCord had an imposing residence, "Temple Grove", built on Côte-des-Neiges.

Modelled after Greek temples with an extended wing surrounded by a portico on three sides, it was one of the rare examples of Greek Revival—then popular in the United States[2]—in Quebec architecture. The residence was bequeathed to David Ross McCord in 1865 and later won renown for the quality of its Canadian history collections. In 1919, David Ross McCord donated them to McGill University, thus forming the initial nucleus of the present-day McCord Museum.[3]

Dorothy Farr situated the perspective of this watercolour based on the above biographical information. Given the presence of the two towers on Notre-Dame de Montréal church and the disappearance of that of the former parish church, we have dated it post-1843. James Duncan also painted a panoramic view of Montreal from the terrace of "Temple Grove."[4] Cotton was not as ambitious as Duncan—

his landscape was not descriptive. However, he did spontaneously capture a real-life fragment of Montreal bathed in high-summer sunlight. Evidence of this is the treatment in which nothing seems to have been pre-constructed. Only a very quick pencil sketch establishes the outline. Layers of colour washes have been generously applied, effortlessly and without regard for the contours of the drawing. The faded red of the chair in the foreground and the neutral beige tones on the door and terrace serve solely to highlight the cold, predominant blues and greens of the vegetation and the river's waters. The artist has used graphite to darken the foliage and accentuate the luminosity still further.

This leaves the frame, or to be more precise, the frame within the frame, for what Henry Cotton shows us first and foremost is a double door, opened so as to give a sweeping view of the outdoors, and whose left side seems to be held in place by the back of a chair. Although refreshingly novel, given the absence of such compositions in the watercolours of this period in Quebec, this type of presentation is nonetheless quite old. The view through an open door is a throwback to the Dutch pictorial tradition developed primarily by Pieter Saenredam (1597-1665)[5]. But this is really no more than a

reference, for Cotton had other intentions. By the conspicuousness of the chair which obstructs the exit, by the hat which awaits the unexpected visitor's departure, it is the passage from interior to exterior that is being suggested. His layout creates an effect of intimacy and arouses in us a desire to cross the threshold. Thus the illusory strength of the drawing is due less to its geometrical structure than to the quiet confidence that it establishes with the viewer.

D.P.

Notes
1. The ROM possesses four views of Quebec City, in graphite, copied from the lithographs of Sarony & Major (ALLODI 1974/1, Vol. II, No. 2142-2145); the John Ross Robertson Collection of the Metropolitan Toronto Library contains a panorama of Quebec City in brown ink (JRR 1971).
2. GAGNON-PRATTE 1980, p. 57, and HARPER 1962/1, p. 53, No. 77.
3. On this question, see Isabel Barclay Dobell's brief introduction in HARPER 1962/1, p. 9. David Ross McCord was active in setting up the museum, whose first registers he organized.
4. HARPER 1962/1, p. 45, No. 60 (Repr.).
5. See Gary Schwartz and Marten Jan Bok, *Pieter Saenredam. The Painter and His Time* (The Hague: Gary Schwartz/SDU Publishers, 1990), p. 237, Fig. 252.

BORN IN LIMERICK, IRELAND, George Russell Dartnell was the son of John Dartnell and Alice Russell. On November 30, 1820, after an apprenticeship at the South Infirmary Hospital in Cork, Dartnell joined the British army as a nurse in Chatham, England. He was appointed assistant surgeon five years later, after studying at St. George's Hospital in London. Dartnell arrived in India on August 25, 1826, where he served for five years. In 1832, after spending time in Bengal, he returned to the United Kingdom for health reasons. He left for Canada on June 12, 1835, and arrived in Montreal, his first posting, on July 21, where he remained until June 1836. Dartnell visited Toronto and Niagara in 1836, on his way to Penetanguishene. He arrived in Quebec City for the first time in July 1838, and stayed until May 1839, when he was appointed a surgeon with the 2nd battalion of the Royal First Regiment. He went back to join his unit in Montreal in July 1839. Dartnell was later stationed in London and Toronto; he also spent some time in Port Talbot and Niagara Falls. It was during this period that he became friends with Captain Daniel Lysons, another topographical artist.

At the beginning of November 1843, Dartnell and Lysons set sail from Quebec City for the West Indies. However, only a few days later, on November 4, their transport, the *Premier,* was shipwrecked near Cap-Chat, in the Gulf of St. Lawrence. Forced to return briefly to Quebec City, Dartnell left for England the following February.

The year after his return to Great Britain, Dartnell was named director of the Military Lunatic Asylum in Great Yarmouth. On November 24, 1854, he was promoted inspector general of hospitals. Less than three years later, in January 1857, he retired from the army with half pay. From 1858 to 1876, Dartnell owned the Arden House Private Lunatic Asylum in Henley-in-Arden, but this did not prevent him from taking part in the exhibitions of the Royal Birmingham Society of Artists between 1867 and 1873. George Russell Dartnell finally retired at Leamington Spa in 1876, where he died on July 22, 1878.

GEORGE RUSSELL
DARTNELL
1799/1800-1878

Main sources
DE PENCIER 1987/1; DE PENCIER 1987/2.

MQ, NGC

84.
Ice Shove at Montreal c. 1836
Watercolour, pen and brown ink over graphite on paper, 23.1 × 34.7 cm

Inscription
(l.r.) *Ice Shove, Montreal.*

Provenance
Descendants of the artist; private collection, Toronto.

Exhibition
Toronto 1987-1988, No. 21.

Bibliography
DE PENCIER *1987/1*, pp. 10, 32 and 99, No. 21 (Repr.)

Collection
Private collection, Toronto

G EORGE RUSSELL DARTNELL is one of the rare watercolourists for whom a relatively complete monograph exists. Honor de Pencier's works and the Royal Ontario Museum's 1987 exhibition on Dartnell did much to bring into the limelight an artist who until then had been virtually unknown.[1]

Between his first visit in the summer of 1835 and his return to England in February 1844, Dartnell's stays in Quebec were for the most part brief: Montreal (August 1835-June 1836); Quebec City (July 1838-May 1839); Montreal (July 1839-May 1840); and Quebec City for part of winter 1843-1844. His portrayals of the ice jams in Montreal harbour in

spring 1836 are perhaps among the most spectacular of his early works. *Masses of Ice Thrown up on the Wharf at Montreal by the Great Shove of the St. Lawrence* (Fig. 84A), a watercolour from this series dated April 26, 1836, is owned by the National Gallery of Canada. The work is a particularly breathtaking detail of the jam formed by ice that has submerged the wharf and piled up alongside the road. The watercolour presented here is from the same series.[2] *Ice Shove at Montreal* is a clearly panoramic view of the same natural phenomenon. Dartnell used graphite to draw the buildings, creating a long strip of sombre facades that serves to bring out the whiteness of the paper support. Out-

lined in pen and brown ink, the ice on the river takes shape as large floes or chunks broken up by obstacles. A minimum of means are used to render this manifestation of nature's impressive strength. The discreet vertical section of wall on the left frames the composition and provides one of the rare elements of stability. Conversely, the piece of wood jutting through the blanket of ice in the foreground looms as a potential threat behind the two tiny figures watching the turbulent river.

George Russell Dartnell's true flair as an artist enabled him to portray the effects of winter in such a manner. Before him, James Pattison Cockburn had primarily striven to render the variations of

Fig. 84A.
George Russell Dartnell,
*Masses of Ice Thrown Up on to the Wharf
at Montreal by the Great Shove
of the St. Lawrence* 1836;
watercolour and gouache over pen and brown
ink and graphite on paper, 21.9 × 29.2 cm.
National Gallery of Canada, Ottawa (28039).

VAG, AGNS, MMFA

85.
Snowshowers Crossing the Saint Lawrence Near Montreal, 1839
Watercolour over graphite with touches of gouache on grey paper, 15.7 × 23 cm

Inscriptions
(l.c. on the mount, in graphite) ICE ROAD OVER ST.
LAURENCE NEAR MONTREAL, *1839;* (below the
previous mount, on a piece of cardboard from an
old mount, in pen and black ink, by another
hand) *Ice Road over the St Laurence near Montreal.
1839.*

Provenance
Dr. Sigmund Samuel, Toronto; gift to the Royal
Ontario Museum, Toronto, 1952.

Exhibition
Toronto 1987-1988, No. 99.

Bibliography
ALLODI 1974/1, Vol. I, No. 640; DE PENCIER *1987/
1,* cover p., 54 and 104, No. 99 (Repr.)

Collection
Royal Ontario Museum, Toronto (952.87.6)

light and colour on snow by superimposing shades of watercolours to create vibrating mauves and pinks on bluish ice.[3] In a predominantly blue-toned composition executed a few years later, William Robert Herries (Cat. 141) successfully captured the vastness of the countryside by portraying it as if frozen in time by the cold and strong winds. There is something of these two themes in *Snowshoers Crossing the Saint Lawrence Near Montreal.* Dartnell does not portray daily winter activities, such as people strolling along the streets, engaging in conversation or walking across the ice bridge between Quebec City and Lévis. Rather, he imposes himself as a skilled colourist who conveys his images

through the harmonious use of colour. The mauve shadows on the ice-covered peaks are enhanced by various shades of green that are in turn picked up by the green of the trees indicating the path across the ice. The brown and red clothing of the two snowshoers repeats the colours of the sunset. The white gouache used to highlight the masses of ice three or four times the size of the figures catches the last rays of sunlight. The snowshoers are penetrating into a hostile environment, an image reminiscent of Herries. The essence of the subject matter is concentrated in the lower third of the page, confining the observer to the narrow foreground. The diagonal line formed by the tracks in the snow,

framed by the two fir trees and blocked by the wall of ice, constantly reduces the image to this single triangle, a remarkable feat considering that Dartnell manages to condense a broad view of winter life using a minimum number of motifs.

The name George Russell Dartnell cannot be dissociated from the dramatic event that occurred when the artist left Quebec with his regiment. On October 31, 1843, Dartnell and the Royals boarded the *Premier,* bound for the British West Indies. The transport, which was carrying 350 passengers, was shipwrecked off Cap-Chat bay during the night of November 3.[4] The captain showed a good deal of confidence in allowing the pilot who was to

MQ, NGC

86.
Rescue Boat Trying To Land in Cap Chat Bay, 1843
Pen and brown ink with brown wash over graphite on paper with traces of scraping out,
12.0 × 20.0 cm

Inscription
(u.l.) *Wreck of the Premier Transport in Cape Chatte Bay - 4 No.v. 1843.*
Provenance
Descendants of the artist; private collection, Toronto.
Exhibition
Toronto 1987-1988, No. 172.
Bibliography
DE PENCIER 1987/1, pp. 82, 83 and 108, No. 172 (Repr.)
Collection
Private collection, Toronto

have guided the ship to the mouth of the St. Lawrence to disembark near Ile Verte. The weather, which had been clement thus far, rapidly deteriorated in the hours that followed. The *Premier,* thrown off course by rough seas, ran aground a few cable lengths offshore. The following is Dartnell's account of what happened when the ship's keel first hit bottom:

A heavy gale was blowing, and thick driving snow, the night intensely dark, the sea running mountain high, and bursting in floods over the decks; the ship plunged and laboured dreadfully, as if struggling like an ensnared animal to free herself, but in vain, her bottom violently striking against the ground with a most frightful and indescribable sensation, and the sails slatting, with thundering sound, against the bending masts, whilst the shrieks of the women and children mingled with the howlings of the wind.[5]

A rescue operation mounted at dawn was made perilous by the turbulent sea. Dartnell's **Rescue Boat Trying To Land in Cap Chat Bay** shows a tiny boat, half hidden behind a wave, attempting to reach a group of fishermen on shore in the hope

of organizing the rescue. Meanwhile, waves sweep across the deck of the *Premier,* dismasted and aground, compromising the passengers' survival. A rope was finally stretched between the shore and the *Premier* in order to guide the fishing boats, which freed the passengers in six hours. Within a few days, the whole regiment was taken back to Quebec City, where it had to spend the winter because it was too late in the season to attempt another crossing. Dartnell probably used the time to begin writing a new manuscript that was published in 1845: *A Brief Narrative of the Shipwreck of the Transport "Premier", Near the Mouth of the River St. Lawrence, On the 4th November, 1843, Having on Board the Head-Quarter Wing of the Second Battalion of the First or Royal Regiment, Proceeding from North America to the West Indies.*[6] The work was sponsored by a public subscription of three hundred names, including those of several well-known personalities and military figures: Captain Bayfield, Lord Charles Beauclerck, Sir Henry Caldwell, Archibald Campbell,

the Cary bookstore and publishing house of Quebec City, Lieutenant-Colonel Thomas Chaplin, Sir George Murray and Jonathan Sewell.[7]

D.P.

Notes
1. DE PENCIER 1987/1.
2. Five works were done depicting various aspects of the same phenomenon (DE PENCIER 1987/1, p. 99, No. 20-24).
3. We are referring in particular to *Entrance to the Ice from Cul de Sac,* a watercolour owned by the MSQ. (CAMERON AND TRUDEL 1976, p. 49, Repr.).
4. DE PENCIER 1987/1, pp. 81-87, and DE PENCIER 1987/2, pp. 22-24.
5. Quoted from DE PENCIER 1987/2, p.22.
6. The work was published by Jeremiah How of London, and illustrated with lithographs produced either from drawings done at the scene of the shipwreck, or from reproductions of these drawings (DE PENCIER 1987/1, p. 82).
7. The complete list of subscribers is provided in the introductory pages of the book (pp. vii-xv).

VITAL DESROCHERS was the third child of sculptor Urbain Desrochers (1781-1860). One of the earliest mentions of Desrochers as an artist can be traced back to the May 19, 1836 edition of *La Minerve,* in which Desrochers advertised himself as a portraitist who also specialized in church paintings. His studio was located near the Montreal courthouse. In fall 1836, he settled in Pointe-aux-Trembles for the winter and took out an advertisement offering home portraits. Also in 1836, he signed one of his few religious works, a Sacred Heart for the church in Saint-Eustache. In fact, several of Desrochers' works adorn the church, including an 1840 portrait of Father Jacques Paquin, one of a series of portraits of clergymen Desrochers is thought to have done based on the memories of parishioners. In 1841 and 1842, at the request of the priest in Saint-Eustache, Desrochers sculpted— he had probably learned the art from his father—a sacristy cupboard, a paschal candelabrum and altar candelabra. No subsequent record of Desrochers can be found until August 14, 1845, when he advertised in *La Minerve* (virtually the same text appeared in *L'Aurore des Canadas* on the same date) as a portraitist specialized in daguerreotype portraits and nut oil paintings. Desrochers further stated that he "had obtained one of the best achromatic devices for making daguerreotypes at the national manufacturing plant in New York" (*Translation*) and that he "had practised for a time under Plumb and Ferry, the city's two great masters." (*Translation*) In the same edition of *La Minerve,* a columnist referred to the advertisement in the following manner:

Monsieur Desrochers, a student of one of our greatest artists, Monsieur Plamondon of Quebec City, has advertised his services as an artist specialized in painted and daguerreotype portraits. Although still young, Monsieur Desrochers has already earned a reputation worthy of the master under whom he studied. We have had a look at some of his early daguerreotypes, and they do not suffer from comparison with the best of what we have seen in Montreal. (*Translation*)

Desrochers appears to have received his training as a painter from Plamondon and to have studied the art of daguerreotype in the United States around 1843-1845. Aside from a few references to Desrochers in 1845 and 1846, nothing more is known about him.

VITAL DESROCHERS

active between 1836 and 1846

Main sources
HARPER *1970;* LESSARD *1982.*

87.
Mrs. Barthélemy Joliette, née Marie-Charlotte Tarieu Taillant de Lanaudière, 1838
Oil on canvas, 72.5 × 61 cm

Inscription
(s.d., b.) *tiré par V Des Rochers, 1838.*

Provenance
Séminaire de Joliette; on deposit at the Musée d'art de Joliette, 1972.

Bibliography
CORBEIL 1971, pp. 241-242; CORBEIL 1978, pp. 69 and 97 (Repr.); LACROIX 1989/2, p. 16 (Repr.); TRÉPANIER 1989, p. 4 (Repr.).

Collection
Musée d'art de Joliette. Deposit from the Clercs de Saint-Viateur (L-72.016-P)

Fig. 87A.
Vital Desrochers,
Barthélemy Joliette, 1838;
oil on canvas, 72.5 × 61 cm.
Musée d'art de Joliette. Deposit from the Clercs de Saint-Viateur (L-72.004-P).

D ressed as a true lady of the manor, with her face framed by a delicately embroidered wimple, Madame Joliette remains the discreet provider of the village of l'Industrie. (*Translation*)

It was in these terms that the late Wilfrid Corbeil (1893-1979) once described the portrait of Marie-Charlotte Tarieu Taillant de Lanaudière done in 1838 by Vital Desrochers, an obscure itinerant artist. Daughter of the seigneur of Lavaltrie, Marie-Charlotte married Barthélemy Joliette (Fig. 87A) in September 1813. Twenty-five years later, her husband had become an important figure in the area, serving as an officer in the militia, a notary, seigneur, politician, businessman and justice of the peace. Joliette founded the village of l'Industrie, which was officially named after him in 1863.

In its edition of October 15, 1846, *Le Journal de Québec* summarized as follows the "many important services" (*Translation*) Joliette rendered to his village:

Monsieur Joliette has built a beautiful church and established an academy for boys and a convent for girls, all at his own expense. When the largest glass factory in the country opens in l'Industrie next spring, the village will certainly have earned its name. (*Translation*)

The author further wrote:

Not only does Monsieur Joliette build temples to God, but he also wants them decorated in a manner befitting a king. Commissioned by Monsieur Joliette himself, our own Monsieur Plamondon recently finished a superb painting of a high altar representing St. Charles Boromeo giving communion to victims of the plague in Milan. The work is eleven feet high and at least eight feet wide; the figures are almost life-

Fig. 87B.
Antoine Plamondon after Pierre Mignard,
*Saint Charles Borromeo giving Communion
to the Plague Victims of Milan*, 1846;
oil on canvas, approximately 335 × 244 cm.
Cathédrale de Joliette.

size. Although the composition is from Mignard, the colours were produced entirely by the brush of Monsieur Plamondon, whose skills as a colourist are well known. (Fig. 87B)

This striking work is a credit to the artist and to the man who so generously promised it to the church of l'Industrie.

Anyone wishing to see the painting will have to hurry, for in just a few days it will be taken to its intended destination. (*Translation*)

Eight years earlier, however, Joliette had commissioned a disciple of Plamondon, Vital Desrochers, to do his portrait. Today, the work hangs in the Musée d'art de Joliette, alongside the portrait of Joliette's wife, Marie-Charlotte. In comparison, however, Joliette's portrait is distinguished by its relative simplicity.

In a head-and-shoulders portrait set against a neutral background, Madame Joliette appears in all her finery. Her attire is as rich as it is studied; the many accessories bear witness to her prestigious social status and to her husband's financial success. One suspects her of a desire to impose her style on her contemporaries or to leave her mark on posterity with her overdone—bedecked as it is with ribbons, plaits and embroidery—yet fanciful coif and array of valuable jewellery (drop earrings, double-stranded necklace, broach, loop-pin and long chain with what appears to be a magnifying glass on the end). Nevertheless, such accoutrements do not succeed in softening the underlying severity of Madame Joliette's features. If the portrait is a good likeness, which is plausible, it suggests a haughty woman with little sensitivity.

It should, however, be pointed out that the man who immortalized her was clearly more comfortable in rendering meticulous decorative detail than in providing insight into psychological character. Apparent in Desrochers' painting are a number of simplistic elements such as an additive composition, a hieratic pose and a schematization of components.

The essence and treatment of Madame Barthélemy Joliette's portrait are very similar to the work of a contemporary artist such as Jean-Baptiste Roy-Audy. In fact, one could justifiably ask whether some of the many canvases attributed to the latter might not have been produced instead by the applied hand of Vital Desrochers, that other itinerant painter, who was clearly less favoured by the vagaries of destiny.

J.R.P.

ANSON DICKINSON

1779-1852

 NSON DICKINSON was born on April 19, 1779 in Milton, near Litchfield, Connecticut. Around 1790 he was apprenticed to a goldsmith named Isaac Thompson (or Thomson). Dickinson eventually abandoned the trade and, in May 1802, established himself as a miniaturist in New Haven. In 1804-1805, he settled in New York, but although this was Dickinson's base, his career took him to other cities such as Philadelphia, Montreal, Charleston, Baltimore, and Washington. During his first stay in New York, he met another American miniaturist, Edward Greene Malbone (1777-1807), who did his portrait and influenced his style.

Dickinson showed his works on several occasions. For example, he exhibited at the Pennsylvania Academy of Fine Arts in Philadelphia in 1811 and at the American Academy of Fine Arts in New York in 1816, where he showed one of his most remarkable paintings, *Cupid and the Graces*. He also had showings at the National Academy of Design in New York in 1826 and at the Boston Athenaeum Gallery in 1827-1828.

Dickinson began recording his activities from the outset of his career in September 1803. Consequently, today we know of a large number of his works and can trace his many trips over the years, including a stay in Canada between 1811 and 1825. After 1833, he appears to have settled in New Haven, although he did make a few trips in the Litchfield area and to New York state. In 1846, Dickinson returned to his birthplace, where he died on March 9, 1852, at the age of 73.

Main source
DEARBORN 1983.

MQ, NGC

88.

George Hervey, Lieutenant, First Battalion, 60th Regiment or King's Royal Rifle Corps 1822

Watercolour and gum arabic on ivory,
7.5 × 6.1 cm

Inscriptions
(b., printed business card) *A. Dickinson/ MINIATURE PAINTER/49 Chamber S[t]./New York.;* (all around the card, written in ink) *Taken Novr 1822./Montreal/at 22 years & 8 months of Age.*

Provenance
Marie de Bellefeuille, Mascouche; acquired by the Musée de la Province de Québec, Quebec City, 1957.

Exhibition
Hartford 1983, No. 42.

Bibliography
DEARBORN 1983, pp. 13, 14, 26 and 82, No. 42 (Repr.).

Collection
Musée du Québec, Quebec City (57.241)

N OT ONLY DID AMERICAN MINIATURIST Anson Dickinson produce many quality paintings,[1] he also kept numerous documents authenticating several of his works. Among other things, Dickinson kept a record of his customers in which he noted with relative accuracy the name of the item sold, the place and date of execution and, occasionally, the selling price.[2] Based on such records, his output is estimated today at more than 1500 miniatures painted in over 20 locations in North America.[3]

The first miniature in our exhibition had always been thought to represent Eustache Lambert-Dumont, an ancestor of the De Bellefeuille family, from whom the Musée du Québec acquired the work. According to archival records, however, the only Eustache Lambert-Dumont, seigneur des Mille-Isles, lived in the 18th century and could therefore not be the person in the miniature. Furthermore, because of the military uniform, the painting cannot possibly be of any member of the Lambert-Dumont family. Identification was made possible through analysis of various historical facts; for instance, the business card Dickinson used from 1822 to 1826 when he had a studio at 49 Chamber Street, in New York, appears on the back of the miniature.[4] According to an inscription, the portrait was done in Montreal in November 1822. During his two-month stay in Montreal in fall of the same year, Dickinson recorded only 11 names, including a "Mr. Harvy", who sat for him in early November.[5] The entry probably refers to George Hervey, who became a lieutenant in the 1st battalion of the 60th regiment on July 25, 1822. "Mr." was correct usage in referring to junior officers, as rank was used as a courtesy title reserved for senior officers only.[6] Analysis of the uniform worn by this particular rifle corps of the British army confirms the identification. The uniform is comprised of a dark green dolman with scarlet collar and facings; three rows of round, silver buttons; and black braids and embroidery—exactly the uniform worn by the figure in the miniature. The matter is put to rest with the postings of the regiment. The 1st battalion of the 60th regiment was garrisoned at Montreal in 1821 and 1822, before being stationed in Kingston in 1823 and called back to England in June 1824.[7] The young soldier who, according to the inscription, was close to 23 years of age at the time, perhaps befriended the Lambert-Dumont family or the Berthelet family, their relatives, and left them a souvenir of his stay in Canada.

Another, better-known soldier also took advantage of Dickinson's stay in Canada. Charles-Michel d'Irumberry de Salaberry (1778-1829) is famous for his role in the War of 1812. When hostilities escalated, he mobilized a provincial light infantry corps, the *Voltigeurs Canadiens,* at the request of Major-General Sir George Prevost. On the shores of the Châteauguay river on October 26, 1813, Salaberry, backed by 250 men from his regiment, members of the sedentary militia, the Canadian Fencibles and Amerindians, managed to turn back the American troops poised to attack Montreal. The battle promptly took on the proportions of a myth and became one of the greatest examples of bravery in French Canadian history. In 1816, Salaberry received a medal commemorating the battle of Châteauguay and, in 1817, was named a companion of the Order of Bath.[8] When Salaberry had his portrait done by Dickinson in 1824 and again in 1825, the two decorations were pinned to his *Voltigeurs Canadiens* uniform—a green dolman with black collar and facings, and three rows of black buttons joined by black braiding across the chest—styled after the rifle corps uniform of the 60th regiment. Dickinson's records show that "Col. Salaberry" sat for his portrait on September 7 and 12, 1824. The name "Col. DeSalaberry" is again entered on July 10 of the following year.[10] Two portraits must have been done. The first was apparently commissioned by Jacques Viger and would account for the two dates entered in September 1824, while the second was probably done in July 1825 for Salaberry himself or his family. It is the latter of the two works that the Château Ramezay is supposed to have acquired in 1898 at the same time as the paintings of Lieutenant-Colonel Ignace-Michel-Louis-Antoine d'Irumberry de Salaberry (1752-1828), the father of the "Hero of Châteauguay," and Julie Hertel Rouville (1788-1855), his mother. All three works are attributed to Dickinson. The miniatures apparently came from the Salaberry family, who still owned them when the Numismatic and Antiquarian Society of Montreal held its exhibition in 1887.[11]

The work commissioned by collector Jacques Viger in 1824 is well documented.[12] According to an article published in *La Bibliothèque Canadienne* in May 1826, Viger had "the portrait done in 1824 by Mr. Dickinson, an American painter, as part of his collection of portraits of Canadian and foreign men having distinguished themselves in Canada."[13] (*Translation*) Viger had intended to have Salaberry's

VAG, AGNS, MMFA

89.

Charles-Michel d'Irumberry de Salaberry, 1825

Watercolour and gum arabic on ivory, 7.9 × 6.6 cm

Provenance
Salaberry Family; acquired by subscription by Château Ramezay, Montreal, 1898.

Exhibitions
Montreal 1887, No. 298; Hartford 1983, No. 49; Montreal 1987/2, No. 68; Montreal 1989-1990.

Bibliography
CATALOGUE *1887*, p. 45, No. 298; MCR, *Registre des acquisitions 1895-1974*, p. 56, No. 1360, November 22, 1898; O'LEARY *1901*, p. 49, No. 89; O'LEARY *1903*, p. 53, No. 80; *Le Bulletin des recherches historiques*, Vol. X, No. 8 (August 1904), p. 245 (Repr.); O'LEARY *1907*, p. 49, No. 80; O'LEARY *1917*, p. 47, No. 80; O'LEARY *1920*, p. 48, No. 79; O'LEARY *1922*, p. 50, No. 79; O'LEARY *1923*, p. 48, No. 79; O'LEARY *1926*, p. 54, No. 79; CATALOGUE *1927/2*, p. 54, No. 79; CATALOGUE *1928*, p. 54, No. 79; LEYMARIE *1929*, p. 33; CATALOGUE *1931*, p. 76, No. 79; CATALOGUE *1936*, p. 78, No. 79; CATALOGUE *1937*, p. 75, No. 79; CATALOGUE *1948*, p. 78, No. 79; CATALOGUE *1954*, p. 78, No. 79; CATALOGUE *1956*, p. 78, No. 79; CARRIER *1957*, p. 130, No. 1815; MORISSET *1960/1*, p. 138; CARRIER AND LEFEBVRE *1962*, p. 141, No. 1815; DEARBORN *1983*, pp. 13, 26, 92 and 153, No. 49 (Repr.); GUITARD *1983*, p. 96 (Repr.); WOHLER *1984*, p. 128; SELECTED CATALOGUE *1985*, p. 61, No. 141 (entry by Roslyn Rosenfeld); GUITARD *1987*, p. 379; TÉMOIGNAGES *1987*, No. 68.

Collection
Musée du Château Ramezay, Montreal (CR1360)

portrait engraved by New York artist Asher Brown Durand (1796-1886). A long series of letters recorded by Viger in his *Saberdache* explains the story behind the commission and proves that the miniature in his possession is not that of the Château Ramezay. The letters are also full of details concerning the realization and dissemination of the plate (Fig. 89A). They further reveal that Viger exercised strict control over the project; in fact, he even had Dickinson supervise the impression of the engraving.[14]

In a letter dated July 27, 1825, Viger informed one of his friends, New York merchant Lewis Willcocks, that Dickinson had delivered the portrait of Lt. Col. De Salaberry for him the previous year, adding that De Salaberry and Dickinson were to leave together for New York on Thursday of the following week, and might well pay a visit to Monsieur Durand. In the same letter, Viger gave instructions regarding the content of the

engraving and its adornments. Viger draws the engraver's attention to a specific point:

I beg to call your attention particularly to one circonstance. You must observe in the Portrait, that, for waist of room, the whole of the Sabre does not appear, especially as it is on that side all in the Shade, which seems to have an awkward effect. Now, I would consider it a great improvement if you could contrive to give so much room as to let the whole Saber appear.[15]

Two things are apparent from this letter. First, Salaberry definitely met Dickinson in July 1825. Second, the miniature submitted to the engraver by Viger shows important differences—e.g. the presence of a sabre—with respect to the Château Ramezay version.

Upon receipt of the first proofs in early 1826, Viger sought the opinion of several people regarding the quality of execution and the degree of likeness.[16] The following is an excerpt from a letter from Thomas Douglas, a Quebec City government employee, dated February 26:

I paid a visit to the worthy senior De Salaberry, a letter and the proof of the engraving in hand. The letter was read in the presence of the young ladies and the Colonel of the *Voltigeurs*. Afterward, we unrolled the proof and compared it to another portrait. The good father and his children found Monsieur Durand's engraving to be a perfect likeness, although not particularly flattering. (*Translation*)

This shows that as early as 1826 the Salaberry family had another portrait of the "Hero of Châteauguay" it could use to compare the engraving. At the time, the miniature commissioned by Viger was still in New York. In fact, on May 11, 1826 Dickinson solicited permission from Viger to have the miniature on loan:

There is now opening in N. York a national academy of fine Arts for the purpose of exhibiting works of living Artists, and to exclude all others, and a spur of ambition stimulates me to enter the list as a candidate for fame.

I do therefore consider it one of the greatest favours you can restore to allow me the liberty of exhibiting the Portrait of Col. De Salaberry

Fig. 89A.
Asher Brown Durand after Anson Dickinson,
Charles-Michel d'Irrumbery de Salaberry, 1826;
engraving, 28.3 × 23 cm.
Musée du Québec, Quebec City (81.317).

with my collection, until the 4th of July, when the exhibition closes; after which it shall be delivered according to your orders.

Dickinson did indeed show the work in New York City in 1826.[17] As noted by Viger, permission was granted and the portrait "was greatly admired." (*Translation*)

Two versions of the miniature of Charles-Michel de Salaberry clearly existed. What, then, happened to the work that belonged to Viger? The Séminaire de Québec, where most of the Viger bequest is located, does not own it. Furthermore, the plate of the engraving has never been located despite a note in one of the records kept by Father Hospice-Anthelme Verreau, who purchased the fund in 1860. Whatever happened, Dickinson's work and Durand's engraving bear witness to the role played by a sponsor in propagating a historical cult through art or, in other words, in the making of a hero.[18]
P.B.

Notes

1. Dickinson's paintings exemplify the esthetic changes undergone by the miniature in the 19th century. Initially influenced by the more delicate, aerial and decorative style of his first master, Edward Greene Malbone (1777-1807), and of English miniaturists in general, Dickinson eventually began producing more densely coloured miniatures. Through increased use of gum arabic, Dickinson created impastos and textures reminiscent of oil painting. In the 1820s, he adopted the rectangular format for his miniatures, creating framed works suitable for exhibition rather than miniatures used as jewellery. See Robin Bolton-Smith's text in *DEARBORN 1983*, pp. xxii-xxviii, as well as Robin Bolton-Smith and Dale T. Johnson's article entitled "The Miniature in America" in *Antiques*, Vol. CXXXVIII, No. 5 (November 1990), pp. 1042-1055.

2. The register, known as "Workbook", is apparently still part of a private collection. It was retranscribed first in Mary Helen Kidder, *List of Miniatures painted by Anson Dickinson, 1803-1851*, Hartford, Connecticut Historical Society, 1937, then in *DEARBORN 1983*, pp. 155-168. The Litchfield Historical Society has another workbook, called "Sitter's Book", which is actually a collection of sketches containing descriptions of the artist's use of colours and his technique.

3. This information also enables the artist's itinerary to be traced. Dickinson visited Lower Canada at least five times: from September to December 1811 (Montreal), from September to December 1820 (Montreal), from July to December 1821 (Quebec City and possibly Trois-Rivières), from October to November 1822 (Montreal) and from August 1824 to July 1825 (Montreal, Quebec City and possibly Trois-Rivières). See *DEARBORN 1983*, pp. 158, 160, 161 and 162. Other works by Dickinson from his last stay in Canada are mentioned in the "Workbook" and conserved in a private collection and in a collection of the McCord Museum of Canadian History. The portrait of *Charlotte Genvevay, née Mount* (M968.92.8) is an example.

4. *DEARBORN 1983*, pp. 146-150.

5. *DEARBORN 1983*, p. 161.

6. We would like to thank René Chartrand, Head Curator at the Interpretation Branch of Environment Canada, Canadian Parks Service, in Ottawa, for providing the information that led to the identification of the figure in the miniature.

7. Nesbit Willoughby Wallace, *A Regimental Chronicle and List of Officers of the 60th, or the King's Royal Rifle Corps, formerly the 62nd, or the Royal American Regiment of Foot* (London: Harrison, 1879), pp. 25 and 52.

8. *GUITARD 1987*, pp. 375-380.

9. Jack L. Summers and René Chartrand, *L'uniforme militaire au Canada, 1665-1970* (Ottawa: National Museums of Canada, 1981), pp. 67-69.

10. *DEARBORN 1983*, p. 162.

11. This is at least what can be gathered from a handwritten note by Gérard Morisset in the catalogue belonging to the Musée du Québec. We do not know the sources of the art historian, who indicated the origin of several of the works in this exhibition (see *CATALOGUE 1887*).

12. Jacques Viger served as a captain under Salaberry and befriended his former commander.

13. "Portrait de L'Hon. Charles de Salaberry", *La Bibliothèque Canadienne*, Vol. II, No. 6 (May 1826), p. 229 (this article also appears in *BIBAUD 1891*, p. 261, and *ROY 1895*, p. 191). As early as September 22, 1824, Viger was attempting to obtain the patronage of Francis Nathaniel Burton, Lieutenant-Governor of Lower Canada, to have the portrait engraved. On that date, he already claimed "to have in his possession a faithful, well-executed portrait of Lieut. Col. Charles de Salaberry." (*Translation*) In 1824, the *Voltigeurs Canadiens* had been demobilized for more than nine years, and Salaberry was a legislative councillor. That the portrait was intended to be commemorative is confirmed by the military uniform.

14. It would be too long and tedious here to provide a complete list of the documentation pertaining to this commission. It should, however, be mentioned that the *Saberdache* (Vol. VI and, in particular, Vol. VII) contains more than 20 letters relative to the commission (two originals are located at the New York Public Library) that were transcribed by Viger himself. Such a list is expected to be the topic of a subsequent, more in-depth article.

15. Viger also made the following revealing comment about his opinion of the esthetic value of the work: "I would also beg that you would be more careful in the drapery than the Portrait-Painter has been, especially with regard to the regularity of the embroidery. The Cuffs and Collar were Velvet; the Stock around the Neck was of black silk; the scabbard of the Sword was steel." He criticized American painters, and Dickinson in particular, for the lack of finish respecting this aspect of their works. On February 25, 1826, he made the following remark to his friend Lewis Willcocks: "Everyone who saw the engravings found the treatment of the clothing to lack finesse. I fear that this cannot be corrected. It is my contention that all your artists make the mistake of worrying only about heads and neglecting the rest, which they perceive as merely accessory and not worthy of the time spent finishing the former. I have never succeeded in dissuading Dickinson from this misleading approach. He, too, did a fine job on the head but, strangely, neglected the rest." (*Translation*)

16. Charles-Michel de Salaberry himself responded on March 7, 1826, expressing the same reservations as his peers: "In answer to your questions, I have to say that people generally hold nothing back when it comes to this unfortunate nose. May I suggest that you perform a small operation on it if you do not wish to see something untoward, such as an amputation, happen to it [...] Like many others, I feel this cursed nose is a smidgen too big." (*Translation*)

17. *COWDREY 1943*, p. 123.

18. See *MARTIN 1988*.

LOUIS DULONGPRÉ

(See biographical note)
on page 149)

90.
Joseph Papineau, 1825
Oil on canvas, 76.2 × 61 cm

Provenance
Commissioned by Louis-Joseph Papineau, Montreal, 1825; Descendants of the Papineau family; Louis-Joseph Papineau, Hudson, by inheritance; acquired by the Public Archives of Canada, Ottawa, 1977.

Exhibitions
Ottawa 1986-1987, No. 2; Ottawa 1988; Montreal 1988-1989.

Bibliography
AMMCH, Box XII, "Photocopy of a letter from Louis-Joseph Papineau to his sister Rosalie", April 18, 1825; NAC, MG 24, B2, Vol. XXXIX, dossier 1, "Receipt from Louis Dulongpré to Louis-Joseph Papineau", June 24, 1825; NGC, dossier *Portrait de Joseph Papineau*, "Excerpt from *Mémoires* de L.-J.-A. Papineau", p. 13; BAZIN *1934*; SIMARD *1952*, p. 3 (Repr.); MORISSET *1960/1*, p. 68; PARIZEAU *1975*, pp. 382, 402-403 and 546-547 (Repr.); *Nos racines*, No. 44 (1979), p. 867; BARIBEAU *1988*, p. 7, No. 1; WILSON *1988*, pp. 176-177 (Repr.); DEROME, BOURASSA AND CHAGNON *1988*, pp. 5, 9, 26, 30, 32, 33, 34, 36, 44, 46, 59, 86, 91 and 93 (Repr.); KLEMPAN *1989*, pp. 18-19 (Repr.); (?) LEBLANC *1989*, p. 98 (Repr.).

Collection
National Archives of Canada,
Ottawa (1978-39-8)

O F HUMBLE DESCENT, Joseph Papineau (1752-1841) was the springboard for his family's formidable social climb. Through his determination and perseverance, he led a successful career as a surveyor, notary, politician and seigneur. During the changes in the social hierarchy in the early 19th century, Papineau represented the very incarnation of a certain ambivalence in the bourgeoisie. On the political scene, he earned a reputation as a moderate liberal, whereas in the socioeconomic sphere he exhibited aristocratic and noble aspirations. At the time of his death he owned a collection of more than 200 volumes which included, in addition to French and English law books, the books which were at the source of his sociopolitical beliefs: the theoreticians of English parliamentary government and the French philosophers of the 18th century.

In his portrait, Joseph Papineau is seated in front of a bookcase which is partially hidden by a heavy curtain. His elbow resting on his work table, on which an inkwell and two quills are placed, Papineau poses in a relaxed manner.

It was in 1825 that Louis Dulongpré received the commission for four portraits of Joseph Papineau from the latter's son, the famous tribune, Louis-Joseph Papineau (Cat. 188 and 248). Louis-Joseph related the circumstances surrounding the transaction in a letter addressed to his sister, Rosalie, on April 18, 1825:

Just a short note to say that I will have the pleasure, when I see you next, of making you a present of something you will like very much—the portrait of our beloved father. Mr. Dulongpré came to see him a couple of times on the pretext of talking business, but in actual fact to study his features. He did a good job—I ordered four copies. Having had my dear father and the family and several guests to dine with me yesterday, only one of the paintings was advanced enough to have it brought in after the dinner. Ls. and Jacques Viger, who also wish to have his portrait, had papa and Mr. Dulongpré over to dinner, and he successfully produced many studies. (*Translation*)

Louis-Joseph-Amédée Papineau, son of the aforementioned and grandson of the subject of the portraits, also relates the same events in great detail in his unpublished *Mémoires:*

He (Louis Dulongpré) often went to Grandpapa's to play chess or backgammon. No sooner was the game over than the painter ran off to his studio to work with his palette. After several days like this, he brought the painting to my father's house. Everyone was delighted with it. The likeness was perfect. As soon as it had been framed, Father invited to dinner the closest family and friends. The meal was very cheerful, and after the desert Jacques Viger struck up an appropriate song—a prelude to the scene that was about to follow. We all left the table, and Grandfather was the first to go into the salon, my mother on his arm. Directly opposite the front door his portrait stared back at him! He was greatly astonished, and the company burst into shrieks of joy and admiration in order to nip in the bud any contrariety that Grandfather might show and to force him

Fig. 90A.
Katherine Jane Ellice,
Joseph Papineau, 1838;
watercolour over graphite on paper,
21 × 16.7 cm.
National Archives of Canada,
Ottawa (C-13387).

to laugh along with the rest of us. Dulongpré must have been quite satisfied with his work and with the compliments it brought him. (*Translation*)

Another document provides conclusive evidence of this: the receipt signed by the artist and dated June 24, 1825, acknowledging payment of the four versions of the portrait—for which Louis-Joseph Papineau paid out £30 two and a half months after the presentation of the first version to his father.

It seems that the original of the portrait is the version shown here. It comes from direct descendants of the Papineau family, and both visual and radiographic analysis reveal that it has been touched up many times, particularly around the face, thus supporting the hypothesis of a first production carried out over several days and tied to the constraints of the contract. A second replica belonging to the National Gallery of Canada demonstrates a quicker and less careful execution. This canvas comes from the descendants of Jean Dessaulles, a nobleman from Saint-Hyacinthe, and his wife, Rosalie Papineau. In his letter, Louis-Joseph promised his sister a portrait of their father and he no doubt gave her one of the three copies done by the artist. Napoléon Bourassa also produced a copy of the portrait for his father-in-law, but it could not possibly be one of the Ottawa versions.[1] Furthermore, Dulongpré supplemented his commission with an assortment of portraits of Papineau's

spouse, Rosalie Cherrier. These portraits reveal the artist's style, but the differences in execution and dimensions prove that they were not produced at the same time as those of Papineau.

The story goes on as concerns the portrait of Papineau. The version belonging to the Dessaulles family came very close to being attacked! Recalling certain events that took place during the 1837-1838 uprising, Louis-Joseph-Amédée relates the sorry feats—robbery, vandalism and intimidation—of Dr. Daniel Arnoldi junior with regard to members of his family:

It was the same villain who, catching sight of the portrait of Grandpapa at St-Hyacinthe, threatened it with his sabre while expressing the desire to cut off not only Grandpapa's head, but Papa's as well.[2] (*Translation*)

The version belonging to the Papineau family seems to have met with the same fate as the exiles, following Louis-Joseph to France from 1839 to 1845. The father died in 1841, and this ultimate separation, intensified as it was by his situation as an exile, caused Louis-Joseph a great deal of grief. It is consequently with bitterness that he expressed his affliction to his cousin, Louis-Michel Viger, while contemplating the portrait of the venerable patriarch:

How many heartbreaks have I suffered here in this so very painful exile, alone, below the portrait of my dear father hanging over my desk![3] (*Translation*)

The vast amount of information concerning this commission is exceptional in Quebec art history. Nonetheless, this portrait raises other questions which we should touch on. Amongst other things, the composition of the painting takes up pictorial conventions which, other than in the portrait of Thomas McCord (1816, MMCH),[4] Dulongpré rarely used. The bookcase, with its large volumes and registers, and the inkwell are obvious allusions to Joseph Papineau's offices but also recall the more general concept of learning, the privilege of the educated. Prior to 1810, Dulongpré appears not to have used this method of classifying his subject, choosing, instead, to focus on a few isolated elements (a book, a flower, a cane, etc.) to give his model more individuality. Here, he renders his portrait official, as it were, by depicting not a familiar object, but a decor which identifies the individual with his offices and his social status. It is possible that Dulongpré adopted this tradition through contact with portraits of dignitaries in Lower Canada, which were complying increasingly with this norm. In his treatment of the figure, on the other hand, Dulongpré remained true to character, concentrating on textural and spatial effects. The same is true for the subtle treatment of the blacks of the waistcoat and the reddish ochres of the drapery. The play of shadows and the relief of the jabot, the shirt and the hands are particularly well executed. The face, on the other hand, with its deep lines and flagging jowls, is detrimental to a just appreciation of the work. Probably genuinely portraying his model's unflattering physical appearance (Fig. 90A), this portrait is nonetheless a good example of the last works of portraiture by Dulongpré, then aged 66.

P.B.

Notes

1. *BOURASSA 1968*, p.15
2. NAC, MG 24, B2, Vol. XXIV, Papineau family collection, Louis-Joseph-Amédée Papineau, *Mon pèlerinage au Canada en 1840*, 35 pages of Vol. IV of the *Journal d'un Fils de la Liberté réfugié aux États-Unis par suite de l'Insurrection canadienne de 1837* with separate pagination, p. 22.
3. Letter from Louis-Joseph Papineau to Louis-Michel Viger, Paris, August 22, 1841, quoted by his son Louis-Joseph-Amédée Papineau in *Journal d'un Fils de la Liberté...*, Vol. IV, p. 757.
4. *DEROME, BOURASSA AND CHAGNON 1988*, p. 20 (Repr.).

JAMES D.
DUNCAN

1806-1881

BORN IN COLERAINE (Northern Ireland) in 1806, James D. Duncan emigrated to Lower Canada in the summer of 1830. Upon settling in Montreal, he began a career as an artist and drawing master. He experimented with different techniques—pen-and-ink and pencil drawings, oil painting and even lithography—but was especially renowned for his watercolours of cityscapes and scenes of city life.

Among his first commissions were those from Jacques Viger. The albums compiled by the latter contain several of Duncan's works: some views of Montreal, scenes of an historical nature, such as *First Encounter with the Illinois, Montreal in 1693*, as well as a series of portraits of prominent figures in Canadian history. Duncan also produced for Viger an album of the habits worn by Canadian nuns. The known works that can be attributed with certainty to his career as a painter are still few. Several of his compositions were published in the form of engravings or lithographs. In 1839, Duncan had numerous scenes of Montreal engraved for Newton Bosworth's book *Hochelaga Depicta: The Early and Present State of the City and Island of Montreal*. Six other views of the city, which he himself lithographed, were printed by George Matthews around 1850. He also contributed illustrations to the *Illustrated London News* and the *Canadian Illustrated News* on several occasions.

Besides teaching in various establishments in Montreal, Duncan showed his work in many exhibitions. He participated in the foundation of the Montreal Society of Artists and exhibited with Cornelius Krieghoff, Andrew Morris, Martin Somerville and William Sawyer. In 1867, he helped found the Society of Canadian Artists, where he exhibited from 1867 to 1872. He presented his works at provincial exhibitions held in Montreal between 1863 and 1865, at the Art Association of Montreal from 1865 to 1879, and at the Royal Canadian Academy of Arts in 1881, as an associate member. James Duncan died in Montreal on September 28, 1881.

Main sources
TODD 1982; COOKE 1983; OKO 1984.

Provenance
William D. Lighthall, before 1937; McCord Museum, Montreal, before 1966.

Exhibitions
Vancouver 1966, No. 33; Montreal 1967/1, No. 7; Montreal 1967/2.

Bibliography
La Minerve, Vol. v, No. 6 (March 3, 1831), p. 3; AMMCH, W.D. Lighthal, Donations, etc. 1913-1942, file 9, "Letter from William D. Lighthall to Eric Brown, Director of the National Gallery of Canada", November 2, 1937, "Letter from Eric Brown to W. D. Lighthall", November 2, 1937, "Letter from Eric Brown to W. D. Lighthall", November 29, 1937; *Shadbolt 1966,* No. 33; *Carter 1967,* No. 308 (Repr.); *Harper 1979,* p. 58; *Todd 1982,* p. 313; *Webster 1984,* p. 46, No. 7 (Repr.)

Collection
McCord Museum of Canadian History, Montreal (M966.61)

91.
Montreal From the Mountain, 1830-1831
Oil on canvas mounted on plywood, 150.5 × 241.9 cm

J AMES DUNCAN had a predilection for panoramic views of Montreal as seen from the slopes of Mount Royal. The version belonging to the McCord Museum, ***Montreal From the Mountain,*** is not only the most impressive but also the oldest in the series. In fact, the recent discovery of a paragraph which appeared in the newspaper *La Minerve* on March 3, 1831, put to rest any doubts surrounding the work's attribution and dating. The canvas was exhibited at the Montreal Law Courts:

On display this week, free of charge, in the lawyers' chamber, at the City Law Courts, a painting of some 8 feet by 5 feet, depicting the view of Montreal as seen from the foot of the mountain. It is a polished work which gives a very favourable impression of the artist, Mr. DUNCAN, who arrived from Ireland last summer. He invites members of the public to go and judge his work for themselves.[1] (*Translation*)

Of all the known views of Montreal, the version belonging to the McCord is the only one which matches the dimensions indicated by the journalist. It is an ambitious work, as much in its size as in the quality of the topographical view that it offers. Notre-Dame de Montréal church can be recognized immediately, even without its two frontal towers, which were not completed until 1841 and 1843 respectively. The slender steeple rising to its right recalls the presence of "La Paroisse," the first Notre-Dame church built in the 17th century. It is an element which

dominated the panorama of Montreal from the mountain for about fifteen years, since the church was not demolished until 1843. The spire of the Anglican Christ Church stands out left of Notre-Dame. By producing this canvas and exposing it to the judgement of Montrealers, James Duncan no doubt wanted to show his skill. For an artist who had only arrived the previous summer, the wish to drum up some business must have also played a part in his initiative.

We should take a moment to consider the date at which Duncan arrived in Canada, since a great deal of uncertainty prevails in the matter. Although there is generally a consensus that Duncan was present in Montreal in 1830—a fact that is notably confirmed by the advertisements which appeared in the newspapers—the exact moment of his arrival varies between 1825, 1827 and 1830, depending on the author. Nonetheless, the oldest documents, such as that of Robert Campbell in 1887, are categorical: "He (Duncan) became a citizen of Montreal in 1830, and immediately began the practice of his profession, as an artist and teacher of drawing."[2] According to the sources known to us, it seems to have been Francis St. George Spendlove who, in 1958, introduced the first deviation from this chronology: "came to Canada about 1825, settling in Montreal, where he became a professional artist and lithographer as well as a teacher of art."[3] This information was taken up again by John Russell Harper in 1962, still with-

out any evidence, to our knowledge, to back it up: "coming to Canada in 1825 and settling in Montreal 1827 where he spent the balance of his life."[4] In her master's thesis on the artist submitted to Concordia University in 1978, Patricia Ann Todd upheld certain of Harper's claims, also situating Duncan's arrival in Canada in 1825, but maintaining that he settled in Montreal in 1830.[5] All of this gives rise to a great deal of confusion, particularly if we add the painting *Montreal From the Mountain* (Cat. 238) which bears the artist's signature and was produced before 1830. Until such time as a serious study of the artist is carried out, we must base our comments on those elements which are beyond doubt. The mention made in the newspaper *La Minerve* seems to us to be one such element. If the journalist maintains that Duncan arrived from Ireland in the summer of 1830, nothing at present allows us to doubt his assertion as it probably comes from the artist himself. To refute it would require unearthing new documents and demonstrating, proof in hand, that Duncan had made a previous trip to Montreal.[6]

Given the above, ***Montreal From the Mountain*** is particularly important. Correctly dated, this large canvas provides a sure point of reference for reconstructing Duncan's first years in North America. Its composition and the assurance of its treatment tell us that it is the work of an already mature artist. In this painting, Duncan skilfully capitalizes on the move

MQ, NGC

92.
Montreal Viewed from the East Side of Mount Royal, 1860-1862

Watercolour over graphite on paper, 41.1 × 63.5 cm

Inscription
(s., l.r.) *J Duncan.*

Provenance
J. Wolferston Thomas; acquired by the Château Ramezay, Montreal, before 1917.

Exhibitions
(?) Montreal 1879, No. 345; Montreal 1987/2, No. 86.

Bibliography
(?) CATALOGUE *1879,* No. 345; (?) *Canadian Illustrated News,* May 31,1879, p. 339; O'LEARY *1917,* p. 88, No. 26; O'LEARY *1920,* p. 90, No. 26; O'LEARY *1922,* p. 96, No. 26; O'LEARY *1923,* p. 90, No. 26; O'LEARY *1926,* p. 101, No. 26; CATALOGUE *1927/2,* p. 101, No. 26; CATALOGUE *1928,* p. 101, No. 26; CATALOGUE *1931,* p. 97, No. 26; CATALOGUE *1936,* p. 88, No. 26; CATALOGUE *1937,* p. 85, No. 26; (?) MORISSET *1941/3,* p. 898; CATALOGUE *1948,* p. 87, No. 26; CATALOGUE *1954,* p. 87, No. 26; CATALOGUE *1956,* p. 87, No. 26; CARRIER *1957,* p. 77, No. 758; BAZIN *1959,* p. 29; (?) MORISSET *1960/1,* p. 150; CARRIER AND LEFEBVRE *1962,* p. 83, No. 758; TODD *1978,* p. 177; SELECTED CATALOGUE *1985,* p. 14, No. 23 (entry by Patricia A. Todd); *TÉMOIGNAGES 1987,* No. 86.

Collection
Musée du Château Ramezay, Montreal (CRX 987.1)

into the distance to create an impression of vastness. The imposing dark triangle of the slope of the mountain, in the foreground, sets the scale and enables the development of a panoramic view made up of a succession of horizontal parallel planes which, in order to create greater dynamism, are intercepted in the middle ground by a succession of diagonal lines formed by the enclosures of the fields. In the foreground, two large trees frame the scene and their curved branches direct one's gaze towards the animals and the group of farmers in the full light. The alternation of light and dark areas shapes the passages and leads the eye towards the city. Duncan skilfully handles the transition between the barrier of the forest on the one hand, and the urban centre on the other, by using a pictorial device: a tree, which has one broken branch and another which curves towards Notre-Dame church, serving to link the parts. Some may find the device rather crude. It seems to us, however, that the delicate problem of the imposing wooded area, which forms part of the topography of the scene, is thereby resolved by means of a visual dialogue between the two levels of the picture. All of this corroborates the opinion expressed by the journalist from *La Minerve* when he spoke of a "polished work."

This view of Montreal, correctly dated 1830-1831, also becomes one of the privileged records of the development of the city at a time when visual documents were rare. The Montreal of 1830 is no longer the Montreal of James Peachey (Cat. 43). The city has broken out of its walls and spilled freely into the surrounding countryside. However, as pointed out

in the work of Jean-Claude Robert,[7] the distinction between the city and the suburbs is deeply rooted in the mind of the viewer. Thus, in drafting a lengthy description of the old city along Rue Notre-Dame and Rue St-Paul, Joseph Bouchette, in 1832, ended his text by clearly portraying the mountain as an external entity:

The environs of Montreal exhibit as rich, as fertile, and as finely diversified a country as can well be imagined. At the distance of a mile and a half from the town [...] is a very picturesque height, whose most elevated point at the furthest extremity is about 550 feet above the level of the river [...] The summit, to which there is a good road of every easy ascent, commands a grand and most magnificent prospect, including every variety that can embellish a landscape [...] The space near the town, and all round the lower part of the mountain is chiefly occupied by orchards and garden-grounds; the latter producing vegetables of every description, and excellent in quality, affording a profuse supply for the consumption of the city.[8]

The incontestable merit of the large canvas belonging to the McCord Museum is that it situates Duncan's work at a precise point in time. By way of contrast, and for the purpose of demonstrating the permanence of such a manner of viewing things, we can now compare this landscape with a watercolour which, though dealing with the same subject, is clearly from a later period. The Château Ramezay's **Montreal Viewed From the East Side of Mount Royal,** produced around 1860-1862, adopts the same division of space: the first ridge of the mountain, brought into the foreground as a triangle of land, situates the viewer in front of the spectacle of the city which lies down below. In a

good number of his works, Duncan seemed to rely similarly on techniques learned and mastered in his youth. Although his style certainly evolved toward a greater sensitivity—to the point of achieving true brilliance in the use of colourful rhymes, as in the case of *Saint Paul's Bay* (Cat. 99)—, a good many compositions show very little innovation. Apart from the presence of the new building of the Hôtel-Dieu—occupied at the beginning of the 1860s[9]—which can be seen in the foreground of **Montreal Viewed From the East Side of Mount Royal,** the watercolour can be viewed as a continuation of the large McCord canvas. This long echoing of the rules of topographic portrayal, developed in accordance with composition techniques that were established in the 1830s, is one of the aspects of Duncan's work which makes its analysis extremely complicated.
D.P.

Notes
1. *La Minerve,* March 3, 1831, p.3
2. Robert Campbell, *A History of the Scotch Presbyterian Church, St. Gabriel Street, Montreal* (Montreal: W. Drysdale, 1887), p. 630.
3. SPENDLOVE *1958,* p.65
4. HARPER *1962/1,* p.44
5. TODD *1978,* pp. 11-12
6. Even though Patricia Ann Todd mentions that the parish archives, compiled in Dublin in the early 1900s, were lost in fires around 1920 and 1930 (*Ibid.,* p. 10), it seems to us that research in Ireland, using different sources, would be necessary to provide additional information.
7. Jean-Claude Robert, *Montreal 1821-1871: Aspects de l'urbanisation,* doctoral thesis submitted to the École des Hautes Études en Sciences Sociales, Paris, March 1977.
8. BOUCHETTE *1832,* pp. 230-231.
9. LAHAISE *1980,* pp. 98-102.

MQ, NGC

93.

The Old Market, Montreal, c. 1840-1845

Watercolour over graphite highlighted with gouache on paper,
23.5 × 33.5 cm

Inscriptions
(l.c., in graphite) *Old Market, Montreal;* (u.r., on a sign, above the door)
Police Station A.

Provenance
Maggs Bros.; acquired by the Royal Ontario Museum, Toronto, 1951.

Bibliography
HARPER 1952, p. 164 (Repr.) attr. to Cornelius Krieghoff; *ALLODI 1974/1*,
Vol. I, No. 702; *TODD 1978*, pp. 29 and 105.

Collection
Royal Ontario Museum, Toronto (951.158.12)

MQ, NGC

94.

The Quebec Tandem Club, Champ de Mars, Montreal, after 1847

Watercolour over charcoal highlighted with gouache and gum
arabic on paper, 31.6 × 47.1 cm

Inscriptions
(s., l.l, in graphite) *J. Duncan;* (typed label, mounted on the back of the
base) FROM THE COLLECTION OF GENERAL *L.G. PHILLIPS./*GRENADIER
GUARDS...WHO WAS STATIONED/IN CANADA ABOUT *1840.*

Provenance
Acquired by the Royal Ontario Museum, Toronto, 1951.

Exhibitions
(?) Montreal 1870, No. 49; Banff 1988, No. 21.

Bibliography
(?) *CATALOGUE 1870*, No. 49; *ALLODI 1974/1*, Vol. I, No. 678 (Repr.); *ALLODI
1974/2*, cover p. and title p. (Repr.); *TODD 1978*, pp. ii, 31-32, 162, 224
and 224a (Repr.); *CAUFIELD 1987*, p. 191 (Repr.); *CLAVELL AND REID 1988*,
pp. 8 and 21 (Repr.)

Collection
Royal Ontario Museum, Toronto (953.186.1)

J AMES DUNCAN was a faithful observer of Montreal life in the mid-19th century. The marketplace, for example, was one of his favourite places for sketching picturesque scenes. The old market in Montreal was located between Rue Notre-Dame and Rue St-Paul in line with the Nelson monument. Before the construction of Bonsecours market in 1848, it played a very active role in the retail business, as attested to by Joseph Bouchette:

In the middle of it are ranges of stalls for butchers, covered in by a roof supported on wooden pillars: great care is taken to enforce the regulations to ensure cleanliness. On the two principal market-days in each week, the market is well supplied with every necessary, and nearly every luxury for the table, in great abundance, at prices extremely moderate. The produce of the upper part of this fertile district is almost wholly brought hither for sale, besides a great quantity from the American states,

particularly during the winter, when fish frequently comes from Boston and the adjacent parts.[1]

The watercolour *The Old Market, Montreal* comes from a sketchbook, today taken apart, that was originally composed of thirty-six studies in watercolour,[2] all dealing with the city of Montreal or its surroundings—such as the scenes of Indian camps. Based on research done by Mary Allodi and re-used by Patricia Ann Todd, we have retained the dates 1840-1845 for its production, that is to say the dates corresponding to the dress depicted. James Duncan used these drawings as sources of inspiration for subsequent versions, some of which can be found in a book of drawings kept in a private London collection[3] and which, going by the date of certain works, dates from approximately 1847. It is also likely that Duncan gave certain sheets to his students to copy, as

attested by a drawing of Amelia Frederica Dyneley.[4] The watercolour shown here nonetheless falls midway between the studies of isolated groups and the more ambitious compositions like the parades on Rue Notre-Dame.[5] The buildings in the background serve as a backdrop to the scene. They are treated in neutral hues so that the tones of the clothing of the groups portrayed appears even more brilliant. Duncan was above all a skilful drawer. By repeating the same stroke, a style which lends greater dynamism to the interaction of the figures, he constructed the form in motion. In contrast are the figures of James Pattison Cockburn (Cat. 72), drawn individually and scattered throughout the picture so as to inject life into the architecture.

The Quebec Tandem Club, Champ de Mars, Montreal is quite different from the market scene, in terms of both the social groups depicted and the treatment.

VAG, AGNS, MMFA

Fig. 95A.
Alexander Henderson,
*Back View of
"St. Antoine Hall",
Montreal;*
photograph.
Notman photographic
archives.. McCord
Museum of Canadian
History, Montreal
(MP010 [26]).

95.
"Saint-Antoine Hall", Montreal, 1850
Watercolour, gouache, pen and black ink over graphite on paper,
48.8 × 68.5 cm

Inscription
(s.d., l.l. brown wash) *J. Duncan/Montreal./1850.*
Watermark
J. Whatman, Turkey Mill 1848.
Provenance
Laing Galleries, Toronto; acquired by the Royal
Ontario Museum, Toronto, 1957.
Exhibition
Toronto 1981.
Bibliography
ALLODI 1974/1, Vol. I, No. 679 (Repr.); *TODD
1978,* p. 160; *HOUSE PORTRAITS 1981,* p. 54 (Repr.)
Collection
Royal Ontario Museum, Toronto (957.17.1)

The battleground was located to the north
of Rue Notre-Dame, opposite the marketplace. As its name indicates, it was
originally the site of military exercises. But,
its location being inappropriate, it was
quickly put to other uses:

The Champ de Mars, from being originally
very circumscribed, and quite inadequate as a
place of military exercise, has been made level,
and carried on nearly to the canal, forming a
space 227 yards by 114. It is now an excellent
parade as well as an agreeable promenade for
the inhabitants: seats are fixed for the accommodation of the public, and trees planted in
various part of it. From this spot there is a fine
view of the well cultivated grounds, beautiful
orchards, and country houses towards the
mountain.[6]

*The Quebec Tandem Club, Champ
de Mars, Montreal* has often been dated
circa 1840, in accordance with the inscription on the back. However, when Duncan
depicted the profile of Montreal from the
Champ de Mars, the panorama had

changed considerably. The presence of St.
Patrick's church, in particular, pushes the
date of this drawing back to after 1847.
The drawing is more controlled than *The
Old Market, Montreal,* especially in regard
to the essential forms: the sleds and the
human figures. The colour, too, is more
attentive to the play of textures. The furs
are done with small tight stokes on light
washes. Although the work received harsh
treatment over the years, the play of light
on the snow, which blends the grey-mauve
shadows with the brown tracks of the
runners, is still evident. In this watercolour,
Duncan succeeds in rendering a keen observation of the effects of light on a cold,
sunny day.

"Saint-Antoine Hall", Montreal
can be qualified as a unique piece in Duncan's work. Its owner, John Torrance, was
a merchant and an entrepreneur specializing in the grocery trade and in the tea
business,[7] importing tea from China and
India with no middlemen. The house that
Duncan drew in 1850 was built in two
stages on Rue Saint-Antoine.[8] The central
part dates from 1823, whereas the two
wings, in keeping with the Palladian neo-
classicism of the original building, were
added by John Ostell in 1839. Duncan
reproduced "Saint-Antoine Hall" very
faithfully. Comparison with Alexander
Henderson's photo (Fig. 95A) reveals that
he took no liberties whatsoever. His perspective, however, gave a wider view of
the surroundings of the house, and thus
showed off John Torrance's passion for
horticulture:

Gardening was Torrance's favourite pastime,
and, in 1849, he was active in the creation of
the Société d'horticulture de Montréal. He lived
on Rue Saint-Antoine, which was very elegant
at the time, in a 42-room house, on a property
renowned for its enormous gardens, its green-
houses for flowers and vines, and its orchards.[9]

D.P.

Notes

1. *BOUCHETTE 1832,* p. 229
2. *ALLODI 1974/1,* Vol. I, No. 691 to 726. See
also *TODD 1978,* pp. 97-118. This album had already been attributed to Cornelius Krieghoff in
HARPER 1952. Harper, however, corrected his attribution in his monograph on Krieghoff, while
briefly explaining the hoax to which he had fallen
victim (*HARPER 1979,* p. 178). However, all links
between Krieghoff and Duncan need to be studied.
3. This book is commonly called the "Redford
Sketchbook" after the name of its previous owner
who put it up for sale at Sotheby's in Toronto,
May 28, 1968 (*TODD 1978,* pp. 119-134).
4. She copied *Scène de marché à Montréal:
quartiers de moutons gelés* (NAC, 1970-188-2185)
from one of Duncan's watercolours belonging to
the ROM.
5. *ALLODI 1974/1,* Vol. I, No. 713 (Repr.), *St.
Patrick's Society Parade* and No. 714 (Repr.), *St.
Andrew's Society Parade.*
6. *BOUCHETTE 1832,* p. 229.
7. Frederick H. Armstrong, DCB, Vol. IX (1977).
8. Nathalie Clerk, *Le style palladien dans
l'architecture au Canada* (Ottawa: Parks Canada,
1984), p. 116, and Ellen James, *John Ostell, Architecte, Arpenteur* (Cat.) (Montreal: McCord
Museum, 1985), pp. 20, 22 and 109.
9. Frederick H. Armstrong, *Op. cit.*

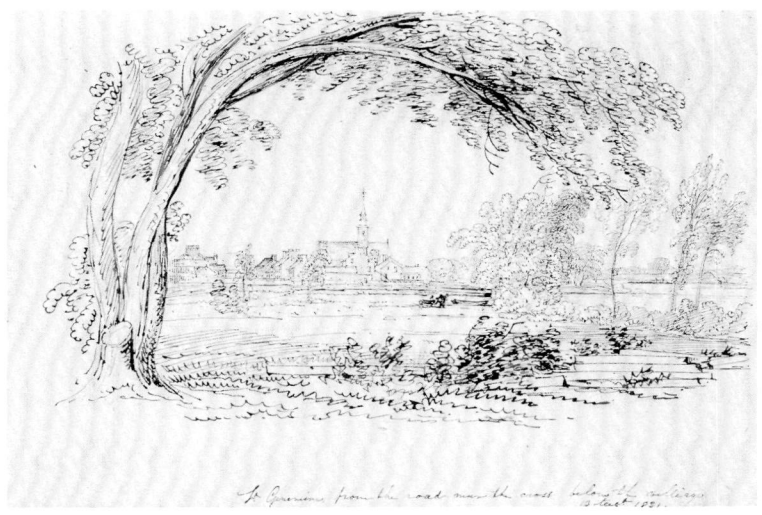

VAG, AGNS, MMFA

96.
Sainte-Geneviève, 1831
Pen and brown ink over graphite on paper, 25.4 × 37.8 cm

MQ, NGC

97.
Bout de l'Île From the Bridge above
Rivière des Prairies, 1831
Pen and brown ink over graphite on paper, 25.8 × 37.5 cm

Inscription
(l.c., in pen and brown ink, in the artist's hand) *S*. *Genevieve, from the road near the cross below the village/13 Aug*. *1831.*

Provenance
(?) Commissioned by Samuel McCord, 1831; David Ross McCord, Montreal; McCord Museum, Montreal.

Exhibition
Montreal 1962-1963, No. 90.

Bibliography
HARPER *1962/1*, p. 64, No. 90; TODD *1978*, p. 135.

Collection
McCord Museum of Canadian History, Montreal (M688)

Inscription
(l.c., in pen and brown ink, in the artist's hand) *Bout de Lisle from the Bridge above the/riviere des Prairies - Breakfast 14 Aug*. *31.*

Provenance
(?) Commissioned by Samuel McCord, 1831; David Ross McCord, Montreal; McCord Museum, Montreal.

Collection
McCord Museum of Canadian History, Montreal (M690)

I N THE SUMMER OF 1831, James Duncan made a short trip to the western extremity of the island of Montreal, visiting Sault-au-Récollet, Sainte-Geneviève, Fort Senneville, Rivière des Prairies and the tip of the island (Cat. 96 and 97). The sketches that he made in his sketchbook are today among his first known drawings. The technique used— quill and brown ink—is worth noting as it may well constitute one of the rare possible links with the artist's formative years in Europe. Perhaps Duncan was familiar with some of the landscapes of Rembrandt (1606-1669) and used the same facture.[1] The stroke which nervously alters the foreground of *Sainte-Geneviève* or which marks the bank in *Bout de l'Ile From the Bridge Above Rivière-des-Prairies* may well have been inspired by a study of the famous painter's works. Similarly, note the manner of working the trees as wholes, their leafy masses being rounded at the

ends. The use of the quill and brown ink as a method of open-air drawing may have been taught to Duncan from Dutch models.

In the two landscapes presented here, the drawing concisely captures the essence of the site while preserving the lighting intensities. *Sainte-Geneviève* is a perfect illustration. Duncan shows us the houses in the village grouped around the church which, built between 1749 and 1752, was replaced by a new building in 1836.[2] The drawing is an important record of an 18th-century building, characterized by the steeple situated at the transept crossing. Its composition is nevertheless not dictated by a concern for the topography. The large tree, which leans all the way across the foreground, embraces the village like a treasured possession.[3]

Duncan quickly abandoned the quill in favour of watercolours for open-air drawing. *Saint-Clément de Beauharnois*

had the same purpose as the drawings from the summer of 1831, that is, to produce a precise record of well-known beauty spots. Furthermore, it is not impossible that this watercolour was commissioned by Jacques Viger, since the registers kept in the historical archives of the Musée du Séminaire du Québec[4] confirm that it belonged to his collection. Duncan chose a perspective set back beyond the river and the waterfall in order to situate the church in its surroundings. This new church was completed in 1845, and the old one, seen to the left of it, was converted into a college in 1847.[5] Using a limited range of colours— essentially blues, greens and light browns— , Duncan captured the essence of what he saw.

Saint Paul's Bay shows Duncan's talent as a colourist. This superb work is among his greatest successes. In it, Duncan meticulously renders the atmospheric effects and the play of light on the waters

MQ, NGC

VAG, AGNS, MMFA

98.

Saint-Clément de Beauharnois, c. 1845

Watercolour over graphite with traces of scraping out on paper, 13.4 × 18 cm (image); 18.3 × 23.9 cm (sheet)

Inscriptions
(l.c., in graphite) *S. Clement de Beauharnois;* (u.r., in ink) *e.*

Provenance
Jacques Viger, Montreal; damsels Lennox, 1858; acquired by Abbé Hospice-Anthelme Verreau, Quebec City, 1860; bequeathed to the Séminaire de Québec, 1901; on deposit at the Société du Musée du Séminaire de Québec, 1983.

Bibliography
TODD *1978*, p. 150.

Collection
Musée du Séminaire de Québec (Pf 985.37)

99.

Saint Paul's Bay, c. 1854

Watercolour over graphite highlighted with gouache on paper, 32.5 × 48.5 cm

Inscription
(s., l.l., over-written in pen and brown ink over graphite) *J. Duncan.*

Provenance
Acquired by the Royal Ontario Museum, Toronto, before 1960.

Exhibition
Montreal 1981-1982, No. 7.

Bibliography
ALLODI *1974/1*, Vol. I, No. 673 (Repr.); TODD *1978*, p. 170; BAKER *1981*, pp. 17 and 108 (Repr.).

Collection
Royal Ontario Museum, Toronto (960x276.85)

of the bay. The coloured passages blend, while playing with the grain of the paper, thus giving the effect of pastel work. The light hatchings in white gouache, on the tips of the waves and on the houses of Baie-Saint-Paul in the distance, heighten the overall effect. And Duncan once again uses very few colours: blues, greens and yellows. The spectrum of shades, from the foreground toward the peaks of the mountains, is nonetheless remarkable. The bright hues in the foreground are taken up again even brighter in the forest on the left. The two wooded triangles, in the middle distance, are separated by waters of a deep blue. This dark band accentuates the village and the foothills in full light against the almost mauve decor of the mountainous barrier which frames the composition. A date as early as the 1840s is therefore difficult to accept. Patricia Ann

Todd dated this landscape around 1854 and Victoria Baker did likewise, taking it for granted that it was painted during Duncan's first trip to Baie-Saint-Paul.[6] For lack of harder evidence regarding Duncan's works, we will go along with this date. However, we should recall that he exhibited views of La Malbaie and Baie-Saint-Paul in 1868 and 1881.[7] Should then this watercolour be situated at such a late date? Only an in-depth analysis of Duncan's stylistic evolution will enable us to come up with some clearer answers.

D.P.

Notes

1. Frederik J. Duparc, *Le paysage en perspective. Dessins de Rembrandt et de ses contemporains* (Cat.) (Montreal: Montreal Museum of Fine Art, 1988), pp. 180 and 182, No. 72 and 74 (Repr.).

2. NOPPEN *1977*, p. 156

3. Duncan made a watercolour reproduction of this drawing for Jacques Viger's album (plate 216).

4. It is one of a set of three watercolours which depict village churches. *Alongside Saint-Clément de Beauharnois,* one should place *Châteauguay* (908) and *Saint-Timothée* (909).

5. Yvon Julien, *Le patrimoine architectural et historique de Beauharnois* (Beauharnois, Québec: Y. Julien, 1984), pp. 13 and 19.

6. Victoria Baker refers to Patricia Ann Todd's text, which does not mention a 1854 visit.

7. *Murray Bay* (No. 31) and *The Village of Murray Bay* (No. 35) were exhibited at the Society of Canadian Artists in 1868 (quoted from TODD *1978*, p. 211) and *Bay St. Paul, below Quebec* (No. 73) was shown at the Canadian Academy of Arts in 1881.

AUGUSTIN ÉDOUART was born Augustin Amant Constant Fidèle Édouart in Dunkirk, France, on January 27, 1788. He served in the army during the Napoleonic Wars until 1813-1814 and fled Europe following the French withdrawal from Holland, turning up in England in August 1814. Édouart gave French lessons at the outset, but then became interested in art. He is believed to have painted miniatures of animals and landscapes, and may even have exhibited at the Royal Academy. He did not really begin to do portraits using the silhouette technique until after 1825. Édouart showed great natural skill, always working freehand, without the aid of a physiognotrace. He rapidly gained recognition, and through his work the term "silhouette" gained acceptance in his adopted country; his services were sought by many notables, including members of the royal family.

Édouart always made two copies of his silhouettes; he would keep one for himself and was thus able to compile numerous albums containing detailed lists and indexes. In 1835, he wrote *A Treatise on Silhouette Likenesses,* which was published in London the same year and constituted a sort of autobiographical resumé of his already prolific career as a silhouettist. He also used his collection as promotional material, exhibiting samples of his art in the various places he visited to make his work known. In this way, he travelled to several towns and cities in Great Britain.

In 1839, Édouart left England to continue his artistic career in America. He travelled throughout the United States, from New England to New Orleans, stopping at cities such as Boston, Washington, Baltimore, Louisville (Kentucky), Philadelphia and New York. He spent several summers in Saratoga Springs, a New York State resort, where he found many customers. It was here that he seems to have met a certain number of Canadians who had their silhouettes done.

The advent of photography forced Édouart to give up his career as a silhouettist and, in 1849, he left for England. His vessel was shipwrecked on the coast of Guernsey, and he lost his material and much of his collection. Discouraged, Édouart eventually returned to France to end his days. He died in Guínes, near Calais, in 1861.

AUGUSTIN ÉDOUART

1789-1861

Main sources
MARTIN AND GRANDBOIS 1991; UN MOMENT 1991.

VAG, AGNS, MMFA

100.
The Wescott Family, 1840
Black paper cutout sepia ink with white highlights and graphite on paper, 31.4 × 46.7 cm

Inscriptions

(s.d., l.r.) *aug.ⁿ Edouart, fecit 1840.;* (b.,l., vertically, in pen and black ink) *James R. Westcott./ James R. Westcott junior.;* (b.,r., vertically, in pen and black ink) *Caroline Elizabeth Pilkin who married James* [Ho]*cum./Eleanor Ellis - wife of James R. Westcott.;* (b., on the frame, in ink) *James R. Westcott/James R. Westcott, junior son of Eleanor (Ellis) and James R. Westcott,/Mary Eleanor Westcott daughter of Eleanor (Ellis) and James R. Westcott/Saratoga Springs. New York/Mary Wayland, second wife of James R. Westcott./She was an English woman, very just and kind but very/exacting; a foe to idleness and is well represented with her knitting/in her hand.*

Provenance

Boutique aux mémoires antiquités Inc., Quebec City; acquired by the Musée du Québec, Quebec City, 1987.

Exhibition

Quebec City 1991/1, No. 14.

Bibliography

LA CHRONIQUE 1983, p. 23, No. 129 (Repr.); *BÉLAND AND BOURASSA 1990,* pp. 6, 8 and 70 (Repr.); *MARTIN AND GRANDBOIS 1991,* pp. 71-73, No. 14 (entry by Denis Martin) (Repr.); *UN MOMENT 1991,* pp. 197-198 and 200 (Repr.); *NADEAU 1991,* p. 60 (Repr.).

Collection

Musée du Québec, Quebec City (87.35)

A UGUSTIN AMANT CONSTANT FIDELE ÉDOUART was one of the most famous and prolific silhouettists in the first half of the 19th century.

Cut-out profiles, called "shadows" in England in the early 1800s, became quite fashionable in the time of Augustin Édouart. These contour figures, which were less costly than painted portraits, were also called "silhouettes," in reference to Étienne de Silhouette (1710-1767), a French finance minister who was ridiculed for his restrictive tax reforms. Édouart carved out a niche for himself in this art form, which was within the reach of many social classes and which, in its fundamentally "democratic" nature, prefigured the advent of photography several years later. Although he remained faithful to the ideals of the French Revolution, Édouart did not hesitate to make his services available to the crowned heads of Europe. The portraits attributed to him include 78 silhouettes of people in the court of Louis

XVIII who were exiled in England and numerous profiles of the English, Scottish and Irish aristocracy.[1] After 1835, Édouart practised his profession in several European centres, especially in Scotland and Ireland. From 1839 to 1849, he travelled throughout America. Research has established that Édouart produced 3 800 signed and dated silhouettes during his stay in the United States.[2] In all, the famous "shadow cutter" is thought to have made nearly 100 000 silhouettes throughout his long career.[3]

Augustin Édouart's work stands out from that done by other "shadow cutters" living at the same time not only in its sheer volume, but also due to the virtuosity of the scissor-work of each silhouette. Unlike many itinerant silhouettists who used a "physiognotrace" (a machine which enabled them to trace back-lit profiles) or a pantograph (to reduce the scale of a figure), Édouart worked freehand, handling his scissors with singular dexteri-

ty and often completing a portrait in less than two minutes. To keep a record of his work, the artist always made two copies of each silhouette by folding the sheet of black paper in two before he started to cut along the outline and snip out the interior details. His astonishing technique enabled him to represent the tiniest objects, such as glasses or knitting needles, and clothing accessories, directly on the paper; other silhouettists were satisfied with simply adding such details in ink. One of the telling features of Édouart's skill and the pains he took to perfect his silhouettes is the white collar worn by many of his subjects. Rather than being stuck on to the portrait at the end, this collar was snipped directly from the main figure and a piece of white paper glued behind it. To make his profile portraits more lifelike and exact, Édouart used silver paint to highlight the hair styles, buttons and ornaments worn by his sitters.[4] The finished silhouettes were often glued to a background representing a

MQ, NGC

101.
James R. Wescott and His Son James Wescott Junior, 1840
Black paper cutout sepia ink and graphite on paper,
31.8 × 23.4 cm

Inscriptions
(s.d., l.r..) *aug^n. Edouart fecit 1840.;* (b.,u.c., in graphite) *3/-;* (b.,l.r., reversed, in graphite) *3 Size* [?]; (b.,l.c.) artist's identification mark in ink with the letters A and E interlaced in an oval; (b., on paper mounted on the protective panel) [T]*he only kind of/likeness we had of/my dear brother Jimmy/(dear father with him)/taken form his cloak and [...] cup worn by a boy of/[...] size./James G. Westcott/died March 1841.*

Provenance
Boutique aux mémoires antiquités Inc., Quebec City; acquired by the Musée du Québec, Quebec City, 1987.

Bibliography
MARTIN AND GRANDBOIS *1991*, pp. 72 and 73 (Repr.).

Collection
Musée du Québec, Quebec City (87.36)

landscape or interior, drawn in ink and sepia wash.

When Augustin Édouart arrived in the United States in 1839, the way had already been opened for him by a talented predecessor, silhouettist Charles Balthazar Julien Févret de Saint-Mémin (1770-1852). This French nobleman, who had fled with his family to New York during the Reign of Terror in 1793, produced nearly one thousand profiles, either life-sized and drawn by hand or reduced with a pantograph. His work was very influential in spreading the fashion for these relatively inexpensive portraits throughout the young American republic. Édouart therefore found himself in a promising situation for practising his artistic talents in the same field.

Between 1840 and 1845, when his silhouettist's career came to an end, Augustin Édouart spent every summer in Saratoga Springs in the state of New York. This resort, which was very popular with the wealthy middle class in the eastern states, also attracted affluent citizens from Upper and Lower Canada. Naturally, this population of summer visitors to Saratoga represented an ideal clientele for Édouart.

During the same period, some of the exiled French-Canadian *Patriotes* were living in Saratoga. Among them was Louis-Joseph-Amédée Papineau (1819-1903), the eldest son of the famous Louis-Joseph Papineau. He had espoused the cause of the *Patriotes* and followed his father when he sought refuge in the United States in the fall of 1837. On the basis of his diary, *Journal d'un Fils de la Liberté,* it is possible to trace the comings and goings of the young Papineau throughout his entire exile—during which time he called himself Monsieur "Montigny," a name his Papineau ancestors had used to designate their place of origin, the village of Montigny in France. In December of 1837, Louis-Joseph-Amédée was in Burlington; the following month he had moved to Sara-

toga, where he started to study law under Mr. Ellsworth. While Louis-Joseph travelled a great deal between Albany, New York and Philadelphia before leaving for France in 1839, his son took lodgings in Saratoga and gradually became part of the town's polite society. Between 1838 and 1841, as well as studying law, he was employed as a French teacher in the Miss Wayland Academy for young girls.

It is not known exactly when during his stay in Saratoga Amédée became friendly with the family of James R. Wescott—or Westcott, according to some documents—but his *Journal* records that he met Mary Eleanor, James Wescott's daughter, at the beginning of 1839; from that time on, he diligently cultivated his relationship with this family. In 1841, Louis-Joseph-Amédée was called to the bar and set up practice in New York. The following year, he became an American citizen and travelled to Paris for a few months to see his family again. It was not until

Fig. 100-101A.
Augustin Édouart,
Louis-Joseph-Amédée Papineau, 1840;
Black paper cutout and graphite on paper,
23.6 × 19.3 cm.
National Archives of Canada,
Ottawa (C-135399).

1845, when his father returned from exile to Canada, that Amédée could ask for Mary Eleanor Wescott's hand in marriage. They were wed the next year.

The group portrait *The Wescott Family,* shown here, was done in Saratoga at a time when the famous silhouettist's reputation was already well established. The portrait is a true conversation piece in which the artist displays his full talent and his ability to invent a scene. Full-length silhouettes of the Wescott family are set off against the background of a well-appointed sitting room drawn in sepia. Standing, from right to left, we can see James R. Wescott, his son James Wescott junior, and his daughter Mary Eleanor; the children's mother was Eleanor Ellis, Wescott's first wife. The woman shown seated here is his second wife, Mary Wayland, an Englishwoman. The intricate work of which Édouart was capable is evident in such details as young Wescott's bow and arrow, the slender knitting needles in Mary Wayland's hands, and the bouquet held by the young woman.

This work by Augustin Édouart, as well as two others representing members of the Wescott family and dated 1840—*James R. Wescott and His son James Wescott Junior* and *James Wescott Junior*—were acquired by the Musée du Québec in 1987. They were obtained from the Papineau family. It is likely that the distinguished American's daughter kept them as family mementos after her marriage in 1846 to the young lawyer from Canada. Augustin Édouart also did individual silhouettes of James R. Wescott, his wife, and his daughter in August of 1841.[5] Coincidentally, Louis-Joseph-Amédée himself met Augustin Édouart several times during the summer of 1840. Papineau recorded his first meeting with the celebrated Saratoga artist in a diary entry dated July 15, 1840:

I have visited a Frenchman, Mr. Édouart, a skilled silhouettist, who insists on doing my profile with an autograph, to add to his immense collection, & on giving me a copy of it.[6] (*Translation*)

This silhouette portrait of Amédée Papineau, then 21 years old, was placed by the young *Patriote* at the back of his *Journal*, which is now kept in the National Archives of Canada in Ottawa (Fig. 100-101A). Papineau playfully added the following tongue-in-cheek note:

Here I am, with my long hair, my waistcoat, my bamboo cane & my straw hat, for it's summer. As is the custom with all the great modern authors, it is quite fitting, I would even say essential, that my portrait and autograph appear at the front of my Works, Hem! Hem![7] (*Translation*)

During the summer of 1841, Amédée saw Édouart several more times and introduced him to his exiled friends, in particular, Jules Lamothe, who also sat for a profile by the artist.[8]

The two portraits, *The Wescott Family* and *James R. Wescott and His Son James Wescott Junior* are still in their original frames of bird's-eye maple. Édouart considered that this was the only wood suitable for framing his work, since it harmonized with the sepia tones of his backgrounds; to give his silhouettes a personal touch, especially when they were intended for someone wealthy, he employed a craftsman who made frames according to his instructions.[9]

Although Édouart did most of his work in New England, it appears that he made a short trip to Canada, since the catalogue drawn up by Mrs. F. Nevill Jackson includes the silhouette of a certain C.G. Hamilton, done in Halifax.[10] How-

ever, it was during his stays in Saratoga that Édouart produced most of his portraits of Canadian notables, clergymen and business men. There are some 800 catalogued silhouettes done by Édouart at Saratoga, and a few of them are of Canadians, such as Mr. and Mrs. Léger Lambers, who came from as far away as Rivière-du-Loup;[11] Edward Webb, an Englishman living in Montreal; the Reverend R. Whitwell, a minister at the Anglican Church in Saint-Armand-Ouest (in the present-day county of Sherbrooke);[12] and Miss Sophia Wilkins of Quebec City.[13]

In 1849, when Augustin Édouart returned to France, his ship was wrecked off the island of Guernsey, and he lost the better part of the some 50 000 silhouette "doubles" he had made throughout his long career. Sixteen albums were saved from the catastrophe; they included nearly 4000 silhouettes of Americans done between 1839 and 1849. These portraits were kept by the Lukis family of Guernsey until 1911, when they were acquired by Emily Jackson (Mrs. F. Nevill Jackson), one of the first historians to take an interest in the art of silhouette-making.[14] She was able to catalogue the collection using the precious information that Édouart always recorded about his silhouettes (the subject's name and profession, and the place and date at which the silhouette was done). Jackson then donated or sold many of the silhouettes to various museums and institutions in the United States, Great Britain and Canada, depending on the interest that the person in the portrait represented for their historical or artistic collections. In this way, the National Archives of Canada in Ottawa acquired sixteen silhouettes by Augustin Édouart in 1912. They included portraits, done in Saratoga, of banker Peter McGill of Montreal; merchants Jean-Baptiste Beaudry and Frederick Wyse of Quebec City; civil servants Dominick Daly, Edward Dowling and Thomas C. Murdochs; and Montreal sheriff John Boston.[15] The silhouettes acquired by the National Archives also include the portrait entitled *Louis-Misaël Archambault, Curate of Saint-Jacques-de-l'Achigan, and J.E. Ross.* Louis-Misaël Archambault, who was born in 1812 in Saint-Antoine-sur-Richelieu and died in 1894 in Saint-Hugues, was ordained as a priest in 1837 and appointed vicar in the parish of Saint-Jacques-de-l'Achigan, where he remained until 1840, the year that Édouart cut the young clergyman's silhouette while he was staying at Saratoga Springs.[16] Less is known about J.E. Ross, of Quebec City, but it may be

VAG, AGNS, MMFA

102.
Louis-Misaël Archambault, Curate of Saint-Jacques-de-l'Achigan, and J. E. Ross, 1832 and 1840
Black paper cutout and black ink on paper, 25.6 × 35.8 cm

Inscriptions
(l.l., under the profile of Abbé Archambault, in pen and black ink) *A. Edouardus hoc fecit/Louis Misail Archambaut Pretre Vicaire de Ste Jacques/ l'Achiganne à S^t. Antoine Riviére Chambly/Bas Canada/Saratoga 17 Aout 1840;* (l.r., under the profile of J. E. Ross, in graphite) *J.E. Ross Esqr/ Quebec/taken in Glasgow 12 March 1832*; (u.r., vertically in pen and black ink) *96.;* (b.,u.l., vertically in pen and black ink) *95.*

Provenance
Mrs. Emily Jackson, London; acquired by the Public Archives of Canada, Ottawa, 1912.

Bibliography
UN MOMENT 1991, p. 198.

Collection
National Archives of Canada, Ottawa (1983-25-4ax and 1983-25-4bx)

supposed that he was a merchant, since his silhouette was done in Glasgow, a city which had an important position in Quebec City's trade relations, especially in the construction timber sector.

Like the portraits of Peter McGill and John Boston of Montreal and Frederick Wyse of Quebec City, done in Saratoga in 1843 and also placed together on a page of one of Édouart's albums, the full-length silhouettes of Louis-Misaël Archambault and J.E. Ross bear witness to the French shade-cutter's meticulous craftsmanship. The two silhouette "doubles" on this page were actually done eight years apart, one in 1832 and the other in 1840. These two examples, as well as the portraits of the Wescott family and of Amédée Papineau, display an constant feature of Édouart's art: the tapered shape which the artist gave to feet, making his models look somehow lighter and endowing them with a certain air of dignity. Within the world of 19th century silhouettists, this particularity is a distinguishing mark in the work of Augustin Édouart.
D.M.

Notes

1. See the introduction by A. Hyatt Mayor in Andrew Oliver, *Auguste Édouart's Silhouettes of Eminent Americans, 1939-1844,* Charlottesville, University Press of Virginia/National Portrait Gallery, 1977, p. xiii.

2. *Catalogue of 3800 named and dated American Silhouettes portraits by Edouart (1789-1861). Discovered by F. Nevill Jackson,* London, undated.

3. Alice Van Leer Carrick, *A History of American Silhouettes. A Collector's Guide—1790-1840,* Rutland (Vermont), Charles E. Tuttle Co., 1968, p. 140.

4. Andrew Oliver, *op. cit.,* p. viii.

5. Individual silhouettes of James R. Wescott, his daughter Mary Eleanor, and his wife are found in the catalogue of 3 800 American subjects "cut out" by Édouart, but the family scene presented here is not included in the book. See *Complete List of 3 800 Silhouette Portraits of American Citizens Taken Between 1839-1849 by Auguste Edouart During his Tour in the United States* in an appendix to Andrew Oliver's work, *op. cit.* p. 547. For more information on the Wescott family's silhouettes, see also *MARTIN AND GRANDBOIS 1991,* pp. 71-73, as well as Lydia Foy's note on "Auguste Édouart (1788-1861)" in *UN MOMENT 1991,* pp. 197-198.

6. NAC, MG 24, B2, Vol. XXIV, Papineau family collection, *Journal d'un fils de la Liberté,*

manuscript, undated (c. 1837-1855), p. 30. The portrait of Amédée Papineau is included in the list of silhouettes done by Édouart in the United States (See *Complete List of 3 800 Silhouette Portraits,* in an appendix to Andrew Oliver's work, *op. cit.,* p. 536).

7. NAC, MG 24, B2, Vol. XXXVII, Papineau family collection, *Appendix au Journal d'un Fils de la Liberté,* unpaginated.

8. "I went with Lamothe to see Mr. Édouart, who took his profile…" (*Translation*) (*Journal d'un Fils de la Liberté,* Thursday, July 16, 1840, p. 30). Lamothe's silhouette, like that of Papineau, is preserved at the NAC. See *UN MOMENT 1991,* p. 200 (Repr.).

9. *Ibid.,* pp. 185-186. To our knowledge, only a very few silhouettes of this quality and of this type (with an inside setting or a landscape as a background) are found in Canadian public collections. The National Archives of Canada owns only one, the silhouette of *George Ramsay, 9th Earl of Dalhousie,* done by J. Hankes in about 1828; the background for this portrait is a panoramic view of Quebec City done in watercolour. For more information, see *WEBSTER 1984,* p. 205, No. 244, (Repr.).

10. See *Complete List of 3 800 Silhouette Portraits,* in an appendix to Andrew Oliver's work, *op. cit.,* p. 525.

11. Done on August 19, 1843 (*ibid.,* p. 530).

12. *Ibid.,* pp. 546 and 547.

13. Édouart did her silhouette on August 24, 1844 (*ibid.,* p. 548).

14. See the note by Lydia Foy in *UN MOMENT 1991,* p. 199.

15. *Ibid.,* pp. 198-199.

16. J.-B.-A. Allaire, *Dictionnaire biographique du clergé canadien-français. Les anciens,* Montreal, Imprimerie de l'École Catholique des Sourds-Muets, 1910, p. 14.

KATHERINE JANE
ELLICE
?-1864

IT WOULD SEEM THAT Katherine Jane Ellice was born in Scotland, the daughter of general Robert Balfour. In 1834, she married Edward Ellice junior, who helped manage his father's business matters, which included several investments as well as immense properties in North America. However, it was political events that brought Edward and his wife to Canada: Edward's father persuaded him to accompany Lord Durham, the new governor general of Canada, as his private secretary. During their stay of several months, the couple travelled with Durham on visits to Upper and Lower Canada, and resided in Montreal, Quebec City, and at the Seigneury of Beauharnois, which had belonged to the Ellice family since 1795. It was at this seigneury that Katherine Jane and her husband were captured by the rebels in 1838.

Katherine Jane was already accomplished in drawing, but her style was much influenced by the fact that she spent part of this voyage in the company of John Richard Coke Smyth, a drawing master in Lord Durham's party. Katherine Jane Ellice did views of Quebec City and Beauharnois, and kept a diary during her Canadian visit (NAC). Her husband Edward, like his father, was a member of parliament in London for a long time; he was also involved in trade and became deputy governor of the Hudson Bay Company in 1858. When the Seigneury of Beauharnois was sold in 1867, the ties which had linked the Ellice family with Canada since the 1770s were severed.

Main sources
HARPER 1970; BELL 1972.

VAG, AGNS, MMFA

103.
Drawing Room and Front Door, Beauharnois, 1838
Watercolour over graphite on paper, 17 × 23.1 cm

Inscriptions
(b.,l.r., in graphite) *Beauharnois/Jane's* [bedroom?]; (b., in graphite) a few geometric composition lines; (on the old mount, l.c., in pen and black ink) *Drawing Room a front door. Beauharnois.*

Provenance
Descendants of the Ellice family; Edward C. Ellice, London; acquired by the Public Archives of Canada, Ottawa, 1928.

Collection
National Archives of Canada, Ottawa (1990-215-15RX)

K ATHERINE JANE ELLICE was a member of Lord Durham's suite when he came to Quebec in 1838; her husband, Edward Ellice, had been appointed private secretary to the governor general of Upper and Lower Canada. The Ellice family already had strong ties with North America. Edward's grandfather, Alexander Ellice, had made his fortune in the fur trade in the late 18th century.[1] A wise financier, he bought large tracts of land in the United States and Lower Canada, including the Seigneury of Beauharnois. When he died in Bath, England, in 1805, his business concerns were taken over by his third son, Edward, who saw to it that they flourished even though he, himself, remained in England, playing an active role in English political life, especially in the field of Canadian affairs. The family's previous links to Canada were no doubt an asset to Edward Ellice junior fils in his new responsibilities. However, as well as having knowledge of Quebec which was useful to Lord Durham, he had an interest in his family's affairs.

Katherine Jane Ellice's diary is much more helpful than the one kept by Lady Durham in informing us about what happened during this trip of a few months in the summer and fall of 1838.[2] The ocean crossing from Portsmouth to Quebec City on board the *HMS Hastings* took thirty-four days, from April 24 to May 27, 1839. Lord Durham was travelling with his wife and his two daughters, Lady Mary Lambton and Lady Emily Lambton (Fig. 103-104A). He had also brought along John Richard Coke Smyth, their drawing master (Cat. 214 and 215). The travellers passed the time on board preparing a play entitled *Tom Thumb*,[3] which was presented a few days before their arrival and for which Coke Smyth painted some of the stage sets.[4] Katherine Jane Ellice also recorded certain moments in the crossing in sketches, such as one done on May 11 of two rabbits which were allowed to exercise on the deck:

Very foggy most part of the day. They say it is always so near the Banks of Newfoundland where we hope to be tomorrow. Mr. Bouverie and C. Bullar read aloud 'Paradise Lost' to us, while we sketched the rabbits (Fig. 103-104B) which were allowed to run about the deck to stretch their legs. Poor things, from their close confinement they have nearly lost the use of them.[5]

This short passage demonstrates the very lively style in which the diary as a whole is written. Katherine Jane Ellice was particularly good at turning out incisive description in a few words, as evidenced by the following comment about John Richard Coke Smyth: "Mary drove us in the pony chair to Mr. Smythe's Studio where she, Emily & Mrs Grey are being painted. Not much likeness as yet."[6]

Ellice's drawings, which she referred to as "scrabbles," have become precious documents, full of information about this period. Her interior scenes are particularly important, since such subjects were rarely painted by Quebec watercolourists. *Drawing Room and Front Door, Beauharnois* is one such drawing.[7] It would be impossible, however, on the basis of Ellice's drawings alone to determine the characteristic features of room layouts and furnishings in Quebec houses. Her interiors represent an individual case, as did, for example, Lady Aylmer's arrangements at the Château Saint-Louis in 1831.[8] Katherine Jane probably brought material and a few pieces of furniture from England in order to spruce the manor up, as this comment in her diary seems to indicate: "Tina & I made new covers for a dirty looking Sofa & Arm Chair, not to mention Muslin Curtains for 2 or 3 rooms. So much for an Invereshie upbringing."[9] Lord and Lady Durham stopped off at Beauharnois in July, on their way back from

MQ, NGC

104.
Ladie's Cabin "Charlevoix", Oct. 29th, Quebec to Montreal, 1838
Watercolour over graphite on paper, 15.8 × 23 cm (irregular dimensions)

Inscriptions
(l.l., in pen and black ink, in the artist's hand[?])
*Ladies Cabin - Charlevoix./Oct. 29th Quebec to
Montreal;* (on the old mount, b.,l.r., in graphite)
Misc. Ships (Merchant)/"Charlevoix".

Provenance
Descendants of the Ellice family; Edward C. Ellice,
London; acquired by the Public Archives of
Canada, Ottawa, 1928.

Collection
National Archives of Canada,
Ottawa (1990-215-22X)

Niagara Falls and Toronto. Lady Durham's impressions of the house were recorded quite differently in her personal diary:

The cottage in which they lived & which in general was occupied by the Agent, was so small that they were obliged to remove out of it themselves in order to accommodate us—they took the greatest pains to make us comfortable & succeeded very well [...] Mrs. Ellice had contrived with a little English Furniture & good arrangement, to make it look very nice for the time.[10]

In her watercolour ***Drawing Room and Front Door, Beauharnois*** Katherine Jane Ellice has recorded a moment in daily life. The picture divides space in a surprising manner expressing a clear desire to draw from nature and a refusal to work out any composition other than that imposed by basic rules of geometry. The immediate surroundings are situated in a rapidly sketched plan, structured around a central vanishing point. The front door opens directly onto the countryside, which is delicately painted in blues and yellows. The cramped proportions of the two rooms shown is evident from the way the armchair is cut in half in the right foreground, suggesting that the artist could not move back far enough to place it entirely in her layout. The secret of the drawing's success lies in its perfect colour contrasts. The grey walls form large empty expanses that are restful for the eye and allow the strong colours to be fully appreciated. The faded reds of the carpet set off the clear reds of

the shawl in the foreground and of the table mat in the further room. The straw yellows of the hats and bag hanging on the wall find an echo in the dress of the woman leaning on the windowsill and grass parched by the sun's heat beyond the door. Katherine Jane Ellice is a colourist. The same qualities are evident in her watercolour work as a whole.

Ellice spent a few days in Quebec City at the end of October visiting Lord and Lady Durham before they returned to England. She left for Beauharnois on October 28 on the steamship *Charlevoix*. According to a diary entry, she had little esteem for this vessel: "got on board the Charlevoix—a steamer of no good reputation, but as it was the only one we had no choice."[11] A watercolour dated October 29, 1838, shows ***Ladies' Cabin "Charlevoix", Oct. 29th, Quebec to Montreal***. Along the back wall are individual bunks which could be closed off with curtains. Promiscuity sometimes led to unexpected situations, such as on the evening of October 28:

One of the *female* passengers meanwhile coolly commenced undressing & got into her berth. Fortunately she drew the curtains so that she was concealed from our view, but still I died of it! Spent half the night in *thinking*—t' would be better for me if I did so oftener. [12]

Their cabin-mate disembarked at Trois-Rivières leaving Jane Ellice and her sister Tina alone.[13] It may well have been at this point that the watercolourist decided

to make a sketch of the cabin, perhaps as a souvenir of the previous evening.

Almost immediately after she returned to Beauharnois, she found herself in the midst of the rebellion of November 1838. The night of November 3 was especially turbulent:

He [Edward Ellice] opened the window & listened, but all was still, & just as he was getting into bed a yell like the Indian war cry burst close to the house & guns fired at the same moment; struck the house on all sides, breaking the windows &c. Edward jumped *into* his clothes & drag'd Tina & I *en chemise*, without shoes or stockings, down stairs & put us thro' a trap door into the cellar. The house was surrounded on all sides; Edward & Mr. Brown taken prisoners, and were carried off we knew nor where, leaving Tina & I alone, *en chemise*, in the middle of a group of the most *'Robespierre'* looking ruffians, all armed with guns, long knives & pikes, without a single creature to advise us, every respectable person in the village being taken prisoner. What a day we passed, sitting hand in hand, in the midst of a heap of confusion, comforting each other & praying for protection to Him who orders all things well. But it was a severe trial. The ruffian looking men coming in every now & then, quite drunk. In the evening the Priest came to see us & we got leave to come to his house. What a wretched day, & yet how much worse it might have been. Poor Edward, how miserable he must be about us.[14]

Katherine Jane Ellice and the members of her household remained at the priest's house for the next seven days, by which time the rebellion had come to an end. Edward Ellice, who had been

Fig. 103-104A.
Katherine Jane Ellice,
*Lady Mary Lambton
and Lady Emily
Lambton*, 1838;
watercolour over
graphite,
18.9 × 13.5 cm.
National Archives
of Canada,
Ottawa (C-13385).

Fig. 103-104B.
Katherine Jane Ellice,
*Rabbits on Board
HMS Hastings*, 1838;
watercolour,
13 × 16.2 cm.
National Archives of
Canada,
Ottawa (C-13375).

imprisoned at Châteauguay, was released on November 11. One week later, the couple left Montreal for New York to take a ship to England. Katherine Jane never returned to Quebec.

Katherine Jane had an album in which she kept her drawings. Some of them were intended to illustrate her diary and give a visual rhythm to the text. However, this album appears to have been more than just a book in which its owner tucked away an expression of her talents. It might even be termed a meeting place. Early on in the trip, on board the *HMS Hastings*, John Richard Coke Smyth had drawn the ship's bell in it.[15] Later, in September of 1838 at Niagara Falls, Katherine Jane Ellice met Henry William Barnard (Cat. 59 to 62), whom she had probably known since her arrival in Quebec City. On September 27, Barnard stopped at Beauharnois on his way back to Quebec City. He stayed there for a while and spent his evenings at the seigneury manor. He also showed his drawings to Katherine Jane Ellice: "*Looked at all Col. Barnard's* beautiful sketches & he at ours, which he was polite enough to praise."[16] Katherine Jane Ellice's sister Tina copied some of Barnard's drawings, "in which she succeeded very well."[17] Before leaving, Barnard added some of his own drawings to Katherine Jane Ellice's album: "Col. Barnard made some funny sketches in my little book this evening & we have some music."[18] Examples of this type of impromptu exchange abound; for instance,

Jane Ellice painted in Lady Catherine Harcourt's album.[19] Amateur painters' custom of sharing their art reflected an attitude also shown by the British royal family. A passing reference in Katherine Jane Ellice's diary on October 2, 1838, is evidence of this practice:

Worked, Sang & chatted through the evening. Ly C. [Lady Catherine Harcourt] told us a good deal about the Queen—her wonderful memory; talent for *drawing;* singing etc. Amiability, kindness, self possession. A very interesting character even if she were not Queen of England.[20]

D.P.

Notes

1. James M. Colthart, DCB, Vol. V (1983), pp. 327-330.
2. *The Diary of Katherine Jane Ellice*, edited by Patricia Godsell, was published by Oberon Press in 1975. Lady Durham's diary was published by the Literary and Historical Society of Quebec in 1915.
3. According to Patricia Godsell, *op. cit.*, p. 177, the play, *Tragedy of Tom Thumb: The Tragedy of Tragedies or The Life and Death of Tom Thumb the Great,* was written by Henry Fielding in 1730.
4. "SATURDAY, 26 MAY, 1838. [...] Very busy helping to make the dresses for the Actors. Anchor'd at 1/2 past 7. The Quarter deck was all covered in. Mr. Smythe painted some very pretty scenes. At 10, the performance began—The Critic & Tom Thumb—were really *well* acted. C. Bullar as '*Puff'* was *perfect.* The scenes painted by Mr. Smythe". Charles Bullar was Lord Durham's Chief Secretary and a member of his Special Council. Katherine Jane Ellice also designed some of the costumes for the play (NAC, I-10).
5. Patricia Godsell, *op. cit.*, pp. 24 and 174. Edward Pleydell-Bouverie was in Lord Durham's party. He married Katherine Jane Ellice's younger sister. John Milton's *Paradise Lost,* published in 1669, had a significant influence on this period, particularly on William Wordsworth. See Jonathan Wordsworth, Michael C. Jaye and Robert Woof, *William Wordsworth and the Age of English Romanticism,* New Brunswick and London, Rutgers University Press and Grasmere, Dove Cottage, The Wordsworth Trust, 1987, pp. 145 and 230, No. 256.
6. Mary and Emily were Lord Durham's daughters; Mrs. Grey was the wife of Colonel Charles Grey, Lady Durham's brother.
7. There is another matching watercolour of these rooms viewed, however, from the opposite direction (NAC, I-6). A remark made by Katherine Jane Ellice hints that she painted other interior scenes which have remained unknown: "Drew the interior of the drawing room with the funny little staircase". (Patricia Godsell, *op. cit.*, p. 116).
8. "I have had all the horse hair sofas covered and plenty of Easy arm chairs, I found in Various parts of the house, have been collected and all covered with the strip'd linen, which we brought from England". This quotation comes from the transcription of Lady Aylmer's diary, *Recollections of Canada,* in the *Rapport de l'archiviste de la Province de Québec pour 1934-1935,* Quebec, Rédempti Paradis, 1935, p. 293.
9. Patricia Godsell, *op. cit.*, p. 58. Invereshie was the Scottish estate belonging to Katherine Jane Ellice's family, the Balfours.
10. *Lady Durham's Journal, op. cit.*, p. 33.
11. Patricia Godsell, *op. cit.*, p.118.
12. *Ibid.*, p. 126.
13. Eglantine Charlotte Louisa Balfour.
14. Patricia Godsell, *op. cit.*, pp. 130-131.
15. NAC, 1990-215-28X.
16. Patricia Godsell, *op. cit.*, p. 109.
17. *Ibid.*, p. 110.
18. *Ibid.*, p. 111.
19. Lady Catherine Harcourt was the daughter of the Earl of Liverpool. She was also a lady's companion to the Duchess of Kent (*Ibid.*, p. 183).
20. *Ibid.*, pp. 111-112.

GEROME
FASSIO

(?1789-1851)

GEROME FASSIO was born in Italy, probably in Rome, around 1789. Little more is known about his life prior to his arrival in Canada, other than the fact that he had at least one son, named Eugenio, born in 1825 or 1826. Fassio came to Montreal from New York in the spring of 1834 and travelled between the three major centres in Lower Canada, advertising himself as a miniaturist. The first year, 1834, he remained in Montreal. The following year, he went to Trois-Rivières, but by August of 1835 he had already moved to Quebec City. Towards the end of the same year, he offered courses for young people in drawing and miniature painting. In spring 1836, he announced he was returning to Montreal and by August, he had begun offering drawing courses as he had in Quebec City, one for young ladies and one for young men. He stayed in Montreal until early summer 1838, when he returned to Quebec City. He continued to give private lessons, but also taught drawing at the Séminaire de Québec during the 1839-1840 school year. In 1839 as well, he exhibited a piece of his work at Joseph Légaré's gallery. The piece was a large-scale miniature representing an allegory of Great Britain, with the four corners of the earth, being presented a figure personifying Canada. Fassio is also known to have done a few small landscapes, which were placed in albums belonging to various people (Montreal Municipal Library, NAC, MMCH). As well, Fassio made a lithograph of a portrait of Pope Gregory XVI and, in 1844, marketed a lithograph representing Louis-Joseph Papineau. Both lithographs were printed by Napoléon Aubin, with whom Fassio also worked on a project for making a collection of lithograph portraits.

Throughout the 1840s, Fassio was obliged to lower his rates, probably because of competition from the daguerreotype. In December of 1843, he lost all his possessions in a fire which destroyed his home. He eventually decided to return to Italy in the spring of 1848, but did not leave until June 1849. In October 1850, he was already back in Quebec City, no doubt because of the political turmoil in his homeland at the time. He finally moved to in Bytown, where he died on January 1, 1851.

Main source
KAREL 1988.

VAG, AGNS, MMFA

VAG, AGNS, MMFA

Fig. 105-106A.
Gerome Fassio,
François-Xavier Paquet's Aunt, c. 1838-1840;
watercolour on paper.
McCord Museum of
Canadian History,
Montreal (M16015).

105.
Michel Paquet, c. 1838-1840
Watercolour and traces of graphite on
paper, 10.8 × 8.9 cm

Provenance
Descendants of the Paquet family; François-Xavier
Paquet, Ottawa; acquired by the Musée du
Château Ramezay, 1932.

Bibliography
MCR, *Registre des acquisitions 1895-1974*, p. 363,
No. 4844, May 1932; *SELECTED CATALOGUE 1985*,
p. 57, No. 132 (entry by Roslyn Rosenfeld).

Collection
Musée du Château Ramezay, Montreal (CR4844)

106.
*Mrs. Michel Paquet, née Marie-Joseph
Badeau,* c. 1838-1840
Watercolour and highlighted with white
gouache on paper, 10.8 × 8.9 cm

Provenance
Descendants of the Paquet family; François-Xavier
Paquet, Ottawa; acquired by the Musée du
Château Ramezay, 1932.

Bibliography
MCR, *Registre des acquisitions 1895-1974*, p. 363,
No. 4845, May 1932; *SELECTED CATALOGUE 1985*,
p. 57, No. 131 (entry by Roslyn Rosenfeld).

Collection
Musée du Château Ramezay, Montreal (CR4845)

MICHEL PAQUET, a merchant, and Marie-Joseph Badeau were married in the church of Saint-Roch in Quebec City in 1837. Their miniature portraits were bequeathed by their son, François-Xavier (1845-1932), a well-known numismatist, to the Musée du Château de Ramezay. Unlike most miniatures, which are usually oval and framed in a black case with ring on top, the portraits of Paquet and his wife are rectangular and placed in a cloth box, or holder, originally with a cover. The rectangular shape and the type of frame also characterize another miniature, held by the McCord Museum, representing an older woman, who is thought to be a close relative of Paquet's (Fig. 105-106A).

Michel Paquet and his wife, presented three-quarter length and turned slightly to the right, are dressed in clothes that were fashionable around 1840. The miniatures may well have been painted shortly after the couple's marriage, as it was customary at the time for newlyweds to have their portraits done. In her right hand Marie-Joseph Badeau holds a rose, which could be an allusion to her wedding. Certain other portraits of women done in this period also show the subject wearing a rose (Cat. 116).

Michel Paquet has his right hand raised to his chest, with his thumb inserted inside his jacket. The stiffness of the couple's pose and the resulting loss of expressiveness is echoed in two other portraits, done by Fassio in 1848, *Jean-Baptiste Godin* and *Joseph Rouleau* (Cat. 109 and 110). In particular, the rigid stance and position of the right hand in the couple's portraits is very like the treatment of the hand in the portraits of Godin and Rouleau. The four portraits show other similarities; not only are the models posed

in the same way, but the paintings also have a common problem with volume and depth. This problem is related to the linearity of the artist's style, which is marked by a certain stiffness, as well as to the very particular techniques he used. The background, face, lace and some details of clothing have been built up with a series of brush strokes applied in tiny dots, while dark-toned clothes and hair have been given a flat treatment with strong contrasts created by highlights along the folds and contours. In these portraits, Fassio displayed both precise draughtsmanship—with firm, almost severe, lines—and rich colouring with subtle, transparent tones. The artist began his portrait of Michel Paquet by sketching his model in pencil, as is shown by the marks on the margin left at the bottom of the paper, while, for that of Marie-Joseph Badeau, he highlighted certain elements, such as her collar and bonnet, with white gouache. A magnifying glass is necessary to truly appreciate the precision of Fassio's work; the naked eye misses the virtuosity displayed in the extremely fine brush strokes that render the tracery of veins on the hands, the reflections of light on the jewellery, and the delicate patterns of the lace and of rose petals.

On the basis of these formal and technical characteristics, two other portraits should be attributed to Fassio. In 1987, we identified these two miniatures as being portraits of Jean-Casimir Bruneau (1801-1880) and his wife, Marie-Reine Dupuy (1799-1874).[1] However, according to the family tree belonging to their last owner, the subjects should rather be identified as the future judge Pierre-Antoine Doucet (1815-1878) and his wife, Delphine Bruneau (1829-1910), the daughter of Jean-Casimir Bruneau. Doucet, born in Quebec City, was called to the bar on February 10, 1838.[2] Throughout his career, he was successively appointed Clerk of the Court of Appeal at Lotbinière

MQ, NGC

107.

(?) *Pierre-Antoine Doucet,* c. 1835

Watercolour, gum arabic and gouache on ivory, 6.5 × 5 cm

Provenance
Descendants of the Bruneau, Doucet, Cimon, Verge and Bigué families; Mrs. Michel Morel, née Lucie Bigué, Quebec City; acquired by the Musée du Québec, Quebec City, 1987.

Bibliography
BÉLAND 1988, p. 65 (Repr.).

Collection
Musée du Québec, Quebec City (87.27)

VAG, AGNS, MMFA

108. (See colour reproduction, p. 105)

(?) *Mrs. Pierre-Antoine Doucet, née Delphine Bruneau,* c. 1848

Watercolour on cardboard, 7.5 × 6 cm

Inscription
(b., recent) *Delphine Bruneau.*

Provenance
Descendants of the Bruneau, Doucet, Cimon, Verge and Bigué families; Mrs. Michel Morel, née Lucie Bigué, Sillery; acquired by the Musée du Québec, Quebec City, 1987.

Bibliography
BÉLAND 1988, p. 65 (Repr.).

Collection
Musée du Québec, Quebec City (87.28)

(1839), Clerk of the Dorchester District Court (1842), and Clerk of the Peace in Quebec City (1848); he married Delphine Bruneau on August 2, 1848.

The two models appear to be both about 20 years old, meaning that the portraits must have been done some ten years apart. That of Pierre-Antoine Doucet was probably done between 1835 and 1838, during his student years leading up to his call to the bar, while that of Delphine Bruneau was most likely done around 1848, the year of her marriage. If this is the case, the roses in her hair might be symbolic of her being a bride. According to the story handed down in the family, both portraits were done on this occasion.

Noticeable differences between the two paintings with respect to size, support—one is on ivory, the other on cardboard—and above all treatment, led us at first to believe that they had been done by

two different artists, as yet unidentified. In fact, these differences are related to stylistic and technical developments in Fassio's work. The portrait of Pierre-Antoine Doucet is similar in support and treatment to two miniatures on ivory painted by the artist in Montreal in 1834. These paintings, which represent Marie-Angélique Chaboillez and her daughter Amelia Berthelet, were recently acquired by the National Gallery of Canada.[3] In comparison, the treatment used in the portrait of Delphine Bruneau calls to mind the miniatures of Godin and Rouleau, signed in 1848. In the earlier group, folds and contours are rendered by fine hatching and cross-hatching, while, in the later group, the same elements are produced with clean, emphatic lines. The two groups are representative of the two approaches taken by Fassio in his Canadian production: an early, more spirited style at the beginning

(around 1835) and a later, more painstaking style at the end (around 1848). The ivory support used for earlier miniatures lends a remarkable transparency and luminosity to the flesh tones; this is especially true of Pierre-Antoine Doucet's portrait, in which the expression and the treatment of the face display much romantic sensitivity.

These examples of Fassio's work testify to the Italian miniaturist's sure technique and his solid reputation as a draughtsman and colourist. During his stay in Canada, the newspapers promoted these qualities enthusiastically, as can be seen in this dithyrambic article in *Le Canadien* on September 14, 1835:

When strangers, instead of bringing us their vices, poverty and diseases, provide us with science, art and industry, as well as the charm and affability of their manners, they have the right to all our favours, all our homage, and all our encouragement. A man of genius, responding to an appreciation of his talents, has decided to settle among us. He represents a conquest of the Old World: the art which he transmits to a New Land is truly perfect.

We have visited the studio of the famous artist, Mr. FASIO; the marvels which we saw there lead us to recommend him to our fellow citizens. The striking likeness of his miniature portraits defies description. There can be no better occasion for anyone who wishes to have a keepsake of a dear one's face, whether father, mother, brother, child or sweetheart. For a few piastres, they will have not only the features, but also the expression, the smile and the muscles of those they love. Everyone can appreciate the excellence of the work, for one need not be a connoisseur to recognize nature. Any eye can see a heart that beats, a vein that throbs, a lip that curves into a smile; for such is the magic of Mr. Fasio's brush that one believes that these objects are really before one's eyes. And then, what fresh, life-like colouring! What nuance, what gentle shading, what perfection in the drawing! It may seem unbelievable, but these tiny masterpieces are completed in two sittings, with possibly another sitting for the likeness, and one day for colouring and accessories. Mr. Fasio will spend the winter in Quebec City if he meets with encouragement. It must be professed that he will certainly have plenty. (*Translation*)

M.B.

Notes

1. See *BÉLAND 1988*, p. 65. The works were acquired in 1987.

2. Pierre-Georges Roy, *Fils de Québec,* Lévis, 1933, p. 5, and *Le Bulletin de recherches historiques,* Vol. XXXIX, No. 3 (March 1933), p. 161.

3. NGA, 35514 and 35515. The portrait of *Amelia Berthelet* has the following inscription in back:" *November* [number?] [...] / [M]r *Fassio* 10[...] / *one pair of* [M?] *of* [obliterated] *one pair of* [...]".

MQ, NGC

109.
Jean-Baptiste Godin, 1848
Watercolour on cardboard, 9.1 × 7.5 cm

Inscriptions
(b., in graphite) *5;* (on a paper protecting the back of the work, in ink, 1st side) *Mon portrait/fut commencé le/7 mars & terminé le 19/-1848-par Signor Fassio/1848/J'avais alors 22 ans & 8 mois/mars-1848/J. Bte Godin/commis marchand;* (2nd side) *Ce portrait a/été reconnu par/toutes les personnes/qui l'ont vu/ce qui prouve* [struck off:*son*]/*l'exacte ressemblance J. Bte.. Godin/1848-.*

Provenance
Mrs. Eve Edouard Tremblay; gift to the Musée de la Société historique du Saguenay, Chicoutimi, 1937; transferred to the Musée du Saguenay, Chicoutimi, 1972.

Exhibition
Quebec City 1952, No. 33.

Bibliography
MORISSET *1950/3,* pp. 26 and 38 (Repr.); MORISSET *1952,* p. 29, No. 33; KAREL *1985,* p. 321; BÉLAND *1988,* p. 65; LACROIX *1989/4,* p. 180 (Repr.); BÉLAND AND BOURASSA *1990,* p. 98.

Collection
Musée du Saguenay-Lac-Saint-Jean, Chicoutimi (75.580)

T HE ITALIAN Gerome Fassio is probably the best known of the many foreign miniaturists who travelled throughout Lower Canada in the first half of the 19th century. His career in Canada is fairly well documented, thanks to advertisements and articles published in Quebec City and Montreal newspapers between 1834 and 1851. Until quite recently, however, knowledge of his production was limited to certain arbitrary attributions and a few particular works, such as the view of *Genève des paquis* and the portrait of *Napoléon I,* which are in the Jacques Viger album conserved at the Montreal Municipal Library.[1] Miniatures that can be attributed with certainty to the artist include the portraits of *Marie-Angélique Chaboillez* and her daughter *Amelia Berthelet,* which were painted in Montreal around 1834 (See Cat. 105 to 108); the portraits of three members of the Cazeau family—who took Fassio in when his studio burned down in 1846;[2] and the portraits of ***Jean-Baptiste Godin*** and ***Joseph Rouleau,*** dating from 1848.

On the backs of the two portraits ***Jean-Baptiste Godin*** and ***Joseph Rouleau*** are inscriptions which give exceptionally precise information identifying not only the

subjects, but also the artist and the dates at which both works were done. These instructive notes are signed by the models themselves, Joseph Rouleau (1825-1901) and the merchant Jean-Baptiste Godin respectively, both of Quebec City. The inscriptions also state that the portraits were painted by Signor—or Senior!—Fassio. It is quite rare to find the painter's name written on a miniature portrait. In this case, it is also stated that Godin's portrait was done between March 7 and 19, 1848, when the subject was 22 years and 8 months old, while Rouleau's was painted between March 19 and 28 of the same year, when the model was 20.[3] The works must have therefore been painted one after the other, with the artist beginning on Rouleau's portrait the same day that he finished Godin's. It can also be calculated that it took the artist 12 days of work to complete the first miniature and 9 days for the second.

Both miniatures are half-length portraits presenting the model in a nearly three-quarter profile. As well, both poses are similar in a curious detail: the subject has a hand raised to his chest, and the thumb of this hand is inserted through a buttonhole in the jacket. The models also

both show the stiffness characterizing Fassio's work. Nonetheless, the two miniatures testify to Fassio's great technical mastery and the high quality of his craftsmanship. These attributes were reported in the newspapers of the time, as well as by Maximilien Bibeau in *L'Encyclopédie canadienne* (October 1842). For example, in *Le Journal de Québec* of February 7, 1846, it is mentioned that:

We have recently seen some of this artist's portraits, which are of a remarkable quality; if his talent had not already taken him so far towards perfection, we would really have to say that he had made new conquests. (*Translation*).

The artist had no doubt, as he advertised himself in the newspapers, achieved "perfect likeness," (*Translation*) an accomplishment which is vouched for in the note written by Jean-Baptiste Godin on the back of his miniature: "This portrait has been recognized by everyone who has seen it, which proves it to be an exact likeness." (*Translation*)

On December 4, 1847, Fassio announced in *Le Journal de Québec* that he intended to return to his native land the next spring and offered, "for the last time, his services [for] lovely miniature portraits […] for the modest sum of four piastres."

MQ, NGC

110. (See colour reproduction, p. 105)
Joseph Rouleau, 1848
Watercolour on cardboard, 9 × 7.5 cm

Inscription
(on a paper protecting the back of the work, in ink) *Senior Fassio/à commencé mon/portrait le 19 mars/1848 et l'a fini le 28/du même mois, j'étais/alors agé de 20 ans/Joseph Rouleau.*

Provenance
Descendants of the Rouleau family; Mrs. Bertrand, née Eva Rouleau; Marie-Paule Michon, Quebec City, 1971; gift to the Musée du Québec, Quebec City, 1987.

Bibliography
BÉLAND 1988, p. 65 (Repr.); BÉLAND AND BOURASSA 1990, pp. 6, 8 and 98 (Repr.).

Collection
Musée du Québec, Quebec City (87.151).

(*Translation*) On the following February 18, he advertised in *L'Ami de la religion et de la patrie,* saying that he had again lowered his fee and that it was now only "three piastres." The fee sought by Fassio does not seem very profitable for the time involved, considering that one month later he earned a meagre six piastres for the three weeks and more spent on painting the portraits of Godin and Rouleau. Fassio had, in fact, begun to reduce his fees by nearly half as early as the mid-1840s: this trend began with an advertisement he placed in *Le Journal de Québec* of February 29, 1844, and became more marked after November 6, 1845:

The miniature has incontestable advantages. When one has relatives or friends who are far away, does one not feel the need to send them one's likeness, or that of their wife, or husband, or child, etc. especially when the price is within everyone's reach. (*Translation*)

The truth is that the miniaturist was increasingly confronted with growing competition from the daguerreotype photograph portrait, which also guaranteed a "perfect likeness" for a modest sum, but in addition could be done very rapidly with little time required for posing. Throughout

the 1840s the daguerreotype, which impressed people with its exact image, gained ground in Lower Canada. As early as June 21, 1841, *Le Canadien* announced: "Ladies and gentlemen, if you wish to be painted by *nature,* it can be done for four piastres." (*Translation*) It is telling that the first French Canadian to call himself a "daguerreotypist" was a painter, Vital Desrochers (Cat. 87), who advertised in *La Minerve* of December 4, 1845. The same issue of *Le Canadien* that reported Fassio's return after an absence of 16 months also announced a "New Canadian daguerreotype establishment" (*Translation*) belonging to Léon-Antoine Lemire. The establishment appears to have been the first business in Quebec City entirely devoted this art form. Fassio had probably used up his potential clientele—apparently comprised of young people and members of the middle class like Rouleau and Godin—during his two advertising campaigns offering low prices in 1847 and 1848 before his departure for Italy. In fact, his portraits of Rouleau and Godin may well be among the last of Fassio's works done in Quebec City, if not in his career. By the end of the 1840s, his miniatures, which

were intended to be widely affordable, were superseded by the daguerreotype in this trend towards egalitarian portraiture. Faced with strong competition from photography, Fassio was obliged to move to Bytown, a newly established town, at the end of November, 1850, in the hope of finding new customers. He died less than two months later. Today, his miniature portraits of members of the middle class remain extremely interesting examples in the history of portraiture.

M.B.

Notes
1. MORISSET 1950/2 (Repr.).
2. MQ, 82.46, 82.47, 82.48. See LE MUSÉE DU QUÉBEC 1983 p. 75, Nos. 72-74 (entry by Claude Thibault, Luc Noppen and Michel Doyon). The subjects were the teacher Clément Cazeau; his wife, née Julie Hamelin; and his mother Madame Jean Cazeau, née Geneviève-Victoire Chabot. All three of them lived in a house on the corner of Rue Couillard and Rue Sainte-Famille in Quebec City.
3. Oddly enough, if the dates are correct for the period in which Rouleau's portrait was done, the subject should have actually been 22 years old in March of 1848, since he was born on December 13, 1825.

T HE FIRST RECORDED REFERENCE to Charles Ramus Forrest concerns his enlistment as lieutenant in the 3rd Foot of the British army on November 18, 1802. Six years later, C.R. Forrest married Ellen St. Leger, daughter of Lieutenant-General William St. Leger. Shortly after his marriage, Forrest travelled with his wife to India to join his father-in-law as aide-de-camp. In 1812, he participated in the Spanish War, and in 1814-1815, he travelled to America for the first time as part of an expedition against New Orleans. His appointment to the position of head of quartermaster general services led him to update the nautical and land charts. After being appointed honourary lieutenant-colonel in June 1815, he served in Ireland and stayed in Bordeaux, France, in 1820 and 1821. During this period, he entered into the service of Lord Dalhousie, Governor of Canada, first as aide-de-camp (December 25, 1820), and then as assistant military secretary (June 25, 1821). He lived with his family in Quebec City from June 1821 to July 1823, at which time Lord Dalhousie was obliged to relieve him of his duties. His companions and friends, James Pattison Cockburn and military doctor John Jeremiah Bigsby (1792-1881), with whom he drew occasionally, mentioned Forrest's sometimes strange behaviour.

Upon his return to England he was without a posting and received, in June 1826, half-pay as lieutenant-colonel. In 1824 he produced, with the assistance of publisher Rudolph Ackermann, six monthly issues of *A Picturesque Tour along the Rivers Ganges and Jumna, in India...* which contained 24 of his aquatints. The following year, Ackermann also published *Picturesque Tour through the Provinces of Lower and Upper Canada*, in eight monthly issues illustrated with 48 colour lithographs. Forrest died in March 1827, in Bath, England, leaving behind views of India, Spain, the West Indies, and South America (NGC). He produced several paintings of Canadian landscapes ranging from the Newfoundland coast to lakes Huron and Superior.

CHARLES RAMUS
FORREST

circa 1787-1827

Sources principales
ALLODI 1974/1 ; COOKE 1983.

MQ, NGC

Fig. 111A.
Charles Ramus Forrest,
Quebec City and Montmorency Falls, 1823;
watercolour over graphite on three sheets of paper, 31.8 × 117.3 cm.
National Gallery of Canada, Ottawa (18495).

Fig. 111B.
Francis Towne,
Lake Albano with Castel Gandolfo, 1781;
watercolour, pen and ink on two sheets of paper, 32.1 × 70.2 cm.
British Museum, London (1972.U.646; L.B. Album III [II]).

111. (See colour reproduction, p. 85)
Falls of the Saint Anne River, 1823
Watercolour over graphite on paper, 66.8 × 49.8 cm

Inscription
(b.,l.c., in the artist's hand, entered in the file before the mount covered the inscription) *Canadian Views No. 50-/Third or Lower Fall on the Ste. Anne or Grande River. Paris St. Joachim/ 32 Miles below Quebec./July 1823.*

Provenance
Descendants of the artist; Cliff Sinclair, Australia (sold by Sotheby's Belgravia, London, November 4, 1975, No. 18); acquired by the National Gallery of Canada, Ottawa, 1975.

Bibliography
TOPOGRAPHICAL PAINTINGS 1975, p. 8, No. 18 (Repr.); *HILL AND LANDRY 1988,* p. 381 (Repr.); *UN MOMENT 1991,* pp. 86 and 87 (Repr.).

Collection
National Gallery of Canada, Ottawa (18509)

T HE WORKS PRODUCED by Charles Ramus Forrest during his stay in Quebec—large-scale landscapes which focus on simplifying the complex elements of nature—are spectacular. Forrest's vision of space is clear and accurate; he imposes a certain order on the wild of nature. In keeping with this concept, his compositions follow a basic symmetry. The drawing, which situates the masses in relation to one another, ensures the composition's coherence. Colour, subordinate to form, was added on the artist's return to his studio.

These works are unequalled by any watercolourist working in Quebec during the same period, be it John Elliott Woolford or James Pattison Cockburn, who admired Forrest's work but did not imitate it. The profound simplicity of these landscapes is indeed astonishing; to understand its source, we must go back a few years to when Forrest lived in England.

Charles Ramus Forrest arrived in Quebec City on June 18, 1821, to assume his duties as aide-de-camp to Lord Dalhousie, then governor of British North America. This new position put an end to several years of inactivity in the officer's career. On June 25, 1817, Forrest had been named major of the 34th Foot and placed on half-pay.[1] He spent the first years (1817-1820) of this retirement in Devon, near Exeter, before leaving for the Pyrenees where drawings bear witness to his presence in July 1820.[2] We cannot be certain that he remained in southwestern France until his departure for North America, but his arrival in Quebec City on the brig *Ann*[3] in "58 days from Bordeaux" leads us to think so. The three years Forrest spent near Exeter are nonetheless crucial to understanding the works he produced in Quebec.

In the early 19th century, Exeter was a secondary town, which meant that artists residing there could not hope to gain exposure in London, as they might have had they lived in Norwich. However, the watercolourists living in Exeter were fairly active, especially under the influence of Francis Towne (1739/1740-1816). Towne, who was born in Exeter, gave drawing classes, trained a number of students, and made copies of his own watercolours done during his visit to Italy to meet the demands of collectors in the Exeter area. He thus had a decisive influence on a number of artists in the area, among them John White Abbott (1763-1851).[4]

Fig. 111C.
Charles Ramus Forrest,
Panoramic View of the Basin of Québec taken from the Grand Battery, 1823;
watercolour, graphite, pen and brown ink on 12 sheets of paper, 43.8 × 263.8 cm.
National Gallery of Canada, Ottawa (18492).

Fig. 111D.
Francis Towne,
A View of the Cascade at Ambleside;
watercolour, pen and ink on paper,
37.7 × 26.5 cm.
Ashmolean Museum, Oxford.

Fig. 111E.
John White Abbott,
Kerswell, Devon;
watercolour on paper,
43.8 × 37.5 cm.
Victoria and Albert Museum, London
(P. 59-1923).

Following his death in 1816, some of these painters perpetuated his style in their own works.

Forrest, who arrived in Exeter in this particular context, already had experience in topographical drawing, which he used to great advantage during his visit to India.[5] His encounter with the works of Towne and his imitators profoundly changed his approach to landscape painting. Francis Towne had developed an original style, a clear method of depicting the shape and structure of landscapes. His works are by no means anecdotal, nor do they contain effects created by brush strokes mixing the washes.

Forrest's large panoramic view of Montmorency falls with Quebec City in the distance (Fig. 111A) is largely influenced by Towne's Italian works, such as *Lake Albano with Castel Gandolfo* (Fig. 111B). The perfect understanding of the shapes of the Quebec landscape, the refined portrayal of the land and the vegetation, where nothing mars the appreciation of the work as a whole, the focus on the light to the detriment of the atmospheric effects, are all indications that Charles Ramus Forrest was influenced by these Italian models. It also appears that Forrest was used to doing his watercolours on

several sheets of paper, just as Francis Towne and John Abbott did. *Quebec City and Montmorency Falls* is done on three sheets, while the *Panoramic View of the Basin of Quebec taken from the Grand Battery* (Fig. 111C) is done on twelve. This last work, which remained unfinished at the time of Forrest's departure in July 1823, is invaluable in that it reflects a working method which hails directly from John White Abbott. Forrest worked outdoors on small sheets of paper, on which he sketched his landscape in pencil. Upon his return to the studio, he put them together to obtain a complete overview of his landscape. The lack of coherence between the sheets bearing the watercolour washes confirms that the colour was applied in the studio, rather than in the presence of the landscape; hence the need to keep in mind the colours observed during the sketching session, either by taking notes or by doing the washes as quickly as possible. Forrest had to leave Quebec City rather hurriedly, which may explain why this panoramic landscape remained unfinished.

The watercolour *Falls of the Sainte-Anne River* is an example of what distinguished Forrest's style from that of Towne and Abbott. The composition is

fairly similar; Forrest must have been familiar with Towne's *A View of the Cascade at Ambleside* (Fig. 111D). The trees, which jut out over the falls, also bear a resemblance in both cases: the curving trunks are crowned with slender leafy branches, and the texture of the bark and the effects of the light are depicted using parallel strokes. However, Forrest's approach to nature is very different. He follows the lessons he has learned, but uses decorative effects to their maximum. John White Abbott had already influenced Francis Towne in this way. In his watercolour entitled *Kerswell, Devon* (Fig. 111E) held at the Victoria and Albert Museum, he has added a great deal more vegetation in the foreground and given the foliage a feather-like appearance, ignoring the pared-down portrayal of the masses which is the mainstay of Towne's landscapes. Forrest goes a step further with the sinuous portrayal of the vegetation and the churning waters of the Sainte-Anne river. The hues confirm his quest for subtlety by focusing on the colour play between the rocks and the vegetation in a palette of browns, blue-greens, khakis, and greys. The Quebec outdoors thus becomes part of an esthetic codification which bears witness to the divergence between reality and the portrayal thereof.

D.P.

Notes

1. COOKE 1983, p. 82.

2. HILL AND LANDRY 1988, p. 375, 18857 and 18858 (Repr.).

3. *Quebec Gazette,* June 21, 1821.

4. On this topic, see Martin Hardie, *Watercolour Painting in Britain. The Eighteenth Century,* 1975, Vol. I, pp. 118-128.

5. *India Observed. India as viewed by British Artists, 1760-1860* (Cat.), (London: Victoria and Albert Museum, 1982), No. 49 (repr.), and Sotheby's Belgravia sales catalogue, London, November 4, 1975, No. 7 (repr.).

JEAN-JOSEPH GIROUARD

(see biographical note on page 159)

MQ, NGC

VAG, AGNS, MMFA

112.
Robert-Shore-Milnes Bouchette, 1838

Graphite and crayon on paper,
24.6 × 18.8 cm

Inscription
(l.c., in graphite) *R S.M Bouchette.*

Provenance
(?) Album belonging to Adèle Berthelot, wife of
L.-H. La Fontaine; William P. Wolfe, Montreal;
acquired by the Musée de la Province de Québec,
Quebec City, 1959.

Exhibition
Quebec City 1983-1984, No. 305.

Bibliography
LE MUSÉE DU QUÉBEC 1983, p. 246, No. 305 (entry
by Guy Paradis) (Repr.); *TARDIF-CÔTÉ 1985,*
pp. 12-13; *BÉLAND AND BOURASSA 1990,* pp. 6, 8,
60 and 62 (Repr.); *MARTIN AND GRANDBOIS 1991,*
p. 15 (Repr.); *UN MOMENT 1991,* pp. 194 and 195
(Repr.).

Collection
Musée du Québec, Quebec City (59.350)

113.
Wolfred Nelson, 1838

Graphite on paper, 25 × 18.7 cm

Inscriptions
(l.c., in graphite) *Nouvelle Prison, Mars 1838;*
(lower down, by another hand) *Wolfred Nelson.*

Provenance
(?) Album belonging to Adèle Berthelot, wife of
L.-H. La Fontaine; William P. Wolfe, Montreal;
acquired by the Musée de la Province de Québec,
Québec, 1959.

Bibliography
BÉLAND AND BOURASSA 1990, p. 60.

Collection
Musée du Québec, Quebec City (59.349)

D OCTOR Wolfred Nelson (1791-1863), lawyer Robert-Shore-Milnes Bouchette (1805-1879), and notary Jean-Joseph Girouard (1794-1855)[1] were among the *Patriotes* imprisoned in the Montreal jail in 1838, at the age of 47, 33 and 44 respectively.

Wolfred Nelson, doctor in Saint-Denis-sur-Richelieu and convert to reformist beliefs, asserted himself as an opponent of the poor British administration in Canada and champion of the civil rights of French Canadians. He became active in politics in 1827 as a member of the *Parti patriote* and was elected the same year member of William Henry (now Sorel) county, constituency of the government party. Nelson then became increasingly radical; one of the few non-French-Canadian members of the *Patriotes,* he was furthermore extremely vocal in the conflict with the constitutional party, composed mainly of English-speaking members. In October 1837 he was made president of the *Assemblée des six comtés,* and on November 16, he was convicted of high treason by a government warrant. Nelson and Louis-Joseph Papineau, who had joined him in Saint-Denis, subsequently decided to resist arrest, provide arms and ammunition to the people, and declare Lower Canada independent. After a preliminary victory over the British brigade on November 23, which conferred on him the status of hero among the *Patriotes,* Nelson was forced to flee on December 1. Ten days later, he was captured and imprisoned for seven months in the new Montreal jail, called the Pied-du-Courant.[2]

Upon his return to Canada in 1834, following a long stay in Europe,[3] Robert-Shore-Milnes Bouchette became involved in politics, joining the *Patriote* liberals. Along with Nelson, he was one of the few English-speaking members of this party. In 1836, he ran as candidate in the county of Saguenay but was defeated. He participated actively in the meetings held in the Quebec City area and founded, on June 17, 1837, in conjunction with artist Joseph Légaré, a bilingual newspaper entitled *Le Libéral/The Liberal*. Following the issuing of warrants against the presidents of *Patriote* committees, Bouchette was arrested and then released on bail. In December, he led the advance guard of a small troop to Moore's Corner (Saint-Armand-Station) where, injured and ill, he was taken to the Montreal jail.

Rallied to the *Patriote* cause, Jean-Joseph Girouard was unanimously elected member of the new riding of Deux-Montagnes in 1831, and became a fervent supporter of Papineau. In 1834, he wholeheartedly backed the Ninety-Two Resolutions and was once again elected member for the *Parti canadien* in the same riding. Very active at the Patriote meetings, Girouard was acknowledged, along with his friend Jean-Olivier Chénier, as one of the leaders of the resistance movement in the Lac des Deux-Montagnes area. On December 1, 1837, his name appeared on the list of outlaws and a reward was offered for his capture. Girouard fled Saint-Benoît, which was then pillaged and burned. The notary finally decided to give himself up to the authorities in order to offer his services to his friends who were already in the Montreal jail.

Girouard was first jailed from December 29, 1837 to July 16, 1838, and then from November 4 to December 22 of the same year, having been freed on bail during the summer. He continued to lead an active life behind bars, compiling notes, addressing personal letters to families of convicts, and even drawing a map of the prison layout. Thanks to this map, we know that the cells in the central section, which were larger, were reserved for the Patriote leaders, and that Girouard's

cell was next to that of Bouchette. Bouchette's cell seems to have been fairly comfortable, judging by the four views (three in watercolour) he painted from its interior (Cat. 65 and 66). Girouard also defended a number of Patriotes and refused to sign any confession, unlike Bouchette and Nelson who, for this reason, were condemned in June 1838 to exile in Bermuda with five other "Sons of Liberty."[4] Girouard, who had managed to procure a small table to work at, as well as pencils and sketching paper, seems to have transformed his cell into a veritable notary's office and artist's studio. During his two prison terms, he masterfully executed some 90 portraits of his companions in captivity (Fig. 112-113A).

The Musée du Québec owns four of these portraits done by Girouard during his prison terms in the Montreal jail— those of Wolfred Nelson, R.-S.-M. Bouchette, Joseph-Amable Berthelot, and captain P. Jalbert—while the National Archives of Canada have a series of some one hundred drawings.[5] Thanks to studies published by Diane Tardif-Côté (1985), and more recently by Lucie Dorais (1991), we now possess considerable information on the notary's artistic production during 1838. Most of this article is in fact a summary of the results of their research.[6]

The National Archives collection includes 95 works, one of which is a view of the ruins of the village of Saint-Benoît done by Girouard in summer 1838 after he was released,[7] and 90 portraits: 87 of *Patriotes,* one each of the jailer and the prison accountant, and one of an engraving editor in New York. Most of these portraits (67) were produced during Girouard's first prison term, that is, between December 29, 1837, and July 16, 1838. This means that Nelson and Bouchette must have been painted during this period, because they were deported to Bermuda in June 1838. Most of the drawings dated during this first prison term bear at the bottom of the portrait original inscriptions and more recent notes, probably written by judge Joseph-Amable Berthelot. The models are all identified this way, sometimes by Girouard, but generally with the model's signature. However, the portraits of Nelson and Bouchette at the Musée du Québec are believed to have been identified by judge Berthelot. The inscriptions also indicate the age or place of residence of the sitter, his trade or profession, his date of imprisonment and, more rarely, the date the portrait was done, as in the case of **Wolfred Nelson,** which bears the

Fig. 112-113A.
François-Marie-Thomas Chevalier de Lorimier (attr. to),
Jean-Joseph Girouard, 1838.
National Archives of Canada,
Ottawa (C-123497).

inscription "*Mars 1838*" (March 1838). According to Lucie Dorais, it is nonetheless practically impossible to determine exactly when all the works were painted. The portraits done in lead pencil, most of which are touched up with charcoal and blurred with a stump (especially the clothing) or with a grease pencil, are on sheets of paper approximately 20×25 cm. Girouard used different types of paper of varying quality. Since paper was hard to come by in prison, he was sometimes forced to cut the sheets in half. Although a number of portraits were done on onionskin paper, tracing paper (25), coloured paper or baling paper, most of them were drawn on quality sketching paper, often embossed.

Most of the portraits are half-length and show the model in profile. In some cases, a network of crisscross lines suggests the background, while a zigzag stroke or a group of clouds done with a stump closes off the bottom of the bust. Some of the portraits are different, such as that of Francis Desrosiers, "the victim of the dungeons" (*Translation*), who is portrayed lying on his bed wearing his nightcap, or that of Neil Scott, who is depicted with a dog in his lap, or those of Joseph-Amable Berthelot, Ignace Dumouchel, Pierre-Amable Boucher of Boucherville, Louis-H. La Fontaine and Wolfred Nelson, portrayed three-quarter length. Three profiles show more than one person in the same drawing: the triple portrait of Jean-Baptiste Dumouchel and his two sons, as well as two double portraits of Joseph Robillard and Luc. H. Masson, each with their respective sons.

As is the case for **Wolfred Nelson** and **Robert-Shore-Milnes Bouchette**, almost all the portraits show the subject's left profile, since this is the profile more naturally drawn by right-handed artists. In many cases, the original drawing displays a faint, slightly wavering outline. According to Lucie Dorais, the notary had his subjects sit in a candlelit room before a wall on which hung a sheet of paper; he would then rapidly trace the silhouette projected by their shadow. Incorrectly situated, wavering light would thus explain the hesitant strokes of the outline and the elongated shape of many of the faces. However, this hypothesis does not allow for the fact that the portraits are reduced, that is, half life-size. Furthermore, many of the drawings bear, at the top of the sheet, holes probably made by needles. These perforations would seem to indicate that some of the sheets were pinned together so that a double of the portrait could be done. Girouard also did, at the request of visitors, portraits of spouses, fathers or sons. As a result, in addition to the original series he did for himself, he was thus able to produce copies of certain portraits, which were given to relatives of the convicts or the convicts themselves. Upon close examination, the portraits of Nelson and Bouchette in the Musée du Québec collection reveal, in the outline and the use of the stump, a more applied and finished product than those at the Archives, which bear witness to a certain spontaneity more in keeping with drawing from nature (Fig. 112A and 113A). However, both series have the thin, wavering outline, while 25 of the Archives drawings are done, as already mentioned, on tracing paper. It is therefore difficult to distinguish the copies from the originals.

Whatever the case may be, this series of portraits of the Patriotes done by Girouard in prison is an invaluable visual record of the key players in the uprisings of 1837-1838, such as Joseph Légaré (Fig. 112-113B), Denis-Benjamin Viger, Jean-Olivier Chenier, and Louis-Hippolyte La Fontaine, to name only a few.   M.B.

Fig. 112A.
Jean-Joseph Girouard,
Robert-Shore-Milnes Bouchette, 1838;
graphite and charcoal on paper,
23.5 × 19 cm.
National Archives of Canada, Ottawa
(C-133448).

Fig. 113A.
Jean-Joseph Girouard,
Wolfred Nelson, 1838;
graphite and charcoal on paper, 24 × 18 cm.
National Archives of Canada, Ottawa
(C-18427).

Fig. 112-113B.
Jean-Joseph Girouard,
Joseph Légaré, 1838;
graphite and charcoal on paper, 29.4 × 21.3 cm.
National Archives of Canada, Ottawa (C-18492).

Notes

1. On Nelson, Bouchette and Girouard, see their respective biographies in John Beswarick Thompson, DCB, Vol. IX (1977); Yves Tessier, DCB, Vol. X (1972); CHASSÉ 1985.

2. All his life, Nelson carried out humanitarian actions; for example, he acted as prison doctor to his companions in misfortune. He later continued to practice medicine in addition to being member for Richelieu (1844-1851), and the first elected mayor of Montreal (1854-1856). In 1838 Théophile Hamel painted his portrait, which is now part of the McCord Museum collection (VÉZINA 1975/1, p. 68, Repr.).

3. During his visit to London in 1830, he frequented the English nobility and bourgeoisie and had his portrait done on December 10, 1830 by Armenius Meyer (NAC).

4. The crossing from Quebec City to Bermuda during July enabled Bouchette and Nelson to compile a list of grievances of the Canadians.

5. Acquired in 1959, the drawings of the Musée du Québec came, according to Gérard Morisset, then director, from the album of Adèle Berthelot, wife of L.-H. La Fontaine and daughter of Joseph-Amable Berthelot, who had his portrait done by his friend Girouard. This portrait bears the inscription "*Mon Père J.A. Berthelot, père du Juge Berthelot*", thereby making Morisset's hypothesis plausible. The series acquired by the National Archives of Canada in 1984 from a descendant of Girouard also came from judge Joseph-Amable Berthelot (1815-1897), Girouard's friend and brother-in-law. The complete collection was published in 1973. See LAURIN 1973. A dozen portraits of notaries, members of the *Parti patriote*, were also reproduced in LAFORTUNE 1986, pp. 38-39.

6. See TARDIF-CÔTÉ 1985, and the entry by Lucie Dorais in UN MOMENT 1991.

7. When he was released in the summer, Girouard had lost everything; his two houses had been burned and his filing cabinet, bookshelves, and pastel and miniature materials had all been pillaged or burned. See "État estimatif des pertes souffertes par Jean-Joseph Girouard, notaire de la paroisse de Saint-Benoît," *Revue d'histoire de l'Amérique française*, Vol. XXI (December 1907), pp. 478-479.

E LIZABETH FRANCES HALE was born in England in 1774, the daughter of Lieutenant General William Amherst. She married John Hale, former aide-de-camp and military secretary to the Duke of Kent in Canada. She thus became the sister-in-law of Edward Hale, seigneur de Portneuf (cat. 243). In June 1799, barely two months after her marriage in London, she left for Canada where her husband had been appointed assistant treasurer-paymaster general of the British Army. The couple took up residence in Quebec City where John Hall held important political positions including that of President of the Legislative Council and of Receiver-General of Lower Canada. In 1819 the Hales purchased the Sainte-Anne-de-la-Pérade seigniory where the family spent the summer months. They also made a few trips to England.

Like other young girls from well-to-do families who had received a good education, Elizabeth Frances Hale had some artistic knowledge. She was interested in the places she visited or lived in, such as the region of Sainte-Anne-de-la-Pérade. Elizabeth Frances Hale died in Quebec City on June 18, 1826 following a lengthy illness.

ELIZABETH FRANCES HALE

1774-1826

Main sources
HARPER 1970; COOKE 1983; LANDRY 1987.

114.

Sketchbook, c. 1824-1825 and 1834

Pen and brown ink, grey wash, graphite with traces of scraping out on paper, 12.8 × 20.6 cm

Provenance
Descendants of the Hale family; J. Beverley McLaughlin, Ottawa; acquired by the Public Archives of Canada, Ottawa, 1939.

Exhibition
Ottawa 1988 (1 sheet).

Bibliography
COOKE 1983, p. 44; WILSON 1988, p. 130; MARTIN AND GRANDBOIS 1991, p. 51.

Collection
National Archives of Canada, Ottawa (1939-252)

E LIZABETH FRANCES HALE, *née* Amherst, married John Hale (1764-1838) in London in April of 1799 and returned to Canada with him as he resumed the post of Deputy Paymaster General of British forces, after which he pursued a successful career in the Public Service. Because of her family's station, she received an aristocratic upbringing and education, wherein she would have also received instruction in the accomplishments of drawing as well as music, dance and French. She lived half of her lifetime in Quebec City and due to her husband's position, it would be expected that she associated with the upper middle class of Quebec. Her sons were educated in England, where she herself returned with the rest of the children at the start of the War of 1812, going back to Quebec in April 1816. The Hales raised a family of 9 children and took up residence at 5 Rue St. Louis, and after the war at 50 Rue des Carrières (Cat. B), where Elizabeth looked to maintaining and improving her situation in life as well as ambitiously securing a substantial future for them.[1] What we know of E.F. Hale's education in drawing must be surmised from her station and education in life, from the evidence of her work and the very pertinent comments she makes about her life and drawing in letters to her brother Lord Amherst (1773-1857).[2]

Through her letters, she inadvertently gives us a fascinating and true self-portrait and speaks revealingly about her drawing. Elizabeth Frances Hale was an intelligent, energetic, adventuresome, and loving person. She was conservatively religious, a dutiful wife, a caring mother, and a very conscientious homemaker. By nature she was optimistic and had a delightful sense of humour with a rather snobbish air in society. As an ambitious woman, acutely aware of the world she lived in, she incessantly tried to use her strong social position for the advancement of her husband and her children. She loved music and dancing, the latest fashions, gossip, parties and picnics, country outings and drawing. The letters also mention the fact that her brother and his wife were both quite adept at drawing. She frequently sent them floor plans and sketches of the houses she occupied as well as sketches done by others. She was constantly procuring things for herself and her family through her brother and eventually asked him to send her "some brown mixture" which she found superior to bistre or any other sort of brown. She also asked for some "good drawing paper for straining on a board or

frame and some good brushes" which she was used to and which she could not get in Quebec. Later, she criticized the poor quality of paper which was sent and mentioned that, on trial, she ruined two very large drawings. On several occasions, she states how well her sister-in-law drew figures and how inadequate she was at making likenesses. In fact, she criticizes a view of Quebec she sent to her brother on June 17, 1811, and asks him to excuse the faults in her style of drawing, but to accept its absolute accuracy and truth of detail. Of her son Edward, who is studying in England by this time, she tells us of his penchant for drawing which she would like to encourage as it would keep him amused and out of mischief. She also expresses the fact that for her, drawing is but a hobby and that she cherishes it because "it is so amusing years and years afterwards to look over sketches of places one has seen, and recollect different occurrences of the moment". Her sketchbook is a remarkable volume of drawings for several reasons. It is unique amongst the handful of sketchbooks from this period surviving intact in Canadian collections and certainly the earliest from the hand of a woman, as many early sketchbooks have met the sad end of being broken up. Its subject matter, exterior views of the residences of four generations of the Hale family, is also unique, since most sketchbooks from this period are by British military topographers who rarely treat such subject matter.

Generally speaking, the sketchbook as a drawing tool was used considerably by English artists who came to North America in the 18th and 19th centuries. The use of the sketchbook emerged as protected paper manufacturing in England became cheaper.[3] Also, the fashion for travel into the English countryside and abroad increased the desire to record the much-valued personal experience of other lands and cultures.[4] To prepare one for such an undertaking, generations of young aristocrats were taught the discipline of drawing as an accomplishment which would prove a useful practice for communication and entertainment. The sketchbook was as personal and intimate an object as was the traveller's journal or diary or letters. Military officers were taught drawing skills as a practical tool in the field.[5] Drawing in a sketchbook was an efficient and unique form of capturing and collating information. The sequential event of proceeding through the book, when turning the pages, offered the possibility of capturing a multiplicity of views of the same

MQ

A. *Views of the Saint Anne River and the Hale Seigneury at Sainte-Anne-de-la-Pérade* (Fol. 4v and 5r), c. 1825
Brush and brown wash over graphite on paper (Fol. 4v); pen and brown ink over graphite on paper (Fol. 5r).

NGC

B. *The House My Father Bought, No. 50 Des Carrières St., Quebec* (Fol. 22v and 23r), c. 1825
Brush, pen and brown wash over graphite on paper

Inscription
(l., Fol. 22v, in graphite) *The House my Father bought/No. 50 des Carriers St. Que./E.R.H.*

subject, often within a time frame which conveyed simultaneity as well as movement through space and time and thus achieved a unique sense of space which the single sheet does not afford.

This small sketchbook came to the collections of the National Archives of Canada from the Hale family through the dealer, Mr. J. Beverly MacLaughlin of Ottawa, on July 3, 1939, as being from the hand of Colonel Hale.[6] The sketchbook is half bound with red leather on the spine and corners, with blue marble papers on the outside of the boards. The spine has five lines of gold tooling imitating sewn cords. There is a pencil holder in the form of two leather straps extending from the fore-edge inside the back cover. The book has an integrated binding, the six sections

being sewn all along two cords and sewn through the boards. It is flat-backed with no headbands. The case holds six sections made up of sixteen leaves folded into thirty-two folios comprising sixty-four pages. The first and last sections consist of two leaves and the second through the fifth sections consist of three leaves each. The paper is woven and cream in colour. At the fore-edge of twelve of the folios are pinholes in the upper and lower corners. Five drawings carry a small pencilled x in one of the corners.[7]

Most of the drawings are meticulously executed in brush and brown wash while a few are carefully rendered in pen and brown ink over pencil, and even fewer are done in brush and grey wash. Three are in pencil and one a combination of

brush and grey wash and pen and brown ink. Her style of drawing when using pen and brush remains faithful to the canons of the Picturesque. When using pen and brown ink, however, a sense of naturalism and realism enters her work. It reveals a conflict between the world observed as it is and the world idealized for art's sake, which often coexists in a talent somewhat trained but too little exercized. The first ten of twenty-four separate drawings in the sketchbook alternate from page to page in a peculiar counterpoint of technique, from pen and brown ink to brush and brown wash, and then continues in an irregular pattern (Cat. A and E). Except for one or two, each of the forty-four drawings is painstakingly executed, almost overworked, and one should hesitate to call

VAG

C. *View of Quebec from the Hale's Residence* (Fol. 27v and 28r), c. 1825
Pen and brown ink over graphite on paper

Inscriptions
(u.r., Fol. 27v, in graphite) *St. Joseph;* (u.c., Fol. 28r, in graphite) *P. Levis.*
Exhibition
Ottawa 1988.
Bibliography
WILSON 1988, pp. 130 and 131 (Repr.).

AGNS

D. *Views of the Chateau Saint Louis from the Parliament Building and from the Citadel* (Fol. 17v and 18r), c. 1825
Brush and brown wash over graphite on paper (Fol. 17v); brush and brown ink over graphite on paper (Fol. 18v).

them sketches, but rather finished drawings, each remaining self-contained and independent. The ten last folios were left blank.

The sketchbook is neither signed nor dated and is only attributed to Mrs. Hale, yet it contains several revealing inscriptions. One of the many pencil inscriptions identifying specific places and buildings depicted throughout the sketchbook is initialled "*E.R.H.*", Mrs. Hale's great-grandson Edward Russel Hale (b.1870-d.-?-), who presumably inherited the sketchbook.[8] From the Hale letters we know that Mrs. Hale's children also drew, and exchanged drawings by post and en-

couraged each other in their efforts to draw well.[9] The only inscription we know to be from the hand of Mrs.Hale, frugal housewife that she was, is a list of expenditures on the inside back cover. It is an accounting of the cost of a journey from Ste. Anne de La Pérade to Quebec City, with references to three of her younger children: Fanny (Frances Isabella), Mary and George. On the back of folio 13 one can see, faintly but clearly, profile pencil sketches of three children. The 1823 watermark found in several sheets of the sketchbook tells us approximately when the paper and possibly the actual book itself was made. As Mrs Hale died of breast cancer on June 18,

1826, we may then conclude that the drawings were most likely executed somewhere between 1824 and 1825.

In studying the subject matter of the sketchbook a little closer, we are able to extend the time frame for the sketchbook and perhaps acknowledge the definite presence of another artist's hand. The first twenty-four drawings describe the manor house of the seigneurie at Ste. Anne de La Pérade (Cat. A and E), her summer home, still partially standing today, purchased in 1819.[10] These views are all picturesque compositions depicting the house at a distance and from all sides and some of the surrounding landscape. The next six-

MMFA

E. *Views of the Hale Seigneury at Sainte-Anne-de-la-Pérade* (Fol. 1v and 2r), c. 1825
Brush and brown wash over graphite on paper (Fol. 1v); pen and brown ink over graphite on paper (Fol. 2r).

Inscription
(u.l, Fol. 1r, in graphite) *St Anne/Below Montreal/Hale Seigneury.*

Fig. 114
Edward Hale,
"Sleepy Hollow", Residence of Edward Hale in Sherbrooke, after 1833;
brush and brown wash over graphite on paper (Fol. 29v); pen and brown ink over graphite on paper (Fol. 30r).
National Archives of Canada, Ottawa (C-137991).

teen drawings describe her house and its surroundings at 50 Rue des Carrières in Quebec City (Cat. B. and D). Suddenly, without a break, we are presented with a full two-page panoramic view of the port of Quebec, taken from high above, near the Citadel where des Carrières is situated. These drawings are much more highly structured than the previous views of Ste. Anne and it is not unlikely that they were drawn with the aid of a *camera lucida*. We also find a double-page panoramic view of Sherbrooke and two landscapes with a house identified as "Sleepy Hollow", her son Edward's home which is still standing today (Fig. 114A). He returned to Cana-

da from India in 1829 after his mother's death and only by 1834 did he settle near Sherbrooke.[11] Obviously, these sheets could not have been executed by his mother and were probably done by Edward himself. Yet, whoever drew them not only respected the style of the previous drawings, but also adhered to the same painting technique and remained consistent with the subject matter. The last landscape in the sketchbook is of "The Plantation", (formerly "Tockets" Hall), a few kilometres north of Guisborough, in Yorkshire, England. This was the Hale ancestral home where General John Hale (1728-1806) lived and where John Hale was born.[12] The manner

of painting on this page remains closer to that of the Sherbrooke drawings. Hinged onto the inside of the back cover is a small quarter page drawing of the La Puce Falls.

Five of the Quebec City views from the sketchbook can also be found in the oeuvre of James Pattison Cockburn (Cat. 72-82). The academic tradition of copying works from other artists for instruction or pleasure is long-standing in Western art. Several artists in Quebec City indulged in such activity, as demonstrated by the work of James Peachey (Cat. 42 to 45), Philip John Bainbrigge (Cat. 54 to 58), George St. Vincent Whitmore (active in Quebec City c. 1822), Fanny Amelia

Bayfield (active in Quebec City 1838-1841) and Millicent Mary Chaplin (Cat. 68 to 71). There is evidence that Mrs. Hale may have copied watercolours by the artist Edward Walsh (1766-1832).[13] Although Cockburn did work with brown wash, stylistically he remains a far superior and much more competent artist.

Mrs. Hale drew with very specific purposes in mind and her letters shed some light on this matter. In several of the letters to her brother Lord Amherst and his wife, regarding the purchase of the seigneurie in 1819, she often refers to a small sketch she had enclosed or was promising, so that they would have a better idea of the location of the house she had just described. The sketchbook comes after the letters but the evidence of Mrs. Hale's earlier work, dated 1805, indicates that she had been actively drawing and painting since her arrival in North America.[14] The direct relationship between her letters, and her drawings is quite clear: one is the very extension of the other. Her drawings are an attempt to convey in the fullest possible sense her experiences of life in Canada to her family in England which she ardently pined for. Like the letters, the drawings concern themselves with family matters. They express a pride in wealth and material success that generations of Hales

achieved through their ownership of property. Although the work of E.F. Hale (et. al.) does not reveal a great artistic imagination nor creative and innovative technical skill, we value it rather because of its rare, intimate description of a very private world which, more often than not, remained unexpressed by most artists and quite inaccessible to us. We respect her and her collaborators for having taken the care in observing and describing some of the poetic reality of their existence, which we can perceive through her letters and know through the humble drawings contained in this sketchbook.

G.G.

Notes

1. *Cooke 1983*, p. 99

2. Letters by Elizabeth Frances Hale and John Hale are located in NAC, RG 23,(G II 18); U of T, Thomas Fisher Rare Book Library, Mss.Colln. 90; India Office Records;10R Mss Eur F140/160A, copied on NAC, Mss.Div., microfilm A1085.

The only surviving drawings she sent with her letters that we know of are the floor plans for the house at 5 Rue St. Louis, in letter of May 16, 1801, and October 28, 1805. There is also a small floor plan drawn in pencil on the last page of the sketchbook. It should be noted that Professor Roger Hall, University of Western Ontario,

is presently editing the Hale annotated letters which will be publish by the Champlain Society. I wish to thank him for kindly making the manuscript available to me.

3. Philip Haskel, *A New Introduction to Bibilography* (Oxford University Press: New York and Oxford, 1972).

4. *Finley 1983*, Chapter I.

5. *Bell and Cooke 1978*.

6. NAC, RG 37, C series, 1938-8.

7. The appearance of pinholes and x is unclear to us. Evidence from other sketchbooks suggests that the pinholes may have to do with the use of a mechanical device such as a camera obscura or lucida. The x could be a personal notation of which drawings were copied and sent off at a later date.

8. NAC, Artist file 705-101, genealogical chart.

9. NAC, MG 23,(G II 18) Vol.4, p. 264 & 2947.

10. John Bigsby, *Shoe and Canoe*, London, 1850 (Grangerized volume); Rare Book Library, NAC. An earlier drawing, in pen and brown ink over pencil, of the manor house of the Seigneurie of Ste. Anne done in 1822 can be found opposite page 36 of Vol. 1. Cornelius Krieghoff painted the same scene; see *Harper 1979*, p. 18 (Repr.).

11. Louis-Philippe Audet, DCB, Vol. X (1982), pp. 356-357.

12. For a similar view with an inscription identifying The Plantation, Guisborough, Yorkshire, England see NAC, Hensley collection, 1979-14-29.

13. *Cooke 1983*, p.p. 200-202.

14. *Cooke 1983*, p. 99.

B ORN NOVEMBER 8, 1817, Théophile Hamel was the son of François-Xavier Hamel, a farmer from Sainte-Foy (near Quebec City). On May 16, 1834, at age 16, he became an apprentice to Antoine Plamondon, under whom he studied for six years. In 1840, he opened his own atelier on Rue Buade and painted his first known portraits. As early as 1842, he painted two large religious canvases inspired by known compositions for the church at Saint-Ours. On June 10, 1843, after three years on his own, he left for Europe; he was the first Quebec artist to travel to Italy. His first stop was Rome, where he remained from summer 1843 to summer 1845. From there, he went directly to Venice. Although we do not know the names of the specific ateliers Hamel visited, he is believed to have studied, among other places, at the Accademia di San Luca. After visiting several cities throughout Italy, he travelled north, to Antwerp, in Flanders. His influences were varied; he copied paintings by masters such as Titian and Rubens (Cat. 123), and produced an increasing number of drawings, which he kept in a sketchbook (Cat. 118).

On his return to Canada in summer 1846, he settled in Quebec City. Having returned from Europe with a number of his "Italian and Belgian" works, he displayed them in his atelier. Included among these works were *Academic Study of a Seated Man Depicted in Left Profile with Head Resting on the Right Hand* (Cat. 119) and *The Pilgrim* (Cat. 122). He also showed his works in Montreal—the seat of government at the time—when he moved there in fall 1847. It was during his stay in Montreal that he took on Napoléon Bourassa as his pupil. He returned to Quebec City in fall 1851 and was inundated with orders.

Hamel's talent as a portraitist was officially recognized in June 1853, when he was commissioned by the government to do a series of portraits of the speakers of the assemblies and legislative councils. In a sense, this commission made him the official portraitist of the government, which he followed as far as Toronto for the sessions of 1856-1857 and 1858. However, he continued to be sought after by the elite in the Quebec City area. On September 9, 1857, at the age of 39, he married Georgina-Mathilde Faribault, daughter of Georges-Barthélemi Faribault (Cat. 237).

While his studies in Europe may have prepared him for painting a wider variety of subject matter, it was in portraiture that he really made his mark. The rare landscapes or history paintings known to have been done by Hamel include *Typhus* (circa 1849, Notre-Dame de Bonsecours chapel), commissioned privately by Monseigneur Ignace Bourget, *Virgin and Child* and *Sainte Geneviève*, painted in 1867 for the *Exposition universelle de Paris*. Hamel also painted a few historical figures, such as *Jacques Cartier* (Cat. 127). To date, some forty religious compositions have been catalogued.

Théophile Hamel met with undeniable success, which allowed him to maintain a high standard of living; in fact, he was so secure financially that on many occasions, he readily extended loans to parish councils and individuals. He exercised his talent as a master portraitist for over 20 years. Certain characteristics of his style were perpetuated, with varying degrees of success, by some of his pupils, particularly Eugène Hamel, Ludger Ruelland and Napoléon Bourassa. Théophile Hamel died in Quebec City on December 23, 1870.

THÉOPHILE HAMEL
1817-1870

Main sources
VÉZINA 1975/1; VÉZINA 1976/1; VÉZINA 1977.

115.
Saint Mary Magdeleine, c. 1840
After an Unidentified Artist, France, 18th Century.
Oil on canvas, 61.5 × 48.4 cm

Provenance
Descendants of the artist; Mrs. Théophile Hamel, née Georgina Faribault, before 1871; Mrs. Gustave Hamel, née Amélie Duchesnay, Quebec City, before 1922; Mrs. Berthe Lessard, née Lemay, Maniwaki, before 1976; Mrs. Louise Lessard-Boivin, Montreal; gift to the Musée du Québec, Quebec City, 1989.

Exhibitions
Quebec City 1991/2.

Bibliography
ANQQ, Notarial Records of Samuel Glackemeyer, "Inventaire des biens de la succesion de feu F. X. Théophile Hamel", March 9, 1871 (No. 5789); *MAGNAN 1922-1923*, p. 352; *BELLERIVE 1925*, p. 49; *VÉZINA 1975/1*, p. 126; *VÉZINA 1976/1*, p. 47, No. 335; *BÉLAND 1989/3*, p. 69; *BÉLAND AND BOURASSA 1990*, p. 36.

Collection
Musée du Québec, Quebec City. Restored in 1991 with the assistance of the Amis du Musée du Québec (89.23)

A LONG WITH Jean-Baptiste Roy-Audy (Cat. 201), who was attracted early in his career by the theme of the repentant Magdalene, Théophile Hamel copied the painting sent to Canada by Father Philippe-Jean-Louis Desjardins (Cat. 202) which hung in the Quebec Picture Gallery, owned by Joseph Légaré.[1] Like Roy-Audy, Hamel's copy was done at the start of his career; unlike him, however, it was done as part of Hamel's training and was not meant to be sold. In fact, it was found in the artist's studio following his death.

The muted colours, the softening of the features through a more detailed rendering and the polished finish clearly show that copies are not only a means of showcasing an artist's talent, but they also reveal differences in taste and artistic approach. While Roy-Audy was content to merely depict a religious subject, Hamel was concerned with painting a work of art.

L.L.

Note
1. Joseph Légaré owned the canvas in 1829, when it was exhibited at the Literary and Historical Society of Quebec. It is mentioned by Joseph Bourne, who published the list of works displayed. John R. Porter advances the hypothesis that Légaré, too, copied it, exhibiting his copy in October 1848 in the House of Assembly in Quebec City (*PORTER 1978/1*, p. 131, No. 174).

116.
Portrait of a Young Woman Holding a Rose c. 1840
Oil on canvas, 85.7 × 71.5 cm

Inscription
(s., c.l.) *T. Hamel P*.

Provenance
Descendants of the artist; Dr. Henri Hamel, Quebec City; acquired by the Musée du Québec, Quebec City, 1967.

Bibliography
HUBBARD 1970, p. 90; *VÉZINA 1973-1974*, p. 49; *VÉZINA 1975/1*, pp. 175, 186, 187, 191, 202, 206, 217 and 218 (Repr.); *VÉZINA 1975/4*, p. 8; *VÉZINA 1976/1*, p. 18, No. 99.

Collection
Musée du Québec, Quebec City. Restored in 1991, with the assistance of the Amis du Musée du Québec (67.08)

T HIS UNIDENTIFIED YOUNG WOMAN may have been related to Théophile Hamel, as the portrait was acquired from a family descendant. *Portrait of a Young Man* (Fig. 116A), of similar format, completes this enigmatic duo. Since the subjects are not presented in complementary poses, it is questionable whether they actually constitute a pair. It should be noted, however, that the concept of symmetry was not always demonstrated in Hamel's work. Further doubts are raised on examining the signatures. While the portrait of the young man bears the inscription *"Peint par T. Ham[el] 1840"* (Painted by T. Ham[el] 1840) in fine black

lettering, the painting of the young woman bears a bold signature painted in bright red. Nonetheless, we can conclude that the two portraits were painted at approximately the same time and were related inasmuch as the compositions are similar and the paint layer and finish show comparable signs of age, making it likely that the portrait of the young woman was painted circa 1840. Other factors support this theory, which may eventually be confirmed by historical research into the sitters' identities.

A study of the clothing allows us to date the portrait with some degree of certitude. The young woman's gown has

a large ribbon round the waist and the décolleté bodice, which crosses over in the front, allows a glimpse of her chemise or tucker of shirred lace. The low shoulder of the leg-o'-mutton sleeve is gathered at her arm and wrist with an aglet or cord. Lace cuffs and a bonnet with cascading ruches and long strings of lace complete her ensemble. Her hair is loosely parted down the middle and arranged in ringlets. All these elements, particularly the size of the sleeve, which begins not at the shoulder but at the elbow, are characteristic of changes in fashion which occurred in the early 1840s, further confirming the proposed date. Moreover, several features of

Fig. 116A.
Théophile Hamel,
Portrait of a Young Man, 1840;
oil on canvas, 89.9 × 71.2 cm.
Musée du Québec, Quebec City (67.07).

Fig. 116B.
Théophile Hamel,
Mrs. Michel Bilodeau, née Luce McNeil, 1842;
oil on canvas, 83.8 × 71.1 cm.
Musée du Séminaire de Québec (Pc983.15).

the same fashion can be found in the portrait *Mrs. Charles-Hilaire Têtu, née Elizabeth O'Brien and her son Eugène*, dated 1841 (MMFA).

In terms of technique and style, this canvas is characteristic of the artist's early works. Having already received a solid grounding in painting, Hamel was seeking the same textural qualities as those found in the works of his master, Antoine Plamondon. Although he was successful, his portrait does not boast the economy of means that mark the work of an accomplished artist. The folds of the gown are stiff, lacking the desired brilliance, assurance and artistry, while the texture of the lace is exaggeratedly coarse. These characteristics can be found in another work, the portrait of *Mrs. Michel Bilodeau, née Luce McNeil* (Fig. 116B), dated 1842.

Portrait of a Young Woman Holding a Rose was painted before Théophile Hamel's trip to Europe and reflects the conventions learned while studying under Plamondon. He adhered closely to the standards of the day: a nearly full-face pose, with the shoulders at a slight angle and the arms placed in such a way as to give the figure an elliptical appearance, while giving the impression of depth. The position of the right hand almost centred in the foreground at the bottom of the canvas is typical of many of Hamel's portraits during this period. Accessories are another constant that can also be seen in Plamondon's work: books, handkerchiefs and documents were the three elements most often used to give the sitter a certain bearing. The rose, which is representative of the sitter in this portrait, was a much rarer motif. Coupled with the handkerchief, it could be seen as a symbol of the purity and innocence of the young woman, newly married if the wedding band and ring are any indication. The draperies, while used to great effect in later years, were a convention rarely employed by Hamel before 1843.

When he was to return from Europe, Hamel would abandon this more formal representation of his subjects and seek rather to focus on their individuality, grace and elegance.

P.B.

Provenance
(?) Léocadie Hamel-Lockwell, Quebec City; Omer Lockwell, Quebec City; Mrs. Omer Lockwell, Quebec City; acquired by the Séminaire de Québec, 1912; on deposit at the Société du Musée du Séminaire de Québec, 1983.

Exhibitions
Detroit 1946, No. 227; Richmond 1949, No. 29; Ottawa 1953, No. 22; Ottawa 1959, No. 25; Mexico City 1960-1961, No. 90; Vancouver 1966, No. 40; Ottawa 1967/1, No. 84; Ottawa 1970, No. 42; Quebec City 1973.

Bibliography
ASQ, *Manuscrit 34*, Vol. IX, p. 9, April 26, 1912; *UNIVERSITÉ LAVAL 1913*, p. 47, No. 199; *UNIVERSITÉ LAVAL 1923*, p. 54, No. 199; (?) *BELLERIVE 1925*, p. 45; *UNIVERSITÉ LAVAL 1933*, p. 91, No. 339; *MORISSET 1934/5*, p. 122; *MORISSET 1936-1937*, Vol. II, p. 161; *MORISSET 1941/1*, p. 73; (?) *COLGATE 1943*, p. 11; *HUBBARD AND BARBEAU 1946*, p. 48, No. 227; *PAINTERS OF CANADA 1949*, p. 5, No. 29; *EXHIBITION 1953*, pp. 11 and 25, No. 22 (Repr.); *MORISSET 1953/4*, p. 657; *BARBEAU 1957* (Repr.); *HARPER 1957*, pp. 22 and 27-28 (Repr.); *MORISSET 1959/2*, No. 25 (Repr.); *ARTE CANADIENSE 1960*, No. 90 (Repr.); *MORISSET 1960/1*, p. 114; *HARPER 1962/2*, pp. 33 and 34 (Repr.); *HARPER 1962/3*, p. 415 (Repr.); *HUBBARD 1963*, p. 58 (Repr.); *SHADBOLT 1966*, No. 40; *HARPER 1966*, p. 90 (Repr.); *HUBBARD AND OSTIGUY 1967*, pp. 52 and 53, No. 84 (Repr.); *HUBBARD 1970*, pp. 34-35 and 89, No. 42 (Repr.); *BAZIN 1971*, p. 15 (Repr.); *HUBBARD AND FRYE 1973*, pp. 9 and 11 (Repr.); *REID 1973*, pp. 50 and 50a (Repr.); *THIBAULT 1973/1*, p. 168; *LORD 1974*, p. 41 (Repr.); *SOUCY AND THIBAULT 1974*, p. 105; *VÉZINA 1975/1*, pp. 24, 48a, 160, 160d, 175, 183, 200, 204, 205, 208, 209 and 212 (Repr.); *VÉZINA 1975/3*, p. 52; *VÉZINA 1976/1*, pp. 21-22, No. 128; *GODSELL 1976*, pp. 54-55 (Repr.); *VÉZINA 1977*, p. 397; *Nos racines*, No. 114 (1982), front. p. and pp. 2270-2271 (Repr.); *STACEY 1983*, pp. 19 and 20 (Repr.); *VÉZINA 1987*, p. 881; *BOURASSA 1989-1990*, p. 43 (Repr.); *TÊTU DE LABSADE 1990*, pp. 243 and 244 (Repr.).

Collection
Musée du Séminaire de Québec (Pc983.12)

117. (See colour reproduction, p. 99)
Self-Portrait with a Landscape, c. 1841-1843
Oil on canvas, 122.5 × 101.7 cm

I N THIS SELF-PORTRAIT, painted early in his career, Théophile Hamel portrays himself wearing an artist's smock and a Renaissance-style cap. Seated before a landscape, he is holding his portfolio of sketches in one hand and a mechanical pencil in the other. There is at once a desire to promote the image of the artist and a desire to display his elegance. From the large lapels of his vest, accentuated by the black silk cravat tied in a simple knot around a turned-down collar, to the gold fob, which subtly suggests the presence of a pocket watch, each detail is designed to convey the image of a man concerned about his appearance.

To the best of our knowledge, Théophile Hamel is the only 19th-century Canadian painter to have done at least three self-portraits.[1] Although they are all unsigned, it is easy to identify both subject and artist since Hamel is known to us through photographs and the paintings came from members of the artist's family. *Self-Portrait with a Landscape* was acquired by the Séminaire de Québec in 1912. It probably belonged to Hamel's younger sister, Léocadie Hamel, wife of André-Théophile-Honoré Lockwell, before passing into the hands of her son, Omer Lockwell. It was Omer's widow who offered the work to the Séminaire. At the

time of the acquisition, Léocadie was still alive and was able to provide the little information we have about this self-portrait. Her words were reported in the Journal of the Séminaire de Québec. On April 26, 1912, the columnist noted that the Superior purchased a "portrait of the late Théophile Hamel, Canadian artist, painted by himself at around age 22 or 23. [...] Mrs. Lockwell, mother of Omer and still alive at age 82, says that this portrait is accurate for the age at which the artist painted it." (*Translation*)

Based on this assertion, the work would have been painted circa 1839-1840. While it is difficult to doubt Léocadie

Fig. 117A.
Antoine Plamondon,
Study of a Woman, c. 1826;
oil on canvas, 72.5 × 58.9 cm.
National Gallery of Canada, Ottawa (9866).

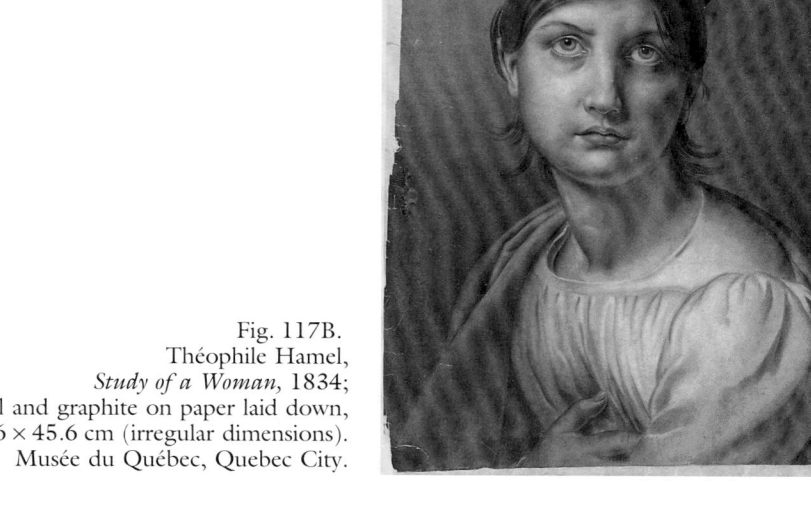

Fig. 117B.
Théophile Hamel,
Study of a Woman, 1834;
charcoal and graphite on paper laid down,
60.6 × 45.6 cm (irregular dimensions).
Musée du Québec, Quebec City.

Hamel given her direct ties to the painter, her assertion that he painted it "around age 22 or 23" warrants further examination. This statement provides an indication of the date, but leaves room for conjecture. Born in 1830, Léocadie was 13 when her brother left for Europe. This event, likely a momentous occasion for the family, would have been too important for the young girl to have confused the image of her brother before and after the trip. It can therefore be assumed that Léocadie was instead simply trying to indicate that it was painted in his younger years, before his stay in Europe. When he left the country, the artist may have entrusted the self-portrait to his parents given the planned length of his absence.[2] In addition to corroborating Léocadie's statement, this theory is plausible and would explain the silence surrounding the work until its acquisition by the Séminaire. However, if it was indeed painted circa 1839-1840, why did no newspaper mention this work, which could hardly have passed unnoticed? On October 27, 1840, a journalist with the *Quebec Mercury* remarked on the quality of a "portrait of an old gentleman," done by Hamel and on the careful execution of a "portrait of a Reverend Ecclesiastic of this neighbourhood." On July 5 of the following year, another reporter, this time from *Le Canadien,* visited Hamel's studio and discussed his recent works reported to

be "from parishes east of Quebec City." (*Translation*) This information would be repeated two weeks later in *Le Fantasque,* run by Napoléon Aubin (Fig. 120A), who knew the artist well. While the reports remain fairly general, we believe that had *Self-Portrait with a Landscape* been located in the studio, certainly some comment would have been warranted. The genre was so uncommon at the time and the portrait so large that it would definitely have made some impact. The stubborn silence of the journalists leads us to conclude that the canvas could not have been painted prior to July 1841 or after 1843 given the comments of the artist's sister.

Self-Portrait with a Landscape was the first in a series of self-portraits painted by Hamel. At the time, the artist had already achieved a reputation as a skilled draughtsman; as a matter of fact, he taught drawing at the Séminaire de Québec during the 1842-1843 school year.[3] Moreover, the exercises he did while apprenticed to Antoine Plamondon from 1834 to 1840 clearly show that Hamel had already mastered this technique. During the first year of his apprenticeship, Hamel did a charcoal copy of the *Study of a Woman* which Plamondon had brought back from France (Fig. 117A and 117B). While the work is, in itself, a compelling example of the passing on of knowledge from master to pupil, it also testifies to the brilliant talent

of the young Hamel, who was only 16 or 17 at the time. A series of studies of the apostles from Leonardo Da Vinci's *Last Supper* (Fig. 117C) were likely another assignment given to the young apprentice; once again, Hamel showed himself to be an accomplished draughtsman.[4]

In his self-portrait, Hamel clearly emphasizes this aspect of his artistic talent by including his portfolio of sketches and mechanical pencil. Even the painting technique used reveals an approach more often employed when drawing, with the forms structured more through the use of line than colour. In addition, the academic principles learned by Hamel have been put into practice in the imaginary landscape, in which the various planes, the meandering of the river, the lighting in the sky at the horizon and the clouds all serve to demonstrate the painter's mastery of linear and atmospheric perspective.

This portrait also proves that Hamel possessed an innate talent for painting. Indeed, even before leaving for Europe, his technique was so exceptional that he had only to refine it.[5] Although he had already mastered texture and light by 1840, he still did not paint with the ease of a fully experienced artist. In his portrait of *Mrs. Michel Bilodeau, née Luce McNeil* (Fig. 116B) and his *Portrait of a Young Woman Holding a Rose* (Cat. 116), the painter succeeded in rendering the whispering of

Fig. 117C.
Théophile Hamel,
The Apostle Judas, c. 1834;
charcoal and graphite on paper laid down, 54.6 × 42.9 cm (irregular dimensions).
Musée du Québec, Quebec City.

the fabric and the airy quality of the lace, cascading freely from the cap. The flesh tones are subtly defined by the lighting, which contributes to the ambience of these works. While these same qualities can be seen in *Self-Portrait with a Landscape,* the inclusion of a landscape in the latter work creates a unique feeling that sets it apart from most of the works done during the same period. It also differs from the artist's usual style, as Hamel routinely accorded little importance to this element. The motif of three mountains in the far distance is repeated in the portrait of *Mrs. Charles-Hilaire Têtu and her son Eugène* (MMFA); however, here it is treated as little more than a decorative element of the composition. This is obviously not the artist's intention in his self-portrait, where the landscape occupies a large portion of the canvas. Nonetheless, certain elements can be likened to those used by his contemporaries. The freely brushed foliage can be seen in the portrait of Louis de Lagrave, done by Antoine Plamondon in 1836, while Hamel was his apprentice (Fig. 194B). The addition of the tree trunk motif to balance the composition was a technique often employed by Joseph Légaré (Cat. 153). Overall, the landscape and the manner in which it is represented show the extent of Hamel's talents and prove he was indeed the equal of the eminent painters of the day.

Despite the inherent qualities of *Self-Portrait with a Landscape,* there is nevertheless a certain stiffness to the body, a slightly dry facture and some awkwardness in the anatomy, such as the disproportionate arms, back and right shoulder, which the fabric of the smock, stiffly rendered, cannot conceal. The same shortcomings can be seen in the portrait of *Mrs. Michel Bilodeau, née Luce McNeil* and the *Portrait of a Young Woman Holding a Rose.* After 1846, the artist's style was more fluid and his use of colour, while never really dominating the composition, became freer, witness *Self-Portrait in the Studio* (Cat. 129), done six or seven years later.

One might wonder what prompted Hamel to paint this self-portrait and promote himself in such a spectacular manner. His inspiration may have come from his decision to go abroad and perfect his training in Europe, or it may have been the social recognition that came with his position as drawing master. Although we will never know exactly what inspired him, one thing is certain: this painting breaks with the existing convention in its composition, format and the emotional feeling it conveys, that is, the pride of a painter who is aware of his talents and who has come into his own as an artist.

J.C. and P.B.

Notes

1. In addition to the *Self-Portrait in the Studio* (Cat. 129) and the one held at the National Gallery of Canada (circa 1857), there may be another self-portrait, painted during Hamel's stay in Italy. A comment in the *Journal de Québec* of September 17, 1846 (p. 2), leads us to believe this is the case. It says, "His studies from nature are generally very realistic; the one which attracted particular notice was the young Canadian seated amid the ruins of Rome; his pose being quite natural and abandoned." (*Translation*)

2. Léocadie may have gotten the portrait from her parents; as far as we know, she owned none of her brother's other paintings.

3. He shared this task with Antoine Plamondon. See ASQ, *Séminaire 129,* No. 306, "Received from Jean Holmes, priest, for drawing lessons for the 1842-1843 school year," (*Translation*) T. Hamel, June 8, 1843.

4. The Musée du Québec has two other unpublished drawings which may also be by Hamel: *The Apostle Matthew* and *The Apostles Thomas and Jacques le Majeur.*

5. Advertisements and short newspaper items published before his departure and upon his return, as well as works he brought back from Europe (Cat. 119, 122 and 123) indicate that Hamel was indeed going to further his training and, in fact, his main goal was to "round out his artistic studies in the lands of the great masters and models." (*Translation*) See *L'Aurore des Canadas,* April 25, 1843, p. 3.

118.
Sketchbook, c. 1843-1845

22 × 28.5 cm

Inscription
(on endleaf of the upper inside cover, in graphite)
Th: Hamel, Peintre.

Watermark
PM topping an *F.*

Provenance
Descendants of the artist; Madeleine Hamel, Quebec City, before 1975; acquired by the Musée du Québec, Quebec City, 1981.

Bibliography
VÉZINA *1975/1,* pp. 79 and 81; VÉZINA *1976/1,* p. 13, nos. 1 to 38; BÉLAND AND BOURASSA *1990,* p. 78.

Collection
Musée du Québec, Quebec City (81.295)

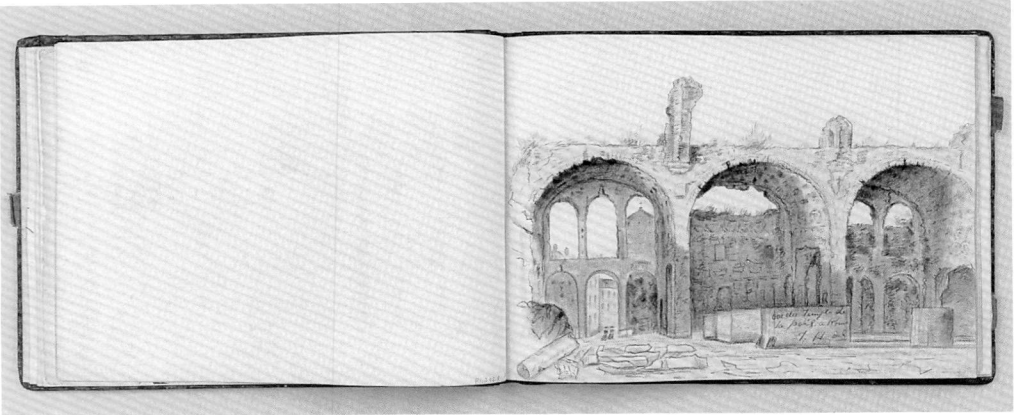

MQ

A. *View of the Temple of the Peace* (81.295.09), c. 1843-1845
Charcoal on paper, 21 × 28.4 cm

Inscription
(i. and titled, l.c. in graphite) *Vue du Temple de/la Paix à Rome/T.H. del.*

Bibliography
VÉZINA *1975/1,* p. 39 (Repr.); VÉZINA *1976/1,* p. 13, No. 10; BÉLAND AND BOURASSA *1990,* p. 78.

T HE SKETCHBOOK used by Théophile Hamel during his stay in Italy from 1843 to 1845 provides a digest of his training and artistic experiences. It includes graphic annotations on works of art (paintings and sculptures) as well as drawings of buildings, sites and landscapes.[1] The book allows us to roughly trace Hamel's artistic pilgrimage from the Roman monuments to the Italian countryside. While the book was not used consistently—perhaps Hamel drew in other books—it does attest to a certain curriculum and an interest in anatomical studies, figure drawing (nude and caricatures) and classical architecture. There does not appear to be any systematic approach to using it. The sketches of other works of art seem to have been done with the page upright, while landscapes were drawn horizontally. Sometimes two drawings appear on the same page (81.295.10 and 81.295.18), while at others, a single drawing might take up two facing pages (81.295.22 to 81.295.24). Once or twice, the same theme is dealt with on successive pages (the Laocoon, the Écorché, the mountainous countryside).

The book is half-bound with kid leather, the rest being covered in green paper mottled with black flecks. It was originally held closed with three cords which, when placed at the end of the plates, held a pencil. The paper bears a watermark in the form of the letters "PM" above an "F". When it was originally acquired, it contained several smaller booklets; its current state makes it difficult to study systematically. In the beginning, it probably held 11 booklets of 4 sheets each.[2] Several pages are missing[3] and booklets 4 and 11 have 5 and 6 sheets respectively. Of the 88 pages (both sides) which the book likely held originally, only 64 are left. They contain 38 drawings, which means the artist used only just over half the available space. This number increases to 40 if we count the two endpapers of the inside covers, which also have sketches on them.

The majority of these drawings are done in pencil, sometimes highlighted with charcoal. On several occasions, the charcoal completely obscures the light pencil marks: *Head of the Laocoon* (Cat. B), studies of *The Écorché of Houdon* (Cat. C), and *View of the Temple of the Peace* (Cat. A). The strokes are long and the crosshatching picks out the volume and shadows. More attention seems to have been lavished on specific drawings, and it is easy to imagine Hamel carrying the sketchbook with him on his visits and excursions. While the stereotypical treatment of certain monuments leads us to believe they may have been drawn from engravings (*Trevi Fountain; Tombe de Cecilia Metella*), the angle and vantage point adopted for other scenes is more original. Hamel drew buildings freehand, seeking to master their linear perspective, which he also wished to do with the atmospheric perspective of landscapes.

The endpaper of the inside front cover is neatly signed "*Th: Hamel, Peintre*" (Th. Hamel, Painter). This signature is juxtaposed with calculations, clearly showing that the book was used to make notes. The first drawings in the sketchbook are details of sculptures, combining anatomical studies with expressive figures—the method suggested in most academic study programs. The *Laocoon,* discovered in 1506, is housed in the Vatican collection. Considered to be the most spectacular group sculpture of classical times, it was copied and reproduced time and again.[4] Hamel drew the outline of the central figure, the father, his right arm upraised, as it had been reconstructed (81.295.02v). The torso is rendered in detailed strokes. The study of the *Head of the Laocoon*

Fig. 118A
Théophile Hamel,
Stel for Giovanni Volpato,
graphite on paper.
Musée du Québec, Quebec City (81.295.13).

NGC

B. ***Head of the Laocoon*** (81.295.03),
c. 1843-1845

Charcoal on paper, 21 × 28.4 cm

Bibliography
VÉZINA   1975/1,   pp. 41 and 79   (Repr.);
VÉZINA 1976/1, p. 13, No. 4.

Fig. 118B.
Théophile Hamel,
Temple of Castor and Pollux,
graphite on paper.
Musée du Québec, Quebec City (81.295.08).

(Cat. B) was probably done from a mould, as suggested by the close perspective and the contour line which cuts the figure off just above the shoulders. In this drawing, a stump was used to give the drawing volume, while a finer line was used for the more expressive details.

The next few pages are devoted to drawings of the most admired anatomical study in the history of sculpture, *The Écorché* by Jean-Antoine Houdon (1741-1828), done in 1766-1767 as a preparatory study for the *Saint John the Baptist* in the Santa Maria degli Angeli church in Rome.[5] Charles Natoire, director of the Académie de France in Rome, recognized the study's merit and requested authorization for Marigny to purchase a cast to be used by all students, saying that "there is no school of drawing in which this skeleton would not be of great use for studies by young students." (*Translation*) Hamel made two sketches, showing left (Cat. C) and right profiles of the figure from the knees up, with an accompanying sketch of the lower leg (81.295.4v, 81.295.5v). The figure is supported by the base of a tree trunk, as in the sculpture of *Saint John the Baptist*.

One final drawing based on a sculpture can be found several pages fur-

ther on, in the fifth booklet (Fig. 118A). It is the *Stel for Giovanni Volpato*, placed in the Santi Apostoli church in Rome by Antonio Canova (1757-1822) in 1807. The sculptor was paying hommage to his friend and patron Volpato, engraver and porcelain factory owner. Canova had the monument erected in the courtyard of the Santi Apostoli church along with his already-famous *Monument funéraire à Clément XIV*. Hamel concentrated on the placement of the figure on the polished stela.[6] The artist seems to have focused his drawing on the flowing robes of this classical figure, since Volpato's features are only roughly sketched.

His study of the human figure is timidly pursued in a pale sketch of a nude, with the left hand resting on the chest (81.295.17v). Lines through the drawing may express either Hamel's dissatisfaction with his rendition of the figure or his desire to censor the subject, even in a private sketchbook.

Two pages of the sketchbook contain caricatures (81.295.28r and the endpaper of the back cover). The first page shows a woman's head viewed from the back, a profile of a man's head with horns and a profile with the face crossed out,

with a crudely drawn face above it bearing the identification "*Théophilus Hamel/Artiste de Rome*" (Théophile Hamel/Roman artist). Could this have been the story of a love triangle in which one of the two men had been cuckolded? The endpaper itself contains drawings of the heads of three men with very prominent noses and ears. A drawing of three children's heads arranged in a circle and placed within a rectangle seems to have been a preliminary sketch for a painting (81.295.01). Hamel, who was to do several children's portraits in his day (Cat. 136), became interested in this type of work during his stay in Rome, as shown in *The ABC* (1845, PC). The sketchbook ends with three roughly sketched street scenes (81.295.31v) showing a group of women fussing around a child, a woman carrying a baby and, the third, a man holding a stick (or perhaps an oar?).

Architectural drawings and landscapes make up the majority of the subjects in the book. There are representations of Ancient Roman monuments and of medieval and baroque buildings. *The Temple of Vesta* (81.295.06) near the Tiber, designated as such because of its circular form recalling the Temple of Vesta in the Forum,

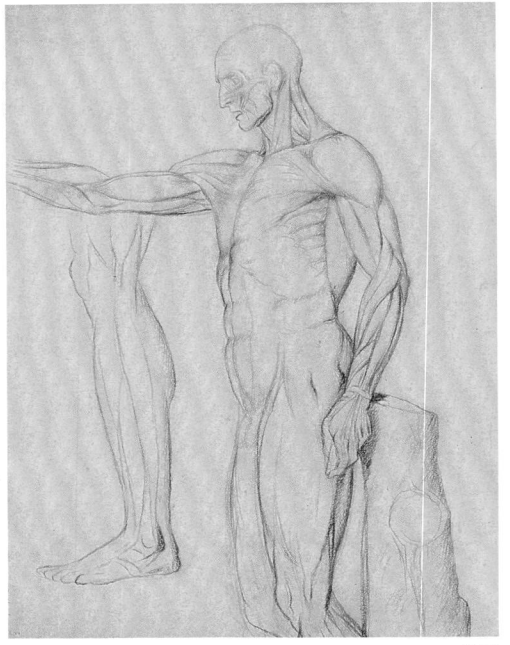

C. *The Écorché of Houdon* (81.295.04v),
c. 1843-1845

Graphite and charcoal on paper,
21 × 28.4 cm

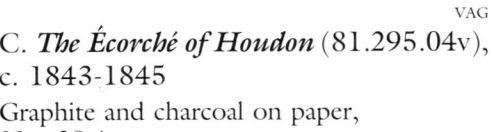

Bibliography
VÉZINA 1975/1, p. 41 (Repr.); VÉZINA 1976/1,
p. 13, No. 5.

Fig. 118C.
Théophile Hamel,
*Deacon Laurent
presenting the Poors to
the Prefect of Rome;*
oil on canvas,
67.8 × 89.1 cm.
Musée du Québec,
Quebec City
(66.151).

was actually dedicated to Hercules. Erected in the late 2nd century BC, it is the oldest marble temple in Rome and remains a spectacular sight, with its 20 fluted corinthian columns and cylindrical scella.

Several vestiges of the Forum can also be found in the sketchbook. The three marble columns, which are all that remain of the *Temple of Castor and Pollux* (Fig. 118B), in a sense symbolize the Imperial Forum itself. The next drawing depicts a **View of the Temple of the Peace,** or of Vespasian (Cat. A), erected a stone's throw away in 71-75. This sketch is particularly noteworthy for its heavy use of charcoal.

In the centre of the Forum is *Column of Phocas* (81.295.10), built in 608 in honour of the emperor of the same name. It is a fluted column from a 1st- or 2nd-century building—the last monument to be erected in the Forum. It is represented on the same page as *Le Temple de la Fortune virile,* a temple dedicated to Portunus located near the Tiber. Despite its modest size, it is a building of majestic allure dating from the 1st century BC.[7]

Two monuments along the Appian Way were also drawn: *La Tombe de Cecilia Metella* (81.295.11)[8], a famous mausoleum 20 metres in diameter located at the far end of the Appian Way, and *Le Bois de la nymphe Égérie* (81.295.15) near the Saint-Sébastien basilica, with its fountain and grottoes. Hamel even included a fragment of a statue from a sarcophagus.

More modern Rome, embodied by the Canova sculpture, is represented by the *Trevi Fountain* (opened in 1762). The famous monument by Nicola Salvi was built at the request of Pope Clement XII. The custom of foreign visitors throwing a coin into the fountain to ensure the return of power to Rome is very old.

Several drawings (81.295.12, 81.295.26 and 81.295.27), inspired by the classical and medieval architecture of unidentified buildings, can be likened to those found in the background of the history painting *Deacon Laurent presenting the Poors to the Prefect of Rome.* Both the oil paint sketch and the canvas (Fig. 118C) belong to the Musée du Québec collec-

tion. They tend to prove that the sketchbook could well have been used to collect notes and ideas for future compositions.

A number of drawings show architectural elements that have been integrated into the natural landscape, such as this view of a tree clinging to the stairs of a street built on a mountainside (81.295.17r). Another, showing a similar street, has been drawn on the same page as an aqueduct (Cat. E) and is probably based on Olevano Romano, a small town located southeast of Rome, in the Sabine mountains. Much appreciated by the Nazarenes, this location was painted by, among others, Franz Horny (1798-1824) and Joseph Anton Koch (1768-1839). It would seem that Hamel made the pilgrimage with his friend Jean-Mathieu Nisen (Cat. 121) before continuing on to Subiaco, magnificently reproduced in a panoramic view, drawn from a high vantage point, which takes up two pages in his sketchbook (Cat. D). The landscapes showing a monastery (81.259.19), an oratory (Fig. 118D) and a village perched on

D. *Subiaco* (81.295.20v and 21r), c. 1843-1845
Graphite, 21 × 28.4 cm (each sheet)

Inscriptions
(l.l., in graphite) *24;* (b.,l.r., in graphite) *25.*

Bibliography
VÉZINA *1975/1,* pp. 42-43 (Repr.); VÉZINA *1976/1,* p. 13, No. 24.

the edge of a mountainside (81.295.20r), the numerous studies of mountain chains (81.295.22v and 23r [Fig. 118E]; 81.295.23v and 24r) and the waterfalls drawn by the artist (81.295.32) may have been inspired by this region in central Italy. For confirmation, the question would have to be studied in greater depth. The hillside landscape (81.295.16) seems to have been inspired by the more bucolic villages around Rome.

Only four drawings were based on painted works, leading us to believe painting played a secondary role in this book. Three of the drawings were inspired by the iconography on the Virgin. The first shows the figure of the woman who has fainted in *The Deposition,* a masterpiece by Daniele da Volterra (1509-1566) which hangs in the Trinité-des-Monts church in Rome (81.295.30). The second shows the Annunciation—Mary, seated on a cushion, humbly accepting her mission (81.295.14). The image seems to have been borrowed from the Nazarenes, as is the full-length figure of the apostle

Fig. 118D.
Théophile Hamel,
Oratory in a Mountain Village;
graphite on paper.
Musée du Québec,
Quebec City
(81.295.25).

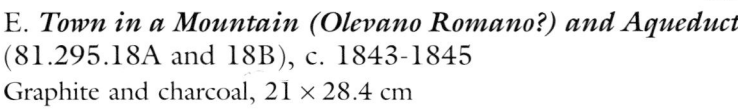

MMFA

Fig. 118E.
Théophile Hamel,
Mountain Landscape;
graphite on paper.
Musée du Québec, Quebec City (81.295.22v and 81.295.23r).

E. *Town in a Mountain (Olevano Romano?) and Aqueduct*
(81.295.18A and 18B), c. 1843-1845
Graphite and charcoal, 21 × 28.4 cm

Inscriptions
(l.l, left section, in graphite) *20;* (l.l., right section, in graphite) *21.*
Bibliography
VÉZINA *1975/1*, p. 45 (Repr.); VÉZINA *1976/1*, p. 13, nos. 20 and 21.

(81.295.22r), inspired by the works of Friedrich Overbeck (1789-1869) after Dürer.[10] A final sketch shows three busts drawn after painted works. In the centre is Saint Cecilia, after Raphaël's *Saint Cecilia with Saint Paul, John the Evangelist, Augustin and Mary Magdeleine* (Bologna, Pinacoteca Nazionale), flanked by an executioner drawn after *The Martyrdom of Saint Agnes* by Domenichino (Bologna, Pinacoteca Nazionale) and a Virgin of the Annunciation after Francesco Raibolini (Francia), also at the Pinacoteca Nazionale in Bologna. This page would seem to indicate that Hamel stopped in Bologna on his way to Belgium.

Hamel's sketchbook shows a complex universe inspired both by nature and by the work of other artists. It deserves to be examined in relation to the other works known to have been done by him in Europe in order that we may better understand the skills and knowledge acquired by the artist during his three years in Italy.
L.L.

Notes

1. The choice of site and the angle from which it was drawn was apparently common among artists visiting Rome. The similarity between Hamel's drawings and those of Belgian artists is striking. See the examples reproduced in Denis Cockelberghs, *Les peintres belges à Rome de 1700 à 1830* (Institut historique belge de Rome, 1976), Tome III, Chap. V, "Les paysagistes et les "vedutistes" de la fin du XVIIIᵉ siècle et du début du XIXᵉ siècle," pp. 297-357.

2. It is the thickness of the back that leads us to make this assumption. Though the restorer was able to respect the order of the booklets during the restoration, the arrangement of the detached pages is factitious. The booklets are currently organized as follows: booklet 1: 2 pages; booklet 2: 3 pages; booklet 3: 2 pages; booklet 4: 5 pages; booklet 5: 4 pages; booklet 6: 3 pages; booklet 7: 2 pages; booklet 8: 4 pages; booklet 9: 2 pages; booklet 10: 3 pages; booklet 11: 6 pages.

3. These pages might correspond to drawings obtained by the Musée du Québec and which are similar in terms of technique, subject matter and the format of the paper on which they are executed; 81.311, *Pompey [sic]*, VÉZINA *1975/1*, p. 55 (Repr.); 81.312, *La contandina greco* [sic], VÉZINA *1975/1*, p. 84 (Repr.); 81.299, *Study of a*

woman; 81.309, *Carmelito costume;* 81.310, *Monk at Rest*, VÉZINA *1975/1*, p. 86 (Repr.).

4. For more on this subject, see Francis Haskell and Nicholas Penny, *Taste and the Antique* (New Haven: Yale University Press, 1982), pp. 243-247.

5. H.H. Anderson details the completion of *The Écorché* and its reception. See *Jean-Antoine Houdon. Le plus grand sculpteur français du XVIIIᵉ siècle* (Lausanne: Edita, Denoel, 1976), pp. 14-15 (Repr.).

6. An analysis of this monument is presented in the work by Fred Licht, *Canova* (New York: Abbeville Press 1983), pp. 83, 87, Repr. Fig. 44.

7. VÉZINA *1975/1*, p. 52 (Repr.).

8. *Ibid.*

9. VÉZINA *1975/1*, p. 45 (Repr.) reversed.

10. The inventory of Hamel's estate lists "a small painting after Overbeck, worth five piastres" (ANQQ, Notarial register of S. Glackemeyer, March 9, 1871, No. 5789).

119.
*Academic Study of a Seated Man Depicted in Left Profile
with Head Resting on the Right Hand,* 1843 or 1845
Oil on canvas, 61 × 48.2 cm

Inscription
(s.d., l.l.) *T. Hamel./Roma 184* [3 or 5].

Provenance
Descendants of the artist; Mrs. Jean Hamel, née
Thérèse Toupin, Montreal; acquired by the Musée
du Québec, Quebec City, 1975.

Bibliography
ANQQ, Notarial Records of Samuel Glackemeyer,
"Inventaire des biens de la succession de feu
F. X. Théophile Hamel", March 9, 1871
(No. 5789); *VÉZINA 1976/1*, p. 57, No. 379; *DE
ROUSSAN 1982*, p. 33 (Repr.); *BÉLAND AND
BOURASSA 1990*, pp. 5, 8 and 82 (Repr.).

Collection
Musée du Québec, Quebec City (75.292)

THE INSCRIPTION at the bottom of this
painting leads us to believe it may
have been placed there some time
after the work was completed. The final
number in the date, which could be either
a 3 or a 5, corresponds to the years Hamel
spent in Rome. Assuming the date is 1843,
the study would have been done within
four months of the artist's arrival. This is
possible given the information provided by
Raymond Vézina: "In his letter of August
26, 1843, Théophile Hamel said he had
been admitted into various Roman academies but preferred working at the Acadé-

mie de France, where they used live models
and objects of classical art. He also worked
in the galleries of the Vatican palace [Cat.
118B], the Borghese palace and the Corsini
palace."[1] (*Translation*) This means that just
a few weeks after arriving in the Eternal
City, Hamel would have had access to a
live model at the Académie de France in
Rome. However, this is hardly likely, giv-
en how difficult it was to be admitted to
the academy, even to the *atelier libre.*[2]
Furthermore, the theory takes neither Roman habits nor the summer climate into
account, the latter heralding a slowdown
in activity during which students would
take time to travel.

While Hamel could have painted
this type of study in the private studio of a
painting master, he appears to have
shunned such resources, probably due to a
lack of funds. On the other hand, he may
well have studied for eight months at the
Accademia di San Luca in Rome.[3] This
academy was easier to get into and the
Quebec painter would have been able to
pursue his drawing and painting there.

Although Hamel had years of study
under Antoine Plamondon behind him as
well as several years of practice, he had
never had the opportunity in Quebec to
draw or paint from a live model. He
therefore saw this trip as an opportunity
to hone his skills and study famous works
without following a specific program. The
study shown here—the only one of its kind
still in existence—bears witness, as do certain drawings (Cat. 118), copies (Cat. 123),
sketches and a few original compositions
(Cat. 122), to the freedom available to the
artist. He took full advantage of the works
and subjects that inspired him during his
visits and although he sought lessons from
a variety of masters and styles, he did not
limit himself to one specific type of teaching.

The skill apparent in this study
demonstrates a basic grasp of anatomy,
drawing and light. The light filters in from
the left, striking the model, who is presented in a relaxed, comfortable pose. The
man, seated on a crate, has his left leg and
arm outstretched. His right arm is resting
on his raised thigh, his foot supported by
a box. The intensity of the light creates
strong shadows, providing little relief in
the musculature. Hamel, although already
a fairly capable portraitist, chose an angle
that would allow him to avoid having to
paint the face. He focused instead on the
articulation of the limbs, which occupied
several levels and two planes; the foreshortened torso and forearm cover the

chest, enabling Hamel to avoid some of the difficulties inherent in anatomical drawings.

    The paint is applied without impasto, even on the areas with more light. The paint layer, applied directly to the unprepared canvas, is thin, priority being given to the drawing, and the palette is dominated by browns and greens. The absence of movement in the contours and the smooth finish are in keeping with the pose, the only background being a halo of light surrounding the sitter.

    Quebec artists wishing to make a career of painting considered it essential to study for a time in Europe. The trip allowed them to perfect their technique while gaining legitimacy and credibility in the eyes of their future clients.[4] Biographical essays would laud the importance of such trips, which provided artists with an opportunity to benefit from the high regard and prestige for the art of France and Italy among Canadian enthusiasts. The likes of Plamondon, Falardeau and Bourassa all travelled to Europe to improve their skills.

L.L.

VAG, AGNS, MMFA

120.
Alphonse Colas, 184[5?]
Graphite on paper, 27.1 × 21.7 cm
(irregular dimensions)

Fig. 120A.
Napoléon Aubin after Théophile Hamel,
Napoléon Aubin, 1841;
lithograph, 25.7 × 19.1 cm.
Musée du Québec, Quebec City (88.132).

Notes

1. *VÉZINA 1975/1*, p. 47.

2. Victor Schnetz was director of the Académie de France in Rome from 1841 to 1846. The academy's records for these years show that the institution was experiencing financial difficulties and that there was a lack of space (Henry Lapauze, *Histoire de l'Académie de France à Rome*, Tome II (1802-1910) (Paris: Plon, 1924), pp. 262-287.

3. *Le Courrier du Canada*, December 26, 1870; *VÉZINA 1975/1*, p. 47. The inventory of Hamel's estate lists two studies, paintings valued at 20 piastres each (ANQQ, Notarial register of S. Glackemeyer, March 9, 1871, No. 5789).

4. Hamel's trip, financed in part by a public subscription in 1844, was proof of the support he received from certain members of the community, who shared this educational ideal.

Inscriptions
(i., l.l., in graphite) *T.H.;* (l.r., in graphite, by another hand) *A. Colas/184* [5?].

Provenance
Descendants of the artist; Mrs. Madeleine Hamel, Quebec City, before 1975; Mrs. Jacques Desjardins (née Marie Hamel), Mrs. Dubravko Raos (née Suzanne Hamel), Mrs. Mark Stein (née Louise Hamel), Montreal; acquired by the Musée du Québec, Quebec City, 1981.

Exhibitions
Quebec City 1983-1984, No. 309; Quebec City 1991/1, No. 15.

Bibliography
VÉZINA 1975/1, pp. 80 and 81, 183, 207 (Repr.); *VÉZINA 1976/1*, p. 13, No. 39; p. 35, No. 216; *GAY 1976*, p. 16; *ALLODI 1980*, p. 145; *LE MUSÉE DU QUÉBEC 1983*, p. 247, No. 309 (entry by Guy Paradis) (Repr.); *MARTIN AND GRANDBOIS 1991*, pp. 19 and 74-76, No. 15 (entry by Denis Martin) (Repr.).

Collection
Musée du Québec, Quebec City (81.301)

O NLY A FEW DRAWINGS FROM the works produced by Théophile Hamel in Quebec can be attributed to him with certainty; however, several sheets and a sketchbook (Cat. 118) from his European trip show that he was an accomplished and prolific draughtsman.

    The drawing of **Alphonse Colas** (1818-1887)[2] was, until very recently, thought to be of Napoléon Aubin (1812-1890)[3], being considered a sort of companion piece to the lithograph published in 1841 (Fig. 120A) by the famous writer and journalist.[4] However, it is not a likeness of Aubin, an important figure and active member of Quebec's cultural life as of 1835, but rather of a young artist from Lille whom Hamel met in Rome, as reported by Raymond Vézina quoting Hamel, "He made a few good friends, like young Colas, a pensioner of the French government and a student from Belgium."[5] (*Translation*)

    While the pencil lines and composition may be reminiscent of the style of portrait made famous by Ingres, the drawing shows neither the economy of means, nor the expressiveness of the master's drawings. Here, the space, which is defined by an almost uniform line outlining the figure, is filled with a series of quick, repetitive strokes indicating texture and shadow. The empty surface of the paper emphasizes the lighting and the pale tones of the shirt and vest. The pose is comfortable and hints at a somewhat dull personality; the delicate face shows little expression. The subject, turned toward the

MQ, NGC

121.
Jean-Mathieu Nisen, c. 1845
Graphite on paper, 22.5 × 16.6 cm

Inscriptions
(i., l.l., in graphite) *T.H.;* (l.c., in graphite, by another hand) *JM Nisen.*

Provenance
Descendants of the artist; Mrs. Madeleine Hamel, Quebec City, before 1975; Mrs. Jacques Desjardins (née Marie Hamel), Mrs. Dubravko Raos (née Suzanne Hamel), Mrs. Mark Stein (née Louise Hamel), Montreal; acquired by the Musée du Québec, Quebec City, 1981.

Exhibition
Quebec City 1983-1984, No. 308.

Bibliography
VÉZINA 1975/1, pp. 81 and 82 (Repr.); *VÉZINA 1976/1,* p. 14, No. 49; *LE MUSÉE DU QUÉBEC 1983,* p. 247, No. 308 (entry by Guy Paradis) (Repr.); *MARTIN AND GRANDBOIS 1991,* p. 76.

Collection
Musée du Québec, Quebec City (81.300)

viewer, gives the impression of having been distracted and turned his head.

The portrait of *Jean-Mathieu Nisen* is also done in pencil, but on parchment, which produces smoother lines. The facial features are conveyed by a series of tight strokes. A variety of graphic techniques—hatching, stumping and highlighting—show an excellent grasp of the medium and understanding of the different shades of black. The relaxed pose of the elegantly dressed model is vibrantly rendered, while the clothing and hands are only roughly sketched out.

"The Belgian student" (*Translation*) that Hamel counted among his circle of friends is identified here as Jean-Mathieu Nisen (1819-1885), also known as Jean-Baptiste, who resided in Rome from 1840 to 1845 after studying with his father Félix Nisen and other Belgian artists (Van Brée, Gustaf Wappers and Van Roy). While in Rome, he studied with German artist Friedrich Overbeck, one of the founders of the Nazarene movement, which took shape in Rome begining in 1810. After returning to Liège, Nisen taught at the city's art academy and attracted some attention, winning several commissions for religious works[6] and portraits. It was through Nisen that Hamel came into closer contact with the Nazarene school (Cat. 122), whose goal was to initiate a revival of religious painting in Italy and Germany in the first half of the 19th century. It was probably also at Nisen's urging that Hamel extended his study tour to include Belgium, which he visited in 1846, before returning to Canada.

The names Colas and Nisen appearing on the two sketches read as autographs. The fact that the two men had their portraits done suggests that Hamel belonged to an artist colony during his stay in Rome. It was common practice for artists to take turns posing for one another. In addition to providing personal mementos, these sketches were excellent exercises in observation. The caricatures found in Hamel's *Sketchbook* (Cat. 118) were likely a result of this type of activity, and stand as evidence of a certain familiarity between the artists.

L.L.

Notes

1. Several drawings and watercolours are reproduced in *VÉZINA 1975/1.*

2. In 1843, Alphonse Colas' talent was recognized and he was sent to Rome as a pensioner of the City of Lille. He returned to Lille in 1848 and, in 1851, began teaching at the city's art academy, which he would later run. According to Hervé Oursel (*Le Musée des beaux-arts de Lille* (Paris, 1984), pp. 61-62), Colas would become a sought-after portraitist and the most important religious painter in Lille at the time. He is responsible, among other works, for a large *Erection of the Cross* (1847, Musée des beaux-arts de Lille), four paintings depicting the life of the Virgin for Saint-André church in Lille, *The Coronation of the Virgin* at Notre-Dame de Roubaix church and several paintings of the tutelary saint of the Saint-Jacques de Douai church. See L. Quarré-Reybourbon, *Alphonse Colas. Peintre d'histoire 1818-1887* (Paris, 1904).

3. See *MARTIN AND GRANDBOIS 1991,* pp. 74-76.

4. *MORISSET 1960/1,* p. 129; *VÉZINA 1975/1,* pp. 81, 162 and 254. "In 1840, Aubin purchased a lithographic press; the first to be commercially used in Quebec City, according to him. [...] Aubin produced a lithograph of his own portrait and placed it in a supplement to the May 10, 1841 issue of the *Fantasque.* [...] A pencil sketch by Hamel, apparently of Aubin, still exists; it was probably done later since Aubin is shown with a beard, moustache and glasses" (*Translation*) (*ALLODI 1980,* p. 145).

5. *VÉZINA 1975/1,* p. 44, letter from Théophile Hamel to Abraham Hamel, Venice, August 31, 1846.

6. Saint-Nicolas-Outremeuse church, Liège; Soeurs de Notre-Dame chapel, Namur; Spa church.

122.
The Pilgrim, 1844 ou 1846
Oil on canvas, 96.5 × 74.4 cm

Inscription
(i.d., c.l.) *T.H. 184* [4 or 6].

Provenance
Descendants of the artist; Mrs. Gustave Hamel, née Amélie Duchesnay, Quebec City, before 1927; Mrs. Madeleine Hamel, Quebec City, before 1975; Mrs. Jacques Desjardins (née Marie Hamel), Mrs. Dubravko Raos (née Suzanne Hamel), Mrs. Mark Stein (née Louise Hamel), Montreal; acquired by the Musée du Québec, Quebec City, 1980.

Exhibition
Quebec City 1936.

Bibliography
ANQQ, Notarial Records of Samuel Glackemeyer, "Inventaire des biens de la succession de feu F. X. Théophile Hamel", March 9, 1871 (No. 5789); *BELLERIVE 1925*, p. 50; *MORISSET 1936/3*, p. 9; *MORISSET 1936-1937*, Vol. II, p. 159; *LESAGE 1946*, p. 45; *VÉZINA 1975/1*, p. 126; *VÉZINA 1976/1*, pp. 47-48, No. 336; *VÉZINA 1977*, p. 398; *ART DU QUÉBEC 1981*, p. 36 (Repr.); *Nos racines*, No. 114 (1982), p. 2278 (Repr.).

Collection
Musée du Québec, Quebec City. Restored in 1991, with the assistance of the Ámis du Musée du Québec (80.12)

T HE AUTHOR OF "Chronique artistique" (Artistic Journal) fully grasped the allegorical nature of the painting *The Pilgrim,* which can be seen as Hamel's reflections on his years in Europe:

After spending several years studying under Monsieur Plamondon, of Quebec City, the young artistic pilgrim, sensing what bearing it could have on his future to work under the great masters and refine his budding talents, did not hesitate to make any sacrifice. The gauntlet was taken up, he travelled to Europe, spending two years in Rome studying in the finest schools, where his work and compositions received more than passing recognition. Monsieur Hamel then travelled throughout Italy, stopping along the way in Pisa, Milan, Florence, Bologna, Venice and Naples before moving on to Paris and Antwerp to bring back a few souvenirs from the French and Flemish schools. After three years of intensive study, he finally returned to his homeland, which welcomed him with open arms.[1] (*Translation*)

The Quebec artist is comparing himself to the pilgrim who, through his solitary adventure and contact with exemplary models, seeks unequivocal answers and constant improvement. Although his home base was in Rome, Hamel took advantage of his time in Europe to visit other cities. He travelled to Naples in 1844 and it could very well have been the local countryside that inspired the landscape visible in the background of *The Pilgrim.* Two years later, Hamel travelled to France and Belgium.

The painting was not meant to be sold, and the fact that Hamel made two replicas (MQ and MAJ) of it underscores its importance to him.[2] The face is a stunning example of an archetype—the old, bald man with a long white beard. The traveller has removed his hat and joined his hands in prayer. The pilgrim bears the usual trappings: shell, walking stick, gourd and basket. Hamel seems to have gone to considerable trouble to render the two shells set against the dark cape, using iridescence to re-create the richness of a pale colour scheme. The cross at the end of the walking stick, decorated with a ribbon, is picked out against the sky. It dominates the landscape and is the focus of the pilgrim's devotions. The feeling of the canvas and its size, despite the narrative nature of the scene, are akin to a history painting. The subject is presented close up, as if an imposing heroic figure.

A still life and landscape complete the composition. The gourd, with a drinking cup attached, and wicker basket are prominently located at the left, while a composite Mediterranean landscape can be

seen in the distance. A tower and colonnade, remnants of classical buildings, rest near the horizon and may have been inspired by the Appian Way. Further back, at the foot of the mountains, is sketched an isolated village containing more-modern buildings. As evidence of meticulous research, the canvas contains two important pentimentos: the first, just behind the subject's head and the second, a hat held in the right hand.

By choosing the pilgrim as his subject, Hamel is demonstrating his understanding of an important theme in Nazarene painting, which was influenced by German artists living in Rome at the turn of the century. The latter were taking part in a movement to rediscover primitive painters and were developing new poetic figures in which man is in harmony with his natural surroundings.[3] The theme is evocative of the medieval period, when pilgrimages were popular—most of them being to Jerusalem, Rome or Compostela, the Spanish city containing the remains of Saint James. By choosing a subject with a religious connotation alluding to this distant Christian era, Hamel is suggesting a paradigm. He is announcing the superiority of Christian art over all other forms,[4] a concept which he, himself, would not pursue, but which to an extent foreshadowed the career of his future pupil, Napoléon Bourassa, whom he would begin teaching in 1848.

L.L.

Notes

1. Quote from "Chronique artistique," an undated document, transcribed in the records of artist Théophile Hamel, Fonds de l'inventaire des oeuvres d'art (Musée du Québec, Centre de documentation). It was impossible to trace the origin of this text, likely written by Napoléon Aubin.

2. "Le repos du Pellerin," estimated to be worth 100 piastres, and a "copy of Le repos du Pellerin", estimated at 20 piastres, were found in the inventory of the artist's estate (ANQQ, Notarial registers of S. Glackemeyer, March 9, 1871, No. 5789).

3. For more on this subject, see the essay by Gianna Piantoni "Considerazioni su alcuni aspetti della teoria Nazarena," *I Nazareni a Roma* (Rome: De Luca editore, 1981), pp. 30-38.

4. Several of Hamel's early works dealt specifically with religious painting (*VÉZINA 1976/1*, pp. 45-49). He made several copies and, during his stay in Rome, worked on a composition of several figures entitled *Deacon Laurent presenting the Poors to the Prefect of Rome,* known from a sketch and canvas belonging to the Musée du Québec collection (54.285 and 66.151, Fig. 118C).

123.
The Education of the Virgin, c. 1845-1846

After Pieter Paul Rubens
Oil on canvas, 43.5 × 36 cm

Provenance
Descendants of the artist; Mrs. Berthe Lemay-Lessard, Maniwaki, before 1976; acquired by the Montreal Museum of Fine Arts, 1982.

Exhibition
Montreal 1983-1984.

Bibliography
ANQQ, Notarial Records of Samuel Glackemeyer, "Inventaire des biens de la succession de feu F. X. Théophile Hamel", March 9, 1871 (No. 5789); *MAGNAN 1922-1923*, p. 353; *BELLERIVE 1925*, p. 49; *HARPER 1966*, p. 90; *VÉZINA 1976/1*, p. 47, No. 332; MMFA, *Rapport annuel 1981-1982*, p. 22; *CLOUTIER 1983/1*, pp. 1-3 (Repr.); *CLOUTIER 1983/2*, p. 1; *BÉDARD AND CLOUTIER 1985*, pp. 42-43 (Repr.); *NIXON 1988*, p. 116.

Collection
Montreal Museum of Fine Arts. Purchase, Horsley and Annie Townsend Bequest (1982.8)

124. (See colour reproduction, p. 86)
The Education of the Virgin, 1849

After Pieter Paul Rubens
Oil on canvas, 121 × 90.5 cm

Inscription
(i.d., c.r.) *T.H 1849.*

Provenance
Estate of the artist, 1871; chapel of the Congrégation Notre-Dame, Montreal, before 1874; Maison Saint-Gabriel, Montreal.

Bibliography
(?) ANQQ, Notarial Records of Samuel Glackemeyer, "Inventaire des biens de la succession de feu F. X. Théophile Hamel", March 9, 1871 (No. 5789); *VÉZINA 1975/1*, p. 126; *VÉZINA 1976/1*, p. 47, No. 331; *LAHAISE 1980*, pp. 197 and 198; *CLOUTIER 1982*, pp. 217-218 and 468-471 (Repr.); *CLOUTIER 1983/1*, pp. 2 and 3; *BÉDARD AND CLOUTIER 1985*, pp. 42 and 43.

Collection
Congrégation de Notre-Dame. Musée de la Maison Saint-Gabriel, Montreal

A CCORDING TO the Apocryphal evangelists and the Golden Legend, Mary left her parents at the age of three to be consecrated to God's service in the Temple cloister. This makes it difficult to imagine how Saint Anne could have taught her the alphabet using the Bible. This latter-day theme was without scriptural foundation, appearing toward the end of the Middle Ages. It became popular only early in the 16th century and, according to Louis Réau, could be explained by the growth of a cult surrounding Saint Anne, who was popularly believed to have had a hand in educating the Virgin Mary.[1] In Quebec, where this cult was very popular, no less than half the representations of Saint Anne focused on the theme of the education of the Virgin.[2] Many of these works were based on the famous painting by Pieter Paul Rubens (1577-1640) held at the Musée royal des beaux-arts d'Anvers (Fig. 123-124A). Dated circa 1625, Rubens' composition was apparently introduced in New France as early as 1666 in the form of an anonymous work kept at Sainte-Anne-de-Beaupré and known as the *Ex-voto du Marquis de Tracy*. However, it was not until the 19th century that the Rubens composition would receive more

Fig. 123-124A.
Pieter Paul Rubens,
The Education of the Virgin, c. 1625;
oil on canvas, 194 × 140 cm.
Antwerp Royal Museum of Fine Arts.

widespread notice due, among other things, to the paintings of François Baillairgé (1800, Saint-Pierre de l'Ile d'Orléans), Jean-Baptiste Roy-Audy (1820, MQ), Antoine Plamondon (1854, Saint-François de l'Ile d'Orléans), Théophile Hamel (circa 1845-1846, MMFA; 1849, Maison Saint-Gabriel) and Eugène Hamel (1871, Saint-Édouard-de-Bécancour).

While the majority of these artists were likely first introduced to Rubens' work through engravings—which explains why certain works mentioned above are mirror-images of the original or are very different in terms of composition and colour—, such is not the case with Théophile Hamel, who likely admired Rubens' *The Education of the Virgin* in Antwerp during his stay in Belgium in 1845-1846. It was there that he did a small copy of the work that would be easy to transport. He brought the copy back with him to Quebec City and kept it in his studio until his death;[3] it was acquired by the Montreal Museum of Fine Arts in 1982.

On August 10, 1846, *Le Canadien* reported that Théophile Hamel, arriving from Europe, where he had spent three-years "completing his artistic studies," (*Translation*), returned with "a magnificent collection of paintings assembled in Italy and Belgium for his studio." (*Trans-*

lation) It should be pointed out that the "collection" in question was a series of copies Hamel did on site and not a "collection" of original works acquired in Europe. This practice was very common in the 19th century, at a time when artistic masterpieces were often known only through engravings or copies. *The Education of the Virgin* was, in this sense, an important testimony to Théophile Hamel's artistic training; moreover, very few of the small copies brought back from Europe by our artists can be traced (See Cat. 182).

A comparison between Rubens' painting and Hamel's smaller version has convinced us that Hamel strove primarily to make as faithful a reproduction as possible in terms of composition, colouring and even pictorial quality. The same cannot be said of *The Education of the Virgin* held at the Musée de la Maison Saint-Gabriel and painted by Hamel in 1849 after his first copy. Much more conventional, this work could quite easily be the same one reported in the estate inventory drawn up on March 9, 1871, especially since no record of its being held by the Congrégation de Notre-Dame nuns was made until the 1870s.[4] Regardless, we are unable to explain what prompted Théophile Hamel in 1849 to replace the book originally held by the Virgin with a

parchment scroll. On the other hand, given the era and who the work was intended for, it is much easier to explain why the painter deemed it prudent, in his larger work, to at least partially obscure the nudity of the cherubs located in the upper portion of the composition.

Y.L.

Notes

1. Louis Réau, *Iconographie de l'art chrétien, tome second: Iconographie de la Bible, II: Nouveau Testament* (Paris: Presses universitaires de France, 1957), p. 168.

2. Among the 143 works catalogued in *CLOUTIER 1982,* 71 deal with the education of the Virgin. It should be noted that this list is by no means exhaustive.

3. The inventory drawn up after Théophile Hamel's death included fifty or so paintings by the artist, among which were two versions of *The Education of the Virgin* "after Rubens." One, valued at "30 piastres", is now owned by the Montreal Museum of Fine Arts. The other, evaluated at "150 piastres", may be the painting held at the Musée de la Maison Saint-Gabriel.

4. Photographs from the 1870s found in the Congrégation de Notre-Dame archives reveal that the painting was hung above the right side altar of the chapel of the old motherhouse on Rue Saint-Jean-Baptiste in Old Montreal. One of these photographs is reproduced in *LAHAISE 1980,* p. 198.

Fig. 125A.
Théophile Hamel,
Monseigneur Joseph Signay, c. 1843;
oil on canvas, 114 × 99.1 cm.
Séminaire de Nicolet (TA-8).

125.
Monseigneur Joseph Signay, 1847
Oil on canvas, 106.7 × 88.4 cm

Inscription
(s.d., l.l.) *Th. Hamel pinxt./1847.*

Exhibitions
Ottawa 1970, No. 64; Quebec City 1974, No. 32; Quebec City 1984-1985, No. XI (exhibited at the Musée du Séminaire de Québec).

Bibliography
TÉTU 1896, p. 298; *HUBBARD 1970,* pp. 94, 79 and 169 (Repr.); *DUMAS 1970,* p. 21; *THIBAULT 1974,* pp. 16 and 42, No. 32 (Repr.); *VÉZINA 1975/1,* pp. 96, 97, 196 and 197 (Repr.); *VÉZINA 1976/1,* p. 43, No. 289; *LE GRAND HÉRITAGE 1984,* p. 342, No. XI (entry by Magella Paradis) (Repr.); *LESSARD 1987,* p. 18; *LESSARD 1987/2,* pp. 37 and 53 (Repr.).

Collection
Archevêché de Québec

A COMPARISON between this harmonious portrait of Monseigneur Joseph Signay by Théophile Hamel and the one painted by Antoine Plamondon eleven years earlier (Cat. 189) shows several obvious differences. The composition is much lighter, leaving more room for accessories. Paradoxically, this provides no less insight into the psychological character of the sitter; on the contrary, the lavish, flowing robes of the white-haired, elderly man only serve to accentuate his fragility. Contrasting with the sharp angles of the double bands, the large curvilinear surface of the cape, its border set off with two rows of ochre fabric, provides a magnificent foil for the gold and brown tones of the rosary of buttons, rich pectoral cross and fine girdle. Added to this is a magnificent stole embroidered with elaborate green and red floral motifs. From beneath all these garments, the delicate hands of the archbishop emerge from the sleeves of his white rochet. With the fingers of one hand he holds a small book open; the reddish spots and blue veins standing out on the other reveal the sitter's age.

Monseigneur Signay seems somewhat lost in the large, heavy armchair decorated with scrollwork in which Hamel has painted him. The artist used the same chair one year earlier for his portrait of the eminent René-Édouard Caron (Fig. 188A). Distracted, apathetic and tired of the incessant difficulties encountered in carrying out the duties of his position, Signay has the disillusioned air of someone who, nearing the end of his days, is measuring his life by the empty trappings of honour and material wealth.

The lavishness and depth of this portrait distinguish it from the earlier and more official portrait of Signay housed in the Séminaire de Nicolet (Fig, 125A). The essence of the latter work and its composition situate it somewhere between Plamondon's portrait of Monseigneur Signay and this one, both kept at the Archdiocese of Quebec.

J.R.P.

126.
Archibald Campbell, 1847
Oil on canvas, 99.8 × 81.6 cm

Inscription
(i.d., l.l., on the arm of the armchair) *T.H. 1847.*

Provenance
Litterary and Historical Society of Quebec, Quebec City (sold by Christie's, Montreal, April 16, 1969, No. 82); William P. Wolfe, Montreal, 1969; acquired by the Musée du Québec, Quebec City, 1969.

Exhibition
Ottawa 1970, No. 65.

Bibliography
PICTURES *1969,* pp. 50-51, No. 82 (Repr.); HUBBARD *1970,* pp. 99-100, No. 65; *Bulletin du Centre de recherche en civilisation canadienne-française de l'Université d'Ottawa,* Vol. IV, No. 2 (April 1974), p. 16 (Repr.); VÉZINA *1973-1974,* p. 46; VÉZINA *1975/1,* pp. 160, 161, 165, 175, 183, 194, 202, 207, 208, 209, 216 and 218 (Repr.); VÉZINA *1976/1,* p. 17, No. 88; VÉZINA *1977,* p. 400; PORTER AND BÉLISLE *1986,* p. 311; BÉLAND AND BOURASSA *1990,* pp. 6, 8 and 94 (Repr.).

Collection
Musée du Québec, Quebec City (69.358)

A DMITTED TO THE BAR in 1812, appointed royal notary in 1821 and becoming seigneur of Bic the following year, Archibald Campbell (1790-1862) practised law in Quebec City for 50 years. Among other things, he was responsible for drawing up a number of shipbuilding contracts. His clerk from 1825 to 1830 was future historian François-Xavier Garneau (1809-1866), of whom Campbell became a friend and patron.

Very active on the cultural scene, Campbell was a member of every musical association in Quebec City and, in 1831, was one of the charter members of the Literary and Historical Society of Quebec. Along with architect Thomas Baillairgé, colleague François-X. Garneau, man of letters P.-J.-O. Chauveau and painters Antoine Plamondon and Joseph Légaré, he was part of the committee set up in 1840 to establish the Vattemare Institute, an organization designed to unite already-existing cultural agencies. He also belonged to a group whose noteworthy members included Joseph Légaré, journalist Napoléon Aubin and judge and art collector Édouard Bacquet; their goal was to found a national gallery in Quebec City. An art enthusiast, he maintained ties with many famous painters. For example, in 1844, Joseph Légaré exhibited a number of works from the notary's collection at his studio, among them, a copy of *Queen Victoria* by Thomas Sully, which Campbell had acquired around 1840. As reported in *Le Castor* of April 18, 1844, Campbell also purchased Légaré's *The Engagement of an*

Indian Girl and *The Despair of an Indian Woman* (Cat. 167), even before the artist had completed them. The notary encouraged more than one young artist and was responsible for facilitating painter Antoine-Sébastien Falardeau's trip to Italy. He was so popular in shipping circles that in 1857 François Valin christened one of his ships the Archibald Campbell and had a sculpture of the eminent personality done for its figurehead.[1] Following Campbell's death at the Bic seigneury, at age 72, Quebec City newspapers sang the praises of the royal notary. The July 18, 1862 edition of *Le Courrier du Canada* stressed his role as a patron of the arts:

Mr. Campbell had fine artistic taste and knew how to encourage talent in others. More than one of our young countrymen owes his future to him, and no need was ever made known to him that he did not strive to answer. He was able to uncover their god-given talents and always seemed to be on the lookout for opportunities that would be useful to them or would get them started on their career; and we could provide several examples of this that would bring the greatest honour to his memory. We have heard, from the lips of strangers to our country, the highest praises for his noble qualities. (*Translation*)

Indeed, his splendid funeral service attracted the cream of Quebec City society.[2]

The portrait of Archibald Campbell, like that of *Reverend Daniel Wilkie* painted by Samuel Palmer in 1843 (Cat. 176), comes from the Literary and Historical Society of Quebec, both men having been founding members of the philanthropic organization. The canvas was painted by Théophile Hamel during the year his studio was temporarily located in Quebec City, at the city hall on Rue Saint-Louis. During this transitional year, between his return from Europe in August 1846 and his departure for Montreal in October 1847, Hamel executed no less that a dozen portraits. The artist also completed a painting of *Madonna of the Rosary* for the parish of Grondines.

Campbell is shown in a pose often favoured by the artist; using a red curtain as a backdrop, the subject is presented in a three-quarter profile, sitting in an armchair, his left arm resting on a table and his right hand relaxed. His profession is subtly indicated by the pen held in his right hand[3] and by the ink pot and manuscript resting on the table. Also on the cloth-draped table are two books, probably legal texts.[4] The artist concentrated on other details as well, such as the tiepin, made either of white metal or pavé diamonds. To the right, through a window, the viewer encounters a seascape featuring a storm-tossed sailing ship on what could easily be the St. Lawrence River looking toward the North Shore, opposite Bic. This artistic convention, in which the viewer is given a glimpse of a landscape or seascape, had been used by Hamel in other portraits, particularly those of women. Despite their rather cursory treatment, certain of these landscapes are easily identified, while others are purely imaginary. This window view alludes directly to Campbell's occupation and to his notarial activities in the shipping industry. In this respect, the positioning of the subject, the attributes, and the window-reference alluding to the sitter's occupation, show a strong resemblance to the portrait of Dr. Arnoldi, painted by Krieghoff the same year (Cat. 149).

Done shortly after Théophile Hamel's return from Europe, the portrait of Archibald Campbell—like those of the Caron couple—mark an intermediary period for the artist between the basic portraits of the early 1840s and the more lavish ones of the mid-1850s. Despite all the attributes indicating the sitter's prestige and importance, Hamel still managed to produce a portrait that promotes understanding and reveals a strong personality. An as-yet-unidentified artist produced a simplified version now housed in the McCord Museum of Canadian History in Montreal.

M.B.

Notes

1. *Le Journal de Québec*, October 8, 1857, p. 2.

2. Pierre Savard, DCB, Vol. IX (1977).

3. This was a change made later by the artist, the quill originally having been in the ink pot.

4. Similar attributes—quill, ink pot and books—were also placed on a table in the official portraits of *René-Édouard Caron,* painted the previous year (Fig. 188A), and *James Stuart,* done in 1852 (NAC).

127.
Jacques Cartier, 1848
Oil on canvas, 130 × 97.3 cm

Inscription
(i.d., l.r.) *Cop. par T. H. 1848.*

Provenance
Gift of the artist to L'Institut Canadien de Québec, 1870.

Bibliography
"Letter from Alfonse Leclerc to Théophile Hamel", April 27, 1870 (quoted by VÉZINA *1976/1*, p. 54); *Le Journal de Québec*, April 9, 1870; (?) MORISSET *1934/1*, p. 2; (?) MORISSET *1936-1937*, Vol. I, p. 3; (?) HARPER *1966*, p. 91; (?) HARPER *1970*, p. 142; VÉZINA *1975/1*, p. 146; VÉZINA *1976/1*, p. 54, No. 367; VÉZINA *1977*, p. 397; NOPPEN *1984*, pp. 23 and 24 (Repr.); TOPOGRAPHICAL PAINTINGS *1987*, p. 14; MARTIN *1988*, pp. 80-81 and 82 (Repr.); VILLENEUVE *1989*, pp. 124-127.

Collection
L'Institut Canadien de Québec

T HE PORTRAIT OF *Jacques Cartier* is one in a series of portraits of historical figures Théophile Hamel began in 1847 that includes Champlain, generals Montcalm, Lévis, Wolfe and Murray, and the man who, in the 19th century, was called the "father" of the history of New France, Jesuit priest François-Xavier de Charlevoix.[1] Hamel's *Jacques Cartier*, which stands, as it were, as an "archetype" of early Quebec history painting, is not only an example of copying, a phenomenon that was to influence Quebec portraitists, but also of the creation of iconographic models, the importance of which would lead to the establishment

of a national portrait gallery at a time when nationalism was to take a marked turn toward commemoration. Like Samuel de Champlain, Maisonneuve and Frontenac, whom this movement would ultimately honour with portraits, *Jacques Cartier* by Théophile Hamel actually formed the basis of a propaganda movement and was widely disseminated.

Of the 19th-century portraits of Jacques Cartier deemed to be authentic, the most famous was painted in 1839 (Fig. 127A) by François Riss (1804-circa 1866) for the city hall in Saint-Malo, Brittany, the birthplace of the discoverer of Canada. Riss' portrait, which was the inspiration

for Théophile Hamel's *Jacques Cartier*, was apparently based on an early portrait (now lost) held in Saint-Malo. In his work, which was doubtless based more on imagination than reality, Riss showed the Saint-Malo navigator leaning over the rails of his ship, gazing off into the distance, right hand on his hip. The City of Saint-Malo had commissioned Riss to do the portrait as part of a series of portraits of famous local figure to decorate the city hall. Riss' canvas was destroyed during the American attack on Saint-Malo in 1944 and was replaced by a replica dated 1895. Earlier copies exist, however, particularly in Canada, which made this portrait of

Fig. 127A.
François Riss,
Jacques Cartier, 1839 (work destroyed in 1944
in Saint-Malo, in Brittany);
oil on canvas, unknown dimensions. Photo
published in Joseph Dumais, *Le Capitaine
Malouin, Jacques Cartier. Découvreur officiel du
Canada. Récit anecdotique de sa vie, de ses
voyages et aventures...*, new ed., Quebec City,
1934, p. [III].

Fig. 127B.
Francis Davignon after Théophile Hamel,
Jacques Cartier, 1848;
lithograph, 43.7 × 34.6 cm.
Musée du Québec, Quebec City (55.112).

Fig. 127C.
François-Xavier Berlinguet,
Jacques Cartier, c. 1860;
polychrome wood, 206 cm.
Musée du Québec, Quebec City (76.180).

Jacques Cartier extremely popular, thanks to the diligence of the eminent Georges-Barthélemi Faribault (Cat. 237) and his son-in-law, painter Théophile Hamel.

As early as 1835, Faribault was one of the promoters of a plan to erect a monument commemorating the tricentennial of Jacques Cartier's landing in Quebec City and his stay in a harbour on the Saint-Charles river during the winter of 1535-1536. Various designs were submitted, but only the one by architect George Brown included an imaginary representation of the Saint-Malo navigator. No monument was ever built, but Faribault nonetheless continued his research on

Cartier. In 1843, the Literary and Historical Society of Quebec, of which Faribault was an honourary librarian, reissued the *Voyages de Cartier*. Faribault sent a copy to the mayor of Saint-Malo, who would inform him, in ensuing correspondence, of the existence of the portrait of Cartier by François Riss. Faribault negotiated to have a copy of the work done in Paris in fall 1846 by painter Louis-Félix Amiel.[2]

In April 1847, the copy of Riss' portrait, donated to the Literary & Historical Society by the City of Saint-Malo, arrived at Quebec. Exhibited at the Parliament Building upon its arrival, the work was an immediate success. That same year,

Théophile Hamel completed a copy in charcoal and two painted copies. Quebec City newspapers began a subscription to produce lithographed copies of Hamel's work. On November 2, *L'Aurore des Canadas* related that Hamel had the "brilliant idea" (*Translation*) of creating a lithograph of Cartier's portrait after the two copies he had already painted, commenting that "the two paintings are almost indistinguishable from the original" (*Translation*) drawing destined for lithographic impression. An article in *La Minerve* on November 4, 1847, had the following to say about the portrait of Jacques Cartier:

We have learned, to our great delight, that Monsieur Hamel, distinguished artist, who copied the portrait of the illustrious French navigator from the original, which is in Saint-Malo, is proposing to have it lithographed. Monsieur Hamel is in Montreal and this evening leaves for New York, where the work will be completed. The announcement also states that a subscription has been begun to underwrite this effort and we hope that everyone will hasten to acquire a copy of this portrait of the able European navigator, who was the first to sail the river to Montreal. (*Translation*)

In late 1848, the portrait of Jacques Cartier, printed in New York by F. Davignon (Fig. 127B), was registered at the provincial legislature and put up for sale soon thereafter. The same year, according to the April 10 edition of *La Minerve*, Hamel's painting had already been copied in a daguerreotype. His *Jacques Cartier* would henceforth be copied by engravers many times over.[3]

In 1864, Father Henri-Raymond Casgrain, in his *Histoire de la Vénérable Mère Marie de l'Incarnation*, recounted the amazing success of the portrait of Jacques Cartier in French Canada:

The portrait of the illustrious mariner, kept in the city of his birth, has found great popularity here. The artist who drew the picture truly understood Cartier's greatness. The hero's meditative attitude, his dynamic features and the passionate intensity of his gaze, fixed on the horizon, convincingly convey the idealism and dignity of this hero who appears to us across the ages.[4] (*Translation*)

To meet this incredible demand, Théophile Hamel did several more copies of his portrait of Jacques Cartier, among them, a watercolour for the *Album* of Montreal historian and "antiquarian" Jacques Viger, between 1847 and 1856, and a copy painted for the House of Assembly in Ottawa in 1860.[5] A copy dated 1848 was acquired by Lord Elgin[6] and another was offered to the Literary and Historical Society of Quebec in 1870 to replace the French canvas, which was destroyed in the fire at the Parliament Building in 1854. The latter was undoubtedly a studio copy which the artist used for his other copies. The Quebec artist even sold a copy of *Jacques Cartier* to the Richelieu and Ontario Navigation Company, which used it to decorate one of the rooms on its steamship, the "Jacques Cartier"; in 1897, the work was offered to the Château Ramezay.[7] The Ursulines of Quebec City also owned a copy of Hamel's work. Another copy of the painting, completed in 1847 and acquired by Sir Allan McNab, seems to have disappeared.[8]

Théophile Hamel's portrait of *Jacques Cartier* after François Riss, widely distributed as an engraving, inspired the numerous plans for statues and monuments honouring the discoverer throughout the second half of the 19th century in French Canada. The impact of Hamel's *Jacques Cartier*, as one of the very first history paintings done by a French-Canadian painter in the 19th century, tells us much about that era. In 1858, Napoléon Bourassa, basing his creation on the model developed by Hamel, completed a bust of Cartier which won great public admiration. The work, presented that same year at the Exposition provinciale de Québec, was cast in plaster in 1861. Many artists were to follow Bourassa's lead, basing their work on the official likeness of the hero; among them, François-Xavier Berlinguet, of Quebec City (Fig. 127C), Charles-Olivier Dauphin, of Montreal, French sculptor Louis Rochet, the architect of the Quebec Parliament Building, Eugène-Étienne Taché, and sculptor J.-Arthur Vincent. From 1850 on, the portrait of Jacques Cartier would hold a place of honour at all historic and commemorative events occurring in Quebec. A mascaron, sculpted sometime between 1870 and 1880 for a business establishment on Rue Saint-Pierre, in Quebec City, demonstrated its continued popularity.

It is unlikely we will ever know what the discoverer of Canada truly looked like. His actual appearance is obscured by history itself and by the 19th-century image of the navigator who was mandated by François I to explore "new lands" (*Translation*). This image spoke to the collective unconscious of Quebeckers and, as a result, has become the accepted likeness of the great man. The few existing maps published following Cartier's voyages to the New World tell us nothing about the navigator's appearance, despite many historians' belief that they provided a genuine likeness of him. Except for rudimentary portraits and hypothetical likenesses of the discoverer, it appears that no "contemporary" portrait of Jacques Cartier can be authenticated with certitude.[9] Posterity and, more importantly, the hero cult which began in Lower Canada in the first half of the 19th century, served to make up for this lack.

D.M.

Notes

1. The majority of this text is extracted from several entries on drawn, painted and sculpted likenesses of Jacques Cartier in *MARTIN 1988*, pp. 75-89. This book contains many bibliographical references on the dissemination of the portrait of *Jacques Cartier* by Théophile Hamel.

2. For more on this subject, see Jacques Robert, "L'invention d'un héros," *Le Monde de Jacques Cartier. L'aventure au XVIᵉ siècle* (under the direction of Fernand Braudel), (Paris/Montreal, Berger-Levrault/Libre-Expression, 1984), pp. 295-299. The plans for the Cartier monument by George Browne are reproduced in this work, p. 295. See also *MARTIN 1988*, p. 86.

3. Known copies include one on a steel plate done by Samuel Freeman in 1849, one engraved by Rebel in 1865 for a book by Father Étienne-Michel Faillon, and another engraved the following year by O'Neill for the English edition of Father Charlevoix's *Histoire et Description Générale de la Nouvelle-France*, by John Gilmary Shea.

4. Henri-Raymond Casgrain, *Histoire de la Vénérable Mère Marie de l'Incarnation, première supérieure des Ursulines de la Nouvelle-France* (Quebec: Léger Brousseau, 1882), Tome I, pp. 23-24.

5. *La Minerve*, March 31, 1860, p. 2. This canvas is now at the National Archives of Canada in Ottawa.

6. *TOPOGRAPHICAL PAINTINGS 1987*, p. 14, No. 25.

7. *La Minerve*, March 26, 1897, p. 4.

8. *Le Journal de Québec*, October 26, 1847. See *TOPOGRAPHICAL PAINTINGS 1987*, p. 14, No. 25. The work by François Riss, copied by Théophile Hamel and made popular in the form of engravings, was reproduced in most illustrated school books and history books in the second half of the 19th century and early 20th century, on dollar bills, postage stamps and even on certain traditional items such as sugar moulds. Its popularity has almost caused us to forget that the portrait was completed three centuries after Cartier's discovery of Canada. A commemorative portrait engraved in 1934 by Pierre Gandon is a more modern testimony to the historic persistence of the model created in 1839.

9. Such as those appearing almost ten years after Jacques Cartier's death, on the plans for Hochelaga in a work by Giovanni Battista Ramusio; on the *Harleian map*, circa 1542, and the 1550 *Mappemonde*, both by Dieppe cartographer Pierre Desceliers; and finally, on a map of North America appearing in the *Atlas* by Nicholas Vallard, completed between 1543 and 1547.

128.
*Portrait of a Young Man of the Taché
Family,* 1848
Oil on canvas, 70.4 × 51.5 cm

Inscription
(s.d., l.r., on the base of the table) *T. Hamel. 1848.*
Provenance
Descendants of the Taché and Kane families;
Harriet Sarah Kane, Westmount, great-
granddaughter of Sir Étienne-Paschal Taché; gift
to the Public Archives of Canada, Ottawa, 1954.
Exhibition
Ottawa 1984-1989, No. 28.
Bibliography
VÉZINA 1975/1, pp. 162, 178, 180, 196 and 202
(Repr.); *VÉZINA 1976/1*, p. 27, No. 149;
SCHOENHERR 1984, p. 18 (Repr.); *LE PASSÉ EN
PEINTURE 1984*, pp. 47-49, No. 28 (entry by Lydia
Foy) (Repr.).
Collection
National Archives of Canada, Ottawa (1954-97)

F OR THÉOPHILE HAMEL, 1848 and 1849 marked a period of transition, with the artist settling temporarily in Quebec City in 1847 and then moving briefly to Toronto in 1850. Shortly after his return from Europe, the artist decided to settle in Montreal, which had become the permanent seat of government. Opening a studio on Rue Notre-Dame, the portraitist found a large number and wide range of clients in his adopted city. During his two-year stay, he received various commissions from prominent citizens of Montreal and Quebec City, his home town, and painted a dozen or so portraits of government officials, members of the clergy and prosperous members of the bourgeoisie.

It was in Montreal that Hamel executed this superb portrait of a member of the Taché family who, until recently, was wrongly identified as Sir Étienne-Paschal Taché (1795-1870). The painting was acquired from descendants of the family along with a full-length portrait of the same size of Madame Étienne-Paschal Taché (a photograph by William Notman coloured by John Fraser). However, as shown by Lydia Foy in 1984, the portrait in question could not be Sir Étienne-Paschal because the latter would have been 53 in 1848. The doctor and politician was immortalized twice by Hamel, first in 1850 (NGC), and again in 1856 (Parliament Buildings, Ottawa). Both portraits show him as an older man, while the 1848 portrait depicts a young man, apparently in his twenties. According to Lydia Foy, the sitter could be one of Sir Étienne-Paschal's nephews, possibly Joseph-Charles Taché (1820-1894), who was also a doctor and politician. In 1848, at age 28, the young politician took his seat in the Legislative Assembly of Canada in Montreal for the first time. The portrait may have been commissioned in recognition of this achievement shortly after his arrival for the new session of Parliament. One thing is certain, however: there is a striking similarity between the facial features and expression of the young Taché and those of his uncle in the two portraits done of him.

This is one of the most sophisticated portraits done by Théophile Hamel, being full-length and set against an elegant decor. Among the hundreds of portraits done by the artist, only a few present a full-length view of the subject in a richly decorated interior setting. Of these, all are large-format, official portraits, usually commissioned by the community in honour of the subject (Cat. 137). Unlike these

stuffy portraits, the one of Taché appears to be an unpretentious, intimate profile of the sitter, both because of its small size and because of the absence of attributes testifying to Taché's occupation, personal activities or accomplishments.

Elegantly dressed and surrounded by exquisite furnishings, the young man appears relatively relaxed, legs crossed, left arm at his side and right arm resting on the back of an armchair. His dark silhouette stands out against a pale green wall, brightly lit and decorated with mouldings. Behind him and to his right is a curtain with a floral pattern partially obscuring a collection of books,[1] while to his left a mullion window looks out over an expanse of grey sky and a snowy treetop, a motif which the artist would use again in 1850 in his portrait of the Molson family (Cat. 132). These two direct, but subtle, allusions to the Canadian winter are the only ones to be found in the artist's entire oeuvre. The interior backdrop includes two pieces of furniture, a Regency-style chair, the back and seat in red, floral-print upholstery, and a pedestal table. A top hat and cane lay on the table alongside two books and a sheet of paper. The bourgeois environment, tasteful furnishings and fashionable clothing indicate the young man is clearly financially well off. The importance of the sitter is accentuated by the complex play of light, creating strong diagonals from two sources located to the left of the composition, one from the ceiling, the other from the floor. Here, Hamel has achieved a highly polished portrait, which nonetheless remains enigmatic in terms of its subject, significance and social impact.

M.B.

Notes
1. In 1841, Hamel used slightly raised drapery revealing a well-stocked bookcase in his portrait *Young Man (Panet)* (MQ), mimicking an element used by Antoine Plamondon in his 1836 portrait of *Louis-Joseph Papineau* (Cat. 188) and by Jean-Baptiste Roy-Audy in his 1838 portrait of *Monseigneur Rémi Gaulin* (Cat. 208).

129.
Self-Portrait in the Studio, c. 1849-1850
Oil on canvas, 53.5 × 41.3 cm

Provenance
Descendants of the artist; Mrs. Gustave Hamel, née Amélie Duchesnay, Quebec City; acquired by the Musée de la Province de Québec, Quebec City, 1934.

Exhibitions
(?) Paris 1867; (?) Quebec City 1919; Quebec City 1936; Toronto 1945, No. 44; Albany 1946, No. 22; Windsor 1947-1948, No. 1; Quebec City 1948; Quebec City 1952, No. 46; Hamilton 1953-1954, No. 17; Winnipeg 1956, No. 147; Vancouver 1959, No. 147; Ottawa 1959, No. 21; Bordeaux 1962, No. 13; Quebec City 1967, No. 24; Ottawa 1970, No. 60; Sherbrooke 1975, No. 17; Quebec City 1983-1984, No. 78.

Bibliography
(?) *Le Canadien,* February 15, 1867; (?) *Le Journal de Québec,* February 16, 1867; (?) *Le Journal de Québec,* May 21, 1867; (?) BELLERIVE 1925, p. 45; MORISSET 1934/5, p. 122; MORISSET 1936/3, p. 9; MORISSET 1936-1937, Vol. II, p. 161; HUBBARD 1945, pp. 18 and 20, No. 44 (Repr.); PAINTING IN CANADA 1946, p. 26, No. 22; LESAGE 1946, p. 43; FRENCH-CANADIAN ART 1947, No. 1; MORISSET 1952, p. 31, No. 46; INAUGURAL EXHIBITION 1953, No. 17 (Repr.); PORTRAITS MIRROR OF MAN 1956, p. 10, No. 147; HUBBARD 1957, pp. 26 and 28 (Repr.); MORISSET 1959/1, p. 45, No. 147; MORISSET 1959/2, No. 21 (Repr.); MORISSET 1960/1, pp. 114-115; MARTIN-MÉRY 1962, p. 13, No. 13; HARPER 1962/3, p. 415; HUBBARD 1963, pp. 58-59 (Repr.); HARPER 1966, pp. 90-91 (Repr.); TRUDEL, JUNEAU AND MASSEY 1967, pp. 50-51, No. 24 (Repr.); COLLECTIONS 1967, No. 35 (Repr.); *Vie des arts,* 1967, p. 10 (Repr.); HUBBARD 1970, pp. 3, 36-37, 97 and 156, No. 60 (Repr.); HAMEL 1971/1, pp. 48 and 48a (Repr.); REID 1973, pp. 41-42 (Repr.); VÉZINA 1973-1974, pp. 45 and 47; LORD 1974, pp. 41-42 (Repr.); PORTRAITS ANCIENS 1975, No. 17; VÉZINA 1975/1, pp. 32a, 34, 145, 175, 200, 206, 207 and 268 (Repr.); VÉZINA 1975/3, p. 52; VÉZINA 1975/4, p. 2; VÉZINA 1976/1, pp. 18-19, No. 103; VÉZINA 1977, p. 397; ROBERT 1978, p. 27 (Repr.); LE MUSÉE DU QUÉBEC 1978, pp. 40-41 (Repr.); *Nos racines,* No. 114 (1982), p. 2275 (Repr.); LE MUSÉE DU QUÉBEC 1983, p. 78, No. 78 (entry by Claude Thibault, Luc Noppen and Michel Doyon) (Repr.); STACEY 1983, pp. 19-20 (Repr.); TREMBLAY 1987, p. 92 (Repr.); BOURASSA 1989-1990, pp. 42-47 (Repr.); BÉLAND AND BOURASSA 1990, pp. 5, 8 and 100 (Repr.); NADEAU 1991, p. 17 (Repr.).

Collection
Musée du Québec, Quebec City (34.237)

U NEQUALLED by any other painting done during the same era, this self-portrait can rightfully be considered one of the most fascinating Canadian works of the 19th century. A work of major significance, this canvas, executed toward the middle of the century, marked a turning point in Théophile Hamel's career. The 1850s witnessed the artist's last major works in which elements of the Romantic style assimilated during Hamel's stay in Europe would come to the fore.

The artist is depicted in his studio and in the background are two works already perceived as pivotal in terms of his career: *The Typhus,* which all of Montreal heralded in 1849 (Notre-Dame-de-Bonsecours chapel in Montreal) and the portrait of *Melchior-Alphonse d'Irumberry de Salaberry* (Cat. 133). A version of this latter canvas, dated 1850, was shown at the Exposition universelle de Paris in 1867. The inclusion of these two works in Hamel's self-portrait allows us to date it circa 1849-1850. Moreover, the self-portrait may have been exhibited at the Exposition universelle de Paris along with the portrait of De Salaberry. Although notes in the exhibition catalogue, as well as brief items in the local newspapers mention the quality of Hamel's works—quality at that time being equated with "striking resemblance" (*Translation*)—they do not confirm whether it was, in fact, this particular self-portrait being described. Nonetheless, the detailed iconography, including a reproduction of the portrait of De Salaberry, which was presented as part of the same exhibition, would seem to support this theory. Indeed, the smaller size of the canvas and its composition lead us to believe that it might have been intended as a study to be displayed as part of a major exhibition, unlike *Self-Portrait with a Landscape* (Cat. 117), which was intended to reaffirm the status of a young painter confident of his abilities. The third portrait of the artist, done with that of his wife around 1857 (NGC)—which, according to some, Hamel considered sending to Paris in 1867[1]—received a much more intimate treatment and does not show the mastery of his *Self-Portrait in the Studio.*

Hamel is shown seated, wearing a cap and a red and black coat shot with gold thread. The presence of a portfolio of sketches may hark back to his first self-portrait or may symbolize the work involved in designing a painting. Holding palette, brush and mahlstick, the artist poses in front of a canvas sitting on his easel, a canvas which is none other than the self-portrait in progress. Because of the "traps" of working with mirror images, the artist has had to do a double reversal, the first when painting his own image, and the second when painting the image of his self-portrait, which is thus facing right and not left. However, the canvases appearing in the background are not reversed, spoiling the accuracy of the specular image. For example, was the artist right-handed or left-handed? Did he play with his reflected image so that it resembled him more closely? In any case, the result is that the purely narrative aspect of the canvas—a portrait of the painter in his studio—is downplayed in order to stress the question of representation in a broader sense. Other elements warrant mention. The palette, which the artist made sure was plainly visible, is truly symbolic insofar as it constitutes the basic tool of the painter's art—a flat surface on which colours are mixed. Neither can one ignore the care Hamel took to make the viewer aware of the colours used in the painting as well as their specific textures. He also chose a light source, or rather lighting, that would charge each element with dramatic potential, creating a veritable tapestry of diagonals to enliven the geometric character of the composition. All these subterfuges—the borrowed elements, the portrait within a portrait, the dramatic effects of lighting, colour, texture and composition—are keys enabling us to unlock the rationale behind this painting, i.e. to present the painter's art and not simply the painter himself. This rhetorical figure reveals Théophile Hamel's talent, his aspirations and his artistic pretensions.

P.B.

Note
1. VÉZINA 1975/1, p. 140.

130.
Charles Wilson, 1849
Oil on canvas, 101 × 83.2 cm

Inscriptions
(s.d., c.l.) *T. Hamel. 1849;* (b., on the frame) *Chas. Wilson Esq. painted by Théophile Hamel 1849.*

Provenance
Descendants of the Wilson family; Miss Pauline Jacques, Longueuil (great-grandniece of Charles Wilson); acquired by the Montreal Museum of Fine Arts, 1963.

Exhibitions
Montreal 1966; Montreal 1967/1, No. 105; Ottawa 1970, No. 70.

Bibliography
(?) *MORISSET 1941/1,* p. 91; *CARTER 1967,* No. 105 (Repr.); *HUBBARD 1970,* pp. 102 and 152 (Repr.); *VÉZINA 1975/1,* pp. 115, 124, 162, 170, 175, 183, 202, 216 and 218 (Repr.); *VÉZINA 1976/1,* p. 22, No. 134; *VÉZINA 1977,* pp. 397, 399 and 400.

Collection
Montreal Museum of Fine Arts. Purchase, Horsley and Annie Townsend Bequest (1963.1423)

A CCORDING TO HIS BIOGRAPHER, Charles Wilson (1808-1877) alone represented something of a cross-section of Canadian society. Through his father, customs officer Alexander Wilson, he was a member of the Scottish community, while through his mother, a D'Ailleboust, he had very deep roots in New France. When, on May19, 1835, he married Ann Tracey, sister of Dr. Daniel Tracey, founder of the *Vindicator and Canadian Advertiser* (Montreal), he allied himself with the Irish community as well.[1]

Wilson enjoyed a relatively important political career built on connections made during his career in business. As a merchant, in 1834 he became proprietor of a hardware store which he made very successful. Director of the Scottish Provincial Insurance Company, he was also a member of the St. Patrick's Society. He was elected to his first term as mayor of Montreal in 1851, being re-elected in 1852[2] and 1853. Member of the Legislative Council in 1852, he was later named senator for the riding of Rigaud.

Théophile Hamel moved to Montreal in 1847 to fill orders from members and employees of the government, which had been seated in Montreal since 1844 (Cat. 128). Hamel's talents were sought after by eminent figures and politicians who had recently come into power and who saw a commissioned portrait as another way of affirming their social position. It was during his stay in Montreal that Hamel did this portrait of Charles Wilson, though we know little else about the circumstances surrounding the commission. A member of the Anglophone establishment, Wilson was also a friend of Louis-Hippolyte La Fontaine and on April 26, 1849, he became involved in the scuffle which rocked the city of Montreal following the adoption of a bill that would compensate victims of the 1837-1838 rebellions. The portrait gives no hint of the upheaval occurring at the time: it shows a self-assured man of action, whose haughty mein and hands set off against a dark background symbolize his rectitude.

The medal proudly worn by the future mayor of Montreal is the cross of the Order of Saint-Gregory the Great, of which he was made commander by Pie IX in September 1855.[3] This means that it must have been added at least six years after the portrait was originally painted, both to bring the latter up to date and to confirm its official nature. Indeed, the stark white shirtfront seemed to cry out for such a decoration.[4] The title of Commander of

the Order of Saint Gregory the Great was undoubtedly meant to recompense Wilson for his role in the Gavazzi uprising, which occurred on June 9, 1853 during his term as mayor of Montreal (Cat. 249). Accused of having ordered shots to be fired into the crowd, Wilson was exonerated of the death of the protestant Walsh. At the time of the trial, the apostolic nuncio to Brazil, Monseigneur Cajetan Bedini, was in Montreal as a guest of the magistrate.[5] The bestowal of this medal dispelled any lingering doubts about the former mayor's innocence.

L.L.

Notes
1. Philippe Sylvain, DCB, Vol. X (1972).
2. In 1851, Théophile Hamel received a commission, paid for by public subscription, for a full-length portrait of the Montreal mayor. The portrait was unveiled by Peter McGill on January 13, 1852 (*VÉZINA 1976/1,* p. 37, No. 238) and was described as follows: "His Worship is drawn with his chain of office round his neck, standing near a column, with an open back ground in which may be seen the most conspicuous objects which from the foreground of the city looking towards the wharves," (*Montreal Herald,* January 13, 1852). The undiscovered painting was probably destroyed in 1853 following the Gavazzi riots (*LEBLOND DE BRUMATH 1890,* p. 394). Wilson was also unfortunate with another portrait, commissioned from Italian artist, G. de Feo, which we know was destroyed before the artist was even paid (*Montreal Herald,* November 20, 1858, *La Minerve,* November 24 and 27, 1858).
3. Philippe Sylvain, *op. cit.*
4. The decoration is described as follows: "A gold, eight-pointed star, enamelled in red and bearing a gold likeness of Saint Gregory in the centre on a field of enamelled blue and bearing the words *S. Gregorius Magnus.* On the back is the Order's motto: *Pro Deo et Principe* on a field of azure. The cross is topped [...] by a laurel crown in green enamel for civilians" (*Translation*) (Victor Morin, *Les Ordres de Chevalerie religieuse au Canada* (Hull: Imprimerie Leclerc, 1940), p. 21).
5. Philippe Sylvain, *Clerc, Garibaldien Prédicant des Deux Mondes, Alessandro Gavazzi (1809-1889),* Tome II, (Quebec City: Le Centre Pédagogique, 1962), p. 434.

131. (See colour reproduction, p. 94)
Portrait of a Young Indian Girl, 1850
Oil on canvas, 90.1 × 76.8 cm

Inscription
(i.d., l.r., on one of the rocks) *T.H. 1850.*

Provenance
Descendants of the Masson family, Terrebonne; private collection, Montreal, c. 1965.

Bibliography
(?) *Le Journal de Québec,* February 5, 1853, p. 2 and May 10, 1853, p. 2; (?) *The Quebec Morning Chronicle,* May 9, 1853, p. 2.

Collection
Private collection, Montreal

T HIS UNPUBLISHED WORK showing a young Indian girl was painted by Théophile Hamel in 1850, the year the artist followed the government from Montreal to Toronto to Quebec City. In 1851, Quebec City became the permanent seat of government. Because of his constant travelling, Hamel's artistic production suffered somewhat; compared with previous years, he completed only a small number of portraits.

As reported in *La Minerve* on October 21, 1850, and in *Le Canadien* and *Le Journal de Québec* the following day, Hamel also showed a few works at the provincial industrial fair in Montreal, works which might have included the ***Portrait of a Young Indian Girl.*** Three years later, on February 5, 1853, *Le Journal de Québec* reported that at a ball organized during the carnival and held in the main ballroom of the Russell Hotel, one could see:

On one of the side walls [...] surrounded by ornaments, the portrait of Jacques Cartier [and] on the opposite side, a painting, a charming work by our own Canadian artist, Monsieur-Théophile Hamel, depicting a young Indian girl from Canada who lived at the same time as the famous navigator from Saint-Malo. (*Translation*)

Three months later, at another ball, this time given at the Music Hall by the Speaker of the Lower Chamber, J. Sandfield Macdonald, *Le Journal de Québec* stated, in its May 10 edition, that "on one of the walls of the room was the portrait of a young Indian girl, and opposite it, that of Jacques Cartier." (*Translation*) It is interesting to note that in both cases, the portraits of the Indian girl and of Cartier were displayed along with large, full-length portraits of Queen Victoria and Governor General Lord Elgin. The exhibition of these two canvases in official locations would no doubt breathe new life into the portraitist's

career in Quebec City. Unfortunately, we have no idea if "the portrait of a young Indian girl" in question refers to the painting shown here. Moreover, we know little about who the previous owners of the work were or the circumstances surrounding its execution. It is possible that the artist completed it after the fashion of his portrait of Jacques Cartier, not as a specific commission but to attract the notice of potential clients—particularly members of the government—and to showcase his skills as an artist and painter. In terms of subject matter, this portrait is not characteristic of Hamel's oeuvre in general.

Théophile Hamel has depicted the Indian girl in a relatively atypical composition for him. The teenage girl is standing and is presented in a three-quarter-length view; her body is turned slightly to the right and she is looking straight at the viewer. Her ebony hair hangs to her hips

Fig. 131A.
Théophile Hamel,
Young Indian Girls in Lorette, 1865;
oil on canvas, 63.8 × 47.2 cm.
Musée du Québec, Quebec City (77.28).

and she is wearing a white shirt belted at the waist and decorated with several pieces of jewellery: a brooch trimmed with small beads and pinned at the base of the collar, a necklace made up of three rows of round stones of different colours and long drop earrings also made of small beads. Bearing a quiver of arrows held in place by a bandolier on her back, the young girl is holding a bow and arrow in her left hand while the back of her right hand is resting on her hip—an uncommon pose in Hamel's portraits. Finally, the subject is shown against a landscape which, with its rapids and evergreen forest is conspicuously Canadian. The natural surroundings also provide some indication of the Native girl's origin—the rapids on the Saint-Charles river in the Village-des-Hurons in Jeune-Lorette. Along with the portrait of missionary Amable Charest (1866, PC), with its scenery reminiscent of the shores of the St. Lawrence, this could be one of the few

works done by Hamel in which the sitter was placed in a real landscape rather than an imaginary one. From *Joseph Brant* by Berczy (circa 1807, NGC) and *Josephte Ourné* (Cat. 166) by Légaré, to *Zacharie Vincent* by Plamondon (Cat. 194), oil portraits of Native Indians from the first half of the 19th century generally show the subject in outdoor surroundings, indicating the close tie existing between the so-called "savages" and nature.

As reported in *Le Journal de Québec* in 1853, the **Portrait of a Young Indian Girl** may have been a logical counterpart to the portrait of *Jacques Cartier* (Cat. 127), the two works being of similar format and composition. Could it have been, like the portrait of *Jacques Cartier,* a history painting of "a young Indian girl who lived at the same time as the famous navigator from Saint-Malo" or, on the contrary, was it simply, like the portraits of *Zacharie Vincent* and *Josephte Ourné,* an actual

portrait of a young Huron? Like Josephte Ourné, the young Indian is portrayed with accoutrements related to hunting, an activity essential to the Native way of life. More than merely another historical or individual portrait, Hamel's canvas seems to have been conceived both as a symbolic image and as a romantic view of a proud and beautiful people. In this painting of the young Indian girl, portrayed as Diana the Huntress, Hamel is following the great North American tradition of idealized portraits of our Native peoples. He would do the same again in 1865, in his painting of two young Huron girls hunting in the great outdoors. The painting embodied this same idealism, but fell into the category of genre scene rather than portraiture (Fig. 131A).

M.B.

132.
Portrait of a Lady of the Molson Family and Her Three Children, 1850
Oil on canvas, 109.2 × 82.9 cm

Inscription
(i.d., c.l.) *T.H. pt/1850.*

Provenance
Descendants of the Molson family; MacDonald House Antiques, Vancouver; acquired by the Vancouver Art Gallery, 1967.

Exhibition
Ottawa 1970, No. 71.

Bibliography
Bulletin of the Vancouver Art Gallery, 1967 (Repr.); HUBBARD *1970*, pp. 102-103, 163, No. 71 (Repr.); DUMAS *1970*, p. 21; DUMAS *1974*, p. 42 (Repr.); DUVAL *1974*, p. 17; VÉZINA *1975/1*, pp. 199 and 211; VÉZINA *1976/1*, p. 31, No. 182; BÉLAND AND BOURASSA *1990*, p. 106; NICOLAÏ *1990*, pp. 61, 72-73, 81, 93 and 115 (Repr.).

Collection
Vancouver Art Gallery. Gift of Dr. and of Mrs. Ben Kanee (67.16)

I T WAS UNDOUBTEDLY at his Montreal studio that Théophile Hamel painted this group portrait of one of the Molson women and her three children. Though we do not know the exact identities of the four family members, we do know that the portrait belonged to members of the Molson family living in Montreal at the turn of the century. Indeed, a 1912 photograph by the Notman studios in Montreal shows the canvas hanging on the wall of the Molson family dining room (Fig. 132A). Placed above a buffet, the work apparently did not have the customary companion piece showing the father.

The portrait shows a seated woman surrounded by her three children. Mrs. Molson is depicted holding a young baby on her lap; her two daughters are placed just a little behind her and on either side. All three children are wearing lovely embroidered outfits, which leave the young girls' shoulders largely bare. Unlike most

Fig. 132A.
Notman studio of Montreal,
Dining Room of the Molson Family, 1912.
Notman photographic archives,
McCord Museum of Canadian History, Montreal.

Fig. 132B.
Théophile Hamel,
Mrs. Jean-Baptiste Renaud and her Children,
1853;
oil on canvas, 115.1 × 87.2 cm.
Musée du Québec, Quebec City (53.169).

adult females painted by Hamel—with the exception of *Mrs. Lemoine-Angers* (1854, NGC) and *Mrs. René-Édouard Caron and Her Daughter* (MQ)—young girls are occassionally shown in gowns revealing, quite innocently, their shoulders or arms. Comfortably ensconced in his mother's lap, the bald-headed baby clutches his mother's pendant, seemingly fascinated by the play of light. Eugène, son of Madame Charles-Hilaire Têtu (1841, NGC), and Caroline, daughter of Cyrice Têtu (Cat. 135) also play with their parents' jewellery—in both cases a pocket watch with a fob chain—while young Emma, daughter of Madame Jean-Baptiste Renaud (Fig. 132B), plays with one of her shoes, which she has removed. During a moment of rest, the oldest of the Molson children looks up from her embroidery, a needle and piece of delicate fabric in her hand. In a group portrait of his four nieces (Fig. 136A), Hamel showed the oldest girl, Noémie, interrupting her sewing to glance at her uncle; sewing and embroidery were considered proper activities for young girls during this period. Finally, the other Molson daughter is turned away and is resting on the back of the chair, her head slightly tilted.

The interior against which the small group is depicted is very sparse, the main accessory being a large curtain almost completely obscuring a harp, an instrument suggesting the Molson's interest in music. With the exception of the piano found in the portrait of *Mrs. Louis-Joseph Papineau* (Cat. 187), musical instruments were relatively rare in portraits done at this time. The large harp overlaps a window opening out onto a cloudy sky and snow-covered tree branches similar to those seen in the *Portrait of a Young Man of the Taché Family* (Cat. 128).

The four Molsons form a compact group in limited space. In this composition, the sitters' heads create an inverse triangle. This painting constitutes one of Hamel's most elaborate group portraits: as far as it is known, the artist painted only three other portraits with four people in them. These group portraits should actually be seen as a group of individual portraits; in fact, as Raymond Vézina so aptly notes in his monography on the artist:

The true group portrait requires that there be some reason for several people to be brought together and interact among themselves and with the viewer; this could be a meal, a hunt, a walk, a religious ceremony or any type of work. If the people have no relationship with the viewer, it is an extension of the individual portrait rather than a true group portrait. This is exactly the approach adopted by Théophile Hamel; the sitters addressing a single interlocutor located directly in front of them.[1] (*Translation*)

M.B.

Note

1. *VÉZINA 1975/1*, p. 199.

133.
**Melchior-Alphonse d'Irumberry de
Salaberry, 1850**
Oil on canvas, 120 × 89 cm

Fig. 133A.
Théophile Hamel,
Abbé Édouard Faucher, 1855;
oil on canvas, 107 × 81 cm.
Église Saint-Louis de Lotbinière.

Inscription
(s.d., l.r., on the belt of the subject) *T. Hamel
1850.*

Provenance
Descendants of the Irumberry de Salaberry, Bossé
and Tracey families; Walter Tracey, great-grandson
of the subject; Monastère des Ursulines de Québec
(given to Juliette Bossé, order of Mère Marie-de-
la-Nativité, granddaughter of the subject), 1954.

Exhibition
Quebec City 1973.

Bibliography
Le Canadien, February 15, 1867; *Le Journal de
Québec*, February 16, and May 21, 1867; THIBAULT
1971/1, p. 101; VÉZINA *1975/1*, pp. 140, 202,
203, 207, 212, 213 and 221 (Repr.); VÉZINA
1976/1, pp. 32-33, No. 190; VÉZINA *1977*, pp. 399
and 400; BOURASSA *1989-1990*, pp. 44, 45 and 46
(Repr.); BÉLAND AND BOURASSA *1990*, p. 100.

Collection
Musée des Ursulines de Québec (CM-80-134-P)

T HÉOPHILE HAMEL's talent was at its
peak when he painted this portrait,
considered one of his masterpieces, in 1850. The imposing presence of the
subject and the harmonious use of colour
could make this work the military companion piece to the typical ecclesiastical
portrait of Father Édouard Faucher (Fig.
133A) painted by the artist five years earlier. There is no question as to the importance Hamel, himself, placed on this
portrait of De Salaberry given its inclusion
in the *Self-Portrait in the Studio* (Cat. 129)
and the fact that it is one of the three
paintings the artist chose to exhibit at the
Exposition universelle de Paris in 1867.

While Hamel's painting may be of
exceptional quality, the same cannot be
said of his subject's career. Son of Charles-
Michel d'Irumberry de Salaberry (Cat. 89),
victor of the famous battle of Châteauguay,
Melchior-Alphonse (1813-1867) profited
from his father's prestige and fame
throughout his life. Having been brought
up in a family with considerable social
standing, the seigneur's son quickly became
enmeshed in the circles of power and his
unwavering loyalty to the British colonial
government would allow him to benefit
immensely from the various positions of
responsibility granted him. In June 1848,
he gave up the practice of law to take a
position he would hold until his death,

that of assistant adjutant general for the
provincial militia of Lower Canada. It is
arrayed in the uniform of this position that
he would pose two years later for the most
famous Canadian portraitist of the day.

Shown standing and from the waist
up before a mountainous horizon and a
grey sky faintly coloured by the last rays of
the setting sun, De Salaberry exudes power.
Framed by muttonchop whiskers, his face
wears a proud and distant expression with
a hint of bonhomie. The portrait is dominated by his barrel chest shrouded in a
bright red uniform, the striking colour
being further accentuated by the glittering
play of oak leaves on the collar, the fringed
epaulettes, the double row of buttons and
the rich braiding on the sleeves. Added to
all this splendour is a double-tassled cord,
a sheathed sword worn military style and a
fanciful helmet with feathers cascading from
the top held firmly in his hand.

Given such skill in rendering detail,
we should remember that Hamel was
trained at the right school, that of his first
teacher, Antoine Plamondon, who was
recognized for the excellence of his military
portraits. During a speech given to members of the Literary and Historical Society
of Quebec in December 1833, Reverend
Daniel Wilkie (Cat. 176) recognized the
artist's merit in the following terms:

Above all, I would recommend to military men
a sitting to Mr. P's pencil; for his 'soldier likenesses' are really *chef d'oeuvres*, displaying as they
do so much of characterizing spirited touch &
splendour of the colouring. Even in the minor
essential of such portraits he is astonishingly
great—the very epaulettes he paints being absolute pictures in themselves seeming to shine
and flicker in the sunlight in all the bright and
gorgeous splendour of their golden reality.[1]

Alas, none of these pictorial marvels
by Plamondon is known to us; undoubtedly the artist's clients took the paintings,
along with their bags and baggage, back
to England when their stint in Canada was
done. Given such a situation it is easy to
understand why a work such as Hamel's
Salaberry stands as a remarkable witness
to a period in Quebec portraiture not yet
fully understood, that is, the first half of
the 19th century.

J.R.P.

Note
1. *Quebec Gazette*, December 13, 1833, p. 2.

134. (See colour reproduction, p. 109)
Mrs. Cyrice Têtu, née Caroline Dionne, and Her Son Amable,
1852
Oil on canvas, 122.2 × 90.8 cm

Inscription
(i.d., c.l., on the base of the column) *T.H. 1852.*

Provenance
Descendants of the Têtu family, Quebec City; Mrs. H.-J. Juchereau-Duchesnay, née Caroline Têtu, c. 1890; Mrs. Gustave Hamel, née Amélie Duchesnay, Quebec City, before 1936; Mrs. P.-A. Piuze, née Jeanne H. Duchesnay, Foster (Brome); acquired by the Musée de la Province de Québec, Quebec City, 1954.

Exhibitions
Quebec City 1936; Quebec City 1967, No. 28; Ottawa 1970, No. 74; Sherbrooke 1975, No. 19; Montreal 1975; Quebec City 1983-1984, No. 81.

Bibliography
BELLERIVE 1925, p. 46; *MORISSET 1936/4*, p. 9; *MORISSET 1936-1937*, Vol. II, pp. 162-163; *MORISSET 1941/1*, p. 74; *HUBBARD 1957/2*, p. 28; *MORISSET 1960/1*, p. 119; *TRUDEL, JUNEAU AND MASSEY 1967*, pp. 58-59, No. 28 (Repr.); *HUBBARD 1970*, pp. 39, 104 and 165, No. 74 (Repr.); *VÉZINA 1973-1974*, p. 46; *PORTRAITS ANCIENS 1975*, No. 19; *VÉZINA 1975/1*, pp. 48b, 48c, 168, 175, 194, 199 and 218 (Repr.); *VÉZINA 1976/1*, p. 20, No. 119; *VÉZINA 1977*, pp. 397 and 399; *Nos racines*, No. 80 (1979), p. 1600b (Repr.); *LE MUSÉE DU QUÉBEC 1983*, p. 80, No. 81 (entry by Claude Thibault, Luc Noppen and Michel Doyon) (Repr.); *TREMBLAY 1987*, p. 94 (Repr.); *NADEAU 1988*, p. 68; *BÉLAND AND BOURASSA 1990*, p. 106; *NICOLAÏ 1990*, pp. 68-71, 91-92 and 115 (Repr.).

Collection
Musée du Québec, Quebec City. Restored in 1991, with the assistance of the Amis du Musée du Québec (54.109)

135. (See colour reproduction, p. 109)
Cyrice Têtu and His Daughter Caroline, 1852
Oil on canvas, 121.9 × 91.5 cm

Inscription
(i.d., l.r.) *T.H. 1852.*

Provenance
Descendants of the Têtu family, Quebec City; Mrs. H.-J. Juchereau-Duchesnay, née Caroline Têtu, c. 1890; Mrs. Gustave Hamel, née Amélie Duchesnay, Quebec City, before 1936; Mrs. P.-A. Piuze, née Jeanne H. Duchesnay, Foster (Brome); acquired by the Musée de la Province de Québec, Quebec City, 1954.

Exhibitions
Quebec City 1936; Quebec City 1967, No. 27; Ottawa 1970, No. 73; Sherbrooke 1975, No. 18; Montreal 1975; Quebec City 1983-1984, No. 80.

Bibliography
BELLERIVE 1925, p. 46; *MORISSET 1936/4*, p. 9 (Repr.); *MORISSET 1936-1937*, Vol. II, pp. 162-163; *MORISSET 1941/1*, p. 74; *HUBBARD 1957/2*, p. 28; *MORISSET 1960/1*, p. 119; *TRUDEL, JUNEAU AND MASSEY 1967*, pp. 56-57, No. 27 (Repr.); *HUBBARD 1970*, pp. 103-104 and 164, No. 73 (Repr.); *VÉZINA 1973-1974*, p. 46; *PORTRAITS ANCIENS 1975*, No. 18 (Repr.); *VÉZINA 1975/1*, pp. 115, 160, 169, 175, 183, 199, 202 and 218 (Repr.); *VÉZINA 1976/1*, p. 20, No. 118; *VÉZINA 1977*, p. 397; *Nos racines*, No. 82 (1979), p. 1640b (Repr.); *LE MUSÉE DU QUÉBEC 1983*, p. 80, No. 80 (entry by Claude Thibault, Luc Noppen and Michel Doyon) (Repr.); *NADEAU 1988*, p. 68 (Repr.); *BÉLAND AND BOURASSA 1990*, p. 106; *NICOLAÏ 1990*, pp. 59, 68-72, 91, 92 and 115 (Repr.).

Collection
Musée du Québec, Quebec City. Restored in 1991, with the assistance of the Amis du Musée du Québec (54.108)

T HIS PAIR OF PORTRAITS of members of the Têtu family are among the most-reproduced works in the Musée du Québec's collection; they show Cyrice Têtu and his daughter Caroline, and his wife, née Caroline Dionne, and her son Amable.

Son of François Têtu of Saint-Thomas de Montmagny, Cyrice Têtu (1818-1890) came from an influential and wealthy family from the South Shore. According to their biographer, "family members included a priest, a notary, a doctor, five merchants and four farmers. Almost all of them tall, all intelligent and well-educated, they were certainly one of the most attractive Canadian families."[1] (*Translation*) Around the age of 15, Cyrice went to join his brother Laurent as a clerk at M. Boisseau & Cie., located on Rue Saint-Jean, in Quebec City. In 1845, still with his brother, he founded an import business called L. & C. Têtu. The two brothers had both their home and business on Rue Saint-Jean. On December 14, 1846, Cyrice married Caroline Dionne, daughter of The Honourable Amable Dionne of Kamouraska. The newlyweds honeymooned in Europe, another indication of their financial prosperity. In 1854, the Têtu brothers moved their business to Rue Saint-Pierre, where they had a large shop built. In addition, they both bought houses on Rue Sainte-Geneviève, a stone's throw away from one another. In 1852, Cyrice hired Charles Baillairgé, then the most important architect in the city, to design a mansion in the neo-classical style.[2]

During this period, the Têtu's business became one of the most successful in Quebec City. The two brothers conducted numerous transactions in Canada, as well as England, and soon found themselves quite wealthy. Throughout the 1860s, Cyrice's lifestyle reflected his means; in 1867, he went to Europe with his wife and two children. He may even have visited the *Exposition universelle de Paris* with Laurent and admired several works by his friend Théophile Hamel. Both Cyrice, with a fortune of at least $150,000, and his brother later had the misfortune to embark on a venture in the lumber industry which would ruin them. In his biography, Monseigneur Henri Têtu explains this misadventure in a bitingly candid portrait of the subject:

Very enterprising, too self-assured, following none but his own impulses and never listening to the advice of others, he launched himself full tilt into speculations which led him to lose almost his entire fortune [...]. Monsieur Têtu was certainly incautious and it is always a mistake to have unlimited confidence in one's own talents. It led him to take an imperious tone with his underlings and assume a certain haughty air with those who disagreed with him. (*Translation*)

After living what was still a relatively comfortable life, he died in Montreal at age 71. Cyrice Têtu and Caroline Dionne had six children; the first two, Cyrice-Amable and Marie-Caroline, were baptised on January 9, 1848 and March 25, 1849 respectively. From her marriage to Henri-Jules Juchereau-Duchesnay, Caroline Têtu had ten children, one of whom, Marie-Caroline-Amélie, married Gustave Hamel, the only surviving son of the painter, in 1890. Thus, the two paintings remained in the family until they were acquired by the Musée de la Province in 1954.

In 1852, the year he retained Charles Baillairgé to build his home, Cyrice Têtu also called upon the services of the most prominent portraitist in Quebec City to complete two family portraits. Cyrice had been a great friend of Théophile Hamel's for a long time. In 1841, during a trip to the Lower St. Lawrence early in his career, Hamel painted portraits of Têtu's parents, François Têtu and Charlotte Bonenfant (PC), his two brothers, David-Henri (Fig. 186A) and Charles-Hilaire (MMFA) and his future in-laws, Amable Dionne and his wife Catherine, née Perreault (MQ). In fact, during his stay in Italy, the artist wrote Têtu a letter from Rome on June 10, 1844. The portraits of Cyrice Têtu and his wife were done the year after Hamel finally settled permanently in Quebec City. In 1852, the latter took up residence at 56 Rue Saint-Jean and was admitted to the Institut canadien. This seems to indicate that he enjoyed an excellent reputation and financial position which allowed him, among other things, to extend loans to certain parish churches. It was at this time and under these circumstances that Hamel painted the portraits of Cyrice Têtu and his wife. We are unsure whether the portraits were commissioned by the rich bourgeois merchant or whether they were a gift from the artist to his friend. In any case, they are considered to be among the artist's finest works.

A rarity in the 19th century, these two family portraits, after the fashion of those of the Williamsons, painted by Krieghoff in Toronto circa 1845-1846 (ROM), show a mother with her son and a father with his daughter. This makes it the only Quebec painting of the era to show a man and his child, except for that of *Zacharie Vincent and His Son Cyprien* (Fig. 194A), which is more a self-portrait than a family portrait. Indeed, portraits illustrating a woman with one or more children were usually the counterpart to a portrait of the husband alone; or were simply designed to stand on their own, without a companion piece. Rarely were all the members of one family shown in the same portrait.

Cyrice Têtu and His Daughter Caroline and ***Mrs. Cyrice Têtu, née Caroline Dionne, and Her Son Amable*** are obviously meant to be an inseparable pair. The parents, each seated in an armchair, are facing one another, their backs toward the outside edges of the two works, while the children, also seated, are turned toward the centre of this symmetrical composition. The subjects are shown in a contrived setting composed of elements prized by the artist; in the upper, outside corners are two brownish red draperies, at the left, two enormous marble columns— one fluted, the other plain and encircled by a heavy cord—as well as a sketchy glimpse of the outdoors. Most of these elements can be found in the portrait of Father J.-D. Déziel, painted the same year (Fig. 137B). The subjects themselves are painted in a very individualized manner.

Cyrice Têtu has his arm around his daughter Caroline, who is seated on a raised, cloth-covered table. He is wearing a dark suit, contrasting with his daughter's bright yellow dress. The three-year-old Caroline has one hand on her father's shoulder, while the other is holding a gold pocket watch with a fob, a pose similar to that struck by Eugène in the portrait of Madame Charles-Hilaire Têtu (MMFA). Madame Cyrice Têtu has her hands tenderly placed on the shoulder and arm of her son Amable, who is seated awkwardly on the arm of her chair. Four-year-old Amable is using his finger to mark his place in the book lying open on his lap as he patiently waits for his mother to read to him. Caroline Dionne is dressed in a dark black gown and white blouse with a delicate lace collar and cuffs. It is decorated with a number of pieces of gold jewellery:

a pendant around her neck, a bracelet set with stones and charms at her wrist and a brooch at the neckline of her gown. The brooch, showing a beaver seated on a branch of maple leaves, seems to have been relatively popular among the bourgeoisie of the era, as proven by the portraits of *Mrs. René-Édouard Caron* (MQ) and *Mrs. Narcisse-Fortunat Belleau* (MUCH), both painted by Hamel in 1847. The son is wearing a chinese tunic embroidered with a number of decorative motifs. This fanciful, oriental-style garment must have been brought back from one of Cyrice's many trips to Europe. The portraits of the two adults correspond to the physical and psychological descriptions of them left by Monseigneur Henri Têtu:

Moreover, he was an excellent man, always a devout Catholic, very charitable, generous and hospitable, loving his wife and children and being dearly loved in return [...]. He always enjoyed perfect health. He was a fine-figure of a man, the Napoleon type, with strong colouring and an aura of distinction surrounding him [...]. Madame [...] was a beautiful, sainted lady, well-educated and a talented painter and musician. She had a nervous constitution and a character which might be called less than strong. Her husband had enough for both of them. (*Translation*)

These classical-inspired portraits have given rise to various interpretations in terms of style and composition. Certain art historians see them as reminiscent of the painter's stay in Italy and as a manifestation of the Têtu's taste for revival art, which was in vogue at the time, as evidenced, among other things, by their luxurious neo-Greek residence. Unlike the portraits of Monsieur and Madame René-Édouard Caron, which displayed, and to some extent justified, the wealth and social status of the subjects, these were in-

tended as intimate portraits of the artist's close friends. Indeed, even while revealing the refined tastes of those being portrayed (decor, clothing and jewellery), the portraits focus more on the relationship between the parents and their children. This relationship, manifesting warmth, trust and gentleness, is conveyed by the affectionate, tender gestures made by the sitters. The subjects' ease and elegance, accentuated by the detailed drawing and rendering of the textures and colours, also show the highly developed sensitivity and technical skill of the painter as a portraitist at the height of his career. The placement of the subjects within this setting, the balance of volume and line in the composition, the quality of the execution and, finally, an analysis of physiognomy and emotion reveal that these two portraits by Hamel rank among the artist's best work.[3]

M.B.

Notes

1. See the biographies of the various members of the Têtu family in *Têtu 1898/1*.

2. This sumptuous home was equipped with the latest conveniences of the day: gas lighting, bathrooms, central heating. The rooms were decorated and furnished in the best of taste, especially the main hall and immense double drawing room with its numerous sculpted ornaments. The Têtu house, today located at 25 Rue Saint-Geneviève is recognized for its cultural importance by the Historic Sites and Monuments Board of Canada and has been the subject of many studies and articles.

3. We should mention that Cyrice Têtu and his wife are widely believed to be the two people posing seated in a sleigh before the Montmorency falls in winter in a landscape done by painter and photographer Joseph Dynes (MQ) circa 1860.

Provenance
Pierre-Joseph-Olivier Chauveau, before 1884; Mrs. Arthur Vallée, née Honorine Chauveau; Descendants of the Vallée family; Pierre Vallée, Quebec City; acquired by the Musée du Québec, Quebec City, 1970.

Exhibitions
Toronto 1971, No. 6; Stratford 1976, No. 32.

Bibliography
LEFEBVRE *1963*, p. 170; VÉZINA *1973-1974*, p. 49; VÉZINA *1975/1*, pp. 151, 158, 160, 160c, 175, 183, 200, 204, 221 and cover p. (Repr.); VÉZINA *1976/1*, p. 17, No. 91; ASPECTS *1976*, No. 32 (Repr.); VÉZINA *1977*, p. 399; ROBERT *1978*, p. 27 (Repr.); *Nos racines*, No. 81 (1979), p. 1620b (Repr.); VÉZINA *1980*, pp. 128-131; NADEAU *1988*, pp. 58 and 66 (Repr.); NICOLAÏ *1990*, pp. 78-79 and 116 (Repr.).

Collection
Musée du Québec, Quebec City (70.95)

136.
Flore and Olympe Chauveau, c. 1852
Oil on canvas, 74.7 × 88.9 cm

WHILE SOME ARTISTS, such as Antoine Plamondon and Samuel Palmer, produced superb portraits of children, example *Cyprien Tanguay* (Cat. 184) and *James Ferdinand Turnbull and His Brother* (Cat. 177), Théophile Hamel undeniably warrants the title of foremost children's portraitist of the 19th century. He painted some 25 children in all, sometimes with a parent, usually the mother (Cat. 132 and 134), but occasionally the father (Cat. 135). In the absence of adults, the children are shown in pairs or groups of four. In several cases, they are the artist's own children (Fig. 136A and 136B) or his nephews and nieces (Fig. 136C). They are shown either in serious poses, playing with toys, petting animals or holding fruit or flowers. As Gérard Morisset wrote in 1960, "it is obvious the artist adored children and he used a brighter palette when painting them, bringing out the golds and reds and putting away all the blacks and whites." (Translation) With the portrait of the artist's four nieces (Fig. 136C) and that of Dominick Daly O'Meara,[1] the painting of Flore and Olympe Chauveau is among Hamel's finest works of this type.

It was Raymond Vézina who, in the mid-1970s, identified the two Chauveau girls, who had been unknown until then. Indeed, knowing the provenance of the portrait allowed us to trace the geneal-ogy back to Pierre-Joseph-Olivier Chauveau (1820-1890), superintendent of education and first premier of Quebec.[2] In his will, drawn up on September 12, 1884, Chauveau left his daughter Honorine *Saint-Ferreol Falls,* a landscape by Joseph Légaré (MQ), along with "the portrait of my daughters Flore and Olympe, painted by Hamel." (*Translation*)

Called to the bar in 1841, P.-J.-O. Chauveau became president of the Literary and Historical Society of Quebec in 1843. The following year, he was elected to the Assembly for the district of Quebec for Louis-Hippolyte La Fontaine's reformist party. In 1850, he was appointed Solicitor General, a position with a lower profile but which ensured recognition, prestige and a steady income. The following year, he was once again elected to the Assembly for the Quebec City riding. In 1851-1852, Chauveau was president of the Institut canadien and in 1853, he published *Charles Guérin: roman de moeurs canadiennes.*[3] In personal terms, however, Chauveau was going through a sad and difficult time, marked, among other things, by the illness of his daughter Olympe, who had tuberculosis. It was during this time that he commissioned the portrait of his two daughters from Théophile Hamel who, in 1852, was admitted to the Institut canadien. It was apparently during that same year that the painter completed the work since Flore and Olympe, born respectively on October 26, 1842 and January 31, 1844, appear to be around 10 and 8 years old.

Serious and earnest, the two young girls, whose silky blonde hair frames innocent young faces, are seated close together on a large armchair placed at an angle. The older of the two girls, turned slightly to the right, is looking beyond the picture frame while the younger, in a full-frontal view, is gazing at the viewer. These different positions create a dynamic composition. Flore's hands are resting on Olympe's left shoulder and hand, an affectionate gesture attesting to the sisters' closeness and one found in other children's portraits of the era. Elegant and graceful, the two girls are dressed in white gowns which reveal their shoulders, a style which can be seen in other children's portraits by Hamel (see the portrait of Madame Molson, Cat. 132) and which is characteristic of a more permissive attitude toward children in Victorian society. The clothing worn by the two little girls is differentiated by the colour of ribbons, pink for Olympe and blue for Flore, located at the shoulders and waist. The younger girl, her hair in ringlets, has her dress hitched up in her right hand so that she might hold some fruit and flowers, treated as a true still life. Hamel painted only one still-life (*Fruit Basket,* MQ) and rarely integrated this element

Fig. 136B.
Théophile Hamel,
*Gustave and Hermine Hamel, Children
of the Artist,* c. 1865;
oil on canvas, 66.2 × 86.5 cm.
Musée du Québec, Quebec City (54.107).

Fig. 136C.
Théophile Hamel,
*Noémie, Eugénie, Antoinette and Séphora
Hamel, Nieces of the Artist,* c. 1854;
oil on canvas, 74 × 96.8 cm.
Musée du Québec, Quebec City (76.370).

Fig. 136A.
Théophile Hamel,
Georges Hamel, Son of the Artist, 1859;
oil on canvas, 61 × 48 cm.
Musée du Québec, Quebec City (80.09).

into his portraits. Nevertheless, this idea was used again in the 1859 portrait of *Georges Hamel* (Fig. 136A), in which his son, like Olympe Chauveau, is holding the bottom of his gown in order to contain bunches of grapes and cherries. Indeed, only a few portraits of women (*Mrs. René-Édouard Caron,* 1846, MQ; *Mrs. Siméon Lelièvre,* 1858, MQ) and a few official portraits include a grouping of objects which constitute a type of still life. On either side of the girls are a cluster of flowers, to the left, and to the right, some wild ivy, an artificial pictorial device which recalls the fronds running up one side of the portraits of Madame Cyrice Têtu (Cat. 134), Father Joseph-David Déziel (Fig. 137B) and Madame Lemoine-Angers (1854, NGC), executed during the same period.

Finally, the girls are depicted in an outdoor setting, one of the rare times Hamel used a natural setting as a backdrop for a portrait. Though slightly idealized, as with his first self-portrait (Cat. 117), this landscape is nonetheless less imaginary and conventional than previously thought. Like the landscapes found in the painting of Father Amable Charest (?1866, PC) and in the *Portrait of a Young Indian Girl* (Cat. 131), this could easily correspond to a real location. The grove, the solitary tree and the dirt road are vaguely reminiscent of a summer residence owned by the Chau-

veaus, while the mountain range in the background could easily be the Laurentians.[4]

Its composition and layout distinguish this double portrait from other canvases showing two children, since children were usually painted from the shoulders up against a neutral background, as in the painting of the Turnbull siblings by Samuel Palmer (Cat. 177 and Fig. 177A), the Mailhot sisters by Frederick W. Lock (1856, MQ) and the Pelletier sisters (1838, NAC), which have always been cautiously attributed to Hamel. Here, the two children are shown inside—uncharacteristic of Hamel's oeuvre in general—like *Gustave and Hermine Hamel* (Fig. 136B), who are seated on a bed. Despite the strong diagonal created by the arm of the chair, the position of their heads and the dirt road, the composition of **Flore and Olympe Chauveau** remains relatively static in comparison to the portrait of the artist's four nieces, painted at the same time, which is full of movement and has a very natural quality about it (Fig. 136C). Finally, the portrait, neatly and precisely sketched, with bright, and even luminous, colours reveals a highly skilled execution. Undoubtedly, this portrait constitutes one of Théophile Hamel's greatest achievements in the field of children's portraiture and in Canadian painting in the 19th century as a whole. M.B.

Notes

1. For more on this painting, attributed to Théophile Hamel, see VILLENEUVE 1991, pp. 49-50 (Repr.).

2. See his biography in Jean Hamelin and Pierre Poulin, DCB, Vol. XI (1982).

3. The novel first appeared in 1846 and 1847 as an anonymous serial in a literary and musical review. With its social and political ramifications, this novel established Chauveau as the best prose-writer of his generation and allowed him to contribute to the intellectual culture of Quebec City.

4. Several of Hamel's portraits depict the subject in an indoor setting with a window opening onto an easily identifiable landscape: the bay at La Malbaie in the portrait of *Mrs. Charles-Hilaire Têtu* (MMFA), the mountains in Montérégie in the one of *Mrs. Jean-Roch Rolland* (MMCH), the St. Lawrence River and North Shore in the one of *Archibald Campbell* (Cat. 126), Cap Tourmente and the tip of Ile d'Orléans in the portrait of *Gustave and Hermine Hamel, Children of The Artist* (Fig. 136B), not to mention the views of Quebec City (N.F. Belleau and Lord Elgin, Cat. 137 and 138), Lévis (Father J.-D. Déziel, Fig. 137B) or Montreal (*The Typhus*). Though these cursory landscapes show no concern for topographical accuracy on Hamel's part, they do show the artist's intention to indicate, in his portraits, a reference to a real and familiar site. The setting in the portrait of the Chauveau girls is clearly less artificial and fanciful than the ones in the portraits of *Peter McLeod* (1854, NAC) and of *M.-A. de Salaberry* (Cat. 133), for example. Indeed, **Flore and Olympe Chauveau** is the only painting, along with that of the young O'Meara boy, to depict children in a landscape setting, the latter being, moreover, extremely elaborate.

137.
Narcisse-Fortunat Belleau, 1853
Oil on canvas mounted on plywood, 243.8 × 152.4 cm

Inscription
(i.d., on the document held by the subject)
Aqueduc./N. F. Belleau Maire./Membres du Comité/D. *J. Morrin President./ F. X. Paradis / D.* *J. Sewell / J. Maguire./ D.* *G. Robitaille/ H. Murray//} Esq.//T.H. p.* 1853.

Provenance
Commissioned by public subscription, City of Quebec, 1853.

Bibliography
Le Journal de Québec, January 11, 1853, p. 2, January 29, 1853, p. 3, June 25, 1853, p. 2, June 28, 1853, p. 2; *Quebec Mercury,* June 25, 1853, p. 2; *Le Canadien,* June 27, 1853, p. 2; *DRAPEAU 1883,* p. 9; (?) *HARPER 1966,* p. 91; *VÉZINA 1977,* p. 397; *BÉLAND AND BOURASSA 1990,* p. 52.

Collection
City of Quebec

I N KEEPING WITH A PRACTICE that was relatively common between 1820 and 1860, this portrait was paid for by a public subscription and offered to the eminent subject in acknowledgement of his contribution to the community. As a rule, the likeness of the person in such portraits would be relatively official and the attributes of his position and nature of his accomplishments would be highlighted. The work presented here is exceptional because of its format and relative complexity.

In January 1853, the residents of Quebec City's Saint-Jean parish had already raised "a tidy sum to have the portrait of the mayor, their municipal councillor, the Honourable N.F. Belleau, painted," (*Translation*) when residents in other parts of the city made known their intention to "join with them to increase the subscription and produce something more complete." (*Translation*) As far as we can ascertain, the fundraising went well since, five months later, they were able to present Belleau, then former mayor, with a large, full-length portrait. The portrait was offi-

Fig. 137A.
Théophile Hamel,
Abbé Patrick McMahon, 1847;
oil on canvas, 229 × 143.8 cm.
Musée du Québec, Quebec City (67.300).

sanitation and fire-fighting problems resulting from flaws in the existing waterworks system. A dam and water tower were built in the municipality of Jeune-Lorette at the confluence of the Saint-Charles river and the lake by the same name. The long pipeline reached the city limits in 1852. The completion of this ambitious project has to have been the City of Quebec's most important accomplishment in the 19th century.

The iconography of the large portrait of Belleau is intimately linked with his main contribution as mayor of Quebec. Soberly dressed in black, the eminent gentleman is shown standing, in a three-quarter profile, his body held upright, his chest thrust slightly forward and his left foot pointing toward the viewer. Even without the official pose, the subject's distinction, prestige and influence are apparent. His left arm hangs by his side and he is wearing a ring on his little finger; his right hand is resting on an ornate table, holding down a list of the names of the municipal council members who sat on the aqueduct committee. A book and an inkstand are also visible on the table, while underneath it is a large register on a splendid rug, whose highly decorative foliage lends a splendiferous air to the whole composition. The background also is quite interesting due to the play of successive planes. From right to left, we move from a large black leather—or horsehair—upholstered armchair of rather exaggerated proportions with a beaver carved on the back, to generous draperies and monumental columns, the latter ultimately giving way to a window affording a view outside. This convenient opening helps to explain the meaning and impact of the document held by Belleau, since it allows us to see, in succession, water sparkling in a large, three-tiered fountain, the Saint-Charles river, a schematic drawing of an aboveground aqueduct and a familiar view of the Laurentians under a grey-tinged sky.

To fully understand the place this portrait holds in the work of Théophile Hamel, we must put it into perspective and remember that the artist first explored the possibilities of the full-length portrait in 1846-1847. His likeness of Father Patrick McMahon (Fig. 137A) was the first opportunity he had to use the leitmotivs of the armchair, table, unrolled document, large draped curtain and window providing a panoramic view in the background. After a more modest, less formal variation in 1848 (*Portrait of a Young Man of the Taché Family,* Cat. 128), Hamel had to

Fig. 137B.
Théophile Hamel,
Abbé Joseph-David Déziel, 1852;
oil on canvas, 122.7 × 130 cm.
Fabrique Notre-Dame de Lévis.

wait three years before doing four successive, large official portraits: that of Mayor Charles Wilson, in 1851 (destroyed), that of Father Joseph-David Déziel (Fig. 137B) painted in 1852 but unveiled in March 1853, that of Governor Elgin (Cat. 138) in May and that of Mayor Belleau in June. Despite their unique features, the last three paintings were very similar in terms of layout and specific graphic elements. In the same way the Déziel portrait ressembles the 1846 McMahon painting, the Belleau portrait resembles that of Elgin. This same observation can be made about the general composition, attributes and colour scheme used in the two paintings.

In retrospect, we are now able to fully assess the iconological impact of the full-length portraits of Déziel, Elgin and Belleau. From one commission to the next, Hamel was in effect called upon to render, in the space of a few months, the distinctive traits of the cream of Quebec society: the clerical power of an ultramontane Church whose moral and institutional power continued to increase; the political and military power of an English city which

cially unveiled on June 24, the national holiday of Saint-Jean-Baptiste, at the Quebec city hall in the presence of many subscribers. The Honourable Louis Panet gave a speech stressing the invaluable services Belleau had provided to the city during his term in office and the fact that the portrait had been painted "by one of our finest Canadian artists," (*Translation*) Théophile Hamel.[1] After the usual expressions of gratitude, Belleau invited all the subscribers to a champagne reception at the Russell hotel.

Narcisse-Fortunat Belleau's (1808-1894) Christian names suited him well and it was no great hardship for him to throw such a reception. A prosperous lawyer and businessman, he began his long political career in 1848 when he ran and lost under the Reform Party banner. That same year, he met with greater success in municipal politics, being elected councillor of the Saint-Jean parish. In 1850, he won his way into the mayor's seat in Quebec City, a position he occupied until February 4, 1853. His mandate was marked by major work on a sewer system designed to solve maintained its privileges despite the recent recognition of the principle of responsible government in the colony; and the power of a prosperous, cultivated and industrious Canadian bourgeoisie involved in politics, business and land management.

It is also easy to imagine that the successive completion of four large, full-length portraits would have helped increase Hamel's standing between 1851 and 1853. By thus providing eloquent proof of his efficiency, his abilities as a painter and his versatility as a portraitist, he managed to conclusively prove he measured up to his chief rivals, particularly the French-born, Toronto painter Georges Théodore Berthon (1806-1892). It may be as a result of these portraits that Hamel won the coveted government contract to paint a gallery of portraits of the speakers of the legislative assemblies and legislative councils in June 1853. Undoubtedly though, the conventional, routine nature of the portraits commissioned would not have provided Hamel with great artistic inspiration over the next eight years!

The large portrait of Mayor Narcisse-Fortunat Belleau still hangs in the council chambers in the Quebec city hall. It is in its original gilded frame, a lovely piece made by John Smith, decorated along the upper portion with a historical inset corresponding to the former arms of the City of Quebec as designed by painter Joseph Légaré for the first seal of the new municipal corporation in 1833. It should be noted, in passing, that Légaré and Belleau had known one another quite well for about twenty years,[2] ever since Légaré had joined the latter on the benches of the Legislative Council.[3] To this day, they remain associates through the offices of Hamel's painting.

J.R.P.

Notes

1. In 1847, Hamel had already painted the head-and-shoulders portraits of Belleau and his wife. These works are now at the McCord Museum of Canadian History.

2. *PORTER 1981*, pp. 134, 135, 143, 150, 191, 195, 277 and 278.

3. During the painter's funeral a few months later, Belleau, along with Premier Étienne-Paschal Taché and legislative councillor Louis Panet, was one of the three eminent gentlemen asked to sign the register of civil status of Notre-Dame de Québec parish.

138. (See colour reproduction, p. 108)

James Bruce, 8th Earl of Elgin and 12th Earl of Kincardine, 1854

Oil on canvas, 76.9 × 49 cm

Inscription
(s.d., c.r.) *T. Hamel. 1854.*

Provenance

James Bruce, 8th Earl of Elgin and 12th Earl of Kincardine, England; offered as a gift to Louis-Hyppolite La Fontaine; Mrs. Dorion, daughter of La Fontaine; acquired by the Château Ramezay, Montreal, 1909.

Bibliography

MCR, *The Numismatic and Antiquarian Society of Montreal Minutes of Council Began 8th January 1904, Finished 16th May 1922* (minutes of the regular meetings of the Council), p. 111, November 9, 1909; *Registre des acquisitions 1895-1974*, p. 224, No. 2396, November 19, 1909; *O'LEARY 1907*, p. 24, No. 127; *O'LEARY 1917*, p. 26, No. 127; *O'LEARY 1920*, p. 26, No. 127; *O'LEARY 1922*, p. 26, No. 127; *O'LEARY 1923*, p. 26, No. 127; *O'LEARY 1926*, p. 28, No. 127; *CATALOGUE 1927/2*, p. 28, No. 127; *CATALOGUE 1928*, p. 29, No. 127; *CATALOGUE 1931*, p. 30, No. 127; *CATALOGUE 1936*, p. 30, No. 127; *CATALOGUE 1937*, p. 30, No. 127; *CATALOGUE 1948*, p. 30, No. 127; *CATALOGUE 1954*, p. 30, No. 127; *CATALOGUE 1956*, p. 30, No. 127; *CARRIER 1957*, p. 26, No. 125; *CARRIER AND LEFEBVRE 1962*, p. 32, No. 125; (?) *HARPER 1966*, p. 91; (?) *HARPER 1970*, p. 142; *SOUCY AND THIBAULT 1974*, p. 105; *VÉZINA 1975/1*, pp. 115, 124, 161, 175, 176, 180, 197, 202, 206, 212 and 213 (Repr.); *VÉZINA 1975/4*, p. 8; *VÉZINA 1976/1*, pp. 27-28, No. 151; *Nos Racines*, No. 80 (1979), p. 1958 (Repr.); (?) *HARPER 1979*, p. 57; *LE PASSÉ EN PEINTURE 1984*, p. 48; *SELECTED CATALOGUE 1985*, p. 15, No. 31 (entry by Susan Feindel).

Collection
Musée du Château Ramezay, Montreal (CR2396)

J AMES BRUCE (1811-1863), Earl of Elgin and Kincardine, was governor of Canada from October 1846 to December 1854. The story behind his portraits done by Théophile Hamel has, until recently, been the subject of controversy, which is why something must be said about the paintings leading up to the 1854 portrait owned by the Château Ramezay before discussing it.

On June 4, 1849, the Montreal newspaper *L'ami de la religion et de la patrie* informed its readers that Hamel was planning to paint a portrait of Elgin with the intention of making lithographs to be sold at a later date. On February 18 of the following year, *La Minerve* confirmed the project, stating that the lithograph had just been completed by Francis Davignon of New York City (Fig. 138A). In all probability, the prototype used by the engraver was the painting which today hangs in the Château Ramezay (Fig. 138B). In it, the governor is shown from the waist up and in a three-quarter profile wearing dark clothing, saved from austerity by a sash and a large four-pointed star combined with a St. Andrew's cross. This very prestigious decoration made of silver, with the emblem of the Scottish thistle in the middle and the motto "NEMO ME IMPUNE LACESSIT" (No one attacks me with impunity) proves his association to the Order of the Thistle, which is reserved for Scots who have rendered exceptional service to the British Crown.[1] A large-format version (109.2 x 82.5 cm) of this portrait is part of the McCord Museum collection. J. Russell Harper noted in the collection a copy done by Cornelius Krieghoff after the lithograph by Davignon and dated it 1847. However, this is difficult to reconcile with the information we have today; in our opinion, the copy is more likely another work by Hamel himself.[2] On the other hand, there is no doubt whatsoever that Joseph Légaré used Davignon's lithograph in 1852 to execute his small, full-length portrait of Elgin, which now belongs to the Musée du Séminaire de Québec.

The engraved portrait of Elgin was greeted with immediate and widespread success, proving the public's affection for the governor. It should be pointed out that it was under his enlightened leadership that responsible government was instituted in 1848 and that, despite violent protest from Montreal's English-speaking community, the legislature adopted the Rebellion Losses Bill. In 1854, Elgin also supported the signing of the Reciprocity Treaty with the United States.

Fig. 138A.
Francis Davignon after Théophile Hamel,
*James Bruce, 8th Earl of Elgin
and 12th Earl of Kincardine*, 1849-1850;
lithograph, 22.5 × 23 cm (image).
Archives nationales du Québec, Quebec City
(P 600-6/GH 1271-16).

Fig. 138B.
Théophile Hamel,
*James Bruce, 8th Earl of Elgin
and 12th Earl of Kincardine*, 1849;
oil on canvas, 32.3 × 27.3 cm.
Musée du Château Ramezay, Montreal
(CRX 978.26.1).

That being said, it was an earlier accomplishment of another nature altogether that led Théophile Hamel to paint a new portrait of Governor Elgin in the fall of 1852. A resolution adopted by the authorities of the Séminaire de Québec and recorded by the institution on October 21 of that year indicate the reasons:

In order that the Séminaire may show His Excellency the Governor General its appreciation for his support in raising the Séminaire's status to that of a University, we ask His Excellency to allow a full-length portrait of him to be executed and hung in the main hall of the future University in recognition of the first members of that Institution. (*Translation*)

The task fell to Théophile Hamel, who would do two versions of the portrait. The first one, a smaller version, was begun in 1852, while the larger one, the commissioned work, was completed in the spring of 1853, at least according to an article in the *Quebec Morning Chronicle* of May 6. It was apparently exhibited some days later in the music room of the Parliament Building during the annual Speaker's ball, hosted by John Sandfield Macdonald, Speaker of the Legislative Assembly. Particularly proud of his work, the artist was given permission to delay delivery so that he could continue to display it in one of the Legislative Council chambers.[3] Unfortunately, he was struck by bad

luck the following year when the work was destroyed in a fire at the Parliament Building in Quebec City. In 1854, Hamel used the smaller version kept at his studio as a basis for a new portrait of the same size. It is quite possible that the latter painting was commissioned from him to be offered to Elgin at the end of his term as governor general of Canada. This would explain why the canvas ended up in England for a short time before being returned as a personal gift from Elgin to Louis-Hippolyte La Fontaine. In 1907, La Fontaine's daughter offered to sell it to the Château Ramezay along with Hamel's portraits of the two other men who paved the way for responsible government, La Fontaine and Baldwin.[4] As for the small version painted in 1852, the artist left it to Sir Francis Hincks who, in a curious turn of events, donated it to Université Laval in Quebec City in December 1876.[5] Today, the work hangs on a free-standing wall at the Musée du Séminaire de Québec.

An examination of the Séminaire de Québec and Château Ramezay versions shows that the state portrait of Governor Elgin was one of the most ambitious works ever undertaken by Théophile Hamel. Not only is it one of his rare full-length portraits, but it also incorporated numerous accessories and detail. Wearing his admiral's uniform, Elgin is shown full-length in the

centre of the canvas. The black of his Windsor uniform particularly sets off an oak leaf collar, epaulettes, aiguillette, sash, double tassled belt, richly decorated cuffs and the silk braiding on his pant leg. His right hand grasps a tricorn hat, while the left is resting on a document "which is unrolled and falling from an ornately carved table." (*Translation*) The document is "the royal charter which [raised] the Séminaire de Québec to the status of a University" (*Translation*) in 1852. Fixed to a baldric, the governor's sword is resting against the legal text. Sitting on the table, the legs carved to resemble elegantly swirled palm fronds, are a portfolio, inkstand, seal and circular ink tray. In the background, beyond two layers of flowered draperies enveloping the shaft of a marble column, can be seen Cap Diamant, dominated by the promenade and the fortified outer walls of the Citadel, above which flies the Union Jack, symbol of British military force in North America. This is not the only example of a window or opening looking out over a panorama of Quebec to be found in paintings done during this period, witness the portrait of Alfred Hawkins painted by Samuel Palmer circa 1842 (Cat. 175). The left side of Hamel's composition is adorned with the tori and lower portion of a colossal column disproportionate to the first. Indeed, its base is hidden by a massive throne, one leg obscured by a panache of plumes resting on a luxurious carpet. Under normal circumstances, the vice-regal throne was kept in the Upper Chamber or council rooms in the southern end of the east room on the second floor of the Parliament Building. Completed in 1852 by master-sculptor Louis-Thomas Berlinguet and his son Louis-Flavien after the plans by carpenter William Drum of Quebec City, the chair was "a sublime example of sculpture." (*Translation*) Upholstered in red, its back bears "the Royal coat of arms in gold, magnificently embroidered by the Sisters of Charity" of Quebec City.[6]

Despite the rich colour scheme, this very official portrait is cold, heavy and even pompous. Apparently the abundance of accessories and relative complexity of the composition monopolized the artist's full attention. If the painting lacks emotional content, it should nonetheless be recognized as a real show of bravura for Hamel, executed as it was just prior to his obtaining the famous government contract of June 1853. Compared to Henry Daniel Thielcke's full-face portrait of Governor Archibald Acheson, Earl of Gosford (MCR), dated 1836,[7] Hamel appears to have been inventive in terms of arranging decorative elements. The prestigious canvas was one in a long tradition of portraits of monarchs and high-ranking dignitaries. In this respect, his painting is more than slightly reminiscent of the famous portrait *Napoleon Bonaparte, First Consul,* which Jean-Dominique Ingres (1780-1867) began in 1803 and which was offered to the City of Liège the following year. Coincidence or not, an engraving after this work was published in 1851, just one year before Hamel did the first version of his portrait of Elgin.

Furthermore, it should be remembered that Elgin was a lover of enlightened art who, in his own way, knew how to take advantage of the modest resources in the colony at that time. After underwriting the publication of four lithographs of Canadian scenes by Krieghoff in 1848 and visiting Joseph Légaré's third Picture Gallery in September 1852, Elgin returned to England with three of Théophile Hamel's paintings: his own portrait, that of Jacques Cartier (Cat. 127) and that of Peter McLeod and three Indian chiefs. This proved him to be somewhat humbler than his father, Thomas Bruce (1766-1841), who, while ambassador to Turkey at the turn of the century, had part of the frieze of the Parthenon shipped to the British Museum!

J.R.P.

Notes

1. We would like to thank Ginette Laroche for having clarified the significance of this decoration.

2. Toronto painter George T. Berthon probably based his 1884 copy on this version held at the McCord Museum. See Fern Bayer, *The Ontario Collection,* Markham, Fitzhenry & Whiteside for the Ontario Heritage Foundation, 1984, pp. 197-199 (Repr.).

3. For more on this version, see the *Quebec Mercury Chronicle,* May 6, 1853, p. 2 and May 9, 1853, p. 2; *La Minerve,* May 12, 1853, p. 2; *Le Journal de Québec,* May 10, 1853, p. 2 and June 14, 1853, p. 2.

4. The work apparently came into the hands of the Château Ramezay in 1907, but was not purchased outright until 1909, following a successful subscription funded by eight Montreal notables. However, we do not rule out the possibility that the portrait of Elgin obtained from La Fontaine's daughter was the one spoken of earlier. Because of inaccuracies in the Musée du Château Ramezay archives, we were unfortunately unable to determine whether this is actually the case.

5. See, in particular, *Le Journal de Québec,* December 28, 1876, p. 2; *Quebec Morning Chronicle,* December 28, 1876.

6. In its August 31, 1852 edition, the *Quebec Mercury* published a good description of the Legislative Assembly building, which was translated for *Le Journal de Québec* on September 9 of the same year. In terms of the role played by Drum and the Berlinguets, we examined a contract registered in the notarial registers of Joseph Petit-clerc as No. 6532 (March 6, 1852).

7. In a letter to Jacques Viger dated December 6, 1839, Joseph Légaré offered to make him a copy of the portrait, which he considered to be a "good likeness." (*Translation*)

THE SILHOUETTE ARTIST who called himself Master Hankes can be identified as Jarvis (or Jervis) F. Hankes, born in 1799 in Pittsford, Ostego County, New York. He began as a sign and ornament painter in 1817, and by 1826 had produced his first portrait paintings. During this time, he also began cutting silhouettes and in 1827 became associated with the Hubard Gallery, an English silhouette emporium that had arrived in the United States in 1824. Hankes appears to have included some of the Hubard Gallery's elaborate architectural silhouettes in his own silhouette gallery, which he brought to Canada in 1827. Billing himself as "Master Hankes," he arrived in Toronto in July 1827 and then moved to Montreal where he conducted business from August 20 until early September. The following announcement was placed in the *Gazette* on 22 August 1827:

NOVEL AND INTERESTING EXHIBITION – THE PAPYROTOMIA, A GALLERY OF PAPER CUTTINGS, executed in a style which has astonished the first artists in Europe, and attracted admiring crowds in all the principal cities in Great Britain and America, will for a very short time be exhibited in the BALL ROOM, at the MANSION HOUSE in this City.

The Cuttings are Trees, Flowers, Landscapes, Perspective views, Architectural, Military and Sporting pieces, Family Groups, Portraits of distinguished individuals & c. & c.

Admission 2s. 6d. Children half price. Each visitor is presented with a correct likeness, cut in a few seconds, by Master HANKES, a boy who possesses the rare talent of delineating every object in nature or art with a pair of common Scissors.

Although "Master" is a form of address usually reserved for young boys, two separate accounts dating from 1829 and 1831 confirm that Hankes was a grown man, perhaps as old as thirty. He probably tried to pass himself off as a young prodigy in order to boost business.

Following his trip to Toronto and Montreal, Hankes went to Charleston, South Carolina, where he briefly joined the Hubard Gallery, replacing "Master Hubard" (William James Hubard, 1807-1862) for whom the gallery was named and who had left the attraction. By July 1828, Hankes too had left the Hubard Gallery and was working in partnership with a Mr. Reynolds in Salem, Massachusetts under the name Reynolds, Hankes & Co. Reynolds was responsible for adding bronze-coloured detailing to Hankes' silhouettes. In contemporary references and advertisements he is referred to simply as "Mr. Reynolds."

Hankes returned to Canada in the winter of 1830-1831 with Reynolds. They went to New Brunswick and Nova Scotia, setting up their gallery first at Saint John from late November until early December, and then at Halifax from about December 15 until the end of January 1831. The following April, thirty-two works by Hankes appeared in an art exhibition held at Dalhousie College, Halifax. According to the exhibition catalogue, none were silhouettes, but included were twenty-three portraits and several religious subjects. A review of the exhibition in *The Halifax Monthly Magazine* for June 1831 severely criticized Hankes' drawings and suggested he stick to his scissors. The exhibition also included works by E. Reynolds and J. Hubard, which suggests that Mr. Reynolds could be Emanuel Reynolds (active 1822-1837), an English-born miniaturist, who would no doubt be capable of adding the fine bronzing details on Hankes' silhouettes. Hankes exhibited portraits at the National Academy of Design in New York in 1828, 1829 and 1834, and from 1838 to 1852 he apparently lived in Cleveland where he painted portraits. Nothing is known of his activities after this date.

L.F.

JARVIS F. HANKES

1799 – after 1852

Main sources

COWDREY 1943; GROCE AND WALLACE 1957; HARPER 1970; BURANT 1980; ROSENFELD 1981; BURANT 1982; MCKECHNIE 1978; FOY 1986.

MQ, NGC

139.
*George Ramsay, 9th Earl
of Dalhousie*, c. 1828
Black paper cutout highlighted with bronze
paint and grey wash on paper,
35.4 × 22 cm

Provenance
Mrs. K. Denny Polson, East Twickenham,
England; acquired by the Public Archives of
Canada, Ottawa, 1959.

Collection
National Archives of Canada,
Ottawa (1959-11-8)

T HE EARL OF DALHOUSIE[1] was born in
Scotland in 1770 and enjoyed a
lengthy military career which cul-
minated in his service under Wellington
during the Napoleonic Wars. He then pursued a career as a colonial administrator
and served as lieutenant-governor of Nova
Scotia from 1816 to 1819 and governor-
in-chief of Canada (Upper and Lower
Canada) from 1820 to 1828, during which
time he resided at Quebec City. He took a
great interest in the development and settlement of the Canadas and was conscientious regarding his duties. However, his
exacting manner and dour disposition hindered his ability to engender the cooperation of the Legislative Assembly of Lower
Canada (Quebec). He came into conflict
with Louis-Joseph Papineau, whom he
considered ill-tempered, though clever, and
grew increasingly suspicious of the political
machinations he believed were conspiring
against his well-intentioned efforts. He was
also convinced that the British government's indifference and lack of support was
at the root of many of the problems in the
colonies. Nonetheless, it was his peevish
nature and belief in the supremacy of his
office that were at least partly responsible
for many of his difficulties.

Despite these political drawbacks,
Lord Dalhousie did make significant contributions to the social and cultural life of
Quebec. He supported a number of educational institutions and was instrumental
in founding the Literary and Historical
Society of Quebec in 1824. As a record of
his Canadian activities and interests, he
acquired a large collection of paintings,
watercolours, prints, maps and plans, many
of which he commissioned from members
of his staff. A number of these valuable
items have recently been acquired from the
Dalhousie family in Scotland and can now
be found in the collections of the National
Archives of Canada, the Nova Scotia Museum, the Provincial Archives of New
Brunswick and the National Gallery of
Canada.[2]

The Countess of Dalhousie was a
constant companion to her husband and a
devoted and valuable helpmate. As well as
fulfilling her viceregal role, she was a patron of the arts and shared an interest in
natural science with the Earl. She collected
plant specimens which she carefully identified and in 1826 she presented a paper on
Canadian plants to the Literary and Historical Society of Quebec. At the time, this
was a rather unconventional occupation for

a woman, and attests to the inquisitive nature of both herself and her husband.

After leaving Canada in 1828, Dalhousie became commander-in-chief of the
British Army in India, but retired to Britain
in 1832 due to ill health. He died in 1838
and his beloved "Lady D" passed away the
following year.

The silhouettes of Lord and Lady
Dalhousie presented here were done by
"*Master Hankes*" (stamped on the back of
the silhouette of Lady Dalhousie). Since
silhouette artists often had to move from
town to town in search of work, it is possible to trace their activities by the advertisements they placed in newspapers to
announce their services. From such an-
nouncements, we know that Hankes had
worked in the United States before he made
his first visit to Canada in 1827, when he
stopped in Toronto in July and Montreal
in August. He may have visited Quebec
City shortly thereafter and presumably cut
the silhouettes of the Dalhousies, but this
cannot be substantiated. He made a second
trip to Canada during the winter of 1830-
1831, this time visiting Saint John, New
Brunswick and Halifax, Nova Scotia. During this trip, Hankes was accompanied by
a Mr. Reynolds who worked in partnership

Inscriptions
(u.c., in black ink, in the artist's hand[?]) *La Countess Dalhousie/182* [?] - *Quebec -;* (b.,u.c., in pen and black ink) *Richardson;* (b.,c., twice, stamp of J. Hankes) *Gallery of Cuttings/Cut by/Master Hankes/with common scissors.*

Provenance
Mrs. K. Denny Polson, East Twickenham, England; acquired by the Public Archives of Canada, Ottawa, 1959.

Collection
National Archives of Canada, Ottawa (1959-11-7)

VAG, AGNS, MMFA

140.
Lady Dalhousie, née Christian Broun, c. 1828
Black paper cutout highlighted with bronze paint and grey wash on paper, 35.2 × 21.9 cm

with Hankes and was responsible for adding the details of hair and clothing in gold-coloured paint, called "bronzing," to the black silhouettes cut by Hankes.

In August 1828, on the eve of his departure from Canada, Lord Dalhousie ordered five pairs of plain and five pairs of bronzed silhouettes of himself and Lady Dalhousie from Hankes and Reynolds who were then in business in Salem, Massachusetts.[3] Like most silhouette cutters, Hankes kept duplicate copies of all of his silhouettes from which he could make additional silhouettes on demand. Presumably, he filled Dalhousie's order using such a duplicate. Hankes and Reynolds charged Dalhousie three dollars each for the plain silhouettes and five dollars each for the bronzed ones. Dalhousie no doubt had the silhouettes made in order to give them away as mementos to staff and colleagues before leaving Canada. This may explain why there are at least three copies of the Dalhousie silhouette to be found in public collections (two in the National Archives, including the one presented here, and one in the Metropolitan Toronto Library). This silhouette of Lady Dalhousie, however, is the only known copy.

Hankes did not resort to the use of tracing machines or other such aids when cutting his silhouettes; instead he cut them freehand using ordinary scissors. His best work is demonstrated in his full-figure silhouettes, like that of Lord Dalhousie. The inclusion of details such as the cane and the irregular shapes indicating the necktie and the puckered coat front add interest to the profile. The bronzing done by Reynolds fills in other features of Dalhousie's costume, such as the Order of Bath which he wears on his chest and the glove he holds in his hand. The bronzing is also used to add shading to the figure and gives a sense of volume to the otherwise flat surface of the black paper profile. Lady Dalhousie's silhouette is set at an awkward angle; her head is in profile, while her body is in frontal position. This advantageous, though unusual, type of profile allowed the most interesting part of the dress, the front, to be described in bronzing details. Lady Dalhousie appears in a very fashionable gown with her hair in an elaborate pile of curls and ribbons. Aside from being portraits, silhouettes are a valuable source of information about costumes.

The present silhouettes are from the collection of William Denny, a British military officer who served in Canada from 1824 to 1831. During this time he married Eweretta Richardson, the daughter of John Richardson, a prominent Montreal politician and founder of the Bank of Montreal. It is possible that Denny or John Richardson (the word "Richardson" appears on the back of the Countess of Dalhousie silhouette) was given one of the pairs of silhouettes ordered by Dalhousie. The silhouettes were acquired by the National Archives of Canada from a family descendent along with Denny's Canadian drawing and diaries.

L.F.

Notes
1. Peter Burroughs, DCB, Vol. VII (1988), pp. 781-799.
2. Marie Elwood, "The study and repatriation of the Lord Dalhousie Collection", *Archiveria*, No 24 (Summer 1987), pp. 108-116.
3. NAC, Dalhousie Papers, MG24 A12, reel A-538, Vol. 11, no 593, account submitted to Dalhousie by Reynolds, Hankes & Co., dated August 1, 1828, at Salem, Massachusetts.
4. NAC, William Denny Papers, MG24 F33, p. 1, printed genealogical chart titled *Table of Descents of "The Denny's", Receipts of Royal Presents;* p. 1.

WILLIAM ROBERT HERRIES

1818-1845

SECOND-ELDEST SON OF British statesman John Charles Herries, William Robert Herries enlisted as an ensign in the 43rd regiment on March 6, 1835. In June of the same year, he sailed to Canada. Stationed first in Saint John, New Brunswick, then in Fredericton, Herries, like James Wandesford Butler, belonged to one of the three regiments that undertook the long march from New Brunswick to Montreal during the winter of 1837-1838, when the threats of revolt were particularly strong. Herries was part of the same army corps as Sir Richard George Augustus Levinge, who also produced a series of watercolours during his stay in the country. They were together during short postings in Niagara, Drummondville and Amherstburg, a city in Upper Canada that had been attacked four times by William Lyon MacKenzie's rebels. While in Canada, Herries was promoted lieutenant of the 43rd regiment. After Canada, he spent some time in South Africa. He attained the ranks of captain of the 43rd regiment (1842) and captain of the 3rd Dragoons (1843). In 1843, while aide-de-camp to General Thackwell, he distinguished himself during the battle of Maharajpur, following which the governor general of India hired him as his aide-de-camp. However, before he was able to reach his destination, he was killed during the battle of Moodkee (India) on December 28, 1845.

Main source
Oko 1984.

141. (See colour reproduction, p. 90)
The 43rd Regiment on March from New Brunswick to Canada Across the Madawaska Portage, 1837
Watercolour over graphite with scraping out and touches of gum arabic on paper, 31.9 × 44.5 cm

Provenance
Ibarcord Group, London (sold by Sotheby's, London, May 28, 1981, No. 89); acquired by the Royal Ontario Museum, Toronto, 1982.
Bibliography
TOPOGRAPHICAL PAINTINGS 1981, p. 39, No. 89 (Repr.) entitled *Soldiers Descending a Hill to Settlement on a Frozen Lake.*
Collection
Royal Ontario Museum, Toronto (982.90.1)

T O PREPARE FOR the feared scale of revolutionary action in the Montreal area, in the wake of the battle of Saint-Denis on November 23, 1837 and the victory of the *Patriotes,* Sir John Colborne ordered several regiments in Novia Scotia and New Brunswick to march to Quebec. We know of the route taken by the soldiers through the journal kept by James Wandesford Butler (Cat. 67), who recorded the troops' daily progress. Richard George Augustus Levinge (1811-1884), who was in the same regiment as William Robert Herries, also related the events of the expedition in his *Echoes from the Backwoods,* published in 1846, a few years after his return to England. Butler's and Levinge's accounts are actually astonishing complements to Herries' watercolours, which convey in images what the written accounts leave unsaid. Together, they provide a fuller understanding of the soldiers' journey that winter.

The thirteen-day, forced march followed along the Saint John River as far as Quebec City.[1] The leading companies of the 43rd light infantry corps, stationed in Fredericton, were the first to set out on December 12, 1837. A new detachment left every day for the next five days; Butler, stationed in Saint John, followed on December 21.[2] While Butler left a detailed account of the journey itself, Levinge added a touch of local colour, such as his description of the soldiers' uniform:

Our costumes—self, *par example,* wore four pairs of socks, (i.e. when I started) then mocassins, over which I had large worsted sort of long boots; P trousers, thick P P coat, over that a coat made of seal-skin, rather *outré,* but very warm and comfortable; then a buffalo-skin muff, fur cap, ear covers, and lots of gloves, miths, boas, &c., oceans of baccy, and a short Indian pipe; to this we added a buffalo skin, to keep our legs warm, and we were each served out with a couple of blankets.[3]

The soldiers no doubt saw the expedition as a real exploit, which, in fact, is exactly how their arrival was described:

Their arrival at Quebec was hailed as next to a miracle, and their exploits in performing such a march in the depth of a North American winter were the theme of universal admiration at the time.[4]

Herries has left a rare visual testament to the march. The first of his views, which we have entitled **The 43rd Regiment on March from New Brunswick to Canada Across the Madawaska Portage,** depicts one of the climaxes of the expedition. This watercolour is today mounted on a double support, making it impossible to verify the inscription on the back. It was sold through Sotheby's in London in 1981 under the general title *Soldiers Descending a Hill to a Settlement on a Frozen Lake.* Its comparison with a similar watercolour by Levinge (Fig. 141A) entitled *First View of the River St. Lawrence by the leading Company 43rd Reg^{t}. on March from New Brunswick to Canada across the Madawaska Portage, 23rd dec^{r}. 1837* for the first time established a connection with the December 1837 expedition. This information would have remained general in nature, however, if Douglas Schoenherr had not identified a third version of the same view in the "Townshend Album", housed in the National Archives of Canada.[5] The album was put together by Caroline Estcourt (1809-1886)[6] and contains, alongside original works by Herries, a few of her own copies, such as the watercolour entitled *First view of the St. Lawrence after crossing the Portage/St. André/copied from Mr Herries.*[7] The *"Portage"* in question is probably the one

Fig. 141A.
Sir George Richard Augustus Levinge,
First View of the River St. Lawrence
by the leading Company 43ᵈ Regᵗ.
on March from New Brunswick
to Canada across the Madawaska Portage,
23ᵈ decʳ. 1837, 1837;
watercolour on paper, 20.3 × 25.7 cm.
National Archives of Canada, Ottawa (C-5207).

at Lake Témiscouata, as mentioned by Butler:

On approaching ye outlet of lake Tamasquatha we left yᵉ ice wʰ was not considered very safe, the portage was very bad—ye hills and cahots very abrupt. My horse got very violent and attempted to jump from one hillock to another. He succeeded in breaking ye sleigh.[8]

The village of Saint-André was the companies' rallying point after reaching the St. Lawrence River. As soon as one company arrived, it waited for the next in order to form a unit of a hundred or so sleighs before continuing on to Quebec City.

Their arrival at the shores of the St. Lawrence was no doubt a special moment for the soldiers, after marching several days through the mountains in the bitter winter cold. It is in this light that Herries' watercolour should be seen. The particularly skilful composition at once makes the viewer aware of the vastness of the river and the forces of nature. Two thin, windswept figures contemplate the panoramic view over the St. Lawrence. The fan-shaped foreground overlooks the few houses in the village below and forms two large diagonals, with the one on the right depicting the action: the tight rows of soldiers slowly make their way forward against the gusting winds. A long diagonal beginning on the lower left side cuts across the page to join the mountaintop in the background on the right, marking the blanket of ice blocking the river. This series of dynamic lines is strengthened by the addition of horizontals, formed by the flow of the ice downriver and the row of mountain peaks in the background. Incisive scratch marks and the use of colour emphasize the grandeur of the site. In this respect, Levinge's composition is less skilful than Herries'. The addition of extraneous motifs such as the fence, the oversimplicity of the figures and the conventional depiction of the ice floes, aligned as they are in parallel strips, makes Levinge's work less successful overall. Consequently, it was initially thought that Herries' watercolour was a studio copy of Levinge's drawing from nature. However, after closer study, it would seem that the two soldiers drew together on site. The spacial arrangement of the planes, the contour of the mountains and the construction of the snowy hills on which the two officers are standing differ enough to support the theory that the two watercolours are independent works.

Their composition is nevertheless similar. Part of the reason most certainly lies in the site itself, as described by Butler:

One league away before our eyes flows the majestic St. Lawrence. The left shore is the highest—the clearly elevated land is sprinkled with snow. Small Islands divide the course to the West, but no obstacle hindered the flow of this mighty River. For maybe two hundred ells along the right shore huge mounds of jagged ice made for a strange and novel appearance. Unfortunately a west wind forced me sit back in my sleigh and cover myself up. I descended the hill and continued on my way along the river.[9] (*Translation*)

As well, the depiction of icy landscapes, mountains and southern seas had undergone some degree of codification since the late 18th century.[10] In this respect, the two watercolours can be compared to certain views of the Alps by John Robert Cozens (1752-1797),[11] the first British watercolourist to truly convey the notion of infinite space and the feeling of sublimeness one gets from alpine landscapes. Herries and Levinge take these principles and apply them to their panoramic views, the treatment of the foreground and the near-monochromatic

VAG, AGNS, MMFA

142.
Advanced Guards, Second Division, Passing the Saint Maurice River, 1838
Watercolour, pen and brown ink with scraping out and touches of gum arabic over
graphite on paper, 29 × 44.4 cm (irregular dimensions)

Provenance
Ibarcord Group, London (sold by Sotheby's,
London, May 28, 1981, No. 94); acquired by
the Royal Ontario Museum, Toronto, 1982.

Bibliography
TOPOGRAPHICAL PAINTINGS *1981;* p. 42, No. 94
(Repr.).

Collection
Royal Ontario Museum, Toronto (982.90.3)

colour scheme, while the compositional arrangement remains conventional. Cozens especially broke with the tradition of dividing the composition into three parallel planes and placing the horizon two thirds of the way up the page. By making the houses smaller in their watercolours, Herries and Levinge were also seeking to convey the vastness of the landscape. In this way, they have succeeded in capturing one of the fundamental characteristics of the notion of sublime and making it tangible.

The troops' arrival at Quebec City was followed by nine days of rest, before continuing their journey to Sorel. On January 7, 1838, Herries arrived in Trois-Rivières, as shown in *Advanced Guards, Second Division, Passing the Saint Maurice River.* This watercolour differs slightly from the preceding work, notably in the overall colour tonality. *The 43rd Regiment on March from New Brunswick to Canada Across the Madawaska Portage* varied from bright blues to blue-greys set against the white of the surface left blank. Herries stresses the powerfulness of nature and the river, which has shoved the ice floes up against the shore where the sleighs

must force their way through. He shows a particularly keen sense of observation: pale purples blend with grey-soaked greens to create clashing masses of ice; pen is used to highlight the rough patches of brown to draw the eye to the sharp ridges of the ice. The same colour tones brush the sky diagonally, suggesting bad weather accompanied the soldiers on their journey. Although the composition differs, it shows a similar interest in depicting the place reserved for man, reduced to tiny figures left powerless by the forces of nature.

D.P.

Notes

1. Large excerpts from Levinge's journal are quoted in BELL *1973/1,* pp. 91-94.

2. *March from S'. Johns, N.B. to Quebec undertaken in consequence of the disturbances in Canada in the year 1837,* Fol. 1. Quoted from the handwritten journal.

3. BELL *1973/1,* p. 93. Levinge quotes part of a letter from a soldier to friends in England.

4. BELL *1973/1,* p. 92.

5. NAC, "William Robert Herries" file. This information is taken from a letter, dated June 7, 1982, to Mary Allodi from Douglas Schoenherr.

6. Lady Caroline Bucknall Estcourt married Sir James B. Bucknall Estcourt (1802-1855) in 1837. She accompanied her husband on his posting to Canada in 1838-1839 and 1844-1847 (*Harper 1970,* p. 106).

7. Quoted from information provided by Douglas Schoenherr.

8. *March from S'. Johns, N.B. to Quebec…,* Fol. 11.

9. *Ibid.,* Fol. 14. This passage is in French in the original text.

10. Barbara Maria Stafford, *Voyage into Substance: Art, Science, Nature, and the Illustrated Travel Account, 1760-1840* (Cambridge: The MIT Press, 1984). This book provides numerous illustrations to this effect. An excellent overview of mountain landscapes can also be found in *Découverte et sentiment de la montagne, 1740-1840* (Cat.) (Annecy: Conservatoire d'Art et d'Histoire de la Haute-Savoie, 1986).

11. Kim Sloan, *Alexander and John Robert Cozens. The Poetry of Landscape* (New Haven: Yale University Press, 1986), pp. 115-125. With respect to the influence of Cozens' composition grid, we are thinking in particular here of his *Pays de Valais* reproduced in Andrew Wilson, *The Art of Alexander and John Robert Cozens* (New Haven: Yale Center for British Art, 1980), Fig. 135.

JAMES HOPE-WALLACE

1807-1854

THE SON OF JAMES HOPE, fourth Earl of Hopetoun, James Hope-Wallace was born in England on June 7, 1807. Following in his father's footsteps, the young Hope chose a career in the military, enlisting in the Coldstream Guards at age seventeen. At the same time as his entry into politics—as member for Linlithgow—he was promoted lieutenant-colonel in 1837. Five months earlier he had married Mary Frances Nugent, daughter of the Earl of Westmeath, in London. Around the same time, he was assigned to the 2nd battalion of the Coldstream Guards, in service in Quebec City, which he joined in July 1838. As of the following November, the commander-in-chief of the Canadian British army, Sir John Colborne, appointed him to the post of staff commander of a brand-new regiment, the *Volontaires de Québec*. He held this position until March 1840. He obtained a first leave the following year and a second from October 9, 1841 to October 9, 1842. Hope returned to England shortly thereafter to join his unit, which had departed October 5, 1842. He left the army two years later and succeeded his uncle, Lord Wallace, whose name and coat of arms he took over. He died in England on January 7, 1854.

Main sources
ALLODI 1974/1; COOKE 1983.

MQ, NGC

143.
Mont-Carmel Street, Quebec,
Looking Towards the River, c. 1839
Watercolour over graphite highlighted with gouache on paper,
25.9 × 31 cm

Provenance
Clark Galleries; acquired by the Royal Ontario Museum, Toronto, 1951.
Exhibition
Toronto 1981.
Bibliography
ALLODI *1974/1,* Vol. I, No. 882.
Collection
Royal Ontario Museum, Toronto (951.45.5)

VAG, AGNS, MMFA

144.
Wolfe and Montcalm Monument, Quebec, 1841
Watercolour over traces of graphite on paper, 22.5 × 32.6 cm

Inscriptions
(l.l, brush and brown wash, in the artist's hand[?]) *12 June 1841;* (l.l.) seal
indicating property of Canada Steamship Lines; (b.,u.l., in graphite) *By the*
Hon. James Hope–
Provenance
W. H. Coverdale, Manoir Richelieu, Tadoussac; acquired by the Public
Archives of Canada, Ottawa, 1970.
Bibliography
BELL *1973/1,* p. 68 (Repr.).
Collection
National Archives of Canada, Ottawa (1970-188-438)

J AMES HOPE-WALLACE must be giv-
en a special place among the British watercolourists who arrived in
Quebec in 1838. The second son of General John Hope, who became the fourth
Earl of Hopetoun in 1816, he embodied
the prestige of a titled family. Several generations of earls of Hopetoun had done
the "Grand Tour," thus amassing an impressive collection of paintings for the
family castle. James Hope was thus raised
in an environment where art was of considerable importance, as shown by his
father's decision to have the entire collection evaluated by Andrew Wilson (1780-
1848) in 1817.[1] This artist, born in
Edinburgh, had a decisive influence on the
collection, which included several hundred
works. He eliminated some, organized new
hangings, and finally became an active
agent in Italy beginning in 1826, in order
to track down new works for Hopetoun.[2]
The earls of Hopetoun also gave commissions to contemporary artists. Gavin
Hamilton (1723-1798) had painted a *The*

Death of Lucrecia, while Andrew Wilson
painted a large landscape of Hopetoun
House in 1820, in the style of Claude
Lorrain.[3] Walter Geikie (1795-1837) also
painted a number of genre scenes. The
visit of King George IV to Hopetoun
House on August 29, 1822, should be
mentioned. This is not the place to emphasize the importance of this royal visit,
prepared by Walter Scott with a view to
reconciling England and Scotland; let us
simply point out that highly symbolic ceremonies were planned and that the king
visited Hopetoun House at the very end
of his trip to knight two people, one of
whom was portraitist Henry Raeburn
(1756-1823).[4]
    This family backdrop is important
to understanding James Hope-Wallace. It
would be incorrect to consider him solely
as an officer trained for a military career.
His past attests to a different type of education, and his enlistment in the army at
age seventeen was perhaps more the result
of his obligation as the family's second son.

When he arrived in Quebec City in July
1838, he was not only lieutenant-colonel
in the Coldstream Guards regiment, but
also member for the Scottish riding of
Linlithgow; he resigned from the army
when he succeeded his uncle, Lord Wallace, in 1844. Therefore, James Hope-
Wallace is obviously not a man with a single
vocation, unlike John Philip Bainbrigge,
for example, who entered the military
academy of Woolwich as a student and
ended his career there as professor of fortifications. Let it simply be said that his
works bear witness to a different vision
from that of the other military topographers present in Quebec City. His perception resembles more that of an art
enthusiast who discovers a country while
travelling, than that of an officer in a garrison who identifies areas for strategic
purposes.
    James Hope-Wallace carefully dat-
ed most of his works, specifying the day,
month and year, as did James Pattison
Cockburn. Thanks to these references and

VAG, AGNS, MMFA

145.
Falls of the Saint Anne River, 1839
Watercolour over faint graphite lines on paper, 22.9 × 33.2 cm

Inscription
(l.r., in pen and black ink) *S'. Anne'.s/13 Sept 1839.*
Provenance
Clark Galleries; acquired by the Royal Ontario Museum, Toronto, 1951.
Bibliography
ALLODI *1974/1,* Vol. I, No. 865.
Collection
Royal Ontario Museum, Toronto (951.45.50)

the album at the Royal Ontario Museum, we have an understanding of the development of his artistic production. The album, which has now been taken apart, was designed in January 1841 by Hope-Wallace's wife, Mary Frances Hope.[5] It includes 69 watercolours, some fifty of which are dated and which mark the highlights of his stay in Quebec City, from July 1838 to October 1841. During this period, he made only a few trips to the surrounding area and a longer journey to Niagara Falls in 1841. The most striking thing in his watercolours is the extreme ease with which he approaches a new country and portrays vast expanses. The town comes into play as a terrace from which the artist observes the distant landscape, looking toward the river or the Saint-Roch district. His perception differs from that of other topographical artists in that the city plays a secondary role to the countryside. Dated July 11, 1838, the first known watercolour, *Saint Roch Suburb Seen from Quebec Rooftops* (Fig. 143-145A), is a composition which was to appear repeatedly during the first two years of the artist's activity. A panorama unfolds beyond an imposing foreground, framed at the side

by the vertical plane of a building or a tree. Figures, although not indispensable to the composition, are sometimes present. James Hope-Wallace's main concern seems to have been to depict the dimensions of the country in his watercolours. This applies not only to his large-scale landscapes, but also to his few smaller watercolours.

Mont-Carmel Street, Quebec Looking, Towards the River, although of a strictly topographical nature, is far from banal. This street, one of the city's oldest, became part of Quebec City's defense system in the 17th century, with a platform of cannons at its westernmost end.[6] Cockburn portrayed it in 1831, capturing its architecture in two pencil drawings.[7] Hope-Wallace's approach is entirely different; his vision is not descriptive but selective. He chose to ignore the street's military past, selecting a lower vantage point than that used by Cockburn, across from the house built in 1820-1821 for Thomas Hunt. This residence, of which we can see part of the facade on the left, was occupied at the time by Dr. Thomas Fargues.[8] Apparently, the impressive three-storey building was what interested Hope-Wallace. In the early 1830s, architect

George Browne erected it in the space left empty between the Fargues home and the oldest residence on the street, built around 1740 at the corner of Mont-Carmel and Haldimand streets. This is the building we see in the middle distance and to which Elzéar Bédard added a storey in 1830.[9] Hope-Wallace has done a very free portrayal, beginning with the long palisade at the right, which serves as a foil for the main architecture. Brown washes have been rapidly applied to the street, disregarding the lateral vistas to create stronger light effects. Echoed in white gouache on the ochre facade of the main house, the light reflects its openings and makes it the centre of the composition.

James Hope-Wallace's talent for composition is just as obvious in *Wolfe and Montcalm Monument, Quebec.* A majestic stand of trees appears in the right foreground, which is bisected by a visual vanishing point opening onto the south shore. In the centre, the monument raises its chalk-coloured profile against a cursorily outlined backdrop. The artist's style is clear and concise. Only the obelisk and its pedestal are clearly outlined, with the secondary motifs traced more vaguely. The

Fig. 143-145A.
James Hope-Wallace,
Saint-Roch Suburb Seen from Quebec Rooftops,
1838;
watercolour over graphite, 22.7 × 32.0 cm.
Royal Ontario Museum, Toronto (951.45.17).

Fig. 145A.
James Pattison Cockburn,
Falls of the Saint Anne River, 1827;
Sepia on paper, 34.8 × 52.9 cm.
Musée du Québec, Quebec City (69.74).

Fig. 145B.
James Hope-Wallace,
Falls of the Saint Anne River, 1839;
watercolour over graphite, 33 × 22.8 cm.
Royal Ontario Museum, Toronto (951.45.42).

strength of the work is in its colour, applied gradually from pale to darker shades. The yellows, for example, absorb the pale greens to produce the olive tone so often present in landscapes. A slightly darker shade is added to the colour scheme, creating the shadow which looms over the entire foreground. Finally, the brush outlines the tree branches in brown, highlighting the luminous sheen of the birch bark in the foreground, produced by the white of the paper. This is far different from Henry William Barnard's vision of the same site (Cat. 60). Although James Hope-Wallace's canvas perpetuates the topographical tradition, it is far more than a description. Firmly rooted in the ground and looking over the river, the monument exudes permanence.

The ability to summarize, characteristic of Hope-Wallace's watercolours, is most evident in the series of waterfalls on the Sainte-Anne, Sault-à-la-Puce and Saint-Ferréol rivers, done during an outing in September 1839. The landscape is pared down to a minimum in a two-tone montage of brown and green. Great masses of rock frame the waterfall, rendered essentially by the white of the paper, and serve as a foil for the vegetation which occupies the entire background. Unlike Cockburn's version, done some ten years earlier (Fig. 145A), it is the vitality of the shapes which dominates this composition. Hope-Wallace manages to convey this effect of grandeur not only through his sparing use of techniques, but also by giving the impression that the motif shown is only part of much more vast natural surroundings. This quest for the sublime is even more striking in another view of the same falls, sketched the same day (Fig. 145B). The line barely suggests the shape, which has been filled in with the paintbrush. The large masses of colour emerge vertically to form a deep, narrow gorge where the frenzy of the torrent expends itself. Here, Hope-Wallace uses colour and light contrasts to suggest the innate organization of nature and its primal strength. James Hope-Wallace owes this "topography of the sublime" to the landscapes of Scotland, which resemble those of Quebec. There is no doubt that the works of his youth, of which we know nothing, prepared him for his experience with Quebec nature.
D.P.

Notes

1. Basil Skinner, "Andrew Wilson and the Hopetoun Collection," *Country Life,* August 15, 1968, pp. 370-372.
2. With regard to the role played by Andrew Wilson in Italy, see Hugh Brigstocke, *William Buchanan and the 19th Century Art Trade: 100 Letters to His Agents in London and Italy* (London: The Paul Mellon Centre for Studies in British Art, 1982), pp. 20-24.
3. For A. Wilson, see John Harris, *The Artist and the Country House* (London: Sotheby Parke Bernet, 1979), p. 342, fig. 390. For G. Hamilton, see B. Skinner, *op. cit.* Geikie's commission is mentioned by E.D.H. Johnson in *Paintings of the British Social Scene from Hogarth to Sickert* (New York: Rizzoli, 1986), p. 153.
4. Gerald Finley, *Turner and George the Fourth in Edinburgh, 1822* (cat.), (London: The Tate Gallery), pp. 13-14 and 65.
5. *ALLODI 1974/1,* Vol. I (under the name of James Hope-Wallace).
6. *CHARBONNEAU, DESLOGES AND LAFRANCE 1982,* p. 36.
7. NAC, *Album Wiggin* (I-55 and I-172). One of them is reproduced by *CAMERON AND TRUDEL 1976,* p. 86.
8. See Luc Noppen, "Maison Feldman et ancienne écurie," in *LES CHEMINS DE LA MÉMOIRE 1990,* t. I, pp. 137-138.
9. Luc Noppen, "Maison Bédard," in *LES CHEMINS DE LA MÉMOIRE 1990,* t. I, pp. 135-136.

MQ, NGC

146. (See colour reproduction, p. 107)
Camping Near Quebec 1840
Watercolour over graphite highlighted with gouache and traces of scraping out on paper, 19,3 × 34,2 cm

Inscriptions
(on the mount, l.l., in graphite over-written in pen) *Night of 22ᵈ Feby 1840;* (on the mount, c., in graphite) *Hᵒⁿ James Hope, Lady Mary Hope, Hᵒⁿ Louis Hope & Lt Col & Mʳˢ Codrington. Camping Nʳ Quebec* (inscriptions over-written on the back of the mount).

Provenance
Kennedy & Co.; acquired by the Royal Ontario Museum, Toronto, 1951.

Exhibition
Toronto 1979.

Bibliography
ALLODI 1974/1, Vol. I, No. 933 (Repr.); *ALLODI 1974/2*, pp. 30-31 (Repr.).

Collection
Royal Ontario Museum, Toronto (951.188.1)

T HIS CAMPING SCENE is rare and exceptional: rare because of its subject, and exceptional in comparison
to the rest of James Hope-Wallace's work.
We have already seen that this artist dated
most of his works, and in this particular
case, he has been even more specific,
marking "night of February 22, 1840."
The night must have been particularly
memorable for it to have merited such
mention, especially since the names of those
present are included; all that is missing is a
record of the temperature! However, it is
currently impossible to determine the exact
circumstances: our hypothesis is that this
excursion was linked to the moose hunt in
which James Hope-Wallace participated,
which began February 25 and extended
into the early days of March.[1] This night
of camping under a makeshift shelter was
perhaps a foretaste of a major outing.

Whatever the case, this is not a
work drawn from nature. Hope-Wallace
has reproduced, probably at a much later
date, a sketch done on-site that has since
disappeared. As Mary Allodi pointed out,
the Royal Ontario Museum owns a small
watercolour entitled *Building a Shelter in
the Quebec Woods in Winter* (Fig. 146A),
which shows elements in common with
this work. The location, action and number
of figures, both men and women, point to
it as being the preliminary stage to the
night spent camping in the forest. The
facture, sweeping and spontaneous, is
echoed in the sketches of forest excursions
(Cat. 145). The pen drawings of the
hunting trip exude the same feeling. The
preparation of the shelter for the night
(Fig. 146B) and the wait for dinner (Fig.
146C) are descriptive records, with no
other objective than to keep alive the

Fig. 146A.
James Hope-Wallace,
Building a Shelter in the Quebec Woods in Winter, c. 1840;
watercolour over graphite on paper, 10 × 14.4 cm.
Royal Ontario Museum, Toronto (951.45.2).

Fig. 146B.
James Hope-Wallace, *Cabanning*, 1840;
ink and graphite on paper, 18.2 × 23 cm.
Musée du Québec, Quebec City (81.279).

Fig. 146C.
James Hope-Wallace, *Waiting for Dinner*, 1840;
ink and graphite on paper, 20.1 × 31.8 cm.
Musée du Québec, Quebec City (81.280).

memory of an event uncommon for British natives.

The strength of ***Camping Near Quebec*** lies elsewhere. This watercolour, the composition of which is particularly polished, no longer has any merit as a direct recording. Hope-Wallace has distributed the figures in a large ellipse, marked at either end by two standing figures with their heads lowered. The seated figures in the foreground are balanced by the tightly massed figures in the middle ground. The man in the foreground with his back to us who is preparing to light the fire closes off the circle toward the warmth of the blaze. This plastic structure is echoed by the colour effects. The dark background, with its slate-blue opening toward the night in the upper right-hand corner, serves not only as a backdrop, but draws our eye to the rich hues—olive, yellow and orange—in the foreground. In the same way, the group of women seated in the middle ground wearing blue-grey checkered coats, with a beige dress that can be glimpsed in the centre, contrasts sharply with the woman seated across from them, whose red dress is bright against her near-black coat. Details such as the bundle of covers, the white sleeve of the shirt worn by the man on the left, and the women's dress collars, all reflect the light. For this night of camping is first and foremost a chiaroscuro scene. The fire in the centre of the composition backlights the figures. The technique of scraping is skilfully used to suggest the intensity of the light and warmth along the left profile of the man in the foreground. However, despite the refinement of this portrayal, it is not the execution which stands out: an effort must be made to fully appreciate the work's logic and complex harmony. The location—a cabin built of branches in the midst of the forest—and the serenity of the facial expressions imbue this work with an apparent simplicity.

D.P.

Note

1. The Musée du Québec owns a series of nine ink drawings which depict the highlights of this excursion (81.274 to 81.282, see *Béland 1991*). The Royal Ontario Museum also houses a drawing from the same series, dated February 27, 1840 and entitled *My first Shot at a Moose* (966.2.9).

CORNELIUS
KRIEGHOFF

1815-1872

CORNELIUS DAVID KRIEGHOFF was born in Amsterdam on June 19, 1815. Several years later, his family moved to Düsseldorf, where his father made wallpaper. Krieghoff probably studied at the painting academy in this city in around the 1830s and later travelled in Europe. He emigrated to America when he was around 21 and, accompanied by his younger brother, arrived in New York. On July 7, 1837, during the war against the Seminole Indians of Florida, Krieghoff enlisted in the American army for three years. It was then that he met and married Émilie Gauthier dit Saint-Germain, a French Canadian from Boucherville, near Montreal. Krieghoff retired from the American army on May 5, 1840. The young couple then settled in Boucherville, where Émilie gave birth to two children. Krieghoff returned to the United States around 1842-1843. He set up a studio and exhibited history paintings in Rochester, New York, where he also became friends with James Bowman. In 1844, Krieghoff returned to Europe to continue his artistic training. He studied with the history painter and portraitist Michel-Martin Drolling (1786-1851) in Paris. In October 1844, he was granted permission to copy works at the Louvre. Returning to Canada in 1845, he first worked in Toronto, settling in Longueuil the following year. He later lived in Montreal.

In 1847, Krieghoff helped to found the Montreal Society of Artists and participated in a major exhibition of works by this group. His paintings were shown beside those of Martin Somerville, William Sawyer, Andrew Morris, and so forth. The same year, Krieghoff exhibited works with the Irish painter Paul Kane at the Salon of the Toronto Society of Artists. In 1847-1848, he published his first series of lithographs, dedicated to Lord Elgin. Krieghoff was hired to give painting and drawing classes at Miss Plimsoll's school for young ladies in 1849.

At the urging of his friend John Budden, an auctioneer for A. J. Maxham & Company, Krieghoff moved to Quebec City in 1853. This marked a turning point in his career: his genre scenes became very popular, particularly with English-speaking merchants and members of the military. Krieghoff's most prolific period was 1853-1863. It was then that he produced his most evocative works, such as *Merrymaking* (1860, BAG).

Two major sales of Krieghoff's works and belongings were organized in 1862-1863. The first presented some of his paintings while the second, many of his personal effects, including a large library of some 1200 volumes, his collection of birds, coins and Chinese curios. After 1863, Krieghoff travelled again in Europe. He exhibited some of his works at the Paris Exhibition of 1867, which also presented paintings by Théophile Hamel and Napoléon Bourrassa. Back in the United States in 1867, he lived with his daughter in Chicago. After visiting Quebec City briefly in 1871, he died of heart failure in Chicago on March 8 the following year.

Main sources
DE JOUVANCOURT 1971; VÉZINA 1972/1; VÉZINA 1972/2; HARPER 1979.

147.
An Officer's Room in Montreal 1846
Oil on canvas, 46 × 65 cm

Inscriptions

(s.d., l.l.) *C. Krieghoff./1846;* (l.l., on one of the gloves) *AAS;* (b.,l.c., on the vertical cross-piece of the stretcher in ink) *From the/Collection of/Hon Mary/Mac Donald/(daughter of/Canada's first/ prime minister);* (b.u.c., on the vertical cross-piece of the sketch, on a damaged label, in graphite) [illegible] *his Huntin...* [?]/[illegible] *Canada. He was/*[illegible] *ask a Governor/*[illegible] *a Crouds* [?] *Colony -/...icture was sold by./...dy Macdonald in/*[?].

Provenance

(?) Commissioned from the artist by Dr. A. A. Staunton; Lieutenant John MacDonnell, Montreal and London; Watson Art Galleries, Montreal; Mrs. Helen Norton, Coaticook, 1936; Dr. Sigmund Samuel, Toronto; gift to the Royal Ontario Museum, Toronto, 1954.

Exhibitions

Montreal 1847, No. 103; Vancouver 1966, No. 38; Toronto 1979; Toronto 1982-1983.

Bibliography

The Montreal Gazette, January 15, 1847; *The Pilot and Journal of Commerce,* January 29, 1847; *Montreal Transcript and Commercial Advertiser,* February 11, 1847; CATALOGUE *1847,* p. 12, No. 103; NGC, W.R. Watson Fund, Sales Record, Ledger No. 2 (1928-1955), No. 2127, April 11, 1936; SPENDLOVE *1958,* p. 75; BARBEAU *1962,* [p. 23] (Repr.) entitled *Lord Elgin's Montreal Office;* HARPER *1962/3,* p. 412 (Repr.); *The Auctioneer,* Vol. VIII, No. 3 (April 1966), p. 7 (Repr.); SHADBOLT *1966,* No. 38; DE JOUVANCOURT *1971,* p. 8a (Repr.); *Perspectives,* October 2, 1971, p. 22 (Repr.); VÉZINA *1972/1,* pp. 102, 171, 178 and 213 (Repr.); DE JOUVANCOURT *1979,* p. 5 (Repr.); HARPER *1979,* pp. 20-21, 22, 26, 44, 47, 182 and 193 (Repr.); DUBÉ *1986,* pp. 105 and 312 (Repr.); TRUDEL *1990/1,* pp. 6-7 (Repr.); TRUDEL *1990/2,* pp. 62-63 (Repr.).

Collection

Royal Ontario Museum, Toronto (954.188.2)

J OHN RUSSELL HARPER deserves the credit for having solved part of the riddle of this painting in his major study on Krieghoff. Harper suggested that the figure seated in the middle of the room full of exotic objects, works of art and books be identified as Andrew Anthony Staunton, who was assistant surgeon of the British army and had been stationed in Montreal since 1845.

More recent research has furthered our understanding of this work, which is a veritable painting within a painting, presenting an eclectic assortment of objects.[1] The recent discovery of the catalogue for the 1847 exhibition of the Montreal Society of Artists has made it possible to identify the canvas' original title: *An Officer's Room in Montreal.*[2] Krieghoff presented 47 other works at this exhibition, some of

Fig. 147A.
Diagram of *An Officer's Room in M*

which are illustrated in the painting itself. It constitutes as it were not only an illustrated catalogue but also a display of his recent work.

Based on the subject of some of the paintings illustrated in this picture (see diagram, Fig. 147A), it seems to have been a sort of tribute by Krieghoff to his friend Staunton, an amateur artist, collector and honorary member of the Montreal Society of Artists. Krieghoff had already worked on the theme of the collector in the *The Antiquarian*[3] in 1845, and **An Officer's Room in Montreal** is the Canadian pendant to this scene. A copy of the latter painting occupies the place of honour (No. 1) at the top of the wall over the fireplace, since it was part of the officer's collection. Six other paintings are copies by Krieghoff after some of Staunton's drawings.[4] The painting directly over the fireplace (No. 11) is a copy of work No. 41 in the 1847 catalogue: *Caravanserai in Mesopotamia; from an original Sketch*. Its composition is identical to that of the engraved drawing in Francis Rawdon Chesney's work, *Narrative of the Euphrates Expedition Carried on by Order of the British Government during the years 1835, 1836 and 1837,* published in London in 1868. The two portraits at the top of the left wall (Nos. 17 and 18) are also based on works by Staunton; listed as Nos. 39 and 40 in the 1847 catalogue, they were

entitled *Portrait of Sheikh Ibrahim, Chief of the Whahabees, from an original Sketch taken by Dr. Staunton, R.A.* and *Portrait of Douab, Chief of the Anazi Bedouis; from an original Sketch by Dr. Staunton, R.A.* Apparently, Krieghoff copied sketches that Staunton had drawn while he was in the Middle East. Neither these two paintings nor the two small desert landscapes (Nos. 9 and 10) over the fireplace have been located. *The Plains of Babylon; from a Sketch,* listed as No. 42 in the 1847 catalogue, might correspond to one of these works. The painting beside the straw hat on the left wall (No. 23) has been identified as a work by Krieghoff; part of the Power Corporation of Canada Collection, it bears the inscription "Landscape on the Nile after Staunton" (Fig. 147B).

Krieghoff included not only paintings based on Staunton's works in this gallery of 26 pictures but also some of his own copies. The large painting on the left wall (No. 16) can be identified as work No. 32 in the 1847 exhibition, which was described as follows: *German Winter Scene; a Prussian Forester talking to children in a Sleigh. From the original by Wickengerg; in the Musée du Luxembourg, Paris, by Mr. Krieghoff.* Actually, it corresponds to the central part of the painting by Petter Gabriel Wickenberg (1812-1846), now housed in the Louvre (Fig. 147C). This scene, which Krieghoff copied in the Lux-

embourg museum during his trip to Europe in 1844-1845, is reminiscent of several of the artist's own compositions, in which the figures are grouped around a sleigh in a winter setting. Similarly, the painting of a face in profile on the left wall (No. 24) is a prototype of Krieghoff's many head-and-shoulders portraits of *habitants*. Finally, there is every indication that Staunton is surrounded by some of the Krieghoff's own works: the small painting above the door (No. 19), ironically surrounded by antlers, reproduces scenes in which a jealous husband surprises his wife in the arms of a military officer.[5] The large landscape on the far wall (No. 15) and the painting of a canoe descending the rapids beside it (No. 14) are probably also two of Krieghoff's own compositions. However, attempts to relate these paintings to known works have been inconclusive. As for the painting depicting the upper body of a woman holding a candle (No. 4), it can be associated with another canvas on the same subject, *Lady with a Candle,* sold in Montreal in 1976 and attributed at the time to François Beaucourt.[6] Even though Krieghoff was familiar with this kind of composition, with its artificial lighting, it is hard to definitely attribute this particular work to him.

Several paintings on the right wall portray cavalry scenes. Horses ridden by one (Nos. 6, 12 and 13) or two people

Fig. 147C.
Petter Gabriel Wickenberg,
Winter Scene;
oil on canvas.
Musée du Louvre, Paris (8527).

Fig. 147B.
Cornelius Krieghoff after A.A. Staunton,
Landscape on the Nile; oil on canvas.
Power Corporation of Canada/Power Corporation du Canada, Montreal.

(Nos. 2 and 5) and a cavalcade (No. 8) bear witness to Staunton's passion for horses. A wide range of saddlery articles are shown on the far wall. This room, which is a veritable showcase of curios, is decorated with objects whose origin indicates that their owner visited several different countries. The many Amerindian artifacts (headdresses, embroidered bags, weapons) and stuffed local animals—Staunton was also reputed to be a naturalist—indicate that he was interested not only in arts and science but also in local customs. The telescope, balanced somewhat precariously on the edge of the table, the travel books on the shelves, and the conspicuously placed bust of Shakespeare[7] also reveal the officer's curiosity. Snowshoes, skates and a toboggan in the foreground indicate the kind of sports played in Canada and, along with the fur coat, boots, fire in the hearth, and the officer's warm clothing, confirm that the scene takes place in winter.

This painting is structured like a theatre set. The floor, embellished with a painted motif and rugs, is sharply inclined, while the walls are laid out at obtuse angles. Although no particular source of light is indicated, the scene is shrouded in a soft atmosphere that accentuates the domestic comfort of this idyllic place. The room depicted is indeed a product of the artist's imagination for Staunton did not have the means to pay for such a decor. With the officer's help, Krieghoff created a cultural microcosm combining the emblems of various countries and attesting to the conditions of cultural imperialism and colonial adventure under which collections were accumulated in the 19th century. Staunton's interest in leather objects, such as shoes and gloves, is particularly obvious. Moreover, a pair of gloves bearing his initials provided the key to the identity of the model.

It is impossible to fully study this painting, with its complex iconography and wide range of associations, within the limits of this text. Both the spirit and central theme of the work seem to be summarized by the relationship between the two large paintings over the fireplace, one depicting the officer's room and the other a caravansary. Located in countries at opposite ends of the world, these two spots, one designed for rest and the other for study, bear witness to the cultural and scientific changes that marked the development of natural and social sciences in the 19th century. The active role of Cornelius Krieghoff in the art world after 1846 had a decisive influence on the changes that occurred over the next decade. His themes, like his technique, helped to define the tastes and sensitivity of Quebec society in the mid-19th century.

L.L.

Notes

1. This research was conducted by Mrs. Jean Bruce and the author of this catalogue entry while this painting was being re-created by the Canadian Museum of Civilization.

2. This painting was very well received. An article on the exhibition in *The Montreal Gazette* of January 15, 1847 described precisely this work: "There is a great deal of merit in his [Krieghoff] interiors, particularly one of 'an officer's apartment,' (we think it is called), in which there is much skilful and characteristic grouping of inanimate objects, and great soundness and transparency of colouring, which, indeed, seems to be his leading characteristic. But it is unreasonable to expect all the merits of an original picture in a place where no one seems to have any notion of the great bodily and intellectual labour, and the adequate remuneration for it, required in producing such a work."

3. *HARPER 1979*, p. 23 (Repr.).

4. Several of Staunton's drawings were lost in the wreck of the *Tigris.* (*Biographical records of Officers,* p. 553).

5. *HARPER 1979,* p. 32 (Repr.).

6. Fraser Bros. Ltd. sale, June 1976, Lot 285b. See *MAJOR-FRÉGEAU 1979,* p. 99 (Repr.).

7. Staunton and Krieghoff both belonged to the "Shakespear Club" (*HARPER 1979.* p. 21). Elinor Kyte Senior's study, *British Regulars in Montreal: An Imperial Garrison* (Montreal: McGill-Queen's University Press, 1981), focuses on the life of British soldiers in Montreal.

Fig. 148A.
Diagram of *Still Life with Flowers, Fruits and Corn Cob.*

Legend of the diagram
1.   Althæa rosea
2.   Fritillaria imperialis
3.   Papaver somniferum
4.   Delphinium sp
5.   Tulipa
6.   Syringa vulgaris
7.   Callistephu chinensis
8.   Calendula officinalis
9.   Anemone sp
10. Primula auricula
11. Rosa sp
12. Convolvulus tricolor
13. See 11
14. Cucurrus melo
15. Vitis sp
16. Prunus sp
17. Prunus persica
18. Ribes pativum
19. Vitis sp
20. Zea mays
21. Citrus limon

148.
Still Life with Flowers, Fruits and Corn Cob, 1846
Oil on canvas, 97.7 × 78 cm

Inscription
(s.d., l.r.) *C. Krieghoff, 1846.*

Provenance
Berry-Hill Galleries, New York City; acquired by the Montreal Museum of Fine Arts, 1967.

Exhibitions
Montreal 1847, No. 118; Montreal 1967/1, No. 194; Quebec City 1971, No. 20.

Bibliography
CATALOGUE 1847, p. 13, No. 118; *CARTER 1967*, No. 194 (Repr.); *LA CHRONIQUE 1968*, p. 40, No. 164 (Repr.); *DE JOUVANCOURT 1971*, pp. 48 and 61 (Repr.); *JUNEAU 1971*, No. 20 (Repr.); *VÉZINA 1972/1*, pp. 164, 165, 177 and 216 (Repr.); *KELLY 1972*, pp. 15 and 17 (Repr.); *DE JOUVANCOURT 1979*, pp. 81 and 99 (Repr.); *HARPER 1979*, p. 195.

Collection
Montreal Museum of Fine Arts. Purchase, Horsley and Annie Townsend Bequest (1967.1549)

A T THE 1847 exhibition of the Montreal Society of Artists, Cornelius Krieghoff presented a still life that was described as follows in the catalogue (No. 118): *Flower and Fruit-Piece. Composition from Several Paintings in the Louvre, by Van Huysum, Van Spanendonk, De Heem, Mignon and from Nature.*[1] With the recent publication of the catalogue, it has been possible to identify the sources used by the artist for this composition. John Russell Harper suggested that Krieghoff "borrowed heavily from a canvas by Jan van Os (1744-1808); minor variations not found in the original, such as a

Fig. 148B.
Jan van Huysum,
Still Life with Flowers (Stillaven met bloemen)
1725;
oil on canvas.
Rijksmuseum, Amsterdam (A 188).

Fig. 148C.
Cornelis van Spaedonck,
Still Life with Flowers, 1789,
oil on canvas.
Musée du Louvre, Paris (1857).

cob of corn, are introduced in deference to the need for some North American flavour."[2]

The corn cob motif[3] was found in Dutch still lifes as of the 18th century.[4] While its presence reflects a knowledge of American flora, the corncob was adapted by European painters to symbolize the death of Christ and his resurrection, the buried kernels signifying rebirth, as it were.

According to the entry in the 1847 catalogue, Krieghoff's still life was based on works by 17th- and 18th-century painters from the northern school whose paintings were in the Louvre and were copied by Krieghoff during his trip to Europe in 1844-1845. While a comparison of his still life with paintings by Jan van Huysum (1682-1749), Gérard van Spaedonck (1746-1822)[5] and his brother Cornelius (1756-1840), Jan Davidsz de Heem (1606-1683/1684), and Abraham Mignon (1640-1679) sheds some light on this question, it reveals above all the composite nature of Krieghoff's painting.

The way in which the flowers have been arranged in an earthenware vase surrounded by fruit and corn on a marble table is typical of Huysum's still-lifes. The prominent position of the slightly diagonal Crown Imperial (*Fritillaria imperialis*) (No. 2, Fig. 148A) is a common feature of this artist's work (Fig. 148B). This flower also appears in a painting by Cornelis van Spaedonck in the Louvre (Fig. 148C). The position and arrangement of the tulips (No. 5) and roses (No. 11) are based primarily on paintings by Abraham Mignon. The tulips and asters (No. 7) form a triangle around the central axis of roses and hollyhocks (No. 1). While the lush flower arrangement is very regular, the fruit around the base of the vase lends considerable stability to the composition as a whole.

Drawing inspiration from other works rather than from nature, Krieghoff has presented a timeless arrangement, despite the presence of a butterfly, believed to mark a specific, ephemeral point in time. Spring and summer flowers are mixed with ripe fruit and vegetables harvested in the fall. Despite the presence of a rose bud on the edge of the marble table and the rough texture of the melon (No. 14), this painting should not be seen as a reflection on the contrast between vegetable and mineral or organic and inorganic. Rather, it concerns the life cycle from awakening or birth, symbolized by the roses (No. 13) and the morning glory (No. 12) still in bud, to sleep or death, evoked by the poppy capsule (No. 3).

L.L.

Notes
1. *Trudel 1990/2*, p. 86.
2. *Harper 1979*, p. 13.
3. Krieghoff included a corncob in another still life, *Still Life with Roses, Delphinia, Tulip and Others in a Glass Vase*, 1845; oil on canvas, 58.4 × 44.4 cm. Art market, Halifax, 1980.
4. For example, Abraham Mignon, *Still Life*, Musée Granet, Aix-en-Provence, and *Früchtestilleben mit Tieren*, Wallraf-Richartz Museum, Cologne; Alessandro Coosemans (1627-1689), *Still Life with a Snail*, Enschende, Rijksmuseum Twenthe.
5. At the 1785 Salon, critics remarked that Spaedonck based his work on Huysum. See Jacques Foucart, *De David à Delacroix* (Cat.) (Paris, Réunion des musées nationaux, 1974), p. 610. According to Foucart (p. 609), three of Spaedonck's four paintings owned by the Louvre in the mid-19th century disappeared to Saint-Cloud in 1870-1871 and to Berlin during World War II.

149.

Doctor Daniel Arnoldi, 1847

Oil on canvas, 123.8 × 103.5 cm

Inscriptions

(s., l.r.) *C. Krieghoff,* (l.r, on the volume placed on the table) *PARISS PHARMACOLGIA/VOL. II;* (c.r., on the volume placed on the window) *ANATOMY.*

Provenance

Collège des Médecins, École de Médecine de Québec, 1849; on deposit at the Université Laval (Séminaire de Québec), 1912; given back to the Collège des Médecins, Montréal, 1934.

Exhibition

Ottawa 1934, No. 146.

Bibliography

ASQ, *Université 176,* No. 62, "Letter from Dr J. Gauvreau to Mgr Amédée-E. Gosselin", April 27, 1912; *Manuscrit 34,* Vol. IX, p. 11, April 29, 1912; *UNIVERSITÉ LAVAL 1913,* pp. 38-39, No. 150; *LAVAL UNIVERSITY 1923,* p. 44, No. 150; *UNIVERSITÉ LAVAL 1933,* pp. 35-36, No. 144; ASQ, *Université 211,* No. 39a, "Letter from H.-O. McCurry to Mgr François Pelletier", January 19, 1934; *Université 251,* No. 1, "Letter from Dr J. Gauvreau to Mgr Camille Roy", May 1st, 1934; *Université 251,* No. 4 and *Université 211,* No. 39c, "Letter from Mgr Camille Roy to Dr J. Gauvreau", May 4,1934; *Université 211,* No. 39b, "Letter from Paul Rainville to Mgr François Pelletier", January 26, 1934; *Université 251,* No. 16, "Letter from Dr J. Gauvreau to Mgr C. Roy", May 17, 1934; (?) *BARBEAU 1934,* p. 130; *EXHIBITION 1934,* p. 20, No. 146, entitled *Portrait of Dr. Arnold;* DE JOUVANCOURT 1971, p. 60; THIBAULT 1973/1, pp. 168-169; DE JOUVANCOURT 1979, p. 101.

Collection

Corporation professionnelle des Médecins du Québec, Montréal

D ANIEL ARNOLDI (1774-1849) obtained a license to practise medicine in 1795 and soon attracted a large and wealthy clientele. He associated with Montreal's upper middle class and enjoyed a most enviable reputation. Appointed doctor of the Montreal jail in 1833, he was accused by some of having failed to look after the *Patriotes* following their imprisonment in 1837-1838, while others praised him for his humanity (see Cat. 65, 66, 112 and 113). A political conservative and a loyalist, and a reformer in his profession, Arnoldi was a member and even chairman of the Board of Examiners for the district of Montreal between 1812 and 1823 and from 1839 to 1847. In 1843, the Board set up a committee to study the possibility of regulating more strictly the teaching and practice of medicine. This led to the passage in 1847 of an act regarded as the great charter of medicine, and to the creation of the College of Physicians and Surgeons of Lower Canada. Arnoldi was appointed chancellor of the college by the governor; he died of cholera, however, two years later.[1]

Although Cornelius Krieghoff was renowned for his genre scenes and landscapes based on Canadian subjects, he also engaged in the art of portraiture at different times in his career. A distinction should be made, however, between the portraits he painted of individuals from nature and his innumerable paintings of stereotyped personages such as hunters, snowshoers, basket and moccasin vendors, pipe smokers and, especially, *habitants.* Such works have more in common with genre scenes. In addition to a self-portrait (1855, NGC), John Russell Harper has inventoried around a dozen copies, including that of a portrait of young Joseph-Ferdinand Turnbull (see Cat. 177), and around 20 portraits drawn from models.[2] The art historian did not mention, however, this striking portrait of *Doctor Daniel Arnoldi,* whose trace had been lost since it was exhibited in Ottawa and Montreal in 1934.

This portrait seems to have been given to Arnoldi by the signatories of the charter of medicine adopted in 1847, the year the doctor was appointed chancellor of the College of Physicians and Surgeons of Lower Canada.[3] Krieghoff therefore signed the painting the year after he had moved to Montreal. It was also the year in which he established himself as an artist by taking part in two major exhibitions, one by the Montreal Society of Artists and the other by the Toronto Society of Artists.

Arnoldi, who was 74 when his portrait was painted, is depicted sitting in a slightly rigid pose in a chair, with his right arm on the armrest, his glasses in his right hand, and his left hand on an open book. The elderly man is surrounded by medical books, two of which are clearly identified: one is a treatise on pharmacology, lying on the table, while the other is a treatise on anatomy, located on the window sill. The window overlooks a mountain in the distance, whose profile is similar to that of Mount Royal and thereby evokes the city where the surgeon practised. The purple cloth covering the table counterbalances the drapery behind the doctor. Both the lighting and composition of the portrait are designed to highlight the face and hands of the practitioner as well as the various attributes of the researcher and scientist. As in the portrait of *Archibald Campbell* painted by Théophile Hamel (Cat. 126) the same year, the composition and, in particular, the various accessories present are designed to reveal and emphasize the occupation of the person portrayed.

In his monograph, Russell Harper mentions seven portraits of fairly different style and composition dating from the early years of Krieghoff's career (1845-1853), when the artist lived in Toronto and Montreal. According to Harper, Krieghoff engaged in portrait painting without a great deal of enthusiasm, believing that this kind of work was basically geared to earning a living. The art historian also declared that Krieghoff's first portraits are generally lifeless and conventional, except for those of Mr. and Mrs. William Williamson and their children (1845-1846, ROM) and that of the auctioneer John Budden, a close friend of the artist (PC). The portrait of Dr. Arnoldi, which may be associated with these high-quality portraits, reveals the influence of two major schools: while its composition complies with certain classical conventions used by Hamel and Plamondon, the freer treatment of the head and, in particular, of the hair and jabot, is reminiscent of the romantic English style of such artists as Samuel Palmer (Cat. 178). Above all, the portrait of *Doctor Daniel Arnoldi* reveals the true personality of a man who, although still actively involved in his career, had nevertheless reached the end of a long professional life.

M.B.

Notes

1. Gilles Janson, DCB, Vol. VII (1988), pp. 25-27.

2. *HARPER 1979,* pp. 194-195.

3. ASQ, *Université 251,* No. 1. When Arnoldi died, his portrait was bequeathed to the College of Physicians and Surgeons, who entrusted it to the care of the Quebec school of medicine. The college recovered the portrait shortly after the exhibition of 1934.

150.
Caughnawaga Indian Encampment, c. 1848
Oil on canvas, 35.6 × 53.3 cm

Inscription
(s., l.r.) *C. Krieghoff.*

Provenance
Mrs. W.W.C. Wilson, Montreal; Leslie W. Lewis of the Haynes Art Gallery, Toronto; Dr. Sigmund Samuel, Toronto; gift to the Royal Ontario Museum, Toronto, 1949.

Exhibitions
Toronto 1979; Toronto 1982-1983.

Bibliography
BARBEAU *1934*, p. 132; BARBEAU *1948*, p. 5 (Repr.); VÉZINA *1972/1*, p. 177; HARPER *1979*, pp. 45, 46 and 191 (Repr.).

Collection
Royal Ontario Museum, Toronto (949.39.17)

C ORNELIUS KRIEGHOFF'S choice of popular subjects, the liveliness of his interpretation, the brilliance of his autumn and winter landscapes, and the sheer volume of his output guaranteed him a last━━━ ━━━━ ━━ ━━━ ━━━━━━ ━━ ━━━━dian paint⎜   ⎜ In-
dian⎜   ⎜ the
Mon⎜   ⎜ch a
good⎜   ⎜out
one ⎜   ⎜de-
voted⎜   ⎜hib-
ited⎜   ⎜nent
scene⎜   ⎜ures
domi⎜   ⎜st a
carefully detailed forest grove. In later years his scenery became more naturalistic, and the figures smaller and more integrated into the landscape.

The subject of the life and customs of the North American Indians was of intense interest in Europe during the 18th century; because few artists had visited the New World, engravings in 18th century publications were often borrowed from images used in much earlier books—with the result that imaginary Indians were depicted either as wild savages or as ancient classical figures.[2] By the 19th century art-

ists were travelling the continent, sketching Indians from life. In 1830 the American artist George Catlin (1796-1872) began a long career of painting Indians; in Canada, Paul Kane (1810-1871) of Toronto first travelled west to record Indian life in 1846, and dedicated the rest of his working years to this subject. In Quebec, British military artists such as Thomas Davies, George Heriot and John Crawford Young (Cat. 236) included sketches of Indians in their watercolour portfolios, and professional painters such as Martin Somerville (Cat. 217) and James Duncan drew figure studies of Indians whom they observed in downtown Montreal.

However, it was Cornelius Krieghoff who captured the popular imagination by portraying Indians in a storytelling way. His vivid oil paintings show the native people shooting rapids in bark canoes, and returning from the hunt to tell tales around the campfire in idyllic woodland settings. His paintings are detailed in style of presentation, yet romantic in mood. The costumes and artifacts are generalized, and the Indians are not portraits of individuals. This painting is titled as a Caughnawaga encampment, depict-

ing the Mohawks of the Iroquois confederacy who lived in Caughnawaga village near Montreal; however, the bark-covered conical lodge in the background is of the Algonkian type. This is not surprising, since Krieghoff was in the habit of borrowing details for his paintings from prints, and adapting them to his own use. In some of his Indian encampment paintings, figures were taken directly from lithographs after John Richard Coke Smyth. At other times he copied Bartlett engravings, Currier & Ives lithographs, and drawings by Martin Somerville.[3] Rather than being documentary records, his paintings of Indian life reflect the current tastes of his time for romantic and anecdotal themes.

M.A.

Notes
1. HARPER *1979*, p. 44.
2. Hugh Honour, *The European Vision of America* (Cleveland: The Cleveland Museum of Art, 1975) and François-Marc Gagnon, *Ces hommes dits sauvages* (Montreal: Éditions Libre Expression, 1984).
3. HARPER *1979*, pp. 44-53.

Provenance
Mrs. J. W. Rowat, Montreal; Watson Art Galleries, Montreal, 1955; Pierre Rinfret, Quebec City, 1955; Maurice Bellemare, Montreal; Galerie Bernard Desroches, Montreal, 1981; acquired by the Musée du Québec, Quebec City, 1982.

Bibliography
NGC, W.R. Watson Fund, Inventory Book, No. 2 (1955), p. 194, No. 15529, November 28, Sales Record, Ledger No. 2 (1928-1955), No. 15529, November 27, 1955; HARPER *1979,* pp. 92 and 195.

Collection
Musée du Québec, Quebec City (82.15)

151.
Noontime, c. 1853
After John Frederick Herring
Oil on canvas, 31.7 × 35.7 cm

O N JANUARY 29, 1847, a columnist for the *Pilot and Journal of Commerce* made the following comment with regard to the exhibition of the Montreal Society of Artists:

By referring to the catalogue, we find that a great number of the paintings are copies. We are not in the least astonished, that in so short a time some of the artists and amateurs were not fully prepared to furnish originals.

This remark is interesting in that, although the columnist was not surprised to see a number of copies in the exhibition, he seems to have preferred original works. It might be asked whether this attitude denotes a change in the tastes of art enthusiasts, who were more able to appreciate the talent needed to produce an original composition. Nevertheless, copying remained a common and accepted practice throughout the 19th century. Krieghoff, a prolific painter, did not neglect this lucrative market. Throughout his career, he made copies after popular prints, paintings he had seen in European museums, or sketches by friends (Cat. 148). Some of his works were based directly on William Notman's photographs.[1]

John Frederick Herring (1795-1865) was renowned for his horse paintings. George IV, William IV and Queen Victoria each commissioned him to paint portraits of their favourite animal (see Cat. 152). During the 1840s, he integrated horses into more sentimental scenes, such as *Feeding the horse.* Several copies of this scene were executed for Herring, probably with the assistance of the members of his large studio.[2] Krieghoff, who was a meticulous painter interested in details and materials, made a copy in which he paid special attention to the horses' shiny coat and the tam-o'-shanter on the man's head.

The scene takes place on an old farm with a medieval decor. The two saddle horses, one white and the other black, are accompanied by a couple whose clothing does not indicate, however, that they owned or rode the animals. While the black horse is eating grain from the container held by the seated man, the white horse is eating grass from the young woman's hand.

Chickens and other birds in the foreground peck at seeds that have fallen on the ground. Like many genre scenes from the 17th century onwards, this painting has erotic overtones.

After identifying the source of this painting, William Watson, who wrote the certificate of authenticity formerly on the back of the work, made the following comment: "Here, Krieghoff has painted his pretty wife Louise in one of the best portraits we have of her." In reality, however, Krieghoff based this painting directly on Herring's work. The myth that Marius Barbeau created around Krieghoff's wife, Émilie Gauthier, from 1934 onward led Watson tobelieve that she was associated with this scene.   L.L.

Notes
1. Examples have been reproduced in HARPER *1979,* pp. 6, 10, 106, 108, 109 and 140.
2. The Leicestershire Museum and Art Gallery (Leicester, England), which owns one of the versions of this painting, has pointed out the existence of seven other replicas.

152. (See colour reproduction, p. 103)
"Fraser", With Mr. Miller Up, 1854
Oil on canvas, 64 × 79.5 cm

Inscriptions
(s.d., l.r.) *C. Krieghoff pxt/Quebec 1854.*; (b.,l.r., before the new backing covered the inscription) *Portrait of Fraser rode by Mr. Miller./painted by C. Krieghoff. Quebec 1854.*

Provenance
Descendants of the Kirwin family, Bedford; Dominion Gallery, Montreal, before 1961; acquired by the National Gallery of Canada, Ottawa, 1964.

Exhibitions
Fredericton 1961, No. 8; Ottawa 1967/1, No. 115; Ottawa 1969-1970, No. 11; Quebec City 1971, No. 4; Calgary 1976, No. 11.

Bibliography
CORNELIUS KRIEGHOFF 1961, No. 8 (Repr.); *HUBBARD AND OSTIGUY 1967,* pp. 72 and 73, No. 115 (Repr.); *READY 1969,* No. 11; *DE JOUVANCOURT 1971,* p. 98a (Repr.); *JUNEAU 1971,* p. 10, No. 4 (Repr.); *VÉZINA 1972/1,* pp. 103, 109, 165 and 214 (Repr.); *DUVAL 1974,* p. 13; *THROUGH CANADIAN EYES 1976,* No. 12 (Repr.); *DE JOUVANCOURT 1979,* p. 195 (Repr.); *HARPER 1979,* pp. 96, 104 and 193 (Repr.); *GUAY 1987,* p. 24 (Repr.).

Collection
National Gallery of Canada, Ottawa (14609)

I N 1854, Mr. Kirwin commissioned Cornelius Krieghoff to do a painting of his horse "Fraser." Kirwin may have chosen Krieghoff owing to the absence of Robert Clow Todd, who was famous for his equestrian portraits. At the time, Krieghoff was the most prominent artist in the Anglophone community of Quebec City, where he had settled in 1853.

Horse racing was an English tradition that made its appearance in Canada after the Conquest. It clearly reflected the notion that leisure activities enabled the sportsmanly gentleman to enhance his social standing. The Plains of Abraham were the prime location for these social events, which became especially popular as of the 19th century and were often presided over by the Governor-General himself.[1] Cash prizes, or purses, were awarded according to the different categories of races, the most

Fig. 152A.
John Frederick Herring,
Memnon, 1825; engraving, 31.8 × 41.6 cm.
Glenbow Museum, Calgary (63.55.18).

prestigious of which was the Queen's Plate. The horse "Fraser", then owned by Captain Fane, came second in the Turf Club Purse on July 5, 1853; first in the Lumberman's Purse the next day; and second in the Merchant's Plate on July 7.[2] The following year, the seven-year-old horse belonged to W. Kirwin, who entered him in several races. "Fraser" finished second in the Turf Club Purse and first in the Hurdle race. Kirwin also entered him in the Merchant's Plate which, however, did not take place, owing to a lack of participants.[3] The Hurdel Race, which was two miles long and included nine hedges of three and a half feet, offered the winner a prize of £40. According to a journalist with *The Morning Chronicle,* the race was very close:

"Fraser" took a strong lead from the start, striking the first hurdle slightly. He took the second hurdle 29 lengths in advance, "Lady Franklin" second, "Broker" third, and "Sucker" last. The pace must have mended from this, for on rounding into the home stretch "Lady Franklin" had picked up the leader coming past the stand only a length behind. At the 6th hurdle "Fraser" stumbled, but the rider recovered himself handsomely, and brought his horse into his stride on the top of the hill, about a length behind "Lady Franklin." On coming past the Marchmont fence, in the last round the same positions were maintained, but "Fraser" collared "Lady Franklin" at the distance. The last leap was taken at the same moment by both horses, and a beautiful run terminated the victory in favor of "Fraser" by a bare length.

Perhaps Mr. Kirwin asked Krieghoff to paint "Fraser," one of the finest horses in his stable, to commemorate this spectacular victory. He certainly owned several horses since he entered two others in races on the Plains the same year. As indicated by an inscription on the back of the painting, "Fraser" was ridden by a jockey named

Miller. Wearing his owner's colours—a black riding cap and a crimson jacket—he struck a majestic pose with his mount on the Plains of Abraham. The St. Lawrence River and the south shore, probably near Saint-Romuald, can be seen in the background. This painting reveals not only the artist's skills but also his lack of knowledge about horses. Obvious alterations to the animal's head indicate that Krieghoff hesitated when drawing its anatomy. He is also responsible for certain defects in the horse's body, unless they were actually exhibited by the animal itself: for example, the bulging and poorly situated eye, the knock knees and unrealistic neck and stifle. Such problems are certainly not encountered in *"Corbeau," A Trotting Horse* (Cat. 224) by Robert C. Todd. Krieghoff also had to redo certain parts of the harness, in particular, the martingale with rings, attaching the collar, saddle girth and bridle together and intended to prevent the horse from raising its head too high. Other weaknesses can be detected in the way he has drawn the headstall and throatlatch, which allow the bridle to be attached to the horse's head. However, despite the fact that he was new to this type of painting, Krieghoff nevertheless displayed great technical skill, if only in the manner in which he rendered the shiny coat of this gelded chestnut.

This equestrian portrait reflects a British tradition that emerged in aristocratic circles in the 17th century. George Stubbs (1724-1806), among other artists, gave the impetus to this tradition on the eve of the 19th century. This type of portrait complied with very rigid conventions, leaving little room for variation. John Frederick Herring (Fig. 152A) largely exploited the theme of the steed ridden by his jockey, and Krieghoff drew inspiration from Herring's work on at least one occasion (Cat. 151). Pursuing an endeavour initiated some forty years earlier by George Stubbs, Herring disseminated his work widely through the engravings of his series of portraits of the winners of the Derby and St. Leger races. Krieghoff probably had access to one of these portraits, using it to elaborate the composition of the painting shown here; he simply changed the jockey and the surrounding landscape.

P.B.

Notes
1. See *GUAY 1987,* pp. 23-25.
2. *The Morning Chronicle,* July 6, 7 and 8, 1853.
3. *The Morning Chronicle,* August 17, 18, 19 and 21, 1854.

JOSEPH LÉGARÉ

1795-1855

JOSEPH LÉGARÉ was born in Quebec City on March 10, 1795. After attending the Séminaire de Québec for one year (1810-1811), he began working as an apprentice for Moses Pierce, a "painter and glazier." His training prepared him for a wide range of tasks including carriage-painting, sign-painting, interior decoration and restoring paintings. In 1817, he hired his first apprentice, Henry Dolsealwhite, as a painter and glazier. The same year, with the arrival of the first lot of paintings acquired by Father Philippe-Jean-Louis Desjardins in Quebec City, Légaré had an opportunity to do restoration work and thus practice his painting skills. The artist hired another apprentice, Antoine Plamondon, in 1819. During the early years of his career, Légaré gained recognition for his copies of religious paintings; his first signed works date from 1820. Henceforth, the diversity of his artistic production was quite exceptional for the period. Probably under the influence of British topographical painters, Légaré was the first Canadian artist to show a lasting interest in landscape painting. He was also renowned for his history paintings, genre scenes, still lifes, allegories, and so forth. Around 1828, Légaré painted a work of his own composition, *Massacre of Hurons by the Iroquois* (Cat. 157). Henceforth, he never ceased to take an interest in both historical subjects and contemporary events, such as the landslide at Cap Diamant in 1841 and the fires in Quebec City in 1845 (Cat. 168).

Légaré was not only a prolific artist but also an informed art enthusiast. He soon developed a taste for collecting art. One of his first acquisitions included some 30 paintings from the collection imported by Father Desjardins. Légaré's own collection also included a number of European engravings. In 1833, he opened the first art gallery in Lower Canada, the Quebec Picture Gallery. The gallery was closed and then reopened several times over the years and even moved to other locations as Légaré sought support from the Government and municipal authorities for his national gallery project. As an artist and collector, Légaré was aware of the importance of grouping works together in this way so as to encourage citizens to develop a taste for painting. Légaré carried out his gallery project in association with the lawyer Thomas Amiot. Moreover, in September 1838, he invited the painter Henry David Thielcke to give drawing and painting classes at the gallery. He also allowed the Italian miniaturist Gerome Fassio to exhibit some of his works in 1839.

Respected and esteemed by his fellow citizens, Joseph Légaré led a very active social and political life. He was a member of Quebec City's first municipal council from 1833 to 1836 as well as one of the founding members of the Quebec City chapter of the Société Saint-Jean-Baptiste in 1842. He was also very active in the Literary and Historical Society of Quebec. A supporter of Louis-Joseph Papineau, Légaré took part in the 1837-1838 uprisings. He later ran in the by-elections of 1848 and 1850.

Légaré died at age 60 on June 21, 1855, only a few months after being appointed to the Legislative Council.

Main sources
PORTER 1978/1; PORTER 1985.

153. (See colour reproduction, p. 87)
The Vision of Saint Roch
After Matthias Stomer
Oil on canvas, 78.2 × 115.3 cm

Provenance
Fabrique de L'Ancienne-Lorette; acquired by the Musée du Québec, Quebec City, 1973.

Bibliography
FÊTES SOLENNELLES 1910, p. 8; *MORISSET 1934/3*, p. 2; *MORISSET 1936/2*, p. 116; *PORTER 1978/1*, pp. 128-129, No. 166 (entry by John R. Porter) (Repr.); *BÉLAND AND BOURASSA 1990*, pp. 5, 6, 9 and 44 (Repr.).

Collection
Musée du Québec, Quebec City. Restored in 1991, with the assistance of the Amis du Musée du Québec (73.220)

JOSEPH LÉGARÉ acquired the painting *Elijah Throwing his Mantle to the Prophet Elisha* when it arrived in Quebec City with the second shipment of paintings for Father Philippe-Jean-Louis Desjardins in 1820. Légaré's two known versions of this work attest to the ease with which the Quebec painter interpreted his sources. From 1825 onward, he made fewer literal copies, but combined motifs instead, thereby creating his own compositions. Since the subject matter of the original painting was not very suited to popular devotion, Légaré changed the main figure into Saint Roch to meet the needs of the parish of Ancienne-Lorette.

The prophets Elijah and Elisha were worshipped mainly by the Carmelite Order. The passage illustrated by the European painting was taken from *The Second Book of Kings* (2, 1-14) and recalls the Carmelites' dual mission of prayer and action.[1] The scene takes place on the banks of the Jordan River: Elijah is being transported to heaven on a horse-drawn chariot of fire; the passing of his mantle to Elisha symbolizes the transfer of authority and Elijah's disappearance from the face of the earth. A dog witnessing the spectacle barks with surprise and fear.

The theme of Elijah throwing his mantle to Elisha was illustrated on several occasions in the 17th century by various schools of art. Valdes Leal (1622-1690) painted the theme in the Carmelite convent in Cordoba, while Palma il Giovane (1544-1628, Atheneum, Helsinki) and Giovanni Battista Piazzetta (1682-1754, National Gallery of Art, Washington) made it famous in Italy. However, it was primarily the Flemish and Dutch schools that showed an interest in this theme (Abraham Bloemaert, 1564-1651; Tartarius, mid-17th century; Van des Schuer, 1628-1707).

154.
Elijah Throwing his Mantle to the Prophet Elisha
Matthias Stomer
Oil on canvas, 160.2 × 130 cm

Provenance
Desjardins painting shipment, 1820; Joseph Légaré, Quebec City; Joseph Légaré and Thomas Amiot, Quebec City, 1836; Séminaire de Québec, from the Joseph Légaré estate, 1874; on deposit at the Société du Musée du Séminaire de Québec, 1983.

Bibliography
Bourne 1829, No. 43 attr. to Plurtorst; *Le Canadien*, July 27, 1838, No. 34; *Catalogue 1852*, p. 4, No. 9 attr. to Albert Van Ouwater; ASQ, *Séminaire 12*, No. 41, 1874, No. 76 attr. to Albert Van Ouwater; *Peintures du Séminaire 1874-1875*, p. 3, No. 79; *Lemoine 1876*, p. 365, No. 79; *Laval University 1880*, p. 4, No. 32 attr. to Albert Van Ouwater; *Université Laval 1883-1884*, p. 12, No. 32 attr. to Albert Van Ouwater; *Laval University 1883-1884*, p. 12, No. 32 attr. to Albert Van Ouwater; *Université Laval 1887*, p. 12, No. 32 attr. to Albert Van Ouwater; *Laval University 1887*, p. 12, No. 32 attr. to Albert Van Ouwater; *Université Laval 1889*, p. 12, No. 32 attr. to Albert Van Ouwater; *Université Laval 1893*, p. 12, No. 32 attr. to Albert Van Ouwater; *Laval University 1894*, p. 12, No. 32 attr. to Albert Van Ouwater; *Laval University 1898*, p. 14, No. 32 attr. to Albert Van Ouwater; *Laval University 1901*, p. 14, No. 32 attr. to Albert Van Ouwater; *Université Laval 1903*, p. 18, No. 86 [twice] attr. to Albert Van Ouwater; *Laval University 1905*, p. 18, No. 87 attr. to Albert Van Ouwater; *Université Laval 1906*, p. 24, No. 87 attr. to Albert Van Ouwater; *Université Laval 1908*, p. 24, No. 87 attr. to Albert Van Ouwater; *Carter 1908*, pp. 27, 27a, 192 and 205, No. 87 (Repr.) attr. to Philippe de Champaigne; *Carter 1909*, pp. 8 and 8a, No. 87 (Repr.) attr. to Philippe de Champaigne; *Laval University 1909*, p. 27, No. 87 attr. to Philippe de Champaigne; *Université Laval 1909*, p. 25, No. 87 attr. to Philippe de Champaigne; *Université Laval 1913*, p. 43, No. 176 attr. to Philippe de Champaigne; *Laval University 1923*, p. 49, No. 176 attr. to Philippe de Champaigne; *Université Laval 1933*, p. 41, No. 153 attr. to Philippe de Champaigne; *Morisset 1934/3*, p. 2; *Morisset 1934/4*, p. 2; *Morisset 1936/2*, pp. 114-116 attr. to Gaspard de Crayer; *Porter 1978/1*, pp. 128-129, No. 166; *Nicolson 1979*, p. 93; *Lefebvre 1982*, p. IX.

Collection
Musée du Séminaire de Québec (Pe983.3)

Fig. 153-154A,
Joseph Légaré,
The Virgin Mary appearing to Saint Roch,
c. 1825, after Matthias Stomer (detail);
oil on canvas, approximately 180 × 110 cm.
Église Saint-Philippe de Trois-Rivières.

While French art historian Charles Sterling[2] believed that Mayno had painted this work, Pierre Rosenberg[3] suggested it be attributed to Matthias Stomer (ca. 1600 - 1650). Rosenberg's hypothesis was confirmed by Benedict Nicolson in 1979. Even though the stylistic and pictorial treatment do not reflect Stomer's more refined style, reminiscent of Caravaggio's work, they are nonetheless typical of Stomer's approach. The naturalism and rendering of Elisha's anatomy and the drapery are characteristic of Stomer. It is not easy to observe the artist's qualities as a colourist, however, for the surface of the work has been largely repainted, as revealed by scientific analysis. The very tight framing of the composition suggests that the edges of the painting may have been trimmed during previous handling.

In copying this work, Légaré inflicted a wound on Elisha's knee, thereby disguising him as Saint Roch, the patron saint of plague victims. Cholera ravaged the population of Quebec City on two occasions, and people constantly sought protection from the disease. In the painting ***The Vision of Saint Roch,*** formerly kept in the church of Ancienne-Lorette, Légaré extended the landscape to the left so as to make the composition horizontal. He also made certain changes to the tree trunk and the dog, which he depicted with a piece of bread in its mouth. By replacing the mantle with a thick cloud, he merely suggested the vision experienced by Saint Roch. The figure's attributes, namely his wounded knee and dog, alone reveal his true identity. His facial features and expression have not been depicted, since his head is turned so far away that his face is no longer visible.[4]

L.L.

Notes
1. Gilles Chazal, *L'art du XVIIe siècle dans les Carmels de France* (Paris, 1982), p. 122.
2. MSQ, painting file notes, 1933.
3. MSQ, painting file notes and personal communication, 1975.
4. Légaré painted the same subject for the church of Saint-Philippe; he retained, however, the vertical format of the original work and replaced Elijah with the Virgin (Fig. 153-154A). See *Porter 1978/1*, p. 129. No. 167 (Repr.).

155.
Still Life with Grapes, before 1826
After an unidentified artist, Italy, 17th century
Oil on canvas, 95 × 126.5 cm

Inscriptions
(s., l.l., on the tree trunk) *J*⁰ˢ.. LÉGARÉ *pinxit;*
(b.,l.c.,on the canvas, in the hand of Triaud,
hidden under a whitewashing before backing,
which covers the inscription) *Peint par Légaré/
retoucher par Triaud 1826.*

Provenance
Herbert T. Schwartz, Montreal; acquired by the
National Gallery of Canada, Ottawa, 1968.

Exhibitions
(?) Quebec City 1845; (?) Quebec City 1848;
Ottawa 1972/3, No. 16; Ottawa 1978-1979/1,
No. 68.

Bibliography
(?)*Quebec Mercury,* May 6, 1845, p. 2, October
5, 1848, p. 3, No. 4; (?)*Le Canadien,* October 2,
1848, p. 3, No. 4; (?)*L'Ami de la Religion et de
la Patrie,* October 4, 1848, p. 655, No. 4; (?)*Le
Journal de Québec,* October 5, 1848, p. 3, No. 4;
(?) BELLERIVE *1925,* p. 14; STOLOW *1972,* p. 26,
No. 16; GODSELL *1976,* pp. 46-47 (Repr.); PORTER
1978/1, pp. 87 and 90, No. 68 (entry by John R.
Porter) (Repr.); LEVENSON *1983,* pp. 33, 34, 36
and 37; BÉLAND AND BOURASSA *1990,* pp. 42 and
64.

Collection
National Gallery of Canada, Ottawa (15684)

J AMES PURVES CARTER, art expert and
restorer, attributed the painting
Vines and Grapes to Michelangelo
Pace *dit* Il Campidoglio (1610-1670) in
1908. Although it is impossible to confirm that he was the author of the work,
there is every reason to believe that it was
painted by an artist active in Rome around
1650.[1] The subject is treated in an original
manner in that it depicts only one type of
fruit in an outdoor environment. This more
naturalistic approach was unusual at the
time, for still life painters usually preferred
to mix several types of fruit together in an
indoor setting. Michelangelo Cerquozzi
(1602-1660) was one of the first artists to
paint grapes in different colours while they
were still on the vine.[2]

156.
Vines and Grapes, c. 1650
Unidentified Artist, Italy, 18th Centuy
Oil on canvas, 88.3 × 73.9 cm

Provenance
Jean-Baptiste-Édouard Bacquet Collection, c. 1823; Descendants of the Bacquet family, 1853; Sœurs de la Charité de Québec; gift to the Séminaire de Québec, 1886; on deposit at the Société du Musée du Séminaire de Québec, 1983.

Exhibition
Quebec City 1973.

Bibliography
ANNUAIRE *1887*, p. 104, No. 31; UNIVERSITÉ LAVAL *1893*, p. 19, No. 135; UNIVERSITÉ LAVAL *1901*, p. 14, No. 36 attr. to the Italian school; UNIVERSITÉ LAVAL *1903*, p. 14, No. 36 attr. to the Italian school; LAVAL UNIVERSITY *1905*, p. 13, No. 36 attr. to the Italian school; UNIVERSITÉ LAVAL *1906*, p. 18, No. 36; UNIVERSITÉ LAVAL *1908*, p. 18, No. 36 attr. to the Italian school; CARTER *1908*, p. 23, No. 36 attr. to Campidoglio; CARTER *1909*, p. 18, No. 36 attr. to Campidoglio; UNIVERSITÉ LAVAL *1909*, p. 18, No. 36 attr. to Campidoglio; LAVAL UNIVERSITY *1909*, p. 19, No. 36 attr. to Campidoglio; UNIVERSITÉ LAVAL *1913*, p. 31, No. 99 attr. to Campidoglio; LAVAL UNIVERSITY *1923*, p. 33, No. 99 attr. to Campidoglio; UNIVERSITÉ LAVAL *1933*, p. 24, No. 74 attr. to Campidoglio; MORISSET *1935/2*, p. 4 attr. to Campidoglio; MORISSET *1936-1937*, Vol. I, p. 177 attr. to Campidoglio; TRUDEL, JUNEAU AND MASSEY *1967*, p. 78 attr. to Campidoglio; ZERI AND FREDERICKSEN *1972*, p. 626; PORTER *1978/1*, pp. 86, 87 and 89 (Repr.) attr. to Campidoglio; PORTER *1990/1*, p. 923; BÉLAND AND BOURASSA *1990*, p. 64 attr. to Campidoglio.

Collection
Musée du Séminaire de Québec (Pe983.47)

The fruit-laden vine fills the entire canvas as it falls to the ground in front of a tree trunk. With its abundant ripe fruit and yellow leaves, the work resembles a *vanitas* painting, or to use the phrase coined by André Chastel, a "moralized still life."[3] (*Translation*) By presenting such a quantity of superb, sumptuous fruit whose beauty is essentially divine but whose earthly enjoyment is ephemeral and transient, *vanitas* paintings invited the viewer to recognize the miracle of creation while detaching himself from the material world so as to achieve divine glory.

The vine also evokes a very popular Christian symbol, namely, the blood of Christ shed for the salvation of mankind. While outwardly portraying a secular subject, the still life has religious significance. The magnificent fruit, whose nearness to the ground indicates that it is ready to eat, symbolizes the Eucharist. The popularity of this theme in Lower Canada indicates that collectors were probably highly aware of the message it conveyed. In purchasing such a painting, they not only acquired a beautiful still life but, owing to their education and religious beliefs, they understood the symbolic content of the work, which thus became all the more acceptable. Three copies of this subject have been identified in Quebec, two of which are by Légaré and one by Plamondon (Cat. 193),

Contrary to what was long believed on the basis of a copy by Légaré, the painting *Vines and Grapes* did not come into the possession of the Séminaire de Québec as part of Joseph Légaré's collection.[4] Rather, it was offered to the seminary in 1886 by the Sisters of Charity of Quebec,[5] who had acquired it from one of the heirs of the estate of Judge Jean-Baptiste-Édouard Bacquet *dit* Lamontagne (1794-1853).[6] Called to the bar in 1818, Bacquet practised in Quebec City. He became one of the first 10 justices of the Superior Court of Quebec on January 1, 1852.

The Séminaire de Québec acquired most of the 70 paintings and "around twelve good engravings"[7] from Bacquet's collection, which consisted mainly of landscapes and seascapes (30), but also still lifes (13), genre scenes and drawings of heads illustrating different expressions. The circumstances under which Bacquet acquired *Vines and Grapes* are unknown; however, in the event that he did not purchase it from or exchange it with the painter and collector Joseph Légaré,[8] he probably bought it in one of the many auctions held regularly in Quebec City.[9] Bacquet seems to have collected mainly European paintings even though he kept company with Quebec artists and granted them access to his collection, as the copies of this painting seem to indicate. His involvement in the art world led him to work with Joseph Légaré and Napoléon Aubin in 1845 on the project to set up a national gallery in Quebec City.[10]

If the inscription visible on the back of Joseph Légaré's painting prior to its remounting by the National Gallery of Canada in 1969 is authentic, this copy would date from before 1826. The phrase "Painted by Légaré/retouched by Triaud 1826" (*Translation*) indicates that Louis-Hubert Triaud restored or touched up the

Fig. 155A.
Joseph Légaré,
After an Unidentified Artist, Italy 17th Century
Still Life with Grapes;
oil on canvas, 88.9 × 73.8 cm.
Musée du Québec, Quebec City (51.122).

work *Still Life with Grapes* that year. To have needed retouching, the painting must have been done several years earlier; moreover, it must no longer have been in the artist's possession, for he would certainly have done the necessary work himself. Based on Father Louis-Joseph Desjardin's correspondence, Triaud knew how to clean and remount paintings.[11] However, his actual contribution to this work remains unknown. Touching up a painting involves working on its paint surface. According to Rustin Levenson, X-ray analysis of *Still Life with Grapes* revealed an underlying drawing, perhaps a landscape.[12] Therefore, the current painting is actually a complex amalgamation of Légaré's original copy, his final composition and Triaud's work.

This painting is more than just a copy of the work that belonged to the lawyer Bacquet[13] since, in accordance with his usual working methods (Cat. 153 and 154), Légaré changed it somewhat to produce an original composition. While he retained the idea of rendering the grapes as if they were viewed in nature, he added the vista of a landscape on the left side of the painting. Departing from the original work, Légaré included a branch in the upper left-hand corner, thereby integrating the tree trunk into the blue sky, which he in turn used to highlight the vine leaves. The work is organized around two conflicting, juxtaposed vantage points without any foreshortening: one overlooks the city in the background[14] while the other the grapes in the foreground. A tree trunk encloses the composition on the left, framing the view in the distance.[15] By adding a landscape, Légaré accentuated the realism of the scene and, by treating the grapes as a plant motif, he robbed the work of part of its symbolic content. While the Italian still life he used as a model sanctified the vine, or the symbol of the blood of Christ, by making it the only subject, Légaré rejected part of its original meaning by making it part of the landscape. Nevertheless, Légaré's work may still be considered a *vanitas* painting owing to the addition of a butterfly, symbol of frivolity and inconsistency and whose metamorphoses evoke the ephemeral quality of life.

Légaré made another copy of *Vines and Grapes* (Fig. 155A) without making any changes. This version may have been exhibited in Quebec City in October 1848 along with other works that were to be sold in a lottery in the House of Assembly.[16] It should be noted that while this copy, listed as item No. 4 in the sale, and another copy, the *Return of Jacob*, were valued at £20 and £30 respectively, the painting *Landscape with Wolfe Monument* (Cat. 161) was valued at only £7. It might be asked whether Légaré prized his copies more highly than his own compositions or simply adapted his prices according to the popularity and interest of the subject matter.

L.L

Notes

1. Certain painters in Pace's entourage come to mind here: Mario Nuzzi dei Fiori (1603-1674), Alessandro Coosemans (1627-1689) and Abraham Brueghel (1631-1697). For further reading, see Luigi Salerno, *La natura morta italiana* (Rome: Ugo Bozi Editore, 1984) and the catalogue *Stilleben in Europa* (Münster: Westfalisches Landesmuseum für Kunst und Kulturgeschichte, 1979).

2. Examples of this artist's work are reproduced in Luigi Salerno, *op.cit.*, p. 166, Fig. 41.1, and p. 167, Fig. 41.2. Three types of grapes can be seen in the painting discussed here.

3. In his text "Glorieuses vanités", published in the catalogue *Les Vanités dans la peinture au XVIIᵉ siècle* (Paris: Réunion des musées nationaux, 1990), p. 13.

4. *PORTER 1978/1*, p. 86, No. 67 (Repr.).

5. ASQ, *Université 49*, No. 18. On December 17, 1886, Soeur Marie du Sacré-Coeur, mother superior of the Sisters of Charity, wrote to the reverend Père E. Méthot, superior of the Séminaire de Québec and rector of Université Laval: "Father Superior, we are pleased to ask you to accept, as a small token of our profound gratitude, the collection of paintings left to us by Miss Bacquet. Since she was so attached to these works, we would not have been able to dispose of them while she was still alive." It was through Miss Bacquet, therefore, that the 70 paintings from Judge Bacquet's estate came into the possession of the Séminaire de Québec.

6. Item No. 10 of the inventory of Jean-Baptiste Édouard Bacquet's estate bore the title: "Grappes de raisins à deux livres." (ANQQ, Notarial records of O.C. de la Chevrotière, April 18-22 and May 7, 1853, No. 383, April 26-30 and May 2, 1853, No. 384) Judge Bacquet's four sisters—Sophie, Nathalie, Olivette and Adelaïde—were named universal legatees. This information as well as that on the provenance of this work were provided by Didier Prioul.

7. ASQ. Séminaire 9, No. 51a. Of the paintings listed in the inventory of Judge Bacquet's estate, *Grappes de raisins* (No. 10) was valued at £25. Its price had increased tenfold from 1853 to 1886.

8. According to the inventory of Bacquet's estate, he and Légaré jointly owned 17 paintings; these works were exhibited at Légaré's gallery.

9. The following item was included in Joseph Cary's sale announced in the *Quebec Mercury*, August 26, 1823: "No. 105: A fruit Piece."

10. In 1838, Bacquet was one of the 58 subscribers to Joseph Légaré's "Quebec Picture Gallery" (ASQ, *Polygraphie 31*, No. 19A). For further reading on the national gallery project, see *PORTER 1977/2*.

11. AMUQ, Fonds Desjardins, Desj. 1, 77 and n.d. Desj. II, 22, Letters from Louis-Joseph Desjardins to Mère Saint-Henry, March 25, 1839. In 1829-1830, Triaud "repainted" the *Saint Anthony of Padoua* above the right lateral altar in the exterior chapel of the convent of the Augustines de l'Hôtel-Dieu de Québec. See *BOISCLAIR 1977*, pp. 103-105, No. 152 (Repr.).

12. *LEVENSON 1983*, p. 37.

13. Even though the provenance of the painting definitely indicates that it was in the possession of Judge Bacquet at the time of his death in 1853, this in no way invalidates the hypothesis that Joseph Légaré owned the painting at an earlier date.

14. This type of landscape in the distance, consisting of a town located beside a body of water at the foot of a mountain, is also found in Louis-Hubert Triaud's painting *The Martyrdom of Saint Andrew* (1821, church of Saint-André de Kamouraska).

15. In his three copies of the *The Rapture of Saint Paul*, Légaré also enclosed the composition with tree trunks blending into the sides of the painting and forming an integral part of the frame (1820, church of Saint-Roch-des-Aulnaies; 1821, church of Bécancour; 1822, church of Saint-Philippe in Trois-Rivières; see *PORTER 1978/1*, pp. 125-126, Nos. 156-158, Repr.).

16. *L'Ami de la Religion et de la Patrie*, October 4, 1848, p. 655. The list of works in question here was published in English in the *Quebec Mercury* on October 5, 1848.

157.
Massacre of Hurons by the Iroquois, c. 1828
Oil on canvas, 63.5 × 84.2 cm

Inscription
(b., on a piece of newspaper, today lost)
334 bataille de Sauvages. Légaré.

Provenance
Séminaire de Québec, from the Joseph Légaré estate, 1874; antiquaire Jean Gilbert, Quebec City, 1957; acquired by the Musée de la Province de Québec, Quebec City, 1957.

Exhibitions
Paris 1958; Vancouver 1959, No. 171; Mexico City 1960-1961, No. 81; Toronto 1966; Ottawa 1978-1979/1, No. 12; La Rochelle 1982-1983, No. 218.

Bibliography
La Bibliothèque Canadienne, March 1828, p. 159; *La Minerve,* April 9, 1829, p. 4; ASQ, *Séminaire 12,* No. 41, 1874, Fol. 6, No. 235; *Peintures du Séminaire 1874-1875,* p. 4, No. 141; *Annuaire 1875,* p. 59, No. 141; *Lemoine 1876,* p. 366, No. 141; *Laval University 1880,* p. 12, No. 12; *Université Laval 1883-1884,* p. 31, No. 14; *Laval University 1883-1884,* p. 31, No. 14; *Université Laval 1887,* p. 31, No. 14; *Laval University 1887,* p. 31, No. 14; *Université Laval 1889,* p. 31, No. 14; *Université Laval 1893,* p. 32, No. 14; *Laval University 1894,* p. 29, No. 14; *Université Laval 1898,* p. 32, No. 16; *Harris 1898,* p. 355; *Laval University 1901,* p. 21, No. 144; *Gallery 1902,* p. 17, No. 24; *Université Laval 1903,* p. 30, No. 24; *Laval University 1905,* p. 32, No. 24; *Université Laval 1906,* p. 45, No. 55; *Carter 1908,* p. 87, No. 255; *Laval University 1909,* p. 50, No. 255; *Université Laval 1913,* p. 62, No. 334; *Laval University,* 1923, p. 71, No. 334; *Bellerive 1925,* p. 16; *Université Laval 1933,* p. 80, No. 226; *Colgate 1943,* p. 109; *Morisset 1959/1,* pp. 47 and 53, No. 171 (Repr.); *Arte Canadiense 1960,* No. 81 (Repr.); *Morisset 1960/1,* p. 98; *Harper 1966,* p. 82; *Cauchon 1968,* p. 2; *Tremblay 1972,* pp. 41-42, 44 and 59; *Lord 1974,* p. 49; *Porter 1977/1,* pp. 15b-17 (Repr.); *Porter 1978/1,* pp. 16-17, 33-35 and 75, No. 12 (entry by Jean Trudel) (Repr.); *Porter 1978/2,* pp. 3 and 4 (Repr.); *Porter 1978/4,* p. 63; *Derome 1978,* p. 28; *Derome and Leclerc 1978,* pp. 1 and 8, No. 2; *Robert 1978,* pp. 24-25 (Repr.); *The Legacy 1978,* p. 13 (Repr.); *Lehmann 1979,* p. D-4; *Nixon 1979,* p. 16; *Nos racines,* No. 8 (1979), pp. 150-151 and cover p. (Repr.); *Toupin 1979,* p. E-19; *Gagnon 1980,* p. 42; *Légaré 1980,* p. 13; *Porter 1981,* pp. 13, 53-55 and 57; *Une autre Amérique 1982,* p. 134, No. 218 (Repr.); *Davis 1982,* p. 14; *Lacroix 1982,* p. 36; *Levenson 1983,* pp. 24 and 33; *Comeau 1983,* p. 160; *Stacey 1983,* p. 60; *Trudel 1985,* pp. 158-159 (Repr.); *Porter 1985,* p. 548; *Porter 1987/3,* p. 1088; *Jacquin 1987,* pp. 40-41 and 186 (Repr.); *Iroquois Wars 1988,* p. 1095 (Repr.); *Têtu de Labsade 1990,* p. 248.

Collection
Musée du Québec, Quebec City (57.204)

assacre of Hurons by the Iroquois is one of Légaré's best-documented paintings as well as one of the most important for studying his oeuvre. Jean Trudel traced the history of this painting in 1978 for an exhibition of the artist's works in Ottawa.[1] His main findings will be summarized in this section. In October 1827, the members of the Society for the Encouragement of Art and Science in Canada set up three committees or "Classes" for the purpose of launching a public competition.[2] Based on "a method sanctioned by the experience of enlightened nations" (*Translation*), the main goals of the competition were as follows:

to foster praiseworthy emulation among studious, educated youth, by rewarding efforts of genius [...] to celebrate merit wherever it emerges and to pay tribute to successful endeavours in all genres.[3] (*Translation*)

Légaré competed in the "Literary Class" by satisfying the requirement to produce an oil painting whose design and composition were of the artist's own invention.[4] The rules also stipulated that each entry had to be accompanied "by a sealed letter containing the name and address of the artist and bearing, on the back, the description to be placed above the work."[5] (*Translation*) When the prizes were awarded in March 1828, Légaré received an honourary medal for "the original design of an oil painting representing the barbarous character of the savage fighting between the Hurons and the Iroquois."[6] (*Translation*) There is reason to believe that this description corresponds exactly to that provided by the artist.

In commenting on the circumstances surrounding Légaré's award, Jean Trudel called into question the quality of his painting. According to Trudel, by granting Légaré an honorary medal, the jury made a distinction between the way in which he had rendered the subject matter and its originality, since the latter quality alone was worthy of encouragement. He based this statement on the fact that no first prize was awarded for painting in the "Literary Class." We believe, however, that the conditions of the competition, as described in *La Bibliothèque Canadienne*, should be reconsidered. Candidates were allowed to submit entries on any of the various subjects listed in each class. Successful entries were awarded prizes according to class rather than subject. Two works of equal merit tied for first place in the "Commercial Class" and both received a medal.[7] James Smillie won first prize in the "Literary Class" for "an engraving of a map

of a valley,"[8] the fifth subject of the competition. It is not known why Légaré did not win first prize like his competitor. We can only suggest another hypothesis which in no way questions his painting.

Although the membership lists of the Society for the Encouragement of Art and Science in Canada are not available for the years at issue here, we cannot dismiss the hypothesis that Légaré belonged to this society. We know that he was a member of the Literary and Historical Society of Quebec in 1831 and that the Society for the Encouragement of Art and Science had amalgamated with this society in 1829. Perhaps the jury for the 1827 competition preferred to make a distinction between its own members and competitors from outside the society, who alone were eligible for prizes. It therefore merely imitated Napoléon Aubin who made a similar decision in 1843 to avoid "using patronage for purposes of exclusion"[9] (*Translation*) when Joseph Légaré submitted banner designs for a celebration organized by the Société Saint-Jean-Baptiste. If our reasoning is correct, the fact the Légaré was awarded an honourary medal does not question the quality of his painting but rather the status he enjoyed within the Society for the Encouragement of Art and Science in Canada. This hypothesis is reinforced by the fact that another honourary medal was awarded to Joseph Bouchette Jr., whose father Joseph and brother Robert-Shore-Milnes were president and assistant secretary of the Society in 1827. It is also interesting to note that, James Smillie, who won first prize in the "Literary Class," did not join the Society until February 26, 1829.[10]

Massacre of Hurons by the Iroquois was Légaré's first large-format work on a secular subject as well as his first major composition. The fact that Légaré decided to participate in the 1827 competition and submit this work to his contemporaries for judgment influenced its design. The painting pursues research the artist began in *The Martyrdom of Françoise Brunon-Gonannhatenha*,[11] executed in November or December 1827. Lacking confidence in his drawing skills and creative ability, Légaré looked to various sources for inspiration. We believe that it is important to discuss the various components of this picture individually, even though such an approach may be a bit tedious. It is essential to understanding Légaré's work as a whole.

In the Ottawa exhibition catalogue entry (1978), Jean Trudel wrote that "the picture as a whole is clumsy in the ex-

treme. The composition is confused, with no sight-lines. The background, with the landscape, has no depth."[12] Admittedly, the composition is not outstanding; nevertheless, Légaré tried to organize the subject matter coherently. The painting is structured on two separate planes: the frieze of figures in the foreground is separated by a line of trees from the valley and mountains in the background. This organization seems to have been borrowed from an anonymous engraving (Fig. 157A) after a painting by Charles Le Brun (1619-1690), *Porus fighting* or *The Defeat of Porus*.[13] Légaré has attempted to organize the various motifs fairly rigorously, although admittedly without much success. In the engraving after Le Brun, the figures form a pyramid whose apex is occupied by Porus on his elephant. Légaré has tried to organize his figures according to the same principle, but the result is somewhat awkward. Jean Trudel states that "the chief of the attackers seems to be the figure in the background, left of centre, who, holding a bow in his right hand, makes an imperious gesture with his left arm."[14] As in the source work, the viewer's attention is directed toward this Amerindian by a diagonal that links him to the lower right-hand corner of the painting. Another diagonal links the Amerindian lying on the ground in the left-hand side of the work with the central figure. Légaré imitated the original composition by framing his painting with two trees, one on the right and another on the left, and the background with a hill and mountains. However, compared to the model, which reflects the artist's knowledge and skills, Légaré's composition reveals his lack of experience. In imitating Le Brun's work, Légaré was nevertheless attempted to elaborate a skilful composition.

Légaré borrowed figures from various sources for this painting. For example, the two warriors in the lower right-hand corner were taken from *Porus fighting* (Fig. 157B). Their clothing was replaced by loincloths and the sword by a short-handled knife with a curved blade. Only one piece of material, covering the upper left leg of the standing figure, was retained. Légaré seems to have copied these figures in isolation, without paying attention to the change in scale. The struggling figures seem to be the same size as those in the engraving and are therefore too small for the larger painting. The light shining diagonally from the left foreground is distributed accordingly, in a pattern fairly similar to, although more rigid than, that of the engraving.

Fig. 157A.
Unidentified engraver after Charles Le Brun,
Porus fighting or *The Defeat of Porus;*
burin, 18.2 × 42 cm (image).
Musée du Séminaire de Québec (P986.12A).

Fig. 157B.
Detail of the right portion of *Porus fighting* or
The Defeat of Porus

Fig. 157C.
Detail of the left portion of *Porus fighting* or
The Defeat of Porus.

Légaré also borrowed the second group of warriors fighting in the left foreground of the engraving after Le Brun (Fig. 157C). However, he separated the two figures in his own composition. He retained only the upper body, arm movements and club of the standing figure, which he placed behind the tree on the right. As for the other warrior, Légaré made a partial, but inverted copy, representing him as a Huron pinned to the ground by an Amerindian with a tomahawk. In this case, the borrowing is much freer, since Légaré was merely looking for a suitable pose for the figure attempting to fight off his assailant; in fact, it is necessary to refer to the model to understand that Légaré meant to depict a hand at the end of the figure's right arm. The drawing would probably have been more coherent if he had replaced the shield with a weapon, but perhaps he wanted to indicate that the warrior had been disarmed.

An engraving by Carlo Antonini after Salvator Rosa (1615-1673), *The Death of Attilius Regulus* (Fig. 157D), provided Légaré with a model for the Amerindian wielding a tomahawk in the middle right-hand side of his painting. He borrowed the kneeling figure raising his right arm in the centre right foreground of the engraving. The artist copied the general pose,

making certain changes. While retaining the upper body, right thigh and arm movements, he turned the face to the right, presenting a three-quarter view instead of a perfect profile. To adapt the figure to his own composition, Légaré drew him without clothing and lengthened the left arm grasping the head of the Huron on the ground. Instead of designing the figures as a group and creating a coherent whole, Légaré juxtaposed two separate elements, as shown by the lengthening of the arm. For the Amerindian in front of the Iroquois chief in the central left side of his painting, he borrowed the general pose of the bending figure hammering a peg into the barrel in the middle left side of *The Death of Attilius Regulus.* Oddly, however, Légaré forgot to draw the figure's left arm. Consequently, the viewer is obliged to mentally reconstruct and understand the figure on the basis of only a few elements. Finally, the assailant in the middle foreground comes from *Massacre of the Innocents* (Fig. 157E), an engraving after one of the three Vatican tapestries based on drawings by students of Raphaël (1483-1520). Légaré literally copied the assassin in the right foreground and largely simplified the rendering of the child on the ground. He merely retained the child's

head, which he suggested rather than drew in detail. He imitated the luminous qualities of his model and added more vegetation.

Between 1820 and 1827, Joseph Légaré developed his working methods by copying works by other artists. This certainly did not prepare him to approach landscape painting as a novel, original adventure. It is not surprising, therefore, that his first efforts in this field were merely an extension of his religious works. It is hardly a coincidence that he imitated Rubens' (1577-1640) religious composition, *The Martyrdom of Saint Lawrence,*[15] in painting *The Martyrdom of Françoise Brunon.* His earlier works had familiarized him with compositions organized on a minimum number of planes, where the figures themselves played a leading role. The techniques commonly applied in religious painting had a decisive influence on Légaré's first secular works (1827 - ca. 1839): the figures were depicted in a setting where the landscape served merely as a backdrop. In both *Massacre of Hurons by the Iroquois* and *Le Canadien* (Cat. 159), the figures acted out their various roles in front of the landscape.

A distinction must be made, however, with regard to the rendering of these works. Late 1827 and early 1828 mark a veritable turning point in the development of Légaré's style. Instead of subordinating all elements to the figures, which was common in religious paintings, Légaré began to pursue a new approach, learned by copying a painting from his own collection, *Peasants playing Cards* (Fig. 157F), which he attributed to Salvator Rosa.[16] Rather than applying paint with smooth brush strokes, as in his religious works, Légaré attempted to create a textured effect. Stylistically, this small canvas had a profound impact on his first landscapes. In *Massacre of Hurons by the Iroquois,* he coated his brush with a thick layer of paint and outlined the figures' clothing with luminous impastos. This pictorial device, which heightened the relief of the various motifs, characterized Légaré's style for many years. It can be seen again in the shirt of the figure in *Le Canadien* (Cat. 159) and later in *The Caldwell Manor and the Etchemin Mills,* executed around 1843 (MQ). Moreover, Légaré sometimes used this highly evocative technique in landscapes,

Fig. 157D.
Carlo Antonini after
Salvator Rosa,
*The Death of Attilius
Regulus*, 1780;
etching, 46.8 × 70 cm
(image).
Musée du Séminaire
de Québec
(P983.63.23).

Fig. 157E.
Unidentified engraver after the drawings
of the pupils of Raphaël,
Massacre of the Innocents;
burin, 38.9 × 27.8 cm (image).
Musée du Séminaire de Québec
(portfolio 80-G, Fol. 66).

emphasizing the light on the foliage with thick daubs of paint.

In copying *Peasants playing Cards,* Légaré came to understand that drawing was not the only way to render figures. His copy reflects a new-found freedom compared to the more rigid approach adopted by the artist in *Saint Francis of Paola in Prayer,* painted for the Hôpital général de Québec in 1824. Although Légaré partially resolved the problems related to rendering nudes through borrowing, he fully applied the lessons learned from the Italian painting in working on secondary figures. He used the interplay of light and shadow to depict facial features: round faces with sunken eye sockets and noses highlighted with luminous paint. The faces of the Indians in **Massacre of the Hurons by the Iroquois** have been rendered in this way. Perhaps Légaré had accepted the fact that he was more a colourist than a draughtsman. This hypothesis is supported by the fact that, henceforth, he chose models where colour played a more preponderant role than drawing.

D.P.

Notes

1. PORTER *1978/1*, pp. 33-35, No. 12.
2. The competition was divided into three classes: Literary, Philosophical and Commercial. The "Literary Class" included literature, in the strict sense of the word, public speaking and fine arts. Participants wishing to compete in scientific categories (zoology, mineralogy or botany) had to register in the "Philosophical Class." The "Commercial Class" dealt with economic issues such as business and agriculture.
3. *La Bibliothèque Canadienne,* Vol. V, No. 5 (October 1827), p. 192.
4. *Ibid.*
5. *Ibid.,* p. 193.
6. *La Bibliothèque Canadienne,* Vol. VI, No. 4 (March 1828), p. 159. As mentioned by Jean

Trudel, the subject of this painting may have been taken from Lafiteau's book *Moeurs des sauvages,* which Légaré had in his library. It should also be mentioned that the documents we consulted did not allow us to confirm the statement made by J. R. Harper (1966) and repeated by M. Cauchon (1968) and B. Lord (1974) to the effect that Légaré was described as the first artist to paint Canadian history scenes when he received this medal.
7. The entries referred to here were two essays on agriculture. (ibid. p. 158).
8. *Ibid.,* p. 158. See ALLODI AND TOVELL 1989, pp. 64-65, 107 and No. 54 for a reproduction of the map entitled *Sketch of the Great Valley of the River St. John.*
9. *Le Canadien,* June 9, 1843, p. 3.
10. ALLODI AND TOVELL *1989,* p. 100.
11. MMFA (1979.7), see PORTER *1978/1,* p. 143, No. 230 (Repr.). Légaré drew the inspiration for this small oil on paper from the story "L'Iroquoise, Histoire ou nouvelle historique," published in *La Bibliothèque Canadienne* in October and November 1827. This is one of the very first instances where a literary text was translated into a painting in Quebec.
12. PORTER *1978/1,* p. 34.
13. This engraving was done after Le Brun's modello for *Porus fighting,* which is no longer in existence, or after a copy by François Verdier (1651-1730).
14. PORTER *1978/1,* p. 34.
15. Engraving by Lucas Vorsterman, dated 1621, Musée du Séminaire de Québec (Portfolio 69-G, Fol. 42).
16. It is impossible to attribute all of the paintings and engravings under the name of Salvator Rosa in the Légaré collection in the Musée du Séminaire de Québec to Rosa. Some of the engravings are copies and certain paintings are pastiches, while other works have absolutely no relationship to Rosa. It is ironic to note that while Légaré believed he was in contact with and imitating the work of this Neapolitan artist, he only had access to copies. *Peasants playing Cards* is especially interesting in that it is a pastiche, probably from the early 18th century, of a work done by Rosa in his youth. See Luigi Salerno, *L'opera completa di Salvator Rosa* (Milan: Rizzoli, 1975), No. 2 (Repr.).

Fig. 157F.
Unidentified artist,
Peasants playing Cards, Italy, early 18th century;
oil on canvas, 38 × 34 cm.
Musée du Séminaire de Québec (83).

158.
Cholera Plague, Quebec, c. 1832
Oil on canvas, 82.2 × 111.7 cm

Provenance
Séminaire de Québec, from the Joseph Légaré estate, 1874; antiquaire Jean Gilbert, Quebec City, 1957; William P. Wolfe, Montreal, 1957; acquired by the National Gallery of Canada, Ottawa, 1959.

Exhibition
Ottawa 1978-1979/1, No. 19.

Bibliography
Le Canadien, May 21, 1832, p. 16, July 6, 1832, p. 2, July 9, 1832, p. 2, September 12, 1834, pp. 2-3; *Quebec Mercury,* March 10, 1832, p. 3, April 21, 1832, p. 1, July 7, 1832, p. 2; ASQ, *Séminaire 12,* No. 41, 1874, p. 7 (No. 267); UNIVERSITÉ LAVAL *1913,* p. 63, No. 350; LAVAL UNIVERSITY *1923,* p. 72, No. 350; LES PEINTURES DE LÉGARÉ *1926,* p. 432; BELLERIVE *1925,* p. 15; ROBSON *1932,* p. 20; (?) MORISSET *1934/6,* p. 23 entitled *Cathédrale de Québec au clair de lune;* UNIVERSITÉ LAVAL *1933,* p. 81, No. 242; COLGATE *1943,* p. 108; SIMARD *1952,* p. 37 (Repr.); HUBBARD *1963,* p. 56 (Repr.); HARPER *1966,* p. 82; HARPER *1967,* p. 70; CAUCHON *1968,* p. 2; HARPER *1970,* p. 194; HUBBARD *1970,* p. 15; HARPER *1971,* pp. 8 and 9-10; ANDREWS *1972,* p. 14 (Repr.); GIROUX *1972,* pp. 3-12 (Repr.); TREMBLAY *1972,* pp. 57-60, 120 and 163 (Repr.); LORD *1974,* pp. 49-53 and 128c (Repr.); VÉZINA *1974,* p. 49; VÉZINA *1975/3,* p. 53; GODSELL *1976,* p. 46; PORTER *1978/1,* pp. 40-42, No. 19 (entry by John R. Porter) (Repr.); PORTER *1978/2,* p. 6; PORTER *1978/3,* pp. 64 and 66 (Repr.); DEROME *1978,* p. 28; *Le Nouvelliste,* October 2, 1978, p. 21; *L'Information médicale et paramédicale,* January 16, 1979, p. 30; VIAU *1979,* p. 25; MURRAY *1979,* p. 92; SIMARD *1979,* p. 274; NOPPEN, PAULETTE AND TREMBLAY *1979,* p. 325 (Repr.); *Nos racines,* No. 61 (1979), p. 1206 (Repr.); GAGNON-PRATTE *1980,* pp. 50 and 167 (Repr.); BILSON *1980,* cover p. (Repr.); LÉGARÉ *1980,* p. 13; PORTER *1981,* pp. 82, 83, 84, 88, 106, 107 and 115; MELLEN *1981,* p. 28; DAVIS *1982,* pp. 13 and 14 (Repr.); LACROIX *1982,* p. 40; PORTER *1985,* p. 549; TRUDEL *1985,* pp. 168 and 169 (Repr.); KOBAYASHI AND BIRD *1985,* p. 126 (Repr.); CORBIN AND LESSARD *1986,* p. 38 (Repr.); PORTER *1987/2,* p. 1088; BROWN AND LINTEAU *1988,* p. 267 (Repr.)

Collection
National Gallery of Canada, Ottawa (7157)

S INCE ITS ACQUISITION by the National Gallery of Canada in 1959 and, especially, over the past 20 years, Joseph Légaré's work *Cholera Plague, Quebec* has taken on the status of an icon as it were. Historians have taken advantage of a wide range of publications to disseminate a both rare and striking illustration evoking the terrible epidemic that ravaged the capital of British North America in 1832.

Thousands of destitute immigrants from England, Scotland and Ireland brought cholera to the shores of the St. Lawrence River. Some 3 451 people, more than two thirds of whom were of local extraction, died in Quebec City alone. The capital not only lost one tenth of its population but also experienced serious disruption of its daily activities. Citizens fled to the countryside and business activities

Fig. 158A.
William Walton after Robert A. Sproule,
View of the Market Place and Catholic Church, Taken from the Barracks,
Fabrique Street (Quebec, Lower-Canada), 1832; engraving, 26.8 × 38 cm.
Musée du Séminaire de Québec (portfolio 160-G, Fol. 9)

were reduced to a minimum. Churches were closed, industry paralysed and property values fell.

From June 6 to November 7, 1832, the newspaper *Le Canadien* published numerous articles and a wide range of information on the disease. In particular, it discussed the incessant activities of the board of health set up by the Governor and of which Joseph Légaré was a member. The board inspected and monitored the salubrity of houses, introduced regulations for inns and grocers' shops and for the transportation and burial of the dead, appointed municipal health wardens, informed the public on the progress of the disease and, above all, set up an efficient quarantine system in and around Quebec City. The epidemic was still raging on July 5, when a relief committee was created to help orphans and needy families afflicted with the disease. Two days later, Joseph Légaré joined the committee and, with the merchant Robert Symes (Cat. 220) and the lawyer René-Édouard Caron, (Fig.

188A) took charge of raising funds in the Palais quarter.

Such information is precious in that it reveals the motives that probably led Légaré to paint *Cholera Plague, Quebec.* This work is one of the first major examples of the link that existed between several of his paintings and his socio-political activities. However, in addition to this aspect and the historical interest of the work, it is essential to consider the picture's impact on the history of Quebec painting. Part chronicle, part history painting, this work is innovative on account of the genre it exploits. It stands out not only because of its dramatic intensity but also because it is one of the first night scenes in the history of Quebec art. Shrouded in an atmosphere of sadness and despair, *Cholera Plague, Quebec* depicts the market place in Upper Town in the dead of night, surrounded by fumigating fires and illuminated by a cold, menacing moon. Despite the late hour, the marketplace is bustling with activity: a priest is leaving the cathedral

to minister to the dying, while a funeral procession follows a hearse. Closer to the foreground, Légaré has drawn a veritable human frieze depicting different aspects of the tragedy caused by cholera: scenes of crying and despair, a figure suddenly smitten with the disease, the dying being crammed into a cart, and so forth.

Légaré drew inspiration for the architectural setting of his painting from an engraving executed in 1832 by William Walton after a work by Robert A. Sproule (Fig. 158A). However, he changed the atmosphere radically. He also borrowed certain figures and motifs from Walton's engraving. It is doubtful, in fact, that he drew any of the figures from nature. More probably, he once again consulted his books of European engravings, in search of figures he could borrow or copy for his work. This practice was not unusual for Légaré and sheds light on his development as a self-taught painter, highly aware of his surroundings. Strictly speaking, Légaré made few innovations in the course of his career. On the other hand, he never ceased to reinvent on the basis of what others had created before him. In *Cholera Plague, Quebec,* he did not slavishly copy Walton's engraving insofar as he created a painting whose ultimate significance is the antithesis of that of his original source.

An artist such as Légaré may be appreciated not so much for subtle or spontaneous compositions or refined style as for his curiosity, his desire to transcend the limits of his craft, and his receptiveness to pictorial stimuli. Even when his rendering is somewhat awkward, when weaknesses can be detected in the foreshortening of a figure or other element, when certain combinations are somewhat naïve or he has made errors of perspective, Légaré always demonstrates an ability to observe, refine, make choices, assimilate, reuse, transform, associate, combine, recreate, and invent in a highly personal manner.

Moreover, Légaré's vision of Lower Canada does not appear to have been neutral. It went beyond the mere search for anecdotes or the picturesque. Linked not only to the ideology of the emerging French-Canadian middle class but to contemporary pictorial sources from abroad and to ancient western art, it constantly oscillated between the quest for originality and the burden of models with which he had to comply. In this sense, *Cholera Plague, Quebec* provides valuable insight into the colonial context in which Légaré evolved throughout his career.

J.R.P.

Fig. 159A.
Bartolomeo Pinelli,
Trasteverini giocando alla Ruzzica, 1809;
etching, 19.9 × 29.1 cm (image).
Musée du Séminaire de Québec
(Fonds ancien, 202).

159.
Le Canadien, 1833
Oil on canvas, 16.8 × 24.2 cm

Inscription
(u.c., partially erased) *LE CANADIEN.*

Provenance
Louis Mulligan, Montreal; Jean Palardy, Montreal; acquired by the Musée du Québec, Quebec City, 1972.

Exhibition
Ottawa 1978-1979/1, No. 22.

Bibliography
PORTER 1978/1, pp. 16, 17, 44, 45-46, 86 and 141, No. 22 (entry by Jean Trudel) (Repr.); *PORTER 1978/2*, p. 6; *DEROME AND LECLERC 1978*, pp. 1 and 12, No. 22; *PORTER 1981*, pp. 14, 107-108 and 129; *DAVIS 1982*, p. 14; *LEVENSON 1983*, pp. 34 and 37; *PORTER 1985*, pp. 548 and 549; *DEROME, BOURASSA AND CHAGNON 1988*, pp. 65 and 80; *GAGNON AND LACASSE 1989*, pp. 74 and 75 (Repr.).

Collection
Musée du Québec, Quebec City. Restored in 1991, with the assistance of the Amis du Musée du Québec (72.43)

O N MAY 17, 1833, the newspaper *Le Canadien* announced that it intended to change its typographical presentation and embellish its title page with an illustration of:

[…] a Canadian farmer in the middle of his field. His oxen and his plough are beside him, and he himself is resting or smoking his pipe, which in common parlance means the same thing. In the background, the beginning of a Canadian village can be seen, and on the other side, the view ends in a forest and mountains.[1]

Le Canadien came out three times a week in 1833. Under the direction of Étienne Parent and Jean-Baptiste Fréchette, it aired the opinions of French Canadians in an effort to counterbalance the views expressed in the *Quebec Mercury*.[2] As mentioned by Jean Trudel in 1978, Légaré was probably commissioned to do the painting shown here by the owners of the newspaper.[3] On account of the subject matter, namely, a *Canadien*, Légaré was obliged to paint a male figure. Not very skilled in drawing the human body, he turned to his collection of engravings in search of an appropriate model. He found a solution in Bartolomeo Pinelli's (1781-1835) anthology *Raccolta di Cinquanta Costumi Pittoreschi*, published in Rome in 1809.[4] Légaré borrowed from the figure lying down in the right middle ground in an etching entitled *Trasteverini giocando alla Ruzzica* (Fig. 159A). In copying the

figure, Légaré was generally faithful to the original, changing only minor details: he replaced the fedora with a peaked cap and the buckled shoes with boots. In the source work, the pipe appears in the subject's left hand.[5]

However, closer examination reveals subtle changes that explain the discomfort experienced by the viewer as he observes the stiff figure of the *Canadien*. The fact that the personage is seated in the foreground is not the only reason. The relaxed appearance of the figure in Pinelli's *Trasteverino* stems not only from the lie of the land—a series of small mounds next to a path—but also from the natural position of the slightly bent leg. The Roman is resting on one of the mounds during a game of quoits. Although the main purpose of Légaré's landscape was to show the figure off to advantage, he has awkwardly integrated the topography into the composition. He retained only one mound, simply because the position of borrowed figure obliged him to do so. An alteration in the lower right-hand corner of the work indicates that he originally intended to extend the mound toward the bottom of the painting. Légaré seems to have simply copied Bartolomeo Pinelli without much concern for coherence in the landscape. The impression of discomfort conveyed by the Canadien stems mainly from the fact that he seems to be leaning on a mound that does not continue behind him. In addition, the oxen are not only too small in relation to the main figure but also too close. Despite these problems, Légaré has observed the details of the hands well, more carefully, in fact, than those of the face. He has replaced the fine angular features of the model with a simpler oval.

Le Canadien has a number of affinities with works from the first years of Joseph Légaré's career, when he was apprenticed to Moses Pierce as of spring 1812. Although Pierce is still a somewhat enigmatic figure, we do know that he undertook to teach Légaré the rudiments of a type of painting only casually related to the noble art, that is, decorating carriages, coats of arms and signs.[6] The importance attached to his artistic training must have been very limited, if not, nil. However, it should be mentioned that the craft of sign painting is not very well known. Perhaps it provided the budding artist with an opportunity to go beyond simple lettering and try his hand at motifs. *Le Canadien* bears certain similarities to the type of painting Légaré learned as an apprentice, which usually focused on one main subject—a common figure or object—and was embellished with short inscriptions.

D.P.

Notes

1. *Porter 1978/1*, pp. 45-46. Légaré's painting was engraved without being inverted for the newspaper *Le Canadien*, which printed the illustration until November 11, 1836. The newspaper also used the engraving as a vignette, making several minor changes to the sky and mountains in the background as well as to position of the figure, which it depicted leaning further back.

2. André Beaulieu and Jean Hamelin, *La presse québécoise des origines à nos jours* (Quebec City: Les Presses de l'Université Laval, 1973), Vol. I, pp. 15-17.

3. *Porter 1978/1*, p. 46.

4. The full title of the work is *Raccolta di Cinquanta Costumi Pittoreschi. Incisi all'Acqua Forte da Bartolomeo Pinelli Romano*. It appeared for the first time in *Catalogue 1852*, p. 15, No. 20. Légaré may have purchased it, however, in 1822 during Joseph Cary's sale (See *Quebec Mercury*, September 10, 1822, under the title "Raccolta di Costumi in Roma"). This anthology, which came into the possession of the Séminaire de Québec with the artist's entire collection in 1874, is now in the Musée du Séminaire de Québec. It is interesting to note that Bartolomeo Pinelli engraved the outlines of James P. Cockburn's drawings of Pompei for the work *Delineations of the celebrated City of Pompei...*

5. Légaré may have consulted another engraving in this anthology, namely, *Baccanale di Roma in Testaccio* (Fol. 2). A figure in a similar position smokes a pipe in the right foreground.

6. *Porter 1981*, pp. 28-31.

160.
George IV, 1834
After Sir Thomas Lawrence
Oil on canvas, 58.3 × 46 cm

Inscriptions
(l.c., on the frame, on a recent metal plate) King George IV/By Joseph Légaré/Presented To Louis-Joseph Papineau, Seigneur/By Hon. Jacques Viger, Mayor of Montreal, 1834; (b.,l.r., on the frame, in graphite) *Papineau/491 Argyle Ave.*

Provenance
Commissioned by Jacques Viger, Montreal, 1834; Amédée Papineau, Montreal; Descendants of the Papineau family; John L. Russell, Ganonoque, Ontario; Beaver Hall Antiques; acquired by the Royal Ontario Museum, Toronto, 1980.

Exhibitions
Ottawa 1973-1974, No. 42; Ottawa 1978-1979/1, No. 25.

Bibliography
ROM, "Letter from Joseph Légaré to Jacques Viger", June 14,1834; *Morisset 1960/1*, p. 97; *Tremblay 1972*, pp. 54-55; *Harper 1973*, pp. 66 and 67, No. 42 (Repr.); *Porter 1978/1*, pp. 35, 47 and 48-50, No. 25 (entry by John R. Porter) (Repr.); *Porter 1978/2*, p. 3; *Allodi 1978*, p. 24; *L'Information médicale et paramédicale*, January 16, 1979, p. 30; *Légaré 1980*, p. 13; *Porter 1981*, pp. 55-57, 105 and 106; *Stacey 1983*, p. 60; *Porter 1985*, p. 548; *Allodi and Tovell 1989*, p. 122.

Collection
Royal Ontario Museum, Toronto (980.104.1)

 n June 14, 1834, Joseph Légaré wrote the following letter to Jacques Viger, mayor of Montreal:

Sir,

I take the liberty of sending you by the Steamboat Eagle the small painting of His late Majesty George the Fourth, to be presented by you to the oldest son of the Honourable J.-L. Papineau, Speaker of the House of Assembly, as you were good enough to promise during the conversation that I had the honour to have with you on this subject last winter.

I was not able to send it to you sooner, having been delayed by the workman who made the frame.

I beg you at the same time to present my respects to the Hon. Papineau and believe me, Sir,

Your very humble and obedient servant,

Joseph Légaré

(*Translation*)

According to this letter, Jacques Viger seems to have ordered a portrait of George IV (1762-1830) from Légaré in winter 1834 as a gift for Louis-Joseph Papineau's eldest son (Cat. 188), Amédée (1819-1903).[1] The painting remained in the Papineau family for many years and was still hanging in their old seigneurial manor of Montebello when it was acquired by the collector who eventually sold it to the Royal Ontario Museum in 1980.

On August 4, 1829, the *Quebec Mercury* announced that a portrait of George IV—king of England from 1820-1830—was to be exhibited in the premises of the Literary and Historical Society of Quebec. The public was invited to come and admire the painting, which was a copy by the English painter Wheatley after a work by his master, Sir Thomas Lawrence (1769-1830). A long description of the portrait appeared in the same edition of the newspaper:

Portrait of His Majesty

Mr Jones arrived from Montreal yesterday, with a splendid full length portrait of His Majesty which is exhibiting in the rooms of the Literary and Historical Society, in the Union Buildings. This picture possesses high merit, and is a copy of the famous portrait painted by Sir Thomas Lawrence, immediately after the Coronation, which is now at Oxford.—It is by Mr. Wheatley, an artist who paints under Sir Thomas Lawrence, and who executes the draperies and other subordinate parts of the great artist's portraits, the face therefore in the picture now exhibiting may properly be said to be the only part copied, the robes, decorations and crown being by the same hand which executed the same parts of the Oxford picture. His Majesty is represented standing in an easy dignified posture, his right hand extended to a table on which stands the Crown, manufactured for the Coronation by Messrs. Rundell & Bridge, and for which they received £20,000 for the use of the jewels, and £3,000 for the workmanship.

The whole figure of His Majesty is graceful and expressive of that natural ease and dignity for which he has always been so conspicuous. The face is a striking likeness, though at first sight it appears somewhat young for a man of His Majesty's years, yet, on close inspection the marks incidental to advanced life are plainly discoverable. The arrangement of the robes is particularly happy, concealing the corpulency which, of later years, has taken somewhat from the symmetry of His Majesty's person; the richness of the velvet and the shining gloss of the satin are admirably shewn, and the embroidery on the robe appears absolutely worked in gold.—The Collars of the several orders with which His Majesty is decorated have the like appearance of reality, and by the happy introduction of a dark back ground of extraordinary depth, the jewels of the Crown are so admirably brought out, that were a second Colonel Blood present they would tempt his fingers to purloin the pictured gems, so exquisite is the imitation. The picture is one which must please every one, the connoisseur sees in it the skill of the artist who has contrived so wonderfully to subdue the glaring colours and light parts, and produce from these unfriendly materials a chaste and harmonized effect which could only be achieved by the hand of a master. Those who enter into details will admire the fidelity with which the gems and precious stones are made to glitter, the gold to beam in its massive richness, and the soft lustre of the velvet and satin in which the portrait is decked—whilst those who have seen our beloved monarch will esteem it for the true portrait of Him who is "Aye every inch a King."—The picture we understand is for sale; and we hope that it will not be permitted to leave the province, it ought to remain in the metropolis of British North America whether considered as a work of art, or as the portrait of a monarch who lives in the hearts of his subjects.

At the time this article appeared, Légaré was a member of the Literary and Historical Society of Quebec, to which he had lent his personal collection of paintings for an exhibition in the Union Hotel. This is where Wheatley's George IV was hung in August 1829. On November 7 of the same year, the *Quebec Mercury* announced that Légaré had almost completed a copy of this painting. This news was immediately repeated by the editor of *La Bibliothèque Canadienne*, who added some comments of his own:

A PORTRAIT OF THE KING

We were glad to see the copy of His Majesty's portrait that Mr. Légaré of this town is now copying from that of Mr. Wheatley, after the original by Sir Thomas Lawrence. Mr. Légaré has succeeded perfectly in catching the tone of the picture he is studying, and the drapery as well as the jewels and the gold embroidery are remarkably well imitated. The picture is nearly completed, and it is a fine example of the skill of this Canadian artist, who had only his good taste and his natural talents to guide him in the art that he has cultivated and which he practices with honour for himself and for his country. We would be pleased to learn that he feels enough encouragement to induce him to continue to follow the lofty paths of his profession; we are sure that a little instruc-

tion and the opportunity to study the great masters would place Mr. Légaré well above a mediocre painter.

Mercury

We have ourselves had the opportunity of seeing Mr. Légaré's work. It was then only a sketch; but the part that was completed seemed to us a perfect imitation of Mr. Wheatley's copy. We even detected an improvement in the face: appearing too young in the work of the English painter, it seemed in that of our compatriot more in keeping with the age of His Majesty, at the time of his coronation.

Editor (Translation)

On November 23, the *Quebec Gazette* in turn congratulated the artist on his copy, emphasizing the fact that it had been seen and admired by Governor Kempt and Lieutenant-Colonel James P. Cockburn, a connoisseur in the matter. The newspaper also took the opportunity to announce the impending acquisition of Légaré's painting for the Legislative Council Chamber, a purchase that was confirmed a few days later. In January 1830, the painter Jean-Baptiste Roy-Audy also made a copy of Wheatley's portrait of George IV, which had just been acquired for decorating the chamber of the Legislative Assembly.[2]

Légaré's work was destroyed in 1854 when the Parliament Building in Quebec City burned down. Fortunately, his small version of 1834 gives some idea of what the larger portrait was like. It corresponds perfectly with the description of Wheatley's painting that appeared in the *Quebec Mercury* on August 4, 1829. Légaré skilfully surmounted the problems involved in copying a royal portrait, rich in textures and brimming with detail.

The preceding text repeats almost exactly what we wrote in 1978 for the first retrospective of Légaré's work. However, we would like to complete this catalogue entry with two observations. The first concerns Légaré's status as an artist. Based on the various clichés published in the newspapers about his large portrait of George IV, Légaré was perceived in his own milieu as a talented self-taught artist who, however, needed additional instruction. On the one hand, critics delighted in pointing out "the skill of this Canadian artist, who had only his good taste and his natural talents to guide him in the art that he has cultivated and which he practices with honour for himself and for his country." (*Translation*) On the other hand, they hoped that he would feel "enough encouragement to induce him to continue to follow the lofty paths of his profession; [they were] sure that a little instruction

and the opportunity to study the great masters would place Mr. Légaré well above a mediocre painter." (*Translation*) Contrary to such artists as Antoine Plamondon and Théophile Hamel, Légaré never went to Europe to develop his skills. He preferred to pursue his artistic training alone, a decision which no doubt affected his career and production. His refusal to study elsewhere condemned him to bear the label for the rest of his life of a self-taught artist who "never had the advantage of studying the divine art of painting beneath other skies."[3] (*Translation*) While this handicap made some of his contemporaries acknowledge his merits even more and admire him for his artistic knowledge, it lessened his prestige in the eyes of others.

In another line of thought, it might seem paradoxical that a Papineau supporter, opposed to the abuses of the colonial system, would agree to paint portraits of British sovereigns: he executed a portrait of George III in 1830 and two of Queen Victoria in 1839. It might also seem ironic that one of these portraits was intended for the oldest son of the patriotic orator. There is no paradox, however, since Lower Canadian elites linked to the *Parti canadien* had looked on British institutions and therefore the monarchy with unbounded admiration for many years. Even in the 1830s, Papineau and his supporters remained faithful to English institutions as long as the latter served their political interests. Although French-speaking members of the liberal professions defined their nation as the antithesis of the Anglophone bourgeoisie, for several, this in no way diminished their loyalty to Great Britain. In this sense, the King was not perceived as the enemy of the *Canadiens* but as a figure who would protect them from the local English-speaking minority.

J.R.P.

Notes

1. Not "Lactance" as we stated incorrectly in our 1978 catalogue.

2. A painting by Andrew Morris (Cat. 173) also bears many similarities to Wheatley's work. Moreover, it proves that even the setting of Légaré's smaller portrait of George IV was the same as that of his model.

3. *Le Journal de Québec*, June 15, 1852, p. 2.

161.
Landscape with Wolfe Monument, c. 1840

Oil on canvas, 132 × 175.8 cm

Inscriptions
(i., l.l., at the foot of the tree almost illegible) *JL;*
(c., on the pedestal of the statue) *J.WO.*

Provenance
Mrs. Jean Rousseau, Quebec City; acquired by
the Musée de la Province de Québec, Quebec
City, 1955.

Exhibitions
Quebec City 1848; London 1965; Ottawa 1967/
1, No. 91; Montreal 1974, No. 42; Ottawa 1978-
1979/1, No. 42; Berlin 1982-1983, No. 2;
Quebec City 1983-1984, No. 65.

Bibliography
Le Canadien, October 2, 1848, p. 3, No. 7;
L'Ami de la Religion et de la Patrie, October
4, 1848, p. 655, No. 7; *Quebec Mercury,* October
5, 1848, p. 3, No. 7; *Le Journal de Québec,*
October 5, 1848, p. 3, No. 7; *RECENT
ACQUISITIONS 1956,* p. 295; *MORISSET 1960/1,*
pp. 64d and 99 (Repr.); *HARPER 1962/3,* p. 418
(Repr.); *HARPER 1966,* pp. 81 and 82 (Repr.);
COLLECTIONS 1967, No. 33 (Repr.); *HUBBARD AND
OSTIGUY 1967,* pp. 56 and 57, No. 91 (Repr.);
PALL MALL 1967, p. 344 (Repr.); *TRUDEL 1970,*
pp. 36 and 37 (Repr.); *TREMBLAY 1972,* pp. 196-
199 (Repr.); *REID 1973,* p. 47; *LORD 1974,* p. 54;
JUNEAU AND THIBAULT 1974, No. 42; *DUMAS 1974,*
p. 40 (Repr.); *LE MUSÉE DU QUÉBEC 1978,* pp. 35-
36 (Repr.); *PORTER 1978/1,* pp. 15, 50, 64-65 and
82, No. 42 (entry by Jean Trudel) (Repr.); *PORTER
1978/2,* pp. 4, 6 and 7 (Repr.); *DEROME 1978,*
p. 29; *DEROME AND LECLERC 1978,* p. 13, No. 42;
THIBAULT 1978, pp. 15 and 16 (Repr.); *TOUPIN
1979,* p. E-19; *MONTPETIT 1979,* p. 295; *MURRAY
1979,* pp. 92-93 (Repr.); *GAGNON 1979-1980,*
pp. 11-14 (Repr.); *GAGNON 1980,* pp. 44-45;
GAGNON-PRATTE 1980, pp. 90 and 169 (Repr.);
PORTER 1981, pp. 250-254; *LACROIX 1982,* pp. 38,

39 and 124, No. 2; *LEVENSON 1983,* pp. 33 and 36;
LE MUSÉE DU QUÉBEC 1983, p. 69, No. 65 (entry
by Claude Thibault, Luc Noppen and Michel
Doyon) (Repr.); *PORTER 1985,* p. 549; *PORTER
1986,* p. 196; *TRUDEL 1987,* pp. 103-104; *DEROME,
BOURASSA AND CHAGNON 1988,* pp. 65 and 80;
GAGNON AND LACASSE 1989, pp. 73-75 (Repr.);
BÉLAND AND BOURASSA 1990, pp. 6, 7, 9 and 72
(Repr.).

Collection
Musée du Québec, Quebec City (55.109)

T HIS PAINTING was long considered a
model of a typically Canadian
landscape, albeit with some reservations. Gérard Morisset fully endorsed this
idea:

The artist must have taken many walks in Canadian forests—where white birch was the
dominant species one hundred and twenty five
years ago—to produce such a faithful, skilful,
sensitive, and rich painting of this environment.[1]
(*Translation*)

This notion was rectified to a certain extent by John Russell Harper who
qualified **Landscape with Wolfe Monument**
as a Canadian version of a "Salvator-Rosa-
style" landscape.[2] (*Translation*) His intui-
tion was correct since John R. Porter
identified one of Rosa's works, now in the
Séminaire de Québec collection, as a model
for this painting.

Except for the figures, all the elements in this landscape were copied from
the engraving *Mercury Putting Argus to
Sleep* (Fig. 161A) made by Emile Carlier
after Salvator Rosa's painting. However,
Légaré changed his model in several ways,
modifying, in particular, the atmosphere
of the natural setting. He accentuated the
division between the various planes by focusing on the dead tree in the right foreground. By elongating the stump, drawing
sharply pointed branches in the foreground
and playing with patterns of light, he emphasized their role as repoussoirs. In addition, by placing the statue of Wolfe in
the visual field and distributing the light
more dramatically and sparingly, he
shrouded the landscape in a very different
atmosphere. The statue commands attention and prevents the eye from exploring
the existing space.

Not a great deal can be said about
the way in which Légaré has copied the
figure of Wolfe from a work by Richard
Houston.[3] He merely borrowed the outline of the model, without reproducing all
of its subtle details. The facial features, especially the large eye near the top of the
head, bear only a superficial resemblance
to the person portrayed. The fullness and
folds of the clothing can be attributed more
to convention than to careful observation:
the cuffs, outline of the right arm and hand,
which is out of proportion in relation to
the model, confirm this statement.[4] Légaré
referred once again to his collection of
engravings for the figure of the Indian.
He literally borrowed the figure of Vulcan
from a painting by François Boucher
(1703-1770), *Vulcan presenting Venus with
Weapons for Aenas* (Fig. 161B),[5] in turn
engraved by Jacques Danzel (1737-1809).
He traced the outline of the body and face
exactly,[6] and reproduced the pattern of
light and shadow on the torso. An alteration to the right arm suggests the problems Légaré had to resolve in completing
the figure. By making the elbow rounder,
he initially increased the size of the arm.
However, he later abandoned this idea
since he would have had to straighten the
head and chest and thereby jeopardize the
coherency of the figure as a whole. Légaré
also borrowed other elements from the
French engraving, such as the mound on
which the figure is seated and certain attributes, which he simplified. This is the
case, for example, of the quiver full arrows
and the axe; the hammer, for its part, was
replaced by a tomahawk. Légaré impro-
vised the bow in the Amerindian's hand
using Vulcan's sword as a model. Finally,

he borrowed the general arrangement of the figures from the engraving after Boucher: the position of James Wolfe in relation to the Indian is similar to that of Venus in relation to Vulcan. This observation makes the true significance of **Landscape with Wolfe Monument** much more complex.

If we are to present the various interpretations advanced with regard to this work, the question of its significance must be reviewed in full. While John R. Porter's discovery of Carlier's engraving (Fig. 161A) refuted Gérard Morisset's assertion, it sparked a controversy about the iconography of Légaré's painting. It should be recalled that *Mercury Putting Argus to Sleep* refers to Ovid's work, *Metamorphoses*. Mercury, who is seated on a rock, is playing a flute to put Argus, the 100-eyed giant, to sleep. Argus is guarding the nymph Io, whom Zeus had changed into a heifer to protect her from the wrath of Hera, his wife. According to Jean Trudel:

If we assume that the cow Io is replaced by the bark canoe, the shepherd Argus is replaced by the Indian, and Mercury by the Wolfe Monument, the allegory is linked to Légaré's political ideas after the troubles of 1837 [...] it must not be forgotten that the newspaper that defended the interests of the English-speaking population (and the rival of the newspaper *Le Canadien*, with which Légaré was connected) was *The Mercury*.[7]

François-Marc Gagnon rectified this interpretation. In his opinion, "the Indian takes the place of Mercury; the statue of Wolfe, that of Argus; and the tip of the canoe, that of the heifer. This is logical, for who else could better symbolize the power of England than the 100-eyed colossus?"[8] (*Translation*) Although John R. Porter acknowledges the attractiveness of this hypothesis, he cannot subscribe to it since it is "incompatible with Légaré's state of mind after the events of 1837 [...] Like Jean Trudel, I believe that we must associate Wolfe with Mercury."[9] (*Translation*)

We agree with Jean Trudel, François-Marc Gagnon and John R. Porter about the allegorical nature of the landscape. However, we also believe that it is too limiting to try to establish a one-to-one correspondence between Salvator Rosa's figures and those of Légaré. Légaré borrowed only the landscape from Émile Carlier's engraving; his figures, however, come from Boucher. Consequently, there is reason to believe that we must look to the engraving after Boucher to identify corresponding subject matter. *Vulcan presenting Venus With Weapons for Aeanas*

illustrates a passage from the eighth book of the Aeneid, in which Venus uses her powers of seduction to convince her husband Vulcan to forge weapons for her son Aeneas. Boucher's painting illustrates the moment when Vulcan gives the weapons to Venus. How did Légaré interpret this gesture? Perhaps he saw it merely as an offering. On the other hand, he may also have been familiar with Virgil's poem and the way in which Venus obtained the weapons, that is, by subjecting Vulcan to her will through her powers of seduction. Obviously, the interpretation of this painting is very different depending on the which of these alternatives is considered correct.

It should above all be recognized that many of the elements needed to settle this question are lacking. It should first be noted that, stylistically, the painting **Landscape with Wolfe Monument** belongs to the 1838-1839 period. It demonstrates how Légaré's treatment of his subject matter had changed gradually with the models he had chosen over the previous decade. Late 1837 and early 1838 were difficult for the artist socially speaking. In Quebec City, Légaré was quite deeply involved in the activities that would lead to the uprising in the Montreal region. The stand he took did not go unnoticed when the authorities gained control of the situation. He was arrested and imprisoned from November 13 to November 18, 1837. His trial, which was to have been held the following year, was eventually postponed. The experience was no doubt painful for Légaré. It not only affected his health,[10] but, in particular, marked the failure of his political ideas. It resulted in a real loss of social prestige and was detrimental to his painting career. As John R. Porter shrewdly remarked, it was in this context that "Joseph Légaré deemed it wise to quietly return to his paintbrushes and his collection."[11] (*Translation*)

The various hypotheses surrounding **Landscape with Wolfe Monument** must be formulated with the above points in mind. It must first be asked whether or not Légaré intended to paint "a tribute to Wolfe." It should not be forgotten that his political leanings in around 1839 did not prevent him from copying a portrait of Queen Victoria by Thomas Sully.[12] Moreover, when his landscape was exhibited in 1848,[13] it bore the title *Wolfe's Monument* and was hung beside the portrait of Queen Victoria. This exhibition was organized by Légaré for the purpose of holding a lottery. There is reason to

believe, therefore, that the artist also identified the paintings on display. In our opinion, it is revealing that the painting was entitled *Wolfe's Monument*, which, in Légaré's eyes, was the real subject of the painting, rather than *Landscape*.[14] Furthermore, why would he have exhibited a "subversive" work amidst paintings for which the newspapers, both French and English, had nothing but praise? It must be noted that when Légaré painted an allegorical representation of St. Lawrence on the banner for the first section of the Société Saint-Jean-Baptiste de Québec in 1843,[15] he used an iconography that was very similar to that of the painting in the Musée du Québec:

An Indian seated on the riverbank with a jug in one hand and his instruments of war, arrows, tomahawk, etc., nearby, offers a necklace and a peace pipe to Saint Lawrence with the other hand, as a token of the alliance contracted by Canada with the Faith. The frame is surmounted by the crown of England, as a mark of its sovereignty over the country through which the river flows. (*Translation*)

It might be asked whether **Landscape with Wolfe Monument** should not be interpreted in a similar light. The Indian, symbol of Canada or French Canadians, offers his bow to Wolfe, the incarnation of British power in North America. With this gesture, he professes his allegiance to the British Crown. The birchbark canoe is merely an additional attribute, like the various weapons surrounding Vulcan in François Boucher's painting.[16]

This preliminary and literal interpretation of Légaré's painting does not necessarily reveal the full significance of the work. If we accept that Légaré was familiar with the myth illustrated by François Boucher in which Venus seduced and deceived Vulcan to make him provide her with weapons, a similar relationship can then be established between the Indian and Wolfe on his pedestal. French Canadians were also deceived by the British Crown, to which they had reasserted their loyalty after the failure of the Rebellion of 1837-1838. Lord Durham's *Report on the Affairs of British North America,* published in London in early 1839, recommended that French Canadians be assimilated into British culture and that the two Canadas be united. Any hopes still cherished by French Canadians were crushed. Is it exaggerated, therefore, to believe that Légaré used his **Landscape with Wolfe Monument** to make a political statement? He depicted an Amerindian declaring his allegiance to the representative of the British Crown, commemorated by a statue. In our opinion,

Fig. 161A.
Émile Carlier after Salvator Rosa,
Mercury Putting Argus to Sleep, 1768;
etching, 24.4 × 39.6 cm.
Musée du Séminaire de Québec (portfolio 70-G, Fol. 15).

Fig. 161B.
Jacques Danzel after François Boucher,
Vulcan presenting Venus with Weapons for Aeneas;
burin, 49.5 × 63.4 cm (image).
Musée du Séminaire de Québec (P 984.569).

the references to the engraving after François Boucher support the argument advanced by John R. Porter:

At the time, he [Légaré] was plagued with the anxiety and deep despair afflicting the French Canadian elite as a whole. Étienne Parent expressed their pessimism well in 1839: "Some people, including ourselves, believed that, with the support and favour of England, French Canadians could profess to be able to preserve and promote their nationality so as to eventually form an independent country [...] Given England's current plan [to unite the two Canadas], it would be the height of folly and blindness for French Canadians to stubbornly continue to remain a separate nation in this part of the continent.[17] (*Translation*)

Légaré was surely disillusioned by the political game that had just come to an end. The gesture of the Amerindian (French Canadian), which is not at all spontaneous or voluntary, suggests Légaré's state of mind. That he should use this painting to reflect his emotions is totally in keeping with his creative approach. His work expressed simple beliefs, deeply rooted in the everyday events he depicted. This painting must also be considered from the perspective of the social prestige it conferred on the artist. Based on the title Légaré gave to his painting in 1848, we believe that Légaré enjoyed playing on the ambivalence of his ***Landscape with Wolfe Monument.*** It must not have displeased him that his work was perceived by some people simply as a tribute to the hero. It is also very probable that others, particularly

friends who shared his political ideas, fully understood the renunciation expressed by the Indian's gesture. We do not believe, however, that anything more should be read into Légaré's painting. Nor do we believe, as François-Marc Gagnon brilliantly tried to demonstrate,[18] that ***Landscape with Wolfe Monument*** was inspired by François-Xavier Garneau's poem, *Le Dernier Huron.* If limits should be set on the interpretation of Légaré's work, we believe that he should not be considered a "painter-philosopher."

D.P.

Notes

1. *MORISSET 1960/1,* p. 99.
2. *HARPER 1966,* pp. 81-82.
3. For a reproduction of this work, see *PORTER 1978/1,* p. 64, Fig. 42b. For detailed information on this borrowing, see *TRUDEL 1970,* pp. 34-37.
4. It is impossible to definitely identify the model used for the pedestal of this full-length portrait which Légaré elevated to the rank of a statue. However, the artist may have drawn inspiration from engravings by Marco Ricci (1676-1730) or from others in his collection based on works by Gian Paolo Panini (1691-1765).
5. We have used the title under which Légaré knew this painting. However, its correct title is given in the François Boucher catalogue: *Vénus dans la forge de Vulcain (François Boucher, 1703-1770,* Cat. (Paris: Grand Palais, 1986-1987), pp. 274-279, No. 67).
6. This is a very rare example of Légaré's working methods: the lines he drew in tracing the figures are visible on the back of this engraving.

7. *PORTER 1978/1,* p. 65
8. *TRUDEL 1980,* p. 45.
9. *PORTER 1981,* p. 252.
10. *Le Fantasque,* November 1837.
11. *PORTER 1981,* p. 152.
12. For further information on the circumstances under which Légaré copied this portrait and on its coverage in the press, see *PORTER 1978/1,* pp. 59-61.
13. *Quebec Mercury,* October 5, 1848, p. 3.
14. To be exact, we would have had to replace the present title of the painting, ***Landscape with Wolfe Monument,*** with the title used by the artist at the time, *Monument du général Wolf.* However, for the sake of convenience, we have decided to use the title under which it has been known since it was acquired by the Musée du Québec, even though we are fully aware that it is not really correct. It should also be mentioned that we do not wish to speculate on the pun created by the omission of the final "e" in the name of the victor of the battle of the Plains of Abraham. It was probably a simple typographical error by the newspaper *Le Canadien;* such mistakes were frequent at the time.
15. *Le Canadien,* June 28, 1843, p. 3. For more on the subject, see *Le Fantasque,* July 3, 1843, p. 3.
16. In support of this argument, it should be added that the Indian is wearing a medal bearing the monogram of King George III around his neck. French Canadians had admired this monarch since the Conquest and they honoured him as their ally when he died in 1820 (see the eulogy written by Louis-Joseph Papineau in the *Quebec Gazette,* July 10, 1820). The presence of a beaver in the foreground on the mound to the left of the tree supports the theory that the Amerindian represents French Canadians.
17. *PORTER 1981,* p. 252.
18. *GAGNON AND LACASSE 1989,* pp. 73-74.

Fig. 162A.
Robert Coulson,
Québec seen from Pointe Lévis, 1839-1842;
watercolour on paper, 25.7 × 35.6 cm.
Private collection.

162. (See colour reproduction, p. 96)
Quebec Viewed from Pointe Lévis, c. 1840-1842
Oil on canvas, 90 × 120 cm

Provenance
Philippe Gagnon, Loretteville; Berthe Gagnon, Loretteville; Dr. Conrad Brouillette, Loretteville, 1979; acquired by the Montreal Museum of Fine Arts, 1980.

Exhibitions
Berlin 1982-1983, No. 3; Montreal 1984/2.

Bibliography
(?) MORISSET 1960/1, p. 99; ŒUVRE MAGISTRALE 1980, p. 1; *The Museologist*, No. 161 (summer 1982), cover. p. and title p. (Repr.); LACROIX 1982, pp. 38, 39 and 124, No. 3 (Repr.); CLOUTIER 1984, p. 2; NAUBERT-RISER 1989, p. 867 (Repr.).

Collection
Montreal Museum of Fine Arts. Gift of the J.-A. DeSève estate and the Horsley and Annie Townsend Bequest(1980.3)

T HIS UNSIGNED, undated landscape came to light after the exhibition in Ottawa in 1978. Available historical documents had made no mention of the work. It illustrates a large farmhouse with a panoramic view of Quebec City in the background and represents the view from the heights of Pointe-Lévis. It is a superb landscape painting and, like *The Martyrdom of Fathers Brébeuf and Lalemant* (Cat. 165) is one of Légaré's best works.

Once again, the success of this painting is indissociable from the model that lent the overall tone to the composition. Before the model was identified, this landscape was said to resemble, although with some reservations, James Duncan's large panoramic views of Montreal (Cat. 91 and 92). All uncertainty was dispelled recently when a series of watercolours by Captain Robert Coulson (ca. 1805-1849) were put on sale in London.[1] A member of the Grenadier Guards, Coulson came to Quebec in 1839 and lived there until 1842. One of his watercolours definitely served as a model for Légaré's painting; oddly, however, the title *Quebec from the Fall of Montmorenci* is written on the back of Coulson's work (Fig. 162A). Not only is the vantage point identical to that of Légaré's landscape, but the foreground is organized in a similar manner: in both paintings, it consists of two overlapping triangles of land crossed by a diagonal that directs the viewer's attention. The link between the two works is further confirmed by way in which the composition has been framed: by a group of young trees on the left and by a tall fir tree on the right. Compared with Coulson's watercolour, however, all the planes in Légaré's work are equally important. Consequently, there is not enough depth and, owing to a lack of proportion, the motifs are "overpowered." The middle ground is too narrow, while the overly prominent vegetation gives

the impression that the landscape is located right in front of the city. These features are typical of many of Légaré's landscapes; the painting *Falls of the Chaudière River,* in a private collection in London, also illustrates this type of composition.[2]

The particularly meticulous facture of **Quebec Viewed from Pointe Lévis** represents an amalgamation of techniques used in previous landscape paintings and oil-on-paper sketches. The detailed brushwork is reminiscent of that of *The Martyrdom of Fathers Brébeuf and Lalemant* (Cat. 165) while the smooth brush strokes on the field in the middle ground foreshadow the artist's later works (Cat. 169). However, even greater similarities can be seen between the trees in the foreground and certain parts of Légaré's two oil-on-paper works, *Hôpital général de Québec* (Fig. 164A: left side) and *The Old Water Mill of the Hôpital général de Québec* (Cat. 164: right side). In the first work, the more supple brushwork creates smoother, less angular forms, thereby emphasizing their shape and volume. In the second, the brush strokes are both light and vibrant, and more refined than in **Quebec Viewed from Pointe Lévis.** Contrary to *Massacre of Hurons by the Iroquois* (Cat, 157) and *Landscape with Wolfe Monument* (Cat. 161), in which Légaré depicted the foliage by drawing the leaves individually, the foliage in this landscape has been painted as a single mass, with individual leaves drawn only on the periphery. Based on these characteristics, it is possible to attribute this view of Quebec City to Légaré and to date it from around 1842-1843, or the same period as Coulson's watercolour.

The discovery of this drawing adds a new perspective to the very complex question of the influence of British landscape artists on Légaré's work. James Pattison Cockburn made a profound impression on the artist in the early years of his career. As a result, Légaré created landscapes in which a certain equilibrium was achieved only through the addition of numerous plant motifs or figures. He also used tall trees as repoussoirs in this more idealized approach to nature (Cat. 165). Légaré employed these devices in oils on canvas until the end of his career. In later years, however, he was confronted with the work of watercolourists who had a totally different view of nature: for example, Henry William Barnard (Cat. 59 to 62) and James Hope-Wallace (Cat. 143 to 146). During the years 1839 to 1843, Légaré radically changed his approach to landscape painting, at least with regard to works on paper. He adopted a more supple, less laborious approach, lowered the horizon line and made his compositions more open (Cat. 169). The artist asserted his skills through truly masterful works in which nature was devoid of artificial elements.[3] While he never seems to have grasped the subtle interplay of diagonals that allowed James Pattison Cockburn to gradually extend the planes of his composition into the distance, Légaré seems to have better understood the style of British artists from the 1830-1840 period. Perhaps he appreciated their less rational approach to nature, expressed in simpler compositions. The studied negligence of their watercolours was certainly more in keeping with his tastes as a colourist.

D.P.

Notes

1. *Pictures, Drawings, Watercolours, Prints and Sculptures,* Christie's sale, South Kensington (London), October 29, 1987, Lot 69 (Repr.). These works were originally part of an album put up for sale at Christie's on October 29, 1980 (Lot 41). For further reading on Coulson and for reproductions of his work, see G. Blair Laing, *Memoirs of an Art Dealer 2* (Toronto: McClelland and Stewart, 1982), p. 56, Figs. 18 and 19.

2. *PORTER 1978/1,* p. 83, No. 61 (Repr.).

3. See *PORTER 1978/1,* pp. 38, 43, 60, Nos. 16, 21 and 38 for examples.

163. (See colour reproduction, p. 101)
Country House of Philippe Panet on the Little Saint Charles River, before 1838
Oil and gouache on paper, 35.4 × 46.2 cm

Inscriptions
(b.,u.r., in graphite) *Residence de M͏ʳ. Panet, Petite Rivière/(St. Charles).;* (b.,l.r., in graphite) *Residence de M͏ʳ Panet/Petite Rivière.*

Provenance
Séminaire de Québec, from the Joseph Légaré estate, 1874; on deposit at the Société du Musée du Séminaire de Québec, 1983.

Exhibitions
Ottawa 1978-1979/1, No. 17; Quebec City 1980/2, No. 16.

Bibliography
PORTER 1978/1, pp. 39-40, No. 17 (entry by John R. Porter) (Repr.); *PORTER 1978/2,* pp. 6 and 7 (Repr.); *PORTER 1978/4,* p. 21; *DEROME 1978,* p. 28; *DEROME AND LECLERC 1978,* p. 14, No. 17; *L'information médicale et paramédicale,* January 16, 1979, p. 30 (Repr.); *GAGNON-PRATTE 1980,* pp. 93, 94 and 169 (Repr.); *PORTER 1981,* p. 115; *LACROIX 1982,* p. 38.

Collection
Musée du Séminaire de Québec (Pc983.70)

L IKE SEVERAL leading citizens of Quebec City, such as Henry Atkinson, who had built "Carouge" (Cat. 76) 10 years earlier, Philippe Panet settled on the fringe of the inhabited zone, between the city and the country. He chose a site on the banks of the Saint-Charles River, near Scott Bridge (Cat. 209) to build "*Le Bocage*" in late summer 1830.

This country house is the first example of the influence of the Italian Renaissance on villa architecture in Quebec.[1] The original building contract, located by John R. Porter, described the residence as follows:

A three-storied residence, twenty-two feet in width by fifty feet in depth including the two ends which will be five-foot projections of semi-hexagonal form in each of which there will be nine openings and two on the long sides [...] Two wings joining the main building, which will be only two stories in height and each twenty feet wide by forty feet in depth.[2]

The architecture of "*Le Bocage*", which was surmounted by a roof terrace, reflects early developments in the Picturesque movement at the beginning of the 19th century. Its overly rigid geometry is offset by projecting façades with cut-off corners and windows opening onto the surrounding countryside. The site of the building played a predominant role, and Légaré fully understood its importance by making it a prominent part of his painting. Philippe Panet's villa is relegated to the background, nestled in a clump of trees. Owing to its location above the river, it dominates the natural spectacle offered by the surrounding "*bocage*", or mixture of woodland and fields. This landscape occupies more than half of the composition

Fig. 164A.
Joseph Légaré,
Hôpital général de Québec, c. 1842-1843;
oil on paper, 35.1 × 51.1 cm.
Musée du Séminaire de Québec (Pc983.36).

164.
The Old Water Mill of the Hôpital général de Québec, c. 1842-1843
Oil and graphite on paper, 34.6 × 50.8 cm (irregular dimensions)

Inscription
(b.,u.c., in graphite) *Hopital général.*

Provenance
Séminaire de Québec, from the Joseph Légaré estate, 1874; on deposit at the Société du Musée du Séminaire de Québec, 1983.

Exhibition
Ottawa 1978-1979/1, No. 29.

Bibliography
PORTER 1978/1, pp. 51-53, No. 29 (entry by John R. Porter) (Repr.); PORTER 1978/4, p. 19; DEROME 1978, p. 29 (Repr.); DEROME AND LECLERC 1978, p. 16, No. 29; PORTER 1981, p. 113.

Collection
Musée du Séminaire de Québec (Pc990.3)

and employs almost all the components of Picturesque vocabulary: water, vegetation, a small bridge, and such pastoral elements as a cowherd and his cattle. This landscape foreshadows later works by Légaré and probably dates from before 1838. It is very hard to distinguish, however, between pictures painted outdoors and those executed in the artist's studio.[3]

Compared with Légaré's other oils on paper, **The Old Water Mill of the Hôpital général de Québec** is exceptionally well executed. Located on the banks of the Saint-Charles River, the Hôpital général was founded in the 17th century by Monseigneur de Saint-Vallier, Bishop of Quebec.[4] Its water mill built in 1702 was replaced by a windmill only eight years later because of a lack of water in the stream supplying the structure. The small building was then used for extra lodgings and as a laundry. The Hôpital général often attracted the attention of British landscape artists. James Pattison Cockburn drew this group of buildings on many occasions,[5] in both summer and winter. His works provide a very good idea of how the various

structures were organized and where the water mill was located. Hidden by a clump of slender trees, the mill stood behind and below the hospital's main building. Légaré depicted the water mill in another painting (Fig. 164A) which focused primarily on the façade of the main building. In our opinion, however, the artist was more interested in the natural environment as such than in the historical value of the building. This oil-on-paper is one of his most skilfully executed works, owing, in particular, to the way in which he has rendered the masses of foliage rustling in the gentle breeze, their leaves shimmering in the light. The harmonious use of light and colour and coherent integration of forms in space bear witness to the high quality Légaré's oil-on-paper landscapes from 1842 to 1843. These works are characterized by a common stylistic device: the contrast between, on the one hand, the sharp, clear lines and precise brush strokes used to draw the buildings and, on the other hand, the broad sweeping strokes used to paint the foreground. Henceforth, Légaré applied the lessons learned from some of Henry

William Barnard's watercolours, such as *View from the Backyard of the Jesuit Barracks, Quebec* (Cat. 62). His new compositions were simple and precise.[6] As in **The Old Water Mill of the Hôpital général de Québec**, Légaré structured his works horizontally, adding vertical architectural lines sometimes offset by the diagonals of the surrounding landscape. However, the link between Légaré and foreign landscape artists from the 1840s should not be analyzed in terms of specific models which the artist copied, as in the case of *The Martyrdom of Fathers Brébeuf and Lalemant* (Cat. 165) where he drew inspiration from Cockburn. Rather, this link should be considered in terms of the spiritual affinity that Légaré felt for these artists.

D.P.

Notes

1. *GAGNON-PRATTE 1980*, pp. 93-95 and 268-269.

2. *PORTER 1978/1*, p. 39.

3. To deal with this question fully, we would have to discuss it at length. May it simply be said that a distinction can be made between Légaré's first oil-on-paper landscapes, i.e. those in the Viger and Maguire albums (*PORTER 1978/1*, p. 68, No. 46, Repr.; pp. 71 and 73, No. 51, Repr.; pp. 137 and 138, No. 205, Repr.; p. 138, No. 209, Repr.; p. 139, No. 210, Repr.) and their known copies (*PORTER 1978/1*, pp. 67 and 68, No. 45, Repr.; pp. 70-71 and 72, No. 50, Repr.; pp. 35-36 and 37, No. 35, Repr.) which we consider studio works that the artist executed to master new techniques. We situate this period around 1838, prior to the major developments of the years 1840-1843.

4. *NOPPEN, PAULETTE AND TREMBLAY 1979*, pp. 203-207.

5. *CAMERON AND TRUDEL 1976*, pp. 156-159, Nos. 143-146 (Repr.).

6. In addition to **The Old Water Mill of the Hôpital général de Québec**, these works include *Hôpital général de Québec* (Fig. 164a), *The Church of Sainte-Foy, Quebec viewed from Sainte-Petronille Point, Ile d'Orléans, Chateau Haldimand and the Citadel* and *Saint Paul's Bay* (*PORTER 1978/1*, pp. 43, 32, 49 and 28, Nos. 21, 10, 27 and 6, Repr.).

165.
The Martyrdom of Fathers Brébeuf and Lalemant, c. 1843

Oil on canvas, 67.7 × 97.2 cm

Provenance
Private collection (sold by Jacoby's House of Antiques, Montreal, October 22, 1969, No. 161); Mrs. Mary Barriere, Westmount, 1969; acquired by the National Gallery of Canada, Ottawa, 1977.

Exhibitions
Ottawa, 1978-1979/1, No. 53; La Rochelle 1982-1983, No. 217.

Bibliography
HIGHLY IMPORTANT 1969, pp. 118, 119 and cover p., No. 161 (Repr.); *PORTER 1978/1,* pp. 16, 73 and 75, No. 53 (entry by Jean Trudel) (Repr.); *PORTER 1978/2,* p. 7; *DEROME 1978,* pp. 29 and 30 (Repr.); *DEROME AND LECLERC 1978,* p. 9, No. 53; *La Presse,* September 26, 1978 (Repr.); *Le Devoir,* September 26, 1978, p. 12; *Le Quotidien,* September 26, 1978, p. A-10; *Le Nouvelliste,* October 2, 1978, p. 21; *NIXON 1979,* p. 16; *VÉZINA 1979,* p. 44 (Repr.); *GAGNON 1980,* p. 42; *PORTER 1981,* pp. 113-114 and 260; *UNE AUTRE AMÉRIQUE 1982,* p. 134, No. 217 (Repr.); *DAVIS 1982,* p. 6; *LACROIX 1982,* pp. 38-39 (Repr.); *LEVENSON 1983,* pp. 33 and 37; *PORTER 1985,* p. 550; *MARTIN 1988,* p. 33.

Collection
National Gallery of Canada, Ottawa (18795)

A LTHOUGH *The Martyrdom of Fathers Brébeuf and Lalemant* is undated and its provenance can be traced back only as far as 1969, its creation has rightly been associated with the return of the Society of Jesus to Canada in 1842.[1] The society's participation in a retreat led by a Jesuit priest at the Séminaire de Québec the following year marked an important stage in the reestablishment of ties within the group. To commemorate their reunion and revive the past, the priests who took part in the retreat commissioned Joseph Légaré to paint a picture for the Jesuit father.[2] Père Félix Martin accurately described this painting entitled *Memorials of the Jesuits of New France:*

In the foreground, the life-size copy of a silver bust of Father de Brébeuf can be seen, kept with an important relic in one of the Quebec communities. All the memorials relating to local history and productions are near him, and in the distance can be seen the martyrdom of this heroic man and his selfless companions.

Even the frame is a precious object to us: it was the fine ornament of one of the pictures belonging to the church of our College in Quebec City.[3] (*Translation*)

The last comment is interesting from an historical perspective. The Jesuits' church was destroyed during the Conquest, the bombardments having left only the building's shell. The fact that the picture's frame was rescued from the debris and preserved for 80 years elevates it to the rank of a tangible historical record, even more so than the image it contained. It is not surprising that in *The Martyrdom of Fathers Brébeuf and Lalemant* Légaré continued in the same vein as in *Memorials of the Jesuits of New France;* the composition of the former work was merely an extension of the scene depicted in the background of the latter. Did Légaré paint the picture of fathers Brébeuf and Lalemant to fulfil another order by the Jesuits, as Jean Trudel suggested?[4] Or did he decide

Fig. 165A.
James Pattison Cockburn,
Quebec from Point a Pizeau, c. 1830;
Sepia over graphite on paper, 39.9 × 55.1 cm.
Musée du Séminaire de Québec (Pf 986.59).

Fig. 165B.
Joseph Légaré,
*The Martyrdom of Fathers Brébeuf and
Lalemant.*
Photograph of the painting taken
under infrared light.

Fig. 165C.
C. Hunt after James Pattison Cockburn,
*Cape Diamond and Wolfe's Cove
from Point a Pizeau*, 1833;
aquatint, 52 × 71 cm (plate size).
Musée du Québec, Quebec City (66.165.01).

to create an historical pendant to the commemorative work on his own initiative in view of the priests' favourable response to his first painting? While a number of hypotheses are possible, none can be confirmed. One thing is certain, however; like *Quebec Viewed from Pointe Lévis* (Cat. 162), this landscape is one of Légaré's most successful works. He was obviously careful not to disappoint his clients, perhaps because of the prestigious nature of the commission or because the work might be sold. Lacking confidence in his own creative abilities, he again had recourse to models he admired.

We will briefly discuss the central group of figures. It is well known that they were copied from an engraving by Grégoire Huret, *The Martyrdom of the Jesuits Fathers*.[5] This engraving depicts the death of 10 martyrs, each of whom is identified by a number. Légaré borrowed the figures in the middle ground: Jean de Brébeuf (No. 6) on the right, killed by the Iroquois in 1649; and Gabriel Lalemant (No. 7), killed the same year and depicted with his hands tied to a stake. He copied the figures quite carefully and accurately, only innovating by adding a feather in the Iroquois' headbands.

Based on imitation and borrowing, **The Martyrdom of Fathers Brébeuf and Lalemant** is certainly one of Légaré's most complicated works from the viewpoint of design. The essential elements of the landscape were inspired by a sepia drawing by James Pattison Cockburn, *Quebec from Point a Pizeau* (Fig. 165A), which was part

of Légaré's own collection.[6] It should be mentioned that even if Légaré painted this work for a commission, the conditions set by his client must not have been very restrictive since he took tremendous liberties with the story: Brébeuf and Lalemant were martyred in Huronia, which is now the Midland area, in Ontario. Légaré retained the general organization of his model, that is, a central vista overlooking Quebec City in the distance. He borrowed the most picturesque motifs from Cockburn's sepia drawing: the broken tree and the tree with the scrubby branches on the left. As for the right side of the painting, it seems to have been taken from another source. An infrared photograph (Fig. 165B) of Légaré's work reveals an important change to the initial composition. The original motif, still visible to the naked eye, seems to have been taken from an engraving by C. Hunt after Cockburn's drawing, *Cape Diamond and Wolfe's Cove from Point a Pizeau* (Fig. 165C), in which two trees frame the right-hand side of the composition. Légaré also borrowed the clearing and the pattern of light in the foreground from Hunt's engraving. He may have originally intended to make the composition more open by leaning the trees toward the edge of the painting. However, realizing that this would upset the balance of his composition, he ultimately had to rework this section by adding other elements.

Like *The Despair of an Indian Woman* (Cat. 167), **The Martyrdom of Fathers Brébeuf and Lalemant** represents

the final version of an idea that might almost be qualified as complex. In both works, the various elements setting the scene of activity have been chosen with great care. It might be logical to think, therefore, that these works were the outcome of a fairly long reflective process. Let us consider, in particular, the link between Légaré's oil sketches and large landscape paintings. Some of his oils on paper (Cat. 163 and 164) are works in their own right and differ from the finished paintings only in the support they were painted on. Others, however, such as *The Engagement of an Indian Girl* (167B), are clearly no more than preparatory sketches. **The Martyrdom of Fathers Brébeuf and Lalemant** makes it possible, however, to pose the problem from a different perspective. A small sketch in the Musée du Séminaire de Québec, *Landscape* (Fig. 165D), definitely served as a model for this painting. The tree on the bow-shaped rock and another mound of rock to the right were taken from this sketch and included in the left foreground of the painting in Ottawa. The interplay of light and shadow, the mountains in the distance, and the two dead trees leaning to the right are also echoed in the historical landscape. In light of these similarities, it might be asked whether this sketch should be considered a preparatory work for the composition of **The Martyrdom of Fathers Brébeuf and Lalemant.** We would certainly like to think so since it would provide unique proof that Légaré worked out a final painting by gradually developing a

Fig. 165D.
Joseph Légaré,
Landscape, c. 1841-1842;
oil on paper, 26 × 45.6 cm.
Musée du Séminaire de Québec (Pc983.38).

Fig. 165E.
Unidentified artist,
Gust of Wind;
oil on canvas, 71.7 × 92.5 cm.
Musée du Séminaire de Québec (Pe988.1).

preliminary idea and borrowing motifs and stylistic devices in the process. Unfortunately, however, we must adopt a more cautious approach. This *Landscape* was probably no more than a reference sketch or a work that, for some unknown reason, Légaré had left unfinished and remembered a few years later. He then reused the left-hand side of the drawing, rearranging certain elements. In addition, by borrowing elements from Cockburn and from a painting attributed to Andrea Locatelli (1695-1741),[7] he embellished the desert landscape so as to make it less forbidding.

Up to the end of his career, Légaré referred to his collection of European paintings in executing major works. For example, the facture of **The Martyrdom of Fathers Brébeuf and Lalemant** imitates that of the painting *Gust of Wind* (Fig. 165E), attributed by Légaré to Andrea Locatelli. The influence of the Italian model is evident in the way that Légaré has drawn the branches against the light. Although the foliage in his work is more open and less luxuriant, allowing the light to filter through, the long, heavy brush strokes on the oblong leaves have been derived from *Gust of Wind*. Compared to other works by Légaré, the colours is this painting are unique; the artist has tried to appropriate the palette of an Italian landscape artist from the 18th century. He has chosen a decorative approach in which the calm blue of the sky contrasts with the lime green foliage and copper-coloured carnations. Similarly, the dark, crowded foreground is very different from the open

background, which is shrouded in a more lyrical atmosphere. As Jean Trudel pointed out in 1978, the juxtaposition of this atmosphere with the tragic nature of the subject matter is somewhat surprising: "this contrast between the beauty and serenity of the landscape and the violence of the Jesuits' suffering was intentional on Légaré's part: it creates a balance that makes the main subject of the painting endurable."[8] The artist was obviously acting deliberately for, in other paintings, such as *The Despair of an Indian Woman* (Cat. 167) and the series of works on fires in Quebec City (Cat 168), he created the opposite effect by accentuating the dramatic nature of his subject matter. However, should this be considered a decision based merely on esthetics? By situating the action in an almost idyllic setting, the artist above all transcended the particular event—the torture of the two Jesuit missionaries—in order to emphasize their heroism in the face of death. Légaré is known to have been familiar with religious iconography, owing to the many copies he made during the earlier years of his career. Perhaps the pure blue of the sky in this work, which is unique in Légaré's landscapes as a whole, should be seen as a symbol of the martyrs' detachment from earthly values.

D.P.

Notes

1. *PORTER 1978/1*, p. 73 and *PORTER 1981*, pp. 259-260.

2. For a reproduction of Légaré's painting *Memorials of the Jesuits of New France,* see *PORTER 1978/1*, pp. 71-73, No. 52 (Repr.).

3. *PORTER 1978/1*, p. 71 and *PORTER 1981*, pp. 259-260.

4. *PORTER 1978/1*, p. 73.

5. For a reproduction of this work, see *PORTER 1978/1*, p. 75, Fig. 53a. For a recent study of the theme of martyred Canadian saints, see *MARTIN 1988*, pp. 29-35.

6. The influence of James Pattison Cockburn on Joseph Légaré is particularly complex. Légaré seems to have studied Cockburn's work regularly, not only making literal copies but also borrowing certain elements and imitating technique and style.

7. This landscape cannot be identified in the artist's collection until 1852, when it was listed as No. 128 in *CATALOGUE 1852* under the heading "Landscape, by... Andrea Lucatelli." It is not known when Légaré added it to his collection. However, it is tempting to see a connection between this event and the appearance of an item (No. 5) in the sale announced by Joseph Cary in the *Quebec Mercury* on July 3, 1821: "italian landscape by Locatelli." Whatever the case may be, the attribution of this work to Locatelli has been rejected by Maria-Maddalena Mosco in "Les trois manières d'Andrea Locatelli," *Revue de l'art*, No. 7 (1970), p. 39, and by Andrea Busiri-Vici in *Andrea Locatelli e il paesaggio del Settecento* (Rome: Ugo Bozzi Editore, 1976), p. 439.

8. *PORTER 1978/1*, p. 73.

166. (See colour reproduction, p. 92)
Josephte Ourné, c. 1844
Oil on canvas, 131.2 × 95.5 cm

Inscription
(b.,u.c., before the new backing covered the inscription) *Josephte Ourné* [...] *agée de* [...]/*fille d'un Chef Sauvage d'Ocnawaga.*

Provenance
Séminaire de Québec, from the Joseph Légaré estate, 1874; antiquaire Jean Gilbert, Quebec City, 1958; Bernard Desroches, Montreal; acquired by the National Gallery of Canada, Ottawa, 1975.

Exhibitions
Toronto 1907, No. 31; Ottawa 1978-1979/1, No. 56; Berlin 1982-1983, No. 4.

Bibliography
Le Castor, June 4, 1844, p. 3 (repeated June 13, July 9, 25 and 30, August 1st and 6, September 19, 24 and 26, and October 9 and 17, 1844); *Quebec Mercury,* October 5, 1848, p. 3, No. 6; *Le Canadien,* October 2, 1848, p. 3, No. 6; *L'Ami de la Religion et de la Patrie,* October 4, 1848, p. 655, No. 6; *Le Journal de Québec,* October 5, 1848, p. 3, No. 6; ASQ, *Séminaire 12,* No. 41, 1874, p. 5, No. 179; *Peintures du Séminaire 1874-1875,* p. 4; *Lemoine 1876,* p. 367, No. 152; *Laval University 1880,* p. 7, No. 126; *Université Laval 1883-1884,* p. 19, No. 126; *Laval University 1883-1884,* p. 19, No. 126; *Université Laval 1887,* p. 19, No. 126; *Laval University 1887,* p. 19, No. 126; *Université Laval 1889,* p. 19, No. 126; *Université Laval 1893,* p. 19, No. 126; *Laval University 1894,* p. 19, No. 126; *Université Laval 1898,* p. 21, No. 126; *Laval University 1901,* p. 21, No. 126; *Gallery 1902,* p. 14, No. 6; *Université Laval 1903,* p. 27, No. 6; *Laval University 1905,* p. 27, No. 6; *Université Laval 1906,* p. 36, No. 6; *Canadian National Exhibition 1907,* p. 11, No. 31; *Carter 1908,* p. 87, No. 156; *Laval University 1909,* p. 38, No. 156; *Université Laval 1913,* p. 63, No. 364; *Laval University 1923,* p. 73, No. 364; *Bellerive 1925,* p. 16; *Université Laval 1933,* p. 82, No. 256; *Morisset 1935/9,* p. 2; *Morisset 1936-1937,* Vol. II, p. 76; *Colgate 1943,* p. 109; *Morisset 1960/ 1,* p. 98; *Tremblay 1972,* p. 196; *Nelson 1975,* p. 22; *La Presse,* December 30, 1975, p. A-11 (Repr.); *The Gazette,* January 3, 1976, p. 13 (Repr.); *Le Nouvelliste,* January 5, 1976, p. 18 (Repr.); *Galerie nationale 1976,* p. 97 (Repr.); *Godsell 1976,* p. 45, 46 and 49 (Repr.); *Porter 1978/1,* pp. 75-76, No. 56 (entry by Jean Trudel) (Repr.); *Porter 1978/2,* pp. 1, 2 and 7 (Repr.); *Robert 1978,* pp. 24 and 25 (Repr.); *The Legacy 1978,* p. 11 (Repr.); *Toupin 1978,* p. D-1 (Repr.); *L'Information médicale et paramédicale,* January 16, 1979, p. 30; *Toupin 1979,* p. E-19; *Viau 1979,* p. 25 (Repr.); *Nixon 1979,* p. 16; *Lehmann 1979,* p. D-4 (Repr.); *Murray 1979,* p. 94; *Vézina 1979,* p. 45; *Samuel 1980,* p. 186 (Repr.); *Gagnon 1980,* pp. 43 and 44; *Lacroix 1982,* pp. 36 and 124, No. 4; *Porter 1987/2,* p. 1088 (Repr.); *Gagnon and Lacasse 1989,* pp. 74, 76-77 and 79 (Repr.).

Collection
National Gallery of Canada, Ottawa (18309)

J EAN TRUDEL wrote the following eloquent description of *Josephte Ourné,* a fascinating portrait that raises a number of questions:

Standing before a background of dense and sombre forest, Josephte Ourné holds a fishing rod in her left hand, on the line of which two trout are hooked, and in her right hand a bird. The painter originally had her hold a catfish in her right hand, but for some reason changed the fish to a bird. With feathers in her hair, Josephte Ourné is adorned in all her finery, with her flower-embroidered dress, her necklace, her earrings, and her silver *couette.* She thus displays pieces of jewellery that the fur traders exchanged with the Indians.

More than a portrait of an Indian, unique in Légaré's work, it was perhaps his own notion of the Indian that he had wished to convey in this painting. While the proud and fine figure standing before her forest is tinged with ro-

manticism, the attributes with which she is adorned relate directly to fishing, hunting, and trade with the White man. (*Translation*)

The first question raised by this portrait is the identity of the person portrayed. Despite considerable research, we still do not know who this 25-year-old woman is; historical documents refer to her as "the daughter of an Indian chief." (*Translation*) The identity of her father also remains a mystery: was he Abenaki, as some old catalogues indicate, or a Mohawk from Caughnawaga, as suggested by a plausible interpretation of an inscription on the back of the work?[1]

It is also difficult to fully appreciate some of the painting's stylistic features owing to the major restoration work done in 1972-1973 to repair severe previous

damage. The subject matter in the top left corner had almost disappeared, perhaps in a fire. Analysis of the painting under ultraviolet light (Fig. 166A) revealed that the background had been almost totally obliterated while the figure had been retouched on several occasions.

Under these circumstances, it seems rather hard to compare this nonetheless exceptional work with various other more conventional portraits associated, rightly or wrongly, with Légaré. The question of whether he should really be considered a portraitist is not unusual in itself. Lacking reliable points of reference such as signed canvases, we must fall back on the logical assumption that portraits of family members and very close friends can probably be attributed to him: in particular, those of his sister Marie-Louise and brother-in-

Fig. 166A.
Joseph Légaré,
Josephte Ourné.
Photograph of the painting taken under
ultraviolet flourescence

Fig. 166B.
Joseph Légaré (attr. to),
Charles Jourdain;
oil on canvas, 68.5 × 58.5 cm.
Musée du Québec, Quebec City (80.08).

law Charles-Maxime De Foy, and of master mason Charles Jourdain (Cat. 166B), all of which are in the Musée du Québec collection. However, owing to the diligent, laborious way in which these portraits were painted, they contrast sharply with a work believed to be Légaré's self-portrait. In fact, it would probably be more wise to associate the latter work with the portraits of *John Neilson* (Cat. 53), *Joseph Rémi Vallières de Saint-Réal* (Fig. 53B) or *Hector-Simon Huot*, attributed to Louis-Hubert Triaud. In short, with certain exceptions, Légaré never made a career as a portraitist. In fact, his most remarkable portraits were copies of paintings by other artists (George IV, Cat. 160).

Historical documents must be consulted to attribute *Josephte Ourné* to Légaré. They reveal that "the portrait of an Indian chief's daughter" (*Translation*) was put up for sale in the notary Archibald Campbell's office (Cat. 125) on Rue Saint-Paul from June 4 to October 17, 1844. The titles of the other paintings in the sale indicate that they belonged to Légaré's personal collection or were works that he himself had painted (e.g. the full-length portrait of Queen Victoria). The docu-

ments also reveal that a painting entitled *An Indian Woman* was one of the 31 canvases Légaré exhibited in the House of Assembly in 1848. It should be noted that the hairstyle, clothing and ornaments of Josephte Ourné bear a definite resemblance to those of the female figure in the painting *The Engagement of an Indian Girl,* which the artist executed in 1844.[2]

Another important question remains to be answered: that of how to interpret Légaré's portrait, which was and still is an exceptional work. Jean Trudel suggested that it illustrates the artist's notion of the Indian. François-Marc Gagnon is more inclined to interpret it as the female counterpart of *Zacharie Vincent* painted by Plamondon in 1838 (Cat. 194), with the difference, however, that Légaré used his subject to express defiance rather than resignation. Of course, it is also possible that Légaré's interest in the past prompted him to paint, as Théophile Hamel did several years later (Cat. 131), the handsome profile of an Amerindian from New France.[3]

It should also be recalled, however, that Légaré's perception of Amerindians, like that of his contemporaries, was basi-

cally ambivalent. In depicting Amerindian customs, he was sometimes inspired by the romantic European notion of the "noble savage" and sometimes by the typically American notion of the "barbaric savage." As for his attitude toward the survivors of "the once large and powerful tribes of the Six Nations," (*Translation*) it was probably one of curiosity. Like Thielcke, Krieghoff, Somerville (Cat. 217) and many other artists, Légaré was no doubt attracted by the picturesque lifestyle, traditional activities and "primitive coquetry" of these Amerindians who, year after year, persisted in living on the fringe of the White man's civilization.

J.R.P

Notes

1. This interpretation is based on a partial transcript made when the painting was remounted.
2. *Porter 1978/1*, pp. 76-78, No. 57.
3. This hypothesis is contradicted to an extent by the presence of silver trade; it should be mentioned, however, that Légaré committed a number of anachronisms in his history paintings.

167.

The Despair of an Indian Woman, 1844-1848

Oil on canvas, 134.6 × 178.8 cm

Provenance

Séminaire de Québec, from the Joseph Légaré estate, 1874; antiquaire Jean Gilbert, Quebec City, 1958; Brigitte Gilbert, Quebec City; acquired by the Musée du Québec, Quebec City, 1965.

Exhibitions

Quebec City 1848; Quebec City 1967, No. 37; Ottawa 1978-1979/1, No. 59; Quebec City 1983-1984, No. 69.

Bibliography

The Quebec Spectator, October 6, 1848, p. 2; *Le Canadien*, October 13, 1848, p. 2; ASQ, *Séminaire 12*, No. 41, 1874, Fol. 3, No. 98; *Université Laval 1874-1875*, Fol. 1, No. 3; *Peintures du Séminaire 1874-1875*, p. 2, No. 3; *Annuaire 1875*, p. 56, No. 3; *Galerie 1875*, p. 91; *Lemoine 1876*, p. 363, No. 3; *Laval University 1880*, p. 5, No. 4; *Université Laval 1883-1884*, p. 13, No. 44; *Laval University 1883-1884*, p. 13, No. 44; *Université Laval 1887*, p. 13, No. 44; *Laval University 1887*, p. 13, No. 44; *Université Laval 1889*, p. 13, No. 44; *Université Laval 1893*, p. 13, No. 44; *Laval University 1894*, p. 13, No. 44; *Université Laval 1898*, p. 15, No. 44; *Laval University 1901*, p. 15, No. 44; *Gallery 1902*, p. 14, No. 7; *Université Laval 1903*, p. 27, No. 7; *Laval University 1905*, p. 28, No. 7; *Université Laval 1906*, p. 36, No. 7; *Carter 1908*, p. 87, No. 157; *Laval University 1909*, p. 37, No. 157; *Université Laval 1913*, p. 63, No. 363; *Laval University 1923*, p. 73, No. 363; *Bellerive 1925*, p. 16; *Université Laval 1933*, p. 82, No. 255; *Colgate 1943*, p. 109; *Morisset 1960/1*, p. 98; *Hubbard 1963*, p. 56; *Trudel, Juneau and Massey 1967*, pp. 72-73, No. 37 (Repr.); *Ostiguy 1970*, p. 106; *Tremblay 1972*, pp. 39-41 and 196; *Derome and Leclerc 1978*, p. 8, No. 59; *Porter 1978/1*, pp. 17, 75, 78, 79-80 and 81, No. 59 (entry by Jean Trudel) (Repr.); *Porter 1978/2*, p. 7; *Lehman 1979*, p. D-4; *Viau 1979*, p. 25; *Gagnon 1980*, pp. 43-44; *Légaré 1980*, p. 14 (Repr.); *Porter 1981*, pp. 16, 234, 241-242, 245-246, 254-255 and 385; *Levenson 1983*, pp. 33, 34 and 36; *Comeau 1983*, p. 160; *Le Musée du Québec 1983*, p. 72, No. 69 (entry by Claude Thibault, Luc Noppen and Michel Doyon) (Repr.); *Béland and Prioul 1988*, p. 85; *Béland 1989/2*, p. 75; *Béland and Bourassa 1990*, pp. 6, 7, 9 and 92 (Repr.).

Collection

Musée du Québec, Quebec City (65.90)

T HE INSPIRATION for this painting and its pendant, *The Engagement of an Indian Girl* (Fig. 167A) in the Wellington County Museum in Fergus, was drawn from a story written by Pierre Boitard (1789-1859) and published by Napoléon Aubin under the title "Kosato, le Pied Noir, Fragment d'une histoire à faire" in the *Mélanges Littéraires* section of the Quebec City newspaper *Le Castor*.[1]

The history of these two paintings is fairly complex. According to an anonymous article published by Napoléon Aubin in *Le Castor* on April 18, 1844, they were purchased by the notary Archibald Campbell (Cat. 126) even before they were finished. A few years later, in 1848, two paintings depicting the same subjects as the works acquired by Campbell were in Légaré's possession and exhibited in the House of Assembly in Quebec City; they were not for sale, however.[2] Légaré still owned a version of each of these works at the time of his death.[3] Two hypotheses may be advanced to unravel this imbroglio. First, in view of the enthusiastic response to the two paintings purchased by his friend the notary, Légaré may have made replicas. Or second, for some unknown reason, Légaré may have resumed possession of Campbell's paintings. Upon further analysis, the first hypothesis would seem more correct.

Although Légaré did not paint a specific scene from "Kosato, le Pied Noir," he nevertheless drew inspiration from this story, published between March 28 and April 11, 1844. Less than a month, or precisely 20 days, later, the same newspaper, *Le Castor,* announced that Campbell had purchased the paintings; it also specified that "those who wish to see these

Fig. 167A.
Joseph Légaré,
The Engagement of an Indian Girl, 1844-1848;
oil on canvas, 120 × 158 cm.
Wellington County Museum, Fergus (Ontario).

Fig. 167B.
Joseph Légaré,
The Engagement of an Indian Girl, 1844;
oil on paper, 15.2 × 18.8 cm.
National Gallery of Canada, Ottawa (23397).

Fig. 167C.
Joseph Légaré,
*Biblical Scene in a Landscape
with an Ancient Ark,* 1842-1843;
oil on canvas, 72 × 92 cm.
Musée du Québec, Quebec City (87.163).

pictures should hurry since they will be delivered very shortly." (*Translation*) Although the works were unfinished, they must have been sufficiently well advanced to elicit such a warm response from art enthusiasts. Even though it is not known whether Légaré worked quickly or not, it is unlikely that he would have painted such large pictures in such a short time. Had he actually painted these works in 1844, they would have to have been smaller.

Even if we suppose that Campbell refused the two paintings at the last minute, why did Légaré wait until 1848 to show them to the public? They were not included in the works put up for sale by the artist on June 4, 1844, in the premises placed at his disposal by Archibald Campbell.[4] Given the enthusiastic response to these paintings, Légaré would only have benefited from including them in the sale, which offered the public a unique opportunity to appreciate these works. This argument is even more convincing when we consider that the artist tried to sell one of his two copies of the portrait of Queen Victoria at the exhibition, although without much success.[5] Finally, given that these two landscapes were considered major works, it is hard to understand why, if Légaré had painted them in 1844, they were not exhibited on May 6, 1845 in his joint show with Antoine Plamondon and Jean-Baptiste Roy Audy at the Mechanic's Institute of Quebec.[6] The most plausible explanation seems to be that the two paintings had, in fact, been purchased by Archibald Campbell in 1844 and that Légaré made replicas of them at a later date; the artist often worked this way. It is these replicas, then, that were shown for the first time in 1848 and that later remained in Légaré's collec-

tion. Moreover, it is these replicas that we know today. The hypothesis that the much smaller *modello* of *The Engagement,* an oil-on-paper sketch (Fig. 167B), was one of the Campbell pendants should also be dismissed. The fact that a painting on this subject was mentioned in the newspaper in 1844 does not provide definite proof. Art terms were often used incorrectly at the time, and it was not common for an oil sketch to be called a painting. It is unlikely, however, that the notary Campbell, a patron of the arts and a collector, would have made this kind of mistake. He is said to have valued the two paintings very highly even before they were finished. In our opinion, it is unlikely that he would have considered this small sketch, which according to contemporary esthetic criteria was a hasty and "negligent" piece, as a "future monument to the first works of the Canadian school." (*Translation*)

If these arguments are valid, the two paintings shown here, *The Engagement of an Indian Girl* (Fig. 167A) and **The Despair of an Indian Woman** (Fig. 167), correspond to the replicas Légaré painted of Campbell's purchases between 1844 and 1848. The other work (Fig. 167B) is a preparatory sketch that he did for *The Engagement.* Consequently, we still have to locate the oil-on-paper *modello* for **The Despair,** if it ever existed, and the two original Campbell pendants painted in 1844.

Despite the problems related to the history of these works, they are important with regard to both their subject matter and style. An article published on April 18, 1844 reveals the scene on which they were based: "anyone planning to go and see Mr. Légaré's painting should first read

the fine scene in which Kitchy sings a funeral chant beside the bloodstained body of her husband." (*Translation*) This scene was published in the April 9 edition of *Le Castor.* Légaré illustrated the moment where Kosato took shelter at Kitchy's side after scalping an enemy:

He returned to the trench in the camp. However, at that very moment, a bullet pierced his forehead and he fell into the pit […] Kitchy, who was sitting at the bottom of the trench, laid her husband's head on her knees, washing his wounds with her tears and wiping the blood with her long hair. (*Translation*)

A brief examination of the painting immediately reveals that Légaré did not reproduce this pathetic scene with absolute faithfulness. Basically, he recreated the general setting, beginning with the teepee "hidden in a dense thicket of willow trees." (*Translation*) The large mound of rock served the same purpose. It appeared at the beginning of the story, when Boitard described the region through which he was travelling: "there is an unusual rock that stands as straight as a lighthouse and that travellers call the Chimney." (*Translation*) The rock and the teepee, however, are only a few of the main elements around which Légaré organized his composition; he also drew inspiration from various paintings in his collection.

The composition of the final version of *The Engagement* (Fig. 167A) is similar to that of the preparatory sketch (Fig. 167B). Initially, Légaré borrowed elements from a religious painting of his own composition,[7] *Biblical Scene in a Landscape with an Ancient Ark* (Fig. 167C), painted around 1842-1843. He completely transformed the arch in the sketch for *The Engagement:* its vault was replaced by foliage

Fig. 167D.
Joseph Légaré,
Tree and Castle, c. 1838;
oil on paper, 59 × 46.7 cm.
Musée du Séminaire de Québec (Pc983.68).

and was framed by two vistas, while its left pillar was replaced by three large tree trunks. The right pillar, decorated with a bas relief, and the coffered ceiling, decorated with religious scenes, became a column of rock, trees and a leafy bower. The open space on the right and, especially, the trees behind the pillar are echoed in both works. The link between them is further confirmed by what might seem to be an insignificant detail: in both the sketch and the painting, a dead branch in the top right corner droops toward a dead tree. The organization of the foreground in *The Engagement* also suggests that this work was derived from Légaré's *Biblical Scene*. The version on canvas in the Fergus museum (Fig. 167A) follows the paper sketch fairly closely, with a few minor variations. Légaré enlarged the column of rock behind the teepees and made the foliage less dense so as to provide the viewer with a glimpse of the radiant light outside the wooded oasis. He more or less repeated this structure in *The Despair of an Indian Woman*. The two large trees on the right and in the left middle ground are merely borrowings from previous sketches. Once again, Légaré copied the tree from the small sketch *Paysage* (Fig. 165D), previously used in *The Martyrdom of Fathers Brébeuf and Lalemant* (Cat. 165). The birch tree framing the composition on the

left was borrowed from a major tree study (Fig. 167D) painted around 1838.

The question of the source of the figures was resolved only recently. Although it was commonly agreed that they had been borrowed from another work, it was impossible to identify which one. In 1988, the Musée du Québec acquired a painting *The Brazen Serpent*[8] (Fig, 167E), attributed at the time to Gérard de Lairesse (1640-1711). Although it had previously belonged to Justice Jonathan Sewell, the work disappeared after Sewell's death in 1839. Owing to his special relationship with the Sewell family, Légaré may have had access to the painting in 1844. Whatever the case, he borrowed the figure in the left foreground for Kitchy in *The Engagement* and two figures from the central group for *The Despair of an Indian Woman*. He also drew inspiration, for the latter work, from the highly contrasted light in the European model. To eliminate any confusion, it should also be mentioned that, in our opinion, Légaré could not possibly have borrowed the idea for the central column of rock from *The Brazen Serpent*. When he first defined the main elements of his composition in the sketch for *The Engagement*, he does not seem to have had the European painting in mind, since the two figures bear no relationship to those in this latter work. Based on his usual working method, it is more likely that Légaré defined his composition before looking for suitable models that would fit in with his subject matter. A difficult question remains unsettled: namely, what prompted Légaré to paint these scenes in particular. Obviously, they do not correspond to simple illustrations such as *Lost in the Wood* (Cat. 190) or *The Little Savoyards* (Cat. 199) by Plamondon. An article by Napoléon Aubin on *The Engagement* and *The Despair of an Indian Woman* in *Le Castor*, seems to herald a new, although short-lived, approach to Légaré's work. In alluding to the artist's creative ability, it mentions a quality that was rarely discussed:

An artist from this city has traced in no less eloquent characters two scenes taken from the life of savages and which depict both its sweet ease and terrifying energy [...] As an *objet d'art* and a philosophical painting of the customs of those nations which peopled the land of America before the Europeans arrived, the second painting [*The Despair of an Indian Woman*] offers a terrifying contrast to the previous work [...] Through sheer talent and imagination, the painter has used the same subject to portray a scene as beautiful and touching as that described by the author, yet even more painful and poignant and therefore more lasting. (*Translation*)

Fig. 167E.
Unidentified artist,
The Brazen Serpent;
oil on canvas, 63.8 × 49.3 cm.
Musée du Québec, Quebec City (88.09).

To our knowledge, this is the first time that Légaré's paintings were discussed without merely referring to their "truth to life." Consequently, based on what we know about his other works, we hesitate to affirm that Légaré was responsible for the philosophical content of these two paintings.

D.P.

Notes

1. This story was published in five issues: March 28, April 2, 4, 9 and 11, 1844, pp. 1-2. The name of the author, Boitard, appeared in the last issue.

2. *The Quebec Spectator*, October 6, 1848, p. 2.

3. The inventory of the estate of Légaré's widow, drawn up in 1874, lists these two paintings (Fol. 12v and Fol. 13r).

4. *Le Castor*, June 4, 1844, p. 3

5. For further reading on the Queen Victoria portraits, see Porter 1978/1, pp. 59-61 and 136, Nos. 40 and 199. These two paintings are now in the collections of the Musée du Séminaire de Québec.

6. *Quebec Mercury*, May 1, 1845, p. 3 and May 6, 1845, p. 2.

7. This painting was acquired by the Musée du Québec in 1988. See Béland and Prioul 1988, p. 85.

8. This work is no longer attributed to Gérard de Lairesse. See Béland 1989/2, p. 75.

168.
Fire in the Saint-Jean Quarter, Quebec, Seen looking Westward, 1845-1848
Oil on canvas, 82 × 111 cm

Provenance
Séminaire de Québec, from the Joseph Légaré estate, 1874; antiquaire Jean Gilbert, Quebec City, 1958; acquired by the Musée de la Province de Québec, Quebec City, 1958.

Exhibitions
Montreal 1848; Quebec City 1848; Quebec City 1967, No. 38; Toronto 1971, No. 7; Ottawa 1978-1979/1, No. 72; Quebec City 1983-1984, No. 70.

Bibliography
L'Avenir, September 6, 1848, p. 3; *La Minerve,* September 7, 1848; *L'Ami de la Religion et de la Patrie,* September 8, 1848, p. 566; *The Quebec Spectator,* October 6, 1848, p. 2; *Le Journal de Québec,* October 10, 1848, p. 2; ANQQ, Notarial Records of J.-B. Delâge, December 6, 1872, No. 2921; ASQ, *Séminaire 12,* No. 41, 1874; *Peintures du Séminaire 1874-1875,* p. 1; *Lemoine 1876,* p. 362; *Laval University 1880,* p. 11, No. 2; *Université Laval 1883-1884,* p. 30, No. 2; *Laval University 1883-1884,* p. 30, No. 2; *Université Laval 1887,* p. 30, No. 2; *Laval University 1887,* p. 30, No. 2; *Université Laval 1889,* p. 30, No. 2; *Université Laval 1893,* p. 30, No. 2; *Université Laval 1906,* p. 11, No. 7; *Bellerive 1925,* p. 15; *Colgate 1943,* p. 108; *Morisset 1960/1,* p. 100; *Trudel, Juneau and Massey 1967,* pp. 74-75, No. 38 (Repr.); *Cauchon 1968,* pp. 1-4 (Repr.); *Lessard and Marquis 1971,* pp. 462 and 464 (Repr.); *Giroux 1972,* p. 3; *Tremblay 1972,* pp. 159-161; *Reid 1973,* pp. 48a and 49 (Repr.); *Lord 1974,* pp. 51-52; *Porter 1978/1,* pp. 16, 88, 92-93 and 94 (entry by Jean Trudel) (Repr.); *Robert 1978,* p. 25 (Repr.); *Noppen, Paulette and Tremblay 1979,* p. 325 (Repr.); *Nos racines,* No. 80 (1979), p. 1585 (Repr.); *Légaré 1980,* p. front. (Repr.); *Porter 1981,* pp. 244-246, 272-274 and 454-455; *Art du Québec 1982,* p. 48 (Repr.); *Le Musée du Québec 1983,* p. 73, No. 70 (entry by Claude Thibault, Luc Noppen and Michel Doyon) (Repr.); *Huard 1986/2,* p. 32 (Repr.); *Jean and Lebel 1987,* p. 23 (Repr.); *Béland and Bourassa 1990,* pp. 7, 9 and 88 (Repr.); *Musée 1990,* p. 239; *Nadeau 1991,* p. 16 (Repr.).

Collection
Musée du Québec, Quebec City. Restored in 1991, with the assistance of the Amis du Musée du Québec (58.470)

L IKE THE TERRIBLE CHOLERA epidemics of 1832 (Cat. 158) and 1834, the major fires of 1845 were one of the worst catastrophes to afflict Quebec City in the first half of the 19th century. While the epidemics were costly in terms of human life, the fires were disastrous from a material viewpoint since two-thirds of the city was destroyed. The first fire, on May 28, in the Saint-Roch quarter destroyed 1650 houses, leaving some 12 000 people homeless and around 20 dead. One month later, on June 28, the Saint-Jean quarter was in turn destroyed by fire. This time 1 315 houses were lost, while 10 000 people were thrown onto the street. This was the case of Joseph Légaré's brother-in-law, the notary Michel Tessier, in whose house the fire had started. The artist himself lost a house that he rented out, while his former apprentice, Antoine Plamondon, who lived at 90, Rue Richelieu, declared himself ruined after all his personal belongings were destroyed.[1]

Since the two consecutive fires of May and June 1845 had thrown the city into a state of confusion, a general relief committee for fire victims was rapidly set up. This committee was responsible for seeking financial assistance from Quebec merchants and residents as well as from England and the United States. From 1845 to 1847, Légaré took part in around 30 committee meetings and promoted fundraising activities for fire victims, including a diorama exhibition for which he and Plamondon expressed great enthusiasm.

Once again, Légaré's social concerns were tangibly reflected in his artistic work. His series of panoramic views of the Saint-Roch and Saint-Jean fires are definitely some of his best works.[2] As in the case of the Saint-Roch fires, he painted two complementary views of the fires in Saint-Jean. While the east view shows the ruins left by the blaze, the west view depicts the fire at its height, thereby echoing a description that appeared in the *Quebec Mercury* on July 12, 1845:

During the height of the fire, the scene was awfully grand. An area of about half a mile was at one time in flames, the lucid volume precluding any view beyond. As the several buildings fell, a shower of bright sparks shot up into the air, and were carried onward in their career of devastation. At day break, the scene was truly magnificent to an uninterested spectator. The whole horizon was illuminated, the valley of the St. Charles was as distinct to the view as at mid-day, and the meandering river of that name reflected an unearthly light. Ever and anon, as the flames shot upwards, might be seen crowds of people congregated on the heights in rear of St. John's suburb, on the

Fig. 168A.
Joseph Légaré,
Fire in the Saint-Jean Quarter, seen looking westward
(partial reproduction);
oil on paper.
Private collection, Quebec City.

Fig. 168B.
Unidentified artist, (?)Europe, 18th century,
Fire Scene in a Fortified City;
oil on cardboard, 13.7 × 18.6 cm.
Séminaire de Nicolet (Ta-67).

glacis adjoining the city wall, and on the ramparts themselves. The thoroughfares were impeded by the refugees. Every species of vehicle was in requisition for the transport of goods. The hoarse cry of the firemen and soldiery mingled with the despairing wail of the sufferers: such a scene of despair has seldom been witnessed.

Légaré painted *Fire in the Saint-Jean Quarter, Quebec, Seen Looking Westward* from the vantage point of the ramparts near St. John's Gate. Despite its very strong horizontal registers and the importance of its central axis, the painting is very animated. Twisted columns of fire and smoke spewing sparks into the night sky tower above the sinister rows of burning houses, whose profiles change with the different alignments of Saint-Joachim, Saint-Jean and D'Aiguillon streets. In the foreground, the artist has depicted a large crowd of fire victims in the passageway leading to St. John's Gate. The passageway is aligned with the vanishing point formed by Rue Saint-Jean, where a few valiant firefighters are still trying to contain the blaze. The slightly curved diagonal of the passageway breaks up the somewhat symmetrical plan of the composition. Its entrance is guarded by a detachment of soldiers standing between the large retaining walls that surround the gentle, grass-covered slopes of the glacis. Dotted with soldiers ensuring that no one approaches the burning buildings, the glacis is high-

lighted in the foreground by the irregular string of personal belongings that vigilant survivors have managed to rescue from the flames. Finally, the striking appearance of the painting can be attributed to a simple, yet effective, colour scheme in which fiery reds are set off by deep greens.

Without doubt, *Fire in the Saint-Jean Quarter, Quebec, Seen Looking Westward* is one of the most perfect compositions in the series of pictures Légaré painted on the fires in Quebec City. The artist must have been aware of this since he produced three different versions of the composition. In addition to the painting just discussed, he executed a larger, more accurate, but less spontaneous work, which belongs to the Art Gallery of Ontario, and another very small, preliminary oil-on-paper sketch that he gave to the wife of his friend Joseph-Ulric Tessier around 1850 to adorn an album (Fig. 168A).[3]

However, in addition to the fact that Légaré's composition has undeniable qualities, it may well be related in some way, like several of his other works, to earlier pictorial sources. Two small oil-on-cardboard paintings of fire scenes in a European fortified town have recently come to light in the Séminaire de Nicolet. These anonymous works, whose large scratches attest to their poor state of preservation, formerly belonged to the priest of Nicolet, Father Jean Raimbault (1770-1841), a

Frenchman who had fled to Lower Canada to escape the French Revolution and who later commissioned Légaré to paint *The Corpus Christ Procession at Nicolet* (Fig. 228A). A comparison of one of the small oil paintings (Fig. 168B) in the Séminaire de Nicolet with *Fire in the Saint-Jean Quarter* reveals a number of striking similarities, from the reddish smoke in the night sky to the treatment of the haggard silhouettes and arrangement of certain sight lines. It is very likely therefore that, through channels still unknown, the small oil on cardboard in Nicolet influenced the creative endeavours of Légaré the chronicler, that intuitive synthesizer always on the lookout for new pictorial ideas.

J.R.P.

Notes

1. Except for the studio he had occupied in the old Château Saint-Louis since April 1845 and where he kept, among other things, his collection of six paintings by European masters.

2. These works were exhibited in Montreal and Quebec City in 1848. See PORTER *1978/1*, pp. 87-94 and 142, Nos. 69-73 and 227.

3. Compiled as of January 1, 1846, this album included another version of an oil painting by Légaré, *The Martyrdom of Françoise Brugnon-Gonannhatenha*, (1850), as well as a drawing by Théophile Hamel and unpublished texts by P.-J.-O. Chauveau, F.-X. Garneau and J.-C. Taché.

169.
Election Scene at Château-Richer, c. 1851
Oil on canvas, 64.5 × 95.5 cm

Provenance
Séminaire de Québec, from the Joseph Légaré estate, 1874; on deposit at the Société du Musée du Séminaire de Québec, 1983.

Exhibitions
Quebec City 1948; Vancouver 1959, No. 172; Ottawa 1965, No. 51; Quebec City 1973; Ottawa 1978-1979/1, No. 78.

Bibliography
GALLERY 1902, p. 14, No. 3; UNIVERSITÉ LAVAL 1903, p. 27, No. 3; LAVAL UNIVERSITY 1905, p. 27, No. 3; UNIVERSITÉ LAVAL 1906, p. 36, No. 11; UNIVERSITÉ LAVAL 1913, p. 63, No. 353; LAVAL UNIVERSITY 1923, p. 72, No. 353 attr. to an unknown artist; BELLERIVE 1925, p. 16; UNIVERSITÉ LAVAL 1933, p. 81, No. 245; COLGATE 1943, p. 109; DÉSILETS 1949, p. 47; MORISSET 1959/1, p. 47, No. 172; MORISSET 1960/1, p. 99; HARPER AND HUBBARD 1965, p. 51, No. 51 (Repr.); HARPER 1966, p. 82; HARPER 1967, p. 70; CAUCHON 1968, p. 2; HARPER 1970, p. 194; OSTIGUY 1970, p. 106; GIROUX 1972, p. 3; TREMBLAY 1972, pp. 187-191 and 199 (Repr.); SOUCY AND THIBAULT 1974, p. 105; LORD 1974, pp. 53 and 54 (Repr.); PORTER 1978/1, pp. 97-100, No. 78 (entry by Jean Trudel) (Repr.); PORTER 1978/2, pp. 5 and 6 (Repr.); PORTER 1978/3, p. 64; DEROME 1978, p. 31; DEROME AND LECLERC 1978, pp. 1 and 13, No. 78; NIXON 1979, p. 16; *Nos racines,* No. 79 (1979), p. 1573 (Repr.); TOUPIN 1979, p. E-19; LÉGARÉ 1980, p. 13; PORTER 1981, pp. 17, 339-340 and 356; LACROIX 1982, p. 39; PORTER 1985, p. 549; *Revue parlementaire canadienne,* Vol. XI, No. 3 (fall 1988), cover. p. and table of contents p. (Repr.).

Collection
Musée du Séminaire de Québec (Pc983.33)

T HE CAREER of Joseph Légaré was unusual in that he did not limit himself to the kinds of activities usually pursued by Canadian painters of the period. A fairly wealthy landowner, Légaré distinguished himself through both varied and lasting commitments at the social, cultural and political level. Moreover, many of his most interesting paintings were based on, and even motivated by, specific socio-political experiences. This was the case, for example, of **Election Scene at Château-Richer,** a beautiful landscape whose rich content resembles both an historical account and an allegory. It also constitutes a genre scene that faithfully describes electoral practices in Quebec in the mid-19th century. Although the events depicted by the artist took place in November 1851, it is essential to consider what happened in August 1848 to clearly understand why Légaré painted this picture.

Delighted with the return of Louis-Joseph Papineau (Cat. 188) to the

Fig. 169A.
Unidentified artist.
Grande Chasse du Sault-à-la-Puce (tableau allégorique), c. 1848;
lithograph, 30 × 26.5 cm.
Bibliothèque municipale de Montréal (C. 4/42097).

Canadian political scene, Légaré agreed to run in a by-election in Quebec City in spring 1848. Throughout the election campaign, he was the victim of demagogic attacks by Joseph-Édouard Cauchon, member of Parliament for Montmorency and owner of the *Journal de Québec*. Légaré was eventually defeated on the day of the election, June 6; however, the political battle continued in the newspapers over the next few weeks. On August 1, the journalist Napoléon Aubin, Dr. Édouard Rousseau and the lawyer Marc-Aurèle Plamondon, all members of the Légaré camp, attended a constituents' meeting in Montmorency riding. During the meeting, organized by the lawyer Jacques-Philippe Rhéaume, the participants condemned the iniquitous provisions of the Act of Union imposed by England in 1840. They also denounced Cauchon for preventing the adoption of electoral reforms compatible with proportional representation of the people. It was therefore declared that he had "lost the confidence of those who had invested him with their mandate." (*Translation*) The meeting turned sour when the member for Montmorency arrived with around 20 young men. A scuffle broke out between this group and Rhéaume's men. After losing the fight, Cauchon managed with great difficulty to take refuge in a neighbouring farm, where he was held captive under the watchful eye of Rhéaume's friends. In desperation, Cauchon's supporters sent for Joseph Légaré in Quebec City. When the artist

arrived at the farm, he managed to convince Rhéaume to release the member of Parliament.[1]

This incredible episode was evoked shortly afterwards in a naïve caricature ironically entitled *Grande Chasse du Sault à la Puce (tableau allégorique)* (Fig. 169A). It portrays the representative Cauchon as a pig branded with the letters "M.P.P." for *Membre du Parlement Provincial* (Provincial Member of Parliament). One of his pursuers takes pleasure in trampling a copy of the *Journal de Québec* while, in the background, the artist has depicted the fenced-in fields on the hills along the Beaupré coast and the rough outlines of the Sault-à-la-Puce Hotel. This building on the banks of the Sault-à-la-Puce River was often used for political meetings in Montmorency riding.

In January 1850, Légaré was again defeated in a by-election in which he ran under the annexationist banner. This defeat was even more bitter than the first for he was a victim of many vile personal attacks. The editor of the *Journal de Québec* lost all restraint and even criticized his artistic abilities: "we are no longer living in an era," he said, "where an artist merely has to sketch the rough outlines of a piece of wood and daub paint on a canvas to exhibit his works and gain the approval of an adoring public."[2] (*Translation*) This was not the end, however, of Légaré's problems. The same year, a caricature depicted him in an artist's smock accompanied by his main supporters (Fig. 169B).

Disappointed by the defeats of 1848 and 1850, Légaré decided not to run in the 1851 elections. He nonetheless probably took part in certain electoral debates, particularly in Montmorency riding, where his sworn enemy, the influential and crafty Cauchon, was again candidate. Hesitant to advocate sweeping reforms and fiercely opposed to "socialism," Cauchon expressed reservations with regard to liberals while increasing his support for conservatives. Through impertinent attacks on his political opponents, he again sparked heated debate in the press. He was formally denounced for his conduct during a meeting to nominate candidates for Montmorency riding, in which Légaré's friend, Joseph Larose, actively participated on Saturday, November 29. Larose had come with other voters to support the candidature of Cauchon's opponent, Germain Guay. It may well be that Légaré also took part in the meeting,[3] for he was a friend of the notary Guay. Whatever the case, the nomination of candidates in Château-Richer on November 29 degenerated into a violent brawl that pitted a number of braggarts from both camps against one another. At least this is what emerges from the conflicting reports published soon afterwards in *Le Journal de Québec* and *Le Canadien*.[4]

Influenced by his political opinions, Légaré believed that Cauchon and his supporters were entirely responsible for the fight. In painting the event, he took pleasure in translating into visual terms the puns of which Cauchon was commonly a

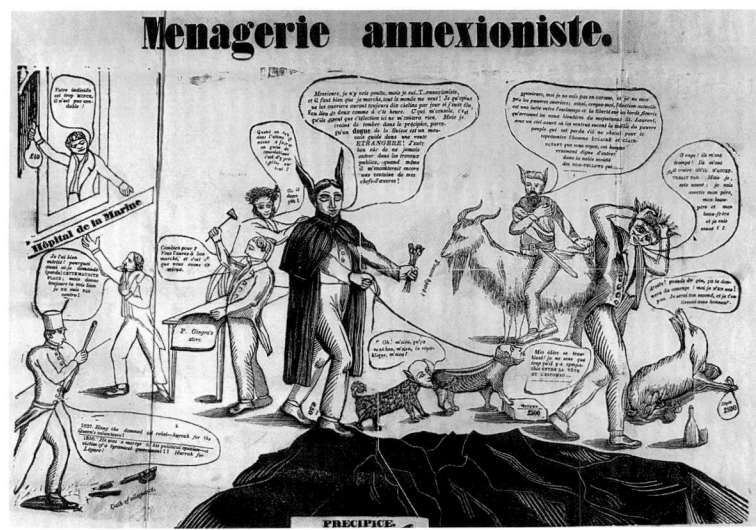

Fig. 169B.
Unidentified artist,
Ménagerie annexionniste, 1850;
engraving on wood, 43 × 60.7 cm.
Musée du Québec, Quebec City (87.221).

victim at the time. In the foreground of *Election Scene at Château-Richer,* he drew an enormous pig (Cauchon) leading a group of four children holding a slingshot, a stick and a bow. These children, who represent Cauchon's henchmen, are running towards a fifth child who, alone and armed with a stick, seems to be trying to protect a herd of sheep, probably symbolizing voters susceptible to intimidation. Behind this allegorical group of children, a battle rages between the unequally matched supporters and opponents of the member of Parliament for Montmorency.[5]

A preliminary examination of the general composition of *Election Scene at Château-Richer* readily reveals how the 1848 caricature must have influenced Légaré as he worked on this painting. It not only includes the group pursuing the pig in the foreground but also the assailants climbing the hill behind the Sault-à-la-Puce Hotel. Légaré, therefore, was familiar with the caricature, which he deliberately used in his painting. Moreover, he was thoroughly acquainted with the topography of the area. As previously illustrated by Thomas Davies (Cat. 20), the houses were closely aligned along the road on the narrow strip of land between the river and the hills along the Beaupré coast. Légaré had studied these features closely, even noticing the bridge over the Sault-à-la-Puce River. However, perhaps he intended to do more than simply depict the site accurately in order to place his subject matter in its proper setting. Is it merely a coincidence that the composition is organized

around the road winding through Château-Richer at the bottom of the hill and that, as in an ideally composed Italian landscape, the diagonal row of trees intersects the diagonal formed by the road? Perhaps, but Légaré rarely achieved such a well-balanced composition on his own and there is reason to believe that he was inspired by a model.[6]

Election Scene at Château-Richer is an amalgamation of the main characteristics of Légaré's later works. Over the years, he had mastered the technique of extending his perspectives toward an increasingly distant horizon. His later landscapes always had a diagonal opening on the left-hand side; in *Election Scene at Château-Richer,* the opening is formed by the St. Lawrence River as it flows towards the vanishing point on the horizon. This composition was based on *Ruins after the Fire in the Saint Jean Quarter, Looking Eastward.*[7] Apparently, the scope of the work required by the series of fire pictures influenced had more of an impact on Légaré's future painting than might be imagined. Henceforth, Légaré no longer thought in terms of values, as in *Massacre of Hurons by the Iroquois* (Cat. 157) or *Landscape with Wolfe Monument* (Cat. 161), but in terms of volumes that balanced one another. Be it the tree in *Villa "Clermont" at Sillery*[8] or the road leading to the fight in *Election Scene at Château-Richer,* a strong diagonal directs the viewer's eye toward the main subject. In conclusion, Légaré's later works all have a certain geometrical precision created by

such features as a clearly defined perspective grid, a central vanishing point and a very low horizon.

J.R.P. and D.P.

Notes

1. *Le Canadien,* July 26, 1848, p. 3 and August 2, 1848, p. 2; *L'Ami de la religion et de la patrie,* August 2, 1848, p. 438 and August 4, 1848, p. 466; Jacques Monet, *The Last Cannon Shot* (Toronto: University of Toronto Press, 1969), pp. 297-298.

2. *Le Journal de Québec,* January 15, 1850, p. 2.

3. It is not absolutely certain that Joseph Légaré attended this meeting. Contrary to what our colleague Jean Trudel believed (*PORTER 1978/1,* pp. 97-100, No. 78), Légaré is not mentioned in an article discussing the meeting to nominate candidates and published in *Le Canadien* on December 3, 1851 (p. 2). Instead, the article is referring to the lawyer Pierre Légaré, a friend of Cauchon and a supporter of Joseph Légaré's opponent in the by-election of January 1850. This was revealed by another article published in *Le Journal de Québec* on January 2, 1851 (p. 2).

4. *Le Journal de Québec,* December 2, 1851, p. 2; *Le Canadien,* December 3, 1851, p. 2.

5. Cauchon defeated his opponent by 963 votes to 523 in this election.

6. Contrary to what John Russell Harper and Barry Lord have said, we do not know of any painting in Légaré's collection which could have served as a model for this work.

7. *PORTER 1978/1,* p. 95, No. 73 (Repr.) (AGO).

8. *PORTER 1978/1,* p. 99, No. 77 (Repr.).

WILLIAM EDMOND
LOGAN

1798-1875

WILLIAM EDMOND LOGAN was born April 20, 1798 in Montreal, of Scottish parents. Although born in Lower Canada, his profession took him to Great Britain, where he stayed until age 44, after his parents sent him to Edinburgh to study at age 16. During the twenty-odd years that followed, he worked with his uncle, Hart Logan, a prosperous businessman. His duties at this time enabled him to gain experience in the fields of cartography and geology, and he also took courses in drawing, languages and mathematics. Logan's geological maps of southern Wales bear witness to his scientific expertise. In spring 1842, the Société d'histoire naturelle de Montréal and the Literary and Historical Society of Quebec, having received government subsidies, called on Logan—whose reputation had preceded him—to carry out geological studies. He thus became the first director and prime contractor of the Geological Survey of Canada, whose principal mandate was to discover the country's geological riches.

In spring 1844, he exhibited his collections in a house he had rented on Rue Saint-Jacques. Later, in 1851 and 1855, he enjoyed considerable success with the mineral collections he made up for the London and Paris exhibitions. The analyses he conducted in 1846 on the ice dams on the St. Lawrence were particularly useful to engineers during construction of the Victoria Bridge. In 1860, he observed an orogeny in the Quebec City area which was subsequently christened "Logan's Fault." In addition to compiling scientific data, writing reports and drawing geological maps of the regions he visited on his travels throughout the country, Logan published *Geology of Canada* in 1863 and, two years later, a colour atlas of geological maps.

Over the years he accumulated various honours and was knighted by Queen Victoria in 1856. Logan stepped down from his position as director of the Geological Survey of Canada in November 1869 and took up residence in his sister's home, Castle Malgwyn, in Wales. He returned a number of times to Canada to do geological work. William Edmond Logan died a bachelor in 1875 in Cilgerran, Wales.

Main source
WINDER 1972.

170.
Gaspésiea (Notebook), 1844
10.6 × 17.5 × 2 cm

Inscription
(Identified on the back in gold letters against a black background) Gaspé/*1844*/W.E.Logan.
Collection
National Archives of Canada, Ottawa (RG 45, Vol. CLVIII)

MQ

A. *Gros-Morne* (Fol. 60v-61r)

Bibliography
Chartrand, Duchesne, and Gingras *1987,* p. 134 (Repr.).

I T MAY COME AS A surprise to see the name of Sir Edmond William Logan included in a work devoted mainly to professional and amateur artists, but by doing so we hope to illustrate the difficulties in establishing a hard-and-fast definition of the concept of topography during this period. We are also including Logan[1] here in order to situate his "landscape drawings" in their initial context. In addition to the analysis of a site for purposes of military defense or the preparation of nautical charts, as was the case for James Peachey (Cat. 42 to 45), there exists another very different vision that focuses on observation and the portrayal of natural elements and their oft-hidden aspects. It is from this perspective that we will be looking at Logan's work.

Before being appointed geologist for the Province of Canada in 1842, Logan had already carved out a solid reputation for himself in England.[2] His work in geology was originally linked to the development of the mining industry, since the discovery of significant coal deposits guar-

anteed both work for miners and a constant supply for mining companies. To achieve these results, Logan undertook a comprehensive survey of the region of Wales in which he was living at the time. He recorded his geological observations—depth and continuity of the deposits, internal rocky bedding—on existing topographical maps. The concern for detail taught in drawing classes seems, in Logan's case, to have served mainly scientific purposes, although such training was the type commonly received by all amateur artists at that time.

The link between the need to step up geological research in Canada and the benefits foreseen for the mining industry can be traced back to the early 1820s.[3] Logan's arrival was in keeping with this concern for continuity, and the mandate of the Geological Survey of Canada and of its first director was to produce "a complete and scientific description of the country's rock, soils and minerals, to prepare maps and diagrams, to do drawings, and to gather samples to illustrate the various

sites."[4] But here again, there was a serious lack of topographical maps for use as reference, so Logan enlisted the services of a retired cartographer, Alexander Murray, to do on-site surveys.

Logan travelled to the Gaspé in summer 1844 to conduct the first topographical and geological survey of the peninsula. The drawings he made in his notebook, although extremely detailed and accurate, were obviously not meant to be esthetically pleasing. In addition to conserving the memory of the site observed intact, the drawings enabled him to record in images what words could not convey. For example, in *Gros-Morne,* Logan isolated the coastline on a page of his notebook, taking care to scrupulously indicate the pattern of the rocky strata formed by folds in the earth's crust. The tiny figures, indicated by a thickening of the pen strokes in the fore- and middle ground, serve no other purpose than to indicate scale. It is tempting to see the sketches of *L'Anse-Pleureuse* (Fig. 170A) as works of leisure in an otherwise austere notebook, which

Fig. 170A.
William Edmond Logan,
L'Anse-Pleureuse (Fol. 61v-62r).
National Archives of Canada (C-137943).

Fig. 170B.
William Edmond Logan,
L'Anse à Claude (Fol. 63v-64r).
National Archives of Canada, Ottawa (C-137944).

was covered with fine, detailed annotations. Although we do not know Logan's exact working method or claim to be science historians, there does appear to be a link to cartography here. The overview of the right-hand folio positions the bay and the mountains, forming a valley, while the left-hand folio repeats the same subject in detail. The same is true for *L'Anse à Claude* (Fig. 170B), which Logan visited on June 25, 1844. This time, he remarked, in words and images, on the curious nature of the sandstone folds.

Logan's interest lay primarily in analyzing visible elements for scientific ends. He relied on a minimum of methods and techniques: pen and pencil were used indiscriminately for drawing and writing. He knew nothing of pictorial standards; at the most, he would occasionally add a wash to emphasize shadows and atmospheric perspective. His objective was not an artistic one: just as a soldier makes up a battle plan[5] following strategic standards, so Logan broke nature down into its basic components with a view to writing the geological history of a new continent.

D.P.

Notes

1. It is probably due to this work as draughtsman that Logan's name can be found in HARPER 1970, p. 200, or in Blake McKendry, *Folk Artists in Canada from the 17th Century to the Present*

(Elginburg: Blake McKendry Limited, 1988), p. 140.

2. Logan was the object of a biographical entry by WINDER 1972. We are indebted to the latter for all our information.

3. This is a whole separate issue concerning the importance of British officers—and more particularly scientists—which we will not deal with here. John Jeremiah Bigsby (1792-1881), military doctor and amateur artist, published a number of geological studies in the United States and England. The same is true for Henry Woolsey Bayfield (1795-1885), land surveyor. This issue is studied by CHARTRAND, DUCHESNE AND GINGRAS 1987, pp. 127-131. For Logan and the Geological Survey, see pp. 131-146.

4. WINDER 1972, p. 488.

5. We are thinking especially of Thomas Davies (HUBBARD 1972/2, pp. 82-84, No. 9-11. (Repr.).

ALEXANDER CAVALIÉ MERCER

1783-1868

BORN IN HULL (Yorkshire, England) on March 28, 1783, the son of General Alexander Mercer, Alexander Cavalié Mercer followed in his father's footsteps, choosing a career in the military. Despite some difficulty, he was accepted to the Royal Military Academy in Woolwich (London) in 1798. On graduating in 1799, he joined the royal artillery as second lieutenant, and was later promoted colonel (1846) and then general (1865).

From 1801 to 1805, Mercer served in Ireland; a few years later, he travelled to South America as part of an expedition to Buenos Aires. In 1815, he took part in the famous Battle of Waterloo but was reduced to half-pay the following year. In 1823, he took command of the 5th battalion of the royal artillery in Quebec City. His postings in Canada included Quebec City, Montreal and Kingston. Apart from an authorized leave from 1825 to 1827, Mercer remained in the colony until his departure for England in 1829, returning to Canada eight years later as lieutenant-colonel. He was stationed in Halifax, Nova Scotia, at the time of the Maine-New Brunswick border dispute and, during his posting, inspected Maritime defense systems on several occasions.

On August 16, 1842, Mercer returned to Ireland. His last years were spent in southern England close to Exeter, where he died on November 9, 1868 at age 85. Two years later, in 1870, the diary he had kept during the Waterloo campaign was published.

Main sources
BELL 1972; BELL 1977.

VAG, AGNS, MMFA

171.
Daybreak, Quebec, 1824
Watercolour with traces of scraping out on paper, 16 × 21.9 cm

Inscription
(b., in graphite, in the artist's hand) *Quebec Jan^r 21. 1824/about an hour after day break -/Moon Setting -/The peculiar Crimson Band of Vapour/I observed for nearly a Fortnight afterward./every day, both after Sunset & before Sun rise./& always in the opposite* [? *greater*].

Provenance
Private collection (sold by Sotheby's, Toronto, May 27, 1968, No. 25); William P. Wolfe, Montreal, 1968; acquired by the Public Archives of Canada, Ottawa, 1968.

Exhibition
Ottawa 1972-1975, No. 67.

Bibliography
CATALOGUE 1968, p. 8, No. 25; *BELL 1972*, No. 67 (Repr.).

Collection
National Archives of Canada, Ottawa (1968-67-1)

A MONG THE watercolourists who produced works in Quebec in the mid-1820s, Alexander Cavalié Mercer warrants particular mention as his choice of subjects and sensitive rendering of nature expressed a new vision.

Mercer entered the Woolwich military academy in 1797 and was taught by Thomas Paul Sandby (?-1832), who had recently taken over from his father as drawing master. After a few short months in Argentina (1807-1808), Mercer distinguished himself in the Battle of Waterloo (June 1815) by quashing Marshal Ney's last stand. From July 1815 to January 1816, he took part in the siege of Paris, keeping a diary that revealed his curiosity, keen observation of Parisian customs and sense of humour in describing the oddities of a society with which he had come into contact for the first time.[1] Mercer was posted in Quebec in June 1823 after several years of inactivity, having been reduced to half-pay since his return to England.

The fact that very few of Mercer's works from the 1820s are known to us is not necessarily due to a disinterest in drawing on his part, his assignment to Halifax, from 1837 to 1842, having left obvious traces.[2] *Daybreak, Quebec* and *Effect of A Snow Storm, Lower Town, Quebec* are surprising works, both in the novelty of their subject matter and the quality of the finished product.

Mercer's interest was not restricted to topographical drawing and his topographical renderings differ considerably from those of contemporaries James Pattison Cockburn (Cat. 72 to 82) and Charles Ramus Forrest (Cat. 111). *Island of St. Helen's, opposite Montreal* (Fig. 171-172A) is a good example. Ile Sainte-Hélène is no more than a thin strip of wooded land underlining the horizon, the foreground occupying more than half of the work. The two empty chairs, which replace the traditional spectators, break with the rules governing this genre. Mercer appears patently disinterested in creating "nature compositions" in which nature is recomposed based on ideals. Instead, he concentrates on unexpected occurrences and the arbitrariness of changing light. This concept existed as early as the 18th century but took on increasing importance at the turn of the 19th.[3] This, then, is the first element governing the context in which Mercer worked. The second is more closely related to the two works shown here. The inscriptions on the watercolours, especially *Daybreak, Quebec,* in which the artist took great pains to indicate the precise moment and exact phenomenon observed, reflect

MQ, NGC

172.
Effect of Snow Storm, Lower Town, Quebec, 1828
Watercolour over graphite on paper, 30.9 × 20.2 cm

Inscription
(b.,c., in pen and black ink, in the artist's hand)
Quebec -/Effect of a Snow Storm in the Lower Town under/Cape Diamond near the Anse-des-mères -/ 1828.

Provenance
Private collection (sold by Sotheby's, Toronto, October 24, 1973, No. 265); acquired by the Public Archives of Canada, Ottawa, 1973.

Bibliography
CATALOGUE *1973*, p. 88, No. 265.

Collection
National Archives of Canada, Ottawa (1973-83R)

Fig. 171-172A.
Alexander Cavalié Mercer,
Island of St. Helen's, opposite Montreal, 1829;
watercolour over graphite on paper,
19.9 × 26.3 cm.
National Gallery of Canada, Ottawa (28030).

the interest in atmospheric phenomena typical of the period.[4] From Constable to Turner, studies of clouds and rainbows mark the early 19th century, a period which also witnessed specialized publications including *Researches about Atmospheric Phenomena*[5] by Thomas Forster (1789-1860). In observing uniquely North American phenomena of this sort, Mercer demonstrates a similar interest.

Mercer's range of colours—a combination of dark browns to olive greens—in *Effect of A Snow Storm, Lower Town, Quebec,* seeks to pinpoint the instant when the blizzard masks shape and colour. The driven snow, an effect created using a partially dry brush, lends an oblique angle to the whole composition. Bundled up in his coat, the soldier is bent over, depicted at a point when the wind has taken his breath away. *Daybreak, Quebec*

does not reveal the same effect of the near-overpowering force of nature. The artist's keen sense of observation is revealed in the alternating streaks of bistre, indigo and grey, and in the moon, painted in a mix of grey and yellow tones on a white background to suggest its contrasting craters and mountains. The originality of these works must not, however, overshadow the fundamental fact that Mercer did not do pure atmospheric studies. In *Daybreak, Quebec,* the viewer's eye is drawn to the narrow strip of hills in the foreground, indicating that this is indeed a landscape. As Ank C. Esmeijer[6] observed of the works of Henri de Valenciennes (1750-1819), Mercer's is a variant of the panoramic view. Like Valenciennes, Mercer uses a strip of land in the lower portion of his composition to indicate the vantage point.
D.P.

Notes
1. *Journal of the Waterloo campaign kept throughout the campaign of 1815.* This work was published in London in 1870 by Mercer's son.
2. The NAC holds 97 watercolours from this period.
3. Roger de Piles, *Cour de peinture par principes,* Paris, 1708 (republished in 1791). Pierre-Henri de Valenciennes, *Éléments de perspective pratique à l'usage des artistes,* Paris, 1820. See also Paula Rea Radisich, "Eighteenth-Century *Plein-Air* Painting and the Sketches of Pierre Henri de Valenciennes", *The Art Bulletin,* Vol. LXIV, No. 1 (March 1982), pp. 98-104.
4. See Barbara Maria Stafford, *Voyage into Substance, Art, Science, Nature, and the Illustrated Travel Account, 1760-1840,* Cambridge and London: MIT Press, 1984.
5. Work published in London in 1813 (republished in 1815) with illustrations by Frederick Christian Lewis.
6. "Cloudscapes in theory and practice", *Simiolus,* Vol. IX, No. 3 (1977), pp. 137-138, Fig. 7.

ANDREW
MORRIS

active between 1844 and 1852

ACCORDING TO NEWSPAPERS OF THE DAY, Andrew Morris was born in Kilmarnock, Scotland. In 1844, he had already been living in Montreal for some time but the exact year of his arrival in Canada is unknown, as are the date and place of his death. Although he produced portraits and paintings of historical subjects, Morris is best known for the two large allegorical paintings commissioned in 1844 by the Speaker of the Assembly, which had been sitting in Montreal since the unification of the two Canadas. This commission had given rise to some controversy over the government's commitment to art.

In 1847, Andrew Morris was president of the Montreal Society of Artists when he participated in a group exhibition with James Duncan, Cornelius Krieghoff, William F. Wilson, William Sawyer and Martin Somerville. The following year, Morris exhibited his work once again, this time in Toronto, and won first prize for his rendering of Jacques Cartier meeting an Indian chief in Hochelaga in 1535. At the time, it was called "the best historical drawing of Canada" and was later lithographed in Toronto (Fig. 254B). In fact, Morris himself may have gone there to oversee the task. Although he appears to have resided in New York from 1848 to 1852—in 1848 he exhibited two portraits at the American Art Union, an association for Scottish-born artists—we know nothing of his comings and goings after 1852.

Main sources

GROCE & WALLACE 1957; HARPER 1970; TRUDEL 1990/2.

Before Restoration

173.
Sir Charles Metcalfe Opening Parliament in Montreal, 1845
Oil on canvas, 55.8 × 76.2 cm

Inscription
(s.d., l.l.) *Andrew Morris. Fecṭ 1845.*

Provenance
Sir Charles Metcalfe by way of his private secretary, Captain Higginson; Sir James MacAuley Higginson; acquired by the Public Archives of Canada, Ottawa, 1933.

Exhibition
Charlottetown 1964, No. 25.

Bibliography
NAC, RG 7, G20, Correspondence of the Governors-general, Vol. CDXIII, No. 634, "Letter from Andrew Morris to Captain Higginson", March 13, 1845; DOUGHTY *1934,* p. vii; HARPER *1964,* pp. 25-26 and *27,* No. 25 (Repr.); MACLENNAN 1965, p. 27 (Repr.); HARPER *1970,* p. 230; *Nos racines,* No. 79 (1979), p. 1569 (Repr.); NOPPEN AND DESCHÊNES *1986,* p. 36 (repr.).

Collection
National Archives of Canada, Ottawa (1990-481-1X)

O N NOVEMBER 28, 1844, following the November 12 elections, Sir Charles Metcalfe declared the first session of the second Parliament of the United Provinces of Canada open. For the first time, the Legislative Council and the Assembly sat in Montreal, having been located in Kingston from 1841 to 1843. The Act of Union of 1841 united Upper and Lower Canada under one government, and Montreal, the centre of the country's economy, trade and road network, was chosen as the new capital, rather than having the seat of government alternate between different cities. Parliament was set up in a building erected in 1833 by architect George Brown for the Rue Sainte-Anne market (Fig. 173A). Leblond de Brumath described the division of functions in the building which "measured 342 feet in length and 50 in width. [...] On the first floor [...] in the left wing, the Legislative Council Chamber, [...] and, in the south wing, the Legislative Assembly Chamber."[1] (*Translation*)

Morris' canvas shows Governor Charles Theophilius Metcalfe (1785-1846)[2] addressing the members of the Council and the Assembly on November 29. The previous day, he had appeared before the same men but postponed his speech until the Assembly had elected a Speaker. The beginning of this session was disturbed by the election of Sir Allan McNab as Speaker of the Assembly with a three-vote majority over Augustin-Norbert Morin. Two of these votes came from Francophone members, one of whom was Denis-Benjamin Papineau.[3]

Fig. 173A.
A. Kollner,
Parliament House, Montreal, 1848;
watercolour on paper.
National Archives of Canada,
Ottawa (C-13425).

Fig. 173B.
James Duncan,
The House of Assembly, Montreal, c. 1848;
watercolour, and gouache over graphite on
paper, 27.7 × 40 cm.
National Gallery of Canada, Ottawa (28066).

Notes

1. Adrien Leblond de Brumath, *Histoire popu-laire de Montréal depuis son origine jusqu'à nos jours* (Montreal: Granger Frères, 1890), pp. 379-380. On the history of the various parliamentary buildings see Michel Desgagnés, *Les édifices parlementaires depuis 1792* (Quebec City: National Assembly, 1978) and NOPPEN AND DESCHENES 1986.

2. Sir Charles Metcalfe was appointed governor on February 24, 1843. He left the country, seriously ill, after only a short stay, on November 23, 1845. *L'Aurore des Canadas* of August 31, 1844 announced that a certain "Mr. Bredish, portraitist, has recently completed what is said to be one of the best likenesses done to date of Sir Charles Metcalfe. The work is permanently displayed at the artist"s studio, on Rue Notre-Dame." (*Translation*)

3. For the minutes of the stormy debates, see *La Minerve*—edited by Ludger Duvernay—of November 28, 1844.

4. We have been unable to establish whether or not William Morris, receiver general, and Andrew Morris, the artist, were related.

5. *George III*, on the left, is a copy after Joshua Reynolds. Joseph Légaré and Roy-Audy had copied it in 1830. *George IV* is after the work by Sir Thomas Lawrence—a version of it by Wheatley arrived in Quebec City in 1829. Légaré copied it the same year (Cat. 160) and Roy-Audy, the following year.

6. This commission was the subject of a debate between *Le Journal de Québec and The Montreal Gazette*, which had announced and encouraged it, on the pretext that local artists could not produce sketches worthy of being judged in a public contest. It was even suggested that canvases be ordered from Europe to be used as models for local painters. *Le Journal de Québec* contested this viewpoint, pointing out that since this commission was paid from the public coffers, it should be the object of a competition. The following was written on August 31, 1844: "Such encouragement is worthy when it encourages the arts and not one particular artist. We are surprised that the speaker of the house did not open this commission up to a competition in order to elicit not only paintings but the best paintings possible". On September 12, 1844, *Le Journal de Québec* told its readers: "The only thing local artists are lacking is encouragement, emulation by competition; the government and the legislature alone can produce the desired results." (*Translation*) See PORTER 1977/1, pp. 13-24.

7. *Le Journal de Québec* of April 18, 1846 (p. 3.) noted: "N.B. Notice to artists. The two famous paintings that Mr. Cuvillier left to the country to punish it for having had the audacity to exempt him from being elected and from the speaker"s chair, continue to decorate our legislature's walls and bear crying witness to the poor taste of that individual who claimed the right to "choose his painter"." (*Translation*)

8. These categories are based on the subjects of works shown in the 1847 exhibition of the Montreal Society of Artists. See TRUDEL 1990/2.

La Minerve of December 2, 1844 described the pomp marking the November 28 ceremony, and which no doubt continued the next day, as follows:

At one o'clock, the council reconvened. The Honourable Adam Ferrie and L. Morris,[4] receiver general, took their seats after having been sworn in as usual. His Excellency the Governor's arrival at and departure from the parliament buildings was heralded by the firing of a cannon. Such pomp and circumstance had not marked the last parliamentary session which was held in Kingston—Montreal being deserving of more solemnity! The governor was accompanied by a considerable train. The seats of honour were reserved for the upper court, inside the sessions chamber, to the right of the throne—the justices in attendance were the Honourable Vallières de St. Réal, J.R. Rolland, Gale, Day and McCord. (*Translation*)

In the crowd portrayed by Morris, flanking the governor are the Speaker, the Honourable René-Édouard Caron (Fig. 188A), and high-ranking military men. The justices and members of the Legislative Council are seated and the elected members stand behind the Bar. The female guests are in three rows either side of the chamber, which is lit by large bay windows and semicircular openings in the vaulted ceiling. The chamber of the Legislative Council had recently been decorated: a huge canopy, curtains and portraits of kings George III and George IV[5] imparted a solemn air to the renovated room. This building and its contents were destroyed on April 25, 1849, following riots protesting the compensation voted by the Assembly for losses incurred by the citizens of Lower Canada during the 1837-1838 rebellions (Cat. 130).

Andrew Morris, an artist of Scottish origin, had good reason for being award-

ed the commission for this work. In fall 1844, he had obtained an initial order for two allegorical paintings representing *Commerce* and *Agriculture* to decorate the sessions chamber of the Legislative Assembly.[6] These works were commissioned by the Speaker of the Assembly, Augustin Cuvillier.[7] The location of these two canvases, which were also destroyed in 1849, is shown in James Duncan's watercolour of the Assembly in session (Fig. 173B).

On March 13, 1845, Andrew Morris addressed the following letter of thanks to Captain Higginson, secretary to Governor Metcalfe, confirming the viceregal's order and the nature of the relations the artists were to maintain with their clients:

I have the honor to acknowledge receipt of Your Note enclosing a check of £50 being the price of the Painting representing the opening of the first Provincial Parliament held in Montreal, and for the high honor conferred on me by His Excellency Lord Metcalfe in being the purchaser of my picture I can only return sincere thanks: not only as regards myself but for the liberal and substantial mark of his Excellency's endeavours to promote the progress of the fine Arts in Canada. I sincerely trust he may long continue to be their distinguished Patron.

Landscape artist, history painter and painter of genre scenes,[8] Andrew Morris was a prolific artist whose work is, nevertheless, not well known. As founding member and president of the Montreal Society of Artists, Morris played an important role in awakening public recognition of the artist's professional status in Lower Canada.

L.L.

R EPORTEDLY OF IRISH ORIGIN, John Murray is thought to have been born in 1810, have immigrated to Canada in 1836 and have married in Quebec City. As is the case for many other foreign artists who came to Canada to ply their trade, little is known about Murray and what he did. His earliest known works—a series of engravings of views of Montreal—were produced circa 1843-1844 and were printed by Adolphus Bourne and George Matthews. Other works include a sketch of the fire in Quebec City's Saint-Roch district in 1845, which was lithographed by Endicott in New York and distributed by Bourne. Murray's view of Montreal from atop Mount Royal (Cat. 174) is the only canvas known to us at date. In an article published on April 30, 1850, *Le Journal de Québec* reported that Murray was also an architect who had recently completed plans for a Gothic church. Murray is said to have given lessons in drawing, perspective and the art of colour in Quebec City in 1864 and taught Quebec goldsmith Pierre Lespérance (1819-1892).

JOHN MURRAY

1810 – after 1868

Main sources
HARPER 1970; ALLODI 1980.

174.
Montreal From the Mountain, 1851
Oil on canvas, 90.5 × 133.5 cm

Inscription
(s., l.l.) *J⁰ Murray.*
Provenance
Andrew Dow estate, Montreal; acquired by the Château Ramezay, Montreal, 1902.

Bibliography
MCR, Registre des acquisitions 1895-1974, p. 140, No. 2170, March 20, 1902; *O'LEARY 1907,* p. 78, No. 75; *O'LEARY 1917,* p. 87, No. 11; *O'LEARY 1920,* p. 89, No. 11; *O'LEARY 1922,* p. 95, No. 11; *O'LEARY 1923,* p. 89, No. 11; *O'LEARY 1926,* p. 100, No. 11; *CATALOGUE 1927/2,* p. 100, No. 11; *CATALOGUE 1928,* p. 100, No. 11; *CATALOGUE 1931,* p. 97, No. 11; *CATALOGUE 1936,* p. 87, No. 11; *CATALOGUE 1937,* p. 84, No. 11; *CATALOGUE 1948,* p. 87, No. 11; *CATALOGUE 1954,* p. 87, No. 11; *CATALOGUE 1956,* p. 87, No. 11; *CARRIER 1957,* p. 69, No. 751; *CARRIER AND LEFEBVRE 1962,* p. 82, No. 751.

Collection
Musée du Château Ramezay, Montreal (CR2170)

T HIS PAINTING gives us insight into yet another stage in the growth of Montreal. The towers of Notre-Dame church have been completed since James Duncan did his *Montreal From the Mountain* (Cat. 91). St. Patrick's church, completed in 1847, is set disproportionately far back and Bonsecours market (1848) can be made out in the direction of Ile Sainte-Hélène. The land between Sherbrooke Street and the foot of the mountain also boast new buildings. In 1838-1839, architect John Ostell (1813-1892) was commissioned to build the first building for McGill University.[1] The project was carried out in two stages: when Murray painted this panoramic view, only the Fine Arts building and the eastern wing (Dawson building) had been completed (1843). These buildings stood near "Burnside", James McGill's summer residence, and it may be this imposing residence, with its fire walls, that can be seen in the right foreground.

As indicated by the information provided on the provenance of this work, it may have been commissioned by Andrew Dow. The latter died in 1853 and his brother, William Dow, took in his widow and four daughters.[2] It is entirely possible that Andrew Dow and his wife Mary are the figures shown from the back in the foreground. This canvas, dated circa 1850-1851, coincides with Murray's departure for Quebec City, where he worked with Robert Clow Todd in 1852 on the decoration of the legislative palace.

The five tiny windows close to the speaker's chair have been transformed into semicircular openings. This has extended the galleries either side of the speaker's chair and considerably increased the amount of light which enters and is softened by magnificent transparent openwork motifs portraying the cities of Quebec, Montreal, Toronto and Kingston and painted by Mr. Todd and Mr. Murray of this city.[3] (*Translation*)

John Murray is clearly not James Duncan. His composition is less assured and his topography shakier. Murray separates his planes, and the main link he creates—by significantly lightening the land extending past the fence of James McGill's estate—serves to turn the viewer's gaze away from, rather than towards, the city. He indicates two parallel views leading into the distance. The first, the overriding one, is marked by the figures, one of whose arms indicates the line to follow. The second is created by the spotted cow and by the excessively imposing scale of the house, the only lit facade in an island of dark green. Murray thus divides his composition into two very different planes. The first plays on lighting contrasts while the second displays uniform lighting. This distinction influences the manner in which motifs are dispersed in the secondary planes. The decreasing size of the buildings as they are located farther off in the distance is poorly rendered. We do not know whether Murray wished to rival Duncan; we do know, however, that in 1843-1844, he engraved a series of views of Montreal just as Duncan did.[4] Also, Murray settled in Quebec City in the early 1850s to pursue his career there. Perhaps he had decided that the market was more promising in the capital.

D.P.

Notes

1. Ellen James, *John Ostell, Architecte, Arpenteur* (Cat.), (Montreal: McCord Museum, 1985), pp. 34-42, Fig. 16 and 19.
2. François Rémillard and Brian Merrett, *Demeures bourgeoises de Montréal, le Mille carré doré, 1850-1930,* (Montreal: Éditions du Méridien, 1986), pp. 74-76.
3. *Le Journal de Québec,* September 9, 1852, p. 1.
4. *ALLODI 1980,* pp. 172-185 for the Duncan series (1843-1844); pp. 190-199 for the Murray series (circa 1843-1844).

SAMUEL PALMER

active between 1834 and 1845

L ITTLE IS KNOWN to date about Samuel Palmer, who was often confused with the British artist of the same name (London, 1805—Reigate, 1881). His origins are uncertain and the first mention of him in Canada dates from April 26, 1834, when he ran an advertisement in the *New Brunswick Courier*. At the time, he was in Saint John offering his services as a portraitist of the living and of the deceased. According to the information contained in his ads, he arrived in the United States in fall 1834 to study American painting. The following summer he announced, in the same newspaper, his intention to travel to Europe. There is no further mention of him until 1842, when another ad appeared in the May 14, 1842 edition of *The Montreal Gazette* indicating Palmer's arrival in Montreal. As was the custom, he vaunted his talent to the public, mentioning, however, that he did not paint portraits of children under the age of 3.

Palmer settled in Quebec City in mid-July 1842 and spent three consecutive winters there punctuated by trips outside the city, notably to Kingston in late summer 1842. His stay in Quebec City seems to have been profitable, since most of his known works date from this period and portray principally members of the English-speaking community.

Main source
HARPER 1970.

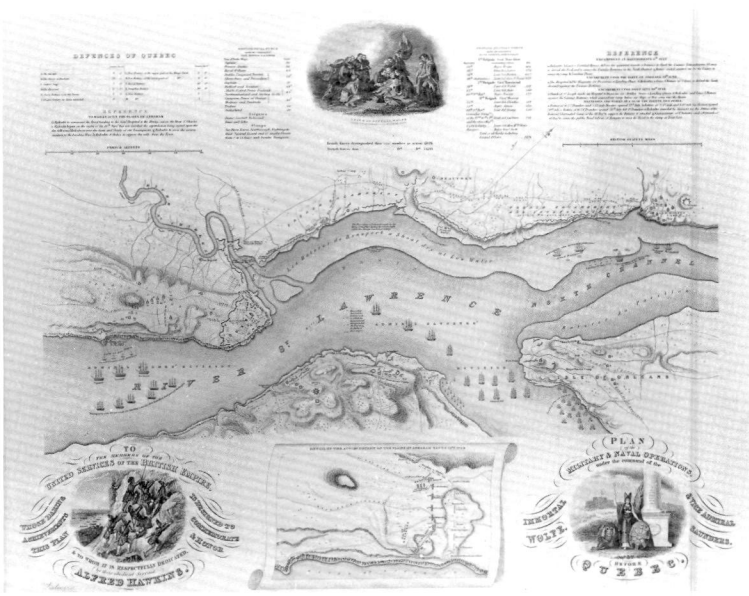

Fig. 175A.
James Wyld after John Grant (published by Alfred Hawkins),
Plan of the Military & Naval Operations under the Command of the Immortal Wolfe & Vice Admiral Saunders, Before Quebec, 1841; engraved map, 59 × 73 cm.
Archives nationales du Québec, Quebec City (P600-6/C-962-Québec-1759 O.).

175.
Alfred Hawkins, c. 1842
Oil on canvas, 62 × 50 cm

Inscription
(s., l.l.) *PALMER.*

Provenance
Descendants of the Hawkins family; Norah Curry; gift to the City of Quebec, 1944.

Bibliography
(?) *Quebec Mercury,* August 18, 1842, p. 2; RYDER *1985,* p. 428.

Collection
City of Quebec

A LFRED HAWKINS (1792-1854) was born in England and settled in Quebec City around 1817 as a merchant of wine and spirits. Active in various municipal organizations (Quebec Assembly, Bourse de Québec, Banque de Québec, Société du feu de Québec), he played an important role in society. In 1834, when a growing interest in history manifested itself, he published *Hawkins' Picture of Quebec: with Historical Recollections,* which depicted the great moments in the history of Quebec City from its discovery to the time it won municipal

status in 1832, the year before Elzéar Bédard was elected its first mayor (Cat. 197). Hawkins also had the first plan of the new incorporated city engraved in 1835, had it republished in 1840 and 1845, and commissioned a topographical survey of the military operations for the Battle of the Plains of Abraham, which he had published in London in 1841. His name is also associated with Quebec City's first two directories, which he compiled and published in 1844 and 1847, and he founded a commercial newspaper, the *Morning Herald and Commercial Advertiser,* which was published from April 1837 to March 1838. Hawkins died of cholera in 1854 when he was Shipping Master of the port of Quebec.

The portrait housed in the Quebec city hall, the perfect location for this individual who played such a propagandist role in favour of the municipality, shows Hawkins sitting in an armchair holding a partially unrolled map in his right hand. Behind him, to the left, is a desk complete

with inkwell, parchment paper and books. Partially hidden behind two large columns and a curtain draped whimsically, to say the least, is a view of the Quebec City promontory. In this theatrical setting, Hawkins' activities connected to Quebec City as cartographer and historian are obvious.

During the early months of Samuel Palmer's stay in Quebec City, a *Quebec Mercury* editor published the following on August 18, 1842:

MR. PALMER, *Portrait Painter.*—We were invited yesterday, to visit the *atelier* of this talented artist, who has recently arrived in Quebec, and has, as yet, painted but two portraits, both of gentlemen well known in this city. The one is a three- quarter picture, as large as life, the other a full length of cabinet size; they are in oils and highly finished. The tone of the colouring of these pictures has seldom been equalled in this Province, whilst the likeness of each individual is so well preserved that it is immediately recognized.

This article tells us that Palmer did at least two types of portraits: life-size,

Fig. 175B.
Samuel Palmer,
James Turnbull Senior, c. 1842-1845;
oil on canvas, 59.1 × 46.8 cm.
Musée du Québec, Quebec City (56.221).

head-and-shoulders portraits and full-length "cabinet size" portraits. The painting of Hawkins is a perfect example of the latter—a small portrait showing the subject full-length, although seated. The term "cabinet size" referred to works for semi-public use, usually hung on the walls of an office.[1] It is entirely possible that Hawkins' portrait was the one shown in Palmer's studio at the time. The *Quebec Mercury* article appeared shortly after Hawkins' publication of his *Plan of the Military & Naval Operations under the Command of the Immortal Wolfe & Vice Admiral Saunders, Before Quebec* (Fig. 175A). This map can be easily recognized in the portrait in part through the legends symbolizing the valour and victory of the British: Wolfe's death, after the famous painting by Benjamin West, the climb up Cap Diamant by the various army corps, and an allegory (*Britannia* leaning on a lion) of the victorious British beside a column dedicated to Wolfe. The idea for the map dates from 1837, when Hawkins exhibited the original pen drawing by John Grant (active between 1825 and 1845) and indicated that he would have it engraved by a first-class artist if he received the encouragement deserving of such an undertaking.[2] In 1839, he published a prospectus announcing his project complete with a list of subscribers.[3] Finally, Hawkins ran an ad in *Le Canadien* on November 3, 1841 indicating that the map would be available soon; however, it was April 11, 1842 before copies were ready for delivery. To mark the publication of this "work that was honoured by more than 1000 subscribers", Hawkins' advertisement listed the

names of the most prestigious individuals and organizations, topped by "Her very Gracious Majesty the Queen". (*Translation*) He also reproduced several letters of congratulations from the city councils of Montreal, Quebec City and Kingston.[4]

It therefore seems logical to think that this portrait was painted shortly after the publicity campaign surrounding the publication of his map—something of a crowning glory. Since Palmer arrived in Quebec City only in July 1842, the portrait mentioned in the article of August 18 of that same year—the "full length of cabinet size"—may well be that of Hawkins.

Palmer probably painted other similar portraits. Another unpublished work, the portrait of *James Turnbull Senior* (Fig 175B), may also be attributed to him. This work is similar to that of Hawkins in its composition, handling and format. Both share a number of stylistic traits: the same very gestural method of highlighting the drapes with bright red, the same sweeping rendering of the hair and the chair details, and the same unique style of lengthening shapes to give the subject a tapered look. Palmer offered Quebec City residents a new type of portrait offering an innovative type of iconography that was much more elaborate than a simple three-quarter profile. In the United States, certain artists made this their specialty. From 1829 to 1832, William James Hubard (1807-1862), who first made his reputation as a silhouettist, exhibited portraits described as "small whole length" at the Pennsylvania Academy of Fine Arts.[5] Palmer may have seen these works in winter 1834 since on September 24 of that year, he thanked his

clients of Saint John—where he had worked for two years—in the *New Brunswick Courrier* and announced his intention to leave the region for a short time:

Mr. P. expects to return in the Spring, and in the mean time, he hopes to have the advantage of studying the best specimens of Painting in America, and thus render himself more worthy of the patronage of an enlightened public.

Through these works, Samuel Palmer shows the increasing presence of an Anglo-American style of painting in the country. The style and technique of this type of painting differ from that of an artist like Théophile Hamel, who also made use of theatrical settings.

P.B.

Notes

1. This term would also be used by photographers some twenty years later to designate small-size photos that could be exhibited or collected in an album.

2. *Le Canadien*, September 18, 1837, p. 3.

3. *Quebec Mercury*, October 19, 1839, p. 2.

4. *Le Canadien*, April 11, 1842, p. 2.

5. The following can be recognized among these small oil paintings of approximately 60 × 40 cm: Vice-President John C. Calhoun (Corcoran Gallery of Art), Senator Henry Clay (University of Virginia) and Attorney General John Marshall (National Portrait Gallery). These show the same conventions as those used by Palmer: seated subjects, shown full length in a furnished room with a backdrop of drapes and then a landscape. See Margaret C.S. Christman, *Fifty American Faces from the Collection of the National Portrait Gallery* (Washington: Smithsonian Institute Press, 1978), pp. 85-89 (Repr).

176.
Reverend Daniel Wilkie, 1843
Oil on canvas, 91.6 × 76.5 cm

Inscription
(s.d., c.l.) *Painted by* [S. Palmer?] *Quebec 1843.*

Provenance
Descendants of the Wilkie family; D. R. Wilkie; Patricia B. Keir, Victoria, great-granddaughter of the subject, 1956; Litterary and Historical Society of Quebec, 1959 (withdrawn from sale by Christie's, Montreal, April 16, 1969, No. 85); Patricia B. Keir, Victoria, 1969; gift to the National Gallery of Canada, Ottawa, 1969.

Bibliography
Quebec Mercury, December 29, 1842, p. 2, February 4, 1843, p. 3; PICTURES *1969*, p. 55, No. 85; LAMBERT *1986*, p. 17 (Repr.).

Collection
National Gallery of Canada, Ottawa. Gift from Patricia B. Keir, 1969 (15819)

I T IS DUE IN PART to the capriciousness of the Quebec winter and the early halting of navigation in December 1842 that this work exists. Delayed by certain commissions, Samuel Palmer decided to extend his stay in Quebec City and take up lodging in the Payne hotel to be more accessible to the public.[1] The former students of Reverend Daniel Wilkie (ca. 1777-1851) decided to take advantage of this opportunity to commission Palmer to paint their teacher's portrait.

An article in the *Quebec Mercury* of December 29, 1842 gave the details of this unique commission:

The pupils who attended the school for so many years past, existing under the auspices of the able and much respected Dr. Wilkie, have requested their venerable preceptor's acceptance of some gift by which they might mark the esteem in which he is held by them, as well as their sense of the education benefits they have derived from his superintendance and instruction. Their flattering wish has been kindly acceded to, and Dr. Wilkie has consented to sit for his portrait to Mr. Palmer, the talented artist now on a stay in town. This is as it should be; and will afford this reverend scholar, now in the decline of years, a gratifying token of the appreciation of that zeal, and those abilities, which have contributed to the perfection, in past years, of many of these minds which now adorn the bar, the pulpit, and the medical profession, in various parts of the province.

The canvas was officially presented to Dr. Wilkie's wife on January 30, 1843 during a small ceremony organized to mark her husband's official retirement from the teaching duties he had assumed for some 40 years.

This portrait, with its very English composition and handling, is typical of Palmer's technique. Wilkie is presented in three-quarter profile, seated in a red armchair, in front of a heavy brown curtain. Wearing a black redingote and waistcoat, the elderly gentleman with the determined look and dishevelled hair is holding an open book in his right hand. One might almost think that he was eager to get back to reading after this unfortunate interruption! In the right background, the curtains are pulled back to show a miniature landscape with a setting sun over a street scene containing what might be a temple or school. Like the book, this motif is clearly wrought with the symbolism of Reverend Wilkie's twofold career. In this rather sombre composition, the head of the sixty-year-old is defined by a high stand-up collar and cravat. These elements help draw the viewer's eye to the sitter's face, which is still manly despite the drawn features and

Fig. 176A.
Samuel Palmer,
Mrs. Daniel Wilkie,
1843; oil on canvas, 92.2 × 76.2 cm.
National Gallery of Canada, Ottawa.
Gift from Patricia B. Keir, 1969 (15820).

the sagging jowls. With its sensitive rendering, use of light and shadow, and contrasting colours, this powerful portrait with its spirited brushwork, definitely reveals considerable dexterity and great technical control. Its counterpart is a painting of Mrs. Wilkie which, although unsigned, was probably done by the same artist shortly thereafter (Fig. 176A).

A native of Scotland, Daniel Wilkie, educator and Presbyterian minister, settled in British North America in 1803. His choice quite naturally fell on Quebec City, which was outstanding due to its status as the capital and its quality intellectual and cultural life. Among Wilkie's preferred haunts during his prolific career was the Literary & Historical Society of Quebec, better known as the "Lit", founded by Lord Dalhousie (Cat. 139) in 1824. Twelve years later, Wilkie became its pres-

ident and took up the torch of "advancing literature, the sciences and the arts among all classes of citizens." (*Translation*) Hence, it is not surprising that he openly supported the initiatives of collector Joseph Légaré when the latter opened an art gallery in Quebec City in 1833 and 1838. Later on, Wilkie also promoted the establishment of the Vattemare Institute and a museum of fine arts in Quebec City in 1840 and 1845 respectively.[2]

An art lover, Wilkie the humanist closely followed the careers of two Quebec City painters. In a paper presented before members of the "Lit" in December 1833, he extolled the merits and perseverance of Légaré and Plamondon, exhorting the organization and the public in general to encourage them as much as possible. He acknowledged Légaré's interest in Canada's picturesque landscapes

and enthusiastically lauded Plamondon's talent, promise and skill in his military portraits.[3] Wilkie's enlightened and subtle comments still help us today in understanding and better appreciating the important facets of the evolution of Quebec painting in the years 1820-1850.

J.R.P.

Notes

1. *Quebec Mercury,* December 1, 1842 (advertisement also run on December 3, 6 and 8, 1842); *Le Canadien,* December 9, 1842 (advertisement also run on December 12, 14, 21, 26 and 30, 1842 and January 4, 1843).

2. Several first-hand documents related to Wilkie are cited in our doctoral thesis on Joseph Légaré. See PORTER *1981,* pp. 109, 117, 118, 120, 122, 123, 171, 228, 230 and 231.

3. *Quebec Gazette,* December 13, 1833, p. 2; *Quebec Mercury,* December 19, 1833, p. 1.

Provenance
Jeffery-Hale Hospital, Quebec City; acquired by the Musée de la Province de Québec, Quebec City, 1956.

Bibliography
FAIRCHILD 1907, pp. 159-160; MORISSET 1941/1, p. 80; MORISSET 1960/1, p. 138; HARPER 1966, p. 117; DE JOUVANCOURT 1979, p. 102; HARPER 1979, p. 195; *Nos racines*, No. 106 (1981), p. 2120b (Repr.); ART DU QUÉBEC 1981, p. 6 (Repr.); NADEAU 1988, p. 90 (Repr.); BÉLAND AND BOURASSA 1990, pp. 6, 9 and 84 (Repr.).

Collection
Musée du Québec, Quebec City. Restored in 1991, with the assistance of the Amis du Musée du Québec (56.220)

177.
James Ferdinand Turnbull and His Brother, c. 1843
Oil on canvas, 77.2 × 64.2 cm

T HIS PORTRAIT shows James Ferdinand Turnbull (1835-1917) and his older brother—despite research in various archives, we were unable to unearth additional information on the latter.[1] He was probably 10 to 12 years old when this portrait was painted, because his younger brother was 8. James Ferdinand was born in England and was one year old when his parents moved to Quebec City in 1836. He began working as a clerk in a trading company and in 1855 embarked on a long, brilliant military career mainly within the cavalry. After marrying in 1867, he travelled extensively abroad to perfect himself in this area. He was promoted to the rank of lieutenant-colonel in 1874 and, on returning to Canada in 1883, headed the Cavalry school the Canadian Government had recently opened in Quebec City. He participated in the Northwest campaign in 1885 during the Riel Rebellion and retired in 1895 after serving as inspector of the Canadian Armed Forces in Toronto.

James Ferdinand Turnbull is immortalized in at least three portraits: this one by Palmer showing him with his older brother and two works attributed to Cornelius Krieghoff. One of Krieghoff's works shows Turnbull in his early twenties—thus situating it around 1855. It belongs to a private collection and is known to us through a photograph only.[2] The other canvas is the property of the Musée du Québec and bears the initials "CK". It is attributed to Krieghoff despite its style, which is unlike that of the artist and the unusual written form of the initials. It is a partial copy of Palmer's painting showing only James Ferdinand, without his brother. The copyist, indicating his debt to the author of the original work through the mention "*After Palmer*", thus allows us to authenticate the original.

All three of these portraits come from Quebec City's Jeffery Hale Hospital. Five other works by Samuel Palmer also belonged to this establishment and were

acquired by the Musée du Québec in 1956. They were: two portraits of James Turnbull senior (one in three-quarter length and the other a full-length cabinet size, Fig. 175B), one of Caroline Oldaker, his wife, one of their two unidentified daughters (Fig. 177A) and one of James McKenzie (1788-1859), James Ferdinand Turnbull's father-in-law.[3]

In the portrait by Palmer, the two young Turnbull brothers are shown in an affectionate pose, the elder pulling his younger brother James Ferdinand close to him by the shoulder. The pose presents some problems, however, as James Ferdinand's right shoulder practically becomes part of his brother's torso. This shortcoming implies that the subjects probably sat for separate portraits which Palmer later used to paint a single work.

Palmer built his composition on the immutable principle of the triangle which, in this case, is not a perfect equilateral but whose centre is slightly off to the left over

Fig. 177A.
Samuel Palmer,
Misses Turnbull, Daughters of James Turnbull, 1843;
oil on canvas, 92.1 × 76.5 cm.
Musée du Québec, Quebec City (56.219).

the head of the older boy. Thus the artist has breathed life into his canvas and stressed the informal nature of the subject. He draws the viewer's attention to the sitters's faces, which are subtly rendered to create a focus which also sets off the sketched treatment of the background and clothing. To ensure the figures stand out, Palmer has used broad brush strokes to create a cloud-like background in shades of black, brown, brick red and blue-grey. The black attire with its red highlights creates a unified effect that is promptly shattered by the small white ruffs in order to emphasize the flesh tones. This dress is typical of that worn by boys over six at the time and, like the background, it has been rendered rather cursorily in the lower portion.

This painting was clearly done in the same spirit as that of the Turnbull sisters: the pose, composition and even harmonious colour scheme is the same. Unlike many portraits from this period, these were

not designed to be set in a medallion since, no matter how the works are turned, some white would show. This intended *non finito* effect harks back to the English tradition that endows children with the idyllic qualities of innocence and purity. In this, Palmer's two canvases resemble Joshua Reynolds' *The Gawler Boys,* painted in 1777.[4]

The portrait of the Turnbull boys is somewhat exceptional in Palmer's work, however, in that the facial contours are more polished than for the two sisters. Usually, the artist painted faces less meticulously, using broader strokes to practically sculpture the flesh from his coloured oils. This is particularly true of the portrait of Daniel Wilkie (Cat. 176). It would thus appear that Palmer used somewhat different techniques to confer upon his works a certain expressiveness in keeping with the sitter's age or character. In the case of the young Turnbull boys, beauty and innocence dictated a soft rendering to accentu-

ate the sensual charm of a child's face while evoking Arcadian youthfulness.

P.B.

Notes

1. The information provided by the parish archives of St. Andrew's Presbyterian Church in Quebec City and Lévis is not sufficient to allow us to establish definite links.

2. COOKE 1961, No. 12.

3. Jeffery-Hale hospital received large donations from the Turnbull and McKenzie families. To date, a great deal of confusion has surrounded the identification of these portraits. In fact, James McKenzie and James Turnbull were mistaken for one another when the works were acquired in 1956. Furthermore, the work that was mistakenly believed to be the half-length portrait of McKenzie was attributed to Ludger Ruelland and dated 1854, and the cabinet-size version was thought to have been done by Samuel Hawksett.

4. Ellis K. Waterhouse, *Reynolds* (London: Kegan, Paul, Trench, Trubner & Co. Ltd.), Pl. 188.

178.
Peter Patterson, 1844
Oil on canvas, 90 × 75 cm

Inscription
(s.d., l.l.) *Painted by/S. Palmer/Québec 1844.*

Provenance
Descendants of George Benson Hall, son-in-law of the subject; P. Lindsay Hall; gift to Manoir Montmorency, Beauport, 1979.

Exhibition
Quebec City 1980/2, No. 8.

Collection
Société des établissements de plein air du Québec (Manoir Montmorency), Quebec City

A S HE MOVED FROM PLACE TO PLACE in Lower Canada between 1842 and 1845, Samuel Palmer earned himself a solid reputation as a portraitist for a distinguished clientele. After painting the likenesses of various members of Quebec City's elite in 1842 and 1843 (Cat. 175 to 176)—and enjoying press coverage of his efforts—Palmer ran a notice in the *Quebec Mercury* from March 9 to November 28, 1844 stating that he was staying in the Albion hotel in Quebec City and that he was prepared to take more orders for portraits. It was during one of his short stays in the Old Capital that he painted Peter Patterson (1768-1851) and his son-in-law, George Benson Hall (1810-1876) (Fig. 178A).[1]

A wealthy landowner and successful timber merchant, Peter Patterson was highly esteemed in Quebec City business circles. His activities were centered around Montmorency where, in 1815, he had purchased the former summer residence of Governor Haldimand and the Duke of Kent. On May 27, 1844, Patterson bought the seigneury of Beauport, thus coming to own the two shores of the Montmorency river virtually in their entirety. The many real estate transactions he carried out in 1843 and 1844 show how successful he had been and how much capital he had accumulated. At the height of his glory, but at the end of his career, Patterson, aged 76, had his portrait done at the same time as that of his young son-in-law. In 1843, George Benson Hall had married Mary Jane, Patterson's only child who, when her father died eight years later, inherited his entire fortune. Hall applied himself, his intelligence and his energy to extend the activities of the family business even further, buying numerous mills and acquiring new concessions.[2]

Looking somewhat severe, Peter Patterson is presented in a three-quarter profile sitting in an armchair whose red back stands out against the plain brown background. The latter lacks uniformity: to the left of the table is the suggestion of architectural forms—the shaft and base of a column—, perhaps an afterthought on the part of the artist. The life-size portrait shows Patterson turned to the left, but gazing at the viewer. The sitter has slipped his right hand inside his buttoned-up, double-breasted black redingote. The opening at the collar allows a glimpse of a black vest and a white ascot tied around a very high collar. Such dark clothing is typical of the decade 1840-1850, the beginning of the Victorian era. Apart from the very discreet presence of the armchair, there

Fig. 178A.
Samuel Palmer,
George Benson Hall, 1844;
oil on canvas, 90 × 75 cm.
Société des établissements de plein air du Québec (Manoir
Montmorency), Quebec City.

is no ornament or attribute revealing the functions or social status of the wealthy merchant.

The portrait has clearly been designed to draw the viewer's attention to the subject's facial features and expression. The light hues of the head and vest collar contrast markedly with the dark, Spartan setting consisting of the coat, armchair and backdrop. The vitality of the face and its well-defined features are skilfully rendered, particularly in the anatomy and the flesh tones. Unlike precise line drawings, the use of very liquid oils and a finely shaded colour scheme create a play of light and shadow that serve to set off the haggard features of the toothless old man with hollow cheeks, high cheekbones, aquiline nose, protruding, elongated ears, high forehead, thinning hair, and unevenly grey sideburns. The rest of the composition—dress, furni-

ture and background—are secondary, if not entirely unimportant. Clearly, by portraying the sitter's age so realistically, the artist was aiming to produce a "faithful likeness," as guaranteed in his advertisements of December 1842 and January 1843 in the *Quebec Mercury* and *Le Canadien.*

To a certain extent, this work must be viewed in conjunction with the portrait of George Benson Hall, although the latter shows considerable differences in composition. Hall's portrait depicts a young man of 35, standing, hands clasped, and body turned toward the right, that is, in a position totally opposite to that of Hall's father-in-law, who is seated with his hands hidden. Reminiscent of certain effects proper to miniatures, the principal lines and contours of the redingote have been rendered in broad strokes, typical of Palmer's work. As in the previous portrait,

though, the artist has sought to draw our attention to the sitter's upper torso, and especially the head. Although the painting contrasts with that of Patterson in expressing the subject's age, it gives no additional information as to either the sitter's activities or his social standing. In addition to portraying two of the most influential English-speaking merchants of the 19th century, Palmer's two canvases boast definite esthetic qualities and are remarkably forceful.

M.B

Notes

1. In a paper on Palmer submitted to Université Laval in 1980, Pierre B. Landry, present assistant curator with the National Gallery of Canada, analyzed the two portraits in depth.
2. See the respective biographies of Patterson and Hall in John Keyes, DCB, Vol. VIII (1985), and Andrée Désilets, DCB, Vol. X (1972).

HENRY HUGH MANVERS
PERCY

1817-1877

THIRD SON OF THE DUKE OF Northumberland, Henry Hugh Manvers Percy was born at Burlwood House (Surrey, England) on August 22, 1817. After completing his classical studies at Eton, near London, he joined the army on July 1, 1836 as ensign in the Grenadier Guards. Two years later, in June 1838, he arrived in Canada aboard the *Inconstant,* with the second battalion of the Grenadier Guards, British reinforcements sent to Canada to quash the 1837-1838 rebellions. He stayed mainly in La Prairie, Montreal and Quebec City, taking several leaves between postings.

Later promoted captain and lieutenant-colonel, Percy served in the same regiment during the Crimean War in 1854 and 1855. On November 5, 1854, he distinguished himself in the battle of Inkerman and his valour earned him the Victoria Cross in May 1857. From 1855 until February 1865, he was aide-de-camp to the Queen. In 1861, Percy's duties took him to New Brunswick as part of a 15000-man contingent that London sent to Canada during the *Trent* Affair, which left England and the United States on the brink of war during the American Civil War. Percy had been promoted to the rank of major the previous year and now commanded the first battalion of the Grenadier Guards. In October 1862, he retired from military service and was later honoured with the titles of colonel (1874) and general (1877) in recognition of his work in the army. Percy died a bachelor in London on December 3, 1877.

Main source
HARPER 1970.

179.
Album "America", 1838-1840
53 × 39 cm

Inscriptions
(on the back, gold letters) AMERICA/LIEUT. COL./
HON. H. PERCY; (u.l., opposite Fol. 1, in graphite)
*53 Watercolour Drawings: Montreal, Quebec, etc./
by General Sir Henry Percy (1817-77) who served
in Canada/during the Insurrection of 1838.*

Provenance
Dr. Gustave Lanctôt, archivist; acquired by the
Public Archives of Canada, Ottawa, 1939.

Collection
National Archives of Canada, Ottawa (1939-399)

MQ

A. *Montreal* (Fol. 4), c. 1838
Watercolour over graphite on paper laid down, 20.5 × 30.4 cm

Inscriptions
(l.c., on the mount, in graphite, in the artist's hand[?]) *Montreal;* (u.l., vertically, in graphite, by another
hand) *Montreal.*

T HE SECOND BATTALION of Grenadier Guards arrived in Quebec City in June 1838 aboard the *Inconstant*. Among the men was Henry Hugh Manvers Percy, who had entered the regiment as an ensign two years earlier. Aged 21, he was just beginning his military career. A student at Eton from 1832 to 1835, he was probably taught by William Evans (1797/1798-1877), the college's drawing master since 1818[1], after David Cox (1783-1859) and Peter de Wint (1784-1849). Like his predecessors, Evans espoused a flexible technique that combined subtle detail with more lavish washes.

Percy thus did not arrive in Quebec a rigorously trained British topographer accustomed to mapping a site for strategic purposes. Eton had given him a different type of training and his drawing lessons, although certainly less practical, had made him a cultivated amateur instead. This is virtually all we know about Henry Hugh Manvers Percy. He has never been the subject of a separate study, either for bio-

graphical purposes or for his work. Many questions remain unanswered, including those regarding his family life, which no doubt played an important role during the youth of this soldier-to-be.

The tangible evidence Percy's stay in Quebec is a dark green cardboard compendium with reinforced corners underlined in gilt filigree and originally containing some fifty watercolours divided into 45 folios. The military ranking "LIEUT. COL/HON. H. PERCY" in gilt letters on the back of the album lead us to believe that he compiled it between July 19, 1865—when he entered the British Parliament as a member for North Northumberland, hence the abbreviation Hon. preceding his name—and May 28, 1874, when he was promoted to the rank of colonel in recognition of his military service.[2] Basically, this portfolio is a digest of his many trips abroad. Similar evidence of his participation in the Crimean War in 1854 and his travels to New Brunswick in 1861 during the *Trent* Affair may exist, but to date

no works have been found to corroborate this fact.

Percy's *America Album* is doubly important in that it is a single compendium bearing witness to the discoveries of youth. Alongside conventional sites such as *Montreal* and *Quebec From the South Shore of the Saint Lawrence River* (Cat. 179A and 179B.) or *Montmorency Falls* (Cat. 179D), Percy broke new ground in authoring a series of drawings on locations hitherto ignored, i.e. *Grosse-Île* (Cat. 179C). For a long time, the island was simply one of many possible moorings along the St. Lawrence; such was its role in the watercolours by James Peachey (Cat. 45).[3] However, a legislative act passed by Lower Canada in February 1832 gave the island a new vocation, i.e. the site of official quarantine for immigrants.[4] Sadly, the cholera epidemic of summer 1832 (Cat. 158) immediately won the island renown for the lack of means available to health authorities. A hospital and lodgings were subsequently built to more adequately

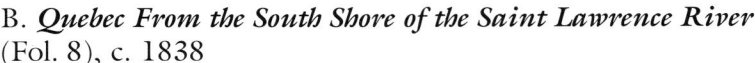

NGC

VAG

B. ***Quebec From the South Shore of the Saint Lawrence River***
(Fol. 8), c. 1838
Watercolour over graphite with traces of scraping out on paper
laid down, 20.8 × 33 cm

Inscriptions
(l.c., on the mount, in graphite, in the artist's hand[?]) *Quebec;* (u.l., vertically,
in graphite, by another hand) *Quebec.*

C. ***Grosse-Île*** (Fol. 19), c. 1838
Watercolour over graphite on paper laid down 26.8 × 36.4 cm

Inscription
(l.c., on the mount, in graphite, in the artist's hand[?]) *Grosse Isle.*

Bibliography
LEMOINE *1985,* p. 11 (Repr.); VAUGEOIS *1990,* p. 33 (Repr.).

counter another onslaught of the disease in 1834. This was the Grosse-Île that Percy discovered in approximately 1838-1840, not as someone quarantined there, but as a visitor.[5] He devoted six watercolours to it which he placed here and there in his album (Fol. 18-22 and 28). Although a few cut trees create clearings in the forest hither and yon, the rest of the island remains in its natural state. In this respect, the work shown here is perfectly representative of the series: in the foreground, a trail runs through trees and underbrush to a rocky headland topped by a semaphore. The goat which has clambered atop the outcropping may belong to the wildlife inhabiting the isle. It is associated with a whole decorative vocabulary, particularly valued at the time, on how to embellish landscapes. Early-17th-century Flemish artists included the goat in their mountainous landscapes, its agility calling to mind these wilderness sites.[6] However, in the late 18th and early 19th centuries, the British elevated this technique to the rank

of a veritable codification. In his *Three Essays: on Picturesque Beauty, on Picturesque Travel; and on Sketching Landscape,* William Gilpin voiced one of the first steps in this codification:

Living animals, like man, are beautiful in nature and on canvas. We admire in the horse (as a real object) the elegance of its form, the proud nature of its look, the lightness of its movements and the lustre of its skin. We also admire it in a representation, but as an object of picturesque beauty we prefer an old cart horse, a cow, a goat or a donkey. Their uneven contours and the roughness of their skin are much more suitable for bringing out the elegance of a brush [...] Animals with too even a coat cannot produce a picturesque effect. (*Free translation).*[7]

In 1838, this harmony figured prominently in the landscapes painted by amateur artists, and drawing manuals were quite vocal on the various means of portrayal. The goat, with its rough coat and angular form, naturally identified jagged, steep landforms. By comparison, the flowing lines of the sheep were associated

with pastoral views. This interpretation of Percy's scene of Grosse-Ile is reinforced by the artist's handling of the subject matter and use of colour. Rather than employing the transparency and softness made possible by watercolour, Percy has used strong hues—a range of greens, mauves and pinks. The use of a brown wash specifically for the goat and the log in the foreground makes the contrast even more striking. The same is true of the diminutive vessel on the horizon and the choice of light of the setting sun. Percy has endeavoured to impart a sublime quality to this hostile environment and has skilfully employed the effect of confinement. Thus, through the associations with this particular location, the viewer is filled with emotion.

Sainte-Geneviève Church (Cat. 179E) is worlds apart from this concept.[8] This composition's balance, interrupted by parallel planes through the play of shadow, depicts an entirely different view of nature. Here, the landscape is tightly controlled, especially in its development: the

AGNS

MMFA

D. *Montmorency Falls* (Fol. 27), c. 1838
Watercolour over graphite with traces of scraping out
on paper laid down, 23.4 × 34.3 cm

E. *Sainte-Geneviève Church* (Fol. 36b), c. 1838
Watercolour over graphite on paper laid down, 14 × 23.3 cm

artist has done a detailed drawing in pencil before applying the watercolour. Percy's other works generally concentrate on the essential, foregoing detail in favour of broad brushstokes, sometimes playing with the paper's grain to create lighting effects as in *Quebec From the South Shore of the Saint Lawrence River* (Cat. 179B). *Sainte-Geneviève Church* is unlike Percy's other works in that it is based on another artist's drawing, namely an ink sketch by James Duncan (Cat. 96). In it, the same majestic tree bends to form an arbour in the foreground and frame the church in the far distance. It is difficult to pinpoint the exact circumstances surrounding this copy. Perhaps fate placed the original in Percy's hands, or perhaps he took private drawing lessons from Duncan. To complicate matters even further, Duncan reproduced his drawing for Jacques Viger's album in 1839, and a fourth version of *Sainte-Geneviève Church* is still catalogued "artist unknown" in the National Archives of Canada.[9] Given the lack of solid facts, our questions

remain unanswered. However, it is tempting to see in these works, which were copied on more than one occasion, a network of exchanges that went far beyond the mere teaching of drawing by a master.

D.P.

Notes

1. Four generations of the Evans family held this position between 1796 and 1922. William Evans, known as Evans of Eton, belonged to the second generation.

2. Leslie Stephen and Sidney Lee, eds. *Dictionary of National Biography,* London, 1908-1909, Vol. XV, p. 862.

3. At the same time as Percy, Henry Francis Ainslie gives a similar picture; see BELL *1973/1,* p. 48 (Repr.). George Russell Dartnell was one of the few watercolourists to do inland views of the is-

land in 1838 (DE PENCIER *1987/1*, p. 52-53 and 103, No. 84-87, Fig. 86).

4. On the history of Grosse-Ile, see Louise Bisson, *La Grosse-Ile,* paper presented to the Department of Geography, Université Laval, for a bachelor's degree in geography, December 1978; and Marianna O'Gallagher, *La Grosse-Ile: porte d'entrée du Canada, 1832-1937* (Sainte-Foy: Carraig Books, 1987).

5. In UN MOMENT 1991 (p.77, Note 6), Susan North transcribes a passage from the *Quebec Mercury* of August 15, 1835 relating a day trip of soldiers from the garrison to Grosse-Ile.

6. This is true for *Landscape with Flight to Egypt* by Paul Bril, reproduced in Yvonne Thiery, *Les peintres flamands de paysage au XVIIᵉ siècle. Des précurseurs à Rubens.* (Brussels: Lefebvre and Gillet, 1986), p. 103.

7. William Gilpin, *Three Essays: on Picturesque Beauty, on Picturesque Travel, and on Sketching Landscape.*

8. This same folio includes another view of Sainte-Geneviève as seen from Ile Bizard.

9. Unidentified artist, *Sainte-Geneviève Church,* watercolour over pencil, 19 × 30.6 cm. National Archives of Canada, Ottawa (1979-46-76). The work is erroneously identified as a view of Montreal and dated 1820.

ANTOINE PLAMONDON

1804-1895

 NTOINE PLAMONDON was born in Ancienne-Lorette, near Quebec City, on February 29, 1804. On March 1, 1819, he was apprenticed to painter Joseph Légaré, under whom he trained for six years. In March 1825, Plamondon opened his own studio in Quebec City on Rue Saint-Hélène (Rue McMahon). In July of the following year, he embarked for France, where he was to complete his artistic training in the company of his cousin, Ignace Plamondon. Both studied in the studio of Jean-Baptiste Guérin, dit Paulin-Guérin, the official painter of King Charles x. Plamondon left France during the July revolution in 1830, which effectively ended the reign of Charles X. Upon his return, he attempted to compel recognition and monopolize the Quebec City market, taking advantage of the prestige attached to being the pupil of "the painter to the king of France." (*Translation*) His ambition grew, touching off several disputes with competitors, especially foreign artists who came to carve out a career for themselves in this country. Such painters included James Bowman and Henry D. Thielcke, about whom he published several barbed comments. Plamondon soon acquired a reputation as a highly talented painter, which caused the Reverend Daniel Wilkie (Cat. 176) to say in December 1833 that he was both a skilled copyist and a masterly portrait painter. In summer 1836, Plamondon travelled to Montreal to meet the demand of a large clientele. There he completed several remarkable portraits (Cat. 187, 188, 191 and 192) and was commissioned to execute the new paintings of the Stations of the Cross for the Notre-Dame church (Cat. 195). In this he was assisted by the two apprentices he hired in 1834, François Matte and Théophile Hamel. Although he had difficulty in completing all his Montreal commissions, he returned to Quebec City three years later.

In the 1840s, he gave drawing lessons at the Séminaire de Québec and to the novices at the Hôpital général (Cat. 196). He was also involved in various social and cultural activities, especially as a musician, and in the project to establish a Vattemare Institute in Quebec City. However, the mid-1840s represented a difficult turning point for him, both on the financial level, with the burning of his home, and on the professional level, with the return from Europe of his former pupil and new competitor, Théophile Hamel. In spring 1851, having lost his studio at the Château Saint-Louis, he decided to move to the property he had owned at Pointe-aux-Trembles (Neuville) since 1842.

Despite his many civic responsibilities and farming duties, Plamondon did not in any way relinquish his artistic endeavours. Taking advantage of his huge studio, he completed his famous work, *The Pigeon Hunt* (Cat. 266), and executed several large religious paintings. However, he showed signs of slowing down in the 1860s; Plamondon again criticized the importation of European works, and later the commissions which church authorities awarded directly to Italian painters. During this period, he nevertheless completed a few original secular works, including *The Flutist,* of which he made at least five copies. Plamondon did not stop painting until 1885, the year in which he put his studio collection up for sale. He lived for another ten years before dying on September 4, 1895 at Pointe-aux-Trembles at the age of 91. Antoine Plamondon remained a bachelor throughout his life.

Main source
PORTER *1990/1*

180.
The Ecstasy of Saint Francis of Assisi, 1825
Oil on canvas mounted on plywood, 66.8 × 54.6 cm

Inscription
(s.d., l.l.) *Ant: Plamondon/Pinxit. 1825.*

Provenance
Séminaire de Québec, before 1934; on deposit at the Société du Musée du Séminaire de Québec, 1983.

Bibliography
Université Laval 1933, No. 480; *Morisset 1935/1*, p. 53; *Morisset 1935/2*, p. 4; *Morisset 1935/3*, p. 4; *Morisset 1936-1937*, Vol. I, pp. 12-13; *Morisset 1944*, pp. 53 and 112, No. 49; *Bourassa 1986*, p. 212.

Collection
Musée du Séminaire de Québec (Pc983.63)

I T IS NOT KNOWN HOW OR WHEN this work, dating from Antoine Plamondon's youth, became part of the collection of the Séminaire de Québec. It seems unlikely that the painting was acquired after 1874, the year in which Université Laval purchased Joseph Légaré's Picture Gallery. The institution's yearbooks, usually so loquacious with regard to donations made to the art gallery, remain silent about this work, and the archives reveal nothing about a possible purchase after that date.[1] Although the origins of Canadian paintings in the Musée du Séminaire are generally traced, those of certain canvases by Plamondon remain a mystery. Such is the case for *The Ecstasy of Saint Francis of Assisi,* completed in 1825. Given the artist's ties to the Séminaire de Québec and the commissions he received from that institution, it is possible that this work became part of the collection during the years in which Plamondon gave drawing lessons there, namely, between 1833 and 1835, and between 1840 and 1851. This hypothesis is plausible, but remains unproven, since research in the archives has yielded nothing. Only one thing is known about this painting: when Gérard Morisset visited the institution in 1934, *The Ecstasy of Saint Francis of Assisi* was hanging in the refectory of the Grand Séminaire.

It is easy for art historians to draw a parallel between *The Ecstasy of Saint Francis of Assisi* at the Séminaire de

Québec and the oval work to the right of the high altar in the retable of the chapel at the Hôpital général in the same city. Indeed, the works are identical and were painted simultaneously by Plamondon. According to Morisset, tradition has it that "in 1824, when the Hospitalières had their chapel restored, they gave Plamondon the original of Saint Francis of Assisi (it was in poor condition), on the condition that the artist paint another copy which was as faithful as possible."[2] (*Translation*) The painter therefore completed the painting for the Augustines' retable and took the opportunity to make another copy. The Hôpital général's commission thus helps us trace the origin of the work, but not its model. We are more hesitant than Morisset to conclude that the original of these works was a painting by Frère Luc which he examined at the Sulpicians' establishment in Montreal.[3] This canvas cannot have served as Plamondon's model because the iconography of the saint is very simplified and the construction is awkward. The dimensions of the canvas are also too small for the medallion of the Hôpital général retable.[4]

By means of a more thorough study of this retable, we can trace its evolution and, consequently, understand *The Ecstasy of Saint Francis of Assisi's* place in it. It should be noted that the paintings on either side of *The Assumption of the Virgin* by Frère Luc were commissioned in 1697, as the annals indicate:

It was that same year that panelling was installed around the Pulpit, the arch of the Retable, two paintings on either side of the Retable, one of St. Augustine and one of St. Magdalene, the Sanctuary Baluster, and the Retable was done in the manner in which it appears today. Paintings were also done in the panels of the panelling.[5] (*Translation*)

Despite the fact that no reference was made to the medallion of St. Francis of Assisi and its companion piece, St. Francis of Sales, these paintings were probably executed at the same time. If this is the case, the model used by Plamondon could not have been a work painted by

Frère Luc, since it had already been returned to France by that date. Whatever the case may be, when Plamondon "replaced" the St. Francis of Assisi in 1825, the nuns had just undertaken the second phase of their renovation and commissioned nine paintings from Joseph Légaré. It is not known whether Plamondon collaborated with his former master in completing this set, but he was indeed the one who painted *The Ecstasy of Saint Francis of Assisi*, probably one of his first works.

This work corresponds to the codifications promoted during the Counter-Reformation. In fact, the iconography of St. Francis of Assisi (1182-1226)[6] was disseminated shortly after his death, and borrowed many themes from episodes commonly related in traditional hagiographical texts; but it was with the Council of Trent that the themes became more specific and the concepts of asceticism and ecstasy preferred. As in Plamondon's work, the saint wears a cowl attached to the waist by a cord characteristic of the Order of Friars Minor.[7] A scourge used for flagellation is evocative of his attitude of mortification. Often associated with Christ crucified, St. Francis is depicted with his arms crossed on his chest, enabling viewers to see his stigmata. The crucifix, symbol of his entreaty and devotion to, as well as his identification with Christ, is also reminiscent of the ecstatic vision of stigmatization. This entire iconography dates directly back to the austere outlook of the 17th century, when mortification and ecstasy were intertwined within the same spiritual fervour.

In this regard, it is plausible that the Plamondon's model was French in origin, partly because the saint was undoubtedly very popular in France during the 17th century and partly because the strong current of devotion and piety flowing through the country resulted in austere depictions which became examples to be followed by members of orders in their quest for grace.

J.C. and P.B.

Notes

1. Our knowledge of this collection leads us to believe that the institution rarely purchased Canadian works at that time. In this context, the 1912 purchase of Théophile Hamel's *Self-Portrait with a Landscape* (Cat. 117) is an exception. The Séminaire more commonly commissioned the portraits of the seminary's clergymen.

2. MORISSET 1935/3, p. 4. Research conducted more recently, however, has not uncovered the source of this tradition.

3. To explain how the painting of the Hôpital général de Québec ended up in Montreal after being in Plamondon's possession, Morisset forged the various fragments together and came up with an astute solution: "We know that Plamondon undertook in 1832 [*sic*] the execution of a monumental set of the Stations of the Cross for the Notre-Dame church in Montreal. About this vast set [...] Plamondon had a brush with Father Vincent Quiblier, priest at Montreal's Notre-Dame, who had doubts about the artist's liturgical orthodoxy. Did Plamondon try to mollify the recalcitrant priest by giving him Frère Luc's painting? Maybe...." (*Translation*) See MORISSET 1935/3, p. 4.

4. The medallion of the painting of Montreal's Notre-Dame church measures 59 cm × 49.5 cm, while that of the Hôpital général measures 69 cm × 54 cm.

5. Archives du monastère des Augustines de l'Hôpital général de Québec, 13.14.1.1/1.9.1 *Annales du monastère Notre-Dame-des-Anges de l'Hôpital-Général de Québec*, Vol. I, 1693-1743, year 1697.

6. It should be remembered that Francis of Assisi was the founder of the Order of Friars Minor or the Franciscans. Dedicated to mendicant poverty and the glorification of Christ through evangelism, "Poverello" was one of the great mystics of Christian history, his most famous ecstasy being the seraphic vision of Christ on the cross, who imprinted stigmata on him. He was canonized only two years after his death. The story of his life is modeled on Christ's. On the iconography of St. Francis of Assisi, see Émile Mâle, *L'Art religieux de la fin du XVI* siècle, du XVII* siècle et du XVIII* siècle. Étude sur l'iconographie après le Concile de Trente*, 2nd edition (Paris: Librairie Armand Colin, 1951), pp. 171-179; Louis Réau, *Iconographie de l'art chrétien, tome III, Iconographie des saints*, Vol. I (Paris: Presses Universitaires de France, 1958), pp. 516-531; *L'immagine di San Francesco nella Controriforma* (Rome: Edizioni Quasar, 1982).

7. Although it does not appear in Plamondon's work, this belt is usually depicted with three knots which symbolize the vows of poverty, chastity and obedience taken by the Franciscans.

181.
Monseigneur Joseph-Octave Plessis, 1826
Oil on canvas, 90 × 76.5 cm

Inscriptions
(s.d., l.r.) *Ant Plamondon/pinxit Québec 1826;* (l.r., on the volume) *B.V./R*

Provenance
Descendants of the Ranvoyzé and Rousseau families; Marie-Louise Rousseau-Joncas estate, Quebec City; acquired through Louis Joncas by the National Gallery of Canada, Ottawa, 1978.

Exhibition
Montreal 1980-1981.

Bibliography
MORISSET 1935/2, p. 2; MORISSET 1935/9, p. 2; MORISSET 1936-1937, Vol. II, p. 76; MORISSET 1960/1, p. 103; MORISSET 1960/2, p. 14; ROULEAU-ROSS 1983, pp. 99, 124-128 and 227 (Repr.).

Collection
National Gallery of Canada, Ottawa (23168)

ALTHOUGH the portrait of the eleventh bishop of Quebec City held at the National Gallery of Canada cannot be defined as a post-mortem portrait, it was indeed executed after the death of Monseigneur Joseph-Octave Plessis (1763-1825), who passed away on December 4, 1825.[1] Plamondon, who completed his training with Légaré in March of that year, was then seeking commissions in order to establish his market and his reputation among enthusiasts.[2] Producing a portrait of the deceased prelate, whose memory still lived on, was a means of attracting attention. Plamondon seemed to have taken advantage not only of the interest raised by the archbishop's death, but also of the publicity surrounding the presentation to Monseigneur Plessis, by the parishioners of Saint-Roch of Quebec City, of his portrait painted by John James[3] (Fig. 181A) in late January 1825.

An initial version of this portrait, completed by Plamondon and dated 1825, was purchased by Father Jean Raimbault, superior of the Séminaire de Nicolet[4] (Fig. 181B). It is unlikely that Monseigneur Plessis posed for the Nicolet version, because his state of health deteriorated considerably over the course of the year. Plamondon's composition is based on James' portrait, which hung in the rectory of the Saint-Roch church in Quebec City. The young painter nevertheless made a major change to the prelate's iconography, depicting him with a stole,[5] his breviary in hand. The stole, richly embroidered with patterns of flowers and leaves, is decorated with lace. Here, Plamondon was not depicting the administrator or the archbishop, but rather the pastor, former priest of the influential parish of Notre-Dame de Québec (1792-1805) and founder of ecclesiastical services in the Saint-Roch district. The devout Catholic seems less distant and more human. Plamondon portrayed a less authoritarian figure than that suggested by James in his full-length portrait. Nicolet's version, which is a half-length of Monseigneur Plessis, is more intimate, even though the face is severe[6] and the subject continues to wear his pectoral cross.

The second version—preserved at the National Gallery of Canada—is more ambitious, and differentiates from James' prototype in the arrangement of the hands. In this portrait, Monseigneur Plessis is holding the hand clasped around the breviary against his body and lets his right hand bearing the episcopal ring hang from the armrest. The gilt-edged breviary bears a title piece and decoration in gold bands. The surplice sleeve, as in James' painting, is tapered in the forearm and decorated with lace. Another important element, the signature, is written in large, cursive letters like an advertisement on the armrest, on which the name, city and year are also indicated. Plamondon's style is also different from James' in other respects; except for the background, which is solid, Plamondon preferred to decorate all parts of the painted surface. For example, he folded the stole in order to fill the space at the bottom of the painting and suggest resistance against the leg. His interest in brighter colours is omnipresent: in the flesh tints, in the shimmering ripples of the taffeta

Fig. 181A.
Antoine Plamondon,
Monseigneur Joseph-Octave Plessis, 1825;
oil on canvas, 72.1 × 58.1 cm.
Séminaire de Nicolet (TA-24).

Fig. 181B.
John James,
Monseigneur Joseph-Octave Plessis, 1824-1825;
oil on canvas, 229 × 157 cm.
Musée du Québec, Quebec City (76.153).

mozzetta, in the richness of the embroidery, in the highlights of the material on the gilded tassels.

There are 29 known portraits of Monseigneur Plessis, but only a few can be dated from his lifetime.[7] This means he became an object of veneration after his death, touching off an avalanche of copies of his image. A clever strategist—he was a member of the Legislative Council between 1817 and 1825—and indefatigable worker, he performed the tasks of coadjutor beginning in 1801, bishop from 1806 to 1819 and finally archbishop of the Diocese of Quebec from 1819 to 1825, which earned him many tributes. The fad for portrait galleries in religious institutions[8] gave rise to many replicas, variants and copies.

Monseigneur Plessis considered religious art another means of asserting his authority and respect for the moral and religious values of which he was the guardian.[8] Not only did he ensure that the architectural rules were complied with in the construction of new churches, but he also encouraged the decoration of religious buildings and was himself a modest collector. He took European art, based on rules of clarity and symmetry, as his model and considered it the norm. He was also one of the instigators of the shipment of 120 Desjardins paintings in 1817 and brought

back another lot of 60 works upon his return from Europe in 1820. By promoting church decoration, he indirectly stimulated the market for Quebec painters. In fact, several church authorities who could not obtain imported works commissioned them from local artists. Monseigneur Plessis often set himself up as a censor, his fear being that the compositions of artists ill trained in drawing, with their bizarrely rendered subjects smeared with poorly harmonized, garish colours, would distract the faithful, rather than stimulating their piety.   L.L.

Notes

1. See in this regard the texts of historian James H. Lambert, whose excellent notice was published in the DCB, Vol. XI (1987).

2. He composed for the Cap-Santé church a history painting representing *Saint Anne Saving Shipwreck Victims*. See *MORISSET 1980*, pp. 47-49 and 134-139 (Repr.).

3. *La Gazette de Québec*, January 31, 1825; *Le Canadien*, February 2, 1825; Archives de l'archevêché de Québec, Registre des lettres, Vol. XII, p. 186, letter from Monseigneur J.-O. Plessis to Monseigneur de Telemesse (J.-J. Lartigue), February 14, 1825.

4. *ROULEAU-ROSS 1983*, pp. 124-128 and 226-227 (Repr.). Mgr. Plessis had founded the Séminaire de Nicolet in 1806.

5. John James had painted in 1824 the portrait of Curé Joseph Signay, in a surplice, wearing the stole and holding a breviary (Fabrique Notre-Dame de Québec, MSQ deposit). The stole seems to be a characteristic feature with which the priests of Notre-Dame de Québec are depicted, including Father Augustin-David Hubert (1751-1792), priest from 1775 to 1792. Plamondon and Hamel used this element in the other portraits of the priests of Notre-Dame de Québec, and also for those of other parishes. See, for example, the illustrations in *THIBAULT 1974*, pp. 57-58; *VÉZINA 1975/1*, pp. 97-99 and 102.

6. This severity is accentuated by the rigid line of the lips and the dark eyebrows. According to his biographer, Father Bois, Monseigneur Plessis powdered his hair but it had not turned grey.

7. Since Mme. Rouleau-Ross completed her inventory in 1983, two more portraits of Monseigneur Plessis have been recorded (MQ and Archdiocese of Ottawa). Other than the portrait painted by John James, only an anonymous portrait housed in the Hôpital général de Québec and attributed to Louis Dulongpré, an aquatint completed around 1820 by Gerritt Schipper (see Cat. 47 to 50) and a medallion portrait decorating a snuffbox (Diocese of Quebec) can be considered as works completed before 1825.

8. Locations where a portrait of Monseigneur Plessis can be found include: the rectory of Saint-Eustache, the seminaries of Trois-Rivières, Nicolet, La Pocatière, Montreal and Quebec City; the convents of the Ursulines and the Hôtel-Dieu de Québec; the archdioceses of Montreal, Quebec City and Ottawa.

9. See in this regard the section on the artistic taste of the bishop of Quebec City and his influence on the arts in the early 19th century in *ROULEAU-ROSS 1983*, pp. 49-64.

Fig. 182A.
Antoine Plamondon after Jean-Baptiste Guérin,
Abbé Philippe Jean-Louis Desjardins, 1826-1830;
oil on canvas, 72.3 × 60.3 cm.
Musée des Augustines de Hôtel-Dieu de
Québec.

182.
The Despair of Cain, 1826-1830
After Jean-Baptiste Guérin, dit Paulin-Guérin
Oil on canvas, 64.6 × 80.8 cm

Inscription
(s., l.r.) *A. Plamondon.*

Provenance
Baby Collection; Séminaire de Québec, c. 1910;
on deposit at the Société du Musée du Séminaire
de Québec, 1983.

Bibliography
Le Fantasque, July 28, 1838, pp. 136-138;
Université Laval 1913, p. 63, No. 356 entitled
Adam et Ève; Laval University 1923, p. 72,
No. 356 entitled *Adam and Eve's Despair*;
Bellerive 1925, p. 30; Université Laval 1933,
No. 248 entitled *Adam et Ève*.

Collection
Musée du Séminaire de Québec (Pc983.59)

H ISTORY STILL SHROUDS in mystery
Antoine Plamondon's study tour
in Europe following his appren-
ticeship under the young tutor, Joseph
Légaré. At any rate, we know that he left
Quebec City in July 1826, probably with
his cousin Ignace Plamondon (Cat. 200).
They had letters of recommendation from
Father Louis-Joseph Desjardins, chaplain
to the nuns of the Hôtel-Dieu de Québec
hospital, to his brother, Father Philippe-
Jean-Louis Desjardins, the vicar general of
Paris, under whose protection they remained while studying in the studio of
Jean-Baptiste Guérin, *dit* Paulin-Guérin
(1783-1855), the official painter of
Charles X. Not being very resourceful, they
were apparently a burden to their protector, who went so far as to call them "babes
in arms." (*Translation*) Terrorized by the
July revolution of 1830, Antoine hastened
to return to Quebec City in the fall,
bringing with him the visual fruits of his
new training, in this case, paintings, drawings and engravings. These included two
copies completed in Paris after works by
his master Guérin: one, a portrait of his
protector, Father Philippe-Jean-Louis
Desjardins (Fig. 182A), after a work executed in 1828;[1] the other, ***The Despair of
Cain***, copied from a famous canvas which
had been exhibited at the Salon de 1812
(No. 454) with the title *Cain after the
Murder of Abel*. As a gesture of gratitude,
Plamondon donated the first work to Father Louis-Joseph Desjardins, but kept the
second. Journalist and drawer Napoléon
Aubin thus had the opportunity to view it

in July 1838 during a visit to Plamondon's
new studio at the Hôtel-Dieu de Québec.
Professing himself drawn to the few masters in the artist's possession,[2] Aubin proved
agreeably surprised by the quality of the
copy of Guérin's work, as can be seen in
this extract from the account of his visit
published in *Le Fantasque* of July 28, 1838:

Mr. Plamondon possesses excellent copies by
his own hand; we can cite a Virgin by Raphael
for the daintiness of its strokes, the delicacy
and brightness of the colours, and the transparency of the skin; the crown of thorns for its
vigour and expression; and especially a small
copy of the great work by Guérin, Cain's despair, in which the copyist skilfully managed to
reproduce the hideous tinge of horror, remorse
and affliction spread to the slightest detail, but
especially on the face of the guilty man, author
of the first murder; the fiery sky, skilfully contrasted with dark clouds, seems to reflect within Cain's haggard eye the glimmer of blood,
the sorrow stamped on the face of his wife at
his feet is an expression of despair analogous to
her sex; she seems overcome in the midst of
this upheaval of nature. Cain adds curses to his
remorse. In a word, this painting renders all
the grandeur of a beautiful design within a
small copy. (*Translation*)

Fig. 182B.
Jean-Baptiste Guérin,
Cain after the Murder of Abel, c. 1812;
oil on canvas, 46 × 55.7 cm.
Musée d'art et d'histoire de Rochefort (France).
Gift from M. Lesson, 1890 (No. 103).

Fig. 182C.
Antoine Plamondon,
Sainte Anne saving Shipwreck Victims, 1843
(detail);
oil on canvas, approximately 220 × 164 cm.
Église de Sainte-Marie de Beauce.

This mention of a "small copy" of a "great work" is significant in that it confirms that the work copied by Plamondon was indeed the large version painted by Guérin (2.91 m × 3.90 m), which was exhibited at the salons of 1812 and 1814, transferred by the French government to the Musée de Toulon in 1872 and destroyed during the bombings of 1943-1944.[3] Fortunately, the Musée d'art et d'histoire de Rochefort has preserved an advanced study (Fig. 182B) which corresponds perfectly to Aubin's description of Plamondon's copy and to the description given in the catalogue of the Salon de 1812:

Cain, a fugitive, followed by his wife and children, is stopped at the edge of a precipice. The thunder bursting above his head fills him with fear and awakens his remorse. Satan, who urged him to commit fratricide, is attached to his feet in the form of a serpent. The bloody bank of clouds is reminiscent of his crime, and his children cry in the arms of their mother who is fainting from fatigue and sorrow, entreating divine clemency.[4] (*Translation*)

In fact, save for the latter's breasts, which the prudent Plamondon chastely hid, the copy is very close to the Rochefort's version in terms of iconography and plastic qualities.

At the end of his description of the work painted by Guérin's disciple, the editor of *Le Fantasque* said he "regretted that some church had not yet commissioned Mr. Plamondon to paint a large

copy of this beautiful work. This subject would be highly suitable for such a place, both for the horror it inspires against the first man who spilled innocent blood, and because it would give a Canadian artist the opportunity to use all his talent in recreating, so to speak, his master's inspiration." (*Translation*)

To our knowledge, Plamondon never had such an opportunity; however, he borrowed elements from his small copy for three of the twelve versions of the *Saint Anne Saving Shipwreck Victims* that are known to us. In those for Baie-Saint-Paul and Sainte-Marie de Beauce (Fig. 182C), he repeated the group consisting of Cain's wife and children, while for the work at Saint-Jean on the Ile d'Orléans, he was content to merely use Cain's bust. This practice, which is typical of a colonial art which was attempting to assert itself and develop by means of borrowing, is proof of the deep attachment felt by the Quebec painter for his former master, the portraitist Guérin. It should not be forgotten that it was through Guérin that Plamondon could claim to be a part of the great classical tradition of Raphael, Poussin and Louis-Antoine David.[8] Given this context, it is highly revealing that in 1871 he was still fond of introducing himself as "the pupil of Paulin Guérin, the painter to Charles X in Paris."[6] (*Translation*)

J.R.P.

Notes

1. This painting is now preserved at the Musée des Augustines de l'Hôtel-Dieu de Québec. Copies by Plamondon exist at the Congrégation de Notre-Dame in Montreal, the Musée des Ursulines in Quebec City and the Séminaire de Nicolet. Guérin's original work has disappeared, but we are familiar with it thanks to an engraving—reversed—by Belliard.

2. In 1845, Plamondon was forced to say that he was "obliged to part with" (*Translation*) his small but valuable collection following the fire of June 28. The works he then possessed were attributed to Van Ostade, Murillo, Rubens, Poussin, Peeter Tays and Sneyder (*Le Canadien,* August 18, 1845, p. 2). Two years earlier, the artist had in vain offered his Rubens—a *Decapitation of Saint John the Baptist* measuring 1.45 × 2.3 m—to collector and politician Denis-Benjamin Viger (Musée du Québec, Centre de documentation, artist's file, letter from Antoine Plamondon, to D.-B. Viger, June 10, 1843). During his visit to Plamondon's studio, Aubin became especially interested in this painting, *The Martyrdom of Saint Erasmus* by Poussin and *The Birth of Hercules* attributed to Albani, which were not mentioned in the newspapers of August 1845.

3. The collections of the Musée de Toulon still include a small oil on wood (26.5 × 31 cm) which is fairly close to Guérin's composition, but whose colour scheme does not seem to conform with his palette.

4. Description given by Marie-Pascale Bault, curator at the Musée d'art et d'histoire de Rochefort, through our colleague Louise d'Argencourt, curator at the Montreal Museum of Fine Arts, whom we would like to thank.

5. Early in his career, Guérin was the protégé of François Gérard (1770-1837), who had himself benefitted from the David's protection in his younger days.

6. *Le Courrier du Canada,* March 17, 1871, p. 3.

183.
Mrs. Thomas Pod, née Julie Blais,
c. 1831
Oil on canvas, 72.7 × 59.7 cm

Inscription
(i., l.l.) *A.P.*

Provenance
Descendants of the Pouliot and Lemieux families;
Claude R. Lemieux, Noranda, great-grandson of
the goddaughter of the subject; acquired by the
Montreal Museum of Fine Arts, 1967.

Exhibitions
Sarasota 1966-1967, No. 71; Montreal 1967/1,
No. 98; Ottawa 1970, No. 6.

Bibliography
CARTER *1966*, pp. 29 and 30 No. 71 (Repr.);
CARTER *1967*, No. 98 (Repr.); HUBBARD *1970*,
pp. 25, 66-67 and 119, No. 6 (Repr.); DUMAS
1970, p. 21.

Collection
Montreal Museum of Fine Arts. Mr. and
Mrs. Maurice Corbeil Fund(1962.1341)

F ARMER'S DAUGHTER, Julie Blais married in Sainte-Foy on March 29, 1800 one "Thomas Pod[1], merchant innkeeper from Quebec City, a boy of age born in England knowing neither his father or his mother, whom he lost in his childhood and having come to this country shortly after, while still a child." (*Translation*) Thanks to the diary of Juliana Pouliot, their goddaughter, written in the late 19th century (PC), we know that Thomas Pod was born in England in the 1760s. He lost his parents at the age of 12 and was claimed by his navigator cousins. He then became a sailor and decided to move to Canada. After spending a few years "selling trifles" (*Translation*), he opened his own business in the stairway of Rue Champlain in Quebec City. He probably lived a short time in Beaumont, where he owned a house, before returning to Quebec City to his goddaughter's home, where he died some 25 years later at the age of 84. It was not possible to find information regarding his wife. All we know is that she had a daughter, who was named Julie after herself, on July 31, 1803.

The portrait of ***Mrs. Thomas Pod, née Julie Blais*** was probably completed the same year as that of her husband, which was signed and dated by Plamondon in 1831 (MMFA). Both paintings were executed when the couple was living with Mrs. Pod's goddaughter in Quebec City. A study of the clothing bears this date out. With her immense Alsatian cap and the leg-o'-mutton sleeves of her gown, typical of the 1830s, Mrs. Pod takes up the entire painting. The lines of the bodice, lace ruff and coiffure, consisting of wide curls, all provide a fullness which highlights the subject's severe face. A stylistic analysis also confirms the suggested date, since the artist's style was not yet fully developed. Some rather less-than-successful effects betray the artist's unsureness. Certain areas around the neck and the upper lip lack assurance, and the artist had difficulty integrating the subject within a tangible space in the arrangement of the lighting. Nevertheless, skill and sureness of strokes dominate the execution of the lace and fabrics. The background, seemingly monochromatic and even, is in fact subtly worked with a myriad of strokes which texture a very thin, finely shaded surface, making the canvas appear to be lying beneath the subject in several areas.

Completed shortly after the artist's return from Paris, the portrait of Mrs. Pod marks an important step in Plamondon's experimentation which lasted until 1835. By using this very direct approach to the human face, which dominates the space of the painting, the artist is attempting to create an effect of monumentality, both with proportions and style. He generates maximum tension between the subject and the spectator, given the model's frontality and proximity, enhanced by dramatic lighting and stark background. Plamondon was to experiment with different ways of incorporating his subject into space, sometimes using a dark background as in this painting, and sometimes lighting it to provide a clearer outline of the side of the face left in shadow, and sometimes suggesting in certain cases a discreet drape used as a foil. The portrait of *Mrs. Amable*

Fig. 183A.
Antoine Plamondon,
Mrs. Amable Dionne, née Catherine Perreault,
1834;
oil on canvas, 68.6 × 55.9 cm.
Musée du Québec, Quebec City (34.506).

Dionne, née Catherine Perreault, dating from 1834 (Fig. 183A), is an example of the second method. Although the clothing is more sober and only the coiffure crowns the subject's head, this portrait closely resembles that of Mrs. Pod. In one, the starkness harmonizes with the face's softness and allows the subject's personality to shine through; in the other, the amplitude of the effects accentuates the character's gravity. A *Portrait of a Lady*, also dating from 1834 and recently acquired by the National Gallery of Canada—of which a copy dating from 1835 is preserved at the Montreal Museum of Fine Arts—constitutes an excellent example of the third method developed for these half-length portraits. The treatment of the clothing and the background takes on new importance here, which, in some extent, runs contrary to the austerity and intensity sought in these works. Having exhausted the resources of this approach, the artist was then to give the subject the space needed to show his or her personality more fully, by using a less restrictive composition and employing the subject's pose and gestures as a means of expression.

P.B.

Note
1. To date, his name has been written "Podd" or "Paud," but all documents consulted, including several which were signed, indicate that the name was indeed spelled "Pod."

184.
Cyprien Tanguay, 1832
Oil on canvas, 73 × 59.9 cm

Inscriptions
(s.d., l.r.) *Ant. Plamondon/pinxit 1832.;* (l.r., on the book) *CICERON/I;* (l.c., on the sheet) *Cicero...* [illegible]; (b.,u.c., in black ink) *Cyprien Tanguay Etud./agé de 12 ans. 1832.*

Provenance
Mgr Cyprien Tanguay, Quebec City; bequeathed to the Séminaire de Québec, 1902; on deposit at the Société du Musée du Séminaire, 1983.

Exhibition
Quebec City 1952, No. 79; Ottawa 1959, No. 12; Bordeaux 1962, No. 24; Ottawa 1970, No. 7; Quebec City 1973; Ottawa 1979, No. 2.

Bibliography
(?) *Quebec Mercury,* July 27, 1833, p. 3; ASQ, *Manuscrit 34,* Vol. VI, p. 279, December 27, 1902; *UNIVERSITÉ LAVAL 1913,* p. 63, No. 361 dated 1852; *UNIVERSITÉ LAVAL 1923,* p. 73, No. 361 dated 1852; *BELLERIVE 1925,* p. 33 dated 1852; *UNIVERSITÉ LAVAL 1933,* p. 82, No. 253 dated 1852; *MORISSET 1935/2,* p. 4; *MORISSET 1935/6,* p. 6; *MORISSET 1941/1,* pp. 73 and 84e (Repr.); *COLGATE 1943,* p. 110; *MORISSET 1952,* p. 37, No. 79 (Repr.); *MORISSET 1953/1,* p. 39; *MORISSET 1956/2,* pp. 11 and 13 (Repr.); *HUBBARD 1957/2,* pp. 21 and 24 (Repr.); *BARBEAU 1957* (Repr.); *MORISSET 1959/2,* No. 12 (Repr.); *MORISSET 1960/1,* p. 107; *MORISSET 1960/2,* p. 14; *MARTIN-MÉRY 1962,* p. 19, No. 24; *HARPER 1966,* p. 83; *Forces,* No. 9 (fall 1969), p. 16a (Repr.); *HUBBARD 1970,* pp. 25, 67 and 120, No. 7 (Repr.); *DUMAS 1970,* p. 21; *HAMEL 1971/1,* p. 47; *HAMEL 1971/2,* p. 15; *THIBAULT 1973/1,* pp. 153, 160 and 165 (Repr.); *THIBAULT 1973/2,* p. 8 (Repr.); *LORD 1974,* pp. 35 and 36 (Repr.); *SOUCY AND THIBAULT 1974,* p. 105; *Nos racines,* No. 58 (1979), p. 1180b (Repr.); *CONRAD-BURY AND LEBEL 1979,* pp. 4, 5, 6 and 13, No. 2; *Weekend Magazine,* February 17, 1979, p. 10 (Repr.); *LAMOUREUX 1984,* p. 52; *GALARNEAU 1988,* pp. 7 and 10 (Repr.); *PORTER 1984,* p. 1; *NICOLAÏ 1990,* pp. 29, 30, 31-39, 44, 57, 76, 94 and 119 (Repr.); *LACROIX 1990,* p. 20.

Collection
Musée du Séminaire de Québec (Pc983.9)

U PON HIS DEATH IN 1902, Monseigneur Cyprien Tanguay (1819-1902) bequeathed to his *alma mater,* the Séminaire de Québec, his portrait painted by Antoine Plamondon in 1832 when he was taking classical studies at that institution. At that time, he had the fierce determination of a 13-year-old adolescent discovering the fascinating universe of the humanities with a conscientious and docile avidity.

The young Cyprien is shown face-on, writing on a table covered in dark-green baize. This continuous horizontal plane takes up approximately one quarter of the painting's surface and is treated in such a way that three sides of the table cannot be seen by the spectator, thereby creating, with its bird's-eye view of the props, a feeling of presence and promoting a dialogue between the spectator and the subject which goes beyond the boundaries of time.[1] Young Tanguay's left fist rests on a book with "French" binding whose spine reveals the name of Cicero. Opposite, beside two books—one with "English" binding—are large sheets of paper, whose diagonal surface is curled in one corner, and on which can be seen the first two words which the young student inscribed thereon with his goose quill, after having dipped it in the pewter inkwell resting on the table in the foreground. Above, the pyramidal torso of the adoles-cent stands out against a dark, solid background. He is wearing a dark blue seminarian's uniform with white piping, adorned with a lace jabot and a white ruff of irregular design. The horizontal lighting used by the artist highlights a serious and concentrated face in which large, attentive eyes shine. All-in-all, this is a simple, frank and sensitive work whose highly classical structure cannot be considered static. On the contrary, this animated canvas uses light which plays as subtly on the flesh tints and the edges of objects as on the contrasting textures of fabrics and the disparities within a sober palette of colours. In short, Gérard Morisset was justified in exclaiming, "What fluidity in the execution of this pleasant canvas and what harmony in its tones! Other children, boys and girls, were to pose for the artist; he was not to do any better." (*Translation*) In fact, this canvas clearly surpasses in intensity the *Joseph-Octave Fortier* of the Séminaire de Trois-Rivières painted by the same artist during the same year. Not only does it not have the same foreground as *Cyprien Tanguay* but, what is more, its subject seems awkward and nervous (Fig. 184A).

Underlying the obvious pictorial qualities of this portrait belonging to the Musée du Séminaire de Québec is a strong evocative power, which subtly translates the values and realities of Quebec society at that time. If it can be assumed that all the objects resting on the table represent to some extent student Cyprien Tanguay's attributes, is it not revealing that Cyprien Tanguay bases his education on a book containing texts by Cicero, a famous personage in Ancient Rome who, despite his modest origins, managed to distinguish himself through his talents as an orator and through his constant defense of moral values? Then too, it was not by chance that the first word inscribed by Cyprien is "Cicero." This is entirely symbolic of the acceptance, recognition and transmission of values which transcend time and space. As well, the depiction of two books, one with "French 18th-century binding" and the other with binding "of an English style, with a deeply etched relief decoration," (*Translation*) on the same table also seems significant. As our colleague Laurier Lacroix so rightly pointed out, this duality summarizes to some extent the cultural and political reality of Lower Canada in which an ancient French heritage and foreign realities associated with English colonial power encounter, confront and mingle with each other. And on another level, such a serious student as Cyprien Tanguay, already studying the ideas and knowledge inherited from the great men of the past, can also be seen as an archetype of the male universe which was parallel to the female horizons of one Ézilda Papineau, still under her mother's supervision and who, like the

Fig. 184A.
Antoine Plamondon,
Joseph-Octave Fortier, 1832;
oil on canvas, 66 × 58.4 cm.
Musée Pierre-Boucher (deposit from the
Séminaire de Trois-Rivières). Gift from Abbé
Dusablon.

Fig. 184B.
James Bowman,
Cyprien Tanguay, 1830;
oil on cardboard, 55.8 × 45.5 cm.
Collège Sainte-Anne-de-la-Pocatière.

latter, is preparing to assume with dignity her future responsibilities as hostess and housewife sensitive to the decorative arts (Cat. 187). All of which goes to show that the painted portrait is never far from social reality....

That being said, the portrait of Cyprien Tanguay by Plamondon remains an outstanding work whose very commission raises questions. Some would certainly be tempted to consider this work premonitory. In fact, it is not unsurprising that this student, surrounded by his tools of knowledge and already so aware of the values of tradition, was destined to become many years later a great archivist and a renowned genealogist, whose *Dictionnaire généalogique des familles canadiennes-françaises* (1871-1890) is still today a compulsory reference work. Nor is it surprising that there is a previous portrait of Cyprien Tanguay, painted in 1830 when he was only 9 years old (Fig. 184B). The work of American James Bowman, this oil on cardboard is today preserved at the Collège de Sainte-Anne-de-la-Pocatière, the institution at which the young Cyprien stayed briefly for three months in 1830.[2] It is certainly permissible to think that his parents, who were very attached to their son, wanted to be able to evoke his image in their Quebec City residence in his absence through this portrait. However, why then commission a second portrait two

years later? Dissatisfaction with the relative inadequacy of the first likeness? Maybe, although another hypothesis can be made. It should be remembered that 1832 was a terrible year for Quebec because of the cholera epidemic (Cat. 158), which decimated its inhabitants. Given this context, in which life probably seemed tenuous, the unchanging image of a loved one must have been of considerable value.

These hypotheses and the obvious differences in quality between Bowman's and Plamondon's *Cyprien Tanguay* aside, it is entirely logical to see in these portrayals an indication of the competition and rivalry existing between the two artists. Since his arrival in Quebec City in the early 1830s, Bowman had endeavoured to carve out a niche in the portrait and religious painting market in addition to assuming the duties of drawing master to the Ursulines. To Plamondon, jealous of the prestige of his recent European training and anxious to continue increasing his clientele, the American artist represented a definite threat. He was therefore pleased to finally find the dreamed-of opportunity to get back at him during the summer of 1833, when the editor of the *Quebec Mercury* said he much appreciated a diorama or "perspective painting" representing "the interior of the Capuchin Chapel in Rome" which Bowman was exhibiting in Quebec City. In the same breath, he solicited the opin-

ion of Plamondon who, in keeping with his disposition, needed no coaxing to ridicule Bowman's work. Through the sometimes scathing journalistic exchanges, it seems obvious that our artist's contemporaries appreciated his talents despite his jealous and quarrelsome temperament. In an article published on July 27, 1833, the editor of the *Mercury* indicated that he had recently seen in the painter's studio "some portraits of uncommon merit," including one of a respected leading citizen and another "of a student of the Seminary," two paintings deemed valuable both as works of art and as portraits. If the artist was flattered by the compliment, he did not show it. On the contrary, he reproached the journalist for not having said anything about the "9 religious history paintings"— probably religious copies—and for being content to discuss two "simple half-length portraits" which he considered "the least of [his] collection."[3] (*Translation*) Should the "portrait of a student of the Seminary" discussed in the *Mercury* be indeed that of Cyprien Tanguay, there is no doubt that, in his comments, the artist's main intention was to have the last word, at the risk of seeming to minimize the plastic qualities of one of the best portraits he had painted since his return from Europe in 1830. Throughout his career, his esthetic appreciation of his own work and that of his competitors fluctuated widely depending on the circumstances, his primary criterion being, as always, the defense of his personal interests and the preservation of his market.

J.R.P.

Notes

1. The composition of this painting naturally calls for a comparison with that of *Self-Portrait*, which the artist painted in 1882 from a photograph. The formula is basically the same, but the integration of the props in the foreground was clearly better in 1832.

2. We would like to thank Denis Castonguay for pointing out the existence of this work. The back of this painting bears the inscription: "*Cyprien Tanguay/âgé de 9 ans/Bowman pinxit 1830*" (Cyprien Tanguay/aged 9/painted by Bowman 1830). There is a copy of the same format— apparently a later copy—of this portrait in the collection of the works on paper of the Musée du Séminaire de Québec. It was also painted on cardboard, but completed with coats-of-arms corresponding to the status of "camerarius a secretis" conferred upon Monseigneur Tanguay by the Pope in 1887.

3. *Le Canadien,* August 7, 1833, p. 1.

185.
Saint Francis Xavier Preaching in India, 1834
Oil on canvas, 226.2 × 162.5 cm

Inscription
(s.d., l.r.) *Ant Plamondon p-xit/1834.*

Provenance
Acquired by Fabrique de Saint-Augustin de Portneuf, 1836; deposit at the Grand Séminaire de Québec, university campus, 1962; acquired by the National Gallery of Canada, Ottawa, 1976.

Exhibition
Quebec City 1984-1985, No. 51.

Bibliography
Le Journal de Québec, December 16, 1874, p. 2; BÉCHARD *1885,* p. 198; EAST *1934,* p. 5; MORISSET *1935/2,* p. 4; *LE GRAND HÉRITAGE 1984,* pp. 35 and 52, No. 51 (entry by Yves Lacasse) (Repr.); BOURASSA *1987,* p. 121; LAROCHE-JOLY *1990,* pp. 337 and 380-381.

Collection
National Gallery of Canada, Ottawa (18616)

THIS WORK painted by Antoine Plamondon in 1834 and purchased two years later by the Fabrique de Saint-Augustin de Portneuf is in fact a copy of an anonymous work which the Saint-François-Xavier de Batiscan parish had ordered from France in 1733 and is now on deposit at the Musée du Québec. Antoine Plamondon painted at least three other versions of it: the first dates from 1833 and was completed for the Saint-Jean parish on the Ile d'Orléans; the second was delivered to Saint-Charles-de-Bellechasse at an undetermined date; and the third, of unknown origin but now housed at the Musée du Québec, has also been attributed to him. A similar copy, although now considered anonymous, can be found at Saint-Jean-Chrysostome de Lévis. On the same subject, highly popular during the first half of the 19th century, we can mention the works by François Baillairgé (around 1802-1805, Sainte-Famille, Ile d'Orléans), an unidentified artist (1805, MQ), and Yves Tessier (around 1830, Sainte-Élizabeth de Joliette and Diocese of Sherbrooke). Finally, several works depict St. Francis Xavier alone, preaching near a river bank.

Batiscan's original work, which is the source of Plamondon's painting, is in very poor condition and was almost entirely repainted. It is therefore difficult to know exactly how much original input the artist had in this composition. One thing that is certain, his style is recognizable, especially the way in which the paint is applied: the artist uses a very wide stroke and a fairly clear paste in certain areas, while in others the texture is richer and he uses a fine brush to paint the beard or to create thick areas of white or gold which make the paint layer vibrate in the highlights.

Plamondon seemed to hold this painting in great esteem, along with the set he delivered to Saint-Augustin. In fact, he used these works as an example some forty years after their completion (in 1874) when he virulently attacked Martino, a painter-set painter, and he cited the churches which he and his team had "slapped paint on":

And you, Saint-Augustin, my neighbour [he was writing from Neuville], the band of fine arts marauders visited you and murdered you; but they could not destroy you entirely because, for many years, you have been decorated with excellent paintings: a St. Michael, a St. Francis Xavier, a St. Augustine and four paintings of saints have protected you from this horde of barbarians.... (*Translation*)

Canonized in 1622, some 70 years after his death, St. Francis Xavier is among the most representative saints of the Counter-Reformation. His worship and iconography were quickly propagated, thereby confirming two practices promulgated by the Council of Trent: the worship of saints and the worship of images. In Canada, his image was disseminated very early. Second patron of the country after St. Joseph, the companion of Ignatius Loyola found his place in this missionary land, incarnating the dynamic dimension of the Society of Jesus. Obviously, it was the Jesuits who, before the Conquest, encouraged devotion to the one who was called the apostle of India. Curiously, this devotion experienced an upsurge in popularity just at the time when the Jesuits left the country (between 1800 and 1843). The socio-religious situation explains this phenomenon to some extent. However, there are other reasons behind the propagation of a Jesuit iconography in the early 19th century. Upon the death of the last Canadian Jesuits—Jean-Baptiste Well in Montreal in 1792 and Jean-Joseph Casot in Quebec City in 1800—certain rites, practices and customs, such as the novena to St. Francis Xavier, were taken up by other religious communities. Perhaps in a spirit of solidarity, but also in reaction to the Protestant threat which had grown since the Conquest, the survival of religious communities in Canada and, by extension, that of the Jesuits, was fiercely promoted. Thanks to the Sulpicians, the Jesuits returned to Canada in 1843.[1] The missionary revival became a veritable leitmotif for the clergy, engaged in a struggle for survival and the expansion of Catholicism in North America. This struggle was the physical manifestation of a resurgence of the spirit which had driven the Jesuits in the early days of the Counter-Reformation.

Given these facts, the iconography disseminated can be seen in a whole new light. The two scenes propagated from the life of St. Francis Xavier—his preaching in India and his death, alone and abandoned on Shangch'uan Shan (St. John Island) off the coast of China—were significant in a movement aimed at asserting the Catholic presence in Canada by mobilizing the faithful and fighting against Protestant proselytism, both in schools and in missions.

As regards the novena in honour of the saint, the clergy seemed to prefer the depiction of St. Francis Xavier's death, which provided the faithful with an image of a threatened clergy, and a model of virtue which reminded them of the imminence of death, the primacy of spiritual

values and the marvels of salvation. Conducive to meditation and internalization, this imagery was particularly well suited to the saying of the novena, although the scene of St. Francis Xavier preaching was also used in this same context, as evidenced by the painting which Plamondon sold to the Saint-Jean parish on the Ile d'Orléans in 1833. The parish priest tells us that:

In November 1832, I informed my parishioners who asked me for the novena (of St. Francis-Xavier) that it would be appropriate, if we were to obtain this advantage, to put something towards a painting of the St. The proposal was welcomed, a collection in the amount of £16.15 was soon taken up. The success of this venture changed our initial plan entirely, which was to have only a small painting of 3 or 4 feet in height. I therefore came to an agreement with Mr. Plamondon, Painter, of Quebec City for a painting of 9 by 11 feet for the price of £30. Said Painting must consist of 12 subjects, namely, St. Frs X (life size), a small clergyman in a surplice, 10 Indian listeners and finally a rigged vessel in the distance.[2] (*Translation*)

This description corresponds perfectly to the painting by Plamondon, who changed his composition slightly from the Batiscan canvas by adding a few ships sailing on a calm sea in the background and by not depicting the figure at the left, of whom only the face can be seen in the other versions.

The iconography of St. Francis Xavier preaching, with its motivational dynamism, can also be linked to another contemporary phenomenon, the *Oeuvre de la Propagation de la Foi* (project to propagate the faith), established on December 28, 1836 in the Diocese of Quebec by Monseigneur Joseph Signay (Cat. 125 and 189) and in February 1838 in the Diocese of Montreal by Monseigneur Jean-Jacques Lartigue (Cat. 242). This movement was the tangible result of the missionary activities undertaken for several years, especially in the Northwest Territories, at Monseigneur Joseph-Norbert Provencher's instigation.[3] The goal of this association—a veritable army organized in "centuries" and "sections"—was to economically support missionaries and was under the protection of St. Francis Xavier.[4]

This organization perhaps made up for the shortfall resulting from the government's refusal as of 1837 to pay the salary of missionaries from the funds derived from the liquidation of the Jesuits' property.[5] Whatever the case may be, all these elements give us a context for the dissemination of the imagery associated with St. Francis Xavier. The early 19th-century portrayal of a Jesuit saint which enhanced

the dynamism and apostolic zeal of an order which no longer functioned in Canada was not, after all, so surprising, given that it provided a model for the faithful and the clergy, recently mobilized by a similar mission.

P.B.

Notes

1. Georges-Émile Giguère, "Restauration de la Compagnie de Jésus au Canada," *Société canadienne d'histoire de l'Église catholique* [*Canadian Catholic Historical Association*], Vol. XXXVI (1969), pp. 67-73.

2. Archives de la Fabrique de Saint-Jean, île d'Orléans, *Livres de comptes 1788-1849*, handwritten notes of Father Antoine Gosselin, p. 68.

3. Father G. Dugas, *Monseigneur Provencher et la mission de la Rivière Rouge* (Montreal: Beauchemin, 1889), pp. 161-162.

4. *Rapport sur les missions du diocèse de Québec 1839-1845 qui sont secourues par l'Association de la Propagation de la Foi*, Vol. I, 1839-1841, pp. iii-iv. Although the St. Francis Xavier guild had been turned down by the Sacred Congregation for Divine Worship in 1843, only to be accepted in 1904, Monseigneur Signay's mandate specified that a plenary indulgence would be granted on "the feast day of St. Francis-Xavier, patron of the Association, on December 3." (*Translation*) See *Mandements, lettres pastorales et circulaires des évêques de Québec* published by Monseigneur Têtu and Father C.O. Gagnon (Quebec City: A. Côté et Cie, 1888), Vol. III, p. 348, and *LAROCHE-JOLY 1990*, pp. 343 and 368, Note 11.

5. Archives de l'archevêché de Québec, Registre des lettres, Vol. XVIII, p. 52, "Lettre de Mgr. Joseph Signay à Mgr. Jean-Jacques Lartigue," March 28, 1837 quoted in *Rapport de l'archiviste de la Province de Québec*, Vol. XVIII (1937-1938), p. 192. See also *Mandements..., op. cit.*, p. 341.

186.
Abbé David-Henri Têtu, 1835
Oil on canvas, 122 × 101.5 cm

Inscriptions
(s.d., l.r., on the parchment) *Ant. Plamondon pinxit/1835;* (lower, on the same parchment, almost erased) [Québec]; (l.r., on the volumes) IMITAT/DE/ JESUS-C; HISTOI/SAINT.

Provenance
Descendants of the Têtu family, Saint-Thomas de Montmagny; Colonel J.-Georges Garneau, Westmount; acquired by the National Gallery of Canada, Ottawa, 1966.

Exhibition
Ottawa 1970, No. 12.

Bibliography
TÊTU *1898/1,* p. 202; TÊTU *1898/2,* pp. 68-69; RAPPORT ANNUEL *1966-1967* (Repr.); LA CHRONIQUE *1967,* p. 49, No. 189 (Repr.); HUBBARD *1970,* pp. 28, 70 and 123, No. 12 (Repr.); LACROIX *1990,* p. 20.

Collection
National Gallery of Canada, Ottawa (14895)

F ATHER DAVID-HENRI TÊTU (1807-1875) was the brother of Charles-Hilaire and Cyrice Têtu (Cat. 135). Born in Saint-Thomas de Montmagny, he was educated at the Collège de Saint-Hyacinthe. After his ordination in 1829, he was appointed vicar, then, in 1833, priest to the Saint-Roch parish in Quebec City. In 1839, he became parish priest to Saint-Roch-des-Aulnaies, where he remained until his death. He was buried in the crypt of the parish church.[1] This portrait comes from the descendants of the Têtu family in Montmagny, David-Henri's birthplace. As reported in 1898 by his nephew and biographer, Monseigneur Henri Têtu, the portrait was then in "the Saint-Thomas family home." (*Translation*) The portrait may have been commissioned by a close relative shortly after the vicar was appointed to the Saint-Roch parish in Quebec City. The abbé was then 28 years old.

The three-quarter-length portrait shows the young priest upright and almost face-on. Clothed in his black soutane and standing in front of a background of red drapes, he is lit from the upper left corner. Like Napoleon, his right hand is depicted slipped inside the opening of his soutane—a convention frequently used in portraiture at that time—while his left hand rests on a pile of four books, near which are sheets of paper, an inkwell and a quill. Reading and writing are an integral part of this classically educated individual. The books form a pyramid and two of them are clearly identified: *Imitation de Jésus-Christ* and *Histoire Sainte.*

The painting was signed and dated by Antoine Plamondon five years after his return from France. Beginning in the mid-1830s, Plamondon acquired a solid reputation in the field of portraiture, with Reverend Daniel Wilkie (Cat. 176) even stressing his excellence as a portraitist in 1833. The following year, the artist announced that he had at his disposal "an apartment in the magnificent provincial parliament building in which to do his paintings." (*Translation*) That same year, he also hired two young apprentices,

François Matte and Théophile Hamel. Plamondon apparently executed the portrait of Father Têtu in this studio and in the presence of his young students the following year.

Plamondon, like Hamel after him, is known for having executed several portraits of members of the upper and lower clergy (see Cat. 181 and 189). His portrait of *Abbé David-Henri Têtu* stands out in many ways from the rest of his work in general and from his portraits of clergymen in particular. Along with the portrait of Zacharie Vincent (Cat. 194), this portrait is one of the few in which the model is portrayed upright from the knees up. Moreover, the artist rarely made the background seem entirely covered in large drapes (See *Portrait of a Lady,* 1834, MMFA; *Joseph Laurin,* 1841 and *François-Xavier Paradis,* 1842, MQ).

Between 1834 and 1838, Father David-Henri Têtu's vicar at Saint-Roch was Charles Chiniquy. In *Cinquante ans dans l'Église romaine* (*Fifty Years in the Roman Catholic Church*), which was first published

Fig. 186A.
Théophile Hamel,
Abbé David-Henri Têtu, 1841;
oil on canvas, 84 × 71. cm.
Musée du Québec, Quebec City (76.160).

in English in 1886 and translated around 1903, the famous defrocked priest and renegade describes, not without a few pithy comments, the physique of his former priest:

He had a very beautiful appearance: tall and well-proportioned, wide forehead, blue eyes, a remarkably handsome nose, pink lips. He had very white skin, too white even for a man; but his short sideburns...corrected what could have been too feminine in his face and gave his entire person both a virility and pleasantness. (*Translation*)

The portrait painted by Plamondon, which corresponds to this description in every way, was not greatly appreciated by David-Henri Têtu's biographer. Although he only knew his uncle when the latter was already well advanced in years, Monseigneur Henri Têtu considered the portrait very unlike the subject, especially compared with the two other portraits of the same individual. In fact, this somewhat effeminate image of this young priest with fine features and clear skin did not correspond with Monseigneur Têtu's ideal image of the members of his strong, robust family:

There are three large portraits of M. Têtu. One is at the Saint-Thomas family home, but while the painting is quite good, the likeness is not. Another, in the sacristy of Saint-Roch de Québec, seems excellent to me, as is the one which graces the sacristy of Saint-Roch des Aulnaies. (*Translation*)

As we have already mentioned, the portrait at the Saint-Thomas family home is the one which is today housed at the National Gallery of Canada; the second, signed and dated by Théophile Hamel in 1841, was acquired by the Musée du

Québec in 1976 (Fig. 186A); and the third portrait, which still hangs at the Saint-Roch-des-Aulnaies church, was executed by Eugène Hamel, nephew of Théophile, in 1874. Besides these oils, there is a photograph taken at the time of the last painting, in which the subject's pose is identical to that in Plamondon's work.

It is interesting to compare the portraits completed within six years of each other by the master and his former apprentice. Hamel's work—one of the first signed by the artist—was painted the year following his apprenticeship with Plamondon. Unfortunately, we do not know all the circumstances surrounding the commission and execution of this work. What is more, this portrait, until recently housed at the Saint-Roch church, was painted two years after the priest left this parish.[2] Whatever the case may be, Hamel utilizes several conventions in the composition of his subject used at the same time by Plamondon in his portraits of the clergy. The 1841 portrait shows the priest seated, dressed in his liturgical clothing, his left hand inside the opening of his soutane and his right hand holding a book half open. The priests Baillargeon, Bédard and Chiniquy painted by Plamondon are also portrayed in this way, seated and dressed in surplice and stole, and holding a book (in the case of the latter two). The 1835 portrait, in its simplicity of composition but great evocative power, stands as the half-way point in Plamondon's work between his stark paintings of the early 1830s and the more sophisticated works of the early 1840s. It also stands out from the other portraits of clergymen executed by the artist in Quebec City at that time. In

these works, the subject is portrayed either half-length and close up (*Abbé Pierre-Flavien Turgeon,* circa 1830, HDQ), or seated further back (*Abbé Charles Chiniquy,* 1842, PC; *Abbé Laurent-Thomas Bédard,* 1842, HGQ; and *Abbé Charles-François Baillargeon,* 1850, Fabrique Notre-Dame de Québec). Likewise, of the portraits of parish priests of this period, the portrait of a young, educated, city-dwelling priest is, to some extent, midway between the very sober portrait of the country priest (*Abbé Louis Delaunay,* Cat. 204) and the large, official, full-length portrait presented as a token of gratitude by parishioners (Théophile Hamel, *Abbé Patrick McMahon,* Fig 137A, and *Abbé Joseph-David Déziel,* Fig. 137B).

M.B.

Notes

1. See the biographies of TÊTU 1898/1; TÊTU 1898/2 and Father J.-B.-A. Allaire, *Dictionnaire biographique du clergé canadien-français. Les anciens* (Montreal: Imprimerie catholique des sourds-muets, 1910), p. 512.

2. There was nothing in the archives of the Fabrique de Saint-Roch de Québec about the portraits painted by Plamondon and Hamel. We know through newspapers that Hamel toured the Lower St. Lawrence area in 1841, where he executed a certain number of portraits, including those of François Têtu and his wife (PC) of Montmagny, as well as those of their son Charles-Hilaire and his wife (MMFA) of Rivière-Ouelle. During this trip, the artist probably painted the portrait of another member of the same family, recently appointed parish priest to Saint-Roch-des-Aulnaies. It is therefore possible that Father David-Henri Têtu had, as a souvenir, given this painting to his former parishioners in Quebec City.

187. (See colour reproduction, p. 88)
Mrs. Louis-Joseph Papineau, née Julie Bruneau, and Her Daughter Ézilda, 1836
Oil on canvas, 122 × 106.7 cm

Inscriptions
(s.d., l.l., on the arm of the armchair) *A. Plamondon 1836;* (l.c., on the sheet of music) *Ézilda.*

Provenance
(?) Miss. Ézilda Papineau, Montreal, before 1867; Descendants of the Papineau family; Mrs. Westcott Papineau, Montreal, before 1970; J. R. Westcott Papineau estate, Montreal, 1972 (on deposit at the National Gallery of Canada since 1971); acquired by the National Gallery of Canada, 1974.

Exhibitions
Montreal 1960, No. 14; Ottawa 1970, No. 22.

Bibliography
Le Canadien, October 10, 1836, p. 2; *Onze artistes 1960,* No. 14; *Collard 1960-1961,* pp. 8-9 (Repr.); *Lefebvre 1963,* pp. 160-163; *Hubbard 1970,* pp. 28, 75 and 130, No. 22 (Repr.); *Dumas 1970,* p. 21; *Lord 1974,* pp. 36, 37 and 90 (Repr.); *Galerie nationale 1975,* p. 72, No. 37 (Repr.); *Porter 1975,* p. 6; *Amtmann 1976,* p. 352 (Repr.); *Rumilly 1977,* p. 182; *Nos racines,* No. 65 (1979), p. 1218 (Repr.); *Lacasse 1983/1,* pp. 28 and 91; *Fox 1986,* pp. 25-26 (Repr.); *Villeneuve 1987,* pp. 105 and 117 (Repr.); *Brown and Linteau 1988,* p. 321 (Repr.); *Derome, Bourassa and Chagnon 1988,* p. 74; *Porter 1990/1,* p. 922; *Nicolaï 1990,* pp. 59-62, 63, 65, 114 and 147 (Repr.).

Collection
National Gallery of Canada, Ottawa (17920)

188.
Louis-Joseph Papineau, 1836
Oil on canvas, 122 × 106.5 cm

Inscriptions
(s.d., l.l., on the table-cloth) *A. Plamondon/1836;* (on the library books *économie politique*/T. II; *desmosth*/T. I; *aristote*/T. III; *jefferson* T. I; *esprit des lois*/T. I; *fox speech*/T. X; (on the book held by the subject) *C. ONIS/OP.RA;* (b., on the stretcher) *Président (Orateur) de l'Assemblée du Bas-Canada/de 1815 à 1840.*

Provenance
(?) Louis-Joseph-Amédée Papineau, Montreal, before 1867; Descendants of the Papineau family; Mrs. Westcott Papineau, Montreal, before 1970; J. R. Westcott Papineau estate, Montreal, 1972 (on deposit at the National Gallery of Canada since 1971); acquired by the National Gallery of Canada, 1974.

Exhibitions
(?) Montreal 1887, No. 218; (?) Montreal 1892, No. 434; Montreal 1960, No. 13; Ottawa 1970, No. 21.

Bibliography
Le Canadien, October 10, 1836, p. 2; MQ, Fonds de la famille Hébert, "Letter from Louis-Joseph-Amédée Papineau to Louis-Philippe Hébert", August 18, 1887; (?) *Catalogue 1887,* p. 40, No. 218; (?) *MacDonald 1892,* p. 29, No. 434; *Simard 1952,* p. 62 (Repr.); *Onze artistes 1960,* No. 13; *Collard 1960-1961,* pp. 8-9 (Repr.); *Lefebvre 1963,* pp. 160-163; *Hubbard 1970,* pp. 28, 74-75 and 129, No. 21 (Repr.); *Dumas 1970,* p. 21; *White 1971,* p. 43 (Repr.); *Lord 1974,* pp. 36 and 90 (Repr.); *Galerie nationale 1975,* p. 73, No. 38 (Repr.) identified as *Portrait de Joseph Papineau* painted by Louis Dulongpré; *Nos racines,* No. 61 (1979), p. 1205 (Repr.); *Lacasse 1983/1,* pp. 28 and 91; *Villeneuve 1987,* pp. 105 and 117 (Repr.); *Derome, Bourassa and Chagnon 1988,* p. 74; *Porter 1990/1,* p. 922; *Lacroix 1990,* p. 20.

Collection
National Gallery of Canada, Ottawa (17919)

F OR ANTOINE PLAMONDON, 1836 was a busy year. Although a wide range of commissions flowed in from every direction, it was his talents as a portraitist which were most appreciated. Henceforth, Plamondon's reputation was to spill over the boundaries of the capital of Lower Canada. In June, he was proud to inform his usual clients "that at the repeated urging of several of Montreal's leading citizens, he must leave Quebec City to practise his art in that city for a few weeks."[1] (*Translation*) On the 27th of that month, he used *La Minerve* to inform the Montreal public that he was lodging "with M. Augier *Café Français* Rue Notre-Dame, across from the Houses of Government." (*Translation*) In the same issue, the newspaper editor commented on the artist's arrival in highly flattering terms:

We went to see our fellow countryman Mr. Plamondon, who arrived from our capital three or four days ago to spend some time in Montreal and practise his art here. We have always heard that Mr. Plamondon was a skilful artist. A few connoisseurs, who have had the opportunity to view his paintings, have praised them very highly. We are ourselves convinced that these reports have not been in any way exaggerated, and we do not hesitate to proclaim Mr. Plamondon as the country's leading talent in painting. We strongly encourage enthusiasts and those who wish to study this art to take advantage of this opportunity. (*Translation*)

With such an opinion, Plamondon enjoyed great success in Montreal, to the point where he was not able to meet the demand. In addition to landing the major contract for the 14 large canvases of the Stations of the Cross for the Notre-Dame church (Cat. 195), he executed a number of "family portraits" (*Translation*), including that of Louis-Joseph Papineau, with its companion piece, a portrait of his wife Julie and his daughter Ézilda. This commission was very prestigious, given Papineau's political status and his current public reputation. Upon his return to Quebec City in early October, Plamondon, who constantly took care to advertise himself and preserve his artistic aura, found the means to inform the public of his return through the editor of *Le Canadien*, dated October 10:

The public can now view in his studio portraits of M. and Mme. Papineau, with one of their young Daughters, lacking only a few final touches. We are not afraid to say that M. Plamondon is the first to have given us a good portrait of the great *Patriote*. (*Translation*)

It should be remembered in passing that it was thanks to the generosity of the Speaker of the House of Assembly, Louis-Joseph Papineau himself, that the artist had occupied since April 1834 "an apartment in the magnificent provincial parliament building in which to do his paintings."[2] (*Translation*) His neighbour was British portraitist Henry Daniel Thielcke, who enjoyed the same privileges.

The two portraits commissioned by Papineau in 1836 are in many respects indissociable. Not only do the large red drapes in each portrait complement one other and the subjects face one other, but these portraits should be viewed together. In fact, we do not think it would be going too far to refer to them as a diptych. These works are as ambitious as they are novel in their composition, setting and rich accessories. With these paintings, Plamondon made one of his rare uses of a design which his disciple Théophile Hamel was later to turn to advantage: the presence of child next to her mother. It should be remembered that, except in a few cases, the artists of Lower Canada would not portray a couple in a single painting, preferring to use separate works. Such a decision often resulted in a simple juxtaposition of two half-length portraits of the same format. Given this context, the integration effort inherent in the Papineau portraits leaps to the eye, the dynamism of these companion pieces being an essential criterion in their appreciation, over and above the individual qualities of each work.

The left portion of our "diptych" could have been entitled "the interrupted music lesson," but it bears the less imaginative and more explicit title of **Mrs. Louis-Joseph Papineau, née Julie Bruneau, and Her Daughter Ézilda.** Daughter of a Quebec City merchant and member of the Assembly, Julie Bruneau (1795-1862) had married Papineau in April 1818. They had three sons and two daughters, of whom Ézilda (1828-1894) was the elder.[3] Plamondon depicted the eight-year-old young lady in the right half of his painting. Seated at her piano, she still has her hands on the keyboard, but has interrupted the monotonous rhythm of her scales for a moment to cast a curious glance at the spectator. Her carefully groomed coiffure explodes into a mass of ringlets at the wide neckline of her bodice. Her crinoline gown sports a large blue bow at the back of her waist. She is also wearing pantalettes falling to her ankles, an item of clothing not reserved to young girls, as can be seen in the portrait painted by Théophile Hamel in 1852 of Mrs. Cyrice Têtu and her son Amable (Cat. 134). On the wall in the background is a lyre, which can be associated with poetry or with young Ézilda's activity. Between her and her mother, the artist painted a charming bouquet which both rounds out the composition and ensures a harmonious, if not symbolic, transition.

Mrs. Papineau is shown seated, resting her arms on the arms of a chair. Two rings adorn her right hand: the first, set with an emerald, graces her index finger, while the second, a ruby, encircles her middle finger. In her left hand she holds a small piece of paper marked with Ézilda's name on which the artist, ever a great lover of music, has carefully written a score which seems to correspond to scales. Drawing Mrs. Papineau's left hand seems to have given Plamondon some difficulty, but the artist managed to make up for it in the rendering of the attire of this rich member of the bourgeoisie. She is wearing a sumptuous gown of yellow satin shot through with brown and green patterns, with a pleated bodice ending in a boned point above an enormous crinoline skirt. Her huge leg-o'-mutton sleeves taper in at the elbows and extend to the wrists, which are decorated with a fabric bow and ruffles that partially cover the hand. This highly sophisticated costume, which was no longer the latest in fashion,[4] is complemented by a chiffon scarf or mantilla embroidered with silvered leafy patterns. Mme. Papineau's high neckline brings out the brilliance of a gold chain, while another chain, from which hangs a cross set with topazes, decorates the bodice. If the lady's set face shows every one of her 40 years, it is perhaps because of her sophisticated, yet heavy coiffure in which mother-of-pearl flowers and leaves are entwined in the coils of hair, which are topped with a huge comb resembling a crown or diadem.

This latter detail would not go unnoticed at the time, as can be seen in this satirical commentary in Montreal's *Le Populaire* of August 4, 1837, shortly before the first *Patriote* insurrections:

We have seen a portrait of Queen Victoria, produced by one of the American newspapers. Our sovereign seems to be endowed with a gentle, yet noble face, and her hair forms a beautiful crown. We have seen in Quebec City a portrait of Mme. Papineau who, except for her figure and age, mimics that of our Queen. It seems that this lady, very involved in the future plans of her illustrious husband, wanted to see if a crown would sit as well on her head, and she took care to be painted with a comb which makes her look like she is wearing a diadem. Many people, upon seeing this painting, will exclaim "*It is still too soon!*" but, as a great man once said, *things move quickly in Canada*. (*Translation*)

Fig. 188A.
Théophile Hamel,
René-Édouard Caron, 1846;
oil on canvas, 124.3 × 100.3.
Musée du Québec, Quebec City (47.128).

Fig. 188B.
C. Hamburger after Robert A. Sproule,
Louis-Joseph Papineau, 1832;
lithograph, 20 × 15.9 cm (image).
Musée du Séminaire de Québec (portfolio 6-G,
Fol. 49).

Fig. 188C.
C. Hamburger,
The Honourable Denis-Benjamin Viger, 1832;
lithograph, 20.4 × 16.5 cm (image).
Musée du Séminaire de Québec (portfolio 6-G,
Fol. 93).

Behind the irony, we can see that Plamondon's composition is all the more open to criticism because Mrs. Papineau seems to be seated beneath a dais of hangings draped in a valance, somewhat as if she were sitting on a throne....

For his part, Louis-Joseph Papineau is attempting to compel recognition from the viewer. Like his wife, he is seated diagonally in an armchair and occupies the centre of the composition. Behind him, the tiled floor and great fringed drapes, from which hang two large ropes decorated with golden tassels only serves to enhance the subject and the accoutrements of his occupation. As Speaker of the House of Assembly, he is gowned in a long black robe which contrasts with the spill of his jabot and double lawyer's bands. Papineau seemingly wanted to appear as a man of government. In his left hand, he is holding upright against his thigh a speckled leather book with a heavy binding and a traditional spine; his right hand is resting on a

document placed on his work table, on which a few undecipherable lines are written. Also on the table, but in the background, are six large books either lying flat, standing upright or inclined, as well as a very rich circular inkwell tray, from which a fine white quill is protruding. In the background, the large draped curtain gives us a glimpse of the shelves of a well-stocked bookcase. All in all, the work has a very clever construction, a complete opposite of the *Monseigneur Rémi Gaulin* (Cat. 208) which Jean-Baptiste Roy-Audy was to paint two years later using basically the same props.

This portrait by Plamondon is as important in its own way as its companion piece because the artist used a type of composition which was to have significant repercussions both in his work, and in that of the most famous of his future competitors. We are referring here to *Elzéar Bédard* (Cat. 197), which Plamondon was to paint in 1842, and to *René-Édouard Caron*

(Fig. 188A), which Théophile Hamel was to execute in 1846. Moreover, these two paintings, as well as that of Papineau, cannot be contemplated without taking into account the probable influence of two engravings published in 1832 of Louis-Joseph Papineau, after a drawing by Robert A. Sproule (Fig. 188B) and Denis-Benjamin Viger, after a drawing by C. Hamburger (Fig. 188C).

At another level, it is important to recall the political scene in which Papineau was a key player at the time in order to understand the scope of his image. *Patriote* party leader, he was widely supported by Canadian middle classes, which were dominated by merchants and professionals. Little by little, he came to oppose the Anglophone merchant bourgeoisie, bureaucracy and the colonial government, in a political climate dominated by serious economic difficulties, demographic pressures and massive immigration. All these phenomena served to intensify nationalist fervour, and the Legislative Council—whose members were appointed by colonial authorities—soon became a symbol of exploitation and the root of all evil. In short, the *Patriote* leader's effort at ideological renewal gradually led to his considering the principle of making all government bodies answerable to the people through elections of primary importance and consequently to his questioning of British institutions and the English colonial system. Following the *Ninety-Two Resolutions* of 1834, the end result of a radicalization process begun in 1828, Papineau wanted to undermine the economic foundations of the power of his Anglophone adversaries. At the time when Plamondon painted his portrait, he was advocating that business relations to be broken off with them and their products boycotted; at the same time, he tried to weaken bureaucrats by advocating the refusal of subsidies, an action which led to a freeze in the salaries of civil servants and a considerable reduction in the colonial government's leeway in terms of public spending.

In light of this information, we can better understand the meaning or scope of certain iconographic components in Plamondon's work, such as the books on the work table. These include the works of Aristotle and Demosthenes, two great names in the history of Ancient Greece, the first a philosopher and father of logic, and the second an orator and politician who praised democracy. Next appears the first volume of the "Esprit des lois," a work by the 18th-century French moralist, thinker and philosopher Montesquieu, who studied the political organization of nations and advocated equitable reforms with regard to individuals. The name of American Thomas Jefferson is associated with democratic and republican ideals, as well as the writing of the Declaration of Independence of 1776. The presence of "Speech" by Englishman Charles Fox, that defender of the American colonies, is explained by Papineau's loyalty to English institutions when they met his objectives. He wrote:

One can find, he wrote, [...] in the speeches of Fox and others, the sublime maxims of public right and liberty [...] to the extent that the enemies of the Canadian name who want to lay down such narrow boundaries to English freedom would do well to read them.[5] (*Translation*)

Finally, the inscription "Économie politique" refers to a work in three volumes published in Paris in 1834 by Vicomte Alban de Villeneuve-Bargemont (1784-1850), a work whose full title reveals its underlying ideology: *Économie politique chrétienne, ou Recherches sur la nature et les causes du paupérisme, en France et en Europe, et sur les moyens de la soulager et de la prévenir.*[6] By including the names of all these authors in his portrait, Papineau was probably trying to explain the tenets of his thinking, legitimize his political activities and include himself to some extent with the line or tradition of thinkers, orators, legislators and men of government who have left their mark on humanity. Given this context, the composition used by Plamondon faithfully portrays the ambitions and pretensions of the great speaker and patriot Papineau, although his thinking and political activities were not entirely devoid of paradoxes and inconsistencies.

On another level altogether, and in referring back to the two sections of the "diptych" painted by the artist, we cannot fail to appreciate its iconological scope. This is a pictorial dialogue between two distinct, yet indissociable spaces, which oppose, yet complement one another. The very duality of this portrait, which represents a microcosm of Canadian middle classes, seems significant in that it contrasts family with society, private life with public life, or the role of women as instructors with that of men responsible for providing the essentials. From an iconographical point of view, this dialectic contrasts the colour scheme and extravagance of the gowns with the austere black of the robe of office, the piano with the desk, the bouquet and lyre with the bookcase, and the musical score with a legal text.... In short, we have on the one hand the comfortable setting and safety of the family circle in which the main concerns are education, decorative arts and poetry and on the other, the working world, in which reflection and politics fully absorb the man of conscience, who faces his collective responsibilities alone.

To conclude, a final observation can be made regarding the feeling dominating the portraits commissioned from Plamondon by Papineau. Evidently, these works focus more on appearances, rather than on spontaneity. Even the domestic intimacy of the portrait of Mme. Plamondon and her daughter fools no one. There is no warmth, no easy flow between the subjects, only a cold distance, reserve and self-control. The corollary of painting's starched nature and affectation is the care given to the rendering of the attire and accessories, to the point where the reddish flesh tones are somewhat artificial. When compared with the romantic intimacy of the double portrait (Cat. 219) painted the same year by Plamondon's neighbour, the Englishman Thielcke, the "Frenchness"—that is, the traditional and official nature—of the images of the Papineaus is obvious. In fact, it could be said that the artist was not able to grasp the character or temperament of Louis-Joseph and Julie, as if social distance prevented him from penetrating the wall of proprieties and appearances. The artist usually proved to be a great psychologist when he felt he "dominated" his subject. He surpassed himself with *Cyprien Tanguay* (Cat. 184) and *Soeur Sainte-Anne* (Cat. 196). When, on the contrary, he felt intimidated by the imposing bearing of his impenetrable models, he carried it off with great panache, but without managing to convey the desired intensity, as in his portrait of Monseigneur Signay (Cat. 189) painted in 1836, shortly before or after his portraits of the Papineaus. With regard to the latter, only the impish, gamin face of young Ézilda saved the whole. This eight-year-old child could not intimidate "the country's leading talent in painting!" (*Translation*)

J.R.P.

Notes

1. *Le Canadien*, June 10, 1836, p. 3. See also *Le Canadien*, June 17, 1836, p. 3.
2. *Le Canadien*, April 21, 1834, p. 2.
3. Her sister Azélie (1834-1869) married painter Napoléon Bourassa in 1857. After Azélie's death, Ézilda agreed to take charge of educating the children of her brother-in-law. He painted a portrait of Ézilda (1869) preserved at the Musée du Québec. This portrait shows a strong resemblance to the face painted by Plamondon.
4. Beginning in 1836, fashion demanded that leg-o'-mutton sleeves be puffed only at the elbow, and tapered up top and toward the bottom.
5. Papineau quoted by Fernand Ouellet, DBC, Vol. X (1972), p. 628.
6. Two theories can be advanced to account for the inscription appearing on the back of the volume held by Papineau, "C. ONIS/OP.RA." This title may be an abbreviation of "Ciceronis/opera," a collection of works by Cicero. In a portrait of James Stuart (NAC) painted by Théophile Hamel, the subject is holding a volume bearing this title (see *VÉZINA 1975/1*, p. 167). This inscription could also be a reference to Don Luis de Onis (1762-1827), a Spanish diplomat who was the ambassador plenipotentiary to the United States and whose principal indexed writings were entitled *Mémoires sur les négociations entre l'Espagne et les États-Unis d'Amérique qui amenèrent le traité de 1819.*

189.
Monseigneur Joseph Signay, 1836
Oil on canvas, 76.2 × 63.5 cm

Inscription
(s.d., l.l.) *Plamondon/1836.*

Exhibitions
(?) Montreal 1887, No. 692; (?) Montreal 1892, No. 64; Ottawa 1970, No. 20.

Bibliography
(?) *Catalogue 1887,* p. 5, No. 692; (?) *MacDonald 1892,* p. 7, No. 64; *Tétu 1896,* p. 294; *Magnan 1922-1923,* p. 351; *Bellerive 1925,* p. 30; *Morisset 1935/2,* p. 4; *Morisset 1935/5,* p. 2; *Morisset 1935/9,* p. 2; *Morisset 1936-1937,* Vol. I, p. 145, Vol. II, p. 76; (?) *Lambert 1947,* p. 36; *Morisset 1960/2,* p. 15; *Hubbard 1970,* pp. 28, 74, 99 and 128, No. 20 (Repr.); *Porter 1990/1,* p. 922.

Collection
Archevêché de Québec

MONSEIGNEUR JOSEPH SIGNAY (1778-1850) was the thirteenth bishop and third archbishop of Quebec from 1833 to 1850. He also became the first metropolitan of the new ecclesiastical province of Quebec City in May 1844. In a period when the Quebec Church was marked by sweeping changes, it seems that Monseigneur Signay's conservative, hesitant, prudent and stubborn temperament put him somewhat at a disadvantage, although these character traits were offset by his zeal, charitableness and decided liking for beautiful ceremonies. In short, and to use the words of Maximilien Bibaud, "although this prelate did not pass for a superior man, his face and his entire person were very imposing, and his manners very distinguished."[1] (*Translation*) Signay was also a member of the Literary and Historical Society of Quebec, and the first subscriber to Joseph Légaré's Picture Gallery in 1838.

There is a fairly wide range of portraits of Monseigneur Signay. Several of them were formerly attributed to Antoine Plamondon, but the one of interest to us is the only one which can be formally associated with his brush, since it was signed and dated 1836. That year was very profitable for the artist, and the significant addition of a new prestigious commission from the highest episcopal authority must have flattered his pride and encouraged him to surpass himself.

Plamondon's work is distinguished by its official nature and classical qualities. Within a tight composition, Signay's bust seems to dominate the viewer. He has the proud, haughty mien of an ecclesiastical dignitary of a past century. Here again, the artist's brush portrays the cold presence and bearing rather than providing a psychological and sensitive treatment of the subject. However, the dark, pinkish complexion and beautiful modelling of the bishop's aristocratic face, the blue and violet highlights playing on the rich taffeta mozzetta and the delicate rendering of the patterns embroidered on the tight-sleeved rochet can still be appreciated.

J.R.P.

Note

1. *Bibaud 1891,* pp. 264-265.

190. (See colour reproduction, p. 102)
Lost in the Wood, 1836
Oil on canvas, 74 × 63.8 cm

Inscription
(s.d., l.l.) *A. Plamondon/fecit. 1836.*

Provenance
(?) Edward Burroughs, Quebec City; John Burroughs, Quebec City; Burroughs Pelletier, Quebec City; Louis Pelletier, Sillery; acquired by the Musée du Québec, Quebec City, 1982.

Exhibition
Quebec City 1983-1984, No. 61.

Bibliography
Vie des arts, 1983, p. 96a (Repr.); LA CHRONIQUE *1983,* p. 21, No. 114 (Repr.); ACQUISITIONS *1983,* p. 231, No. 34 (Repr.); LE MUSÉE DU QUÉBEC *1983,* p. 65, No. 61 (entry by Claude Thibault, Luc Noppen and Michel Doyon) (Repr.); NADEAU *1988,* p. 96 (Repr.); BÉLAND AND BOURASSA *1990,* pp. 7, 9, 54 and 114 (Repr.); NICOLAÏ *1990,* p. 95; PORTER *1990/1,* p. 922.

Collection
Musée du Québec, Quebec City (82.14)

I MMEDIATELY UPON MOVING to Rue Notre-Dame in Montreal in summer 1836, Antoine Plamondon published in *La Minerve* of June 27 an advertisement informing the public "that he would be pleased to execute all works of PAINTING that anyone would like to commission, such as portraits, church works, genre scenes, fantasy pictures, etc." (*Translation*)

This was apparently when Louis-Joseph Papineau (Cat. 188) purchased from him a copy of Titian's *Femme au miroir,* executed by the artist at the Louvre while he was studying in Paris. This canvas soon found its way into the hands of Edward Burroughs (1790-1871), and then his son John Burroughs (1824-1904), both of whom were employees of the

clerk's office of the Superior Court and prothonotaries of the district of Quebec.[1] It was at the home of one of these two Anglophone lawyers that the work now entitled *Lost in the Wood* was found. Unfortunately, we do not know the exact circumstances of the Burroughs' acquisition of this unique painting. It is not known whether the lawyers, who met Plamondon on several occasions, purchased the work following a specific commission, or during a visit to the painter's studio. Nor are we sure as to whether the artist executed the work in Montreal or during the months preceding or following his stay in that city. What we do know, however, is that the painting remained in the Burroughs family until it became part of the Musée du Québec collection in the early 1980s.

Lost in the Wood was one of the first genre scenes executed by Plamondon during his career. Obviously, this work, with such an atypical subject for Plamondon, belongs to the category of "genre scenes, fantasy pictures" announced by the painter in Montreal. Within this general classification adopted by the artist, we are inclined to include works whose subjects are as diverse as *The Little Savoyards* (Cat. 199), *The Pigeon Hunt* (Cat. 266) and *The Little Gardeners* (Cat. 267). All these secular works have something in common: they portray children or young adolescents in an outdoor setting.

This painting depicts two young children who, while out picking wild fruit, have lost their way and have been taken by surprise by nightfall. Exhausted by the fresh air and their walk in the middle of the woods, the two careless children are dozing at the foot of a tree, against a moss-covered embankment or rock. The elder of the two children, holding a branch of wild berries, is sleeping so soundly that he is not even aware of a small bird singing, perched on his left shoulder.

Like *The Little Gardeners,* this touching adventure engenders a feeling of innocence which could not fail to satisfy the era's sensibilities. This type of anecdotal and sentimental imagery, which was not without some mawkishness, was based on folk tales and stories, highly prized by the bourgeoisie and, consequently, widely disseminated in various forms of illustrations. It is therefore entirely plausible that, like Légaré in the design of some of his works (Cat. 167), Plamondon was inspired by such literary or iconographic sources to complete his composition,[2] as he was for *The Little Savoyards* and *The Little Gardeners.*

In any case, Plamondon showed ingenuity with *Lost in the Wood,* attracting attention to these children, camped out in the middle of a twilit landscape. The artist accentuated the picturesque and romantic nature of the scene by means of strong contrasts between the various planes of the composition and a complex interplay between light and colour. The details of the meticulously treated foreground—with its moss, rocks, grass and flowers—stand out against the dark background of unclearly rendered undergrowth. The luminous colours of the middle distance, especially the greens of the vegetation and the browns of the soil, also bring out the dark tones of the background. Finally, the rays of the setting sun break through from the upper left corner, giving the painting a wonderful sense of depth. All these pictorial devices were probably added at that time to enhance the painting's effectiveness and the emotional charge associated with the drama experienced by the two children.

M.B.

Notes
1. ANQQ, Collection Papineau-Bourassa, letter from John Burroughs to L.-J.-Amédée Papineau, August 1891, and reply from A. Papineau to J. Burroughs, August 16, 1891.
2. Research conducted by Louise d'Argencourt, curator at the Montreal Museum of Fine Arts, through correspondence with European curators did not yield any results regarding a possible engraved source used by Plamondon. According to a letter dated April 20, 1991 from Dr. Christa Pieske of Lübeck (Germany) to Mme. d'Argencourt, the model or the composition could be German, Austrian or Swiss, perhaps English or French. *Lost in the Wood* could be associated with the imagery of the Guardian Angel watching over children sleeping in the woods, or with the fairy tale of Hansel and Gretel.

Inscription
(s.d., l.r.) *A. Plamondon/1836.*

Provenance
Descendants of the Wragg, Cumming and Cullin families; Angela A. Cullin, great-granddaughter of the subject; Patricia Price Antiques, Manchester, Ontario, 1982; acquired by the Art Gallery of Ontario, Toronto, 1982.

Bibliography
LACASSE 1983/1, p. 28 (Repr.); FOX 1986, p. 26; LACROIX 1990, p. 21.

Collection
Art Gallery of Ontario, Toronto (82.147)

191. (See colour reproduction, p. 89)
Mrs. Thomas B. Wragg, née Mary Ann Wilkins, 1836
Oil on canvas, 88.2 × 73.5 cm

PLAMONDON'S TEMPORARY MOVE to Montreal in 1836 opened up a whole new market in this rapidly growing city. There was, so to speak, no portraitist with an established reputation in the city, since Louis Dulongpré had, for all intents and purposes, retired, and only a few itinerants offered their services on a temporary basis. This stay produced a large body of work, including some dozen portraits. Those of **Mrs. Thomas B. Wragg, née Mary Ann Wilkins** and **Mrs. John Redpath, née Jane Drummond** are representative of this work. Although these works go together with the portraits of the subjects' husbands, Plamondon was not necessarily trying to create an effect of absolute symmetry, as he did with the portraits of the Papineaus executed that same year. Thus, even though Mr. Redpath and his wife are each seated at one end of a sofa, different sources of light and slightly

different vantage points indicate that they cannot correspond to the same spatial reality. That year, when Plamondon painted the portraits of Mr. and Mrs. Louis de Lagrave (MMFA), he depicted the wife seated on a sofa, like her two fellow citizens, while her husband is shown half-length, against a forest background, a rare proceeding in Plamondon's work (Fig. 194B).

At the time when Plamondon painted their portraits, the Redpaths and the Wraggs were worthy representatives of the Montreal Anglophone business community. Jane Drummond (1815-1907) had married two years previously, becoming the second wife of John Redpath (1796-1869). She wed a businessman who had already enjoyed success and amassed a fortune, thanks to the construction of the Lachine and Rideau canals. In 1833, he gravitated towards high finance and sat on the board

of directors of the Bank of Montreal. In subsequent years, he was to increase his fortune with numerous investments, finally building Canada's first sugar refinery in 1854. Mary Ann Wilkins (1805-1880) was a native of Upper Canada, as was her husband Thomas Busby Wragg (1799-1876), whom she married on July 21, 1823 at Carrying Place, Bay of Quinte in Upper Canada. It is not known exactly when they moved to Montreal, but during the 1840s, Thomas B. Wragg owned a nail factory on Rue Saint-Paul, while his father-in-law was a shareholder in the import firm Shuter & Wilkins, whose Montreal branch was also located on Rue Saint-Paul. His brother-in-law Peter McGill also had a business on the same street. In 1871, the Wraggs returned to Ontario and settled in Belleville.

Both ladies, of the same social class, are dressed and adorned in a similar manner. They are wearing gowns with puffed

192.
Mrs. John Redpath, née Jane Drummond, 1836
Oil on canvas, 87 × 73.8 cm

Inscription
(s.d., l.l., on the armchair) *A.. Plamondon 1836.*

Provenance
Descendants of the Redpath and Bovey families; Jean Bovey, Montreal, granddaugher of the subject; Gift to the McGill University, Montreal, 1942.

Bibliography
La Tribune, November 4, 1942; LACASSE *1983/1,* p. 28; PORTER *1990/1,* p. 922.

Collection
McGill University, Montreal

sleeves and their waists are drawn in with a wide sash. Mrs. Redpath's gown sports a sharply pointed cape, gathered on the chest and covering the shoulders (jockei); Mrs. Wragg's gown has short, frothy sleeves, and is trimmed with a collarless lace cape with floral patterns, forming epaulettes and transparent leg-o'-mutton sleeves which completely cover her arms. Both women's coiffures consist of wide curls; the first woman is wearing a lace cap decorated with feathers, flowers and knots of ribbon, while the second is wearing a large tortoiseshell comb as her only ornament. Both are sporting long earrings, a brooch, a band, a ring and a chain, to which is attached a chatelaine and a pendant watch tucked under the sash.

Of all the bourgeois couples painted by Plamondon, the Wraggs and the Redpaths are most representative of the new style adopted by the artist after 1835. Although the subjects still take up most of the space in the painting, their poses are more varied, contrasting with the obstinate frontality of Plamondon's half-length portraits of the preceding period. The face is still placed very high on the canvas, with the headdress touching the upper edge of the portrait. Both women are seated slightly diagonally, with their shoulders almost parallel to the painting's plane and one elbow resting on the arm of the chair; both hold an octavo, with the index finger placed inside to mark the page, as if they had suddenly stopped reading. Mrs. Redpath is resting her other hand on a white handkerchief, whose presence seems somewhat artificial. In fact, it seems that the artist changed his composition. Originally, the book was held in the left hand and not in the right; the handkerchief was perhaps added to conceal this alteration. The background is neutral, but sof-tened by the light placed slightly above and falling across the subject diagonally. Despite a somewhat faulty effect near Mrs. Redpath's left shoulder, the crisscross brushstrokes are of a richness and chromatic modulation which presage the works of the years 1840-1845. Already hinted at in some works of the preceding period, the treatment of the clothing, fabric and accessories is even more opulent here. The artist's self-expression is evident in these accessories, as Plamondon brilliantly suggests the shimmer of heavy fabrics, the lightness of diaphanous lace, the substance of jewels; the strokes are wide, fine or generous. All these effects combined with the highly classical structure of these portraits help magnify their subjects, although their gravity, by the same token, is outweighed by the painting's decorativ⸱⸱ pects.

P.B.

193.
Still Life with Grapes 1838
After an unidentified artist, Italy,
18th century
Oil on canvas, 91.8 × 75.3 cm

Inscription
(s.d., l.l.) *Plamondon/1838.*

Provenance
Duquet family, Quebec City, before 1925; Jean Soucy, Quebec City; acquired by the Musée du Québec, Quebec City, 1976.

Bibliography
L'Aurore des Canadas, August 24, 1843, p. 2; *Le Journal de Québec,* September 12, 1843, p. 2; BELLERIVE *1925,* pp. 31-32; MORISSET *1935/2,* p. 4; MORISSET *1936-1937,* Vol. I, p. 86; DUMAS *1970,* p. 20; PORTER *1978/1,* p. 86; LACASSE *1983/1,* pp. 29, 30 and 92 (Repr.); BÉLAND AND BOURASSA *1990,* pp. 5, 6, 9, 42, 64 and cover. p. (Repr.).

Collection
Musée du Québec, Quebec City. Restored in 1991, with the assistance of the Amis du Musée du Québec (76.175)

A LTHOUGH ANTOINE PLAMONDON attempted to gain a reputation as an original creator, an illustrious "student of Paris"[1] (*Translation*), after his return to Canada, he was not above copying, and several of his compositions are inspired by European engravings or paintings (Cat. 185, 195 and 199).

Eager to meet all market expectations, Plamondon executed religious paintings, portraits and still lifes for a wide range of clients, including members of the clergy and the bourgeoisie. The copy of the painting in the possession of attorney Jean-Baptiste-Édouard Bacquet (Cat. 156) was completed during an extremely productive period for the artist.[2] Perhaps it was for the benefit of his apprentices that Plamondon copied this still life, which, with its subtle contrasts of light and values, poses some specific problems. This copy is especially convincing and the editor of *L'Aurore des Canadas* was so taken by it that he wrote on August 24, 1843:

Behold how beautiful these grapes are, so juicy that if one was alone and slightly greedy this small painting would be in grave danger of being munched; because, short of snatching God's work away from Him, it is impossible to do better. Ah, Mr. Plamondon, if only you could give your grapes flavour, the Creator Himself could well be jealous of you! (*Translation*)

These sentences refer to the famous anecdote about Zeuxis' grapes, recounted by Pliny in book XXXV of his *Natural History.* Like the grapes which the Greek artist Zeuxis painted so perfectly that birds were fooled by them and tried to peck them, these grapes were so well done that our enthusiast wanted to bite them from the canvas, since they lacked nothing but their juice. But would this Quebec journalist have used this image if he had known the outcome of the story? Pliny went on to explain that Zeuxis' rival, Parrhasius, taking advantage of his absence, painted a curtain in trompe-l'oeil over the painting depicting the grapes. Upon his return, Zeuxis, in trying to raise the curtain to show his work, had to admit the superiority of Parrhasius, who was capable of fooling an artist, while he, an artist, had only fooled animals.

The columnist's account, like the interest raised by the work in the Bacquet collection, shows the value attached to artists' technical skill and the importance accorded to *mimesis,* that is, the role of imitating nature. As Pierre Georgel wrote, "genuine imitation had [...] long passed for the ultimate in art: for the people, it was almost magic; for learned people, it was the fruit of a scientific approach enhanced by exceptional talent."[3] (*Transla-*

tion) Quebec collectors, by preferring portraits and landscapes, were seeking images whose referents were part of their reality, images which can now be interpreted as "idealized," transformed by the relations of creators and collectors to this environment. Faithfulness to nature was the primary criterion. The painting in the Bacquet collection was considered a model for imitating nature; by successfully reproducing it, artists proved this superiority. They demonstrated both their adherence to the rule of *mimesis* and their ability to reproduce what, in art, was the most conformist.

L.L.

Notes
1. The expression is taken from the newspaper *Le Canadien,* October 17, 1832, p. 2. Plamondon had a very high opinion of himself, which he unhesitatingly displayed.
2. LACASSE *1983/1,* pp. 330-332.
3. Pierre Georgel, *La peinture dans la peinture* (Dijon: Musée des beaux-arts de Dijon, 1982), p. 153.

194. (See colour reproduction, p. 93)
Zacharie Vincent, 1838
Oil on canvas, 114.3 × 96.5 cm

Inscription
(b., before the new backing covered the inscription) *Le Tableau est le Portrait du dernier des Hurons de Lorette, il se nome Zacarie Vincent, il est agée de 23, Peint par Ant Plamondon a québec 1838.*

Provenance
John George Lambton, lst Earl of Durham, Quebec City, 1838; Descendants of the Lambton family, England; John Frederick Lambton, 5th Earl of Durham, Lambton Castle, England, 1929; private collection, London, 1932; private collection, Toronto, 1982.

Exhibitions
Quebec City 1838; Toronto 1988-1989, No. 1.

Bibliography
Le Canadien, April 30, 1838, p. 3 and August 12, 1838, p. 1; *Le Populaire*, May 14, 1838, p. 3; AMUQ, Papiers Desjardins II, Letters from 1831 to 1838, letter from abbé Louis-Joseph Desjardins to R. M. St-Henry, November lst 1838; *L'Ami du peuple*, May 5, 1840, p. 3; *Le Journal de Québec*, June 9, 1855, p. 1; *Journal de l'Instruction publique*, No. 10 (February 1866), pp. 17-18 and 29; MAGNAN 1922-1923, p. 351; (?) BELLERIVE 1925, p. 31; MORISSET 1935/2, p. 4; MORISSET 1935/9, p. 2; MORISSET 1936-1937, Vol. II, pp. 76-77 and 108; MORISSET 1941/1, p. 77; COLGATE 1943, p. 110; AYRE 1956, p. 16 (note by Gérard Morisset); MORISSET 1960/1, pp. 98 and 125; MORISSET 1961, p. 6; HARPER 1966, p. 86; HUBBARD 1970, pp. 28-29; HUBBARD 1973, p. 72; LORD 1974, p. 44; DUMAS 1974, p. 43; PORTER 1975, p. 8; PORTER 1977/1, pp. 17-18; LABELLE AND THIVIERGE 1981, p. 326; KAREL, LABELLE AND THIVIERGE 1981, p. 1002; LACASSE 1983/1, pp. 29, 30, 32 and 92 (Repr.); PORTER 1987/3, p. 1511; REID 1988/1, pp. 8 and 14-15, No. 1 (Repr.); REID 1988/2, pp. 11 and 13 (Repr.); GAGNON AND LACASSE 1989, pp. 68-79 (Repr.); BÉLAND AND BOURASSA 1990, p. 64; PORTER 1990/1, p. 922; PORTER 1990/2, p. 404.

Collection
Private collection, Toronto

Z ACHARIE VINCENT TELARI-O-LIN, which means "unmixed" or "undivided," was born on January 28, 1815 in Village-des-Hurons, near Loretteville, a community in which he possibly lived for most of his life. On August 14, 1848, he married Marie Falardeau, an Iroquois woman. Of this union were born four children: three sons and a daughter. Vincent died on October 9, 1886 in Quebec City.

Although the features of the "last of the Hurons" are familiar, the famous portrait of Zacharie Vincent painted by Antoine Plamondon in 1838 is not in any way responsible for this familiarity, since it was discovered and reproduced only recently. Instead, credit goes to the many self portraits—there are nearly ten—which this amateur artist left us (Fig. 194A). It should be noted, however, that Plamondon's canvas probably played a major role in launching Vincent's artistic career.

The portrait of *Zacharie Vincent* by Antoine Plamondon apparently was painted specifically to be submitted to a contest organized by the Literary and His-torical Society of Quebec in April 1838. By winning the first-class medal "for an original work" (*Translation*) with his portrait, which is also called *The Last of the Hurons,* Plamondon broke the isolation in which the major commission to paint the Stations of the Cross for the Notre-Dame de Montréal church (Cat. 195) had held him for several months. Initially made public in Quebec City in *Le Canadien* of April 30, 1838, the painter's resounding success was to be echoed in Montreal papers the following month. Plamondon's greatest triumph was probably having John George Lambton, 1st Earl of Durham (1792-1840), new governor-general of the British North American colonies, who had landed in Quebec City on May 29, 1838, purchase his painting. Leaving Quebec City for England barely five months after his arrival, Lord Durham took the portrait back with him to London.

Nothing is more enlightening with regard to the political and cultural context in which Plamondon's work was produced and received than this article published in *Le Canadien* of April 30, 1838, following the awarding of the medal which was won by the painter for his portrait of *Zacharie Vincent:*

Last Thursday, the Literary and Historical Society of Quebec presented Mr. Antoine Plamondon, Canadian artist and pupil of Paulin Guérin, one of its first-class medals. Mr. Plamondon won this token of esteem by reproducing on canvas with all the grace and naturalness of his brilliant palette the features of the last purebred Huron Indian to live in this Province; and who is probably the last of this entire savage and warlike race.

The last of the Hurons! That in itself is an interesting, artistic and truly Canadian subject and Mr. Plamondon took full advantage of it. He has depicted his savage standing in an imposing, warrior-like and meditative manner, his arms crossed on his breast, his forehead raised to the sky; he has placed him in the middle of his woods, to which he seems to be saying a final, solemn farewell, for himself and for his entire race; in a word, he has truly painted the last of the Hurons. When one gazes for the first time on his long black, flowing hair, curling on his shoulders, his eminently characteristic features, his coppered flesh, his sparkling eyes, the beautiful fabric of his coat, his sash from which his cutlass hangs, one recognizes him for the son of *free men,* the hunter and

Fig. 194A.
Zacharie Vincent,
Zacharie Vincent and his Son Cyprien, c. 1845;
oil on canvas, 48.5 × 41.2 cm.
Musée du Québec, Quebec City (47.156).

Fig. 194B.
Antoine Plamondon,
Louis de Lagrave, 1836;
oil on canvas, 81.3 × 68.9 cm.
Montreal Museum of Fine Arts. Gift from
Miss Juliette Courteau (1947.989).

warrior of our vast forests, the canoeist of great lakes, the last offshoot of a noble and intrepid nation, which has disappeared before our very eyes like the beaver from our rivers, the elk from our woods; as perhaps we ourselves will disappear, giving way to a more powerful nation. The strong hunt the weak, that is basically the story of Adam's sons, and Mr. Plamondon's work reveals a tiny element of this truth.

It is to be hoped that this gentleman will not stop there, that our beautiful country will yield up other subjects no less picturesque, and that often, Mr. Editor, you will have similar articles to insert. May all our fellow countrymen work in this way, each in his own field! May we raise some monuments of ourselves before we are engulfed in a wave of immigration! Then we would no longer ask ourselves: when will the day come when Canada emerges from its obscurity, and when will arts and sciences flourish here as elsewhere? Let us admit it frankly, although our national future is very uncertain, there is much hope for us yet, more than one star has begun to shine; who knows whether we will one day point as other peoples to our glorious authors, learned people and artists. Courage! and onward young Canadians. (*Translation*)

As François-Marc Gagnon noted in his article on this work,

To understanding the meaning of this naive, incisive prose...we must understand the ideological outlook of the times. At the time when this article was written, in late April 1838, the Rebellion of 1837 was over. Even though Robert Nelson, taking refuge in Vermont with some 300 of his men, had just proclaimed the independence of Lower Canada and established the Republic on February 28, 1838, the atmosphere in Lower Canada was more despair-

ing than defiant. When the author of the *Le Canadien* article wondered if, like the Hurons, we were going to "disappear" in turn, "giving way to a more powerful nation," hunted "by the strong," "engulfed in a wave of immigration," he was not just speaking rhetorically. He was expressing the concern of the majority about "our national future." He also explained the fascination at the root of Plamondon's work. Was not this "last of the Hurons," if not just like ourselves, at least what we could become? And just as his "noble and intrepid nation" had given way to ours, so was ours at risk of giving way "to a more powerful nation," especially as this nation had just demonstrated this power by crushing the rebellion of the "Fils de la Liberté."[1] (*Translation*)

It would be surprising, however, if Lord Durham, upon purchasing the painting, had seen it as something other than a particularly well done "ethnographic" portrait of an Amerindian, let alone the "last of the Hurons." The proof is that it was upon the sadly famous recommendations by this governor that, in July 1840, Queen Victoria approved the Act of Union, which backed the supporters of a united Canada and imperiled the very survival of the French-Canadian nation.

A fierce adversary of the Act of Union, François-Xavier Garneau (1809-1866) then composed a long poem entitled "Le Dernier Huron," which was to be published in *Le Canada* of August 12, 1840. In this poem, the poet and historian bombastically exploited the dangers threatening the Huron race, doomed to extinction. By way of an introduction, and after having explicitly acknowledged his

debt to Plamondon, whose work served as his source of inspiration, Garneau insisted on the fact that "if the thoughts of the young Huron are indeed so sorrowful, this man provides us with a touching spectacle of the vicissitudes of peoples." (*Translation*) Upon the death of its author in February 1866, a revised version of the poem "Le Dernier Huron" was published by the *Journal de l'Instruction publique,* which specified that:

At the time when M. Garneau published this short poem, our race had everything to fear, and this can be sensed in the poet's touching verses as a sombre mental reservation, as one of those allegories which are so frequent in the poetry of sacred books. (*Translation*)

The portrait of **Zacharie Vincent** seems to have made a very strong impression on those who could admire the work during the few months it was in Quebec City. Like the poem "Le Dernier Huron" by Garneau a few years earlier, the very beautiful portrait of *Josephte Ourné* (Cat. 166) painted circa 1844 by Joseph Légaré was probably the latter's reaction to the portrait of **Zacharie Vincent:**

Légaré's intention seems clear to us. It must be remembered that in 1844, Plamondon's work was no longer in Quebec. How can we not suspect that Légaré was tempted to fill the void, if that word can be used, created by the departure of Plamondon's work for England? And, in fact, there are certain similarities between the two works.[2] (*Translation*)

Plamondon's painting was to be discussed again some ten years later when, deploring the absence of works by A. Plamondon, Légaré and Hamel from the 1855 *Exposition universelle* in Paris, Joseph-Charles Taché (1820-1894), who acted as Canada's representative at this event, mentioned in *Le Journal de Québec* in June of that year that he would have liked "to see in the Fine Arts galleries some of their paintings, such as, for example, M. Plamondon's 'last of the Hurons.'"[3] (*Translation*) Although none of them had seen the work, most art historians interested in Antoine Plamondon during the 20th century unfailingly referred to the portrait of **Zacharie Vincent**. Since the work was repatriated from England in 1982 by its current owners, we have been given the opportunity to appraise its originality and appreciate its plastic qualities. Of the hundred or so portraits of men left to us by Plamondon, that of **Zacharie Vincent** is, to the best of our knowledge, the only one in which the subject is not a member of the clergy or the bourgeoisie. It was also unusual for the painter to place his subject in an outdoor setting, although this choice is easily explained by the relationship between Amerindians and nature. Except for paintings such as *The Flutist* (of which there are several versions) and *The Pigeon Hunt* (Cat. 266) which are considered genre scenes, there is only one other known portrait by Plamondon in which the subject is placed outdoors in the style of English portraits: the portrait of *Louis de Lagrave* (Fig. 194B). The portrait of **Zacharie Vincent** also draws our attention, both for the subject's pose and for the layout of its composition. Most of Plamondon's portraits are either half-length, with the subjects standing, or they depict the subject seated. However, in *Abbé David-Henri Têtu* (Cat. 186), the model, like Zacharie Vincent, is portrayed standing up and the portrait is three-quarters-length. In the painting studied here, the subject's pose—arms proudly crossed on the chest and eyes fixed in the distance—has no equivalent in Plamondon's body of work. It is obvious that the artist did not attempt to paint a conventional portrait, but to immortalize an archetype, the "last of the Hurons of Lorette" (*Translation*), as he himself indicated on the back of his painting.

Y.L.

Notes

1. *GAGNON ET LACASSE 1989*, p. 71.

2. *Ibid.*, p. 74.

3. Letter from Joseph-Charles Taché dated May 24, 1855, reprinted in *Le Journal de Québec* of June 9, 1855 (p. 1).

195.
The Arrest of Christ, 1839
After Jacques Stella
Oil on canvas, 153.2 × 240.7 cm

Inscription
(s.d., l.c.) *A. Plamondon p. 1839.*

Provenance
Commissioned by Joseph-Vincent Quiblier, Fabrique Notre-Dame de Montreal, 1839; St. Patrick's Church, Montreal, 1847; Institution des Sourds-Muets, Montreal, 1929; acquired by the Montreal Museum of Fine Arts, 1961.

Exhibitions
Quebec City 1839; Montreal 1967/1, No. 31; Ottawa 1970, No. 25; Quebec City 1977 (presented solely at the MMFA); Montreal 1984/1, No. 1.

Bibliography
Quebec Mercury, November 26, 1839, p. 2; *Le Canadien,* November 27, 1839, p. 2 and December 6, 1839, p. 2; *HARPER 1966*, pp. 86 and 87 (Repr.) entitled *Kiss of Judas; CARTER 1967*, No. 31 (Repr.); *La Presse,* March 1st 1967; *Le Soleil,* March 2, 1967; *HUBBARD 1970*, pp. 26, 77-78 and 132, No. 25 (Repr.); *DUMAS 1970*, p. 20; *ROSENBERG 1971*, p. 10 (Repr.); *UN SANCTUAIRE 1973*, p. 13; *LACASSE 1983/1*, pp. 54-57 and 74 (Repr.); *NIXON 1988*, p. 141.

Collection
Montreal Museum of Fine Arts. Purchase, Horsley and Annie Townsend bequest (1961.1321)

*T*he Arrest of Christ is the second of the fourteen Stations of the Cross which Antoine Plamondon painted for the Notre-Dame de Montréal church in the late 1830s; this group of paintings is the most consistent and masterful the artist ever executed.[1] An initial set of the Stations of the Cross had been commissioned in 1834 from painter James Bowman after he had finished the six paintings for the side chapels of this church.[2] However, discouraged by the sheer magnitude of the work to be done, Bowman quickly abandoned the task. In summer 1836, the superior of the Sulpicians, Joseph-Vincent Quiblier (1796-1852), called on Plamondon so that the Notre-Dame parishioners could finally benefit from all the privileges and indulgences associated with the devotion to the Stations of the Cross. Completed in 1839, the fourteen works of the Stations of the Cross were then exhibited at the House of Assembly in Quebec City (Fig. 195A) and earned Plamondon the most enthusiastic accolades. Despite a unanimously favourable review of his work, the ecclesiastical authorities, for reasons of religious orthodoxy, were obliged to refuse the fourteen paintings: the Passion scenes selected by Plamondon did not correspond to the usual scenes depicted in the Stations of the Cross. The fate of this set of paintings was as curious as it was eventful. First stored in the painter's studio, then transported to Montreal, the Stations of the Cross subsequently graced the nave of the new St. Patrick's church in 1847. In the late 19th century, the works were again stored, and it was probably at this time that eight of them disappeared. In 1929, the six remaining paintings took their place on the walls of the parlour of the Institution des Sourds-Muets on Rue Saint-

EXHIBITION
DE LA PASSION DE N. S. JÉSUS-CHRIST
EN 14 TABLEAUX,
DE 8 PIEDS DE LARGE SUR 5 DE HAUT
PEINT PAR
ANT. PLAMONDON, Artiste.

LES sujets suivants sont maintenant exposés à la GARDE ROBE de la CHAMBRE d'ASSEMBLÉE pour quelques jours seulement :

I. Tableau,—Mon Père, détournez, s'il vous plaît de moi ce calice. Néanmoins que ma volonté ne se fasse point, mais la vôtre.   St. Luc ch. 22 v. 42.

II.—Quoi ! Judas, avec un baiser, vous livrez le fils de l'homme.   St. Luc ch. 22 v. 48.

III.—Si j'ai bien parlé ; pourquoi me frappez-vous ?
          St. Jean ch. 18 v. 23.

IV.—Une servante vint à lui, qui lui dit ; vous étiez aussi avec Jésus de Nazareth.   St. Mat. ch. 26 v. 69.

V.—Hérode le fit revêtir par moquerie d'une robe blanche.   St. Luc ch. 23 v. 11.

VI.—Pilate fit prendre Jésus, et le fit flageller.
          St. Jean ch. 17 v. 1.

VII.—Puis entrelaçant des épines, ils en firent une couronne qu'ils lui mirent sur la tête ; ils lui mirent aussi un roseau à la main droite.   St. Mat. ch. 27 v. 29.

VIII.—Pilate dit : Voilà que je vous l'amène dehors, afin que vous sachiez que je ne trouve en lui aucun sujet de condamnation. Jésus sortit donc, portant une couronne d'épines et un manteau de pourpre, et Pilate leur dit ; Voilà l'homme.   St. Jean ch. 19 v. 4 et 5.

IX.—Pilate se lavant les mains dit : je suis net du sang de cet homme juste.   St. Mat. ch. 27 v. 24.

X.—Jésus portant sa croix, alla au lieu appelé Calvaire, qui se nomme en hébreu Golgotha.
          St. Jean ch. 19 v. 17.

—Mais Jésus, déjà épuisé de forces et de sang, succomba bientôt sous le faix,

XI.—Est-il une douleur semblable à la mienne ?
          Jéré. Lam. ch. 1 v. 12.

—Ce fut à la troisième heure du jour qu'ils l'attachèrent à la croix. Ils crucifièrent avec lui deux voleurs, un à sa droite et l'autre à sa gauche, et Jésus au milieu.

XII.—Mon Père, je remets mon ame entre vos mains, et disant ces paroles, et baissant la tête il rendit l'esprit.   St. Jean ch. 19 v. 30.

XIII.—Joseph (d'Arimathie) vint trouver Pilate, et obtint de lui le corps de Jésus. Il le descendit de la croix.   St. Luc ch. 24 v. 52 53.

XIV. Et dernier tableau. Joseph prit le corps, et le mit dans le sépulchre qu'il avait fait tailler dans le roc.
          St. Mat. ch. 27 v. 59 60.

Prix d'admission, 1s. 3d.
Québec 26 Novembre 1839.

Fig. 195A.
"Exhibition de la Passion de N.S. Jesus Christ" in *Le Canadien*, November 27, 1829, p. 2.
1839

Fig. 195B.
Claudine Bouzonnet-Stella after Jacques Stella, *The Arrest of Christ;*
engraving, 46.5 × 35.3 cm.
Cabinet des estampes de la Bibliothèque Nationale, Paris.

Laurent in Montreal,[3] and then became part of the collections of the Montreal Museum of Fine Arts in 1961.

Pierre Rosenberg was the first to associate three of Plamondon's paintings of the Stations of the Cross which have come down to us—namely, the second, fifth and sixth Stations—with the compositions of French painter Jacques Stella (1596-1657), compositions made popular through a Passion series in 14 plates engraved by Claudine Bouzonnet-Stella (1641-1697). Antoine Plamondon probably owned a series of these plates, which he likely acquired either in Europe or in Quebec City itself. At the time, the drawing of these engravings was mistakenly attributed to Nicolas Poussin (1594-1665). Given Plamondon's great admiration for this painter, it is not surprising that he tried to use these compositions as much as possible in executing Quiblier's sizeable

commission. Since the series by Claudine Bouzonnet-Stella could not have been complete—it originally was to contain 30 subjects—Plamondon must have also referred to other painted or engraved sources to execute his Stations of the Cross. These sources include an anonymous work preserved in Oka, a copy of a work by Jean Jouvenet (1644-1717) (8th Station), and two engravings: the first after a work by Ludovico Cardi, *dit* Cigoli (1559-1613) (10th Station) and the second after a painting by Pierre Mignard (1612-1695) (13th Station).

As related by the four evangelists, Jesus' arrest consisted of two major events: Judas' kiss and the arrest itself. When he painted his *The Arrest of Christ*, with which we are familiar today thanks to the engraving by his niece (Fig. 195B), Jacques Stella did not fail to include in his scene the episode of Malchus having his ear cut

off, as related by St. Luke, and the episode of the naked young man who ran away, of whom only St. Mark spoke. In copying the Bouzonnet-Stella engraving, Plamondon changed the composition only slightly. Because of the horizontal format of his painting, he was content to merely remove the vegetation, which partially cut the scene in the right foreground. A tree trunk also had to be added at each side of the painting. By using an engraved source, Plamondon was also able to display his undeniable talents as a colourist.

Y.L.

Notes

1. On this set, see *LACASSE 1983/1*.

2. See *LACASSE 1983/2*.

3. Anonymous, "Six tableaux d'Antoine Plamondon. Leur histoire," *L'ami des sourds-muets*, June 1954, pp. 134-135.

Inscriptions
(s.d., l.r., on the arm of the armchair, almost erased) *1841/A. Plamondon* (b.,l.c., on a sheet glued to the canvas, in black ink) *Née le 1 […] 1823/ Mathilde G. Tourangeau est entrée à/l'Hôpital Général le 28 Mai 1840. Elle a pris/le voile blanc le 17 oct 1840. Elle a fait/profession sout le titre de Mere Sᵉ Anne/le 21 Oct 1841//Son portrait a été fait par Mʳ Ant Plamondon/le 10 Sept 1841.*

Provenance
Tourangeau family, Quebec City; Hôpital général de Québec.

Exhibition
Quebec City 1959.

Bibliography
Le Canadien, August 20, 1841, p. 2; *Le Fantasque,* August 23, 1841, pp. 436-439; MORISSET *1935/2,* p. 4; MORISSET *1935/10,* p. 5 (Repr.); MORISSET *1936-1937,* Vol. I, pp. 147-157 (Repr.); Archives du monastère des Augustines de l'Hôpital général de Québec, "Journal du Musée", t. I (1938-1957), pp. 19, 20, 27, 32 and 66, t. II (1958-à aujourd'hui), p. 6; MORISSET *1941/1,* p. 73; MORISSET *1945,* p. 4; LAMBERT *1947,* p. 36; MORISSET *1960/2,* p. 15; HARPER *1962/3,* p. 415; HARPER *1966,* pp. 83 and 86 (Repr.); HUBBARD *1970,* pp. 19 and 29 (Repr.); DUMAS *1970,* p. 21; PORTER *1975,* pp. 6, 10, 17, 18 and 28 (Repr.); BOULIZON *1976,* Vol. II (Repr.); LE GRAND HÉRITAGE *1984,* p. 122; PORTER *1987/4,* p. 1511; BÉLAND AND BOURASSA *1990,* p. 74; PORTER *1990/1,* p. 923; LACROIX *1990,* p. 21.

Collection
Musée de l'Hôpital Général de Québec

196. (See colour reproduction, p. 98)
Sœur Sainte-Anne, 1841
Oil on canvas, 88.9 × 71.1 cm

O NE NEVER GROWS WEARY of examining, comparing and admiring the three portraits of nuns from the Hôpital général de Québec, which Plamondon painted for their parents in 1841, because they represent an undisputable pinnacle in the development of art in Quebec. Of the three, the most famous is that of *Soeur Saint-Alphonse* at the National Gallery of Canada, not because of any degree of superiority, but simply because of the collection, of which it became part in 1937. Since then, it has largely benefitted from the institution's prestige and from several exhibitions both at home and abroad, to such an extent that it now holds a considerable, if not inordinate, place in the historiography of Canadian art. At the same time, the paintings *Soeur Saint-Joseph* and ***Soeur Sainte-Anne*** quietly graced the walls of the Hôpital général de Québec, apparently since the first decades

of the 20th century, thanks to a donation by the heirs or descendants of their sponsor in 1841.

Sisters Saint-Joseph and Sainte-Anne were from the same family. Daughters of Joseph Guillet *dit* Tourangeau and Judith Kemner-Laflamme, they were christened Flore (1821-1850) and Marie-Mathilde (1823-1908). Their father was a very prosperous butcher in the Saint-Roch quarter, and his affluence and commitment to municipal affairs made him a respected leading citizen. As proud of his children as he was of his social success, he was, after the portraits of his daughters Flore and Marie-Mathilde were executed, to commission Plamondon to complete several other portraits in 1842.[1] Sister Saint-Joseph did not enjoy a long religious career. Born on September 17, 1821, she entered the community on July 22, 1839, took the veil on October 15, pronounced her per-

petual vows on October 19 of the following year and died on November 16, 1850. In 1842, in view of her natural inclinations, she was one of two Hôpital général nuns chosen by the Mother Superior to take courses in "théréum drawing" (pochoir painting?) given by French artist Victor Ernette, so that she could subsequently teach this technique to the institution's boarders. As for Sister Sainte-Anne, she set a record for longevity within the institution. Born on September 1, 1823, she entered as a postulant on May 28, 1840, took her white novice's veil on October 19, pronounced her solemn vows on October 21 of the following year and continued her religious career until October 2, 1908. Just before her death, she was the "venerated dean" of the institution, a "relic of the good old days" (*Translation*), in the words of the annalist. Like her sister, she was made drawing mistress,

Fig. 196A.
Nicolas de Largillière,
Elizabeth Throckmorton, 1729;
oil on canvas, 81.3 × 65.7 cm.
National Gallery of Art,
Washington, D.C. (1964.20.1 [1929]).

and also assumed the task of supervising students until the Hôpital général boarding school was closed in 1868. According to the writer of "the annual letter for the year 1908," "Soeur Saint-Anne was extremely scrupulous in her feelings and methods," distinguishing herself, among other ways, "by acts of generous humility." (*Translation*)

Her open, attentive and intelligent disposition can also be seen in the beautiful image conveyed by Plamondon in his portrait of Sister Sainte-Anne. These characteristics distinguish her from the pensive face of Sister Saint-Joseph and the proud assurance of Sister Saint-Alphonse. It can also be noted in passing that the young woman's features strongly resembled those of her father.[2] Besides these peculiarities, a few minor variations and the fact that Sister Sainte-Anne is the only one sporting the white veil worn by novices, the three portraits of the nuns basically draw on the same type of composition and the same range of plastic and formal qualities. A white headband covers their foreheads and a wimple surrounds the rest of their faces, widening out below their chins and descending to their chests. Although only a part of the lining appears in the painting, their veil gives the composition its triangular structure. The fact that they are seated on an armchair which is discreetly depicted on an angle on the right and that the bottom of the composition corresponds to the top of their laps gives the three paintings a great deal of density. The painter's clever rendering of the remainder of the Augustines' clothing, in this case, the white linen rochet, the white wool robe and the black wool serge cope, must also

be emphasized. To this can be added the beautiful contrasts, the subtle play of light and the fine variations which the artist used in drawing the hands of the nuns holding the red book of the *Constitutions* of their order, under the silvered profile of their pectoral crosses. In short, these three portraits are very well constructed.

With a very sure touch, Plamondon managed to render the roundness of the contours. Essentially limiting his palette to red, black and white, he relied on limpid tones and subtle contrasts to portray the relative austerity of his subjects. By conferring a sort of immateriality to the lighting in his portraits, he achieved a classic purity which transcends mere likeness. Here, the result of his originality is a faithfulness to the grand tradition of portraits of nuns instituted in Europe in the 17th century, a faithfulness illustrated by the way in which parallels can be drawn between his three canvases and that of *Elizabeth Throckmorton* by Nicolas de Largillière, an image of a nun painted in 1729 (Fig. 196A). Of Plamondon's three nuns, art historian Gérard Morisset confessed his preference for *Soeur Sainte-Anne*. He considered it a masterpiece or "at least the most beautiful work of the 19th-century Canadian school." (*Translation*) He especially appreciated the tension of the feeling and expression, the seductiveness of the face, the contours of the skin, and the sweep of fabric. We, in turn, would like to stress the freshness, presence and spirituality of the subject. Over and above her undeniable charm, an intense wave of creative inspiration can be felt beneath the swelling folds of the beautiful white veil of the 18-year-old novice.

Plamondon was definitely aware that he had surpassed himself with this type of painting. He probably recalled the portrait of *Soeur Sainte-Claire* (Musée de l'Hôpital général), which he had painted seven years earlier, but without attaining the same degree of mastery, sensitivity and fluidity. This time, he was so proud of his work that, even before he had completed the painting, he wanted to publicize it in the newspapers. His mentor, Joseph-Édouard Cauchon, agreed to publish a long, open letter in *Le Canadien* of August 20, 1841. While shedding light on the problems with regard to face and costume the artist had to overcome, our anonymous "friend of painting" (*Translation*) warmly congratulated the painter for his incomparable sense of colour, even going so far as to call him, for all intents and purposes, the "premier colourist of the New World." (*Translation*) This one-sided opinion, however, was not unanimous and "a friend of painters" (*Translation*) hastened to respond in *Le Fantasque* of August 23. The author of this second letter roundly denounced the Plamondon-Cauchon tactic, and the "pompous, pedantic tone" (*Translation*) of the text published in *Le Canadien*. If he was criticizing Plamondon's three portraits, which he nevertheless recognized as being "certainly entitled to some praise," it was because he could not tolerate the artist's attacks and "his desire to harm other colleagues through [uncalled-for] comparisons." (*Translation*)

Once again, we can see the jealous rivalry between the proud Plamondon and his competitors, and the controversial atmosphere he frequently created through

Fig. 196B.
(?) Émilie Tourangeau
after Michel Dessaillant,
*Mère Louise Soumande
de Saint-Augustin*, c. 1842;
watercolour on paper.
Archives du Séminaire de Québec.

his untimely statements and the epistolary excesses of his mentor. At the time when he painted the portraits of Sister Sainte-Anne, Sister Saint-Joseph and Sister Saint-Alphonse, the artist had access to the Hôpital général as drawing master to the novices. However, he was unable to meet his clients' expectations in this capacity, as can be seen in this passage from the "Journal du noviciat," dated July 19, 1841:

This gentleman showed us only how to draw faces according to the rules of drawing, without explaining where shade, light, reflection and shadow should be placed; that is what we learned later as will be seen. But another important thing which he could not show us was the miniature and we waited for Providence to intervene, and our wait was not in vain. This same Mr. Plamondon offered to show us oil painting, but since this is expensive and in a convent lessons take place one after another, in the time we would have spent arranging our paintings one lesson would be over and we would have been obliged to set them aside, and everything would have been lost or partially wasted. (*Translation*)

On February 5, 1842, the nuns' expectations were satisfied when French artist Victor Ernette introduced himself at the Hôpital général "with drawing samples, and offered his services to teach [them] théréum drawing in six lessons, for 22 piastres." (*Translation*) The author of the "Journal du noviciat" went on to write that:

This gentleman also demonstrated the miniature; but since the roads were very bad, and our men and horses very busy, we could not send someone round to pick up this gentlemen, since the price of his lessons was greatly reduced when we sent someone round. We were in sad straits, [...] but Providence came to our rescue; two of our friends, Mr. P. Pelle-

tier and Mr. J. Tourangeau offered, one to bring him down to us and the other to take him back to Upper Town all the time we were taking lessons. (*Translation*)

It can be easily understood why Plamondon's lightning bolts were unleashed two months later upon the unfortunate head of Victor Ernette.[3] Not only did the latter replace him as drawing master to the novices at the Hôpital général but, even worse, he did so with the help of two excellent clients, merchant Pierre Pelletier and butcher Joseph Tourangeau, both of whom had just recently commissioned from him portraits of their respective daughters, namely, Sister Saint-Alphonse, Sister Saint-Joseph and Sister Sainte-Anne. Besides Plamondon's discontent, what should be remembered here is Joseph Tourangeau's interest in the art of drawing and painting. One of the subscribers to Joseph Légaré's second Picture Gallery, he had not failed to notice the artistic talent with which several of his children were endowed. Proof positive: not only did Sister Saint-Joseph and Sister Sainte-Anne teach drawing to the boarders at the Hôpital général, but their younger sisters Joséphine and Émilie also distinguished themselves in this regard.[4] The latter may even have been the author of a small portrait of Mother Louise Soumande de Saint-Augustin, first superior of the Hôpital général de Québec, preserved in the album "Ma Saberdache," compiled by collector Jacques Viger (Fig. 196B). Evidently, this was a copy of a small, post-mortem portrait painted by Michel Dessaillant in 1708 (Musée de l'Hôpital général), a copy rendered in the fashions of the 19th century and based on one of the portraits painted by Plamondon in

1841, probably the one of Sister Saint-Joseph.[5] From the brush of Largillière to that of a young boarder at the Hôpital général de Québec, by way of the brushes of Plamondon and his rival Ernette, it can certainly be said that the avenues of creation and imitation followed unusual routes!

J.R.P.

Notes

1. Perhaps these were the portraits discussed in an article by M. Bibaud published in *L'Encyclopédie canadienne* of Montreal in October 1842. During a visit to the artist's studio, the editor was especially impressed by the quality of the half-length portraits "of an entire Quebec City family, father, mother, son, daughter, etc." (*Translation*) The Musée du Québec today houses some of them, including those of the sponsor and his wife.

2. The portrait Plamondon painted of him in 1842 is preserved at the Musée du Québec (53.77).

3. See *Le Canadien*, March 14 and 30, p. 2, and *Le Fantasque*, April 7, 1842, p.

4. Joséphine (1833-1866) was to be the subject of a portrait by Plamondon in 1854 (MQ) before entering the Quebec City Ursuline community, where she took the name of Soeur Sainte-Marguerite; one of his oil paintings is discussed in the "Journal du Musée" of the Hôpital général (Vol. I, January 22, 1940, p. 58). Émilie (born in 1829) won the first-class award for "théréum" drawing during the formal distribution of awards to the young boarders at the Hôpital général de Québec on July 25, 1844. See *Le Journal de Québec*, July 30, 1844, p. 1.

5. At the time, the institution's boarders also took their inspiration from a portrait of the institution's founder, Monseigneur de Saint-Vallier, who was depicted in prayer in a large painting preserved in the chapel.

197.
Elzéar Bédard, 1842
Oil on canvas mounted on fibreboard, 123.5 × 98 cm

Inscriptions
(s.d., l.l.) *A. Plamondon/1842;* (c.l., on the book) BLAC[K]/[?]/LAW/I.

Provenance
John L. Russell, Montreal, before1959 (on deposit at the Art Gallery of Hamilton, 1969); acquired by the Art Gallery of Hamilton, 1973.

Exhibitions
Montreal 1960, No. 17; Montreal 1967/1, No. 104; Ottawa 1970, No. 32.

Bibliography
Le Bulletin des recherches historiques, Vol. XI, No. 8 (August 1905), p. 243 (Repr.); ROY *1933,* p. 40 (Repr.); ONZE ARTISTES *1960,* No. 17; CARTER *1967,* No. 104 (Repr.); CARTER *1967-1968,* p. 18; HUBBARD *1970,* pp. 30, 81-82 and 138, No. 32 (Repr.); DUMAS *1970,* p. 21; *Nos racines,* No. 62 (1979), p. 1232 (Repr.); HARE, LAFRANCE AND RUDDEL *1987,* p. 235 (Repr.); LACROIX *1990,* p. 22.

Collection
Art Gallery of Hamilton. Gift of the Volunteer Committee, 1973 (1969.88.R)

A FTER BEING FULLY ABSORBED for almost four years in painting the Stations of the Cross for the Notre-Dame church in Montreal (Cat. 195), Antoine Plamondon returned to portraiture in the early 1840s. At that time, he executed the portraits of three nuns of the Hôpital général de Québec (Cat. 196), members of the Tourangeau family (MQ) and Elzéar Bédard (1799-1849) and his wife, née Julie-Henriette Marett. Bédard studied at the Séminaire de Nicolet, then at the Petit Séminaire de Québec, where he was destined for the priesthood. He finally opted for law and, like many of his colleagues, soon became interested in politics. Member of Parliament for Montmorency in 1832 and 1834, he first sided with Louis-Joseph Papineau (Cat. 188) and presented at the House of Assembly the Ninety-Two Resolutions, drafted at his home with the assistance of Louis Bourdages (Cat. 205), among oth-

ers. He subsequently distanced himself from the radical wing of the Patriote party, siding with the moderates. In the meantime, he was also involved in municipal politics and became, in 1833, the first mayor of the new incorporated City of Quebec. His mandate lasted only a single year and he subsequently sat as an ordinary councillor until 1835. His appointment as a justice of the Court of King's Bench in 1836 was considered an act of corruption and cowardice by his former political colleagues. Bédard nevertheless proved his integrity in 1838 when he acquiesced to a writ of *habeas corpus,* thereby going against the orders of the Special Council. Suspended for two years, he continued his career as a justice in Quebec City until 1848, then in Montreal, where he died the following year following a cholera epidemic.

Painted two years after the justice's reinstatement, this portrait, in which he is

depicted wearing an ermine robe, to some extent reprises a composition scheme with which Plamondon had already experimented in the portrait of Louis-Joseph Papineau (Cat. 188). However, unlike what he had done in the latter portrait, the artist did not place the subject's head in the centre, but rather slightly back and to the right. In this way, he corrected the imbalance created by the position of the subject who, in the 1836 work, was confined to the left half of the painting, thereby obliging Plamondon to resort to some rather less than successful subterfuges in composition (drapery and floor tiling). The harmony of Bédard's portrait is ensured by the arrangement of forms on the painting's diagonals and by the distribution of books, thereby establishing a sort of eurhythmics despite the eccentric position of the face. The same props featured in the portrait of his former political ally, namely, an inkwell and a goose quill, also

198.
Mrs. Elzéar Bédard, née Julie-Henriette Marett, 1842
Oil on canvas mounted on fibreboard, 123.5 × 98 cm

Inscription
(s.d., l.l.) *A Plamondon/1842.*

Provenance
John L. Russell, Montreal, before 1959 (on deposit at the Art Gallery of Hamilton, 1969); acquired by the Art Gallery of Hamilton, 1973.

Exhibitions
Ottawa 1959, No. 17; Montreal 1960, No. 18; Montreal 1967/1, No. 103; Ottawa 1970, No. 33.

Bibliography
MORISSET *1959/2,* No. 17 (Repr.); ONZE ARTISTES *1960,* No. 17; CARTER *1967,* No. 103 (Repr.); CARTER *1967-1968,* p. 18; HUBBARD *1970,* pp. 30, 82 and 138, No. 33 (Repr.); DUMAS *1970,* p. 21; *Nos racines,* No. 62 (1979), p. 1232 (Repr.).

Collection
Art Gallery of Hamilton. Gift of the Volunteer Committee, 1973 (1969.88.Q)

appear here, albeit in less detail, along with a book and a document held in much the same manner, but in the opposite order. The same goes for the drapery opening onto a bookshelf which is seen in perspective. The treatment as a whole seems more realistic and better executed; the whites of the ermine in particular are finely textured and lit thanks to the use of a lightly tinted dense mixture and the myriad strokes applied with a wide, short brush. Plamondon also skilfully rendered the transparency and rigidity of the bands and collar, using a more sparkling white and blended strokes.

Mrs. Bédard's portrait is based on a subtle balance between the almost frontal position of her body and the diagonal created by the armchair and setting. Like the long ringlets framing Mrs. Bédard's face, her body takes on a sinuous shape, reflected in the movement of her hands, arms, torso and head. The subject is wearing a red gown with a fitted bodice topped by a black-lace bertha and tapering to a sharp point, from which hang two long tassels. The short sleeves are caught up above the elbows and adorned with lace cuffs which partially cover the forearms. Her outfit is complemented by a pair of dress gloves. A brooch worn on the bodice, a wedding ring and a wide bracelet are her only ornaments. The setting serves to enhance the subject. The armchair, placed slightly on a diagonal and disappearing off the canvas to the right, integrates the subject in space. Even the draperies fulfil this function, since the left tassel appears closer than the right. The composition opens onto an atypical landscape painted to complement the turquoise and greenish hues of the armchair and curtain.

With the coming of the 1840s, Antoine Plamondon fully mastered space in his paintings. In his works of the preceding decade, the subject took up almost all the painted surface, overpowering the viewer. By setting his subjects farther back, the artist incorporated greater autonomy into his work and his subject, thereby giving himself greater freedom of expression which enabled him to give freer rein to his vast talent. Although the construction of these portraits remains classical, they play on the balance between shape and colour, while offering a variety of poses which were often absent from his previous works. With their more fully developed background, these portraits are an excellent example of this style. The portraits of Joseph Guillet dit Tourangeau and his wife (MQ) dating from the same year demonstrate the artist's mastery with regard to subjects placed on a background enhanced solely by light.

P.B.

199.
The Little Savoyards, 1844
After Joseph Hornung
Oil on canvas, 91.4 × 76.2 cm

Inscription
(s.d., l.l.) *A. Plamondon/1844.*

Provenance
Denis-Benjamin Viger, Montreal, 1847; Sir Louis-Amable Jetté; Mrs. Rodolphe Lemieux, née Jetté; Mrs. Alfred Thibaudeau, née Lemieux, Westmount; gift to the Montreal Museum of Fine Arts, 1963.

Exhibitions
Quebec City 1845; Montreal 1857.

Bibliography
L'Aurore des Canadas, August 24, 1843, p. 2 and November 23, 1847, p. 2; *Le Journal de Québec,* September 12, p. 3, October 3, 1843, pp. 2-3 and November 16, 1847, p. 3; *Quebec Mercury,* May 6, 1845, p. 2; *Le Canadien,* November 19, 1847, p. 2; *Mélanges Religieux,* November 19, 1847, p. 77; *La Minerve,* August 25, 1857, p. 2; MORISSET 1936-1937, Vol. I, pp. 177-178; MORISSET 1960/2, p. 15; PORTER 1990/1, p. 923; NICOLAÏ 1990, p. 95; POMERLEAU 1990, p. 286 (Repr.); BÉLAND AND BOURASSA 1990, p. 54.

Collection
Montreal Museum of Fine Arts. Gift from Mrs. Alfred Thibaudeau (1963.1393).

A LTHOUGH THE PAINTING *The Little Savoyards* dates from 1844, the editor of *L'Aurore des Canadas* was able to admire the work in Plamondon's studio as early as August 24, 1843. The following is his rather colourful description:

I will begin with *The Little Savoyards,* a pretty work which has just been completed and which would be enough to make the artist's reputation if he had not already accomplished that long ago. The two children are sitting in the cottage, glasses filled with an excellent Bordeaux in hand, and a bundle of sticks and a pretty dog which seems to be regarding them with satisfaction in their drunkenness at their feet. A beam of sheer joy is spread across the face of the elder, while the other's lips are curved into a calm, sweet smile. These two faces reveal two different souls, but they have such an effect on you that you have to be in a really ill humour to look at them for a full minute without getting caught up in their beatitude; you could almost say that they are

laughing at the hand which has just created them! As always, Mr. Plamondon has imbued the painting with charm and colour, a poetry of imagination in the painting's background, a beauty and naturalness of character, truthfulness and a happy facial expression which already made his *Tableau de Pape,* which all Montreal went to see some time ago, a truly superior piece; unfortunately, it is still in his studio. (*Translation*)

The Little Savoyards did not remain in the artist's studio for long, however, since *Le Canadien* of November 19, 1847 tells us that:

The Honourable D.B. Viger, for whom M. Plamondon executed the great painting of Tobias of which we spoke recently, has just purchased the delightful copy made by this same artist after an engraving of the charming painting by M. Hornung of Geneva, entitled *Happy as a King,* which is today known as *The Little Savoyards.* (*Translation*)

This paragraph gives us two pieces of important information for our study of this painting: the name of the first owner of the work, and Plamondon's source. In the first case, it was attorney, journalist, essayist and politician Denis-Benjamin Viger (1774-1861); counted as one of the leading landowners in the city of Montreal, Viger also owned a "beautiful collection of paintings."[1] (*Translation*) "M. Hornung of Geneva," discussed in the *Le Canadien* article, can only refer to Joseph Hornung, "history and genre painter, born in Geneva on January 25, 1792, and died in the same city on February 4, 1870" (*Translation*), recorded in the Bénézit. However, we have not been able to trace this artist's painting *Happy as a King,* on which our work is based. An engraving taken from the painting in question was found at the Hôpital général de Québec

Fig. 199A.
Unidentified engraver after Joseph Hornung,
Happy as a King;
engraving (attached to a screen).
Hôpital général de Québec.

(Fig. 199A). This is likely the source used by Plamondon when copying Hornung's composition, which has its own roots in the famous *Mangeurs de melon* by Murillo (1618-1682).

As Guy Barbichon and Gérald Collomb noted:

Among the seasonal migrant workers, the Savoyard chimney sweep was a conspicuous player on the Parisian scene until the turn of the century. Parisian society found him a tender, picturesque subject and fully cultivated in image and song.

Exiled, poor, exploited by adults, beggar and public entertainer, busker with performing marmots, he is depicted sometimes in sordid surroundings as a pitiable victim, sometimes as the blackened, yet naive hero of the uplifting stories of good peasants, and sometimes as the impish figure of a street urchin from the mountains.[2] (*Translation*)

It was not without some condescension that an admirer of Plamondon's painting admitted in *Le Journal de Québec* of October 3, 1843 that he could not "contain his hilarity in seeing the transports of joy experienced by these small orphans upon the sight of a good meal, and they indeed know the true worth of a good meal! because they are accustomed to often being hungry." (*Translation*)

Since Plamondon's canvas is inspired by a European work, one could think that, as far as its subject is concerned, there is nothing Canadian about it. Nevertheless, young Savoyards did work as chimney sweeps in New France, as was mentioned on many occasions. In 1729, Governor Beauharnois and Intendant Hocquart asked that four Savoyards between the ages of twelve and fourteen be sent "because the two sent a few years ago

are now too big to get into the chimneys."[3] (*Translation*) Small Savoyard children often worked in twos: one of the children would enter the chimney armed with a scraper to scrape off the soot, while the other, posted on the roof, would hold the first with a rope.   Y.L.

Notes

1. *Le Journal de Québec*, November 16, 1847, p. 2. According to Louis-Joseph-Amédée Papineau, Viger's library and painting gallery were probably, in 1852, two of the most beautiful collections in Canada. See Fernand Ouellet and André Lefort, DCB, Vol. IX (1977).
2. Guy Barbichon and Gérald Collomb, "Sur le thème du petit ramoneur savoyard...," *Ethnologie française*, Vol. X, No. 2 (1980), pp. 178-180.
3. Pierre-Georges Roy, "Les Savoyards dans la Nouvelle-France," *Le Bulletin des recherches historiques*, Vol. XXXIV, No. 9 (September 1928), p. 536.

IGNACE
PLAMONDON

1796-1835

I GNACE PLAMONDON was born at Ancienne-Lorette on February 7, 1796. His artistic career remains somewhat of a mystery. He may have studied under Joseph Légaré, like his cousin Antoine Plamondon, with whom he also took lessons from painter Paulin-Guérin in Paris starting in 1827. Ignace stayed on in Europe, however, after Antoine returned home in 1830. In a letter dated March 14, 1831, Father Philippe-Jean-Louis Desjardins mentions that he thinks Ignace Plamondon was in Switzerland at the time. In all likelihood, he spent some time with the Jesuits in Fribourg, probably returning to Canada in 1831, since in 1832 he took up a teaching position at Chambly college. An article in the June 10, 1833 edition of *La Minerve* provides a few details on the subject:

> Monsieur Ignace Plamondon teaches drawing. This young Canadian spent seven years in Europe, attending the best ateliers in France and Switzerland, from which he bene-fitted immensely, acquiring knowledge and skills that he can now pass on to his pupils at Chambly. I have seen several samples of his work and I can assure you they show such taste and talent that they honour him and make him worthy of your encouragement. (*Translation*)

In the fall of 1833, Ignace Plamondon entered the Séminaire de Saint-Hyacinthe, whose administration was pleased to be able to "train a teacher in this field" (*Translation*) as candidates of such calibre were few and far between in Lower Canada. We have no information on his activities from 1833 until his early death at age 39, on June 14, 1835, at his birthplace, Ancienne-Lorette. Virtually nothing is known about the artistic production of this "extremely humble [and] particularly excellent Christian artist" (*Translation*), as he was described in his obituary.

Main source
HARPER 1970.

200.
*François Langlois dit Ciartres
(The Bagpiper)*, c. 1820-1825
After Anton Van Dyck
Oil on canvas, 81.3 × 65 cm

Inscription
(b.,u.r., on the stretcher, upper cross-piece, recent inscription) *Joueur de cornemuse/d'aprèsVan Dyck A. Plamondon.*

Provenance
Ulric-Joseph Tessier, Quebec City; Cyrille Tessier, Quebec City; Mrs. Hélène Gagné, Quebec City, 1948; acquired by the Musée du Québec, Quebec City, 1989.

Exhibitions
Quebec City 1848; Quebec City 1920.

Bibliography
Le Canadien, October 2, 1848, p. 3, No. 27; *L'Ami de la Religion et de la Patrie*, October 4, 1848, p. 655, No. 27; *Quebec Mercury*, October 5, 1848, p. 3, No. 27; *Le Journal de Québec*, October 5, 1848, p. 3, No. 27; *Le Canadien*, October 13, 1848, p. 2; EXHIBITION *1920*, p. 3; BÉLAND *1989/3*, p. 69; BÉLAND AND BOURASSA *1990*, pp. 6, 9 and 42 (Repr.); LA CHRONIQUE *1990*, p. 36, No. 175 (Repr.).

Collection
Musée du Québec, Quebec City. Restored in 1991, with the assistance of the Amis du Musée du Québec (89.28)

Fig. 200A.
Unidentified artist after Anton Van Dyck, *François Langlois (The Bagpiper)*; oil on canvas, 78 × 61.5 cm. Musée du Séminaire de Québec (444).

T HE PAINTINGS sent from France by Father Philippe-Jean-Louis Desjardins included, as far as is known, only three secular works. They were part of the collection sent in 1820 and were purchased by Joseph Légaré. The copy of this painting by Anton Van Dyck (1599-1641) from the Légaré collection was attributed to Jan Mienze Molenaer (Fig. 200A). It is not known whether there was originally an inscription on the painting making it possible to attribute it to Molenaer with such certitude.

This genre portrait, whose composition reflects literary and mythological themes, inspired Ignace Plamondon to produce an excellent copy of similar format.

The attribution to Ignace Plamondon is based on an article by Polymétis published in *Le Canadien* of October 13, 1848, which stated: "An admirable copy of a bagpiper after an admiral original painting done by the late Plamondon under the supervision of Monsieur Légaré." (*Translation*) The canvas was displayed in the House of Assembly and was to be a prize in a lottery organized by Légaré. The artist could therefore not be Antoine Plamondon as originally thought, but rather is Ignace Plamondon, who had died thirteen years earlier. Antoine was too loquacious and too visible on the Quebec art scene for Polymétis to have confused the two artists. Moreover, following the appearance of Ignace Plamondon's obituary in *Le Canadien* of June 19, 1835, his op-

portunist cousin Antoine, always looking for publicity, had the following item published:

We would like to take this opportunity to rectify a false impression existing among the population as a result of the obituary of Mr. Ignace Plamondon, also an artist and pupil of Mr. Guérin. The deceased was only the cousin of the artist by the name of Antoine Plamondon, who is still very much alive, and willing to paint the likeness of anyone wishing to have their portrait immortalized for posterity. We would further like to take this opportunity to draw your attention to one of Mr. Antoine Plamondon's most recent works. (*Translation*)

Regrettably, we know of no other definite work by Ignace Plamondon, since as well as being a talented restorer—these talents were countless times extolled by Father Desjardins[1]—, he boasted a keen sense of observation and was a skilled colourist. Although nothing is known about the circumstances surrounding Ignace's initial artistic training, we do know it was done in Quebec City. He went to Paris with his cousin Antoine in 1826 and at the time of his death was considered a master draughtsman.

In North America, this allegorical portrait was to be considered a genre scene known as *François Langlois dit Ciartres (The Bagpiper)*.[2] It is one of the rare copies of profane subject matter done by a Lower Canadian artist. The model who inspired Van Dyck was François Langlois (1588-1647), known by the name of Ciartres because he was born in the city of

Chartres. A reputable art dealer, Langlois was primarily a bookseller and publisher. He founded the *Colonnes d'Hercule*, a publishing concern known for its books and prints and which, thanks to the work and talent of the Langlois and Mariette dynasties, continued to exist until the 18th century. In addition to Van Dyck, Claude Vignon (1593-1670) also immortalized on canvas this great friend to all artists and disseminator of the arts (PC, Wellesley College Museum deposit, United States). *François Langlois dit Ciartres (The Bagpiper)* does not stand as an alternative or proposal for a rebirth of portraiture, but rather as an exotic subject in which Scottish legend and religious connotations inhabit the same canvas. The shepherds in *The Adoration of the Shepherds* are often depicted with bagpipes, an unpretentious musical instrument. It was the vivacious expression and contrasts in lighting that would seem to have attracted Ignace Plamondon.

L.L.

Notes
1. Father Louis-Joseph Desjardins recalls how Ignace Plamondon restored a tear using a piece of canvas and some wax and how he remounted a canvas (AMUQ, letter from L.-J. Desjardins to Reverend Mother Saint-Henri, January 20, 1840).
2. For more on the iconography on François Langlois, see Marianne Frote-Langlois, "Iconographie de François Langlois dit Ciartres", *Gazette des beaux-arts*, Tome CII (October 1983), pp. 119-120.

JEAN-BAPTISTE
ROY-AUDY

1778 – before 1848

JEAN-BAPTISTE ROY-AUDY was born November 15, 1778 in Quebec City, into a family of woodworkers (joiners, carpenters, and cabinetmakers). He trained with François Baillairgé and then in his father's workshop. In spring 1802, when he ceased being a dependent of his father, he opened his own workshop in the Saint-Jean-Baptiste quarter, where he practised the trades of woodworker, cabinetmaker, and wheelwright, besides painting carriages and signs. On July 27 of the same year, he married Julie Vézina in Quebec City. In 1805, he built the organ case of the Notre-Dame church in Montreal, while Louis Dulongpré was commissioned to paint, gild and decorate it.

Roy-Audy's business prospered and, in 1811, he hired his first two apprentices. However, by 1816, severe financial problems forced him to declare bankruptcy and sell his assets. This misfortune likely encouraged Roy-Audy to abandon woodworking completely in order to devote himself entirely to painting. *The Holy Family resting in Egypt* (Boucherville, 1817) is one of his first works to be signed and dated. In 1819, Roy-Audy took on Yves Tessier as an apprentice and taught him the art of painting. The following year, he formed an association with European-born artist Louis-Hubert Triaud. The exact contribution of each painter is still not known, but together they produced a large canvas entitled *The Baptism of Christ*. They also advertised themselves as portraitists, miniaturists and history painters, and offered to give courses in drawing and painting "based on the method used in the English and French academies." (*Translation*) Obviously, this statement could not truthfully be applied to Roy-Audy.

Over the following years, Roy-Audy produced several religious paintings for churches in various regions around Quebec City, such as Louiseville (five paintings, 1820), Saint-Augustin-de-Desmaures (1823), and Saint-Roch-de-l'Achigan (1823). Most of these works are faithful reproductions of specific subjects, except perhaps *Saul sur le chemin de Damas* (Verchères church, circa 1825), which shows an attempt at originality. In 1828, he left Quebec City for Montreal. He returned in 1830, and then settled again in Montreal circa 1833-1834. Most of his known portraits date from this period.

The end of Roy-Audy's career remains obscure. After 1838, there seem to be no further trace of him. His death is mentioned in a document dated April 26, 1848, in which his widow authorizes Joseph Légaré to sell two portraits painted by her husband. Roy-Audy may also have died outside Quebec well before this date, because in January 1845, during the signing of a document notarized by his wife, he is mentioned as being an artist from Quebec City, but "absent from the province" (*Translation*) at the time.

Main sources
CAUCHON 1971; CAUCHON 1988.

201.
Saint Mary Magdeleine, 1819
After an Unidentified Artist, France, 18th Century
Oil on canvas, 67.4 × 56 cm

Inscription
(s.d., l.l.) *J.B.R. Audy/P. 1819.*

Provenance
Denis Pinard, Amqui; acquired by the Musée du Québec, Quebec City, 1980.

Bibliography
BÉLAND 1989/3, p. 69; BÉLAND AND BOURASSA 1990, pp. 6, 9 and 36 (Repr.).

Collection
Musée du Québec, Quebec City. Restored in 1991, with the assistance of the Amis du Musée du Québec (80.04)

I N 1818, Jean-Baptiste Roy-Audy, who was just beginning his career as a painter, copied some of the European works imported to Quebec City by Father Louis-Joseph Desjardins.[1] The artist, who was attempting to make a living from his art, was seeking models as inspiration. He therefore copied in 1818 (PC), and then in 1819, this repentant Mary Magdalene. The work enabled him to gain experience in portraying anatomy and draperies; furthermore, given the work's small size and subject, he was guaranteed to find buyers. Roy-Audy, like his contemporaries Légaré and Plamondon, but unlike artists of the following generation, combined two trades: instead of making copies of masters with the sole objective of gaining experience, as suggested by academic methods, he attempted to obtain commissions for them.

The interest on the part of Roy-Audy, Hamel (Cat. 115) and likely Légaré[2] in copying this Mary Magdalene was due to several factors. The painting, easy to trace freehand, did not take much time to copy, although the artists obviously took great pleasure in portraying the detail in the subject's hair. The original was probably still in Father Desjardins' possession when Roy-Audy copied it in almost identical dimensions. To emphasize the work's picturesque quality, the artist focused on the rustic aspect of the cross held by the saint. In addition to this detail, he obviously felt the need to justify her tearful gaze to the left by adding a background of clouds and piercing them with a ray of light.

The original work was attributed to Louis-Antoine David (1648-1730) by Joseph Légaré. This attribution does not appear in documents on the Desjardins

collection. In 1829, Bourne was the first to mention the work with a reference to David, but with no first name. The 1852 catalogue for the Légaré collection gives Louis-Antoine David (1648-1728/1730). Is this an error, and did Légaré see similarities between this painting and works by neo-classical artist Jacques-Louis David (1748-1825)? The attribution to Louis-Antoine David is surprising, to say the least. This artist, who supposedly was born and died in Lugano, Switzerland, left no works for comparison. How could the name of such a little-known artist come to be associated with this painting? The model's classic physiognomy is more typical of the late than of the early 18th century.

The size of the work corresponds to a religious picture, and the subject's expression conveys fear mingled with repentance. It is interesting to compare the

202.
Saint Mary Magdeleine, après 1750
Unidentified artist France, 18th century
Oil on canvas, 59.8 × 48 cm

Provenance
Desjardins painting shipment 1817; Joseph Légaré, before 1829; Séminaire de Québec, from the Joseph Légaré estate, 1874; on deposit at the Société du Musée du Séminaire de Québec, 1983.

Exhibition
Quebec City 1988.

Bibliography
BOURNE 1829, No. 9, attributed to David; CATALOGUE 1852, p. 5, No. 22, attributed to Louis-Antoine David; PEINTURES DU SÉMINAIRE 1874-1875, p. 3, No. 107; LEMOINE 1876, p. 366, No. 107; LAVAL UNIVERSITY 1880, p. 5, No. 42; UNIVERSITÉ LAVAL 1883-1884, p. 13, No. 42; LAVAL UNIVERSITY 1883-1884, p. 13, No. 42; UNIVERSITÉ LAVAL 1887, p. 13, No. 42; LAVAL UNIVERSITY 1887, p. 13, No. 42; UNIVERSITÉ LAVAL 1889, p. 13, No. 42; UNIVERSITÉ LAVAL 1893, p. 12, No. 42; LAVAL UNIVERSITY 1894, p. 13, No. 42; UNIVERSITÉ LAVAL 1898, p. 15, No. 42; LAVAL UNIVERSITY 1901, p. 15, No. 42; UNIVERSITÉ LAVAL 1903, p. 13, No. 31; LAVAL UNIVERSITY 1905, p. 13, No. 31; UNIVERSITÉ LAVAL 1908, p. 17, No. 31; CARTER 1908, p. 39, No. 31; UNIVERSITÉ LAVAL 1909, p. 18, No. 31; LAVAL UNIVERSITY 1909, p. 18, No. 31; UNIVERSITÉ LAVAL 1913, p. 33, No. 122; LAVAL UNIVERSITY 1923, p. 36, No. 122; (?) MAGNAN 1926, p. 99; UNIVERSITÉ LAVAL 1933, p. 17, No. 40; PORTER 1978/1, p. 131; BÉLAND 1989/3, p. 69; BÉLAND AND BOURASSA 1990, p. 36.

Collection
Musée du Séminaire de Québec (Pe990.1)

version of both Quebec copyists. Roy-Audy, in the work at the Musée du Québec, has intensified the model's remorse by emphasizing her tears, while Hamel, by softening the facial features, portrays the saint's contrition as a tender melancholy. The two copies show the changes made to the neckline of the model's garments. The work at the Séminaire shows a considerable loss of paint, which the restorer filled in with no knowledge of the early copies which all depict the neckline's original zigzag in the same fashion.

Roy-Audy's copy bears witness to another phenomenon, that of censorship, as evidenced by its modesty overpainting which was done on works considered too

suggestive. Father Louis-Joseph Desjardins ensured that the works he put on the market complied with Catholic chastity standards. He had thus veiled any naked parts of the body. Here, the work, representing a religious subject, shows a beautiful woman with a dimpled arm whose breasts are quite apparent, even in these loose robes. Did Roy-Audy dress the repentant sinner while painting the work, or were the sleeve and heavy torso covering added later? The same phenomenon can be observed in the signed version dated 1818, in which the saint wears a long-sleeved, lace-trimmed dress with lace at the neckline.[3]

L.L.

Notes
1. Examples of this are *The Pentecost* after Philippe de Champaigne, 1818, and *Christ among The Doctors* after Samuel Massé, 1821, Sainte-Anne-de-Varennes church; *Saint Peter Freed from His Prison*, 1819, and *Christ on the Cross*, after Charles Monnet, 1825, Sainte-Famille church in Boucherville.
2. PORTER 1978/1, p. 131, No. 174.
3. Could one of these copies be that mentioned in the accounts book of the Fabrique de Sainte-Famille in Boucherville? The following order from Monseigneur Lartigue was recorded May 25, 1829, in this book: "We order that the canvas of Saint Magdalene which hangs in the choir on the altar side be made more decent, in compliance with the judgement to be handed down by Mr. Le Grand Vicaire Deguise after changes are made in said canvas." (*Translation*) Roy-Audy received several commissions for paintings from this church between 1819 and 1825.

203.
The Baptism of Christ, 1824
After Claude-Guy Hallé
Oil on canvas, 83 × 67.3 cm

Inscription
(s.d., l.r.) *JB.R. Audy. P.. 1824.*

Provenance
Fabrique de Saint-Joseph de Deschambault; on deposit at the Musée du Québec, Quebec City, 1969.

Exhibitions
Quebec City 1972; Quebec City 1984-1985, No. 219.

Bibliography
MORISSET 1951/1, p. 18; MORISSET 1960/1, p. 88; BOISSAY 1966, p. 28; HARPER 1966, pp. 93 and 94

(Repr.); CAUCHON 1971, pp. 71, 75, 78, 81, 83 and 126 (Repr.); NOPPEN 1977, p. 104; LE GRAND HÉRITAGE 1984, p. 246, No. 219 (entry by Laurier Lacroix)(Repr.); VANIER-SHEPHERD 1986, p. 47; BÉLAND AND BOURASSA 1990, pp. 5, 6, 9 and 40 (Repr.); LES CHEMINS DE LA MÉMOIRE 1990, p. 314.

Collection
Musée du Québec, Quebec City. Deposit from the Fabrique de Saint-Joseph de Deschambault. Restored in 1991, with the assistance of the Amis du Musée du Québec (L 69.17)

T HE SCENE OF CHRIST'S BAPTISM, the first episode in Jesus's public life, was recounted by the four Apostles.[1] From these stories, it appears that this episode was composed of two separate events: Jesus' purification in the waters of the river and the theophany, or the manifestation on Earth of the Holy Spirit. This scene, portrayed countless times, became the preferred adornment for baptistries, baptismal chapels and fonts themselves; it was also the subject of paintings which hung above the high altar in a number of churches dedicated to St. John the Baptist. From the early days of the colony, the Catholic Church played a decisive role in implementing and disseminating the iconography of Christ's baptism. The *Extrait du Rituel de Québec,* published by Monseigneur Joseph Signay (Cat. 125 and 189) in 1836, stipulated that fonts should be decorated with a "painting depicting the baptism of Our Lord by St. John the Baptist." (*Translation*) Thanks to these numerous holy ordinances setting out the standards to be followed with regard to the location and decoration of baptistries, the Quebec City diocese offered our artists, during the entire first half of the 19th century, a golden opportunity to put their talents to good use.

Research done to date has turned up some one hundred portrayals of this theme in Quebec art, the majority of which are painted works. Most of these works portray, based on the iconographic tradition, two main figures, Christ and John the Baptist, often joined by the Holy Spirit in the shape of a dove. Angels and cherub's heads are frequently added to fill out and balance the composition. Some parish churches, lacking in resources, had to settle for decorating their baptistries with a simple engraving, which at a later date would hopefully be replaced with a more elaborate painted or sculpted work. The engraving could then serve as a model for the artist, as was the case in 1789 for Louis-Chrétien de Heer in a work he did for the Saint-Charles-de-Bellechasse church. Painters and sculptors were fierce rivals when it came time to solicit commissions from church authorities, as shown by the heated argument which was carried on in the newspapers between Antoine Plamondon and Thomas Fournier. The following riposte, which Plamondon penned to the sculptor, appeared in the April 4, 1850, edition of *Le Journal de Québec:* "As concerns images of Christ's baptism sculpted in wood [...] I must say that they bring you nothing but shame, so little do they resemble the human form." (*Translation*)

Fig. 203A.
Jean-Baptiste Roy-Audy,
The Baptism of Christ, 1821;
oil on canvas, 213.3 × 116.8 cm.
Musée du Québec, Quebec City (76.677).

Most works produced in Québec were based on two prestigious models. The first is an engraving by Gérard Audran (1640-1703) based on a composition by French painter Pierre Mignard (1612-1695), a copy of which still adorns the baptistry of the church in L'Islet. Mignard's work, engraved on several occasions, was very popular and gave rise to a dozen painted or sculpted portrayals. The second model is a work by French painter Claude-Guy Hallé (1652-1736), one of the first paintings sent to Lower Canada in 1817 by Father Philippe-Jean-Louis Desjardins. This large-scale painting (approximately 3 m × 1.5 m) first hung in the chapel of

the Séminaire de Québec until 1888, when fire destroyed the building. The painting, which emerged unscathed, was then hung in Quebec City's Notre-Dame cathedral, where it was destroyed by fire in 1922. This canvas is only known to us thanks to the many copies—some 25 versions—painted by Quebec artists, who have reproduced Hallé's work almost identically. As Laurier Lacroix has pointed out, the canvas gained prestige and authority due to its place in the Séminaire de Québec, while its bright, energetic composition successfully combines both the natural and the spiritual worlds. For various reasons, this version of the ***Baptism of Christ*** became the most legitimate and popular model with the clergy and, consequently, the one most frequently copied by artists of the first half of the 19th century.

Jean-Baptiste Roy-Audy is believed to have been the first painter to copy the work by Claude-Guy Hallé. At the beginning of his career, that is, around 1820, he painted jointly with Louis-Hubert Triaud, newly arrived in Quebec City, a version of the *Baptism of Christ* which is now conserved at the Saint-Charles-Borromée church in Garthby. As shown by an advertisement appearing in the January 4, 1820 edition of the *Quebec Gazette,* these two artists worked together, offering their services as painters of portraits, miniatures and history paintings, that is, religious works. The Garthby *Baptism of Christ* appears to be the only known example of their brief association. Between 1818 and 1824, Roy-Audy, who lived temporarily in Saint-Augustin de Portneuf, was active both in the Montreal and Quebec City areas. He painted, this time on his own, five additional copies of the *Baptism of Christ:* one for Louiseville (destroyed) and one for Saint-Antoine de Longueuil (disappeared), in 1820; one for Saint-Augustin de Portneuf (today at the Musée du Québec), the following year (Fig. 203A); one for Saint-Louis de Lotbinière around the same date; and finally, one for Saint-Joseph de Deschambault, in 1824.[2] The latter work, which was probably destined for the font, ended up in the sacristy, likely following the building of a new baptistry in 1856. The artist had already produced in 1820, for the Deschambault parish, near his home, three canvases which subsequently ended up in a shed attached to the church: *The Education of the Virgin, Saint Joseph and the Child-Jesus,* and *Saint Jean de Pathmos* (MQ). During the same period, he is also thought to have painted an *The Adoration*

of the Magi and an *The Adoration of the Shepherds,* as well as a *Saint Charles Borromeo* which was sold in 1851, perhaps to the church in Grondines.

The Baptism of Christ, signed and dated in 1824, was likely produced during a transitional year in the artist's career. On September 2, 1824, Roy-Audy announced in the *Quebec Gazette* that he had returned to settle in Quebec City, spurred on by the encouragement of priests, church-wardens and other members of religious communities. Roy-Audy was not the only Quebec artist to be inspired by Hallé's *Baptism of Christ:* Joseph Légaré and Antoine Plamondon are both believed to have produced a total of seven copies of the painting, between 1828 and 1850 and 1840 and 1858 respectively, and there are a number of anonymous versions as well as a later transposition by Joseph Dynes in 1878. The inventory remains to be completed and the attributions to be confirmed. Although all use Hallé's original composition, there are considerable differences, especially with regard to size, colour schemes and drawings. The same goes for the size and handling of the various versions by Roy-Audy which have reached us. Some of them were produced either on-site—in the Séminaire chapel directly from the original—or in the studio, using copies, sketches or another of the artist's studies.

M.B.

Notes
1. Matthew 3, 13-17; Mark 1, 9-13; Luke 3, 21-22; and John 1, 29-32. Our discussion of the theme of Christ's baptism is a summary of Yves Lacasse's article, "Le Baptême du Christ," *LE GRAND HÉRITAGE 1984,* pp. 239-243, and of the article by Philippe Dautrey and Marie-Agnès Sonrier entitled *Saint-Jean Baptiste, prophète et missionnaire* (Musée de Chaumont, 1990).
2. Another version, held at the Musée d'art de Joliette and which probably came from the Soeurs de Jésus-Marie convent in Sillery, is also attributed to Roy-Audy. The painting in the Garthby church is signed "*Audy*" and "*Triaud*" and likely corresponds to the unidentified work mentioned in *Le Bulletin de recherches historiques,* Vol. XIV, No. 6 (June 1908), p. 192, while the canvas in the Saint-Augustin church is signed solely "*Audy.*" According to the parish archives, the latter work was acquired from the artist in 1821, along with a *Christ on the Cross.* The Lotbinière painting was attributed and dated by Gérard Morisset based on the Saint-Augustin archives. As concerns the Louiseville and Longueuil paintings, see *CAUCHON 1971,* pp. 59-61 and 124.

204
Abbé Louis Delaunay, 1832
Oil on canvas, 92 × 81.5 cm

Inscription
(s.d., b.,l.r., in black ink) *JB^te R. Audy/Pin^t 1832.*

Provenance
Mgr Albert Tessier, Trois-Rivières; Séminaire de Trois-Rivières; on deposit at the Musée Pierre-Boucher, Trois-Rivières, 1977.

Exhibition
Quebec City 1972.

Bibliography
MORISSET 1935/6, p. 6; *MORISSET 1935/9,* p. 2; *MORISSET 1936-1937,* Vol. II, p. 78; *MORISSET 1941/1,* p. 74; *MORISSET 1953/2,* p. 449; *MORISSET 1953/3,* p. 546.; *CAUCHON 1971,* pp. 15, 17, 60, 105 and 128 (Repr.); *LE GRAND HÉRITAGE 1984,* pp. 110 and 111 (Repr.).

Collection
Musée Pierre-Boucher. Deposit from the Séminaire de Trois-Rivières (L-77.55-P)

F ATHER LOUIS DELAUNAY (1761-1837) was 71 years of age when he posed for Jean-Baptiste Roy-Audy. The portrait, modest in size and soberly handled, is in keeping with the subject's unremarkable career. It is interesting to compare the life of Father Delaunay with that of Jérôme Demers and Pierre-Olivier Langlois-Germain, who were ordained on the same date as Delaunay, that is, August 24, 1798. Father Demers was a brilliant professor and administrator at the Séminaire de Québec, while Father Langlois dit Germain was priest of the Château-Richer parish. The decisions of their diocese superior, which determined

the course of their vocation, were assuredly based on his observation of their intellectual predispositions and social background.

Father Delaunay's entire career unfolded in the parish of Saint-Léon-le-Grand (Maskinongé county), where he was appointed priest in 1805, a position he held until his death on May 7, 1837, at the age of 75 years and 9 months.[1] The parish historian wrote, somewhat cynically, "From 1807 to 1818 the records show nothing remarkable." (*Translation*) This situation was probably the same in a number of other villages, where everyday life was marked only by the changing seasons. To Delaunay's credit, in 1823, the first church was built to replace the chapel, erected in 1798. His years of service were also marked by the founding in 1819 of the Sacré-Coeur brotherhood.

Did Roy-Audy grasp the simplicity, isolation and resignation of this man, or do we, as viewers, tend to attribute these qualities to the artist's methods? The features of the sitter's static face are thickened by the drawing. The black skullcap[2] covering the top of the model's head destroys any illusion of relief. This absence of volume undoubtedly indicates baldness, but also the artist's inability to depict volume when using darker shades. Despite this, the white hues of the hair and the outline of the bands are portrayed subtly, creating a transparent effect. Recent restoration has revealed alterations in the length of the fingers, which were shortened, and in the left contour of the head, which was corrected. These alterations

suggest that the artist followed his own personal code of proportions and rules.

The head is separated from the body by a turned-down white collar, the curving outline of which overlaps the bands. The most dynamic pictorial effects can be seen where the torso meets the head, in the superposition of the bands and in the line of the collar. The hand, which traces a faint diagonal in the composition, rests awkwardly on the model's stomach, and is as tense as the facial features. Despite these difficulties, Roy-Audy has succeeded in bringing his subject to life. The painting attracts our attention and arouses our sympathy as much for the problems experienced by the artist in breathing life into his subject as for the unique physiognomy which is the result. The accumulation of these quirks provides a unique portrait imbued with the presence of both artist and model.

L.L.

Notes

1. Monseigneur Cyprien Tanguay, *Répertoire général du clergé canadien* (Montreal: E. Senécal & fils, 1893), p. 165, provides a background for these biographical notes, which were updated in light of the text by Amanda Plourde entitled *Notes historiques sur la paroisse de Saint-Léon-le-Grand,* Trois-Rivières, Le Bien Public, 1916, pp. 2-7.

2. The unique shape of the skullcap, which covers the entire crown of the head and forms a point near the front, can also be found in other portraits of the clergy done during the same era. See, for example, the portrait of *Monseigneur Jean-Jacques Lartigue* (Cat. 242).

205.
Louis Bourdages, c. 1834
Oil on canvas, 67.2 × 56.2 cm

Inscription
(s., l.l., on the parchment) *Audy P./Convention/Conseil législatif,/électif tous les quatre ans.*

Provenance
Maurice Corbeil, Montreal; acquired by the Musée du Québec, Quebec City, 1977.

Exhibitions
Vancouver 1966, No. 26; Quebec City 1972; Ottawa 1973, No. 16.

Bibliography
SHADBOLT *1966*, No. 26 (Repr.); BOISSAY *1966*, p. 29 (Repr.); CAUCHON *1971*, p. 130; HUBBARD *1973*, pp. 68-69, No. 16 (Repr.); BÉLAND *1987*, p. 66; BOURASSA *1990*, p. 84; BÉLAND AND BOURASSA *1990*, p. 56.

Collection
Musée du Québec, Quebec City (77.27)

U PON COMPLETING HIS STUDIES at the Petit Séminaire de Québec, Louis Bourdages (1764-1835) practised various trades before settling in Saint-Denis-sur-Richelieu in 1790. In the years that followed, he purchased land that enabled him not only to fulfil his family's needs, but also to begin practising law as a notary, around 1800. Bourdages played an important role in his community, where he managed to rise to the top of the hierarchy by carrying out various representative duties; promoted to the rank of major in 1812, he was made lieutenant-colonel of the Saint-Denis militia battalion the following year. By the end of the decade, he was one of the leading landowners in his community. However, it was first and foremost in the political arena that Bourdages cemented his prestige and authority. His rise through the social ranks was in keeping with the upsurge of the liberal professions in Canadian society in

the early 19th century and with the creation within this group of a liberal, nationalist ideology.

Bourdages' political career began at a time when the House of Assembly was mainly composed of members of the liberal professions and small business owners who espoused the cause of Canadian nationalism by denouncing the colonial leaders, most of whom were English-speaking. These new leaders began to express themselves within an organized party, called the *Parti canadien,* of which Bourdages became a member. He was in turn elected member for the riding of Richelieu, between 1804 and 1814, for the riding of Buckingham in 1820, and finally for the riding of Nicolet from 1830 to the time of his death. A skilful technician and an eloquent, persuasive speaker, Bourdages rapidly established himself as a seasoned parliamentarian. Gifted for debates and popular in his riding, he was

entrusted with a number of important tasks in the House of Assembly. In 1806, he was one of the founders of the newspaper *Le Canadien.* In 1826, the *Parti canadien* became the *Parti patriote* and created its own newspaper, *La Minerve.* At first opposed to the appointment of the new party leader, Louis-Joseph Papineau, he later rallied unconditionally to his ideas; in fact, on a number of issues, Bourdages was even more radical than Papineau. His last important political gesture was to participate in the drafting and dissemination in 1834 of the Ninety-Two Resolutions, which set out the demands of the House of Assembly and its complaints with respect to the British government.[1] These resolutions also served as an electoral platform in the fall of the same year.

This portrait must have been painted after February 1834; the inscription on the parchment held by the subject refers to one of the main resolutions demanding

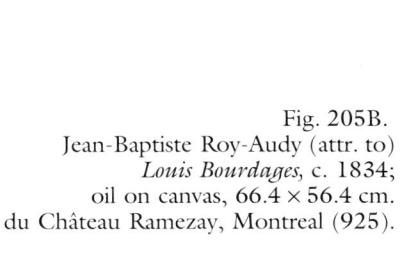

Fig. 205A.
Jean-Baptiste Roy-Audy,
Ludger Duvernay, 1832;
oil on canvas.
Société Saint-Jean-Baptiste de Montréal,
Maison Ludger-Duvernay.

Fig. 205B.
Jean-Baptiste Roy-Audy (attr. to)
Louis Bourdages, c. 1834;
oil on canvas, 66.4 × 56.4 cm.
Musée du Château Ramezay, Montreal (925).

that members be elected to the Legislative Council. The word *"Convention"* may refer either to the extraordinary assembly called to amend the constitution, or to the United States Constitution, since Papineau's and Bourdages' admiration for American institutions knew no bounds.

Louis Bourdages was typical of a considerable portion of the lower middle class of the era, which sought to change the colonial political system without revamping the social structure. This lower middle class, composed of professionals, merchants, seigneurs, landowners, and members of the clergy, formed most of Roy-Audy's and Dulongpré's clientele during the first third of the 19th century. The two artists, both officers in the militia, travelled from town to town or to rural areas to meet the demands of this social class for portraits and religious paintings. Thus, around 1835, Roy-Audy practised his trade as much in the urban centres of Quebec City and Montreal as in rural communities; he therefore could have painted Bourdages either in the capital of Lower Canada—seat of the Legislative Assembly—in his role as politician, or in the village of Saint-Denis, in his role as landowner and notary. In 1831, Roy-Audy completed two religious paintings for the church in Saint-Antoine de Longueuil, situated near Saint-Denis. The following year, he produced portraits of Father Louis Delaunay, priest of Saint-Léon-le-Grand (Cat. 204), and of Patriote Ludger Duvernay, editor and owner of the Montreal newspaper *La Minerve* (Fig. 205A). Roy-Audy seems to have been sympathetic to Papineau's followers: not only was he present, along with R.-S.-M. Bouchette

(Cat. 112), Joseph Légaré and Louis-Thomas Berlinguet, at a patriotic meeting held in Quebec City on May 26, 1837, but he is also believed to have painted the portraits of other well-known Patriotes.

Bourdages is depicted half-length in three-quarter profile against what appears to be an interior background, in this case two roughly sketched, monumental columns which could represent the Parliament building. This pictorial device, although common in early 19th-century American portraits, was infrequently used in Canadian works of the same period.[2] This architectural element did not become a common artifice in Quebec portraiture until some years later. Along with the parchment, clearly displayed, the two columns were obviously meant to represent the subject's authority and prestige. This simple yet effective setting was designed to emphasize the rise through the social ranks and current standing of the subject, a longtime officer in the militia and member of the House of Assembly. Furthermore, this painting was done when Bourdages was 70 years of age, only a few months before his death. Similar devices, such as a window with bars and a manuscript of *La Minerve*, can be seen in the portrait of Duvernay, painted the year the popular hero was imprisoned following the publication in his newspaper of one of his virulent attacks on the Legislative Council.

A number of formal elements, specific to Roy-Audy's style, can be found in the portrait of Louis Bourdages, especially the stiff features, the piercing gaze, the Windsor tie knotted with a hint of coquetry, the awkward foreshortening and junction of the arm and the left shoulder,

and the tapered, crooked thumb. The artist's meticulous rendering of the wrinkles and warts on the subject's eyelid reflects the clients' quest for resemblance. Despite his concern for realism, Roy-Audy sought to surpass and counterbalance this resemblance, as seen by the formal elegance of certain physical and vestimentary elements, such as the lines of the coat, which appears as a veritable decorative motif. Bourdages' personality is apparent even to today's viewers, so intensely has the artist depicted his presence and veracity. There does in fact exist a simplified version of this portrait, in which not only the columns, but also the warts and wrinkles, have been eliminated. This work is attributed to the same artist and is part of the collection of the Musée du Château Ramezay (Fig. 205B).[3]

M.B.

Notes

1. Richard Chabot, DCB, Vol. VI (1987).

2. See the portrait of *Stephen Burroughs* done by an unknown artist circa 1810-1820, and recently acquired by the Musée du Québec (*BOURASSA 1990*, p. 84, repr.).

3. First attributed to Louis Dulongpré in the Musée catalogue (*O'LEARY 1901*, No. 113), and in *MORISSET 1960/1* (p. 68), this work was recently attributed to Roy-Audy; see *DEROME, BOURASSA AND CHAGNON 1988*, p. 72, note 14. As in the case of the portrait of John Neilson (Cat. 53), Théophile Hamel may also have done a version of this portrait (now lost) circa 1865, for the gallery of historical portraits commissioned by the Canadian government. See *VÉZINA 1975/1*, pp. 111-115; *VÉZINA 1976/1*, p. 53; and *VÉZINA 1977*, p. 397.

206.
Portrait of a Lady from Île Perrot,
c. 1835
Oil on canvas, 67.1 × 56.7 cm

Provenance
Mrs. Claude Bertrand, Outremont; acquired by the National Gallery of Canada, Ottawa, 1973.
Bibliography
Perspectives, Vol. XXII, No. 52 (December 27, 1980) (Repr.); LEVENSON *1983,* pp. 2, 4, 36 and 37 (Repr.).
Collection
National Gallery of Canada, Ottawa (17133)

Fig. 206A.
Jean-Baptiste Roy-Audy (attr. to), *Émilie Persillier dit Lachapelle, née Marie-Émilie-Catherine Saint-Omer;* oil on canvas, 73.5 × 60 cm. Royal Ontario Museum, Toronto (984.86.2).

T HIS PORTRAIT of an unidentified woman is believed to have been acquired from a family on Ile-Perrot. The painting, on which we have been unable to gather further information, typifies the problem of attribution to Jean-Baptiste Roy-Audy. The artist, whose style has been qualified in turn as naïve, primitive, provincial and popular, adopted more or less the same attitude as many others with regard to the visible reality, using a conceptual approach in which simplicity, linearity, uniform shades and lighting, concern for detail, anatomical irregularities, etc., are given priority. These factors, present in this painting, complicate the identification process. However, some of the work's stylistic and technical characteristics show similarities to other portraits attributed to Roy-Audy, especially those of Mrs. Ranvoyzé and of the woman with a lace bonnet in the Montreal Museum of Fine Arts, as well as that of Émilie Persillier dit Lachapelle in the Royal Ontario Museum (Fig. 206A). All four women are wearing elaborate lace caps which have been painted in detail, as evidenced by the fine cross-hatching which brings out the diaphanous network of the ground, and by the more defined brush strokes complemented by myriad minuscule lines, which creates the opacity of the edging

and the decoration. The ribbons, more or less opaque, with or without designs, are knotted with precision, while the resplendent jewellery is clearly displayed. The background is neutral and unmodulated, while the draperies of the clothing, usually subtle—except for that of Madame Persillier—are overly stiff. The portrayal of the hands, as in the ***Lady from Ile-Perrot*** (Cat. 206), is laborious: the fingers are long and tapered, and join up awkwardly with the hand. The faces all bear a set expression. The features are depicted with precision, as is the hair, carefully curled and styled. However, there are differences, which make us hesitant to attribute all these works to the same artist without first studying his style more closely to determine its development and influences. For example, the use of grey strokes on the edging of the cap of the lady from Ile-Perrot and the less detailed drawing, as well as the artist's focus on the fingernails and knuckles, vary from the other portraits.

The decorative aspect of the shawl worn by the model is the most attractive element in this portrait. The bright colours of the floral pattern, where greens, reds, pinks and blues mingle, bring the composition to life and break the monotony created by the dark hues and the sitter's frontal position. This element harks back

to another work, which also raises problems concerning attributions to Roy-Audy. A similar shawl appears in the portrait of Mrs. François Poulin de Courval (MQ), dated 1843. However, in this portrait, the portrayal of the face, hand and lace trim is very different from that of the artist's other work; furthermore, Roy-Audy does not seem to have produced any paintings after the year 1838. This piece of clothing, fashionable at the time, can also be seen in a number of American primitive portraits,[1] and lends an element of fancy to this type of composition, which otherwise would suffer from the austerity created by the flattened portrayal of the body.

It is impossible for now to affirm unconditionally that the ***Lady from Ile-Perrot*** was done by Roy-Audy. By the same token, this leads us to wonder about the validity of a number of attributions proposed for an entire body of anonymous female portraits acquired by Canadian museums over the years.

P.B.

Note
1. Jean Lipman, *American Primitive Painting* (New York City: Dover Publications Inc., 1969), p. 35 (repr.).

207.

Portrait of an Elderly Woman,
c. 1835-1840

Oil on canvas mounted on fibreboard,
65 × 55.5 cm

Provenance
Descendants of the Arnoldi family; Charles-Pascal
Arnoldi; Arthur Arnoldi; Paul Arnoldi, Montreal;
acquired by the Musée du Québec, Quebec City,
1986.

Bibliography
BÉLAND 1987, p. 66; *BÉLAND AND BOURASSA 1990*,
p. 9 and 56 (Repr.).

Collection
Musée du Québec, Quebec City (86.41)

T HIS PORTRAIT of a woman, unsigned
and undated, typifies all the problems of research and study (especially attribution, dating and identification)
inherent to a number of portraits done in
the late 18th and early 19th centuries.

The canvas comes from Montreal's
Arnoldi family, several members of which
were silversmiths at the turn of the 19th
century; the silver crucifix worn by the sitter
calls to mind certain pieces crafted by
Michael Arnoldi (1763-1807). However,
the family's genealogy does not permit us
to definitively identify this elderly woman,
or to link her to any of the branches of the
Arnoldi family.

Portrayed against a stark background, the woman is seated in an armchair, elbows resting on the arms of the
chair and hands crossed. This armchair,
the back of which is covered in red fabric,

is an example of a furniture style common
between 1830 and 1840, characterized by
a free interpretation of various styles; the
scrolls carved with plant patterns, for example, are inspired by the Elizabethan era.
The subject is wearing a white lace bonnet
with a double row of pleats, a black shawl,
and a brown dress which appears to be
made of a rich fabric, judging by the sheen
of the sleeves. These three pieces of
clothing, especially the bonnet, were in style
circa 1840, as seen in other contemporary
portraits of women (T. Hamel, *Mrs.
François Têtu*, 1841, PC, or *Mrs. François-
Xavier Hamel*, circa 1843, MQ).

As mentioned earlier, the elderly
woman wears only a single piece of "jewellery," in this case a silver crucifix with
the tips in the form of a fleur-de-lys. Worn
mainly by nuns (see Cat. 12, 25 and 196),
this cross may be either a family memento
of the Arnoldi silversmiths, or a symbol of
the subject's social standing. The elderly
woman's combination of civil clothing and
the crucifix shows that she may also have
belonged to a secular order or charity, such
as the Association de Charité de Montréal,
which was created in 1828, recognized by
canon in 1844, and commonly known
since that time as the community of the
Soeurs de la Providence. This group of
women, headed by Mother Superior Émilie
Gamelin, visited the poor and kept a house
for elderly, disabled women who were also
underprivileged. These historical references, as well as the detail of the clothing and
the armchair, lead us to believe that the
portrait was produced circa 1835-1840 in
the Montreal area.

Close scrutiny of the formal and
technical elements of the painting enable
us to attribute it definitively to Jean-Baptiste Roy-Audy, who visited the Montreal
area several times during the 1830s. In the
portraits he painted during this period,
Roy-Audy used a number of formulas
which have become identified with this so-
called "naïve" or "primitive" artist. Obviously, this self-taught painter had difficulty
mastering the complex rules of perspective
and anatomy, as seen by the unsteady position of the sitter in the chair, the awkward foreshortening of the arms and
twisted hands, and especially the head itself,
which, positioned clumsily on the shoulders, seems almost to have been added as
an afterthought. However, he artfully
manages to draw our attention away from
these flaws by meticulously portraying
certain details such as the chair back with
its scrolls and studs in the form of gilt
rosettes. This eye to detail is also apparent

Fig. 207A.
Jean-Baptiste Roy-Audy,
Mrs. Charles-Auguste Globenski, (?) 1823;
oil on canvas, 63.3 × 55.1 cm.
Private collection, Montreal.

in the harmonious curves of the bonnet
ribbons and lace and the transparent crown
with embroidered patterns. Some of the
elements are portrayed in a purely decorative fashion, such as the folds and reflections in the dress sleeves which recall the
portrait of *Mrs. Charles-Auguste Globenski,*
by the same artist (Fig. 207A).

This decorative painter's eye for
detail is more noticeable in the portrayal
of the face, a veritable stereotyped mask
with its fixed smile and haunting gaze.
Bathed in a garish, uniform light, the features of the elderly woman are accented—
and therefore highly personalized—thanks
to the flattened treatment and firm, linear
outline of closed shapes with clearly defined
contours. Not a single fold in the chin or
wrinkle in the cheek or forehead have es-
caped the portraitist's scrutiny, and the
eyes, which seem to glow with life, literally
pierce the canvas and freeze the viewer in
his tracks. The painter thus focuses all our
attention on the subject's facial expression
and gaze. Despite her stiff, austere appearance, Roy-Audy accurately grasps the
character and personality of this elderly
lady, whose identity remains unknown.
During this era, the very purpose of portraits demanded that they resemble their
subject as closely as possible, but Roy-Audy
went beyond this criterion by providing
an overall physical and psychological picture
of the sitter which was as penetrating as it
was authentic.

M.B.

208. (See colour reproduction, p. 104)
Monseigneur Rémi Gaulin, 1838
Oil on canvas, 84.5 × 71.3 cm

Inscriptions
(s.d., l.l., on the arm of the armchair) CAP.. ROY AUDY FECIT AND PINXIT *1838.;* (on the books on the top shelf) HOLY/BIBLE; MILNERS/CONT; (on the books on the second shelf) DROIT/CAN. volumes I to VI; [WM AMON?] volume upside down; (on the books of the third shelf) HIST/ECCLES; BRÉV/ROM. volumes I to IV; LIVES/OF/THE STS. volumes VI and VII; on the books on the fourth shelf) JNST/OL. on the first; JNST/THEOL. on the two others.

Provenance
Fabrique de L'Assomption; Jean Palardy, Montreal; acquired by the Musée de la Province de Québec, Quebec City, 1956.

Exhibitions
Toronto 1966; Quebec City 1967, No. 49; Toronto 1971, No. 9; Quebec City 1972; Montreal 1974, No. 56; Montreal 1975; Sherbrooke 1975, No. 29; Quebec City 1983-1984, No. 62; Quebec City 1984-1985, No. 62.

Bibliography
Morisset 1941/1, p. 74; *Morisset 1953/2,* p. 450; *Morisset 1953/3,* pp. 545-546 (Repr.); *Morisset 1960/1,* pp. 89-90; *Harper 1966,* pp. 94 and 97 (Repr.); *Trudel, Juneau and Massey 1967,* pp. 94-95, No. 49 (Repr.); *Collections 1967,* No. 28 (Repr.); *Cauchon 1971,* pp. 31, 101, 102, 104, 106 and 129 (Repr.); *Juneau and Thibault 1974,* pp. 8, 9 and 26, No. 56 (Repr.); *Lord 1974,* p. 35 (Repr.); *Portraits anciens 1975,* No. 29; *Vézina 1975/1,* p. 162; *Le Musée du Québec 1983,* pp. 60 and 66, No. 62 (entry by Claude Thibault, Luc Noppen and Michel Doyon) (Repr.); *Le Grand Héritage 1984,* p. 124, No. 101 (entry by John R. Porter) (Repr.); *Béland 1987,* p. 66; *Béland and Bourassa 1990,* pp. 6, 9, 56 and 68 (Repr.); *Lacroix 1990,* pp. 19 and 20 (Repr.); *Nadeau 1991,* p. 15 (Repr.).

Collection
Musée du Québec, Quebec City (56.469)

THIS PORTRAIT is probably the most ambitious ever produced by Roy-Audy, and the one which best represents the artist's naivete, based on the very fact that he attempts to imitate academic art. For Roy-Audy probably completed this affected portrayal of his subject, then coadjutor to the bishop of Kingston, with some great portrait of state in the classical French style in mind. The portrait of Monseigneur Gaspard-Charles-Guillaume de Vintimille, bishop of Marseille, painted by Nicolas de Largillière and engraved by Coussin, could well have had a certain influence. In both works, the position and gestures of the subjects are similar, although considerably simplified in the case of Monseigneur Gaulin; it is also quite apparent that Roy-Audy tried stubbornly to depict the artificial folds of the surplice, cape and curtain draperies.[1] Roy-Audy was a self-taught artist, and this is reflected in his use of "tricks of the trade," even when, as in this case, he adopts a number of commonly used pictorial devices, or when he imitates a work. In this respect, he differs little from his American colleagues, such as Horace Bundy (1814-1883) who, in his portrait entitled *Homme de loi du Vermont,*[2] used the processes of sophisticated/scholarly art without truly mastering its techniques. In his work, Roy-Audy portrays each detail—the lace of the surplice, the pectoral cross and rope, and the books—with almost obsessive scrupulousness. He even devoted special attention to his signature, using the title of captain of the militia which he had obtained 1833. Taken separately, these shreds of "bravura" have a certain charm; as a whole, they reflect the artist's shortcomings: anatomical disproportion, distorted perspective, linear drawing, garish colours and a certain stiffness on the part of the subject. Ironically, although he sought to make his work decorative, Roy-Audy imposed a certain severity on his models.

Monseigneur Rémi Gaulin (1787-1857) was ordained priest in 1811. After a stay in the Maritimes, he was assigned to various parishes in the Montreal area. Consecrated bishop in 1833 and named coadjutor to Monseigneur McDonnell in Kingston, Gaulin was to ensure the administration of the entire diocese as of 1835. Upon Monseigneur McDonnell's death, Gaulin became bishop of Kingston. Physical and mental problems, however, overshadowed his episcopacy, and in 1843 he was forced to abandon the administration of his diocese, although he tried several times until 1852 to regain control.

Meanwhile, he had been appointed vicar-general of the Montreal diocese and priest of L'Assomption in 1845.

In Roy-Audy's painting, Monseigneur Gaulin is depicted wearing priestly garb, seated in front of his well-stocked library, pointing to a document with his left hand. The document is perhaps the report of his pastoral visit to western Upper Canada, published the same year this portrait was painted. His library contains a bible, a Roman breviary, works on theology and canon law, the lives of saints, an ecclesiastical history, and two unidentified works (Milners and Amon?). The fact that many of the titles are in English is significant; Monseigneur Gaulin was bishop of a diocese with an English-speaking majority, mostly people of Irish and Scottish descent, and it was therefore normal that he possess English-language works. This detail also allows us to assume that Roy-Audy painted this portrait in Kingston. In fact, there is no proof that Monseigneur Gaulin was in Québec at all in 1838. As an itinerant artist and with a view to obtaining additional commissions, Roy-Audy may well have travelled as far as Kingston, which was one of the largest centres on Lake Ontario's north shore. On August 7 of the same year, he placed an advertisement in The Patriot of Toronto, stating his intention to stay awhile in this town "to accomplish such orders as he may be favoured with in his profession." The portrait of Monseigneur Gaulin, probably done during this trip, is one of Roy-Audy's last known works and probably marks the end of his artistic career. After that we lose trace of him, but certain information leads us to believe that he died outside of Québec, perhaps in Rochester, where he is believed to have painted a number of portraits two years earlier.[3]

P.B.

Notes
1. Myra Nan Rosenfeld, *Largillière, portraitiste du dix-huitième siècle* (Montreal: Montreal Museum of Fine Arts, 1981), p. 389 (repr.).

2. *Peintures naïves américaines, XVIIIᵉ-XIXᵉ siècles. Cent onze tableaux de la collection Edgar William et Bernice Chrysler Garbisch* (cat.), (Paris: Grand Palais, 1968), p. 83, (repr.).

3. "Roy-Audy [...] made his temporary residence here in the year 1836. He painted a few pictures, among wich was a full-lenght portrait of Elisha Johnson, one of our most prominent citizens. [...] Mr. Audy soon left, and has not since visited the city professionally". William F. Peck, *The Semi-Centennial History of the City of Rochester* (Syracuse: D. Mason & Co. Publishers, 1884), p. 520.

GEORGE SETON was born in London on March 18, 1819. In July 1838, at age 19, he joined the army as an ensign and became a member of the 93rd Foot, the Sutherland High-landers. In May 1842, he was promoted lieutenant. Landing in Halifax on April 14, 1844, he went on to Quebec City and then Montreal, where he arrived in May of the same year. He remained in Montreal with his regiment until July 1846. Between June and September 1844, Seton apparently travelled to Kingston and Niagara, if a series of sketches held at the National Archives of Canada are any indication. From July 1846 until his regiment's return to England in early August 1848, Seton lived in Quebec City. In November 1853, he joined the Royal Canadian Rifles. Back in Canada in 1854, he was apparently stationed in Kingston, where his two sons were born. In 1857 and 1858, he was posted in Fort Garry (present-day Winnipeg), site of the Canadian head office of the Hudson's Bay Company. At the time, he was commander of the Royal Canadian Rifles volunteers, who had been requested to assist the Hudson's Bay Company. This led to his helping geologist and naturalist Henry Youle Hind (1823-1908) explore the Red, Assiniboine and Saskatchewan rivers. George Seton retired from the army in September 1858 and announced his plans to return to England that fall. He died in England in 1905.

GEORGE SETON

1819-1905

Main source

UN MOMENT 1991.

VAG, AGNS, MMFA

MQ, NGC

209.
Scott's Bridge Across the Saint Charles River, 1847-1850
Brown and blue wash over graphite on paper, 21 × 31.8 cm

Inscriptions
(b.,u.r., in pen and brown ink, in the artist's hand) *Scotts' Bridge across the S'. Charles River near Quebec Canada East./19' October 1847*; (below, in graphite, in the same hand) *1847*; (b,l.l., in pen and black ink, in the same hand) *22' Feb'. '50*; (below, in graphite, in the same hand) *22 Feby 50*.

Watermark
J. WHATMAN/TURKEY MILL.

Provenance
Old Print Shop, New York; acquired by the Royal Ontario Museum, Toronto, 1953.

Bibliography
ALLODI 1974/1, Vol. II, No. 1492.

Collection
Royal Ontario Museum, Toronto (953.132.38)

210.
Durham Terrace, 1848
Watercolour over graphite on paper, 24.2 × 34.8 cm

Inscriptions
(b.,l.r., in pen and black ink, in the artist's hand) *The "Platform", Quebec Canada/28' April '48;* (b.,l.l., over-written in pen and black ink on inscription in graphite, in the same hand) *14' Sept '48;* (b.,l.r., in graphite, in the same hand) *28 April 48.*

Provenance
Old Print Shop, New York; acquired by the Royal Ontario Museum, Toronto, 1953.

Exhibition
London 1981.

Bibliography
ALLODI 1974/1, Vol. II, No. 155 (Repr.); *ALLODI 1974/2*, pp. 32-33 (Repr.); *FAIR 1981*, pp. 21 and 22 (Repr.).

Collection
Royal Ontario Museum, Toronto (953.132.35)

G EORGE SETON arrived in Quebec City in July 1846 after a two-year stay in the Montreal area, where he was stationed with his regiment, the 93rd Sutherland Highlanders. The city was recovering from two fires, in May and June 1845, that had destroyed Saint-Roch and Saint-Jean parishes (Cat. 168). It is in this context that a scene as unique as *Scott's Bridge Across the Saint Charles River* must be viewed. The bridge had been built in 1790,[1] across the ford of Petite Rivière (Rivière Saint-Charles) to facilitate travel to Charlesbourg and Saint-Ambroise de la Jeune-Lorette. Thomas Scott had ceded part of his land to enable the bridge's construction, which is why the structure was commonly referred to as Scott's Bridge. Built of wood, it was often repaired before being replaced in 1845. It is not known whether it simply deteriorated over the years or whether it was destroyed in the fire that hit Saint-Roch parish. Regardless, on June 23, 1845, Frederick Hacker

(ca. 1802-1846) submitted a plan to notary Louis Prévost for a new bridge to be built from scratch.[2] The three-span bridge was to be supported by two central piles anchored to the riverbed. As Luc Noppen and Marc Grignon showed, what made the design so new was primarily the parapet of X-shaped trusses, a system which was originally designed in the United States in 1841 and known as the Howe Truss, after its inventor, William Howe. Hacker provided a detailed view of the bridge's components in the plan he submitted for approval (Fig. 209A): the trusses are secured inside the upper and lower chords by a series of vertical metal armatures that distribute the tension. However, it would appear that this new design did not meet with the owners' approval since there is no trace of it in Seton's drawing: the tension thrusts are spread across a series of diagonal buttresses located between the deck and the piles. The purpose of the railing, then, is more decorative than structural in

nature. Yet it is the railing that Seton chose to emphasize in his drawing. The large triangle of the riverbank in the foreground, accentuated by the use of the darker brown wash to indicate vegetation serves as a foil for the bridge, which takes up the entire middle distance. The drawing is analytical, as is all of Seton's work; he showed little inclination for depicting pure landscape. Whether he was drawing churches, such as the one in Beauport or the Aubigny church at Pointe-Lévis, or an entire parish, such as Saint-Roch,[3] this military artist took a descriptive approach and was concerned mainly with producing a visual record of the representative elements of a given site.

This same clear, concise manner of depicting a site can be found in Seton's *Durham Terrace, Quebec.* In June 1838, *Le Canadien* informed its readers that "The Earl of Durham has ordered that the garden on Cap Diamant, behind the Wolfe and Montcalm monument, be opened to the public for use as a boardwalk."[4]

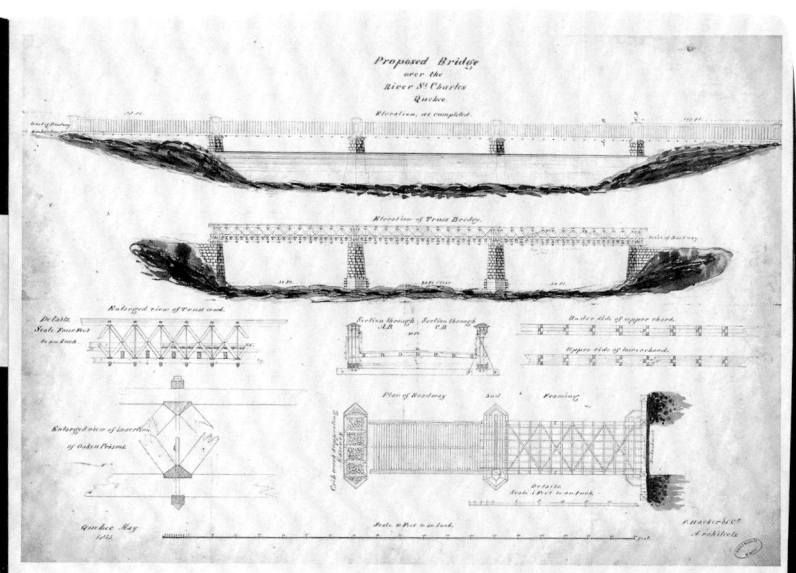

Fig. 209A.
Frederick Hacker,
Proposed Bridge over the Saint Charles River, 1845;
ink and wash on paper, 60 × 81.3 cm.
Archives nationales du Québec,
Quebec City.
Fonds Louis Prévost (CN1-232).

(*Translation*) The newspaper further reported that:

measures are to be taken to remove the ruins of Château Saint-Louis, which for four and a half years have borne witness to the fire that destroyed this building, which do little to promote the dignity of the British representative, and which so deface the horizon of Place d'Armes by blocking the view of the river and the countryside to the southeast.[5] (*Translation*)

Lord Durham's wishes must have been carried out in the summer since, in its October 1 edition, *Le Canadien* reported that:

His Excellency has just declared the site and yard of the burned-down Château [a public boardwalk], which will unquestionably make this the most beautiful walk and public square in all of Canada. The portion overlooking the river has been decorated with a lovely wrought-iron railing.[6] (*Translation*)

This watercolour by Seton is one of the earliest representations of the terrace.[7] In keeping with his usual practice, he began by outlining the basic composition—a pencil drawing on the back of the watercolour represents the artists preliminary sketch of the scene—before going back to complete the drawing at a later date.

This particular method of working warrants further comment. Seton used a double dating system. The first date corresponded to the drawing from nature or survey of the site to be represented; the second referred to the date on which the resultant drawing or watercolour was completed. The majority of Seton's known drawings were completed once the artist had returned to England. Seton sailed from Quebec City on August 1, 1848 aboard

the *Resistance*.[8] The same day, he completed the watercolour entitled *Montmorency Falls,* for which he had done the preliminary drawing a year earlier.[9] In this particular case, it is possible that the choice of colour washes was determined by the artist's direct observation from on board the *Resistance* as it was leaving shore. However, this is certainly not the case with Scott's Bridge, for which the drawing was done on October 19, 1847 and highlighted with blue wash to define the Saint-Charles river on February 22, 1850. An addition of this kind is in keeping with pure topographical convention. Should we question the accuracy of the colours used in the watercolour of Durham Terrace, dated September 14, 1848? If the figures are more a decorative addition than they are faithful portraits, the site was still fresh enough in Seton's mind to recognize more than a mere coloured drawing. Ten years after the terrace's construction, one can assume that the wooden planks of the walk, half separated, would indeed be somewhat worn.

Although we are dealing here with the work of a topographical artist in the strict sense of the term, Seton's watercolours must be placed in a different category from those of James Pattison Cockburn. Punctilious, controlled observation leaves little room for extraneous elements. The principal theme—the solidity of Scott's Bridge or the size of Durham Terrace—dominates the entire composition. Seton does not conform to the use of multiple vanishing points or the embellishment of a foreground through an attractive motif. His clear view implies a genuine concern for objectivity. Furthermore, Seton is a scru-

pulous draughtsman, skilled at capturing the essential with a minimum of means, as evidenced by the numerous panoramic views sold through Sotheby's in Toronto in 1985.[10] Taking up three or six sheets of paper, the views employ the same technique of coloured drawings as in *Scott's Bridge:* the application of brown wash over a pencil drawing, then highlighted with blue wash. Nothing is known about Seton's youth prior to his obtaining an ensign's brevet in July 1838. However, an approach such as this leads us to believe that he was trained from the outset to record a strict, faithful representation of the natural setting for military purposes. The pre-eminence of line, the essentially symbolic use of colour and the extreme accuracy of the datings on the works—differentiating what was drawn from nature from later additions—are in keeping with the principles taught in military academies such as the one at Woolwich and disseminated through teaching manuals on topographical drawing for strategic purposes.

D.P.

Notes

1. "Les ponts de la rivière Saint-Charles", *Le Bulletin des recherches historiques,* Vol. XLVI, No. 3 (March 1940), pp. 89-90, and Antonio Drolet, *La ville de Québec, histoire municipale,* Tome II (Quebec City: La Société historique de Québec, 1965), pp. 97-98.
2. NOPPEN AND GRIGNON 1983, pp. 226-227, No. 68 (Repr.). For information on the biography of Frederick Hacker, see RICHARDSON ET AL. 1984, pp. 301 and 308-309.
3. ALLODI 1974/1, Vol. II, No. 1493, 1495 and 1494 (Repr.).
4. *Le Canadien,* June 8, 1838, p. 2.
5. *Ibid.*
6. *Le Canadien,* October 1, 1838, p. 2. While passing through Quebec City in the summer of 1838, William Henry Bartlett did a drawing of the terrace's ongoing construction. See DE VOLPI 1971, p. 120 (Repr.).
7. Joseph Légaré had depicted it around 1843 in an oil on paper held at the MSQ (Pc 983.35). See PORTER 1978/1, No. 27 (Repr.). Still, the most well-known representation of Durham Terrace is the lithograph by Sarony & Major, *View from Parliament Building, Quebec,* published in New York circa 1850. See DE VOLPI 1971, p. 127 (Repr.), and Gloria Gilda Deak, *Picturing America, 1497-1899* (Princeton: Princeton University Press, 1988), p. 421, No. 622 (Repr.).
8. UN MOMENT 1991, p. 92 (entry by Jennifer Devine).
9. ROM, 953.132.46. The first drawing is dated July 28, 1847.
10. Sotheby's, Toronto, sale of May 28, 1985, lots 911 to 914. *Panoramic View of Quebec City from Pointe Lévis* (lot 911) was purchased by the National Archives of Canada. See UN MOMENT 1991, No. 30 (Repr.).

WILLIAM SMITH
SEWELL

1798-1866

W ILLIAM SMITH SEWELL was born in Quebec City on May 28, 1798 and grew up in cultivated social circles. His father was Jonathan Sewell, Attorney General and Chief Justice of Lower Canada. The latter was known for his talents in theatre, music and painting, and was the first president of the Literary and Historical Society of Quebec. Another of his sons, Edmund Willoughby, was also a drawer and painter and produced many views of Quebec City (NAC, MMFA, MMCH). The numerous relations maintained by the Chief Justice may have allowed his sons to find affinities and exchange viewpoints with members of the local art community; miniaturist Gerome Fassio, for example, lived with the Sewells in 1838. In addition to the occasional painting, William Sewell produced the illustrations for Alfred Hawkins' *Hawkin's Picture of Quebec,* published in 1834, and those of the fire that destroyed the city's Saint-Roch district in 1845. Sewell made his career in law. His father had him appointed sheriff of the District of Quebec on November 13, 1822, after the dismissal of Philippe Aubert de Gaspé, which was greeted with protest from the Assembly. He held this position for over forty years.

Main sources
HARPER 1970; GREENWOOD AND LAMBERT 1988.

211.
View of Sainte-Ursule, Street Quebec, 1842
Oil on cardboard, 22.7 × 29.9 cm

Inscription
(b.,c.,) *La rue St-Ursule à Québec/designe pour le Col et Mrs. Chapelin/par William Sewell/artiste/ Québec sept. 1842.*

Provenance
Private collection, London (sold by Christie's, Manson & Woods, London, July 2 and 3, 1968, No. 3); Daniel Lafond, Quebec City; acquired by the Musée du Québec, Quebec City, 1982.

Bibliography
Christie, Manson & Woods, London, July 2 & 3 1968, p. 12, No. 3; HUARD 1986/1, p. 50 (Repr.); BRIERLEY 1988, p. 388 (Repr.); BÉLAND AND BOURASSA 1990, pp. 7, 9 and 76 (Repr.); LES CHEMINS DE LA MÉMOIRE 1990, p. 81 (Repr.).

Collection
Musée du Québec, Quebec City (82.53)

W ILLIAM S. SEWELL did this view of Rue Sainte-Ursule in 1842. It is one of the very few oils by Sewell that have survived. As indicated in the inscription on the back of the support,[1] this small oil on cardboard was painted in September 1842 for Lieutenant-Colonel Thomas Chaplin and his wife, Millicent Mary Chaplin, a landscape watercolourist. The work was actually designed to portray the Chaplins' home (second building from the right) from 1838 to September 1842 and situate its location. Millicent Mary did her own watercolour of the facade of the house (Cat. 68). Sewell's work, then, could either have been done at the request of the British officer and his wife, or offered to them by the amateur painter as a gift or a souvenir of their stay in Lower Canada. In this regard, it must be remembered that, like many other artworks belonging to the British colonialists, this painting was probably taken back to England by its owners, where it was discovered only in 1968.

Rather than depicting each building in detail, this picturesque view, opening as it does onto a view of the Laurentians and the village of Charlesbourg in the far distance, depicts the alignment of the building facades and portrays the characteristic lighting of early fall, with its warm hues reflected on the roughcast walls. A few soldiers in uniform—the Coldstream Guards, members of Chaplin's regiment, including an orderly standing at attention in front of the colonel's residence, is a reminder of the strong presence of the British garrison in the city's streets following the 1837-1838 rebellions. In this respect, the painting clearly evokes the posting of Chaplin and his wife, temporarily residing on Rue Sainte-Ursule, which was built after the Conquest and provided a direct link between the Artillery and Citadel barracks. It would seem that British military and French-Canadian residents mingled peacefully without necessarily maintaining cordial relations. The light touches of red on their respective apparel serve to highlight and enliven the overall colour tone of the landscape, which is dominated by sallow shades of yellow and brown ochre.

M.B.

Note
1. A watercolour sold at the auction in 1987 entitled *Château St. Louis, Québec* bears a similar inscription: "*Painted for Col. William Foster Coffin by William S. Sewell 1834*". See auction catalogue *John L. Russell. Collection of Canadiana,* Toronto, Sotheby's, November 12, 1987, No. 68.

JOHN RICHARD COKE SMYTH

1808-1882

T HE ONLY SON OF Richard Smyth and Elizabeth Coke, John Richard Coke Smyth was born in England in 1808. He took several trips to various European countries, staying in Constantinople in 1835 and 1836. Shortly afterwards, John George Lambton, Earl of Durham, retained his services as drawing master. In this capacity, he embarked for Canada in April 1838 aboard the *HMS Hastings,* since Lord Durham had just been appointed governor of the colony. His brief stay, which lasted until October of that year, enabled Coke Smyth to get to know a few regions in Canada and to publish in London in 1840 *Sketches in the Canadas,* an album containing 23 lithographs dedicated to Durham. As private drawing master, his pupils were the daughters of Lord Durham, including Lady Mary Louisa Lambton (1819-1898, later Lady Elgin), and perhaps Lord Durham himself, along with Katherine Jane Ellice, the wife of Edward Ellice, secretary to Lord Durham during his stay in Canada.

Upon his return to England, Coke Smyth continued his career, primarily becoming involved in portraiture, architecture and costume design. Victoria had even commissioned from him a series of illustrations of the queen's masked ball costumes, which were published in 1843. This interest was also revealed in his attempt to have *Prospectus & Specimen of a Proposed Work on the Costume of the Principal Nations of Europe from the Beginning of the 13th to the End of the 17th Century* published. Coke Smyth also regularly exhibited at the Royal Academy of Arts between 1842 and 1855, as well as at the British Institution and Society of British Artists until 1867. In 1871, he illustrated *A Comprehensive History of India,* published by Henry Beveridge. Coke Smyth died in 1882.

Main sources
ALLODI 1974/1; COOKE 1983.

VAG, AGNS, MMFA

212.
The Cathedral, Quebec, 1838
Watercolour and graphite on paper,
35.9 × 25.8 cm

Inscriptions
(u.r., in graphite) *Quebec/June 3ʳᵈ 1838;* (l.l., in graphite) *W.H. Bartlett.*

Provenance
Frank T. Sabin Gallery, London; acquired by the Royal Ontario Museum, Toronto, 1950.

Exhibition
Ottawa 1967/1, No. 88.

Bibliography
SPENDLOVE 1958, pp. xvii and 42a (Repr.); HUBBARD 1959, p. 128 (Repr.); HUBBARD AND OSTIGUY 1967, pp. 54 and 55, No. 88 (Repr.); ALLODI 1974/1, Vol. II, No. 1545.

Collection
Royal Ontario Museum, Toronto (950.114.5)

MQ, NGC

213.
Lower Town, From the Chateau, 1838
Watercolour and graphite on paper, 26 × 36.3 cm

Inscriptions
(l.l., in graphite) *W. H. Bartlett/Chateau./Quebec/June 1838;* (l.r., on the mount, in graphite, by another hand) *Chateau Quebec.*

Provenance
Frank T. Sabin Gallery, London; acquired by the Royal Ontario Museum, Toronto, 1950.

Bibliography
ALLODI 1974/1, Vol. II, No. 1546.

Collection
Royal Ontario Museum, Toronto (950.114.3)

W HAT WE KNOW about John Richard Coke Smyth has long been limited to a single album of lithographs, *Sketches in the Canadas,* published in London in 1840.[1] It was also through this volume, dedicated to the Earl of Durham, that the relationship between these two individuals was established. Research has yielded new information: Mary Allodi began reconstructing his body of work by identifying the artist's composition among a set of drawings bearing the signature of William Henry Bartlett.[2] This theory has been amply proven and cannot be questioned. We will therefore not go over it in detail. Let us simply say that these 52 pieces from the Royal Ontario Museum collection form a coherent set of lead pencil and wa-tercolour drawings, all taken from nature. Some of them, such as *Lower Town, Quebec, From the Chateau,* were to be used in the preparation of the 1840 lithographs (Fig. 213A). They were glued to the pages of an album with a watermark dated 1838, which indicates that they were mounted by Coke Smyth upon his return to England.

John Richard Coke Smyth was an artist in the truest sense of the word. As such, he was hired by John George Lambton, 1st Earl of Durham, around 1837. In his capacity as drawing master, he followed Durham to Quebec in April 1838. No stranger to travelling (Coke Smyth had just returned from Constantinople, where he stayed between 1835 and 1836), he probably did not consider this departure a drawback. Their voyage is known to us from the personal journals of Lady Durham and Katherine Jane Ellice,[3] who was accompanying her husband, Edward Ellice, personal secretary to Lord Durham. Durham's stay was of short duration: arriving in Quebec City on May 27, 1838, he was to embark for Plymouth on November 1 aboard the *HMS Inconstant.* In the meantime, he travelled through the Canadas. Through James Richard Coke Smyth's drawings, we can follow his travels from Quebec City to Sorel, Montreal, Beauharnois, Cornwall, Kingston, Toronto and Niagara Falls.

These drawings are remarkable for their spontaneity and the economy of

Fig. 213A.
John Richard Coke Smyth,
Quebec from the Chateau, 1840;
lithograph, 38.2 × 54.6 cm.
Musée du Québec, Quebec City (54.61.06).

Fig. 212-213A.
John Richard Coke Smyth,
Dickenson's Landing, 1838;
graphite on paper, 10.6 × 14.4 cm.
Royal Ontario Museum, Toronto (950.114.37).

Fig. 212-213B.
Richard Parkes Bonington,
Trees and a Cottage by a River Pond, 1827,
graphite on paper, 16 × 20.3 cm.
Yale Centre for British Art, New Haven. Paul
Mellon Collection (B1977.14.4657).

means they employ. They are the fruit of a vigorous style which goes directly to the heart of the subject while attempting to maintain the spontaneity of the first impression. In attempting to understand the style of these drawings, the name of Richard Parkes Bonington (1802-1828) immediately springs to mind. We know nothing about the youth and training of Coke Smyth, who was twenty years of age when Bonington died. But Bonington's influence was considerable during the 1830s. Martin Hardie mentioned in late 1838 that:

over 160 oil paintings, over 300 water-colours, and more than 900 sketches in black-and-white or with slight tint, had passed under Bonington's name through the sale-rooms in England and France.[4]

Obviously, fakes and imitations had been mixed in with his originals. In addition, a large number of artists, probably including Coke Smyth, copied his works as a technical exercise.[5] Coke Smyth's *Dickenson's Landing* (Fig. 212-213A) depicts the motif in short, parallel hatchings, much like Bonington's style in *Trees and a Cottage by a River Pond* (Fig. 212-213B).

But Bonington's influence was only one element in a much more complex whole in understanding the general feel of works such as ***Lower Town, Quebec, From the Chateau*** and ***The Cathedral, Quebec.*** The portfolio of twenty-six lithographs, published in 1838 after drawings executed in Constantinople in 1835-1836,[6] show an artist sure of his craft. These drawings from nature must have been very forceful and vigorous since, according to Andrew

Wilton, they engendered in John Frederick Lewis (1805-1876) an enthusiasm for Arabic countries and the Middle East.[7]

Like many of his predecessors who passed through North America, Coke Smyth visited the same sites and rendered the same subjects. However, he did not view them in the same manner. His vision was like his drawing: clear and incisive. The composition of the view of Lower Town, Quebec, from the Château Saint-Louis deliberately plays on contrasts with the inclusion of an abrupt diagonal in the foreground, without a stable point of reference for the spectator. The compact mass of houses and the tangle of roofs blend in with the horizontal of the background, while the great empty diagonal in the foreground accentuates the effect of domination, making the ruins of Château Saint-Louis seem like an eagle's nest perched above the city. Only a wastewater pipe serves as foil in the left foreground. The 1840 engraving (Fig. 213A) was to cover it in greenery and hide it behind the "*beau motif*" of the parapet, symbol of English military might. The façade of the Quebec City cathedral possesses all the qualities of topographical accuracy. Coke Smyth skilfully adjusts the layout to minimize the effect of the imbalance created by the absence of the second tower. He was more interested in seeking harmonies by means of colour, contrasting the beaten earth of Rue Buade with the crépi of the façade and playing on the ochred hues on the facing stones. The topographer's eye, consistently deft throughout the work, does not make it possible to approach this

drawing on a poetic level. He achieves this goal by simplifying secondary motifs which would otherwise reduce the picturesque into an overly rigid site.

D.P.

Notes

1. Although the title page does not mention it directly, it can be assumed that Coke Smyth transposed his drawings on stone, thereby collaborating with publisher Thomas McLean and printer Alfred Ducôté in the album's publication. In 1837, McLean and Ducôté had already worked together in publishing the drawings of Thomas Miles Richardson (1813-1890), *Sketches in Italy, Switzerland, France, &*, which the latter had lithographed on their presses (Joan M. Friedman, *Color Printing in England, 1486-1870*), cat. [New Haven: Yale Center for British Art, 1978, p. 45, No. 127]). A similar undertaking may have occurred with Coke Smyth.

2. *ALLODI 1968*.

3. *Lady Durham's Journal* (Quebec City: The Telegraph Printing Co., 1915 [Ninth Series of Historical Documents]), pp. 7-61. For Katherine Jane Ellice, see Cat. 103 and 104.

4. Martin Hardie, *Water-Colour Painting in Britain*, Vol. II, *The Romantic Period* (London: B.T. Betsford Ltd., 1979), p. 181.

5. For Bonington, see Marcia Pointon, *Bonington, Francia & Wyld.*, (London: B.T. Betsford Ltd., 1985), pp. 33-64 and Nos. 16-26.

6. *Lewis's Illustrations of Constantinople made during a Residence in that city in the years 1835-6, arranged and drawn on stone from the original Sketches of Coke Smyth by John F. Lewis*. See also Michael Twyman, *Lithography 1800-1850* (London: Oxford University Press, 1970), p. 210 and Fig. 117.

7. Andrew Wilton, *British Watercolours 1750 to 1850* (Oxford: Phaidon Press Limited, 1977), p. 51.

MQ, NGC

214. (See colour reproduction, p. 106)
The Pulpit of the Church of the Ursuline Convent, Quebec, 1838
Watercolour over graphite highlighted with gouache and pastel on paper, 25.5 × 28.5 cm

Inscriptions
(b.,u.c., on an old mount cutout and mounted, in graphite) *Interior of the Church belonging to the Ursuline Convent at Quebec.*; (b.,c., on the panel protecting the back, in graphite) *No. 9* [crossed out]/*No. 6/No. 2;* (b.,c,on the panel vertically, in black ink) *Interior of the church belonging/to the Ursuline/Convent Quebec/Coke Smyth 1838.*

Provenance
Lady Mary Louisa Lambton, daughter of the Earl Durham and later wife of James Bruce, 8th Earl of Elgin and 12th Earl of Kincardine; Descendants of the Bruce family (sold by Sotheby's, London, November 4, 1987, No. 27); private collection, Toronto.

Bibliography
TOPOGRAPHICAL PAINTINGS 1987, pp. 16 and 17, No. 27 (Repr.).

Collection
Private collection, Toronto

THESE TWO WATERCOLOURS, which came up for sale in London in 1987 with the entire estate of the 8th Earl of Elgin, are a real find. We are presenting them here for the first time thanks to the kindness of their current owner.

It is quite likely that when she married James Bruce in 1846, Mary Louisa Lambton kept not only her own works executed during her stay in Canada in 1838, but also those which were given to her. It is on this basis that these two

VAG, AGNS, MMFA

215.

Interior of the Church of the Ursuline Convent, 1838
Watercolour over graphite highlighted with gouache and pastel on paper, 25 × 21.5 cm

Inscriptions
(b.,u.c., on an old mount cutout and mounted,
in graphite) *Interior of the Church belonging to the
Ursuline Convent, Quebec.;* (b.,c., on the panel
protecting the back, in graphite) *No. 4/No. 2/
[Interior] of the Church belonging/to the Ursuline
Convent/at Quebec/Coke Smyth 1838.;* (b.,c, on the
panel, in black ink) *Interior of the Church
belonging/to the Ursuline Convent/at Quebec/Coke
Smyth 1838;* (b.,l.l., on a label, print characters)
LB.

Provenance
Lady Mary Louisa Lambton, daughter of the Earl
of Durham and later wife of James Bruce, 8th Earl
of Elgin and 12th Earl of Kincardine; Descendants
of the Bruce family (sold by Sotheby's, London,
November 4, 1987, No. 28); private collection,
Toronto.

Bibliography
TOPOGRAPHICAL PAINTINGS 1987, pp. 16 and 17,
No. 28 (Repr.).

Collection
Private collection, Toronto

renovated in 1902: the 1722 building was
demolished and replaced by a new building.
However, the interior decor was preserved
and used again in the new church, a proceeding which earned the nuns the praise
of Monseigneur Lionel Lindsay during the
inauguration of the new chapel: "Friends
of art history will be grateful to them for
having so carefully preserved these relics
of the past and for having so painstakingly
enshrined them in the new temple."[4]
(*Translation*)

The first watercolour features the
pulpit and its steps with a straight handrail
leading to the pulpit itself, topped by the
canopy, which is in turn crowned by the
angel blowing on a trumpet. In the rest of
the work, the viewer can see part of the
retable of the Sacré-Coeur chapel and the
left wing of the main retable. The balustrade closing off the chancel structures this
spectacular layout on a diagonal. The second page is primarily a detail study, which
again features the left wing of the main
retable and focuses on the *Saint Augustin*
and the crimson curtain which filters the
light.[5] The large painting hanging on the
right wall of the Sacré-Coeur chapel cannot
go unnoticed, since Coke Smyth made it
one of the points of interest in his composition, especially in the second version.
George Bourne mentioned it for the first
time in 1829, referring to it as *A Mater
Dolorosa* and attributing it to Anton van
Dyck (1599-1641).[6] It was mentioned
again on August 7, 1838 in a paragraph of
the Actes de l'Assemblée capitulaire of the
Quebec City Ursulines:

watercolours became part of the Elgin collection, since John Richard Coke Smyth
was Lady Lambton's drawing master (Cat.
212 and 213).

These views are remarkable, especially with regard to their subject, because
interiors are very rare in topographical
representations in Quebec. Those of the
Jesuit and Récollet churches, engraved
following the Conquest after the drawings
of Richard Short, did not initiate a trend.[1]
There are, of course, the naive pieces by
R.S.M. Bouchette (Cat. 65 and 66), and a
few pages from Katherine Jane Ellice's
sketchbook, showing the interior of the
ship which brought her to Quebec (Cat.
103) and the drawing-room of her residence in Beauharnois (Cat. 104), but there

is nothing remarkable. These two interiors
of the Ursuline chapel are therefore an
exception. It must be stressed that, apart
from a late 19th-century photograph,[2] the
Ursuline chapel is known to us only by
written accounts. These two watercolours
therefore visually translate the superlatives
encountered in the accounts of travellers
who were especially taken with the quality
of the sculpture of the retable and the
brilliance of the gilding.[3]

Coke Smyth shows us the interior
of the Ursuline chapel in its original condition, at a time when the sculpture works
executed by Pierre-Noël Levasseur (1690-
1770) over a ten-year period had made it
one of the most prestigious decorative sites
in Quebec. The chapel was subsequently

Fig. 214-215A.
John Richard
Coke Smyth,
*The Private Chapel of
the Ursuline Convent,*
1840;
lithograph,
38.2 × 54.6 cm.
Musée du Québec,
Quebec City
(54.61.23).

as in the balustrade under the pulpit. An abundance of light enters through the open window, picked up by highlights of white gouache and spread riotously across the page to invade the crépi of the walls in a splash of bluish grey. This same light, filtered in red by the curtain covering the window opening onto the chancel, permeates the column of the retable and stains the *Saint Augustin.* Coke Smyth's style is rapid and sure, as he deftly uses chrome yellow to pick out the details of the gilding on the fluting of the column and the pilaster, the canopy and the balusters. Colour fashions shape, transforming the surface of the paper into a sumptuous decor. Is this then a pretext for virtuosity, with the artist sacrificing attention to detail for brilliance of style? It would probably be erroneous to believe this, because the drawing chosen for the album of lithographs, *The Private Chapel of the Ursuline Convent* (Fig. 214-215A), just as deftly combines the candour of direct observation with the recollection of radiance.

D.P.

Mère Supérieure S Adélaïde de S Gabriel convened the chapter in order to present two proposals. [...] The second was to change the painting of our Lord taken down from the Cross for a Nativity. Since this work is a gift from My Lord Desjardins, who would like it returned, the chapter agreed to both proposals.[7] (*Translation*)

However, it is difficult to determine whether this *Deposition* was indeed taken down within the next few days. On August 22, Father Louis-Joseph Desjardins wrote to Mother Superior Saint-Henry to tell her to keep the painting, but, on March 25 of the following year, asked her to "deliver to bearer of this letter The Moulded frame, which was used for the Painting of our dead Sav., attributed to Vandike? we hope to be use it for the Wayside Altar of S Patrice."[8] (*Translation*) We know that the Ursulines kept the canvas, since Thielcke asked permission to borrow it on March 10, 1842 in order to copy the shroud depicted in it.[9]

In all this confusion, one fact nevertheless remains clear: the frame was indeed taken from the painting. The "Moulded frame" certainly corresponds to the one adorning the *Deposition* in Coke Smyth's watercolours. We are very inclined to believe that the initial decision made on August 7 was indeed carried out after his works were executed. It can be assumed from Father Desjardins' wording when he spoke of the frame in the past tense on March 25, 1839 that, due to a lack of space, the painting was subsequently taken from its frame and stored. If this premise

is acceptable, it can be then assumed that Coke Smyth executed these two interiors of the Ursuline chapel between late May, the date of his arrival in Quebec City, and early August 1838.

The cautious use of coloured washes in previous drawings (Cat. 212 and 213) did not prepare us for such mastery of colour. The power of these two works comes through in the complex interplay between light and texture. During the period in which Coke Smyth was active, watercolours were no longer what they were in the late 18th century and in the first decade of the following century—a technique considered secondary to oils and exhibited as such in London at the Royal Academy and at the Society of Painters in Watercolours. The explorations in technique undertaken by Joseph Mallord William Turner (1775-1851) and John Sell Cotman (1782-1842) aimed at giving more body to the transparency of watercolours, along with those of Richard Parkes Bonington (1802-1828), William Henry Hunt (1790-1864) and John Frederick Lewis (1805-1876), focusing on the joint use of watercolours and gouache, had made watercolours the equivalent of oils when it came to the power of suggestion. From a technical point of view, these two views of the interior of the Ursuline chapel are quite clearly part of this revival.

The extreme attention to detail and texture is rendered by successive sweeps of the brush in a thick layer of pigments, which become progressively more concentrated to suggest the depth of shadows,

Notes

1. *DE VOLPI 1971,* Pl. 19 and 24.

2. Jean Trudel, *Un chef-d'oeuvre de l'art ancien du Québec. La chapelle des Ursulines* (Quebec City: Les Presses de l'Université Laval, 1972), pp. 14-15.

3. Jean Trudel cites the visit of Joseph Samson to the Ursuline chapel in 1817, about which he published an account in London in 1820 in *Travels in Lower Canada:* "An old priest said Mass before a magnificent retable, a tabernacle of uncommon splendour" (*Ibid.,* p. 95) (*Translation*).

4. Jean Trudel, *op. cit.,* p. 24. The raising of the supporting wall of the retable and the removal of the left side window considerably changed its visual impact inside the chapel (*Ibid.,* pp. 50-51).

5. We can assume from these two drawings that perhaps a broader visual "sweep" of the interior of the chapel was made. It seems unlikely that Coke Smyth decided not to keep at least a view of the entire main retable. Nor has the preliminary drawing for the engraving of the private chapel of the Ursuline convent been found (Fig. 214-215A).

6. *BOURNE 1829.* In a letter from Father Louis-Joseph Desjardins to Mother Superior Saint-Henry, it was entitled *Suaire* and attributed to the same artist. Father Desjardins asked the nun if he could borrow the painting so that he could give it to François Matte to be copied. (AMUQ, Correspondance de l'abbé L.-J. Desjardins II, 29, p. 2). We would like to thank Laurier Lacroix for allowing us to use his research on this painting belonging to Father Desjardins in our entry.

7. AMUQ, Actes de l'Assemblée capitulaire, August 7, 1838, p. 139.

8. AMUQ, Correspondance de Abbé L.-J. Desjardins II, 32.

9. *Ibid.,* 25, p. 2.

216.
View of Quebec, 1839-1840
Oil on canvas, 89.8 × 181 cm

Provenance
Canada Steamship Lines; acquired by Power Corporation of Canada, Montreal, 1981.

Collection
Power Corporation of Canada/Power Corporation du Canada, Montreal

J OHN RICHARD COKE SMYTH left Quebec shortly after Lord Durham's departure, or at least that is what can be understood from the comment which Katherine Jane Ellice wrote in her journal on October 30, 1838:

What more shall I say? Oh! we left Georgine in Montreal to pack up our Butin (or what the Yankees call Plunder), to go to England in the Athole with Bobby & Ld. D.'s servants. Mr. Smythe would not like to hear himself so called.[1]

He took with him a large number of lead pencil drawings, sketched on site, which he used in preparing the album of lithographs which he dedicated to Lord Durham in 1840. This unsigned, undated *View of Quebec* must be placed within this context.[2]

This original work was acquired in 1981 by the Power Corporation of Canada when Canada Steamship Lines was purchased. However, it is difficult to verify whether it came from the William Hugh Coverdale collection, because it is not identified in any of the catalogues compiled by Percy F. Godenrath.[3] The fact that it

was attributed to John Richard Coke Smyth and that it was commissioned by Lord Durham in 1838 is therefore based on the single comment on the form accompanying the painting in the Power Corporation collection. The information is obviously not first-hand. However, given the lack of information directly related to the work, it is probable that the person who catalogued it merely transcribed an older reference.

If this *View of Quebec* was indeed commissioned by Lord Durham, it can be assumed that the artist executed it within the space of a few months, because Durham died on July 28, 1840.[4] There is nothing surprising in the fact that Durham commissioned a painting as a keepsake of his sojourn in Canada and that Coke Smyth received the mandate to execute it. Not only was the artist attached to the Lambton household even before their departure for Canada, but the relationship continued after their return to England, as evidenced by the dedication which accompanied the album of lithographs:

To the R. Hon.The Earl of Durham, &c. &c. &c. This Volume of Canadien Sketches, is most respectfully dedicated with permission, by His Lordships Most obliged, & obedient, humble Servant, Coke Smyth.

This can be seen as a simple acknowledgement, partly obligated,[5] partly

self-seeking, which helped promote the sale of the portfolio of engravings by flaunting a prestigious name. It can also be seen as real gratitude for Lord Durham's patronage. But this is only a theory. Given the current stage of research on the painting's background, the possibility that it might simply have been painted by Coke Smyth to portray an especially spectacular site, and not to fulfil a specific commission, cannot be rejected out of hand.

This work shows the Quebec City skyline as it appeared in autumn 1838. Château Saint-Louis, which burned down in January 1834, remained in ruins until 1838. On Durham's orders, its remains were razed to make way for a terrace, inaugurated in October of that same year.[6] Its foundation can be very clearly seen in Coke Smyth's work: supported by the buttresses of the old chateau, it is bordered at left by the old outbuildings, attached to the greenhouse, and at rear by Château Haldimand, which became the Governor's official residence. The painting is of solid composition: the strong diagonal in the foreground is counterbalanced by the imposing horizontal of the Quebec City cliff, intercepted in the middle distance by the two great three-masters. The most impressive of the two, at right, extends the energy of the foreground; the second is apparently parallel to the city. The two

Fig. 216A.
John Richard Coke Smyth,
Quebec Citadel, 1840;
lithograph, 38.2 × 54.6 cm.
Musée du Québec, Quebec City (54.61.08).

Fig. 216B.
John Richard Coke Smyth,
The Quebec Citadel seen from the Ferry Landing at Lévis;
graphite and watercolour on paper, 17.6 × 26 cm.
Royal Ontario Museum, Toronto (950.114.10).

side vistas show Quebec City as an impregnable fortress which controls the river.

View of Quebec is closely related to Coke Smyth's watercolour drawings and the lithographs he made of them. *Quebec Citadel* (Fig. 216A), lithographed in 1840, is based on a drawing (Fig. 216B) whose foreground motif, sketched from nature, was faithfully engraved. However, the background could not have been sufficiently clear to obtain such coherence between the buildings, and Coke Smyth probably used other drawings to verify the distribution of houses along the bank. Proof that such sketches existed in larger quantities was given to us by Mary Allodi, who established links with the engravings for seven drawings only, while the portfolio contains 23 lithographs.[7] This discrepancy leads us to believe that there is an entire section of the artist's work which is still unknown and on which he certainly relied to compose this large panoramic view. By examining his drawings, his engravings and this painting together, we can verify that Coke Smyth was indeed the artist.

The energetic style of this artist who drew on stone is evident in the way in which the brush was used and the colour applied to especially highlight the rocks supporting the King's bastion at the far end of the Citadel. The tight cluster of houses, overlapping roofs and façades, can

be seen in *Quebec from the Chateau* (Fig. 213A). There again, the style, which emphasizes textures, stone walls and roofs, is counterbalanced by the heavy thickening creating cohesiveness between the buildings along Côte de la Montagne. The colour used also attests to this painting's relationship with the drawings and engravings. Coke Smyth did not use a very extensive palette and the yellow-green tones of the earth, the beiges and ochre of the houses can be easily compared to the watercolour washes in the drawings. This painting is therefore not a radical departure from what we know about his drawn or engraved words. The figures in the foreground, for example, whether it be the peddlar on the pontoon with his baggage on his back, or the individuals in the small craft approaching the far end of the jetty, share with their counterparts in the lithographs (Fig. 216C) a squat aspect and the unique characteristic of having faces half-hidden by the brims of their hats.

The charm of this landscape nevertheless resides in its foreground and in the dynamic contrast it offers to the stability of Cap Diamant.[8] The surprising foreshortening in perspective of the craft carrying a Grenadier Guard, while the oarsman attempts to manoeuvre the craft close to the jetty using a boathook, is the sole focus of peril. Although the subject is

exceptional in Quebec painting, Coke Smyth was not the first to experiment with this genre. This technique is apparent in the painting which Joseph Mallord William Turner exhibited in 1803 at the Royal Academy, *Calais Pier with French Poissard Preparing for Sea: An English Packet Arriving* (Fig. 216D). Coke Smyth repeats the diagonal of the jetty, moving it to the centre of his composition. He also duplicates its precarious aspect by drawing attention to the moorings sliced through by the water and the backwash of the foam. Should the presence of the sailboat at left, perpendicular to the jetty, be seen as a mere coincidence? In Turner's work, this same motif, placed on the horizon, is one of the few notes of stability in a dramatic composition. It is not impossible that Coke Smyth wanted to accentuate contrasts in the same way.

Within the same context, this painting also conjures up another consideration. Is it only a simple depiction of a sublime panorama or should we see a deeper meaning? First, it must be recognized that *View of Quebec* does not describe an historic moment. At most, we can see an allusion to the events which marked the departure of Lord Durham in the troubled waters and the wind which sweeps the clouds above the mouth of the Saint-Charles river towards England. It

Fig. 216C.
John Richard Coke Smyth,
Cape Tourmente from Château-Richer, 1840;
lithograph, 38.2 × 54.6 cm.
Musée du Québec, Quebec City (54.61.04).

Fig. 216D.
Joseph Mallord William Turner,
Calais Pier with French Poissard Preparing for Sea: English Packet Arriving;
oil on canvas. National Gallery, London (472).

should be remembered that the decisions made by Durham regarding the political prisoners arrested following the Rebellion of 1837 quickly earned him the repudiation of the members of his own party and the British government, headed by Lord Melbourne. On June 28, 1838, by edict, Durham exiled ordinary prisoners to Bermuda without a trial. Moreover, he imposed the death penalty on escaping Patriotes. As a result of these decisions, which overstepped his jurisdiction, he lost his London support. He was forced to resign on October 9, 1838 and returned directly to England,[9] refusing to stop in the United States on his way home although this trip, undertaken on a private basis, would have enabled him to be received as a personal guest of the President[10] and thereby regain credibility with the English political class. If he was the sponsor of this large *View of Quebec,* it can be easily understood why he did not want a painting which underscored such an episode. Only the large three-master in the middle of the channel could possibly be the *Inconstant.*[11] But does the abundant white smoke concealing the bridge truly correspond to the firing of salvos from the frigate's cannon, saluting the city at the time of departure?[12] Although this hypothesis cannot be set aside, it is not the only one that can be formulated. There are too many uncertainties to fully support a single theory. John Richard Coke Smyth, while executing his lithographs, may have simply wanted a

larger composition which would enable him to create a new synthesis from his drawings. The addition of the figurative group and the agitation of the river in the foreground, contrasting with the calm water at the edge of the city, imbue *View of Quebec* with meaning. In an attempt not to see it as a specific metaphor, we can only repeat its similarity to Turner's work. The latter is firmly situated within the tradition of 17th-century Dutch and Flemish seascapes. Such works did not always illustrate an event, but instead established a visual analogy between actual fact and its various connotations. Turner took these associations to an especially high level of complexity,[13] combining an analysis of the human experience with topographical representations. Did Coke Smyth wish to underscore the political climate of 1838-1839? We will leave this question unanswered, but will reiterate that such an attempt would be entirely in keeping with artistic trends of that era.

D.P.

Notes

1. Patricia Godsell, ed., *The Diary of Jane Ellice* (Oberon Press, 1975), p. 127.

2. The painting was inexpertly relined, with the canvas clumsily cut along the lower edge. The retouches are abundant on the entire perimeter of the canvas and in the sky. Despite this condition, we had to present it because it marks a major point in landscape art of this period.

3. However, it is not impossible that the painting passed through the hands of L. Kashnor, the bookseller of the Museum Book Store of London. The information comes from the J.R. Coke Smyth file in the National Archives of Canada. Kashnor owned the albums of drawings by James P. Cockburn in 1927, which he offered for sale to the National Archives (See. Cat. 76).

4. Fernand Ouellet, DCB, Vol. VII (1988), p. 515.

5. This is what we must understand from Katherine J. Ellice's comment.

6. "Promenades Publiques," *Le Canadien,* October 1, 1838, p. 3.

7. ALLODI *1968,* p. 12.

8. Coke Smyth used it in the same way in his *View of Quebec,* in which the river, churned into high waves by a squall, makes the crossing dangerous for a small craft (DE VOLPI *1971,* Pl. 105).

9. Fernand Ouellet, DCB, Vol. III (1980), p. 518.

10. *Lady Durham's Journal* (Québec City: The Telegraph Printing Co., 1915 [Ninth Series of Historical Documents]), p. 50.

11. We do not know of any representation of it, but Lady Durham mentioned its arrival in Quebec City on October 5 and identified it as a frigate (*Lady Durham's Journal,* p. 47).

12. Lady Durham did not mention it in her Journal. Moreover, she does mention that a firm alarm was sounded on board at the moment of embarkation which did not, however, delay the departure (*Ibid.,* pp. 53-54).

13. For Dutch and Flemish art, see Lawrence Otto Goedde, *Tempest and Shipwreck in Dutch and Flemish Art. Convention, Rhetoric and Interpretation* (University Park: The Pennsylvania State University Press, 1989). For Turner, see Eric Shanes, *Turner's Human Landscape* (London: William Heinemann Ltd., 1990).

MARTIN SOMERVILLE is thought to have been born around 1796-1797. By 1839, he had left England and arrived in Canada. Once settled in Montreal, he offered his services as a painting master in both oils and watercolours and taught many genres: history painting, landscape painting and simple floral designs. He was also a drawing master, teaching freehand and perspective techniques in a school for young ladies. He linked up with other artists, notably, Cornelius Krieghoff who, around 1846, had taken a studio in the same building as Somerville.

In 1847, Somerville exhibited at the gallery of the newly founded Montreal Society of Artists. In 1849 and 1850, the *Illustrated London News* ran some of his drawings of American Indians and views of Montreal. Nothing indicated that Somerville owned a residence in Quebec City, but he was a tenant in one of the houses owned by Joseph Légaré. He died in Quebec City on May 31, 1856, at age 59.

MARTIN SOMERVILLE

circa 1796/1797-1856

Main sources
HARPER 1985; TRUDEL 1990/2.

217.
Mocassin Vendor, 1852
Oil on canvas, 30.5 × 25.7 cm

Inscriptions
(s.d., l.r) *M. Somerville. Montreal. 1852.;* (b., on the stretcher) *Painted by M. Somerville, Montreal 1852-.*

Provenance
Berry-Hill Galleries, New York; Dominion Gallery, Montreal, 1958; Misters Keable Ltd., Les Méchins (Matane), 1958; Maurice Duplessis, Trois-Rivières, 1959; gift of the Maurice Duplessis estate to the Musée de la Province de Québec, Quebec City, 1959.

Bibliography
BÉLAND *1991*, p. 54; KAREL *1991*, p. 20.

Collection
Musée du Québec, Quebec City (59.611)

A T THE 1847 EXHIBITION of the Montreal Society of Artists, the 21 works of Martin Somerville stood out for their eclecticism. Among them were copies of European and American landscapes, studies of flowers and trees, religious subjects, portraits and genre paintings. Number 30, *The Chief's Daughter* suggests that the artist was already painting Amerindian subjects. Two years later, he worked with Cornelius Krieghoff to complete the portraits of three Chippewa chiefs who visited Lord Elgin.[1]

In fact, beginning in 1846, Somerville and Krieghoff had studios in the same building on Rue Saint-Jacques in Montreal. One work, attributed to Krieghoff by Russell Harper, shows a woman selling moccasins in front of the building displaying the names of the two artists.[2] By associating the subject with their names, the artists' interest in painting Amerindians interacting with the urban environment is shown. Generally, they portrayed Iroquois women from the Kahnawake reserve who found a market for their artwork and crafts among tourists and Montrealers. Whether they appear in works by Krieghoff or those by Somerville, the Native women wear not only moccasins, but also carry embroidered bags decorated with beadwork or dyed porcupine quills.

The street vendor is a dominant theme in genre paintings. Dutch and French artists created very famous works showing the crafts and "*cris,*" who earned this name for their characteristic fashion of calling out what products and services were being offered to the inhabitants of the streets they wandered.[3] Krieghoff and, to a lesser extent, Somerville adapted this tradition to local customs, depicting beggars, artisans and street vendors.[4] The sale of wild fruit and bread, and cutting of wood fell to the habitants; Amerindians were shown selling rush baskets, bags and embroidered leather moccasins.

Despite the fact that these Amerindians were heading for the city, they were only shown en route to it, in an intermediary landscape between the reserve and their destination. They usually carried only a few pairs of moccasins with a bag, indicating their relatively high cost and how long they took to make. Production of moccasins and baskets was reserved for artisans, as was their sale. These ordinary objects were usually intended for tourists or collectors. While the strong, supple moccasins were common footwear in the country, such was not the case in the city.

Somerville shows his subject full-length crossing the frozen river.[5] Blocks of ice and the outstretched shadow display his interest in the effects of subtle shading.

The woman is wearing a skirt with a false hem. A long blouse falls to her thighs. She is enshrouded in a blanket bearing the striped border of the Hudson's Bay Company which she clutches with her mitten-clad hands. Gaiters held up by laces are an extension of her leather moccasins.

L.L.

Notes
1. HARPER *1979*, p. 53. Two of Krieghoff's portraits are reproduced on page 54.
2. This is *A Red Indian Woman outside the Artist's Studio* (PC). See HARPER *1979*, p. X (Repr.).
3. For more on this issue, see the important work by Karen F. Beall, *Kaufrufe und Strassenhandler Cries and Itinerant Trades. A Bibliography* (Hamburg: Dr. Ernst Hauswedell Co., 1975).
4. The recent work by POMERLEAU *1990* provides a rich iconography for these lost arts.
5. The manner in which the woman is presented in the space is more slightly reminiscent of the portrait of *Kateri Tekakwitha*, attributed to Claude Chauchetière and kept at Kahnawake. See *Le Grand Héritage. L'Église catholique et la société au Québec* (Cat.), (Quebec City: Gouvernement du Québec, 1984), p. 40 (Repr.).

YVES TESSIER

1800-1847

Y VES TESSIER was born in Quebec City on December 22, 1800. On September 4, 1819, his father apprenticed him to painter Jean-Baptiste Roy-Audy and his training period probably ended in 1822. When his marriage was announced on February 18, 1830, he was listed as a resident of Montreal and as a history and portrait painter. In fact, Tessier had already captured a portion of the religious painting market just outside Montreal and in the Richelieu Valley. He painted one of his first works for the church at Saint-Denis-sur-Richelieu in 1823. In 1824, he received an important commission from Saint-Marc, another parish in the region. On November 21, "Mr. Tescier, Quebec painter," (*Translation*) delivered two paintings to the parish and received a commission at the same time to complete four more, based on the Passion. Other important commissions came from the parishes of Lachenaie (1825), Saint-Eustache (1825), L'Acadie (1826, 1828), Saint-François-du-Lac (1827), Marieville (1829), Saint-Jacques-de-L'Achigan (1830), Sainte-Rose (1831), Beloeil (1831, 1832) and Sainte-Elizabeth de Joliette (1831, 1833). While moving from place to place, Tessier also completed several smaller works, such as a banner for the Caughnawaga church in 1827 and a frontal for the church in Des Cèdres in 1839. At the same time, he was commissioned to "restore" older paintings, which he seemed content merely to revarnish.

Very few portraits can be attributed to him with any certainty, among them the portrait of Jean-Jacques Lartigue (See Cat. 242). Tessier was not yet 47 when he died in Montreal on October 26, 1847 following a long illness.

Main source

HARPER 1970.

218.
Saint Peter, c. 1820-1823
Oil on canvas, 58.5 × 46.5 cm

Inscription
(b., paper mounted on the back of the canvas, in brown ink) *Ce tableau a été donné/par M*. Tessier jeune/Peintre à la S* Magd. de S* Pierre/par reconnaissance en 1823 ou 24.*

Provenance
Gift of the artist to Soeur Saint-Pierre (née Marie-Madeleine Vocelle), Hôtel-Dieu de Québec, 1823 or 1824.

Exhibition
Quebec City 1972.

Bibliography
MUSÉE HISTORIQUE 1964, p. 2; *BOISCLAIR 1977,* pp. 45-46, No. 65 (Repr.); *CAUCHON 1971,* p. 51 (Repr.).

Collection
Musée des Augustines de l'Hôtel-Dieu de Québec (65)

T HE APOSTLE SAINT PETER is normally presented as bald, white-bearded and holding two keys, one to Heaven and one to Earth, Christ having said to him, "I will give you the keys of the kingdom of heaven, and whatever you bind on earth shall be bound in heaven, and whatever you loose on earth shall be loosed in heaven" (Matt.16:19). Thus, according to popular belief, Saint Peter became Heaven's gatekeeper.

The iconography in Tessier's painting is related to the various series of the twelve apostles, the most famous being those by Pieter Paul Rubens[1] and Anton van Dyck.[2] These apostolic series, in full-length or half-length, were very popular, in Spain for instance, where numerous *Apostolados* were painted by El Greco and Zurbaran. Designed as character sketches, they were often naturalistic portraits in the manner of Caravaggio, being transformed into apostles by the mere addition of certain attributes.[3] The series of twelve apostles were largely distributed as engravings.[4] The 14 larger oil works representing the apostles and two evangelists attributed to Louis Dulongpré—donated to the Hôtel-Dieu de Québec hospital in 1805 by the family of Dr. Jacques Denéchaud (Fig. 26A)—bear witness to the popularity of such works in Canada.

While Tessier's **Saint Peter** can be compared to the canvas by Van Dyck, found in the Hermitage Museum, in what was formerly Leningrad and made familiar through the engraving by Cornelius Van Caukercken,[5] its exact source is unknown. Tessier's work shows Saint Peter hands clasped, eyes raised heavenward. The strong light, which creates harsh shadows, gives the painting an emotional power, accentuating the drama of the scene. The bushy beard, furrowed features, robe and draped clothing give Saint Peter the air of a peasant in prayer lost in some mystical torment, rather than that of a Classical hero lost in thought. In fact, the subject is also reminiscent of the so-called repentance of Saint Peter. El Greco painted a series of such portraits, in which Peter is shown in an identical pose bearing two keys at his waist.[6] However, when shown in a penitent attitude (Fig. 10-11A), the apostle was usually portrayed with a rooster, bringing to mind his denial of Christ (Matt. 27:75 and Mark 14:72). This symbol did not appear until sometime later, in 18th-century Baroque art. The iconography in Tessier's Saint Peter probably harks back to 17th century iconography, which changed

Fig. 218A.
Yves Tessier,
The Descent from the Cross, 1824;
oil on canvas, approximately 290 × 180 cm.
Église Saint-Marc-sur-Richelieu.

slightly once it came into contact with the sensibilities of the following century.

When, in 1819, Yves Tessier was apprenticed to Jean-Baptiste Roy-Audy, he was already 19. When his contract ended, with his attaining the age of majority, he had had only two years of training. We can therefore assume that this small painting, done from an engraving, was an exercise for the young painter. The work is by no means faultless, exhibiting shortcomings in the rendering of the hands and the draped fabric, which lacks realism, and in the rather abrupt variations in the lighting on the flesh. Nonetheless, in it, we already see the artist's partiality for brilliant colours and exaggerated features, preferences which would serve him well in his later religious paintings. The year he gave this painting to Sister Saint-Pierre, it being a portrait of her protector, Yves Tessier produced a painting for the parish of Saint-Denis-sur-Richelieu. The following year, in Saint-Marc-sur-Richelieu:

Mr. Tescier, Quebec painter, delivered two canvases, one of the flagellation and the other of the removal of Jesus' body from the cross, and agreed to do four more, two for the main church and two others to flank the large altar.[7] (*Translation*)

Of this group, only four works have survived, and they are among the artist's finest. *The Descent From the Cross* by Tessier (Fig. 218A), copied from a work at Oka—itself copied from a work by Charles Le Brun, dated approximately 1679 and located at the Musée des beaux-arts in Rennes—shows how the robust style and vivid colours used in **Saint Peter** come into their own in a large-scale work.

It was probably following this important contract that Tessier settled in the Montreal area, where he obtained many commissions from surrounding parishes despite a relatively short career of which little evidence remains.

P.B.

Notes

1. *La peinture flamande au Prado* (Antwerp and Paris: Fonds Mercator and Albin Michel, 1989), pp. 294-295.

2. Alan McNairn, *Le jeune van Dyck* (Cat.) (Ottawa: National Gallery of Canada, 1980), pp. 38-49.

3. Susan Urbach, "Preliminary Remarks on the Sources of the Apostle Series of Rubens and van Dyck," *RACAR*, Vol. VIII, No. 1 (1983), pp. 5-22.

4. We should also mention the two series engraved by Claude Mellan. See *Inventaire du fonds français. Graveurs du XVIIᵉ siècle* (Paris: Bibliothèque nationale, 1988), T. XVII, No. 33-54.

5. Alan McNairn, *op. cit.,* p. 278 (Repr.).

6. José Guidol, *Doménikos Theotokopoulos Le Greco, 1541-1614. Biographie et Catalogue* (Paris: Éditions Weber, 1973) pp. 113 and 244-245.

7. Parish records from Saint-Marc-sur-Richelieu, Account Ledgers II, Fol. 3 and 3 v., 1824.

8. *Boisclair 1977*, pp. 82-84.

HENRY DANIEL
THIELCKE

(?)1787-1874

T HIELCKE IS BELIEVED to have been born in 1787 of German parents, and lived in England at least until his early thirties. He was trained at London's Royal Academy of Arts, where he received honourable mention for his landscapes done from nature, and at the Institution of the Arts and Sciences (British Institution). Between 1805 and 1816, he exhibited portraits and religious and mythological works. During this period, he is thought to have been under the patronage of one of the members of the royal family, having painted the portrait of the Duchess of York. Between 1818 and 1832, we have no record of his commissions or travels.

Upon his arrival in Lower Canada in 1832, Thielcke advertised himself as a portrait painter in both oils and miniatures. In 1834, he was given a studio in the House of Assembly building. One of his first known portraits in Canada portrays Lord Gosford, Governor of Lower Canada (1836, MCR). Besides painting portraits, such as that of *Mrs. William Burns Lindsay, née Maria Jones, and Her Son John* (1836, Cat. 219), Thielcke tried to branch out into the religious painting market, but his efforts provoked biting criticism from Antoine Plamondon. In early September 1838, he opened a school of drawing and painting at the Quebec Picture Gallery, owned by Joseph Légaré and Thomas Amiot. In 1839, he presented two compositions to the Literary and Historical Society of Quebec, one of which portrayed the *Death of Wolfe,* inspired from an engraving after the work by Benjamin West, for which he was awarded a prize.

In 1840, he completed *Presentation of a Newly Elected Chief of the Huron Tribal Council of Lorette* (Cat. 220), his most renowned work. Two years later, he exhibited a number of portraits at New York's National Academy of Design. Thielcke was also a teacher, giving French and drawing classes at the Quebec High School. He worked in the English-speaking community as member of the Church Society of the Diocese of Quebec and assistant secretary (1851), then secretary (1852), of the board of directors of the Literary and Historical Society. In 1854, after fire destroyed the Parliament Building, where the Society had its premises, he left Quebec to settle in Chicago, where he offered his services as portraitist at least until 1864. He died in this city on November 25, 1874.

Main source
Fox 1986.

Fig. 219A.
Sir Joshua Reynolds,
Georgiana, Duchess of Devonshire and her Daughter, Lady Georgiana Cavendish,
1784-1786;
oil on canvas, 113 × 140 cm.
Devonshire Collection, Chatsworth.
Reproduction authorized by
The Chatsworth Settlement Trustees.

219.
Mrs. William Burns Lindsay, née Maria Jones, and Her Son John, 1836
Oil on canvas, 101.5 × 127.2 cm

Inscription
(s.d., b.) *Hʸ. D. Thielcke Pinxit. 1836 Quebec./ Historical Portrait Painter to H.R.H. The late Duchess of York.*

Provenance
Descendants of the Lindsay and Drummond families; Alexander Drummond, Toronto, before 1954; Charles Crawford Lindsay, Saint-Anicet, c. 1972; Robert J. Lindsay, Saint-Anicet; Bernard Sauvé, Saint-Anicet; acquired by the National Gallery of Canada, Ottawa, 1981.

Bibliography
Fox 1986, pp. 20-29; *NICOLAÏ 1990,* pp. 60, 62-63, 65 and 114 (Repr.).

Collection
National Gallery of Canada, Ottawa (26538)

THIS PAINTING is one of the first known works from Thielcke's Canadian career. The portrait shows Maria Jones, second daughter of Colonel Robert Jones and wife of William Burns Lindsay (1796-1862), who was teller at the Quebec branch of the Bank of Montreal, then clerk for the Lower Canada House of Assembly, and finally clerk for the Legislative Assembly. The child portrayed is believed to be John Lindsay, born July 4, 1834, and thus two years of age at the time Thielcke painted this portrait. In

this work, Thielcke has managed to convey comfort, intimacy and sensual charm. His models are placed in a setting characterized by rich textures (fabric and furs), sombre yet warm tones, and subdued lighting. The intimate aspect of this portrait is highlighted by the mother's maternal stance and the child's trusting gesture as he invites her to smell the flower he holds. Thielcke's talents as a colourist are evident here, but he appears to be a less skilful draughtsman. The portrait suffers from flaws in the treatment of the draperies and the portrayal of the sitters' anatomy. However, the artist is more successful in depicting elements of colour and texture, for example in the fur on which the child is seated and in the landscape. Both are painted in a sweeping fashion using impasto and subtle lighting effects. There are also significant shortcomings on a strictly technical level. Thielcke's too-rapid combination of paint with different drying properties—preparation, pigment, glaze, and varnish—and his use of large quantities of bitumen in his primer have caused the paint layers to congeal in masses, giving the canvas the appearance of crocodile skin.

The design and even the handling of this canvas call to mind the portrait of *Georgiana, Duchess of Devonshire and Her*

Daughter, Lady Georgiana Cavendish painted by Joshua Reynolds (1723-1792) in 1784-1786 (Fig. 219A). The layout of the figures, although reversed, and their position, as well as the landscape glimpsed on the right behind a heavy red drapery, are based on a similar composition. The paint effects seen in Thielcke's work also recall the spirited handling and impasto of Reynolds' canvas, evidence of his studies with 17th-century masters of the northern tradition.[1] This work by the first president of the Royal Academy, the "glorious apogee of the baroque style of Reynolds' mature period," in the words of David Mannings, was "the successful result of having studied handling and composition in the style of Rubens."[2] (*Translation*) Thielcke was able to study this canvas at the British Institute, where it was exhibited in 1813. Having received his training in England, Thielcke exhibited some of his own work at the same institution in 1811, 1815 and 1816, as well as at the Royal Academy of Arts between 1805 and 1816.

We know of few works by Henry Thielcke that were actually done in Canada. The one of *Archibald Acheson, 2nd Earl of Gosford,* also painted in 1836, is striking because of the sitter's frontal pose which gives the impression of formality, authority, and even severity. The treatment of the textures is the same as in the portrait of Mrs. Lindsay and her son. Another work by Thielcke, *Presentation of a Newly Elected Chief of the Huron Tribal Council of Lorette* (Cat. 220), is without a doubt the artist's most ambitious work and the one which brought him renown. Comparison of the landscape in each of these works shows the artist's predilection for atmospheric effects and contrasts in tonality modulated by dramatic lighting.

The portrait of Mrs. Lindsay and her son is unique when compared to the rest of this era's pictorial production. Defying the esthetic principles of Antoine Plamondon-style classicism, Thielcke was not long in incurring the wrath of this artist, especially in 1835 when he took the liberty of exhibiting religious works of his own design. This style found less favour with the Canadian bourgeoisie, which was coming into its own and therefore seeking more to glorify itself than to display acquired wealth. In this sense, Plamondon's monumental designs were more in keeping with public expectations. Thielcke, as "*Historical Portrait Painter to H.R.H. the late Duchess of York*," perhaps executed this work in the hope of luring clients away from the famous "student of the French school." (*Translation*) But the English artist appears not to have found an environment conducive to the development of this new style.

P.B.

220. (See colour reproduction, p. 95)
**Presentation of a Newly Elected Chief
of the Huron Tribal Council of Lorette,** 1840
Oil on canvas, 127 × 107 cm

Notes

1. The technical problems observed in Thielcke's canvas recall the results of several experiments by Reynolds with paint, especially his excessive use of bitumen and siccatives. See M. Kirby Talley, Jr., "*Tous les bons tableaux se craquellent*": la technique picturale et l'atelier de Sir Joshua Reynolds" in *Sir Joshua Reynolds* (cat.), (Paris: Éditions de la Réunion des musées nationaux, 1985), pp. 83-114.

2. *Ibid.*, p. 242.

Provenance

Acquired by the Château Ramezay, Montreal, 1913.

Exhibitions

Quebec City 1840; Quebec City 1853; La Rochelle 1982, No. 122; Montreal 1986, No. 35.

Bibliography

Quebec Mercury, September 5, 1840, p. 3; *Le Canadien*, September 7, 1840, p. 3; *Le Fantasque*, September 14, 1840, pp. 309-311; *Quebec Mercury*, September 19, 1840, p. 3, November 11, 1841, p. 2, March 19, 1842, p. 2, August 2, 1842, p. 3, September 10, 1842, p. 3, November 15, 1842, p. 3, and June 9, 1853, p. 3; *Le Journal de Québec*, June 7, 1853, p. 2, and June 18, 1853, p. 2; HARRIS 1898, p. 355; LINDSAY 1900, pp. 240 and 271-273 (repr. - lithograph); MCR, *The Numismatic and Antiquarian Society of Montreal. Minutes of Council. Begin 8th January 1904, Finished 16th May 1922* (minutes of the regular meeting of the Council), p. 176, November 21, 1913; *The Antiquarian and Numismatic Journal*, Vol. XI, No. 1 (1914), p. 47; O'LEARY 1917, p. 40, No. 290; O'LEARY 1922, p. 92, No. 19; O'LEARY 1926, p. 98, No. 19; CATALOGUE 1927/2, p. 98, No. 19; CATALOGUE 1928, p. 98, No. 19; CATALOGUE 1931, p. 89, No. 19; MORISSET 1935/7, p. 2 (repr. - lithograph); MORISSET 1935/9, p. 9; CATALOGUE 1936, p. 93, No. 19; MORISSET 1936-1937, Vol. II, pp. 86 and 100-101; CATALOGUE 1937, p. 90, No. 19; MORISSET 1941/1, p. 80; CATALOGUE 1948, p. 93, No. 19; CATALOGUE 1954, p. 93, No. 93; CATALOGUE 1956, p. 93, No. 19; CARRIER 1957, p. 83, No. 835; MORISSET 1960/1, pp. 138 and 79c (repr. - lithograph of MQ); CARRIER AND LEFEBVRE 1962, p. 88, No. 835; HARPER 1970, p. 307; SOUCY AND THIBAULT 1974, p. 105; *Nos racines*, No. 79 (1979), p. 1568 (Repr.); FREDRICKSON AND GIBB 1980, p. 75 (Repr.); KAREL, LABERGE AND THIVIERGE 1982, p. 1002; UNE AUTRE AMÉRIQUE 1982, p. 99, No. 122 (Repr.); SELECTED CATALOGUE 1985, pp. 37-38, No. 69; VINCENT 1986, cover. p. (Repr.); LAFORTUNE 1986, pp. 48 and 49, No. 35 (Repr.); FOX 1986, p. 27.

Collection

Musée du Château Ramezay, Montreal (CRX978.41.1)

T HE SEPTEMBER 7, 1840 EDITION of the Quebec City newspaper *Le Canadien* informed its readers, and particularly "painting enthusiasts," of the exhibition in the home of the Sewell heirs on Rue Buade of a "very interesting canvas" done by the artist Thielcke, "the subject of which is the presentation of a newly elected chief of the Huron tribal council of Lorette." (*Translation*) Two days earlier, the *Quebec Mercury* had provided more information and remarks on the subject:

Mr. THIELCKE has just completed a very interesting picture, the subject of which is the Presentation of a newly elected Chief to the Council of the Huron Tribe at Lorette. The Indians, and the received Chief, are represented in the grand costume of the tribe, as at present worn, and the painting contains portraits of the principal Chiefs of the Lorette Hurons and other characters who are well known to most of the residents in this city. Amongst these we recognize the portrait of Zachari Vincent, (*Telariholin*), said to be the only remaining pure blooded Huron in that village. The grouping of the picture is good and the portraits are animated and faithful representations of the living characters they are intended to represent.—The picture is now on exhibition, with other pieces from the easel of the same artist, in Buade Street, next door to Mr. Joseph Prior's.—An explanatory key is delivered to each visitor, which fully designates the several individuals, as they appear in the picture and a short notice explains the circumstances it is intended to commemorate, which are highly creditable to the principal character in the group; whose portrait will be easily recognized, but whose name we suppress, lest we should offend the delicacy of his feelings. Mr. Thielcke has exerted himself with great effect in this historical painting, and has produced a piece which fully supports his character as a painter.

In conclusion, the editor of the *Mercury* pointed out that his newspaper had published an account of the enthroning ceremony of the main figure in the canvas in its edition of February 22, 1838.

The long account in question is interesting from more than one viewpoint because it describes the Amerindian festivities which lasted from February 20 to 23, 1838, celebrating the marriage of a Huron woman from Jeune-Lorette—a village located on the banks of the Saint-Charles river not far from Quebec City (Cat. 77)—and the election of two new chiefs to the Huron tribe, in this case one Lieutenant Vivian, and the colourful justice of the peace Robert Symes.[1] The latter, elected Wednesday February 21, was portrayed by Thielcke two years later in the centre of his commemorative canvas. In order to fully appreciate the faithfulness of this work as a history painting, the following passage, taken from the *Mercury* account, should be noted:

The united attraction of these important events was the means of assembling at the village, yesterday in particular, a large amount of the 'beauty and fashion' of Quebec, who entered into the spirit of the different amusements that prevailed, with much glee. Distinctions of rank were laid aside and matrons and spinsters of the city were to be seen in the same set of quadrilles with the sweethearts and wives of the Huron Indians. The whole scene presented, to those who witnessed it, a most novel and striking appearance. The large number of different uniforms of the Volunteers mixed up with the dresses of the Indians, was a means of heightening in a great degree the picturesque nature of the scene. Blanket coats were decidedly at a premium, as may be imagined from the circumstance of numbers of the Rifle and Queen's Own Corps being added to the *capots de couverte* of the Indians and Squaws.

[...] the installation of the worthy Magistrate ['*Monsieur Symes*'] became a matter of much greater importance than that of his predecessor, from the circumstance of the news of Tuesday's proceedings having reached town and induced the townsfolk to the number of some two hundred or so to get themselves conveyed to Lorette. The consequences were such as we have already stated; and the recollection of yesterday will remain in the minds of all the visitors, no doubt, for some time hence.

A majority of the visitors had been informed in town that 10 a.m. was the hour at which Mr. Symes would take his degree, but the event did not take place until 1 p.m. The intervening hours, however, were not lost upon the Quebeckers, who spent them in paying visits to all the houses, and dancing. [...]

As the hour of one approached, great preparations were making at the house of Nicolas Vincent in which Mr. Symes was to 'take a name.' The principal Chiefs were there to be seen donning their finest dresses and bringing to light, their silver bracelets, armlets and the gold and silver medals presented to them by their late Majesties George III and George IV. Having arrayed themselves to the best advantage and the clock having struck one they issued forth in quest of the candidate for Chieftain's honours who was awaiting the summons at another house in the village. After a short absence the Chiefs returned, bringing with them their *brother to be* attired in full costume and looking very like an Indian certainly, followed by a large concourse of persons who filled the installation apartment almost to suffocation. Order having been obtained with some slight difficulty, the ceremony commenced by a peroration in the Huron language from the head Chief, André Romain, accompanied by interjectional exclamations from others of the tribe who formed a circle in the middle floor. Within this circle was placed a huge cauldron of soup 'all hot', flanked by two ten-gallon casks of Racey's best. Having concluded speaking, Nicolas Vincent walked up to Mr. Symes and shook hands at the same time saying '*Hotsawati*', by which name he is to be hereafter known among the Huron tribe. This done, the second Chief André Romain, walked three times round the cauldron with a ram's head in his hands, and chaunting what we took to be a war-song. He then shook hands with *Hotsawati* and the same ceremony was repeated by five or six lesser Chiefs in succession. This portion of the ceremony being concluded, *Hotsawati*'s commission, in the following terms, was read by Eusebe Vincent son of Vincent Ferrier the village school master, in the Huron, French and English languages:

'ROBERT SYMES, Esquire, a friend to our people, was this day created a Chief of our Tribe, and the name *Hotsawati* (he has defended his country) given to him in remembrance of the numerous Acts of Benevolence rendered our Nation by him and his amiable Lady during the prevalence of the Cholera, in the year of

Fig. 220A.
H. Lynch, Day & Hague after Henry Daniel Thielcke,
*Presentation of a newly elected Chief to the Council
of the Huron Tribe*, 1841;
lithograph, 58.7 × 45.7 cm.
Musée du Québec, Quebec City (55.508).

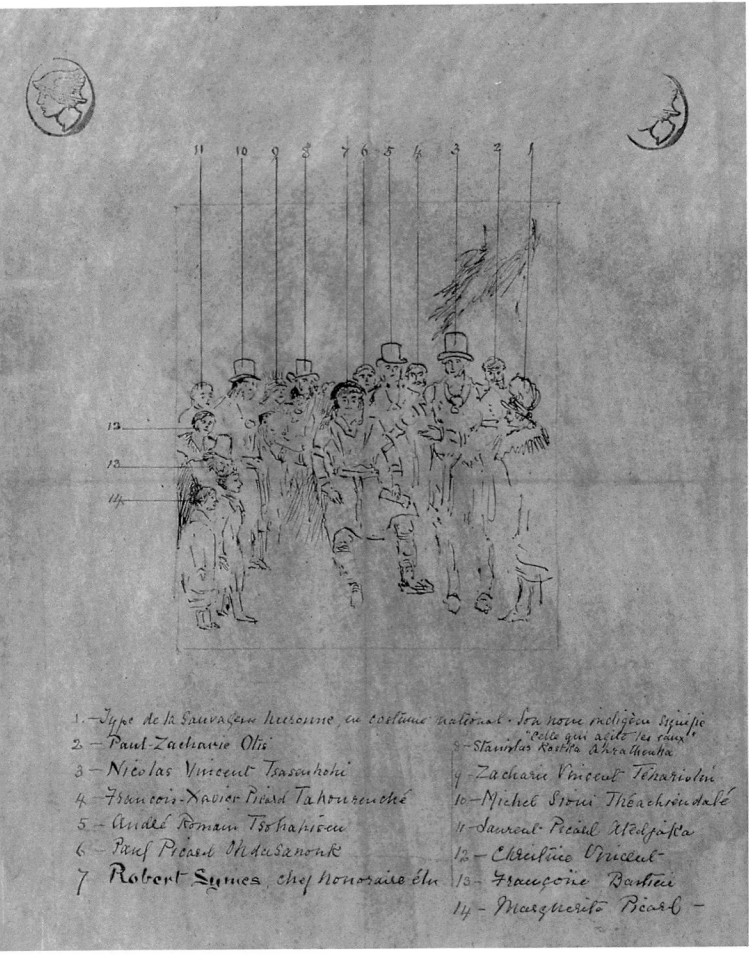

Fig. 220B.
Schema and legend on the back of the lithograph:
Presentation of a newly elected Chief of the Huron Tribal Council of Lorette
Musée du Québec, Quebec City (55.508).

our Lord 1834; and as a token of gratitude for the valuable services he has devoted to our country in his public character as Magistrate of the District of Quebec.

NICHOLAS VINCENT,
ANDRE' ROMAIN,
STANISLAS COSKA,
MICHEL ISIOUI.

Indian Lorette, 21 February, 1838.'

Three times three cheers followed the reading of the commission, in honour of *Hotsawati*, who acknowledged the honour conferred upon him in the following terms:—My Friends,—I receive this mark of distinction which you have been pleased to confer upon me with the greatest pleasure, and if I have at any time been of any service to your people, you have now repaid me a hundred fold, and the kind manner in which you have been pleased to acknowledge the feeble services of myself and Mrs. Symes, will never be effaced from my memory; and I beg to assure you that if at any future time I can assist you, the opportunity

shall never be lost; but the manner in which you have mentioned my public services calls from me the greatest acknowledgment, as it establishes the high character for loyalty to your Sovereign which has always distinguished the Huron Indians of Lorette, and I trust that we shall never be found wanting in this particular, and that we shall always be ready to defend the rights of our Queen to the last drop of our blood. I again return you my sincere thanks for the honor now conferred upon me, and I trust I shall not disgrace the distinguished name which you have now given me.

Loud cheers followed this address from *Hotsawati* who was then considered *de facto* and *de jure* a chief of the Hurons. [...] The name 'Hotsawati,' has a more extensive meaning than the translation given to it in the new chief's commission. It signifies in addition to 'He has defended, &c.' a pacificator—one who acts as a mediator—and is the highest distinction which the Hurons can confer. It is the word or exclamation which their forefathers uttered on first beholding a Christian missionary.

On February 23, 1838, the day following the publication of the account in the *Mercury*, the editor of the *Canadien* published an article which was not only less verbose, but also less flattering to Symes; he even stated, ironically, that "the newly elected chief looked exactly like a savage" at the time of his enthroning, and that his Huron name meant not only "defender of the country" and "peacemaker" but also "informer"! (*Translation*) This last word referred to the questionable role Symes had played with regard to the *Patriote* party in the capital: after having conducted a secret investigation on the directors of the *Le Libéral/The Liberal*, he took advantage of his powers to arrest a number of well-known *Patriotes*, among them his former rival in the municipal elections, artist Joseph Légaré. The November 20, 1837, edition of *Le Libéral* published a reference to "his well-known hostility toward Canadians of French origin, subjects of Her Majesty." (*Translation*) As for the moderate editor of the *Canadien*, Étienne Parent, he described him a month later as a sad-faced Don Quixote showing "signs of mental derangement."[2] (*Translation*) In the months and years that followed, "Robert Symes the 1st," alias "Bobby" or "Robert-the-braggart," (*Translation*) became the protagonist of several satirical texts parodying his failings.[3] In this context, the scathing reception given Thielcke's exhibition of Symes' portrait in September 1840 by Napoléon Aubin, editor of the *Fantasque*, was hardly surprising. In an article entitled "Like misfortune, beasts always come in twos or threes," (*Translation*) Aubin compared the story of Symes' portrait to that of "an immense canvas depicting an enormous crocodile happily munching on a man," which a merchant of the lower town used to entice gawkers into paying thirty sous to see a collection of young, singularly harmless crocodiles:

It is undoubtedly the effect produced on Mr. Symes by the crocodile painted on canvas which gave him the idea of a sign for his store. Having seen that the customers were attracted by the horrible, he immediately came up with the brilliant project of having himself depicted as an Indian chief! No sooner said than done; but before offering up the precious sign to the avid but unforgiving eyes of laymen, he decided, like the merchant that he is, to take advantage of this public gawking. Thus, those passing by the corner of Rue Buade will see a poster inviting them, for the fee of thirty sous, to gaze upon the painting of a Huron chief being received into the tribe. If you are the least bit good-hearted, or if you aspire to the reputation of lover of the fine arts, naturally, you put down the money and enter the shop, where you behold the famous Huron chief, invincible warrior, protector of his race, the terrible Hot-a-sa-wa-tzi! *alias* none other than Robert Symes, Esquire, dealer in ribbons and calico. The immortal hero of the ribbon shop is seated gravely on a rock, dressed in a blue overcoat with red and yellow epaulettes. His legs are enveloped in the traditional *mitas* of the civilized Indian nations, and he is shod with mooseshide boots embroidered with pearls from his own shop; on his head he wears a type of fur cap decorated with feathers which have probably seen many a turkey. His arms are bedecked with magnificent tin-plated bracelets; on his chest shine the medals lent to him by the chiefs of Lorette; and, to top it all off, from his belt hangs an unused hatchet, almost as "untried" as its wearer. The resemblance pays homage to the artist, who threw himself into this extravagant canvas; the rather vibrant colours of the face lead us to believe that the idea for this clownish masquerade came to the subject following a copious meal washed down with quantities of wine.

Around the hero are gathered all the chiefs of the village of Lorette, and it is easy to see that their dreadful grimaces are disguising a desperate attempt to hold back their laughter.

When Mr. Symes has exhibited his canvas, it is probable that he will next put himself on display by placing this work above his door, just like the owner of the crocodiles did for his little monsters. Chances of this are good.

But in all seriousness, as an object of art, and as an honest piece of work, the canvas is quite commendable; but it seems to us that an artist, after having been forced to produce such a ridiculous caricature, should have enough self-respect to refuse to exhibit it publicly. (*Translation*)

Thielcke took no notice of Aubin's advice, especially since the exhibition of this painting enjoyed great success, with several people expressing their desire to purchase an engraved copy. The artist took advantage of this opportunity to collect contributions of five dollars so he could travel to London to supervise the publication of a lithograph. In November 1841, the *Quebec Mercury* quoted an article in a London newspaper on the publication of the engraving. After having analyzed the colourful translations of the names of the main Indians portrayed, the author concluded his article with this anthropological reflection:

The characters are painted in the grand costume of the tribe, as at present worn, and, placed alongside [Benjamin] West's *Death of Wolfe*, enables us at a glance, by looking at the warriors there, to note several of the changes which the Europeans have brought in the Indians. M. Thielcke's picture is valuable, both as a work of art and history. It is a graphic memorial of changes already effected in an interesting people who are passing away.

In March 1842, the lithograph done after Thielcke's painting was put up for sale in Quebec City, printed in monochrome at $2.50 apiece, and in polychrome at $5.00 (Fig. 220A). The popularity of the engravings seems to have contributed greatly to the renown of the original painting. When it was exhibited at Quebec City's Exposition industrielle in 1853, *Le Journal de Québec* pointed out that it had already been exhibited several times, which did not prevent the canvas from being awarded first prize in the painting category.[4] Thielcke thus beat out his eternal rival Plamondon, who was represented by three copies and who merited second prize. The easily offended Antoine was undoubtedly vexed at this, for he informed the editor of *Le Journal de Québec* that his canvases had been exhibited by a friend without his consent and that if he had had the time he

would have exhibited an original! We do not know what became of Thielcke's painting until it was acquired by the Château Ramezay in 1913.[5]

At first glance, it is obvious that the canvas painted in 1840 does not correspond exactly to the honourary ceremony of February 21, 1838, during which Robert Symes received the name Hotsawati. The ceremony actually took place in the home of Chief Nicholas Vincent, where the affluence was so extreme as to be almost suffocating. In Thielcke's version, the crowd is portrayed outdoors, and in springtime to boot; however, the foreground does showcase Symes and the four main chiefs of the tribe identified in the *Mercury* account. The Indians are all wearing top hats and, like Symes, sport navy blue overcoats with red epaulettes and cuffs, a sash, and various ornaments, such as medals, gorgets, armlets and silver bracelets. The mass of humanity in the foreground is made up of some fifteen people, behind whom is sketched a shapeless crowd half-hidden by the smoke from a volley of gunfire. Through this bluish-white haze can be made out the rounded peaks of high mountains which dominate a late-afternoon sky in tones of yellow, grey and blue. Despite the symmetrical positioning of the five main figures, the composition displays certain quirks, such as the shadow mark in the foreground and the three tall conifers in the middle ground. The dark green of these trees contrasts sharply with the brilliance of the many red surfaces and brush strokes that accentuate the human mass of the canvas.

It is now possible for us to identify each of the subjects in this group portrait, thanks to an explanatory sketch on the back of a copy of the 1841 lithograph at the Musée du Québec (Fig. 220B), and to this description which dates from 1900:[6]

Beginning at the right of the canvas, the first model which meets the eye is that of an Indian maid, whose Huron name means "she who stirs up the water." The head in half-tones in the background is that of Paul Zacharie Hôtesse [Otis], whose Huron name means "he who passes over the housetops." His rank is that of warrior chief of the Turtle company; he is the son of a council chief and acts as interpreter of the Iroquois language. Next, our gaze falls on the full-length portrait of the grand chief Nicolas Vincent Tsasenhohi, "the Vulture." His uncle, José Vincent, was grand chief until his death, after which his nephew took over his position after having been elected by the Six Nations, who alone can grant this distinction. The council chiefs are elected by tribe councillors who possess this inherent right, and the warriors choose their chief from among those

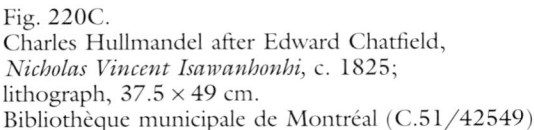

Fig. 220C.
Charles Hullmandel after Edward Chatfield,
Nicholas Vincent Isawanhonhi, c. 1825;
lithograph, 37.5 × 49 cm.
Bibliothèque municipale de Montréal (C.51/42549).

Fig. 220D.
Charles Hullmandel
After Edward Chatfield,
Michel Tsioui, Teacheandale. Chief of the Warriors.
Stanislas Coska, Aharathaha.
Second Chief of the Council. Andre Romain, Tsouhahissen.
Chief of the Council, 1825;
lithograh, 48.2 × 40.4 cm.
Musée du Québec, Quebec City (58.542).

of the company and present him to the council for approval. The grand chief belongs to the Deer company.

Next comes a young warrior chief. His name is François-Xavier Picard Tahourenché, which means "morning dawn." He is from the Wolf company. In front of him stands André Romain Tsohahisen, "he who is close to the road." He is the first council chief and belongs to the Deer company. The head behind the central figure, immediately to the left of André Romain, is that of Paul Picard. He is highly respected by all those who know him. His Huron name is Ohdasanonk, or "he has the river in his mouth." He is married to the sister of the grand chief and his father was council chief. He belongs to the Deer company. Stanislas Kostka, second council chief, is next. His Huron

name, Ahrathenha, means "he who quickly climbed a hill." His father was grand chief. He belongs to the Bear company and is the medicine man of the tribe.

The young Indian wearing a headdress he made himself appears in the painting as the type of Huron whose blood has not been mixed with that of the white man. The artist insisted on this portrayal as a historical reminder of the race. The name of this person is Zacharie Vincent Tehariolin, which means "undivided" or "unmixed." He belongs to the Turtle company. The full-length portrait which comes next is that of Michel Sioui. His Indian name, Théachiendalé, means "he who has two names." He is the third council chief and belongs to the Turtle company. He is depicted introducing a young Indian to whom he is showing, as

a model designed to foster his emulation, a newly elected chief. The figure appearing immediately to the left of Michel Sioui is that of Laurent Picard, whose expressive Huron name is Atedjaka, which means "perfect warrior." He is from the Deer company and, like his brother Paul, is the son of a council chief. In front of him stands Christine Vincent, daughter of the grand chief, whose Huron name Athianonk means "she who cares for the water source." She belongs to the Wolf company. Françoise Bastien, widow of Basile and Laurent Picard, has no Huron name, but belongs to the Deer company. She is leaning forward to draw her child's attention to the portrait's central figure. Little Marguerite's expression conveys both surprise shyness. (*Translation*)

Despite the undeniable appeal of its rich iconographical content, Thielcke's canvas also bears witness to the difficulties he encountered in portraying his many models full-length. The result is a number of pictorial shortcomings, ranging from flaws in scale, to his awkward way of suggesting the sequence of the planes, to the laborious integration of the scene's five protagonists. Thus, the chief Nicolas Vincent, who was responsible for "presenting" Symes, resembles a clown or articulated dummy with his dangling legs and the strange stiffness of his right arm. And what about the drawing of the arms of chief Stanislas Kostka, who is leaning curiously on the barrel of a gun? What about the excessively small feet of his counterpart Sioui, or Zacharie Vincent's head, which seems to be floating on the shoulder of his neighbour? The artist fared much better in the sensitive, spontaneous rendering of the canvas' secondary figures.

These obvious flaws can be explained by the very nature of Symes' commission to Thielcke, which was that of a commemorative work to be reconstituted after the fact rather than the portrayal of a specific event witnessed by the artist. In this context, it is easy to imagine Thielcke seeking a practical way to respond to what must have been, for him, an unprecedented artistic challenge. He did so by laboriously borrowing and recycling figures from two lithographs printed in London in 1825 by Charles Hullmandel after canvases by English artist Edward Chatfield (1802-1839). The first engraving depicted the chief Nicholas Vincent Isawanhonhi (Fig. 220C), while the second portrayed the Huron chiefs Michel Tsioui, Stanislas Coska and André Romain (Fig. 220D). In 1824, these three Hurons had accompanied the grand chief Nicolas Vincent to England where they were to be introduced to King George IV (Cat. 160) on April 7 of the following year. The two engravings in question were clearly Thielcke's saving grace.[7] Following Légaré's example, he tried to use them to the best of their advantage, extracting, adapting, transforming and retouching the faces, clothing and poses of the Amerindian chiefs. Given the length of this entry, we will leave it up to others to analyze in detail this laborious borrowing process, which is an essential element in the composition studied. For now, we will limit ourselves to observing that although the four chiefs in the 1825 version reappeared in the 1840 canvas, one of them, André Romain, must have, through the magic of Thielcke's brush, sacrificed his body to the new chief Hotsawati, alias Robert Symes!

To conclude on a more serious note, the many messages conveyed by ***Presentation of a Newly Elected Chief of the Huron Tribal Council of Lorette*** should be emphasized. In addition to its picturesque and anecdotal nature, the composition is significant for the way it was interpreted during the era, the cultural context it conjured up, the Amerindian image it conveyed, and the pictorial practices it reflects. Not only is it an interesting specimen of colonial art which was well received and widely disseminated, but it is also a history painting lending itself to an anthropological and ideological interpretation as well as a historical and stylistic one. Thielcke's group portrait thus rounds out, in its own way, the unique image of Zacharie Vincent that Plamondon had captured in 1838 (Cat. 194), just as it heralds, by the relative newness of its composition, a formula Québec photographers began to use some fifteen years later.

J.R.P.

Notes

1. In the biography of merchant George Burns Symes (1803-1863), Brian J. Young paints the following portrait of George's brother Robert: "[He] was also active in Quebec City social life. Member of the Société d'horticulture de Québec and payroll clerk for the 6th battalion of the Quebec City militia, he was a lifelong member of the Literary and Historical Society of Quebec, then a founding member of the Association de la salle de tempérance de Québec, and the first treasurer for the Société St. George, founded in 1835 to provide aid to English and Scottish immigrants to encourage them to 'venerate the soil of their ancestors.'" See DCB, Vol. IX (1977). Outgoing councillor for the du Palais quarter, artist Joseph Légaré defeated Symes in the 1835 municipal elections (PORTER 1981, pp. 94 and 101).

2. PORTER 1981, pp. 147-149.

3. See for example the July 28, 1838 and June 17, 1848 editions of *Le Fantasque*.

4. The jury of section D (fine arts) was composed of "J. Carter, W.D. Campbell, H. Gibsone, Capt. Hamilton, T. Hamel, Jos. Légaré, W.S. Sewell, and Thilckie" (*Le Journal de Québec*, June 18, 1853, p. 2). See also the *Quebec Mercury*, June 9, 1853, p. 2. This article states that the works that won first and second prize were sent to the World Fair in New York. We were unable to determine whether or not Thielcke's painting was among them.

5. The records of the Numismatic and Antiquarian Society board state only that the canvas was acquired "at the Museum sale."

6. Like the article published in the *Quebec Mercury* on September 5, 1840, the remark from a London daily which appeared in part in the same newspaper on November 11, 1841 referred to this explanatory note, even quoting some Amerindian names accompanied by their translation. Despite our research, we have not been able to retrace an original copy of the text translated by Lindsay.

7. The artist's use of engravings was not, however, exceptional. He appears to have used them for his 1835 *Baptism of Christ* and, of course, for the *Death of Wolfe*, for which he won a prize from the Literary and Historical Society of Quebec in 1839 (information from David Karel).

ROBERT CLOW
TODD

(?)1809-1866

Robert C. Todd is believed to have been born in 1809 at Berwick-upon-Tweed in northern England near the Scottish border. Before immigrating to Canada at the age of twenty-five, he apparently practised decorative painting in Edinburgh. In 1834, he settled in the Quebec City region, but little is known about his first years of activity in the new country. In the early 1840s, he published advertisements for the opening of an "evening school," hoping, "through his selected collection of models and his approved teaching methods [...] to merit some public encouragement." (*Translation*) In fall 1843, he gave private classes to young men and women, and apparently took Antoine-Sébastien Falardeau as apprentice in 1841. From spring 1845 to 1847, he advertised his services as a sign painter, while also producing easel paintings, especially for his English-speaking clientele.

In 1853, he decided to leave Quebec City for Toronto. In April, before his departure, he announced a sale by lottery of 25 canvases, several of which had been painted after European works. Despite Toronto's booming growth, the city was still too young to have developed an artistic tradition significant enough to allow artists to earn a living doing decorative work, as Clow Todd himself pointed out. Despite this, he remained there for almost thirteen years, until his death May 7, 1866. Although he advertised himself as a "painter of banners, blazons, signs and ornamental works" (*Translation*) while in Toronto, we know little about his production during this period.

Main sources
Harper 1970, Harper 1977/2.

judging from the model's age and costume.[2]

The portrait of Narcisse Belleau is believed to be one of the first works done by British-born Robert Clow Todd, who at the time (circa 1834) had recently arrived in Quebec City, where he offered his services painting signs, carriage emblems and decorative works. This small canvas is, to date, the only known portrait by the artist, primarily reputed for his landscapes and genre scenes, especially his many versions of the *Ice Cone, Montmorency Falls, Quebec* (Cat. 225).[3] The very realistic portrait of Belleau shows a highly personalized handling: the clothing and hair are sketched in rapidly, while the facial features are painted with great refinement. The meticulous brush strokes, thin and smooth, reflect Todd's specialty as a decorative painter, and call to mind the artist's eye for detail in his other types of works. Furthermore, the luminosity and transparency of the flesh tones recall the technique of a number of contemporary miniaturists. In fact, the size and style of the work are closer to the intimate art of the miniature than to the large official portraits of the era. We know of two later portraits of Belleau which fall into the latter category. Both painted by Théophile Hamel, they portray the model carrying out his official duties as mayor of Quebec City between 1850 and 1853 (Cat. 137), and as president of the Legislative Council of Canada, from 1857 to 1862 (House of Commons, Ottawa).

M.B.

221.
Narcisse-Fortunat Belleau, c. 1835
Oil on panel, 28.1 × 22.6 cm

Inscription
(s., l.r.) *R.C. Todd.*

Provenance
Descendants of the Belleau family; Antoinette Belleau, Quebec City; acquired by the Musée du Québec, Quebec City, 1977.

Exhibition
Quebec City 1983-1984, No. 60.

Bibliography
LE MUSÉE DU QUÉBEC 1983, p. 64, No. 60 (entry by Claude Thibault, Luc Noppen and Michel Doyon) (Repr.); BÉLAND 1987, p. 66; BÉLAND AND BOURASSA 1990, pp. 6, 9 and 52 (Repr.).

Collection
Musée du Québec, Quebec City. Restored in 1991, with the assistance of the Amis du Musée du Québec (77.39)

THIS SMALL PORTRAIT depicts Narcisse-Fortunat Belleau (1808-1894). Following his classical studies at the Petit Séminaire de Québec, Narcisse Belleau began training as a lawyer's clerk in 1827 until he was called to the bar on September 26, 1832. Financially comfortable, Belleau married Marie-Reine-Josephte Gauvreau on September 15, 1835.[1] In keeping with a common practice of the times, the young man's portrait may have been done on the occasion of his wedding. A miniature on ivory portraying his wife, acquired by the Musée du Québec in 1987, likely dates from the same time,

Notes
1. Michèle Brassard and Jean Hamelin, DCB, Vol. XII (1990).
2. See *BÉLAND 1987*, p. 66.
3. We should also mention another canvas portraying a bearded figure, crowned with mistletoe, carrying a log on his back and holding a stick and bowl, who could represent Santa Claus or the "old year." This oil on board was acquired in 1987 by the Robert McLaughlin Gallery (Oshawa, Ontario). When selling his collection in 1853, the artist called one of his works "Christmas with his log", (*Translation*) which may be this work (*Le Canadien*, April 4, 1853).

222. (See colour reproduction, p. 97)
The Timber and Shipbuilding Yards of Allan Gilmour and Company at Wolfe's Cove, Viewed from the West, 1840
Oil on canvas, 76.4 × 121.8 cm

Inscriptions
(s.d., l.l, on one of the casks) *R.C. Todd/1840;*
(b.,c., on the frame on a typed label) *Timber Yards, Pollok, Gilmour and Company/Wolfe's Cove St. Lawrence River, Quebec.*

Provenance
Commissioned by Allan Gilmour, Quebec City; Descendants of the Gilmour family, Liverpool;

Sir John Gilmour, Liverpool, before 1966 (sold by Sotheby's, London, October 22, 1986, No. 46); Richard Green, London, 1986; acquired by the National Gallery of Canada, Ottawa, 1987.

Bibliography
HARPER *1966*, pp. 126 and 127 (Repr.); LORD *1974*, p. 45 (Repr.); HARPER *1977*, p. 874 COMEAU *1983*, p. 244; *Sotheby's Preview*, No. 65 (September-October 1986), p. 3 (Repr.); *Sotheby's Art at Auction 1985-87,* pp. 46-47 (Repr.); TOPOGRAPHICAL PAINTINGS *1986*, No. 46 (Repr.); KRAMER *1987*, p. 55 (Repr.); ACQUISITIONS *1988*, p. 214, No. 234 (Repr.); LA CHRONIQUE *1988*, p. 23, No. 128 (Repr.); VILLENEUVE *1991*, p. 50.

Collection
National Gallery of Canada, Ottawa (29696)

T HESE ARE THE FIRST of four canvases Robert Todd is known to have painted on commission from the Scottish-born timber merchant and shipping magnate Allan Gilmour (1805-1884). It is clear from their related themes and virtually identical physical formats that they were conceived as pendant pieces. As iconographic and formal extensions of one another, they are best understood and appreciated together, yet stand equally well as unique and compelling images on their own. They are the earliest and most accomplished extant view paintings by Todd, an artist previously best known for his pictures of Montmorency Falls in winter,

notably *The Ice Cone, Montmorency Falls* (National Gallery of Canada), circa 1845.

Anse au Foulon (Wolfe's Cove), a place of strategic military importance in the mid-18th century, was in the 19th century the principal site of the timber pound and shipbuilding yard of Allan Gilmour & Company, a Quebec branch of the Glasgow-based firm Pollok, Gilmour and Company. Between 1812 and 1835, the Scottish parent company, founded in 1804 by brothers John and Arthur Pollok and Allan Gilmour Sr. (1775-1849), opened six independently managed Canadian branch offices located respectively in Miramichi, Saint-John, Restigouche and

Bathurst (New Brunswick), Montreal and Quebec City. The Quebec City office, established in 1828, was headed by Allan Gilmour Sr.'s nephew and namesake. It was on the recommendation of the younger Allan Gilmour that company operations began at Anse au Foulon in July 1828.[1]

During the 1830s and 1840s, the Gilmour firm enjoyed an unequalled period of expansion and prosperity, reflecting the importance and rapid growth of the North American timber trade in the early 19th century. Quebec, an administrative, social and religious centre, was by 1830 also the hub of the transatlantic trade in

223.
The Timber and Shipbuilding Yards of Allan Gilmour and Company at Wolfe's Cove, Viewed from the South, 1840
Oil on canvas, 76 × 122.3 cm

Inscriptions
(s.d., l.l., on one of the planks of the raft)
R.C. Todd 1840; (b.,l.c., on the frame, on a typed
label) [...] *Yards, Pollok, Gilmour and Company/*
[...] *St. Lawrence River, Quebec.*

Provenance
Commissioned by Allan Gilmour, Quebec City;
Descendants of the Gilmour family, Liverpool;
Sir John Gilmour, Liverpool, before 1966 (sold
by Sotheby's, London, October 22, 1986,
No. 47); Richard Green, London, 1986; acquired
by the National Gallery of Canada, Ottawa, 1987.

Bibliography
HARPER 1977, p. 874; COMEAU 1983, p. 244;
Sotheby's Preview, No. 65 (September-October
1986), p. 3; TOPOGRAPHICAL PAINTINGS 1986,
No. 47 (Repr.); KRAMER 1987, p. 55; ACQUISITIONS
1988, p. 214, No. 234; VILLENEUVE 1991, p. 50.

Collection
National Gallery of Canada, Ottawa (29695)

Canadian timber products. Of the series
of sheltered coves ranging east from Sillery
to Cap Rouge equipped to receive, square,
store and ship timber brought down from
the Gatineau to Quebec as rafts, Anse au
Foulon was the most important. Larger
than neighbouring sites and the last to
freeze, Anse au Foulon provided the most
spacious base of operation with an extended shipping season that gave Allan
Gilmour & Company a crucial competitive
edge. By 1835, the company employed
some 150 men and, under Allan Gilmour's
direct supervision had begun constructing
ships at Anse au Foulon to carry company
goods, principally square timbers, overseas.

The total number of vessels built and
owned by the firm is said to have peaked
at as many as 130 by 1839, reportedly the
largest merchant fleet in the United
Kingdom.[2]

Gilmour's desire for pictures of
Anse au Foulon can be linked to his recall
to Scotland in late 1838 to replace his
retired uncle as a full partner in Pollok,
Gilmour & Company and to take over as
manager of the Glasgow head office. Apart
from occasional business trips to Canada,
Gilmour thereafter permanently resided
in Glasgow with his Canadian wife and
children, his brother John having taken
over the Quebec office. It seems only

natural that he would wish to visually document the prosperous business he had almost single-handed built, the resultant
paintings serving at once as personnal souvenirs of his Quebec years and testimony
to a major business success.

Robert Clow Todd's credentials,
published in the *Quebec Gazette* in 1834,
as a former employee to "many of the first
nobility and gentry in London and Edinburgh," albeit as a "house, sign, carriage
and ornamental painter," was a probable
factor in his winning this obviously important commission from a leading member of the close-knit Scottish-Canadian
community in Quebec.[3] While advertising

Fig. 222-223A.
James Pattison
Cockburn,
*Cape Diamond seen
from Spencer Wood,*
1830;
Sepia over graphite on
paper, 15.4 × 22.6 cm.
Musée du Québec,
Quebec City (53.61).

Fig. 222-223B.
H. Adlard After
William H. Bartlett,
*Timber Depot near
Quebec,* 1840;
engraving,
22.8 × 29.2 cm (plate)
National Gallery of
Canada, Ottawa
(18017.13).

as an ornamental painter, it is evident from the small oil-on-panel *Narcisse-Fortunat Belleau* (Cat.221), dated circa 1835, that Todd was also active as an easel painter from at least his arrival in Quebec City in 1834. His early competence as a portrait and view painter, if not demonstrable through other extant paintings before 1840, may be surmised from Gilmour's confidence in hiring him and the quality of these two views of Anse au Foulon proudly brougth back to Glasgow and kept in the Gilmour family until recent years.

In keeping with his patron's documentary interests, Robert Todd's panoramic views of Wolfe's Cove record with factual accuracy and linear precision the sprawling Gilmour enterprise as seen respectively from the west and the south. The double rendering not only provides a fuller understanding of the contemporary appearance and spatial layout of the subject, but serves more particulary to highlight the dual nature of the Gilmour Company's commercial operations at this location. In *The Timber and Shipbuilding Yards of Allan Gilmour and Company at Wolfe's Cove, Viewed from the West,* the focus is on the company's land-based operations. It shows from ground level the timber storage pound stretching across the cove, the shipbuilding facility in the middle distance featuring a timber ship in drydock for repairs and the hull of another under construction, and backing this the row of worker's homes and company administrative offices lining Chemin de Foulon at the foot of the cliffs. On the other hand, *The Timber and Shipbuilding Yards of Allan Gilmour and Company at Wolfe's Cove, Viewed from the South,* highlights the company's related water-based activities. Viewed from shipboard, we are provided here with a more detailed to and from the site. A close-up of a timber raft

of the kind floated down from the Gatineau neatly balances the unusual perspective study of a timber ship on the near right. It was at Wolfe's Cove that such rafts were disassembled, their individual timber components then stored in the timber pound portrayed in the companion view for processing and, ultimately, shipment overseas.

These are the most accomplished paintings Todd is known to have produced. They demonstrate a level of technical expertise and formal sophistication seemingly beyond the abilities of a decorative artist, as Todd described himself and as he has been historically viewed. The visual dialogue between the tow compositions reflects the careful forethought and knowledge involved in their conception. Working within an established tradition of British topographical painting, Todd evidently undertook a close, empiric study of his complex subject. His choice of a low vatange point in both pictures is in marked contrast to the high prospects preferred in earlier on-the-spot views of Wolfe's Cove by James Pattison Cockburn (1779-1847) (Fig.222-223A) and William Bartlett (1809-1854), the latter published in 1842 as an engraving (Fig.222-223B). Positioned below the cliffs, Todd depicts Wolfe's Cove in more direct terms, with less emphasis on the site's picturesque qualities. To capture the whole of this expansive locale from a low level, the perspective treatment is perforce much sharper. In *View from the West,* forms rapidly recede to the horizon along well-defined diagonal lines; in *View from the South,* they recede in foreshortened planes.

While concerned with optical truth, Todd reveals a conceptual bias in his finished canvases, where external reality is ordered in accordance with tenets of good design. The attention to pictorial design

and propensity to organize and render forms in a mathematically measured, linear and closed manner may be traced to Todd's formative experiences as an ornamental painter of signs, carriages and heraldic devices.[4] These formal traits, characteristic of decorative and folk art, are also common to a school of British marine painting developed in the 18th century by Samuel Scott under the direct influence of the Italian topographical view painter Canaletto. Todd's paintings recall the work of Scott and his artistic heirs, notably the British-American marine painters Robert Salmon (or Salomon, 1775—circa 1843) and William James Bennet, in their strong draughtsmanship, simplified, volumetric forms and steady, clear light and colour. Such details as the titled dory and workmen on dockside in *View from the West* were among standard compositional elements in British marine painting. How direct Todd's contact was with the work of these painters cannot be ascertained, although it is tempting to think that he was aware of Salmon and Bennet, both popular painters active in Boston and area in the 1830s. At the least, the affinities between their work suggest a similar mix of influences from contemporary English and Scottish painting and personal experiences as a decorative painter.

V.B.

Notes

1.John Rankin, *A History of Our Firm,* (Liverpool: Henry Young & Sons, Limited, 1921), pp. 20-23, 90-100; David S. MacMillan, DCB, Vol.XI, (1982), p.382-384.

2.John Rankin, *op.cit.,* p.212; Cowdney C.J. Bond, DCB, Vol. X (1982), p.349.

3.*Quebec Gazette,* January 8, 1834, p .2.

4.*Quebec Gazette,* January 8, 1834, p. 2.

224.
"Corbeau", A Trotting Horse, 1845
Oil on canvas, 51.5 × 64.5 cm

Inscriptions
(s., l.r.) *R.C. Todd. del.;* (d., l.l., on the rock) *CORBEAU./1845;* (b.,l.c., on the frame on a label) *Doig & McKechnie/Picture Restorers, Printsellers/ & Publishers/90 George Street/Edinburgh;* (b.,u.c., on the frame) *CORBEAU/Property of Allan Gilmour, Esq. of/Quebec/and Montrane - Winner of/trotting races Quebec. Subsequently sold to John Pollok, Lismany, Ireland. Where he was used for breeding.*

Provenance
Commissioned by Allan Gilmour, Quebec City; Descendants of the Gilmour family; Sir John Gilmour, Liverpool, before 1962 (sold by Sotheby's, London, November 4, 1987, No. 56); acquired by the National Gallery of Canada, Ottawa, 1987.

Bibliography
HARPER *1962/3,* p. 418 and 419 (Repr.) entitled *The Horse (Corbeau);* HARPER *1966,* p. 129; TOPOGRAPHICAL PAINTINGS *1987,* No. 56 (Repr.); REID *1988/1,* p. 16; VILLENEUVE *1991,* pp. 49 and 50 (Repr.).

Collection
National Gallery of Canada, Ottawa (29783)

A FTER THE PENDANT VIEWS of the Allan Gilmour & Company timber storage ground and shipbuilding yards at Wolfe's Cove, Quebec (Cat. 222 and 223), Allan Gilmour commissioned Robert Todd in 1845 to portray his prize-winning horse Corbeau.[1] During the nearly twenty years the artist resided in Quebec City, he developed a reputation among local breeders for this paintings of prized animals. Gilmour's decision to entrust Todd with portraying yet another of his valued possessions reflects his appreciation for the artist's painterly skills.

Todd produced two paintings in response to Gilmour's commission: this profile view of Corbeau in a verdant

Fig. 224A.
Robert Clow Todd, *"Corbeau" at Montmorency Falls*, 1845; oil on canvas, 53.3 × 66.6 cm.
Private collection, Toronto.

summer landscape along the shores of the St. Lawrence River and another portraying Corbeau in a winter setting (PC, Toronto) (Fig. 224A).[2] Both feature the horse outdoors in the environs of Quebec City, but whereas the painting of Corbeau pulling a sleigh below the frozen Montmorency Falls was conceived in the manner of popular English sporting pictures of the day, the canvas *Corbeau, A Trotting Horse* emulates an equestrian portrait type developed and perfected in British artistic circles in the 18th century. Horse-racing was a popular sport in 19th-century Quebec; indeed, it was probably the most common form of outdoor amusement from the time British immigrants first settled in Quebec. As early as 1789, the Quebec Turf Club had been organized with races held on the Plains of Abraham. The presence of the British military garrisons evidently had an influence on the popularity of equestrian events in British North America. As in England, Canadians and Americans were enthusiastic about the possession of fine horses and racetrack activities.[3] Allan Gilmour, a Scottish immigrant whose Quebec business empire had made him a wealthy

man, not surprisingly was a passionate horse lover and owner. With the trotting horse Corbeau, he enjoyed the thrill of many racing victories. It may have been in commemoration of one particularly memorable match, held on March 19, 1845 in Laprairie, Quebec, that Gilmour commissioned Robert Todd to paint the portrait of Corbeau.

A contemporary description of the race in the *Montreal Gazette* reveals the importance and pride attached to Corbeau's win.

Yesterday the grand trotting match came off on the ice at Laprairie, between the American horse, *Dread*, and the Canadian horse, *Corbeau*. From the high reputation formerly enjoyed by *Dread*, the greatest excitement prevailed on the course, and large sums were freely offered upon his head. Both horses came to scratch in gallant style, and both heats were won by *Corbeau* with the greatest ease. The faces of the knowing ones fell several degrees upon the termination of the race—such trotting as was displayed by the latter had not been seen on the ice for many a day. For a Canadian Poney (sic) to beat the fastest horse in British North America, is certainly something to boast of, and the owner of *Dread* will be "dreadfully" afraid to challenge British North

America with the same horse again. Time: one mile, lst heat 2 min. 45 sec. Do. Do. 2nd do. 2 min. 39 sec.[4]

When his racing days were over, Corbeau was sold for breeding to John Pollok, senior partner of Gilmour and Company, and spent his remaining life on the sprawling Irish estate of Lismany that Pollok purchased in 1853.

The compositional affinities between this equine portrait and any number of contemporary British examples reveal Todd's familiarity with equestrian painting probably based on direct study during his formative years in London and Edinburgh as well as through popular prints after the work of fashionable British horse painters. True to type, Corbeau is depicted in full profile view displayed in an open panoramic landscape. As an individual touch in the lower left foreground, a large rock, enveloped in a decorative spray of local vegetation, is inscribed "Corbeau 1845" (a similar inscription is found on a foreground block of ice in *"Corbeau" at Montmorency Falls*). This artificial pictorial device, which recalls Todd's work as a decorative artist, contrasts formally with the naturalistic rendering of Corbeau and surrounding landscape.

Like the 1840 views of Wolfe's Cove, with which it bears a significant historical relationship, this painting is a rare and particularly fine example of Robert Todd's later work as an easel painter. It displays a similar degree of formal sophistication suggesting an awareness of mainstream artistic developments and forcing a re-evaluation of Todd as primarily a decorative painter. Clearly, when working closely from a living model, he could rise above the limits of a non-academic training to produce pictures notable for their naturalism. This depiction of Corbeau is all the more remarkable for being the earliest extant equestrian portrait canvas in the history of Canadian art. It predates Cornelius Kreighoff's canvas *"Fraser" with Mr. Miller, Up* (NGC) painted for the Quebec breeder Mr. Kirwan in 1854, within months of Todd's permanent departure for Toronto.

V.B.

Notes

1. NAC, J. Russell Harper Papers, Letter from Sir John Gilmour to J. Russell, June 18, 1962.
2. *Ibid.*
3. Nancy Howell and Maxwell L. Howell, *Sports and Games in Canadian Life: 1700 to the Present* (Toronto: Macmillan of Canada, 1969), pp. 19-20.
4. "The Trotting Match," *The Gazette* (Montreal), March 20, 1845, p. 2.

225.
The Ice Cone, Montmorency Falls, c. 1840-1850
Oil on canvas, 51.2 × 68.1 cm

Inscription
(s., l.r.) *R.C. Todd del.*

Provenance
Henry Strachey, London; acquired by the Art Gallery of Ontario, Toronto, 1987.

Exhibition
Toronto 1990.

Bibliography
BLODGETT *1990*, pp. 73 and 76 (Repr.); MUSÉE *1990*, p. 238 (Repr.).

Collection
Art Gallery of Ontario, Toronto. Purchased with the assistance of the Government of Canada under the Cultural Property Export and Import Act (87.94)

T HE ICE CONE which forms in winter at the foot of Montmorency Falls became, early on, a major attraction on the outskirts of Quebec City. As of 1785, it appeared in the series of aquatints James Peachey had engraved in London[1], and was portrayed regularly throughout the 19th century.

James Pattison Cockburn, for example, depicted it spectacularly in the aquatint he had published in 1833.[2] By viewing it from a different angle, he was one of the few watercolourists to disregard its decorative, somewhat stereotyped character, portraying instead the way this imposing mass is formed. Author Joseph Bouchette pointed out the geological phenomenon represented by these falls "nearly 250 ft. high, being 100 ft. higher than the Falls of Niagara."[3] The same year, in 1832, he recopied in *The British Dominions of North America* a passage from the conference given by William Green before the members of the Literary and Historical Society of Quebec:

When the river St. Lawrence is frozen below the Falls, the level ice becomes a support, on which the freezing spray descends as sleet; it there remains, and gradually enlarges its base and its height, assuming an irregularly conical form; its dimensions thus continually enlarg-ing, become towards the close of the winter, stupendous; [...] The face of the cone next the Fall presents a stalactitical structure, not apparent elsewhere, and there occasioned by the dashing of water against it, which, freezing in its descent, assumes the form which characterizes it under such circumstances. The whole cone is slightly, yet very perceptibly, tinged with an earthly hue, which it can only have derived from infinitely comminuted portions of the bed of the Montmorenci, attracted by the torrent, and conveyed into the atmosphere with the spray.[4]

Robert Clow Todd was a bit of an outsider with regard to this landscape tradition, whether purely topographical or imbued with a more complex feeling for nature. His falls were first and foremost a backdrop for his characters. Although the work at the Art Gallery of Ontario (AGO) is the best example, the same link can be seen between the groups of people and the grandiose background in many similar works. Several paintings have been attributed to Todd, and this is part of the problem; since no other artists could be recognized in the countless portrayals of Montmorency Falls in winter, they were all attributed to him. Analysis of this series of paintings was called for in order to correctly attribute the works.

We know of nine such paintings, either directly or through photographs. First, the work entitled *"Corbeau" at Montmorency Falls* (Fig. 224A) must be ranked with the AGO painting. These are the only two canvases in which the hand of the artist can be identified unmistakably. The Power Corporation version (Fig. 225A) also belongs to this first group and resembles the AGO work, to the extent that we are tempted to consider the latter a copy with minor variations. The work entitled *The Ice Cone, Montmorency Falls, Quebec* at the National Gallery of Canada[5] poses some problems of attribution. Although elements in this painting resemble those in preceding works, especially the portrayal of the trees, it is surprising to note the bareness of the foreground, the rigid distribution of the groups of people to mark the planes, and the location of the shadow marks. The case of the Winnipeg painting[6] is less mysterious. Although it is a less successful version of *"Corbeau" at Montmorency Falls*, we must discount Robert Clow Todd as author: the wooden surface, the elongated hill at the right, the pile of ice blocks depicted as an overly evident foil, and the relaxed handling point to another style. Four versions of the

Fig. 225A.
Robert Clow Todd,
The Ice Cone, Montmorency Falls,
c. 1840-1850;
oil on canvas, 45.4 × 61.2 cm.
Power Corporation of Canada/
Power Corporation du Canada, Montreal (225).

The copy of the address [...] was printed on white satin, in a very handsome manner, at the Literary Transcript Office in this city. On the reverse was a splendid representation of the Arms of the Earl and Countess of Durham, on purple satin, from the attelier of Mr Todd, whose talents in Herald painting are well known to be of a very superior order?[11]

Is this mention of an "attelier" merely referring to Todd's place of work, or does it imply a professional structure of which we are currently unaware? Along the same lines, how much credibility should be granted Georges Bellerive when he affirms that Antoine Sébastien Falardeau:

started with Mr. Todd as a sign painter where he finally began to develop his artistic talent. He remained there two years, becoming so skilful that his master was highly gratified, and proudly showed his work to his friends. (*Translation*)[12]

Although we possess few indications, *The Ice Cone, Montmorency Falls, Quebec* is an important piece in the puzzle. In the foreground we see a pair of horses at rest, the first of which is held by a groom. A figure is seated in the sled astride a lion's head, while the pelt of a black bear is carelessly tossed over the back seat. There are a number of foils in the immediate foreground: ice blocks with jagged edges, a pine branch, and two children with a sled. Several secondary groups can be seen in the intermediate planes: a pair of horses in full gallop, on the left, is the only dynamic movement in the entire composition; on the right, half hidden by the main pair of horses, a team at rest, its sled laden with fox pelts, patiently awaits the return of its owner. Three admirers, in the centre of the painting, direct our gaze toward the ice cone. A cursory glance immediately reveals the lack of coherence between the main subject and the rest of the composition: the horses and the sled with the lion's head seem to have been added merely to fill the empty space in the foreground. This oddity was explained in the restoration report. When it was acquired in 1987, the canvas bore a long slash stretching from the ice block in the foreground to the belly of the horse, near the sled. Close study showed that this entire group covered a layer of paint, thereby proving that the work had been done in two relatively close stages. The landscape appears to have been painted first; the artist added the figures later on.

A working method of this kind leaves little room for conjecture. It indicates that Todd must have had in his studio one or more models which he submitted to his client for approval. Once an agreement was reached on the basic composition, the painter adjusted the content to the client's demands, painting a portrait onto the landscape. He then rounded out the whole with the motifs agreed upon, horse-drawn sleds and people out for a stroll.[13] The painting in the Power Corporation collection (Fig. 225A) was perhaps one of these reference compositions. It is not a coincidence that this work contains all the elements of the Toronto version: the outline of the background and the foils at the right; the same team of horses with the groom clearly obvious in the centre; the sled with the fox furs which echoes the group at rest on the left and marks the middle ground on the right; the three admirers in the centre and the minuscule sled in the background. Surprisingly, the main sled is empty, as if put there merely as a reference point in the composition. The groom and the horses are also almost identical in the two cases. The poor quality of the original drawing in the AGO painting bears out our theory of a repertory of motifs used for various purposes: the bodies of these horses are overly large in comparison to their short heads and exaggeratedly slim legs. Contrary to popular opinion, the flattened buttocks and the heads do not correspond to those of Arab thoroughbreds, but rather those of English thoroughbreds.[14] Furthermore, these horses have undergone an operation which consists of removing their buttocks, thereby reducing the length of their tail. This was a common practice at the time for parade horses.

In light of such an observation, the question can no longer be avoided: how can an experienced artist like Todd have painted both *Corbeau, A Trotting Horse* (Cat. 224) and this obviously flawed team of horses? Corbeau is a stallion in the truest sense of the word; in fact, Todd took special care to emphasize its attributes and convey the energy radiating from the animal. The horse is well proportioned and its muscles are powerful, albeit somewhat exaggerated around the neck. This is the result of close observation, and the final version can only be the result of countless drawings, done when the horse was in its stall in the stable. This indicates that Todd was familiar with horses and, with Corbeau, he reveals a genuine talent for drawing. In this area, it can be said that he masters his art better than did Krieghoff painting Fraser (Cat. 152). How, then, do we explain the difference between Corbeau and the pair of horses in the AGO work? There are two plausible theories. The first

subject remain: along with this canvas, formerly in a Toronto collection,[7] we must include that of the Musée d'art de Joliette[8] and the two works put up for sale on the art market in Montreal[9] and London.[10] All of these paintings seem to have borrowed their main subject—a pair of spirited horses drawing a sled—from the work belonging to the National Gallery of Canada. Given the few signed paintings and our lack of information on Robert Clow Todd, it is preferable to exclude them from his body of work. In light of the renewed demands of his English-speaking clientele who wished to conserve a souvenir of this renowned site, the painter probably inspired a number of imitators. Are the resulting works studio productions or out-and-out pastiches? Are we dealing with a single imitator, or were several artists responsible? It is currently impossible to resolve these questions. In fact, Todd's entire body of work requires in-depth analysis. What are we to think, for example, of the paragraph published in the November 3, 1838 edition of the *Quebec Mercury,* which gives the address offered by Quebec City printers to Lord Durham upon his departure:

is based on the existence of the studio which Todd seems to have had at his disposal. Perhaps he mandated an assistant to draw the horses, doing only the sled and the portrait of the client himself. This would explain the poor quality of the drawing, but also forces us to question the buyer's perspicacity. The second theory is based on the artist's years of training. When he advertised his services in 1842, Todd mentioned that he possessed a series of models for teaching purposes.[15] We can thus conclude that he brought with him to Quebec a number of drawings which he had previously used to execute commissions in England.[16] The visible shortcomings in the horses' anatomy could thus be due to Todd's having copied an earlier drawing—possibly even a work from his youth—at a time when he did not fully master the art of draughtsmanship. The portrayal of a double team of parade horses would thus explain why the owner accepted the work, associating the prestige of his own portrayal with that of a fine pair of horses. For it is obvious that the horses and sled were not originally part of the same painting, as evidenced by the blatant disproportion between the scale of the figure seated on the lionskin and the horses held by the groom. The officer, seated on the lionskin in the sled, probably posed in the studio for the artist, who then reworked the ensemble, painting in the team of horses and adding the shadow marks.[17] Although this is a polished work in many respects, it does not come close to the harmony of "*Corbeau*" *at Montmorency Falls*.

The date the work was painted remains to be determined. All the views of Montmorency Falls in winter attributed to Robert Clow Todd are invariably situated circa 1845, despite lack of evidence. Only the version of "*Corbeau*" *at Montmorency Falls* is actually dated 1845, leading us to believe that it served as a reference for the rest of the works. However, Todd arrived in Quebec City circa 1834 and stayed for some twenty years. Around 1835, he painted the portrait of Narcisse Belleau (Cat. 221); in 1840 he produced the two large landscapes which are now at the National Gallery of Canada (Cat. 222 and 223); and in 1850 he completed the antependium at the Musée du Séminaire de Québec (Cat. 226). So what are we to think? Given the talent for drawing which is apparent in these works, we can hardly confine the production of the Toronto work to the years immediately preceding and following 1845. Only the identity of

the officer seated in the sled might enable us to date the landscape with more accuracy, but research conducted at the Art Gallery of Ontario when the painting was acquired[18] and the working hypotheses advanced provide no clear answers.

For these reasons, we prefer to date the work within a ten-year period, between 1840 and 1850. Todd could have painted this *Ice Cone, Montmorency Falls, Quebec* as part of the double commission of the views of Allan Gilmour's shipyard in 1840. In the same way, the quality of "*Corbeau*" *at Montmorency Falls* may have resulted in greater demand on the part of the British after 1845. Finally, it must be recalled that in April 1853, when he contributed 25 canvases to a lottery, Todd included two views of Montmorency Falls, one painted in summer and one in winter.[19] This indicates that the subject was still popular. But at the time, Todd's imagery was probably outdated. Cornelius Krieghoff had portrayed the site in 1852 using another style, in a more ambitious composition which had nothing in common with the theatrical settings of the preceding decade.[20]

D.P.

Notes

1. *DE VOLPI 1971*, Pl. 30 (Repr.). It must be pointed out that Montmorency Falls warrant an exhibition all to themselves, to demonstrate their importance in the imagery of the late 18th century.
2. *DE VOLPI 1971*, Pl. 81 (Repr.).
3. *BOUCHETTE 1832*, entitled "Montmorenci river".
4. *BOUCHETTE 1832*, pp. 280-281.
5. *GODSELL 1976*, p. 67 (Repr.).
6. *Selected Works from the Winnipeg Art Gallery Collection* (Winnipeg: Winnipeg Art Gallery, 1971), p. 93 (Repr.).
7. *HARPER 1973*, Fig. 102. The canvas was put up for sale at Sotheby's in Toronto on May 31, 1988, lot 199. The signature and date "R.C.T. 1841" are highly unconvincing.
8. The canvas was sold at Jacoby's House of Antiques in Montreal during its sale held from October 21-23, 1970, lot 62 (Repr.). It was likely acquired by the Galerie Michel de Kerdour, which advertised it in *Vie des arts* Vol. XXIV, No. 97 (winter 1979-1980), p. 3. Meanwhile, it underwent drastic restoration which completely trans-

formed it, to the extent that it was no longer possible to recognize Todd's style. In October 1978, after close examination of the work, John R. Harper reached the same conclusions.
9. Jacoby's House of Antiques, sale of October 22, 1970, lot 163 (Repr.). We are familiar with this work only through a photograph, but the presence of a double ice cone and the quality of the figures clearly points to the work of an imitator. The canvas is currently part of a private collection in Toronto.
10. Sale at Sotheby's in London, February 10, 1982, lot 100 (Repr.). The canvas was marked as being a copy after Todd.
11. In 1851, Todd was also commissioned to paint Lord Elgin's coat of arms. In a ceremony organized in his honour, "a triumphal arch is being erected at the corner of Wolfe, at the top of which are to be placed the coat of arms of the illustrious Elgin family, painted by Mr. Todd". (*Le Journal de Québec*, October 9, 1851, p. 2). (*Translation*)
12. *BELLERIVE 1825*, p. 44. Bellerive confirms the statements of Abbé Casgrain, who published a biography of Falardeau in 1862. John R. Harper situates Falardeau's visit to Todd's home in 1838, when Falardeau was only sixteen (*HARPER 1970*, p. 108).
13. The relationship between the main subject and the rest of the landscape is similar in the version at the National Gallery of Canada and in "*Corbeau*" *at Montmorency Falls*. This disproves the theory that the AGO work was copied from a damaged, recycled canvas, and that the artist tried clumsily to disguise the slashes in it by adding the team of horses in the foreground.
14. We would like to thank Paul Bélanger, certified instructor with the Equestrian Federation of Canada, for having studied these various horses and teaching us about their characteristics.
15. See Cat. 226, note 7.
16. When he advertised himself as a "painter of buildings, signs, vehicles and ornaments," (*Translation*) in the January 8, 1834 edition of *La Gazette de Québec* (p. 2), he specified that he had been employed for several years by the "high society and nobility of London and Edinburgh." (*Translation*)
17. This practice was commonly used later on in photographers' studios in order to suggest outdoor activities. See *THOMAS 1979*, p. 74, fig. 43 and 44.
18. According to the person who sold it, the canvas was purchased in Canada by Captain Walter Holbech of the 60th Rifle Regiment and kept in the family. The seller also insists that the figure portrayed is not Captain Holbech (letter addressed to Dennis Reid on March 17, 1988 and kept in the file of the work).
19. *Le Canadien*, April 4, 1853, p. 3, No. 11 and 12.
20. See the canvas in the Thomson collection reproduced in *HARPER 1979*, fig. 61. Another artist who espoused this new interpretation of the site was Joseph Dynes (1825-1897), who produced a version of *Montmorency Falls in Winter* dated 1856, in a private Quebec collection, and another, painted in 1860, which is at the Musée du Québec (*BÉLAND 1991*, p. 54 Repr.).

226.
Antependium with the Adoration of the Shepherds, 1850

Oil on canvas, 75.3 × 182.3 cm

Inscriptions
(s.d., l.l) *R.C. Todd del. 1850.;* (u.c.)
GLORIA IN EXCELSIS DEO.

Provenance
Commissioned by the Séminaire de Québec, 1850;
on deposit at the Société du Musée du Séminaire
de Québec, 1988.

Bibliography
ASQ, *Manuscrit 34*, December 23, 1850, p. 97.

Collection
Musée du Séminaire de Québec (Pc990.2)

T HIS ANTEPENDIUM, or altar ornament, was designed to decorate the
chapel altar of the Séminaire de
Québec congregation (Fig. 226A). Already
in 1824, the institution had commissioned
sculptor Thomas Baillairgé to produce a
tabernacle, which he surmounted with a
sculpture in the round representing *The
Assumption of the Virgin*. Baillairgé's work
was supported by an altar monument
containing ornaments which changed with
the liturgical ritual. It seems only natural
that a chapel dedicated to the Virgin have
a quality antependium to celebrate the
Nativity, the moment which symbolized
the link between the Son of God and His
mother. The *Antependium with the Adoration of the Shepherds* was probably en-
visaged with this in mind. To our
knowledge, this was Robert Clow Todd's
first commission from the Séminaire de
Québec.

On Monday, December 23, 1850,
the Séminaire "had pipes installed to
channel gaslight onto the congregation

altar." (*Translation*) This reference in the
Séminaire de Québec newspaper accom-
panies the description of the altar and in-
forms us of the effect produced by the
antependium when it was unveiled for the
first time:

Tuesday. Christmas Eve. [...] The congregation
rose at 11:35 p.m. for the midnight mass. On
each side of the statue [*The Assumption of the
Virgin*] was a half-circle of gas jets, 20 or 30,
for the best effect. On the pews there were 3
large gas jets on a tripod with glass vases
[crossed-out s] flared at the top. In addition to
this there were six large candles and a multitude
of small ones, the light of which appeared pale
beside the gas: they were not arranged symmetrically enough. The front of the altar is a
beautiful transparency painted by one Mr. Todd
for 14 piastres: the adoration of the shepherds,
the Holy Virgin and Joseph. Well done. it is
illuminated by two gas jets placed under the
altar. (*Translation*)

Installed in the depths of the altar
monument, the gas jets illuminated the
transparency from behind, creating a
stained-glass effect. Apparently, the commission for the transparency was the last
step in the installation of the gas lighting,
which had been terminated since fall 1849
inside the Séminaire buildings.

The antependium faithfully reproduces the *The Adoration of the Shepherds*
by Guido Reni (1575-1642).[1] This Italian
canvas was not unknown in Quebec: there
were two versions of it in the first group
of works sent by Father Desjardins in
1817.[2] Catalogued as a "copy of the Guido Reni," (*Translation*) one of the two

versions was acquired by the Fabrique
Notre-Dame de Québec and displayed in
the cathedral until fire destroyed it in
1922.[3] This leads us to believe that it is
this very model which gave the priests of
the Séminaire de Québec the idea of
commissioning a version for their chapel.

Robert Clow Todd skilfully over-
came the difficulty inherent in the shape
of the antependium—a rectangle two and
a half times as long as it is wide—by placing
his composition within an elongated oval.
The overall balance is ensured by the in-
sertion of the main subject inside a frame
which is decorated on both sides with palm
branches and foliage. This was not a new
method; many embroidered antependia
also included a central inset showing the
main theme, often flanked by secondary
subjects and decorative elements such as
foliated scrolls, garlands of foliage or cas-
cades of flowers. If Todd was at first un-
familiar with the principle, he had only to
study the impressive collection of the Ursulines de Québec[4] or, more directly,
consult with Joseph Légaré.[5] However, in
order to understand the organization of
the front of the altar, we are obliged to
refer to the work by Guido Reni. Octagonal in shape, it was engraved in an identical format (Fig. 226B) in the 17th century
by François de Poilly (1623-1683)[6], and we
believe we are correct in stating that Robert
Clow Todd copied this engraving for his
antependium.[7] The fact that the figures in
this *The Adoration of the Shepherds* are
placed the other way around bears out the

Fig. 226A.
Anonymous photograph,
*Chapel of the Congregation in 1936
with its Christmas Decorations* 1936;
photograph, 20.5 × 26.5 cm.
Archives du Séminaire de Québec (drawer 33).

Fig. 226B.
François de Poilly
After Guido Reni,
The Adoration of the Shepherds; engraving.
Albertina Graphic Collection,
Vienna (AAB 14, 118).

theory that they were copied from an engraved model.[8] Furthermore, and as a result of this, it is not mere coincidence that Todd chose to work with an oblong shape: the octagon made it easier for him to copy. All that remained was for him to flesh out the draperies and extend the buildings.

The copy is of fine quality and confirms that Robert Clow Todd was an accomplished draughtsman. The outline is sure, without alterations. The liberties taken by the artist are minor and serve primarily to redistribute the subject in a less confined space. The two angels, carrying the banner, are portrayed here in the sky rather than against the buildings. Saint Joseph, who is set slightly apart from the rest of the group, is alone in the foreground, leaving a larger space for the lamb which symbolizes the sacrifice to be made. The background motifs have been eliminated, leaving only a few mountains. Todd took all these variations from the canvas in the Quebec City cathedral, thereby proving that he did not consult it merely for its colour scheme. The colours are applied in thin layers within the drawn outline, and the shadows are faithfully copied from those in the engraving, thereby confirming the close link between Todd's final work and his model.

This transparency is one of the rare known works which bears witness to a technique and a style of production that were very common in the 19th century.[9] The cause of the rapid deterioration of these works, painted on resin-coated paper or very thin fabric, is certainly due to the fragility of their surfaces. The artist or art enthusiast was obliged to take particular care in drawing the motifs, the outlines of which were generally traced. Since the transparency was placed before a light source, any flaw was accentuated, thereby leaving the artist little leeway for correcting his errors. The colour, usually watercolour

or gouache, was not supposed to "dry in a crust"[10] (*Translation*) and thus damage the transparency. Instead, the use of bright colours, applied in broad sweeping strokes without superposing the hues, was recommended to obtain the maximum effect. Journalists of the era often remarked on the use of these transparencies, frequently placed in windows during ceremonies of great pomp and circumstance which included a procession in the streets. This ***Antependium with the Adoration of the Shepherds*** is in keeping with this festive spirit: designed for a private chapel, it commemorated each year the birth of Christ until very recently, for the Musée du Séminaire did not acquire it until 1988.

D.P. and J.C.

Notes

1. The work by Guido Reni, painted between 1639 and 1640, is now in Moscow at the Pushkin State Museum of Fine Arts, after having passed through England as part of Horace Walpole's collection. See Stephen Pepper, *Guido Reni. A Complete Catalogue of His Works with an Introductory Text* (Oxford: Phaidon, 1984), p. 287, No. 190.
2. There were two Desjardins paintings portraying the *Adoration of the Shepherds* (*La Nativité* according to the inventory title) after Guido Reni. No. 36 (5'11" × 3'11" according to the inventory), acquired by Notre-Dame de Québec in 1817, was destroyed in the 1922 fire; a photo of it exists in the Fonds Livernois of the ANQQ. This appears to be the canvas which Légaré copied twice. No. 44 (4'3"×3'3"), entitled *Nativité* and described in the inventory as another copy after the Guide, was acquired by the Fabrique de Cap-Saint-Ignace in 1817 and disappeared at an unknown date.
3. Joseph Légaré did two copies of this canvas, one of which is still at the Augustine convent of the Hôpital général de Québec (*PORTER 1978/1*, p. 108, No. 89 and 90, repr.).
4. See *LE GRAND HÉRITAGE 1984*, p. 96, No. 84.

5. In 1850, Joseph Légaré rented accommodation to Todd (*PORTER 1981*, p. 17). He also did antependia for the Charlesbourg, Cap-Santé and St. Patrick churches (*PORTER 1978/1*, pp. 263-265).
6. See *Guido Reni e l'Europa. Fama e Fortuna* (cat.), (Frankfurt: Schirn Kunsthalle, 1988), pp. 425-426, No. C-14 (repr.).
7. It may be useful to recall that, also in 1850, Todd presented a watercolour entitled *L'Aurore* at the first bazaar in Quebec City. This drawing, today at the NGC (28311), is a partial copy after the fresco done by Guido Reni for one of the pavilions of the Scipion Borghese garden in Rome (today the Rospigliosi-Pallavicini palace). This fresco was widely disseminated through engraving, and became a source of inspiration for neoclassical artists. See *Guido Reni e l'Europa, op. cit.,* pp. 289-291, No. B-12 and B-13 for the drawing, and pp. 429-430, No. C-17, for the engraving. The artist's sustained interest in Reni leads us to believe that Todd may have owned his own collection of prints, on which he drew according to his needs. When he advertised the opening of a school of drawing and painting in October 1842, he announced that he owned "selected collections of models," (*Translation*) to be used in his instruction (*Le Canadien*, October 31, 1842, p. 2).
8. A canvas by Guido Reni, published in 1848 in Paris to illustrate the fourth edition of the *Évangiles traduction nouvelle* by Félicité Robert de Lamennais, must be discounted. The variations are too marked to stand comparison. See *In Praesepio. Immagini della Natività nelle incisioni dei secoli XVI-XIX* (cat.), (Rome: Biblioteca Casanatense, 1987), No. 100 (Repr.).
9. The transparencies appeared in several publications in England in the early 19th century. One of the earliest is the one by Edward Orme entitled *An Essay on Transparent Prints;* this work, published in London in 1807, was accompanied by engraved plates illustrating the applications of transparencies. See John Krill, *English Artists Paper. Renaissance to Regency* (London: Trefoil Publications Ltd., 1987), pp. 116-117 and bibliography.
10. The expression is from Henry Guedy (*Nouveau manuel complet de peinture à l'aquarelle,* reprinting of the Encyclopédie Roret du XIXe siècle Inter-Livres, 1988, p. 99).

LOUIS-HUBERT
TRIAUD

1790-1836

L OUIS-HUBERT TRIAUD was born in London in 1790 of French parents. Nothing is known of his training, except that he exhibited some works at the Royal Academy of Arts in London, among them a *Self-Portrait*, shown in 1811. Upon his arrival in Lower Canada in 1820, Triaud formed a partnership with Jean-Baptiste Roy-Audy. A *Baptism of Christ* (Garthby church, Wolfe county) signed by the two artists bears witness to this cooperative effort, which at the time was uncommon.

He was one of the principal protégés of Father Louis-Joseph Desjardins. The latter benefited greatly from the technical knowledge of the artist, who was particularly active in the field of restoration, and took every opportunity to laud Triaud's ability to produce quality work rapidly. Currently, except for a *Saint André* painted in 1821 for the church in Saint-André de Kamouraska, and *The Corpus Christi Procession in Quebec* (Cat. 228), we know of very few original works by the artist.

As concerns his restoration activities, we know that Triaud worked at Saint-Michel de Bellechasse in 1823 with the assistance of Antoine Plamondon, and then at the convent of the Ursulines de Québec circa 1824-1825, and later at the Hôtel-Dieu de Québec hospital. At the same time, he produced a number of decorative works; for example, in 1827, he was commissioned to paint the coat of arms of the Duchesse d'Aiguillon, founder of the Hôtel-Dieu de Québec (Cat. 229). He also painted theatre sets for the Théâtre Royal de Québec, first in 1830 and then in 1832, when he was assisted by another foreign artist, J.-F. Schinotti. It is difficult to find traces of the artist's activities after this date; we know only that he passed away some years later, on January 14, 1836, at the age of 46.

Main source
KAREL 1988.

227.
The Death of Mary Magdeleine, 1824
After Carle Vanloo
Oil on canvas, 118.5 × 132.8 cm

Inscription
(b.,c., on the canvas) *Triaud Pin^{ct}/1824.*
Provenance
Ursulines de Québec, c. 1825.
Bibliography
THIBAULT 1973/1, p. 99.
Collection
Musée des Ursulines de Québec (CM-80-62-P)

T HE PAINTING BY TRIAUD housed at the Ursulines convent is based on a composition after the now missing work by Carle Vanloo (1705-1765), entitled *La Madeleine dans le désert,* known through the drawing done by Gabriel de Saint-Aubin.[1] Diderot saw this painting at the Salon de 1761 and ridiculed it for what he considered its exaggerated bucolic qualities:

The grass is too green [he wrote] and too soft; the cavern seems more a refuge for happy lovers than a retreat for a sorrowing, penitent woman. Beautiful saint, come, let us enter this grotto, where we will perhaps recall certain moments from your first life.[2] (*Translation*)

The canvas sent to Quebec City was not the original by Vanloo, as seen by comparing its dimensions (8'3" × 11') with those of the work exhibited in 1761. Number 7 in the booklet gives the measurements of this canvas destined for the

Saint-Louis du Louvre church: 8 feet high by 5 feet wide. The composition was done vertically, while the Quebec City version is done on the horizontal. In the latter version, the cherubim heads, which hovered in the upper section of the 1761 composition, are located further to the right.

Despite Diderot's criticism, the subject is less idyllic than it appears, since the imagery depicts the saint's last moments isolated in a "horrible desert", (*Translation*) after *The Golden Legend,*[3] which quotes:

in this place, there was no resource, neither water, trees, nor grass [...]. However, every day, at the stroke of seven, she was taken by angels to the heavens where she heard, with her whole being, charming concerts sung by heavenly choirs. (*Translation*)

This version of the painting by Carle Vanloo arrived in 1817 with the first batch of canvases sent by the abbés

Desjardins (no. 98 of the inventory). Louis-Joseph Desjardins spoke highly of this work, which he was unable to sell, in 1817. On January 25, 1818, he informed his brother of offers he had supposedly received from the United States to purchase this canvas: "The academies of these large cities themselves are perhaps interested in acquiring originals. I was contacted via New York concerning the purchase of the Magdalene by Carl-Venloo. But it would be such a shame for Canada to lose it!"[4] (*Translation*)

Triaud probably copied the work before it found its way into the hands of Father Louis-Marie Cadieux;[5] the Ursulines acquired this copy shortly after it was completed. An inventory provides the following description:

1. In the common room of our lay Sisters: painting of St. Mary Magdalene in the Sainte-Baume. Purchased circa 1825, thanks to various

tasks done by the sisters, for the main St. Mary Magdalene room, occupied then and until 1854 by the day boarders,[6] and now, in 1899, a recreation and study hall for students at the École Normale.[7] (*Translation*)

From the time of his arrival in Quebec City in 1820, Triaud was in close contact with the Ursulines. He taught the nuns in spring 1821, and is believed to have painted *The Corpus Christi Procession in Quebec* (Cat. 228) during the same year; in 1824, he restored a number of their canvases.[8] He was greatly sought after for this type of work, and was responsible for the conservation of several canvases.[9] The version by Triaud bears witness to the work by Vanloo and to the influence of the Desjardins Paintings. It is part of the phenomenon of the dissemination of the iconography of St. Mary Magdalene (see Cat. 115, 201 and 202), who was a popular devotional figure in the French regime.

L.L.

228.
The Corpus Christi Procession in Quebec, 1824
Oil on canvas, 75.5 × 107.5 cm

Notes

1. Marie-Catherine Sahut, *Carle Vanloo* (cat.), (Nice: Musée Cheret, 1977), p. 97, no. 236.
2. Diderot, *Salon de 1761*, Seznec ed., 1975, p. 110.
3. On this topic, see Martha Mel Edmunds, "La Sainte-Baume and the Iconography of Mary Magdalene", *Gazette des beaux-arts*, Vol. CXI, (July-August 1989), pp. 11-28.
4. Bibliothèque Saint-Sulpice, Paris, Carton Desjardins, fol. 57, p. 2, taken from a letter from Louis-Joseph Desjardins to Philippe Jean-Louis Desjardins, Quebec City, January 25, 1818.
5. The canvas was acquired by Father Louis-Marie Cadieux (who was in Trois-Rivières from 1823 to 1835, and in Rivière-Ouelle from 1835 to 1838) before becoming part of the collection of Joseph Légaré and Thomas Amiot (1838), and then of Joseph Légaré. We lose trace of it after this date.
6. "The Ursuline convent in Quebec City is without a doubt North America's premier educational institution for girls, and especially for the underprivileged. There are now over fifty schoolgirls who are boarders or day boarders there, and two hundred and fifty day students, almost half of whom who will be taking their first communion this year. Education is free of charge for the day students, with the exception of a piastre or two each year to cover the cost of firewood and classroom upkeep. Students learn to read, write, count and sew. The boarders receive instruction in all branches suitable for girls" (Le Canadien, May 16, 1821, p. 136). (*Translation*)
7. AMUQ, *Notes historiques sur l'église du Monastère*, 1899, p. 20, "other paintings in the house". (*Translation*)
8. AMUQ, Journal V (1820-1836), March 1824 receipts and expenditures (*THIBAULT 1973/1*, p. 87, repr.).
9. *KAREL 1988*, p. 942.

Inscription
(b. on the canvas before the new backing covered the inscription, according to *THIBAULT 1973/2*) 1824.

Provenance
Ursulines de Québec, c. 1825.

Exhibitions
Albany 1946, No. 19; Ottawa 1965, No. 41; Vancouver 1966, No. 28; Ottawa 1967/1, No. 57; Toronto 1984, No. 164.

Bibliography
MORISSET 1935/9, p. 9; *AU MUSÉE 1936*, p. 19, No. 49; *MORISSET 1936-1937*, Vol. II, pp. 80-81; *MORISSET 1941/1*, p. 65; *PAINTING IN CANADA 1946*, p. 25, No. 19 (Repr.); *MORISSET 1950/3*, p. 50 (Repr.); *HUBBARD 1957*, pp. 19 and 23 (Repr.); *MORISSET 1960/1*, p. 94; *HUBBARD 1960*, p. 50 (Repr.); *HUBBARD 1963*, p. 55; *MACLENNAN 1965*, p. 22 (Repr.); *HARPER AND HUBBARD 1965*, p. 48, No. 41 (Repr.); *SHADBOLT 1966*, No. 28 (Repr.); *HARPER 1966*, pp. 81 and 84 (Repr.); *WADE 1966*, p. 153 (Repr.); *HARPER 1967*, p. 70; *TRUDEL, JUNEAU AND MASSEY 1967*, p. 112; *HUBBARD AND OSTIGUY 1967*, pp. 40 and 41, No. 57 (Repr.); *THIBAULT 1973/1*, pp. 90 and 99 (Repr.); *THIBAULT 1973/2*, p. 8 (Repr.); *Nos racines*, No. 78 (1979), cover. p. and pp. 1544-1545 (Repr.); *COMEAU 1983*, p. 247; *WEBSTER 1984*, p. 159, No. 164 (Repr.); *BROWN AND LINTEAU 1988*, p. 288f (Repr.); *KAREL 1988*, p. 942.

Collection
Musée des Ursulines de Québec (CM-80-70-P)

T HE "NOTES HISTORIQUES" on the "Peintures au Réfectoire des Religieuses" of the Ursuline convent in Quebec City, written in 1899, refer to a:

Procession of the Holy Sacrament parading before the Basilique. Work believed to be by Mr. Briand (who gave painting lessons to the community in 1821 and 1822). This canvas arouses our interest because of its faithfulness. Everything appears natural: the bright clothing of the priests and clergymen, the women's costumes, their hats in the style of 1820, the peasants hastening to the site, the citizens joining in the procession, etc. (*Translation*)

This is the earliest known reference to this painting in the Ursuline convent and to its attribution to a Mr. "Briand", which can be read as "Triaud", according to the information which holds that the author of this work taught at the Ursuline convent in 1821. Since the work is not signed, and given the absence of information prior to 1899 in the archives, we must rely on word of mouth for this attribution to Louis-Hubert Triaud. Even the date was long a bone of contention: Morisset, Hubbard and Harper, who published the canvas several times, put the date at 1821, the year Triaud taught at the convent. Claude Thibault, in *Trésors des communautés religieuses* (p. 99) in 1973, discovered the date 1824 inscribed on the back of the canvas. Given its esthetics and handling,

Fig. 228A.
Joseph Légaré,
The Corpus Cristi Procession in Nicolet, c. 1832;
oil on canvas, 40 × 62.2 cm.
National Gallery of Canada, Ottawa (6459).

this work is not easy to relate to the rather sketchy body of works known to be by Triaud: the large-scale religious paintings (Saint-André de Kamouraska, Hôtel-Dieu de Québec), more functional works (theatre sets, coats of arms), and his supposed self-portrait (MQ) which make up this body of work have little in common with this reconstitution of a June Sunday in the Notre-Dame market square.

The artist attempts to convey, through the regular, geometrical portrayal of the square, the liveliness of a holiday. The plunging perspective and the layout, which create the impression of depth through long diagonals, the miniaturization of the figures and meticulous detail, lend a startling aspect to the work. Was Triaud attempting to reach a different market by combining an urban landscape with a memorable event? For, although views of Quebec City were popular with art enthusiasts and travellers, this work also depicts a Catholic tradition, a typical aspect of life in Lower Canada. Does the fact that the work is not in possession of the Notre-Dame de Québec church authorities mean that it was not met with favour by the client targeted? Were the Ursulines, whom the rules of their order forbade to participate in public events, seeking to obtain a view of their city, disguised as a religious holiday? These still unanswered

questions do not allow us to definitely attribute the work to Triaud. Examination of the style does, however, indicate that the artist was versed in the rudiments of geometrical perspective, but that he had trouble connecting the planes in a coherent ensemble. The buildings stand out against an almost disproportionate sky. This break in space is intensified by the artist's linear handling of the outlines and his difficulty in rendering volume. In short, his status as a landscape artist was obviously not yet established. However, as noted by the nun in charge of cataloguing: "this work attracts viewers because of its faithfulness." (*Translation*) The meticulous portrayal of the market square and the crowd encourages the viewer to examine the hustle and bustle more closely, thereby breaking it down into its various components. By choosing a vantage point from the two-storey house located at the corner of Rue de la Fabrique and Rue Sainte-Famille, the artist looks down on the crowd and places his horizon line so as to disappear into the procession. The perspective is framed on the left by the front of the cathedral, which is portrayed full-length, including the bell tower. The building, rebuilt in 1771, determines the scale of the composition. The front was renovated circa 1810 by François Baillairgé. A pediment has been outlined on the gable of

the facade, and the new rough coat emphasizes the toothed quoins which separate the church into sections. Notre-Dame de Québec looks out onto the market square of the same name, whose central covered marketplace, erected in 1818, closes off the composition on the right. Behind this building is the former Jesuit college, at the time transformed into a barracks. The square is bordered at the furthest point by Rue Buade. The building fronts on this street, which are two or three storeys high, are lined up in orderly fashion and present a decorative aspect with their alternating plaster and dimension stone fronts, signs and shutters, and roofs in tinplate or tile dotted with dormer windows. The elegant bell tower of the Anglican Cathedral of the Holy Trinity, which was completed in 1804, thrusts skyward above the roofs.

This setting was the theatre for a religious ceremony, the Fête-Dieu (Feast of Corpus Christi), which marked the beginning of summer. The Sunday following Pentecost, each church organized a procession through the streets of its parish. The Notre-Dame de Québec procession stopped in the main chapels of the Upper Town where wayside altars were set up. In this work, the procession is already well advanced because the painter chose to portray the moment when the priest leaves the church. Under a canopy carried by four men and flanked by two acolytes, Father Joseph Signay (Cat. 125 and 189), priest of Notre-Dame de Québec, is depicted holding the paten which contains the host. The choirboys, dressed in white, precede him, and five of them are preparing to parade backwards to mark their respect and veneration given the presence of Christ in the host. They follow a group of men, probably members of a religious brotherhood.

The procession route is lined with conifers, and the houses on Rue Buade are decorated with greenery. James P. Cockburn, in an 1831 watercolour portraying the Fête-Dieu, shows the same decorations.1 On either side of the procession, in homage, a tightly massed crowd has gathered. Despite the small scale of the figures, the artist devoted particular attention to the costumes, especially the hats worn by the women—straw hats with a light, wide brim—and the stance of the spectators in the street and at their windows. Despite the imposing architecture and grandiose procession, the subject is portrayed in miniature, since the artist was not willing to sacrifice a single detail by using a small-scale canvas. The sky takes up two-thirds of the canvas, thereby detracting somewhat from the main subject. This is definitely an urban portrayal, an important public religious event, a summer holiday, even if the crowd is quite civilized. The overpowering grey sky tinged with yellow emphasizes the explosion of colour in the procession. Such disproportion conveys a feeling for the grandeur and fragility of nature, rather than for the harmony between social and cultural life and this vast expanse.

Using different means, Joseph Légaré, whose *The Corpus Christi Procession, Nicolet* portrays a similar scene (Fig 228A), also combines the forces of nature with a religious event. He portrays the scene from a ground angle, emphasizing yet distancing the sacred subject, while nature takes up half the composition and the entire foreground. It is wild, as shown by the untamed thicket where the villagers kneel in prayer, and yet cultivated, like the orderly rows of trees which set the stage for the monuments and the procession. Nature is even part of the mystery of religion, as evidenced by the tree on the left which, given the height of the painting, is forced to bow down before the church.   L.L.

Note
1. *Cameron and Trudel 1976*, p. 121, No. 99 (repr.). See also the essay by John R. Porter, "Processions et défilés," *Le Grand Héritage 1984*, pp. 257-266.

229.
Coat of Arms of the Duchesse d'Aiguillon, 1827
Oil on panel 71.7 × 56.2 cm

Inscription
(f., in oil) *Mᵉ La Duchesse Daiguillon./Fᵉ de. L'Hᴸ. Dieu./1639.*

Provenance
Hôtel-Dieu de Québec, 1827.

Bibliography
Archives du monastère de l'Hôtel-Dieu de Québec, Recettes et dépenses, 1825 à 1857, p. 38; *Musée HISTORIQUE 1964*, p. 2, No. P-78; *Thibault 1973/1*, p. 34; *Boisclair 1977*, p. 53, No. 78 (Repr.); *Karel 1988*, p. 942.

Collection
Musée des Augustines de l'Hôtel-Dieu de Québec (P-78)

I N A SOCIETY where the practice of art was less subject to a ranking system than in Europe, it is difficult to assess to what extent the production of signs, posters, letters, coats of arms, etc., ruled the distribution of tasks and organization of work in a painter's trade. Were these activities secondary to the artist's craft? They certainly did not have the same importance they do in today's society, where they are almost exclusively monopolized by graphic artists and where renowned artists are asked to put their signature on a product or trademark to grant it some of the plus-value associated with their name.

The second half of the 19th century saw an increased demand for these types of products, as a result of their industrialization and marketing. This era corresponds to the development of the trade of commercial artist, taught in the schools of the Arts and Trade Councils and in specialized schools. Prior to this, merchants and wheelwrights had to commission artists, who possessed the required materials and technique, to do signs and decorative work. Although artists tended to accept more of these types of commissions when they were starting out, they nonetheless did them to a certain extent throughout their career. In the case of Jean-Baptiste Roy-Audy, for example, this was his official trade before practising as an artist, rounding out his carpentry activities. In the March 25, 1802 edition of the *Quebec Gazette,* he announced that he "painted signs with gilt or coloured letters and mottos according to individual tastes." (*Translation*) This specialty was confirmed in 1807 in the same newspaper, on May 14 and June 4: "He exercises carpentry in all its branches, and furniture making; he makes carriages, paints and varnishes and emblazons them, and paints and varnishes signs." (*Translation*) As demonstrated by Michel Cauchon,[1] this period in Roy-Audy's career, before 1817, centres around this painstaking, specialized trade which enabled him to make a name for himself in Quebec's high society. Although he received several commissions after 1818 for portraits and history paintings, he continued to advertise his work "in different branches of art, such as Paintings, Coats of Arms, Signs, Carriages, & C."[2] (*Translation*) Many artists were forced to accept, as a supplement to their work as portrait, landscape or history painters, commissions for other more utilitarian works.[3]

On May 19, 1812, Joseph Légaré signed an apprenticeship contract with Moses Pierce, itinerant painter and glazier. His illustrious career shows that, on a number of occasions, he did work relating to this trade of sign and transparency painter.[4] The increase in the demand for this type of work was such that the *Quebec Directory for 1822*[5] listed five artists who identified themselves as "painter and glazier." They were William Bradford, Simon Elstob, Robert Gain, Meredith McConnell and William Synott. The advertisement published by Elstob (p. 131) reads: "Sign and Ornemental Painter [...] Coat of Arms, Masonic Aprons, and Ships Likeness painted in the neatest manner. Canvas prepared for Portraits and other painting."

The commission for a coat of arms for Marie de Vignerot, wife of Combalet, niece of the Cardinal de Richelieu and Duchesse d'Aiguillon (1601-1675), founder of the Augustines of the Hôtel-Dieu de Québec, is mentioned in 1827,[6] but nothing in the way of anniversary or celebration can be found to justify this commission. It was too early for the trend of historicism which was to mark the 1840s, when intensive research into archives breathed new life into characters from the French Regime, who were subsequently raised to the rank of hero (Cat. 127).[7] The production of the Duchesse's coat of arms was, nonetheless, linked to several events and their commemoration. When they learned of her death at the age of 71, on April 17, 1675, the Hospitalières, as reported by annalist Soeur Jean-Françoise Juchereau de Saint-Ignace, had said for her:

Several long masses, and one especially where we invited everyone, and which we carried out with as much grandeur as possible. We decorated the entire church in black, from the arch to the very bottom. In the middle, there was a mausoleum raised on several steps and surrounded by a multitude of lights, with the coat of arms of Madame la Duchesse D'Aiguillon painted and hung everywhere.[8] (*Translation*)

Other coats of arms for the Duchesse were produced in 1889, for the celebration of the 250th anniversary of the founding of the Hôtel-Dieu de Québec;[9] another version was done by Gauthier and Son of Quebec City in 1908, for the tricentennial of the founding of Quebec City.[10]

The coat of arms assigned to the Duchesse D'Aiguillon by letters patent of Louis XIII on January 1, 1638, bore "on the 1st and 4th de Vignerot (three boar's heads in gold) and on the 2nd and 3rd de Richelieu (three chevrons in silver) with the supports of duke and peer."[11] (*Translation*) Triaud added in serif characters the identity of the founder of the Hôtel-Dieu hospital and the date the institution was founded.

Louis-Hubert Triaud was a protégé of Father Louis-Joseph Desjardins, chaplain of the Hôtel-Dieu de Québec hospital, who used his influence a number of times with members of the religious communities to obtain employment for Triaud. The artist's training in London seems to have prepared him to meet the demands made to Lower Canada artists for various types of artwork. Triaud executed religious paintings, genre scenes, portraits, and theatre sets. He taught drawing and restored canvases. Other pictorial productions for special occasions have been documented, such as a painting on satin done in 1833 for the brotherhood of the Imprimeurs de Québec. It showed "a printing press mounted on a globe, decorated with the appropriate inscriptions."[12] (*Translation*) Triaud also did a coat of arms for Lord Dalhousie in 1825, which was subsequently engraved by James Smillie to serve as a book plate for the governor.[13]

L.L.

Notes

1. *Cauchon 1971,* pp. 25-26.
2. *Quebec Gazette,* September 2, 1824.
3. For example, Louis Dulongpré opened in 1812 "a factory for manufacturing carpets painted in oils" (*Quebec Gazette,* April 23, 1812), (*Translation*) while William Berczy seems to have produced this same type of work in 1809 for the freemasons of Quebec City (Archives de l'Université de Montréal, Collection Baby, p. 58, letter from William Berczy to his wife, March 19, 1809). In 1834, Robert C. Todd advertised himself as a "painter of buildings, carriages, signs and ornaments." (*Translation*)
4. *Porter 1978/1,* pp. 148-149, No. 263-265.
5. Thomas Henri Gleason, *The Quebec Directory for 1822* (Quebec City: Neilson & Cowan, 1822).
6. The reference in the archives reads as follows: "A.M. Triaud to paint the coat of arms of the Duchesse d'Eguillon, our founder, £2-10." (*Translation*)
7. See *Martin 1988.*
8. Dom Albert Jamet, ed., *Les Annales de l'Hôtel-Dieu de Québec 1636-1716* (Montreal: Presses de Garden City, 1939), pp. 179-180.
9. Gérard Morisset, *Nomenclature des tableaux conservés à l'Hôtel-Dieu de Québec,* typed manuscript, 1932, no. 102. *Boisclair 1977* (p. 95, No. 138) notes that "these coat of arms, those of the Duchesse d'Aiguillon, are missing from the inventory of the Musée." (*Translation*)
10. *Boisclair 1977,* No. 81 (Repr.).
11. Dom Albert Jamet, ed. *op. cit.,* p. 180.
12. *Karel 1988,* p. 942.
13. *Allodi and Tovell 1989,* p. 54 (Repr.).

HENRY JAMES
WARRE

1819-1898

S ON OF LIEUTENANT-GENERAL Sir William Warre, Henry James Warre was born January 12, 1819 in Cape of Good Hope (South Africa), where his father had been posted. In February 1837, he entered the army as ensign with the 54th Royal Infantry Regiment. Shortly thereafter, he obtained a six-month leave to study in Paris, not only the French language but also the works in the Louvre. His position as aide-de-camp to his uncle, Sir Richard Downes Jackson, commander of the English troops in Canada, brought him to this country in fall 1839. Throughout his stay in America he had the opportunity to make several trips, during which he developed his talent for drawing; he also kept several annotated and illustrated journals of his expeditions (NAC). From May 1845 to July 1846, Warre carried out his last important mission for the British army, namely, a visit to Oregon in order to assess the defensive potential of this region, since the Canada-U.S. border was the object of fierce rivalry at the time. Warre sailed for England in August 1846. Promoted to various ranks of officer, including colonel in 1858 and general in December 1880, he served in different areas of the world, including Ireland, the Crimea, India and New Zealand. After giving up his position as commander-in-chief in Bombay in 1811, he completed a round-the-world tour, returning by the Pacific via the United States and Canada.

A number of his works were published as lithographs, especially his views of the Rockies done during his trip to Oregon, in *Sketches in North America and Oregon Territory,* in 1848. *Sketches in the Crimea* was published in 1856, and *Historical Records of the Fifty-seventh, or, West Middlesex Regiment of Foot...,* in 1878. Warre died in London on April 3, 1898.

Main source
COOKE 1983.

230.
Journal of an Expedition in Sarch of 'Moose Deer' on the Saint Maurice River, c. 1842

Ink on paper, 21.8 × 27.6 × 2.5 cm

Inscriptions
(Fol. 1r, Pen and black ink in the artist's hand) *March 1842;* (Fol. 1v, in graphite in the artist's hand) *Journal of an/Expedition in search of "Moose Deer"/on the St Maurice River/called by the Indians/Me˜ta˜-be˜-bo to -No. - Ze˜-be^u./March 1842.*

Provenance
Descendants of the Warre family; Michael Warre, London, England; acquired by the Public Archives of Canada, Ottawa, 1965.

Bibliography
COOKE 1983, p. 204.

Collection
National Archives of Canada, Ottawa (1965-76)

MQ

A- *Walking with Snow Shoes* (Fol. 27)
Sepia on paper

*A*s the moose were to the hunters, so were the salmon to the fishermen.[1] With this short but accurate formula, John Russell Harper summed up the importance of hunting and fishing expeditions in the 19th century. Quebec rivers, especially the Jacques-Cartier near Quebec City, were renowned for their great recreational fishing potential. Watercolours by James Pattison Cockburn,[2] James Hope-Wallace and Henry William Barnard conjure up days spent in the forest on the banks of rivers replete with salmon. In *The Sportsman in Canada*, published in London in 1845,[3] Frederic Tolfrey wrote fiery articles on the fierce rivalry among fishermen and the challenges they set one another. Often, the same people could be found in pursuit of duck and woodcock in summer, and tracking big game in winter.

Portrayals of moose hunting are traditionally associated with the works of Cornelius Krieghoff: the animal lying dead in the snow, the hunters grouped around their catch preparing to take home trophies, or the return from the hunt after long hours spent tracking the game.[4] However, these same subjects, which were portrayed later on in photographs, existed well before Krieghoff arrived. For example, in 1840, with *Moose Hunter,* John Richard Coke Smyth included the moose in his series of lithographs. An enormous dead moose, lying on its side, takes up half the picture, while an Amerindian is seated on a rock in the centre of the composition, his dog at his side. This emblematic motif, present in popular imagery, bears witness

to a marked interest in a particularly spectacular type of game. For it must be understood that hunting expeditions had nothing to do with subsistence. The goal was purely recreational: to fire a few successful shots.

Such was the context for the *Journal of an Expedition in Search of "Moose Deer" on the Saint Maurice River* by Henry James Warre. This manuscript is especially interesting because of the spontaneity of the writing, although an important point should be made. Two versions of this voyage exist. The first is a small sketchbook, with the following title appearing on the cover: "*March 1842. / Moose deer Hunting / on the Snow / up the three Rivers.*"[5] It contains an account of the same moose hunt, followed by sketches done directly from nature. Based on these daily notes, Warre made up the journal of his expedition, a comprehensive document which aimed to be more than a simple souvenir of a memorable hunting trip. A rapid look at its content leads us to believe that Warre attempted to polish it up, perhaps with a view to publication. The text-image arrangement is particularly skilful, Warre having played on certain dynamic compositions, like in folio 27 (Cat. A), where he portrays people snowshoeing through deep snow. But the written account is what convinces us that this manuscript targeted publication. The text is written in black ink, with countless crossouts and additions put in by the artist to complete an idea or correct a hasty statement. The journal also contains correc-

tions with purple chalk, but it is impossible to tell without further research whether they were made by the artist or by someone else. Despite this, the work remains unfinished. It should be noted that Warre chose a used sketchbook for this account of the moose hunt. Originally used backwards, under the title *Sketches and Scraps in North Americas from 1839 to 1843*, the notebook contains, in no particular order, sketches made of various events, such as a sleigh ride from Montreal to Quebec City in January 1840. The *Journal of an Expedition in Search of "Moose Deer" on the Saint Maurice River* thus takes up only the first folios of the volume, from 1 to 77. Furthermore, the artist evidences a certain lassitude beginning at folio 58: less care is taken with the drawings, and the sepia washes which accentuated the first illustrations are absent. However, this is only a technical detail, definitely important for the understanding of the context in which the manuscript was produced, but which takes nothing away from the account itself.

The expedition, which left from Montreal, lasted from March 12 to March 29, 1842. Captain Bush of the 7th Hussard accompanied Warre. They were joined in Berthier by Captain Jenkinson of the 68th Infantry Regiment, who was quartered in Sorel, before moving on to Trois-Rivières. Travelling winter routes was not easy, and the first pages of the account are sprinkled with remarks on the obstacles encountered: "The snow was drifted in some places to a great height; and the inequalities in the

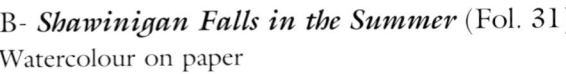

NGC

B- ***Shawinigan Falls in the Summer*** (Fol. 31)
Watercolour on paper

VAG

C- ***Our Temporary Camp in the Forest*** (Fol. 35)
Sepia on paper

Road (called, 'Cahôts') were as distressing to the Passengers, as to the Horses." (Fol. 19)[6] With two images entitled *Sleighing in the Country* and *Sleighing in the City (my Sleigh) of Montreal*, Henry James Warre contrasted the two modes of transport, thereby setting the tone for the rest of his account. The illustrations, done as an integral part of the account, punctuate the main links in the text, translating words into images.

Their arrival in Trois-Rivières signalled the true departure toward the Saint-Maurice ironworks where an Amerindian guide, Tomaqua, was in charge of leading the men through the forest and picking out moose tracks. The sled soon had to be abandoned and the route continued on foot. Despite their experience, the guides sometimes chose to deviate from the initial route in search of a shortcut. The same type of decision explains the anachronism of the portrayal of ***Shawinigan Falls*** (Cat. B) in summer, whereas the expedition took place in March. Warre skilfully justified the drawing's presence, thereby showing his intention of addressing readers:

By the Route we had taken, we avoided a very considerable bend of the S Maurice River, but we lost the Winter view of the Falls of Sho! Winnigan which I consider, second only to Niagara; and as I made an Expedition in the Summer on purpose to see them; I introduce the Sketch, altho not quite in keeping with Winter Scenery. (Fol. 31)

Learning how to walk on snow-shoes over long distances was no easy task (Cat. A):

Although we had practised walking upon the Snow *Shoes*, without which, it would have been impossible to have gone a mile, through the soft & very deep snow; we found it by no means easy to avoid roots & other little inequalities which caught the end of the Shoe; & as a natural consequence disturb the equilibrium of the Wearer; However we got on tolerable well for Amateurs. (Fol. 27 and 29)

But injuries caused by the "*mal de racket*" (Fol. 35) were quickly mitigated by the new experience of a night in the forest (Cat. C):

enveloped in Snow; the cheering influence of the Fire, & the air of comfort of our temporary 'Camp', caused us to forget our minor evils & we smoked our Pipes, and drank our Brandy & Water, 'hot'—with as much comfort as if we were luxuriating in a well furnished Drawing Room, instead of being under the bright blue Sky of Heaven with Thermometer 20 degrees below the Freezing point. (Fol. 35 and 37)

When the chafing became worse, Amerindian remedies—although quite drastic—relieved the pain:

It would be impossible to realize the real pain of walking, particularly after a short rest. The action of the foot upon the Sinew, of which the Snow Shoe is made, had rendered the sole of the Foot, one immense Blister; [and] we were advised to apply the common turpentine,

gathered from the Pine Trees; which produces the most agonizing torture for a few moments, but happily has the desired effect. (Fol. 39)

But accommodations were sometimes uncertain, like on the day a snow-storm prevented the group from reaching their planned refuge (Cat. D):

The track of the leading file, was filled as soon as made [...] We took refuge under the shelter of some thick Fir trees till Morning.—Here we remained, wrapped in our Blankets, enveloped in Snow, till the Sun rising in all its unclouded glory. [...] and the Snow, having fallen very heavily during the night, our resurrection in the Morning, resembled that of Ghosts from the Tomb.; enshrouded in our fleecy Mantles. Many a bitter invective against the p*leasures!* of Moose Hunting in such a climate, was uttered during the night, 'not loud, but deep. (Fol. 43, 45, 47 and 49)

Finally, the actual hunt did not begin until March 18 when Tomaqua and the Amerindian guides discovered fresh tracks in the snow:

being eager for the châsse Jenkinson and I started 'a la bonne héure.' on our first attempt against the gigantic Moose Deer. [...] walked for 3 or 4 hours without a symptom of Game; now crossing over an undulating Country, then traversing small Lakes [...] we were in despair [...] We told the Indian (Zavier) to go on & return to us, if he saw any signs of the Game.— In less than 10 minutes this Indian returned having crossed the track of three Moose, altho they had evidently passed some days, their 'trail' being scarcely visible under the fresh fallen

AGNS

D- *Our Meeting with a Large Party of Lumberers, Saint Maurice River* (Fol. 48)
Sepia over graphite on paper

MMFA

E- *A Lucky Chance!* (Fol. 65)
Pen and black ink over graphite on paper

snow. [..] in about two hours I was delighted to hear a shout, and nearly at the same moment, three splendid Moose Deer, rushed through the Snow, within about 40 Yards— and had it not been for the other Indian Zavier who could not resist bellowing at these enormous denizens of the Forest, rushed would have passed within a few Yards of me. As it happened they turned; & I was only able to take my Rifle from its case, in time to get a flying shot at the last, which I wounded severely, as it instantly turned, & left its companions. Reloading as quickly as possible, I started a pursuit of the two, [but] more than an hours hard running up hill & down dale, was necessary, before I could get another shot— I then fired at the largest, a magnificent male or Bull Moose: and dropped him at the first shot, giving him the 'Coup de grâce' with the second barrel. In my hurry to reload & follow the third, I twisted my Snow Shoe, the consequence was a complete summersault in the snow: and the escape of the animal. (Fol. 54-58)

The pursuit continued the next day, when Tomaqua identified the tracks of three other moose. After a first clumsy shot, which he had to repeat three times before the moose finally went down, Warre went in hot pursuit of the two moose that had fled (Cat. E):

The other two Animals had gained much ground upon me, during the interim; but trusting to being able to return by retracing my Steps, away I again started and as the Moose were almost as tired as myself; In less than half an hour I again caught sight of them, laboring through the deep snow, I was quickly alongside, taking a deliberate shot at each, I had the satisfaction of seeing one roll to the *right*, & the other to the *left*, as the smoke cleared from the alternate muzzles. (Fol. 64 and 65)

All that remained was to take the trophies—the moose tongues—to prove that the hunters had truly gunned them down. Gourmets reserved the moose's lips for themselves, since these parts were considered a delicacy (Fol. 61).

Henry James Warre deemed the expedition a success because the total catch was impressive: "Thirteen Moose Deer twenty Martens and sundry Hares, small Birds &c.—of which I fortunately obtained the greater share killing Six Moose to my own Gun" (Fol. 72). Interestingly enough, he ends his account with a veiled warning to readers wishing to organize such an expedition:

On the 29th we dismissed our Men, and settled our accounts, which are rather exorbitant, when one takes into consideration the immense fatigue which Master as well as Man, undergoes in pursuit of the formers amusement. Each Bourgeoise, i e, Gentleman. must at least have one attendant; not merely as Valet but to carry his share of Provisions [*&c*] his Clothes Ammunition &c.—this attendant is usually accompanied by one or more dogs, which are harnessed to the Tebaugins or 'light sleighs' that carry the 'plunder'—and are the scape goat for every article of provision that is purloined from our Mess or Camp. (Fol. 76 and 77)

D.P.

Notes

1. *HARPER 1979*, p. 113.

2. *CAMERON AND TRUDEL 1976*, p. 155, No. 142 (Repr.).

3. The work was translated and presented by Paul-Louis Martin under the title *Tolfrey, un aristocrate au Bas-Canada* (Montreal: Boréal Express, 1979). Frederic Tolfrey arrived in Quebec City in 1816 as an officer with the British army. He remained for two years and travelled in Upper Canada in 1817.

4. *HARPER 1979*, Fig. 94, 95, 97-99 and 101.

5. NAC, 1971-1986. Hardcover sketchbook, reinforced corners and spine, measuring 14.6 × 24.1 × 1 cm. This sketchbook bears the stamp of the Ackermann & Co. Repository Arts.

6. These quotes are from the transcription of the manuscript done by the National Archives of Canada. However, in order to make reading easier, we have left out any notes made by Henry James Warre, keeping only the preliminary version of the text. To shorten the references, we have indicated the page numbers of the original text following each quote.

WILLIAM F.
WILSON

active between 1842 et 1854

W E HAVE LITTLE INFORMATION on the period William F. Wilson spent in Canada. An advertisement published in the November 10, 1842 edition of the *Montreal Gazette* indicated his presence in this city, that he was born in England, the son of a former officer, and that as a young boy, he had spent time in an asylum for the blind and deaf in London. Wilson also points out that he learned to paint in France, having studied with an "eminent Flemish painter." He advertised himself as specializing in portrait painting, although he also painted landscapes. He settled in Montreal at the home of William Footner, a German-born architect who is best known for having won the competition for the design of the Bonsecours market in Montreal.

In 1847, Wilson exhibited some of his works along with Krieghoff, Morris, Somerville, Sawyer and others at the "Galerie de Tableaux" on Rue Saint-Jacques owned by the Montreal Society of Artists, of which he was a member. Wilson probably settled in Quebec City that same year, where he remained until 1851. We lose track of him after his stay in Boston between 1852 and 1854.

Main sources
COLLARD *1969*, HARPER *1970*.

231.
View of Quebec, 1851
Oil on canvas, 76.3 × 107 cm

Inscription
(s.d., l.l) *W.F. Wilson/Quebec 1851.*

Provenance
N. Newman Ltd., London; acquired by the McCord Museum, Montreal, 1980.

Exhibition
Montreal 1981-1983.

Collection
McCord Museum of Canadian History, Montreal. Purchased with the assistance of the Government of Canada under the Cultural Property Export and Import Act (M980.75)

T HIS AMBITIOUS COMPOSITION is an example of the type of commissions painters could aspire to in the mid-19th century, and bears witness to the interests and tastes of a rapidly growing public that was becoming increasingly aware of artistic issues. Wilson's *View of Quebec* combines the landscape with a group portrait and a genre scene. Panoramic views of towns and picturesque sites often included various scenes and figures in the foreground. This landscape by Wilson includes the sleigh ride characteristic of winter landscapes, with the addition of a harbour scene and a family of Amerindians. A couple and their son are riding in the sleigh, and the arrangement and detail in the portrayal of their faces resemble that of portraits. The prototype for this type of composition goes back to Heriot (Cat. 35 and 225), but was not to become popular

until the 1850s. Krieghoff painted a number of works portraying bundled-up couples in their sleighs with Quebec City as a backdrop.[1]

In this painting, Wilson used elements of contrast which provided a complex portrait of the Quebec sociocultural community. The British flag waves over the Citadel on the left side of the canvas, while the French flag is hoisted on the mast of the ship at the right. The regularity of the urban landscape in the background contrasts sharply with a fence made of poles and tree trunks which frames the composition in the front. The forest is not far off, as evidenced by the presence of a couple of Amerindians shod with snowshoes on the right. The man is carrying a hunting rifle and pulling a toboggan loaded with bundles, while the woman carries a child on her back. They are about to pass the

Fig. 231A.
William F. Wilson,
View of Montreal from the Priest's Farm, c. 1848;
oil on canvas, 51.4 × 66.7 cm.
The Beaverbrook Foundation, Beaverbrook Art Gallery, Fredericton.

sleigh pulled by two magnificent horses. The cultural and social situation, the power relationships and the feelings of the residents with regard to the various components of the colony are summed up in this proximity of elements, which clearly depicts the key players and limits of this society.

First, Wilson paints a magnificent landscape. Quebec City is bathed in a superb bluish light typical of a late afternoon in winter. This shows that Wilson was a keen observer of atmospheric conditions and a painstaking colourist. Unfortunately, excessive restoration has eliminated a number of subtleties in the treatment of the paint layers, and flattened the impasto which at one time must have caught the light.

This urban landscape was probably commissioned by the family seated in the sleigh. The pair of horses and the carriage take up, on the surface of the canvas, about the same length as does Quebec City in the distance. Although the three figures seated in the sleigh are depicted in typical portrait style, we have no source attesting to their identity. Could the man be an officer on holiday, or are they a bourgeoisie family practising one of the favourite sports of this social class? The fact that this sleigh is being followed by another in the distance reinforces the hypothesis of a recreational activity, an outing among friends. However, it is obviously a weekday, judging from the activity on the ice bridge and the two habitants loading logs onto a sled. The Quebec Driving Club (or Tandem Club) brought together members of families of Quebec City high society who had the means to maintain stables of several horses. Louisa Anne Call, wife of Baron Aylmer, governor of Lower Canada, sponsored the Quebec Driving Club. She

describes the pleasure of a winter outing on the south shore across from Quebec City as follows:

Tomorrow we are going across the magnificent frozen St Lawrence [...] and the drive on the opposite side of the River though now covered with snow, yet owing to the quantity of firs and precipitous ground toward the River, it is very picturesque and the situation of Quebec, on its Elevated promontory, is very fine from the other side of the River.[2]

Compared to these detailed physiognomies, those of the Amerindian family are stereotyped and do no more than add local colour through their dress, mode of transportation and as a source of information concerning the distribution of work in Amerindian society. This is not so much the portrayal of a specific couple as an emblem, an iconographical motif, just as the topographical contours of the city's outline enable us to identify the landscape. There were no reserves on the south shore close to Quebec City, and the Abenakis are hardly ever portrayed in paintings. However, Amerindians are often depicted in views of Quebec City from the Lévis shore.

Although it was not until 1842 that he arrived in Canada and advertised his services as portraitist, Wilson must have come to the capital relatively early on. He was not immune to the charms of Quebec City and the surrounding area, because he showed *The Falls of Montmorency, from Nature* and *A Landscape, near Quebec* at the Montreal Society of Artists exhibition in January 1847. His presence in Quebec City was indicated in *Mackay's Quebec Directory* of 1848-1849, as well as in the 1850 edition, but his name was absent from the 1852 publication.

This landscape is the only known work dating from Wilson's stay in Quebec City. The treatment is superior to that of the *View of Montreal from the Priest's Farm*, dated circa 1848 (Fig. 231A): the imposing St. Patrick's church, which was completed in 1847, is undoubtedly responsible for such a late dating. This work, with its traditional vantage point and more geometric treatment of the perspective, vegetation and clouds, is worlds away from the one dealt with above. The quality of *View of Quebec* far exceeded the expectations of the critics of the 1847 exhibition[3] who, while praising Wilson's talent as a portraitist, also suggested that he hone his landscape skills. A work of such stylistic and iconographic importance warrants a more appropriate place for Wilson within the history of landscapes no longer subject to topographical constraints, but which provide an interpretation of life in Canada.

L.L.

Notes

1. Such works by Cornelius Krieghoff include *Captain Alfred Torrens and his Wife Caroline (née Price) on the Ice in front of the Citadel at Québec*, circa 1854 (sale at Christie's South Kensington, June 9, 1988, lot 99); *Tandem Driving, Quebec*, 1858, collection of the Hon. K. R. Thomson, Toronto (HARPER 1979, p. 69, Repr.). Joseph Dynes (1825-1897) took his inspiration from this work for his own *View of Montmorency Falls* (c. 1856, MQ) and Charles Huot (1855-1930) used it for one of his first compositions; *Promenade devant Québec* (1873, PC). See Jean-René Ostiguy, *Charles Huot* (Ottawa: National Gallery of Canada, 1979), p. 31.

2. Quoted in *ALLODI 1980*, p. 121.

3. The article published in *The Pilot and Journal of Commerce* on January 29, 1847 is initialled H.N.

CHARLES WOODLEY

active between 1830 et 1839

F ROM 1824 TO 1827, one C. Woodley, architect and miniaturist, exhibited at the Royal Academy of Arts in London. In 1825, he presented a portrait—a drawing or a miniature—to the Royal Society of British Artists. Five years later, in June 1830, a portrait painter by the name of Woodley advertised his services in the pages of the *Quebec Gazette;* he had recently arrived from London. He requested the support of Quebec City residents, planning to remain in the city for two or three months. He invited the public to examine "a wide assortment of drawings," and mentioned that he was prepared to teach in this field. In 1832, he was chosen to design the backdrop of the new Théâtre royal de Québec, which was painted by Louis-Hubert Triaud and J.-F. Schinotti; Joseph Légaré had also done work for this theatre. On July 15, 1833, he offered his services in Montreal, specifying that his works included "Portraits in Miniature […] from eight to thirty piastres, Landscapes, Views from nature, and a large collection of Drawings in many other styles, the result of several years of application and study." (*Translation*) In January 1834, he returned to Quebec City. Records show that his work consisted mainly of painting miniatures and teaching drawing; in fact, he taught at the Séminaire de Québec from 1835 to 1839. It is not known what became of him after this date.

Main sources
HARPER 1970, PORTER 1981.

MQ, NGC

232.

Portrait of an Unknown Man, 1834
Watercolour, gouache and gum arabic on cardboard, 16 × 12.8 cm

Inscription
(s.d., b.,l.l., in ink) *W* [covered] *Cha¹.. Woodley fect/1834.*

Provenance
Damsels Painchaud, Quebec City; acquired by M⁸ʳ François Pelletier, Quebec City, 1941; gift to the Université Laval, 1942; Séminaire de Québec; on deposit at the Société du Musée du Séminaire, 1983.

Bibliography
ANNUAIRE 1942.

Collection
Musée du Séminaire de Québec (Pf 986.1)

T HIS ORIGINAL MINIATURE was acquired by Université Laval in 1942 under the title *Portrait of Doctor Joseph Painchaud.* Such an identification was interesting because Dr. Painchaud was an eminent Quebec City physician during the 19th century. It was also highly plausible, since the watercolour was acquired by the doctor's descendants. A year after having acquired the work, the *Laval Médical*[1] published, with the permission of the Painchaud family, an oil on canvas[2] which also portrayed the former president of the Société médicale de Québec. However, this work raised a problem because, in all evidence, the two portraits were not of the same man! A photograph

in the *Galerie des Contemporains,* published by the Livernois studio in 1866, helps us solve the mystery[3]: only the oil on canvas actually depicts Dr. Painchaud. This means that the original identification of the miniature is incorrect.

It is certainly gratifying to be able to identify sitters portrayed by artists, but portraits are interesting for other reasons. This miniature is significant in that it is the only known example of Charles Woodley's work. The watercolour convincingly illustrates the artist's mastery of the technique of portrait painting. The refined execution of the face, contoured to highlight the features, bears witness to a sure hand. The colour scheme contributes to the quality of the work in the portrayal of the shadows, the subtlety of the contrasting tones of the hair, and certainly in the effect produced by the sitter's immense blue eyes with their limpid, pensive gaze. However, the artist's shortcomings are obvious: his portrayal of anatomy and fabric textures is downright clumsy, as seen in the overly long neck, the small, drooping left shoulder, the arms awkwardly attached to the body and the hastily sketched clothing. The difference between the refined portrayal of the face and the roughness of the rest of the composition is striking; it is almost as if the painting had been done by two different artists.

Woodley's career remains obscure, but we do know that he taught drawing from 1835 to 1839 at the Séminaire de Québec. For eighteen years, that is, from 1833 to 1851[4], the institution entrusted this course to professional artists. We know very little about how these courses were carried out, except that anyone could register and that they were taught two hours a week.[5] Antoine Plamondon was the uncontested *Maître* of the Séminaire, since he held this position for thirteen years.[6] However, he left his job temporarily, which is why, on December 18, 1835, it was "Resolved that the Séminaire will give Drawing Master Mr. Woodley £18 ...— approximately—with the students paying the rest".[7] (*Translation*) It appears that Woodley was hired only temporarily,[8] at a time when Plamondon had decided to try his luck in Montreal for the commission of the Chemin de croix for the Notre-Dame church.[9] Still, Woodley participated in Séminaire activities for four years. Could this explain the acquisition by Université Laval of the *Portrait of an Unknown Man* in 1942? The initial identification of the portrait of Dr. Painchaud is certainly linked to the purchase of the miniature.[10] But it

is possible that an informed art enthusiast, such as Monseigneur François Pelletier (1858-1944),[11] acquired this watercolour because it was by Charles Woodley, which meant that it not only portrayed a former professor of the School of Medicine, but was also done by a *Maître de dessin* (drawing master) of the Séminaire de Québec.

J.C.

Notes

1. *Laval Médical,* Vol. VIII, No. 1 (January 1943), p. 88 (Repr.), reprinted in *Laval Médical,* Vol. XVII, No. 6 (June 1952), p. 835, (Repr.).

2. This anonymous oil on canvas is in storage at the Musée du Québec.

3. LESSARD 1987/2, p. 84 (Repr.). In the photograph, Dr. Painchaud appears in the third row, at centre left in the top portion of the image.

4. As of 1851, the clergy of the Séminaire took full responsibility for the drawing class.

5. "Today from 4h to 6h, drawing class, by M. Antoine Plamondon. There are 21 students registered to date. They pay one piastre for the whole year, and there are two hours of classes per week". (*Translation*) (ASQ, *Manuscrit 34,* October 2, 1850, p. 84). The class must have functioned much the same way while Woodley was teaching.

6. He taught there from 1833 to 1835 and from 1840 to 1851; in 1842-1843, he shared the position with Théophile Hamel, and then in 1848-1849 with Thomas Fournier.

7. ASQ, *Séminaire 12,* No. 48.

8. The same could probably be said for the hiring of Gerome Fassio, who took over from Woodley for 1839-1840.

9. As concerns this commission, see Cat. 195. When Plamondon completed his *Station of the Cross* (Cat. 195), he resumed his position at the Séminaire until he decided to leave Quebec City to settle in Neuville.

10. Already in 1917, when Monseigneur Pelletier was head of the Séminaire, the institution purchased "a small portrait (pastel) of Dr. Naud, former professor at the university." (ASQ, *Manuscrit 34,* November 17, 1917, p. 123). (*Translation*)

11. Monseigneur Pelletier was head of the Séminaire and also in charge of the Pinacothèque of Université Laval. He distinguished himself through his judicious purchases of both European and Canadian paintings. Although the list of works acquired by Monseigneur Pelletier is incomplete, see THIBAULT 1973/1, pp. 162-163 and 170.

J OHN ELLIOTT WOOLFORD was born in London in 1778. He is believed to have studied drawing at the Tower of London and perhaps at the Royal Military Academy in Woolwich. We do know for sure that he was posted to the 2nd Royal Infantry Regiment in 1797. He took part in a number of campaigns during the Napoleonic Wars, such as the one in Egypt where George Ramsay, ninth Earl of Dalhousie and avid art enthusiast, noticed his talent for drawing. He left army ranks in 1803 on half-pay and settled in Edinburgh, where he became renowned as a landscape painter. Twelve years later, Lord Dalhousie enlisted his services, making him official draughtsman of his entourage, which was to accompany him to Canada. Dalhousie arrived in Nova Scotia in October 1816 to carry out his duties as lieutenant-governor.

In Nova Scotia, Woolford produced several views of villages and landscapes which he discovered on his excursions with Dalhousie. He published a series of them as aquatints based on his drawings, doing the engravings himself. In July 1819, Woolford accompanied Dalhousie on a tour which took them to York.

In November 1819, Dalhousie was named governor-in-chief of the Canadas (1820-1828), and was subsequently transferred to Quebec City. Woolford joined him there in 1821 and accompanied him on a tour through Upper and Lower Canada, still as official draughtsman.

In 1823, Woolford was posted to Saint John, New Brunswick, and was then appointed master general of barracks at the Fredericton headquarters, a position he held until 1859. His career as an artist continued during this period: Woolford produced architectural blueprints for buildings such as the governor's new residence in Fredericton, King's College (1828), and the local prison (1830). He associated with several artists working in Fredericton, such as Alexander Cavalié Mercer, Robert Petley (circa 1809-1869), and Edward Thomas Coke (1807-1888). He also participated in at least two exhibitions, at the Mechanic's Institute in Saint John in 1842, and at the 1852 Provincial Exhibition held in the same city. He died in Fredericton in 1866.

JOHN ELLIOTT WOOLFORD
1778-1866

Main sources
MacKay 1977; Un moment 1991.

MQ, NGC

MQ, NGC

233.
Old French Ferry Place, Pointe Lévis, 1819 or 1821
Sepia over graphite on paper, 12.9 × 21.8 cm

Inscription
(b.,l.r., in graphite, in the artist's hand) *Old French Ferry Place/Pointe Levis.*
Provenance
Royal Ontario Museum, Toronto, 1963.
Bibliography
ALLODI *1974/1*, Vol. II, No. 2072.
Collection
Royal Ontario Museum, Toronto (960.273.5)

234.
Old French Ferry Place, Pointe Lévis 1819 or 1821
Watercolour over graphite on paper, 22.3 × 34.3 cm

Inscription
(l.l., in pen and in ink) *Major J.E. Woolford, Del. 1824.*
Provenance
Charlotte H. Perley; Toronto Public Library, Toronto, 1902.
Bibliography
TORONTO *1964*, p. 45, No. 942; ALLODI *1974/1*, Vol. II, No. 2072.
Collection
Metropolitan Toronto Reference Library (902-1-27)

N EAR THE END OF HIS LIFE, John Elliott Woolford wrote a brief memoir to James Ramsay, tenth Earl of Dalhousie, recounting the main stages of his career.[1] This manuscript detailed his first postings to the 2nd Royal Infantry Regiment commanded by George Ramsay, future Governor of British North America. Woolford was sent to Ireland in 1798 to quash the rebellion, and participated in an expedition to Holland (1799) before joining the Egyptian campaign in 1801-1802. This moment seems to have marked a turning point in Woolford's professional career, because he points out to James Ramsay that his father:

had found out that I was somewhat skilful in Sketching & painting & had employed me during any leisure in those pursuits on leaving Egypt for Minorca, Malta, & Gibraltar I was still so employed and received repeated Acts of kindness from His Lordship who left the Regiment at Gibraltar and brought me to Dalhousie castle were I continued to be employed in finishing the [*various, many: two words crossed out*] different Sketches & models I had collected among the preceding periods.[2]

It is John Elliott Woolford's presence at Lord Dalhousie's side which inter-ests us here. When the latter applied for the position of lieutenant-governor of Nova Scotia in 1816, he had Woolford accompany him. A passage from Dalhousie's diary sheds light on the nature of their relationship: "I am glad I have brought my draftsman Woolford with me. He shall be kept hard at work during my rambles in Canada, so that hereafter I may refer to his sketches for the beauties of the Country."[3] Dalhousie wrote these lines on July 3, 1819. At this time, Woolford was accompanying him on a tour of a few weeks which was to take them to York. For the moment, the visit to Chaudière falls allowed them to make concessions to the discovery of a grandiose site which, in comparison, showed "how little & how utterly insignificant are all the works of man."[4] Was it on this occasion that Woolford did the small sepia drawing which is now part of the ROM collection? It is possible, because Dalhousie mentioned that he returned to Quebec City by crossing the river from Pointe-Lévis. However, we cannot confirm this, because Dalhousie took the same trip in 1821 as part of an inspection tour, after becoming Governor of British North America. Woolford had just joined him in Quebec City to make a visual record of this tour. Thus, there is a certain ambiguity with regard to the dates 1819 and 1821. Until further proof is found, we prefer to retain both dates, even though the second appears more plausible. In any case, this changes nothing in our analysis because the drawings of Quebec are somewhat of an exception in a body of work devoted mainly to Nova Scotia (1816-1823) and New Brunswick (1824-1866).

These drawings are an especially good example of work subject to the criteria of a commission. The choice of subjects seems mainly linked to the demands of Lord Dalhousie, as shown by his journal accounts. On July 7, 1819, at Les Cèdres, he wrote: "At Sunset I made Woolford try to sketch it, but I much fear is not equal to it."[5] On August 7, 1821, on the shores of Lake Superior, he noted: "I noted the scene in a pencil memo which at same time I made Woolford sit by me & sketch correctly."[6] These drawings thus served as a visual record, just as a few lines written in a personal diary can help revive a vague memory.

VAG, AGNS, MMFA

235.
Village of the Cedars on the Saint Lawrence, 1819 or 1821
Watercolour and gum arabic over graphite on paper laid on cardboard, 15 × 23.8 cm

Inscription
(l.l., on the mount, in pen and black ink, in the hand of Lord Dalhousie)
Village of the Cedars on St. Lawrence.

Provenance
George Ramsay, 9th Earl of Dalhousie, Québec, 1828; Descendants of the Ramsay and Lindsay families, Scotland; Captain Colin Broun-Lindsay, Colston, Haddington, Scotland; acquired by the National Gallery of Canada, Ottawa, 1979.

Collection
National Gallery of Canada, Ottawa (23419)

Fig. 233-234A.
John Elliott Woolford,
View of Point Lévi, the Fall of Montmorency in the Distance
1819 or 1821;
brown wash over graphite on paper laid, 20.6 × 30.8 cm.
National Archives of Canada, Ottawa (C-99525).

The sketches also had to be completed fairly quickly, since the travellers could make only brief stops. A rapid sketch was done in pencil to outline the motif and situate the masses. Next, monochrome washes were applied to distribute the light. This drawing from nature can be seen in *Old French Ferry Place, Pointe Lévis.* Through its composition and chiaroscuro effect, this work conforms to the standards of picturesque topography. Woolford approached landscape painting with the general principles of William Gilpin (1724-1804) in mind, choosing motifs "capable of being portrayed in painting."[7] (*Translation*) Watercolour is applied later, correcting details without reworking the composition. What, then, is to be made of the drawing at the National Archives of Canada (Fig. 233-234A), which is similar in composition? Should it be situated somewhere between the preliminary sketch and the large finished watercolour? The dimensions and some of the motifs, such as the boat washed up on the riverbank, lead us to think so.

Woolford collected these works in various albums which he presented to Lord Dalhousie in 1823, when he was appoint-ed assistant to the master general of barracks in St. John, New Brunswick. Later, most of them were conserved in the libraries of Lord Dalhousie's heirs. The watercolour *Village of the Cedars on the Saint Lawrence,* which appeared in one of these now dismantled albums, displays the same characteristics as the preceding works. The technique echoes the spontaneity of the original sketch, and the final product bears witness to initial difficulties, especially the artist's attempt to link the various planes along the road using graduated bands of colour. Les Cèdres was considered one of the compulsory stops along the route to Upper Canada. During his first visit in 1819, Dalhousie described his impression of it in his journal, in the entry dated July 7:

Our road from Vaudreuil again touched the back of St. Lawrence at the rapids called the Cèdres. There it is truly a grand rapid river [...] Here the river tumultuous & broken is divided by several islands richly wooded into the very stream.[8]

D.P.

Notes

1. Archives of the University of New Brunswick, Fredericton, Saunders Family papers, Mil. 1857, letter from J.E. Woolford to James Ramsay, tenth Earl of Dalhousie: "Woolfords account of his services in the army 1797 to 1860."

2. *Ibid.* The sixty-four watercolours, as well as maps, are included in an album acquired by the National Gallery of Canada in 1985 (29213.1 to 29213.70).

3. Marjory Whitelaw, ed., *The Dalhousie Journals* (Ottawa: Oberon Press, 1978), Vol. I, p. 120.

4. *Ibid.*

5. *Ibid.,* p. 125.

6. *Ibid.,* Vol. II, p. 86.

7. William Gilpin, *Three Essays: on Picturesque Beauty; on Picturesque Travel; and on Sketching Landscape: to which is added a Poem, on Landscape Painting* (London, 1794), second edition, p. 3.

8. Marjory Whitelaw, *op. cit.,* p. 125. The National Gallery of Canada owns a small watercolour which corresponds fairly closely to this description (23422).

JOHN CRAWFORD
YOUNG

1788 – circa 1859

J OHN CRAWFORD YOUNG was born in Dalkeith, Scotland, on April 15, 1788, and was an officer by trade. At the age of 16, he entered the 91st Royal Infantry Regiment as an ensign. Promoted captain in October 1813, he was transferred four years later, with the same rank, to the 79th Royal Infantry Regiment (the Queen's Cameron Highlanders). From 1808 to 1814 he participated in the Spanish War. In October 1825, he took up duties at the general headquarters of the 79th Regiment in Quebec City. Between October 1826 and June 1827, he served as aide-de-camp to Lord Dalhousie, who was then governor-in-chief of the Canadas; this position as aide-de-camp had been held a few years before by Charles Ramus Forrest. In October 1827, Young submitted a project—which was accepted by the ad hoc committee, of which James Pattison Cockburn was a member—for the monument to Wolfe and Montcalm which was to be erected near the Château Saint-Louis. In the end, the monument was raised in the Jardin des Gouverneurs.

Young was posted to various parts of the country: Ile-aux-Noix in 1828, Kingston in 1829 and, finally, York in 1830. He took leave a number of times to see to personal matters. In summer 1834 he was in Quebec City, but returned to Edinburgh in May 1835, where he married Sarah Riddell.

Main sources
ALLODI 1974/1; COOKE 1983.

236.
American Portfolio No. 1, 1825-1827
45.6 × 60.8 × 2.5 cm

Inscriptions
(on the edge of the cover, laid down) ex-libris of
Lord Dalhousie by James Smillie, etching on wove
paper, 10.1 × 7.9 cm; (inscribed on the plate) TRIA
JUNCTA IN UNA/ICH DIEN/ORA AND LABORA.

Provenance
George Ramsay, 9th Earl of Dalhousie, Quebec
City, 1827; descendants of the Ramsay and
Lindsay families, Scotland; Captain Colin Broun-
Lindsay, Colston, Haddington, Scotland; acquired
by the National Gallery of Canada, Ottawa, 1985.

Collection
National Gallery of Canada, Ottawa. Purchased
with the assistance of the Government of Canada
under the Cultural Property Export and Import
Act (29214).

NGC

A- *Indian and French Canadian,*
Market Place, Quebec, 1825-1827
(29214.2)
Watercolour over graphite on paper,
27 × 21.8 cm

Inscriptions
(i., l.r., in brown wash, almost erased) *J.C.Y.;*
(l.r., on the mount, in pen and black ink, in the
artist's hand) *Indian an French Canadian./Market
Place - Quebec.*

Kingfisher (Fol. 57) or for their travels
through the Outaouais in August 1827
(Fol. 23, 29, 47, 63, 65, 67 and 69).

A large number of the works,
however, are totally independent of Dalhousie's travels, and are simply the result
of the artist's presence in Quebec, such as
the views of the city or the figure studies.
They were likely done between October
1825 and June 1827, when John Crawford Young presented them to Lord Dalhousie. In any case, the actual works are
what enable us to situate the artist in his
proper context, that is, as one of the art
enthusiasts who benefited from Lord Dalhousie's patronage.

The immediate impression received
upon consulting the album is that of an
eclectic artist. First, because of his choice
of subjects: pure landscapes (Fol. 29, 63)
jostle portraits (Fol. 57) and figure studies
(Fol. 9, 31, 49, 53, 57). Genre scenes
(Fol. 1, 5, 13, 17, 39) are interspersed
with topographical views (Fol. 3, 7, 11,
15, 33, 37, 41, 45, 55, 59, 69) and portrayals of events (Fol. 27, 43). Second,
because of his combination of styles: certain characteristics of style, especially his
treatment of the foregrounds and framing
of the composition, recall the landscapes
of James Pattison Cockburn.[7]

But these are not the only elements
which characterize the album. Even in his
topographical views, Young devotes particular attention to the human figure. Almost all his works have this in common
and show that the artist, attentive to detail, is a keen observer. Any attempt to
retrace the origin of the album would be
foolhardy, given our lack of knowledge of
John Crawford Young's life and work. We
know that he was born in Scotland and
lived in Edinburgh, since he was married
there in 1835, but this period is too late
to be of any use to us. We know nothing
of the years preceding his arrival in Quebec.
Like Charles Ramus Forrest, Young was
put on half-pay in 1816 with the reduction
of the military staff. Assigned to the 79th
Infantry Regiment in October 1817, he
did not resume active service again until
September 1, 1825, when he was posted
to Canada. Did he spend the interim in
Edinburgh? If he did, then we must look
to the Scottish tradition of Sir David Wilkie
(1785-1841) or Hugh William Williams
(1773-1829) for influences. The contrast
in the topographical views such as that of
*Below Cape Diamond, Lower Town Quebec
– in the Distance No. 1 Tower* (Fig. 236B),
the nervous treatment, the complexity of
the plans connected using a series of walk-

U NTIL RECENTLY, we knew of only a
few works by John Crawford
Young, mostly housed in Toronto
at the Royal Ontario Museum. It was
purely by chance that Marie Elwood, while
doing research on John Elliott Woolford
(Cat. 235) in the library of Lord Dalhousie in Haddington, Scotland, discovered
an album containing some forty drawings
by John Crawford Young. The album, to
which Lord Dalhousie gave the title
American Portfolio No. 1, was acquired by
the National Gallery of Canada in 1985.
It is a half-bound book with the back and
corners in green leather, decorated with
gold thread. The front cover, in marbled
green paper, bears Lord Dalhousie's
bookplate in its centre, drawn by James
Smillie circa 1826.[1] It includes forty watercolours and brown wash drawings, distributed in no particular order among
sixty-nine folios.[2] As Rosemarie L. Tovell
observed,[3] the drawings can be grouped in
several different ways according to the
travels of Lord Dalhousie.

Young arrived in Quebec in October 1825 and served as acting aide-de-camp

to Lord Dalhousie from October 1826 to
June 1827. As part of his duties, he accompanied the governor on many of his
inspection tours throughout Canada.
However, it appears that Young had the
opportunity to accompany him well before
his official appointment, as evidenced by
the four watercolours of Gaspésie fishermen
and fish salters. In July and August 1826,
Dalhousie travelled through Nova Scotia
and New Brunswick.[4] On their way back,
off the coast of Bonaventure Island and
Percé rock, they noticed intensive offshore
and inshore fishing activities. Lord Dalhousie gazed at this activity through his
telescope "until he was nearly blind."[5]
(*Translation*) The entry in his journal could
apply to Young's watercolour entitled *Fish
Curers, Bay of Chaleur* (Fig. 236A):

Others were dressing & stretching the cod to
dry on the clean shingle beach. Others spreading the herring nests & cleaning the catch of
the last night. An abominable smell of fish &
boiling oil, however, impregnated the air on
this most delightful day.[6]

Other such text-image links can be
established for the launching of the brig

Fig. 236A.
John Crawford Young,
Fish Curers, Bay of Chaleur, 1826;
watercolour over graphite
on paper, 18.4 × 13.3 cm.
National Gallery of Canada,
Ottawa (29214.4).

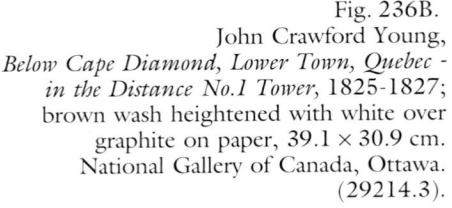

Fig. 236B.
John Crawford Young,
*Below Cape Diamond, Lower Town, Quebec -
in the Distance No.1 Tower,* 1825-1827;
brown wash heightened with white over
graphite on paper, 39.1 × 30.9 cm.
National Gallery of Canada, Ottawa.
(29214.3).

ways, the bustling activity, all this is the antithesis of the topographical tradition developed by Paul Sandby (1731-1809). John Crawford Young follows more in the wake of watercolourist Samuel Prout (1783-1852) and artists who travelled to Normandy when the boundaries were opened (1819-1820). The appeal of these new towns, the overlapping of the houses and their roofs, the picturesque yet decrepit nature of the architecture and the element of human activity all enabled Young to see Quebec City as no topographer ever had.

How, then, should we analyze the fine work ***Indian and French Canadian, Market Place, Quebec?*** An Amerindian, seated among his baskets, waits patiently. Beside him, a coachman (?) smokes placidly, whip in hand. In the middle ground, the activity of the location is suggested by three figures in animated discussion. Colour plays a predominant role, bearing witness to Young's mastery of colour palettes. The white clothing mixed with beige—or trimmed with blue in the case of the Amerindian—is luminous against the mauve backdrop of the architecture. Colour also brightens the secondary groups, such as the figure in the middle ground

carrying a stick, traced in blue so as to match the sky. Young is as skilful with the subtlety of the harmony: he distributes white highlights (ground, walls and knees) to suggest arctic cold, and streaks the snow with mauve under the feet of the figures.

A question remains: was Young merely trying to convey to us his interest in everyday life? We suspect not, based on the revival of the theory of associations in the work by Archibald Allison, entitled *Essays on the Nature and Principles of Taste.* Allison sets himself apart from his predecessors, who believed that only certain objects in nature possess characteristics inherent to beauty, the picturesque or the sublime, and that the recognition of these objective qualities resulted in a mental association of corresponding ideas. For Allison, on the other hand, the imagination is the ultimate authority. Consequently, it is impossible for some objects to possess absolute qualities and for others to have none at all. Samuel H. Monk summarized the basis of this theory in a sentence which opposes these two viewpoints: "In one case, we perceive only the qualities that objects present to the senses; in the other, we see the values implied, the experiences to which

they are allied, their significance—in other words we see imaginatively."[8] The central position of the Indian, his disproportionate size and the intensity of his gaze confront us, despite ourselves, with his status in society. The image thus touches us more deeply than we at first realize.

D.P.

Notes

1. *Allodi and Tovell 1989,* No. 41 (repr.).

2. The folia are numbered recto/verso. The first folio is not numbered.

3. NGC, artist's file, document dated May 1985.

4. Marjorie Whitelaw, ed., *The Dalhousie Journals* (Oberon Press: 1982), Vol. III, pp. 58-70.

5. *Ibid.,* p. 68.

6. *Ibid.*

7. It must be recalled that all these artists were part of Lord Dalhousie's entourage. See *Allodi and Tovell 1989,* pp. 5-8. In the same light, what were the links between Andrew Brown (active in Quebec City between 1825 and 1828) and John Crawford Young? It cannot be proved conclusively that only the latter influenced the former.

8. Samuel H. Monk, *The Sublime. A Study of Critical Theories in XVIII-Century England* (Ann Arbor: The University of Michigan Press [Ann Arbor Paperback No. 40], 1960), p. 149.

UNATTRIBUTED
WORKS

237.
Georges-Barthélemi Faribault, c. 1821
Oil on cardboard, 30.8 × 25.2 cm

Provenance
Descendants of the Théophile Hamel family; Mrs. Jean Hamel, née Thérèse Toupin, Montreal; Galerie Bernard Desroches, Montreal, 1975; acquired by the Musée du Québec, Quebec City, 1983.
Bibliography
VÉZINA 1976/1, p. 29, No. 160.
Collection
Musée du Québec, Quebec City (83.10\

THE ORIGIN OF THIS PAINTING—from a descendent of Théophile Hamel—coupled with the resemblance between this figure and a photograph of Faribault,[1] confirm the sitter's likely identity. Théophile Hamel married Mathilde-Georgina Faribault (1831-1906) on September 9, 1857. She was the only surviving child of Faribault's marriage to Marie-Julie Planté.

Faribault (1789-1866)[2] was a lawyer by trade, but is known primarily for his work as a bibliographer. His interest in Canadian history led him to publish the first bibliography on the subject in 1837, the *Catalogue d'ouvrages sur l'histoire de l'Amérique, et en particulier sur celle du Canada, de la Louisiane, de l'Acadie, et d'autres lieux; avec des notes bibliographiques, critiques et littéraires.*

Hamel painted his father-in-law's portrait twice[3] and the Musée du Québec also holds a portrait of Madame Faribault. However, the work in question here, *George-Barthélimi Faribault,* cannot have been done by the artist: the thicker impasto

and the pictorial treatment, with brush marks visible in the lighting, are not characteristic of Hamel's works.[4] The attention to detail and the precision of the facial features indicate it was done by a specialist in portraiture, possibly an itinerant miniaturist passing through Quebec City at the time.

While it is difficult to place an exact age on the sitter, he is obviously still a young man. It could be a marriage portrait, which would suggest it was painted in 1821, when Faribault was only thirty. The lack of attributes and the forced omission of the hands are, to say the least, surprising. Rather than being shown with book in hand, a familiar object found in many portraits of educated Lower Canadians, Faribault is portrayed as a socialite: nothing attests to his duties either as a senior official (assistant clerk, translator in the House of Assembly) or as a researcher and author. Remarkable attention has been paid to his appearance. The long, aquiline nose is as if balanced by the tuft of hair and sideburns. The viewer's attention is drawn

to Faribault's elegant attire, particularly the rich waistcoat and wide black tie, which contrasts with the colour of the armchair and the drapery completing the composition.

L.L.

Notes
1. *VÉZINA 1975/1,* p. 122, nº 63 (repr.).
2. Yvan Lamonde, DBC, vol. IX (1977), p. 274-276.
3. Le portrait datant de 1861 est connu en deux versions : celle du Musée du Québec et celle de la Bibliothèque nationale du Canada. Cette dernière provient de la Société littéraire et historique de Québec, dont Faribault avait été bibliothécaire honoraire pendant de nombreuses années et président en 1858-1859. Le Musée du Québec conserve un autre portrait daté de 1870.
4. Faribault fut délégué en Angleterre et en France, en 1851 et 1852, pour constituer une bibliothèque parlementaire et nationale destinée à remplacer celle qui fut détruite dans l'incendie du parlement en 1849. Il était alors âgé de plus de soixante ans; le portrait à l'étude n'a donc pas pu être réalisé à cette occasion.

238.
Montreal From the Mountain, c. 1819-1826
Oil on canvas, 68.2 × 84.6 cm

Inscription
(s., l.l.) *J. Duncan.*

Provenance
Louis Carrier, Sainte-Anne-de-Bellevue; acquired by the Musée de la Province de Québec, Quebec City, 1959.

Exhibitions
Albany 1946, No. 23; Vancouver 1959, No. 125; Montreal 1963; Quebec City 1983-1984, No. 64.

Bibliography
PAINTING IN CANADA *1946*, pp. 26-27, No. 23 entitled *Montreal from the Summit of Mount Royal;* MORISSET *1959/1*, p. 43, No. 125; MORISSET *1960/1*, p. 150; HARPER *1966*, p. 189 entitled *Montreal* (Repr.); TODD *1978*, pp. 11, 22-24, 41, 47, 220 and 221 (Repr.); ART DU QUÉBEC *1981*, p. 74 (Repr.); TODD *1982*, p. 313 entitled *View of Montreal;* LE MUSÉE DU QUÉBEC *1983*, p. 68, No. 64 (entry by Claude Thibault, Luc Noppen and Michel Doyon) (Repr.); BÉLAND AND BOURASSA *1990*, pp. 7, 8 and 86 (Repr.); NADEAU *1991*, p. 17 (Repr.).

Collection
Musée du Québec, Quebec City (59.236)

E VER SINCE IT WAS ACQUIRED by the Musée du Québec in 1959, this landscape has been attributed to James Duncan. Gérard Morisset was one of the first to put the attribution in print, followed by John Russell Harper. Patricia Ann Todd, in her masters' thesis, presented it as the artist's first painting, dating it circa 1826. Signed *J. Duncan,* the landscape did, in fact, support the theory of the artist's early arrival in Montreal. A quick glance immediately reveals the absence of Notre-Dame church. Construction on the church began in 1824 and the skeleton was completed three years later. As of 1825-1826, then, once the walls had been erected, the church could be seen from atop Mount Royal.

An anachronism of this kind in the city's topography and the doubts as to Duncan's presence in Montreal understandably raise many questions. In writing his entry, in collaboration with Luc Noppen and Michel Doyon, for the Musée du Québec's exhibition catalogue entitled *500 oeuvres choisies,* Claude Thibault at-

tempted to reconcile the various theories. On the one hand, he hoped that documents would prove Duncan was in Montreal in 1826 before certifying that *Montreal From the Mountain* was indeed painted this same year. On the other, he formulated a new theory in order to situate the landscape circa 1845:

James Duncan painted several historical scenes and used his art to reproduce works or landscapes that had since disappeared, notably to illustrate the Viger album. It is therefore possible that this canvas was painted with a view to re-creating an earlier, idealized view of the city at the turn of the century and that, to attain this goal, the painter adopted a manner or style of execution that differed from his usual works, which depicted his world in a much more descriptive manner.[1] (*Translation*)

Actually, there is a much simpler explanation.

Curiously enough, the signature itself has never been the subject of a separate study. Yet one can only wonder about the surprising written form of the "*J.Duncan*" in question. The first initial and the first letter of the last name are

separated by a period. In addition, the downstroke of the letter J has a slight mark in the middle that could be confused with a capital F. The curve of the letter D resembles signatures of the 1850s, such as the one on *Saint Paul's Bay* (Cat. 99). However, in this case, Duncan has written his first initial and the first letter of his last name so close together that they create a single initial. The imitator who was looking to copy this mark on the Musée du Québec painting did not understand the principle. In separating the J and the D, the person drew a loop in the middle of the J, thereby making a complete error in the shape of the letter. This preliminary visual observation was confirmed using ultraviolet rays, which showed that the signature was located between two layers of varnish, making it unlikely it was the work of the artist. It is not known exactly when this landscape was first attributed to Duncan. One thing is certain, however: the person responsible was very familiar with the artist's watercolours, particularly those of fluid construction. It was apparently the work's obvious stylistic unity with Duncan's oeuvre as a whole that to date eliminated any doubts about the signature.

From the moment **Montreal From the Mountain** is no longer accepted as being the work of Duncan, there is no reason to question its pictorial content, which is actually very coherent and dates the work between 1819-1820 and 1825-1826. Construction on Christ Church, the Anglican cathedral, began in 1805. However, the spire, rising upward in full sunlight just right of centre in the watercolour, was not completed until 1819-1820.[2] The first Notre-Dame church, "La Paroisse," stands alone before the river, indicating that the new parish church cannot yet be seen. A close study of the other buildings would nevertheless be necessary before the date can be narrowed down any further. In this respect, one wonders whether it is really Saint-Jacques cathedral on the far left, caught between the shadow and the light, and whether it is possible to identify the bourgeois homes popping up along Sherbrooke Street. Many questions clearly remain.

Although it is too soon to suggest the name of another painter, this work was clearly done by a skilled artist who treated panoramic views in the same manner as the 17th-century Dutch painters. The heavy sky, with the occasional ray of sunlight shining through to the ground, is reminiscent of Jacob van Ruisdael (circa 1628/1629-1682).[3] It could easily have been done by either a British or American landscape artist passing through Montreal at the time.

D.P.

Notes

1. MUSÉE DU QUÉBEC 1983, p. 68, No. 64 (entry by Claude Thibault, Luc Noppen and Michel Doyon).

2. Nathalie Clerk, *Le style palladien dans l'architecture au Canada* (Ottawa: Parks Canada, 1984), p. 68.

3. See, in particular, *View of Alkmaar* in Peter C. Sutton, *Masters of 17th-Century Dutch Landscape Painting* (Cat.), Amsterdam, Boston and Philadelphia, 1988, pp. 463-465, No. 89 (Repr.).

MQ, NGC

239.
Portrait of a Lady, c. 1825
Watercolour, 9.1 × 7.1 cm

A T FIRST GLANCE, this watercolour miniature stands out for its relative simplicity and somewhat naive or schematic handling. Inscribed in an oval format is the half-length figure of a woman in her thirties whose pale complexion sets off her distinctive features: bare forehead, attentive gaze, aquiline nose, thin lips and the beginnings of a double chin. The sitter's social standing is shown as much through the studied coiffure, with its braid twisted into a chignon, as through her jewellery, in this case an elegant drop earring and a round pin on the bodice of her dress. Despite the plunging neckline revealing an apparently ample bustline, the young woman's costume does meet the standards of decency of the time. The puffed-sleeve dress, the top of the full skirt and the checkered shawl over her shoulders are rendered in large brushstrokes. The large, curved drapery and the more angular elements of the classical-style architecture in the background are similarly roughly sketched out. Aside from the red and blue plaid shawl, the entire setting is painted in fairly neutral tones—black and grey—which partially serves to define the sitter's traits.

Provenance
Miss Pearle LeMesurier, Quebec City; acquired by the Musée du Québec, Quebec City, 1965.

Collection
Musée du Québec, Quebec City (65.187)

While the miniature likely dates back to the mid-1820s, the lack of reliable data or convincing comparisons would make it foolhardy to try and attribute it to any artist in particular. It was undoubtedly done by one of the many itinerant artists who visited Quebec City looking for clients whose portrait they could paint in miniature or whose profile they could "reproduce in a likeness of superior execution."

The question remaining is who is this mysterious lady who had her face immortalized at the request of a relative, friend or spouse. At the risk of being considered audacious, and in light of the origin and probable date of execution, the sitter could possibly be Julie Guérout, daughter of a former member of Parliament and merchant from Saint-Denis-sur-Richelieu, who wed businessman Henry LeMesurier of Quebec City in October 1815. But regardless of whether there is any substance to this theory, this watercolour portrait remains significant in that it bears witness to a common artistic practice and a once-sizeable production of which too few examples have survived.

J.R.P.

MQ, NGC

240.
Portrait of a Man, 1837
Graphite on paper, 19.1 × 14.5 cm

Inscription
(i.d., l.r.) *J.L. 1837.*
Provenance
Galerie Bernard Desroches, Montreal; acquired by the Musée du Québec, Quebec City, 1968.
Exhibitions
Ottawa 1978-1979/1, No. 30; Quebec City 1983-1984, No. 303.
Bibliography
PORTER *1978/1*, pp. 52 and 53, No. 30 (entry by John R. Porter) (Repr.); PORTER *1981*, p. 132; LE MUSÉE DU QUÉBEC *1983*, p. 245, No. 303 (entry by Guy Paradis) (Repr.); MARTIN AND GRANDBOIS *1991*, p. 17.
Collection
Musée du Québec, Quebec City (68.157)

THIS DRAWING SHOWS a head-and-shoulders portrait of a mature man presented at a three-quarter angle. His slightly bent position indicates he is seated and his big eyes enliven his drawn, but determined, facial features. The viewer senses great strength in the subject's searching gaze, straight nose and stern look. Dominated by a lock of hair that recalls the famous coiffure of *Patriotes* party leader Louis-Joseph Papineau (Cat. 188), the balding forehead conveys seriousness and reflexion. The sitter is wearing a dark collar, a plaid, buttoned-up waistcoat and a redingote with sleeves gathered at the shoulders.

The unfinished lower section of the drawing and the unevenly shadowed area in the background help define the presence, indeed the outline of the figure. The overall composition and fine detail in the Musée du Québec drawing show both a sense of observation and technical skill, witness the full use of the graphic possibilities of pencil drawings while the lines, colour gradation, hatching and contrasts help render the facial contours, the awkward waving of the hair and the varied textures of the costume.

One may ask whether such qualities are reconcilable with the often hesitant lines of a self-taught artist such as Joseph Légaré who, as far as it is known, produced no graphic works? It is doubtful, even though the drawing in question has to date been attributed to him based on the inscription in the lower right-hand corner: "*J.L. 1837*". It is also questionable since a recent study shows that the shape of the two initials does not resemble the initials Légaré signed on various documents of the day. Furthermore, an attempt to find another artist with the same initials who was plying his trade in Lower Canada in the 1830s has so far been unsuccessful. Should the inscription actually be authentic, one might wonder whether the initials could belong to the mysterious sitter and whether the latter was involved in the 1837 uprisings? But this would be losing ourselves in conjecture.

Whether or not research will one day allow us to identify the artist of this enigmatic drawing as well as its subject, it remains a nice addition to a small corpus of portraits drawn in the St. Lawrence valley during the period 1820-1850.

J.R.P.

241.
***Panorama of the Beaupré Coast, Île d'Orléans and the South Shore
of the Saint Lawrence from the Parliament Building***, c. 1836-1840
Watercolour over graphite with traces of scraping out on paper, 29.8 × 180.4 cm (4 sheets 29.8 × 45.1 cm)

Inscriptions
(b.,l.l., on the first sheet, in graphite) *No. 1- Back
of Governm'. House & Distant View from Quebec;*
(above, in the same hand, in graphite) *5 cf cf* [?];
(b.,l.l., on the second sheet, in graphite) *No. 2- Isle
of Orleans & part of point Levy near Quebec;* (b.,l.l.,
on the third sheet, in graphite) *No. 3. part of point
Levy & Village opposite the Town of Quebec;* (b.,l.l.,
on the fourth sheet, in graphite) *No. 4- part of the
Village opposite Quebec.*

Provenance
Robert W. Reford estate, Montreal (sold by
Sotheby's, Toronto, May 27, 28, 29, 1968,
No. 83); Manuge Galleries Limited, Halifax;
acquired by the Musée du Québec, Quebec City,
1978.

Exhibition
Quebec City 1978-1979/1, No. 12 (second sheet
- 78.379.02).

Bibliography
CATALOGUE 1968, p. 26 s. (Repr.); *THIBAULT 1978*
(second sheet - 78.379.02) pp. 46 and 47 (Repr.);
ACQUISITIONS 1979-1980, p. 154, nos. 36 and 37
(third and fourth sheets - 78.379.03, 78.379.04);
ART DU QUÉBEC 1983 (third sheet - 78.379.03),
p. 98 (Repr.).

Collection
Musée du Québec, Quebec City (78.379.01 to
78.379.04)

HIS IS THE FIRST TIME ***Panorama of
the Beaupré Coast from Ile
d'Orléans and the South Shore of
the Saint Lawrence from the Parliament
Building*** has been shown in its entirety
since it was acquired by the Musée du
Québec. It is actually a set of four drawings
of similar format which, when put together,
form a panorama almost two metres long.
As indicated in the inscription—"*Back of
Governm' House*"—on the back of the first
drawing, the artist has his back to the seat
of government, then housed in the former
bishop's palace, and is drawing from the
edge of the terrace closest to the river.[1]
Overlooking Côte de la Montagne, Lower
Town and the St. Lawrence, this site offers
a panoramic view of the south shore. In a
sepia drawing contained in Lady Aylmer's
album, James Pattison Cockburn pin-
pointed the location, below Château Saint-
Louis near the wall surrounding the
Séminaire de Québec gardens (Fig. 241A).
The gardens, along with the parapet
crowned by a large battery, serve as a foil
for the overall panoramic view.

The panorama unfolds from the
Beaupré coast, across the tip of Ile
d'Orléans, to the ferry dock at Lévis. The
general composition is restrained; the artist has left out all extraneous detail, as
clearly evidenced by the ships on the river:
the few sailing ships and two timber floats
dragged by steamships are based more on
pictorial convention than on actual observation. Where are the traditional three-
masters from foreign ports, and why does
this view not show the daily activity on
the river? Joseph Bouchette had described

Fig. 241A.
James Pattison Cockburn,
Quebec from the Chateau;
Sepia on paper from the album
Recollections of Canada, by Lady Aylmer.
Archives nationales du Québec,
Quebec City (P363/AQ-29)

the constant comings and goings between
Quebec and Pointe-Lévis back in 1832:

a steam boat ferry-boat plies regularly every
half hour from six o'clock in the morning to
eight in the evening, performing the trip across
in from ten to fifteen minutes. There are also
three horse-boats, to which the preference is
generally given by the country people in
bringing their produce to the market. A great
number of other ferry-boats are likewise continually passing to and fro.[2]

Let us go back to the drawing at
hand to understand the purpose of the

panorama and see that a similar observation could be made by examining the villages bordering the river: row alignment along the Beaupré coast, concentration at Pointe-Lévis and more spread out near the shipyard and ferry departure for Quebec. Only the occasional landmark can be named: the Saint-Joseph-de-la-Pointe-Lévis church, the tower of the Aubigny Anglican church and the ship under repair at the shipyard. The artist has made a point only of defining the sites as they appear in their geographical layout. The sole purpose of the occasional ship on the St. Lawrence is to give an idea of distance, just as the small figure walking along the battery indicates the dimension of the four watercolours.[3]

A concern for a faithful topographical recording of the site is uppermost in the artist's mind and the panorama was certainly done by someone who had sufficient control over his technical means. The scene is well-laid-out and the relative proportions strictly respected. The artist is also a master of technique, applying a layer of monochromatic grey wash overtop the preliminary pencil drawing to indicate shadow. This foundation is then covered with layers of varied tones of watercolour. While this technique indicates strict instruction, probably received in a military academy, it also comes from teachings that had become outdated by the 19th century. Coloured drawings carried on the tradition of the first topographical artists of the 18th century well into the 19th. By circa 1800, most artists had stopped using neutral, grey or brown tones in order to paint shadows directly on the support us-

ing pure colours. Furthermore, the composition shares something with 18th-century construction. The narrow foreground framing the composition on the left can be found in the views of the Thames from the terrace of Somerset House drawn and painted by Canaletto (1697-1768) in England and engraved beginning in 1750-1751.[4] There is no question that the artist of ***Panorama of the Beaupré Coast from Ile d'Orléans and the South Shore of the Saint Lawrence from the Parliament Building*** fully understood the topographical tradition, but the processes employed are hardly progressive for the suggested period of execution, i.e circa 1836-1840.

And that is precisely one of the main problems with this landscape. It has never been attributed to a definite artist and there is not enough data to do so. However, the artist was most certainly familiar with the work of Philip John Bainbrigge. This watercolour reproduces, in particular, Bainbrigge's method of drawing trees using diagonal hatching.[5] And the figure walking along the battery—thin, dark silhouette whose long shadow is cast on the ground—is found in some of his watercolours. Nevertheless, the panorama is much less skilful than Bainbrigge's works as a whole. The almost total lack of spontaneity in the treatment of the vegetation in the left foreground and the too-formal use of hatching to suggest woods on the south shore make it impossible for this work to have been done by a verified landscape artist such as Bainbrigge. It was more likely painted by either a young soldier, fresh out of an academy[6] and who had

not yet had the time to develop his own artistic characteristics given the contact with various influences, or a lesser-known watercolourist whose technique was influenced by the artists arriving during the rebellions of 1837-1838.

D.P.

Notes

1. For a detailed view of Duberger's mock-up showing the site of Government House overlooking Lower Town and the river, see, in particular, NOPPEN, PAULETTE AND TREMBLAY 1979, p. 260, Fig. 33.

2. BOUCHETTE 1832, p. 273.

3. This site today corresponds to the corner of Rue Port-Dauphin and Rue des Ramparts.

4. J.G. Links, *Canaletto and his patrons* (London: Paul Elck Ltd., 1977, p. 71. See also Luke Hermann, *British Landscape Painting of the 18th Century* (London: Faber & Faber, 1973), p. 29 and Pl. 17A and 17B.

5. *La Fabrication du sucre d'érable, Bas-Canada* is a good example. See UN MOMENT 1991, No. 32 (Repr.).

6. Several parallels can be drawn between this watercolour and the construction of certain works by Henry James Warre held at the Provincial Archives of British Columbia, Victoria: unbroken pencil line to accentuate the contour of the mountains, the application of washes in layers for the ground and in soft hatching to indicate spruce trees in the forest, traces of scratching on bodies of water to demarcate land. The issue is far from simple and the case of Warre is only one example of many other artists whose first realizations in Quebec are unknown. The influence of Henry William Barnard could possibly have led to a profound change in his style and manner as of 1840.

Inscription
(l.c., painted in oil) *J.J. LARTIGUE, PREMIER ÉVÊQUE DE MONTREAL, NÉ LE 20 JUIN 1777. DÉCÉDÉ LE 19 AVRIL 1840/L'on vit briller en lui les plus rares vertus/ [D]e cette Ecolle il fut le Fondateur./C'est pourquoi ses enfans, dont il fit le bonheur,/Ne [voudraient] l'oublier. quoiqu'il ne vive plus.*

Provenance
Acquired by subscription (P. O. Tremblay, P. R. Breton, L. W. Sicotte, A. J. Boucher, Henry J. Tiffin, Justice Georges Baby), Château Ramezay, Montreal, 1897.

Exhibition
(?) Montreal 1892, No. 68.

Bibliography
(?) *MACDONALD 1892*, p. 8, No. 68; MCR, *Numismatic & Antiquarian Society Minute Book No. 4. Begin January 19, 1897, Ended December 20, 1907* (Minutes of the regular meetings), p. 14, February 16, 1897; *Registre des acquisitions 1895-1974*, p. 25, No. 710, February 16, 1897; *CATALOGUE s.d.*, p. 3, No. 16; *CATALOGUE 1898*, p. 6, No. 16; *O'LEARY 1901*, p. 23, No. 112; *O'LEARY 1903*, p. 30, No. 127; *O'LEARY 1907*, p. 26, No. 154; *O'LEARY 1917*, p. 28, No. 154; *O'LEARY 1920*, p. 28, No. 154; *O'LEARY 1922*, p. 28, No. 154; *CATALOGUE 1927/2*, p. 31, No. 154; *CATALOGUE 1928*, p. 31, No. 154; *CATALOGUE 1931*, p. 32, No. 154; *CATALOGUE 1936*, p. 31, No. 154; *CATALOGUE 1937*, p. 32, No. 154; *CATALOGUE 1948*, p. 32, No. 154; *CATALOGUE 1954*, p. 32, No. 154; *CATALOGUE 1956*, p. 32, No. 154; *CARRIER 1957*, pp. 29-30, No. 139; *CARRIER AND LEFEBVRE 1962*, p. 36, No. 139; *Nos racines*, No. 66 (1979), p. 1303 (Repr.).

Collection
Musée du Château Ramezay, Montreal (CR710)

242.
Monseigneur Jean-Jacques Lartigue, c. 1840
Oil on canvas, 89.7 × 75 cm

J EAN-JACQUES LARTIGUE (1777-1840) was related to Montreal's most prominent families. Like his cousins Denis-Benjamin Viger (1774-1861) and Louis-Joseph Papineau (Cat. 188), Lartigue started out to become a lawyer. In 1797, however, he opted for priesthood and was ordained in September 1800. Six years later he became a Sulpician and was given oversight of part of the Notre-Dame parish as well as certain "delicate" matters: legality of the establishment of new parishes, appeasement of the rioters in Lachine, etc. In 1819, he was sent to London to represent the Sulpicians in defending the title deeds to their seigneuries. He was accompanied by Monseigneur Joseph-Ocave Plessis (Cat. 181), who was in the midst of trying to obtain authorization to split up his diocese. While the bishop of Quebec did not come home fully satisfied, he did obtain the city's consent and was allowed to appoint four titular and auxiliary bishops. His choice for Montreal was Lartigue, who was appointed to the position in January 1821. Lartigue's bishopric was initially conse-

crated at the consolidation of his Church: Séminaire Saint-Jacques, for theological training, civic recognition of parishes and the establishment, in conjunction with Monseigneur Plessis, of the first ecclesiastic province in Canada. But his bishopric was marked by prolonged conflict with fellow Saint-Sulpice priests who saw his nomination as a threat of interference in the matters of the Séminaire, which was still run by French priests trained in the Gallic spirit. In 1836, without submitting their project to the British authorities beforehand, Monseigneur Lartigue and the Montreal clergy obtained authorization to establish the new Montreal diocese.

Prior to 1829, the bishop and his clergy had supported the social demands of the bourgeoisie. However, the increasing liberalism of the political elite forced Lartigue to protest against the leaders of the Patriote party, a confrontation that came to a head with his pastoral letter of October 24, 1837. History finally proved Lartigue right. The bishop succeeded in rallying the population to his side following the foiled 1837-1838 uprisings, trig-

gering the far-reaching religious movement that was to dominate Quebec society throughout the 19th century. At his death on April 19, 1840, Lartigue was replaced by Monseigneur Ignace Bourget, his secretary for over sixteen years and auxiliary bishop for three. Bourget (1799-1885) continued to lead the religious awakening and headed the new diocese for the next thirty-six years.

Two weeks after the death of Monseigneur Lartigue, the May 2, 1840 edition of *L'Ami du Peuple* notified the public that:

We are pleased to announce that Mr. Yves Tessier, a local painter, [has] gone to New York City to have engraved and lithographed the portrait of our venerable prelate whose passing we lament. The said portrait was executed while Monseigneur Lartigue was still of this world. We have seen the original portrait to be used for the engravings and lithography and we assure you that it is a remarkable likeness, having received the approval of all those who have been invited to see it. The taste and talent of Mr. Tessier are an absolute guarantee of the care that will be given the execution of this work. As a reminder of our history, most likely

Fig. 242A.
George Endicott
After Yves Tessier,
Monseigneur Jean-Jacques Lartigue, 1840;
lithograph, 57 × 37 cm.
Musée du Séminaire de Québec
(portfolio 156-G, Fol. 13).

the portrait, which was widely disseminated through engravings? The question remains unanswered for not enough is know about the works of these artists to be able to make a definite attribution.

The Château Ramezay painting reproduces the exact same composition. One significant point is that it bears an inscription indicating it was done after the bishop's death in 1840 and was probably commissioned by the students at the Séminaire Saint-Jacques, founded by Monseigneur Lartigue in 1825.[2] As in the case of the painting which cannot be traced, James Duncan was suggested as the artist, but this attribution follows the same misguided deduction as Morisset. Again, it is difficult to attribute this work to any artist in particular. It could have been done by either Tessier or Valin, or it could be the work of another artist who painted the figure either based on the original work or an engraving. The numerous existing versions[3] of this portrait make it difficult to understand its dissemination. Although not as many portraits were painted of Monseigneur Lartigue as of Monseigneur Plessis (Cat. 181), it is no less another telling example of the phenomenon of copying portraits of important religious figures.

P.B.

everyone will want to own a copy of this portrait whose merit will be to immortalize the traits of the first bishop of the diocese of Montreal for posterity. (*Translation*)

Bookseller C.-P. Leprohon announced the sale of the lithography on May 30. On the same day, the editor of *L'Ami du peuple* described the work in his own words: "based on the report of its execution, this work surpasses all expectations and is a most appropriate decoration for any Canadian parlour."[1] (*Translation*) The composition of the lithography (Fig. 242A) is exactly the same as most known paintings of Lartigue, including the one held at Château Ramezay. However, the most skilful of these portraits, and the one that probably all the others are copied after cannot be traced. We are familiar with it through a photograph by William Notman that was used to illustrate one of his articles in the series entitled *Portraits of British Americans,* published in July 1865 (Part III) and through the photograph by Gérard Morisset taken in the archbishop's palace in Montreal for the *Inventaire des oeuvres d'art.* Morisset attributed the painting to James Duncan, assuming that the watercolour medallion copy done by Duncan for Jacques Viger's *Album,* was

necessarily copied from one of his own paintings. However there is nothing to support such a theory. Does this mean we can assume Yves Tessier painted the portrait of Monseigneur Lartigue? The letter accompanying the lithographed portrait mentions that it was "Published by Yves Tessier, 1840" (*Translation*), which proves who the publisher was, but not the draughtsman. *L'Ami du Peuple* informed its readers that "the original [...] is of a remarkable likeness" without stating whether or not Tessier is the author. However, the sales ad for the lithography published in *Le Canadien* on June 3, 1840 mentions that the "engraving done in New York City after a painting by M. Ives [sic] Tessier, is now on sale at the Librairie Canadienne." (*Translation*) Three years previously, on October 27, 1837, an editorialist with *Le Canadien* visited Thomas Valin (circa 1810-1857), "pupil of Mr. Bowman," recently back from Michigan. At Valin's workshop, located in the residence of the Grey Nuns, the reporter "admired several portraits of Monseigneur de Montreal in which the traits of the venerable and pious prelate are reproduced with beautiful richness." (*Translation*) So, was it Tessier or Valin who actually did

Notes

1. In 1840, Tessier also had a lithography of Monseigneur Ignace Bourget published. See *Le Grand Héritage 1984,* p. 182, No. 157 (entry by Laurier Lacroix).

2. Gilles Chaussé, *Jean-Jacques Lartigue, premier évêque de Montréal* (Montreal: Éditions Fides) pp. 144-145.

3. Other paintings have the same composition. Unidentified versions can be found in the parish of Boucherville and the Vaudreuil museum (held in trust and belonging to the local parish church). A variation, in which the bishop has no book, but holds a similar pose, belongs to the Saint-Eustache parish church. A second painting belonging to the Château Ramezay is of similar composition. Another portrait of Monseigneur Lartigue, this time with a tighter perspective, hangs in the portrait gallery of bishops of the province of Quebec in the Saint-Sulpice seminary in Montreal; the portraits are of similar format and the one of Monseigneur Joseph Signay—which has the same facial features as in the painting by Théophile Hamel (Cat. 125)—is signed Alfred Boisseau (1833-1901) and dated 1882. Finally, the archbishop of Montreal owns a full-length portrait of the bishop which retains only the characteristic facial expression found in Tessier's work. It is actually an interpretation by the Italian painter Pietro Gagliardi (1809-1890) likely done circa 1864, at the same time as a similar painting of Monseigneur Bourget (*La Minerve,* July 26, 1864, p. 2).

VAG, AGNS, MMFA

243.
Edward Hale of Portneuf, c. 1845
Beige paper cutout on black paper,
36.7 × 32.1 cm (irregular dimensions)

Inscription
(u.l., in pen and black ink) *Honble Edw Hale of
Portneuf L. Canada.*

Provenance
Descendants of the Hale family; Stephanie
Hensley, London, Ontario; acquired by the Public
Archives of Canada, Ottawa, 1978.

Bibliography
ACQUISITIONS 1979-1980, p. 162, No. 97 (Repr.).

Collection
National Archives of Canada,
Ottawa (1979-14-19)

MQ, NGC

244.
Mary Louisa Hale, c. 1845
Beige paper cutout on black paper
35.7 × 26.3 cm (irregular dimensions)

Inscription
(u.l., in pen and black ink) *Mary Louisa Hale/now
M^{rs}. Major R Bethune/of St Andrews Scotland.*

Provenance
Descendants of the Hale family; Stephanie
Hensley, London, Ontario; acquired by the Public
Archives of Canada, Ottawa, 1978.

Collection
National Archives of Canada,
Ottawa (1979-14-23)

T HESE DELIGHTFUL LIFE-SIZE SILHOU-
ETTES show the profiles of Mary
Louisa Hale and her great-uncle
Edward Hale (1789-1862), who was a mill
owner and businessman at Portneuf, near
Quebec City. He was known as Edward
Hale of Portneuf[1] to distinguish him from
his better-known nephew, Edward Hale
(1800-1875), the politician and entrepre-
neur.[2] In 1839 both Edwards sat on the
Special Council considering the union of
Upper and Lower Canada.[3] Edward of
Portneuf never married and left his entire
estate to the children of his brother John
(1765-1838, receiver-general of Lower
Canada).[4] Among these children were
Edward (mentioned above) and William
Amherst Hale (1809-1844),[5] father of
Mary Louisa, the little girl in the present
silhouette. She was born in 1840,[6] which
suggests that her silhouette may have been
done around 1845. In 1865 Mary Louisa
married Major Robert Bethune his native
Scotland and settled in St. Andrews.[7]

Unlike those cut by itinerant silhouette artists such as Eliab Metcalf (Cat.
38-41), Augustin Edouart (Cat. 100-102)
and T.P. Jones (Cat 37), these are amateur
works probably produced by a member of
the Hale family. They would have been
easy to make: the subject was placed near
a wall on which a large sheet of paper was
tacked up, then by the use of a candle or
lamp, a shadow of the person's profile was
cast on the paper. The outline of the
shadow was traced with a pencil and then
cut out with scissors. The outer piece of
paper or the "hollow-cut" was then backed
with black paper to complete the silhouette.

This method was simple, but instead of producing the small intimate
portraits like those produced by the professional silhouette artists, the resulting
silhouettes are large life-size profiles, which
may explain why none of them appears to
have been framed for display. Given the
apparent wear and tear they seemed to
have suffered, it is likely they were kept in

a portfolio or between the pages of an
album, and brought out occasionally to be
passed around for the enjoyment of family
members.

These portraits of Mary Louisa and
Edward Hale are from a collection of eight
large silhouettes all of which appear to have
been done at the same time, perhaps on
the occasion of a family gathering.[8] The
sitters are identified by inscriptions which
were added some years after the silhouettes
were done. The silhouettes, along with
numerous other Hale portraits, were acquired by the National Archives of Canada from a family descendant.

L.F.

Notes
1. NAC, MG23, G II 18, vol. 6, miscellaneous
genealogies, document titled "Genealogy of the
family of Genl. John Hale of Plantation…," lists
Edward "the Baron of Portneuf" among the family
members; also a document titled "the 22 Children of Genl. John Hale…" has a reference to
Edward Hale as "our uncle of Portneuf." There
is also a reference to Edward Hale of Portneuf in
the entry for his nephew in the DCB, see note 2.
2. Louis-Philippe Audet, DCB, Vol. X (1972),
pp. 356-357. This Edward was sometimes referred to as Edward Hale of Sherbrooke, after the
area where he had land holdings.
3. *Macmillan Dictionary of Canadian Biography*
(Toronto, 1978), p. 326.
4. NAC, Hale family papers, Vol. 6, genealogical
notes show that Edward was unmarried and a
genealogical notebook contains a copy of a letter
from John Hale to his brother William Hale, dated 7 January 1827, containing the following information: "…our brother Edward is well and we
are on the best terms. He has not yet met with a
mate to his mind and it is doubtful whether he
now looks much for one—his habits as a single
man being pretty much formed." See the *Macmillan Dictionary of Canadian Biography* (Toronto, 1978), p. 326.
5. NAC, family papers, Vol. 6, document titled
"Genealogy of General John Hale…," gives William Amherst Hale's birth and death dates.
6. NAC, Hale family papers, Vol. 6, document
titled "Children of John Hale and Elizabeth
Frances Amherst…," shows Mary Louisa's birth
date as 4 December 1840.
7. NAC, Hale family papers, Vol. 6, newspaper
clipping announcing Mary Louisa's marriage to
Robert Bethune of Nydie, Fifeshire, the ceremony performed by her uncle, Rev. H. Hotham, on
January 24, in England. The year of the marriage
appears in a document also in Vol. 6, cited in
note 6.
8. Other silhouettes in the collection are of Edward Hale of Sherbrooke (1800-1875, son of
John Hale), Frances Isabella Hale (1804-1882,
unmarried daughter of John Hale), Captain John
Orlebar (married to Elizabeth Harriet Hale,
daughter of John Hale), Mary Caroline Hale
(mother of Mary Louisa and wife of William
Amherst, son of John Hale), and Miss Winslow
(probably Hannah Winslow, the unmarried aunt
of Mary Caroline Hale).

245.

John Bethune, c. 1845

Oil on canvas, 76.5 × 58.5 cm

Provenance

Descendants of the Bethune family; Strachan Bethune, Montreal, before 1902; McGill University, Montreal; McCord Museum, Montreal (transfer from the Visual Arts Committee of McGill University), 1986.

Exhibitions

Montreal 1887, No. 308; Montreal 1892, No. 215; Montreal 1987/1.

Bibliography

CATALOGUE 1887, p. 4, No. 308; *MACDONALD 1892*, p. 12, No. 215; *The McGill University Magazine*, Vol. II, No. 2 (1902) (Repr.); *MILLMAN 1943*, p. 16 (Repr.); *AUDET 1952*, p. 250 (Repr.); *DEROME 1981-1982*, pp. 45 and 46 (Repr.).

Collection

McCord Museum of Canadian History, Montreal (M986.X.137)

J OHN BETHUNE (1791-1872) came from a family of church pastors. Ordained in 1814, Bethune began his career as a missionary before being appointed minister of Montreal's Christ Church Cathedral and first pastor of the city's Anglican parish in 1818. He was named rector *pro tempore* of McGill University in November 1835, succeeding George Jehosaphat Mountain (1789-1863). A difference in opinion with Mountain regarding the strictly Anglican vocation of the University led to Bethune's dismissal in 1846. During his mandate, however, Bethune had the trust fund left by James McGill (Cat. 17) released and used the money to build the initial faculty of arts and sciences building and the rec-

tor's residence, which was completed in 1843. He also introduced new programs of study, which had been limited to medicine since the University's founding in 1829. After leaving McGill, Bethune became a pastor, then dean at Christ Church Cathedral. His ministry continued until his death in 1872.

This portrait of John Bethune, until recently held at McGill University, shows him in his rector's costume, bedecked as he is in his gloves, black sash and hood, black gown with red epaulettes and gold trimming, red robe, and white collar and bands. This indicates the portrait was done after 1835 and cannot be the one painted in 1820 by American artist William Dunlap during his brief stay in Montreal.[1] Actually, the portrait essentially employs the same conventions as those used by Samuel Palmer in his painting of *Alfred Hawkins* (Cat. 175), i.e. a full-length likeness depicting the subject seated in an armchair in a furnished room. However, it would be difficult to attribute this work to Palmer given the stylistic differences between the two works in question. The composition also shows affinities with the portrait of American President James Monroe painted by Charles Bird King (1785-1862) and known through the engraving published by Goodman & Piggot in December 1817 (Fig. 245A). The composition is indeed very similar, with the sitter presented at a three-quarter angle, his body slightly right of centre, leaving room to embellish the background on the left.[2] Unlike these two examples, however, the portrait of Bethune has no opening looking out over the landscape behind. Instead, the artist has preferred to include two paintings, one of which is hidden behind the drapery on the right and the other, apparently a reproduction of Louis Dulongpré's portrait of *James McGill* (Fig. 17A), which is recognizable despite the slight artistic licence taken, i.e. the addition of drapes. As Robert Derome has observed, "this iconographic process is uncommon in the history of Quebec art, and through it Bethune is appropriating the moral and spiritual authority of McGill." The University rector, probably living in his new residence built in 1843 with money from McGill's estate, is possibly paying tribute to the man who enabled its construction.

This portrait has been attributed to William Sawyer (1820-1889) on the basis of a stylistic comparison with the first known works of the Canadian artist. However, not much is known about Sawyer's training or early career. In 1847, he

Fig. 245A.

Goodman & Piggot after Charles Bird King, *President James Monroe*, 1817; engraving, 49.2 × 33.2 cm. National Portrait Gallery, Washington (NPG.79.72).

was already a familiar figure in Montreal, exhibiting his works along with those of Andrew Morris, Cornelius Krieghoff, Martin Somerville and James Duncan as part of the Montreal Society of Artists. Among the paintings shown were copies based on works by Joshua Reynolds, William Collins and Thomas Sully, apparently indicating that Sawyer studied in Europe, most likely in England.

Although the portrait of John Bethune obviously shows some British influence, if only in its composition, the comparison with Sawyer is not altogether convincing. Both the brush strokes and the colour scheme are more vibrant and richer than Sawyer's: the drawing in several of Sawyer's portraits from the 1840s is somewhat weak and the material, dull and flat. Other Anglophone artists, whose work is less known, were also active as portraitists in Montreal during the 1840s. For lack of more solid data, it would be better to leave this portrait anonymous for now.

P.B.

Notes

1. *BAZIN 1972*, p. 20.

2. Andrew F. Cosentino, *The Paintings of Charles Bird King (1785-1862)* (Washington: Smithsonian Institute Press, 1977), pp. 33-37 and 147 (Repr.).

246.
Notre-Dame Church Square, Montreal, c. 1850

After William Henry Bartlett
Oil on canvas, 61.5 × 73.5 cm

Inscriptions
(i., l.l., in a rectangle) *WH* [superposed and forming the only letter H]*B./MONTREAL;* (b.c., on a sign) MONTREAL.

Provenance
(?) Hamburg, Germany; (?) Victor Spark Gallery, New York; R. M. Elliot, Toronto; acquired by the Royal Ontario Museum, Toronto, 1954.

Exhibition
(?) Montreal 1935.

Bibliography
Montreal Star, May 29, 1935; MORISSET 1936-1937, Vol. I, p. 138; BARTEAUX 1945, p. 433; WADE 1966, p. 185 (Repr.); DUVAL 1974, p. 12.

Collection
Royal Ontario Museum, Toronto (954.192.4)

T his luminous and theatrical painting shows a tightrope walker performing at Place d'Armes, Montreal. The view of the square with Notre-Dame church is based on a composition by William Henry Bartlett, which was published as an engraving titled *The Cathedral, Montreal* in 1840-1842 (Fig. 246A).[1] Bartlett was a graphic artist who is not known to have painted in oil; however, steel engravings of his works were widely distributed and were copied by artists in Europe and America. The author of this oil painting has acknowledged his source by including the inscription "*WHB*" in the

view. The unknown artist transformed the topographical view by focusing on a daring acrobatic performance, and also by rendering the buildings in greater detail, which changes them in character. In copying the work by Bartlett, he has moved the viewpoint to the left, which gives an oblique angle to the church and the buildings on Rue Notre Dame. The buildings in the background are taller, narrower, and quite different from those in the engraving. To this view, he has added the dramatic element of a tightrope walker and a crowd of spectators who were not present in the Bartlett view. We see a similar set up in

Fig. 246A.
James Carter
After William Henry Bartlett,
The Cathedral, Montreal, 1838;
engraving published by George Virtue, 19.7 × 27.5 cm.
Musée du Québec, Quebec City (81.321.07).

Fig. 246B.
Unidentified artist
After William Henry Bartlett,
The Market Place, Quebec, c. 1850;
oil on canvas, 38.1 × 45.7 cm.
Royal Ontario Museum, Toronto (954.192.3).

The Market Place, Quebec (Fig. 246B). Judging from the dress of the spectators in the Montreal view (for example, the women's shallow bonnets and skirts with multiple flounces), the painting dates probably from the early 1850s.

This painting is one of a group of nine views of Montreal and Quebec subjects, all seemingly by the same hand. Each painting was based on a Bartlett view, and in most of the works the unknown artist added elements of his own invention. The additions were usually figures in the foreground, but he also used the weather as a feature by introducing stormy skies and choppy seas. These paintings first came to notice in Germany, where they were photographed in 1934.[2] Several of the canvases, now in the collection of the Royal Ontario Museum, have Berlin customs stamps on the reverse.[3] The paintings were exhibited at the Continental Art Gallery in Montreal in 1935. In 1936, they were said to be owned by a resident of Austria; other sources reported that they came from Hamburg, Germany. Whatever their origin, it is possible that they were painted by an artist who never visited the scenes he portrayed.
M.A.

Notes

1. *Willis 1842.* This book was first issued in parts in 1840.

2. Photographs by "Echtermeyer, Berlin", copyrighted in 1934. Information from files of National Archives of Canada.

3. The following canvases are stamped: "*Zollzweigstelle Bahnhof [...] strasse, Berlin*": *Notre-Dame with Books,* 953.194.1; *Market Place Montreal,* 953.194.2; *Quebec from Pointe Levis,* 953.194.3; *Market Place, Quebec,* 954.192.3; and *Quebec from the Citadel,* 953.194.4. The canvas *Notre-Dame Church Square, Montreal* has been relined, so no stamp is visible.

MQ, NGC

247.
Portrait of a Man, 1853
Watercolour over graphite with white
highlights on paper laid on cardboard,
23.3 × 19.2 cm

Inscription
(l.r., on the mount, in pen and black ink) *Québec
1853.*

Provenance
Galerie Bernard Desroches, Montreal; acquired
by the National Gallery of Canada, Ottawa, 1976.

Collection
National Gallery of Canada, Ottawa (18701)

T HIS LEAD PENCIL AND WATERCOLOUR drawing depicts a man in his thirties seated in an apparently austere room overlooking woods and a mountain. Laying on the table to the sitter's right are two books, one of which is opened to fashion illustrations of feathered hats. This distinct iconographic motif no doubt indicates the subject is either a milliner or hatter by trade. An early pen and black ink inscription reveals that the portrait was done in Quebec City in 1853. A lack of historical data, however, makes it impossible to identify either the sitter or the portraitist.

While this watercolour certainly has weaknesses, its polished quality makes it unique in several respects. The hatter is shown in a half-length profile, his body turned slightly away from the centre of the composition. The pervading feeling of nonchalance and contentment is favoured by an airy composition and the graceful line of the right arm, which moulds the contour of the chairback. The sitter's costume is apparently as studied as it is of good quality. The rough lines of the black waistcoat and sienna redingote contrast with the detailed lines of the high collar adorned with a butterfly knot. These elements work together to set off the subject's manly traits. His strong chin, thick lips, thin nose and large eyes, his fine, wavy hair and his sideburns give him undeniable charm, despite his somewhat evasive look.

It seems the table on which the young man is resting his left elbow presented some problems for the artist. While the veins of the wood and details of the fashion illustrations have been rendered with a greater concern for detail, the overall perspective of the table and the books laying on it is somewhat awkward. The same holds true for the jamb and ledge of the large rectangular window above the table. Beneath awkwardly rendered clouds, the unpolished landscape is limited to a mountain, a few scraggy evergreens and a clump of deciduous trees whose foliage curiously resembles the feathers on one of the hats in the fashion illustrations!

The motif of an open window looking out onto nature is neither common nor unusual in Quebec portraiture of the first half of the 19th century. François Beaucourt himself had used nature to embellish part of a famous painting done in the West Indies in 1786 (MMCH). Closer to home, Théophile Hamel used it in a cautious, but conventional manner a dozen times, more often than not combining it with a drapery used as a foil. On the other hand, to our knowledge this motif was never employed in the works of Antoine Plamondon, and yet this portrait has been attributed to him. In our opinion, various other facts argue against such an attribution, from the unique treatment of the facial features and extremely soft line of the hand to the type of composition and date of execution, as Plamondon had retired to Neuville in 1851. Furthermore, Plamondon rarely worked in watercolour; in fact, not much is known about his use of the medium. The Musée du Québec's art collection holds two signed portraits which are dated 1841 and 1850 respectively, but which show numerous formal and stylistic differences with the unsigned—and yet more polished—work in question here.

Some fifteen years ago, quality portraits dating to the first half of the 19th century tended automatically to be attributed to a small circle of well-known Canadian artists. Now that we have greater knowledge on the subject, a practice of this kind is as questionable as it is foolhardy. After close study, it would seem more likely that our hatter was immortalized on paper by a foreign, itinerant artist whose works have not yet been discovered. Just like the fashion books in the portrait, the circulation of ideas and movement of artists was far more extensive in the 19th century than was previously thought.

J.R.P.

PERSPECTIVES
1850-1860

**N**APOLÉON BOURASSA was born in Acadia on October 21, 1827. In the late 1840s, while pursuing his studies in law, the young Bourassa took painting lessons from Théophile Hamel. Beginning in the summer of 1852 and following in the footsteps of his master, he headed for Europe, more precisely Italy. After a short stay in Paris, he travelled first to Florence and then Rome. At the time, he was a devotee of the neo-classical artistic movement led by Hippolyte Flandrin (1809-1864), in which art was inspired by the Italian Renaissance. Bourassa returned to Canada in December 1855. His early career was difficult and he had to limit himself to portraiture. Among his most notable works was one of his father-in-law, Louis-Joseph Papineau (Cat. 248). He also gave lectures on Italian art and began teaching in 1861, first at École normale Jacques-Cartier, then Collège Sainte-Marie and, finally, the Société des artistes canadiens-français (from 1866 to 1871). In 1877, the provincial government sent him to observe the French system of fine arts schools; his report, however, went unheeded.

In 1870-1872, he began to work on the murals of the former Nazareth chapel in Montreal. With the Notre-Dame-de-Lourdes chapel (Montreal, 1872-1880), Bourassa was to establish harmony between interior decoration and architecture, turning the work site into a veritable studio for his apprentices. His other large-scale religious decorative works, for Notre-Dame de Montréal church (1873) and the church in Saint-Hyacinthe (1875-1890), would never be completed. The same held for the decoration of the new Parliament Building in Quebec City (1883). Despite the fact that large iconographic compositions held more interest for him, as confirmed by the incomplete *The Apotheosis of Christopher Colombus* (MQ), he also pursued his easel pictures. Napoléon Bourassa died in Lachenaie on August 27, 1916.

NAPOLÉON
BOURASSA
1827-1916

Main sources
BOURASSA 1968; LEMOINE 1974; VÉZINA 1976/2.

248. (See colour reproduction, p. 111)
Louis-Joseph Papineau, 1858
Oil on canvas, 151.9 × 115 cm

Provenance
Descendants of the Papineau family; Caroline R. Papineau; acquired by the Musée de la Province de Québec, Quebec City, 1952.

Exhibitions
Quebec City 1968; Quebec City 1983-1984, No. 87.

Bibliography
ANQQ, Fonds Papineau-Bourassa, letters from L.-J. Papineau to Mary Wescott, September 9 and 26, 1858, and to Amédée Papineau, February 11, 1859; BOURASSA 1968, pp. 15, 53 and 59 (Repr.); DE ROUSSAN 1969, p. 10 (Repr.); LE MOINE 1974, pp. 48 and 251; DUMAS 1974, p. 41 (Repr.); VÉZINA 1976/2, pp. 26, 131 and 249 (Repr.); VÉZINA 1976/3, pp. 14 and 24; VÉZINA 1978, p. 2 (Repr.); PARIZEAU 1980, p. 318 (Repr.); *Nos racines,* No. 91 (1981), p. 1812 (Repr.); LE MUSÉE DU QUÉBEC 1983, p. 86, No. 87 (entry by Achille Murphy) (Repr.); TRUDEL 1986, p. 1 (Repr.); VILLENEUVE 1987, pp. 113 and 124 (Repr.); BROWN AND LINTEAU 1988, p. 247 (Repr.); PICKERING LEBLANC 1989, pp. 98 and 99 (Repr.); BÉLAND AND BOURASSA 1990, pp. 6, 8 and 110 (Repr.); VEYRON 1990, p. 521 (Repr.); LACROIX 1990, p. 20.

Collection
Musée du Québec, Quebec City (52.58)

N APOLÉON BOURASSA RETURNED in 1855 after three years of studies abroad in Europe and, in the years that followed, produced religious paintings, but concentrated on portraits. While he held portraiture in low esteem, Bourassa nonetheless completed many likenesses. While he gained satisfaction from painting close relatives and friends, many of his works were done on commission (several members of the clergy in Montreal, Ottawa and Saint-Hyacinthe).

On September 17, 1857, Bourassa married Azélie Papineau, daughter of Louis-Joseph (1786-1871). During the winter of 1857-1858, he painted a self-portrait and a portrait of his wife (MQ). For his father-in-law, he copied the portraits of Joseph and Rosalie Papineau, painted by Dulongpré (Cat. 90). The following summer, in the studio set up in the "granary" of the manor at Montebello,[1] he sculpted a bust of Jacques Cartier and attempted to do a large portrait of his famous father-in-law, then aged 71. In September, in two letters addressed to his daughter-in-law, Mary Westcott, the model wrote that the portrait was "excellent" and that he hoped Bourassa would exhibit it, along with the bust of Cartier, at an upcoming exhibition in Montreal. The artist, feeling that the painting still required several retouches, refused. Louis-Joseph explained to his daughter-in-law "that he is careful of his reputation. The portrait seemed to me to be sufficiently complete some time ago. Since then, he has made me sit for three long sessions and each time he has refined the work further."[2] (*Translation*) Once the painting was complete, Papineau wrote to his son Amédée, Mary Westcott's husband:

It is difficult to express to you just how much it resembles me, I am pleased you find the portrait well done for all concerned. Bourassa required more sessions of me to achieve a great success, than other artists, who have done me poorly from time to time.[3] (*Translation*)

Already retired from politics for four years at the time, Papineau was focusing his attention on his Petite-Nation seigneury. The seigneur took an active interest in his fief, keeping a watchful eye on his best interests and strongly protesting the abolition of the seigneurial system. He had always dreamed of settling down in the country, surrounded by his family and his books. However, his two daughters Ézilda and Azélie wanted, on no account, to live on the estate. To entice them into doing so—a vain attempt—he had a luxurious home built in 1850; the Manoir Montebello was equipped, among other things, with an imposing library. From 1850 until his death in 1871, Papineau remained, according to Fernand Ouellet, the advocate of annexation and democracy.[4] This time in his life remained marked by domestic disappointments and unrest. It was in this context that Bourassa painted his portrait of the famous orator.

Papineau had posed for many painters: John James around 1830 (portrait disappeared) and Antoine Plamondon in 1836 (Cat. 188). Théophile Hamel also painted him on two occasions, around 1850 (location unknown) and in 1856 (NAC).[5] Another portrait, by Alfred Boisseau around 1871 (MQ), completes the list. This does not take into account numerous engravings, lithographs and photographs, particularly those by William Notman and Alfred Boisseau.[6] Bourassa also created several sculpted models of his father-in-law, including a bronze bust (MCR), several cameos moulded in plaster (MQ) and at least two oils on canvas. In formal, iconographic and psychological terms, the 1858 portrait is not only the most striking one of Papineau, but also Bourassa's most perceptive work. The famous patriot's correspondence reveals that the artist worked diligently on the painting, particularly on the landscape and the head, where much impasto is apparent.

Standing in a three-quarter profile and shown from the knee up, the model entirely dominates the composition and draws the eye. The bushes, the land in the background and the subject's clothing direct one's attention to and accent the majestic head. The setting Bourassa chose captured Papineau's dignity and bearing, as well as the doctrinarian's contradictions and intransigence. Thus shown, Papineau seems to exude a supernatural glow; he stands as a veritable monument for his contemporaries and for generations to come. The water, the setting sun and the garden, with its large oaks, serve to lessen the Spartan effect of the composition as a whole, endowing the subject with a human element. Holding a book in the hands clasped behind his back, the seigneur is captured in deep thought at his beloved refuge of Montebello. This is one of the few rare portraits of the era to place the model in a realistic natural setting and not an imaginary or artificial one, as was the case with Théophile Hamel's *Self-Portrait with a Landscape* (Cat. 117) and Plamondon's *Zacharie Vincent* (Cat. 194). Bourassa introduced Quebec to a new manner of presenting a subject in a landscape, developing a new esthetic to be applied to the art of portraiture.

M.B.

Notes

1. See his advertisement in *La Minerve* of April 27, 1858: "Painter, Mr. N. Bourassa will be at Petite-Nation until the month of October at his studio there." (*Translation*)

2. ANQQ, Papineau-Bourassa bequest, letters from L.-J. Papineau to Mary Westcott, September 9 and 26, 1858.

3. Letter dated February 11, 1859, quoted in *Bourassa 1968*, p. 15.

4. Fernand Ouellet, DCB, Vol. x (1972).

5. For information on the first, see Pierre Caron, "Antonio Maranzi restaurateur d'oeuvres d'art," *Perspectives*, Vol. xvi, No. 24 (May 25, 1974), pp. 8-9; for the second, see *Hubbard 1970*, pp. 24 and 37, as well as NAC, RG 14, C5, Vol. xii, N75 & 76, "Account of T. Hamel for Portrait of Speakers" (letter from T. Hamel, April 15, 1856).

6. See *Villeneuve 1987*, pp. 103-130.

JAMES D.
DUNCAN

(See biographical note on page 250)

249. (See colour reproduction, p. 112)
The Gavazzi Riot, 1853
Watercolour over graphite with gum arabic highlighted with gouache,
23 × 37.2 cm (image); 32.6 × 41.5 cm (sheet)

Inscriptions
(l.c., in graphite) *Montréal*; (l.r., in blue pencil) *Conenti* [Convention] *de Gavazzi;* (b.,l.r., in graphite) <u>*June 8th 1853*</u>, *reproduit en gravure par J. Walker.*

Provenance
Jacques Viger, Montreal; damsels Lennox, 1858; acquired by Abbé Hospice-Anthelme Verreau, Quebec City, 1860; bequeathed to the Séminaire de Québec, 1901; on deposit at the Société du Musée du Séminaire de Québec, 1983.

Exhibitions
Quebec City 1952, No. 29; Ottawa 1965, No. 40; Montreal 1988.

Bibliography
ASQ, Fonds Verreau, Reg. 0218, Fol. 26; *MORISSET 1952*, p. 28, No. 29; *MORISSET 1960/1*, p. 150; *HARPER AND HUBBARD 1965*, p. 47, No. 40; *TODD 1978*, p. 167; *TODD 1982*, p. 314; *Horizon Canada*, No. 46 (1982), p. 1082 (Repr.); *CAUFIELD 1987*, p. 194.

Collection
Musée du Séminaire de Québec (Pf984.32)

A LTHOUGH THE WORK is not signed, ***The Gavazzi Riot*** has traditionally, and apparently correctly, been attributed to James Duncan. His touch is evident in this panoramic view, which removes the viewer somewhat from the scene, and in the descriptive topographical treatment, which has remained faithful to the essential details of the site, allowing it to be identified. The uncluttered precision of the buildings contrasts with the agitated rendering of the crowds—the people in motion being only roughly sketched, characteristic of Duncan's style. In addition, the archives of the Séminaire de Québec contain a notebook in which Father Verreau (1828-1901)[1] drafted a list of what he felt were the most interesting pieces in Jacques Viger's bequest, then in his possession. The last section of the document contains a descriptive list of the contents of a "Large portfolio with various engravings and sketches" (*Translation*) in which the "View of the Gavazzi riot in Montreal"[2] (*Translation*) is mentioned. This very clear notation therefore indicates that the watercolour first belonged to Jacques Viger (1787-1858).[3] Given that Duncan did a number of works for the Montreal collector and that the watercolourist worked for Viger during the summer of 1853, it is highly likely that the latter was able to acquire ***The Gavazzi Riot.*** At the same time, Duncan was completing *Costumes des communautés religieuses de femmes au Canada* for the album which Viger intended for Monseigneur Cajetan Bedini, apostolic nuncio to Brazil.[4]

Oddly enough, the person for whom the album was intended was directly related to Alessandro Gavazzi (1809-1889), protagonist of the clash which bears his name, a name immortalized by the incident. Indeed, for Monseigneur Bedini, Lower Canada was a haven of peace after his tumultuous stay in America, during

Fig. 249A.
J.W. Orr,
Gavazzi Riot at Montreal - Exterior of Zion Church and *The Lecture*;
engravings (2), 37.1 × 25 cm.
Published in the *Illustrated News*, July 2, 1853.
Archives du Séminaire de Québec (portfolio 86, folio 88).

which Gavazzi had stepped up his actions to discredit him. The latter, an ex-monk from the order of Clerks of St. Paul, took his vengeance on Monseigneur Bedini, who had had him imprisoned in 1848. The facts show that at that time Gavazzi had been participating in the popular revolution against the absolutism of the papacy, which, in addition to never having democratized its political system, refused to liberate Italian territories occupied by Austria. After being freed by Republican friends, Gavazzi fled to England where he organized meetings to rally public opinion to his cause. With the same goal in mind, he set sail for North America in 1853, hoping to garner funds for Italian patriots. Everything went well for the preacher as long as he addressed his anti-papist speeches to Protestant audiences, but then he decided to make the rounds of Lower Canada.

After giving a few speeches in Toronto, Gavazzi left for Quebec City, where his reputation had preceded him. His was able to give his first speech, but was politely asked to speak somewhere other than the Wesleyen temple; and therefore went to Chalmer's Church. A speech on the Inquisition caused things to heat up. Indeed, Gavazzi compared the brutal methods of this tribunal to the contemporary actions of the papacy and Catholic priests. Run out of the conference hall, Gavazzi left for Montreal where he would give three more speeches. There again, tension mounted. The Irish community was up in arms over

the fact that municipal authorities had agreed to rent the Bonsecours market, the location of the city hall, to the "destroyer of papacy". (*Translation*) Given the number of protests and the risk of riot, Mayor Charles Wilson (Cat. 130) changed his mind and eventually refused Gavazzi access to the room. The meetings was therefore held in a congregationalist temple, Zion Church. In his first speech, Gavazzi attempted to convince the audience of "*Le système papal est l'aveuglement.*"[5] That evening, he spoke:

Gavazzi proceeded to Montreal, and announced a lecture in the Zion Church on the evening of the 9th of June, which was well attended by many of the most respectable citizens. [...] At about a quarter to 8 o'clock a band of ruffians attacked and overpowered the police, [...] and proceeded to force their way into the church, from which a body of fifteen or twenty repulsed them, several shots from guns and pistols being fired from both sides. The assaulting party were effectually routed; two or three of their member were left dead or severely wounded.

At the conclusion of the lecture the congregation dispersed, there being considerable noise and hooting, but no apparent disturbance. At this time the troops fired upon the people. It was reported that the firing occurred by order of the Mayor, which he afterwards denied. The consequences were extremely unfortunate. The number of persons shot was about fifty, and of those killed outright or mortally wounded, from ten to twelve. The whole affair created intense excitement at Montreal.[6]

After that evening, Gavazzi returned to New York where he was con-

fronted by an old enemy, Monseigneur Bedini. During that time, in Montreal, an inquiry was underway to determine who was responsible for the tragedy. Since the nine Protestants and ten Catholics acting on the jury would base their vote on their religious affiliation, a controversial verdict was to put an end to the issue. Light would never really be shed on these events.

An analysis of **The Gavazzi Riot** does not really provide answers to the questions posed by the inquiry. It does, however, allow us to determine the site of the turmoil on June 9. Indeed, the precise rendering of the location shown in the watercolour provides a clear framework for the events.[7] The foreground shows the Commissioners Square, with the building that houses the fire station. To the north is the hay market and weighing office. Then, from left to right, we can see St. Andrew's Church, the small neo-classically designed Unitarian Church, imposing St. Patrick's Church and the Collège des Jésuites. The viewpoint adopted by Duncan is stunning; indeed, Zion Church, where Gavazzi's meeting took place, is not shown from the front, but from the side, facing the hay market at the corner of Sainte-Radegonde and Latour. This composition by James Duncan stresses St. Patrick's over Zion Church. Did he, in this manner, wish to signal his allegiance to the Irish community and the Roman Catholic Church? Even if Duncan's usual works do not contain such messages, the

THE GAVAZZI DISTURBANCE AT QUEBEC—REMARKS ON PAGE 4.

Fig. 249B.
J.W. Orr,
The Gavazzi Disturbance at Quebec,
engraving, 21.7 × 25.1 cm.
Published in the *Illustrated News,* July 2, 1853.
Archives du Séminaire de Québec (portfolio 86, folio 88).

event was so emotion-laden that this hypothesis is plausible. One thing is certain, he decided to illustrate the most dramatic moment in the melee: the volley fired by the soldiers of the 26th regiment standing back-to-back. People are running, abandoning dead bodies behind them; the desultory actions being taken by a few of the city's police who, armed with truncheons, are attempting to restore order, occupy the foreground.

The event made newspaper headlines. An engraving by J.W. Orr appeared in the *Illustrated News* (New York) on July 2, 1853 (Fig. 249A). This illustration repeats and interprets the left side of Duncan's work. But was it really this watercolour that served as the model for the engraving? The slight difference in the point of view adopted, showing more of the front of Zion Church to allow a view of the crowd exiting it, leads us to believe that it may have been inspired by another of Duncan's drawings, very similar in composition to the watercolour. The artist might very well have done several sketches of the scene. However, it is interesting to note that the engraving, while reminiscent of Duncan's work, expands on it, making the characters and their actions more sensational. Indeed, the *Illustrated News* refers very generally to the artist who provided the engraving, "Our artist has transmitted to us sketches of the most remarkable scenes at the recent Canadian disturbances."[8] Are they referring to Duncan or Orr? We have no information on the latter, who did not appear to be living in Montreal in 1853. If it was Duncan,

would he also have provided the drawings which formed the basis of the two other engravings accompanying the same article? Let us immediately eliminate the one relating the events in Quebec since it bears absolutely no resemblance to Duncan's works (Fig. 249B). The second, which shows the interior of Zion Church (Fig. 249A), is less clear; it may have been based on a drawing by Duncan, with the engraver retaining only the architectural detail and general composition.

The issue of the use of Duncan's works in magazines raises many questions. Unfortunately, current research does not allow us to determine whether the artist contributed regularly as a reporter and artist. However, we do know of one other engraving published in the *London Illustrated News* on August 7, 1852, patterned after an oil by Duncan showing the *Burning of Hayes House, Dalhousie Square* (MMCH). Like *The Gavazzi Riot,* this work showed a noteworthy event in Montreal news. In addition, the 1852 engraving shows the same characteristics. In it, we find the group composition and viewpoint adopted by the artist, but interpreted in such a way as to provide a journalistic dimension to the event. These two news-related works do not appear to be major achievements in terms of Duncan's career. So what exactly do they represent? Many engravings could have been produced after drawings done by the artist, but as long as comparative works remain unknown to researchers, holes in their knowledge about Duncan will linger.

J.C.

Notes

1. Abbé Hospice-Anthelme Verreau occupied the history chair at the Université Laval in Montreal and was a founding member of the Montreal Historical Society and the Royal Society of Canada. When Jacques Viger died, Abbé Verreau bought a large portion of his collection.

2. ASQ, Verreau bequest, Reg. 0218, Fol. 24 and 26.3. In addition to being a roads inspector in Montreal—one of the most important positions in the public service—Jacques Viger was the first mayor of the city. He is remembered mainly for his active interest in history which led him to collect books, documents and works of art about Canadian history.

4. Monseigneur Bedini had expressed the desire to own such a compendium shortly after his visit to Montreal. For details about this order, see *LE GRAND HÉRITAGE 1984,* pp. 77-94 (entry by John R. Porter).

5. The bulk of the information on the events that took place in Montreal and about Gavazzi are drawn from Robert Sylvain, "Le 9 juin 1853 à Montréal—Encore l'affaire Gavazzi," *Revue d'Histoire de l'Amérique Française,* Vol. XIV, No. 2 (September 1960), pp. 173 to 216, and Armand Yon, "L'Apostat Gavazzi au Canada (1853)," *Le Canada français,* Vol. XXVI, No. 4 (December 1938), pp. 329 to 347.

6. *Illustrated News,* July 2, 1853, p. 4.

7. The site corresponds to today's Victoria Square.

8. *Illustrated News,* July 2, 1853, p. 4.

ANTOINE-SÉBASTIEN FALARDEAU was born on August 13, 1822, in Cap-Santé (Portneuf county). Unfortunately, we have little information on either his childhood or his introduction to painting. Around 1841-1842, he became an apprentice to Robert Clow Todd and then, in 1845, took several lessons from Italian miniaturist Gerome Fassio. On November 14, 1846, he left for Italy, where he eventually settled permanently.

Falardeau first enrolled at the Florence academy of fine arts in 1847-1848 and studied under Giuseppe Calendi and Tommaso Gazzarrini. He visited several cities on the peninsula (Milan, Bologna, Naples, Venice), where he made copies of Old Masters. In 1851, in Parma, he took part in a contest for the best copy of Coreggio's *Saint Jerome*. His work attracted widespread admiration and won first prize from the Parma academy of fine arts. From that moment on, his reputation as a copyist was made. On January 17, 1857, the Duke of Parma gave him the title of Knight of the Order of St. Louis. Once he returned to Florence, this sign of honour in hand, he began to win important commissions; some from prominent people abroad.

Falardeau produced several portraits in addition to his usual copies. He also maintained ties with his homeland, occasionally being visited by compatriots, like Napoléon Bourassa in 1852, and Eugène Hamel in 1869. On September 7, 1861, he married Caterina, daughter of Marquess Francesco Mannucci-Benincasa Capponi. He made only two short trips to Canada, in 1862, and then twenty years later, in 1882. These two stints provided an ideal opportunity for him to offer the Canadian public two extensive collections of his works; he also accepted specific commissions, such as one for the portrait of former premier of Quebec Joseph-Adolphe Chapleau, in 1882. Antoine-Sébastien Falardeau drowned accidentally on July 14, 1889 in the Arno river in Florence.

ANTOINE-SÉBASTIEN FALARDEAU
1822-1889

Main sources
FALARDEAU 1936; VÉZINA 1982; NIXON 1988.

250.
Saint John The Baptist, 1861
After Titian
Oil on canvas, 192.6 × 127.3

Inscription
(b., before the new backing covered the inscription, partial reading) [*Le chevalier Falardeau*].

Provenance
Louis Beaudry, before the 1862 sale by auction; Fabrique Notre-Dame de Montreal.

Bibliography
Le Canadien, June 30, 1862; *Le Courrier du Canada,* July 2, 4 and 23, 1862; *La Minerve,* July 17, 19, 22 and 24, 1862; *Le Pays,* July 17 and 22, 1862; *L'Ordre,* July 21 and 25, 1862; *Le Journal de Québec,* July 22, 1862; FALARDEAU *1936,* pp. 114-120; MUSÉE NOTRE-DAME *1938,* pp. 9 and 10, No. 105 (Repr.) dated 1859; MAURAULT *1949,* p. 159; MUSÉE NOTRE-DAME *1950,* No. 115; NIXON *1988,* pp. 76, 81-83 and 293-294, No. 136.

Collection
Basilique Notre-Dame de Montréal

T HE ART OF copying knew its finest hour in Quebec under Chevalier Antoine-Sébastien Falardeau. From 1846 on, he practised his art in Florence. Twice, in 1862 and 1882, Falardeau profited from the aura surrounding overseas acclaim to return and reap the rewards in the country of his birth. During his first visit he became the subject of the first-ever published work on a Canadian artist, written by Father Henri-Raymond Casgrain (1831-1904), who had visited him in 1858. Despite his physical absence, he remained well-known on the artistic scene throughout the 1850s, mainly due to word-of-mouth information carried back by the many Canadians to visit Italy, among them Torontonian Egerton Ryerson, who, in 1856, commissioned several copies for the museum he planned to build. Napoléon Bourassa, who arrived in Florence in September 1852, gave the following opinion of Falardeau's talent:

The painters he appears to best comprehend are Guido Reni and Carlo Dolci; as for the colorists; I do not believe that he fully understood them [...]. I truly believe that he would have achieved good colouring or could still achieve it by working more closely after nature, or by copying only colourists. At this time, I have to say he has few equals among those who work as copyists in Florence.[1] (*Translation*)

During his artistic studies in Florence, Falardeau discovered the economic potential represented by copying and devoted his career to it. The *Gazzetta di Parma* of December 1, 1851 described him as scouring Italy in search of models, "to do copies of some of the most famous works. He also visited Rome and Bologna."[2] (*Translation*) Though Titian was not his favourite painter, Falardeau, early in his career, copied at least seven other works by the Venetian artist, some of them several times. These somehow found their way to Quebec.[3]

The copies he brought to Canada would lead to the development of a new type of commission, which would benefit Canadian artists. Indeed, during the last quarter of the 19th century, several artists would use these commissions to offset the cost of their studies abroad.[4] The copy continued to dominate the market with clients insisting that copyists work from the original. The availability of information on art history, as well as the custom of travelling abroad, would lead clients to look for copies of recognizable works after famous masters.

Falardeau who, according to his biography, possessed an innate sense of public relations, attended the Saint-Jean celebrations as soon as he landed in Quebec City on June 24, 1862.[5] He organized an exhibition of his work in an old foundry at 138 Rue Saint-Jean and orchestrated a promotional campaign in the press. *Le Courrier du Canada* reported extensively on his stay in the country.

A July 2, 1862 article was extravagant in its praise. The paean was based on an eyewitness account. The journalist, having seen firsthand the artist's success in Europe, could confirm that he was not only a remarkable copyist, but that he also painted original works:

We regret that our friend did not bring some of his own creations, which we had the privilege to see in Florence years ago. The first large painting which meets the eye on crossing the threshold of the small museum on the Rue Saint-Jean—the museum for which Mr. Falardeau is assuming all costs himself—is a magnificent copy of *St. John the Baptist* by Titian, the original of which can be found at the imperial and royal academy in Venice. (*Translation*)

"The Museum of Mr. Falardeau" was the subject of a long article in the same paper, dated July 4, 1862. After describing the composition, the anonymous author concludes in glowing terms saying that the copy, with its narrative and evocative quality, can be confused with the original:

The pose struck by Saint John is dignified and magnificently inspired. His features are of admirable regularity and beauty. His unkempt hair and beard, the extraordinary expression on his lips and sparkle playing off his pupil are prophetically poetic. And what a gorgeous figure study! What perfection in the vigorous torso, in the way the muscles of the right arm join the shoulder! What grace in the motion of the hand when seen in conjunction with the words sitting poised on the prophet's lips about to escape! Add to all of this beauty, the freshness of the flesh tints and the vibrant colours of Titian and you will have some idea of the effect produced by this superb painting. (*Translation*)

Apparently, however, the Quebec City populace did not appreciate this copy which was, nonetheless, perfectly suited to the local socioreligious context. The canvas was put up for sale at a special auction in Montreal on July 19, 1862 with 20 other works by Falardeau.[6] As mentioned in *La Minerve* on July 22, 1862, the work was purchased by Louis Beaudry before being auctioned off. Two days later, the same paper announced that the owner intended to donate it to the Société Saint-Jean-Baptiste, of which he was a member, both to decorate the association's offices and to be placed at the main altar of Notre-Dame church during the parish feast.[7]

The warm welcome Falardeau received would revive the nationalistic leanings, esthetic sensibilities and acerbic pen of Neuville recluse Antoine Plamondon. For one of the last times, Plamondon would lash out, vilifying the quality of his expatriate's inspired painting.

Let us take a tour of Florence and see Saint John the Baptist, the centrepiece! A copy of a masterpiece by Titian. Imagine! Titian in Canada!

Tell me frankly my dear correspondent C.D., is this a religious painting? Saint John the Baptist! Lord have mercy! Dear God! He is a brigand. Yes, a brigand. He lacks only the belt, pistols and dagger to be a brigand in every sense. Do you believe that Titian, who always painted with such depth and with the conviction of his religious beliefs would have painted Saint John the Baptist thus?[8] (*Translation*)

While Falardeau's copies apparently did not receive unanimous approval, certain comments made by enthusiasts indicate what a novelty they were. Their air of authenticity was widely recognized, as confirmed by an article published in *Le Courrier du Canada* on July 2, 1862:

The greatest fault among copyists is the use of purplish hues, the heightened tones making even unenlightened connoisseurs unhesitatingly state, "That is not an original!" Mr. Falardeau is perhaps one of the few Italian artists who avoids this error; he has the ability, in addition to his overall excellence of technique, to imbue his copies with a certain aura of age which, unless subjected to intense scrutiny,

means they can easily be taken for originals. (*Translation*)

The ability to purchase the works of masters for the price of copies shaped the market. In the decades following, the creation of permanent museums dedicated to the fine arts (Pinacothèque de l'Université Laval, 1874; Art Association of Montreal, 1879) and the proliferation of exhibitions in locations other than auction rooms, meant that hitherto barely known facts about art history became available and altered the esthetic appreciation of the moneyed classes desirous of refining their social image.

L.L.

Notes

1. ANQQ, Papineau-Bourassa bequest, letter from N. Bourassa to Théophile Hamel, Florence, December 7, 1853.
2. *NIXON 1988*, p. 27. The information was confirmed by Henri-Raymond Casgrain, "He visited (before 1851) in turn, Milan, Bologna, Parma, Venice, Rome, Naples, spending several months in each city admiring, studying and copying the master works of each school, habituating his brush to the variety of styles, enriching his palette with the ideal tints which would unlock the secrets of the Old Masters." (H.-R. Casgrain, *Oeuvres complètes, Vol. 2, Biographies canadiennes* (Montreal: Beauchemin et Valois, 1885), p. 38).
3. *NIXON 1988*, pp. 289-294. See Cat. No. 125-139. The paintings are: *Flora, Mary Magdeleine, Christ, Bella, Titian's Daughter, Virgin and Child* and *Self-Portrait*.
4. For example, we could mention Charles Gill, Joseph Franchère, Henri Beau, Joseph Saint-Charles, Marc-Aurèle de Foy Suzor-Coté, Clarence Gagnon. See the list in Laurier Lacroix, "Les artistes canadiens copistes au Louvre (1838-1908)," *Journal of Canadian Art History*, Vol. II, No. 1 (Summer 1975), pp. 54-70.
5. *FALARDEAU 1936*, p. 104.
6. The advertising copy appeared in *Le Pays* on July 19, 1862.
7. "We have been informed that M. Louis Beaudry, an officer of the Société Saint-Jean-Baptiste, has acquired this magnificent painting from the Falardeau collection to donate it to our national association if it pleases that organization to accept it. It is a happy thought and we hope that the Société Saint-Jean-Baptiste will be grateful to Mr. Beaudry for his good intentions. Indeed this painting would be the most appropriate decoration for the St. Jean-Baptiste hall, and who would prevent its being shown at the parish church above the main altar on our national feast day? This work of art and piety is undoubtedly better than a banner, as worthy as that may be, and the price is not all that high; and, moreover, it has the advantage of being a work by an illustrious artist whom we may count among our own compatriots. We believe that the Société Saint-Jean-Baptiste will accept, with alacrity, the offer of Mr. Beaudry." (*La Minerve*, July 24, 1862). The information also appeared in *L'Ordre* on July 25, 1862.
8. *Le Journal de Québec*, August 2, 1862.

JOHN ARTHUR
FRASER

1838-1898

(See also the biographical entry on Notman on page 567)

JOHN ARTHUR FRASER was born in London on January 9, 1838. Few verifiable facts remain allowing us to determine his artistic activities before he left London for Canada shortly after his marriage in 1858. In 1860, he arrived in Montreal, where he worked for the Notman company in the newly created artistic division. In practice, his work consisted mainly of adding colour to portraits done on photographic film. Beginning in 1864, he held the most important position at Notman's, that of artistic director.

While he held this position, Fraser exhibited his landscapes at the Art Association of Montreal, among other places. In 1867, he became one of the founding members of the Society of Canadian Artists. The following year, William Notman made him an associate, giving him responsibility for the new shop in Toronto, Notman and Fraser. In 1872, Fraser helped found the Ontario Society of Artists and was elected vice-president of the organization. He exhibited his work there the following year. In 1874, differences forced him to vacate his post in favour of Lucius R. O'Brien (1832-1900). It was during his term as artistic director of the Centennial Photographic Company, created by Notman, that he once again began sketching and painting, presenting a number of works at the Ontario Society of Artists in May 1878. In addition, he helped train such artists as Henry Sandham (1842-1910), Homer R. Watson (1855-1936) and Horatio Walker (1858-1938). In 1880, Fraser became one of the founding members of the Royal Canadian Academy of Arts.

In 1883, the Notman and Fraser studio was liquidated; the following year, Fraser and Sons opened for business. In 1885, Fraser left Toronto, leaving the studio to his sons. He went to live in Boston, where some of his family still dwelt. Fraser and Sons was sold in 1886 and Fraser made his final trip to Canada that year when Canadian Pacific offered him an opportunity to travel all along its railway lines drawing sketches. He finally settled in New York in the early 1890s and became involved in various artistic associations, such as the New York Water Colour Club. John Arthur Fraser died there on January 1, 1898.

Main source
REID 1990.

251.
John Samuel McCord, 1862
John Arthur Fraser and William Notman
Oil on photographic emulsion on paper mounted on canvas,
119 × 90 cm

Inscription
(s.d., l.r.) *Notman phot/J Fraser pinx[t] 1862.*

Provenance
Commissioned by subscription of the graduates and friends of Bishop's University, Lennoxville, 1862.

Bibliography
AMMCH, McCord Family Papers, file 0851; *BAKER 1980*, p. 16.

Collection
Bishop's University, Lennoxville

D URING THE second half of the 19th century, photographers sought the help of painters. Despite the fact that photography was earning its wings, becoming an art form practised by an increasing number of professionals and amateurs, most of its prestige was gained through its association with painting.[1] Though it is no longer common to retouch photographs with watercolours, oil or charcoal, better-equipped photographers, such as Notman in Montreal and the Livernois family in Quebec City,[2] used painters to give their photography the status of a work of art. Several artists received commissions to paint portraits from photographs (Cat. 253), thus elevating photographic reproductions to the level of painted canvases. The daguerreotype would unseat the miniature and technological developments and standardization of production procedures for cartes-de-visite

(2 1/4" × 3 1/2") and cabinet-size portraits (4" × 5 1/2") would provide serious competition to the traditional painted portrait.[3]

Despite the fact that photography was supplanting painting, when it came to formal photographs, the medium owed much to compositions used in portraiture and was even behind the times in terms of the variety and flexibility of poses. Exposure times, which varied from 60 to 90 seconds, forced photographers to use supports to hold the head and hands in place.[4] The technique was comparable to that used when drawing after live models, the sitter being immobilized in a sort of harness which was adjusted using pulleys.

Esthetically speaking, the stiff, unnatural poses adopted by those portrayed in photographs are reminiscent of official portraits of an earlier era. The organization and articulation of facial details and bodily

proportions would have been rendered by the photograph, so the painter's work consisted mainly in reproducing skin tone and opening the eyes (in general, eyes were kept half-closed, in a more comfortable position, during the exposure time).

In 1856, William Notman established a photographic studio in Montreal which gained national and international renown. For more than half a century, the constant search for technological innovation, the acquisition of prestigious contracts, a dynamic sales technique and a long family dynasty ensured Notman studios control over the market in Eastern Canada. Notman offered his clients photos retouched or highlighted with either oils or watercolours. A multitude of artists were employed by him between 1860 and 1870.[5] Notman photographs inspired various artists; Krieghoff, Jacobi (Cat. 255) and Henry Sandham based canvases on

Fig. 251A.
William Notman,
John Samuel McCord, 1861;
Photograph on albumen paper.
Notman photographic Archives, McCord
Museum of Canadian History,
Montreal (2188-I).

his shots. In 1860, at the age of 22, John A. Fraser was hired by Notman. A coloured photo dating back to 1861 documents his early association with Notman's work. He quickly moved up to the position of "artistic director," and could skilfully use watercolours to retouch or repaint portraits which he would then integrate with landscapes.[6]

The portrait of Chancellor McCord was the first oil Fraser worked on with the photographer. The work is extraordinary for its imposing size and the commission was important given the prestige of the subject and reputation of the institution placing the order.[7] John Samuel McCord (1801-1865) was the fourth son of Thomas McCord (1750-1824) and Sarah Solomons (?-1812). In 1805, he emigrat-

ed from Ireland to Montreal with his parents. His father, a prosperous merchant and landowner, was a police magistrate in Montreal. After completing his studies in law in 1823, McCord practised in Montreal and was appointed judge in 1842; it was not until 1857 that he was promoted to judge of the Superior Court of Lower Canada. He married Anne Ross (1807-1870) in 1832 and the couple had six children. His interest in science led him to become a member of local scientific societies and to pursue meteorology, with results from his observations being published in Great Britain. A Freemason, John Samuel McCord was involved in many philanthropic activities. He received an honourary doctorate from Bishop's in 1855 and agreed to hold the positions of vice-chancellor and chancellor for that university until his death in 1858.[8]

Creating such a large photograph from a small negative using a solar enlarger left a very blurred, phantom-like image. It fell to John A. Fraser to give it life and definition.[9] The search for facial resemblance was the essential criteria in portraiture. The blotchy-complexioned face shown here is surely not idealized. Under Fraser's brush, McCord takes on a headstrong and sanguine look. The eyes, which were enlarged, seem to bulge slightly. The purplish hue of his face picks up the blue of his toga and the bright gold tassel of his mortarboard. McCord's hand is resting on a book bound in green. These colours help to relieve the sobriety of the composition with its neutral background to which multidirectional brushstrokes have been applied to capture the light.

The development of new technology and experimental use of it in photographs such as this one meant that photographic portraiture had yet to be mastered. Time constraints involved in posing and the model's absence when facial features were being painted gave birth to a hybrid situated somewhere between the two artistic practices. Neither photography nor painting lived up to its full potential in this portrait. Instead, a work of this type provides us with some indication of the new relationship which was being forged between unique works of art and mechanical reproduction in the second half of the 19th century. In the decorative arts, printmaking and, by extension, fine arts, technological developments would be increasingly called upon to meet the demand for new markets and greater accessibility to art.

L.L.

Notes

1. For more on this subject, see the works of Aaron Scharf, *Art and Photography* (Middlesex: Penguin Books, 1968); Peter Galassi, *Before Photography, Painting and the Invention of Photography* (New York: The Museum of Modern Art, 1981); Heinrich Schwarz, *Art and Photography Forerunners and Influences* (Chicago: The University of Chicago Press, 1985) and THOMAS 1979.

2. LESSARD 1987/2.

3. Artists were often merely required to colour large photographs. "These large prints were sometimes produced from a smaller negative by the use of a solar enlarger, a device which used the rays of the sun as a light source. Sometimes, the larger prints were made by copying a small print directly onto a negative of the larger size required, but many times the portrait was taken directly on an 18×22 inch negative [mammoth plate]" (TRIGGS 1985, p. 141).

4. Jana Bara, "Through the Frosty Lens: William Notman and his Studio Props, 1861-1876," *History of Photography*, Vol. XII, No. 1 (January-March 1988), pp. 23-30.

5. REID 1979, pp. 27-66, and TRIGGS 1985, pp. 141-163.

6. "Fraser's contribution to the output of the Notman studio was substantial. Not only was he one of the foremost watercolourists in Canada, he developed his own style of colouring photographs which was unique in the way it preserved the photographic quality of the original, yet imparted to the monotone print a rich and life-like colour. Portraits coloured by Fraser were in great demand by Notman's wealthier patrons" (TRIGGS 1985, p. 144).

7. "January 20, 1862. Sir: The undersigned, feeling that some token is due from the Alumni and Friends of the University of Bishop's College to their present Chancellor, the HON. J.S. MCCORD, to manifest the high sense which they entertain of the real ability and perseverance which he has shown in promoting the interests of that Institution respectfully request your assistance in obtaining a suitable PORTRAIT of that gentleman, to be presented to the University at the Annual Meeting of Convocation in June. The contributions for the purpose are proposed to be limited as follows: Clergymen and Under-graduates... $1 00 Lay Members of Convocation and other Lay Friends... $2 00. You are requested to send your contribution, at your earliest convenience, prepaid, to the Rev. R. Lindsay, Knowlton, who has kindly consented to act as Treasurer. We remain, &c, &c. J.H. Nicolls, D.D. G Slack, M.A.R. Lindsay, M.A.". McCord Museum of Canadian History archives, McCord Family Papers, File 0851.

8. Biographic details are from Pamela Miller, ed., *McCord Family Papers 1766-1945*, Vol. I, *Inventory* (Montreal: McCord Museum of Canadian History, 1986), n.p.

9. The Notman archives mention three photographs of Chancellor McCord by Notman. Only two of these have been located (Fig. 251A). They were probably all done at the same time with the large portrait Fraser was highlighting in mind.

WILLIAM FREDERICK FRIEND is believed to have been born in the United States, in Washington, D.C.. He left for England with his parents in 1842, returning three years later to settle in Boston, where he opened a private music and drawing school. He was involved in two projects which would cause him to suffer financial reversals: a theatre in Boston—which was devoured by flames in 1847—and a project which was certainly original—a floating museum on the Wabash River (Indiana and Illinois). Following these failures, he rethought his career and, in 1849, moved to Philadelphia, where he managed to convince several financial backers to advance him the funds necessary to carry out another project: the completion of a panorama of Canadian and American landscapes.

From 1849 to 1851, Friend roamed vast stretches of the countryside, making an impressive number of sketches. Even with the help of two assistants, the panorama took several months to complete. The "world premiere" of his *Panorama* was in Quebec City, where it was received with enthusiastic acclaim. A long tour of several North American cities followed and he even travelled to Great Britain, where he presented his work to Queen Victoria.

It was around 1858 that Friend found a way to reap even greater gains from his experience with the publication of his *Guide-Book to Mr. Washington Friend's Great American Tour*. Apart from his participation in the Canadian section of the *Colonial and Indian Exhibition* in London in 1886, the rest of his career remains a mystery. He died on January 6, 1891, in Littlehampton, England.

WILLIAM FREDERICK « WASHINGTON » FRIEND

1820-1891

Main sources
HARPER 1970; COOKE 1983; OKO 1984.

MQ, NGC

252.
View of Quebec From the South Shore of the Saint Lawrence, (?) 1851
Watercolour over graphite highlighted with gouache on paper, 32.9 × 54.6 cm

Inscription
(s., l.r.) *W F Friend.*

Provenance
Private collection (sold by Sotheby's Belgravia, London, May 11, 1976, No. 159); Bert and Barbara Stitt Collection, Toronto, 1976; gift to the Art Gallery of Hamilton, 1984.

Exhibition
Hamilton 1984-1986, No. 27.

Bibliography
TOPOGRAPHICAL PAINTINGS 1976, p. 53, No. 159 (Repr.); *OKO 1984,* pp. 23, 29 and 85, No. 27 (Repr.).

Collection
Art Gallery of Hamilton. Bert and Barbara Stitt Collection (1984.STI.66)

W ILLIAM FREDERICK "WASHINGTON" FRIEND was an uncommon character, undaunted by grand endeavours.[1] After two financial failures, he succeeded in travelling to Philadelphia and raising the money to undertake a two-year voyage during which he would devote his energy to the completion of a gigantic panorama of landscapes of the eastern United States and Canada. The long tour began in the spring of 1849, and fall found Friend in Niagara, where he spent ten months. Following that, he spent five weeks in Queenstown, around May and June 1850. His next stay, Toronto, lasted some eight months (summer 1850-winter 1851) and in spring 1851, he arrived in Montreal via Kingston. His stay in Montreal was quite short. He did, however, have time to contact Lord Elgin, from whom he managed to obtain plans for the Victoria bridge, which would figure, in its completed form, on his panorama. He ended his journey in Quebec City, where he arrived in late spring or early summer 1851.

We do not wish to put too much faith in the brief biographical sketch from which we have obtained most of our knowledge about Washington Friend. Written by the artist himself, it is readily apparent that the document abounds in descriptions of the vicissitudes of his life in order to lend it colour. For example, he describes a time when "having no other cash than New Jersey dollar notes, he proffered one for the payment of his fare, which the conductor refused; consequently he was immediately set down in the midst of a primitive forest."[2] After two days and two nights of wandering, eating only wild strawberries, he was finally aided by hunters. Such is the style of this biography, the title alone constituting a warning, *Friend; or, the Adventures of an Artist: a Biographical Sketch.*

However, we should not underestimate the extent and quality of the work he accomplished. In the preface to the brochure which accompanied his panoramic show, Friend published the following outline of his work in a place of honour:

The observations here made *refer to facts* which have fallen under my own observation, combined with information derived from personal friends who have resided longer than myself at some of the places represented in the Panorama. The whole of the picture is painted by myself, from my own original sketches taken on the spot; the accuracy of the Panorama, therefore, may be relied upon.[3]

It is within this context that we must examine the *View of Quebec from the South Shore of the Saint Lawrence.* Direct observation is confirmed by the cityscape itself, in which the newly completed right wing of the Parliament Building, designed by Thomas Baillairgé,[4] is clearly visible. In the foreground, he stresses local colour—an Indian close to her wigwam carrying her papoose on her back. Was this the watercolour that served directly as a model for the panorama, the one which would be transferred onto canvas? Unfortunately, we cannot be sure. Too much remains unknown about Friend's methods for us to draw hasty conclusions. A similar watercolour with only minor differences in detail was sold at Sotheby's in London in 1985, confirming that the artist repeated his compositions.[5] This is one of the factors which greatly complicates the dating of his works and our overall understanding of them. Martha E. Cooke noted similar problems with his paintings of a view of Niagara Falls.[6]

However, strange as it may seem, such complications are unimportant. This watercolour was nothing more than a preparatory step in the grand, colossal, stupendous final project described in "Leviathan Painting," which can be found in the biographical sketch of Washington Friend. That it would be repeated later in *View of Quebec from the South Shore of the Saint Lawrence* does not in any way alter the fact that it is closely tied to his trip to Quebec City in 1851 and to one of the "panels" in the panorama. This latter point is important. The panorama was made up of a very large canvas which was unrolled from one cylinder to another, relating, in images, the sequence of the journey, beginning with New York. The cities of Rochester, Niagara, Toronto, Kingston, Montreal and Quebec City followed, interspersed with stops at picturesque sites (Trenton falls, Lake Ontario and the Mille-Iles river). In fact, it was a real spectacle, combining movement, commentary, music and singing with visual images. Thus, the *View of Quebec from the South Shore of the Saint Lawrence* appeared before Friend reached Quebec City, while he still had a sweeping view of it and could sing, "By the great St. Lawrence river, on the shore, on the shore, Where the dark and foaming waters loudly roar, loudly roar, I look for my absent husband, o'er the flood, o'er the flood."[7] His arrival in Pointe-Lévis faithfully described what he called the observed facts:

Indians encamped—Their Wigwams—Their curious Manners and Customs. The Wigwams have a very rude appearance, being chiefly built of birch bark, and the skins of animals stretched upon poles. In this scene Mr. Friend will introduce an Indian Papoose and Case, giving the audience a faithful representation of the manner in which the Indians manage their papooses, or babies, (creating roars of laughter.). The ladies are particularly invited to witness this interesting and amusing scene.

Finally, Friend's panorama should not be seen simply as an artistic or commercial undertaking, although that was certainly true in the early stages. After a premiere in Quebec City, where it remained popular for two months, came a tour of several North American cities (Montreal, Washington, Boston, Philadelphia, Baltimore and New York). However, as soon as Friend settled in London and began touring British cities, the panorama became inseparable from the preface which accompanied the explanatory brochure. This prepared the spectator for a 5000 mile voyage in the Far West, as Friend called it, and stressed the opportunities for immigrants. He was, in fact, making a strong case for Canada, and particularly Upper Canada, promised land par excellence. The point in history at which Friend chose to show his panorama in England was particularly propitious. Each year between 1851 and 1857, 20 000 to 50000 Britons immigrated to Canada, most of them settling in Canada West.[8] Thus, despite the fact that it was published later, around 1857-1858, this text played an essential role in understanding the panorama, which was, in fact, a propaganda tool. The following long passages from the text, quoted to preserve the tone, support this contention:

The emigrant who may select this great and rising continent as his future home, will not choose a country whose capabilities are untried, the character of whose soil is unknown, whose climate is uncertain, or where the chance of obtaining a livelihood is a mere lottery, as is the case in going to *Australia* or *California*. [...] Canada may very justly be described as the land of hope and plenty; it is a country where the industrious labourer, mechanic, struggling shop keeper, or small farmer may easily rise, and with a young and growing family around him, speedily become a man of property. As for taxation, it is a mere farce to call it such, so trifling is the amount levied in this country. Education is placed within the reach of all; religious instruction abounds; and there exists absolute freedom in all matters relating to religious opinions. For labourers and artisans and female servants, the rate of wages is high, provisions are low in price, and there is a large demand for labour of all kinds.

Following this was a long description of a farmer with a plot of land to be cleared and cultivated and living in a cabin and his unshakeable confidence in the future. Seven years later, Friend had the opportunity to return to the same place, near the village of Caledonia in Upper Canada:

The little log hut was used as a back-kitchen to a neat two-story frame house painted white. A large barn stood near it, with stock of every description in its yard; the stumps, round which the blades of corn, when I last saw the place, had so much difficulty in springing up, had nearly all disappeared; luxuriant Indian corn had sole possession of the place where the potatoes had so hard a struggle against the briar bushes and the underwood; the forest—dense, impenetrable, though it seemed—had been crushed far back by the energetic hand of man. A garden, bright with flowers, and enclosed in a snake fence, fronted the house; a young orchard spread out in the rear.

A final note was contained as an epilogue:

I have often seen, in different rambles through the Far West, changes take place in rapid succession from the log hut to the farm house; then a village rise up, as it were in a dream, and in a short time become a flourishing little town.[9]

D.P.

Notes

1. Facts about Washington Friend's life are based on the biographical sketch which accompanied the explanatory brochure for the panorama: *Guide-Book to Mr. Washington Friend's Great American Tour of Five Thousand Miles in Canada and the United States, including Niagara and the River St. Lawrence. With the Words of the Songs and Melodies Sung by Him in His unrivalled Entertainment. With Engravings, & Publié à York chez J. Coultas*, n.d., pp. 25-30.

2. *Ibid.*, p. 26.

3. *Ibid.*, p. 3.

4. NOPPEN, PAULETTE AND TREMBLAY *1979*, pp. 264-266.

5. Sale of November 6, 1985, lot 54 (Repr.).

6. COOKE *1983*, p. 88, No. 209 (Repr.). This is why the date is accompanied by a question mark (1851).

7. *Guide Book, op. cit.*, p. 22.

8. Rosario Bilodeau, Robert Corneau, André Gosselin and Denise Julien, *Histoire des Canadas* (Montreal: Hurtubise HMH, 1971), p.418.

9. *Guide Book, op. cit.*, pp. 3, 5 and sq.

THÉOPHILE HAMEL

(See biographical note
on page 283)

Before Restoration

253.
Cécile Bernier, 1858
Oil on canvas, 99.7 × 76.4 cm

Inscription
(i.d., c.r.) *T.H. After/un Dague/1858.*

Provenance
Descendants of the Bernier family; J.-Eugène Bernier, Iberville; acquired by the Musée de la Province de Québec, Quebec City, 1941.

Exhibitions
Sherbrooke 1945, No. 5; Arvida 1946, No. 4; Quebec City 1948; Rimouski 1949, No. 4; Ottawa 1970, No. 85, Montreal 1979.

Bibliography
UN SIÈCLE D'ART CANADIEN *1945,* p. 4, No. 5 entitled *Portrait de jeune fille;* UN SIÈCLE D'ART CANADIEN *1946,* pp. 9-10, No. 4, entitled *Portrait de jeune fille;* UN SIÈCLE D'ART CANADIEN *1949,* p. 3, No. 4 (idem); MORISSET *1960/1,* pp. 120 and 128b (Repr.); HUBBARD *1970,* pp. 40, 109 and 172, No. 85 (Repr.); DUMAS *1970,* p. 21; VÉZINA *1973-1974,* pp. 46 and 47; DUMAS *1974,* p. 43; VÉZINA *1975/1,* pp. 160a, 183, 191, 194, 195, 202 and 206 (Repr.); VÉZINA *1976/1,* p. 17, No. 87; VÉZINA *1977,* pp. 398 and 399; THOMAS *1979,* pp. 68-69 (Repr.); *Nos racines,* No. 83 (1979), p. 1660b (Repr.); COMEAU *1983,* p. 124.

Collection
Musée du Québec, Quebec City. Restored in 1991 with the assistance of the Amis du Musée du Québec (41.119)

THÉOPHILE HAMEL completed the portrait of young Cécile Bernier in 1858. Having settled permanently in Quebec City in 1851, throughout the 1850s, Hamel enjoyed several professional successes; crowned by his becoming the official painter of the government. In 1853, he finished fourteen portraits of successive speakers of the legislative assemblies of Upper and Lower Canada, then, in 1856, fourteen portraits of the speakers of the legislative councils of the two provinces and of Canada. In September 1857, his marriage to Mathilde-Georgina Faribault, daughter of Georges-Barthélemi Faribault (Cat. 237), head of the government library, gave him access to Quebec City's social and intellectual elite. At the end of the 1850s, Hamel, then in his early 40s, had come into his full artistic talents, was at the peak of his career and, moreover, was financially well-off. In fact, the artist loaned a rousing $8 000 to his brothers Abraham and Joseph-Colbert.

The important government contract did not prevent him from continuing to paint members of the bourgeoisie and clergy, as confirmed by the many commissioned works he produced, particularly those completed in 1858 and 1859: *Joseph Morrin* (HDQ), *Mrs. Siméon Lelièvre* (MQ), *Monseigneur Pierre-Flavien Turgeon* (Sisters of Charity of Quebec City), *Antoine Dessane* and the portrait of his wife (MQ), *François Cadoret, Reverend Leach* and one named *Wells* (the last three canvases have not been located). From the same era is a self-portrait, accompanied by one of his wife (NGC), as well as one of his oldest child, Georges (MQ), born in July 1858 (Fig. 136A). These works are of unequal value, varying from richly detailed canvases to simple head-and-shoulders oval portraits, strongly inspired by photography.

In 1858, Hamel, whose studio had been located at the Music Hall on Rue Saint-Louis since the previous fall, took a tour of the Lower-Saint-Lawrence region. It was apparently during this voyage that he received the commission for the portrait of Cécile Bernier. The registers of Saint-Thomas parish reveal that young Bernier, born April 19, 1840, died at age 17, on November 8, 1857.[1] The inscription on the painting indicates that the portrait was painted by Hamel in 1858, after a daguerreotype, making it a posthumous portrait based on a photograph which no longer exists. The painting was therefore intended as a reminder of a young musician with a promising future who died prematurely. The artist thus revived post-

humous portraiture, popular in the previous century (See Cat. 12). However, a certain number of the speakers' portraits, commissioned by the government in 1853 and 1856, were copied after older works, making them the likenesses of men who were already deceased.

The portrait of Cécile Bernier was produced not only to perpetuate the memory of the dead girl, but also to keep alive the image of her as an adolescent. Indeed, in 1960, Gérard Morisset described this Hamel portrait as "one of the most animated [...] the expression is lively, the position of the hands adorable, the pose relaxed and accessories, reduced to a minimum, are portrayed with unequalled agility." (*Translation*) This portrait, overflowing with candour, shows a girl of about fifteen—the subject's age indicates that the daguerreotype was taken around 1855. The young girl, apparently in the pink of health, has an almost perfectly oval face with clear skin, lively black eyes, delicate features and a small mouth with finely chiselled lips. Cécile is wearing a style popular in the mid-1850s. Her black dress is shot with green and brown and has a small double ruff held in place by a pale blue flower and lace sleeves flecked with colour. Her hair is parted in the middle and held to either side by ribbons in the same colours as her gown.

Reminiscent of the portrait of *Mrs. J.S. McDonald* (1850, NAC), the canvas shows a three-quarter view of the subject standing, facing forward, with her hands crossed and her left arm resting on a table covered by a rug with a gold pattern. The composition and, more particularly, the subject's pose, are very unusual for the artist, but quite characteristic of certain daguerreotypes of the era; witness that of Commander Jacques Viger, taken by an unknown photographer around 1855.[2] Set against a neutral background of varying shades of brown and green, the teen poses in a sober decor consisting essentially, besides the subject, of a bare wall, hastily sketched column and red drapes, artificially pleated and decorated with two tassels. This curtain arrangement, placed vertically and on one side, also uncommon in Hamel's work, was likely common to certain photographic studios at the time. Finally, the upper portion of the composition, with rounded corners, calls to mind the slip-frame or arched frame used for photographs in times past.

As Ann Thomas noted in the catalogue, *Canadian Painting and Photography 1860-1900*, this portrait by Hamel, is,

for all intents and purposes, a free interpretation of a photograph rather than a faithful copy:

This portrait of *Cécile Bernier* is not a slavish imitation of the daguerreotype but rather it is a painted image which in pose, relationship to surrounding space and in execution of form, *relates* to the daguerreotype. While offering a fair amount of visual information about its subject it also communicates the human presence of the sitter very strongly. The viewer is not confronted with a mechanically copied image but is brought to share the emotional and formal qualities which Hamel extracted from the daguerreotype.

It was in 1849, in Montreal, while he was painting *Mère Marie-Rose* (Sisters of the Holy Names of Jesus and Mary), that Hamel first used the daguerreotype in conjunction with direct observation of the subject. Unlike the portrait of Cécile Bernier, this is not the translation of a photograph to canvas, but the use of two different sources: the daguerreotype copy and the study of a living model.[3] In addition, as reported by Monseigneur Henri-David Têtu in 1896 about Monseigneur Cajetan Bedini, apostolic nuncio from Rome, and his trip through Quebec City in 1853:

Mr. [George William] Ellison took a daguerreotype portrait of the distinguished visitor. It was reproduced on canvas by Théophile Hamel and was to be given a place of honour in the episcopal palace, which it occupies today.[4] (*Translation*)

Other portraits, which Hamel definitely executed after daguerreotypes all date from 1858. Unlike Plamondon, the artist carefully noted this source below his signature; he did the same for copies of painted portraits. These oval portraits are of Ernest Morriset (MSQ), a student at the Séminaire Saint-Sulpice in Montreal and of Father Antoine Langevin, "grand-vicaire" and benefactor of the Collège Sainte-Anne-de-la-Pocatière. It is interesting to note this last portrait, still kept at the college, was in fact a posthumous portrait, since Father Langevin died the year previous at Saint-David de Madawaska.[5] Finally, the artist's account ledgers show a commission from a woman named Aird, from Ottawa, for a portrait of her husband after a photograph.[6]

Conversely, daguerreotypes were made of a number of Hamel's works and were sometimes highlighted with colour so that they could be reproduced and distributed (Cat. 261).

Cécile Bernier's portrait, completed in the late 1850s, illustrates not only important changes in artists' practices in terms of his painting, but also demonstrates the rising popularity of and competition afforded by photographs during that period. In 1858, during a visit to Hamel's studio, a journalist from the *Morning Chronicle* noted this phenomenon in the July 28 edition of the same year:

Hamel is undoubtedly highly appreciated and valued in Canada, but does he receive such friendly countenance and such substantial support, as he deserves, even in his own city, to which he clings with persisting faithfulness? Daguerreotypes are pretty memorials to possess of absent friends, neat tokens of affection and regard; but they shrink into comparative insignificance before the noble emanations of the canvas and the brush from the hands of polished Artists.

M.B.

Notes

1. ANQQ, *Registre Baptèmes, mariages et sépultures de Saint-Thomas de la Pointe-à-la-Callière (Montmagny)*, Vol. 14, 1852-1862, Fol. 114v and 151v. According to information provided in 1941 by descendants, to Paul Rainville, then to Gérard Morisset, Cécile Bernier was born around 1835 to Siméon Bernier, farmer, who was married to Cécile Couillard-Dupuis, from the parish of Saint-Thomas de Montmagny. According to the same sources, the young Cécile, a talented pianist, was to travel to London to complete her musical training. However, shortly after her portrait was completed and before her departure for Europe, Cécile fell ill and died at about 20 years of age, around 1860.

2. *LESSARD 1987/2*, p. 49 (Repr.).

3. *LE GRAND HÉRITAGE 1984*, pp. 124-125, No. 102 (entry by Laurier Lacroix).

4. *TÉTU 1896*, p. 197, and *LESSARD 1987/2*, pp. 48-49 (Repr.).

5. Archives of the Collège de Sainte-Anne-de-la-Pocatière, *Reçu de Théophile Hamel*, September 25, 1858, "Received from the Reverend Ant. Pilote, Superior of the Collège Sainte Anne, the sum of twelve louis and ten shillings, being the price of a copy of the portrait of the Reverend Ant. Langevin," (*Translation*) and *Reçu de Thomas Fournier, sculpteur-ornamentiste et doreur*, for a gilt frame.

6. MQ, Centre de documentation, artist's file. This canvas could correspond to the portrait of M. Aird, signed and dated in 1852, recently acquired by the Musée d'art de Joliette.

I N ALL LIKELIHOOD, Hawksett was the son of Samuel Hawksett (1776-1851), a native of Belfast (Ireland) who enjoyed modest success as a portraitist during the first half of the 19th century. It can therefore be assumed that Samuel Junior acquired the rudiments of portraiture from his father.

SAMUEL C. HAWKSETT

1827-1903

Samuel C. Hawksett first became known through a signed, dated portrait completed in New York City in 1855. He probably arrived in Quebec City in 1856 and stayed for a few years. In 1859, he was commissioned to do the history painting, *Conference Between Jacques Cartier and the Natives of Stadacona (6 May 1536)* (Cat. 254). He was then to work for two photographic studios, entering into a partnership with Joseph Dynes (1825-1897) in the firm Dynes & Hawksett of Montreal during the first half of the 1860s. A few years later, he was hired by the firm Joseph Archambault & Cie of Quebec City, which had just opened a branch on Rue Saint-Jacques in Montreal, as announced by *La Minerve* of September 11, 1867: "M.A. [Mr. Archambault] having acquired the services of the famous Painter, Mr. Hawksett, will execute all works which one may wish to confer upon him, namely, paintings in oils, watercolours or India ink, at reasonable prices." (*Translation*)

During the 1870s, Hawksett exhibited his works at the Art Association of Montreal (1870-1879), and then displayed them in 1880 at the Royal Canadian Academy and the Dominion Exhibition held in Montreal. He was also to become a member of the Society of Canadian Artists established in the same city. At least two religious institutions, the Séminaire de Saint-Hyacinthe and the Séminaire de Joliette, owned some portraits of clergymen painted by him. Hawksett died in Montreal in 1903.

Main sources
GROCE AND WALLACE 1957; COLLARD 1968; HARPER 1970.

254.
Conference Between Jacques Cartier and the Natives of Stadacona (6 may 1536), 1859
Oil on canvas, 87.8 × 122.9 cm

Inscriptions
(s.d., l.l.) *S. Hawksett/1859-;* (c.r., on the coat of arms of the cross) *Franciscus/Primus Dei/Gratia Fran-/corum Rex/Regnat.;* (c.l. on the stern) *LA GRANDE HERMINE;* (b.,l.c., in brush and black oil) *Painted by/S. Hawksett./Quebec L.C./May 1859-;* (b.,l.r., reversed, in white chalk) *2.*

Provenance
Commissioned by Georges-Barthélemi Faribault, Quebec City, 1859; bequeathed to the Université Laval, 1866; kept at the Séminaire de Québec; on deposit at the Société du Musée du Séminaire de Québec, 1983.

Exhibitions
(?) Montréal 1887; Ottawa 1965, No. 62; Vancouver 1966, No. 45; Quebec City 1986.

Bibliography
Le Journal de Québec, May 24, 1859, p. 2; *ANNUAIRE 1875,* No. 19; *LAVAL UNIVERSITY 1880,* p. 4, No. 33; *UNIVERSITÉ LAVAL 1883-1884,* p. 12, No. 33; *LAVAL UNIVERSITY 1883-1884,* p. 12, No. 33; *UNIVERSITÉ LAVAL 1887,* p. 12, No. 33; *LAVAL UNIVERSITY 1887,* p. 12, No. 33; *Paris-Canada,* 12 janvier 1888, p. 2; *UNIVERSITÉ LAVAL 1889,* p. 12, No. 33; *UNIVERSITÉ LAVAL 1893,* p. 12, No. 33; *LAVAL UNIVERSITY 1894,* p. 12, No. 33; *UNIVERSITÉ LAVAL 1898,* p. 14, No. 33; *LAVAL UNIVERSITY 1901,* p. 14, No. 33; *UNIVERSITÉ LAVAL 1903,* p. 12, No. 23; *LAVAL UNIVERSITY 1905,* p. 12, No. 23; *UNIVERSITÉ LAVAL 1906,* p. 16, No. 23; *UNIVERSITÉ LAVAL 1908,* p. 16, No. 23; *CARTER 1908,* p. 69, No. 23; *UNIVERSITÉ LAVAL 1909,* p. 16, No. 23; *LAVAL UNIVERSITY 1909,* p. 16, No. 23; *UNIVERSITÉ LAVAL 1913,* pp. 54-55, No. 276; *LAVAL UNIVERSITY 1923,* p. 63, No. 276; *UNIVERSITÉ LAVAL 1933,* p. 82, No. 250 entitled *Paysage, Scène champêtre; MORISSET 1941/1,* p. 82; *HARPER AND HUBBARD 1965,* p. 57, No. 62; *SHADBOLT 1966,* No. 45; *COLLARD 1968,* p. 17; *LUCHAIRE 1971,* p. 4 (repr. - lithograph); *NOPPEN 1984,* p. 9 (repr. - lithograph); *QUÉBEC EN PEINTURE 1986,* p. 11 (Repr.).

Collection
Musée du Séminaire de Québec (Pc983.75)

THANKS TO a lithograph (Fig. 254A) which was a part of a series on Jacques Cartier,[1] we are now able to determine the title of the work by Samuel Hawksett. There are slight differences between the print and the painting, which leads us to believe that the lithograph was not done after the original, but rather from a photograph.[2] *Conference Between Jacques Cartier and the Natives of Stadacona (6 May 1536)* was printed in Paris in 1862, three years after the painting was completed. The work was commissioned under the direction of Georges-Barthélemi Faribault (Cat. 237), who was acting on behalf of the Literary and Historical Society of Quebec, and it was apparently the latter who gave the work its name at that time.

Given the title of the work, it is interesting to note what happened on May 6, 1536. On that date, a single entry was made in the accounts of Cartier's voyages: "On Saturday, the sixth day of the month of May, we cast off from Sainte-Croix harbour [Saint-Charles river], and anchored below Ile d'Orléans."[3] (*Translation*) There could not have been a conference on May 6 because Cartier was holding on board Donnacona, Chief of Stadacona, along with nine of his men, all of whom were kidnapped three days earlier. On May 3, Holy Cross Day, the captain had erected within the fort a 35-foot cross which, he hoped, would attract the "savages" and enable him to carry out his plan because "it had been decided to take said Lord Donnacona to France, to recount and tell the King what he had seen in these western countries of the marvels of the world; because he had assured us that he had been in the Land of Saguenay, where there was an infinity of gold, rubies and other riches."[4] (*Translation*) Cartier's stratagem worked and he left for St-Malo with ten Amerindians on board. Obviously, the suggested portrayal is not based on fact. So what then does this painting portray?

Le Journal de Québec of May 24, 1859 gives us some clues about the work:

We have just been to see a work which Mr. Hawksett just painted on Mr. Faribault's orders. It is a canvas 4 feet by 3 feet, depicting the countryside formed by the mouth of the little Lairet river, near Quebec City, and showing the final farewells of Jacques Cartier to the savages of the tiny village of Stadacona.[6] (*Translation*)

It is not surprising to realize what a history buff Faribault was, as sponsor of this work. But what could have caused him to request such a work at a time when Canadian art was as yet uninterested in history painting? The idea may have come from *Jacques Cartier His First Interview with the Indians at Hochelaga now Montreal in 1535,* a lithograph produced in 1850 after the work by Andrew Morris (Fig. 254B). Or did he already have in mind the lithograph series he was to have printed three years later? Whatever the case may be, Faribault's interest in Jacques Cartier was not sudden. In fact, since the celebration of the tricentennial of Cartier's landing in Quebec City in 1835, he had stepped up his efforts to find information on the navigator. Faribault was to be the honorary librarian of the Literary and Historical Society of Quebec, as well as its president in 1844 and from 1849 to 1859. In this capacity, he wrote to the mayor of St-Malo to obtain information on Cartier. It was after these efforts were made that a copy of the so-called portrait of the explorer

arrived in Quebec City in 1847. And the rest is history: Théophile Hamel was asked to paint two copies of the work (Cat. 127) and in 1848, thanks to a public subscription, a lithograph made from Hamel's work was printed in New York City. From that point on, the dissemination of Cartier's image was assured. The navigator became a national hero: copies made from Hamel's work began to be circulated as early as 1849, to such an extent that the Province of Canada even used this image on its fourth stamp issued in 1855.

When Faribault commissioned *Conference Between Jacques Cartier and the Natives of Stadacona (6 May 1536),* the navigator had therefore become a well-known figure, even more so with the Literary and Historical Society's reprinting of Cartier's *Voyages* in 1843.[6] Not only did this publication finally make the navigator's accounts accessible to Lower Canada, but it ended the debate on the question of Cartier's winter home in Quebec City. The new edition boasted a revealing appendix: *Description of Quebec City and Environs in 1608, and Various excerpts related to the Site of Jacque Quartier's Winter Encampment 1535-36.*[7] This publication gave Faribault the information needed to commission a history painting associated with Cartier. But why did Faribault disregard the entry for May 6, 1536, even though it was obviously included in the reprinting? *Le Journal de Québec* of May 24, 1859 helps us answer this question:

Mr. Faribault wanted to have reproduced on canvas the image of this famous site of our historical past before industry, which was snatching up land in this area, changed its picturesque face. The painting is a landscape, with a historical scene painted merely as an embellishment. (*Translation*)

Faribault was therefore interested in a specific site: the confluence of the rivers Lairet and Saint-Charles near Quebec City, where Jacques Cartier wintered during his second voyage in "the new land called New France." (*Translation*) Although this site is now gone, Hawksett succeeded in depicting it in a recognizable manner, since his contemporaries who saw the work could identify it:

The mouth of the river Lairet, at its junction with the Saint-Charles river, with the surrounding slopes and the view of the Stadacona hill in the background, is a charming site and truly an excellent subject to paint.[8] (*Translation*)

However, we, like the 1859 columnist, must recognize that this is an "autumn landscape—although the historical scene took place in spring. The at-

mosphere, water and foliage, tinted with a variety of colours with which we are all familiar, have that warmth of hues that can be seen so often in the beautiful days of late September." (*Translation*) However, the inscription on the back of the work and the article in *Le Journal de Québec* indicate that the work was completed in May 1859. Could Hawksett have painted the landscape the preceding autumn? It is possible, although this implies a long execution time; we should add, however, that we know nothing about how quickly Hawksett worked. Maybe the painter allowed himself one whimsical fancy within an overly restrictive commission? Nevertheless, it seems surprising that Faribault did not insist on this important detail. This entire line of questioning poses once again the basic problem of the initial commission and forces us to continue to analyze the depiction.

By wanting to preserve the visual aspect of a site considered historic, Faribault set the tone for his commission by drawing on his information in the reprinting of Cartier's *Voyages*. Similarly, the presence of the fort on the banks of the Lairet river corresponds to the indications provided by Samuel de Champlain, and published as an appendix to the 1843 work. This publication was indisputably a determining factor, because we can now identify certain elements on the canvas directly from the navigator's accounts. There are three ships in the composition, including one which is partially submerged, reminiscent of the one Cartier had to scuttle, lacking the crew to sail it. On the poop of the most imposing is inscribed LA GRANDE HERMINE. The cross bears France's coat-of-arms and a transcription of the dedication to Francis I, an exact replica of the text indicated in *Voyages*. However, the accounts mention that the cross was raised inside the fort, while in the painting, it is placed in the foreground. Obviously, this position enables the viewer to read the inscription, but it also gives importance to this element, which symbolizes Cartier's taking possession of the land and, by extension, France's dominion over them. As a counterpoint to this statement, it should be noted that the arrangement of the frieze of people has the Amerindian group at the foot of the cross, as if they had accepted *ipso facto* this state of affairs.

An examination of the painting reveals a number of contradictions. The site chosen, the location of the fort, the presence of ships and their descriptions, as well as the coat-of-arms on the cross and the

Fig. 254A.
Étienne David after Samuel Hawksett,
*Conference Between Jacques Cartier and the Natives
of Stadacona (May 6, 1536)*, 1862;
lithograph published in Paris chez Lemercier, 24.4 × 32.1 cm.
Musée du Séminaire de Québec (P984.1513.1).

dedication, correspond in every way to the information provided in the 1843 reprinting of *Voyages*. However, several elements do not correspond to the historical reality which was intended to be conveyed with this work. For example, the peaceful meeting depicted does not in any way relate to the events of May 6, 1536, the season painted does not correspond to the time of year and the cross is not in its original place. This amalgam is probably the result of the requirements and information laid down by the sponsor and Hawksett's interpretation of certain, less well-defined elements. Faribault, however, accepted the work, even to the extent of having lithographs made of it three years later. It is obvious, too, that it was indeed May 6, 1536 that was to be depicted because *Le Journal de Québec* noted: "The historical scene which Mr. Hawksett added to the landscape deals with Jacques Cartier's departure in May 1536." (*Translation*) After giving a description of the painting, the columnist ends his account in the following manner: "We do not know the location well enough to judge the historical accuracy of the work

done by the artist, who managed to give his landscape a remarkable warmth of colour." (*Translation*) To that we can answer that accuracy was certainly sought at the beginning, but Faribault also wanted a painting which was a tribute to Cartier. For this glorification to be credible, the events of May 1536 could not be faithfully related. Faribault wanted to mark Cartier's winter home and underline the symbolism related to the image of the cross. It is clear that, from that point on, the work could no longer be entirely grounded in historical reality.

For similar reasons, the painting contains the same amalgam of verifiable and distorted elements as the historical works of the second half of the 19th century. The first are the result of the excavations which had commenced several decades previously in Lower Canada to feed this yen for discovery which then dominated this field. The second are the direct result of the rising clerical-nationalist ideology which was aimed at a single goal: edification. This interpretation of historical facts led our first historians to embellish and sometimes distort the truth in order

to create an account which corresponded to their aspirations. In itself, Samuel Hawksett's work is indicative of this mindset.

The Musée du Séminaire's collections include, in addition to Hawksett's work, several copies of the lithograph series on Jacques Cartier. It may be supposed that they were part of the lot of archives, books and engravings on Canadian history which Faribault bequeathed to Université Laval in 1866. His will stipulated that Father Charles-Honoré Laverdière (1826-1873), an historian associated with the university, could choose from his library anything which deserved to be preserved by the institution.[9] To our knowledge, ***Conference Between Jacques Cartier and the Natives of Stadacona (6 May 1536)*** was the only painting selected by Laverdière. Is it because the site depicted gives the canvas documentary value? Or is it because this work, given the information and treatise it contains, is primarily considered a "visual document" of history? We do not know. In 1866, when the work was acquired, Université Laval's Galerie de peintures did not yet exist; it was not

Fig. 254B.
Napoléon Sarony after Andrew Morris,
*Jacques Cartier His First Interview with the Indians
at Hochelaga now Montreal in 1535*, 1850;
lithograph.
McCord Museum of Canadian History, Montreal (M19656).

founded until the purchase of the Joseph Légaré collection in 1874. Hawksett's work[10] was to be hung, along with three other paintings and a photograph, in the Premier Salon, an antechamber leading to the Université's Grand Salon.[11] But was this painting presented as a work of art or as a piece of history? In this room, it was placed next to Livernois' *Portrait du Rév. M. J.-B.-A. Ferland*, Théophile Hamel's *Portrait du Dr. Morrin*, Joseph Légaré's *Fire in the Saint-Jean Quarter, Quebec, Viewed from the West* (Cat. 168) and Wilhem Lamprecht's *Portrait du Rév. M.G. Plante*.[12] To Université Laval, these three portraits showed recently deceased distinguished dignitaries. Without further study of the establishment of the Université's painting collection, it would be dangerous to propose an absolute interpretation for this placement. However, we can make an initial hypothesis, based on the historical context. Were officials attempting to raise three contemporary individuals to the level of the national hero, Cartier? Was this a way of showing that recent history also provided excellent examples to follow? To this way of thinking, even the unfortunate event of the fire in the Saint-Jean quarter could be used to symbolize how society managed to overcome such a disaster. Within this context, these contemporary individuals and the glorious past are paid equal tribute, making a single edifying statement.

J.C.

Notes

1. For more information on these series of seven lithographs, see Denis Martin, *Les collections de gravures du Séminaire de Québec (histoire et destins culturels)*, master's thesis submitted to Université Laval, 1980, pp. 112-113.

2. This photograph is attributed to Jules-Isaï Livernois (ASQ, Ph 86.0724 B44C1). Its very small size may have disconcerted the engraver. For example, the mass consisting of the Amerindian seated before the wood fire was interpreted by the engraver as thick smoke.

3. Jacques Cartier, *Voyages en Nouvelle-France* (Ville LaSalle: Cahiers du Québec/Hurtubise HMH, 1977), p. 129 (coll. Documents d'his-

toire); text rewritten in modern French by Robert Lahaise and Marie Couturier with introduction and notes.

4. *Ibid.*, p. 124.

5. *Le Journal de Québec*, May 24, 1859, p. 2.

6. *Voyages de découverte au Canada, entre les années 1534 et 1542, par Jacques Quartier...* (Québec City: William Cowan et fils, 1843) (under the direction of the Literary and Historical Society of Quebec).

7. *Ibid.*

8. *Le Journal de Québec*, May 24, 1859, p. 2.

9. ANQQ, Amable Bélanger notarial records, No. 2239, March 17, 1864. Faribault set a single condition: Laverdière could not take two small seascapes dealing with Cartier because he intended them for his daughter. One of these works could have been *L'Arrivée de Jacques Cartier à Québec (1535)* by Louis-Félix Amiel, which was purchased by the Musée du Québec from one of the descendants of Georgina Faribault-Hamel (80.13).

10. Université Laval was to display it as *L'Arrivée de Jacques Cartier à Stadaconé, et prise de possession au nom du roi de France.*

11. We do not know where the painting was hanging between 1866 and 1875.

12. The titles of the works are given as they appeared in *ANNUAIRE 1875*, No. 19, p. 56.

OTTO REINHOLD JACOBI

1812-1901

TTO REINHOLD JACOBI was born in 1812 in Königsberg, capital of former East Prussia (now Kaliningrad, Russia). It was apparently there that he received his initial artistic training before entering the *Königliche Akademie der Kunste* in Berlin in 1830, at age twenty-eight. He then studied at the academy of arts in Dusseldorf under painter Johann Wilkem Shirmer, after which he exhibited his works in various cities throughout Germany. Around 1840, he entered the court of a German prince, at Wiesbaden (now Hesse), where he remained for some twenty-odd years.

Around 1860, Jacobi emigrated to North America. He initially settled in Montreal, establishing contact with local artists, particularly foreign artists, such as fellow German Adolph Vogt (1812-1871). He opened a studio which he at first shared with one of his sons, a lithographer. Primarily a landscape artist, Jacobi worked in the areas of Montreal, Quebec City, Ottawa and Kingston. He was away from Montreal for varying lengths of time; for example, he stayed in Toronto in 1878 and from 1891 to 1893, and in 1881, he visited Philadelphia. He participated in the annual exhibitions of the Art Association of Montreal and the Royal Canadian Academy (1880-1898). He also had showings in Chicago and Philadelphia, and won second prize for a landscape of non-Canadian subject matter at the Upper Canada Provincial Exhibition held in London in 1865. In 1890 he became president of the Royal Canadian Academy of Arts. Jacobi died in 1901 at Ardoch, Dakota, where some of his children lived.

Main source
REID 1979.

255.
Montmorency River Rapids, 1860
After William Notman
Oil on canvas, 41 × 48.7 cm

Inscription
(s.d., l.l.) *O R Jacobi. 1860.*

Provenance
(?) William Notman, c. 1864; Watson Art Galleries, Montreal; acquired by the Musée de la Province de Québec, Quebec City, 1936.

Exhibitions
(?) Montreal 1864; Sherbrooke 1945, No. 4; Arvida 1946, No. 3; (?) Quebec City 1948; Rimouski 1949, No. 3; Winnipeg 1950-1951, No. 3; Baie Comeau 1951, No. 4; Ottawa 1978-1979/2.

Bibliography
NGC, W.R. Watson Fund, "Sales Record", Ledger No. 2 (1928-1955), No. 2027, July 1936; *MONNIER 1936*; *La Patrie. Journal du Dimanche,* August 30, 1942 (Repr.); *UN SIÈCLE D'ART CANADIEN 1945,* p. 4, No. 4; *UN SIÈCLE D'ART CANADIEN 1946,* p. 9, No. 3; *UN SIÈCLE D'ART CANADIEN 1949,* p. 3, No. 3; *UN SIÈCLE D'ART CANADIEN 1951,* No. 4; *REID 1979,* pp. 68, 70 and 72 (Repr.); *PRINGLE 1985,* pp. 35-36 (Repr.); *BÉLAND AND BOURASSA 1990,* p. 120; *MARTIN AND GRANDBOIS 1991,* p. 85.

Collection
Musée du Québec, Quebec City (36.34)

T HE GROWING NUMBER of immigrants arriving in Canada beginning in the 1850s, coupled with their diverse origins, was to define the plurality of this rapidly developing country. The majority of immigrants came to Montreal, the economic, trade and administrative centre as well as the crossroads, before moving on to other destinations. Of the successive waves of new Canadians from countries other than England, Germans were among the earliest to arrive prior to Confederation

Fig. 255A
Otto R. Jacobi
Montmorency River, 1860
oil on canvas, 41.1 × 48.6 cm
Musée du Québec, Quebec City (36.39)

and they came in the largest numbers.[1] Dennis Reid went so far as to suggest the existence of a community of German artists in Montreal, whose most famous members included William Raphael (1833-1914, arrived in 1858), Otto Jacobi and Adolph Vogt (1842-1871, arrived in 1865).[2] Their production, along with that of the Italian artists, together with the spread of photography, was to have a particular influence on painting in Quebec in the second half of the 19th century.

Jacobi moved to Montreal in 1860. He apparently came to paint a view of *Shawinigan Falls* for a gift to be presented the Prince of Wales during his visit to the city. Although it is highly unlikely, the story has it that not long after his arrival, Jacobi met photographer William Notman, who was also to contribute works for the royal visit. Because of his training at the reputable academies of Berlin and Dusseldorf and his years of experience, Jacobi, despite the fact that he had not been in the city for long, enjoyed a degree of authority that few other artists could claim. Napoléon Bourassa, already familiar with the artistic production of the Nazarenes, spoke very highly of Jacobi's oeuvre.[3]

The view shown here of the Montmorency river rapids, like the matching canvas of the falls painted from another angle (Fig. 255A), was inspired by William Notman's stereogram (Fig. 255B). This pair of stereoscopic pictures was part of the *Maple box:* a large box made of hard maple containing a series of Canadian views by Notman to be offered the Prince of Wales during his royal visit to Montreal. One wonders whether Jacobi, in selecting to paint a Canadian view to be taken back to London, was looking to quickly carve out a place for himself on the local art market. There is question that the two canvases were bought by Notman himself, since a painting entitled *River Montmorenci* and owned by the photographer were shown at the 2nd *conversazione*

Fig. 255B.
William Notman,
Natural Steps, Montmorency Falls,
Québec, c. 1860;
stereogram, 7.5 × 14.2 cm.
Notman photographic archives, McCord
Museum of Canadian History, Montreal
(7515).

organized by the Art Association of Montreal in 1864.

While the entire composition is based on the principles of photography, the artist has offset it by giving it a pictorial treatment. The work lies somewhere between its photographic source and the realist movement in painting under which Jacobi was trained in Germany. The composition is essentially photographic in nature. No painter would have given such importance to the rocks or sought to give a close-up view of the foreground such as in the mass that takes up over half the painting on the right. Jacobi has taken the vertical format of the stereoscopic pictures, less common in painting, and turned it into a painting of horizontal format. This compensation in height and width is conveyed using means borrowed from the esthetics of photography. The fuzzy edges are reminiscent of the out-of-focus areas beyond the camera shot. The detail of the rocks, defined by strong light, and the lack of definition of the flowing river are obtained through the precision of photography and the specific exposure time. Jacobi has given the landscape pictorial treatment by applying soft, individual strokes of colour to a light background. The limited colour scheme recalls the predominant sepia of photographs. The absence of human figures avoids the anecdotal aspect and the temporal precision they can convey in photography. Jacobi draws the viewer's attention to the twofold composition of the painting, in which the vibrant right side blends with the movement of the water, trees and the sky in the distance.
L.L.

Notes
1. In 1871, there were 7963 Germans in Quebec. (Paul-André Linteau, René Durocher, Jean-Claude Robert, *Histoire du Québec contemporain*, Montréal, Boréal Express, 1979, Vol. I, p. 61).
2. *REID 1979*, pp. 80-81.
3. Napoléan Bourassa, "Quelques réflexions critiques à propos de la Art Association", *La Revue Canadienne*, Vol. I (March 1864), pp. 170-182.

CORNELIUS KRIEGHOFF

(See biographical note on page 338

256.
Quebec Viewed from Pointe Lévis, 1853
Oil on canvas, 36.6 × 53.9 cm

Inscription
(s.d., l.r.) *C. Krieghoff 1853.*

Provenance
Alfred Torrens, Quebec City; Descendants of the Torrens and Blair families; Ronald E. Blair, London; acquired by the Musée du Québec, Quebec City, 1983.

Bibliography
ACQUISITIONS 1986, p. 156 (Repr.); *HUARD 1986/ 1*, 44 (Repr.); *DE ROUSSAN 1989*, p. 4 (Repr.); *BÉLAND AND BOURASSA 1990*, pp. 9 and 104 (Repr.).

Collection
Musée du Québec, Quebec City. Purchased with the assistance of the Government of Canada under the Cultural Property Export and Import Act (84.18).

T HESE TWO VIEWS of Quebec City painted three years apart by Cornelius Krieghoff seem, at first glance, to have the same landscape design. The landscape sweeps across the lower half of the painting in three parallel lines, with the foreground taking up most of the space. As in almost all of his work, the artist used widely divergent tones, with light accentuating the colour contrasts. However, a more in-depth examination reveals two different approaches to nature.

In the Musée du Québec work dating from 1853, Quebec City is Krieghoff's main concern.[1] At the top of Côte de la Montagne, at the right, stand the Parliament Buildings, which were to burn down the following year, while the towers of the Quebec City cathedral pierce the skyline behind. At left is the chevet of the Anglican cathedral, then the terrace built in 1838 atop the ruins of the Château Saint-Louis, facing the Château Haldimand. Even further to the left can be seen the obelisk of the monument to Wolfe and Montcalm erected in the Governor's gardens, as well as the rise of the Chalmers-Wesley church. On the lofty heights of Cap Diamant can be seen the Citadel and, finally, Martello tower number 1. At the foot of Côte de la Montagne, at the left, the King's magazine and former customs office round out the identifiable buildings.[2] Krieghoff shows the ties binding the Citadel to the city, Upper Town to Lower Town by means of Côte de la Montagne, Lower Town to the river, and Quebec City to the South Shore. The city is depicted as a strategic site with absolute control over access to the river. To render this cohesiveness, Krieghoff structured his composition using a traditional grid consisting of horizontals formed by the various parallel planes and the few verticals, in the form of trees, placed at the points of recession. This rigid grid is enlivened by the dynamic

Inscription
(s.d., l.l.) *C. Krieghoff 1856.*

Provenance
Scott & Sons, Montreal, c. 1934; private collection, Montreal, by inheritance.

Exhibition
Montreal 1972.

Bibliography
WINKWORTH 1972, No. [19] (Repr.); HARPER 1979, pp. 143, 144 and 194 (Repr.).

Collection
Private collection, Montreal

257.

View of Quebec from the Grand Trunk Railway Station at Pointe Lévis, 1856
Oil on canvas, 61.5 × 41 cm

treatment of the foreground, where the artist used a fairly flexible set of crossed diagonals to make the progression to the river less abrupt.[3] The alternation between light and dark areas which breaks this monotony is clearly of Dutch influence and can be found in the large panoramic landscapes of Philips Koninck (1619-1688).[4]

Three years later (in 1856), Krieghoff used the same subject, but approached it in a different way. By taking a more westerly vantage point, from the Auberivière cliff, he portrays a different profile of Cap Diamant. Few new architectural elements have been added to the scene, other than the extension of the Château Saint-Louis esplanade, known as the Durham terrace, completed in 1854. The Citadel is blended into its surroundings—the ramparts are no longer outlined in white—and the city, confined to the edge of the cape, is no longer depicted as the gateway to the river. Quebec City, which was the actual subject of the 1853 painting, is simply a motif in this painting. In fact, the train station is now the artist's—or his sponsor's—main concern. To obtain this vantage point, Krieghoff took up a position above Tibbits Cove and the Grand Trunk railway station at Pointe Lévis.[5] On January 7, 1852, the Quebec & Richmond Railway Company—which later merged with the Grand Trunk Railway Company—

undertook the construction of a railway connecting Quebec City and Richmond on the Saint-François river and linking up with the St. Lawrence and Atlantic Railroad. On November 13, 1854, the first train entered the new Pointe Lévis station from Longueuil after a 9-hour run.[6] A site plan, prepared in June 1856, makes it possible to identify the buildings appearing in the work executed by Krieghoff that same year. Spectators can make out the Depot, to which is connected the Freight House and, at the bottom of the cove, part of the Hôtel Victoria. Based on this plan, we can determine that Krieghoff accurately depicted the layout of the wharves, pontoons and railway tracks.[7]

To emphasize the depot site, the foreground was reduced to a minimum. The subtle interplay of ridges which punctuate the 1853 landscape gives way here to a tight, overhanging band of earth, divided in the centre by an abrupt path, probably Tibbits Hill, as identified on the 1856 plan. To indicate steepness, a figure is depicted struggling up the slope, clearly exhibiting the effort entailed. This composition style, which draws the spectator into a plunging movement, was widely used in the mid-19th century to blend topographical accuracy with the portrayal of nature on a sweeping scale. The engravings found in travel guides often resorted to this technique.

The reasons why Krieghoff painted this subject and the background of the work are not known. The only clue we have dates back to 1934, when the canvas was photographed by the Notman firm on behalf of Montreal art dealers Scott & Sons,[8] which probably sold it to the Montreal family which owns it today. However, it can be assumed that its sponsor had railway interests. The name James Tibbits naturally springs to mind, as he was part owner of the cove and path which bore his name and led to the station. Tibbits also participated in various operations linked to the railway industry, goods transportation and the ferries which shuttled between Lévis and Quebec City.[9]

In 1862, Krieghoff disseminated his work in the form of a lithograph. It was printed in London and entitled *View of Quebec, Canada, from the Railway Station opposite Quebec, the City.*[10] The title reflects the importance which the artist attached to this composition and the site chosen. In 1863, Krieghoff once again employed the theme of Quebec City viewed from the railway station (Fig. 257A). The site had changed considerably. In fact, on December 16, 1856, "a terrible fire reduced the Grand Trunk railway station at Pointe Lévis to ashes, along with both hotels of Messieurs Lawlor and Dion, as well as three first-class cars, four second-class cars and a quantity of goods."

Fig. 256A.
Cornelius Krieghoff,
Quebec viewed from Pointe Lévis, 1853;
oil on canvas, 36.2 × 53.3 cm.
Royal Ontario Museum, Toronto (955.84)

Fig. 257A.
Cornelius Krieghoff,
Quebec viewed from Pointe Lévis, 1863;
oil on canvas, 34.9 × 82.5 cm.
Montreal Museum of Fine Arts.
Miss Mary Fay Dawson bequest (954.1103)

(*Translation*) The Hôtel Victoria suffered the same fate on April 12, 1859.[11] This is a different site which Krieghoff depicts from a slightly lower vantage point, perhaps halfway down Tibbits Hill. The perspective has changed, and the overhang of the wharves is much less pronounced. Other comparisons between the two works have also proved significant. In 1856, Krieghoff offers a wide perspective of the North Shore, while his later work provides only a partial and less panoramic view of the city. The topographical rendering is less accurate. The excessive elongation of Pointe Quercy, the profile of the cape and the angle of view do not correspond to the site visible from Tibbits Hill. This work was probably composed from memory, with the artist drawing on his recollections of direct observation and repeating motifs already used.[12]

In his views of Quebec City,[13] Krieghoff combines topographical representation with a sensitive approach to nature, in which the selection of vantage point, layout, colour and light all play a part. To a strictly faithful representation, as revealed by the identification of buildings from the 1856 depot plan, he adds his own unique vision which augments the complexity of the levels of interpretation. The artist's interest in the railway and technological progress is indissociable from this pictorial conception.[14]
D.P. and P.B.

Notes

1. A similar version of this work (Fig. 256A), dating from the same year, belongs to the Royal Ontario Museum. Only a few details in the foreground are different. However, the vantage point from the westernmost point of Lévis and the topography of Quebec City remain essentially the same. The Musée du Québec work comes from the family of Captain Alfred Torrens, who was garrisoned in Quebec City in the 1850s. A painting depicting him and his wife in front of the Montmorency Falls in winter was painted by Krieghoff in 1854 (see Cat. 231, Note 1).

2. *NOPPEN, PAULETTE AND TREMBLAY 1979,* pp. 120-127, 152, 160-163, 168, 264-267, 276-278, 306, 407.

3. The use of diagonals to suggest vast spaces and increase the number of planes harkens back to Gaspard Dughet, who more fully developed Nordic and Bolognese influences. See Marie-Nicole Boisclair, *Gaspard Dughet. Sa vie et son oeuvre, 1615-1675* (Paris: Arthéna, 1986), p. 76.

4. See especially *Panoramic Landscape With a Village* from the Collection of Edward William Carter reproduced in *A Mirror of Nature. Dutch Paintings from the Collection of Mr. and Mrs. Edward William Carter* (Cat.) (Los Angeles: Los Angeles County Museum, 1981), No. 16.

5. The Pointe Lévis railway station was located in the cove formed at the foot of Tibbits Hill, which is now known as Côte Rochette.

6. Pierre-Georges Roy, *Dates lévisiennes* (Lévis: 1932), Vol. I, pp. 24 and 62.

7. Plan deposited in the records of notary Noël Hill Bowen, No. 1023, June 1856 and entitled *Terminus of the Quebec & Richmond Raylway at Tibbits Cove* (ANQQ).

8. Reproduced in No. 19 of *WINKWORTH 1972.*

9. A steamship, perhaps the *Grand Trunk Ferry,* launched on July 15, 1856 by Tibbits, can be seen on the river. Earlier, Quebec-bound passengers had to cross in canoes or travel to the Lauzon wharf, where they could take one of the many passing ships. The Lauzon wharf was located in the area now occupied by the ferry and station at Lévis, which were moved to that location in the early 20th century, thereby causing the closure of the Pointe Lévis station. See Pierre-Georges Roy, *La traverse entre Québec et Lévis* (Lévis, 1942), pp. 102-103 and 147.

10. Krieghoff concluded his project, begun in 1848, to disseminate his more popular subjects by means of engravings. See *WINKWORTH 1972,* and *DE VOLPI 1971,* Pl. 132.

11. Pierre-Georges Roy, *op cit.,* Vol. I, pp. 88 and 116.

12. This vantage point was also used later by photographers. Louis-Prudent Vallée photographed the same site circa 1870. See *LE MUSÉE DU QUÉBEC 1983,* p. 295, No. 393 (Repr.).

13. A fifth view of Quebec City entitled *Quebec seen from New Liverpool,* signed and dated 1871— the last year in which Krieghoff was active in Quebec City—was part of Mrs. G.I. Morewood's collection in 1965. New Liverpool was located west of the Etchemin river and is now part of Saint-Romuald. See *HARPER AND HUBBARD 1965,* p. 49, No. 46.

14. In 1858, Krieghoff painted a landscape with a train going by on the horizon. This work was entitled *Tubular Bridge at St. Henry's Falls.* John Russell Harper considered it, like all other paintings featuring the railway, an allegory for the disappearance of the old order. See *HARPER 1979,* pp. 142 and 144 (Repr.).

258.
The Coming Storm, before 1860
Oil on canvas, 30.9 × 46 cm

Inscription
(s., l.l.) *C Krieghoff.*

Provenance
Watson Art Galleries, Montreal; Newton D. Galbreaith, Hamilton; Margaret E. Galbreaith, by inheritance, 1925; Art Gallery of Hamilton, 1949 (on deposit until the final settlement of the estate in 1984).

Exhibitions
Brantford, 1968; Toronto, 1975.

Bibliography
HARPER 1979, pp. 125, 129 and 192 (Repr.).

Collection
Art Gallery of Hamilton. Galbreaith Collection (Galbreaith 13)

K RIEGHOFF'S REPUTATION and art enthusiasts' interest in him rest in part on his talent as an observer and the humour with which he depicted the customs of French-Canadian *habitants.* His body of work, however, also has its serious side. The series on hunted and injured animals, dating from the end of his career, offers a tragic vision of the relationship between man and nature. Some landscapes from the 1850s to some extent foreshadow this more secret aspect of his inspiration.

The Coming Storm, like *The Passing Storm, St. Féréol* (1854, NGC) and *St. Ann's Falls, Looking Downstream from the Grand Rocks* (undated, PC)[1] are landscapes inspired by a specific topography, but interpreted with a romanticism which idealizes nature. Krieghoff used every bit of his knowledge of nature and his technique in the composition of autumn landscapes transfigured by the effects of a storm.

Having learned the lessons of 17th-century Dutch landscapists, such as Jacob I. van Ruysdael (1628-1682),[2] Krieghoff, in this painting, portrays a forest which is luxuriant and varied, yet battered and turbulent. The alternation between dark and light planes which forge this landscape in a series of diagonals, the movement of clouds, the obliques created by the dried or lightning-struck trees which hem in the riverbed at the spot where the river explodes into a fury of rapids, all combine to make this a scene of intense drama.

The presence of three Amerindians leaving the river to carry their canoe and its contents to avoid the rapids imbues the whole with magnificence. Their presence confirms their inherent appropriateness within this environment. One of them is carrying a bundle of furs, while the other two are weighed down by the weight of the birchbark canoe. While Amerindian figures were the main subject of his compositions during the 1840s and the early 1850s (Cat. 150 and *Indians at Portage,* 1850, ROM), Krieghoff now integrates them into the landscape by blending their actions with the movements and forms of nature.

L.L.

Notes
1. *HARPER 1979*, pp. 122 and 124 (Repr.).
2. Krieghoff exhibited at the Montreal Society of Artists in 1847 a copy after Ruysdael, *Approaching Storm* (No. 120).

259.
The Ice Boat, c. 1860
Oil on canvas, 22.8 × 32.8 cm

Inscription
(s., l.r.) *C. Krieghoff.*

Provenance
Musée de la Province de Québec, Quebec City, before 1934.

Exhibitions
Quebec City 1948; Fredericton 1961, No. 53; Ottawa 1965, No. 45; Quebec City 1967, No. 33; Quebec City 1971, No. 110; Montreal 1976; Quebec City 1983-1984, No. 90.

Bibliography
Barbeau 1934, pp. 151-152; *Cooke 1961,* No. 53; *Harper and Hubbard 1965,* p. 49, No. 45; *Collections 1967,* No. 40 (Repr.); *Trudel, Juneau and Massey 1967,* pp. 66-67, No. 33 (Repr.); *Juneau 1971,* p. 65, No. 110; *Vézina 1972/1,* pp. 110 and 174; *Dimanche Matin,* November 14, 1976, p. C-8 (Repr.); *Harper 1979,* pp. 64, 66 and 193 (Repr.); *Nos racines,* No. 84 (1979), p. 1676 (Repr.); *Québec Yachting,* 1981-1982, front p. (Repr.); *Le Musée du Québec 1983,* pp. 86-87, No. 90 (entry by Claude Thibault, Luc Noppen and Michel Doyon) (Repr.); *Art du Québec 1983,* p. 12 (Repr.); *Cap-aux-Diamants,* 1986, front p. and tab.of contents (Repr.); *Huard 1986/1,* p. 134 (Repr.); *de Roussan 1989,* p. 17; *Bouchard 1990,* p. 24 (Repr.); *Béland and Bourassa 1990,* pp. 6, 7, 9 and 118 (Repr.); *Béland 1991,* p. 54.

Collection
Musée du Québec, Quebec City (34.266)

T HIS FAMOUS PAINTING illustrates a winter pastime which had just been taken up by Anglophone officers and members of the bourgeoisie from Quebec City: ice-boating on the St. Lawrence. The boat, sporting a red pennant and the Union Jack, is depicted at the moment when it was passing the Quebec City promontory heading east. The small craft, consisting of a wide, trapezoidal platform on "skates," and equipped with two large sails attached to a mast, glides along the clear ice of the river. However, it was somewhat rare for the icy surfaces of the St. Lawrence to be smooth and clear enough for such a sailboat to be used. Initially, this type of sled on "skates," which originated in northern Europe, was essentially used as a means of transporting goods; but it had become a vehicle used for entertainment and prized for its great speed. The ice boat, along with the toboggan, was considered the quickest winter vehicle. It could travel as fast as a locomotive (see Cat. 262). Similar sailboats were painted by an anonymous artist in Quebec City in 1844 (MMCH) and by William Armstrong on Lake Ontario, near Toronto, circa 1855 (ROM).[1]

The craft takes up almost the entire space of the painting and carries four passengers, dressed in "canadiennes" or fur coats fastened with an arrow sash. At the stern, a French-Canadian *habitant*, wearing moccasins and smoking a plaster pipe, controls the rudder on "skates," while from amidships to the bow, three gentlemen handle the rigging. In the background is a partial profile of Quebec City, from the grounds of the Séminaire in Upper Town to Pointe Quercy in Lower Town. This limited view of the Quebec City skyline gives prominence to three recent public buildings. At the top of the cliff can be seen the Université Laval pavilion, erected in 1855-1856 from the plans of Charles Baillairgé; between the two sails can be seen the customs office built in 1856 from William Thomas' plans, and finally, to the left of the main sail, is a building similar to the Finlay Market built in 1851 based on the plans of Théophile Baillairgé.[2] One of the cannons of the grand battery on the heights of the promontory can even be glimpsed. This view of Quebec City serves only to situate the main element in the foreground within a very evocative context. This was a tried-and-true formula used many times by Krieghoff during his stay in Quebec City between 1853 and 1863. These paintings generally showcase various modes of transportation operating on the icebound river in front of Cap Diamant: *Royal Mail Boat on St. Lawrence, Sleighs Racing in Front of Quebec, Tandem Driving, Ice Harvest*, etc. Unlike the vehicles depicted in these scenes, the ice boat, despite its swelling sails, its Union Jack and pennant floating on the breeze, seems immobilized for the needs of the painter and his composition. The artist was probably inspired by a photographic print taken in 1858 or 1859 by Samuel McLaughlin and widely disseminated at that time (Cat. 262). Thus, the movement of the craft seems rather unconvincing.

The Ice Boat could only have been executed around 1860, after the main buildings identified in the background were built, but before the artist departed for Europe in late 1863 or early 1864. The painting was the subject of *cartes-de-visite* photographs taken around 1863 and enhanced using watercolour. First Marius Barbeau, then John Russell Harper mentioned the presence of an *Ice Boat Sailing on Clear Ice* in two albums containing almost twenty photographs of Krieghoff's works, painted in watercolours and signed by the artist. One of these albums probably belonged to John S. Budden, an auctioneer and a great friend of Krieghoff's; while the other belonged to Mme. Gibbs, whose husband was also an art patron, a collector and a friend of the artist. The photographs in these two albums bear the stamp of photograper George William Ellison of Quebec City and the Moulin firm of Paris respectively.[3] It can therefore be assumed that Krieghoff prized *The Ice Boat*. Photographs of the painting also indicate that the new medium was beginning to replace engravings as a means of reproducing and disseminating original works of art.

The Ice Boat reveals this genre scene painter's interest in depicting the recreational activities of members of the bourgeois and officers of the Quebec City garrison. The painting's subject returns to the theme of sleigh rides, canoe trips, hunting expeditions and toboggan rides illustrated many times by the artist. The work's facture is characteristic of the Dutch painter's style of brilliantly and painstakingly portraying the dress of the four passengers, the general form of the vehicle and the main buildings of this part of the city. This unusual pastime was one of the curiosities which struck Krieghoff's imagination. This very contemporary activity also reveals a new interest on the part of the artist, who was more open to the traditional way of life stamped with a rustic character.

M.B.

Notes

1. For Armstrong, see *Clavel and Reid 1988*, p. 38 (Repr.); the McCord painting bears the inscription "*Ice Boats on the St. Lawrence at Quebec 3 feb 1844.*"
2. See *Noppen, Paulette and Tremblay 1979*, pp. 306-307, 312-313, 354 and 355.
3. See *Barbeau 1934*, p. 134, as well as *Harper 1979*, pp. 153-155 and 179. Budden's album, acquired by the Montreal Museum of Fine Arts in 1981, still contains the photograph of *The Ice Boat* (1981 PH1.12).

LÉON-ANTOINE LEMIRE

active between 1850 and 1856

W E KNOW NOTHING about Lemire's early training. Sometime in late summer 1850, he opened his daguerrean gallery and, as reported in the September 23 edition of *Le Canadien,* it was his "artistic skills, which are [..] a guarantee for persons making use of his services." (*Translation*) A year later, on June 11, 1851, an advertisement published in the same newspaper announced that Lemire's studio had become the *Galerie nationale de daguerréotypie.* Lemire claimed to be able to "take portraits in only a few seconds, with or without colour, whether the day be clear or overcast, using a sky-light, and will also mount in elegant shell, velvet or leather casings, frames, lockets, rings, etc.— Engravings or paintings copied with the greatest faithfulness—Portraits of the ill or deceased taken in the home, a perfect likeness guaranteed." (*Translation*)

In November 1854, Lemire obtained letters patent for a new technique he had developed for polishing daguerreotype plates. In the *McLaughlin's Quebec Business Directory* of 1854-1855, he offered classes in which "equipment and materials used to make daguerreotypes [will be] provided with lessons in this technique, at a very low price." (*Translation*) He apparently then left for Europe. On his return, he planned to produce architectural views and landscapes on paper. In *The Quebec Directory* of 1855-1856, Lemire advertised portraits on glass, or ambrotypes, and continued to offer "courses in the latest techniques in the art of daguerreotypes." (*Translation*) We know nothing about Lemire's activities after 1856.

Main sources
LESSARD 1982; LESSARD 1983; LESSARD 1987/1.

260.
Abbé Antoine Parent, c. 1851
Hand-coloured daguerrotype 8 × 6.7 cm

Exhibition
Quebec City 1987.

Bibliography
LESSARD *1983*, p. 43 (Repr.); LESSARD *1987/1*, p. 16 (Repr.); LESSARD *1987/2*, pp. 34 and 50 (Repr.).

Collection
Séminaire de Nicolet

261.
Portrait of Monseigneur Joseph Signay, by Théophile Hamel, c. 1851
Hand-coloured daguerreotype 8 × 6.7 cm

Exhibition
Quebec City 1987.

Bibliography
LESSARD *1984*, p. 36 (repr. - version of Hôpital général de Québec); LESSARD *1987/1*, p. 18 (Repr.); LESSARD *1987/2*, pp. 37 and 53 (Repr.).

Collection
Séminaire de Nicolet

painted portrait of Monseigneur Joseph Signay by Théophile Hamel (Cat. 125), of which at least one other version belonging to the Hôpital général de Québec is known. Lemire took his copy to the point of reproducing the full colour scheme of Hamel's canvas. On August 31, 1852, a columnist from the *Journal de Québec* acknowledged the "receipt of two magnificent, lithographed portraits after daguerreotype copies by local artist Monsieur Lemire of the late Archbishop Signay and His Grace the current Archbishop of Quebec City." (*Translation*) The lithograph of Monseigneur Signay is not familiar, but this note reveals the various means taken at the time to disseminate pictures of venerated figures. Other portraits were reproduced in daguerreotypes, such as the one of Sir George Prevost painted by Robert Field.[3] Attributed to Jules-Isaï Livernois (1830-1865), the ambrotype of Father Pierre Villeneuve (1802-1856) is another testament to copying. This ambrotype is actually a copy of a daguerreotype that was already a reproduction of an oil on canvas, probably by Théophile Hamel, done by Livernois circa 1858.[4] After 1860, numerous paintings were reproduced in countless *cartes-de- visite,* such as Théophile Hamel's famous portrait gallery of politicians done between 1853 and 1856, or the portraits of Melchior-Alphonse d'Irumberry de Salaberry painted by Hamel in 1850 (Cat. 133) and of his father, Charles-Michel, engraved by Asher B. Durand after the miniature by Anson Dickinson (Cat. 89).[5] In the United States, well-known artists such as Albert Sands Southworth (1811-1894) and Josiah Hawes (1808-1901) made photographed copies of paintings. A daguerreotype reproduction of the famous painting of George Washington by Gilbert Stuart (1755-1828) was done in 1853.[6]

P.B.

T HE CAREER OF Léon-Antoine Lemire spans the period in which the daguerreotype held sway over all other techniques for creating "likenesses", that is, until it was supplanted by processes such as the calotype, ambrotype, salted and albumen paper prints, etc. With its frontal pose and somewhat candid realism, the portrait of Father Antoine Parent (1785-1855), head of the Séminaire de Québec, is a typical example of this artistic production. In order to soften and breathe life into this veritable cornerstone of the Church, Lemire has given the sitter's cheeks a rosy glow. Influenced by painted portraits, the daguerreotype often employed a very similar composition, especially for religious portraits, such as in the photograph of Father Charles-Félix Cazeau taken by Ellison & Cie[1] and, of course, the

one of Mother Saint-Anselme,[2] of the Hôpital général de Québec, taken by Lemire himself. The photograph of Mother Saint-Anselme shows the influence of the portraits of sisters Saint-Alphonse, Saint-Joseph and Sainte-Anne painted by Plamondon (Cat. 196) in 1841 for the same religious community.

The daguerreotype also made it possible to reproduce a famous picture or valuable portrait at a lower cost. Photography was pitted against more than just painting, however: it also had to compete with the other reproduction processes of engraving and lithography. In his advertisement of June 11, 1851, Lemire boasted the daguerreotype's possibilities in this respect: "The most faithful copies of engravings or paintings." (*Translation*) One example is Lemire's daguerreotype of the

Notes

1. See Ralph Greenhill, *Early Photography in Canada* (Toronto: Oxford University Press, 1965), No. 21 (Repr.).

2. *LE GRAND HÉRITAGE 1984*, p. 126, No. 103 (entry by John R. Porter).

3. See colour reproductions in LESSARD *1987/2*, p. 38.

4. See LESSARD *1987/1*, p. 17 (Repr.).

5. See the *cartes-de-visites* portrait reproductions in LESSARD *1987/2*, p. 119.

6. Robert A. Sobieszek and Odette M. Appel, *The Spirit of Fact. The Daguerreotypes of Southworth & Hawes, 1843-1862* (Boston: D.R. Godine, 1976), p. 126, No. 106 (Repr.).

SAMUEL McLAUGHLIN

1826-1914

ORN ON JANUARY 28, 1826, Samuel McLaughlin was a native of Ireland. Upon his arrival in Canada, he settled in Quebec City, where he worked as a clockmaker and publisher. In 1854, he published *McLaughlin's Quebec Directory*, in which he indicated his intention to publish engravings of the city and surrounding area. Around the same period, he also became interested in photography. Between 1858 and 1860, he published the first portfolio of photographic prints produced in Canada, *The Photographic Portfolio: A Monthly Review of Canadian Scenes and Scenery*, in which he combined his talents as publisher and photographer. Over the next few years he took several views of Quebec City and Montreal.

In 1866, he was hired as a photographer by the federal government's Department of Public Works. His first mandate consisted primarily in covering the final phases of the construction of the Parliament Buildings. McLaughlin was to be employed in this capacity until 1893, when he retired and left Ottawa for Los Angeles. Four years after his departure, a fire destroyed the rich photographic material which Samuel McLaughlin had left to his son.

Main sources
KOLTUN 1980; LESSARD 1987/3.

VAG, AGNS, MMFA

262.
The Ice Boat, 1858 or 1859

Photograph on albumen paper mounted on Bristol board, 14 × 19.9 cm (photograph); 31.6 × 38.7 cm (cardboard)

MQ, NGC

263.
Falls of Montmorency (Winter View), 1858 or 1859

Photograph on albumen paper mounted on Bristol board, 14.6 × 20.4 cm (photograph); 31.4 × 38.6 cm (cardboard

Inscriptions
(l.c., in ink, in the artist's hand) *Falls of Montmorency/(Winter View)*; (l.r., in ink) *Photographed/by S. McLaughlin.*; (l.l., oval mark) REYNOLD'S/BRISTOL BOARD surrounding a crown.

Provenance
Séminaire de Québec; on deposit at the Société du Musée du Séminaire de Québec, 1983

Collection
Musée du Séminaire de Québec (Ph987.5).

Inscriptions
(l.l., in ink in the artist's hand) *The Ice Boat.*; (l.r., in ink) *Photographed by/S. McLaughlin.*; (u.r., oval mark) REYNOLDS'S/BRISTOL BOARD surrounding a crown.

Provenance
Séminaire de Québec; on deposit at the Société du Musée du Séminaire de Québec, 1983.

Bibliography
GREENHILL AND BIRRELL *1979*, plate 15; KOLTUN *1980*, p. 26 (repr. - print of the NAC); HARE, LAFRANCE AND RUDDEL *1987*, p. 307 (repr. - print of the NAC); LESSARD *1987/3*, p. 10 (repr. - print of the Bibliothèque municipale de Montréal).

Collection
Musée du Séminaire de Québec (Ph987.4)

B ETWEEN 1858 AND 1859, Samuel McLaughlin published some of his photographs in a series entitled *The Photographic Portfolio: A Monthly View of Canadian Scenes and Scenery.* It was in this manner that he marketed **Falls of Montmorency (Winter View)** and **The Ice Boat.** Although research has not yet enabled us to determine the order in which the prints were published, we can, however, reconstruct the initial set, thanks to two collections. In addition to the two copies reproduced here, the Musée du Séminaire de Québec holds four other prints: *French Cathedral, Wilson's Monument, Valley of the River St-Charles* and *Mount Hermon Cemetery.* Only the latter photograph is missing from the album owned by the Bibliothèque municipale de Montréal, which also has *Spencer Wood, The Harbour, Habitant Cottage Lower Canada, View on Cap Rouge Road, The Natural Steps (on the Montmorenci)* and *Montmorency Falls.* This incomplete album initially led us to believe that McLaughlin had taken only eleven photographs,[1] but we have no choice but to hold that McLaughlin carried out his initial plan of delivering a photographic portfolio for every month.

In publishing this series, McLaughlin used a general presentation format which he employed for each publication. The photographs were delivered inside a portfolio whose cover provided basic information (Fig. 262-263A): the front mentioned the author, the title of the set and the choice of Middleton & Dawson as printers, while the back indicated the cost of the publication and the fact that it was issued the first Monday of the month. The portfolio opened to a flyleaf, which sometimes had the year of production indicated on the back,[2] followed by an albumen paper print mounted

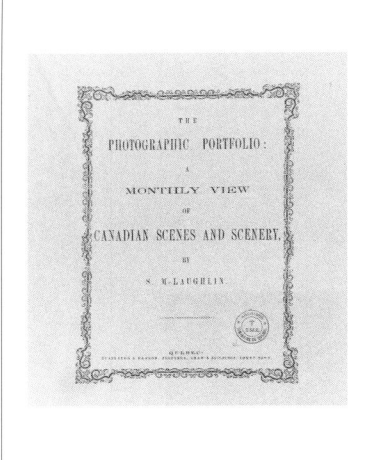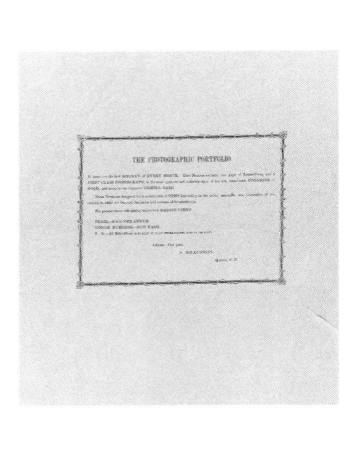

Fig. 262-263A.
Samuel McLaughlin,
*The Photographic Portfolio: A Monthly View
of Canadian Scenes and Scenery* (recto-verso cover).
Musée du Séminaire de Québec.

Fig. 263A.
Samuel McLaughlin,
Montmorency Falls, 1858;
Photograph on albumen paper, 14 × 20 cm.
Bibliothèque municipale de Montréal (D917.1447 M161Ph).

on Bristol board and protected by silk paper. It was generally titled and signed by the artist.[3] Finally, a written notice in English presented and explained in detail the subject photographed. The tone adopted in the text indicates that the publication was primarily intended for a foreign clientele.

In publishing a series of photographs of Canadian views, McLaughlin decided to showcase one of the most popular sites around Quebec City, the Montmorency Falls. He gave them preferential treatment, since two of the prints in the set dealt with this subject. This theme was used very often by 19th-century painters who, by dint of providing often repetitive views, almost managed to make the site commonplace. With *Montmorency Falls* (Fig. 263A), McLaughlin approached his subject from a painterly perspective by framing the space and using a foil in the foreground, thereby setting off the site's worth. He also resorted to devices often employed by painters, such as having a man pose in contemplation of the falls, while another holds a horse hitched to a sled. Such was not the case with *Falls of Montmorency (Winter View),* where the photographer's vision has much more to do with the technical method selected. The observer is distanced from the main subject and automatically seeks the snapshot effect which the photograph's techniques did not as yet permit. Furthermore, McLaughlin's intention was not to compose an image in

this case, but rather to fix a moment in time which the site's reality demanded. In this regard, it is interesting to note that McLaughlin's vantage point accentuates one of the aspects of the site which as yet had been largely ignored, namely, the power capacity of the falls which provided work for the local population. The introductory text which accompanied the photograph closed with an explanation of this distinctive feature:

In the left, near the top, may be seen the mill race, the property of G.B. Hall, Esquire. The water in this mill-race is said to run at the extraordinary rate of 60 miles an hour. The leakage from it forms upon the rocks in galleries of icicles or beaded pillars of a pale green blue color; these sprinkled with snow have a very beautiful appearance when seen within a few hundred feet in sunshine. The foreground of our picture is composed of the cuttings, &c., from the mills in the vicinity, and the horse, sleight, &c., in common use.

With *The Ice Boat,* McLaughlin chose a spectacular subject, which fitted in well with a set intended to represent typically Canadian scenes. The theme was also touched on in oils: Cornelius Krieghoff (Cat. 259) depicted a similar scene, although it is obvious that he was able to take advantage of the flexibility of his medium to simulate the sailboat's movement. Photographic technique did not enable McLaughlin to do likewise; he therefore posed the crew for the time it took to take his plate. He prepared his composition

using parallel planes, placing a felled conifer in the foreground to serve as a foil for the sailboat, which stands out against Cap Diamant, the final element in the scene.

It is fortunate that the texts accompanying the photographs were preserved, because they contain an irreplaceable account of the representation:

The scene which is here represented, an "ice-boat," on the smooth and icy bosom of the majestic St. Lawrence, opposite the city of Quebec, is one which is only to be witnessed occasionally, even in these hyperborean regions, when the river is spanned over by "a bridge" of polished ice. [...]

The "ice-boat" consists of a deck, or floor, of rough boards, joined together, and placed upon a pair of iron runners, or "skates." A bowsprit, and mast, with sails, and a rudder, iron shod, with a tiller, complete the rig. [...] The passengers, who may be as many as the deck will contain, have occasionally to get out upon the ice, to alter the course of the boat, when the ice is uneven, or impeded by snow; but, if it be perfectly smooth, the machine may be tacked and propelled in any direction, except against the wind, and at a speed under favorable circumstances equal to the best railroad time.

J.C.

Notes

1. *LESSARD 1987/3*, p. 12.
2. This is not the case for the prints reproduced here.
3. The Musée du Séminaire du Québec's *Valley of the River St-Charles* is neither signed nor titled.

WILLIAM NOTMAN was born in Paisley (Scotland) on March 8, 1826. As a youth, he first aspired to a career in the arts before his father asked him to join him in the family business: a wholesale dry goods firm. After an unfavourable economic period, the business went bankrupt and, in 1856, Notman emigrated to America. He decided to settle in Montreal and opened a photographic studio in December of that same year. In 1858, he obtained the contract to prepare a photographic record of the construction of the Victoria Bridge by the Grand Trunk Railway Company (Cat. 264 and 265).

Notman offered a variety of products: portraits in carte-de-visite, cabinet or full-length format, enhanced with oils or watercolours; group portraits, sometimes of hundreds of people (sporting clubs or social events); landscapes; stereographs, etc. To help him in his business, Notman hired at various times artists such as William Raphael (1833-1914), John Arthur Fraser and Henry Sandham (1842-1910). In 1868, he opened his first branch in Ottawa, the new Canadian capital, and operated up to seven establishments across Canada—Toronto, Halifax, Saint John (N.B.)—as well as a dozen outside the country.

In addition to developing his own collection of paintings, Notman hosted, in January 1860, the founding meeting of the Art Association of Montreal and, seven years later, that of the Society of Canadian Artists. A favourite meeting place for Montreal artists, his studio was even the site of painting and sculpture exhibitions. In 1863, Notman published *Photographic Selections*, which contained the photographs of 44 works by renowned artists, and repeated this activity in 1864 and 1865. Beginning in 1865, in collaboration with John Fennings Taylor (1817-1882), he published *Portraits of British Americans, with Biographical Sketches,* presenting over 80 biographies of remarkable personalities in Canadian history.

William Notman was assisted by his three sons. When Henry Sandham left the Montreal studio in 1882, one of them, William McFarlam, became his father's partner and took over the business upon his father's death in Montreal on November 25, 1891.

WILLIAM
NOTMAN
1826-1891

Main source
TRIGGS 1990.

Laying the Foundation Stone of N.º 11 Pier, at which Genl Sir W.F. Williams, of Kars, and other Celebrities, were present.

264.
Laying the Foundation Stone, No. 11 Pier, Victoria Bridge, Montreal, 1859
Stereo photograph, 7.5 × 14.2 cm (modern print from an original of the album *Canada East* presented to the Prince of Wales).

Inscriptions
(on the original mount, l.c., in ink) *Laying the Foundation Stone of No. 11 Pier, at wich Genl. Sir/W.F. Williams, of Kars, and other Celebrities, were present.*; (u.c., in ink) <u>30</u>.

Collection
Notman photographic archives, McCord Museum of Canadian History, Montreal (7030).

W ILLIAM NOTMAN'S PHOTOGRAPHIC STUDIO at the foot of Rue Bleury in Montreal had been open barely a year when the Grand Trunk Railway commissioned him to photograph the construction of the Victoria Bridge. From that point onwards, photographers were to be appointed to meet the ever-growing demand to document important events and facts.

In March 1858, Notman took his first photos of the bridge when the city and river were still in the grips of winter. Using a 10 × 12-inch view camera, Notman recorded all the major phases of the project, regardless of the season, until the bridge was completed in December 1859.

Notman, who used collodion-on-glass negatives, always had to take his darkroom with him to treat his negatives immediately, before the emulsion dried (or froze!). In winter, he moved around fairly easily by sled on the ice and set up this darkroom as close as possible to the location where he was working. During the summer, the weather was undoubtedly milder, but the photographer had to carry his equipment from one side of the bridge to the other, or have it transported to Saint-Lambert on board one of the steamships. Existing technology did not enable him to take snapshots in the modern sense. When he photographed events such as this, Notman kept a certain distance from the subject, which gave it monumental grandeur. The sheer magnitude of the construction and engineering projects to some extent demanded this approach, which was comparable to the general vantage points of watercolourists and painters such as Duncan (Cat. 91) or Légaré (Cat. 162). The painter's subjectivity and ability to synthesize the various episodes of a scene, to manipulate and condense the various aspects within a cohesive pictorial record, were replaced by photographic methods. The fragmentation of time and the succession of shots add to the representation's illusion of truthfulness and the greater involvement of the spectator. Notman, inspired by his subject, structured his photographs within a strict framework, using a variety of unusual angles and perspectives. These prints retain a solid, fixed aspect which gives the impression that the construction was posing along with the workers or guests.

Centre Tube and N° 13 Pier

265.
Center Tube and No. 13 Pier, Victoria Bridge, Montreal, 1859
Stéréo photograph, 7.5 × 14.2 cm (modern print à partir d'un original de l'album *Canada East* présenté au prince de Galles).

Inscriptions
(on the original mount, l.c., in ink) *Centre Tube and No. 13 Pier;* (u.c., in ink) 13.
Collection
Notman photographic archives, McCord Museum of Canadian History, Montreal (7013)

William Notman conscientiously recorded the project. His remarkable photographs show the construction of the temporary dams, the laying of the gigantic stone piers, the complicated wooden scaffolding used to erect the cast iron tubes.

In many scenes, one can see the workers busily riveting iron plates, moving stones and operating steam machines. Notman went so far as to descend to the bottom of a temporary dam to photograph the men removing the sand, gravel and mud from the riverbed to obtain a solid base on which the piers would be placed on the rocky substratum.

Celebrations were also caught on Notman's collodion wet plates. We can attend the laying of the foundation stone of the last pier in summer 1859, and the outdoor banquet held at the bridge's entrance on the 17th day of an icy December.

Everyone called the Victoria Bridge the eighth wonder of the world. Highly praised at the time, Notman's images support this claim. They were sold as stereographs and as large copies, and were widely disseminated as engravings and chromolithographs. Of the over 500 images contained in the superb *Maple box* offered to the Prince of Wales on the occasion of his visit to Canada in summer 1860, there were many photographs of the bridge which earned Notman his title of photographer to the Queen.

Perhaps these photographs can be appreciated even more today than at the time they were taken. Their abstraction and their majesty do not pose an obstacle to their being studied in great detail. They help us understand the grandeur and interest of this gigantic undertaking of erecting a bridge on the St. Lawrence River.

After 130 years, these photographs have retained all the freshness and vigour of Notman's vision. They are among the best photographs taken during the 19th century.

S.G.T. and L.L.

ANTOINE
PLAMONDON

(See biographical note
on page 406)

266.
The Pigeon Hunt, 1850-1853
Oil on canvas, 184.2 × 182.9 cm

S OME THIRTY YEARS AGO, art historian Gérard Morisset called *The Pigeon Hunt* the "pièce de résistance of mid-19th century Canadian painting" in the final article he was to write on portraitist Antoine Plamondon. The play on words concerning the pleasures inherent in sampling game aside, Morisset's judgement still seems valid today. *The Pigeon Hunt* is an important and significant painting, not only in Plamondon's work, but also in the development of genre painting in Quebec in the 19th century. Morisset himself showed great interest as of 1936 in reproducing it and using the painting to create a colourful and picturesque account which he quite rightly entitled "The Pigeon Hunt." This text was published first in the *Almanach de l'Action sociale catholique,* and was reprinted that same year in the first volume of *Peintres et tableaux.* An examination of the abundant historiography on the painting reveals that this account had great influence on later interpretations of *The Pigeon Hunt.* The fruits of Morisset's literary imagination, as well as certain liberties taken with history, have, over the years, turned into indisputable fact. Moreover, the erroneous information from the story of the painting's photographic reproduction helps confuse things even further.

To get to the truth of the matter, we should go back to the starting point, that is, the month of October 1850, when Plamondon submitted for the inspection of visitors to the first Exposition artistique, agricole et industrielle de Québec a painting representing a "pigeon hunt." The event in question was evidently organized in haste, which caused many problems, as can be seen in this extract from *Le Canadien* of October 18:

We are convinced that the late date on which this exhibition was announced, on the spur of the moment as it were, was solely responsible for preventing many of our artisans, artists and others from getting to work and exhibiting the

Inscription
(s.d., l.l.) *A. Plamondon/1853.*

Provenance
MM. Larue & Cie, Quebec City, before 1865; Édouard Picher, Quebec City; Achille Picher, Quebec City; Mrs. Paradis, née Sophie Migner first wife of Achille Picher; acquired through F. K. Deschênes by the Art Gallery of Toronto, 1943.

Exhibitions
Quebec City 1850; Montreal 1853; Quebec City 1924; Toronto 1945, No. 45; Montreal 1955; Montreal 1960, No. 19; Mexico City 1960, No. 82; Bordeaux 1962, No. 26; London 1965, No. 319; Vancouver 1966, No. 31; Ottawa 1967/1, No. 113; Ottawa 1970, No. 35.

Bibliography
Le Journal de Québec, October 6, 1850, p. 2, and October 12, 1850, p. 2; *La Minerve*, October 14, 1850, p. 2; *Le Canadien*, October 18, 1850, p. 2; *La Ruche littéraire et politique*, Montreal, 1853, p. 536; *The Anglo-American Magazine*, Vol. III (July-December 1853), p. 535; BIBAUD 1857, p. 256; *Le Canadien*, September 1· 1865, p. 3; BELLERIVE 1925, p. 33 entitled *Groupe d'enfants: Plamondon jeune et ses deux jeunes frères;* MORISSET 1935/2, p. 4; MORISSET 1936/1, pp. 46-48 (Repr.); MORISSET 1936-1937, Vol. I, pp. 195-207 (Repr.); MORISSET 1941/1, p. 64; MORISSET 1941/2, p. 5; COLGATE 1943, p. 110; HUBBARD 1945, p. 18, No. 45; LAMBERT 1947, pp. 35, 36, 37-42 (Repr.); LEMIEUX 1948, pp. 109 and 110 (Repr.); ART GALLERY 1950, p. 27 (Repr.); BUCHANAN 1950, pp. 18 and 18b (Repr.); MORISSET 1953/1, p. 40; MORISSET 1956/2, pp. 8 and 12 (Repr.); HUBBARD 1957, pp. 22, 27 and 28 (Repr.); LES ARTS 1958, pp. 19-20 (Repr.); HUBBARD 1959/1, pp. 41 and 44 (Repr.); PAINTING AND SCULPTURE 1959, p. 32 (Repr.); ONZE ARTISTES 1960, No. 19; MORISSET 1960/1, pp. 96f, 108-109 (Repr.); MORISSET 1960/2, p. 15; ARTE CANADIENSE 1960, No. 82; MARTIN-MÉRY 1962, p. 20, No. 26; *La Revue française*, No. 14 (May 1962), cover. p. and p. 21 (Repr.) attr. to Ignace Plamondon; HUBBARD 1963, p. 58 (Repr.); WADE 1966, p. 312 (Repr.); SHADBOLT 1966, No. 31 (Repr.); HARPER 1966, pp. 86 and 90; HUBBARD AND OSTIGUY 1967, pp. 70 and 71, No. 113 (Repr.); HARPER 1967, pp. 69 and 70 (Repr.); HUBBARD 1970, pp. 31, 35, 59, 83-85 and 139, No. 35 (Repr.); ART GALLERY 1970, pp. 379-380 (Repr.); DUMAS 1970, p. 20; MURRAY 1970, pp. 17 and 18 (Repr.); HAMEL 1971/1, p. 47; HAMEL 1971/2, p. 15; REID 1973, pp. 50 and 51 (Repr.); CATALOGUE 1974, p. 109 (Repr.); PORTER 1975, p. 10; A SELECTION 1977, p. 18 (Repr.); HARPER 1979, p. 137; *Nos racines*, No. 69 (1979), p. 1380b (Repr.); MARTIN 1980, pp. 150 and 215 attr. mistakenly to Théophile Hamel; COMEAU 1983, p. 206; PORTER 1987/3, p. 1511; TRUDEL 1987, p. 104; BRIERLEY 1988, p. 152b (Repr.); DEROME, BOURASSA AND CHAGNON 1988, p. 79; BÉLAND 1989/1, p. 80; NICOLAÏ 1990, p. 26; PORTER 1990/1, p. 924; BÉLAND AND BOURASSA 1990, p. 122; MUSÉE 1990, pp. 46 and 243 (Repr.).

Collection
Art Gallery of Ontario, Toronto. Gift of the Albert H. Robson Memorial Subscription Fund (2601)

---

fruits of their art or their industry, which would have done great honour to the district of Quebec, but whose preparation required more time than they were given. (*Translation*)

This specific context explains why the proud Antoine Plamondon agreed to exhibit an incomplete canvas, which nevertheless earned him a first prize of £5 in the "Painting" category. The description provided in *Le Journal de Québec* of October 12 confirms that this painting is indeed the one which is now housed at the Art Gallery of Ontario:

The painting which attracted the most attention on the part of the many visitors was one of a pigeon hunt, a composition by M. Antoine Plamondon; by the time the judges awarded him first prize, the public had already unanimously awarded him this prize long since. The three young hunters are seated on a knoll at the foot of a tree; however, the one behind is standing up and pointing out pigeons carelessly perched on a tree with dried branches to the one holding the weapon. In the latter's hands, and all around him, are several pigeons already felled by the deadly lead. The subjects are well grouped, and the faces, which are very natural, are extremely mobile. In the painting there is much perspective, depth and especially space. The pigeons which we can see in the foreground are painted with a trueness to life which, in our opinion, is difficult to attain, and even more difficult to surpass. Just look at the tiniest details; that horn, for example, and its transparency and the powder which can be seen across it, impress and surprise the onlooker. The colour scheme of this painting is like everything which comes from the hands of our artist, rich and true. The trees do not have the polish of the rest; but M. Plamondon, taken by surprise like everyone else, will be able to give his painting the final touches, and especially the varnish, without which the most beautiful work in the world cannot fully satisfy the eye. (*Translation*)

Contrary to Morisset's assertion, this painting, which was interesting even to its "tiniest details," was not in any way a "sketch"[1] and it is plausible that the artist only completed, signed and dated it in 1853 in preparation for his participation in another exhibition held this time in Montreal. After all, there was nothing to force him to put the final touches to his work after 1850. Earlier in his career, had he not put aside the great copy after an engraving of Raphael's *Transfiguration* which he had begun in 1832, and which he was to return to in 1855, only to complete it two years later? In short, by all indications this was the same painting—but completed and varnished—which the artist exhibited during the final week of September 1853 during the Exposition industrielle et agricole provinciale presented in Montreal. According to the *Le Journal de Québec* columnist, the "arts were only sparsely represented and were lost in the middle of this immense mass of material products; however, the talent of our artist, M. Plamondon, shone through there, and his hunters ranked first by far; they were awarded first prize." (*Translation*)

Without minimizing Plamondon's twofold success, nor the intrinsic value of

Fig. 266A.
Antoine Plamondon,
Hunting Scene 1863;
graphite on paper, 38.8 × 45 cm.
Musée du Québec, Quebec City (68.263).

Fig. 266B.
William Sidney Mount,
Boys Caught Napping in a Field, 1848;
oil on canvas, 91.7 × 74 cm.
The Brooklyn Museum. Dick S. Ramsay Fund (39.608).

his painting, we have no choice but to acknowledge that he was painting a familiar subject designed to please a wide audience. The following passage should give us more information on this point; it is an extract from the 1980 work by ethnologist Paul-Louis Martin on the *Histoire de la chasse au Québec:*

If there was a species of game which found favour among our ancestors, both young and old, rich and poor, it was the passenger pigeon. The preparations which accompanied the seasonal arrival of pigeons in the St. Lawrence valley for almost three hundred years can be termed a general mobilization, or utter pandemonium. A veritable godsend in food for some, a devastating plague for others, passenger pigeons eventually completely disappeared from America's skies, where once they had completely covered them for months on end. The last one died in captivity in the United States in 1914.

These were large pigeons (*Ectopistes migratorius*), also known as "wild" pigeons. Its ashen plumage and long, pointed tail distinguished it from our rock doves of today. The males had red throats, while the females had a drabber plumage of greyish brown. The young resembled the females, although they had more white on their heads, throats and wingtips.[2] (*Translation*)

In September 1865, **The Pigeon Hunt** was exhibited "in the window of the establishment of MM. Larue et Cie"

(*Translation*) on Rue Saint-Jean in Quebec City. A short article published in *Le Canadien*[3] tells us that the Messieurs Larue were its owners at that time and that they were offering it for sale for the tidy sum of $500. Contrary to what was long believed, the work's first owner was not Édouard Picher, whom Morisset mistakenly associated with the individual at the right in Plamondon's composition. If we must at all costs identify the three young men, it would be more accurate to believe that they are Sifroid Bussière, Charles Bussière and Soferance Denis, the three day labourers in Plamondon's service who lived with him at his home in Neuville.[4] It should be remembered that in 1842, the artist had purchased a lot in this village located some twenty miles upriver from Quebec City. Four years later, he had a two-storey wooden house built there, which boasted an extremely well lit studio with a 16-foot ceiling and a surface area of 18 feet by 30 feet. Plamondon made it his permanent home in spring 1851 after learning that the government needed all of its offices and that he was going to lose the use of his studio in Château Saint-Louis in Quebec City.

Although the hypothesis that Plamondon's three young day labourers were

the three subjects in his painting seems tempting, we do not subscribe to this theory, given what we know about the artist's pictorial practices. In short, we are inclined to believed that some engraved source was the model for the central group painted by the artist. It must be remembered that Plamondon was never known to paint full-length works without subjects borrowed from engravings.[5] By what stroke of genius would he have thrown himself into an original, daring and large-scale work, which posed a whole range of difficulties with which he had never dared to grapple up to that point? Given this context, is it not more likely that **The Pigeon Hunt,** like *Lost in the Wood* (Cat. 190), *The Little Savoyards* (Cat. 199) and *The Little Gardeners* (Cat. 267), was a genre scene or a "fancy picture" taken directly from an as yet unidentified iconographic source? In this regard, the Art Gallery of Ontario painting seems very close in its essence, if not in some of its components,[6] to the curious *Hunting Scene* of European inspiration which the artist sketched in pencil in 1863 (Fig. 266A). There is one final indicator which makes our hypothesis that Plamondon borrowed from another painting more plausible: the direction of the light in the painting or, if one prefers, the direction of

Fig. 266C.
Napoléon Bourassa,
Les Petits Pêcheurs (Fishing Scene), c. 1865;
oil on canvas, 48.6 × 59.2 cm.
Musée du Québec, Quebec City. Gift of the Bourassa estate (43.55.193).

shadows. Save for an inexplicable natural phenomenon or a mysterious caprice on the part of the artist, the group could not have been painted *in situ* at Neuville if the painting's background did indeed consist of the St. Lawrence River and the lands of the South Shore, and that two of the young men are pointing to the east. If this premise were accepted, that would mean that the light falling on the group would come from the north! Unless, of course, the artist borrowed his trio from elsewhere, integrating them—along with their shadows—in the middle of a typically Quebec landscape....

Others before us have undoubtedly noted the unevenness of *The Pigeon Hunt* in terms of composition, since the relative dryness and dullness of the landscape do not measure up to verve and beautiful hues apparent in the treatment of the subjects, props and feathered creatures in the foreground. Obviously, this is not a work painted from nature, but rather a studio painting which is distinguished by its very structured and dynamic composition and by the grid treatment of certain dark zones and planes, such as the ambiguous pictorial rendering of the green knoll. Thus, although the plumage of the pigeons is brilliantly rendered, it is difficult

to understand how the wild birds have come into contact with the neutral, grassed surface on which the artist allegedly placed them.

All these considerations regarding the plastic qualities and the degree of originality of the work aside, the fact remains that *The Pigeon Hunt* shows a new sensitivity on the part of Plamondon to the events which made up daily life in Lower Canadian society. This statement in itself is not insignificant if we recall the rigorous principles which the artist professed to have with regard to painting. That a hunting scene with local flavour finally became worthy of his brush says a great deal about the transformation which had occurred in Quebec painting since the 1820s. That Plamondon took advantage of an engraved source to compose his painting is of little import. What does matter is that he was able to assimilate and recycle the borrowed element and give it new scope, somewhat in the manner of his former master Légaré, or even as in some of his own religious "compositions." Nor should the very nature of *The Pigeon Hunt* be taken lightly. In fact, this is not a sketch, a study on paper, or even a timid attempt on canvas, but rather a large-scale work which asserts its novelty with undeniable

assurance. Within this context, Plamondon's canvas stands as a symbol in that it marks a passage, a transition, an opening onto the world of genre painting, just like Légaré's *Election Scene at Château-Richer* (Cat. 169), or the joyous libations in country inns in which Krieghoff began to be interested in the 1850s.

Finally, this exceptional contribution by Plamondon to the creation of a uniquely Canadian or Quebec iconography cannot be explained without taking into account his openness or his receptiveness to scenes of daily life and anecdotal or sentimental subjects conveyed at that time by magazines, works and illustrated newspapers published abroad. These publications echoed the blossoming of realism and genre painting in the Western art world. Within this context, we cannot help but draw a parallel between the body of work by one of Plamondon's contemporaries, American painter William Sidney Mount (1807-1868), whose 1848 work *Boys Caught Napping in a Field* (Fig. 266B) lends itself well to many obvious comparisons with *The Pigeon Hunt.* Within the context of Canadian painting, Plamondon's work presages *Les Petits Pêcheurs (Fishing Scene)* (Fig. 266C) which Napoléon Bourassa was to paint a dozen years later, but in a much smaller format.[7]

J.R.P.

Notes

1. Morisset—and R. H. Hubbard after him in 1970—referred in 1936 and 1960 to a "sketch," separate from the painting dating from 1853, which had "apparently disappeared" and "was made in 1850."

2. *MARTIN 1980*, p. 205. In its June 3, 1845 edition, *Le Journal de Québec* mentioned the abundance of passenger pigeons and the damage they caused in the fields.

3. On September 1, 1865. The text contains a brief description.

4. According to the census of 1851 (ANQQ, Reel C-1132, Pointe-aux-Trembles, p. 9), they were then aged 15, 19 and 22 respectively.

5. One has only to think of the various versions of his *The Flutist*, which he was to paint in the mid-1860s, a subject which presented fewer difficulties than *The Pigeon Hunt.*

6. See the treatment of the tree trunks, the apparel of the main subject and the hunting caps reminiscent of those of the romantic period. See R. Turner Wilcox, *The Mode in Hats and Headdress* (New York: Charles Scribner's Sons, 1945).

7. Long dated 1860, this painting could well correspond to one of the three paintings—"a fishing scene"—which Bourassa exhibited at the Art Association of Montreal on February 27, 1865. See *REID 1979*, p. 24.

267. (See colour reproduction, p. 110)
The Little Gardeners, 1857
After Edward Magnus
Oil on canvas, 92.7 × 77 cm

Inscription
(s.d., l.l.) *Plamondon 1857.*

Provenance
J.-P.-E. Dussault estate, Quebec City, 1966; Yves Dussault, Loretteville, 1966; Gérard Plamondon, Montreal, 1966; Mrs. Germaine Plamondon, Montreal, 1975; M.r Guy and Mrs. Paule Plamondon, Montreal, 1986; acquired by the Musée du Québec, Quebec City, 1990.

Bibliography
BÉLAND AND BOURASSA 1990, p. 54; *NICOLAÏ 1990*, pp. 95-96; *BÉLAND AND BOURASSA 1991*, p. 77.

Collection
Musée du Québec, Quebec City (90.68)

T HIS UNPUBLISHED WORK by Antoine Plamondon, recently acquired by the Musée du Québec, was examined and appraised in 1966 by Gérard Morisset in the estate of architect J.P.E. Dussault of Quebec City. The art historian titled this genre scene *Allégorie de la jeunesse* and termed it a "sumptuous and pleasant painting." (*Translation*) That same year, one of the painter's grand-nephews acquired the canvas with Morisset's help.[1]

The painting was completed in 1857 by Plamondon, who had by then lived in Neuville for six years. Mayor of the village since 1855, landowner and prosperous farmer, Plamondon had nev-

ertheless remained active on the artistic scene. During the 1850s, some thirty religious copies, mostly large-scale works, left his vast studio for various parishes throughout the province. In 1857, the painter executed three large religious canvases which earned him many praises in the Quebec City newspapers. These paintings were: a *Transfiguration* after Raphael, an *Assumption* after Poussin for the Saint-Jean-Baptiste church in Quebec City (destroyed in the fire of 1881), and a *Sainte Cecilia* after Raphael for the Sainte-Cécile du Bic church (destroyed in the fire of 1890).

Of his other artistic endeavours in 1857, Montreal's *La Minerve* of August 25 reported that, during an exhibition held at Bonaventure Hall in that city, "we noticed two canvases by Plamondon, including one of truly remarkable taste which was not even mentioned in the catalogue: it is said to come from the collection of the Hon. D.B. Viger, who owns another magnificent canvas by the same brush." (*Translation*) If the work belonging to Viger was perhaps *The Little Savoyards* (Cat. 199), it is not known whether the second, unidentified canvas, was this genre scene. Moreover, we know nothing of the circumstances surrounding the execution of

Fig. 267A.
William St. Maur Bingham,
The Swinging Gate, 1858;
oil on canvas, 97.5 × 114 cm.
Musée du Québec, Quebec City (80.05).

this very surprising work on the part of the artist. We do not know if Plamondon, who is known to have painted a few portraits of children (Cat. 184), executed the painting in response to a specific commission or for his own pleasure.

As he had done in 1844 for *The Little Savoyards*, Antoine Plamondon evidently took his inspiration from a then popular illustration to paint the genre scene. In fact, an engraving illustrating this same scene had been published in 1847 in *Marshall's Cabinet of Fashion* and in Suttaby's *Le Souvenir*. A copy of this engraving includes inscriptions mentioning the title of the work, its printer and its author: the scene entitled *The Little Gardeners* was printed by the firm G. Baxter, Northampton Square, London, after a painting by Edward Magnus (1799-1872), a German painter especially active in Berlin.[2] It was therefore through one of these engraved sources that Plamondon executed to some extent a literal copy of Magnus' painting. The painter undoubtedly included this scene, so unusual in his body of work, in what he himself termed "genre scenes, fancy pictures." (*Translation*)

The Little Gardeners depicts, in the foreground, a little girl and a little boy, who could be her younger brother, play-

ing with cut flowers. The two children are depicted in a landscape of autumn colours. Although the meaning of this charming scene remains obscure, it conveys a feeling of freshness and purity which can only correspond to the era's eclectic tastes. This type of sentimental, almost mawkish imagery, stems from the romantic paintings so liked by Victorian society. By dealing with a subject borrowed from a widely distributed, popular illustration, Plamondon was "plugging into" this wave of nostalgia for the carefree and innocent existence of childhood. Children were most often depicted playing or sleeping in a rustic setting, as was the case for *Lost in the Wood*, painted by Plamondon in 1836 (Cat. 190), or as in *Happy as a King*, also called *The Swinging Gate*, successively painted by William Sawyer in 1847, Cornelius Krieghoff circa 1855, and William St. Maur Bingham in 1858 (Fig. 267A). It is interesting to note that these various painters were all inspired by chromolithographs taken from the canvas of English painter William Collins.

Nevertheless, through **The Little Gardeners**, we can appreciate Plamondon's skill in rendering a landscape, an uncommon element in his body of work. Although the artist painted some portraits in

the 1830s with references to nature—especially *Richard-Achille Fortier*, 1835 (MQ); *Louis de Lagrave*, 1836 (Fig. 194B); *Zacharie Vincent* (Cat. 194); *Young Girl Holding a Rose*, circa 1840 (MMFA)—, it is primarily his genre scenes such as *Lost in the Wood* (Cat. 190) and *The Pigeon Hunt* (Cat. 266) can to some extent be compared to this painting. However, with the twenty years' difference between *Lost in the Wood* and **The Little Gardeners**, we can see a clear distinction, if not a certain development, in the artist's approach to the landscape. The romantic nature of the scene is rendered by more diffused, less dramatic lighting, a more vivid palette and broadly painted foliage.

M.B.

Notes

1. Musée du Québec, pre-archives, letters from G. Morisset to Y. Dussault, March 28, 1966; from G. Plamondon to G. Morisset, November 29, 1966; from G. Morisset to G. Plamondon, December 7, 1966; from G. Plamondon to G. Morisset, December 11, 1966; from G. Morisset to G. Plamondon, January 12, 1967.

2. See A. Ball and M. Martin, *The Price Guide to Baxter Prints*, Antique Collector's Club, 1974 (1983), p. 257. Information provided by Mme Victoria Baker of the National Gallery of Canada.

INDEX OF NAMES

INDEX OF NAMES

Artists' names are indicated in italics

BIBLIOGRAPHY

Washington Friend

<u>Bibliography</u>

Adamson (1978) Jeremy
     From Ocean to Ocean
_____

Allodi, Mary C

PUBLICATIONS AND ARTICLES

The titles preceded by an asterisk are bilingual or have an English version

A SELECTION 1977 – *A Selection from the Canadian Collection of the Art Gallery of Ontario,* Toronto, Art Gallery of Ontario, 1977, 31 p.

ACQUISITIONS 1983 – "Acquisitions principales", *RACAR,* Vol. X, No. 2 (1983), pp. 223-245.

ACQUISITIONS 1979-1980 – "Acquisitions principales", *RACAR,* Vol. VII, No. 2 (1979-1980), pp. 147-175.

ACQUISITIONS 1986 – "Acquisitions principales", *RACAR,* Vol. XIII, No. 2 (1986), pp. 1147-165.

ACQUISITIONS 1988 – "Acquisitions principales", *RACAR,* Vol. XV, No. 2 (1988), pp. 181-220.

ADAMSON 1978 – Adamson, Jeremy, *From Ocean to Ocean: Nineteenth Century Water Colour Painting in Canada* (cat.), Toronto, Art Gallery of Ontario, 1978, 20 p.

AGENDA D'ART 1982 – *Agenda d'art 1983. La vie quotidienne au Canada au 19ᵉ siècle,* Ottawa, Éditions Marcel Broquet, 1982.

ALLAIRE 1905 – Allaire, Jean-Baptiste-Arthur, *Histoire de la paroisse Saint-Denis-sur-Richelieu (Canada),* Saint-Hyacinthe, Imprimerie du Courrier de Saint-Hyacinthe, 1905, 543 p.

ALLODI 1968 – Allodi, Mary, "Forgery: Who Signed Bartlett's Name?", *Rotunda,* Vol. 1, No. 1 (Summer 1968), pp. 10-21.

ALLODI 1974/1 – Allodi, Mary, *Canadian Watercolours and Drawings in the Royal Ontario Museum,* Toronto, Royal Ontario Museum, 1974, 2 Vols.

ALLODI 1974/2 – Allodi, Mary, "Our Past in Pictures", *Rotunda,* Vol. 7, No. 4 (Fall 1974), pp. 30-35.

ALLODI 1978 – Allodi, Mary, "Canadian Faces. Some Early Portraits", *Rotunda,* Vol. 11, No. 1 (Spring 1978), pp. 18-25.

*ALLODI 1980 – Allodi, Mary, *Les débuts de l'estampe imprimée au Canada. Vues and portraits,* Toronto, Royal Ontario Museum, 1980, 244 p.

ALLODI 1990 – Allodi, Mary, "The Growing Collections. The ROM Acquires a Rare Early Canadian Portrait", *Rotunda,* Vol. 23, No. 2 (Fall 1990), pp. 5-6.

ALLODI AND TOVELL 1989 – Allodi, Mary and Rosemarie Tovell, *An Engraver's Pilgrimage: James Smillie in Quebec, 1821-1830,* Toronto, Royal Ontario Museum, 1989, 139 p.

ALLODI, MOOGK ANS STOCK 1991 – Allodi, Mary, Peter N. Moogk and Beate Stock, *Berczy* (Cat.), Ottawa, National Gallery of Canada, 1991, 327 p.

AMERICAN FOLK PORTRAITS 1981 – *American Folk Portraits. Paintings and Drawings from the Abby Aldrich Rockefeller Folk Art Center,* Boston, New York Graphic Society in association with the Colonial Williamsburg Foundation, 1981.

AMTMANN 1976 – Amtmann, Willy, *La musique au Québec 1600-1875,* Montreal, Les Éditions de l'Homme, 1976, 420 p.

ANDRE 1967 – andre, John, *William Berczy Co-Founder of Toronto,* [Toronto], [1967], 168 p.

ANDREWS 1972 – andrews, Elizabeth, *Ellen Elliott: A Pioneer,* Ginn and Company, Xerox of Canada Limited, 1972.

ANNUAIRE 1875 – *Annuaire de l'Université Laval pour l'année académique 1875-1876,* Quebec City, Augustin Côté et cie, 1875.

ANNUAIRE 1880 – *Annuaire de Ville-Marie. Origine, utilité et progrès des institutions catholiques de Montréal. Hôpital-Général (suite),* troisième livraison du second volume, Montreal, S. Chapleau et Fils Imprimeurs et Relieurs, 1880, 100 p.

ANNUAIRE 1887 – *Annuaire de l'Université Laval pour l'année académique 1887-1888,* No. 31, Quebec City, Typographie d'Augustin Côté et Cie, 1887, 192 p.

ANNUAIRE 1942 – *Annuaire de l'Université Laval pour l'année académique 1942-1943,* No. 86, Quebec City, L'Action Catholique, 1942, 370 p.

ART GALLERY 1950 – *Art Gallery of Toronto. 50th Anniversary,* [Toronto], The Art Gallery of Toronto, [1950], 36 p.

ART CANADIEN ET EUROPÉEN 1988 – *Art canadien et européeen, mobilier, antiquité and objets de collection,* Montreal, Encans Pinney's, 1988.

ART DU QUÉBEC 1981 – *Art du Québec. Agenda 1982,* Quebec City, Musée du Québec and Éditions Élysée, 1981, 113 p.

ART DU QUÉBEC 1982 – *Art du Québec. Agenda 1983,* Quebec City, Musée du Québec and Éditions Élysée, 1982.

ART DU QUÉBEC 1983 – *Art du Québec. Agenda 1984,* Quebec City, Musée du Québec and Éditions Élysée, 1983.

ART GALLERY 1970 – *Art Gallery of Ontario. The Canadian Collection,* Toronto, McGraw-Hill Company of Canada Limited, 1970, 603 p.

ARTE CANADIENSE 1960 – *Arte Canadiense* (cat.), Museo Nacional de Arte Moderno – Instituto Nacional de Bellas Artes – SEP, Mexico, 1960.

ASPECTS 1976 – *Aspects of the Art of French Canada 1700-1850* (cat.), Stratford, The Gallery, 1976.

AU MUSÉE 1936 – *Au musée du vieux monastère des Ursulines, Québec, 1639-1936,* [1936], 48 p.

AU MUSÉE 1980 – "Au Musée du Québec, le rayon X perce les mystères des œuvres d'art", *Le Droit,* June, 4, 1980.

AUDET 1952 – Audet, Louis-Philippe, *Le système scolaire de la Province de Québec,* Vol. III, *L'Institution Royale. Les débuts: 1801-1825,* Quebec City, Les Presses de l'Université Laval, 1952.

AYRE 1956 – Ayre, Robert, "Painting in Quebec. The Older Traditions", *Vie des arts,* No. 4 (Sept.-Oct. 1956), p. 16.

*BAKER 1980 – Baker, Victoria, *L'art dans les Cantons de l'Est 1800-1950* (cat.), Sherbrooke, Galerie d'art du Centre culturel de l'Université de Sherbrooke, 1980, 63 p.

BAKER 1981 – Baker, Victoria, *Images de Charlevoix 1784-1950* (cat.), Montreal, Montreal Museum of Fine Arts, 1981, 178 p.

BAKER 1947 – Baker, Charles E., "The Story of Two Silhouettes", *The New-York Historical Society Quarterly,* Vol. XXXI, No. 4 (October 1947).

BARBEAU 1934 – Barbeau, Marius, *Cornelius Krieghoff, Pionnier Painter of North America,* Toronto, The MacMillan Company of Canada, 1934, 152 p.

BARBEAU 1948 – Barbeau, Marius, *Cornelius Krieghoff,* Toronto, The Ryerson Press, 1948, 36 p. (Canadian Art Series).

*BARBEAU 1957 – Barbeau, Marius, *J'ai vu Québec,* Quebec City, Librairie Garneau Ltée, 1957 (168 p.).

BARBEAU 1962 – Barbeau, Marius, *Cornelius Krieghoff,* Toronto, McClelland and Stewart Limited, 1962, 15 p. (The Gallery of Canadian Art I).

*BARIBEAU 1988 – Baribeau, Claude, *Papineau et son temps* (cat.), Ottawa, National Archives of Canada, 1988.

BARTEAUX 1945 – Barteaux, Eleanor, "W.H. Bartlett, of "Bartlett Prints"", *Dalhousie Review,* Vol. 24, No. 4 (January 1945), pp. 423-437.

BAZIN 1934 – Bazin, Jules, "Une histoire de la peinture au Canada français (résumé de la thèse soutenue avec éclat par M. Gérard Morisset à l'École du Louvre)", *L'Ordre*, 16, 17, 18, 19 May 1934.

BAZIN 1971 – Bazin, Jules, "Historique de quelques musées", *Vie des arts*, No. 63 (Summer 1971), pp. 14-19.

BAZIN 1972 Bazin, Jules, "Un peintre américain à Montréal en 1820", *Vie des arts*, Vol. XVI, No. 66 (Spring 1972), pp. 19-23.

*BAZIN 1988 – Bazin, Jules, "Dulongpré, Louis", *Dictionnaire biographique du Canada*, Quebec City, Les Presses de l'Université Laval, Vol. VII (1988), pp. 276-278.

BÉCHARD 1885 – Béchard, A., *Histoire de la paroisse de Saint-Augustin (Portneuf)*, Quebec City, Léger Brousseau, 1885, 395 p.

BÉDARD AND CLOUTIER 1985 – Bédard, Rodrique and Nicole Cloutier, "La restauration d'un Théophile Hamel", *Continuité*, No. 26 (Winter 1985), pp. 42-43

BÉLAND 1987 – Béland, Mario, "Acquisitions récentes", *Cap-aux-Diamants*, Vol. 3, No. 3 (Fall 1987), p. 66.

BÉLAND 1988 – Béland, Mario, "Les portraits miniatures", *Cap-aux-Diamants*, Vol. 4, No. 3 (Fall 1988), p. 65.

BÉLAND 1989/1 – Béland, Mario, "Nouveaux venus à la galerie", *Cap-aux-Diamants*, Vol. 5, No. 2 (Summer 1989), p. 80.

BÉLAND 1989/2 – Béland, Mario, "Paysages à l'honneur", *Cap-aux-Diamants*, Vol. 4, No. 4 (Winter 1989), p. 75.

BÉLAND 1989/3 – Béland, Mario, "Deux précieuses copies", *Cap-aux-Diamants*, Vol. 5 No. 3 (Fall 1989), p. 69.

BÉLAND 1991 – Béland, Mario, "La muse hivernale", *Cap-aux-Diamants*, No. 24 (Winter 1991), pp. 50-54.

BÉLAND AND BOURASSA 1990 – Béland, Mario and Paul Bourassa, *Agenda d'art 1991*, Quebec City, Musée du Québec and Les Publications du Québec, 1990, 144 p.

BÉLAND AND BOURASSA 1991 – Béland, Mario and Paul Bourassa, "Tableaux de l'ère victorienne", *Cap-aux-Diamants*, No. 26 (Summer 1991), p. 77.

BÉLAND AND PRIOUL 1988 – Béland, Mario and Didier Prioul, "Acquisitions récentes", *Cap-aux-Diamants*, Vol. 4, No. 2 (Summer 1988), p. 85.

BÉLISLE 1982 – Bélisle, Jean, "La décoration des navires au Québec", *De la voile à la vapeur: la construction de navires dans les environs de Québec et de Montréal*, under the dir. of Victoria A. Baker and Diana Dutton, Saint-Lambert, Le Musée Marsil, 1982, 12 p.

BÉLISLE 1984 – Bélisle, Jean, "François Baillairgé, un sculpteur de proue", *Neptunia*, No. 154 (June 1984), pp. 32-40.

*BELL 1972 – Bell, Michael, *Visage du Canada. Aquarelles et dessins historiques tirés de la collection permanente des National Archives of Canada* (cat.), Ottawa, Archives publiques du Canada, 1972.

BELL 1973/1 – Bell, Michael, *From Annapolis Royal to the Klondike: Painters in a New Land*, Toronto, McClelland and Stewart Limited, 1973, 224 p.

*BELL 1973/2 – Bell, Michael, *La collection Coverdale. Exposition d'un choix de peintures, dessins et gravures sur le Canada* (cat.), Ottawa, National Archives of Canada, 1973.

*BELL 1977 – Bell, Michael, "Mercer, Alexander Cavalié", *Dictionnaire biographique du Canada*, Quebec City, Les Presses de l'Université Laval, Vol. IX (1977), pp. 599-600

*BELL AND COOKE 1975 – Bell, Michael and Martha E. Cooke, *Québec et ses environs. Une exposition d'aquarelles et de dessins par James Pattison Cockburn (1779-1847)* (cat.), Ottawa, National Archives of Canada, [1975].

BELL AND COOKE 1978 – Bell, Michael and Martha E. Cooke, *The Last "Lion"… Rambles in Quebec with James Pattison Cockburn* (cat.), Kingston, The Agnes Etherington Art Centre, 1978, 55 p.

BELLERIVE 1925 – Bellerive, Georges, *Artistes-peintres canadiens-français. Les anciens*, 1st series, Quebec City, Garneau, 1925, 80 p.

BETCHERMAN 1962 – Betcherman, Lita-Rose, *William Von Moll Berczy: His Career as an Artist in Lower Canada, 1805-1812*, Master's thesis, Carleton University, 1962, 125 p.

BIBAUD 1857 – Bibaud, Maximilien, *Dictionnaire des hommes illustres du Canada et de l'Amérique*, Montreal, Bibaud et Richer, 1857, 389 p.

BIBAUD 1891 – Bibaud, Maximilien, *Le Panthéon canadien. Choix de biographies. Nouvelle édition, revue, augmentée et complétée jusqu'à ce jour par Adèle et Victoria Bibaud, nièces de l'auteur*, Montreal, Jos. M. Valois, 1891.

BILSON 1980 – Bilson, Geoffrey, *A Darkened House: Cholera in Nineteenth-Century Canada*, Toronto, University of Toronto Press, 1980, 245 p. (Coll. "Social History of Canada", No. 31).

BLANCHET 1987 – Blanchet, Danielle, *Saint-Roch: un quartier en constante mutation*, Quebec City, Ville de Québec, 1987, 54 p. (Coll. "Les quartiers de Québec").

BLODGETT 1990 – Blodgett, Jean, "Lost Heritage Regained: Works of Art Repatriated with the Assistance of the Government of Canada's Cultural Property Program", *Muse*, Vol. VIII, No. 2 (Summer 1990), pp. 73-77.

BOISCLAIR 1977 – Boisclair, Marie-Nicole, *Catalogue des œuvres peintes conservées au monastère des augustines de l'Hôtel-Dieu de Québec*, Quebec City, Ministère des Affaires culturelles, 1977, 195 p. (Publication No. 24 of the Centre de documentation de l'Inventaire des biens culturels).

BOISSAY 1966 – Boissay, Pauline, "Deux œuvres religieuses certaines de Roy-Audy", *Vie des arts*, No. 42 (Spring 1966), pp. 26-30.

BOUCHARD 1990 – Bouchard, Christian, *Québec sur glace. Sports et divertissements*, Quebec City, Musée de la civilisation, 1990, 30 p.

BOUCHETTE 1815 – Bouchette, Joseph, *A Topographical Description of the Province of Lower Canada with Remarks upon Upper Canada and on the respective Connexion of Both Provinces with the United States of America*, London, W. Faden, 1815, 640 p.

BOUCHETTE 1832 – Bouchette, Joseph, *The British Dominions in North America; Or a Topographical and Statistical Description of the Provinces of Lower and Upper Canada, New Brunswick, Nova Scotia, The Islands of Newfoundland, Prince Edward, and Cape Breton. Including Considerations on Land-Granting and Emigration. To which are Annexed, Statistical Tables and Tables of Distances, &.*, London, Longman, Rees, Orme, Brown, Green and Longman, 1832, 2 Vol.

*BOUDREAU AND LÉPINE 1988 – Boudreau, Claude and Pierre Lépine, "Bouchette, Joseph", *Dictionnaire biographique du Canada*, Quebec City, Les Presses de l'Université Laval, Vol. VII (1988), pp. 103-107.

BOULIZON 1976 – Boulizon, Guy, *Les musées du Québec*, Montreal, Fides, 1976, 2 Vol. (Coll. "Loisirs et culture").

BOURASSA 1968 – Bourassa, Anne, *Un artiste canadien-français, Napoléon Bourassa 1827-1916*, Montreal, 1968, 87 p.

BOURASSA 1986 – Bourassa, Paul, *La diffusion d'un thème iconographique dans l'art au Québec: la mort de saint François Xavier*, Master's thesis, Université du Québec à Montréal, 1986, 448 p.

BOURASSA 1987 – Bourassa, Paul, "La diffusion d'un thème iconographique dans l'art au Québec: la mort de saint François Xavier", *The Journal of Canadian Art History*, Vol. X, No. 2 (1987), pp. 120-152.

BOURASSA 1989-1990 – Bourassa, Paul, "L'Autoportrait dans l'atelier de Théophile Hamel ou l'image de la ressemblance", *Esse*, No. 14 (Winter 1989-90), pp. 42-47.

BOURASSA 1990 – Bourassa, Paul, "Héros et malfaiteur", *Cap-aux-Diamants*, No. 21 (Spring 1990), p. 84.

BOURNE 1829 – Bourne, George, *The Picture of Quebec*, Quebec City, D. & J. Smillie, 1829, 134 p.

BRIERLEY 1988 – Brierley, Jane, *A Man of Sentiment. The Memoirs of Philippe-Joseph Aubert de Gaspé, 1786-1871*, Montreal, Véhicule Press, 1988, 461 p.

*BROWN AND LINTEAU 1988 – Brown, Craig and Paul-André Linteau (under the dir.), *Histoire générale du Canada*, Montreal, Éditions du Boréal, 1988, 694 p.

BUCHANAN 1950 – Buchanan, Donald W., *The Growth of Canadian Painting*, Toronto, William Collins & Sons, 1950, 112 p.

BURANT 1980 – Burant, Jim, "Art in Halifax: Exhibitions and Criticism in 1830 and 1831", *RACAR*, Vol. VII, Nos. 1-2 (1980), pp. 125-135.

BURANT 1982 – Burant, Jim, "Further Notes Concerning the Halifax Art Exhibitions of 1830 and 1831", *RACAR*, Vol. IX, Nos. 1-2 (1982), pp. 78-82.

*CAMERON AND TRUDEL 1976 – Cameron, Christina and Jean Trudel, *Québec au temps de James Patterson Cockburn*, Quebec City, Garneau, 1976, 176 p.

CANADIAN NATIONAL EXHIBITION 1907 – *Canadian National Exhibition* (cat.), Toronto, Department of Fine Arts, 1907.

CARRICK 1928 – Carrick, Alice van Leer, *Shades of Our Ancestors: American Profiles and Profilists*, Boston, Little, Brown and Company, 1928.

CARRIER 1957 – Carrier, Louis, *Catalogue of the Château de Ramezay. Museum and Portrait Gallery*, Montreal, The Antiquarian and Numismatic Society of Montreal, 1957.

CARRIER AND LEFEBVRE 1962 – Carrier, Louis and Jean-Jacques Lefebvre, *Catalogue du Musée du Château de Ramezay de Montréal*, Montreal, Société d'Archéologie et de Numismatique, 1962, 176 p.

CARTER 1908 – Carter, J. Purves, *Descriptive and Historical Catalogue of the Paintings in the Gallery of Laval University, Quebec*, Quebec City, L'Événement Printing Co., 1908, 230 p.

CARTER 1909 – Carter, J. Purves, *Livret officiel de l'exposition spéciale des tableaux récemment restaurés. Musée de peintures université Laval, Québec. Sous la direction de l'association des anciens élèves gradués de l'université Laval à Québec* (translated by Abbé Adolphe Garneau), Quebec City, La Cie d'imprimerie du "Telegraph", 1909, 22 p.

CARTER 1966 – Carter, David-G., *Masterpieces from Montreal* (cat.), Montreal, Montreal Museum of Fine Arts, 1966.

CARTER 1967 – Carter, David-G., *Le peintre et le Nouveau Monde* (cat.), Montreal, Montreal Museum of Fine Arts, 1967.

CARTER 1967-1968 – Carter, David G., "Anatomie d'un hémisphère de 1564 à 1867", *Vie des arts*, No. 49 (Winter 1967-1968), pp. 14-21.

CATALOGUE s.d. – *Catalogue of the Château Ramezay*, Montreal, Gazette Print., s.d.

CATALOGUE 1847 – *Catalogue for the Montreal Gallery of Pictures 1847. Exhibition the First* (cat.), Montreal, Lovell and Gibson, 1847, 16 p.

CATALOGUE 1852 – *Catalogue of the Quebec Gallery of Paintings, Engravings, etc, the Property of Jos. Légaré, St. Angele Street, Corner of St. Helen Street*, Quebec City, E. R. Fréchette, 1852, 16 p.

CATALOGUE 1870 – *Catalogue... Gallery of Art Association ... Montreal, 8thMarch 1870*, Art Association of Montreal 6thExhibition.

CATALOGUE 1879 – *Catalogue... exhibition by the Association on the Occasion of the Opening of the Art Gallery, Phillips Square, May 26th1879*, Montreal, Art Association of Montreal 9thExhibition, 1879.

CATALOGUE 1887 – *Catalogue Raisonné of a Loan Exhibition of Canadian Historical Portraits and Other Objects Relating to Canadian Archaeology: Held in the Natural History Society's Building by the Numismatic and Antiquarian Society of Montreal, In Commemoration of the 25thAnniversary of the Foundation of the Society, on Thursday, December 15th, 1887, And Following Days* (cat.), Montreal, Numismatic and Antiquarian Society of Montreal (The Gazette Printing Company), 1887, 80 p.

CATALOGUE 1898 – *Catalogue of the Château Ramezay Museum*, [Montreal], Woman's Branch of the Numismatic & Antiquarian Society of Montreal, 1898.

CATALOGUE 1927/1 – *Catalogue of Important Drawings by Old Masters...*, London, Sotheby & Co., 1927.

CATALOGUE 1927/2 – *Catalogue of the Chateau Ramezay. Museum and Portrait Gallery*, Montreal, 1927.

CATALOGUE 1928 – *Catalogue of the Chateau de Ramezay. Museum and Portrait Gallery Exhibited by The Antiquarian and Numismatic Society of Montreal*, Montreal, 1928.

CATALOGUE 1931 – *Catalogue du Château de Ramezay. Musée et galerie de portraits*, Montreal, 1931.

CATALOGUE 1936 – *Catalogue of the Château de Ramezay. Museum and Portrait Gallery Exhibited by The Antiquarian and Numismatic Society of Montreal*, 23rd edition, Montreal, 1936.

CATALOGUE 1937 – *Catalogue of the Chateau de Ramezay. Museum and Portrait Gallery Exhibited by The Antiquarian and Numismatic Society of Montreal*, 24th edition, Montreal, 1937.

CATALOGUE 1940 – *Catalogue of a Selection from the Watercolour & Sepia Drawings (1760-1850) in the William H. Coverdale Collection of Historical Canadiana at the Manoir Richelieu, Murray Bay, P.Q. Exhibited at the Galleries of the Art Association of Montreal* (cat.), Montreal, Canada Steamship Lines, 1940, 11 p.

CATALOGUE 1942 – *Catalogue of Canadiana. Being a Selection of Prints, Watercolour Drawings, Oil Paintings and Maps Drawn from the William H. Coverdale Collection of Historical Canadiana at The Manoir Richelieu, Murray Bay, P.Q. Canada. Together with a Group of Oil Paintings by Contemporary Canadian Artists. Exhibited Under the Auspices of the Maple Leaf Fund Inc. at The Grand Central Art Galleries, New York City* (cat.), New York, Grand Central Art Galleries, 1942, 54 p.

CATALOGUE 1948 – *Catalogue du Château de Ramezay. Musée et galerie de portraits*, Montreal, 1948.

CATALOGUE 1954 – *Catalogue du Château de Ramezay. Musée et galerie de portraits*, Montreal, 1954.

CATALOGUE 1956 – *Catalogue du Château de Ramezay. Musée et galerie de portraits*, Montreal, 1956.

CATALOGUE 1962 – *Catalogue of Eighteenth and Nineteenth Century Sculpture, Drawing and Paintings*, London, Sotheby & Co., 1962.

CATALOGUE 1968 – *Catalogue of Watercolours, Prints and Maps from the Collection of Canadiana formed by The late Robert W. Reford of Montreal*, Toronto, Sotheby & Co. (Canada) Ltd., 1968.

CATALOGUE 1973 – *Catalogue of Important Canadian Paintings, Drawings, Watercolours, Books and Prints of the 19th and 20thCenturies*, Toronto, Sotheby & Co. (Canada) Ltd., 1973.

CATALOGUE 1974 – *Catalogue illustré. Art Gallery of Ontario*, Toronto, Art Gallery of Ontario, 1974, 215 p.

CAUCHON 1968 – Cauchon, Michel, "L'incendie du quartier Saint-Roch (28 mai 1845) vue par Joseph Légaré", *Bulletin du Musée du Québec*, No. 10 (October 1968), pp. 1-4.

CAUCHON 1971 – Cauchon, Michel, *Jean-Baptiste Roy-Audy 1778 c. 1848*, Quebec City, Ministère des Affaires culturelles, 1971, 153 p. (Coll. "Civilisation du Québec", No. 8).

*CAUCHON 1988 – Cauchon, Michel, "Roy-Audy, Jean-Baptiste", *Dictionnaire biographique du Canada*, Quebec City, Les Presses de l'Université Laval, Vol. VII (1988), pp. 824-825.

CAUFIELD 1987 – Caufield, Jon, "Three Preconfederation Painters of the Canadian City. Part II. James Duncan", *Revue d'histoire urbaine*, Vol. XVI, No. 2 (October 1987), pp. 190-195.

*CHARBONNEAU, DESLOGES AND LAFRANCE 1982 – Charbonneau, André, Yvon Desloges and Marc Lafrance, *Québec ville fortifiée du XVIIᵉ au XIXᵉ siècles*, Quebec City, Éditions du Pélican, 1982, 491 p.

CHARTRAND 1986-1987 – Chartrand, René, "The Lower Canada Select Embodied Militia Battalions, 1812-15", *Military Illustrated, Past & Present*, No. 4 (December 1986-January 1987), pp. 38-42.

CHARTRAND, DUCHESNE AND GINGRAS 1987 – Chartrand, Luc, Raymond Duchesne and Yves Gingras, *Histoire des sciences au Québec*, Montreal, Les Éditions Boréal, 1987.

CHASSÉ 1985 – Chassé, Béatrice, "Girouard, Jean-Joseph", *Dictionnaire biographique du Canada*, Quebec City, Les Presses de l'Université Laval, Vol. VIII (1985), pp. 366-370.

CHEERS 1980 – Cheers, Pam, "Rembrandt Materpiece Featured in Quebec Museum Exhibition", *Quebec Chronicle Telegraph*, 25 June 1980, p. 13.

*CLAVELL AND REID 1988 – Clavell, Edward and Dennis Reid, *Quand l'hiver était roi: L'image de l'hiver au Canada du XIXᵉ siècle* (cat.), Banff, Altitude Publishing and The Whyte Museum of Canadian Rockies, 1988, 80 p.

CLOUTIER 1982 – Cloutier, Nicole, *L'iconographie de sainte Anne au Québec*, Ph.D. thesis, Université de Montréal, 1982, 792 p.

*CLOUTIER 1983/1 – Cloutier, Nicole, *Au fil des collections. L'Éducation de la Vierge de Théophile Hamel* (cat.), Montreal, Montreal Museum of Fine Arts, 1983, 4 p.

*CLOUTIER 1983/2 – [Cloutier, Nicole], "L'Éducation de la Vierge de Théophile Hamel", *Collage*, Vol. 8, No. 7 (September 1983), p. 1.

*CLOUTIER 1984 – [Cloutier, Nicole], *Au fil des collections. Québec vu par Légaré, Holloway, Krieghoff, Sewell* (Cat.), Montreal, Montreal Museum of Fine Arts, 1984, 6 p.

COLGATE 1943 – Colgate, William G., *Canadian Art: its Origin & Development*, Toronto, The Ryerson Press, 1943, 278 p.

COLLARD 1960-1961 – Collard, Elizabeth A., "An Early French Canadian Artist", *The Seigneur*, Winter 1960-1961, pp. 8-9.

COLLARD 1968 – Collard, Elizabeth A., "A Forgotten Artist: Samuel Hawksett", *Canadian Antiques Collector*, Vol. 3, No. 12 (December 1968), pp. 16-17.

COLLARD 1969 – Collard, Elizabeth A., "The Mystery of W.F. Wilson", *Canadian Antiques Collector*, Vol. 4, No. 7 (July 1969), pp. 22-24.

COLLECTIONS 1967 – *Collections des musées d'état du Québec*, Quebec City, Ministère des Affaires culturelles, 1967, 108 pl.

COMEAU 1983 – Comeau, André, *Artistes plasticiens. Canada (Régime français et Conquête), Bas-Canada et le Québec*, Montreal, Les Éditions Bellarmin, 1983, 261 p.

* CONRAD-BURY AND LEBEL 1979 – Conrad-Bury, Janine G. and Marc Lebel, *Enfants d'autrefois* (Cat.), 2nd edition, Ottawa, National Archives of Canada, 1979, 31 p.

COOKE 1961 – Cooke, Edwy, *Cornelius Krieghoff, ca. 1815-1872* (Cat.), Fredericton, Beaverbrook Art Gallery, 1961, [16 p.].

* COOKE 1983 – Cooke, W. Martha E., *Collection d'œuvre canadiennes de W. H. Coverdale. Peintures, aquarelles et dessins (Collection du Manoir Richelieu)*, Ottawa, National Archives of Canada, 1983, 299 p. and 500 Repr.

* COOKE 1987 – Cooke, W. Martha E., "Fisher, sir George Bulteel", *Dictionnaire biographique du Canada*, Quebec City, Les Presses de l'Université Laval, Vol. VI (1987), pp. 281-283.

CORBEIL 1971 – Corbeil, Wilfrid, *Le Musée d'art de Joliette*, 1971, 291 p.

CORBEIL 1978 – Corbeil, Wilfrid, *Trésors des fabriques du diocèse de Joliette*, [Joliette], Le Musée d'art de Joliette, 1978, 110 p.

CORBIN AND LESSARD 1986 – Corbin, Régis and Rénald Lessard, "Le choléra de 1832: un artisan témoigne", *Cap-aux-Diamants*, Vol. 2, No. 1 (Spring 1986), p. 38.

COURVILLE 1990 – Courville, Serge, *Entre ville et campagne. L'essor du village dans les seigneuries du Bas-Canada*, Quebec City, Les Presses de l'Université Laval, 1990.

COWDREY 1943 – Cowdrey, Mary Barlett, éd., *The National Academy of Design Exhibition Record 1826-1860*, New York, The New-York Historical Society, 1943, 2 Vol.

DAVIS 1982 – Davis, Ann, *A Distant Harmony. Comparaisons in the Painting of Canada and the United States of America* (cat.), Winnipeg, The Winnipeg Art Gallery, 1982, 190 p.

DEARBORN 1983 – Dearborn, Mona Leithiser, *Anson Dickinson. The Celebrated Miniature Painter 1779-1852* (Cat.), Hartford, The Connecticut Historical Society, 1983, 187 p.

DE JOUVANCOURT 1971 – de Jouvancourt, Hugues, *Cornelius Krieghoff*, Montreal, Éditions de la Frégate, 1971.

DE JOUVANCOURT 1979 – de Jouvancourt, Hugues, *Cornelius Krieghoff 1815-1872*, Montreal, Éditions Stanké, 1979, 223 p.

DE PENCIER 1987/1 – De Pencier, Honor, *Posted to Canada. The Watecolours of George Russell Dartnell 1835-1844*, Toronto and Oxford, Dundurn Press, 1987, 112 p.

DE PENCIER 1987/2 – De Pencier, Honor, "The Harrowing Journey of George Russell Dartnell", *Rotunda*, Vol. 20, No. 2 (Fall 1987), pp. 18-26.

DEROME 1976 – Derome, Robert, "Charles Huot et la peinture d'histoire au palais législatif de Québec (1883-1930)", *Bulletin of the National Gallery of Canada*, No. 27 (1976), 42 p.

DEROME 1978 – Derome, Robert, "Joseph Légaré (1795-1855)", *Canadian Collector*, Vol. 13, No. 5 (September-October 1978), pp. 28-31.

DEROME 1981-1982 – Derome, Robert, "Le portrait de James McGill peint par Louis Dulongpré", *Vie des Arts*, Vol. XXVI, No. 105 (Winter 1981-1982), pp. 44-46.

* DEROME AND LECLERC 1978 – Derome, Robert and Denise Leclerc, *Brève introduction à l'œuvre de Joseph Légaré (1795-1855)*, Ottawa, National Gallery of Canada, [1978], 19 p.

* DEROME, BOURASSA AND CHAGNON 1988 – Derome, Robert, Paul Bourassa and Joanne Chagnon, *Dulongpré: de plus près* (Cat.), Montreal, McCord Museum of Canadian History, 1988, 99 p.

DE ROUSSAN 1969 – de Roussan, Jacques, "Les portraits de famille de Napoléon Bourassa", *Perspectives*, April, 5, 1969.

DE ROUSSAN 1975 – de Roussan, Jacques, "François Baillairgé (1759-1830), peintre, sculpteur et architecte", *Perspectives*, March, 22, 1975, pp. 22-24.

DE ROUSSAN 1982 – de Roussan, Jacques, *Le nu dans l'art au Québec*, La Prairie, Éditions Marcel Broquet, 1982, 223 p.

DE ROUSSAN 1989 – de Roussan, Jacques (with the collaboration of Micheline Huard), *Québec en peinture*, Pointe-Claire, Roussan Éditeur, 1989, 167 p.

DÉSILETS 1949 – Désilets, Alphonse, *Les Cent ans de l'Institut Canadien de Québec, 1848-1948. Compte-rendu des fêtes du Centenaire en September 1948*, Quebec City, Institut Canadien de Québec, 1949, 252 p.

* DE VOLPI 1971 – De Volpi, Charles P., *Québec: recueil iconographique. Gravures historiques et illustrations relatives à la ville de Québec, Province de Québec, Canada*, Longman Canada Limited, 1971, 23 p., 188 pl.

DOUGHTY 1934 – Doughty, Arthur G., *Report of the Public Archives for the Year 1933*, Ottawa, J. O. Patenaude, 1934.

DRAPEAU 1883 – Drapeau, Stanislas, *Biographie de Sir N.-F. Belleau*, Quebec City, Léger Brousseau, 1883.

* DUBÉ 1986 – Dubé, Philippe, *Deux cents ans de villégiature dans Charlevoix: l'histoire du pays visité*, Quebec City, Les Presses de l'Université Laval, 1986, 336 p.

* DUCLOS 1987 – Duclos, Laurette, "Coutlée, Thérèse-Geneviève", *Dictionnaire biographique du Canada*, Quebec City, Les Presses de l'Université Laval, Vol. VI (1987), pp. 185-186.

DUMAS 1970 – Dumas, Paul, "Antoine Plamondon (1802-1895) et Théophile Hamel (1817-1870)", *L'information médicale et paramédicale*, December, 15,1970, pp. 20-21.

DUMAS 1974 – Dumas, Paul, "L'histoire de la peinture", *Canadian Antiques Collector*, Vol. 9, No. 3 (May-June 1974), pp. 34-43.

DUVAL 1954 – Duval, Paul, *Canadian Water Colour Painting*, Toronto, Burns and MacEachern, 1954, 102 p.

DUVAL 1974 – Duval, Paul, *High Realism in Canada*, Toronto, Clarke, Irwin & Company Limited, 1974, 175 p.

DUVAL 1977 – Duval, Monique, "Vers une redécouverte de l'œuvre québécoise de Patterson Cockburn", *Le Soleil*, 12 January 1977, p. H-6.

EAST 1934 – East, Charles, "Saint-Augustin de Portneuf", *L'Action Catholique*, 8 September 1934, p. 5.

EXHIBITION 1934 – *Exhibition of Paintings by Cornelius Krieghoff 1815-1872* (Cat.), Ottawa, National Gallery of Canada, 1934, 22 p.

EXHIBITION 1953 – *Exhibition of Canadian Painting to celebrate the Coronation of Her Majesty Queen Elizabth II* (Cat.), Ottawa, National Gallery of Canada, 1953, 39 p.

EXPOSITION 1920 – *Exposition de peintures et dessins à l'Académie commerciale de Québec* (Cat.), Quebec City, Académie commerciale, 25 October 1920, 11 p.

FAILLANT-DUMAS 1980 – Faillant-Dumas, Lola, *Analyse scientifique des œuvres d'art* (Cat.), Quebec City, Musée du Québec, 1980, 82 p.

FAIR 1981 – Fair, D. Barry, *Yesterday's Canada* (Cat.), London (Ont.), London Regional Art Gallery, 1981, 28 p.

FAIRCHILD 1907 – Fairchild, G. M., *From My Quebec Scrap-Book*, Quebec City, Frank Carrel, 1907, 316 p.

FALARDEAU 1936 – Falardeau, Émile, *Un maître de la peinture, Antoine-Sébastien Falardeau*, Montreal, Éditions Albert Lévesque, 1936, 164 p. (Figures canadiennes).

* FARR 1990 – Farr, Dorothy, *L'image de la ville en peinture canadienne* (Cat.), Kingston, Agnes Etherington Art Centre, 1990, 124 p.

* FENWICK AND STACEY 1956 – Fenwick, Kathleen M. and Charles Perry Stacey, "Thomas Davies, Soldier and Painter of Eighteenth-Century Canada", *Canadian Art*, Vol. 13 (1956), pp. 270-276 and 300.

FÊTES SOLENNELLES 1910 – "Fêtes solennelles à l'Ancienne-Lorette", *L'Action sociale*, Vol. III, No. 851 (October, 13, 1910), pp. 1 and 8.

FIELDING 1974 – Fielding, Mantle, *Dictionary of American Painters, Sculptors and Engravers*, Greens Farms, Modern Books and Crafts, 1974, 455 p.

FINLEY 1978 – Finley, Gerald, *George Heriot Postmaster-Painter of the Canadas* (Cat.), Toronto, Buffalo, London, University of Toronto Press, 1983, 72 p.

FINLEY 1979 – Finley, Gerald, *George Heriot 1759-1839*, Ottawa, National Gallery of Canada, 1979, 81 p. (Coll. "Artistes canadiens", No. 5).

FINLEY 1983 – Finley, Gerald, *George Heriot Postmaster-Painter of the Canadas*, Toronto, University of Toronto Press, 1983, 310 p.

* FINLEY 1988 – Finley, Gerald, "Heriot, George", *Dictionnaire biographique du Canada*, Quebec City, Les Presses de l'Université Laval, Vol. VII (1988), pp. 432-436.

* FOX 1986 – Fox, Ross, "Henry D. Thielcke: A Recently Found Portrait and Some Reflections on Thielcke's Links with the English School", *Annual Bulletin* (National Gallery of Canada), No. 8 (1986), pp. 21-29.

* FOY 1986 – Foy, Lydia, "Les ressemblances les plus parfaites", *L'Archiviste*, Vol. 13, No. 5 (September-October 1986), p. 12.

* FRANÇOIS BAILLAIRGÉ 1985 – *François Baillairgé (1759-1830) – Un portefeuille de dessins académiques* (Cat.), Montreal, Galerie d'art Concordia, 1985, 57 p.

*FREDRICKSON AND GIBB 1980 – Fredrickson, N. Jaye and Sandra Gibb, *La chaîne d'alliance: l'orfèvrerie de traite et de cérémonie chez les Indiens* (Cat.), Ottawa, Musée national de l'homme, 1980, 168 p.

FRENCH CANADIAN ART 1947 – *French Canadian Art 1850-1947* (Cat.), Windsor, Willistead Art Gallery, 1947.

GAGNON 1979-1980 – Gagnon, François-Marc, "The Hidden Image of Early French Canadian Nationalism: a Parable", *Arts Canada*, Nos. 232-233 (December 1979-January 1980), pp. 11-14.

GAGNON 1980 – Gagnon, François-Marc, "Joseph Légaré et les indiens", *The Journal of Canadian Art History*, Vol. V, No. 1 (1980), pp. 39-46.

GAGNON AND LACASSE 1989 – Gagnon, FrançoisMarc and Yves Lacasse, "Antoine Plamondon, *Le dernier des Hurons* (1838)", *The Journal of Canadian Art History*, Vol. XII, No. 1 (1989), pp. 68-79.

GAGNON-PRATTE 1980 – Gagnon-Pratte, France, *L'architecture et la nature à Québec au dix-neuvième siècle: les villas* (Cat.), Quebec City, Musée du Québec, 1980, 334 p.

GALARNEAU 1986 – Galarneau, Claude, "Autrefois, le commerce du livre", *Cap-aux-Diamants*, Vol. 2, No. 1 (Spring 1986), pp. 3-7.

GALARNEAU 1988 – Galarneau, Claude, "Un souffle nouveau dans l'enseignement", *Cap-aux-Diamants*, Vol. 4, No. 1 (Spring 1988), pp. 9-12.

GALERIE 1875 – "Galerie de peinture de l'Université-Laval", *Journal de l'instruction publique*, Vol. XIX, No. 6 (June 1875), p. 91.

*GALERIE NATIONALE 1975 – *Galerie nationale du Canada. Septième revue annuelle 1974-1975*, Ottawa, National Gallery of Canada, 1975.

*GALERIE NATIONALE 1976 – *Galerie nationale du Canada. Huitième revue annuelle 1975-1976*, Ottawa, National Gallery of Canada, 1976.

GALLERY 1902 – *Gallery of Paintings*, [1902], 22 p.

GAUTHIER 1988 – Gauthier, Ninon, "Le marché des encans", *Le Collectionneur*, Vol. VI, No. 22 (Spring 1988), pp. 76-82.

GAY 1976 – Gay, Paul, "Théophile Hamel, peintre national", *Le Droit*, April, 3, 1976, p. 16.

*GIROUX 1972 – Giroux, Sylvia, "Le choléra à Québec: un tableau de Joseph Légaré", *Bulletin de la Galerie nationale du Canada*, No. 20, 1972, pp. 3-12

GODENRATH 1939 – Godenrath, Percy F., *Supplemantary Catalogue and an Abridged Index of the Manoir Richelieu, Murray Bay, P.Q., Historical Collection of Canadiana*, Montreal, Canada Steamship Lines, 1939, 46 p.

GODENRATH 1942 – Godenrath, Percy F., *Le Vieux Québec. Exposition de gravures, aquarelles, peintures, plans et cartes de Québec et de ses environs tirés de la collection William H. Coverdale déposée au Manoir-Richelieu, à la Malbaie; meubles anciens du Canada Français provenant de l'Hôtel-Tadoussac prêtés par les Canada Steamship Lines Limited, de Montreal* (Cat.), Montreal, Canada Steamship Lines, 1942, 36 p.

GODSELL 1976 – Godsell, Patricia, *Enjoying Canadian Painting*, Don Mills, General Publishing, 1976, 275 p.

GREENHILL AND BIRRELL 1979 – Greenhill, Ralph and Andrew Birrell, *Canadian Photography: 1839-1920*, Toronto, The Coach House Press, 1979.

*GREENWOOD AND LAMBERT 1988 – Greenwood, F. Murray and James H. Lambert, "Sewell, Jonathan", *Dictionnaire biographique du Canada*, Quebec City, Les Presses de l'Université Laval, Vol. VII (1988), pp. 847-858.

GROCE AND WALLACE 1957 – Groce, George C. and David H. Wallace, *The New-York Historical Society's Dictionnary of Artist's in America, 1564-1860*, New Haven, Yale University Press, 1957, 759 p.

GUITARD 1983 – Guitard, Michelle, *Histoire sociale des miliciens de la bataille de Châteauguay*, Ottawa, Parks Canada, 1983, 150 p.

*GUITARD 1987 – Guitard, Michelle, "Irumberry de Salaberry, Charles-Michel", *Dictionnaire biographique du Canada*, Quebec City, Les Presses de l'Université Laval, Vol. VI (1987), pp. 375-380.

GUAY 1987 – Guay, Donald, "Le sport des rois", *Cap-aux-Diamants*, Vol. 2, No. 4 (Winter 1987), pp. 23-26.

HAMEL 1971/1 – Hamel, Marcel, "En souvenir de Théophile Hamel", *Québec-Histoire*, Vol. 1, No. 1 (February-March 1971), pp. 47, 48 and 50.

HAMEL 1971/2 – Hamel, Marcel, "Rôle de la Capricieuse dans la peinture de Plamondon", *Québec-Histoire*, Vol. 1, No. 2 (April-May-June 1971), pp. 14-15.

*HARE, LAFRANCE AND RUDDEL 1987 – Hare, John, Marc Lafrance and David-Thiery Ruddel, *Histoire de la ville de Québec 1608-1871*, Montreal, Boréal / Musée canadien des civilisations, 1987, 398 p.

HARPER 1952 – Harper, John Russell, "A Sketch-Book of Cornelius Krieghoff", *Canadian Art*, Vol. IX, No. 4 (Summer 1952), pp. 163-164.

*HARPER 1962/1 – Harper, John Russell, *Une imagerie canadienne. Peintures et dessins du Musée McCord de l'université McGill* (Cat.), Ottawa, Imprimeur de la Reine, 1962, 80 p.

HARPER 1962/2 – Harper, John Russell, "Tour d'horizon de l'Art canadien", *Vie des arts*, No. 26 (Spring 1962), pp. 28-37.

HARPER 1962/3 – Harper, John Russell, "Three Centuries of Canadian Painting", *Canadian Art*, Vol. XIX, No. 6 (November-December 1962), pp. 405-452.

*HARPER 1964 – Harper, John Russell, *Un siècle de peinture: l'époque coloniale de la guerre de Sept Ans à la Confédération* (Cat.), Ottawa, Imprimeur de la Reine, 1964, 70 p.

*HARPER 1966 – Harper, John Russell, *La peinture au Canada des origines à nos jours*, Quebec City, Les Presses de l'Université Laval, 1966, 442 p.

HARPER 1967/1 – Harper, John Russell, "Painting in Canada 1604-1867", *Antiques*, Vol. xcii, No. 1 (July 1967), pp. 66-67.

HARPER 1967/2 – Harper, John Russell, "Three Hundred Years of Canadian Art", *Burlington Magazine*, Vol. CIX (August 1967), pp. 461-465.

HARPER 1970 – Harper, John Russell, *Early Painters and Engravers in Canada*, Toronto, University of Toronto Press, 1970, 376 p.

HARPER 1971 – Harper, John Russell, *Paul Kane's Frontier*, Toronto, The University of Toronto Press, 1971, 350 p.

*HARPER 1973 – Harper, John Russell, *L'art populaire: l'art naïf au Canada* (Cat.), Ottawa, National Gallery of Canada, 1973, 167 p.

HARPER 1974 – Harper, John Russell, *A People's Art. Primitive, Naïve, Provincial and Folk Painting in Canada*, Toronto, University of Toronto Press, 1974, 173 p.

HARPER 1977/1 – Harper, John Russell, *Painting in Canada: a History*, second edition, Toronto, University of Toronto Press, 1977, 463 p.

*HARPER 1977/2 – Harper, John Russell, "Todd, Robert Clow", *Dictionnaire biographique du Canada*, Quebec City, Les Presses de l'université Laval, Vol. IX (1977), p. 874.

HARPER 1979 – Harper, John Russell, *Krieghoff*, Toronto, University of Toronto Press, 1979, 204 p.

*HARPER 1985 – Harper, John Russell, "Somerville, Martin", *Dictionnaire biographique du Canada*, Quebec City, Les Presses de l'université Laval, Vol. VIII (1985), p. 926.

*HARPER AND HUBBARD 1965 – Harper, John Russell and Robert H. Hubbard, *Trésors de Québec* (Cat.), Ottawa and Quebec City, National Gallery of Canada and Musée du Québec, 1965, 62 p.

HARRIS 1898 – Harris, Robert, "Art in Quebec and in the Martitime Provinces", *Canada. An Encyclopaedia of the Country. The Canadian Dominion Considered in its Historic Relations, its Natural Resources, its Material Progress, and its National Development* [J. Castell Hopkins, edit.], Toronto, The Linscott Publishing Company, Vol. IV, 1898, pp. 353-364.

HAWKINS 1834 – Hawkins, Alfred, *Picture of Quebec with Historical Recollections*, Quebec City, Neilson and Cowan, 1834, 477 p.

HIGHLY IMPORTANT 1953 – *Highly Important Printed Books and Manuscripts Autograph Letters and some Drawings and Etchings by Old Masters the Property of the Right Honourable The Earl of Derby, M.C.*, London, Christie's, 1953, 56 p.

*HILL AND LANDRY 1988 – Hill, Charles C. and Pierre B. Landry, *Catalogue du Musée des beaux-arts du Canada, Ottawa. Art canadien*, Vol. I A-F, Ottawa, National Gallery of Canada and National Museums of Canada, 1988, 414 p.

HOUSE PORTRAITS 1981 – "House Portraits at Canadianna Building R.O", *Canadian Collector*, Vol. 16, No. 3 (May-June 1981), p. 54.

HUARD 1986/1 – Huard, Micheline, *Québec, patrimoine mondial... Agenda d'art 1987* [Quebec City, Musée du Québec], La Prairie, Éditions Marcel Broquet, 1986, 136 p.

HUARD 1986/2 – Huard, Micheline, "Le regard des artistes", *Cap-aux-Diamants*, Vol. 2, No. 2 (Summer 1986), pp. 29-33.

*HUBBARD 1945 – Hubbard, Robert H., *Le développement de la peinture au Canada 1665-1945* (Cat.), Toronto, The Art Gallery of Toronto, 1945.

HUBBARD 1957 – Hubbard, Robert H., "Primitives with Character: A Quebec School of the Early Nineteenth Century", *The Art Quaterly*, Vol. XX, No. 1 (Summer 1957), pp. 17-29.

HUBBARD 1959/1 – Hubbard, Robert H., "The Discovery of Early Canadian Painting", *Art in America*, Vol. XLVII, No. 3 (1959), pp. 40-47.

HUBBARD 1959/2 – Hubbard, Robert H., "Four New Books on Canadian Art", *Canadian Art*, Vol. XVI, No. 2 (May 1959), pp. 122-129.

HUBBARD 1960 – Hubbard, Robert H., *An Anthology of Canadian Art*, Toronto, Oxford University Press, 1960, 187 p.

HUBBARD 1963 – Hubbard, Robert H., *L'évolution de l'art au Canada*, Ottawa, Imprimeur de la Reine, 1963, 137 p.

*HUBBARD 1970 – Hubbard, Robert H., *Deux peintres de Québec. Antoine Plamondon (1802-1895), Théophile Hamel (1817-1870)* (Cat.), Ottawa, National Gallery of Canada, 1970, 176 p.

HUBBARD 1972/1 – Hubbard, Robert H., *Thomas Davies in Early Canada*, Ottawa, Oberon Press, 1972, 64 p.

HUBBARD 1972/2 – Hubbard, Robert H., *Thomas Davies, c. 1737-1812* (Cat.), Ottawa, National Gallery of Canada, 1972, 255 p.

*HUBBARD 1973 – Hubbard, Robert H., *Peintres du Québec. Collection Maurice et Andrée Corbeil* (Cat.), Ottawa, National Gallery of Canada, 1973, 212 p.

HUBBARD AND BARBEAU 1946 – Hubbard, Robert H. and Marius Barbeau, *The Arts of French Canada 1613-1870* (Cat.), Detroit, Detroit Institute of Arts, 1946, 52 p.

HUBBARD AND FRYE 1973 – Hubbard, Robert H. and Northrop Frye, *The Artist and the Land. Canadian Landscape painting 1670-1930* (Cat.), Madison, Elvehjem Art Center, University of Wisconsin, 1973, 198 p.

*HUBBARD AND OSTIGUY 1967 – Hubbard, Robert H. and Jean-René Ostiguy, *Trois cents ans d'art canadien* (Cat.), Ottawa, National Gallery of Canada, 1967, 254 p.

INAUGURAL EXHIBITION 1953 – *Inaugural Exhibition* (Cat.), Hamilton, Art Gallery of Hamilton, 1953.

IROQUOIS WARS 1988 – "Iroquois Wars", *The Canadian Encyclopedia*, second edition, Edmonton, Hurtig Publishers, 1988, Vol. 2, p. 1095.

JACQUIN 1987 – Jacquin, Philippe, *La terre des Peaux-Rouges*, [Paris], Gallimard, 1987, 192 p. (Coll. "Découvertes Gallimard", No. 14).

JEAN AND LEBEL 1987 – Jean, Michèle and Alyne Lebel, "Pleins feux sur Saint-Jean-Baptiste", *Cap-aux-Diamants*, Vol. 3, No. 1 (Spring 1987), pp. 23-26.

JEFFERYS 1948 – Jefferys, Charles W., *A Catalogue of the Sigmund Samuel Collection: Canadiana and Americana*, Toronto, The Ryerson Press, 1948.

JUNEAU 1971 – Juneau, André, *Cornelius Krieghoff 1815-1872* (Cat.), Quebec City, Musée du Québec, 1971, 80 p.

JUNEAU AND THIBAULT 1974 – Juneau, André and Claude Thibault, *Les arts du Québec* (Cat.), Quebec City, Ministère des Affaires culturelles, 1974, 31 p.

KAREL 1974 – Karel, David, *Teaching of Drawing at the French Royal Academy of Painting and Sculpture from 1760 to 1793*, Ph.D. thesis, The University of Chicago, 1974.

*KAREL 1985 – Karel, David, "Fassio, Gerome", *Dictionnaire biographique du Canada*, Quebec City, Les Presses de l'Université Laval, Vol. VIII (1985), pp. 320-322.

*KAREL 1988 – Karel, David, "Triaud, Louis-Hubert", *Dictionnaire biographique du Canada*, Quebec City, Les Presses de l'Université Laval, Vol. VII (1988), pp. 941-943.

KAREL 1991 – Karel, David, *La collection Duplessis*, Quebec City, Musée du Québec, 1991, 66 p. (Coll. "Le Musée du Québec en Images", No. 4)

*KAREL, LABELLE AND THIVIERGE 1982 – Karel, David, Marie-Dominic Labelle and Sylvie Thivierge, "Vincent, Zacharie", *Dictionnaire biographique du Canada*, Quebec City, Les Presses de l'Université Laval, Vol. XI (1982), pp. 1002-1003.

*KAREL, NOPPEN AND PARADIS 1987 – Karel, David, Luc Noppen and Magella Paradis, "Baillairgé, François", *Dictionnaire biographique du Canada*, Quebec City, Les Presses de l'Université Laval, Vol. VI (1987), pp. 26-31.

KAREL, NOPPEN AND THIBAULT 1975 – Karel, David, Luc Noppen and Claude Thibault, *François Baillairgé et son œuvre (1759-1830)* (Cat.), Quebec City, Université Laval and Musée du Québec, 1975, 85 p.

KELLY 1972 – Kelly, Greta M., "Une tradition de générosité / Legacies Shaping the Future", *M* (Journal of the Montreal Museum of Fine Arts), March 1972, pp. 14-18.

*KLEMPLAN 1989 – Klemplan, Barbara, "La conservation: un nouveau regard sur l'histoire", *L'Archiviste*, Vol. 16, No. 3 (May-June 1989), pp. 18-19.

KOBAYASKI AND BIRD 1985 – Kobayaski, Terry and Michael Bird, *A Compendium of Canadian Folk Artists*, Erin (Ont.), The Boston Mills Press, 1985, 243 p.

KOLTUN 1980 – Koltun, Lilly, "Treasures of Canada's Photographic Past", *Canadian Collector*, Vol. 15, No. 6 (November-December 1980), pp. 23-28.

KRAMER 1987 – Kramer, Miriam, "What's New in the United Kingdom", *Canadian Collector*, Vol. 22, No. 1 (January 1987), p. 55

LABELLE AND THIVIERGE 1981 – Labelle, Marie-Dominic and Sylvie Thivierge, "Un peintre huron du XIXe siècle: Zacharie Vincent", *Recherches amérindiennes du Québec*, Vol. XI, No. 4 (1981), pp. 325-333.

*LACASSE 1983/1 – Lacasse, Yves, *Antoine Plamondon. Le chemin de croix de l'église Notre-Dame de Montréal* (Cat.), Montreal, Montreal Museum of Fine Arts, 1983, 111 p.

LACASSE 1983/2 – Lacasse, Yves, "La contribution du peintre américain James Bowman (1793-1842) au premier décor intérieur de l'église Notre-Dame de Montréal", *The Journal of Canadian Art History*, Vol. VII, No. 1 (1983), pp. 74-91.

LA CHRONIQUE 1963 – "La chronique des arts", *Supplément à la Gazette des beaux-arts*, No. 1129 (February 1963), p. 65.

LA CHRONIQUE 1967 – "La chronique des arts", *Supplément à la Gazette des beaux-arts*, No. 1176 (February 1967), p. 49.

LA CHRONIQUE 1968 – "La chronique des arts", *Supplément à la Gazette des beaux-arts*, No. 1189 (February 1968), p. 40.

LA CHRONIQUE 1979 – "La chronique des arts. Principales acquisitions des musées en 1978", *Supplément à la Gazette des beaux-arts*, No. 1323 (April 1979), p. 30.

LA CHRONIQUE 1983 – "La chronique des arts. Principales acquisitions des musées en 1982", *Supplément à la Gazette des beaux-arts*, No. 1370 (March 1983), p. 21.

LA CHRONIQUE 1988 – "La chronique des arts. Principales acquisitions des musées en 1987", *Gazette des beaux-arts*, No. 1430 (March 1988), p. 23.

LA CHRONIQUE 1990 – "La chronique des arts. Principales acquisitions des musées en 1989", *Gazette des beaux-arts*, No. 1454 (March 1990), p. 36.

LACROIX 1982 – Lacroix, Laurier, "Joseph Légaré", *Okanada Historische Malerei Kanadas* (Cat.), Berlin, Ausstellungen und Veranstaltungen der Akademie der Künste, 1982, pp. 34-41.

LACROIX 1989/1 – Lacroix, Laurier, "Les tableaux Desjardins: un héritage fructueux", *Cap-aux-Diamants*, Vol. 5, No. 3 (Fall 1989), pp. 43-46.

LACROIX 1989/2 – Lacroix, Laurier, "Le musée d'art de Joliette", *Continuité*, No. 43 (Spring 1989), pp. 16-18.

LACROIX 1989/3 – Lacroix, Laurier, "After the Conquest", *A Colonial Portrait Art in Canada to 1871*, Vancouver Open Learning Agency, 1989.

LACROIX 1989/4 – Lacroix, Laurier, "Italian Art and Artists in Nineteenth-Century Quebec: A Few Preliminary Observations", *Arrangiarsi, The Italian Immigration Experience in Canada*, Montreal and Guernica, Roberto Perin ed., 1989, 252 p.

LACROIX 1990 – Lacroix, Laurier, "La reliure telle que représentée dans la peinture au Québec. 1ère partie. Avant 1850", *Le Journal ARQ* (Association des relieurs du Québec), Spring 1990, pp. 16-22.

LAFORTUNE 1986 – Lafortune, Hélène, *Le notaire et la vie quotidienne des origines à 1870* (Cat.), Montreal, Archives nationales du Québec, 1986, 128 p.

LAHAISE 1980 – Lahaise, Robert, *Les édifices conventuels du Vieux Montreal. Aspects ethno-historiques*, Montreal, HMH Hurtubise, 1980, 604 p. (Coll. "Cahiers du Québec").

LAMBERT 1947 – Lambert, R. S., *The Adventure of Canadian Painting*, Toronto, McClelland and Stewart, 1947, 226 p.

LAMBERT 1986 – Lambert, James, "Daniel Wilkie: un humaniste au service de l'éducation", *Cap-aux-Diamants*, Vol. 2, No. 3 (Fall 1986), pp. 17-22.

LAMONTAGNE 1980 – Lamontagne, Ann, "L'abbé Henri Gilbert, restaurateur de tableaux. Trente ans de miracles!", *Perspectives*, February, 16, 1980, pp. 20-21.

LAMOUREUX 1984 – Lamoureux, Georgette, "Mgr Cyprien Tanguay, éminent généalogiste", *Le Droit*, April, 26, 1984, p. 52.

LANDRY 1987 – Landry, Pierre, "Amherst, Elizabeth Frances (Hale)", *Dictionnaire biographique du Canada*, Quebec City, Les Presses de l'Université Laval, Vol. VI (1987), pp. 9-10.

LAROCHE-JOLY 1990 – Laroche-Joly, Ginette, *L'iconographie jésuite et ses implications cultuelles dans l'art et la religion du Québec (1842-1968)*, Ph.D. thesis, Université Laval, 1990, 546 p., 241 ill.

LAURIN 1973 – Laurin, Clément, *J. J. Girouard et les patriotes de 1837-1838. Notes bio-bibliographiques*, Montreal, Bibliophile du Canadiana, 1973, 120 p.

LAVAL UNIVERSITY 1880 – *Laval University*, [1880], 12 p.

LAVAL UNIVERSITY 1883-1884 – *Laval University*, [1883 ou 1884], 32 p.

LAVAL UNIVERSITY 1887 – *Laval University*, Quebec City, L. Brousseau Printer, [1887], 32 p.

LAVAL UNIVERSITY 1894 – *Laval University*, Quebec City, Léger Brousseau, 1894, 30 p.

LAVAL UNIVERSITY 1901 – *Laval University*, Quebec City, Léger Brousseau, 1901, 31 p.

LAVAL UNIVERSITY 1905 – *Laval University*, Quebec City, La Compagnie de l'Événement, 1905, 47 p.

LAVAL UNIVERSITY 1909 – *Laval University*, Quebec City, Telegraph Printing Co., 1909, 84 p.

LAVAL UNIVERSITY 1923 – *Laval University*, Quebec City, L'Action Sociale Ltd, 1923, 97 p.

LEBLANC 1989 – Leblanc, J.-Normand Pickering, *Le Mémorial Papineau*, Montreal, Éditions du Fleuve, 284 p. (Coll. "Généalogie").

LEFEBVRE 1963 – "De quelques testaments", *Rapport des archives du Québec*, Vol. 41 (1963), pp. 154-174.

LEFEBVRE 1982 – Lefebvre, Jacqueline, *L'abbé Philippe Desjardins, un grand ami du Canada, 1753-1833*, Quebec City, Société Historique de Québec, 1982, 288 p.

LÉGARÉ 1980 – Légaré, Jean-Paul, "Joseph Légaré: père des beaux-arts au Canada", *Le Collectionneur*, Vol. II, No. 8 (1980), pp. 11-14.

LE GRAND HÉRITAGE 1984 – *Le Grand Héritage. L'Église catholique et les arts au Québec* (Cat.), Quebec City, Gouvernement du Québec, 1984, 369 p.

LEHMANN 1979 – Lehman, Henry, "Joseph Légaré", *The Montreal Star*, February, 24, 1979, p. D-4.

LEMIEUX 1948 – Lemieux, Jean-Paul, "Quebec City and the Arts", *Canadian Art*, Vol. V, No. 3 (Winter 1948), pp. 108-111.

LEMOINE 1876 – Lemoine, James MacPherson, *Quebec Past and Present. A History of Quebec 1608-1876*, Quebec City, Augustin Côté & Co, 1876, 466 p.

LE MOINE 1974 – Le Moine, Roger, *Napoléon Bourassa l'homme et l'artiste*, Éditions de l'Université d'Ottawa, 1974, 258 p. (Cahiers du Centre de recherche en civilisation canadienne-française).

LEMOINE 1985 – Lemoine, Réjean, "Grosse-Ile: cimetière des immigrants au XIXe siècle", *Cap-aux-Diamants*, Vol. 1, No. 2 (Summer 1985), pp. 9-12.

LE MUSÉE DU QUÉBEC 1978 – *Le Musée du Québec. Œuvres choisies. Renseignements généraux sur les collections*, Quebec City, Musée du Québec, 1978, 151 p.

LE MUSÉE DU QUÉBEC 1983 – *Le Musée du Québec. 500 œuvres choisies* (Cat.), Quebec City, Musée du Québec, 1983, 378 p.

LE PASSÉ EN PEINTURE 1984 – *Le passé en peinture. Un choix d'œuvres de la Division de l'iconographie des Archives publiques du Canada* (Cat.), Ottawa, National Archives of Canada, 1984, 77 p.

LES ARTS 1958 – *Les arts au Canada*, Ottawa, Ministère de la citoyenneté et de l'immigration, 1958, 120 p. (Cahiers de la citoyenneté canadienne, No. 6).

LESAGE 1946 – Lesage, Jules S., *Mélanges. Notes artistiques et propos littéraires*, Quebec City, 1946, 232 p.

LES CHEMINS DE LA MÉMOIRE 1990 – *Les chemins de la mémoire. Monuments et sites historiques du Québec*, Quebec City, Les Publications du Québec, Vol. 1, 1990, 540 p.

LES PEINTURES DE LÉGARÉ 1926 – "Les peintures de Légaré sur Québec", *Bulletin des recherches historiques*, Vol. XXXII, No. 7 (July 1926), p. 432

LESSARD 1982 – Lessard, Michel, "L'époque des miroirs à mémoire (1840-c.1860)", *Photo-Sélection*, Vol. 2, No. 4 (September-October 1982), pp. 52-54.

LESSARD 1983 – Lessard, Michel, "La patente à Lemire. Des daguerréotypes au marsouin…", *Photo-Sélection*, Vol. III, No. 3 (July 1983), pp. 42-43.

LESSARD 1984 – Lessard, Michel, "Impromptu sur le daguerréotype", *Photo-Sélection*, Vol. IV, No. 2 (May 1984), pp. 36-37.

LESSARD 1987/1 – Lessard, Michel, *La photo s'expose: 150 ans de photographie à Québec* (Cat.), Quebec City, 1987, 135 p.

LESSARD 1987/2 – Lessard, Michel, *Les Livernois photographes*, Quebec City, Musée du Québec and Québec Agenda, 1987, 339 p.

LESSARD 1987/3 – Lessard, Michel, "Une première au Canada. Le portfolio photographique de Samuel McLaughlin", *Cap-aux-Diamants*, Vol. 3, No. 2 (Summer 1987), pp. 9-12.

LESSARD 1989 – Lessard, Rénald, "Les déclarations d'étrangers", *Cap-aux-Diamants*, Vol. 5, No. 3 (Fall 1989), p. 57.

LESSARD AND MARQUIS 1971 – Lessard, Michel and Huguette Marquis, *Encyclopédie des antiquités du Québec. Trois siècles de production artisanale*, Montreal, Les Éditions de l'Homme, 1971, 526 p.

LESSER 1984 – Lesser, Gloria, "Portraits de Joseph Brant par William Berczy", *Annual Bulletin 6*, Ottawa, National Gallery of Canada, 1984, pp. 9-28.

LEVENSON 1983 – Levenson, Rustin Steele, "Materials and Techniques of Painters in Québec City, 1760-1850", *The Journal of Canadian Art History*, Vol. VII, No. 1 (1983), pp. 1-54.

LEYMARIE 1929 – Leymarie, Léo-A., *Exhibition rétrospective des colonies françaises de l'Amérique du Nord* (Cat.), Paris, 1929.

LINDSAY 1900 – Lindsay, Abbé Lionel Saint-Georges, *Notre-Dame de la Jeune Lorette*, Montreal, La Cie de Publication de la Revue Canadienne, 1900, 319 p.

LORD 1965 – Lord, Barry, "The Eighteenth-Century Urban View in Canada", *Canadian Art*, Vol. XXII, No. 97 (May-June 1965), pp. 26-29.

LORD 1974 – Lord, Barry, *The History of Painting in Canada: Toward a People's Art*, Toronto, NC Press, 1974, 253 p.

LUCHAIRE 1971 – Luchaire, André, "Jacques Cartier, un tour d'horizon", *Québec-Histoire*, Vol. 1, No. 1 (February-March 1971), pp. 5-9.

MACDONALD 1892 – MacDonald, A. C. de Léry, *A Record of Canadian Historical Portraits and Antiquities Exhibited by the Numismatic and Antiquarian Society of Montreal 15th September 1892. In Commemoration of the 250th Year of the Foundation of Montreal* (Cat.), Montreal, Numismatic and Antiquarian Society of Montreal, 1892, 56 p.

MCDOUGALL 1988 – McDougall, Anne, "L'aquarelliste écossais George Heriot", *Vie des arts*, Vol. XXXII, No. 130 (March 1988 – Spring), pp. 30-33.

MCINNIS 1950 – McInnis, Graham, *Canadian Art*, Toronto, The MacMillan Company of Canada, 1950, 140 p.

MACKAY 1977 – MacKay, Donald C., "Woolford, John Elliott", *Dictionnaire biographique du Canada*, Quebec City, Les Presses de l'Université Laval, Vol. IX (1977), pp. 936-938.

MCKECHNIE 1978 – McKechnie, Sue, *British Silhouette Artists and their Work 1760-1860*, London, Sotheby Parke Bernet Publications, 1978.

MACLENNAN 1965 – MacLennan, Hugh, "Canada", *American Heritage*, Vol. XVII, No. 1 (December 1965), pp. 6-45.

MAGNAN 1922-1923 – Magnan, Hormisdas, "Peintres et sculpteurs du terroir", *Le Terroir*, Vol. III, No. 8 (December 1922), pp. 342-354; Vol. III, No. 9 (January 1923), pp. 410-422.

MAGNAN 1926 – Magnan, Hormisdas, "Liste des tableaux envoyés de Paris au Canada de 1817 à 1820", *Bulletin des recherches historiques*, Vol. 32, No. 2 (February 1926), pp. 93-103.

MAHEUX 1939 – Maheux, Arthur, "William Von Moll Berczy, colonisateur et peintre", *Le Canada Français*, Vol. XXVI, No. 9 (May 1939), pp. 872-886.

MAJOR-FRÉGEAU 1979 – Major-Frégeau, Madeleine, *La vie et l'œuvre de François-Malépart de Beaucourt (1740-1794)*, Quebec City, Ministère des Affaires culturelles, 1979, 196 p. (Coll. "Civilisation du Québec", No. 24).

MAJOR-FRÉGEAU 1980 – Major-Frégeau, Madeleine, "Malépart de Beaucourt, François", *Dictionnaire biographique du Canada*, Quebec City, Les Presses de l'Université Laval, Vol. IV (1980), pp. 548-550.

MARTIN 1980 – Martin, Paul-Louis, *Histoire de la chasse au Québec*, Montreal, Éditions du Boréal Express, 1980.

MARTIN 1988 – Martin, Denis, *Portraits des héros de la Nouvelle-France. Images d'un culte historique*, Montreal, Hurtubise HMH, 1988, 176 p.

MARTIN 1990 – Martin, Denis, *L'estampe importée en Nouvelle-France*, Ph.D. thesis, Université Laval, 1990, 426 p., 324 ill.

MARTIN AND GRANDBOIS 1991 – Martin, Denis and Michèle Grandbois, *La collection des dessins et estampes: 80 œuvres choisies* (Cat.), Quebec City, Musée du Québec, 1991, 214 p.

MARTIN-MÉRY 1962 – Martin-Méry, Gilberte, *L'art au Canada* (Cat.), Bordeaux, Musée des beaux-arts de Bordeaux and Delmas, 1962, 176 p.

MAURAULT 1949 – Maurault, Olivier, "Le Musée de Notre-Dame de Montréal", *Les Cahiers des Dix*, No. 14 (1949), pp. 149-164.

*MELLEN 1981 – Mellen, Peter, *Les grandes étapes de l'art au Canada de la pré-histoire à l'art moderne*, Laprairie, Éditions Marcel Broquet, 1981, 260 p.

MILLMAN 1943 – Milmann, Thomas L., "The Very Rev. Hohn Bethune, D.D., LL.D. Acting Principal of McGill College, 1835-1846", *The McGill News*, Vol. XXIV, No. 4 (Summer 1943), pp. 16-18 and 57.

*MONTPETIT 1979 – Montpetit, Raymond, "[Review of] John Porter, Nicole Cloutier, Jean Trudel, *Joseph Légaré (1795-1855). L'œuvre*", *Livres et auteurs québécois, 1978. Revue critique de l'année littéraire*, Quebec City, Les Presses de l'Université Laval, 1979, pp. 294-295.

MOOGK 1977 – Moogk, Peter N., *Building a House in New France. An Account of the Perplexities of Client and Craftsmen in Early Canada*, Toronto, McClelland and Stewart, 1977, 144 p.

MORISSET 1934/1 – Morisset, Gérard. "Les débuts de la peinture en Nouvelle-France", *Le Canada*, June, 13, 1934, p. 2.

MORISSET 1934/2 – Morisset, Gérard, "Joseph Légaré copiste", *Le Canada*, August, 14, 1934, p. 2.

MORISSET 1934/3 – Morisset, Gérard, "Joseph Légaré copiste", *Le Canada*, September, 12, 1934, p. 2.

MORISSET 1934/4 – Morisset, Gérard, "Joseph Légaré copiste", *Le Canada*, September, 25, 1934, p. 2.

MORISSET 1934/5 – Morisset, Gérard, "La collection Desjardins et les peintures de l'école canadienne à Saint-Roch de Québec ", *Le Canada français*, Vol. 22, No. 2 (October 1934), pp. 115-126.

MORISSET 1934/6 – Morisset, Gérard, "Le Noël de nos artistes", *Le Terroir*, Vol. 16, Nos. 6-7 (November-December 1934), p. 23.

MORISSET 1935/1 – Morisset, Gérard, "Plamondon à Neuville", *Almanach de l'Action sociale catholique*, Vol. 19 (1935), pp. 18, 31 and 46.

MORISSET 1935/2 – Morisset, Gérard, "Les prouesses picturales de Antoine Plamondon (texte d'une causerie donnée à Thetford Mines)", *L'Événement,* January, 15, 1935, p. 4; January, 16, 1935, p. 4; January, 17, 1935, p. 4.

MORISSET 1935/3 – Morisset, Gérard, "Une autre œuvre retrouvée. À propos d'une peinture du Frère Luc", *L'Événement,* March, 21, 1935, p. 4.

MORISSET 1935/4 – Morisset, Gérard, "Portraits de mortes en Nouvelle-France", *Le Canada*, March, 22, 1935 p. 2; March, 25, 1935, p. 2.

MORISSET 1935/5 – Morisset, Gérard, "Les peintures de Plamondon à l'Hôtel-Dieu de Québec", *Le Canada*, May, 28, 1935, p. 2.

MORISSET 1935/6 – Morisset, Gérard, "Un brelan de portraits au Séminaire des Trois-Rivières", *Le Droit*, July, 3, 1935, p. 6.

MORISSET 1935/7 – Morisset, Gérard, "Le peintre américain Thielcke au Bas-Canada", *Le Canada*, July, 10, 1935, p. 2.

MORISSET 1935/8 – Morisset, Gérard, "Un beau portrait: Louis Dulongpré, par Wilhelm von Moll Berczy", *La Renaissance*, July, 27, 1935, p. 5.

MORISSET 1935/9 – Morisset, Gérard, "Le portrait canadien il y a un siècle", *Le Droit*, July, 29, 1935, p. 2; August, 3, 1935, p. 9.

MORISSET 1935/10 – Morisset, Gérard, "Deux chefs-d'œuvre de Plamondon", *La Renaissance*, Vol. 1, No. 10 (August, 24, 1935), p. 5; Vol. 1, No. 11 (August, 31, 1935), p. 5.

MORISSET 1936/1 – Morisset, Gérard, "La chasse aux tourtes", *Almanach de l'Action sociale catholique*, Vol. 20 (1936), pp. 46-48.

MORISSET 1936/2 – Morisset, Gérard, "La collection Desjardins au Musée de l'Université Laval", *Le Canada français*, Vol. 23, No. 5 (January 1936), pp. 446-456; Vol. 24, No. 2 (October 1936), pp. 107-108.

MORISSET 1936/3 – Morisset, Gérard, "L'exposition Théophile Hamel", *Le Soleil*, March, 28, 1936, p. 9.

MORISSET 1936-1937 – Morisset, Gérard, *Peintres et tableaux*, Quebec City, Les éditions du Chevalet, 1936-1937, 2 Vols. (Les arts au Canada français).

MORISSET 1941/1 – Morisset, Gérard, *Coup d'œil sur les arts en Nouvelle-France. Ouvrage orné de 32 gravures*, Quebec City, 1941, 170 p.

MORISSET 1941/2 – Morisset, Gérard, "En marge d'un salon. Marguerite Scott, peintre animalier", *L'Événement*, March, 18, 1941, p. 5.

MORISSET 1941/3 – Morisset, Gérard, "Montreal et ses artisans", *L'Enseignement primaire*, 3rd series, Vol. 1, No. 10 (June 1941), pp. 891-900.

MORISSET 1944 – Morisset, Gérard, *La vie et l'œuvre du Frère Luc*, Quebec City, Médium, 1944, 142 p.

MORISSET 1945 – Morisset, Gérard, "À propos d'une illusion de perspective", *L'Action catholique*, April, 28, 1945, p. 4.

MORISSET 1950/1 – Morisset, Gérard, "Le peintre François Beaucourt", *La Patrie. Journal du Dimanche*, March, 19, 1950, pp. 26 and 50.

MORISSET 1950/2 – Morisset, Gérard, "Giuseppe Fascio, le miniaturiste", *La Patrie. Journal du Dimanche*, April, 9, 1950, pp. 26 and 38.

MORISSET 1950/3 – Morisset, Gérard, "Notre art religieux", *La Patrie. Journal du Dimanche*, August, 27, 1950, pp. 26-27 and 50.

MORISSET 1950/4 – Morisset, Gérard, " Un maître-maçon d'autrefois", *La Patrie. Journal du Dimanche*, September, 24, 1950, pp. 26-27 and 51.

MORISSET 1951/1 – Morisset, Gérard, "L'église de Deschambault", *La Patrie. Journal du Dimanche*, February, 4, 1951, pp. 18-19.

MORISSET 1951/2 – Morisset, Gérard, "Old Churches of Quebec", *Canadian Geographical Journal*, Vol. 43, No. 43 (September 1951), pp. 100-115.

MORISSET 1952 – Morisset, Gérard, *Exposition rétrospective de l'art au Canada français* (Cat.), Quebec City, Musée de la Province de Québec, 1952, 118 p.

MORISSET 1953/1 – Morisset, Gérard, "Trésors d'art de la province", *La Revue française de l'élite européenne*, No. 43 (February 1953), pp. 132-136.

MORISSET 1953/2 – Morisset, Gérard, "Un primitif: Jean-Baptiste Roy-Audy – Son existence", *Technique*, Vol. 28, No. 7 (September 1953), pp. 443-450.

MORISSET 1953/3 – Morisset, Gérard, "Un primitif: Jean-Baptiste Roy-Audy – Son œuvre", *Technique*, Vol. 28, No. 8 (October 1953), pp. 539-546.

MORISSET 1953/4 – Morisset, Gérard, "À bâtons rompus", *Technique*, Vol. 28, No. 10 (December 1953), pp. 657-661.

MORISSET 1956/1 – Morisset, Gérard, "Portraits de cadavres", *Vie des arts*, No. 1 (January-February 1956), pp. 20-23.

MORISSET 1956/2 – Morisset, Gérard, "Antoine Plamondon (1804-1895)", *Vie des arts*, No. 3 (May-June 1956), pp. 7-13.

*MORISSET 1959/1 – Morisset, Gérard, *Les arts au Canada français* (Cat.), Vancouver, Vancouver Art Gallery (printed by Charrier & Dugal Inc., Quebec City), 1959, 96 p.

*MORISSET 1959/2 – Morisset, Gérard, *Portraits canadiens du 18ᵉ et 19ᵉ siècles* (Cat.), Ottawa and Quebec City, National Gallery of Canada and Musée de la Province de Québec, 1959.

MORISSET 1960/1 – Morisset, Gérard, *La peinture traditionnelle au Canada français*, [Ottawa], Le Cercle du Livre de France, 1960, 216 p. (L'Encyclopédie du Canada Français, 2).

MORISSET 1960/2 – Morisset, Gérard, "Un grand portraitiste, Antoine Plamondon", *Coneorde*, Vol. 11, No. 5-6 (May-June 1960), pp. 14-15.

MORISSET 1961 – Morisset, Gérard, "Les archives paroissiales: sources principales de l'histoire de nos arts plastiques", *L'administration paroissiale*, Vol. 1, No. 4 (March-April 1961), p. 6.

MORISSET 1962 – Morisset, Gérard, "L'influence française sur l'art au Canada", *La Revue française de l'élite européenne*, No. 140 (May 1962), pp. 29-37.

MORISSET 1965 – Morisset, Gérard, "Généalogie et petite histoire. Le peintre François Beaucourt", *Mémoires de la Société généalogique canadienne-française*, Vol. 16, No. 4 (October, November, December 1965), pp. 195-199.

MORISSET 1980 – Morisset, Gérard, *Le Cap-Santé, ses églises et son trésor* (reedtion for an exhibition hold at the Montreal Museum of Fine Arts), Montreal, Montreal Museum of Fine Arts, 1980, 401 p.

MORRIS 1980 – Morris, Jerrold, *100 ans de dessins canadiens*, Montreal, Éditions France-Amérique, 1980.

MURRAY 1970 – Murray, Joan, "Victorian Canada – Part two", *Canadian Antiques Collector*, Vol. 5, No. 3 (March 1970), pp. 16-19.

MURRAY 1979 – Murray, Joan, "Joseph Légaré: Rebel Painter with a dash of Edgar Allan Poe", *Arts News*, Vol. 78, No. 2 (February 1979), pp. 92-94

MUSÉE 1990 – Art Gallery of Ontario. Œuvres choisies, Toronto, Art Gallery of Ontario, 1990, 456 p.

MUSÉE HISTORIQUE 1934 – Musée Historique de l'Hôtel-Dieu. Peintures, Quebec City, 1964.

MUSÉE NOTRE-DAME 1938 – Musée Notre-Dame. Catalogue illustré. Souvenirs historiques, tableaux anciens et modernes, ornements et vases sacrés, objets d'art, livres anciens, vieille argenterie, collections diverses, Montreal, 1938, 16 p.

MUSÉE NOTRE-DAME 1950 – Musée Notre-Dame. Catalogue illustré..., 8th édition, Montreal, 1950.

NADEAU 1988 – Nadeau, Michel, Visages d'enfants. Agenda d'art 1989, Quebec City, Musée du Québec and Québec Agenda, 1988, 117 p.

NADEAU 1991 – Nadeau, Michel, Chefs-d'œuvre de la collection, Quebec City, Musée du Québec, 1991, 87 p. (Coll. "Le Musée du Québec en Images" No. 2).

NAUBERT RISER 1989 – Naubert-Riser, Constance, "Vie culturelle. Les arts plastiques et l'architecture. L'art du XVIIe au XIXe siècle", Encyclopædia Universalis, 1989, pp. 866-869.

NELSON 1975 – Nelson, James, "National Gallery gets Rare Quebec Portrait", The Gazette, December, 30, 1975, p. 22 (reprinted in The Vancouver Sun, December, 30, 1975, p. 21).

NICOLAÏ 1990 – Nicolaï, Éric, Portraits of Children in Québec Art, 1800-1860, Master's thesis, Université Laval, 1990, 177 p.

NICOLSON 1979 – Nicolson, Benedict, The International Caravagesque Movement, Oxford, Phaidon, 1979, 264 p.

NIXON 1979 – Nixon, Virginia, "Légaré View of Quebec Life comes across on Painting", The Gazette, February, 23, 1979, p. 16.

NIXON 1988 – Nixon, Virginia, Antoine-Sébastien Falardeau (1822-1889) and the Old Master Copy in the Nineteenth Century, Master's thesis, Concordia University (Montreal), 1988, 304 p.

NOPPEN 1977 – Noppen, Luc, Les églises du Québec (1600-1850), Quebec City, Éditeur officiel du Québec and Fides, 1977, 298 p. (Coll. "Loisirs et culture").

NOPPEN 1984 – Noppen, Luc, Le portrait de Jacques Cartier ou la découverte des découvreurs au XIXᵉ siècle (Cat.), Quebec City, Musée du Québec, 1984, 32 p.

NOPPEN AND DESCHÊNES 1986 – Noppen, Luc and Gaston Deschênes, L'Hôtel du Parlement, témoin de notre histoire, Quebec City, Les Publications du Québec, 1986, 204 p.

NOPPEN AND GRIGNON 1983 – Noppen, Luc and Marc Grignon, L'art de l'architecte. Trois siècles de dessin d'architecture à Québec (Cat.), Quebec City, Musée du Québec and Université Laval, 1983, 293 p.

NOPPEN, PAULETTE AND TREMBLAY 1979 – Noppen, Luc, Claude Paulette and Michel Tremblay, Québec, trois siècles d'architecture, Montreal, Libre Expression, 1979, 440 p.

NYGREN 1986 – Nygren, Edward J., Views and Visions. American Landscapes before 1830, Washington D.C., The Corcoran Gallery of Art, 1986, 311 p.

ŒUVRE MAGISTRALE 1980 – "Œuvre magistrale de Légaré acquise par le musée", Collage, Vol. 5, No. 9 (October 1980), p. 1.

O'GALLAGHER 1979 – O'Gallagher, Marianna, Saint-Patrice de Québec, Quebec City, La Société Historique de Québec, 1979 (Cahiers d'histoire No. 32).

O'GALLAGHER 1981 – O'Gallagher, Marianna, Saint Patrick's Quebec. The Building of a Church and of a Parish 1827 to 1833, Quebec City, Carraig Books, 1981, 124 p.

OKO 1984 – Oko, Andrew J., Le Canada au dix-neuvième siècle: Collection de la famille Bert et Barbara Stitt (Cat.), Hamilton, Art Gallery of Hamilton, 1984, 100 p.

O'LEARY 1901 – O'Leary, Thomas, Catalogue of the Chateau Ramezay. Museum and Portrait Gallery, [Montréal], [1901].

O'LEARY 1903 – O'Leary, Thomas, Catalogue of the Chateau Ramezay. Museum and Portrait Gallery, 2nd edition, Montreal, C. A. Marchand, 1903.

O'LEARY 1907 – O'Leary, Thomas, Catalogue of the Chateau Ramezay. Museum and Portrait Gallery, 5th edition, Montreal,, 1907.

O'LEARY 1917 – O'Leary, Thomas, Catalogue of the Chateau Ramezay. Museum and Portrait Gallery, 10th edition, Montreal, 1917.

O'LEARY 1920 – O'Leary, Thomas, Catalogue of the Chateau Ramezay. Museum and Portrait Gallery, 11th edition, Montreal, 1920.

O'LEARY 1922 – O'Leary, Thomas, Catalogue du Château de Ramezay. Musée et galerie de portraits, 12th edition, Montreal, 1922.

O'LEARY 1923 – O'Leary, Thomas, Catalogue of the Chateau Ramezay. Museum and Portrait Gallery, 13th edition, Montreal, 1923.

O'LEARY 1926 – O'Leary, Thomas, Catalogue of the Chateau Ramezay. Museum and Portrait Gallery, Montreal, 1926.

ONZE ARTISTES 1960 – Onze artistes à Montréal (Cat.), Montreal, Montreal Museum of Fine Arts, 1960.

OSTIGUY 1970 – Ostiguy, Jean-René, "Les arts plastiques", Visages de la civilisation au Canada français (Léopold Lamontagne, edit.), Société royale du Canada, University of Toronto Press and les Presses de l'Université Laval, 1970, p. 100-118.

PAINTERS OF CANADA 1949 – Painters of Canada: Exhibition of Canadian Painting 1668-1948 (Cat.), Richmond, Virginia Museum of Fine Arts, 1949, 14 p.

PAINTING AND SCULPTURE 1959 – Painting and Sculpture. Illustrations of Selected Paintings and Sculpture from the Collection, Toronto, Art Gallery of Toronto, 1959, 95 p.

PAINTING IN CANADA 1946 – Painting in Canada. A Selective Historical Survey (Cat.), Albany, Albany Institute of History and Art, 1946, 46 p.

PALL MALL 1967 – Pall Mall Encyclopaedia of Art, Vol. 1, London, Pall Mall Press, 1967.

PAQUET AND WALLOT 1983 – Paquet, Gilles and Jean-Pierre Wallot, "Structures sociales et niveaux de richesse dans les campagnes du Québec: 1792-1812", Bulletin d'histoire de la culture matérielle, 1983, pp. 25-44.

PARADIS 1979 – Paradis, Magella, Étude stylistique de l'œuvre sculpté de François Baillairgé, Ph.D. thesis, Université de Toulouse–Le-Mirail, 1979, 537 p.

PARIZEAU 1975 – Parizeau, Gérard, La Société canadienne-française au XIXᵉ siècle. Essais sur le milieu, Montreal, Fides, 1975, 551 p.

PARIZEAU 1976 – Parizeau, Gérard, Les Dessaules, seigneurs de Saint-Hyacinthe. Chronique maskoutaine du XIXᵉ siècle, Montreal, Fides, 1976. 159 p.

PARIZEAU 1980 – Parizeau, Gérard, La vie studieuse et obstinée de Denis-Benjamin Viger (1774-1861), Montreal, Fides, 1980, 330 p.

PEINTURES DU SÉMINAIRE 1874-1875 – Peintures du Séminaire de Québec, s.é., [1874 or 1875], 4 p.

PICKERING LEBLANC 1989 – Pickering Leblanc, J.-Normand, Le Mémorial Papineau, Montreal, Éditions du Fleuve, 1989, 284 p.

PICTURES 1969 – Pictures, Drawings, Watercolours & Prints by Canadian Artists French & English Books & Sets in Fine Bindings Rare Canadian, Americana, Books, Manuscripts, Maps & Prints (Cat.), Montreal, Christies, Manson & Woods (Canada) Ltd., 1969.

POMERLEAU 1990 – Pomerleau, Jeanne, Métiers ambulants d'autrefois, Montreal, Guérin Littérature, 1990.

PORTER 1975 – Porter, John R., Antoine Plamondon. Sœur Saint-Alphonse, Ottawa, National Gallery of Canada, 1975, 32 p. (Coll. "Masterpieces in the National Gallery of Canada", No. 4).

PORTER 1977/1 – Porter, John R., "La société québécoise et l'encouragement aux artistes de 1825 à 1850", The Journal of Canadian Art History, Vol. VI, No. 1 (Spring 1977), pp. 13-24.

PORTER 1977/2 – Porter, John R., "Un projet de musée national à Québec à l'époque du peintre Joseph Légaré (1833-1853)", Revue d'histoire de l'Amérique française, Vol. 31, No. 1 (June 1977), pp. 75-82.

PORTER 1978/1 – Porter, John R. (with the collaboration of Nicole Cloutier and Jean Trudel), Joseph Légaré 1795-1855. L'œuvre (Cat.), Ottawa, National Gallery of Canada, 1978, 157 p.

PORTER 1978/2 – Porter, John R., "Joseph Légaré, peintre engagé / Painter and Citizen", Journal of the National Gallery of Canada, No. 29 (September, 21, 1978), 8 p.

PORTER 1978/3 – Porter, John R., "L'apport de Joseph Légaré (1795-1855) dans le renouveau de la peinture québécoise", Vie des Arts, Vol. VIII, No. 92 (Fall 1978), pp. 63-66.

PORTER 1978/4 – Porter, John R., "L'architecture québécoise dans l'œuvre de Joseph Légaré", Bulletin du Conseil des monuments et sites du Québec, No. 6 (May 1978), pp. 19-21.

PORTER 1981 – Porter, John R., Un peintre collectionneur québécois engagé dans son milieu: Joseph Légaré (1795-1855), Ph.D. thesis, Université de Montréal, 1981, 531 p.

PORTER 1984 – Porter, John R., "Antoine Plamondon (1804-1895) et la tableau religieux: perception et valorisation de la copie et de la composition", The Journal of Canadian Art History, Vol. VIII, No. 1 (1984), pp. 1-25.

PORTER 1985 – Porter, John R., "Légaré, Joseph", Dictionnaire biographique du Canada, Quebec City, Les Presses de l'Université Laval, Vol. VIII (1985), pp. 547-552.

PORTER 1986 – Porter, John R., "L'histoire de l'art québécois et la défense des valeurs collectives", *Étude de la construction de la mémoire collective des Québécois au XXᵉ siècle: approches multidisciplinaires* (under the dir. of Jacques Mathieu), Quebec City, Cahiers du CELAT, No. 5 (November 1986), pp. 31-42.

PORTER 1987/1 – Porter, John R., "Le rôle des gens d'Église dans l'évolution de l'art au Québec (XVIIᵉ-XXᵉ siècles)", *Annales de Bretagne et des Pays de l'ouest*, Vol. 95, 4 (1987), pp. 529-539. (Symposium "Clercs et changement matériel travail et cadre de vie (XVᵉ-XXᵉ siècles") held at the Centre d'Histoire Religieuse, Université de Rennes 2, June, 11-12, 1987).

* *PORTER 1987/2* – Porter, John R., "Légaré, Joseph", *L'Encyclopédie du Canada*, Vol. 2, Montreal, Stanké, 1987, pp. 1088.

* *PORTER 1987/3* – Porter, John R., "Plamondon, Antoine", *L'Encyclopédie du Canada*, Vol. 3, Montreal, Stanké, 1987, p. 1511.

* *PORTER 1990/1* – Porter, John R., "Plamondon, Antoine", *Dictionnaire biographique du Canada*, Quebec City, Les Presses de l'Université Laval, Vol. XII (1990), pp. 921-930.

PORTER 1990/2 – Porter, John R., "[Review of] Allodi, Mary and Rosemarie L. Tovell, *An Engraver's Pilgrimage. James Smillie in Quebec 1821-1830...*", *Revue d'histoire de l'Amérique française*, Vol. 43, No. 3 (Winter 1990), pp. 403-405.

PORTER AND BÉLISLE 1986 – Porter, John R. and Jean Bélisle, *La sculpture ancienne au Québec. Trois siècles d'art religieux et profane*, Montreal, Éditions de l'Homme, 1986, 512 p.

PORTRAITS ANCIENS 1975 – *Portraits anciens du Québec* (Cat.), Sherbrooke, Université de Sherbrooke, 1975.

PORTRAITS MIRROR OF MAN 1956 – *Portraits Mirror of Man* (Cat.), Winnipeg, The Winnipeg Art Gallery, 1956.

PRINGLE 1985 – Pringle, Allan, "Robert S. Duncanson in Montreal, 1863-1865", *The American Art Journal*, Vol. XVII, No. 4 (Fall 1985), pp. 28-50.

* *PRIOUL 1988* – Prioul, Didier, "Cockburn, James Pattison", *Dictionnaire biographique du Canada*, Quebec City, Les Presses de l'Université Laval, Vol. VII (1988), pp. 209-212.

QUÉBEC EN PEINTURE 1986 – *Québec en peinture* (Cat.), Quebec City, Bibliothèque Gabrielle-Roy, 1986.

* *RAPPORT ANNUEL 1966-1967* – *Rapport annuel. La Galerie nationale du Canada, 1966/67*, Ottawa, National Gallery of Canada, 1967.

* *READY 1969* – Ready, Wayne J., *Portraits anciens du Canada*, Ottawa, National Gallery of Canada, 1969.

RECENT ACQUISITIONS 1956 – "Recent Acquisitions by Canadian Museums and Art Galleries", *Canadian Art*, Vol. XIII, No. 3 (Spring 1956), pp. 295-296.

RECENT ACQUISITIONS 1957 – "Recent Acquisitions by Canadian Museums and Art Galleries", *Canadian Art*, Vol. XIV, No. 2 (Winter 1957), pp. 51-62.

REID 1973 – Reid, Dennis, *A Concise History of Canadian Painting*, Toronto, Oxford University Press, 1973, 319 p.

* *REID 1979* – Reid, Dennis, *Notre patrie le Canada. Mémoires sur les aspirations nationales des principaux paysagistes de Montréal et de Toronto, 1860-1890*, Ottawa, National Gallery of Canada, 1979, 453 p.

REID 1988/1 – Reid, Dennis, *Collector's Canada. Selection from a Toronto private collection* (Cat.), Toronto, Art Gallery of Ontario, 1988, 83 p.

REID 1988/2 – Reid, Dennis, "Le Canada du collectionneur. Œuvres d'une collection privée d'art canadien", *Muséo Clips*, No. 9 (Fall 1988), pp. 10-15.

* *REID 1990* – Reid, Dennis, "Fraser, John Arthur", *Dictionnaire biographique du Canada*, Quebec City, Les Presses de l'Université Laval, Vol. XII (1990), pp. 921-930.

RICHARDSON AND AL. 1984 – Richardson, A. J. H. and al., *Quebec City: Architects, Artisans and Builders*, Ottawa, National Museum of Man, Parks Canada, 1984, 589 p.

ROBERT 1978 – Robert, Guy, *La peinture au Québec depuis ses origines*, Sainte-Adèle, Iconia, 1978, 221 p.

ROBSON 1932 – Robson, Albert H., *Canadian Landscape Painters*, Toronto, The Ryerson Press, 1932, 227 p.

ROSENBERG 1971 – Rosenberg, Pierre, "Six tableaux de Plamondon d'après Stella, Cigoli, Mignard et Jouvenet", *M* (journal of the Montreal Museum of Fine Arts), Vol. 2, No. 4 (1971), pp. 10-13.

ROSENFELD 1981 – Rosenfeld, Roslyn, *Miniatures and Silhouettes in Montreal 1760-1860*, Master's thesis, Concordia University (Montreal), 1981.

ROULEAU-ROSS 1983 – Rouleau-Ross, Lucille, *Les versions connues du portrait de Monseigneur Joseph-Octave Plessis (1763-1825) et la conjecture des attributions picturales au début du XIXᵉ siècle*, Master's thesis, Concordia University (Montreal), 1983, 236 p.

ROY 1895 – Roy, Pierre-Georges, "Le portrait de Salaberry", *Bulletin des recherches historiques*, Vol. 1, No. 12 (December 1895), p. 191.

ROY 1933 – Roy, Pierre-Georges, *Les juges de la Province de Québec*, Quebec City, Imprimeur du roi, 1933, 588 p.

ROYAL ONTARIO MUSEUM 1988 – *Royal Ontario Museum. Thirthy-Eight Annual Report July 1987 – June 1988*, Toronto, Royal Ontario Museum, 1988.

* *RUDDEL 1987* – Ruddel, David-Thiery, *Québec City, 1765-1832. The Evolution of a Colonial Town*, Hull, Canadian Museum of Civilization, 1987, 291 p. (Coll. "Mercury Series – History Division Papers", No. 41).

RUDDEL 1990 – Ruddel, David-Thierry, "Consumer Trends, Clothing Textiles and Equipment in the Montreal Area, 1792-1835", *Bulletin d'histoire de la culture matérielle*, No. 32 (Fall 1990), pp. 45-64.

RUMILLY 1977 – Rumilly, Robert, *Papineau et son temps*, Montreal, Fides, 1977.

* *RYDER 1985* – Ryder, Dorothy E., "Hawkins, Alfred", *Dictionnaire biographique du Canada*, Quebec City, Les Presses de l'Université Laval, Vol. VIII (1985), pp. 427-428.

SAMUEL 1980 – Samuel, P. and al., *Treasures of Canada*, Toronto, Samuel-Stevens, 1980.

* *SCHOENHERR 1984* – Schoenherr, Douglas E., "Art et histoire: *Le Passé en peinture*", *L'Archiviste*, Vol. 11, No. 4 (July-August 1984), pp. 16-18.

SEARS 1978 – Sears, Stephen W., "The Lion's-Eye View", *American Heritage*, Vol. 29, No. 4 (1978), pp. 98-107.

SELECTED CATALOGUE 1985 – *Selected Catalogue of Works in the Permanent Collection of the Chateau de Ramezay, Montreal* (under the dir. of Sandra Paikowski), Montreal, Concordia University, 1985, 144 p.

SENIOR 1985 – Senior, Elinor Kyte, *Redcoats and Patriotes. The Rebellions in Lower Canada, 1837-38*, Ottawa, Canadian War Museum, 1985.

SHADBOLT 1966 – Shadbold, Doris, *Images for a Canadian Heritage* (Cat.), Vancouver, The Vancouver Art Gallery, 1966.

SIMARD 1952 – Simard, Marc, *Papineau et les Patriotes de 1837*, Ottawa, La Société Canadienne du Livre Limitée, 1952.

SIMARD 1979 – Simard, Sylvain, "[Review of] John Porter, *Joseph Légaré 1795-1855. L'œuvre*", *Revue d'histoire de l'Amérique française*, Vol. 33, No. 2 (September 1979), pp. 273-276.

SIMARD 1989 – Simard, Jean, *Les arts sacrés au Québec*, Ottawa, Éditions de Mortagne, 1989, 319 p.

SMITH 1973 – Smith, Frances K., *Early Canadian Painting. The English Colonial Period and the Early Years of Confederation* (Cat.), Kingston, The Agnes Etherington Art Centre, 1973, 12 p.

SOUCY 1969 – Soucy, Jean, "L'art traditionnel au Musée du Québec", *Canadian Antiques Collector*, November 1969, pp. 39-41.

SOUCY AND THIBAULT 1974 – Soucy, Jean and Claude Thibault, "Quelques musées canadiens et leurs trésors", *Canadian Antiques Collector*, Vol. 9, No. 3 (May-June 1974), pp. 98-105.

SPENDLOVE 1958 – Spendlove, F. St. George, *The Face of Early Canada: Pictures of Canada Wich Have Helpen to Make History*, Toronto, The Ryerson Press, 1958, 162 p.

SPENDLOVE 1967 – Spendlove, F. St. George, "The Wonderful Watercolours of James P. Cockburn", *Canadian Antiques Collector*, Vol. 2, No. 2 (February 1967), pp. 6-10.

STACEY 1983 – Stacey, Robert, *The Hand Holding the Brush. Self Portraits by Canadian Artists* (Cat.), London (Ont.), London Regional Art Gallery, 1983, 130 p.

* *STAGGS 1983* – Staggs, Ronald J., "Berczy, William", *Dictionnaire biographique du Canada*, Quebec City, Les Presses de l'Université Laval, Vol. V (1983), pp. 77-80.

STOCK 1983 – Stock, Beate, "William Berczy in Italy and Switzerland, 1780-1787", *RACAR*, Vol. X/2 (1983), pp. 123-137.

* *STOLOW 1972* – Stolow, Nathan, édit., *Progrès en conservation et en restauration* (Cat.), Ottawa, National Gallery of Canada, 1972.

* *STRONG 1967* – Strong, Roy, *Pages d'histoire du Canada* (Cat.), Ottawa, National Gallery of Canada, 1967, 315 p.

* *TARDIF-CÔTÉ 1985* – Tardif-Côté, Diane, "Portraits des Patriotes de 1837-1838 par Jean-Joseph Girouard (1795-1855)", *L'Archiviste*, Vol. 12, No. 1 (January-February 1985), pp. 11-13.

TÉMOIGNAGES 1987 – Témoignages. 125 ans d'histoire et d'acquisitions (Cat.), Montreal, Société d'Archéologie et de Numismatique de Montréal, 1987.

*TESSIER 1972 – Tessier, Yves, "Bouchette, Robert-Shore-Milnes", *Dictionnaire biographique du Canada*, Quebec City, Les Presses de l'Université Laval, Vol. X (1972), pp. 82-83.

TÉTU 1896 – Têtu, Mgr Henri, *Histoire du palais épiscopal de Québec*, Quebec City, Pruneau & Kirouac, 1896, 304 p.

TÉTU 1898/1 – Têtu, Mgr Henri, *Histoire des familles Têtu*, Quebec City, 1898.

TÉTU 1898/2 – Têtu, Mgr Henri, *Notice biographique. L'abbé David-Henri Têtu, curé de Saint-Roch-des-Aulnaies*, Quebec City, Dussault & Proulx, Imprimeurs, 1898, 94 p.

TÉTU DE LABSADE 1990 – Têtu de Labsade, Françoise, *Le Québec, un pays, une culture*, Quebec City, Les Éditions du Boréal, 1990.

THE LEGACY 1978 – "The Legacy of Légaré", *Weekend Magazine*, September, 23, 1978, pp. 11-13.

THIBAULT 1973/1 – Thibault, Claude, *Trésors des communautés religieuses de la ville de Québec* (Cat.), Quebec City, Ministère des Affaires culturelles, 1973, 200 p.

THIBAULT 1973/2 – Thibault, Claude, "Semaine de l'art québécois. Les trésors des communautés religieuses au Musée du Québec", *Au Fil des Événements*, Vol. 8, No. 22 (March, 1, 1973), p. 8.

THIBAULT 1974 – Thibault, Claude, *Le diocèse de Québec 1674-1974* (Cat.), Quebec City, Ministère des Affaires culturelles, 1974, 59 p.

*THIBAULT 1978 – Thibault, Claude, *L'art du paysage au Québec (1800-1940)* (Cat.), Quebec City, Musée du Québec, 1978, 145 p.

THIBAULT 1981 – Thibault, Claude, "La place de l'art religieux au Musée du Québec", *Musées*, Vol. 4, No. 3 (September 1981), pp. 21-23.

THIBAULT, GALARNEAU AND NOPPEN 1977 – Thibault, Claude, Claude Galarneau and Luc Noppen, *L'art du Québec au lendemain de la Conquête (1760-1790)* (Cat.), Quebec City, Ministère des Affaires culturelles, 1977, 141 p.

*THOMAS 1979 – Thomas, Ann, *Le réel et l'imaginaire: Peinture et photographie canadiennes, 1860-1900* (Cat.), Montreal, McCord Museum, 1979, 116 p.

TODD 1978 – Todd, Patricia-Ann, *James D. Duncan (1806-1881). Catalogue of Works and Introduction to his Art*, Master's thesis, Concordia University (Montreal), 1978, 218 p.

*TODD 1982 – Todd, Patricia-Ann, "Duncan, James D.", *Dictionnaire biographique du Canada*, Quebec City, Les Presses de l'Université Laval, Vol. XI (1982), pp. 313-314.

TOPOGRAPHICAL PAINTINGS 1975 – Topographical Paintings, Drawings, Watercolours and Prints, London, Sotheby's Belgravia, 1975.

TOPOGRAPHICAL PAINTINGS 1976 – Topographical Paintings, Watercolours, Drawings, Prints and Bronzes, London, Sotheby's Belgravia, 1976.

TOPOGRAPHICAL PAINTINGS 1981 – Topographical Paintings, Watercolours, Drawings and Prints, London, Sotheby Parke Bennet & Co., 1981.

TOPOGRAPHICAL PAINTINGS 1986 – Topographical Paintings, Watercolours and Drawings, London, Sotheby's, 1986.

TOPOGRAPHICAL PAINTINGS 1987 – Topographical Paintings, Watercolours and Drawings, London, Sotheby's, 1987.

TORONTO 1964 – Toronto and Early Canada. A Catalogue of the Toronto and Early Canada Picture Collection in the Toronto Public Library. (Landmarks of Canada, Volume 3), Toronto, The Baxter Publishing Company and The Toronto Public Library, 1964, 63 p.

TOUPIN 1977 – Toupin, Gilles, "Québec en 1830", *La Presse*, May, 21, 1977, p. D-19.

TOUPIN 1978 – Toupin, Gilles, "Pour saluer Joseph Légaré et Suzor-Côté", *La Presse*, December, 9, 1978, p. D-1.

TOUPIN 1979 – Toupin, Gilles, "Joseph Légaré ou la fabrication d'un héros", *La Presse*, February, 17, 1979, p. E-19.

TREMBLAY 1972 – Tremblay, Claire, *L'œuvre profane de Joseph Légaré*, Master's thesis, Université de Montréal, 1972, 275 p.

TREMBLAY 1987 – Tremblay, Marie-France, *Portraits d'artistes. Agenda d'art 1988*, Quebec City, Québec Agenda, 1987, 117 p.

TRÉPANIER 1989 – Trépanier, Paul, "L'héritage de Marie-Charlotte", *Continuité*, No. 43 (Spring 1989), p. 4.

TRIGGS 1985 – Triggs, Stanley, *William Notman. The Stamp of a Studio*, Toronto, Art Gallery of Ontario, 1985.

*TRIGGS 1990 – Triggs, Stanley E., "Notman, William", *Dictionnaire biographique du Canada*, Quebec City, Les Presses de l'Université Laval, Vol. XII (1990), pp. 858-862.

TRUDEL 1970 – Trudel, Jean, "À propos de la statue de Wolfe", *Vie des arts*, No. 59 (Summer 1970), pp. 34-37.

*TRUDEL 1976 – Trudel, Jean, *William Berczy. La famille Woolsey*, Ottawa, National Gallery of Canada, 1976, 40 p. (coll. "Masterpieces in the National Gallery of Canada", No. 7).

TRUDEL 1985 – Trudel, Jean, "Joseph Légaré et la bataille de Sainte-Foy", *The Journal of Canadian Art History*, Vol. VIII, No. 2 (1985), pp. 141-177.

TRUDEL 1986 – Trudel, Clément, "Louis-Joseph Papineau (1786-1871). Un tribun victime de l'oppression, de l'injustice et de ses propres erreurs", *Le Devoir*, October, 7, 1986, pp. 1 and 8.

TRUDEL 1987 – Trudel, Jean, "Sans titre", *Parachute*, Vol. 46 (March-April-May 1987), pp. 102-105.

TRUDEL 1990/1 – Trudel, Jean, "L'imaginaire comme objet de curiosité: le *Musée des Traces* d'Irene F. Witthome", *Parachute*, No. 57 (January-February-March 1990), pp. 4-9.

TRUDEL 1990/2 – Trudel, Jean, "*The Montreal Society of Artists*, une galerie d'art contemporain à Montreal en 1847", *The Journal of Canadian Art History*, Vol. XIII/1 (1990), pp. 61-87.

TRUDEL, JUNEAU AND MASSEY 1967 – Trudel, Jean, André Juneau and Georges Massey, *Peinture traditionnelle du Québec* (Cat.), Quebec City, Musée du Québec, 1967, 125 p.

UNE AUTRE AMÉRIQUE 1982 – Une autre Amérique (Cat.), La Rochelle, Le Musée du Nouveau Monde, 1982, 261 p.

UNIVERSITÉ LAVAL 1874-1875 – Université Laval. Pinacothèque, [1874 ou 1875].

UNIVERSITÉ LAVAL 1883-1884 – Université Laval, [1883 ou 1884], 32 p.

UNIVERSITÉ LAVAL 1887 – Université Laval, [1887], 32 p.

UNIVERSITÉ LAVAL 1889 – Université Laval, 1889. 32 p.

UNIVERSITÉ LAVAL 1893 – Université Laval, 1893, 32 p.

UNIVERSITÉ LAVAL 1898 – Université Laval, Quebec City, Léger Brousseau, 1898, 32 p.

UNIVERSITÉ LAVAL 1901 – Université Laval, Quebec City, Léger Brousseau, 1901, 40 p.

UNIVERSITÉ LAVAL 1903 – Université Laval, Quebec City, Léger Brousseau, 1903, 45 p.

UNIVERSITÉ LAVAL 1906 – Université Laval, Quebec City, Éd. Marcotte, 1906, 72 p.

UNIVERSITÉ LAVAL 1908 – Université Laval, Quebec City, Éd. Marcotte, 1908, 72 p.

UNIVERSITÉ LAVAL 1909 – Université Laval, Quebec City, Éd. Marcotte, 1909, 72 p.

UNIVERSITÉ LAVAL 1913 – Université Laval, Quebec City, L'Action Sociale limitée, 1913, 91 p.

UNIVERSITÉ LAVAL 1923 – Université Laval, Quebec City, L'Action Sociale limitée, 1923, 91 p.

UNIVERSITÉ LAVAL 1933 – Université Laval, Quebec City, L'Action Catholique, 1933, 94 p.

*UN MOMENT 1991 – Un Moment dans l'Histoire. Vingt ans d'acquisition de peintures, de dessins et d'estampes aux Archives nationales du Canada (Cat.), Ottawa, National Archives of Canada, 1991, 302 p.

UN SANCTUAIRE 1973 – "Un sanctuaire pour la collection d'art religieux ancien du Québec", *M* (journal of the Montreal Museum of Fine Arts), Vol. 5, No. 2 (Fall 1973), pp. 12-14.

UN SIÈCLE D'ART CANADIEN 1945 – Un siècle d'art canadien (Cat.), Sherbrooke, Chambre de Commerce des Jeunes de Sherbrooke, 1945, 24 p.

UN SIÈCLE D'ART CANADIEN 1946 – Un siècle d'art canadien (Cat.), Arvida, Comité des Arts et Métiers d'Arvida, 1946.

UN SIÈCLE D'ART CANADIEN 1949 – Un siècle d'art canadien. Exposition d'œuvres d'art du Musée de la Province (Cat.), Rimouski, Les Compagnons de l'Art, 1949, 16 p.

UN SIÈCLE D'ART CANADIEN 1951 – Un siècle et demi d'art canadien (Collection du Musée de la Province de Québec) (Cat.), Baie Comeau, 1951.

VANIER-SHEPHERD 1986 – Vanier-Shepherd, Gyde, "L'art de la révélation: la tradition baroque au Québec de 1664 à 1839", *Splendeurs du Vatican. Chefs d'œuvres de l'art baroque*, Ottawa, Musée des beaux-arts du Canada, 1986, pp. 41-48.

VAUGEOIS 1990 – Vaugeois, Denis, "Vaincre la distance et le temps. Une obsession millénaire", *Cap-aux-Diamants*, No. 23 (Fall 1990), pp. 30-33.

VAUGEOIS AND LACOURSIÈRE 1970 – Vaugeois, Denis and Jacques Lacoursière, *Canada Québec: synthèse historique*, Montreal, Éditions du Renouveau Pédagogique, 1970, 619 p.

VEYRON 1990 – Veyron, Michel, *Dictionnaire canadien des noms propres*, Montreal, Éditions Larousse, 1990.

VÉZINA 1972/1 – Vézina, Raymond, *Cornelius Krieghoff. Peintre de mœurs (1815-1877)*, Quebec City, Éditions du Pélican, 1972, 220 p.

* VÉZINA 1972/2 – Vézina, Raymond, "Krieghoff, Cornelius", *Dictionnaire biographique du Canada*, Quebec City, Les Presses de l'Université Laval, Vol. X (1972), pp. 449-455.

VÉZINA 1973-1974 – Vézina, Raymond, "Nos grands-pères au Musée du Québec", *Deuxième mouvement*, Vol. 1, No. 1 (1973-1974), pp. 43-50.

* VÉZINA 1974 – Vézina, Raymond, "Attitude esthétique de Cornelius Krieghoff au sein de la tradition picturale canadienne-française", *RACAR*, Vol. 1, No. 1 (1974), pp. 47-59.

VÉZINA 1975/1 – Vézina, Raymond, *Théophile Hamel, peintre national (1817-1870)*, Montreal, Éditions Élysée, 1975, 301 p.

VÉZINA 1975/2 – Vézina, Raymond, "Evolution of the Lineage of Theophile Hamel 1636-1975. An instance of social advancement due to art", *French Canadian and Acadian Genealogical Review*, Vol. V, Nos. 3-4 (1975), pp. 154-252.

VÉZINA 1975/3 – Vézina, Raymond, "[Review of] Barry Lord, *The History of Painting in Canada*", *RACAR*, Vol. 2, No. 1 (1975), pp. 51-54.

VÉZINA 1975/4 – Vézina, Raymond, "Théophile Hamel, premier peintre du Saguenay", *Saguenayensia*, Vol. 17, No. 1 (Jan.-Feb. 1975), pp. 2-16.

VÉZINA 1976/1 – Vézina, Raymond, *Catalogue des œuvres de Théophile Hamel*, Montreal, Éditions Élysée, 1976, 64 p.

VÉZINA 1976/2 – Vézina, Raymond, *Napoléon Bourassa (1827-1916). Introduction à l'étude de son art*, Montreal, Éditions Élysée, 1976, 262 p. (Coll. "L'art au Canada").

* VÉZINA 1976/3 – Vézina, Raymond, *Napoléon Bourassa (1827-1916). Soixantième anniversaire* (Cat.), Ottawa, National Archives of Canada, 1976, 27 p.

* VÉZINA 1977 – Vézina, Raymond, "Hamel, Théophile", *Dictionnaire biographique du Canada*, Quebec City, Les Presses de l'Université Laval, Vol. IX (1977), pp. 395-401.

VÉZINA 1978 – Vézina, Raymond, "Napoléon Bourassa et la famille Papineau: les liens sociaux"; *La Petite Nation*, 6 April 1978, p. 2.

VÉZINA 1979 – Vézina, Raymond, "Exposition Joseph Légaré", *RACAR*, Vol. VI, No. 1 (1979), pp. 43-45.

VÉZINA 1980 – Vézina, Raymond, "La généalogie et l'histoire de l'art" in *Le rôle de la généalogie dans la société*, 1980, pp. 127-135.

* VÉZINA 1982 – Vézina, Raymond, "Falardeau, Antoine-Sébastien", *Dictionnaire biographique du Canada*, Quebec City, Les Presses de l'Université Laval, Vol. XI (1982), pp. 339-340.

* VÉZINA 1987 – Vézina, Raymond, "Hamel, Théophile", *L'Encyclopédie du Canada*, Vol. 2, Montreal, Stanké, 1987, p. 881.

VIAU 1979 – Viau, René, "Joseph Légaré 1795-1855 / L'œuvre", *Le Devoir*, February, 17, 1979, p. 25.

VILLENEUVE 1987 – Villeneuve, Claudine, "Les portraits de Louis-Joseph Papineau dans l'estampe de 1825 à 1845", *Questions d'art québécois* (under the dir. of John R. Porter), Cahiers du CELAT, No. 6 (February 1987), pp. 103-130.

VILLENEUVE 1991 – Villeneuve, René, "De l'art traditionnel à l'art ancien", *Cap-aux-Diamants*, No. 25 (Spring 1991), pp. 47-50.

VINCENT 1986 – Vincent Thehariolina, Marguerite, *La nation huronne: son histoire, sa culture, son esprit*, Quebec City, Les Éditions du Pélican, 1984, 507 p.

* WADE 1966 – Wade, Mason, *Les Canadiens français de 1760 à nos jours*, Vol. I: 1760-1914, 2nd edition, Montreal, Cercle du Livre de France, 1966, 685 p.

WEBSTER 1984 – Webster, Donald B. (with the collaboration of Micheal S. Cross and Irene Szylinger), *Georgian Canada. Conflict and Culture 1745-1820* (Cat.), Toronto, Royal Ontario Museum, 1984, 225 p.

WHITE 1971 – White, Michael, "Portraits Show the True Faces of Lower Canada", *The Gazette*, February, 6, 1971, p. 43.

WILLIAMSON 1976 – Williamson, Moncrieff, *Through Canadian Eyes, Trends and Influences in Canadian Art 1815-1965* (Cat.), Calgary, Glenbow-Alberta Institute, 1976.

WILLIS 1842 – Willis, Nathaniel Parker, *Canadian Scenery Illustrated*, London, George Virtue, 1842, 2 Vol.

* WILSON 1988 – Wilson, Bruce G., *Identités coloniales. Le Canada de 1760 à 1815* (Cat.), Ottawa, National Archives of Canada, 1988, 236 p. (Coll. "Les documents de notre histoire").

* WINDER 1972 – Winder, C. Gordon, "Logan, sir William Edmond", *Dictionnaire biographique du Canada*, Quebec City, Les Presses de l'Université Laval, Vol. X (1972), pp. 486-492.

WINKWORTH 1972 – Winkworth, Peter, *Exposition d'estampes en l'honneur de C. Krieghoff, 1815-1872* (Cat.), Montreal, McCord Museum, 1972.

WOHLER 1984 – Wohler, J. Patrick, *Charles de Salaberry, Soldier of the Empire, Defender of Quebec*, Toronto and Charlottetown, Dundurn Press, 1984, 159 p.

YOUNG 1968 – Young, William, ed., *A Dictionnary of American Artists, Sculptors and Engravers*, Cambridge, Mass., William Young and Co., 1968.

ZERI AND FREDERICKSEN 1972 – Zeri, Federico and Burton B. Fredericksen, *Census of Pre-Nineteenth Century Italian Paintings in the North American Public Collections*, Cambridge, Harvard University Press, 1972.

EXHIBITIONS

Quebec City 1838 - *Société littéraire et Historique de Québec*, Quebec City, 1838.

Quebec City 1839 - *Exhibition of Paintings of the Passion of Our Saviour Jesus Christ, in fourteen Pictures*, Wardrobe of the House of Assembly, Quebec City, 1839.

Quebec City 1840 - *Exposition de tableaux de Henry-Daniel Thielcke*, Sewell's heirs' House, Rue Buade, Quebec City, 1840.

Quebec City 1845 - *Exposition de tableaux*, Institut des Artisans de Québec, Quebec City, 1845.

Montreal 1847 - *Montreal Gallery of Pictures*, Montreal, 1847. Catalogue.

Montreal 1848 - *Tableaux d'anciens maitres et d'artistes modernes*, Montreal, 1848.

Quebec City 1848 - *Magnifiques tableaux en loterie*, House of Assembly, Quebec City, 1848.

Quebec City 1850 - *Exposition industrielle provinciale*, Quebec City, 1850.

Montreal 1853 - *Exposition provinciale*, Montreal, 1853.

Quebec City 1853 - *Exposition industrielle de Québec*, Quebec City, 1853.

Montreal 1857 - *Les salons de la bâtisse Bonaventure*, Montreal, 1857.

Montreal 1864 - *Conversazione*, Art Association of Montreal, Mechanic's Institute, Montreal, 1864.

Paris 1867 - *Exposition universelle de Paris*, Palais Royal, Paris, 1867.

Montreal 1870 - *Gallery of Art Association of Montreal, 6th Exhibition*, Art Association of Montreal, Montreal, 1870. Catalogue.

Montreal 1879 - *Exhibition by the Association on the Occasion of the Opening of the Art Gallery, Phillips Square, May 26th 1879*, Art Association of Montreal, Montreal, 1879. Catalogue.

Montreal 1880 - *Royal Canadian Academy of Art. First Annual Exhibition*, Art Association of Montreal, Montreal, 1880. Catalogue.

Montreal 1887 - *Catalogue Raisonné of a Loan Exhibition of Canadian Historical Portraits and other Objects Relating to Canadian Archaeology: Held in the Natural History Society's Building by the Numismatic and Antiquarian Society of Montreal. In Commemoration of the 25th Anniversary of the Foundation of the Society, on Thursday, December 15th, 1887, And Following Days*, Numismatic and Antiquarian Society of Montreal, Montreal, 1867. Catalogue.

Montreal 1892 - *A Record of Canadian Historical Portraits and Antiquities Exhibited by the Numismatic and Antiquarian Society of Montreal 15th September 1892. In Commemoration of the 250th Year of the Foundation of Montreal*, Numismatic and Antiquarian Society of Montreal, Montreal, 1892. Catalogue by A. C. de Lery MacDonald.

Toronto 1907 - *Canadian National Exhibition*, Department of Fine Arts, Toronto, 1907. Catalogue.

Quebec City 1918 - *Exposition provinciale*, Palais central de l'Exposition provinciale, Quebec City, 1918.

Quebec City 1919 - *Exposition provinciale*, Quebec City, 1919.

Quebec City 1920 - *Exposition de peinture et dessins à l'Académie commerciale de Québec*, Académie commerciale, Quebec City, 1920. Catalogue

Quebec City 1924 - *Salon du Terroir*, Palais de l'Exposition, Quebec City, 1924.

Ottawa 1934 - *Exhibition of Paintings by Cornelius Krieghoff 1815-1872*, National Gallery of Canada, Ottawa (Exhibition also presented in Montreal), 1934. Catalogue.

Montreal 1935 - *Continental Art Gallery*, Montreal, 1935.

Quebec City 1936 - *Exposition Théophile Hamel*, Musée de la Province de Québec, Quebec City, 1936.

Montreal 1940 - *Catalogue of a Selection from the Watercolour & Sepia Drawings (1760-1850) in the William H. Coverdale Collection of Historical Canadiana at the Manoir Richelieu, Murray Bay, P.Q. Exhibited at the Galleries of the Art Association of Montreal*, Art Association of Montreal, Montreal, 1940. Catalogue.

New York 1942 - *Canadiana. An Exhibition of Historical Prints, Watercolour, Drawings, Oil Paintings and Maps*, Grand Central Art Galleries, New York, 1942. Catalogue.

Quebec City 1942-1943 - *Le Vieux Québec*, Musée de la Province de Québec, Quebec City, 1942-1943. Catalogue by Percy F. Godenrath.

Sherbrooke 1945 - *Un siècle d'art canadien*, Salons du club social du Jeune Commerce de Sherbrooke, Sherbrooke (Exhibition organized by the Musée de la Province de Québec, Quebec City), 1945. Catalogue.

Toronto 1945 - *Le développement de la peinture au Canada 1665-1945*, The Art Gallery of Toronto, Toronto (Exhibition also presented in Ottawa, Montreal and Quebec City), 1945. Catalogue by Robert H. Hubbard.

Albany 1946 - *Painting in Canada. A Selective Historical Survey*, Albany Institute of History and Art, Albany (New York), 1946. Catalogue.

Arvida 1946 - *Un siècle d'art canadien*, Centre de récréation d'Arvida, Arvida (Exhibition organized by the Musée de la Province de Québec, Quebec City), 1946. Catalogue.

Detroit 1946 - *The Arts of French Canada 1613-1870*, The Detroit Institute of Arts, Detroit (Exhibition also presented in Cleveland, Albany, Montreal, Ottawa and Quebec City), 1946. Catalogue by Robert H. Hubbard and Marius Barbeau.

Windsor 1947-1948 - *French Canadian Art 1850-1947*, Willistead Art Gallery, Windsor, 1947-1948. Catalogue.

Quebec City 1948 - *Exposition du Centenaire de l'Institut Canadien de Québec*, Musée de la Province de Québec, Quebec City, 1948.

Richmond 1949 - *Painters of Canada: Exposition of Canadian Painting, 1668-1948*, Virginia Museum of Fine Arts, Richmond (Virginie), 1948. Catalogue.

Rimouski 1949 - *Un siècle d'art canadien. Exhibition d'œuvres d'art du Musée de la Province de Québec de Québec*, Hôtel de ville, Rimouski (Exhibition organized by the Musée de la Province de Québec, Quebec City), 1949. Catalogue.

Winnipeg 1950-1951 - *Un siècle de peinture du Québec*, Western Canada Art Circuit, 1950-1951 (Travelling exhibition organized by the Musée de la Province de Québec, Quebec City and presented at Winnipeg, Edmonton, Nelson, Victoria, Brendon, Lethbridge, Calgary and Saskatoon).

Baie-Comeau 1951 - *Un siècle et demi d'Art Canadien (Collection du Musée de la Province de Québec de Québec)*, Gymnase du Centre sportif, Baie-Comeau, 1951 (Exhibition organized by the Musée de la Province de Québec, Quebec City). Catalogue.

Quebec City 1952 - *Exposition rétrospective de l'art au Canada français*, Musée de la Province de Québec, Quebec City, 1952. Catalogue by Gérard Morisset.

Ottawa 1953 - *Exhibition of Canadian Painting to celebrate the Coronation of Her Majesty Queen Elizabteh II*, National Gallery of Canada, Ottawa, 1953. Catalogue.

Hamilton 1953-1954 - *Inaugural Exhibition*, Art Gallery of Hamilton, Hamilton, 1953-1954. Catalogue.

Montreal 1955 - *Les arts anciens au Canada français*, Montreal Museum of Fine Arts, Montreal, 1955.

Winnipeg 1956 - *Portraits Mirror of Man*, The Winnipeg Art Gallery, Winnipeg, 1956. Catalogue.

Paris 1958 - *Exposition de la Province de Québec (Visages du Canada - Vallée du Saint-Laurent)*, Grands Magasins du Louvre, Paris, 1958 (Exhibition organized by the Musée de la Province de Québec, Quebec City).

Ottawa 1959 - *Portraits canadiens du 18ᵉ et 19ᵉ siècles*, National Gallery of Canada, Ottawa and Musée de la Province de Québec, Quebec City. Catalogue by Gérard Morisset.

Quebec City 1959 - *Exposition d'art religieux en l'honneur de Mgr François de Montmorency de Laval*, Café du Parlement, Quebec City (Exhibition organized by the Musée de la Province de Québec, Quebec City).

Vancouver 1959 - *Les arts au Canada français*, The Vancouver Art Gallery, Vancouver, 1959 (Exhibition organized by the Musée de la Province de Québec, Quebec City and also presented in Winnipeg). Catalogue by Gérard Morisset.

Montreal 1960 - *Onze artistes à Montreal*, Montreal Museum of Fine Arts, Montreal.

Mexico 1960-1961 - *Arte Canadiense*, Museo nacional de Arte Moderno, Mexico, 1960-1961 (Exhibition organized by the National Gallery of Canada, Ottawa and also presented in Guadalajara). Catalogue.

Fredericton 1961 - *Cornelius Krieghoff, ca. 1815-1872*, Beaverbrook Art Gallery, Fredericton, 1961. Catalogue by Edwy Cooke.

Bordeaux 1962 - *L'Art au Canada*, Musée des Beaux-Arts, Bordeaux (France), 1962. Catalogue by Gilberte Martin-Méry.

Montreal 1962-1963 - *Une imagerie canadienne. Peintures et dessins du McCord Museum de McGill University*, McCord Museum, Montreal and National Gallery of Canada, Ottawa, 1962-1963. Catalogue by John Russell Harper.

Montreal 1963 - *Montreal Harbour City 1535-1867*, Montreal Museum of Fine Arts, Montreal, 1963.

Charlottetown 1964 - *Un siècle de peinture: l'époque coloniale de la guerre de Sept Ans à la Confédération*, Art Gallery and Confederation Museum, Charlottetown, 1964 (Exhibition organized by the National Gallery of Canada, Ottawa). Catalogue by John Russell Harper.

London 1965 - *Treasures of Commonwealth Art Exhibition*, Royal Academy, Burlington House, London (England), 1965.

Ottawa 1965 - *Trésors de Québec*, National Gallery of Canada, Ottawa and Musée du Québec, Quebec City. Catalogue by John R. Harper and Robert H. Hubbard.

Montreal 1966 - *Exposition de peinture et mobilier ancien du Canada français*, Montreal Museum of Fine Arts, Montreal, 1966.

Toronto 1966, *Semaine française à Toronto*, Art Gallery of Toronto, Toronto, 1966 (Exhibition organized by the Musée du Québec, Quebec City).

Vancouver 1966 - *Images for a Canadian Heritage*, The Vancouver Art Gallery, Vancouver, 1966. Catalogue by Doris Shadbolt.

Sarasota 1966-1967 - *Masterpieces from Montreal*, Travelling exhibition organized by the Montreal Museum of Fine Arts and also presented in Sarasota (Floride), Buffalo (New York), Rochester (New York), Raleigh (North Carolina), Philadelphie (Pennsylvania), Columbus (Ohio), Pittsburgh (Pennsylvania) and New York. Catalogue by David G. Carter.

Montreal 1967/1 - *Le peintre et le Nouveau Monde*, Montreal Museum of Fine Arts, Montreal, 1967. Catalogue by David G. Carter.

Montreal 1967/2 - *Portraits, People and Places*, Sir George Williams Art Galleries, Montreal, 1967.

Ottawa 1967/1 - *Trois cents ans d'art canadien*, National Gallery of Canada, Ottawa, 1967. Catalogue by Robert H. Hubbard and J.-R. Ostiguy.

Ottawa 1967/2 - *Pages d'histoire du Canada*, National Gallery of Canada, Ottawa, 1967. Catalogue by Roy Strong.

Quebec City 1967 - *Peinture traditionnelle du Québec*, Musée du Québec, Quebec City, 1967. Catalogue by Jean Trudel, André Juneau and Georges Massey.

Windsor 1967-1968 - *La peinture au Canada 1850-1950*, Travelling exhibition organized by the National Gallery of Canada, Ottawa and presented in Windsor, London, Hamilton, Kingston, Stratford, Saskatoon, Edmonton, Victoria, Charlottetown, Saint-John, Fredericton and Quebec City, 1967-1968. Catalogue.

Brantford 1968 - *The World of Cornelius Krieghoff*, Art Gallery of Brantford, 1968.

Toronto 1968 - *William Berczy Exhibition*, Royal Ontario Museum, Toronto, 1968.

Ottawa 1969-1970 - *Portraits anciens du Canada*, National Gallery of Canada, Ottawa, 1969-1970. Catalogue by Wayne J. Ready.

Ottawa 1970 - *Deux peintres de Québec: Antoine Plamondon (1802-1895), Théophile Hamel (1817-1870)*, National Gallery of Canada, Ottawa, 1970 (Exhibition also presented in Quebec City and Montreal). Catalogue by Robert H. Hubbard.

Quebec City 1971 - *Cornelius Krieghoff, 1815-1872*, Musée du Québec, Quebec City, 1971. Catalogue by André Juneau.

Toronto 1971 - *Exposition des peintures "traditionnelles" et "contemporaines" du Québec* (during the du *Festival québécois*), Hart House Gallery, University of Toronto, Toronto, 1971.

Montreal 1972 - *Exposition d'estampes en l'honneur de C. Krieghoff, 1815-1872*, McCord Museum, Montreal. Catalogue by Peter Winkworth.

Ottawa 1972/1 - *Thomas Davies, c. 1737-1812*, National Gallery of Canada, Ottawa, 1972. Catalogue by Robert H. Hubbard.

Ottawa 1972/2 - *Archives. Miroir du passé du Canada*, National Archives of Canada, Ottawa, 1972. Catalogue.

Ottawa 1972/3 - *Progrès en conservation et en restauration*, National Gallery of Canada, Ottawa, 1972. Catalogue by Nathan Stolow.

Quebec City 1972 - *Jean-Baptiste Roy-Audy*, Musée du Québec, Quebec City, 1972.

Sherbrooke 1972 - *Quinzaine québécoise à l'Université de Sherbrooke*, Sherbrooke, 1972.

St-John's 1972 - *Quinzaine québécoise*, Memorial University of Newfoundland, St-John's, 1972 (Exhibition organized by the Musée du Québec, Quebec City).

Ottawa 1972-1975 - *Visages du Canada. Aquarelles et dessins historiques tirés de la collection permanente des Archives nationales du Canada*, National Archives of Canada, Ottawa, 1972-1975 (Exhibition also presented in Montreal, Toronto, Regina, Winnipeg, Calgary, Vancouver, Victoria, St. John's, Fredericton, Charlottetown and Halifax). Catalogue by Michael Bell.

Austin 1973 - *The Artist and the Land. Canadian Landscape Painting 1670-1930*, University Art Museum of Texas, Austin; University of Wisconsin, Elvehjem Centre, Madison (Exhibition organized by the National Gallery of Canada, Ottawa). Catalogue by Robert H. Hubbard and Northrop Frye.

Chicoutimi 1973 - *Peintures anciennes*, La Société des Arts de Chicoutimi, Auditorium Dufour, Chicoutimi, 1973.

Kingston 1973 - *Early Canadian Painting*, Agnes Etherington Art Centre, Kingston, 1973. Catalogue by Frances K. Smith.

Ottawa 1973 - *Peintres du Québec. Collection Maurice et Andrée Corbeil*, National Gallery of Canada, Ottawa, 1973 (Exhibition also presented in Montreal). Catalogue by Robert H. Hubbard.

Quebec City 1973 - *Trésors des communautés religieuses de la ville de Québec*, Musée du Québec, Quebec City, 1973. Catalogue by Claude Thibault.

Ottawa 1973-1974 - *L'art populaire: l'art naïf au Canada*, National Gallery of Canada, Ottawa (Exhibition also presented in Toronto and Vancouver), 1973-1974. Catalogue by John R. Harper.

Ottawa 1973-1977 - *La collection Coverdale. Exposition d'un choix de peintures, dessins et gravures sur le Canada*, National Archives of Canada, Ottawa, 1973-1977 (Exhibition also presented in London, Kingston, Oshawa, Windsor, Guelph, Regina, New York, Revburg Idaho, Washington). Catalogue-poster by Michael Bell.

Montreal 1974 - *Les arts du Québec*, Pavillon du Québec, Terre des Hommes, Montreal, 1974 (Exhibition organized by the Musée du Québec). Catalogue by André Juneau and Claude Thibault.

Quebec City 1974 - *Le diocèse de Québec 1674-1974*, Musée du Québec, Quebec City, 1974. Catalogue by Claude Thibault.

Montreal 1975 - *Les portraitistes du Québec au XIXᵉ siècle*, Place des Arts, Montreal, 1975 (Exhibition organized by the Musée du Québec, Quebec City).

Quebec City 1975 - *François Baillairgé et son œuvre (1759-1830)*, Musée du Québec, Quebec City, 1975. Catalogue by David Karel, Luc Noppen and Claude Thibault.

Sherbrooke 1975 - *Portraits anciens du Québec*, Université de Sherbrooke, Galerie d'art, Centre culturel, Sherbrooke, 1975 (Exhibition organized by the Musée du Québec). Catalogue.

Toronto 1975 - *100 years of Canadiana*, York University, Toronto, 1975.

Ottawa 1975-1976 - *Québec et ses environs*, National Archives of Canada, Ottawa, 1975-1976 (Exhibition also presented in Guelph, London, Montreal, Kingston, Fredericton, Sherbrooke, Charlottetown, St. John and Quebec City). Catalogue-poster by Michael Bell and Martha E. Cooke.

Calgary 1976 - *Through Canadian Eyes, Trends and Influences in Canadian Art 1815-1965*, Glenbow-Alberta Institute, Calgary, 1976. Catalogue.

Montreal 1976 - *Cornelius Krieghoff*, Place des Arts, Montreal, 1976.

Stratford 1976 - *Aspects of the Art of French Canada 1700-1850*, The Gallery, Stratford. Catalogue

Quebec City 1977 - *L'art du Québec au lendemain de la conquête (1760-1790)*, Musée du Québec, Quebec City, 1977 (Exhibition also presented in Montreal). Catalogue by Claude Thibault, Claude Galarneau and Luc Noppen.

Kingston 1978 - *The Last "Lion"... Rambles in Quebec with James Pattison Cockburn*, Agnes Etherington Art Centre, Kingston, 1978. Catalogue by Michael Bell and Martha E. Cooke.

Toronto 1978/1 - *From Ocean to Ocean: Nineteenth Century Water Colour Painting in Canada*, Art Gallery of Ontario, Toronto, 1978. Catalogue by Jeremy Adamson.

Toronto 1978/2 - *Early Canadian Faces - Exhibition of Portrait in Canada 1780-1870*, Royal Ontario Museum, Toronto, 1978.

Kingston 1978-1979 - *George Heriot. Peintre des deux Canadas*, Agnes Etherington Art Centre, Kingston, 1978-1979. Catalogue by Gerald Finley.

Ottawa 1978-1979/1 - *Joseph Légaré 1795-1855*, National Gallery of Canada, Ottawa, 1978-1979 (Exhibition also presented in Montreal and Quebec City). Catalogue by John R. Porter with the collaboration Jean Trudel and Nicole Cloutier.

Ottawa 1978-1979/2 - *Notre patrie, le Canada*, National Gallery of Canada, Ottawa, 1978-1979 (Exhibition also presented in Winnipeg, Vancouver, Toronto and Montreal). Catalogue by Dennis Reid.

Quebec City 1978-1979 - *L'art du paysage au Québec (1800-1940)*, Musée du Québec, Quebec City, 1978-1979 (Exhibition also presented in Halifax, St-John and Fredericton). Catalogue by Claude Thibault.

Montreal 1979 - *Le réel et l'imaginaire: Peinture et photographie canadiennes, 1860-1900*, McCord Museum, Montreal, 1979. Catalogue by Ann Thomas.

Ottawa 1979 - *Enfants d'autrefois*, National Archives of Canada, Ottawa, 1979. Catalogue by Janine G. Conrad-Bury and Marc Lebel.

Toronto 1979 - *Life in Lower Canada (Exhibition Krieghoff)*, Royal Ontario Museum, Toronto, 1979.

Quebec City 1980/1 - *Analyse scientifique des œuvres d'art*, Musée du Québec, Quebec City, 1980. Catalogue by Lola Faillant-Dumas.

Quebec City 1980/2 - *L'architecture et la nature à Québec au dix-neuvième siècle: les villas*, Musée du Québec, Quebec City, 1980. Catalogue by France Gagnon-Pratte.

Montreal 1980-1981 - *L'iconographie de Mgr Plessis*, Sir George Williams Art Galleries, Concordia University, Montreal, 1980-1981.

London 1981 - *Yesterday's Canadians*, London Regional Art Gallery, London (Ont.), 1981. Catalogue by D. Barry Fair.

Montreal 1981 - *Posing for Posterity*, McCord Museum, Montreal, 1981.

Toronto 1981 - *House Proud. Canadian House Portraits*, Royal Ontario Museum, Toronto, 1981.

Montreal 1981-1982 - *Images de Charlevoix 1784-1950*, Montreal Museum of Fine Arts, Montreal, 1981-1982. Catalogue by Victoria Baker.

Montreal 1981-1983 - *Les artisans du Québec*, McCord Museum, Montreal, 1981-1983.

Saint-Lambert 1982 - *De la voile à la vapeur*, Musée Marsil, Saint-Lambert, 1982. Catalogue under the direction of Victoria Baker and Diana Dutton.

Berlin 1982-1983 - *Okanada Historische Malerei Kanadas*, Ausstellungen und Veranstaltungen der Akademie der Künste, Berlin, 1982-1983. Text on Joseph Légaré by Laurier Lacroix.

La Rochelle 1982-1983 - *Une autre Amérique*, Le Musée du Nouveau Monde, Hôtel Fleuriau, La Rochelle, 1982-1983. Catalogue.

Toronto 1982-1983 - *People and Places: Early Canadian Painting*, Royal Ontario Museum, Toronto.

Winnipeg 1982-1983 - *A Distant Harmony. Comparaisons in the Painting of Canada and the United States of America*, The Winnipeg Art Gallery, Winnipeg and The Art Gallery of Hamilton, Hamilton, 1982-1983. Catalogue by Ann Davis.

Hartford 1983 - *Anson Dickinson. The Celebrated Miniature Painter 1779-1852*, The Connecticut Historical Society, Hartford (Conn.), 1983. Catalogue by Mona Leithiser Dearborn.

Montreal 1983-1984 - *Au fil des collections. L'Éducation de la Vierge de Théophile Hamel*, Montreal Museum of Fine Arts, 1983-1984. Catalogue by Nicole Cloutier.

Quebec City 1983-1984 - *Le Musée du Québec, 1933-1983. Cinquante années d'acquisitions*, Musée du Québec, Quebec City, 1983-1984. Catalogue in collaboration.

Montreal 1984/1 - *Antoine Plamondon (1804-1895). Le chemin de croix de l'église Notre-Dame de Montréal*, Montreal Museum of Fine Arts, Montreal, 1984 (Exhibition also presented in Chicoutimi, Sherbrooke, Quebec City). Catalogue by Yves Lacasse.

Montreal 1984/2 - *Au fil des collections. Québec vu par Légaré, Holloway, Krieghoff, Sewell...*, Montreal, Montreal Museum of Fine Arts, 1984. Catalogue by Nicole Cloutier.

Toronto 1984 - *Georgian Canada. Conflict and Culture 1745-1820*, Royal Ontario Museum, Toronto, 1984. Catalogue by Donald B. Webster with the collaboration of Micheal S. Cross and Irene Szylinger.

Quebec City 1984-1985 - *Le Grand Héritage. L'Église catholique et les arts au Québec*, Musée du Québec, Quebec City, 1984-1985. Catalogue in collaboration.

Hamilton 1984-1986 - *Le Canada au dix-neuvième siècle: Collection de la famille Bert et Barbara Stitt*, Art Gallery of Hamilton, Hamilton, 1984. Catalogue by Andrew J. Oko.

Ottawa 1984-1989 - *Le passé en peinture. Un choix d'œuvres de la Division de l'iconographie des Archives publiques du Canada*, National Archives of Canada, Ottawa, 1984-1989 (Exhibition also presented in Vancouver, Montreal and Halifax). Catalogue en collaboration.

Montreal 1985 - *François Baillairgé (1759-1830). Un portefeuille de dessins académiques*, Sir George William Art Galleries, Concordia University, Montreal, 1985. Catalogue in collaboration.

Quebec City 1985 - *Montreal plaque tournante de la traite des fourrures*, Archives nationales du Québec, Quebec City, 1985.

Montreal 1986 - *Le notaire et la vie quotidienne des origines à nos jours*, Archives nationales du Québec, Montreal, 1986. Catalogue by Hélène Lafortune.

Quebec City 1986 - *Québec en peinture*, Institut Canadien de Québec, Bibliothèque Gabrielle-Roy, Quebec City, 1986. Catalogue.

Ottawa 1986-1987 - *Papineau et son temps*, National Archives of Canada, Ottawa. Catalogue by Claude Baribeau.

Montreal 1987/1 - *Face à face avec l'histoire*, McCord Museum, Montreal, 1987.

Montreal 1987/2 - *Témoignages. 125 ans d'histoire et d'acquisitions*, Musée du Château Ramezay, Montreal, 1987.

Quebec City 1987 - *Les Livernois, photographes: 120 ans de studio à Québec*, Musée du Québec, Quebec City, 1987. Catalogue by Michel Lessard.

Toronto 1987-1988 - *Posted to Canada. The Watecolours of George Russell Dartnell 1835-1844*, Royal Ontario Museum, Toronto, 1987-1988. Catalogue by Honor de Pencier.

Banff 1988 - *Quand l'hiver était roi*, The Whyte Museum of Canadian Rockies, Banff, 1988 (Exhibition also presented in London, Ont., Windsor and Montreal). Catalogue by Edward Clavell and Dennis Reid.

Montreal 1988 - *Montreal en couleur*, Musée du Château Ramezay, Montreal, 1988.

Ottawa 1988 - *Identités coloniales. Le Canada de 1760 à 1815*, National Archives of Canada, Ottawa, 1988. Catalogue by Bruce G. Wilson

Montreal 1988-1989 - *Dulongpré: de plus près*, McCord Museum of Canadian History, Montreal, 1988-1989. Catalogue by Robert Derome, Paul Bourassa and Joanne Chagnon.

Toronto 1988-1989 - *Collector's Canada. Selection from a Toronto private collection*, Art Gallery of Ontario, Toronto, 1988-1989 (Exhibition also presented in Quebec City, Vancouver and Saskatoon). Catalogue by Dennis Reid.

Montreal 1989-1990 - *Montreal, le Québec et la révolution française, 1790-1895*, Maison de la culture Frontenac, Montreal and National Archives of Canada, Ottawa, 1988-1989.

Quebec City 1989-1990 - *Thomas Baillairgé*, Musée du Séminaire de Québec, Quebec City, 1989-1990.

Toronto 1990 - *Lost Heritage Regained*, Art Gallery of Ontario, Toronto, 1990.

Kingston 1990-1991, *L'image de la ville en peinture canadienne*, Agnes Etherington Art Centre, Kingston, 1990-1991 (Exhibition also presented in Toronto, Windsor, Montreal and Halifax). Catalogue by Dorothy Farr.

Quebec City 1991/1 - *La collection des dessins et estampes: 80 œuvres choisies*, Musée du Québec, Quebec City, 1991. Catalogue by Denis Martin and Michèle Grandbois.

Quebec City 1991/2 - *Dons au Musée du Québec 1989-1990*, Musée du Québec, Quebec City, 1991.

Ottawa 1991-1992 - *Berczy*, National Gallery of Canada, Ottawa (Exhibition also presented in Quebec City and Calgary). Catalogue by Mary Allodi, Peter N. Moogk and Beate Stock.

PHOTO CREDITS

Agnes Etherington Art Centre, Kingston, ill. 9.

Albertina Graphic Art Collection, Vienne, fig. 226B.

Archives nationales du Québec, Québec, cat. 30, 31; fig. 30-31A, 82A, 138A, 175A, 209A, 241A.

Art Gallery of Hamilton, cat. 197, 198, 252, 258.

Art Gallery of Ontario, Toronto, cat. 190 and colour, 194 and colour, 266; fig. 49A, 224A (CP); Carlo Catenazzi, cat. 225.

Ashmolean Museum, Oxford (Angleterre), fig. 111D.

Bibliothèque Nationale, Cabinet des estampes, Paris, fig. 10B, 11C, 195B.

British Museum, Londres, ill. 48; fig. 111B.

Castle Museum, Norwich (Angleterre), ill. 52, 57.

Centre de conservation du Québec, Québec: Michel Élie, cat. 107 (MQ), 108 and colour (MQ), 110 and colour (MQ).

Christie's, South Kensington, Londres, fig. 162A.

Claudine Villeneuve, fig. 188B, 188C.

Conrad Toussaint, Saint-Jean-Port-Joly, ill. 21 (collège Ste-Anne-de-la-Pocatière); fig. 184B (collège Ste-Anne-de-la-Pocatière).

Courtauld Institute of Art, Londres, fig. 219A.

Glenbow Museum, Calgary, ill. 24; fig. 152A.

Institut Royal du patrimoine artistique, Bruxelles, fig. 123-124A (Musée royal des beaux-arts d'Anvers).

Inventaire des œuvres d'art (ministère des Affaires culturelles), Québec, ill. 11; fig. 196B.

John R. Porter, Québec, fig. 168A.

McCord Museum of Canadian History, Montreal, ill. 41, 67, 68; cat. 39, 40, 48, 63, 78, 83, 91; fig. 17A, 17B, 95A, 105-106A, 251A, 254B; Archives photographiques Notman, cat. 264, 265; fig. 132A, 255B.

Metropolitan Toronto Reference Library, cat. 234.

Ministère des Affaires culturelles, Québec, ill. 10, 11, 14-16, 73-75; fig. 10A, 11A, 11B, 87B, 153-154A, 182C, 184A, 196B, 218A.

Montreal Museum of Fine Arts, Montreal, ill. 13, 30, 39; cat. 23, 130, 148, 183; fig. 194B, 257A; Marilyn Aitken, cat. 123, 195, 199; Yves Bédard, cat. 162 et colour.

Musée d'art et d'histoire de Rochefort (France), fig. 182B.

Musée d'art de Joliette, cat. 87; fig. 87A.

Musée du Château Ramezay, Montréal, fig. 138B.

Musée du Québec, Québec: Patrick Altman, ill. 2 (ASQ), 6 (ASQ), 12 (HGQ), 13 (Basilique Notre-Dame de Montréal), 17, 22, 23 (ASQ), 29, 31-36, 37 (HGQ), 38, 43 (CP), 47, 58, 69 (ASQ); cat. 3-7, 10, 12 (Sœurs grises de Montréal), 14, 15, 17 (Université McGill), 18 (CP), 19 (CP), 25 (Sœurs grises de Montréal), 27, 28 (MSQ), 38 (MCR), 41, 49, 50 (MSQ), 52 (MSQ), 53, 64-66, 73, 75, 88, 89 (MCR), 92 (MCR), 98 (MSQ), 100, 101, 105, 106 (MCR), 109 (Musée Saguenay-Lac-St-Jean), 112, 113, 115, 117 and colour, 119-121, 124 and colour (Congrégation Notre-Dame de Montréal), 125 (Archevêché Québec), 126, 127 (Institut canadien), 131 and colour, 133 (Ursulines de Québec), 136, 137 (Ville de Québec), 138 and colour (MCR), 149 (Corporation des médecins), 151, 153 and colour, 154 (MSQ), 156 (MSQ), 157, 160, 163 and colour, 164, 168, 169, 174 (MCR), 177, 178 (Soc. des établissements de plein air du Québec), 180, 182, 184 (MSQ), 189 (Archevêché Québec), 192 (Université McGill), 193, 196 and colour (HGQ), 201, 202, 204, 205, 207, 211, 216 and colour (jaquette), 217, 218 (HDQ), 220 and colour (MCR), 221, 226 (MSQ), 227 (Ursulines de Québec), 228 (Ursulines de Québec), 229 (ADQ), 232 (MSQ), 238, 239, 241, 242 (MCR), 248 and colour, 249 and colour (MSQ), 250 (Basilique Notre-Dame de Montréal), 251 (Bishop's University), 253, 254 (MSQ), 257, 259, 260 (Séminaire de Nicolet), 261 (Séminaire de Nicolet), 262 (MSQ), 263 (MSQ), 264 (MMC), 265 (MMC); fig. 12A (Sœurs grises de Montréal), 17C (CP), 26A (HDQ), 27A, 52A (CP), 53B, 67A (ASQ), 80A, 89A, 116A, 116B, 118C, 120A, 127B, 127C, 132B, 133A (église Lotbinière), 136A, 136B, 136C, 137A, 145A, 146B, 146C, 155A, 158A, 165C, 166B, 167C, 167E, 168B, 169A, 169B, 177A, 178A (Société des établissements de plein air du Québec), 181A, 183A, 186A, 188A, 194A, 199A, 200A, 205B, 213A, 216C, 220A, 220B, 220C, 220D, 222-223A, 226A, 242A (MSQ), 246A, 249A (MSQ), 249B (MSQ), 254A, 255A, 263A (Bibliothèque municipale de Montréal), 262-263A (MSQ), 266C, 267A; Jean-Guy Kérouac, cat. 2, 11, 22, 36, 116, 118A à 118E, 122, 129, 134 and colour, 135 and colour, 159, 167, 175, 190 and colour, 200, 203, 208 and colour, 237, 250, 255, 256, 267 and colour; fig. 10-11A, 15A, 17D (CP), 38A, 82B, 117B, 117C, 118A, 118B, 118D, 118E, 131A, 137B (église Notre-Dame de Lévis), 175B, 203A, 205A, 205B, 214-215A, 216A; Claude Bureau, fig. 226A; Nicole Savoie, cat. 240.

Musée du Séminaire de Québec: Pierre Soulard, fig. 157A, 157B, 157C, 157D, 157F, 161A, 161B, 164A, 165A, 165D, 165E, 167D; Denis Chalifour, fig. 157E, 159A.

Musées nationaux (Réunion des musées nationaux), Paris, fig. 2A (Musée d'Orsay), 4A (Musée d'Orsay), 147C, (Musée du Louvre), 148C (Musée du Louvre).

National Archives of Canada, Ottawa, ill. 1, 4, 7, 19, 20, 40, 45, 61, 65, 66, 70, 71, 76, 77; cat. 8 (C-15226), 9 (C-15227), 29 and colour (C-10660), 37 (C-95120), 42 (C-1514), 43 (C-2002), 44 (C-2009), 45 (C-2016), 46 (C-132755), 51A (C-14824), 51B (C-14812), 51C (C-14814, 51D (C-14834), 51E (C-14818), 51F (C-14838), 54 (C-100355), 55 (C-11904), 56 (C-11856), 57 (C-11833), 58 (C-11834), 67A (C-30975), 67B (C-30974), 67C (C-30972), 67D (C-30973), 68 (C841), 69 (C-843), 70 (C-893), 71 (C-842), 79 (C-40012), 80 (C-47013), 90 (C-95591), 102 (C-95145), 103 (C-13383), 104 (C-13390), 114A (C-13077-78), 114B (C-13108/C-137990), 114C (C-137988), 114D (C-13100-1), 114E (C-13071-2), 128 (C-70), 139 (C-95137), 140 (C-95110), 144 (C-40297), 170 (C-137942), 171 (C-35970), 172 (C-67189), 173 (C-315), 179A (C-13606), 179B (C-13610), 179C (C-13621), 179D (C-13629), 179E (C-13642), 230A (C-31285), 230B (C-31247), 230C (C-31244), 230D (C-137984), 230E (C-137985), 243 (C-103394), 244 (C-103389); fig. 5A, 8A-8B, 23A, 53A, 54-58A, 54-58B, 54-58C, 65-66A, 67B, 70-71A, 76A, 76B, 90A, 100-101A, 103-104A, 103-104B, 112-113A, 112A, 113A, 112-113B, 114A, 141A, 170A, 170B, 173A, 233-234A.

National Army Museum, Londres, ill. 54 (1589), 55 (13651).

National Gallery, Londres, fig. 216D.

National Gallery of Art, Washington D.C., fig. 196A.

National Gallery of Canada, Ottawa, ill. 3, 18, 27, 42, 44, 46, 49, 72; cat. 1, 16, 20 and colour, 21, 32, 47, 111 and colour, 152 and colour, 155, 158, 165, 166 and colour, 176, 181, 185-187, 188 and colour, 206, 219, 222 and colour, 223, 224, 235, 236A; fig. 5A, 18-19A, 20-21A, 20-21B (CP), 20A, 60A, 61A, 84A, 111A, 111C, 117A, 165B, 166A, 167B, 171-172A, 173B, 176A, 222-223B, 228A, 236A, 236B; Merrett & Harper, Montréal, cat. 24; Saltmarche Visual Communications, Toronto, cat. 247.

National Portrait Gallery (Smithsonian Institution), Washington D.C., fig. 245A.

Parks Canada, Québec, ill. 10.

Paul Bourassa, Québec, fig. 207A.

Power Corporation du Canada/Power Corporation of Canada, Montréal, fig. 147B, 225A.

Rijksmuseum, Amsterdam, fig. 148B.

Royal Ontario Museum, Toronto, ill. 59, 60, 62-64; cat. 13 and colour, 26, 33, 34, 35 and colour, 59 and coul, 60-62, 72, 74, 76, 77, 81 and colour, 82, 84 (CP), 85, 86 (CP), 93-95, 99, 141 and colour, 142, 143, 145, 146 and colour, 147, 150, 160, 209, 210, 212, 213, 233, 246; fig. 19A, 34A, 36A, 41A, 51A, 79-81A, 143-145A, 145B, 146A, 206A, 212-213A, 216B, 246B, 256A.

Séminaire de Nicolet, fig. 126A.

Sotheby's, Londres, cat. 214 and colour (CP), 215 (CP).

The Beaverbrook Canadian Foundation, The Beaverbrook Art Gallery, Fredericton (N.-B.), ill. 25; fig. 231A.

The Brooklyn Museum, New York, fig. 266B.

The Royal Library, Windsor (Angleterre), ill. 56.

The Whitworth Art Gallery, University of Manchester (Angleterre), fig. 33A.

Université Laval (Service de l'audio-visuel), Sainte-Foy, fig. 127A.

University of New Orleans, ill. 53.

Vancouver Art Gallery, cat. 132.

Victoria and Albert Museum, Londres, fig. 111E.

Wellington County Museum, Fergus (Ontario), fig. 167A.

Yale Centre for British Art, New Haven (États-Unis), ill. 50, 51; fig. 212-213B; Richard Caspole, fig. 28A, 29A.

Produced on the presses of
INTERGLOBE Printers Inc.
Beauceville (Québec)
OCTOBER 1992